LIVING WITH ART

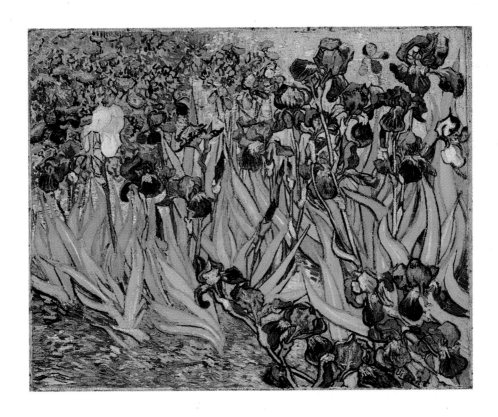

ON THE FRONT COVER:
Vincent van Gogh. *Irises*, detail. 1889.
Oil on canvas, entire work (shown here) $28 \times 36\frac{3}{4}$".
Collection of the J. Paul Getty Museum, Los Angeles, Calif.

ON THE BACK COVER:
Ogata Korin. *Iris and Bridge*, detail of six-fold screen.
Edo Period, Japan, early 18th century.
Ink, color, and gold leaf on paper;
entire screen (shown on page 521) $5'10\frac{1}{2}$" $\times 12'2\frac{1}{4}$".
The Metropolitan Museum of Art, New York
(purchase, Louisa Eldridge McBurney Gift, 1953).

LIVING WITH ART

FIFTH EDITION

Rita Gilbert

Boston, Massachusetts   Burr Ridge, Illinois   Dubuque, Iowa
Madison, Wisconsin   New York, New York   San Francisco, California   St. Louis, Missouri

McGraw-Hill

A Division of The McGraw·Hill Companies

LIVING WITH ART

Copyright © 1998, 1995, 1992 by Rita Gilbert. All rights reserved.
Copyright © 1988, 1985 by Alfred A. Knopf, Inc. All rights reserved.

This book is printed on acid-free paper.

3 4 5 6 7 8 9 0   DOW   DOW   3 2 1 0 9

P/N 0-07-024526-6
PART OF
ISBN 0-07-913212-X

STAFF IN NEW YORK:

Editorial Director: Phillip A. Butcher
Sponsoring Editor: Cynthia Ward
Editing Manager: Curt Berkowitz
Cover Designer: Wanda Lubelska
Text and Related Works Designer: Wanda Kossak
Layout and Contents Designer: Wanda Lubelska
Marketing Director: Margaret Metz
Production Manager: Richard A. Ausburn
Picture Editor: Kathy Bendo
Development Editor: Allison McNamara

STAFF IN BURR RIDGE:

Managing Editor: Jane Lightell
Production Supervisor: Scott Hamilton

Line illustrations: Bill Evans, Denton, Tex.;
   and Vantage Art Studios, Massapequa, N.Y.
Maps: Kelley Graphics, Va.
Compositor: York Graphic Services, Inc., York, Pa.
Color separations: York Graphic Services, Inc., York, Pa.
Cover separation and printing: Lehigh Press Lithographers, Pennsauken, N.J.
Printer and binder: R. R. Donnelley & Sons, Willard, Ohio

Library of Congress Cataloging-in-Publication Data

Gilbert, Rita
    Living with art / Rita Gilbert. —5th ed.
        p.   cm.
    Includes bibliographical references and index.
    ISBN 0-07-913212-X (set)
    1. Art appreciation.   I. Title.
    N7477.G55   1998
    701′.1—dc21   97-11565
                                               CIP

www.mhhe.com

P R E F A C E

Living with Art is a basic art text for college students and other interested readers. It offers a broad introduction to the nature, vocabulary, media, and history of art, showing examples from many cultures.

STRUCTURE OF THE BOOK

As in the four previous editions, I have divided *Living with Art* into five major parts. Part One provides a general overview of the subject of art and its study. In the opening chapter are discussions about what it means to live actively with art, the impulse for art, and the roles of the two essential participants in art—the artist and the observer.

Chapter 2 poses the question "What Is Art?" and gives readers criteria for answering it within their own frames of reference. The chapter considers art's relationship to the audience, to the artist's intention, to beauty, and to the "real" world. This chapter also introduces important concepts of form and content, style, and iconography. Chapter 3 outlines several broad themes that run through the entire history of art, in many cultures, and notes the various purposes art has served and continues to serve.

Part Two is a thorough analysis of the elements and principles of design in art, with detailed explanations and many illustrations. Part Three covers the two-dimensional media and devotes a full chapter to each of the major categories—drawing, painting, prints, the camera arts, and graphic design. In Part Four the same detailed coverage is applied to three-dimensional media—sculpture, crafts, architecture, and environmental design.

Part Five is a brief, but comprehensive, chronological history of art from earliest times to the present. This material now begins with a chapter called "The Ancient World," covering artworks from the oldest cultures we know in various parts of the globe—Africa, Asia, Europe, and Mesoamerica. (The new chapter will be discussed in more detail later in this Preface.) The following chapters trace the development of Western art, and a final chapter surveys art styles in Asia, pre-colonial America, Africa, and Oceania.

ILLUSTRATIONS

Color reproduction of illustrations is a major factor—perhaps *the* major factor—in making an art text useful and attractive to its readers. This fifth edition of *Living with Art* has 575 large color plates and some two hundred "thumbnail" color images used for period identification and visual cross-reference. Except for a handful of photos that proved unobtainable, every artwork that *has* color is reproduced in color. The production managers and I have, together, color-corrected every one of these plates, and we have done our very best to ensure that the reproductions are as nearly faithful to the original works of art as four colors of ink on paper can be.

In all, *Living with Art* has 675 text-size illustrations. Readers will find works of art from many different cultures, works made by women and by men, works as old as civilization and others barely dry. Historical periods have been documented thoroughly. However, because I feel that students often connect particularly well with the art of their own time, one hundred of the works shown in *Living with Art* date from the 1980s and 1990s.

Every work of art in the text is discussed on the two-page spread where the illustration appears. This arrangement is, frankly, quite difficult to achieve with a running text, but I am blessed with two designers who have rare editorial sensitivity and unflappable tolerance for my demands.

FEATURE BOXES

There are four types of feature boxes in *Living with Art*.

"Artists" is a continuation of the feature pioneered in *Living with Art*—single-page biographies of noted artists. Each biography includes a portrait of the artist (usually a self-portrait), a brief life history, and a quotation.

"Art People" focuses on individuals who are not necessarily professional artists but who have had major impact on the world of art. They include collectors, a biographer, an artist's relative, art patrons, even a thief. My recent conversations with the collectors Dorothy and Herbert Vogel resulted in an updating of their feature box and a new photo (page 503).

"Artists on Artists" shows how certain artists have adapted the work of their admired predecessors. The examples include one of Picasso's great studies after Velázquez and Van Gogh's painted version of a print by Hiroshige. A new "Artists on Artists" box in Chapter 10 (page 262) exemplifies *The New Yorker* magazine's less-than-reverent attention to familiar works of art.

"Art Issues" explored in feature boxes include restoration, censorship, public art, and similar topics. Three new "Art Issues" boxes will be described in the following section.

NEW TO THIS EDITION

After a dozen years and four versions of *Living with Art*, I still look for ways to improve the text. About 25 percent of the book has been revised for this edition, and there are changes in every chapter—some subtle, many quite extensive.

The most conspicuous new element in this edition appears throughout Part Five, the chronological history, in the form of toned marginal boxes headed "Related Works." In each box are tiny color plates that function as visual cross-references, with exact page locations, to works in Parts One through Four that relate stylistically and chronologically to the text discussion at that point. I believe these boxes will help to solve a problem that plagues every art appreciation course and text—that is, trying to do two or three things at once. For instance, if I want to discuss Seurat's *Grande Jatte* in Chapter 4 for its optical mixture of color, then I regret its absence from the coverage of Post-Impressionism in Chapter 19. (Repeating all such works full size would not be practical; there are 150 of them.) With the Related Works boxes, instructors and students will know the *Grande Jatte* is in the book and just where to find it. Perhaps the "RW's," as we call them, will make it easier for instructors to plan their lectures and for students to put together the pieces of this multifaceted puzzle that is art history.

Part Five now begins with a new Chapter 14 called "The Ancient World," focusing on the "birthplaces" of art as we know it, on four continents. Two images from the Chauvet cave introduce the chapter, which includes expanded discussions of Mesopotamian and Egyptian art, a section on Nubian art (now a burgeoning field of study), and brief coverage of art from the Indus Valley civilization, Shang and Zhou China, the Olmec culture, and Aegean civilizations. This chapter has a new "Art Issues" box, "Whose Grave Is This Anyway?" (page 359), which explores the complex ethical questions raised by removing artworks from tombs and putting them on display.

Also in Part Five, Classical Greece and Rome now have their own chapter (Chapter 15); Chapter 16 has gained coverage of Early Christian architecture; Chapter 17 treats the Northern Renaissance in greater detail; and Chapter 21 offers much-expanded coverage of North American and African art. Chapter 20 concludes with a section titled "Toward the Millennium," which compares two works of art—one dated c. 1000, the other c. 2000.

Space limitations in the fourth edition led me to cut a section called "The Impulse for Art" from Chapter 1, but several reviewers objected to its disappearance. It is back, with interesting new illustrations. Similarly, the discussion of public art focusing on Serra's *Tilted Arc* has been restored to Chapter 2 in the form of an "Art Issues" box. Chapter 7, "Painting," has a new section on the painting-related techniques of collage and mosaic.

Concerning the discussion of Leonardo's *Last Supper* in Chapter 4, one reviewer made a heartfelt plea for respect owed to "the 20th-century art restorer who has spent her whole life working on preserving/cleaning this mural inch by inch." Dr. Pinan Brambilla Barcilon is the subject of a new "Art Issues" box on restoration (page 115).

My coverage of architecture has now been combined into one chapter (Chapter 13), with a new discussion of Notre-Dame-du-Haut at Ronchamp, plus a few very recent architectural examples and some glorious replacement photos of structures that were already in the book.

PACKAGE AND
ADDITIONAL RESOURCES

Living with Art's "package" consists of four items:

The student handbook, now retitled *Projects Manual and Writing Guide*, has been expanded and completely rewritten to place more emphasis on projects and to provide guidance for specific writing assignments. Although it is still "user-friendly," the Manual contains more challenging material. Instructors who did not use the fourth edition's manual may want to consider class assignments from this new one.

A set of *clear plastic overlays*, coordinated with the Projects Manual, are designed to show students the structure and composition of various artworks. Readers can place these overlays atop specific illustrations and see perspective lines, directional lines, and structural devices such as a triangle. In addition, several blank overlay sheets are provided so that students can draw their own linear analyses, following guidelines in the Projects Manual.

A *Pronunciation Guide* for unfamiliar names—people and places—is printed as a loose card, on heavy paper, that students can insert in the book where they are reading or prop up on the desk in front of them. Several new names have been added to this edition's guide, which is also printed in the text.

A four-page *Time Line*—full color, illustrated, and cross-cultural—is probably the most popular supplement to *Living with Art*. I myself have one tacked on the wall over my desk and refer to it constantly. If students do the same, they may find it easier to keep their bearings while moving through some thirty thousand years of art.

Beyond the supplements described above, *Living with Art* offers certain other resources. There is a bibliography with options for further reading. A glossary of terms summarizes definitions given in the text. An Instructor's Manual is available, in which I suggest teaching strategies and provide sample tests, student projects, ideas for further illustrations, and a list of teaching resources, emphasizing audiovisual materials.

A set of slides of illustrations in the book has been arranged through an independent supplier. Details of the slide package will be explained by local McGraw-Hill representatives.

THE *LIVING WITH ART* TEAM

This is the place where, in each edition, I write admiringly about the creative, intelligent, and hard-working people who make up my book's editorial, design, production, and marketing ensemble. Now I can do something better. I can *show* them to you—albeit in idealized form.

On the last page of this book is reproduced a marvelous work of art—a mixed-media shadow-box construction—titled *The "Living with Art" Team* and created by Jeff Brick, who is one of our number. The original hangs on the wall of my dining room. It was the only artwork I carried by hand when I moved last year from country house to city apartment. It is the art *I* live with.

As I tell on that last page, *The "Living with Art" Team* does not exactly mirror present reality. Some of the people portrayed did not work on this edition of the book, while others, not shown, did. But these are the people who assembled in a flower-filled garden on a gentle spring evening two years ago, for the purpose of declaring group triumph. Jeff Brick's artwork captures the spirit of the team and of that happy gathering.

The "patron" who commissioned this artwork was my sponsoring editor, Cynthia Ward, whom I thank for this splendid gift. I know that she chooses to live with art and that she cares very much about *Living with Art*.

Jane Lightell, managing editor, is the hero of this edition, for she took charge mid-production, when the book was falling apart before my eyes, and calmly helped me put it back together. I deeply value her intelligence, hard work, and good sense.

Development editor Allison McNamara brought a cheerful dedication to the essential jobs of commissioning and analyzing reviews, arranging for the slides and videos, and assisting me on the Instructor's Manual.

I'm not sure this edition would have been published, and I *know* it would not have looked so very fine, if picture editor Kathy Bendo had not pulled off a bravura last-minute rescue of the illustration program. Only a handful of people anywhere have Kathy's array of skills, and I am lucky to benefit from them.

Wanda Siedlecka Kossak brought her usual elegance to the text design of this edition, but even more challenging was her task of creating the Related Works boxes for Part Five. It is *not* easy to take 150 works of art from various sources and sections of the book, choose the whole or a detail, mix them up in a different meaningful order, then arrange them tastefully in boxes with appropriate labels, but Wanda did all this while maintaining outward serenity.

Thanks to Wanda Lubelska, the page layout of this edition is custom-designed to a greater degree than ever before. She and I work closely together, with almost telepathic communication, to nudge pictures and text into exactly the relationships we want. Wanda Lubelska also designed this book's stunning cover. Best of all, she hosted a charming, European-style lunch at her apartment for the inner team, just when our spirits were beginning to flag.

Two production supervisors must be saluted here. Rich Ausburn guided *Living with Art* through two-and-a-half editions, over seven years, maintaining the highest quality standards in the text publishing industry. Scott Hamilton took charge of this edition in mid-production and gave it the same meticulous care. With each of them I ventured to the printer's, in Willard, Ohio, to go sleepless for four days, eat awful food, and color-correct every page on press. Scott's tenure has been brief, but . . . We'll always have Willard.

In previous editions of *Living with Art*, I have referred to editing manager Curt Berkowitz as our "ringmaster" and our "majordomo." Now I will say, simply: He is the one who makes everything work. Curt knows everything there is to know about putting together the millions of pieces that make an art book, and he knows the best spot in Brooklyn for watching the New York Marathon. He has been my ally, my bulwark, and my friend.

NEW YORK CITY, AUGUST 1997   *Rita Gilbert*

REVIEWER ACKNOWLEDGMENTS

As the foregoing Preface should demonstrate, I *do* listen to reviewers whenever I can. Numerous reviewers have helped to shape *Living with Art*. My gratitude goes to the following fifth edition advisors, some of whom also critiqued previous editions: Judith Andraka, Prince George's Community College; John Bell, Blue Ridge Community College; Barbara Bernstein, Ashland University; Roger Churley, Southwestern College; Larry Dellolio, Camden County College; Beverly Dennis, Jones County Junior College; Christina Dinkelacker, University of Memphis; W. Dwaine Greer, University of Arizona; Soo Yun Kang, Chicago State University; John Keller, Harding University; Cher Krause, West Texas A&M University; Anne Lisca, Santa Fe Community College; Robert Llewellyn, Frostburg State University; James May, University of Nebraska, Kearney; Pamela Patton; Lawrence Rakovan, University of Southern Maine; Isabelle Sabau, Northern Illinois University; Diego Sanchez, Virginia Union University; Kathleen Schulz, Raritan Valley Community College; Sally Struthers, Sinclair Community College; Sharon Tetley, Washington State University; and Donald Van Horn, Marshall University.

I do not forget the readers of previous editions, whose counsel continues to enlighten the text. They include: Mary Alice Arnold, Appalachian State University; Gisele Atterberry, Illinois State University; Michelle R. Banks, Memphis State University; Ross Beitzel, Gloucester County College; Kyra Belan, Broward Community College; Catherine Bernard, City College of New York; David Bertolotti, GMI Engineering and Management Institute; Sarah Burns, Indiana University; Carole Calo, University of Massachusetts; George Arnott Civey III; Brian Conley, Golden West College; David Cooper, Butte College; Shelley Cordulack, Millikan University; Jerry Coulter, James Madison University; Patricia Craig, California State University, Fullerton; Betty Disney, Cypress College; Richard T. Doi, Central Washington University; Henry Drewal, Cleveland State University; Steve Eliot, Broward Community College; Robert N. Ewing, California State University, Fullerton; Kathy Flores, New Mexico State University; Elisabeth Flynn, Longwood College; Leonard Folgarait, Vanderbilt University; Lynn Galbraith, University of Nebraska; Douglas George, University of New Mexico; Larry Gleeson, University of North Texas; Paul Grootkerk, Mississippi State University; Janis Hardy, Georgia College; Sharon K. Hopson; Susan Jackson, Marshall University; Ralph Jacobs, Mankato State University; Andrew Jendrzejewski, Vincennes University; Rebecca Jones, University of Texas–Pan American; Karen Kietzman, College of St. Francis; Jan Koot, California State University, Long Beach; Nell Lafaye, University of South Carolina; Pamela Lee, Washington State University; Kathleen Lobley, Butler University; Carolyn Loeb, Central Michigan University; Walter Martin, Concordia University; Robert McGrath, Dartmouth College; Timothy McNiven, Ohio State University; Lynn Metcalf, St. Cloud State University; Joseph Molinaro, Broward Community College; Tim Morris, University of Central Arkansas; Lois Muyskens-Parrott, Richland College; Susan Nelson, Indiana University; Jo Anne Nix, Georgia College; Christie Nuell, Middle Tennessee State University; Helen Phillips, University of Central Arkansas; Robbie Reid, Foothill College; Dominic Ricciotti, Winona State University; John C. Riordan, State University of New York, College at Potsdam; Barbara Kerr Scott, Cameron University; Claire Selkurt, Mankato State University; John Shaak, California State University, Long Beach; Michael J. Smith, Southern Illinois University; Ray Sonnema, Georgia Southern University; Sandra Swenson, University of Texas–Pan American; Thomas Turpin, University of Arkansas; Barbara von Barghahn, George Washington University; Randy Wassell, Colorado State University; Kenneth Weedman, Cumberland College; Rochelle Weinstein, Borough of Manhattan Community College of the City University of New York; and Salli Zimmerman, Nassau Community College.

BRIEF CONTENTS

PART ONE

INTRODUCTION   2

1 LIVING WITH ART   3
2 WHAT IS ART?   18
3 THEMES AND PURPOSES OF ART   46

PART TWO

THE VOCABULARY OF ART   82

4 THE VISUAL ELEMENTS   83
5 PRINCIPLES OF DESIGN IN ART   126

PART THREE

TWO-DIMENSIONAL MEDIA   154

6 DRAWING   155
7 PAINTING   172
8 PRINTS   189
9 THE CAMERA ARTS: PHOTOGRAPHY, FILM, AND VIDEO   215
10 GRAPHIC DESIGN   254

PART FOUR

THREE-DIMENSIONAL MEDIA   264

11 SCULPTURE   265
12 CRAFTS   290
13 ARCHITECTURE   305

PART FIVE

ARTS IN TIME   344

14 THE ANCIENT WORLD   345
15 GREECE AND ROME   365
16 CHRISTIAN ART IN EUROPE: THE EARLY CHURCH, BYZANTIUM, AND THE MIDDLE AGES   380
17 THE RENAISSANCE   395
18 THE 17TH AND 18TH CENTURIES   425
19 THE MODERN WORLD: 1800–1945   448
20 ART SINCE 1945   479
21 ART AROUND THE WORLD   504

C O N T E N T S

PART ONE

INTRODUCTION 2

CHAPTER **1**   **LIVING WITH ART** 3

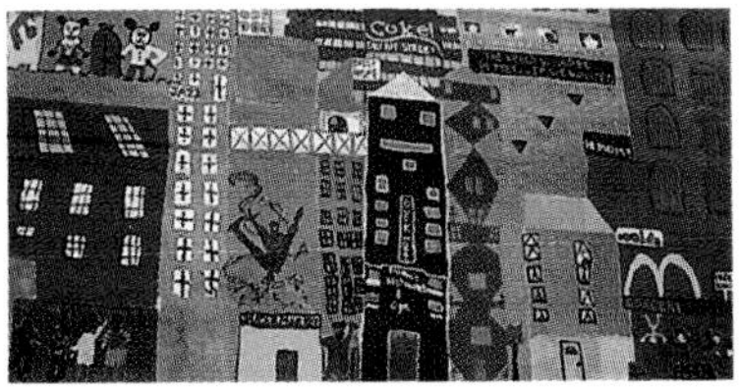

THE IMPULSE FOR ART 4
THE ROLE OF THE ARTIST 7
THE ROLE OF THE OBSERVER 10

ARTISTS   VINCENT VAN GOGH 13
ART PEOPLE   GERTRUDE STEIN 14
ARTISTS   HENRI DE TOULOUSE-LAUTREC 17

CHAPTER **2**   **WHAT IS ART?** 18

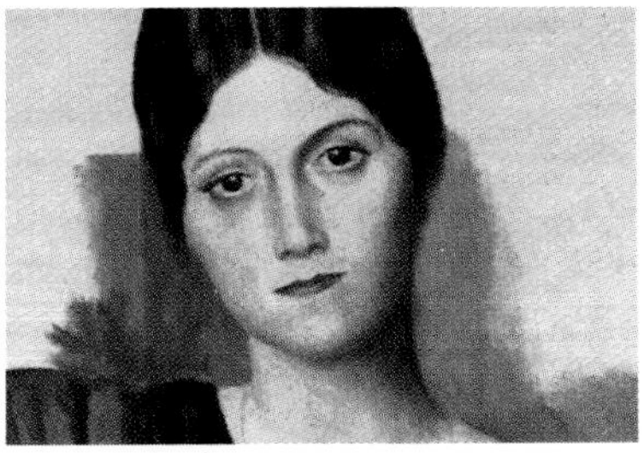

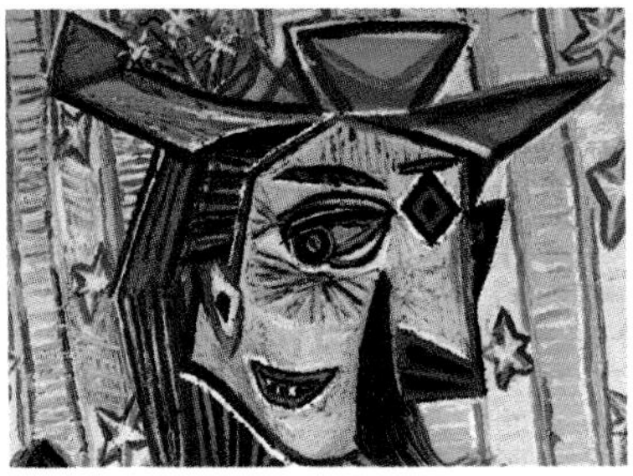

ART AND THE EYE OF THE BEHOLDER 20
Art and the Artist 21
Art and Beauty 24
Art and the "Real" World 25
Representational Art 28
Abstract Art 30
Nonrepresentational Art 31
Art as Expression 31
ART CONCEPTS 36
Form and Content 36
Style 36
Iconography 40

ART ISSUES   PUBLIC ART 23
ARTISTS   HENRI ROUSSEAU 29
ARTISTS   JACKSON POLLOCK 35
ARTISTS   ALBRECHT DÜRER 42
ART PEOPLE   THEO VAN GOGH 45

CHAPTER **3**   **THEMES AND PURPOSES OF ART** 46

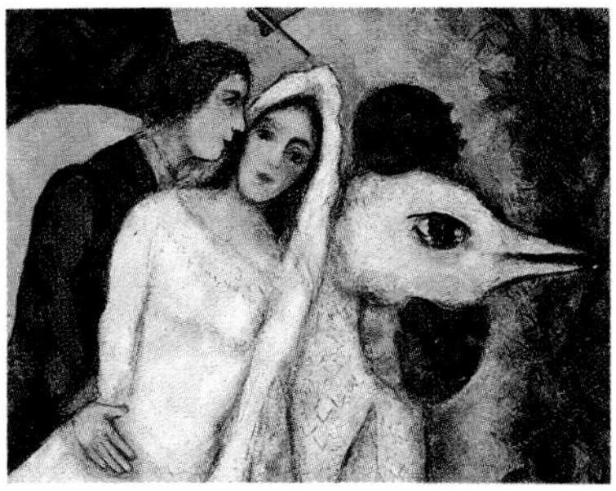

ART IN THE SERVICE OF RELIGION 47
PRIDE AND POLITICS 51
ART AS THE MIRROR OF EVERYDAY LIFE 60
ART AND NATURE 63
IMAGINATION AND FANTASY 70
BIRTH, MARRIAGE, AND DEATH 74

ART ISSUES   PROTECTING A MASTERPIECE: *GUERNICA* 57
ARTISTS   PAUL CÉZANNE 67
ARTISTS   GEORGIA O'KEEFFE 69

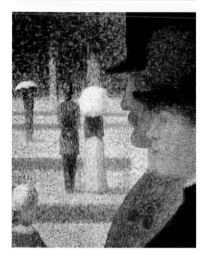

CHAPTER 4 THE VISUAL ELEMENTS 83

LINE 83

Functions of Line 84
Outline and Form 84
Movement and Emphasis 85
Direction 86
Pattern and Texture 87
Shading and Modeling 88

Types of Lines 88
Actual Lines 89
Implied Lines 90
Lines Formed by Edges 90

SHAPE AND MASS 92

LIGHT, VALUE, AND COLOR 94

Light 95
Actual Light 95
The Illusion of Light 96

Value 96

Color 98
Color Theory 99
Color Properties 101
Light and Pigment 101
Color Harmonies 102
Optical Effects of Color 104
Emotional Qualities of Color 105

TEXTURE 107
Actual Texture 108
Visual Texture 108
Pattern 109

SPACE 110
Three-Dimensional Space 110
Two-Dimensional Space 111
Spatial Organization 111
Illusion of Depth 112

TIME AND MOTION 120
Elapsed Time 122
Actual Motion 122
Illusion of Motion 123

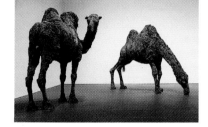

ARTISTS   RAPHAEL 91
ART ISSUES   RESTORATION: *THE LAST SUPPER* 115
ARTISTS   SUZANNE VALADON 121
ART PEOPLE   GIORGIO VASARI 125

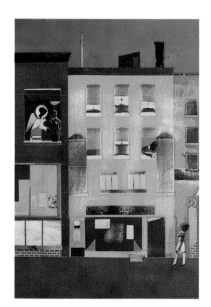

CHAPTER **5**   **PRINCIPLES OF DESIGN IN ART**   **126**

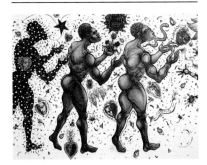

UNITY AND VARIETY 127
BALANCE 131
EMPHASIS AND FOCAL POINT 138
PROPORTION AND SCALE 142
RHYTHM 147
ELEMENTS AND PRINCIPLES: A SUMMARY 152

ARTISTS   HENRI MATISSE 133
ARTISTS   FRANCISCO DE GOYA 141
ART PEOPLE   THE GUERRILLA GIRLS 151

PART THREE

TWO-DIMENSIONAL MEDIA   154

CHAPTER **6**   **DRAWING**   **155**

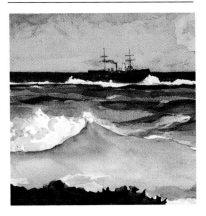

MATERIALS FOR DRAWING 156
Dry Media 157
Pencil 157
Metalpoint 158
Charcoal 159
Chalk and Crayon 159
Liquid Media 161
Pen and Ink 161
Brush and Ink 164
New Drawing Media 166
PURPOSES OF DRAWING 167
Preliminary Study 167
Illustration 168
Expression 169

ARTISTS   REMBRANDT 163
ARTISTS   KÄTHE KOLLWITZ 165
ART ISSUES   WHY DO WE LOSE ART? 171

CHAPTER **7**   **PAINTING**   **172**

ENCAUSTIC 173
FRESCO 173
EGG TEMPERA 175
OIL 178
WATERCOLOR 182
GOUACHE 184
SYNTHETIC MEDIA 184
PAINTING-RELATED TECHNIQUES 187
Collage 187
Mosaic 188

ARTISTS   JACOB LAWRENCE 177
ARTISTS   ALICE NEEL 181

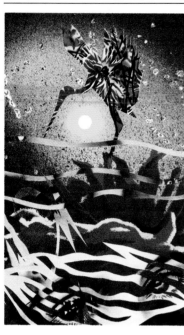

CHAPTER **8** **PRINTS**   **189**

RELIEF 190
Woodcut 191
Linocut 196
Wood Engraving 197

INTAGLIO 198
Engraving 198
Drypoint 199
Mezzotint 200
Etching 200
Aquatint 202

LITHOGRAPHY 203

SCREENPRINTING 209

SPECIAL TECHNIQUES 212

ARTISTS ON ARTISTS   VAN GOGH ON HIROSHIGE 193
ARTISTS   KATSUSHIKA HOKUSAI 195
ARTISTS   EDVARD MUNCH 207
ARTISTS   ROBERT RAUSCHENBERG 208
ARTISTS   ANDY WARHOL 211

CHAPTER **9** **THE CAMERA ARTS:
PHOTOGRAPHY,
FILM, AND VIDEO**   **215**

PHOTOGRAPHY 216
The Still Camera and Its Beginnings 218
Subject Matter in Photography 218
Portraits 218
Landscape 222
Genre 225
Abstraction 227

Purposes of Photography 228
The "Art" Photograph 228
Photojournalism and Editorial Photography 231

Special Effects and Techniques 236
Photography and Motion 239

FILM 241
The Origins of Motion Pictures 241
Films and Filmmakers 242
Special Effects and Animation 250

VIDEO 252

ARTISTS   JULIA MARGARET CAMERON 221
ARTISTS   ALFRED STIEGLITZ 229
ART ISSUES   CENSORSHIP: ROBERT MAPPLETHORPE 232
ARTISTS   ALFRED HITCHCOCK 248

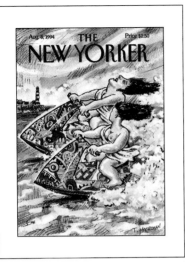

CHAPTER **10**   GRAPHIC DESIGN   **254**

THE TOOLS OF THE GRAPHIC DESIGNER 256
ADVERTISING 258
PRINT MEDIA: BOOKS AND MAGAZINES 259
GRAPHICS AND THE COMPUTER 263

ARTISTS   NORMAN ROCKWELL 261
ARTISTS ON ARTISTS   *THE NEW YORKER* ON PICASSO 262

PART FOUR

THREE-DIMENSIONAL MEDIA   264

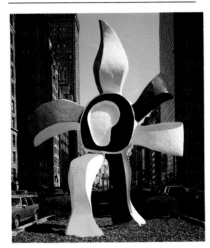

CHAPTER **11**   SCULPTURE   **265**

METHODS OF SCULPTURE 266
Modeling 266
Casting 267
Carving 270
Assembling 273
SCULPTURE AND THE THIRD DIMENSION 278
THE HUMAN FIGURE IN SCULPTURE 280
SCULPTURE AND THE ENVIRONMENT 283
MOTION, LIGHT, AND TIME 288

ARTISTS   HENRY MOORE 271
ARTISTS   DAVID SMITH 275
ARTISTS   LOUISE NEVELSON 276
ARTISTS   CHRISTO AND JEANNE-CLAUDE 287

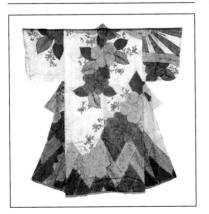

CHAPTER **12**   CRAFTS   **290**

CLAY 291
GLASS 295
METAL 297
WOOD 300
FIBER 302

ARTISTS   MARÍA MARTÍNEZ 293

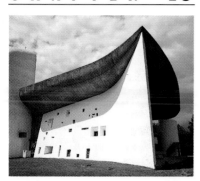

CHAPTER **13** ARCHITECTURE **305**

STRUCTURAL SYSTEMS IN ARCHITECTURE 305
Load-Bearing Construction 306
Post-and-Lintel 307
Round Arch and Vault 308
Pointed Arch and Vault 310
Complex Arches 311
The Dome 312
Cast-Iron Construction 315
Balloon-Frame Construction 317
Steel-Frame Construction 317
Suspension 319
Reinforced-Concrete Construction 320
Geodesic Domes 321

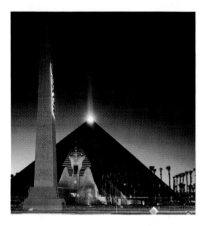

PURPOSES OF ARCHITECTURE 323
Two Houses of Worship 323
Three Museums 326
Three Office Buildings 329
Two Hotels 332
Two Apartment Buildings 334
Three Houses 335

BEYOND THE BUILDING: ENVIRONMENTAL DESIGN 339

ARTISTS   R. BUCKMINSTER FULLER 322
ARTISTS   FRANK LLOYD WRIGHT 337

PART FIVE
ARTS IN TIME   344

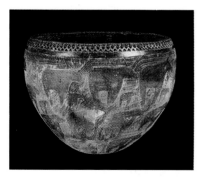

CHAPTER **14** THE ANCIENT WORLD   345

THE OLDEST ART 345
PREHISTORIC ART 348
MESOPOTAMIA 350
EGYPT 354
NUBIA 360
INDUS VALLEY 361
CHINA 361
MESOAMERICA 362
THE AEGEAN 363

ART ISSUES   WHOSE GRAVE IS THIS ANYWAY? 359

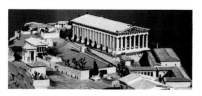

CHAPTER **15** GREECE AND ROME   365

GREECE 365
THE ETRUSCANS 374
ROME 375

ART PEOPLE   PERICLES 369
ART ISSUES   RESTORATION: *LAOCOÖN* 373

CHAPTER 16

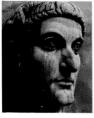
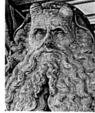

CHRISTIAN ART IN EUROPE:
THE EARLY CHURCH, BYZANTIUM,
AND THE MIDDLE AGES   380

THE EARLY CHRISTIANS 380
BYZANTIUM 382
THE MIDDLE AGES IN EUROPE 384
The Early Middle Ages 385
The High Middle Ages 388
The Late Middle Ages 392

ART PEOPLE   HILDEGARD OF BINGEN 391

CHAPTER 17

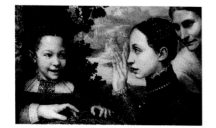

THE RENAISSANCE   395

THE RENAISSANCE IN ITALY 399
THE RENAISSANCE IN THE NORTH 417
LATE 16TH-CENTURY EUROPE 421

ARTISTS   LEONARDO DA VINCI 407
ARTISTS   MICHELANGELO 409
ART PEOPLE   VINCENZO PERUGIA 424

CHAPTER 18

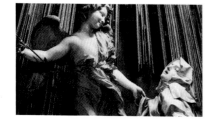

THE 17TH AND 18TH CENTURIES   425

THE BAROQUE STYLE IN EUROPE 425
THE 18TH CENTURY 438
REVOLUTION 445

ARTISTS   GIANLORENZO BERNINI 427
ARTISTS   PETER PAUL RUBENS 432
ARTISTS ON ARTISTS   PICASSO ON VELÁZQUEZ 435
ARTISTS   ELISABETH VIGÉE-LEBRUN 444

CHAPTER 19

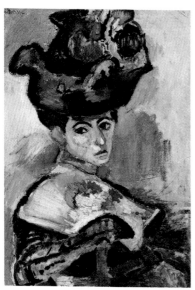

THE MODERN WORLD: 1800–1945   448

FRANCE, EARLY 19TH CENTURY: NEOCLASSICISM,
    ROMANTICISM, REALISM 449
FRANCE, LATE 19TH CENTURY: MANET 454
IMPRESSIONISM AND POST-IMPRESSIONISM 458
BRIDGING THE ATLANTIC: LATE 19TH CENTURY 464
FRANCE, EARLY 20TH CENTURY: FAUVISM, CUBISM,
    AND OTHER MOVEMENTS 466
EARLY 20TH CENTURY: EXPRESSIONISM 470
SYNTHESIS AND AWAKENING: THE ARMORY SHOW 470
NEW YORK IN THE TWENTIES: THE HARLEM RENAISSANCE 473
EUROPE DURING AND AFTER WORLD WAR I:
    DADA AND SURREALISM 475
BETWEEN WORLD WARS: THE BAUHAUS 477

ARTISTS   ROSA BONHEUR 455
ARTISTS   EDOUARD MANET 457
ARTISTS   PAUL GAUGUIN 463
ARTISTS   PABLO PICASSO 468

C H A P T E R **20** **ART SINCE 1945**   **479**

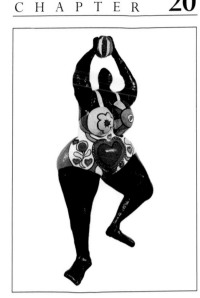

NEW YORK: 1945–1960 479
ART STYLES OF THE SIXTIES AND SEVENTIES 486
Pop Art 486
Minimal Art 487
Realism 489
Conceptual Art and Site Works 491
ART OF THE EIGHTIES AND NINETIES 492
The Figure as Symbol 493
The Figure for Its Own Sake 494
Abstraction 495
Neo-Expressionism 495
Reference, Quotation, and Appropriation 497
Performance, Installations, and Combinations 498
TOWARD THE MILLENNIUM 501

ARTISTS   LEE KRASNER 482
ART PEOPLE   DOROTHY AND HERBERT VOGEL 503

C H A P T E R **21** **ART AROUND THE WORLD**   **504**

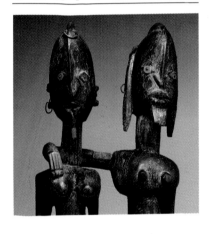

THE ARTS OF ASIA 505
China 505
India and Southeast Asia 512
Japan 517
THE ARTS OF THE AMERICAS 522
Mesoamerica 523
South America 525
North America 526
AFRICA 531
OCEANIA 536

ART ISSUES   RESTORATION: ANGKOR WAT 515

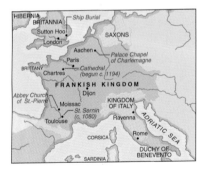

MAPS
THE ANCIENT WORLD 347
THE ANCIENT NEAR EAST 350
GREECE IN THE AGE OF PERICLES 367
THE ROMAN EMPIRE AT ITS HEIGHT 375
EUROPE IN THE AGE OF CHARLEMAGNE 387
EUROPE IN RENAISSANCE 398
EUROPE ON THE BRINK OF REVOLUTION 440
HISTORICAL MAP OF ASIA 505
HISTORICAL MAP OF THE AMERICAS 522
HISTORICAL MAP OF AFRICA 531

PRONUNCIATION GUIDE 537
BIBLIOGRAPHY AND SUGGESTED READINGS 539
NOTES TO THE TEXT 542
GLOSSARY 544
INDEX 549
PHOTOGRAPHIC CREDITS 557
THE "LIVING WITH ART" TEAM 558

LIVING WITH ART

To the Living with Art *Team,*
most particularly Curt, Rich, Wanda, Wanda, Kathy, and Joe.
You will always play on my field of dreams.

INTRODUCTION

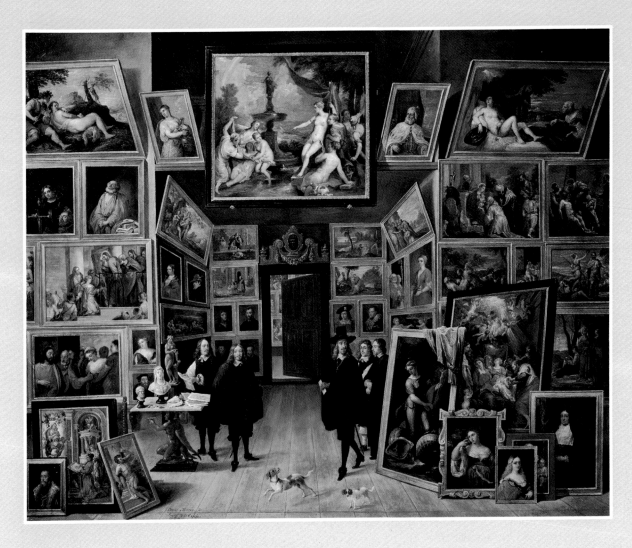

1. David Teniers the Younger. *The Picture Gallery of the Archduke Leopold.*
c. 1650. Oil on canvas, 3'5¾" × 4'2⅞".
Museo del Prado, Madrid.

Living with Art

S OME PEOPLE live with art a little, some a lot. Archduke Leopold Wilhelm, who ruled Belgium in the 17th century, obviously lived with art a *lot*. His court painter, David Teniers the Younger, has left us a fascinating view of the Archduke's private picture gallery **(1)**. Paintings large and small crowd nearly every inch of wall space, butted frame to frame almost to the ceiling, and the overflow works are stacked on the floor. Barely visible through the half-open door at rear is another room, equally crammed with paintings. Even the little dog leaping about in the foreground seems a trifle awed by it all. The Archduke, posed at center wearing a tall hat, has the look of a man pleased and satisfied with his fabulous collection.

Throughout history individuals of wealth and standing have collected art on a grand scale. In the past such collectors tended to be kings and queens, emperors and popes. Today the most ambitious collecting is done by film stars, other entertainers, sports figures, and leaders of industry. None of this latter group would hang their art collections the way Archduke Leopold did; even museums with vast holdings do not. To our modern eyes the Archduke's gallery seems more than a little overdecorated. But this fashion for conspicuous display of art remained popular well into the 20th century.

Relatively few of us have the money or the inclination to acquire great quantities of fine artworks, but that doesn't mean we are not involved with art. Who lives with art? You do. Everybody does. It would be impossible *not* to live with art, because art is inextricably connected to human existence. Art has been with us since the earliest cave dwellers made their first steps toward civilization and will be with us as long as civilized life continues on our planet.

You probably have more art in your life than you realize. If you live in a city or town, artists have designed almost everything in your environment. The buildings in which you live and work, the furniture inside those buildings, the clothes you wear—all were designed by artists in specialized fields. Very likely the walls of your home are decorated with posters, prints, photographs, maybe original paintings, that you have hung to give personal meaning to your world. Perhaps your school or office building has a large-scale sculpture out front or a fabric hanging or mural inside.

Whether we know it or not, all of us make choices—every day, every minute—with respect to art. We choose one product over another, one garment over another, one way to walk from place to place, basing our decisions largely on the visual impact of the preferred option. We choose to study and enjoy particular works of art or to ignore them. We choose to plan encounters with art, as in museums and galleries, or not to do so.

Whatever our degree of involvement with art, we must remember that it *is* a choice. We can go through life like sleepwalkers, ignoring or taking for granted the art around us. Or we can enrich our lives by developing a more active appreciation of the art we live with. This book is about the appreciation of art, which means a combination of understanding and enjoyment. It is possible to heighten our appreciation of art, to learn to see, to take an active interest in the visual world. When we do so, we are only following a basic *aesthetic impulse*—an urge to respond to that which we find beautiful.

THE IMPULSE FOR ART

A few paragraphs ago we said that art is inextricably connected to human existence. Before going on, it might be well to challenge this statement. Is it true? Do we really need art in the same way that, for instance, we need language? In fact, why is there art? Are such things as paintings and sculptures necessary to human life? The history of civilization suggests that we do need art, that it is basic to human expression. This seems equally true for those who make art and those who simply admire it. Let us begin with the artists.

The five illustrations in this section were made either in places where we would not expect to find art or by people whom we would not expect to be making art—in some cases, both. In fact, all were made by people who we might suppose would pay little or no *attention* to art, having far more urgent matters of day-to-day physical survival on their minds. Yet they did make art, and found in this aesthetic expression a way to ensure survival of the spirit.

The earliest people made art, whether they called it that or not. Deep inside certain caves in the mountainous region that is now southern France and northern Spain can be found the oldest paintings known to exist. The illustration **(2)** shows two prancing horses, a detail of the wall paintings in a cave at Lascaux, in France. So lively and vivid are the horses, so lifelike, so convincing in their sprightly gait, that we might think they were painted by a modern artist, but in fact they are some 15,000 years old.

Archaeologists still argue about why these paintings were made. They cannot have been purely decorative; they were not the "living-room art" of their time, for the painted walls are far under the earth, in areas not suitable

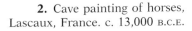

2. Cave painting of horses, Lascaux, France. c. 13,000 B.C.E.

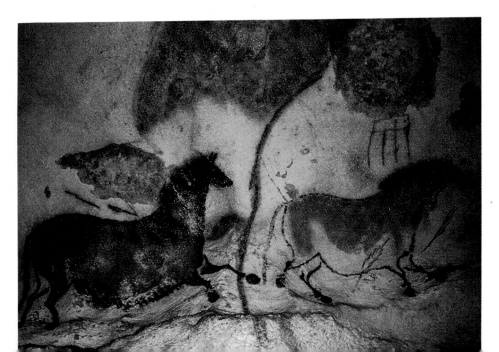

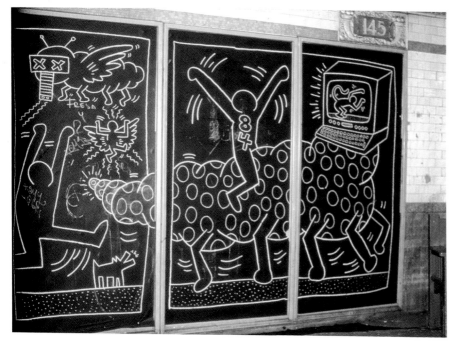

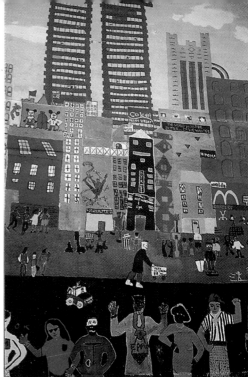

for habitation. Most experts agree the paintings had a magical function—possibly to predict success in the hunt, possibly to forge a bond of some kind with the creatures upon which life depended.

Another underground wall—this one modern and still traveled by—provided a surface for Keith Haring, who began his career in 1981 as a subway graffiti artist. Long before his name was known, Haring's bold outline drawings on blank poster space in the New York subways attracted wide attention **(3)**. The drawings are simple, like cartoons, and they feature instantly recognizable images—a barking dog, a spaceship, a television set, outline people and babies. Short, choppy lines radiating from the figures—a Haring trademark—suggest energy, happiness, exuberance. When Haring's work progressed, he was represented by major New York galleries and appeared in important exhibitions. Still he continued to draw in the same forceful linear style, right up to the time of his death from AIDS in 1990. As a writer for *The New Yorker* put it, "You had to be a chronic sorehead to deny the appeal of this nerdy-looking kid from Kutztown, Pennsylvania, with his round glasses and lantern jaw, his phenomenal energy, and his absurdly joyous ambition to communicate with millions of people who didn't care two beans about art."[1]

Yet another wall provided a surface for people who, perhaps, come most readily and naturally to art: that is, children. Our illustration shows a group effort, a work by many children joining forces to make art. In 1989 seventy-five children collaborated to paint the mural *Calle de Sueños (Dream Street)* on a blank Post Office wall in the East Harlem section of New York City **(4)**. The children ranged in age from five to fifteen, and most of them were homeless, living in city shelters or welfare hotels. Their mural project was supported by New York artist Brookie Maxwell, who had founded the Creative Arts Workshop for Homeless Children.

The children were as free with their colors and forms as with their dreams. A magical Oz-like urban landscape fills the mural, its buildings cheerfully topsy-turvy, its sunny colors as far as possible from the drab surroundings of the real inner city. And what were their dreams for the Calle de Sueños? The dreams of these children were straightforward: McDonald's; unlimited skateboards; free apartments, some meant only for children; no bedtime; no drug dealers; everyone friendly and happy; and, most poignant for these young artists, "Daddy Home." The children cannot create the world they dream of in real life, but they readily embrace the impulse to create that world in art.

left: **3.** Keith Haring.
Subway Drawing. 1983.
Chalk on black paper.
© 1998 The Estate of Keith Haring.

right: **4.** *Calle de Sueños
(Dream Street).* 1989.
Mural, mixed media; $100 \times 50'$.
East 124th Street,
East Harlem, New York.
Project of the Creative
Arts Workshop in affiliation
with Sheltering Arms
Childrens Services 1989.

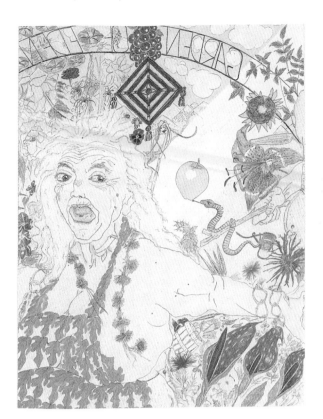

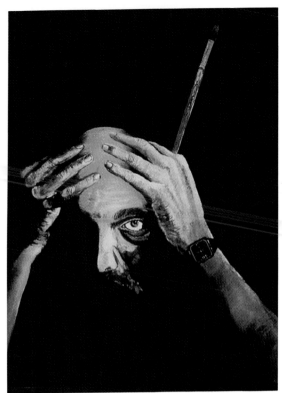

left: 5. Elizabeth Layton. *Garden of Eden.* 1977. Crayon and colored pencil, 28 × 22″. Lawrence Art Center, Lawrence, Kan.

right: 6. Anthony Papa. *15 Years to Life.* 1988. Acrylic, 24 × 18″. Courtesy the artist.

The next two artists took up painting quite consciously as a means of saving their own sanity. Elizabeth Layton found herself, at age sixty-eight, in a state of deep depression and realized she had been severely depressed for more than thirty years. Doctors labeled her condition manic-depressive disorder. She began drawing and painting, she said, because "It was either art, or something more drastic."[2] In powerful works like *Garden of Eden* **(5)** she portrayed her terrified self fleeing a paradise that was for her no refuge. After ten months of work Layton made a startling discovery: She was no longer depressed. Therapists confirmed her belief that the restorative energy of art had "cured" a long-term clinical illness.

Anthony Papa is an inmate at Sing Sing Correctional Facility, a maximum-security prison in New York. He is serving a fifteen-years-to-life sentence for possessing $4\frac{1}{2}$ ounces of cocaine, his first offense. Soon after his arrival at Sing Sing, Papa began to paint, using the very restricted materials allowed him. No oil paints are permitted, so he works in watercolors and acrylics, cleaning his brushes in his cell's toilet bowl. Papa says, "Art has actually saved my life, helped me maintain my humanity." Images like *15 Years to Life* **(6)** have been exhibited outside the prison, notably at an important New York museum. And what are the artist's goals? Apparently, the wall so prominent in this discussion calls to him also. "When I get out of here," Papa says, "my great dream is to paint a huge mural in huge epic proportions."[3]*

So we have seen a remarkably mixed bag of people—prehistoric cave dwellers, a young man doomed to premature death, a group of inner-city children, an older woman suffering profound depression, a convicted felon—all artists, all having elected to follow the aesthetic impulse by *making* art. For whatever reasons—talent or interest or luck—they chose to live with art, actively and deliberately, every day of their lives.

But suppose one does *not* choose to make art. Many people don't, yet they still can participate in the aesthetic impulse. Nonartists can receive and enjoy the gifts that artists give. They, too, can learn to live with art actively and consciously. Any gift is double-sided, valuable to both the giver and the receiver. In the case of art, the giver is the artist, the one who makes art. The receiver is the observer, the one who appreciates art. The balance of this chapter will explore the two roles: artist and observer.

---

*After Papa's art attracted wide attention, the governor of New York granted him clemency. He was released from prison in January 1997.

THE ROLE OF THE ARTIST

WHAT DO ARTISTS DO?

Throughout history artists have filled many different roles, but their value and importance to society have stayed basically the same. To begin with, artists fulfill a practical function, designing virtually every structure and object in the environment. Today this practical role is carried out by artists with specialized training—industrial designers, architects, and fashion designers, among others. But what about the painters and sculptors and photographers? What needs do they meet in our computer age? We can identify at least four basic functions for the artist, all of them age-old, all expanding in complexity.

First, artists *record*. They give us visual images that can be preserved for historical reference. This idea is so obvious that we take it for granted, forgetting how overwhelming our ignorance otherwise would be. Were it not for artists, we would have no idea what people from the past looked like.

Horace Pippin's 1942 painting called *John Brown Going to His Hanging* **(7)** records an event that the artist himself had not witnessed, but which had been described to him in minute detail. During the 1850s the United States was politically and emotionally divided by the conflict between advocates of black slavery and those who deplored the practice of slavery, called abolitionists. Among the most fervent of the abolitionists was a white man named John Brown, whose (sometimes violent) activities in support of freeing the slaves caused him to be arrested and tried for treason in the state of Virginia. Brown was convicted and was hanged on December 2, 1859. The artist Horace Pippin, a descendant of black slaves, was not yet born, but his grandmother was present at the hanging of John Brown, and she pictured the scene, in words, many times. Her grandson later transformed the word-picture into this painting.

We see John Brown at center, silhouetted against the white jailhouse in the background. His arms are bound to his sides, and he is seated on what will be his own coffin. All the occupants of the wagon are dressed in black, but the wagon is drawn by two white horses—surely symbolic of the black-white drama that is being enacted. Directly over Brown's head is a bare tree limb—again, surely symbolic of the tree from which he will soon be hanged. Most of the onlookers are white. They stare at the procession with a kind of morbid fascination, and some chat amiably among themselves. A lone black woman, at far right, turns her back on the scene and stares out fiercely, her arms crossed in anger and accusation. This figure is the artist's grandmother.

7. Horace Pippin.
John Brown Going to His Hanging.
1942. Oil on canvas, $24\frac{1}{8} \times 30\frac{1}{4}''$.
The Pennsylvania Academy
of Fine Arts, Philadelphia
(John Lambert Fund).

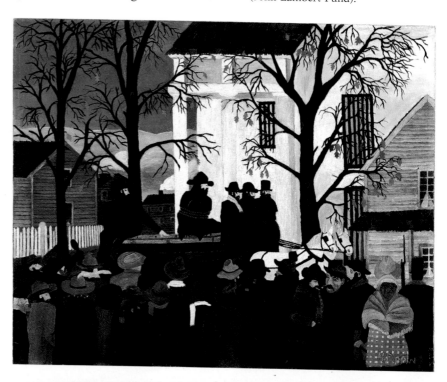

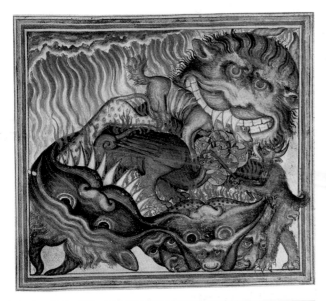

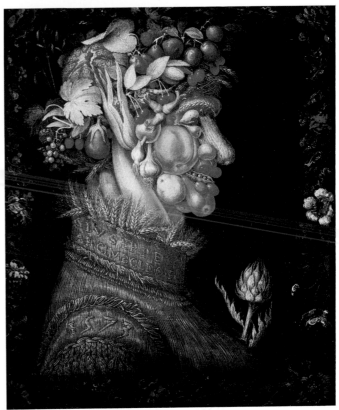

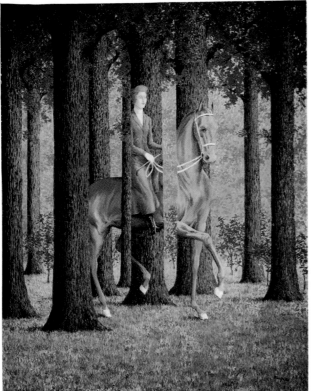

above left: 8. *The Dragon
and the Beasts Cast Into Hell,*
from the *Cloisters Apocalypse* (fol. 35r). c. 1320.
Manuscript illumination: color, gold, silver,
and brown ink on vellum, 12⅛ × 9″.
The Metropolitan Museum of Art, New York
(The Cloisters Collection, 1968).

left: 9. René Magritte.
The Blank Cheque (Le blanc-seing). 1965.
Oil on canvas, 31⅞ × 25¼″.
National Gallery of Art, Washington, D.C.

above: 10. Giuseppe Arcimboldo.
Summer. 1563. Oil on canvas.
Kunsthistorisches Museum, Vienna.

The second thing artists do is *give tangible form to the unknown*. In other words, they attempt to record what cannot be seen with the eyes or what has not yet occurred. This role has been important throughout the history of art. In the early 14th century a painter set out to portray the end of the world, as foretold in the biblical Book of Revelation (Apocalypse). One scene shows the dragon and the beasts being cast into hell, which has a "lake of fire burning with brimstone" **(8)**. For those who fear a final judgment, this vision of evil being consumed by flames would surely bring comfort.

Third, artists *give tangible form to feelings*. These may be the artist's own feelings that are expressed in paint or marble or whatever the medium. But surely they are feelings shared by many people—love, hate, despair, fear, exhilaration, anger. When we pay attention to the emotions a work of art evokes, we are communicating with the artist and with others who have such feelings.

Fourth, artists *offer an innovative way of seeing*, a unique visual "take" on the world. At a glance René Magritte's *The Blank Cheque* **(9)** seems a straightforward picture of a woman riding a horse through the forest. A closer look reveals the sort of bizarre visual disruption in which Magritte delighted. Parts of the figures are hidden by trees, but other parts are hidden by the *space* between trees! The horse's left rear leg comes and goes, defying all natural laws. This is truly an innovative way of seeing forms in space.

To sum up, then, artists perform at least four important functions: they record, they visualize the unknown, they portray feelings, and they stretch one's ability to see. All these functions have to do with communication. Artists are able to fill these roles because they *create* new visual images. The words *creative* and *creativity* will come up often in this book, so it might be well to consider what they really mean.

CREATIVITY

Who is creative? Are artists more creative than other people? If so, how did they get that way? What is creativity? Does everyone start out having it, and do some people then lose it? Is there any way to get it if you don't have it? Can a person become more creative? Less creative? These are fascinating questions to which, unfortunately, there are no definite answers. We can perhaps gain some insight, but nobody will ever write the rules of creativity.

The illustration shows a work by the 16th-century Italian artist Giuseppe Arcimboldo, entitled *Summer* **(10)**. It is a kind of portrait head, made entirely from ripe fruits. Arcimboldo did not limit himself to this fruit-head. Other images from his series (not shown here) included heads formed of vegetables and of sea creatures—fish and shellfish. Clearly, Arcimboldo had a rather bizarre turn of mind. He was preoccupied with the concept of *metamorphosis*— of things changing into other things. Given the oddness of his vision, we cannot help but admire the creative leap that made him first imagine, and then render, a head composed of such diverse natural produce. Nearly every one of us has selected fruit at the market, and sometimes the displays of fruit, with their different colors and textures, are quite attractive. It takes a creative master, however, to visualize these forms in combination, to transform *flora* into *fauna*, to make a human head out of a basic food group.

The last example in this section is a painting by André Derain, called *The Turning Road, l'Estaque* **(11)**. In every respect but one this seems a fairly straightforward landscape. The one exception, needless to say, is the color. Trees and grass in our world are not blood red, nor are people. Clouds and

11. André Derain.
The Turning Road, l'Estaque.
1906. Oil on canvas,
4'3" × 6'4¾".
The Museum of Fine Arts, Houston
(The John A. and
Audrey Jones Beck Collection).

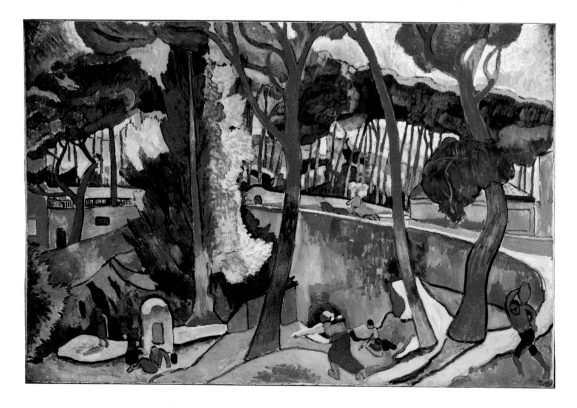

shadows are not vivid purple. Roads seldom are bright yellow (unless they are in Oz). Derain, a member of the Fauve group in France at the early part of this century (Chapter 19), painted in *arbitrary* colors, or colors unrelated to the natural world. He chose to depict nature not as we see it through the window but as he wanted to see it in his painting. Such disregard of natural colors requires a creative twist that was shocking to art viewers of Derain's time.

These two works—the Arcimboldo and the Derain—have certain characteristics in common. Both involved the making of something that had not been before. Both resulted from the artists' suspending judgments about what should be or actually is, in favor of what might be. Both developed as they did because of certain personal preoccupations: for Arcimboldo, the question of metamorphosis; for Derain, color as pure color. Taken together, these characteristics give us clues about the nature of creativity.

The literature on creativity is plentiful. Many writers and educators have tried to analyze creativity and determine what makes a person creative.[4] While the exact nature of creativity remains elusive, there is general agreement that creative people tend to possess certain traits, including:

- *Sensitivity*—heightened awareness of what one sees, hears, and touches, as well as responsiveness to other people and their feelings.
- *Flexibility*—an ability to adapt to new situations and to see their possibilities; willingness to find innovative relationships.
- *Originality*—uncommon responses to situations and to solving problems.
- *Playfulness*—a sense of humor and ability to experiment freely.
- *Productivity*—the ability to generate ideas easily and frequently, and to follow through on those ideas.
- *Fluency*—a readiness to allow the free flow of ideas.
- *Analytical skill*—a talent for exploring problems, taking them apart, and finding out how things work.
- *Organizational skill*—ability to put things back together in a coherent order.

Are artists more creative than other people? Maybe, maybe not. The profession of artist is not the only one that requires creativity. Scientists, mathematicians, writers, teachers, business executives, doctors, lawyers, librarians, computer programmers—people in every line of work, if they are any good, look for ways to be creative. The football coach who invents a new play is being creative, as is the plumber who devises an innovative way to keep the washing machine from leaking. Artists occupy a special place in that they have devoted their lives to opening the channels of *visual* creativity.

Can a person become more creative? Almost certainly, if one allows oneself to be. Being creative, as we said, means making something new. It means learning to trust one's own interests, experiences, and references, and to use them to enhance life and work. Above all, it means discarding rigid notions of what has been or should be in favor of what *could* be. For both the artist and the observer, creativity develops when the eyes and the mind are wide open.

THE ROLE
OF THE OBSERVER

There is a difference between being merely an observer and being an intelligent, *informed* observer. Observers walk through the world letting their eyes record art while their brains are occupied elsewhere. Informed observers, by contrast, have spent the time and energy needed to educate themselves so that their exposure to art will be meaningful.

How, then, do observers of art proceed to educate themselves? As with most areas of life, the more one puts into it, the more one will get out of it.

There are two specific things that can enhance your appreciation of art: exposure and study. Exposure means looking at art, as much as possible, and really seeing it—that is, heightening your perceptions of art. Perception is a complicated process, and if we do not understand its intricacies, a lot of our visual world can slip past us.

PERCEPTION

Our appreciation of art is linked to our individual *patterns of perception*—the ways in which we experience the world around us. Most art depends primarily on visual perception, the process by which our minds interpret the information we collect with our eyes.

In visual perception our eyes take in information in the form of light patterns. Through a complex interaction, the brain processes these visual images to give them meaning. The mechanics of perception work much the same way for everyone, yet in a given situation we do not all see the same things. The human eye cannot take in all available visual information. Our world is too complex, and we are constantly bombarded with an incredible range of visual images. To avoid overloading our mental circuits, the brain responds only to that visual information required to meet our needs at one moment.

Suppose you are motoring along a busy street. Your eyes "see" everything, but what does your brain register? If you are the car's driver, you will see the traffic signs and lights, because awareness of such details is necessary. If you are hungry, your attention may be attracted by fast-food signs. If you are looking for a specific address, you will focus on building numbers and block out nearly everything else. It is easier to cope with our complex visual world if we simplify our perceptions and see according to our immediate needs.

Studies indicate that the brain is often more important than the eyes in determining what each of us sees as we move through the world. The brain's ability to control perception is obvious when we study ambiguous figures, such as the classic one reproduced here **(12)**. When you first look at this drawing, you may see a young woman turning away from you so that only her cheek line, the top of her nose, and her eyelashes are visible. Or you may see a toothless old woman with a large, warty nose, whose chin is buried in a dark collar. For you to be able to see both images, your brain must reorganize the lines in the drawing.

Even after you have been made aware of the two images, you must consciously work at going back and forth between them. You can feel your brain shifting as it organizes the visual information into first one image and then the other. The important thing to remember as you shift your perception back and forth between the young woman and the old is that the visual image *always stays the same*. It is only your perception that changes.

While perception can cause us to miss seeing what is actually present in the visual field, it can also do the reverse: cause us to "see" what is *not* present. In the illustration of wavy forms **(13)** you may see a perfect white circle, but there is no circle. There is only the illusion of a white circle created by breaks in the wavy forms. (If you doubt this, cover up any two adjacent forms and look at the space between them.) This is just another trick our brains play on us as part of the phenomenon of perception. The brain supplies information to create a kind of order it requires, even though that information may not be recorded by the eyes.

Some understanding of perception is extremely helpful to the appreciation of art. When you look at a painting, for example, at least three factors always are operating: the actual, physical substance of the painting; the artist's intention in making the painting; and your own perception of the painting. Each person who looks at that same painting will bring a different perception, so you can see how complex is the communication we call art. To get an idea of how this works, let us study one well-known painting.

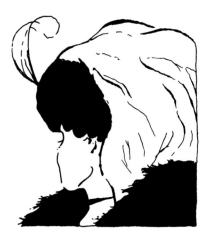

above: **12.** E. G. Boring's ambiguous figure.

below: **13.** The Circle That Isn't There.

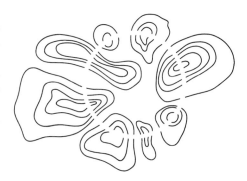

When you look at the image at lower left **(14)**, you will see a layer of paint on canvas, the individual strokes of a brush. This is what you would see if you stood very close to the painting and focused on one area—globs of inert pigment attached to a canvas backing.

Now pull back farther and consider the whole painting **(15)**. You see a brilliantly colored landscape with a tree, a village, a church, and a turbulent sky. This is Vincent van Gogh's masterpiece, called *The Starry Night*. If we limit ourselves to absolute scientific observation, no night sky ever looked like this. Stars do not race about in frenzied whirlpools. What was Van Gogh's perception of the scene that caused him to paint it this way? We know that he was a tormented, intense, and mystical man. Some of the torment, and a kind of ecstasy, are built into the painting.

And what is the viewer's perception? That depends, to a large extent, on the individual's perceptual habits and biases and on past experience. The cosmologist might think *The Starry Night* alludes magnificently to the formation of the universe. A Londoner who experienced the German blitz in World War II might see a bombing raid. Someone who has been in a fever or taken drugs might see a hallucinatory vision. A person with a certain visual disorder might think this is the way a sky always looks. And the individual who views nature in a scientific way might think that Van Gogh was crazy.

The message Van Gogh (or any other artist) sends cannot be precisely the message you receive. Van Gogh brought to his work a whole set of experiences and emotions; no one else can duplicate them exactly. However, if you open yourself to looking at the art, to receiving whatever message it may have for you, then a communication exists. Communication, as we all know, is a two-way process. Two people cannot hold a conversation if one is doing all the talking and the other is sitting there dumbly. Van Gogh poured a lot of himself into *The Starry Night*. If you want to understand and enjoy—to appreciate—his art, then you also must bring something to the experience. This is where *study* comes in.

left: **14.** Vincent van Gogh. *The Starry Night* (detail).

right: **15.** Vincent van Gogh. *The Starry Night*. 1889. Oil on canvas, 29 × 36¼″. The Museum of Modern Art, New York (acquired through the Lillie P. Bliss Bequest).

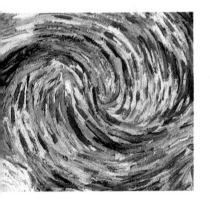

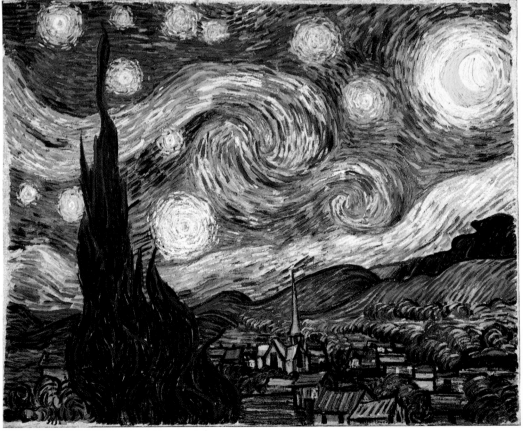

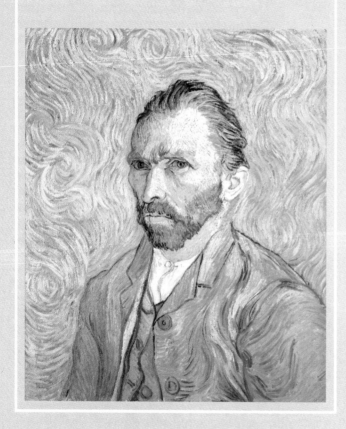

VINCENT van GOGH

1853–1890

THE APPEAL OF Van Gogh for today's art lovers is easy to understand. A painfully disturbed, tormented man who, in spite of his great anguish, managed to create extraordinary art. An intensely private, introspective man who wrote eloquently about art and about life. An erratic, impulsive man who had the self-discipline to construct an enormous body of work in a career that lasted only a decade.

Vincent van Gogh was born in the town of Groot-Zundert, in Holland, the son of a Dutch Protestant minister. His early life was spent in various roles, including those of theological student and lay preacher among the miners of the region. Not until the age of twenty-seven did he begin to take a serious interest in art, and then he had but ten years to live. In 1886 he went to stay in Paris with his brother Theo, an art dealer who was always his closest emotional connection. In Paris Vincent became aware of the new art movements and incorporated aspects of them into his own style, especially by introducing light, brilliant colors into his palette.

Two years later Van Gogh left Paris for the southern provincial city of Arles. There he was joined briefly by the painter Paul Gauguin, with whom Van Gogh hoped to work very closely, creating perfect art in a pure atmosphere of self-expression. However, the two artists quarreled, and, apparently in the aftermath of one intense argument, Van Gogh cut off a portion of his ear and had it delivered to a prostitute.

Soon after that bizarre incident, Van Gogh realized that his instability had gotten out of hand, and he committed himself to an asylum, where—true to form—he continued to work prolifically at his painting. Most of the work we admire so much was done in the last two and a half years. Vincent (as he always signed himself) received much sympathetic encouragement during those years, both from his brother and from an unusually perceptive doctor and art connoisseur, Dr. Gachet, whom he painted several times. Nevertheless, his despair deepened, and in July of 1890 he shot himself to death.

Vincent's letters to his brother Theo represent a unique document in the history of art. They reveal a sensitive, intelligent artist pouring out his thoughts to one especially capable of understanding. In 1883, while still in Holland, he wrote to Theo: "In my opinion, I am often *rich as Croesus*, not in money, but (though it doesn't happen every day) rich, because I have found in my work something to which I can devote myself heart and soul, and which gives inspiration and significance to life. Of course my moods vary, but there is an average of serenity. I have a sure *faith* in art, a sure confidence that it is a powerful stream, which bears a man to harbour, though he himself must do his bit too; and at all events I think it such a great blessing, when a man has found his work, that I cannot count myself among the unfortunate. I mean, I may be in certain relatively great difficulties, and there may be gloomy days in my life, but I shouldn't want to be counted among the unfortunate nor would it be correct."[5]

Vincent van Gogh. *Self-Portrait*. 1889.
Oil on canvas, 25½ × 21½".
Musée d'Orsay, Paris.

GERTRUDE STEIN

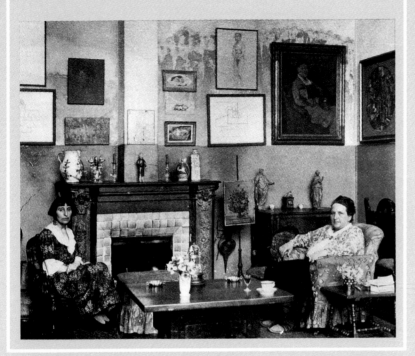

buying innovative art. Their special pets were Pablo Picasso, Henri Matisse, and the Spanish artist Juan Gris, but they also invested in works by Cézanne, Renoir, and others. Perhaps more important, their home soon became a gathering place for the artists and art lovers of the time. Everybody who was anybody came to 27, rue de Fleurus. The Saturday night "at-homes" brought out painters, sculptors, composers, writers, poets, dealers, critics, and all those who wished to meet the foregoing. Picasso and Matisse often came to dine. In later years Gertrude Stein welcomed the American writers Ernest Hemingway and F. Scott Fitzgerald.

Among those who came to the rue de Fleurus was an American named Alice B. Toklas, and, as it turned out, she had come to stay. By 1910 Alice Toklas had moved into the apartment, serving Gertrude Stein as secretary, household manager, and all-purpose useful helpmeet. The two women became inseparable and remained lifelong companions. Some four years later Leo Stein moved out of rue de Fleurus, taking half the art collection with him. The close relationship between brother and sister was over for good.

World War I brought new adventures to Gertrude Stein. France went to war, and so did Stein and Toklas. In a ragtag Ford van nicknamed "Auntie," they traveled all over the countryside delivering supplies in behalf of the American Fund for French Wounded. Stein drove the car. Toklas navigated and handled all necessary paperwork. After the war, most of the women's efforts were directed toward getting Gertrude Stein's writings published—no easy feat, considering their individual and often maddeningly repetitive style. Actually, Stein's only commercial literary success was *The Autobiography of Alice B. Toklas*, which was in fact Gertrude Stein's own autobiography.

When Gertrude Stein died of cancer in 1946, she left her art collection to Alice Toklas, who lived on, with the paintings and her memories, until 1967. The two women are buried together in Paris. After Miss Toklas' death, the Stein family regained control of the collection and sold it for many millions of dollars.

P RACTICALLY NO ONE ever has lived with art so whole-heartedly as Gertrude Stein. Students of literature remember her as a daringly experimental writer, most closely associated with the line: "Rose is a rose is a rose is a rose." But the influence of Gertrude Stein extends far beyond her literary efforts, for she was one of the most ardent collectors of art—and of artists—who ever lived.

Born in Allegheny, Pennsylvania, in 1874, Stein spent her childhood in Europe and in San Francisco. Both parents died when she was a teenager, and thereafter her intimate family would consist of her brother Leo, her oldest brother Michael, and Michael's wife, Sarah—all soon to be art collectors of great importance. Young Gertrude attended Radcliffe and then undertook medical studies at Johns Hopkins, but she never quite finished her medical degree.

In 1903 Gertrude took up residence with Leo at his new apartment in Paris. Their address—27, rue de Fleurus—was destined to become famous in the history of arts and letters. From their combined home and studio, Gertrude and Leo embarked on a fabulous career of

Gertrude Stein **(right)** with Alice B. Toklas in the studio at 27, rue de Fleurus, Paris, 1922, photographed by Man Ray.

STUDYING ART

Art requires intellectual as well as sensory involvement. Your appreciation of art can be greatly improved by knowing how a work of art was made, why it was made, what went before and came after.

The understanding of process—the *how*—often contributes quite a lot to our appreciation of art. Parts Three and Four of this book are largely concerned with this issue. If you understand why painting in watercolor may be different from painting in oil, why clay responds differently to the artist's hands than does wood or glass, why a stone building has different structural needs than one made of poured concrete—you will have a richer appreciation of the artist's expression.

An artist may create a specific work for any of a thousand reasons, and awareness of the *why* can also give the viewer greater understanding. At first glance our next example, a work by the Norwegian artist Edvard Munch **(16)**, registers on the viewer as an image of sorrow. The figures are flat, stark, drawn in truly harsh, acidic colors, each seeming to be a little island of misery. Closer inspection reveals a bed in the background, and we read the title: *Death in the Sickroom*. We know now that someone has died, and the survivors, presumably the family, are frozen in the shock of grief. These facts are available to us from the image and the title, but knowledge about the artist tells us more. Munch suffered two tragedies early in his life—first the death of his mother when he was just five, then the death of his dearly loved older sister nine years later. Both mother and sister died of tuberculosis. *Death in the Sickroom* is a recollection of his sister's death. Munch created this chilling image some twenty years later. If we know about the artist, know that he was haunted by the shadow of death throughout his life, then *Death in the Sickroom* becomes all the more moving.

The historical place of a work of art—*what went before and came after*—can be most interesting. Artists borrow and learn from each other all the time. The myth of the lonely artist—starving in a garret, isolated from human contact, leaving behind a mass of brilliant work that no one had suspected—is mostly that, a myth. There have been a few such cases, but not many. On the whole, artists study each other's work carefully, adapt ideas to serve their own needs, and then bequeath those ideas to future generations of artists. The more you know about this living current of artistic energy, the more interesting will be any specific work of art.

The works illustrated next **(17,18)** have two things in common. Each is a picture of an elegant woman, and each is a *print*—a work designed for multiple reproduction (Chapter 8). But far more than that connects them to the artistic chain letter of seeing, passing along, and adapting.

16. Edvard Munch.
Death in the Sickroom. 1893.
Oil on canvas, 4′5″ × 5′3″.
Munch Museum, Oslo.

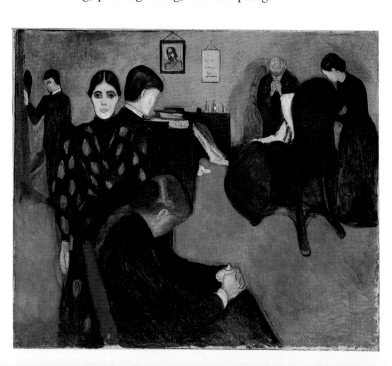

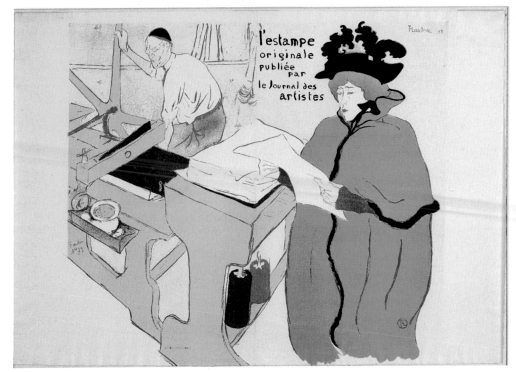

right: 17.
Henri de Toulouse-Lautrec.
L'Estampe originale, cover. 1893.
Color lithograph, $17\frac{3}{4} \times 23\frac{3}{4}''$.
The Metropolitan Museum of Art,
New York (Rogers Fund, 1922).

below: 18.
Ippitsusai Buncho.
The Actor Handayu in a Female Role.
Woodcut, $12\frac{3}{4} \times 6\frac{1}{8}''$.
The Metropolitan Museum
of Art, New York
(The Henry L. Phillips Collection,
bequest of Henry L. Phillips, 1940).

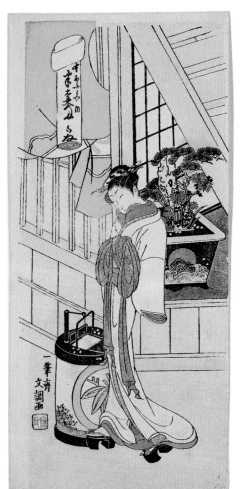

The first print **(17)** is by the French artist Henri de Toulouse-Lautrec. Lautrec was an unexcelled master of the color poster for advertising. The illustration shown here is essentially a print about a print. It shows the entertainer Jane Avril, a close friend of the artist's, examining a freshly printed proof of a poster advertising her performance at the Moulin Rouge nightclub in Paris. This print reveals Lautrec's debt to Japanese art.

In 1853 Commodore Matthew Perry, an American naval officer, had sailed with his fleet into Tokyo Bay and thereby "opened" Japan to the West, ending two centuries of that country's isolation from the rest of the world. Soon afterward, Japanese prints began to flow into Europe, and artists studied them avidly. Lautrec, like many of his colleagues at the time, took from the Japanese images the ideas that were most useful for his own vision. These ideas are evident in a print by Ippitsusai Buncho, created more than a hundred years earlier **(18)**.

Three compositional elements in particular were adapted by Lautrec from Japanese prints like Buncho's. One is the graceful, flowing silhouette line around the figure. Another is the flatness of the figure itself, especially noticeable in the flat color areas of Jane Avril's cloak and the sleeve of the Japanese kimono. And the third is the sharply diagonal composition, here tilting from lower right to upper left **[Overlay 1A].** This last feature became crucial to many artists of Lautrec's generation and was borrowed and explored further by generations of artists who followed them.

As an observer, you will find that familiarity with such artistic currents contributes much to your appreciation of art. Combined with the "how" and the "why," it will move you closer to being an intelligent, informed observer. That is what this book is all about. *Living with Art* is meant to give you a sample of the how, the why, and the when. With this knowledge you should have a much more active enjoyment of the art you live with.

There are great observers as well as great artists. Whatever artists may say, their art is not done just for themselves. It is done for serious observers who, through education and experience, have made themselves sympathetic receivers of the messages of art.

Living with art—living with it actively and positively—does involve some effort, but the effort is worth it. Art stretches our intellectual horizons. It taps our emotions. It deepens our humanity and makes us less alone in the world.

HENRI DE TOULOUSE-LAUTREC

1864–1901

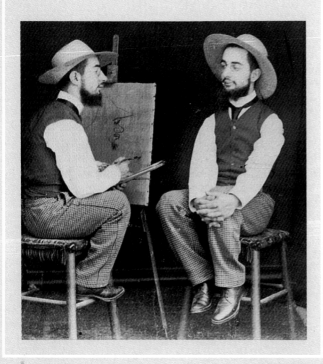

H ENRI MARIE RAYMOND DE TOULOUSE-LAUTREC MONFA was born at Albi, in the south of France, son of an aristocratic French family. From early childhood he showed talent for drawing and painting—a talent his family encouraged. The events that probably shaped the rest of his life and his career as an artist began at the age of thirteen, when he broke his left thigh in a fall. A year later he broke the other thigh. Although he recovered from the injuries, his legs never grew again. As an adult he stood just over 5 feet tall, with a fully developed body but shrunken legs, and he walked with difficulty and pain. In photographs, like the one here, he often stressed his odd appearance.

By the age of seventeen Lautrec had begun serious art studies in Paris. He had also gotten his first taste of Montmartre—the rather seedy part of the city where writers, painters, and students congregated; where the brothels were located; and where soon would open the famed cabaret, the Moulin Rouge. At that time he wrote to his grandmother, "I am against my will leading a truly Bohemian life and am finding it difficult to accustom myself to this milieu." Later, that milieu would be the only one in which he seemed to belong.

The artist gradually began to achieve modest success with his paintings. He also began to accumulate a circle of friends—other artists, writers, intellectuals, performers—who were attracted by his great wit and unflagging high spirits. In 1889 the Moulin Rouge opened and quickly became the focus of this social life, as well as of Lautrec's art. Singers and dancers, prostitutes and poets, the highborn and the lowborn who came to the Moulin Rouge—Lautrec drew them all, with a style and originality that captured the essence of Paris nightlife.

After two years of popularity the Moulin Rouge fell upon hard times, and its owner decided to regroup. He hired new talent, planned a grand reopening, and asked the all-but-resident artist to create a poster announcing the event. The poster Lautrec designed was unlike any Paris had ever seen—colorful, immediate, full of life, focusing on the image, not the printed words. Once again the Moulin Rouge was a sensation, and so were the artist and his poster.

In the years following his triumph as a graphic artist, Lautrec often had no regular home. He lived for periods of time at one or another of the brothels, among the prostitutes. Some of the women were his lovers, many were his friends, and all were potential subjects, whom he painted with sympathy and warmth. His dissipated life notwithstanding, he continued to work prolifically. Little by little, however, he began to drink more and work less, until the situation became so grave his family placed him in a sanitarium. A brief recovery was followed by yet more drinking, and at last the illness took over. In September of 1901, two months short of his thirty-seventh birthday, Lautrec suffered a stroke and died at his family's estate.

Lautrec's art is above all an art of people and life. He explained this after a brief visit to the countryside, meant to improve his health: "Only the human figure exists; landscape is, and should be, no more than an accessory; the painter exclusively of landscape is nothing but a boor. The sole function of landscape is to heighten the intelligibility of the character of the figure."[6]

Maurice Guilbert. *Lautrec par lui-même*. 1890.
Photographic montage. Musée Toulouse-Lautrec, Albi, France.

What Is Art?

Until about a hundred years ago almost no one would have thought to ask the question "What is art?" People who considered art at all assumed they knew what it was. In the 20th century, however, the problem of definition, of deciding what is and is not art, became far more complex, and this is true for several reasons.

For one thing, people today are exposed to art from many different times and places—an available body of art far more varied than at any other period in history. If you walk into a large museum, you will see on display works of art that come from literally all over the world and cover a time span of some 15,000 years. Magazines, newspapers, and television also bring us into contact with different types of art. Each work of art we see is the product of its own culture, with its own prevailing standards of taste. Each represents what the person who made the work—and the audience for whom the work was intended—believed to be art.

Consider, for example, the first three illustrations in this chapter **(19,20,21)**. All three are sculptures, all are rather flat and meant to be seen from one viewpoint, and all depict human figures. The first **(19)** is a marble grave image from the Classical period of ancient Greece, the 5th century B.C.E. The second **(20)** is a brass plaque from the Benin culture that flourished in central Africa during the 16th and 17th centuries. And the third **(21)** is a work by a contemporary American sculptor associated with the Pop Art (or popular art) movement of the 1960s (Chapter 20).

Do all three of these works qualify as art? Certainly the citizen of ancient Athens wouldn't have thought so. Greek art prized perfection of the human form, an idealization of the natural body. Unfamiliar with the elegant stylizations of the Benin sculptor or the amusing satires of Pop artists, our Greek viewer would have found their creations ugly and ridiculous. Modern viewers take a more flexible approach, but even some of us are confounded by the challenge of unfamiliar art.

Before our age of easy worldwide communication, the art produced by any specific culture tended to be relatively homogeneous—much the same in style and expression. We can say, "These are the general characteristics of 5th-century B.C.E. Greek art" (or 16th–17th-century Benin art), and then proceed to list them. Now, not only are we confronted with art from many different cultures, but the art of our own time defies such classification. If you were

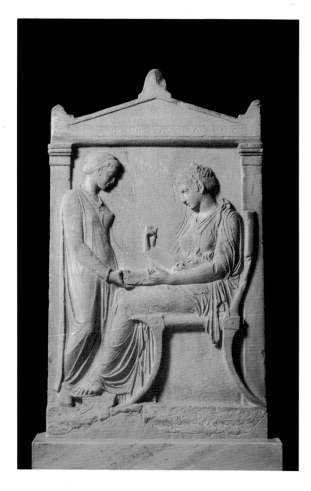

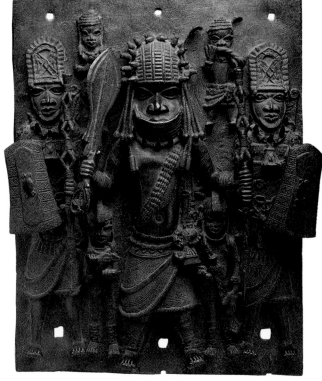

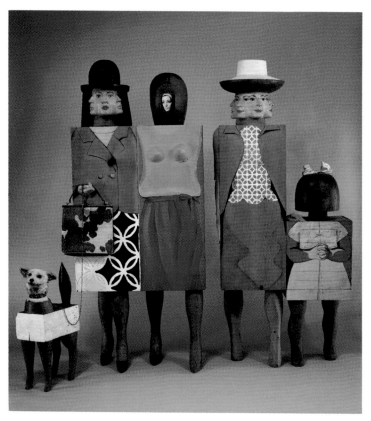

top left: 19. *Grave Stele of Hegeso.*
c. 410–400 B.C.E. Marble, height 4′11″.
National Museum, Athens.

above: 20. *Plaque: Warrior Chief, Warriors,*
and Attendants. Nigeria, Edo, Court of Benin.
16th–17th century. Brass, height 18⅞″.
The Metropolitan Museum of Art, New York
(gift of Mr. and Mrs. Klaus G. Perls, 1990).

left: 21. Marisol. *Women and Dog.*
1964. Wood, plaster, synthetic polymer,
and miscellaneous items; 6′1¼″ × 6′1″ × 2′2¹⁵⁄₁₆″.
Collection of Whitney Museum of American Art,
New York (purchase, with funds from the Friends
of the Whitney Museum of American Art).
© 1998 Marisol/Licensed by VAGA, New York.

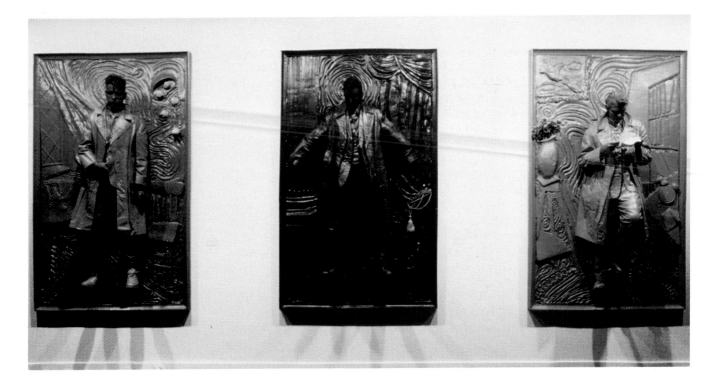

22. Stephen Taylor Woodrow. *The Living Paintings.* The artist and friends, spray-painted and hung on a simulated backdrop. Installation view at the New Museum of Contemporary Art, New York, February 1988.

to tour the art galleries in any major city today and look at all the different works on display, you would be hard-pressed to formulate a definition of art suitable for all of them.

How, for instance, does one categorize a work that consists of the artist and two friends spray-painted and hung (literally hung, by hooks and harnesses) on a "canvas" of simulated drapery **(22)**? Even sophisticated art lovers may be a little perplexed when confronted by a sculpture that climbs down off the wall at night and goes home to dinner.

To further complicate the problem of defining art, we now have works of art created in media undreamed of a mere thirty or forty years ago. Electronic images of all kinds are made and accepted as art. Often, there is no concrete "object," nothing you could hang on the wall or place on a pedestal. Some types of contemporary art are preserved only in the memory banks of computers, and some disappear forever within minutes or hours after they are made. Little wonder, then, that in our era, for the first time, we need to stand back and ask, "What exactly *is* art? How can we tell what is and what isn't?"

This book will not give the definitive answer to either question, about any particular work or about art in general. What it will do, however, is present some guidelines that will help individual viewers make up their minds. It will show what some people have considered to be art in different times and places and what some people consider to be art now. With this information, the viewer should be able to make a better judgment about "What is art *for me?*"

ART AND THE EYE OF THE BEHOLDER

There are any number of tests we could apply to the question "What is art?" None of them is infallible, but all raise interesting issues about the nature of art and the value systems that determine artistic quality. This section explores four of the possible areas we might study in evaluating a particular work: Who made it? Is it beautiful? Does it look natural? What does it say?

ART AND THE ARTIST

Some artists' names are familiar to the public at large. Picasso. Michelangelo. Rembrandt. Leonardo da Vinci. Van Gogh. Mention any one of them, and your listener's brain will probably register "great artist." It follows, therefore, that any work made by one of these people must be "great art"—or, at the very least, unquestionably art. For those with a broader education or interest, the list of "genuine" artists would be much longer. Whether for good or ill, the verdict on "Is this art?" has much to do with another question: Who made it?

This point was made tellingly by a bit of excitement that occurred in New York City in 1996. In the entry foyer of a mansion on Manhattan's Fifth Avenue stands a little statue of a cupid **(23)**. The cupid has occupied that spot for about ninety years, just as thousands of similar statues repose, generally unnoticed, in thousands of buildings. One day, the story goes, an art historian who is expert in 16th-century Italian art walked by the building (or rode by on a bus; accounts vary), saw the cupid through the window, and—essentially—gasped. After extensive study and consultation with other experts, this authority declared the cupid to be a genuine work by Michelangelo!

Needless to say, the media sat up and paid attention. Overnight the little statue's image changed. Whereas previously it had been a miscellaneous bit of decoration (and party-goers had no doubt rested their cocktails and canapés and handbags on the base), now the cupid was roped off, photographed, and exclaimed over. An actual *Michelangelo*, touched by the master's hands!

Writing for *Time* magazine, and considering also a recently "discovered" elegy by Shakespeare, Paul Gray summed up the situation neatly:

> Neither the Cupid nor the elegy is intrinsically different now, in the full glare of worldwide publicity, than a few weeks ago, when both enjoyed obscurity. The only thing that has changed is the attitude we are expected to bring to these objects. What we could safely ignore or overlook before now commands our reverent attention because the names Michelangelo and Shakespeare have been attached to them.[1]

An earlier incident, which also occurred in New York, gives a more frivolous example of the same phenomenon.

In the summer of 1954 artist Willem de Kooning took the three toilet seats from an outhouse on a summer property he was renting and painted the seats in a "marbleized" effect. Apparently, the painting was meant as a joke—whipped off in a few minutes before a croquet party with friends **(24)**. The artist then forgot about it, and so did everyone else. Some thirty years later the summer house was to be sold and the contents dispersed at auction. The auctioneer sensed a good thing and arranged to have the toilet-seat painting authenticated by Elaine de Kooning, Willem de Kooning's wife. The auctioneer therefore had in his possession a certified Willem de Kooning painting, and de Kooning paintings **(541)** sell for millions of dollars. The toilet seats were exhibited and offered for sale. But wait a minute. Is a row of toilet seats, painted just for fun, a work of art because a master artist painted them? Some people think so. Others are outraged.

23. Statue of a cupid, said to be by Michelangelo.

24. Three toilet seats from an outhouse, said to have been painted by Willem de Kooning in 1954.

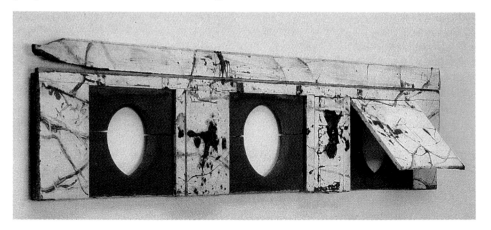

To consider the opposite extreme, is a work *not* great art because a master artist *didn't* paint it? For generations a painting called *The Polish Rider* **(25)** was thought to be a work by Rembrandt and was considered one of the jewels of the Frick Collection, a distinguished small museum in New York City. But now Rembrandt's authorship of this painting—and of numerous other paintings—is in question.

Over the years various experts have tried to determine how many genuine Rembrandts there are in the world. Estimates have ranged from a high of 614 to a low of 48. In 1982 a group of five scholars known collectively as the Rembrandt Research Project, based in the artist's home city of Amsterdam, began work trying to find a definitive answer. Using modern scientific methods, considering such subtleties as brushwork, use of colors, and handling of anatomical forms, the R.R.P. studied paintings thought to be by Rembrandt and presented its conclusions. The task is truly daunting, because judgments of quality are always subjective and unreliable. Even as great a master as Rembrandt must have had Monday mornings when he was not at his best. Nevertheless, the R.R.P. persevered, and for many museums and private collectors the news was bad. The R.R.P. "deattributed" their prized Rembrandts.

Among the deattributed paintings, there is no question of forgery or attempt to deceive. With older paintings it is simply difficult to know for sure who painted them and when. A pupil of Rembrandt's, Willem Drost, is now thought a likely candidate as artist of *The Polish Rider*. Whatever the truth, the effect of deattribution is dramatic. Another Rembrandt work, which came up for auction in 1988, was expected to bring ten million dollars. After the R.R.P. turned its thumbs down, the painting was sold for $800,000—or 8 percent of its previous value.[2]

Through all this questioning, we must remember, *the paintings remain the same.* No matter who painted *The Polish Rider*, it is a splendid, masterful picture. Yet crowds of tourists, who once would have elbowed each other to get a glimpse of it, will now pass it by, looking for the "real" Rembrandts. The student and lover of art should consider seriously how much impact the authorship of a work has to do with one's appreciation of that work.

25. Rembrandt (?). *The Polish Rider.* c. 1655. Oil on canvas, 3′10″ × 4′5⅛″. Copyright The Frick Collection, New York.

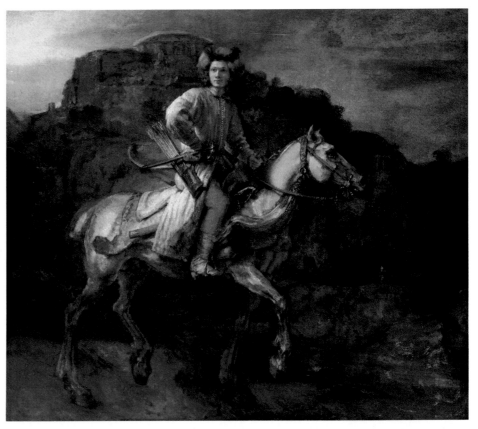

PUBLIC ART

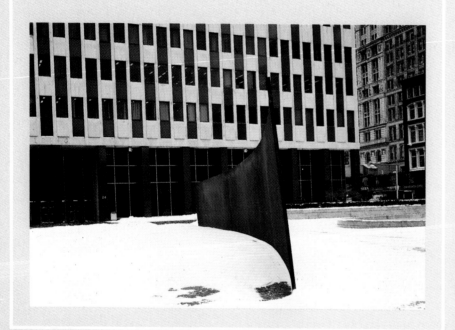

RARELY HAS THE QUESTION "What is art?" caused such a public uproar as in a controversy that erupted in New York City in the early 1980s. At the center of the drama was a monumental sculpture by Richard Serra, entitled *Tilted Arc*, a 12-foot-high, 120-foot-long steel wall installed in a plaza fronting a government building in lower Manhattan.

Commissioned by the Art-in-Architecture division of the General Services Administration, *Tilted Arc* was part of a program that allocates 0.5 percent of the cost of federal buildings to the purchase and installation of public art. Soon after the sculpture's installation, however, the public for whom it was intended spoke out, and their message was a resounding "*That's* not art!" More than 7,000 workers in surrounding buildings signed petitions demanding the sculpture's removal. Opponents of the work had numerous complaints. *Tilted Arc*, they maintained, was ugly, rusty, and a target for graffiti. It blocked the view. It disrupted pedestrian traffic, since one had to walk all the way around it rather than straight across the plaza. It ruined the plaza for concerts and outdoor ceremonies. At a public hearing, one man summed up the opposition view: "I am here today to recommend its relocation to a better site—a metal salvage yard."[3]

Artists, dealers, and critics rushed to the sculpture's defense. The sculptor himself argued vehemently against any attempt to move *Tilted Arc*, maintaining that it had been commissioned specifically for that site and any new location would destroy its artistic integrity.

The battle raged for many months, and, while there were dissenting voices from all sides, it shaped up principally as a struggle between the art establishment (pro) and the general public (con). At last, in an unusual editorial, *The New York Times*—a newspaper that heavily supports the arts—took a stand. "One cannot choose to see or ignore 'Tilted Arc,' as if it were in a museum or a less conspicuous public place. To the complaining workers in Federal Plaza, it is, quite simply, unavoidable. . . . The public has to live with 'Tilted Arc'; therefore the public has a right to say no, not here."[4]

This time the public won, and the question "What is art?" was answered by a kind of popular referendum, a majority decision. *Tilted Arc* was dismantled and removed in March of 1989.

Does this outcome mean that *Tilted Arc* is not art, or that it isn't good art? No, it does not mean either of those things. It means simply that, in this particular circumstance, the people for whom the art was intended chose to reject the art. And similar circumstances have, very likely, occurred since the earliest artists of prehistory began painting on the walls of their caves.

Richard Serra. *Tilted Arc*. 1981.
Cor-Ten steel, 12' × 120' × 2½".
Installed at Federal Plaza, New York;
Collection General Services
Administration (destroyed 1989).

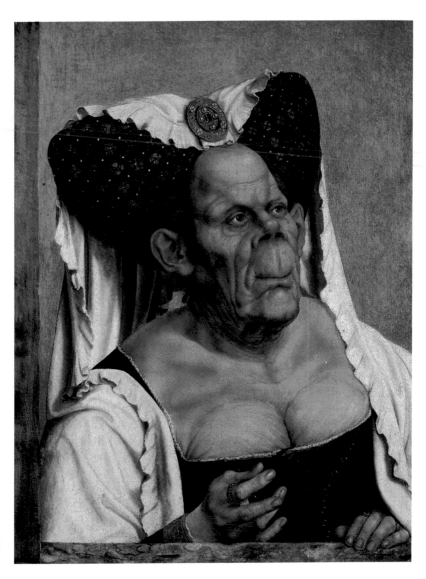

ART AND BEAUTY

Many people assume that all art should be beautiful. They think of art as something to ornament one's home. This approach may cause trouble if you visit a museum, especially an exhibit of 20th-century art. You are sure to find a few things that you consider plain ugly. Why are such objects on display?

We may as well face the question squarely, since it is basic to our whole attitude toward art. Why are there so many "ugly" works of art? There are several possible answers. We might reply that "beauty is in the eye of the beholder." In other words, beauty is subjective, and your personal taste leads you to reject things that might be beautiful to others. Both "beautiful" and "ugly" imply aesthetic value judgments.

Another possibility is that the ugly works of art are failures, which were hung because the museum director didn't look at them carefully or because the artist had a famous name. You might even imagine that you are the victim of a great plot designed to make a fool of you by showing you ugly things as if they were art. All these possibilities depend on the assumption that the artist's proper aim is the creation of beauty.

But there is another possibility. Perhaps the works are successes by artists who were sincerely aiming at something *other than* conventional beauty.

The issue of conventional beauty almost cannot help but come up when we view a painting like Quintin Massys' *Grotesque Old Woman* **(26)**. Even the title challenges our notions about art and beauty with the word "grotesque." Why would an artist paint a subject so ugly, and why would viewers want to look at it? To get an interesting perspective on this problem, we might weigh the opinions of people who live with art all day long. For a 1988 feature article in *Art & Antiques* magazine, writer Catherine Barnett interviewed the guards at several large museums—those whose job it is to protect the art. Here is what two different guards at the National Gallery in London had to say about the Massys painting.

MARGARET: Generally I prefer portraits, but I can't say anything too nice about this one, Quintin Massys's *Grotesque Old Woman*. Visitors walk by and they just say how horrible she is, and I'm inclined to agree. She must be the result of the artist's nightmarish fantasy. . . . It's a bit unnerving. When you dislike a portrait, you feel its eyes on you.

MARIE: When I'm [out] sick I miss the paintings here, especially the *Grotesque Old Woman*. She's one of my favorites and I love her very much. She's very sympathetic. She's got beautiful eyes. Have you ever noticed her eyes? And her hands are lovely. The visitors are always ridiculing her, and that hurts me.[5]

So there we have the opinions of two "experts," who see Massys' work every day. Notice that even Margaret, who doesn't like the portrait, refers to it as "she" and feels the power of the eyes. Neither of the guards is indifferent; both feel some strong connection to the painting. Whether for good or ill, the work evokes a response.

We do not mean to imply that art should *not* be beautiful in the more conventional sense. Many artists aim at creating this kind of beauty. If that is their goal, then we measure their success according to how well they achieve it. The important point for the student of art to learn from the *Grotesque Old Woman* is that art can be many different things, and "beautiful" is only one.

The observer of art should be open to the widest possible range of experience. Art that momentarily pleases the eye offers only one level of experience. Art that touches the intellect and the emotions brings far greater satisfaction.

ART AND THE "REAL" WORLD

Just as many people expect all art to be beautiful, many people expect all art to mimic the real world, to duplicate as closely as possible the appearance of nature. This is another preconception we might examine. If duplicating the natural world is the *only* thing art is supposed to do, why should artists bother? We already have the natural world, so why make another? No one expects this kind of fidelity from the other arts. If, for instance, all works of literature were restricted to a faithful duplication of the real world, there could not be any novels or poems or fairy tales. There probably never was any real Cinderella or Anna Karenina or Tom Sawyer, and if there actually was a King Arthur, we're not sure what he did in his life. The great works of literature are not real, they are made-up stories.

It has often been said that in writing fictional literature you "have to tell a lie to tell the truth." In other words, a made-up story can touch basic truths more vividly than can a strict recitation of facts. In a sense, this is what artists are doing: looking for a basic truth that is more "real" than the everyday world we perceive with our eyes.

Have you ever heard someone say, "That guy's a terrible artist. He can't even draw!" There is a strong feeling among much of the public that a "good" artist should be able to draw well—to make pictures of horses or dogs or people that look like the real thing. To be sure, some modern artists cannot draw lifelike images. But far more of them can—and choose not to. Picasso is a prime example of this situation. By anyone's standard, he was one of the

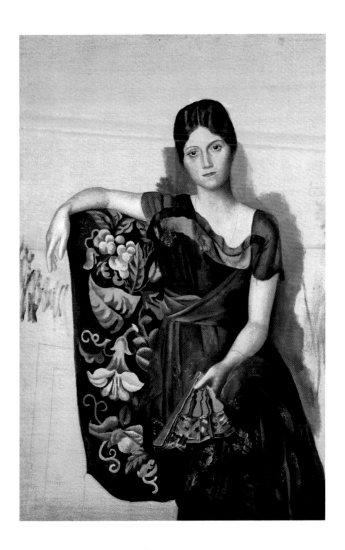

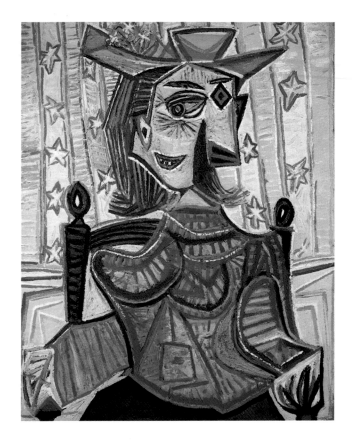

left: **27.** Pablo Picasso.
Olga Picasso in an Armchair.
1917. Oil on canvas,
4'3¼" × 2'10⅝".
Musée Picasso, Paris.

right: **28.** Pablo Picasso.
Dora Maar Sitting. 1939.
Oil on canvas, 28⅝ × 23½".
Courtesy Perls Galleries, New York.

greatest draftsmen who ever lived **(27)**. Nevertheless, through most of his long career he produced works that did not look anything like the "real" world **(28)**.

Picasso himself addressed this problem. He said: "They speak of naturalism in opposition to modern painting. I would like to know if anyone has ever seen a natural work of art. Nature and art, being two different things, cannot be the same thing. Through art we express our conception of what nature is not."[6]

In looking at any work of art, we must always keep in mind that it *is* a work of art. A painting of a horse is not a horse, but daubs of pigment on a backing. A sculpture of a horse is not a horse, but a chunk of metal or wood or stone. The way these works should look is dictated by the artist's aesthetic sense, not by biological laws. Artists are looking for the "lie that tells the truth," for something "realer than real."

Only in Western culture has it been supposed that art should always duplicate the natural world and, at that, only during certain periods of Western culture. We owe this idea to the ancient Greeks and Romans. Plato put forth the notion in *The Republic,* written in Athens in the 4th century B.C.E. He believed that the aim of painters is to create imitations of objects they see before them, as a mirror reflects the appearance of its surroundings. This prescription carried through to later periods in Western art history when Greek and Roman art were much admired—notably the Renaissance in 15th- and 16th-century Europe.

Outside the European tradition there was no similar prejudice. The great artists of Asia, of Africa, of the precolonial Americas generally had much less interest in reproducing the real world. Like so many artists today, they were seeking something "realer than real." In the 15th century the Japanese artist Sesshu painted a study of *Daruma*, the first Zen Buddhist patriarch **(29)**. We may hope this is not what Daruma really looked like. The stark brushwork and the horribly staring eyes are meant to show Daruma's ardent devotion to the Buddha. (Legend tells us that Daruma, while meditating on the Buddha one day, accidentally fell asleep. To punish himself, he cut off his eyelids so that his eyes could never again close on the Buddha.)

We might compare Sesshu's painting with a self-portrait by Picasso, done in 1901 **(30)**. There is an extraordinary resemblance—not in the features, but in the effect. We know that Picasso did not actually look just like this. He did have unusually piercing black eyes, and here he has emphasized that feature. He has also made his face gaunt and almost corpselike. Perhaps we are seeing the intensity of passion in a young man absorbed in his art, just as Daruma was absorbed in his adoration of the Buddha. Both paintings have given us a reality beyond mere illusion.

If we demand realism, therefore, we deny ourselves the pleasure of enjoying a huge portion of the world's art. We would even dismiss a type of art that nearly everyone finds appealing—so-called naive art. Naive art, as the term implies, is made by people who are unsophisticated, lacking in formal art training, direct and fresh in their approach to art. Best known of the naive artists was Henri Rousseau, whose translation into paint of the "real" world was eccentric at best.

Rousseau worked in France during the late 19th and early 20th centuries. He was acquainted with all the up-and-coming artists of the Parisian scene, and sometimes he exhibited with them. In Rousseau's case, the naiveté of his expression came not so much from ignorance of formal art tradition as from

left: 29. Sesshu. *Daruma.* Japan, Ashikaga Period, 15th century. Hanging scroll, ink on paper. Yoshinari Collection, Tokyo.

right: 30. Pablo Picasso. *Self-Portrait.* 1901. Oil on canvas, $31\frac{1}{2} \times 23\frac{5}{8}$″. Musée Picasso, Paris.

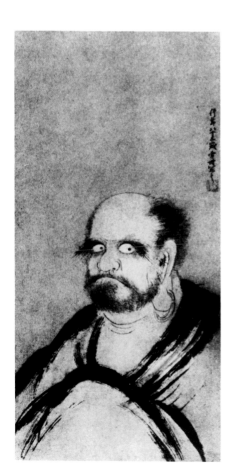

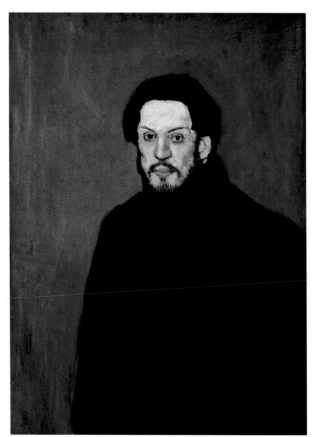

indifference to that tradition. His last work, *The Dream* **(31)**, combines typical elements: a monumental nude perched on a sofa that has no seat; improbable wild animals and birds that never coexist in nature; lush foliage no botanist ever identified; and a dark-skinned "native" (of where?) playing a musical instrument. Rousseau loved to copy plants and animals from books, to fill in from his imagination, to mix and match in a picture as the inspiration took him. He labored over the meticulous rendering of every leaf and stem, yet the rendering is not lifelike at all, for the landscape does not exist; it is a fantasy land. Rousseau's world—which was apparently very real for him—is the paint on canvas that makes a rich, complex design for the viewer's pleasure.

Before we leave this subject of art and the real world, it will be useful to discuss a few terms that will come up throughout the book. All have to do with the relationship between the artistic image and the appearance of objects in the natural world.

REPRESENTATIONAL ART Representational or *naturalistic* images in art are those that look very much like images in the natural world. Picasso's portrait of Olga **(27)** fits this category. You may encounter the term *illusionistic,* which means images so natural they trick us into thinking they are real.

An extreme of illusionism is referred to as *trompe-l'oeil,* the French term for "fool the eye." We generally use this expression when the eye is being fooled into thinking there are three dimensions in a work that is flat.

Trompe-l'oeil illusionism was out of fashion during most of the 20th century, but recently there has been a revival of interest, due largely to the work of Richard Haas. In a number of U.S. cities Haas has used his almost devilish skill to transform blank, depressing, flat walls into fantasy murals that make us question our own senses over and over again. His mural painted on the

31. Henri Rousseau. *The Dream.* 1910. Oil on canvas, 6'8½" × 9'9½". The Museum of Modern Art, New York (gift of Nelson A. Rockefeller).

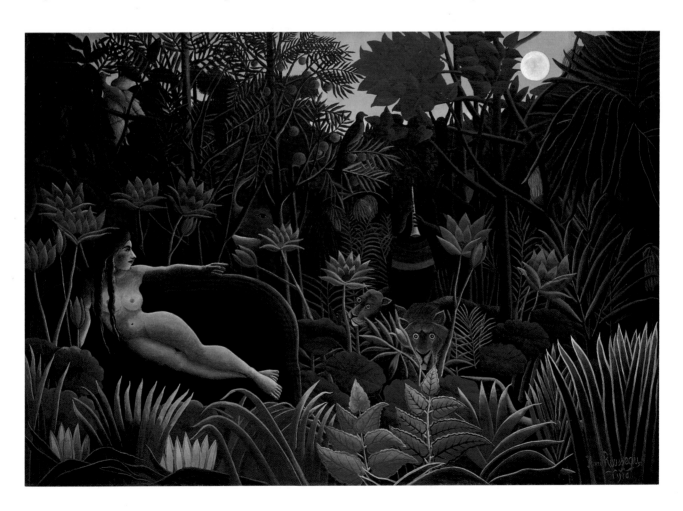

HENRI ROUSSEAU

1844–1910

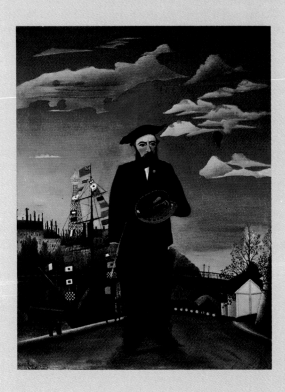

ON THE SURFACE Rousseau was a ridiculous figure. One writer has observed that in the movies he would have been played by Charlie Chaplin. Like the eccentric who thinks he is Napoleon, Rousseau was convinced he was the master painter of his time. He was forever making up stories about his life, and eventually he came to believe them himself. He mingled with the pioneering artists of the day—Picasso, Braque, Kandinsky—who made him rather a pet, an object of half-real/half-mock admiration. Now, of course, the paintings of Picasso and the others are displayed in the world's great museums. So are the paintings of Henri Rousseau.

Born in a town in northwestern France, Rousseau completed secondary school and then enlisted in the army. Later he circulated the story that he had traveled with the infantry to Mexico, where he observed the tropical foliage seen in his mature paintings, but in fact he never left France. After military service, he became a toll collector for the city of Paris, and this too he exaggerated. Because he preferred the much higher rank of *douanier*, or customs inspector, he promoted himself and is often known as "le Douanier Rousseau."

Rousseau began as a Sunday painter, daubing away in his spare time. Then in 1884, at the age of forty, he took a small pension and retired to devote his life to painting. He never had any formal training in art. Instead, he set about teaching himself—copying paintings in the Louvre, studying nature at the botanical gardens in Paris, observing the work of other artists. When drawing figures he would carefully measure the features of his subjects with a tape measure, even though the results never seemed to reflect such precision. Rousseau liked to say that the great and famous art teachers had warned him never to lose the naive quality of his work. And he never did.

In specific details Rousseau's life was a harsh one. He married twice, and both of his wives died early, as did eight of his nine children. He rarely had any money, and sometimes he had to beg for food. Curiously, he seems never to have been unhappy. So convinced was he of his great talent, so caught up in his wonderful visions, so enthralled with the life he had invented for himself—that he floated serenely through the world, much as he appears to float in the self-portrait shown here. Rousseau's death, on the other hand, was a miserable one. A cut on his leg became infected and then gangrenous. "Le Douanier" died virtually alone and was buried in a pauper's grave.

Who was Rousseau? He was a fabulous romantic, a master of the naive, a stolidly middle-class clerk, a disciplined and hard-working painter, a dreamer, a man of simple tastes and magnificent visions. His friend Picasso, even while making jokes at Rousseau's expense, admired and respected the distinctive talent. The highlight of Rousseau's life was a banquet, held in his honor, at Picasso's studio in 1908. All the bohemian artistic world of Paris turned out. Rousseau, enthroned on a chair set atop a packing case, played a composition of his own on the violin. Many toasts were drunk, and the party became quite lively. Near the end, as the story goes, Rousseau staggered up to Picasso and paid what was for Rousseau a splendid tribute: "My dear Picasso," he said, "we are the two greatest painters of our time—you in the Egyptian style and I in the modern style."

Henri Rousseau. *Myself, Portrait-Landscape.* 1890.
Oil on canvas, 4'8¾" × 3'7¼". National Gallery, Prague.

33. Comparison of
abstract and naturalistic figures.

below: *Statuette of a Woman.* Cycladic,
c. 2600–2400 B.C.E. Marble, height 24¾".
The Metropolitan Museum of Art, New York
(gift of Christos G. Bastis, 1968).

bottom: Jean Antoine Houdon.
La Frileuse (Winter). 1787.
Bronze, height 4′9″.
The Metropolitan Museum of Art, New York
(bequest of Kate Trubee Davison, 1962).

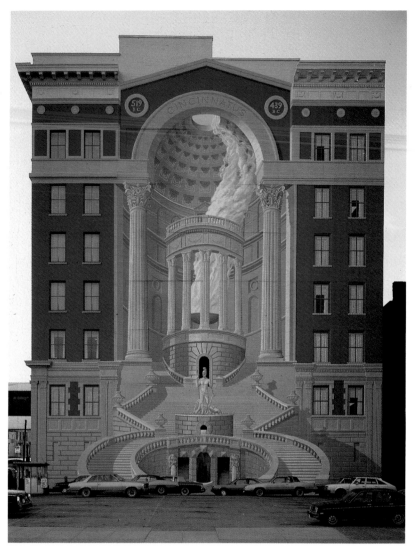

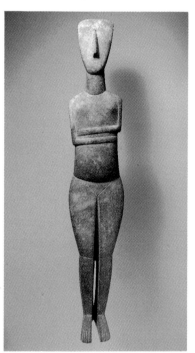

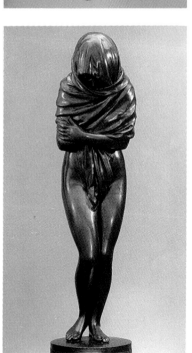

Brotherhood Building in Cincinnati **(32)** offers a spectacular example. Only the windows and the left cornice (roof ornament) are real. Apart from those elements the wall is absolutely flat. The soaring half-dome and columns, projecting porch, and curving stairways are all a painted illusion.

ABSTRACT ART We call a work of art abstract when the art has reference to the natural world but does not try to duplicate it exactly. In the illustration here **(33)** the bottom figure is naturalistic. The figure above it, a sculpture from the ancient culture of the Cyclades Islands, off the coast of Greece, is highly abstract. We have no doubt that the Cycladic image is meant to portray the nude female figure, yet the form has been abstracted to an extreme. The face is a rough triangle, with another jutting triangle for the nose. The crossed arms are flat and geometric. Knees, pubic area, and the curve of the abdomen are suggested by simple incised lines. In a sense, the sculptor of this figure has given us the minimum visual information we need to identify the form. The sculpture thus becomes not any particular female figure, but the *essence* of the female figure.

Stylized is a term closely related to abstract; you may have difficulty separating the two words until you become accustomed to hearing them applied to specific works of art. We are more likely to call a work of art stylized when it shows certain features of a natural form—features closely associated with that form—exaggerated in a special way. In Rousseau's painting **(31)**, for instance, the two big cats, presumably lions, are stylized—their round staring eyes and prominent whiskers not lifelike but a kind of artistic shorthand for "cat." The leaves and flowers are similarly stylized.

NONREPRESENTATIONAL ART   Nonrepresentational art has no reference to the natural world of images. It does not show people or animals or mountains, but simply shapes and sometimes colors. This art bypasses known forms and touches our senses and emotions directly. It does not "represent" anything but itself. In Joan Mitchell's *Lucky Seven* **(34)**, for instance, there is no identifiable imagery. The painting's interest derives from its rich interplay of colors, shapes, and visual textures.

Despite the apparent dissimilarities in these kinds of art, they all share a common trait. They are expressions of the artists who made them.

ART AS EXPRESSION

Until now we have been talking about things that art can be but need not be. At last we come to something that art is always—the expression of the artist. By ***expression*** we mean the artist's unique view of art and of the world, an outward manifestation of the artist's emotions, thoughts, feelings, fears, dreams, and observations. Expression is what the artist—in visual terms—*says* to the viewer or to the world.

Expression means that the artist is always present in the work of art. No matter how straightforward a work may seem, it is influenced tremendously by the artist's own perspective and by his or her culture. This may be a difficult idea to grasp at first. We look at a portrait, for example, especially one painted in earlier centuries, and think, "But that's just the way the person *looks*. The artist isn't expressing anything." Is this really true? To find out, we might compare two portraits of the same person.

34. Joan Mitchell. *Lucky Seven.* 1962. Oil on canvas, 6′7″ × 6′2½″. Hirshhorn Museum and Sculpture Garden, Smithsonian Institution, Washington, D.C. (gift of Joseph H. Hirshhorn, 1966).

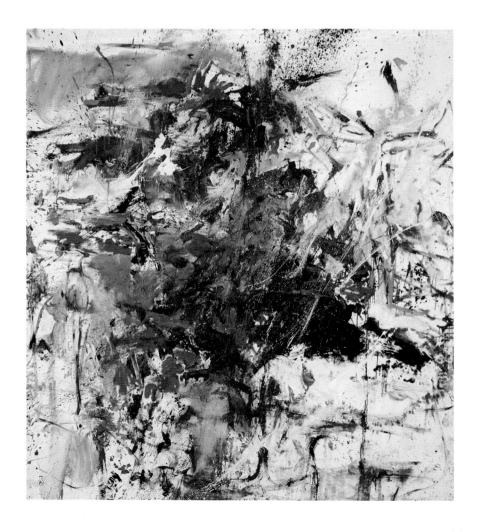

The paintings illustrated next **(35,36)** were done in the same year, and both are portraits of Vincent van Gogh. The first is by Van Gogh's friend Paul Gauguin, and the second is a self-portrait. Without the titles and the background information, almost no one would identify these works as portraits of

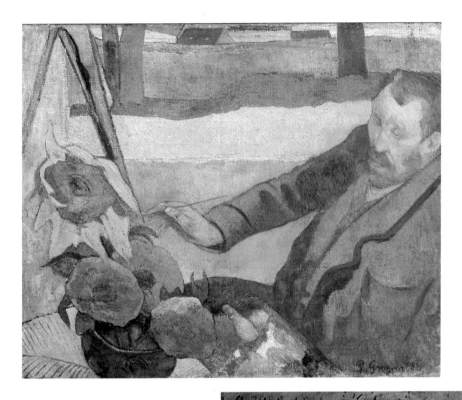

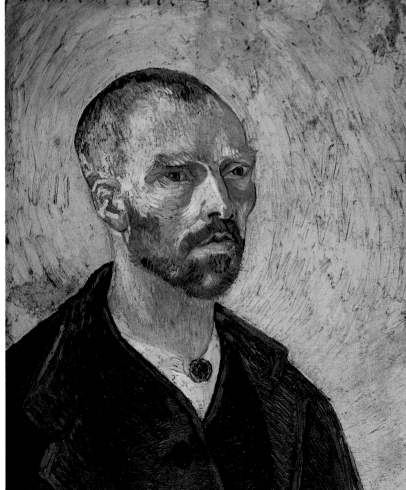

above: 35. Paul Gauguin.
Vincent van Gogh. 1888.
Oil on canvas, 28¾ × 35⅞".
Rijksmuseum Vincent van Gogh,
Amsterdam

right: 36. Vincent van Gogh.
*Self-Portrait Dedicated
to Paul Gauguin.* 1888.
Oil on canvas, 24⅜ × 20½".
Courtesy of The Fogg Art Museum,
Harvard University Art Museums,
Cambridge, Mass.
(bequest from the Collection of
Maurice Wertheim, class of 1906).

the same man at the same time. Each expresses what the artist felt about the subject—in one case, about the self.

Gauguin shows us a rather ordinary, heavy-set, middle-class man at work, delicately painting sunflowers. The subject is shifted far to the right in the composition and balanced against the sunflowers, which assume equal importance. It is as though Van Gogh and his sunflowers are two sides of the same coin. How different is Van Gogh's self-portrait! The artist strips away all background details and presents himself as a gaunt, brooding, almost monk-like figure—totally introspective, totally isolated.

We may be tempted to ask ourselves, which of these two portraits is the more "real"? And the answer must be: both of them. Gauguin's portrait is the *real* Van Gogh as perceived by Gauguin, sifted through his friendship, memories, emotions, and indeed all of Gauguin's life experiences. Van Gogh's self-portrait is equally the *real* Van Gogh, as perceived by himself, sifted through the mental torment we know he endured, colored by the self-image he wanted to express to the world.

Two periods in the recent history of art have so intensely shown us the artist's expression that they have been labeled with the term. ***Expressionism,*** sometimes called ***German Expressionism*** because most of the leading artists worked in Germany, was a movement of the late 19th and early 20th centuries. Above all, this was an art that looked inward, to the soul and psyche. Expressionist artists sought to explore their own emotions, their own passions and terrors. Among the most moving of these artists was Käthe Kollwitz, who worked chiefly in prints. Kollwitz drew images based on her own anguish to express her feelings about a world in which there could be war and brutal death. During her difficult life (p. 165) she witnessed two world wars that tore apart her home country. She endured much personal grief and empathized with the fears and suffering of those around her. *Death and the Mother* **(37)** depicts three figures locked together in a ghastly embrace. We see only one face—the terrified face of the woman, who clutches her child against her breast as the featureless form of Death claims her from behind. We know the woman already belongs to Death and cannot escape; their union is shockingly intimate. Kollwitz' drawing seems simple, yet its expression is universal: the instinct of all mothers to protect their children and the dread felt by all creatures facing their own mortality.

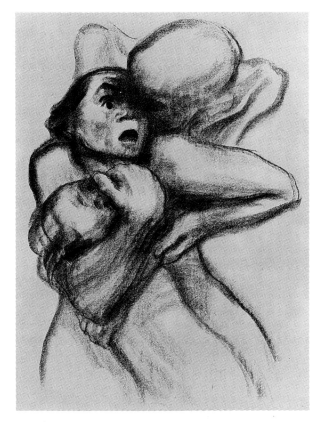

37. Käthe Kollwitz. *Death and the Mother.*
1934. Lithograph, $20\frac{1}{8} \times 14\frac{5}{8}''$.
Courtesy of The Fogg Art Museum,
Harvard University Art Museums,
Cambridge, Mass.
(Gray Collection of Engravings Fund).

Another movement closely linked with the artist's expression came in the mid-20th century and was known as ***Abstract Expressionism*** (Chapter 20). Artists identified with this style also looked inward and sought a direct expression of their emotions. This expression, however, took the form of abstract—often nonrepresentational—images: colors, shapes, lines.

One of the best-known Abstract Expressionists was Jackson Pollock. In the late 1940s and early 1950s Pollock began showing works like *Convergence* **(38)**. His style of painting was unusual, even revolutionary. Pollock set his huge canvases on the floor, stood above them (sometimes walked on them), and flung the paint from brushes, sticks, drippers, and even the paint can itself. The result was an intricate web of lines and colors, with no beginning and no end. A viewer, once drawn into the painting, is led around and through it, with the eye moving continuously through a network of forms. What does the painting express? Movement, color, action, life, vitality—the spirit of the artist. As a matter of fact, many critics referred to this style as ***action painting.*** The artist's action in making the painting is communicated directly to the viewer. If you stand for a while in front of one of Pollock's paintings, you almost want to conduct it, as if it were an orchestra. The expression is available to anyone who is willing to receive it.

So we see that the four questions posed at the beginning of this section—Who made it? Is it beautiful? Does it look natural? What does it say?—all offer interesting material for discussion, but none will provide an absolute litmus test in determining what is or is not art. The thoughtful student should dig a little deeper in exploring the nature of art, should be armed with more information to make reasoned judgments about artworks. The balance of this chapter, then, will present certain basic concepts, common to all art.

38. Jackson Pollock.
Convergence. 1952.
Oil on canvas, 7'11½" × 12'11".
Albright-Knox Art Gallery,
Buffalo, N.Y.
(gift of Seymour H. Knox, 1956).

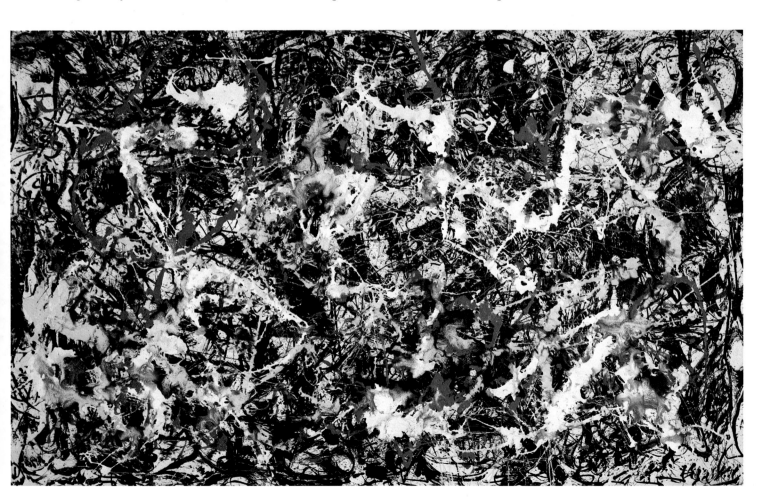

JACKSON POLLOCK

1912–1956

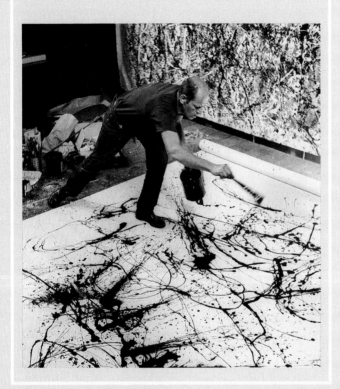

Jackson Pollock was born on a sheep ranch in Cody, Wyoming, the youngest son in a family of five boys. During his youth the family moved around a good deal and led a fairly unstable existence. By the age of fifteen Jackson had begun to show signs of the alcoholism that would plague him all of his life.

In 1930 Pollock went to New York to study at the Art Students League. His principal teacher there was Thomas Hart Benton, a realistic painter of regional Americana, best known for his murals. Later, Pollock would say he was glad to have had the experience with Benton, because he then had to struggle all the harder to make art so very different from that of his mentor.

Money was a critical problem throughout the early years in New York. By 1935 Pollock was employed on the Federal Art Project of the Works Progress Administration—a Depression-era program meant to provide em-ployment for artists. He was required to turn out, every four to eight weeks, one painting suitable for installation in public buildings, for which he was paid a stipend of about $100 a month. Frequent alcoholic binges often interfered with this work, and in 1937 Pollock began psychotherapy in an attempt to overcome his addiction.

Pollock's work was first exhibited in 1942, as part of a group show that also included the work of painter Lee Krasner. Krasner and Pollock soon formed a close relationship, and they were married in 1945. Gradually, Pollock's work began to change, to be freer and more spontaneous, to contain fewer and fewer figural elements. During the late 1940s he began exhibiting works in his mature style.

Some critics praised Pollock as the greatest of all American artists, but the general public was very slow to accept his revolutionary art. *Time* magazine epitomized the bewilderment of the popular press, dubbing him "Jack the Dripper." Nevertheless, there were some collectors willing to invest, so finances became less pressing.

The years 1948 to 1952—Pollock's late thirties—were the artist's prime, when he was at the height of his creative powers. After that, he seemed less sure where to go with his art, and even the sympathetic critics were not so responsive to the work. Pollock began to paint less and drink more. On the night of August 11, 1956, Pollock—along with two young women friends—was driving his convertible near his home when he lost control of the car and rammed into a clump of trees at high speed. Pollock and one of the women were killed instantly. The artist was only forty-four years old.

Pollock drunk could be violent and brutish; Pollock sober was shy, introverted, and uncommunicative. Few ever succeeded in getting him to talk about his art, but there is one quote, reprinted many times, that gives voice to his truly remarkable vision: "On the floor I am more at ease. I feel nearer, more a part of the painting, since this way I can walk around it, work from the four sides and literally be *in* the painting. . . . When I am *in* my painting, I am not aware of what I'm doing. It is only after a sort of 'get acquainted' period that I see what I have been about. I have no fears about making changes, destroying the image, etc., because the painting has a life of its own. I try to let it come through. It is only when I lose contact with the painting that the result is a mess. Otherwise there is pure harmony, an easy give and take, and the painting comes out well."[7]

Jackson Pollock in his studio at East Hampton, N.Y. 1950, photographed by Hans Namuth.

ART CONCEPTS

FORM AND CONTENT

If a good idea were all it took to be a great artist, everyone would be a great artist. The world is full of people who are carrying around in their heads splendid ideas for novels, operas, and paintings. What is lacking is form, and form is essential to any work of art.

In simplest terms, *form* is the way a work of art looks; and **content** is what a work of art says. Form includes everything from the material the artist uses (oil paint, stone, paper, whatever), to the style in which the artist works, to the shapes and lines and colors in the art. It also includes how a work of art is put together—its **composition.**

Content refers to the message communicated by a work of art—what the artist expresses. Sometimes content begins with a story or an event or an image of something we recognize, which we could call the **subject matter.** For instance, in a painting titled, say, *The Battle of Bull Run,* the subject matter would be a battle scene of the Civil War. The content would be a battle scene *and* what the artist wanted to communicate about that battle scene. (You can guess that the content would likely be very different if a Union sympathizer and a Confederate artist were painting the same scene.) Similarly, in a portrait, as in the two portraits of Van Gogh, the content begins with the subject and includes whatever the artist wishes to communicate about the subject.

In other types of art, however, the content may not be so clear. It could be anger or fear or loneliness or joy or, as in the Pollock, action and vitality. For an interesting study in form and content, we might look at Ben Shahn's *Miners' Wives* **(39)**, a painting this American artist made in 1948. In form, *Miners' Wives* is a tempera painting on board with some sharply drawn lines. It is generally representational—we recognize that there are two women and a child inside an enclosure—but many areas are stylized, especially the eyes and hands of the woman at right. The structure is complex **[Overlay 1b].**

As to the painting's content, we have a clue in the title, "miners' wives," but that is only a starting point. Shahn tells us much more about these women than their marital status or their husbands' occupations. The haunted eyes of the woman at right speak of endless days waiting at home to know if her husband will return alive and intact from his dangerous occupation. Her large, clasped hands reveal constant hard work, as well as the grim necessity of carrying on. The other woman, seated at rear and holding a baby, has a mask-like face suggesting numb acceptance of hardship. Through an opening in the brick wall, we see the tiny figures of the men going off to their work. Shahn's picture does not show us *their* reality—every bit as bleak—but the reality of the wives left behind. We might sum up its content this way: "Life is harsh, desolate, frightening, cheerless." And if we know something about the artist's background, know that he was much concerned with social injustice and the suffering of the working classes, we can take the content a step further: "Life is unfair."

Throughout the preceding discussion the word *style* has been used a number of times. Style is a term familiar to us from everyday conversation, but because it is so crucial to an understanding of art, we might consider its meaning as specifically related to art.

STYLE

There are styles of music, styles of dress, styles of interior design, even styles of speaking and walking. When an automobile manufacturer changes the way its cars look from year to year, we speak of the "new style." If a person we know always wears jeans and cowboy boots, or always wears long flowing dresses and flowered prints, we identify that person with his or her particular style of

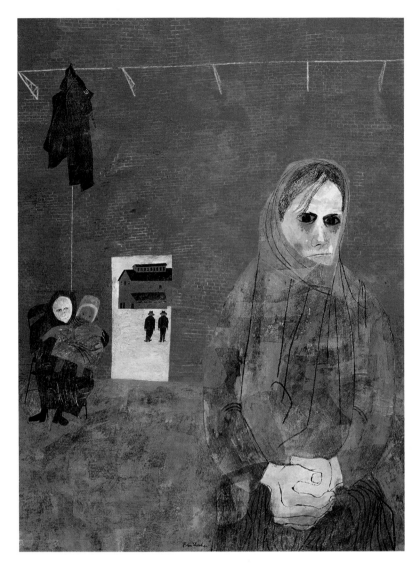

dress. Furthermore, we may say of someone, "She really has style!" Or we might describe the décor of a particular home as "stylish." In the latter two cases, we mean the person or place shows a *desirable* style, one we admire, because everybody and everything has *some* style. But what exactly *is* style?

Above all, **style** is a characteristic or group of characteristics that we can identify as constant, recurring, or coherent. For instance, suppose you have a friend who has very long hair and always wears it in braids; then your friend gets a short haircut. You would call this a sudden change of style. Or perhaps you know a family whose home is entirely decorated with antiques, except for one very modern chair and table in the living room. You would recognize a mix of styles—not necessarily bad, but obvious.

In the visual arts, just as in any other area of life, style indicates a series of choices an artist has made. **Artistic style** is the sum of constant, recurring, or coherent traits identified with a certain individual or group. In painting, for example, a particular style could be composed of many elements—the materials used, the type of brush stroke, the colors, the way forms are handled, the choice of subject matter, the degree of resemblance to the natural world (representational versus abstract style), and so on.

Style may be associated with a whole artistic culture (the Song dynasty style in China); with a particular time and place (the early Renaissance style in Rome); with a group of artists whose work shows similar characteristics (the

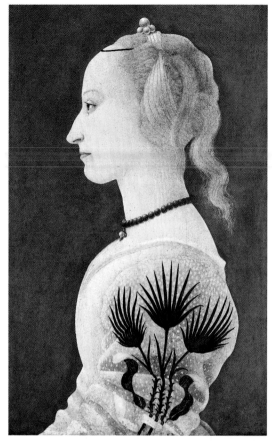

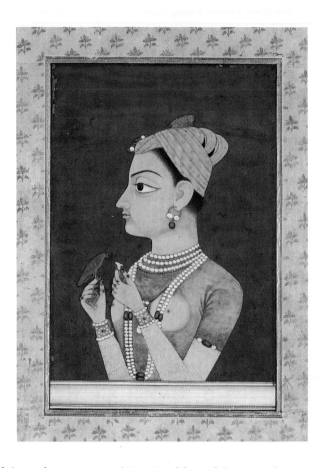

above: **40.** Alesso Baldovinetti.
Portrait of a Lady in Yellow.
c. 1463. Wood panel, 24¾ × 16″.
National Gallery, London
(reproduced by courtesy of the Trustees).

right: **41.** *Lady with a Bird*,
from Hyderabad, India. c. 1730.
Gouache on paper, 13 × 8½″.
Victoria & Albert Museum, London
(by courtesy of the Board of Trustees).

Abstract Expressionist style); with one artist (Van Gogh's style); or with one artist at a certain time (Picasso's Blue period style). In all these instances there are common elements—constant, recurring, coherent—that we can learn to recognize. Once you become familiar with Van Gogh's mature style **(15)**, with its licking, flamelike brush strokes and vivid color, you will probably be able to identify other paintings by Van Gogh, even if you have never seen them before. Some artists develop a style and stick to it; others work in several styles, simultaneously or sequentially.

One way to think of style is to consider it an artist's personal "handwriting." You know that if you give ten people identical pieces of paper and identical pens and tell them to write the same sentence, you'll get ten very different results, because no two people have the same handwriting. Penmanship styles are interesting. Each is absolutely unique, yet there are characteristics we can identify, even if we don't know the person who did the writing. If you study handwriting at all, a given sample should be able to tell you if the writer is male or female, old or young, American or European, and so forth. Much the same is true of artistic styles. Every one is individual, but we may find similarities among artists of a particular time, place, or group.

To get a sense of style variations in art, let us look at three paintings **(40,41,42)** with similar subject matter. Each depicts a woman in profile, from

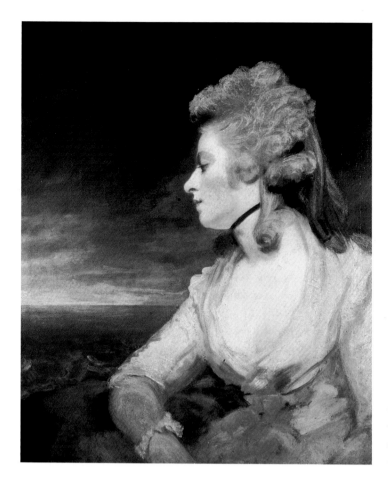

42. Joshua Reynolds.
Mrs. Mary Robinson (Perdita). 1784.
Oil on canvas, 30½ × 25″.
The Wallace Collection, London
(reproduced by permission of the Trustees).

the waist up, but the paintings are very different. Even someone who knows practically nothing about art would observe differences in style, although he or she might not be able to articulate those differences. The first, by Alesso Baldovinetti, was painted in Italy in the 15th century **(40)**. It shows the woman in sharp outline, against a plain blue background, almost as flat as a silhouette. The drawing is lifelike but probably idealized, made to look more beautiful than the subject actually was. All is elegance, from the pure features to the long neck to the prominent leaf pattern on the sleeve.

The second painting **(41)** was made in India in the 18th century. Again the outline is sharp against a plain background, but the subject's pose is even more rigid, almost ritually frozen. The woman holds a bird in one hand and, presumably, the bird's treat in the other, but these are really ornaments for the carefully posed hands. She does not look at the bird but instead stares off into an unseen distance. As was customary in the artistic style of that culture, the artist has bared the woman's breasts and exaggerated her enormous, almond-shaped eyes.

Our third example **(42)**, painted at almost the same time as the Indian picture, is by the great English portraitist Sir Joshua Reynolds. Here we see no flat background but rather the illusion of deep space—a vague and romantic seascape toward which the woman seems to be gazing. Unlike the first two artists, Reynolds invites us into the sitter's mind. She is pensive, perhaps a little sad, perhaps daydreaming or remembering. Her pose is more relaxed than either of the previous two, more dramatic, even a bit theatrical. Colors are softer, the forms slightly blurred.

Three lovely portraits, each by a skilled artist, but markedly different from one another—that is the nature of style. In every case, regardless of the type of art, an artist's style will be influenced by choices related to time, place, and the artist's expressive needs.

In a sense, this whole book—or any book about art—is really about style. Part Two will discuss how an artist's choices of elements affect style, Parts Three and Four will consider styles in the various media, and Part Five will survey styles in art throughout history.

Before going on to these broader issues, however, we should introduce one more term that is important for the study of art. The term is related to style, because if we are to fully understand an artist's style, we must know what is being depicted in a work of art and why—the work's iconography.

ICONOGRAPHY

Loosely, iconography is the "story" within a work of art. Many people find the term confusing, because both subject matter and content could be described in much the same way as iconography. An example may help to clear up the confusion among the three terms. Suppose you see a painting of a boy and a dog. The *subject matter* of that painting is simply "a boy and a dog." Its *content* might be "the love between a boy and his dog." But if you, the observer, see that the dog is a collie, realize that the dog is Lassie, and know the Lassie stories—know that Lassie is an intelligent and heroic dog who often saves people from danger—then you have caught the painting's *iconography*.

Artists around the world always have assumed a certain iconographical knowledge on the part of their audiences. A viewer's comprehension of the iconography includes familiarity with the people, places, and events that are depicted, as well as any symbolism intended by the artist. Much of the history of art has some literary or historical or religious reference. Quite a lot of West-

43. Fra Filippo Lippi.
Nativity. c. 1459.
Tempera on wood, 4'2" × 3'10".
Staatliche Museen, Bildarchiv
Preussischer Kulturbesitz, Berlin.

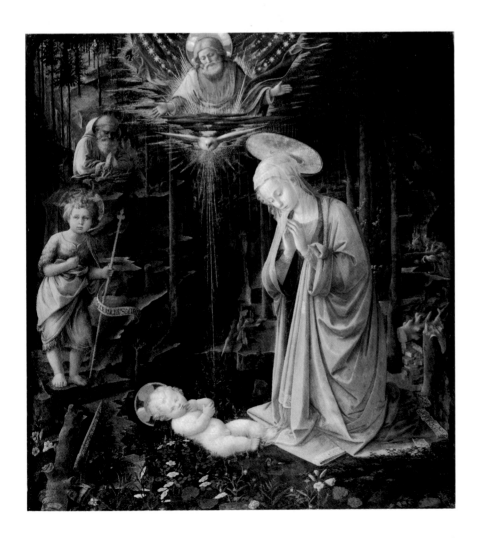

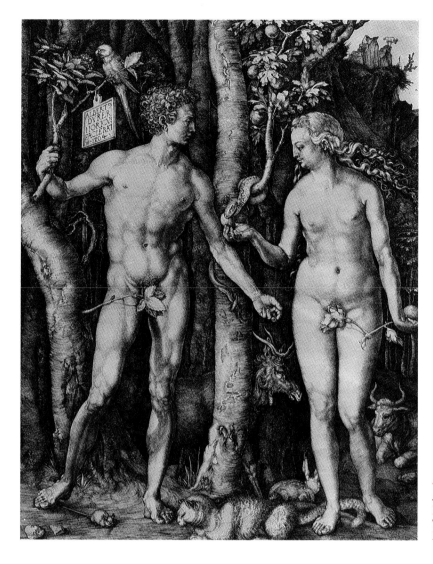

44. Albrecht Dürer.
Adam and Eve. 1504.
Engraving, $9\frac{7}{8} \times 7\frac{5}{8}''$.
The Metropolitan Museum of Art,
New York (Fletcher Fund, 1919).

ern art is based on the Bible. Most of the time an artist's immediate circle of patrons and viewers will grasp the iconography at once. Problems arise, however, when we confront art from other times and places.

Christians around the world are familiar with the story surrounding the birth of Christ. When a person with this background looks at Fra Filippo Lippi's *Nativity* **(43)**, certain things are immediately apparent. There is the child Jesus, watched over by his mother Mary (who wears a halo symbolic of her perfect sinlessness). To the left is a praying saint and, just below, Jesus' cousin John the Baptist, identified by his staff. And at the top are God the Father and the Holy Ghost in the form of a dove, completing the Trinity. Someone with no knowledge of the Christian tradition, however, would probably see a lovely mother-and-child scene and wonder who those other people are and why they are wearing such funny hats. We can try to imagine what an Inca in 15th-century Peru or a samurai in 15th-century Japan (both contemporary with this painting) would see in Filippo Lippi's scene.

Even in the Western culture we have inherited, the iconography can sometimes be unfamiliar. Albrecht Dürer, who worked in Germany during the late 15th and early 16th centuries, was a Christian. Much of his iconography is biblical, but it is overlaid with mystical northern European symbolism. In *Adam and Eve* **(44)** we see that couple about to be banished from the Garden of Eden after their sin of eating the forbidden fruit. Dürer has included symbols of the four humors, or temperaments, which were thought to rule the human body; the elk symbolizes gall; the ox, phlegm; the cat, choler; and the

ALBRECHT DÜRER

1471–1528

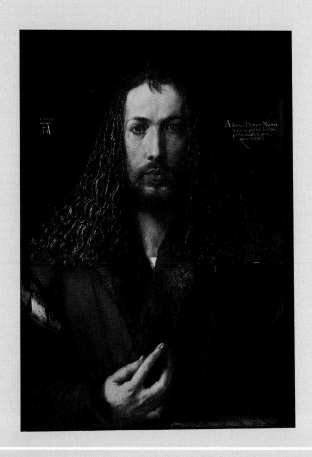

ALBRECHT DÜRER is the first of the northern European artists who seems to us "modern" in his outlook. Unlike most of his colleagues, he had a strong sense of being an *artist*, not a craftsman, and he sought—and received—acceptance in the higher ranks of society. Moreover, Dürer appears to have understood his role in the history of art—sensed that his work would exert great influence on his contemporaries and on artists of the future. This awareness led him to date his works and sign them with the distinctive "AD" (visible in the left background of his self-portrait)—a fairly unusual practice at the time.

Born in the southern German city of Nuremberg, Dürer was the son of a goldsmith, to whom he was apprenticed as a boy. At the age of fifteen young Albrecht was sent to study in the workshop of Michael Wolgemut, then considered a leading painter in Nuremberg. He stayed with Wolgemut for four years, after which he began a four-year period of wandering through northern Europe. In 1494 Dürer's father called him back to Nuremberg for an arranged marriage. (The marriage seems not to have been a happy one and produced no children.) Soon afterward Dürer established himself as a master and opened his own studio.

Dürer made a great many paintings and drawings, but it is his output in prints (engravings, woodcuts, and etchings) that is truly extraordinary. Many people would argue that he was the greatest printmaker who ever lived. His genius derived partly from an ability to unite the best tendencies in northern and southern European art of that period, for Dürer was a well-traveled man. In 1494 he visited Italy, and he returned in 1505, staying two years in Venice, where he operated a studio. This second trip was a huge success, both artistically and socially. The artist received many commissions and enjoyed the high regard of the Venetian painters as well as of important patrons in the city. Upon his return to Germany Dürer took his place among the leading writers and intellectuals of Nuremberg, who seem to have valued him for his knowledge and wit, as well as for his art. In 1515 he was appointed court painter to the Holy Roman Emperor Maximilian I.

The last years of Dürer's life were devoted largely to work on his books and treatises, through which he hoped to teach a scientific approach to painting and drawing. As a Renaissance artist, he was fascinated by perfection and by an ideal of beauty. He wrote: "What beauty is, I know not, though it adheres to many things. When we wish to bring it into our work we find it very hard. We must gather it together from far and wide, and especially in the case of the human figure throughout all its limbs from before and behind. One may often search through two or three hundred men without finding amongst them more than one or two points of beauty which can be made use of. You, therefore, if you desire to compose a fine figure, must take the head from some, the chest, arm, leg, hand, and foot from others; and likewise, search through all members of every kind. For from many beautiful things something good may be gathered, even as honey is gathered from many flowers."[8]

Albrecht Dürer. *Self-Portrait.* 1500.
Wood panel, 25⅝ × 18⅞".
Alte Pinakothek, Munich.

rabbit, blood. Each of these humors, in turn, was associated with a particular sin—avarice, gluttony, cruelty, and lechery—sins to which the fallen Adam and Eve were now susceptible. Dürer's iconography is incredibly rich, and we can only begin to explore it here. For the artist's learned contemporaries it was understandable; for us it is new territory.

Now let us consider a work even further outside the experience of most of us—a painting that portrays an episode from the *Ramáyana*, the classic epic poem of India **(45)**. Probably composed in the 3rd century B.C.E. the *Ramáyana* is an integral part of daily life in India even today. Every character, every incident in the tale is as well known to the Indian public as the details of the Nativity are to practicing Christians.

Briefly, the *Ramáyana* tells the adventures of Rama—a prince who was the seventh incarnation of the god Vishnu—and his beautiful, faithful wife, Sita. Through a trick, the demon-king Ravana manages to abduct Sita and carry her off to his splendid palace at Lanka, which we see in the left half of this illustration. Ravana is so demonic, and so powerful, that he can assume any form he chooses—the worst one being a monster with ten heads and twenty arms. After kidnapping Sita, he gives her one year to renounce Rama and become his consort, and he exiles her to the forest in the keeping of demon-handmaidens. In this episode Ravana is paying Sita a visit to see if she has yet relented, but Sita remains steadfastly true to Rama.

Without this background information we find the painting lovely and exotic, but how much more interesting it becomes when we understand its iconography. Nowadays all of us are exposed to art from cultures other than our own, and it is well worth the effort to learn more about them.

45. *Sita in the Garden of Lanka with Ravana and His Demons.* Guler School, Punjab Hills, India, c. 1720. Gold and color on paper, 21¾ × 31⅛″. © 1996 The Cleveland Museum of Art (gift of George P. Bickford, 1966).

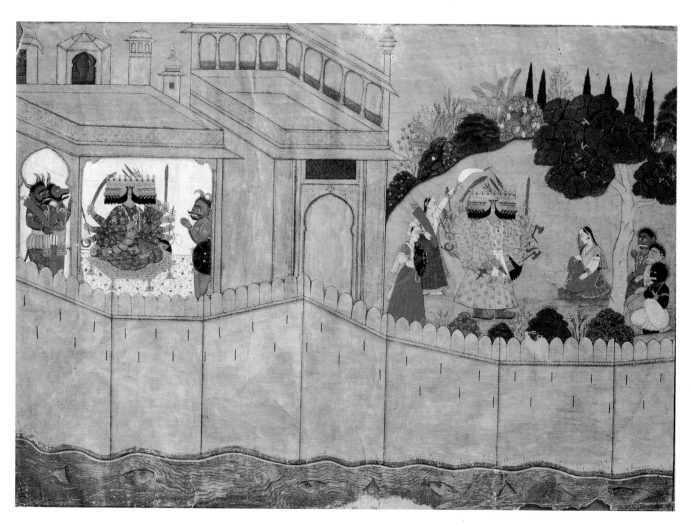

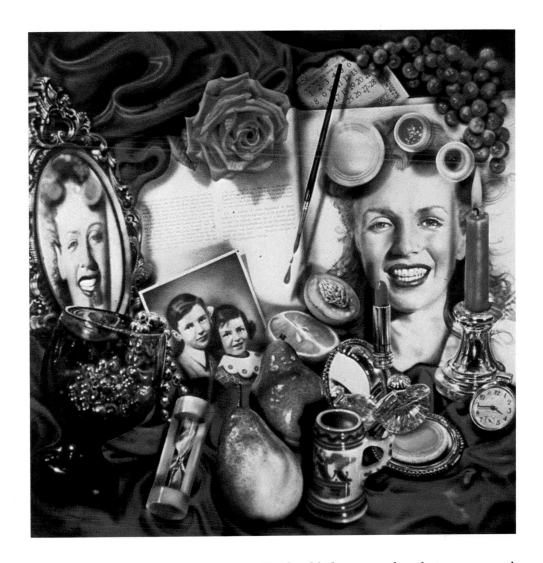

46. Audrey Flack. *Marilyn.* 1977. Oil and acrylic on canvas, 8′ square. University of Arizona Museum of Art, Tucson (Museum purchase with funds provided by the Edward J. Gallagher, Jr., Memorial Fund).

We should also remember that our own culture could be equally mystifying to those outside it. What would Filippo Lippi or Dürer or the painter of the *Ramáyana* make of Audrey Flack's *Marilyn* **(46)**? The details of the tragic film star's life are well known to most Americans, and so we readily accept the symbols of glamour, of artifice, of lushness, and especially of time running out (the candle, watch, calendar, and egg timer). But to someone who has never heard of Marilyn Monroe, the painting would seem a meaningless jumble. A knowledge of any work's iconography, therefore, can enhance our appreciation, as can acquaintance with the culture that produced the art.

And so, to return to the title of this chapter: What is art? It is the "lie that tells the truth." Sometimes it is beautiful, but it may be ugly. It can look like things in the natural world, but frequently it does not. It is always the expression of the artist. It is always a product of the culture that produces it. It is the artist showing us something, telling us something, making us experience something. It is communication—if we but look, listen, think, and feel.

THEO VAN GOGH

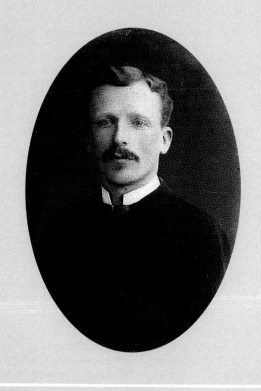

W E THINK OF Theo van Gogh as the sensible one. Mentor and benefactor of his brother, the tormented artist Vincent van Gogh, Theo was nearly everything his brother was not—successful in business, financially solvent, steady and dependable, easy in friendship, a serious family man. Sometimes it is hard to remember that Vincent was the *older* brother, Theo younger by four years. The relationship between them was extraordinary. Without Theo, Vincent van Gogh probably could not have survived as an artist, or survived at all. Without Vincent, Theo probably would have lacked the grand purpose of his life.

Theo was born at the family home in Holland in 1857. When he was a teenager his uncle arranged for him to be apprenticed to a firm of international art dealers, Goupil & Co., as Vincent had been before him. Here the brothers' characters diverged. Vincent soon drifted out of the business. Theo became well established and fairly prosperous, eventually settling in as an art dealer in

Paris. From a young age Theo assumed principal responsibility for Vincent's financial support, and he continued in this role through Vincent's life. Both seemed to accept the arrangement as natural.

The Van Gogh brothers maintained a remarkable intimacy of spirit—surprisingly so, in view of the fact that, except for brief visits, they spent relatively little time in each other's company. They were together in their boyhood, then for two years in Paris, when Vincent stayed with Theo before moving to the south of France. This latter period exhausted Theo; Vincent was never an easy person to live with. Theo described Vincent's presence in the Paris apartment as "unendurable" and was relieved when the artist finally journeyed to Arles.

The thread of Theo and Vincent's connection depended on an immense volume of correspondence. Vincent was compulsive in writing to Theo—his subjects ranging from intensely personal thoughts and emotions through minute descriptions of work in progress. Theo was always there for Vincent. When Vincent finished a series of paintings, he shipped them off to Theo, who did his best to promote and sell the work (with little success). When Vincent was irresponsible, Theo lectured. When Vincent was in financial crisis, Theo sent money. When Vincent was in emotional crisis, Theo arrived to pick up the pieces. Although under no illusion about his brother's difficult temperament, Theo seems to have known from the beginning that Vincent was a brilliant painter and to have considered it his mission to sustain the painter's career.

Theo's marriage to Johanna Bonger in April of 1889 caused a brief strain in the Van Gogh bond. What had been a straight line became a triangle. Vincent suffered over having any of Theo's emotional energy diverted from himself to the new wife. Before long, however, he came to be fond of his sister-in-law and rejoiced in the birth of his nephew.

Vincent shot himself in July of 1890, and Theo was summoned to the deathbed. Three days later Theo wrote to his mother: "One cannot write how grieved one is nor find any solace. . . . Oh, Mother! He was so my own, own brother."[9] Vincent's death left Theo, only thirty-three years old, broken in health and spirits. Within six months he too was dead. The brothers are buried side by side. Afterward, the work of establishing the art of Vincent van Gogh was carried on by Theo's wife and his only child, a son, named Vincent.

Photograph of Theo van Gogh. c. 1888–90.
Amsterdams Historisch Museum.

C H A P T E R   T H R E E

Themes and Purposes of Art

T HERE ARE SEVERAL ways to approach the study of art. A popular one is to trace its history chronologically, from the earliest cave paintings of the Stone Age to the art of our own time. This method offers great advantages, because it places works of art in the context of the cultures from which they emerged and allows one to follow the development of art over the centuries. Part Five of this book will present a brief chronological survey of art.

The chronological approach has one drawback, however, in that we may lose sight of the characteristics that works made by different cultures have in common. For instance, a sculpture produced today and one produced ten thousand years ago may seem very different, and a chronological approach emphasizes the differences by focusing on the cultural aspects that influenced each. But suppose the two sculptures are images honoring political leaders; then we would say they have the same *theme*, so we can make interesting comparisons between them. While it is useful to understand how and why works of art differ, it is also helpful to see how much they are alike, even when thousands of miles and years separate them.

In Chapter 2 we discussed content—the subject matter of a work of art and what the artist means to convey about that subject matter. Content can be considered as theme whenever similar material is treated by many artists at various times and places. A theme is therefore like a thread running through the entire history of art, and there are many such threads. No doubt every person setting out to name the important themes in art would produce a different list. We have chosen to consider these: religion; pride and politics; art as the mirror of everyday life; art and nature; imagination and fantasy; birth, marriage, and death.

The *purpose* of a work of art is what the artist hoped to achieve (or in some cases what the art patron hoped to achieve by commissioning it). Sometimes the two factors—theme and purpose—overlap, so it is difficult to tell them apart, but in other instances we can identify a separate purpose. For example, the theme of a landscape painting would probably be nature and the purpose simply to depict some aspect of nature. But if the artist's goal in painting a landscape is to show the glory of God's creation, then the theme is still nature, but we might consider the purpose to be religion. Let us therefore examine the six themes mentioned, with several examples of each, and see how they lend themselves to various purposes.

ART IN THE SERVICE
OF RELIGION

Since earliest times art has served religion in two important ways. First, artists have erected the sacred temples where believers join to profess their faith and follow the observances faith requires. Second, art attempts to make specific and visible something that is, by its very nature, spiritual, providing images of the religious figures and events that make up the fabric of a faith. In this section we shall explore how the theme of religious art has been adapted for different purposes, for different faiths, in different parts of the world.

A very large portion of the magnificent architecture we have was built in the service of religion. Naturally the architectural style of any religious structure reflects the culture in which it was built, but it is also dependent on the particular needs of a given religion. Three examples will show this.

On a high hill, the Acropolis, overlooking the city of Athens stands the shell of what many consider the most splendid building ever conceived: the Parthenon (47). The Parthenon was erected in the 5th century B.C.E. as a temple to the goddess Athena, patroness of the city, and at one time its core held a colossal statue of the goddess. However, the religion associated with the Parthenon was not confined to worship of a deity. In ancient Greece, veneration of the gods was closely allied to the political and social ideals of a city-state that celebrated its own greatness.

Rising proudly on its hill, visible from almost every corner of the city and for miles around, the Parthenon functioned as a symbol of the citizens' aspirations. Its structure as a religious shrine seems unusual for us in that it turns outward, toward the city, rather than in upon itself. Worshipers were not meant to gather inside the building; actually, only priests could enter the inner chamber, or *cella*, where the statue of Athena stood. Religious ceremonies on festal occasions focused on processions, which began down in the city, wound their way up the steep path on the west side of the Acropolis, and circled the Parthenon and other sacred buildings at the top.

Most of the Parthenon's architectural embellishment was intended for the appreciation of the worshipers outside. All four walls of the exterior were decorated with sculptures high up under the roof, and originally portions of the marble facade were painted a vivid blue and red. In Chapter 13 we shall consider details of the Parthenon's structure; here we concentrate on the theme of religion and on the Parthenon's purpose, which was both religious and political exaltation.

47. Ictinus and Callicrates. Parthenon, Athens. 447–432 B.C.E.

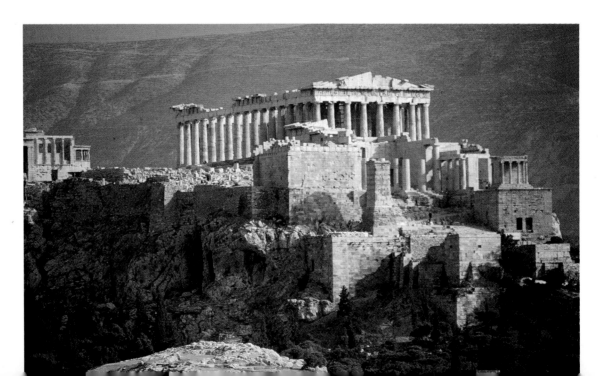

At about the same time the Parthenon was being constructed in Athens, but half a continent away, one of the world's great religions was developing and beginning to form its own architecture. Buddhism derives its principles from the teachings of Gautama Siddhartha, later known as the Buddha, who was born in India about 563 B.C.E. Although of noble birth, the Buddha renounced his princely status and life of ease. When he was about twenty-nine, he began a long period of wandering and meditation, seeking enlightenment. He began with the supposition that humans are predisposed to live out lives of suffering, to die, then to be reborn and repeat the pattern. Ultimately, he worked out a doctrine of moral behavior that he believed could break the painful cycle of life and death, and he attracted many followers.

Buddhism is predominantly a personal religion, and its observances depend less on communal worship than on individual contemplation. It places great emphasis on symbolism, much of it referring to episodes in the Buddha's life. Both of these aspects—the personal and the symbolic—are evident in one of Buddhism's finest early shrines, the Great Stupa at Sanchi, in India (48). Like the Parthenon, the Great Stupa turns more outward than inward, but its moundlike form is more sculptural, intended as a representation of the cosmos. At the top is a three-part "umbrella," symbolizing the three aspects of Buddhism—the Buddha, the Buddha's Law, and the Monastic Order.

Buddhist shrines—the word *stupa* means "shrine"—often housed relics of the Buddha, and worship rituals called for circumambulation ("walking around") of the stupa. Thus, on the outside of the Great Stupa we see a railed pathway, where pilgrims could take the ritual clockwise walk following the Path of Life around the World Mountain. Elsewhere the stupa is embellished richly with carvings and sculpture evoking scenes from the Buddha's life. Every part of the stupa is geared to the pursuit of personal enlightenment and transcendence.

If the Buddhist temple is dedicated to private worship, then its extreme opposite can be found in the total encompassment of a community religious experience: the medieval Christian cathedral. And the supreme example of that ideal is the Cathedral of Notre Dame de Chartres, in France (49). Chartres Cathedral was built, rebuilt, and modified over a period of several hundred years, but the basic structure, which is in the Gothic style (Chapter 16), was established in the 13th century. A cathedral—as opposed to a church—is the bishop's domain and always in a town or city. This one fact is crucial to understanding the nature of Chartres and the role it played in the people's lives.

Our illustration shows that the cathedral towers magnificently over the surrounding city, much as the Parthenon does over Athens, but here the resemblance ends. Whereas the Parthenon is above and apart from the city, accessible only by a steep path, Chartres Cathedral is very much a living presence *within* the city. In the Middle Ages houses and shops clustered right up to

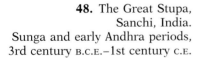

48. The Great Stupa, Sanchi, India. Sunga and early Andhra periods, 3rd century B.C.E.–1st century C.E.

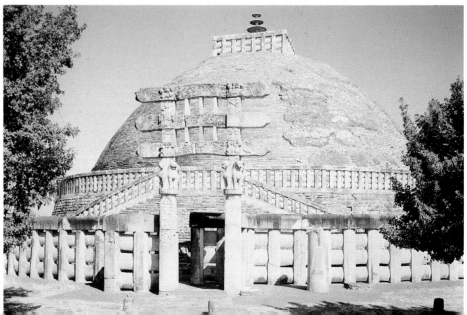

48

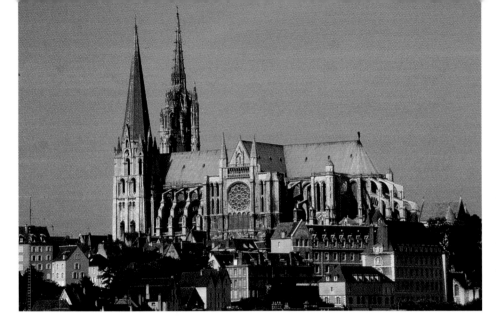

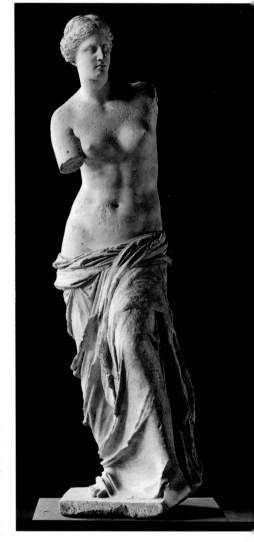

left: 49. Chartres Cathedral, France, view from the southeast. c. 1194–1260.

below: 50.
Aphrodite of Melos
(also called *Venus de Milo*).
c. 150 B.C.E. Marble, height 6'10".
Louvre, Paris.

its walls, and one side of the cathedral formed an edge of the busy marketplace. The cathedral functioned as a hub of all activities, both sacred and secular, within the town.

Medieval France had one dominant religion, and that was the Christianity of Rome. One could assume that almost every resident of the town of Chartres professed exactly the same faith, and so the church was an integral part of everyday life. Its bells tolled the hours of waking, starting work, praying, and retiring for the evening rest. Its feast days were the official holidays. Chartres Cathedral and its counterparts served the populace not only as a setting for religious worship but also as meeting hall, museum, concert stage, and social gathering place. Within its walls business deals were arranged, goods were sold, friends met, young couples courted. Where else but inside the cathedral could the townsfolk hear splendid music? Where else could they see magnificent art?

Three religious structures: the Parthenon, the Great Stupa, and Chartres Cathedral. Each was built in the service of religion, but for each we can find another slightly different purpose. For the Parthenon the purpose is also *political;* for the Great Stupa there is the purely *private* observance of religion; and for Chartres the *social* role is as important as the religious.

Similarly interesting comparisons can be made in the other major aspect of religious art, the creation of imagery. Art provides images of Christ, the Buddha, the whole galaxy of Greek and Roman gods, the saints and angels, and other figures. It portrays the legends, stories, and events connected with a particular faith. Each of these depictions, of course, is the artist's own interpretation of what a certain being or situation looked like. But by giving the faithful an image to focus on, the artist makes religion more concrete, less abstract. Again we will look at art from three faiths.

The first illustration in this series is an example of religious art from ancient Greece, a sculpture called *Aphrodite of Melos* **(50)**, popularly known as the *Venus de Milo*. (Venus was the Roman equivalent of the Greek goddess Aphrodite.) To modern eyes this seems an odd sort of religious statue—a nude woman, undeniably sensuous, shown with provocatively slipping draperies. To understand this work, we should know something about the Greek deities. The gods and goddesses of ancient Greece were grander and stronger than humans, and they possessed powers that humans do not. But they also displayed (to a godlike degree) distinctly human traits, including pride, anger, jealousy, and yes—sexuality. In this context, Aphrodite, the Goddess of Love and Beauty, would naturally be portrayed in the nude, with a body as lovely as the sculptor could make it. The Greeks worshipped her *for* her beauty, and they relished her numerous romantic adventures.

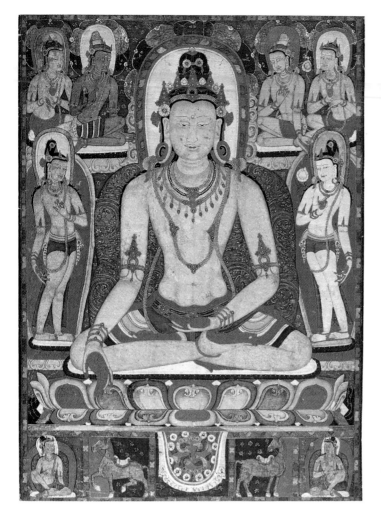

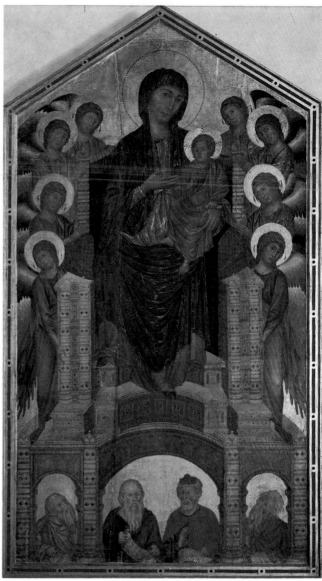

Our next two examples, one Buddhist and one differ-
ent from the Aphrodite, and also different from each other in content. What
may surprise us is how much alike they are in *form*. The works were made at
approximately the same time but some four thousand miles apart.

An image of the Buddha from Tibet or Nepal **(51)** shows the Buddha
seated in the pose of meditation, his hands in a classic *mudra*, or hand posture,
symbolizing the dispensing of gifts. Arranged around him are *bodhisattvas*, or
would-be Buddhas, who have deferred their ultimate goal of *Nirvana*—
freedom from the cycle of birth, death, and rebirth—in order to help others
attain that goal. All wear halos signifying their holiness. The Buddha, being the
most important of the personages depicted, dominates the painting and is
much the largest figure. Typically, he faces straight front, in a pose of tranquil-
ity, while the others around him stand or sit in relaxed postures.

The second example, painted by the 13th-century Italian master
Cimabue, depicts the Virgin Mary, mother of Christ, with her son **(52)**. Mary
sits tranquilly on her throne, her hand in a classic gesture indicating the Christ
child, who is the hope of earth's salvation. On both sides of her are figures of
angels, heavenly beings who assist humankind in its quest for Paradise. Again,
all these wear halos symbolizing their holiness. Yet again, the Virgin, being the
most important figure in this painting, dominates the composition, is the largest, and holds the most serenely frontal posture.

We should not conclude from the remarkable structural similarity of these works that any communication or influence took place between Italy and central Asia. A safer assumption is that two artists of different faiths independently found a format that satisfied their pictorial needs. Both the Buddha and the Virgin are important, serene holy figures. Bodhisattvas and angels, who are always more active, attend them. Therefore, the artists, from their separate points of view, devised similar compositions.

So we see that religious art is deeply affected by many forces: when it was made, where, why, by whom, and for what purpose. The same is true of art that deals with more earthly matters.

PRIDE AND POLITICS

It has been said that everything in life comes down to politics. All the worthy emotions—love, honor, patriotism, charity—have at their root a concern with politics, which means simply possessing the power to achieve one's desired goal. This is not the place to debate whether that theory holds true or not, but it is certainly clear that a great portion of the world's art has had political implications. The queen or pope or president who commissions an artist to make a particular work may have a true love of art, but that patron surely knows that a great masterpiece will enhance the patron's prestige and therefore increase his or her power.

Political art, and those who make it, can be divided between the "ins" and the "outs." The "ins" want to be even more in—to consolidate their power and enhance their prestige. The "outs," by and large, are unhappy with the existing political situation (whatever it may be) and hope to dislodge the "ins" and replace them. Art has traditionally served both ends.

The structures that many consider to be the ultimate in kingly pride, the height of political power, were built four and a half millennia ago and have never been surpassed. At Giza in Egypt rise the three great pyramids, tombs of the pharaohs Mycerinus, Chefren, and Cheops **(53)**. Only an immensely prideful king would divert thousands of workers to the massive chore of erecting a burial mound on this scale. Cheops' pyramid, the largest of the three, is about 450 feet tall (roughly the height of a fifty-story building), covers more than 13 acres, and consists of 2.3 million blocks of stone. Each block had to be quarried with hand tools, dragged to the site, and set in place without mortar.

53. The Great Pyramids, Giza, Egypt.
Pyramid of Mycerinus (c. 2500 B.C.E.);
Pyramid of Chefren (c. 2530 B.C.E.);
Pyramid of Cheops (c. 2570 B.C.E.).

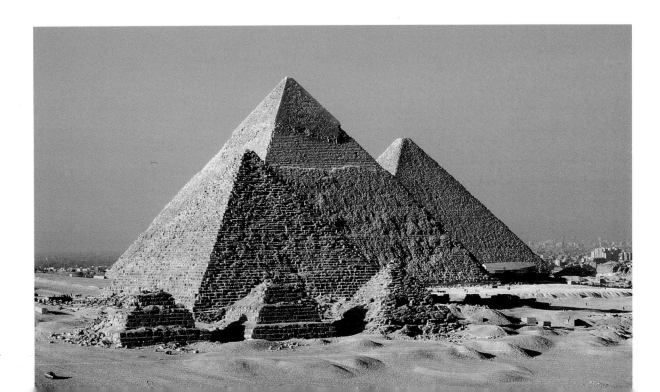

Perhaps even more interesting than the difficulty of the task is the grandiosity of the kings who willed it. The pharaohs planned these pyramids as safe and permanent resting places for themselves and their families in the afterlife. By their logic, the more powerful an individual had been in life, the more dramatic a mark that individual's tomb should make upon the landscape. The great pyramids, therefore, represent an extreme of kingly pride, of a pharaoh saying, in effect, "*My* name will never be forgotten; *my* monument will endure through all the generations to come." And so far, despite the wars and political upheavals and natural disasters the earth has witnessed, they have been right.

We assume the pharaohs, in building their pyramids, were motivated by pride. However, we *know* what motivated another great ruler to undertake an even more ambitious project. The Great Wall of China **(54)** was built along the northern borders of China to repel invasion by barbarians from outside the empire. Sections of the wall may have existed as early as the 5th century B.C.E., but the greatest spurt of building took place by order of Shi Huang Di, the first emperor of China, between about 228 and 204 B.C.E. Constructed entirely by hand of stone and earth, the wall eventually reached a length of more than two thousand miles, curving to follow the contours of rivers, deserts, and mountains. (For comparison, imagine a wall 25 feet high and about 25 feet thick at the base stretching from New York to Denver.) Today much of the Great Wall has crumbled, and what remains is basically a tourist attraction. But in an era before airplanes and missiles, Shi Huang Di and those who followed him could hope to keep themselves politically "in" by keeping everybody else *out*.

Given what we know about the spread of the mighty Roman Empire in the few centuries surrounding the birth of Christ, it is not surprising that some of the most prideful and political art was created at that time. The Roman emperors, who eventually conquered most of the civilized world they knew of, understood the political value of celebrating themselves and their achievements. An example of this approach to art is the statue of Augustus, which is known as the *Augustus of Prima Porta* **(55)**.

54. Great Wall of China. Begun c. 228 B.C.E., completed 17th century C.E. Average height 25′, average thickness at base 25′.

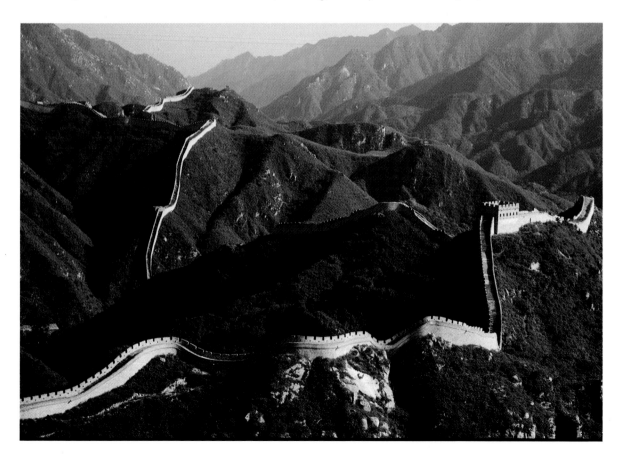

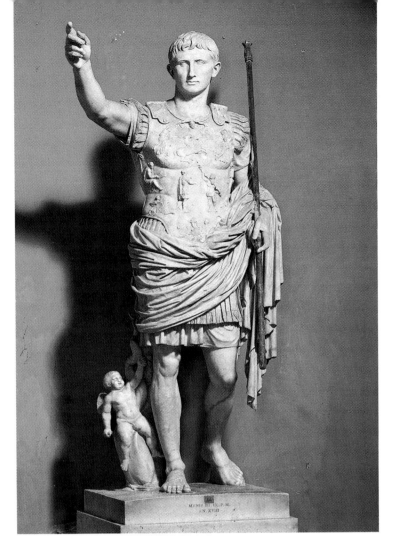

55. *Augustus of Prima Porta.*
c. 20 B.C.E. Marble, height 6'8".
Vatican Museums, Rome.

Augustus came to power in Rome in 31 B.C.E. by virtue of his military successes, and he reigned unchallenged for forty-five years—the first of the great Roman emperors. Under Augustus the empire enjoyed peace, prosperity, administrative order, and a flowering of the arts. In those times the line separating admiration for the ruler and worship of a deity was a fine one; emperors and heroes took on the attributes of gods. (The little figure accompanying Augustus is a cupid, symbol of Venus, the goddess from whom the emperor was supposedly descended.) That Augustus deliberately sought to enhance this godlike image is clear, and recent scholarship provides fascinating clues about how this statue and others played a role in his "public relations" campaign.

Considerable evidence supports the theory that Augustus was in fact much less attractive than he appears here. In life he had unruly hair, a small chin, small eyes, big ears, a bony face, and thin lips. Scholars now believe that in about 27 B.C.E.—seven years before the presumed date of the Prima Porta figure—the emperor commissioned an idealized portrait head, which was to be used as a model for all later sculptures, regardless of the emperor's advancing age. The Prima Porta head was based on this model; not only is it beautiful and godlike, but it also resembles the idealized Greek style. What were Augustus' motives for promoting this idealized portrait? According to those who have studied the question, "the portrait was supposed to show that he had ideal human qualities and, at the same time, that he stood for a culture that combined the best traditions." Also, the Prima Porta style head "was part of a representational program which gave Romans hope for the future under Augustus, as a divinely inspired leader. He claimed to be acting as the agent of the gods on earth."[1] In other words, the emperor's purpose in commissioning this art was a political one—to consolidate his power and ensure its continuity.

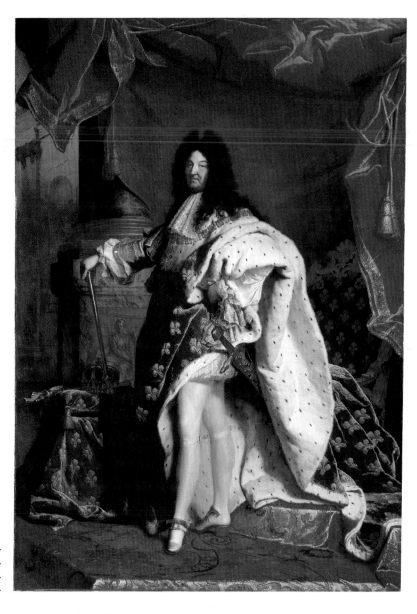

56. Hyacinthe Rigaud.
Louis XIV. 1701.
Oil on canvas, 9'1½" × 6'2⅝".
Louvre, Paris.

For the ultimate in a political portrait, however, we must look many centuries later, to a king who so wholeheartedly embraced his role as divine ruler that he dared to say "L'état, c'est moi" ("I am the state")—Louis XIV of France. Hyacinthe Rigaud's portrait **(56)** captures all the pageantry of a reign that was built on drama as carefully as any full-scale operatic performance might be.

Louis himself commented on the value of visible symbols: "Those who imagine that these are merely matters of ceremony are gravely mistaken. . . . The peoples over whom we reign, being unable to apprehend the basic reality of things, usually derive their opinions from what they can see with their eyes."[2] Louis ruled as the "Sun King" for an amazing seventy-two years, and during that time France experienced a period of political, social, and artistic achievement without parallel. At his death the nation was only seventy-five years away from revolution—a revolution that would bring down the monarchy—but while Louis sat on the throne, he kept all eyes focused on himself as the personification of France in her glory.

To the modern viewer Louis's costume seems absurd, his pose more than a little affected, but his subjects must have found the picture inspiring. No detail that might have contributed to the king's grandeur has been spared, from the lavish ermine-lined robes, to the lush canopy of the backdrop, to the classical Greek column at left. Louis obviously realized that political power rests on illusion. Art that fostered the illusion helped to maintain the power.

So far in this section we have focused on the person who was the *patron* of political art, rather than the artist who made it. Let us turn our attention now to the artist who chooses a specific political ideal and uses his or her talent to realize it. More often than not, such artists are allied with the "outs," not the "ins," of the political scene. Among the most famous of these was the 19th-century French artist Honoré Daumier.

Daumier was a painter, but he achieved greater renown as a political cartoonist, and he possessed all the traits necessary for the latter occupation—righteous anger, an eye for the telling detail, and a pen that could strike like a stiletto. In the early 1830s Daumier's harsh political criticism brought him fame but also got him into trouble with the authorities. One image in particular, widely distributed as a print (Chapter 8), caused official wrath, and that was *Murder in the rue Transnonain* **(57)**.

The title of Daumier's work was enough for his contemporary audience to understand the subject. In 1834 France was rocked by a popular uprising against the government of King Louis Philippe. Working-class people who lived on a certain street in Paris, the rue Transnonain, were suspected of taking part. On April 15 shots were fired from one tenement building, whereupon the civil guard broke in and killed an entire family—without determining their guilt or innocence. Daumier has portrayed the chilling aftermath of that slaughter. The father lies sprawled against a disarrayed bed, nearly covering the body of a dead child. A woman's body, graceless in sudden death, fills the shadows at left, while an old man's blood-spattered head projects into the picture at right.

Daumier's harsh realism gives this image its poignancy. We can't help wondering what these people were doing just a few moments ago, before they were murdered. Were they sleeping? Was the old man sitting in the chair, now overturned? The father's body, bathed in light, has a heroic quality despite the clumsy pose (or perhaps because of it). Daumier's art turned this poor family

57. Honoré Daumier. *Murder in the rue Transnonain,* from *L'Association mensuelle.* 1834. Lithograph, $11\frac{1}{4} \times 17\frac{3}{8}''$. The Metropolitan Museum of Art, New York (Rogers Fund, 1920).

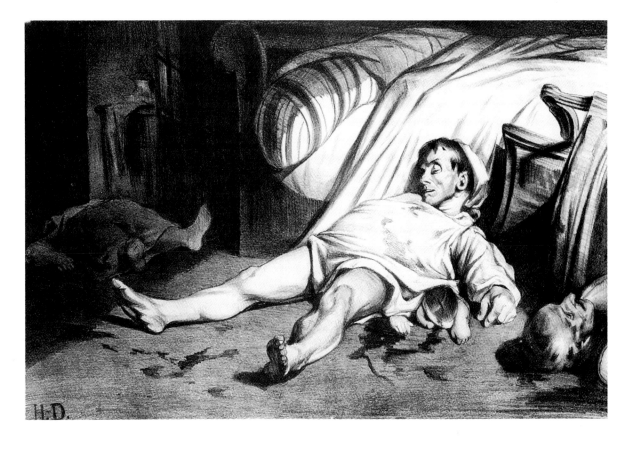

into martyrs for the cause—as the authorities well knew when they confiscated the artist's original and destroyed most of the copies.

Our next example also was created by an artist whose sympathies lay with those not in power, an artist who took up his brush with a sense of fury at the "ins" who caused devastation. From his fury came one of the great masterpieces of 20th-century art. The artist was Picasso, and the painting is called *Guernica* **(58)**.

It is necessary to know the story behind *Guernica* to understand its power. In 1937 Europe was moving toward war, and a trial run, so to speak, occurred in Spain, where the forces of General Francisco Franco waged civil war against the established government. Franco willingly accepted aid from Hitler, and in exchange he allowed the Nazis to test their developing air power. On April 28, 1937, the Germans bombed the town of Guernica, the old Basque capital in northern Spain. There was no real military reason for the raid; it was simply an experiment to see whether aerial bombing could wipe out a whole city. Being totally defenseless, Guernica was devastated and its civilian population massacred.

At the time Picasso, himself a Spaniard, was working in Paris and had been commissioned by his government to paint a mural for the Spanish Pavilion of the Paris World's Fair of 1937. For some time he had procrastinated about fulfilling the commission; then, within days after news of the bombing reached Paris, he started *Guernica* and completed it in little over a month. Despite the speedy execution, however, this was no unreasoning outburst of anger. Picasso controlled his rage, perhaps knowing that it could have better effect in a carefully planned canvas, and he made many preliminary drawings **(197)**. The finished mural had a shocking effect on those who saw it; it remains today a chillingly dramatic protest against the brutality of war.

At first encounter with *Guernica* the viewer is overwhelmed by its presence. The painting is huge—more than 25 feet long and nearly 12 feet high—and its stark, powerful imagery seems to reach out and engulf the observer. Picasso used no colors; the whole painting is done in white and black and shades of gray, possibly to create a "newsprint" quality in reporting the event. Although the artist's symbolism is very personal (and he declined to explain it in detail), we cannot misunderstand the scenes of extreme pain and anguish throughout the canvas. At far left a shrieking mother holds her dead child, and

58. Pablo Picasso. *Guernica.* 1937. Oil on canvas, 11'5½" × 25'5¾". Centro de Arte Reina Sofia, Madrid.

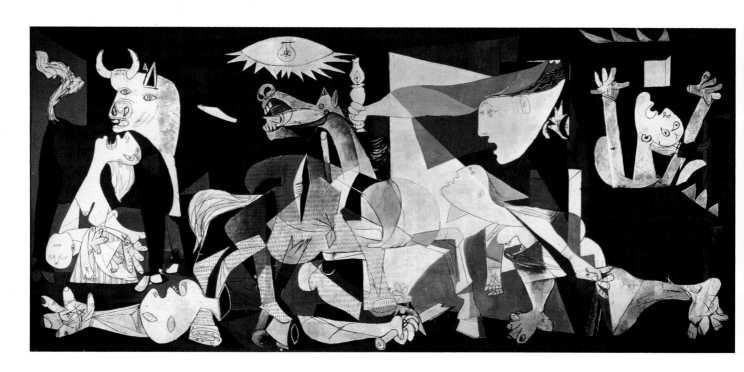

PROTECTING A MASTERPIECE

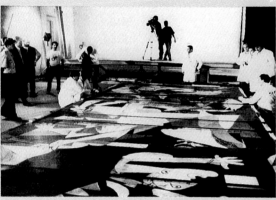

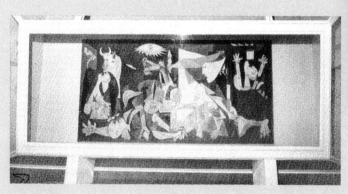

*G*UERNICA IS LIKE no other painting in the world. Enormous in size, stark in its black-and-white tones, shocking in its images of brutality, vehement in its political protest—Picasso's great work stands alone in the history of art. Although Picasso was prolific as an artist, he never made another picture like *Guernica*. This uniqueness, then, presents a problem: How can the painting be kept from harm? How does one protect a one-of-a-kind masterpiece?

Picasso always intended *Guernica* as a gift to the people of Spain, his homeland, but at the time of its creation in 1937, he did not trust the Spanish government. So he shipped the picture off to the Museum of Modern Art in New York, where it was to be held "on extended loan" until such time as a "democratic" government was established in Spain.

In New York, *Guernica* was simply hung on a wall—a large wall, to be sure. Its impact was staggering when the viewer came around a corner and, suddenly, there it was. If the museum guards decided you were all right, and if you held your breath carefully, you could get quite close to the canvas. Or you could stand far back to take in the whole work at a gulp. So the situation remained for forty years. Only one unpleasant event marred the open relationship between artwork and viewers. In 1974 an Iranian artist splashed the *Guernica* with red paint as a political protest, but no permanent damage was done.

By 1981, eight years after Picasso's death, there was general agreement that Spain's government had become sufficiently "democratic" to satisfy the artist's conditions. Under tight security *Guernica* was sent to Madrid, where it was installed in an annex of the Prado museum. The Prado was taking no chances with its newly acquired

masterpiece. *Guernica* was quickly sealed up in what some observers called a "cage"—an immense riot-resistant enclosure under an armor-plated ceiling, with bulletproof glass set some 14 feet in front of the canvas' surface. Obviously, one could no longer move in close to study details. Museum visitors complained that glare on the glass prevented any overall view of the painting. Some grumbled that the protective box dominated the picture, making even a 25-foot-wide painting seem puny. *Guernica* was safe, all right, but at what cost to its expression?

The controversy escalated in 1992, when *Guernica* was moved yet again, this time to the Reina Sofia museum a mile or so from the Prado. This new journey had all the drama of a spy movie. A special steel box, climate-controlled and weighing 3,500 pounds, was built to carry the painting. The transport company practiced its run down the road for weeks in advance, using stand-in paintings. Finally, on the fateful day, an armored truck carried *Guernica* through heavily guarded streets to its new home. The trip took half an hour and cost $200,000. Arriving intact at the Reina Sofia, *Guernica* was once again secured behind bulletproof glass.*

One cannot help wondering what Picasso would have thought about all this hullabaloo. His eldest daughter has accused the Spanish art ministry of "murdering" the *Guernica*. Perhaps "jailing" it would be a better term. The issue is one of balance. If *Guernica* should be damaged or destroyed, there is no way ever to replace it. But what is the point of keeping this masterpiece so *very* safe that no one can properly see it?

---

*After many complaints, the glass was removed in 1995.

---

left: Picasso's *Guernica* in its protective enclosure at the Prado Museum, Madrid.

right: Workers at the Prado Museum in Madrid preparing to move Picasso's *Guernica* to its new location.

at far right another woman, in a burning house, screams in agony. The gaping mouths and clenched hands speak of disbelief at such mindless cruelty.

Another victim is the dying horse to the left of center, speared from above and just as stunned by the carnage as any of the human sufferers. Various writers have interpreted the bull at upper left in different ways. Picasso drew much of his imagery from the bullfight, an ingrained part of his Spanish heritage. Perhaps the bull symbolizes the brutal victory of the Nazis; perhaps it, like the horse, is also a victim of carnage. There is even more confusion about the symbols of the lamp and the light bulb at top center. These may be indications that light is being cast on the horrors of war, or they may be signals of hope. Picasso did not tell us, so we are free to make our own associations.

With *Guernica* Picasso, like Daumier a century earlier, functioned as an artist of the "outs"—a voice crying against those who had power to do something of which he disapproved vehemently. Much political art of our time has this purpose. In the United States one group, black Americans, has a long history of being "out"—out of power, out of work, out of schools, out of the material pleasures of society. No wonder, then, that oppression of blacks should have found expression in art.

Jacob Lawrence, who is himself black, took up this theme in the early 1940s with an ambitious sixty-panel project now called *The Migration Series*. We illustrate here the best-known panel from the series, *One of the Largest Race Riots Occurred in East St. Louis* (59). As a work of social protest, Lawrence's painting can be compared, in concept if not in style, to Picasso's *Guernica*. Rather than depicting realistically the bloody violence of a race riot, Lawrence has transformed the action into a stylized ballet of flat, abstract shapes. Interpreted this way, the conflict takes on universal implications, revealing not just a vicious clash of individuals, but the underlying hatreds of "us" against "them" that mark a pattern throughout human history, in many parts of the world. Lawrence's composition is a masterful geometric arrangement, all forms leading to the clenched fist holding a knife—the one form silhouetted above the horizon line.

59. Jacob Lawrence. *One of the Largest Race Riots Occurred in East St. Louis,* Panel 52 from *The Migration Series.* 1940–41. Tempera on composition board, 12 × 18″. The Museum of Modern Art, New York (gift of Mrs. David M. Levy).

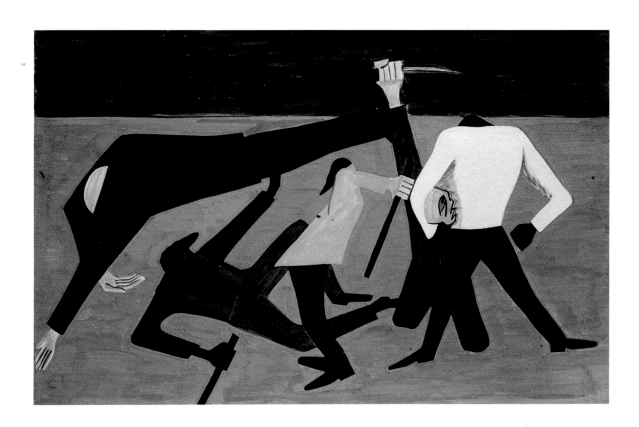

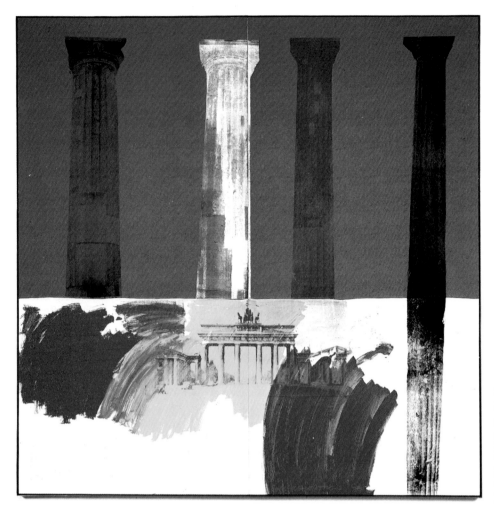

60. Robert Rauschenberg.
Bach's Rocks. 1990.
Acrylic and fabric collage
on plywood panels, 8'3¼" square.
National Gallery of Art,
Washington, D.C. (gift of the Robert
Rauschenberg Foundation, © 1996).
© 1998 Robert Rauschenberg/
Licensed by VAGA, New York.

What happens when the "ins" become "outs," and when the politically unacceptable becomes acceptable? This situation occurred in the late 1980s, when the communist regimes of Europe fell one after another. For decades Europe had been split in two, with democratic and free-market countries in the West, totalitarian and communist countries in the East. A symbol of this division was Berlin—previously one city, then two, cut down the center by the infamous Berlin Wall erected in 1961. How rigid was this division between free West and communist East—and how quickly it changed—can be shown by the experience of one artist, the American Robert Rauschenberg.

For nearly a decade Rauschenberg, through his Rauschenberg Overseas Culture Interchange project (ROCI), had tried repeatedly to mount a show of his work in Berlin. But the exhibition could never be arranged because of the artist's one stipulation: that the show run simultaneously in West Berlin and East Berlin, with access by people from both sides of the wall. The West Berlin museum was willing. The East German government said no.

Then, suddenly, the world changed. On November 9, 1989, the Berlin Wall was opened and began to come down. Rauschenberg hurried to get his exhibition ready, incorporating into works like *Bach's Rocks* **(60)** local references like an image of the Brandenburg Gate, the most famous gate in the wall. The show was planned for East Berlin. No other site was necessary because, astonishingly, Berlin was one city again and everybody could come. As an East German cultural spokesman put it, "An artist—who would be surprised at this?—couldn't breach the wall; a citizens' movement did. But I want to thank [Rauschenberg] for his readiness not to abandon the project despite many failures."[3]

ART AS THE MIRROR
OF EVERYDAY LIFE

When children start to draw and paint, they deal with the images they know best: mother and father, sisters and brothers, the teacher, the house, the dog. Many artists never lose their preoccupation with everyday things, and so we have a rich heritage of art depicting those concerns that are closest to the artist's personal world.

Art that depicts the little moments of everyday life and its surroundings is known as **genre.** Often, its purpose is a simple one—to record, to please the eye, to make us smile. Images like this occur throughout the history of art, in all cultures and parts of the world. A charming example from China is *Court Ladies Preparing Newly Woven Silk* **(61)**, part of a handscroll made in the 12th century but copied from an 8th-century painting. No grand political or social issues are at stake here. Rather, the artist has captured a delightful scene of daily activity: three women and a girl stretch and comb the length of silk, while a little girl peeks underneath as though to see what is going on. The fresh pastel colors of the kimonos, the women's quiet poses, the atmosphere of pleasant shared work—these elements give us a gentle masterpiece of genre.

A series of equally charming genre paintings occurs in an early French manuscript, one page of which we shall examine here. During the Middle Ages wealthy patrons customarily would commission artists to **illuminate,** or hand-illustrate, books, particularly prayer books. In the early 15th century a close relationship existed between the Duc de Berry, brother of the French king, and three artist brothers, the Limbourgs. The Limbourgs painted for the duke what has become one of the most famous illuminated books in the history of art, *Les Très Riches Heures* ("the very rich book of hours").

Meant for daily religious devotion, the *Très Riches Heures* contains a calendar, with each month's painting featuring a typical seasonal activity of either the peasantry or the nobility. Our illustration shows the *February* page **(62)**. At top in the **lunette,** or half-moon shape, the chariot of the Sun is shown

61. *Court Ladies Preparing Newly Woven Silk,* from China, Northern Song Dynasty. Attributed to Emperor Hui-zong (1082–1135) but probably by a court painter. Section of a handscroll; ink, colors, and gold on silk; height 14½". Courtesy Museum of Fine Arts, Boston (Chinese and Japanese Special Fund).

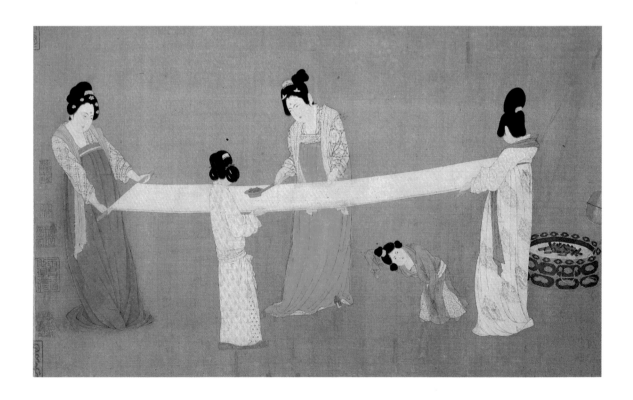

making its progress through the months and signs of the zodiac. Below, the Limbourgs depict their notion of lower-class life in the year's coldest month.

This view of everyday life focuses on a small peasant hut with its occupants clustered around the fire, their garments pulled back to get maximum benefit from the warmth. With a touch of artistic license, the Limbourgs have removed the front wall of the hut so we can look in. Outside the cozy hut we see what may be the earliest snow-covered landscape ever painted. Sheep cluster in their enclosure, a peasant comes rushing across the barnyard pulling his cloak about his face to keep in the warm breath. From there the movement progresses diagonally up the slope to a man chopping firewood, another urging a donkey uphill, and finally the church at the top.

One should bear in mind this is a miniature, only 9 inches high, to appreciate the richness of details. So acute is the Limbourgs' observation, on so tiny a scale, that we understand the condition of each player—the exertion of the woodcutter, the chill of the running figure, the nonchalant poses of men in the hut, and the demure modesty of the lady in blue.

Genre painting has been important in the United States since colonial times. One of its greatest practitioners was Missouri-bred George Caleb Bingham, who in the mid-19th century portrayed scenes of what was then the

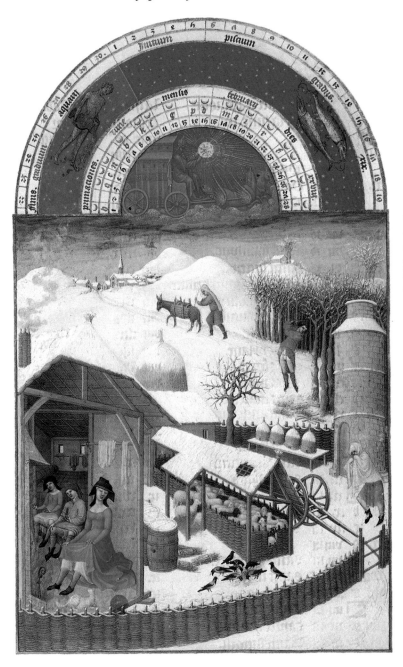

62. Limbourg Brothers. *February* page, from *Les Très Riches Heures du Duc de Berry*. 1416. Illumination, $8\frac{7}{8} \times 5\frac{3}{8}''$. Musée Condé, Chantilly.

American frontier. Bingham's most famous picture, *Fur Traders Descending the Missouri*, shows us an apparently simple subject—a man, a boy, a pet fox, a flat boat floating placidly down the river. At one level we can read the painting as simply capturing a slice of life in the untamed American Midwest **(63)**, but such is Bingham's skill that we find more in the scene as we continue to study it. The serene horizontal of the boat barely making a ripple in the still water,

right: 63. George Caleb Bingham. *Fur Traders Descending the Missouri.* c. 1845. Oil on canvas, 29 × 36½". The Metropolitan Museum of Art, New York (Morris K. Jesup Fund, 1933).

below: 64. Pierre-Auguste Renoir. *Le Moulin de la Galette.* 1876. Oil on canvas, 4'3½" × 5'9". Musée d'Orsay, Paris.

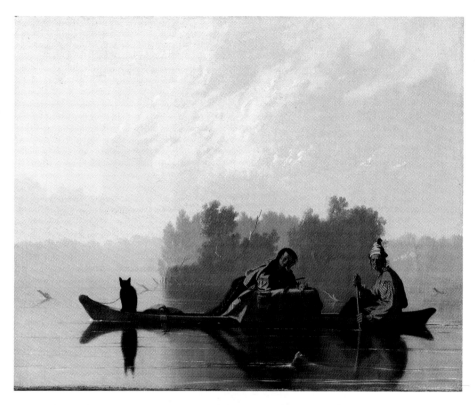

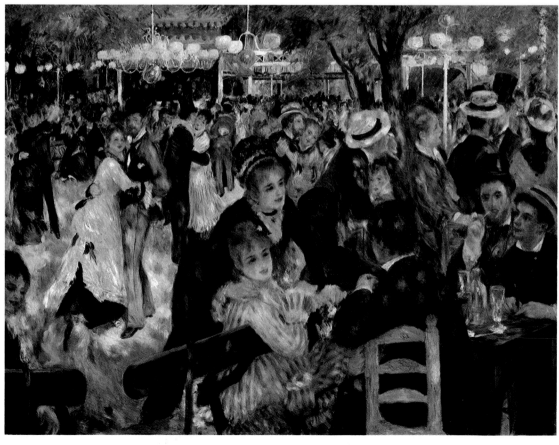

the tranquil poses of the fur traders, the misty (almost mystical) island glimpsed behind them, the cottony clouds in the sky—all these combine to create a poetic vision of people in harmony with nature. One strangely eerie note is the fox, black and motionless, reflected in the mirrorlike river.

French artists of the period were equally interested in portraying life's little moments, the fleeting experiences that last for an instant and then are gone. This type of subject was a particular favorite with the Impressionist painters of the late 19th century, whose goal was to record that which is transitory—an impression (Chapter 19). In Pierre-Auguste Renoir's *Le Moulin de la Galette* (64) young couples meet at the outdoor café, they dance, they fall in love. The viewer has a quick impression of the most delightful of all ways to spend a summer day. As observers, we seem to have glanced briefly at the scene and absorbed its essence, rather than its details. We can almost hear the bright music (a waltz tune unquestionably), feel the warm breezes, sense an atmosphere of innocent flirtation and fun.

The American artist Florine Stettheimer chose everyday life as the main subject of her art—that is, her own glamorous, delicious life. Active from about 1915 into the 1940s, Stettheimer seems to have known every creative person who passed through New York in that era. One of four daughters of a formidable mother, she painted the daily pleasures of her family and friends in a colorful, fanciful, exuberant style all her own. In *Lake Placid* (65) the artist's mother, Rosetta, as always dressed in black, stands at lower left, seeming to cast a disapproving eye on the other happily cavorting figures. To Rosetta's right, the artist herself, in sunhat and robe, tiptoes out of Mother's view to join the fun, while her sisters Carrie and Ettie make two appearances each, as swimmers and sunbathers. Other figures from Stettheimer's circle are readily identifiable. The overall effect is of dazzling sunlight bathing the players in a splashy romp of summer vacation—except, of course, for that one dark figure.

ART AND NATURE

If art is the mirror of everyday life, it is also the mirror of everyday surroundings. Throughout history artists have turned their eyes to nature as an engrossing subject for art. What they have seen depends on many things, including the cultures in which they worked and their own artistic visions.

65. Florine Stettheimer.
Lake Placid. 1919.
Oil on canvas, 40$\frac{1}{8}$ × 50$\frac{1}{8}$″.
Courtesy Museum of Fine Arts, Boston (gift of Miss Ettie Stettheimer).

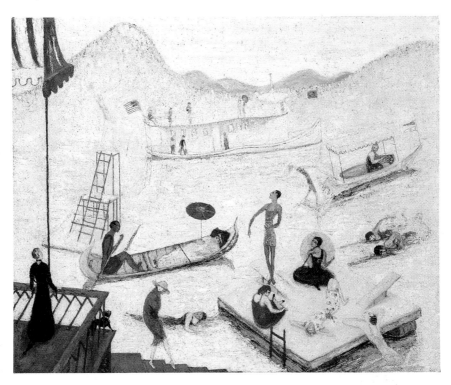

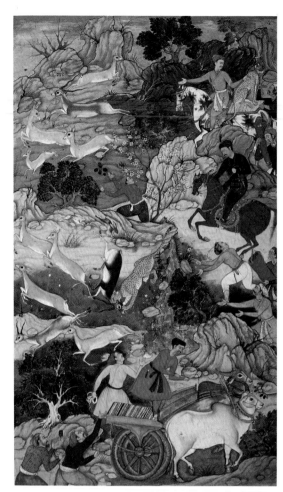

right: 66. Lal and Sanwlah.
*Akbar Hunting with Trained
Cheetahs,* from the *Akbar Nama.*
c. 1590. Gouache on paper,
height 15″.
Victoria & Albert Museum, London
(by courtesy of the Board of Trustees).

below: 67. John Constable.
The White Horse. 1819.
Oil on canvas, 4′3⅝″ × 6′2⅛″.
The Frick Collection,
New York (copyright).

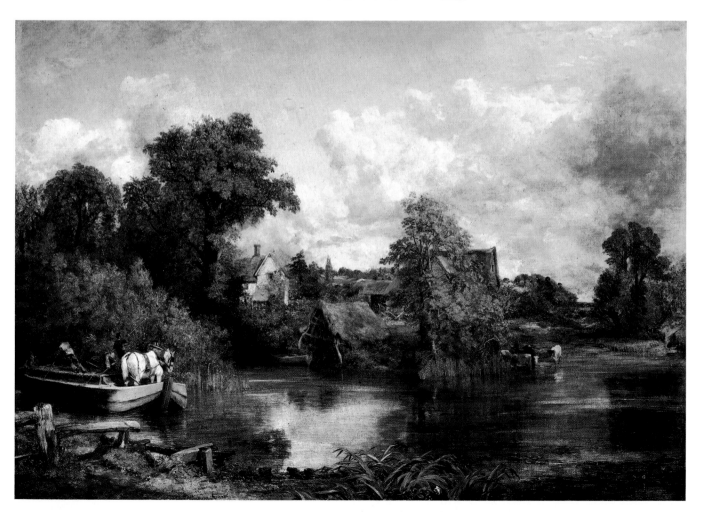

Our first example, a miniature from 16th-century India, is part of the *Akbar Nama,* or history of Akbar. The Mughal emperor Akbar, who ruled India from 1556 to 1605, was both a powerful leader and an enthusiastic patron of the arts. He attracted to his court both Indian and Persian artists, providing them not only with his royal patronage but also with the finest painting materials available, including powdered gold. *Akbar Hunting with Trained Cheetahs* **(66)** shows the emperor at middle right, on a rearing brown horse, watching his cheetah bring down an antelope. The landscape teems with activity. Horses, men, and game rush through the trees and brush, in and around the bulbous, knobby outcroppings of rock. In fact, the trees and rocks themselves seem to be in motion, caught up in the frenzy of the hunt. There is no area of rest for our eyes in this scene. Every inch of the painting is filled with decorative detail and bursting with energy. Were it not for the dominance of natural forms in the composition, we might be tempted to call this a genre scene. But here even the emperor is rendered small amid the turbulent landscape.

England in the first half of the 19th century produced two preeminent landscape artists who were only a year apart in age but light years apart in their approach to the painting of nature. John Constable was concerned with absolute naturalism, a sense of what—for him—the landscape *really* looked like. In a Constable painting, such as *The White Horse* **(67)**, the viewer seems to be surrounded by the natural scene, inside it without taking a step. To stand before this huge canvas is to be transported to another world, a peaceful corner of the rural English countryside. Constable was meticulous about recording details of foliage and other features, but his main fascination lay in transitory effects of light and changing patterns in the sky. The sunlight dapples through the leaves, reflects off the water, and picks out the white horse that gives the painting its name. Clouds scuttling across the sky seem actually to be in motion; we know that a second earlier or later the effect would be different. For all their serenity, Constable's visions capture a moment that will never come again.

Landscapes in the later work of Joseph Mallord William Turner would never be called serene. To be sure, Turner also strove to capture the transitory moment, but his moments are those at the height of the storm, so to speak. Cyclones at sea, huge fires on land, blizzards and tempests and outbursts of *Rockets and Blue Lights* **(68)**—these are the subjects of a Turner landscape, so transformed by the artist's abstraction as to become studies in light and air. Turner's paintings are whirlpools of energy, so compelling we seem to hear dramatic music crashing in the background.

68. J. M. W. Turner. *Rockets and Blue Lights (Close at Hand) to Warn Steamboats of Shoal Water.* 1840. Oil on canvas, 3'1/16" × 4'1/8". © Sterling and Francine Clark Art Institute, Williamstown, Mass.

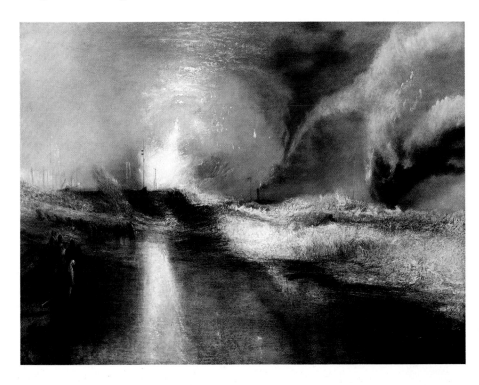

Still another approach to the theme of nature can be found in Paul Cézanne's painting of *Mont Sainte-Victoire* **(69)**, a mountain near the artist's home in the south of France. Through the later years of Cézanne's life, Mont Sainte-Victoire obsessed him; altogether he did some seventy-five painted or drawn versions of the scene. His interest, however, lay not in recording the physical appearance of nature but in searching for a solidity and unity of form in nature, an inherent order that he saw with his painter's eye. Cézanne is famous for his belief that geometry serves as the basis for all forms, including those in the landscape. He sought to discover the forms of geometric solids— the cone, the sphere, the cylinder—in nature and to record them in his art.

To Cézanne, then, nature painting is not an end in itself but rather a vehicle for studying forms in space, much as he would study a human figure for a portrait or a group of objects on a table for a still-life composition **(147)**. Here he portrays Mont Sainte-Victoire as a hulking presence looming over the countryside. We see no animate life—no people or horses or donkeys— and no roads or paths to traverse this landscape. Still, for all its solidity of form, Cézanne's landscape is not static. The artist's brilliant color patches of violet, green, and ochre, set down mainly on the diagonal, cause the surfaces to pulsate and shimmer with living energy.

Nature on a grand scale inspired the artists we have considered so far in this section, but nature rendered on a small scale can be equally compelling.

69. Paul Cézanne. *Mont Sainte-Victoire.* 1902–04. Oil on canvas, $27\frac{1}{2} \times 35\frac{1}{4}''$. Philadelphia Museum of Art (George W. Elkins Collection).

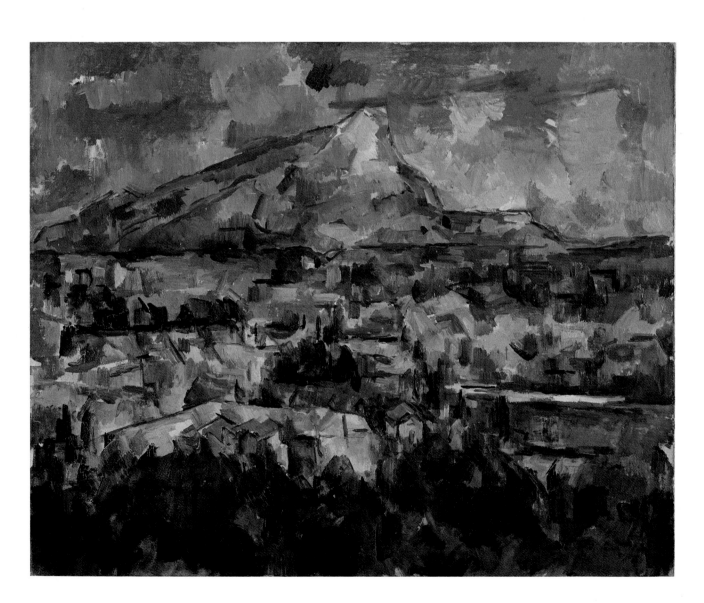

PAUL CÉZANNE

1839–1906

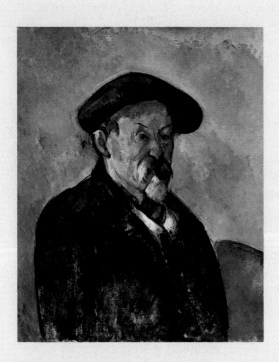

PAUL CÉZANNE remains one of the most enigmatic figures in modern art history, even though the details of his life are well known. A word often used to describe his personality is "difficult." Clearly, he was a man of intelligence and great sensitivity, yet he could be rude to strangers and boorish with his friends. Although he was acquainted with most of the leading artists then working in Paris, he spent the greater part of his life in isolation in the southern French town of Aix-en-Provence, where he was born.

Cézanne's banker father tried to steer his son into his own profession or the law, but the young man showed so little talent and inclination for either that eventually the father gave up and permitted him to undertake art studies. Cézanne's first attempts at exhibiting his work met with disastrous results; the critics' reac-tions ranged from ridicule to outrage. Nevertheless, he persevered, struggling on alone to achieve the form in art that was his vision. Cézanne's paintings are difficult to date, because he worked on many canvases at once and often labored over the same painting for several years. So demanding was he with live models that few sitters were willing to pose for him. One who did pose, the art dealer Ambroise Vollard, reported that he was forced to endure 115 sittings, some lasting three hours or more.

In 1869, while visiting Paris, Cézanne met a young woman, Marie-Hortense Fiquet, and they became lovers. Some three years later their son Paul was born. Cézanne went to extraordinary lengths to conceal this liaison from his domineering father, lest his allowance be cut.

For most of Cézanne's life only the very discerning—and they were few—recognized the genius of his art. After his initial disappointments, the artist stopped ex-hibiting in Paris for twenty years. Then in 1895 Ambroise Vollard decided to mount a show—Cézanne's first one-man exhibition—and asked the artist to send all avail-able work. Cézanne bundled up 150 canvases and shipped them off to Paris from Aix. The show took Paris completely by surprise and was an immediate sensation. From that time until his death the artist gradually ac-quired the recognition he deserved; ironically, he had become so embittered by long neglect that the acclaim gave him little pleasure.

While alternatively mocked and ignored by critics and the general public, Cézanne never lost faith in him-self and his art. In 1874 he wrote this to his mother: "I am beginning to find myself stronger than any of those around me. . . . I must go on working, but not in order to attain a finished perfection, which is so much sought after by imbeciles. And this quality which is commonly so much admired is nothing but the accomplishment of a craftsman, and makes any work produced in that way inartistic and vulgar. I must not try to finish anything except for the pleasure of making it truer and wiser. And you may be sure that there will come a time when I shall come into my own, and that I have admirers who are much more fervent, more steadfast than those who are attracted only by an empty outward appearance."[4]

Paul Cézanne. *Self-Portrait with a Beret*. c. 1906.
Oil on canvas, 25¼ × 21".
Courtesy Museum of Fine Arts, Boston
(Charles H. Bayley Picture and Painting Fund
and partial gift of Elizabeth Paine Metcalf).

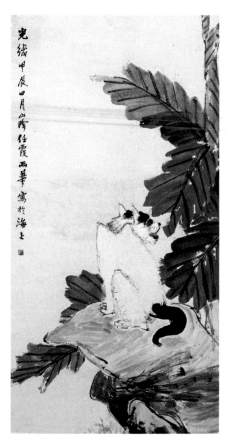

Ren Xia's *Cat on a Rock Beneath Banana Palms* **(70)** is characteristic of nature study popular in China for hundreds of years. Typically, the artist narrows her viewpoint and omits all extraneous details to focus on the elements in her title: the cat, the rock, and the banana leaves. In effect, these natural forms are lifted from their environment and artfully arranged to create a still-life composition. We notice the shapes of the banana leaves thrusting upward and outward, the angular pose of the cat (especially the repeated "peaks" of ears, shoulder, and hind leg), the dramatic curl of the cat's black tail silhouetted against the rock. Trademark elements of Ren Xia's style are her elegant composition and the expressive personality of the animal. This is not a miscellaneous cat, but a cat with *attitude*.

Our next artist zooms in on natural forms even more tightly. The flower paintings of Georgia O'Keeffe, such as *Black Hollyhock, Blue Larkspur* **(71)**, are extreme close-ups, almost to the point of abstraction. O'Keeffe examines every nuance of the form minutely, as though a whole universe were unfolding within the flower. The lush texture of the hollyhock is treated as though it were a circlet of crushed velvet, forming a protective cushion around the gleaming center of the blossom. Much has been made of the apparent sexual symbolism in O'Keeffe's flower paintings. Critics have praised their evocation of ripe female sexuality. The artist scoffed at such interpretations, but there is no denying the sensuous quality in these images.

O'Keeffe's flowers fill nearly every square inch of her canvas, leaving only a little background (non-flower) at the upper edges. For a contrast, we can look at a work that seems to have nothing *but* upper edges, a painting that might have taken up the space that O'Keeffe had left over.

above: 70. Ren Xia.
*Cat on a Rock
Beneath Banana Palms.* 1904.
Hanging scroll, ink on paper;
$40\frac{3}{8} \times 21\frac{7}{8}''$.
Collection Harold Wong, Hong Kong.

right: 71. Georgia O'Keeffe.
Black Hollyhock, Blue Larkspur.
1929. Oil on canvas, 36 × 30″.
The Metropolitan Museum of Art,
New York
(George A. Hearn Fund, 1934).

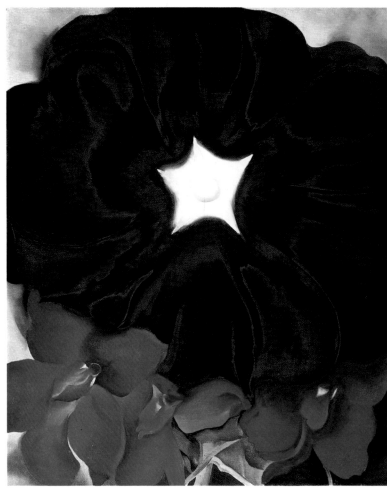

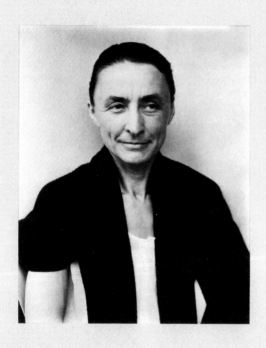

GEORGIA O'KEEFFE

1887–1986

"**A**T LAST! A woman on paper!" According to legend, this was the reaction of the famed photographer and art dealer Alfred Stieglitz, in 1916, when he first saw the work of Georgia O'Keeffe. Whether accurate or not, the quote sums up Stieglitz' view of O'Keeffe as the first great artist to bring to her work the true essence and experience of womanhood. Ultimately, much of the critical art world came to share Stieglitz' opinion.

O'Keeffe was born on a farm in Wisconsin. She received a thorough, if conventional, art training at the School of the Art Institute of Chicago and the Art Students League in New York. During the early years she supported herself by teaching art in schools and colleges. By 1912 she was teaching in Amarillo, Texas—the beginning of a lifelong infatuation with the terrain of the Southwest.

In the winter of 1915–16 O'Keeffe sent a number of drawings to a friend in New York, asking her not to show the drawings to anyone. The friend violated this trust—and no doubt helped to set the path for O'Keeffe's entire life and career. She took the drawings to Stieglitz.

By 1916 Stieglitz had gained considerable fame, not only as a photographer but, through his "291" Gallery, as an exhibitor of the most innovative European and American painters. He was stunned by O'Keeffe's work. Later that year he included her in a group show at "291," and in 1917 he gave her a solo exhibition. This was the beginning of an extraordinary artistic and personal collaboration that would last until Stieglitz' death in 1946.

O'Keeffe moved to New York. Stieglitz left his wife and lived with her. O'Keeffe painted; Stieglitz exhibited her work and made hundreds of photographs of her. The couple married in 1924, but their union was always an unconventional one. For more than a quarter-century their paths crossed and separated. Stieglitz was most at home in New York City and at his family's summer place at Lake George. O'Keeffe was drawn increasingly to the stark landscapes of Texas and New Mexico. O'Keeffe treasured her husband's presence but could paint at her best only in the Southwest. Stieglitz longed for her company but also wanted her paintings for his gallery.

O'Keeffe gained critical acclaim with her first exhibition, and it never entirely left her. Although major showings of her work were rare after Stieglitz died, no one forgot Georgia O'Keeffe. She was part of no "school" or style. Her work took an exceptionally personal path, as did her life. She dressed almost exclusively in black. She came and went as she pleased and accepted into her world only those people whom she found talented and interesting. More than most, O'Keeffe marched to her own drummer.

After 1949 O'Keeffe lived permanently in New Mexico, the area with which she is most closely associated. In 1972, when she was eighty-four years old, a potter in his twenties, Juan Hamilton, came into her life, and they became close companions. Rumors that they married are probably unfounded, but Hamilton remained with the increasingly feeble, almost-blind artist until her death.

Early on, in her thirties, O'Keeffe had expressed her impatience with other people's standards for life and art: "I decided I was a very stupid fool not to at least paint as I wanted to and say what I wanted to when I painted as that seemed to be the only thing I could do that didn't concern anybody but myself—that was nobody's business but my own."[5]

Alfred Stieglitz. *Georgia O'Keeffe*. 1932. Photograph.
The Metropolitan Museum of Art, New York
(Alfred Stieglitz Collection, lent by Georgia O'Keeffe).

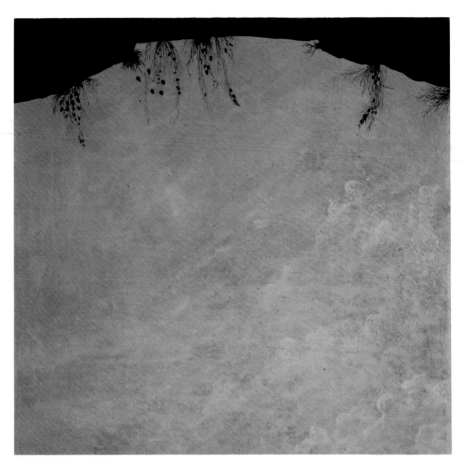

72. Joan Nelson.
Untitled (#227). 1988.
Oil and wax on wood,
12″ square.
Courtesy Robert Miller Gallery,
New York.

Almost the whole of Joan Nelson's tiny painting *Untitled #227* **(72)** consists of sky, showing just a hint of organic forms at the top. The observer of this scene could be in a cave, looking up and out at the clouds, so that the upper rim of the cave obscures the view slightly.

Why did the artist choose such an unusual angle? Why is there much more sky than landscape? The answer gives us clues to the essence of art. In Chapter 2 (p. 26) we said that a painting of a horse is not a horse; horses are flesh and blood, but paintings are daubs of paint on a background. Nelson amplifies this idea. She chooses an image that looks like an unimportant detail from the upper section of, say, a Constable **(67)** and makes it the center of attention. Then she works over her paintings heavily, coating them with wax or varnish, scarring and scraping them to get the quality of an "Old Master" painting that has hung in a museum for generations. Nelson wants us to see that her work is "about" the subject of painting, not "about" the subject of nature. It is the artist's creation, daubs of paint on a background. Of course, every other version of nature painting is the same—as is every painting of every kind. But Nelson drives the point home.

Nelson's art, like all the rest we have seen in this chapter, looks primarily to the outside for inspiration. Our next category focuses on artists who turn inward, to their own brains and psyches, for the genesis of their art.

IMAGINATION AND FANTASY

The purposes of imaginative art are as complex and as individual as imagination itself. An artist may look inward and paint what he or she sees in an attempt to understand this inner life, to purge it of its terrors, or simply because the products of the imagination seem more interesting than the realities of every day. We may be tempted to think of imaginative art as a purely 20th-century phenomenon, a product of the Freudian era or even of the "me generation." Looking closely at one's dreams and fantasies—and then recording them as art—does indeed seem to be a peculiarly modern preoccupation. Nevertheless, we can trace imaginative art back at least to the 16th century, where it flourished in the hands of the Netherlandish artist Hieronymus Bosch.

When we first encounter *The Garden of Earthly Delights* **(73)**, we might think we have wandered into a fun house of a particularly macabre kind. Bosch's large **triptych** (a three-section panel, of which we show only the middle portion) is like a peep into Hell—but this is an X-rated earthly Hell. Hundreds of nude human figures cavort in a fantasy landscape peopled also by giant plants, animals no biologist ever classified, and strange creatures that are part human, part vegetation. Humans ride upon, emerge from, are devoured by, or become part of the plant and animal forms. Bosch has let his imagination and perhaps his dream imagery go wherever it might. He drew upon many sources for his creations, including folklore, literature, astrology, and religious writings, but only his own inventiveness could have constructed an amazing fantasy land like this one.

Artists who deal with the realm of the imagination are often quite interesting as personalities. This was true of Bosch, and it was true also of an

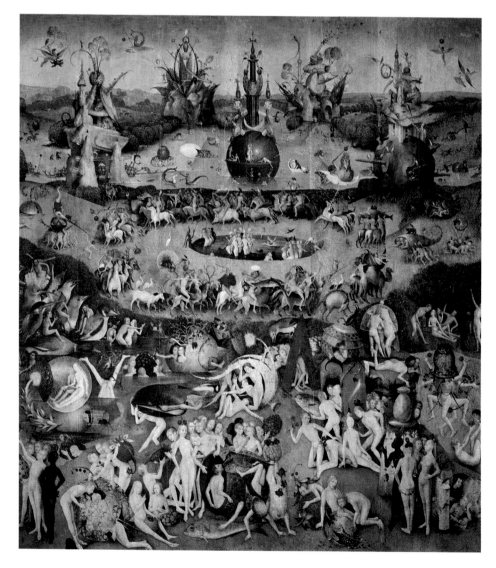

73. Hieronymus Bosch. *The Garden of Earthly Delights,* center section. c. 1505–10. Panel, 7′2⅝″ × 6′4¾″. Museo del Prado, Madrid.

English artist/poet who worked during the late 18th and early 19th centuries. William Blake was, by the standards of his time and most others, a thorough-going eccentric. He was foremost a poet and will be remembered by generations of college literature students for the lines "Tyger! Tyger! burning bright/ In the forests of the night." Much of Blake's production as an artist involved the illustration of books, not only of his own volumes of poetry but also of the Bible, Shakespeare, and Dante. In these he expressed a kind of personal theology, which he claimed had been revealed to him in visions of God, Christ, various angels, and certain notable personages from history.

Typical is his *Satan Watching the Caresses of Adam and Eve* (74), an illustration for John Milton's epic poem, *Paradise Lost.* The scene depicted does not appear in the Scripture or in Milton's poetic version of the fall from grace of Adam and Eve. According to standard Christian doctrine, Adam and Eve were innocent and free of carnal desire before eating the forbidden fruit. William Blake, however, had other ideas, and he followed his own theological and sexual interpretation in this work. Years later, in discussing the illustration, he insisted: "I saw Milton in imagination, and he told me to beware of being misled by his *Paradise Lost.* In particular he wished me to shew the falsehood of his doctrine that the pleasure of sex arose from the Fall. The Fall could not produce any pleasure."[6]

74. William Blake. *Satan Watching the Caresses of Adam and Eve,* illustration for Milton's *Paradise Lost.* 1808. Pen and watercolor on paper, $19\frac{7}{8} \times 15''$. Courtesy Museum of Fine Arts, Boston (gift by subscription, 1890).

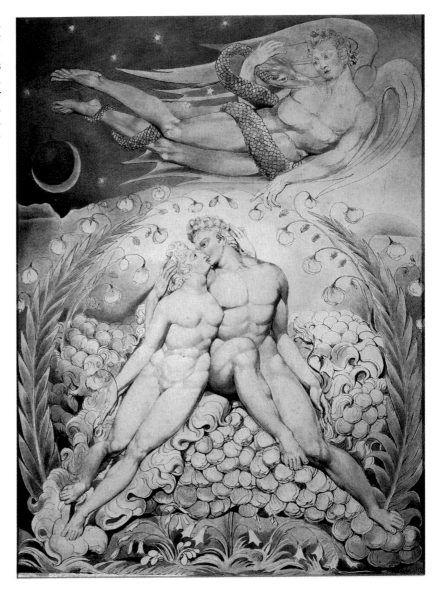

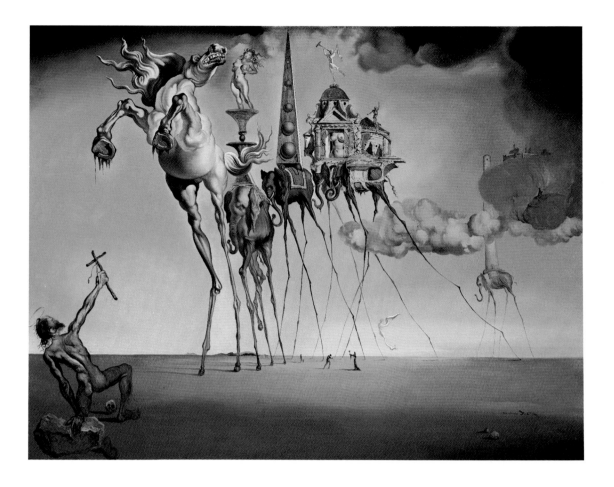

75. Salvador Dali.
The Temptation of Saint Anthony.
1946. Oil on canvas, 35¼ × 47".
Musées Royaux des Beaux-Arts
de Belgique, Brussels
(acquired from Mme Anne-Marie
Robiliart, Brussels, 1965).

Blake's picture, therefore, shows the first couple, still not having touched the apple, still in the Garden of Eden, engaged in a decidedly erotic pursuit. They are enveloped in a lush circle of fantasy foliage, and their bodies are muscular and full-fleshed in the manner of Dürer or Michelangelo, both of whose works were known to the artist. Floating above the pair is the figure of Satan—part angel (it must be remembered that Satan was the fallen angel Lucifer) and part serpent. Soon afterward, Satan, in the guise of a serpent, will tempt Eve to eat the apple, resulting in banishment from the Garden of Eden. Blake's Satan looks down upon the lovers with something rather like jealousy, which puts an entirely different slant on the story of the temptation. The artist's imagery comes not from the Bible, not from Milton, but from his own imagination.

Imaginative treatment of a religious subject also appears in the work of the 20th-century Spanish artist Salvador Dali. In *The Temptation of St. Anthony* **(75)** Dali addresses a subject that had been popular throughout the Middle Ages and early Renaissance. The story concerns efforts by the holy man, St. Anthony, to fend off temptations of the flesh that tormented him in his thoughts and dreams. Earlier representations showed the saint being assailed by all manner of hellish demons and often being lured by a lustful woman or women. Dali has perhaps come closer to the truth by reinterpreting the temptation as a dream/nightmare landscape.

Dali's art, often identified as **Surrealism** (Chapter 19), is predominantly an art of the unconscious. The artist explored his own dreams, studied case histories of psychotic individuals, and even toyed with waking hallucinations, which he claimed he could summon on command. In *The Temptation* St. Anthony appears as a gaunt figure, besieged yet strong, holding off a nightmare parade of fantastic creatures stalking across an endless plain on giant insect legs. Dali's demons are not monsters from Hell, but the demons of the mind.

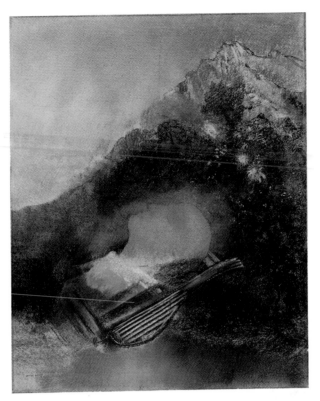

76. Odilon Redon. *Orpheus.* c. 1903–10. Pastel on paper, 27¼ × 22⅜″. © 1996 The Cleveland Museum of Art (gift from J. H. Wade, 1926.25).

The Surrealists drew their inspiration from many sources, among them, very likely, the French artist Odilon Redon, who was a contemporary (but not a colleague) of Cézanne's. Until he was about fifty, Redon worked almost exclusively in black and white, but in later life he adopted the brilliant hues of pastels to portray mythological themes. His mature style is marked by the tense, edgy combination of luscious colors with disturbing subject matter.

Orpheus **(76)** shows the tragic end of the ancient Greek hero-musician whose singing and playing on the lyre were so beautiful that no one could resist being enchanted. After losing his beloved, Eurydice, Orpheus fell into despair and set off to wander in the wilderness. One day he was attacked by a fierce band of Thracian women, who tore him apart and threw his head, still singing, into the river. It is this ghastly scene—the singing, disembodied head with the lyre floating beside it—that Redon finds in his own imagination and presents to us in sparkling, iridescent colors. By dealing with imaginative concepts, the artist himself said he intended to place "the logic of the visible at the service of the invisible."

From the imaginative and fantastic, we turn to the concrete and everyday: the milestones of life. Years ago it was said that a respectable person's name should appear in the newspaper only three times—at birth, marriage, and death. Today other lifetime events are considered properly newsworthy, but those three remain paramount. Two are universal, the third prevalent. And all are valid subjects for art.

BIRTH, MARRIAGE, AND DEATH

It may surprise us to discover that the subject of birth appears so rarely in Western art—the art derived from European traditions. After all, everybody is born, and it is the most important thing that ever happens to us. Many children being born now are photographed and videotaped in the act, and some doctors even provide videotapes of the baby *in utero* through the miracle of ultrasound. But except for religious pictures—images of the birth of Christ are plentiful—birth has not captured the attention of many artists.

Contemporary artist Judy Chicago believes this is so because, historically, most artists have been men, and men do not have babies. Her large-scale enterprise called *The Birth Project* **(77)** was planned to remedy this absence of birth imagery. Its approximately one hundred individual pieces were designed by Chicago and then executed in various forms of fiber craft by 150 volunteer needleworkers, nearly all women. Most forms of traditional "women's craft" are represented—embroidery, quilting, weaving, crochet, petit point—with the needleworkers following Chicago's lushly colored and often anatomically graphic designs. This artist emphasizes the natural continuity from women's sexuality to procreation.

By contrast, a male artist, the Frenchman Jean Dubuffet, depicts *Childbirth* **(78)** as a shocking, almost primitive explosion. In this 1944 painting the baby seems to have popped out of his mother's body to their mutual surprise and dismay. The deliberate flatness of Dubuffet's picture makes the bed on which the woman is lying appear vertical, as though she were standing in a squat to drop the baby on his head.

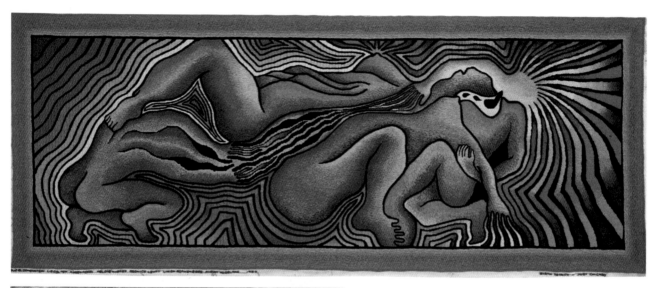

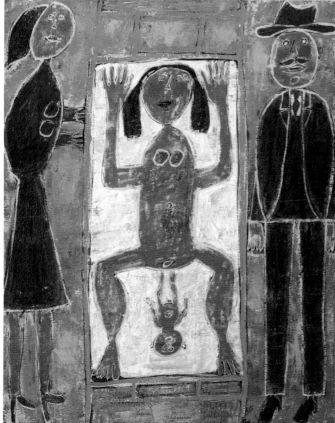

above: 77. Judy Chicago. *Birth Trinity,* from *The Birth Project.* 1983. Needlepoint on 6-mesh canvas, from color study; 3'6" × 10'6". Needlework by "The Teaneck Group." Collection Through the Flower, a nonprofit organization.

left: 78. Jean Dubuffet. *Childbirth,* from the series *Marionettes de la ville et de la campagne.* 1944. Oil on canvas, 39⅜" × 31¾". The Museum of Modern Art, New York (gift of Pierre Matisse in memory of Patricia Kane Matisse).

To understand this unusual imagery, we should know something of the artist's goals. Dubuffet claimed to be drawn to the "banal"—the subject so commonplace as to be trite and boring, which then would be rendered by him in a manner anything but banal. Early in his career he amassed a large collection of artworks by children and the mentally disturbed, which he called *l'Art brut* (brutal art). Certainly in this painting he has cast a rather brutal light on the commonplace event of giving birth. The drawing style is intentionally childlike, and the point of view might well be a child's naive idea of how a baby arrives in the world. But Dubuffet was *not* a child. This sophisticated artist clearly realized that the drawings of children often capture profoundly important experiences and emotions, that children focus on ritual and event. In borrowing these forms, in assuming the mind and eye of a child, he meant to carry human images "onto a plane of seriousness . . . a plane of high ceremony, of solemn office of celebration."[7]

Artists outside the European tradition are more likely than their Western counterparts to view birth and infancy as important aspects of life and therefore as fit subjects for their expression. The art of Africa, Oceania, and Central and South America includes numerous mother-and-baby figures. Our example **(79)** from the Bambara people in what is now Mali, in Africa, shows the mother cradling her newborn child, the infant giving every sign of safety and warmth pressed against its mother's belly. In this sensitive work the sculptor conveys both the power and the nurturing quality of the mother. Her head is large, suggesting intelligence, while her posture, headdress, and thronelike chair indicate high status. The prominent breasts and sheltering curl of the arms emphasize the mother's role as life-giver and provider for the infant.

For a similar treatment in Western art—a rare one—we turn to a painting by Paula Modersohn-Becker called *Mother and Child* **(80)**. What might have been simply a woman nursing her baby has been given a universal quality by Modersohn-Becker, so that the image seems to be *all* mothers nursing all babies since time began. The mother's body, heavy and solid as the earth itself, curves protectively around the child, who in turn curves into the mother's belly. Both figures are anonymous; the baby's face is obscured and the woman's barely articulated. Modersohn-Becker's picture speaks not just of childbearing but of the unbreakable attachment, the primal love, between mother and child.

Marriage is popular with artists from all cultures; in fact, it is the subject of one of the most famous works in Western art, *Portrait of Giovanni Arnolfini and His Wife, Giovanna Cenami* **(81)**. Painted in the 15th century by the northern European artist Jan van Eyck, the "Arnolfini Wedding," as it is sometimes called, is believed by many experts to have had a specific purpose. It apparently served as a marriage document, made to record and legitimize the nuptials between the merchant Arnolfini and his bride. At center in the painting is a mirror reflecting the artist, who has come to bear witness to the ceremony, adding his signature "Jan van Eyck was here, 1434."

To reinforce the solemn nature of the wedding scene, the artist has included many symbols. The little dog at the couple's feet is an emblem of faithfulness. The chandelier at top center has one candle burning—an essential ingredient of the marriage ceremony, because it represents the all-seeing eye of God. Arnolfini has removed his sandals to indicate that he is standing on sacred ground, the ground on which are pledged the holy vows of matrimony. Other symbols relate to the potential fruitfulness of marriage—that is, the hope for many children to come from this union. Actual fruits lying on the windowsill, as well as the marriage bed in the background, express this outcome. Some observers have concluded that the new wife is already pregnant, but her rounded form and the gesture of clasping her gown over her belly are more likely meant as anticipation of offspring who will be conceived. Finally, the couple have joined their hands directly under the mirror, and Arnolfini raises his right forearm. This is the exact moment of oath-taking. The artist Jan van Eyck records it for all time.

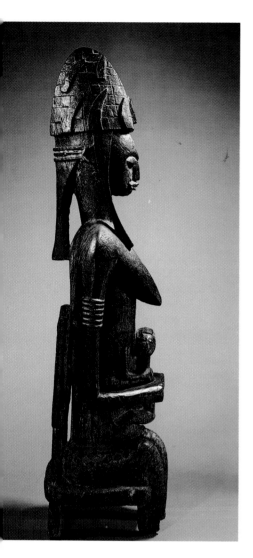

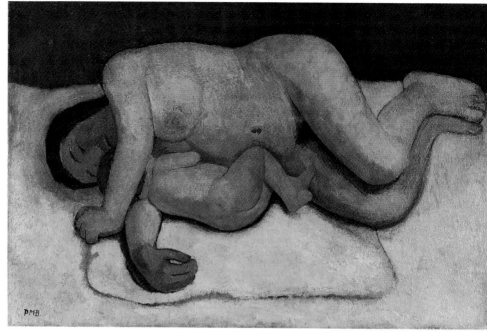

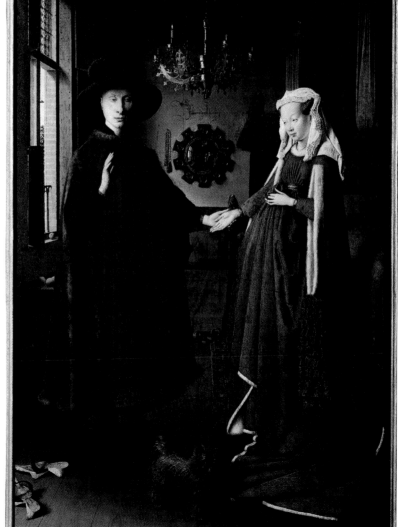

above: 79.
Mother and Child, Bambara,
from Mali. 19th–20th century.
Wood, height 4′5⅝″.
The Metropolitan Museum of Art,
New York (The Michael C.
Rockefeller Collection,
bequest of Nelson A. Rockefeller,
1979).

above right: 80.
Paula Modersohn-Becker.
Mother and Child. 1906.
Oil on canvas, 2′10½″ × 4′1″.
Sammlung Böttcherstrasse, Bremen.

right: 81. Jan van Eyck.
*Portrait of Giovanni Arnolfini(?)
and His Wife, Giovanna Cenami(?)*.
1434. Oil on wood, 33 × 22½″.
The National Gallery, London
(reproduced by courtesy
of the Trustees).

Henri Rousseau's *Wedding in the Country* **(82)** is certainly not the solemn marriage document Van Eyck's was meant to be. Furthermore, given what we know about Rousseau's free exercise of imagination (p. 29), we might take the scene depicted in his painting with a grain of salt. Rousseau poses the bridal couple stiffly—he with his relatives at left, she supported by her relatives at right. The groom gazes fondly at his new wife, but no one, least of all the bride, looks particularly happy on this gala occasion. The two families, in fact, are eyeing each other suspiciously. As though to highlight their wariness, the artist has given each family its own personal forest—two clumps of trees with decidedly different foliage. Can these family trees grow together through the union of marriage? Not even the minister, with his worried frown, would depend on it. Rousseau's painting style may be naive, but he has captured a situation that prevails at all too many weddings.

If Van Eyck's marriage picture is solemn and Rousseau's more than a little grim, Marc Chagall's *Bride and Groom of the Eiffel Tower* **(83)** might best be described as a romantic fantasy. Chagall, who was Russian-born, lived and worked in Paris for long stretches during his career. The Paris skyline was a beloved vista, so he portrays his bride and groom, in their wedding garb, floating past a solid blue version of the Eiffel Tower **(377)**. The couple appear

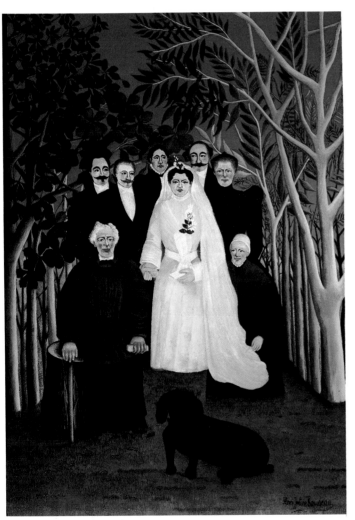

left: 82. Henri Rousseau.
A Wedding in the Country. 1904–05.
Oil on canvas, 5'4¼" × 3'8⅞".
Musée d'Orsay, Paris.

below: 83. Marc Chagall.
The Bride and Groom of the Eiffel Tower. 1938–39.
Oil on canvas, 4'11" × 4'5¾".
Musée National d'Art Moderne, Centre National d'Art et de Culture Georges Pompidou, Paris.

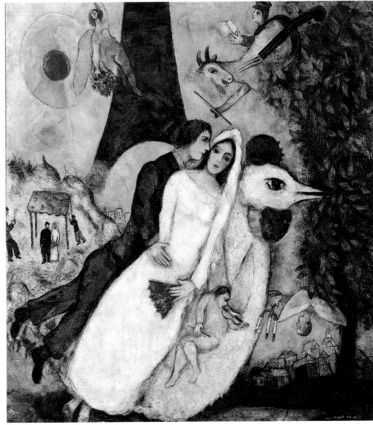

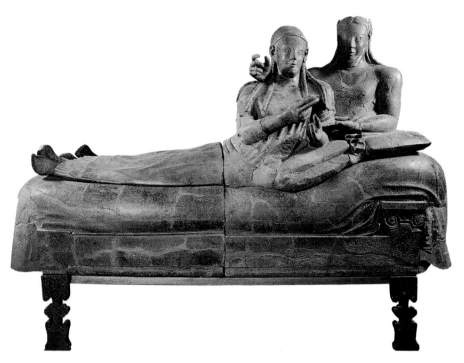

84. *Sarcophagus of the Spouses,*
from Cerveteri. c. 520 B.C.E.
Terra cotta, length 6'7".
Museo Nazionale di Villa Giulia, Rome.

to be carried on the back of a giant bird, a favorite motif of Chagall's, perhaps symbolizing spiritual union. Other images refer to the artist's roots in a Russian-Jewish village. At center left is a tiny rendering of the wedding scene, under the canopy prescribed by Jewish rites. There are two fiddlers—another favorite motif—one superimposed over the bird, one seemingly perched on the tree.

Chagall's art is always imaginative. He ignored conventions of realistic color, size, and placement to create a dreamlike landscape that distilled his many personal references. This painting could equally have been included in our preceding section on fantasy art. It is placed here, however, because the theme of marriage was important to the artist. He painted many wedding scenes—this one being especially warm, charming, and happy.

There is no shortage of death imagery in the history of art. From all times, from all cultures, artworks commemorating death are abundant. We have already seen one such example, the Great Pyramids of Egypt, but the scale of those funeral structures is so grandiose that we placed them in the category of political art. Personal mementos of death are more common, and often they take the form of tomb imagery.

Our first illustration shows a **sarcophagus,** or burial coffin, from the ancient Etruscans—the people who inhabited the Italian peninsula from about the 7th century B.C.E. until the rise of the Roman Empire. From this example **(84)** and many others, we can deduce that the Etruscans held a more serene view of death than most cultures before and after. A couple, presumably husband and wife, recline comfortably on the lid of their sarcophagus, their demeanor suggesting that not only their spirits but their bodies are enjoying the hereafter. Their expressions are those of people at a pleasant dinner party, engaged in animated conversation with other guests, whom we cannot see. This tomb sculpture has a reassuring quality, comforting those left behind with the thought that their loved ones are happy, that the afterlife is not a bad place to be.

The final two works of art in this chapter have much in common. Both commemorate death on a hideously large scale. Both are memorials to *unexpected* death—not the anticipated rest after a long life, but death coming prematurely, striking mostly the young. And both are meant to personalize *each* death among the many, to celebrate the individual life that was amid the mass tragedy that is.

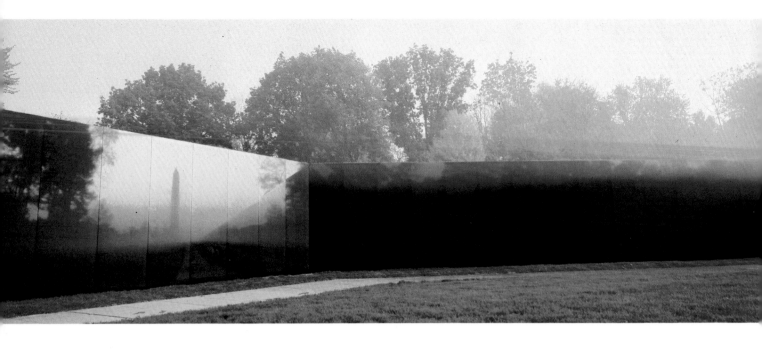

85. Maya Ying Lin. Vietnam Memorial, Washington, D.C. 1982. Black granite, length 492'.

The Vietnam Memorial in Washington, D.C. **(85)**, is the most-visited spot in the nation's capital. Completed in 1982, the memorial was designed by Maya Ying Lin, who was just twenty-two years old when her entry was selected from more than 1,400 submitted for this government commission. When first unveiled to the public, Lin's design was highly controversial. It is, after all, nothing more than two long walls of polished black granite, set into the earth so as to form a V. Many viewers felt "the Wall," as it has come to be called, flouted tradition, that it was not sufficiently respectful of those who fought the bloody Vietnam war. Many thought a statue of a heroic soldier marching off to battle would be more appropriate.

But public opinion changes. In time the American public came to accept this memorial—with its 58,000 names carved into the stark granite walls—as the most fitting tribute to those who died. Visitors from all over, visitors who had no connection with the war, even young people who cannot remember the war, stand quietly before the roster of names—names on a mass tombstone. Many come to find their own personal name, the name of a dead relative chiseled forever into the rock and not to be forgotten. They leave flowers and poems, teddy bears and ribbons, photographs and letters, reminders of the past. Mostly the relatives touch the Wall, running their fingers over the carved letters as though to touch once again the life that is gone.

The Vietnam war is long over; no more names will be added to the Wall. But another wave of unexpected death has swept the nation and the world, also striking primarily the young, and it will not pass soon. The wave of death from AIDS has not even crested. In the United States, San Francisco has been especially hard-hit by the epidemic, and it was there that the Names Project began. The purpose of the Names Project is simple: to memorialize as *individuals* those who have died from AIDS, to remember that each was a unique human being, though all are bound together by a common death. No better means could have been chosen than the AIDS Quilt **(86)**.

The AIDS Quilt consists of hand-sewn panels, each of them 3 by 6 feet, each commemorating one person who has died from AIDS. Some of the panels have a name and a photograph, others just initials or forms symbolizing that person's interests, abilities, and achievements. Most important, each panel tells a story, a story ended too soon, therefore all the more precious in the telling. The choice of a quilt format is especially meaningful. Historically, quilts have often told lifetime stories, incorporating bits of fabric from important life events. Quilts make us think of warmth and protection and nurturing.

And quilting has traditionally been a community activity, so it is natural that a community should form among those grieving death from common illness.

Unlike the Vietnam Memorial, the AIDS Quilt cannot possibly remember all who have died. Only those whose friends or families chose to be involved in the Names Project are represented. Tragically, that number has already created a work of horrific scope. The illustration here shows the quilt spread out in Washington, D.C., in October of 1996. By that time the quilt had grown to more than 37,000 panels and spread out on the Mall for nearly a mile, from the U.S. Capitol to the Washington Monument.

As a work of art, the AIDS Quilt presents many contradictions. Few of its panels, individually, might be considered great art, yet the whole makes a powerful artistic statement. In its entirety, as we watch it grow, the work is incomparably sad, yet each panel is the celebration of a single life. Inevitably, the quilt is a work in progress; it cannot be finished until the plague has been stopped. It is art for the dead—trying to make life bearable for the living.

86. The Names Project, San Francisco. *AIDS Memorial Quilt.* Displayed on the Mall; Washington, D.C., October 1996.

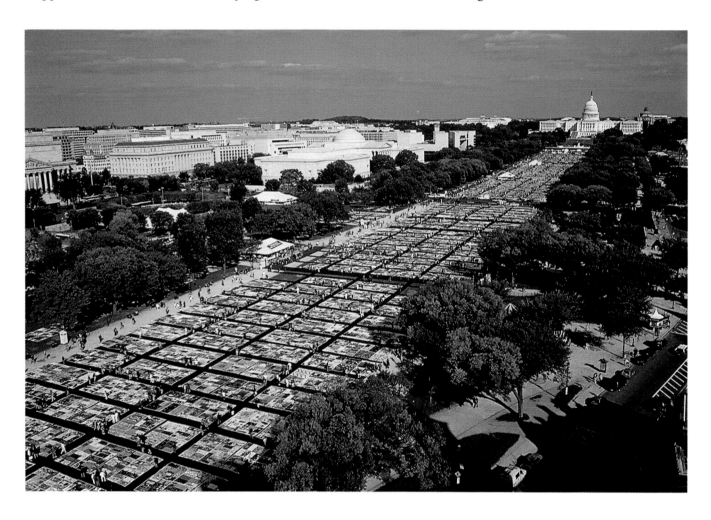

PART TWO

THE VOCABULARY OF ART

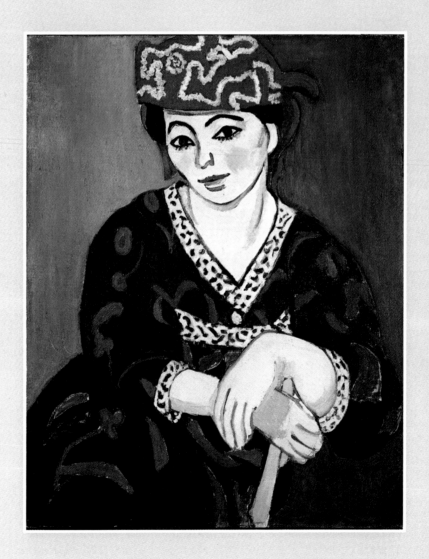

87. Henri Matisse. *Mme Matisse Madras rouge (The Red Madras Headdress).*
1907. Oil on canvas, $39\frac{1}{8} \times 31\frac{3}{4}''$.
Copyright 1996 The Barnes Foundation, Merion, Pa.

The Visual Elements

I F SOMEBODY ASKED YOU what you see in our first illustration **(87)**, you might say something like "a picture of a woman in a red hat." You know it isn't a real woman or even a photograph of one, but a representation in paint on canvas. This is a painting by Henri Matisse, of his wife in costume.

Now look closer and observe how the painting is constructed. You will see that Matisse has used *lines* to define the woman's jawline, her facial features, and the fingers on her hands. He has created the *shape* of the woman's body and set it off against the plainer *space* of the wall behind. The trim on the woman's dress and her turban have a *texture* that contrasts with her smooth skin. *Light* falls on the woman's face and arms, leaving the background in shadow. Matisse employs a range of *colors*—brilliant red and yellow for the headdress, darker red and blue-black for the gown, soft blue for the background, creamy white in the skin. There is also a range of *values*, from lightest in the flesh tones to darkest in the dress.

These seven things that Matisse used to construct his picture—line, shape, light, value, color, texture, and space—are the ingredients an artist has available in making any work of art. They are called the *visual elements*. (As we shall see, some works of art also involve time and motion, so these two are often added to the list.) No matter what kind of art, no matter where or when it was made, the character of these elements and the way they are organized determine what the work of art will be like.

In this chapter we shall look closely at the visual elements—what they are, how they are used, and how they affect a work of art. Chapter 5 deals with organization of these elements according to the principles of design.

LINE

By conventional definition, a line is the path left by a moving point. You put down your pencil on a sheet of paper and *move* its point across the paper to make a line. We can also think of line as an extended mark. Line is so basic to art that it is difficult to conceive of any work of art *not* having lines.

When you sit down to write a check or an examination paper or a note to yourself, you are making lines, whether you think of it that way or not. The letters of the alphabet are lines, and they are also symbols of sounds. Artists, too, use lines as symbols. In Matisse's painting of his wife, the definite line around her chin, for example, acts as a symbol. People's chins don't actually have lines separating them from their surroundings. But at the point where chin visually meets neck, our eyes "see" an imaginary line, so Matisse drew that line in his painting. This task of symbolically outlining form is only one of the many functions line performs in a work of art.

FUNCTIONS OF LINE

OUTLINE AND FORM In Amedeo Modigliani's drawing **(88)** a thin, elegant line describes the shape of a woman's body, viewed from the side. This is called an ***outline drawing.*** There is no interior shading or detail in the figure, and no background. By this extremely economical line the artist convinces us that we see a three-dimensional nude figure seated on an invisible surface. As in Matisse's painting, the line creates a boundary. It marks the point where the woman's body stops and the surrounding area begins. This function of line as outline is extremely important to art. Only in the model's face does Modigliani give us any detail, and even there the features are highly stylized. The almond-shaped eyes and wedge-shaped nose are Modigliani's trademarks.

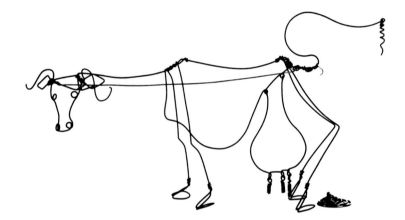

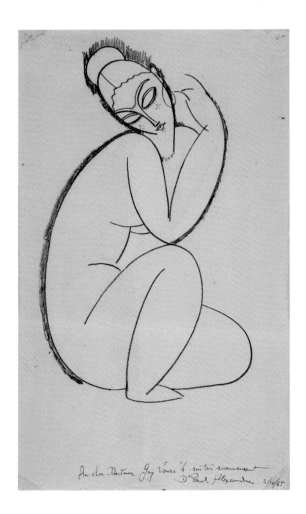

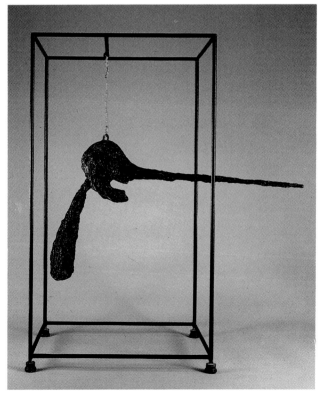

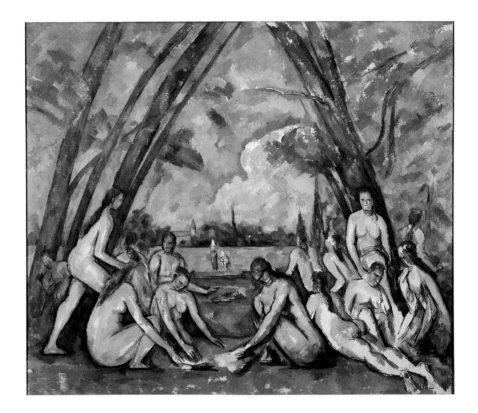

91. Paul Cézanne.
The Large Bathers. 1906.
Oil on canvas, 6'10" × 8'3".
Philadelphia Museum of Art
(purchased: W. P. Wilstach
Collection).

Whereas Modigliani uses line to create the illusion of three-dimensional form, Alexander Calder in his *Cow* **(89)** works with line to create a form that is actually three-dimensional. This witty little sculpture consists of a few pieces of wire welded and twisted together—the wire drawing lines in space. Somehow, Calder makes these few thin lines suggest a cow, placidly standing in the pasture, turning her head to gaze with little interest at us, who have interrupted her grazing. Details drawn in line are the key to this sculpture—one great swoop to show the udder, squiggle lines for the dangling teats, the little curl of hair at the end of the tail, the clumsy feet, the . . . well . . . *cowlike* expression on the face. Line alone, in the hands of a master like Calder, conveys the essence of the beast.

MOVEMENT AND EMPHASIS Line often implies movement, and this is another of its functions. Every line goes somewhere, so the viewer's eye naturally follows it. Alberto Giacometti's *Nose* **(90)** gives us a particularly compelling sculptural line in the form of a Pinocchio figure who has told many lies indeed. The head and torso are suspended, possibly trapped, inside a cage, with only the elongated nose—symbol of the liar—projecting outside. No matter how many times we as viewers try to focus on the face, the sharp line of the nose keeps pulling us away again.

Line also plays a role in creating emphasis in a work of art. In Paul Cézanne's painting *The Large Bathers* **(91)** diagonal lines of trees bend inward to form a triangle in the center of the canvas. The figures lean in such a way as to echo the diagonal lines. By means of this triangle Cézanne focuses attention on the main figures at the bottom center of the composition. His diagonal lines create a frame-within-a-frame, so we concentrate on forms within the triangle.

Cézanne did many paintings showing groups of bathers. (This one is called *The Large Bathers* because the other canvases are smaller.) As with his landscapes **(69)** and still lifes **(147)**, the artist was less concerned with naturalism than with the study of forms and volumes in space. These nudes are not lifelike and certainly are not erotic. Some of them look more like loaves of bread than human females. The brilliance of Cézanne's vision lies in his powerful composition and his conception of the body as a three-dimensional solid expressed on flat canvas.

DIRECTION Most of us have instinctive reactions to the direction of line, which are related to our experience of gravity. Flat, horizontal lines seem placid, like the horizon line or a body in repose. Vertical lines, like those of an upright body or a skyscraper jutting up from the ground, may have an assertive quality; they defy gravity in their upward thrust. But the most dynamic lines are the diagonals, which almost always imply action. Think of a runner hurtling down the track or a skier down the slope. The body leans forward, so that only the forward motion keeps it from toppling over. Diagonal lines in art have the same effect. We sense motion because the lines are unstable; we half expect them to topple over. (One exception is the diagonal line that makes up part of a triangle or pyramid, as in Cézanne's painting [91]; such lines are very

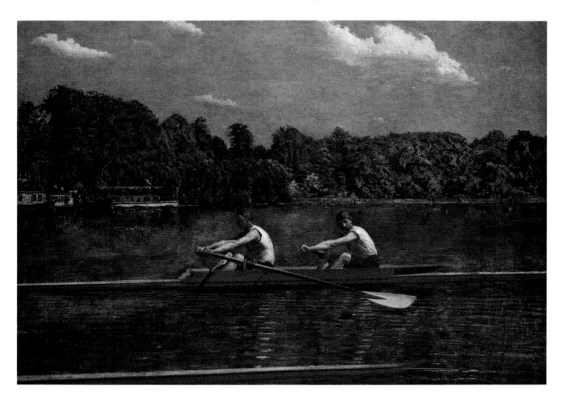

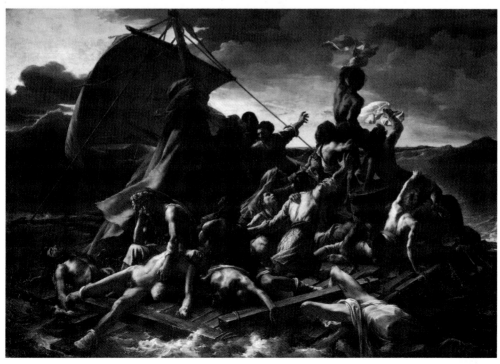

stable because the triangle form is closed and solid.) To see how linear direction works, let us compare two paintings that both show a boat in the water.

In Thomas Eakins' *The Biglin Brothers Racing* **(92)**, nearly all the lines are horizontals **[Overlay 2a]**. The two boats, the shoreline, the ripples on the river, the treetops, even the clouds scuttling across the sky are horizontal. Only the diagonal lines of the oars and rowers' arms and bodies suggest that this is a race. Why should a race be so placid? Eakins has captured the essence of sculling, races involving flat, long-oared boats powered by one or two rowers. Usually done on calm bodies of water, sculling has an odd, streamlined quality in the way the boats knife through the still water. The only apparent motion is in the bodies of the rowers, whose brisk, automaton movements in tandem make them seem, from a distance, like little mechanical toys. Eakins has given his painting an overall serenity, broken only by the diagonals of the men.

There is great contrast in linear direction, and thus in emotional effect, between Eakins' work and our next illustration. Serenity was the last thing Théodore Géricault wanted for his painting *The Raft of the Medusa* **(93)**. Géricault's work is based on an actual event—the wreck of the French government ship *Medusa* off North Africa in 1816. Only a few of those on board survived, some by clinging to a raft. The artist has chosen to depict the dramatic moment when those on the raft sighted a rescue ship. Virtually all the lines in the composition—the men straining forward, the arc of the sail, the bodies of the dead and dying in the foreground—are diagonal **[Overlay 2b]**. Their thrust reinforces the sense of a desperate situation as the raft plunges toward safety. And all these exciting diagonals build toward the climax of the one vertical—the man signaling to the rescue ship.

PATTERN AND TEXTURE   Yet another function of line in art is the creation of pattern and texture. A drawing by Van Gogh, *Old Vineyard with Peasant Woman* **(94)**, consists almost entirely of short, choppy lines, which give the work a rich visual texture. Van Gogh uses wavy, flamelike lines for the trees, rough parallel lines for the sides and roofs of houses and the woman's skirt, and exploding coarse lines to indicate clumps of grass. His washes of soft blue watercolor pull the composition together. Later in the chapter we will consider pattern and texture in more detail.

94. Vincent van Gogh.
Old Vineyard with Peasant Woman,
1890. Pencil, brush, watercolor,
and gouache; $17\frac{1}{4} \times 21\frac{1}{4}''$.
Van Gogh Museum, Amsterdam
(Vincent van Gogh Foundation).

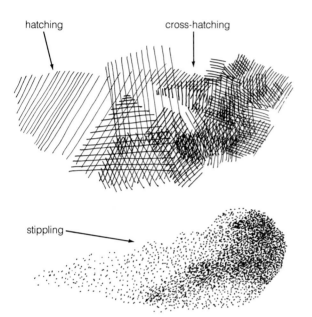

hatching   cross-hatching

stippling

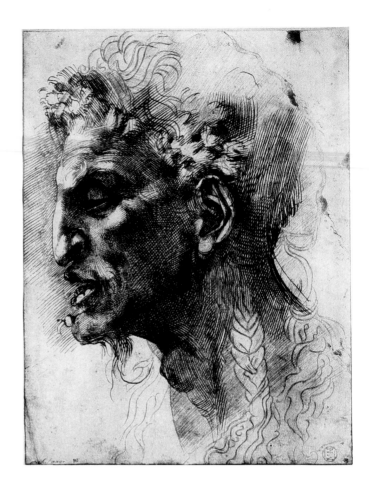

left: 95. Line techniques
to create modeling: hatching,
cross-hatching, and stippling.

right: 96. Michelangelo.
Head of a Satyr.
Pen and ink over chalk,
$10\frac{5}{8} \times 7\frac{7}{8}''$.
Louvre, Paris.

SHADING AND MODELING   One very important function of line, especially in drawing and printmaking, is the creation of shaded effects. Shading is natural to some media, like pencil; the artist can simply use the side of the pencil instead of the point. But with a more "linear" medium, such as pen and ink, this is not possible. Instead the artist will create shaded effects by means of closely spaced short lines **(95)**. There are three basic techniques. *Hatching* is an area of closely spaced parallel lines. *Cross-hatching* is similar except that the parallel lines intersect like a narrow checkerboard. *Stippling* means that the lines are reduced to dots and spaced closer together or farther apart to suggest darker or lighter areas.

Often, the goal of shading is to *model,* or to create the illusion of roundness, of three-dimensionality on a flat surface. We can see this in Michelangelo's *Head of a Satyr* **(96)**. Michelangelo has drawn some areas of hatching, especially in the hair at the right side of the drawing, but most of the modeling is accomplished by cross-hatching. Areas we are meant to perceive as hollows, or depressions in the face, have the densest cross-hatching: the socket of the eye, the back of the nostril, the jawline below the ear, and so forth. Conversely, where we are meant to see a raised area, such as the cheekbone, there is no cross-hatching at all. (If you put your finger over the highlight of the cheekbone, you will see that the face seems flatter.) By the skillful use of line Michelangelo persuades us that the head is three-dimensional.

TYPES OF LINES

The preceding sections have dealt primarily with actual lines—visible marks made in pencil or paint or some other medium. In studying art, however, we often have to take into account other types of lines **(97)**. Actual lines are the most familiar, so we begin with them.

ACTUAL LINES   Actual lines are obvious in Roy Lichtenstein's *Still Life with Crystal Bowl* **(98)**. In fact, they are the dominant element in the composition. Thick parallel bands create a background; the fruits are outlined in bold strokes, while finer lines delineate the shape of the bowl. Working in the Pop Art style with which he is associated—a style deriving its spirit and imagery from the popular culture—Lichtenstein has chosen a familiar item, one that could be found in a great many homes, and transformed it into a precious object, like the gem displayed in a jeweler's window. The strong linear treatment takes the bowl of fruit, so to speak, "outside" itself. We as viewers *must* look at it with fresh eyes, must respond to it for its own sake, rather than as a casual accessory to decorate a dining room table.

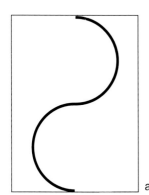 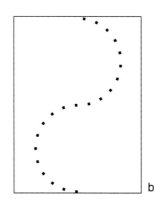 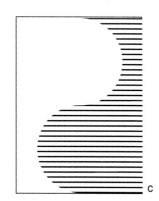 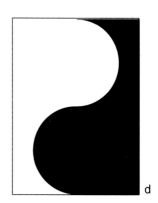

a　　　　　b　　　　　c　　　　　d

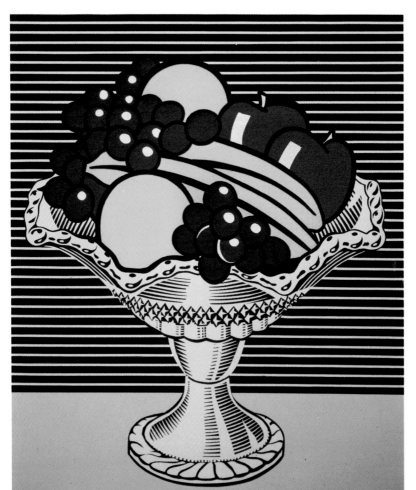

above: **97.** Actual line **(a)**, implied lines **(b,c)**, and line created by edge **(d)**.

left: **98.** Roy Lichtenstein. *Still Life with Crystal Bowl.* 1973. Oil and magna on canvas, 4'4" × 3'6". Collection, Whitney Museum of American Art, New York (purchase, with funds from Frances and Sydney Lewis).

IMPLIED LINES When a person stops on a street corner and gazes upward, other passersby will also stop and look up, following the "line" of sight. When someone points a finger, we automatically follow the direction of the point. Artists often exploit this natural response by using implied lines in their work. In Raphael's painting *The Madonna of the Meadows* **(99)**, the three figures are arranged in a triangular composition **[Overlay 3a]**, with one point of the triangle just above the Madonna's head, another in her extended foot at right, the third beyond the knee of the child at left. Within this greater triangle, however, there is a smaller, implied triangle. Implied lines of sight among the Virgin and the two children help to pull the composition together and direct the eyes of the viewer to the most important figure in the painting—the child Jesus. The Madonna casts her eyes downward toward John the Baptist, who, in turn, gazes upward at the baby Jesus, establishing a triangular flow. As observers, we unconsciously follow these lines of sight around and through the painting, just as we would glance upward if we saw someone in the street staring up. Implied lines give coherence and a subtle sense of movement to the painting.

LINES FORMED BY EDGES If you press the palms of your two hands flat together in a praying gesture, you will see that a "line" seems to form where they meet. There is no line, in reality, but the point where the edge of one form meets the edge of another form creates the impression of a line. This can happen in two-dimensional art as well, wherever one shape or color area meets another shape or color area. Looking again at Raphael's painting **(99)**, we could

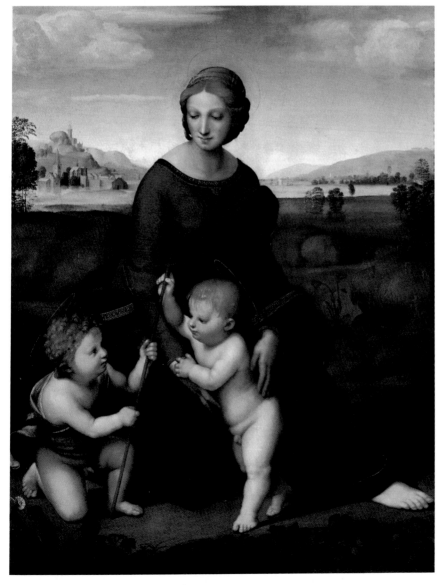

99. Raphael.
The Madonna of the Meadows.
1505. Oil on panel, $44\frac{1}{2} \times 34\frac{1}{4}''$.
Kunsthistorisches Museum, Vienna.

RAPHAEL

1483–1520

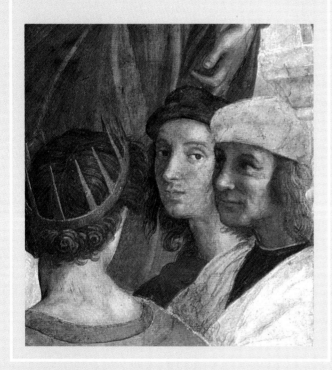

According to the 16th-century biographer Giorgio Vasari, we find in Raphael "an artist as talented as he was gracious," possessed of unbounded "grace, industry, looks, modesty, and excellence of character." Whereas both Michelangelo and Leonardo da Vinci emerge as rather moody, solitary figures, their younger colleague seems to have been the sort of person who charms everybody and to whom success comes as naturally as breathing.

Born in the town of Urbino, Raffaello Sanzio received his first art training from his father, then later became an assistant to the early Renaissance master Pietro Perugino. At twenty-one Raphael struck out on his own, but he continued to study avidly the work of other artists—including Leonardo and Michelangelo, both of whom influenced him greatly. (Vasari claims that Raphael was secretly let into the Sistine Chapel when Michelangelo had temporarily stopped work on the ceiling frescoes so that he could get an advance look at the figures.)

Raphael established his reputation early and throughout his career never lacked for patrons. A major preoccupation was the Madonna-and-child group, of which he made numerous versions. In 1508 Pope Julius II called Raphael to Rome, where the artist began the fresco decoration of four rooms in the Vatican. Among these frescoes was the famous *School of Athens* **(204)**.

By his early thirties Raphael had become a busy person indeed, testing his artistic skills in many areas. Increasingly, the work of carrying out his commissions was delegated to assistants. He had been named chief architect of Saint Peter's Basilica in the Vatican and was also director of excavations for ancient Greek and Roman art in and around the city of Rome. On commission from Pope Leo, Julius' successor, Raphael designed ten huge tapestries for the Sistine Chapel and perhaps executed the cartoons (drawings to guide the weavers) himself, although this point is in dispute.

Raphael's private life seems to have been as full and satisfying as his artistic career. At home in any social situation, sought after as a friend, he played as energetically as he worked. He never married—possibly because he hoped to be made a cardinal of the Church—but he lived for many years with the same woman. The biographer Vasari refers to "secret love affairs" and comments that the artist "pursued his pleasures with no sense of moderation." If we are to believe Vasari, Raphael's death at the tragically premature age of thirty-seven came as the aftermath of such lack of moderation, which brought on a "violent fever" made fatal by unwise medical attention.

Among Raphael's great talents was the ability to please his patrons while at the same time fulfilling his own ideals of art. In about 1514 he wrote this to a noble client: "I should consider myself a great master if [a drawing of Galatea] had half the merits you mention in your letter. However, I perceive in your words the love that you bear me; . . . I am making use of a certain idea which comes into my mind. Whether it is possessed of any artistic excellence I do not know. But I do strive to attain it."[1]

Raphael. *School of Athens,*
detail with presumed self-portrait **(center).** 1510–11.
Fresco. Stanza della Segnatura, Vatican, Rome.

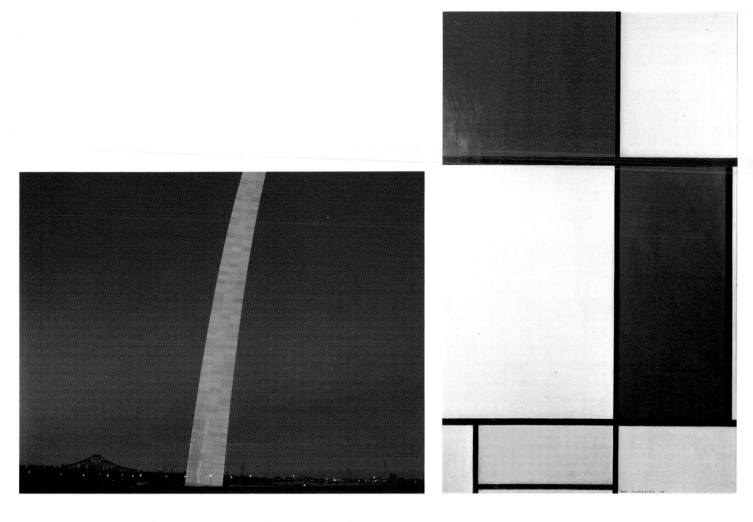

left: 100. Joel Meyerowitz.
St. Louis Gateway Arch. c. 1979.
Photograph.
Courtesy The Bonni Benrubi Gallery.

right: 101. Piet Mondrian.
*Composition with Red, Yellow,
and Blue.* 1928.
Oil on canvas, $4'\frac{3}{4}'' \times 2'7\frac{1}{2}''$.
Collection Stefan Edlis, Chicago.

easily trace a "line" around the Madonna's shoulders and head, as they are set off against the lighter background. The line created by edge is evident in our next illustration—Joel Meyerowitz's photograph of the St. Louis Gateway Arch **(100)**. Meyerowitz focuses on one segment of the enormous arch, thereby turning it into an abstraction. Without the photograph's title, we might have no idea what this form really is, but the illuminated arch creates strong lines where it meets the night sky. The edges of buildings, of sculptures, of any shapes isolated against a plain background fool the eye into seeing lines where none exist.

SHAPE AND MASS

A *shape* is a two-dimensional area with identifiable boundaries. A *mass* is a three-dimensional solid with identifiable boundaries. These definitions are correct as far as they go, and they will make sense to anyone who has studied geometry. Circles and squares are shapes; spheres and cubes are masses. So far, so good. Confusion arises, however, when we try to move beyond these bare-bones statements, and for two reasons. First, there is little consistency in the way the terms are used in everyday conversation; people are just as likely to call a three-dimensional object a "shape." Second, there are at least two other terms—*form* and *volume*—that have similar meanings and overlap the first two. In this section we will try to provide workable definitions that will serve for analysis of the art elements.

A **shape** is a two-dimensional area. Shapes are created by lines, by color areas, by contrasting textures, or by some combination of these. If the artist draws a circle and colors it red inside the line, the result is a round red shape.

Even if there is no line, just a roundish daub of red paint, we still perceive a circular red shape set off from the surrounding space by its red edges.

A *mass* is a three-dimensional solid. It has actual depth in space. An orange is a piece of fruit, and it is also a spherical orange mass. Sometimes the word "mass" implies bulk, density, and weight. We might speak of the mass of a heavy paperweight or the mass of a natural rock formation.

Volume may be synonymous with mass, except that volume can also refer to a void, an empty but enclosed space, whereas mass usually refers to a solid. For example, we might refer to the mass of the Rock of Gibraltar (we might also refer to its volume), but inside a large building, such as the Guggenheim Museum in New York **(126)**, we would talk about the volume enclosed and created by the structure.

Form is the trickiest term of all, because it has so many meanings. It can mean shape or mass. As mentioned in Chapter 2, it can refer generally to the way a work of art looks or the way it is put together. It can also mean composition or structure or even style.

For this discussion of the art elements we have chosen to focus on the terms "shape" and "mass." These two have the most easily restricted definitions and lend themselves more readily to analysis.

It is customary to distinguish two broad categories in both shapes and masses: organic and geometric. **Geometric shapes,** based on the mechanically drawn line, include the square, the rectangle, the circle, and the triangle. **Organic shapes** are based on the forms of nature, which are usually rounded, irregular, and curving.

One artist who devoted a career to exploring the potential of geometric shape was the Dutch painter Piet Mondrian **(101)**. Mondrian's *Composition with Red, Yellow, and Blue* is typical of his mature work and represents the artist's search for what he called a "pure reality." Mondrian felt that certain things are universal, common to all people—the rectangle, the vertical and horizontal, the primary colors red, yellow, and blue, plus black and white. By these means he hoped to cut through cultural differences among people and make a visual statement meaningful to all. Mondrian's canvases, apparently so simple, rest on the hair's-breadth balance of line, shape, and color—the dynamic equilibrium Mondrian achieved with geometric shapes.

Organic shapes prevail in Pedro Perez' *Los Marielitos* **(102)**. This painting has almost no straight lines; it is rather an assemblage of natural forms—animal, human, humanoid, plantlike. Moreover, the forms are interconnected, as though all were branches of a vivid tropical plant. Perez, who was born in Cuba, takes his title from the wave of refugees who entered the United States

102. Pedro F. Perez.
Los Marielitos. 1983.
Oil pastel on black wove paper,
$3'8\frac{1}{4}'' \times 5'$.
The Museum of Fine Arts, Houston
(Museum purchase with funds
provided by Drexel Burnham
Lambert Incorporated).

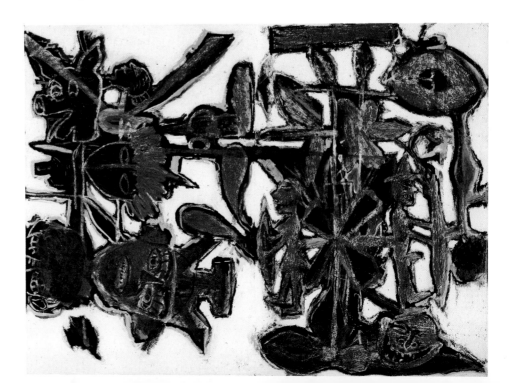

in 1980 from the Cuban port of Mariel. His picture may recall Picasso's *Guernica* **(58)**, in the sense that we know something has *happened* to a group of people, and we feel the magnitude of the event.

Before we complete our discussion of two-dimensional shape, we should touch upon one more aspect of it, and that is the concept of positive/negative shape, sometimes called ***figure-ground relationship***. A painting or other work of two-dimensional art usually has one or more shapes meant to be perceived as positive. In a representational work, they are the shapes of the subject; in a nonrepresentational work, they are the shapes that seem active or dominant. For instance, in Matisse's painting of his wife at the beginning of the chapter **(87)**, the woman and her madras headdress are positive shapes, or figure. Everything else is negative shape, or background. If you compare this with a work by M. C. Escher **(103)**, you will find it hard to decide which are the positive shapes and which are the negative ones. Focus your eyes on the dark figures, and the light ones become ground; focus on the light ones, and the opposite is true. Escher meant this to be a clever visual puzzle, but it makes an important point about art in general. What Escher's drawing emphasizes is that both positive and negative shapes are dynamic elements.

Three-dimensional mass also can be considered either geometric or organic. Nancy Graves' three camels **(104)** take the natural, organic form of that majestic humped beast, whose anatomy the artist had studied in great detail. Apart from their contours, these sculptures are quite literally organic, since Graves used animal skins as part of her construction materials.

LIGHT, VALUE, AND COLOR

Light, value, and color are intimately connected elements. Color is a function of light and therefore directly dependent on its presence. Value, being a measure of lightness or darkness, plays a role in our perception of light and color.

Apart from the purely sensory pleasure we derive from it, color helps to define shape and mass. For example, we notice that the *green* hills are set off

left: 103. M. C. Escher. *Symmetry Drawing E 67 (Study of Regular Division of the Plane with Horsemen).* 1946. India ink and watercolor. Collection, Haags Gemeentemuseum, The Hague, © 1996 Cordon Art-Baarn-Holland. All rights reserved.

right: 104. Nancy Graves. *Camel VI, VII & VIII.* 1968–69. Wood, steel, burlap, polyurethane, animal skin, wax, and oil paint; height of tallest camel 8'. National Gallery of Canada, Ottawa (VII and VIII gift of Allan Bronfman). © 1998 Nancy Graves Foundation/ Licensed by VAGA, New York.

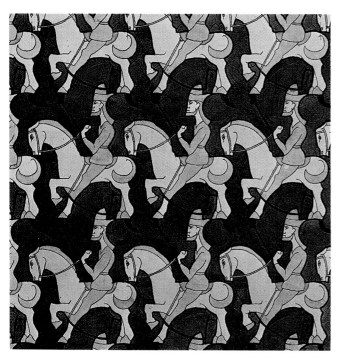

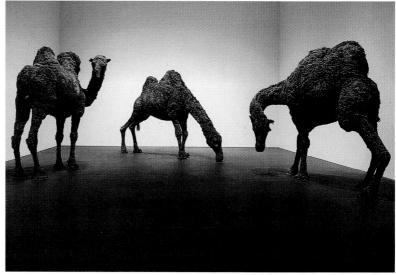

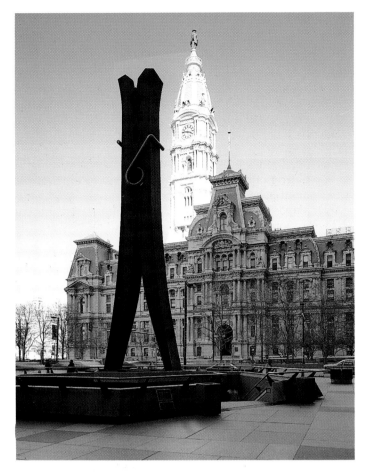
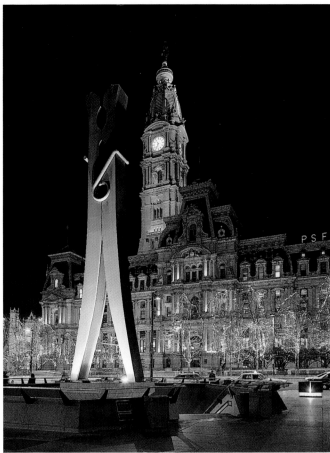

against the *blue* sky. In a nonobjective painting color may be the only means by which we identify shapes and spaces. Color is also used by artists to convey emotion. Value defines shape when, for instance, we see a light shape against a dark background, and it too carries emotional impact. We speak of "dark, brooding" paintings or "light, airy" ones.

In this section we take up the subjects of light, value, and color insofar as they affect our response to art. All involve complex sciences, but only a little of the science is necessary to understand how these elements operate.

105. Claes Oldenburg and Coosje van Bruggen. *Clothespin.* 1976. Cor-Ten steel, height 45'. Centre Square, Philadelphia. **left:** daytime view; **right:** nighttime view.

LIGHT

ACTUAL LIGHT   In architecture and sculpture we are particularly aware of the role played by actual light, whether natural (from daylight) or artificial. Light is the ally of three-dimensional forms. It creates shadows and reflections on their surfaces, gives them solidity and depth, sometimes animates them from within. Consider how different a building looks by day and by night. In the daytime, sunlight bathes the façade to create shadow patterns around windows and ornamental details. At night the windows glow with artificial light, and, if the building has a lot of glass, it may seem like a light sculpture. Our next example shows vividly the different effects of actual light on both sculpture and architecture.

Claes Oldenburg and Coosje van Bruggen's sculpture *Clothespin* **(105)** is a 45-foot-tall steel representation of that humble laundry object. Installed permanently in Philadelphia, it occupies a plaza facing the City Hall. When the scene is photographed in daylight, the sculpture seems flat in color and, from this angle at any rate, makes rather an odd companion for the richly ornate City Hall. By night the view changes dramatically, as the two elements, sculpture and building, are drawn into a warm partnership. The illuminated sculpture takes on a golden glow and appears larger, more heroic. The City Hall has been spotlighted selectively, to emphasize the clock tower and central col-

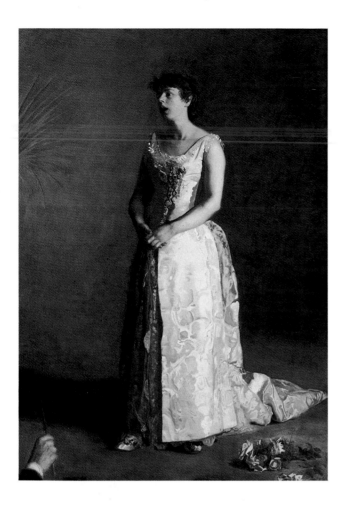

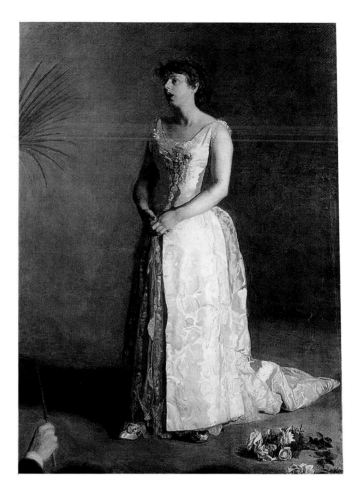

umned arch, leaving other sections in shadow. Even the street lights play a role in this delightfully theatrical setting, picking out the shapes of trees—nature's sculptural forms.

THE ILLUSION OF LIGHT Artists working in two-dimensional art—painting or drawing or prints, for instance—often wish to create the impression of light illuminating their subjects. This apparent light may be daylight evenly illuminating a scene or dappling the leaves in a landscape or the light cast by a lamp, candle, or fire. In some cases the supposed light source is included in the image, as when a painter depicts figures clustered around a lamp. At other times the light source is assumed to be outside the frame of the picture, but we see its effects clearly. A subject bathed in light from a definite angle, with the resultant shadows, may seem more lifelike and three-dimensional. (When light is general and comes from no specific source, figures tend to be flattened.)

We can see how light enhances the sense of depth in Thomas Eakins' painting *The Concert Singer* **(106)**. This work shows the singer Weda Cook in a solo performance. The strong light coming from below and to her left is apparently from a footlight on the concert stage. Eakins obviously was intrigued with the effects of light on form. The lower part of the gown is the most brilliantly illuminated, while more than half the face remains in shadow. Light picks out folds in the dress, hollows in the singer's throat, the musculature of the arms—all of these details contributing to the roundness of the figure.

VALUE

The term *value,* as we have said, means relative lightness or darkness, whether in color or in black and white. Values are perhaps easier to see in black and white than in color; we are accustomed to their effects in classic black-and-white films, photography, and reproductions, such as the ones in this book. When *The Concert Singer* is reproduced in black and white **(107)**, the pale pink on the near side of the dress is seen as a very light gray, the singer's illuminated arm and cheek slightly darker grays, and so on, to the very dark grays that represent the shadows behind the singer and on her right side. Color values are translated into values of gray. In black and white, then, lacking the color cues we have in most situations, we rely to a large extent on contrasts of grays to help us distinguish one from another.

For purposes of analysis, value is usually considered in terms of a value scale **(108)**, ranging from white (the lightest) to black (the darkest), with several gradations in between. (The same value scale can be applied to colors, as we shall see.) Works of art in which light values predominate are called *high-key;* those in which dark values predominate, *low-key.*

Value contrasts—contrasts of light and dark—may be used in a painting or drawing to create the effects of light and shadow in the natural world. This technique is called ***chiaroscuro,*** which literally means "light/dark." In Lorenzo di Credi's *Drapery for a Standing Man* **(109)**, there is no explicit light source, such as a lamp or candle, yet the figure has clearly been modeled as though light were coming from somewhere beyond the man's right shoulder (our left as we look at the drawing). The lightest values are reserved for folds of drapery at the left side of the drawing and on the out-thrust knee. Much darker values appear in folds of drapery that are supposed to be in shadow. These

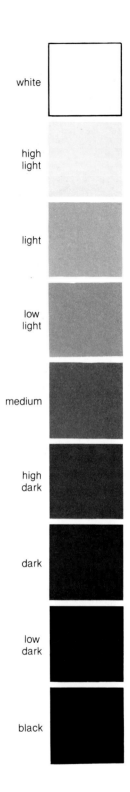

white

high light

light

low light

medium

high dark

dark

low dark

black

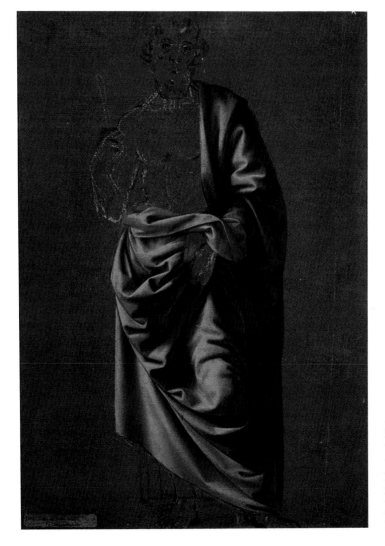

above: 108. Value scale in gray.

left: 109. Lorenzo di Credi.
*Drapery for a Standing Man,
Represented Frontally.*
Late 15th–early 16th century.
Brush and gray wash
on brown paper, $15\frac{1}{4} \times 10\frac{5}{8}''$.
Louvre, Paris.

contrasts and gradations of value give a sense of depth and three-dimensionality to the drapery study. In fact, one of the reasons why the head and torso seem so flat by comparison is that chiaroscuro is not used for this area. The figure seems linear; the drapery looks almost sculptural.

Lorenzo's drawing, while on tinted paper, is primarily black and white. The effects of value, light, and contrast become even more complex when we add color.

COLOR

It is probably safe to say that none of the visual elements give us so much pleasure as color. You will understand this if you have ever been restricted to watching an old black-and-white television and then suddenly have access to a color set. For the same reason certain entrepreneurs have acquired the rights to classic films like *Casablanca* and "colorized" them—applied color by painstaking computer methods to what were originally black-and-white movies. The debate about whether this practice is acceptable, ethically and aesthetically, will continue for many years, but obviously the "colorizers" are hoping to tap a segment of the market that demands full color.

Various studies have demonstrated that color affects a wide range of psychological and physiological responses. Restaurants often are decorated in red, which is believed to increase appetite and therefore food consumption. A common treatment for premature babies born with potentially fatal jaundice is to bathe them in blue light, which, for reasons not fully understood, eliminates the need to transfuse their blood. Blue surroundings also will significantly lower a person's blood pressure, pulse, and respiration rate. In one experiment subjects were asked to identify, by taste, ordinary mashed potatoes colored bright green. Because of the disorienting color cues, they could not say what they were eating. And in one California detention center violent children are routinely placed in an 8-by-4-foot cell painted bubble-gum pink. The children relax, become calmer, and often fall asleep within ten minutes. This color has been dubbed "passive pink." The mechanism involved in these color responses is still unclear, but there can be no doubt that color "works" on the human brain and body in powerful ways.

In this book you will find more than 500 artworks reproduced in full color. This color does not exactly duplicate the colors you would see if you stood in front of the actual works, because mechanical reproduction on paper is never wholly accurate. But you will no doubt look at these color reproductions in preference to the black and whites. Color always draws the eye.

110. Sketch of colors separated by a prism.

At the beginning of this section we said that color is a function of light. Without light there can be no color. The principles of color theory explain why this effect occurs.

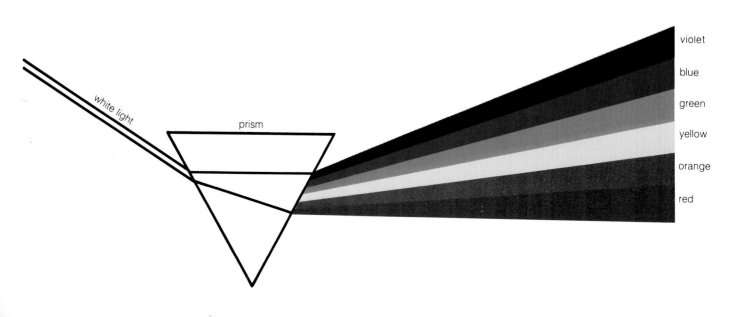

white light

prism

violet

blue

green

yellow

orange

red

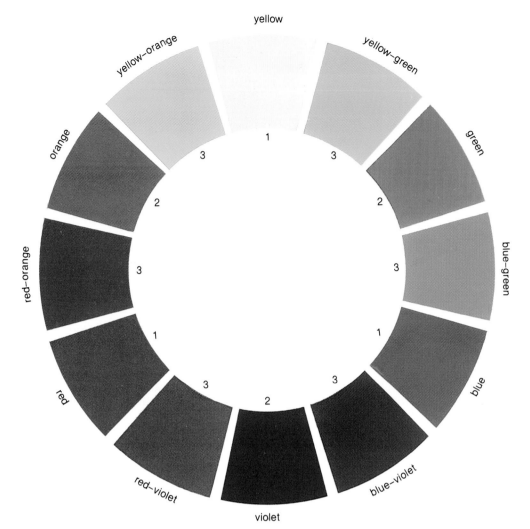

Labels on color wheel (clockwise from top):
yellow, yellow-green, green, blue-green, blue, blue-violet, violet, red-violet, red, red-orange, orange, yellow-orange

111. Color wheel.

COLOR THEORY Much of our present-day color theory can be traced back to experiments made by Sir Isaac Newton, who is better known for his work with the laws of gravity. In 1666 Newton passed a ray of sunlight through a prism, a transparent glass form with nonparallel sides. He observed that the ray of sunlight broke up or *refracted* into different colors, which were arranged in the order of the colors of the rainbow **(110)**. By setting up a second prism Newton found he could recombine the rainbow colors into white light, like the original sunlight. These experiments proved that colors are actually components of light.

In fact, all colors are dependent on light, and no object possesses color intrinsically. You may own a red shirt and a blue pen and a purple chair, but these items have no color in and of themselves. What we perceive as color is reflected light rays. When light strikes the red shirt, for example, the shirt absorbs all the color rays *except* the red ones, which are reflected, so your eye perceives red. The purple chair reflects the purple rays and absorbs all the others, and so on. Both the physiological activity of the human eye and the science of electromagnetic wavelengths take part in this process.

If we take the colors separated out by Newton's prism—red, orange, yellow, green, blue, and violet—add the transitional color red-violet (which does not exist in the rainbow), and arrange these colors in a circle, we have a *color wheel* **(111)**. Different theorists have constructed different color wheels, but the one shown here is fairly standard.

Primary colors—red, yellow, and blue—are labeled with the numeral 1 on the color wheel. They are called primary because (theoretically at least) they cannot be made by any mixture of other colors.

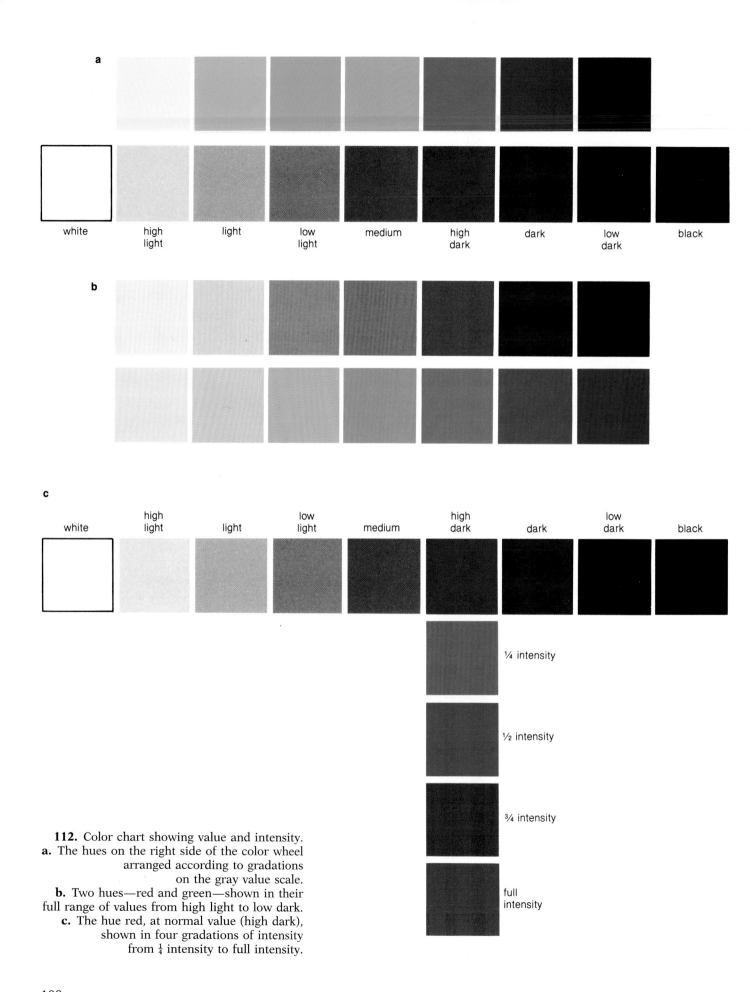

a

white | high light | light | low light | medium | high dark | dark | low dark | black

b

c

white | high light | light | low light | medium | high dark | dark | low dark | black

¼ intensity

½ intensity

¾ intensity

full intensity

112. Color chart showing value and intensity.
a. The hues on the right side of the color wheel
arranged according to gradations
on the gray value scale.
b. Two hues—red and green—shown in their
full range of values from high light to low dark.
c. The hue red, at normal value (high dark),
shown in four gradations of intensity
from ¼ intensity to full intensity.

Secondary colors—orange, green, and violet—are labeled with the numeral 2. Each is made by combining two primary colors. For most of us this information is not new. Even in kindergarten children working with poster paints learn to make green by mixing yellow and blue.

Tertiary colors, labeled number 3, are the product of a primary color and an adjacent secondary color. For instance, mixing yellow with green yields yellow-green.

Complementary colors are those directly opposite one another on the color wheel. They are assumed to be as different from one another as possible. The relationship between complementary colors, as we shall see, is extremely important in such areas as the optical and emotional effects of color.

COLOR PROPERTIES Any color has three properties. They are called hue, value, and intensity.

Hue is the name of the color—green or red or violet-blue. In any serious discussion of color it is important to avoid the poetic color names promoted by the fashion industry, such as "fuchsia"or "topaz." The hues listed on the color wheel and the designations on the color chart **(112)** are meant to be standard, so that people can agree on their meanings. "Autumn red" could mean many things to many people, but "red, high dark, ¾ intensity" is precise; you could pick the correct color out of a box of standard color chips.

Value, again, refers to relative lightness or darkness. Most colors are recognizable in a full range of values; for instance, we identify as "red" everything from palest pink to darkest maroon. In addition, all hues have what is known as a *normal value*—the value at which we expect to find that hue. We think of yellow as a "light" color and violet as a "dark" color, for example, even though each has a full range of values. The top section of the color chart **(112a)** shows the hues on the right side of the color wheel organized according to their normal values in relation to the gray value scale. We could do the same with the left half of the wheel, pairing yellow-orange with light, and so on. The middle section of the color chart **(112b)** shows a full range of values, from high light to low dark, for two hues: red and green.

A color lighter than the hue's normal value is known as a *tint;* for example, pink is a tint of red. A color darker than the hue's normal value is called a *shade;* maroon is a shade of red. (This terminology is specific to color theory and differs from everyday usage of the word "shade" to mean any variation of a color, as in "My coat is a lovely shade of blue.")

Intensity—also called *chroma* or *saturation*—refers to the relative purity of a color. The difference between intensity and value can be a bit difficult to understand until you see how it works on the color chart **(112c)**. Colors may be pure and saturated, as they appear on the color wheel, or they may be grayed and softened to some degree. The purest colors are said to have high intensity; grayer colors, lower intensity. In the color chart **(112c)** we show four intensity gradations of the hue red at normal value. We could construct the same intensity scale for any other hue. To lower the intensity of a color when mixing paints or dyes, the artist may add a combination of black and white (gray) or may add a little of the color's complement.

LIGHT AND PIGMENT Colors behave differently depending on whether the artist is working with light or with pigment. In light, as we said, white light is the sum of all colors. In other words, if you combine all colors, you will get white. This is not true for pigment—artists' colors or dyes. If you mix all these colors, you will get a *neutral*—black or almost colorless brownish-gray.

Artists who work in light need to master a complex technology of light-and-color dynamics. This science applies to photographers, filmmakers, video and computer artists, anyone whose medium involves color as a component of light. One of the fastest-growing areas in art today is the field of computer art, and among its most fascinating branches is fractal imagery.

A *fractal* picture is a computer-generated representation of a complex mathematical formula **(113)**. According to Benoit B. Mandelbrot, the pioneer of fractal mathematics, "Fractals are geometric shapes that are equally complex in their details as in their overall form. That is, if a piece of a fractal is suitably magnified to become of the same size as the whole, it should look like the whole."[2] For the mathematically inclined, fractals are an exciting new world to explore, but considered purely on artistic terms, fractal images are intricate, elegant, usually colorful, and often quite beautiful. Even without understanding their mathematical properties, we can appreciate their visual expressiveness.

Artists using real light usually select their colors mechanically, at a distance, by pushing buttons or choosing filters or adjusting dials. Their work requires a sophisticated knowledge of color science. By contrast, artists who work in pigments—watercolors or oil paints or similar media—usually blend their colors by trial and error, using their own hands. In both cases, familiarity with the color wheel and the color properties can help.

COLOR HARMONIES   A color harmony, sometimes called a ***color scheme,*** is the selective use of two or more colors in a single composition. We tend to think of this especially in relation to interior design; you may say, for instance, "The color scheme in my kitchen is blue and green with touches of brown." But color harmonies also apply to the pictorial arts, although they may be more difficult to spot because of differences in value and intensity.

Usually, an artist's choice of colors is intuitive, so it is only after a work of art has been completed that observers can identify the color harmony involved. These harmonies do, however, help us to understand why certain combinations of colors produce certain visual effects. There are several categories of color harmonies.

Monochromatic harmonies are composed of variations on the same hue, often with differences of value and intensity. A painting all in reds, pinks, and maroons would be considered to have a monochromatic harmony. Arnaldo Roche-Rabell's *Spirit of the Flesh* **(114)**, for instance, is painted entirely in subtle variations of the color blue, to create an eerily brooding, disturbing image of the man's face.

left: 113. Benoit B. Mandelbrot.
A Fractal Dragon. 1982.
Computer-generated image.
Copyright © 1982
by Benoit B. Mandelbrot,
from his book
The Fractal Geometry of Nature.

right: 114.
Arnaldo Roche-Rabell.
The Spirit of the Flesh. 1980.
Oil pastel on paper, 4'2" × 3'4".
Collection Myrna Baez,
Hato Rey, Puerto Rico.

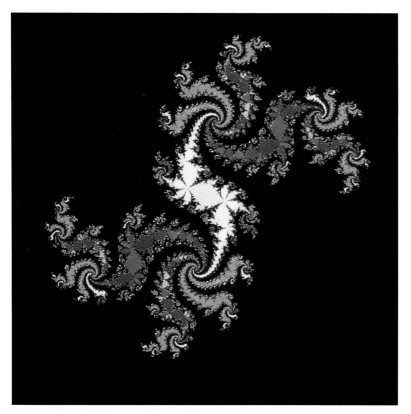

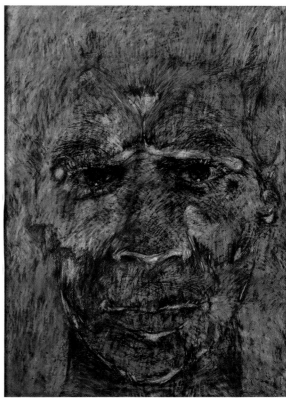

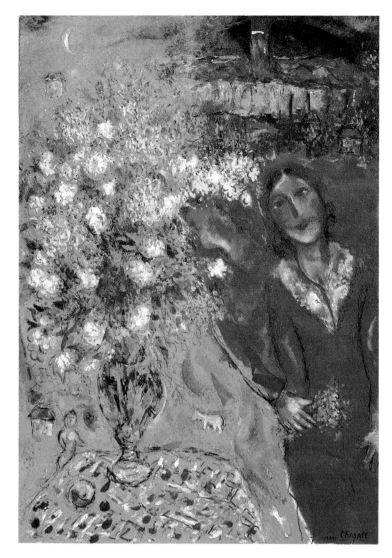

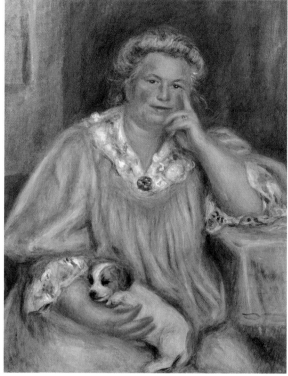

Complementary harmonies involve colors directly opposite one another on the color wheel. The most obvious pairings are red and green, violet and yellow, blue and orange. Complementaries "react" with each other more vividly than other colors. They set up a tension, a dynamic bond of opposites, and thereby intensify each other. Marc Chagall's *Painter and His Wife* **(115)** demonstrates just such a forceful complementary scheme. Chagall has divided his canvas into two sections—the "painter" side, represented by a vase of flowers, in an intense green; the "wife" side in saturated red. The two sections vibrate against one another, suggesting a clear duality, and yet they do not appear to be at war. They seem, in fact, to be two halves of the whole.

Analogous harmonies combine colors adjacent to one another on the color wheel, such as red, red-orange, and orange. In *Portrait of Madame Renoir* **(116)**, Auguste Renoir holds to this scheme to create a warm and charming image of his wife with their small dog. Except for touches of white, nearly all the colors in this work can be found in the upper left third of our color wheel **(111)**, from yellow through the oranges to red.

Triad harmonies use three colors equidistant on the color wheel. The most obvious combination is red, yellow, and blue, as in Mondrian's painting **(101)**. In addition, there are several more complicated color harmonies that are significant mainly to color theorists. For our purposes here it is enough to know that such harmonies exist and that they may sometimes help us to understand why particular colors work together.

left: **115.** Marc Chagall.
The Painter and His Wife. 1969.
Oil on canvas, 36¼ × 28¾".
Private collection,
St. Paul de Vence, France.

right: **116.**
Pierre-Auguste Renoir.
Portrait of Madame Renoir.
c. 1910. Oil on canvas,
31⅞ × 25⅝".
Wadsworth Atheneum, Hartford,
Conn. (The Ella Gallup Sumner
and Mary Catlin Sumner
Collection Fund).

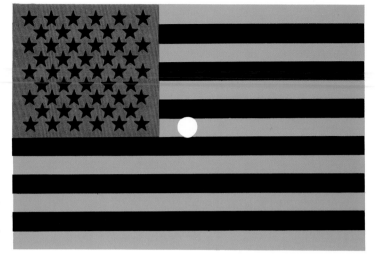

117. Demonstration of the effects of afterimage in colors. Stare at the dot in the center of the flag for at least 30 seconds. Then quickly turn your eyes to a white paper or a white wall. The flag should appear in its usual colors, which are complementary to those shown here.

OPTICAL EFFECTS OF COLOR Certain uses and combinations of colors can "play tricks" on our eyes or, more accurately, on the way we perceive colors registered by our eyes. For one thing, there is the phenomenon known as *simultaneous contrast.* If you place two complementary colors next to each other, both of them will seem more brilliant: red seems redder, green greener, and so forth. Food merchandisers understand this well. Strawberries are nearly always packaged in green, the complement of red, and the meat counter in a grocery store often will have some touch of green. Both the fruit and the meat therefore seem redder and more appetizing. Similarly, the home decorator might create an instant "still life" by piling fresh oranges into a blue bowl on the table; the two colors spark against each other and intrigue the eye.

Another effect associated with complementary colors is *afterimage.* If you stare fixedly at the color areas in the above illustration **(117)** for half a minute and then turn your eyes quickly to a white page or wall, you will see a faint afterimage of the color patches in their complementary colors.

Some colors seem to "advance," others to "recede." Interior designers know that if you place a bright red chair in a room, it will seem larger and farther forward than the same chair upholstered in beige or pale blue. Thus, color can dramatically influence our perceptions of space and size. In general, colors that create the illusion of large size and advancing are those with the warmer hues (red, orange, yellow), high intensity, and dark value; small size and receding are suggested by colors with cooler hues (blue, green), low intensity, and light value.

Colors can be mixed in light or pigment, but they can also be mixed by the eyes. When small patches of different colors are close together, the eye may blend them to produce a new color. This is called *optical color mixture,* and it is an important feature in the painting of Georges Seurat.

Seurat approached painting almost as a science, rather than an art, and he worked out his canvases with great precision, as though they were mathematical exercises. Most artists blend their colors, either on a palette or on the canvas itself, to produce gradations of hue, but Seurat did not. Instead, he laid down his paints by placing many thousands of tiny dots—or points—of pure color next to each other, a process that came to be called *pointillism.* From a distance of a few inches a Seurat painting looks like a meaningless jumble of color dots **(118)**. But as the viewer moves back, the dots merge to form a rich texture of subtly varied tones **(119)**. The painting illustrated here is Seurat's masterpiece, *A Sunday on La Grande Jatte* (**[Overlay 3b]**; see also **188**). Like most of this artist's works, it does not reproduce well in a book, where colors are reduced to ink on paper. Its many verticals of people and trees can make the painting seem static, frozen, lifeless. Seen "in person," however, on the

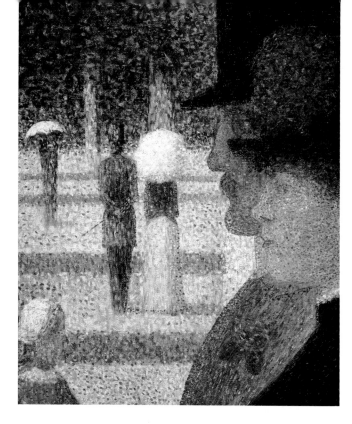

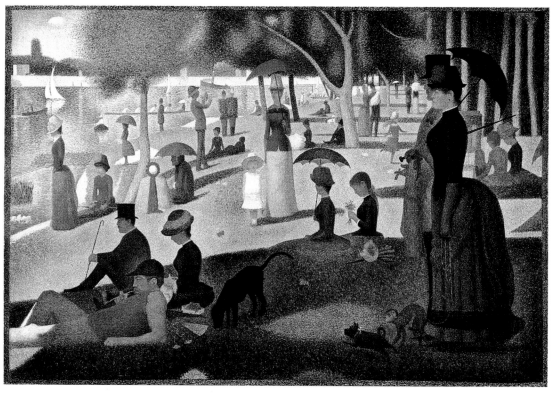

left: 118. Detail of Seurat's
A Sunday on La Grande Jatte, **119.**

below: 119. Georges Seurat.
A Sunday on La Grande Jatte. 1884–86.
Oil on canvas, 6'9¾" × 10'1⅜".
The Art Institute of Chicago
(Helen Brich Bartlett Memorial Collection).

museum wall in Chicago, *La Grande Jatte* sparkles and vibrates with color, comes to life through its myriad little points of light.

EMOTIONAL QUALITIES OF COLOR Endless studies have been undertaken in an attempt to explain the emotional effects of color. Why does a bull chase something red? Why does a person wearing a red shirt or dress attract our attention? (Female political candidates and the wives of male candidates seem to possess vast wardrobes of red garments.) Why are red, white, and silver status colors for an automobile, whereas orange and brown are not? Whatever the reasons, one group of experts—packaging designers—have been aggressive in exploiting these qualities. If you scan the shelves of the supermarket, you will discover that few packages are entirely free of red, because red attracts attention better than any other color. (One exception is foods promoted

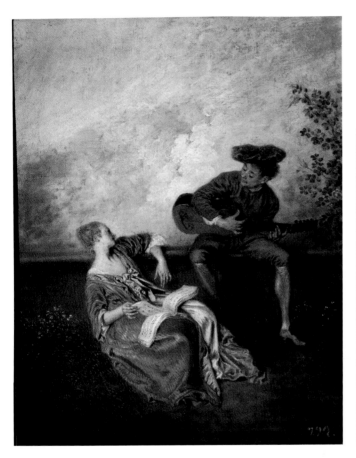

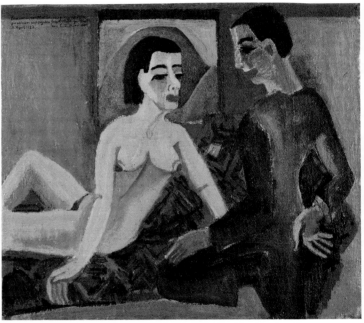

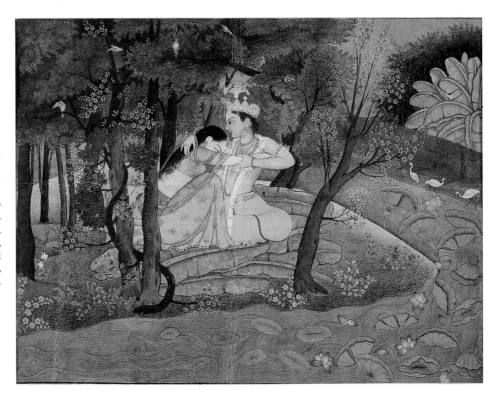

above: 120. Antoine Watteau.
The Singing Lesson.
Early 18th century.
Oil on canvas, 40 × 32″.
Museo del Prado, Madrid.

right: 121. *Krishna and Radha
in a Grove.* c. 1780.
Gouache on paper, 4¾ × 6¾″.
Victoria & Albert Museum,
London (by courtesy of the Board
of Trustees).

above right: 122.
Ernst Ludwig Kirchner.
The Couple. 1923.
Oil on canvas.
Musée National d'Art Moderne,
Centre National d'Art
et de Culture Georges, Pompidou,
Paris.

as being "natural," whose packages usually feature "earth" colors like brown and green.)

In our language we have given specific emotional symbolism to the different color names. Green is associated with envy; blue, with sadness; red, with anger; yellow, with cowardice; and so on. Beyond this, we think of colors as having different "temperatures," as suggested earlier. Red and orange are thought of as being "warm" colors, perhaps because of their association with fire and sunsets. Blue and green are considered "cool."

An artist choosing colors for a particular work will expect those colors to have some emotional impact on the viewer, an impact that supports the intent in that work of art. We can see this by comparing three paintings, each focusing on a couple, with very different emotional qualities.

Antoine Watteau's painting of *The Singing Lesson* **(120)** is an example of the 18th-century style known as **Rococo** (Chapter 18). Watteau's work celebrates an ideal of light-hearted love and frivolity among the French upper classes. No serious concerns intrude in this artist's world. His people are elegant, fashionable, and nearly always portrayed at their delightful leisure. *The Singing Lesson* shows a young man about to play his guitar, smiling down at a lovely woman waiting to sing. The song, we assume, will be a declaration of love between them. (Notice the strong implied line of sight in the lovers' gaze.) Watteau surrounds his couple with a picture-postcard scene, where every leaf and flower is arranged to best effect. His colors are mainly soft pastels, from the fluffy pink-and-blue sky to the buttery yellow of the woman's dress. The mood of this picture is supposed to be light and charming, and Watteau's gentle colors support this mood.

Our second example, a painting from late-18th-century India, shows the Hindu god Krishna in a rendezvous with his beloved, Radha **(121)**. In keeping with the poetic, idyllic mood of the scene, the dominant colors are misty blues and greens, with delicate touches of pink. The shadowy colors also convey an aura of secrecy; this is a clandestine meeting, a few precious moments alone, when no one else is looking. Krishna and Radha seem to float in their own dream landscape, a landscape blurred by soft-focus filters. The only bright colors are in the lovers' garments, suggesting that they alone are real in this magical world.

For our third example we turn to a work by the 20th-century German Expressionist artist Ernst Ludwig Kirchner, called, simply, *The Couple* **(122)**. There is no mistaking that Kirchner has turned up the emotional temperature to "high." Expressionism, as noted elsewhere in this book (Chapters 2 and 19), was an art much interested in psychological exploration, and it was often harsh and pessimistic. These lovers share an emotional and sexual bond, but it is neither light-hearted nor idyllic. Kirchner's colors might best be described as "acid." They shriek and clash, green against orange, setting our teeth on edge. Such colors tell of passion and intensity and lust, but they probably do not predict a happy ending.

These three examples should be enough to demonstrate how potent a force color can be in a work of art, just as it is in life. Our next element is also a major factor in the experience of everyday life, and artists have learned to explore its power in art.

TEXTURE

Texture refers to surface quality—a perception of smooth or rough, flat or bumpy, fine or coarse. Our world would be bland and uninteresting without contrasts of texture. Most of us, when we encounter a dog or cat, are moved to pet the animal, partly because the animal likes it, but also because we enjoy the feel of the fur's texture against our hands. In planning our clothes we instinctively take texture into account. We might put on a thick, nubby sweater over a smooth cotton shirt and enjoy the contrast. We look for this textural interest in all facets of our environment. Few people can resist running their hands over a smooth chunk of marble or a glossy length of silk or a drape of velvet. This is the outstanding feature of texture: it makes us want to touch it.

ACTUAL TEXTURE

All the textures referred to above are *actual* or *tactile;* we experience them through the sense of touch. The rougher the texture, the greater is the difference in surface elevation. If we cannot touch these surfaces, as it is forbidden to touch most sculptures in museums, we understand their actual textures by remembering similar objects we *have* touched.

Actual texture in art is associated with sculpture, architecture, and the crafts. But many paintings also have actual texture. When an artist lays on the paint in thick layers (a technique known as **impasto**), with some areas thicker than others, the painting may have actual surface texture **(209)**. Sometimes, too, an artist may attach three-dimensional objects to a canvas, giving it actual surface texture. More often the textures we see in a painting are visual.

VISUAL TEXTURE

Raoul Dufy's *Regatta at Cowes* **(123)** illustrates the concept of visual texture in painting. If you could touch the surface, you would find it to be primarily flat. Nevertheless, the eye perceives a texture because of the closely spaced, small forms and brush strokes, especially the waves in the sea. This work reminds us of forms in the natural world that do, in fact, have texture, so we apply remembered perceptions of tactile texture to the visual expression.

Sometimes an artist will use visual texture to make a specific expressive point. *Prometheus in Red and Blue* **(124)**, by the Czech artist František Kupka, shows such a device. Prometheus was the ancient Greek god thought to be a particular benefactor to humankind. According to legend, his task was to provide humans with all the resources they would need to survive. Unbeknownst to the ruler god, Zeus—who was angry when he found out—Prometheus flew to heaven and lit a torch from the sun, thus bestowing on humans the special gift of fire. Kupka depicts Prometheus as a virile, energetic figure, master of

123. Raoul Dufy. *Regatta at Cowes.* 1934. Oil on linen, $32\frac{1}{8} \times 39\frac{1}{2}''$. © 1996 Board of Trustees, National Gallery of Art, Washington, D.C. (Ailsa Mellon Bruce Collection).

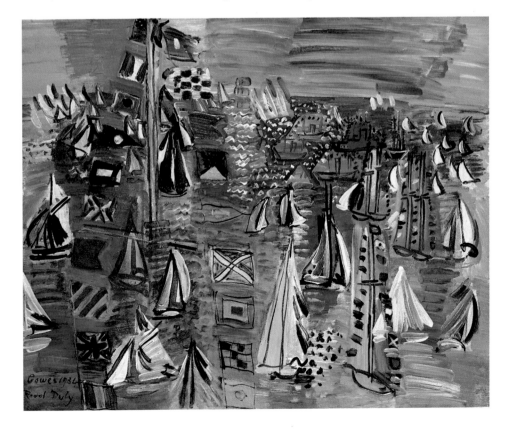

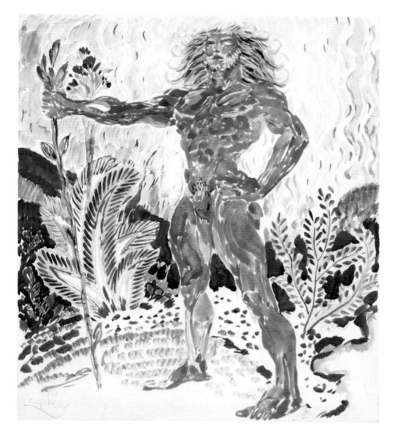

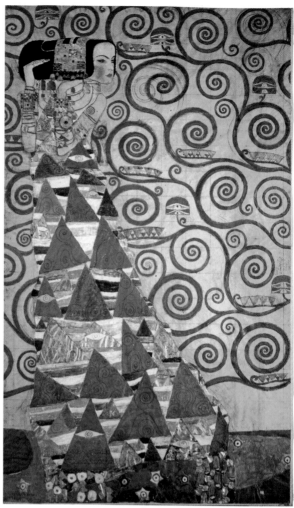

his creation. The lush textures of vegetation around him show that he has done well in ensuring the fruits of the earth. Behind him, flamelike shimmers of yellow symbolize his gift of fire, and his thickly textured yellow hair represents the very sun from which he took it.

A visual texture, therefore, may create an illusion, provide a symbol, or it may exist simply for its own sake, to create visual interest. Either way, the texture helps to enliven a work of art.

PATTERN

Pattern is any decorative, repetitive motif or design. What is the difference between texture and pattern? Pattern nearly always creates visual texture, but texture may not be seen as pattern all the time. When a visual texture is decorative, highly repetitive, and evenly spaced over an area, we are more likely to call it pattern. A good example is the drawing by Gustav Klimt (125). Klimt's subject in this work, a common one for him, is a woman in a long, flowing dress. The dress has been fragmented into a series of irregular triangles. Only this pattern separates the figure from its background, which consists of spiraling plantlike tendrils—another pattern. The figure, then, becomes a point of departure for the overall decorative patterns.

Klimt's drawing is full of movement and energy, thanks to the background spirals, which seem to spin like whirlpools. It is meant to be decorative, not naturalistic. You may observe that there is no impression of roundness in this figure, no distinction of foreground and background, no sense of looking through the "window" of the picture area into a real world. Klimt meant his picture to be "flat," but other artists have had very different goals. This brings us to consideration of the most complex visual element—space.

left: 124. František Kupka. *Prometheus in Red and Blue.* 1908. Watercolor, 12½ × 11⅜". National Gallery, Prague.

right: 125. Gustav Klimt. *Expectation.* c. 1905–09. Mixed media with silver and gold leaf on paper, 6'4" × 3'9⅜". Osterreichisches Museum für Angewandte Kunst, Vienna.

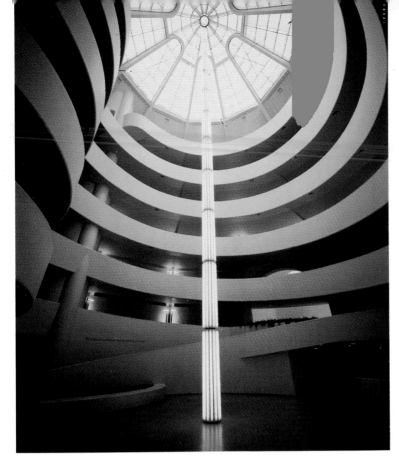

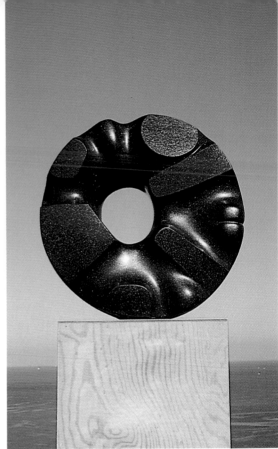

left: **126.** Frank Lloyd Wright. Solomon R. Guggenheim Museum, New York. 1957–59. Interior view with installation by Dan Flavin at the time of the museum's reopening after renovation, June 1992.

right: **127.** Isamu Noguchi. Study for *Black Sun*. 1960–67. Swedish granite. Michio Noguchi, courtesy the Isamu Noguchi Foundation, Inc.

SPACE

The word "space," especially in our technological world, sometimes conveys the idea of nothingness. We think of outer space as a huge void, hostile to human life except when protected by complex support systems. A person who is "spaced out" is blank, unfocused, not really "there." But the space in and around a work of art is not a void, and it is very much there. It is a dynamic visual element that interacts with the lines and shapes and colors and textures of a work of art to give them definition. Consider space in this way: How could there be a line if there were not the spaces on either side of it to mark its edges? How could there be a shape without the space around it to set it off?

In this section we will look at the different types of space an artist deals with and how these spaces affect the other elements.

THREE-DIMENSIONAL SPACE

Sculpture, architecture, and all other forms with mass exist in three-dimensional space—that is, the actual space in which our bodies also stand. These works of art take their character from the individual ways in which they carve out sections of space within and around them.

Architecture, in particular, can be thought of as a means of carving space. Without the walls and the roof of a building, the space would be limitless; with them, the space has boundaries and therefore has volume. For instance, in a very simple house, say a shoebox-shaped house, the walls and roof create a "cube" of space that could be measured in terms of its volume. If the house is subdivided into rooms, then several smaller cubes of space have been created. The interior of the Solomon R. Guggenheim Museum in New York, designed by Frank Lloyd Wright **(126)**, provides a more complex example. Inside the building Wright constructed a huge bubblelike volume enlivened by curved forms cutting in and out and culminating in the skylight dome overhead. Because of this unusual treatment, Wright makes us think of space as active rather than passive, something rather than nothing. From outside we might view the Guggenheim Museum as a *mass;* inside we experience it as *shaped space*. The mass and the space are equal partners, since neither could exist without the other.

Space is also a vital element of sculpture. In Isamu Noguchi's *Black Sun* **(127)** the massive granite circular form takes its character from the rounded opening near the center, which we might be tempted to call a "hole." Certainly it is a hole in the stone, but we can also consider it from the opposite point of view, as a space *encircled* by the granite. The space is not passive; it plays an active role in giving this sculpture its interest and power.

TWO-DIMENSIONAL SPACE

Two-dimensional space refers to the space in a painting, drawing, or print or in some other type of flat art. As the name implies, this kind of space has only height and width, no actual depth. There are two major considerations in dealing with this kind of space. The first is the way in which shapes, lines, and other elements are arranged vertically or horizontally within the space. The second is the possibility of visual depth, or the *illusion* of three-dimensional space on a two-dimensional surface.

SPATIAL ORGANIZATION Working on a picture surface that is flat, the artist has to decide where to place forms in that flat space—high or low, left or right, centered or off to one side. Each time the artist makes a mark of any kind, the space is divided into segments that were not there before.

In Jean Arp's *Collage Arranged According to the Laws of Chance* **(128)**, the square forms have been organized more or less evenly throughout the space. The spaces between squares are similar, as are the top and bottom spaces. Now let us compare the spatial organization in Edgar Degas's *Dancers Practicing at the Barre* **(129)**. The two major forms are crowded into the upper right quadrant of the painting, leaving the rest of the canvas as open space. Why would Degas design such an unusual division of space? Partly because he was influenced by Japanese art, in which asymmetrical balance is common **(159)**. Also partly because he was fascinated by the unexpected angle of vision, such as a viewer might catch by peeping in a window or over a balcony. Even with the eccentric placement of the dancers at upper right, the space below and to

left: 128. Jean Arp. *Collage Arranged According to the Laws of Chance.* 1916–17. Torn and pasted paper, 19⅛ × 13⅝″. The Museum of Modern Art, New York (purchase).

right: 129. Edgar Degas. *Dancers Practicing at the Barre.* 1877. Oil colors, freely mixed with turpentine, on canvas; 29¾ × 32″. The Metropolitan Museum of Art, New York (bequest of Mrs. H. O. Havemeyer, 1929. The H. O. Havemeyer Collection).

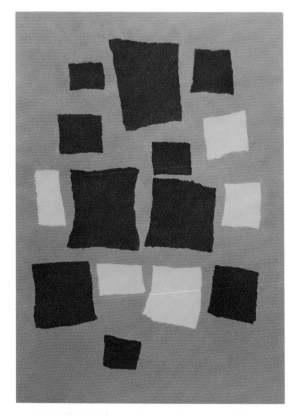

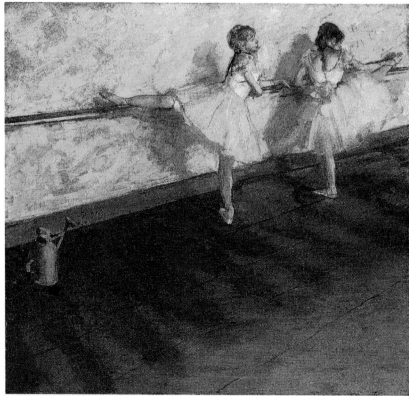

the left does not seem "dead." Quite the opposite—the daring composition and sharp diagonal bring the whole space to life. Notice especially the watering can, which mimics the pose of the dancer at right and which pulls our eyes down into the space of the floor.

ILLUSION OF DEPTH   In some works of art the artist will try to create on a flat surface the illusion of three-dimensional space, as one might see in a natural landscape. This space appears to go backward in depth "behind" the front surface of the painting, which is referred to as the ***picture plane.*** When artists establish illusionary depth, they create the impression that some forms in the composition are farther away than others, and that some forms are in front of or behind others in space.

At different times in history and in different cultures several methods have been used to create the illusion of depth on a two-dimensional surface. One of the simplest of these is ***overlapping.*** If one form overlaps another, that form appears to be in front of the other one. We see this effect in Marie Laurencin's painting, *Group of Artists* **(130)**. Laurencin portrays herself, at top left,

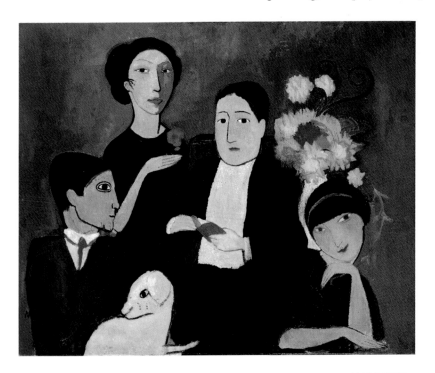

above: 130. Marie Laurencin.
Group of Artists. 1908.
Oil on canvas, $25\frac{1}{2} \times 31\frac{7}{8}$″.
The Baltimore Museum of Art
(The Cone Collection, formed
by Dr. Claribel Cone and Miss Etta Cone
of Baltimore, Maryland).

right: 131. Chiu-Tah, Taos Pueblo.
Taos Round Dance. 1938. Tempera.
Present whereabouts unknown.

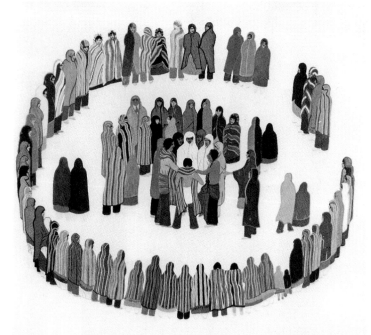

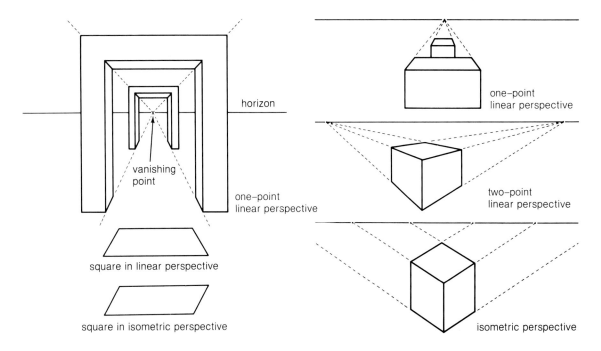

horizon

vanishing point

one-point linear perspective

square in linear perspective

square in isometric perspective

one-point linear perspective

two-point linear perspective

isometric perspective

132. Sketches of linear and isometric perspective.

standing beside her lover, the poet Guillaume Apollinaire (seated, center), along with Pablo Picasso and his dog, Frika (left), and Picasso's lover, Fernande Olivier (right). The space in this group scene is quite shallow, and even the figures are flat, seeming more like cutouts than flesh-and-blood people. Laurencin has slyly given Picasso an "Egyptian" eye, looking straight front in a profile head, much like the eyes he had experimented with in his own paintings. But in spite of the pervasive flatness, we sense some depth because the figures are overlapped. Laurencin is farthest back, overlapped by Picasso and Apollinaire, who are in turn overlapped by the dog and by Fernande Olivier (in her amazing hat) at the picture plane. These layers of depth are very slight, but Laurencin makes them real in the way she arranges her figures.

Another device to show spatial depth is **position.** In this method, pictorial figures that are meant to be understood as farther away are placed *higher* in the composition. We can see this effect clearly in a painting by Chiu-Tah, of the Taos Pueblo, depicting the *Taos Round Dance* **(131).** All the figures in the circle are essentially the same size (except those meant to be children), yet because of their ingenious placement—lowest in the "foreground" gradually moving to highest in the "background"—we have a compelling impression of a circle of people receding into deep space.

During the 15th century in Italy artists perfected the science of **linear perspective**—the most "realistic" method of portraying in two dimensions the visual depth of the natural world. Although linear perspective can be extremely complex and mathematical, it is based on the application of two simple, observable phenomena. In linear perspective:

1. Forms far away from the viewer seem smaller than those close up.
2. Parallel lines receding into the distance seem to converge, until they meet at a point on the horizon line where they disappear. This point is known as the **vanishing point.**

You can visualize this second idea if you remember gazing down a straight highway. As the highway recedes farther from you, the two edges seem to come closer together, until they disappear at the horizon line **(132).** Linear perspective is a translation into drawing principles of these two ideas.

Renaissance artists took up linear perspective with as much delight as a child takes up a new toy. For the first time in the history of civilization (as far as they knew) they could depict absolutely naturalistic scenes, and this was an important goal at the time. Several paintings were done as academic exercises

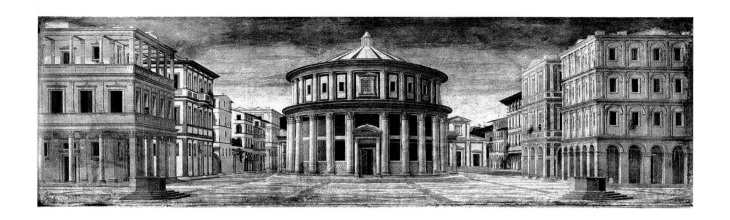

to test the new science of perspective, including *View of an Ideal City* **(133)**. In this work the ground lines, the façades of the buildings, the roof lines, and the protruding architectural elements recede in a perfectly contrived scheme toward a vanishing point somewhere behind the circular building **[Overlay 4a]**.

Once artists had learned to depict deep space in a convincing manner, they could apply that knowledge to their own aesthetic purposes. Some four decades after the *Ideal City* was painted, the great Renaissance artist Leonardo da Vinci used linear perspective to enhance the dramatic and narrative thrust of his masterpiece, *The Last Supper* **(134)**.

Painted on a monastery wall in Milan, *The Last Supper* depicts the final gathering of Jesus Christ with his disciples, the Passover meal they shared before Jesus was brought to trial and crucified. Leonardo captures a particular moment in the story, as related in the Gospel book of Matthew in the Bible. Jesus, shown at the center of the composition, has just said to his followers: "One of you shall betray me." The disciples, Matthew tells us, "were exceeding sorrowful, and began every one of them to say unto him, Lord, is it I?"

Leonardo portrays each of the disciples as individuals, each reacting differently to the terrible prediction. Some are shocked, some dismayed, some puzzled—but only one, only Judas, knows that indeed, it is he. Falling back from Jesus' words, the traitor Judas, seated fourth from the left with his elbow on the table, clutches a bag containing the thirty pieces of silver, his price for handing over his leader to the authorities.

To show this fateful moment, Leonardo places the group in a large banquet hall, its architectural space constructed in careful perspective **[Overlay 4b]**. Cloth hangings on the side walls and panels in the ceiling are drawn so as

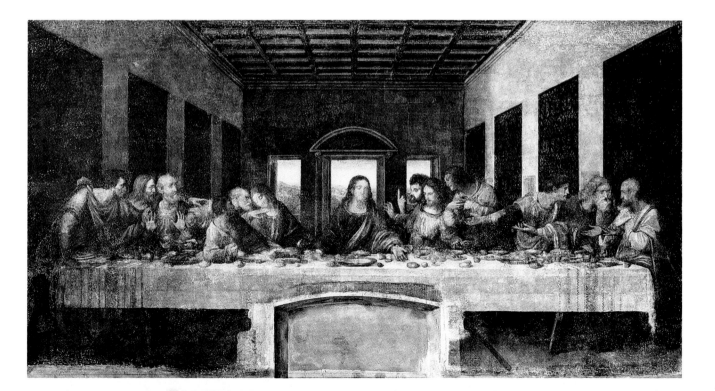

RESTORATION

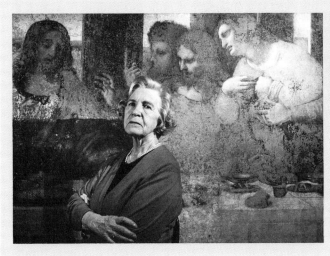 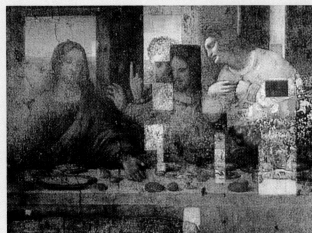

U NWISE RESTORATIONS have been the plague of many a great work of art, and there can be no better example than Leonardo da Vinci's *Last Supper* **(134)**. Leonardo worked on this masterpiece during the years 1495–97. Always a great one for innovation, he bypassed the established wall painting technique and devised an experimental method for this project. For once Leonardo's genius let him down. What may have been his greatest work soon became a ruin. Within ten years the painting was said to be flaking badly; within about fifty years the biographer Giorgio Vasari (p. 125) wrote that "Nothing is visible but a dazzling mass of blots."

The first major restoration was undertaken in 1726, and five others followed. Each of these restorers did more harm than good. One used a harsh solvent that dissolved Leonardo's colors. Another applied a strong glue that attracted dirt. Yet another restorer managed to give one of the Apostles six fingers on one hand.

To make matters worse, the physical environment of *The Last Supper* could scarcely be more precarious. Sharp variations in heat and humidity all but force the paint off the wall, bringing deep cracks in the surface. Sometime in the 18th century well-meaning friars in the monastery installed a curtain across the mural—which had the effect of trapping moisture on the wall and scraping off yet more paint each time the curtain was drawn back. French soldiers of Napoleon who occupied the monastery in 1796 took turns throwing rocks at the mural and climbing ladders to scratch out the Apostles' eyes. A bomb fell on the monastery during World War II, missing the wall by a yard. It's a miracle that anything is left at all, and little is left.

Finally, nearly five hundred years after Leonardo put down his brushes, sensible measures were taken to save the mural. A Milanese restorer, Dr. Pinan Brambilla Barcilon, began a major restoration in 1977; the project would last more than twenty years. Dr. Brambilla had assets earlier restorers lacked—modern microscopes, chemicals, and measuring devices. Through sensitive probing she could determine what was Leonardo's work and what was somebody else's—and remove the latter. In areas where nothing is left of Leonardo's paint, she did not attempt to reconstruct the imagery, but simply painted in a neutral color.

It has not been easy. Dr. Brambilla's eyesight is permanently altered, and she suffers chronic pain in her shoulders and back. She says, "I often have to clean the same piece a second time, or even a third or fourth. The top section of the painting is impregnated with glue. The middle is filled with wax. There are six different kinds of plaster and several varnishes, lacquers, and gums. What worked on the top section doesn't work in the middle. And what worked in the middle won't work on the bottom. It's enough to make a person want to shoot herself."

Inevitably, Dr. Brambilla will have to cope with people who want to shoot *her*. Every art historian in the world will have an opinion about her restoration, and many of those opinions will be negative, even outraged. Still, she remains philosophical about her project. "I am at peace with what I have done here," she says.[3]

---

left: Dr. Pinan Brambilla Barcilon photographed in 1995 with the nearly completed restoration of Leonardo's *Last Supper*.

right: A portion of the mural partially restored.

to recede into space. Their lines converge at a vanishing point behind Jesus' head, at the exact center of the picture. Thus, our attention is directed forcefully toward the most important part of the composition, the face of Jesus. The central opening in the back wall, a rectangular window, also helps to focus our attention on Jesus and creates a "halo" effect around his head.

Leonardo's perspective performs another function as well, in making the scene believable. When thirteen people sit down to dinner, they do not usually cram themselves all on one side of the table, leaving the opposite side empty. But Leonardo needed this odd arrangement to show the personalities and reactions of his characters. Placing the line of figures in deep space helps to take away the oddness, to make the grouping seem more natural. It gives them, pictorially, "more room." You can see how this effect works if you cover up the section of picture above the heads. Without the illusion of space afforded by the perspective, Leonardo's figures would look artificially crowded together.

Linear perspective may seem "correct" to our eyes, but it is not the magic key to perfect art, as some Renaissance artists thought. The perspective works only if the viewer stands motionless and fixes his or her eyes (or, even better, one eye with the other closed) on a particular spot. For this reason the results of academically perfect linear perspective may appear static and lifeless—much like the *Ideal City*, which reminds us less of a living metropolis than of a ghost town. Expanding the perspective to include two or more vanishing points **(132)**, a more complex form of perspective, helps to give a more vital image, but the results may still be rather rigid. Like any other artistic element, perspective is a tool, and its use depends on the artist.

The 18th-century Italian painter Canaletto understood the mathematical precision of linear perspective very well, and he employed that precision to give depth to his many views of Venice. Moreover, he knew how to use it without being rigid or lifeless. In a typically dense canvas, *View of Venice: Grand Canal, Looking Southwest from Near the Rialto Bridge* **(135)**, the expanse of the vista plunges so far into space that the vanishing point never quite seems

135. Canaletto (Giovanni Antonio Canal). *View of Venice: Grand Canal, Looking Southwest from Near the Rialto Bridge.* c. 1730. Oil on canvas, 19¼ × 29". The Museum of Fine Arts, Houston (The Robert Lee Blaffer Memorial Collection, gift of Sarah Campbell Blaffer).

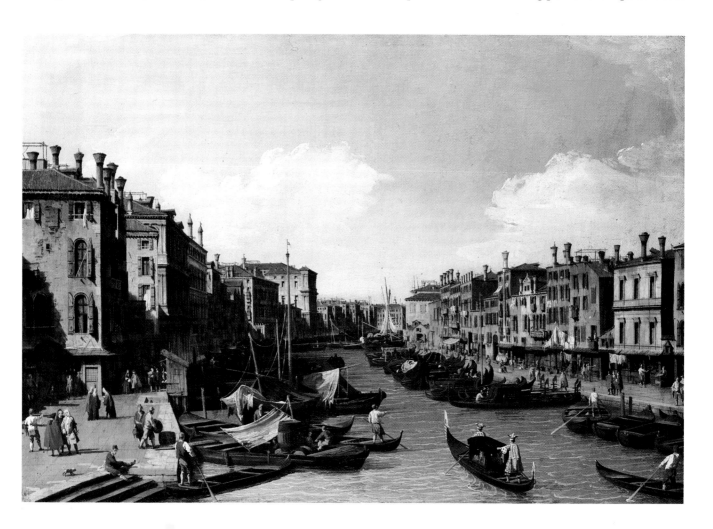

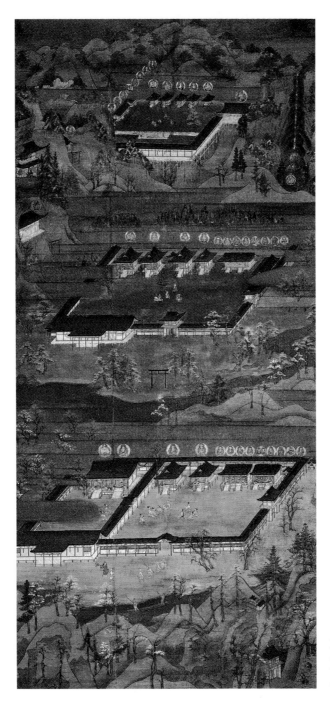

136. *Kumano Mandala.* Japan. Kamakura Period, c. 1300. Color on silk, 4′4¾″ × 2′⅜″. The Cleveland Museum of Art (John L. Severance Fund).

to "vanish" **[Overlay 5a]**. We imagine that if only our vision were sharper, we could see *beyond* Canaletto's vista to yet more buildings, more boats, more people farther down the canal. Much of the life in a Canaletto landscape comes from the thousand details the artist provides: people in all guises and occupations, gondolas in motion or tied up, laundry flapping out of windows, endlessly varied architecture, a little dog barking. For Canaletto, linear perspective creates the framework, but the exuberant life of Venice is the picture.

In Eastern art linear perspective has played much less of a role. Instead, artists often have relied on a system of ***isometric perspective,*** in which distant forms *are* made smaller but parallel lines do not converge. The Shinto shrines depicted in the *Kumano Mandala* **(136)** might be considered the Japanese equivalent of a Renaissance "ideal city." As usual in isometric perspective, lines that would be perpendicular to the picture plane are drawn as sharp diagonals **[Overlay 6a]**. Whereas linear perspective turns the square into a trapezoid, isometric perspective turns the square into a parallelogram **(132)**.

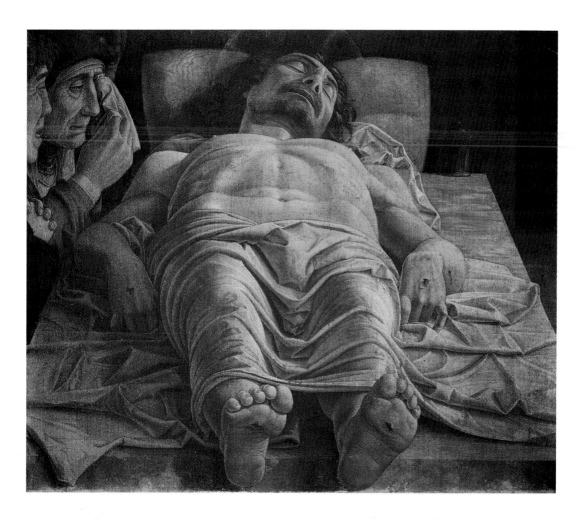

137. Andrea Mantegna. *Dead Christ.* After 1466. Tempera on canvas, 26¾ × 31⅞″. Pinacoteca di Brera, Milan.

In conjunction with linear or isometric perspective, the artist may employ the device of ***atmospheric perspective.*** This means that forms meant to be perceived as far in the distance are blurred, indistinct, and misty—much as the eye perceives distant forms in nature. You can see this effect in many landscape paintings reproduced throughout this book.

To sum up, then, artists can draw upon several devices to create the illusion of three-dimensional depth on a two-dimensional surface. Here are some of the major ones:

Seen as Foreground	Seen as Background
large size	small size
set low in the picture	set high in the picture
parallel lines far apart	parallel lines converging
overlapping other forms	overlapped by other forms
sharply defined forms	blurred forms
intense colors	grayed colors
rough textures	smooth textures

When linear perspective is applied to human or animal forms or to objects receding into depth, the result is called ***foreshortening.*** Literally, the body, or part of it, is "shortened" from its normal vertical height to better convey the appearance of figures that are perpendicular to the picture plane. A classic example of foreshortening is Andrea Mantegna's *Dead Christ* (**137**). If you could lift this figure out of the painting and stand it upright, its proportions would seem very strange indeed. The legs are far too short for the body, and the entire figure would be absurdly short compared with its breadth. Mantegna's composition, however, seems entirely believable given the unusual angle of vision. And his choice of this angle makes the body of the dead Christ all the more poignant and vulnerable.

The aim of all perspective systems, including the device of foreshortening, is to create the impression of realism. Yet once the artist has the *ability* to convey the idea of depth on a flat surface, the question remains, how much sense of depth does he or she want in any given work? Most Renaissance artists would have answered this question by saying "the more the better," the more depth in a painting, the better the artist has succeeded. Later artists, however, have had many different expressive goals, and illusion of depth is only one of them.

The space in Romare Bearden's collage *The Block* (138) is both complicated and ambiguous. This six-part work, of which two panels are shown, depicts the street life of a typical block in the inner city, specifically in Harlem. We see a row of houses and store fronts, with people going about their daily activities. The line of buildings is almost flat, parallel to the picture plane, and even the elements of street life—people, a car, and so forth—seem flattened in this view. Some shallow depth is indicated on the sidewalk, where mourners cluster outside a funeral parlor, but this space seems calculated more to direct our attention to the group than to mimic the natural world. Where the artist gives us peeks into the buildings, these window images, too, seem flat and posterlike. Only at the tops of these panels, above the buildings, is there any indication of depth, a suggestion that the world may continue *behind* this block. Bearden knew how to draw deep space, but in this case he preferred the flatness, perhaps to show that life on the block is a self-contained universe.

138. Romare Bearden.
The Block, detail. 1971.
Collage, cut and pasted papers on Masonite; entire work in six panels, each 49 × 36".
The Metropolitan Museum of Art, New York (gift of Mr. and Mrs. Samuel Shore, 1978).
© 1998 Romare Bearden Foundation/ Licensed by VAGA, New York.

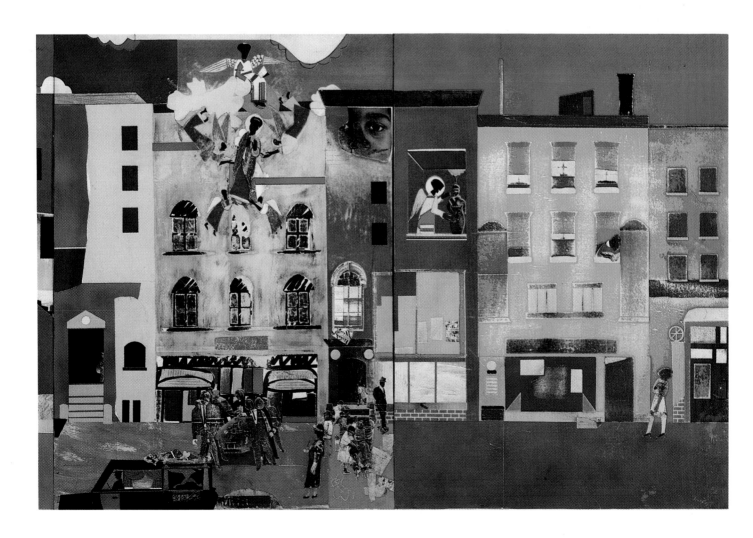

The French artist Suzanne Valadon also knew how to draw deep space, but for her *Reclining Nude* **(139)** she has chosen to keep the space of the painting quite shallow. The figure is posed rather awkwardly on a too-small sofa, with legs crossed and one arm clutched across the breast in a self-protective gesture. This model presents herself for our inspection, but at the same time she pulls away and keeps to herself. Valadon has outlined the figure in a strong black line and concentrated especially on the powerful volumes of thigh and belly and upper arm. But the most fascinating aspect of this painting is its claustrophobic space. We as viewers seem to be very close to the model, who is hemmed in on three sides by the sofa. The tight space creates a tension, a psychological confrontation, between the viewer and the model. She is naked but private; the viewer is perhaps embarrassed and sympathetic, but surely intrigued.

So we see that pictorial depth, or the lack thereof, is a powerful tool that an artist can use for whatever effect is desired. Once the skill is acquired, the possibilities are endless. Yet no matter how skilled the artist, it is not possible to make a painted scene look exactly like a real scene for one simple reason: our world does not stand still. At every moment there is the sense of passing time, the sense of movement. Some works of art, however, do deal with time and motion. We turn finally to a consideration of these two factors.

TIME AND MOTION

The ancient Egyptians undoubtedly would have been puzzled to find time and motion included in a discussion of art. In Egyptian culture, and in many others, art was supposed to be time*less*, motion*less* for all eternity. Our own world, however, is considerably more dynamic. Most of us, especially in the

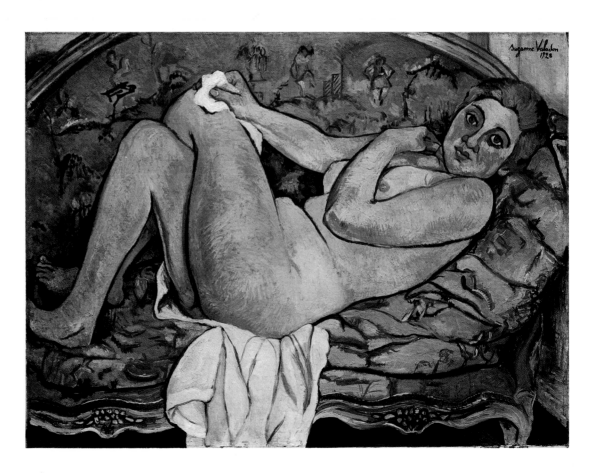

SUZANNE VALADON

1867–1938

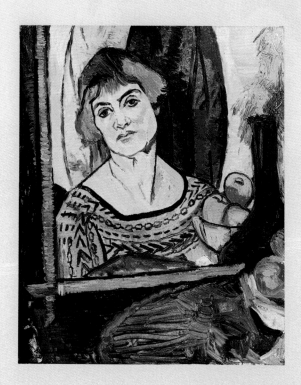

Although she never had a formal lesson, Valadon received much encouragement from her artist-patrons, whose work she was able to study at close range. She began to paint, and then to make prints. By the time she was twenty-eight, she had had her work exhibited by an important dealer and had sold many drawings and etchings. Some compared her painting to that of Paul Gauguin, whom she much admired, yet always she retained an originality and reliance on her own artistic instincts, especially in her use of the bold, definitive outline.

In 1894 Valadon took up with a rich banker, Paul Mousis, and spent the next fourteen years living as his wife—they never were married legally—in a large house in the Paris suburbs. Despite the slightly scandalous nature of their unwed relationship and the presence of Valadon's illegitimate (and alcoholic) son, this proved to be the *least* bohemian period in her colorful life. Valadon continued to work and to exhibit, and she taught Maurice to paint, apparently in the hope that it would help him to overcome his alcoholism. But in 1908 Valadon herself slipped back into what most people considered a bohemian life style. She fell in love with a young painter, André Utter, a friend of Maurice's who was twenty-one years her junior, and went to live with him. On one occasion the three—Valadon, Utter, and Utrillo—held a joint exhibition in Paris, but the public was more interested in the trio's sins than in their art.

Toward the end of her life, Valadon achieved some measure of fame and considerable financial security. Until her last year she continued to paint and to show, in both solo and joint exhibitions. Indeed, death came, in the form of a stroke, while she was at her easel working on a new painting. The mourners at her funeral included virtually the whole Parisian art community, among them Pablo Picasso.

Certainly the details of Valadon's life are interesting, and they mark her as a genuine individual. In her life, as in her art, she followed her own path, copying no one, offering no explanation. She seldom spoke, and never wrote, about her art, but one comment that was recorded seems to sum up her faith in her own vision: "I don't understand the experts, neither their explanations, nor their comparisons. When they speak of technique, balance and values they simply make me dizzy. Only two things exist for me and all others who paint: good pictures and bad pictures, that's all."[4]

I N 1867, IN A small town in central France, was born an illegitimate child named Marie-Clémentine Valade. When Marie was three years old, her mother brought her to Paris, where they lived in extreme poverty, subsisting on vegetables discarded as garbage at the market. Little Marie worked as a laundress and, later, joined a circus as an animal rider and trapeze artist. At the age of eighteen she, in turn, gave birth to an illegitimate child, who would become the painter Maurice Utrillo. During her childhood she taught herself to draw—first with cinders given to her by a coal hauler, then with whatever drawing materials she could find. After an accident at the circus, she became an artist's model, posing for Degas, Renoir, and the young painter Henri de Toulouse-Lautrec. The latter formed a friendship, perhaps a romance, with Marie and is said to have given her a new name— Suzanne Valadon.

Suzanne Valadon. *Self-Portrait*. 1927.
Oil on wood, 24½ × 19¾".
Courtesy Paul Petrides, Paris.

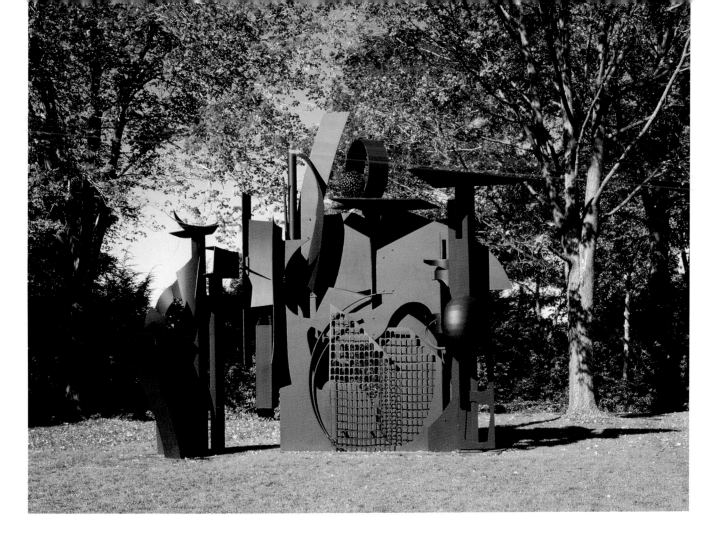

140. Louise Nevelson. *City on a High Mountain.* 1983. Black painted steel, 20′ × 23′ × 13′6″. Storm King Art Center, Mountainville, N.Y. (purchase).

industrialized nations, are obsessed with time, and motion is a fact of everyday life. Both time and motion have come to be viewed as important art elements.

ELAPSED TIME

In the three-dimensional arts, especially sculpture and architecture, time is always a factor in the observer's reaction. When you walk through a building or walk around a sculpture, your viewpoint changes with every split second that elapses. Usually, you *cannot* experience every aspect of the structure from one vantage point or at one moment. You must expend time to accumulate all the different points of view and assemble them into an understanding of the whole. Certainly this is true of Louise Nevelson's massive sculpture *City on a High Mountain* **(140)**.

A single photograph of *City on a High Mountain,* as reproduced here, shows us one particular viewpoint, but that was clearly not the sculptor's intention. This work was meant to be exhibited outdoors, and it is enormous: more than 20 feet high and 23 feet wide at its broadest diameter. Nevelson planned it to be interesting from any angle of approach. Even this one picture should reveal that a walk around the sculpture would present endlessly varied juxtapositions of shape, line, space, texture, and light. And while the sculpture is painted a uniform black, patterns of light and shadow alter the color with time, as one moves around it or as the sun moves across the sky.

ACTUAL MOTION

For Nevelson's sculpture, as for a great many other works of art, time is a factor because the viewer is in motion. In some cases, however, the work of art is also in motion. One sculptor whose special preoccupation has been forms in motion is George Rickey. In a Rickey sculpture the shape of the object is less important than the movements that may be produced by that shape. *Double L Excentric Gyratory II* **(141)** floats above the landscape, its two L-shaped sections set in constant, nonrepetitive motion by the air. The balance of these "excentric" L's makes them receptive to any passing current, from the gentlest summer breeze to the 80-mile-per-hour hurricane-force winds they are designed to withstand. No one can predict exactly what configuration the L's will take at any moment. Their polished surfaces reflect light from above and the colors of their surroundings in an ever-changing pattern.

ILLUSION OF MOTION

Just as artists have long attempted to create the illusion of deep space on a flat surface, so have they often tried to create the illusion of motion where there is none, and, as with spatial depth, the artist has a choice. Some works of art are planned to be rather static and motionless, and a sense of movement would actually be harmful to the artist's intent. Valadon's *Reclining Nude* **(139)** fits this category. In other cases a sense of movement contributes much to the success of the work. Géricault's *The Raft of the Medusa* **(93)** seems dynamic because the artist has created an illusion of the raft plunging through the water, an illusion of motion. We could find many other examples of this situation. Indeed, in Gustav Klimt's drawing **(125)** the illusion of motion—caused by the repetitive pattern of spirals that seem to spin—becomes one of the most important elements in the composition.

The same is true for the two works illustrated here. Bridget Riley's *Current* **(142)**, an example of the style known as **Op Art,** has as its theme the illusion of motion caused by optical effects, a direct response by the retina of the eye to lines and colors arranged in certain ways. The lines in this painting

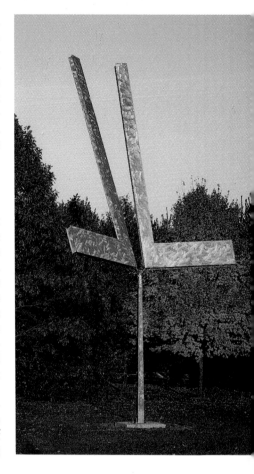

above: **141.** George Rickey.
Double L Excentric Gyratory II.
1981. Stainless steel,
height 27′6″.
PepsiCo Sculpture Gardens,
Purchase, N.Y.
© 1998 George Rickey/
Licensed by VAGA, New York.

left: **142.** Bridget Riley.
Current. 1964.
Synthetic polymer paint
on composition board,
4′10⅜″ × 4′10⅞″.
The Museum of Modern Art,
New York (Philip Johnson Fund).

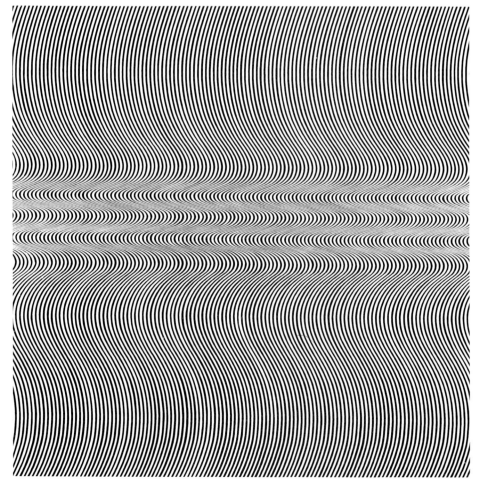

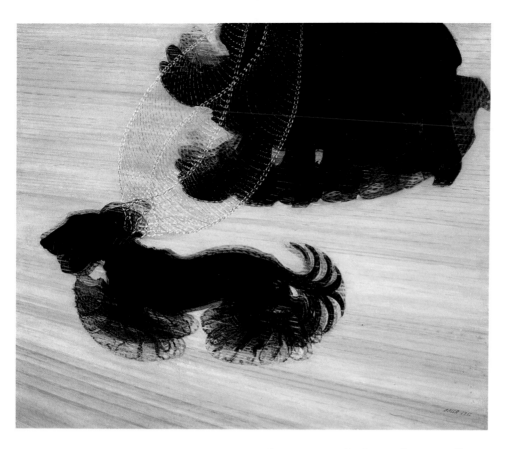

143. Giacomo Balla.
Dynamism of a Dog on a Leash.
1912. Oil on canvas, 35⅜ × 43¼".
Albright-Knox Art Gallery,
Buffalo, N.Y. (bequest of
A. Conger Goodyear and gift
of George F. Goodyear, 1964).
© 1998 Estate of Giacomo Balla/
Licensed by VAGA, New York.

are just that—precisely drawn lines on flat canvas—but as we stare at them they begin to swim before our eyes, and the painting actually seems to be in motion. Some viewers have experienced vertigo or even nausea after spending any length of time in front of an Op canvas, so powerful is the effect on one's central nervous system.

Giacomo Balla's *Dynamism of a Dog on a Leash* **(143)** shows another way in which motion can be suggested. Balla was a member of the ***Futurist*** group that flourished in Italy during the second decade of this century. An important (though short-lived) movement, Futurism, as the name implies, rejected the art forms of the past, which it considered static, in favor of images that conveyed movement and energy. In *Dog on a Leash* Balla has blurred the forms of dog, leash, and dog walker, repeating the feet, tail, and leash many times to set them in motion across the canvas. When we look at this charming painting, we might almost swear we see the dog's tail wagging, its little feet scampering along the ground.

Line, shape and mass, light, value, color, texture, space, time and motion—these are the raw materials, the elements, of a work of art. Some people are troubled by this approach to works of art, taking them apart and putting them back together again like jigsaw puzzles. And how can we justify discussion of the art elements in the face of utterly down-to-earth and commonsensical remarks like Suzanne Valadon's declaration that such analyses of art simply made her "dizzy"?

Whether she cared to talk about the subject or not, Valadon understood the art elements. She had absorbed them into her eye and her hand and her soul as an artist. For the rest of us, a discussion of the elements gives systematic and intellectual order to our aesthetic appreciation of art. With a knowledge of the elements, we begin to understand *why* we love one work of art, why we do not much like another. And then we—along with Valadon—can make intelligent judgments about "good pictures and bad pictures, that's all."

GIORGIO VASARI

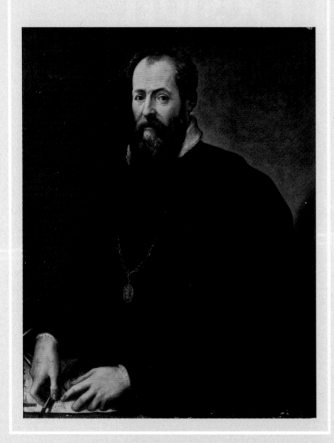

A BIOGRAPHER is by nature a gossip. We value the art of biography because it enables us to better understand the work of noted individuals through knowing their histories. At a more basic level, however, nearly all of us love to learn the details of other people's lives—in other words, gossip. And one of the most delightful gossips in history was Giorgio Vasari.

Vasari was a painter and architect of considerable skill. Born in Arezzo, in the Italian province of Tuscany, in 1511, he pursued the career of artist throughout his life. Many of his paintings still exist, and his major work as an architect, the Uffizi Palace in Florence, is now an important museum. But for two facts, Vasari might today be known as a prominent artist of the Renaissance. The facts are these: Vasari was inevitably overshadowed by the giants at work in Italy at the same time, notably Leonardo da Vinci, Michelangelo, and Raphael. And Vasari's artistic production was overshadowed by his own brilliant literary endeavor—a comprehensive biography of the outstanding Renaissance artists.

The first edition of his masterwork, *Lives of the Most Excellent Architects, Painters, and Sculptors*, was published in 1550, after seven years of hard work. (A revised and expanded edition of the book was published in 1568.) Although other biographies had been written, nothing on this scale had ever been completed. Reading the *Lives* today, we may find the style a trifle precious, but at the time Vasari's approach was considered natural and conversational. For his research, Vasari traveled constantly (on horseback, over bad roads), spoke with anyone he could, viewed works of art whenever possible. Some of his subjects, including Raphael, were long dead when he began the *Lives,* so he depended on secondhand sources. Others, like Michelangelo, were close and respected friends. It is on Michelangelo that Vasari pours out the extremes of his flowery admiration.

Everyone seems to have liked Vasari. He had a vast network of friends, a huge correspondence, a long list of patrons. His genial temperament gave him access to information about all the leading artists. In the *Lives,* Vasari's style is so charming, so enthusiastic, so *cheerful,* that reading him now, more than four hundred years later—we like him too.

Against his extremely busy public life, Vasari's personal life was uneventful. Under pressure from one of his patrons, a cardinal of the Church, he "resolved to do something, which hitherto I had not wished to do, that is to take a wife." In 1550 he married Niccolosa Bacci, always called Cosina, for whom he seems to have had a rather absent-minded affection but little passion. The couple had no children.

As historian and biographer, Vasari must be taken with a grain of salt. His grasp of dates is particularly casual. We should remember, however, that Vasari was breaking new ground. In his day there were no reference books to check facts, no encyclopedias, no public libraries. Under the circumstances, the *Lives* must be viewed as a staggering achievement, giving us a picture of Renaissance artists that is true in its quality if shaky in some specifics. For without Vasari, we would have had little picture at all.

Giorgio Vasari. *Self-Portrait*. c. 1571.
Uffizi, Florence.

Principles of Design in Art

WHEN AN ARTIST sets about making any work, he or she is faced with infinite choices. How big or small? What kinds of lines and where should the lines go? What kinds of shapes? How much space between the shapes? How many colors and how much of each one? What amounts of light and dark values? Somehow, the elements discussed in Chapter 4—line, shape, light, value, color, texture, space, and possibly time and motion—must be organized in such a way as to satisfy the artist's expressive intent. In two-dimensional art this organization is often called **composition,** but the more inclusive term, applicable to all kinds of art, is **design.** The task of making the decisions involved in designing a work of art would be paralyzing were it not for certain guidelines that, once understood, become almost instinctive factors in an artist's repertoire. These guidelines are usually known as the *principles of design.*

All of us have some built-in sense of what looks right or wrong, what "works" or doesn't. Some—including most artists—have a stronger sense of what "works" than others. If two families each decorate a living room, and one room is attractive, welcoming, and pulled together while the other seems drab and uninviting, we might say that the first family has better "taste." Taste is a common term that, in this context, describes how some people make visual selections. What we really mean by "good taste," oftentimes, is that some people have a better grasp of the principles of design and how to apply them in everyday situations.

The principles of design are a natural part of perception. Most of us are not conscious of them in everyday life, but artists usually are very aware of them, because they have trained themselves to be aware. These principles codify, or explain systematically, our sense of "rightness" and help to show why certain designs work better than others. For the artist they offer guidelines for making the most effective choices; for the observer an understanding of the principles of design gives greater insight into works of art.

It must be stressed that the principles of design are not rules or laws. If they were, nearly every great artist would have been guilty of breaking them at one time or another. They are, as we said, guidelines that apply in most situations. There are circumstances, however, in which an artist may choose to violate or ignore these guidelines to achieve a particular effect.

The principles of design most often identified are unity and variety, balance, emphasis and focal point, proportion and scale, and rhythm. This chapter illustrates some thirty-five works of art that show these principles very clearly. But *any* work of art, regardless of its form or the culture in which it was made, could be discussed in terms of the principles of design, for they are integral to all art.

UNITY
AND VARIETY

Unity is a sense of oneness, of things belonging together and making up a coherent whole. Variety is difference, which provides interest. We discuss them together because the two generally coexist in a work of art. A solid wall painted white has unity for sure, but it is not likely to hold your interest for long. Take that same blank wall and ask fifty people each to make a mark on it and you will get plenty of variety, but there probably will be no unity whatever. In fact, there will be so *much* variety that no one can form a meaningful visual impression. Unity and variety exist on a spectrum, with total blandness at one end, total disorder at the other. For most works of art the artist strives to find just the right point on that spectrum—the point at which there is sufficient visual unity enlivened by sufficient variety.

Ben Jones' *In the Spirit* (144) illustrates the way unity and variety work together. This image, part of a larger mixed-media installation, consists of six muscular nude male bodies interspersed with decorative and symbolic motifs that have spiritual significance for the artist. Most of the figures turn in one direction, but the sixth one faces them. In outline and general contours, the figures are almost identical—that is, unified—yet there is extremely rich variation in surface details, colors and patterns, and even in the objects held by and separating the men. If the bodies were not much the same in shape, this work would probably seem chaotic. And without the great variety of details, it could be merely repetitious.

How does an artist achieve unity? One way is by holding one or two elements constant and varying the others. Jones, for *In the Spirit*, kept the elements of shape and space constant and varied the lines, colors, and visual

144. Ben Jones.
In the Spirit. 1994.
Part of the mixed-media
installation *Shango/Changó.*
Jersey City Museum,
Jersey City, N.J.

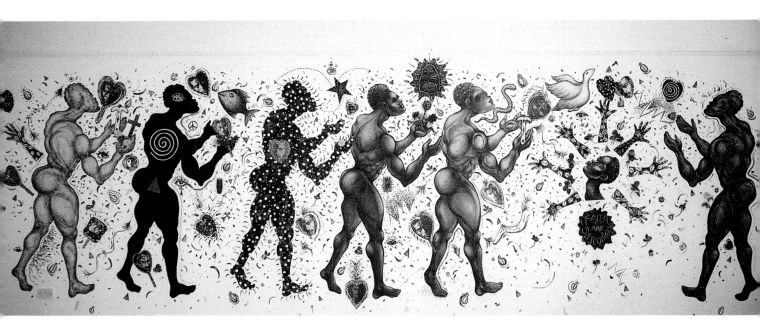

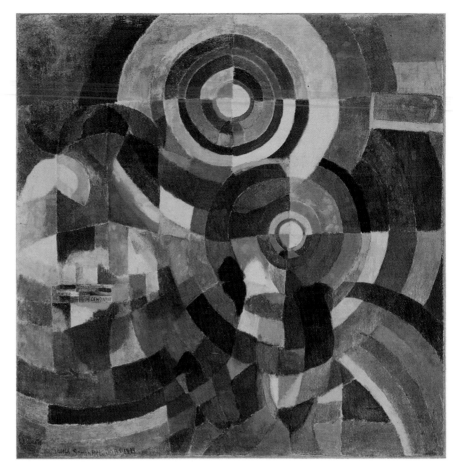

right: 145. Sonia Delaunay.
Electric Prisms. 1914.
Oil on canvas, 7′9¾″ × 8′2¾″.
Musée National d'Art Moderne,
Centre Georges Pompidou, Paris.

below: 146. Henri Matisse.
The Red Studio.
Issy-les-Moulineaux, 1911.
Oil on canvas, 5′11¼″ × 7′2¼″.
The Museum of Modern Art,
New York
(Mrs. Simon Guggenheim Fund).

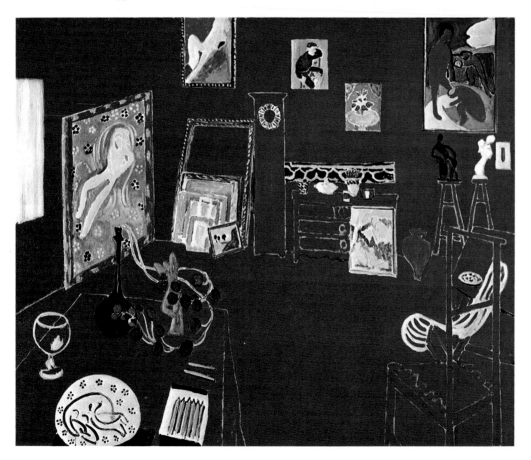

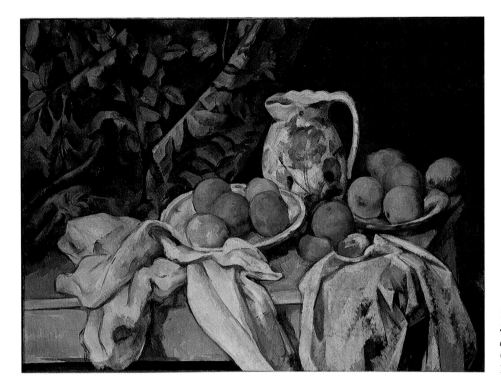

147. Paul Cézanne.
*Still Life with Curtain
and Flowered Pitcher.* c. 1899.
Oil on canvas, 21½ × 29⅛".
Hermitage Museum, St. Petersburg.

textures. Similarly, in Sonia Delaunay's *Electric Prisms* **(145)** shape is the unifying element. Nearly all the shapes in Delaunay's painting are segments of an arc, some of them joined into a bull's-eye arrangement, others suggestive of a larger circle that may continue outside the picture. These arcs convey the dazzling, pulsating effect of bright electric lights. Variations of color, size, placement, and overlapping enhance the throbbing quality of this work, but the unified shapes hold it together.

Henri Matisse used color to unify *The Red Studio* **(146)**. Walls and floor are saturated with a vivid scarlet, and some of the furniture is drawn as though transparent to let the red show through. By this method Matisse controls the variety of what might be any artist's home studio—paintings displayed and stacked against the wall, a clock and bureau, drawing and eating utensils. Although the spatial organization may at first glance seem random, we get a strong sense of unity due largely to the color.

The classic exercise in achieving unity-with-variety is the still-life painting. To make a still life, the artist brings together a number of diverse objects having different colors, shapes, sizes, and textures and arranges them into a pleasing composition. The usual goal is to make these forms belong together, to harmonize with and yet play against one another. A master of this form was Paul Cézanne, whose *Still Life with Curtain and Flowered Pitcher* is shown here **(147)**. The ingredients of this picture are deceptively simple: a table, two plates holding oranges and apples, a pitcher, a patterned drape, some white cloths. An appearance of sculptural solidity unifies this grouping, for each component seems "heavy" and imposing—the rounded fruit, the thick curtain, the artfully crumpled white cloths, the exquisite pitcher. Beyond this, Cézanne has filled his canvas with a gentle, rhythmic motion. For the viewer there is little "stillness" in this still life. The plates seem to tip precariously, perhaps rolling the fruit off the table, and the folds of cloth keep pulling our eyes in different directions. Surprisingly, this very sense of motion, of objects swirling together in their own little universe, helps to unify the composition.

The four works we have just considered show a primarily *visual* unity—unity of shape or space or color or pattern. We should also take into account the potential for *conceptual* unity, or unity of ideas, which may enhance or even replace visual unity. For instance, if Miriam Schapiro's *Children of Paradise* **(148)** reminds you of a patchwork quilt, that is no accident. The quiltlike quality is a major factor in unifying the composition; we perceive all the forms as being of cloth, and we identify the decorative fabric-type designs we would see in a quilt. Even though the little boy's suit and the little girl's dress are not alike in shape or color, we look at them and think "child's outfit." Schapiro is

right: 148. Miriam Schapiro. *Children of Paradise.* 1984. Color lithograph with collage, $31\frac{1}{2} \times 47\frac{1}{4}''$. University of South Florida Art Museum, Tampa, Fla.

below left: 149. Joseph Cornell. *The Hotel Eden.* 1945. Assemblage with music box, $15\frac{1}{8} \times 15\frac{1}{8} \times 4\frac{3}{4}''$. National Gallery of Canada, Ottawa. © The Joseph and Robert Cornell Memorial Foundation.

below right: 150. Andy Warhol. *100 Campbell Soup Cans.* 1962. Oil on canvas, 6′ × 4′4″. Albright-Knox Art Gallery, Buffalo, N.Y. (gift of Seymour H. Knox, 1963).

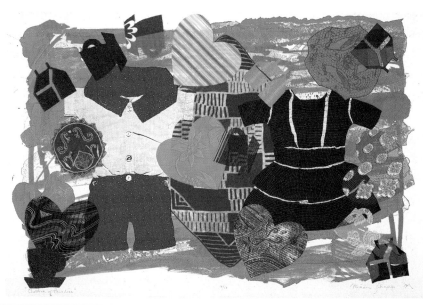

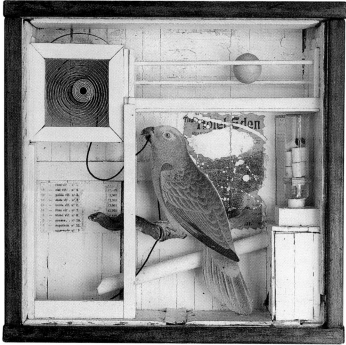

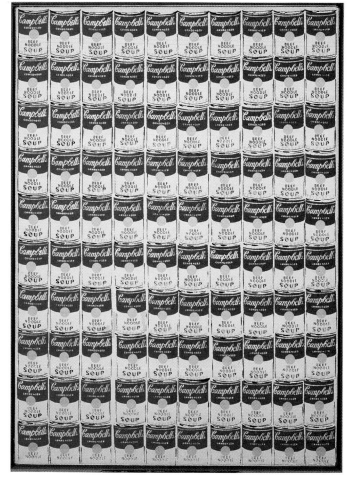

much interested in the handcrafts of 19th-century American women, and she has used this idea to unify her composition. Visual unity is provided by the repeated heart and house motifs, but variety abounds in the colors, patterns, positions, and overlapping of forms.

Conceptual unity predominates in the works of Joseph Cornell, such as *The Hotel Eden* **(149)**. Cornell devoted most of his career to making boxlike structures that enclosed many dissimilar but related objects. Contained within the boxes, these objects build their own private worlds. Cornell collected things, odds and ends, wherever he went. His studio held crates of stuff filed according to a personal system. There were even crates labeled "flotsam" and "jetsam." When making his box sculptures, Cornell would select and arrange these objects to create a conceptual unity that was meaningful to him, based on his dreams, nostalgia, and fantasies. This is not sufficient to provide a *visual* unity, and so the boxed enclosure and the smaller boxes within it take care of the latter.

All the works illustrated so far strike a balance between unity and variety, and this is most often the artist's goal. Sometimes, however, an artist will aim at extreme unity or extreme variety. Andy Warhol's *100 Campbell Soup Cans* **(150)** is an example of the first. No one would question that this composition has unity. It is a precise, grocery-shelf arrangement of one hundred cans of beef noodle soup, painted to be exactly the same. Warhol, like many Pop artists of the 1960s, is commenting on the packaged uniformity of our society. He might be saying that we have sacrificed variety for efficiency, in manufacture and in life, so that this has become our world—row upon row of sameness.

When a composition is as unified as the *100 Campbell Soup Cans,* there is likely to be a side effect in the automatic achievement of compositional balance. In most works of art, however, balance is more subtle and somewhat more difficult to create.

BALANCE

How can a ballet dancer stand, poised on the toes of one foot, with arm and chest thrust out in one direction, extended leg thrust out in the other direction? The answer, of course, is balance. The dancer has instinctively calculated bodily weight so it is dispersed and balanced perfectly around the supporting leg. Even many animals and birds can do this—can arrange their bodies to balance on one leg.

If our bodies were not balanced in standing and walking and running, we would topple over. We have an innate desire for balance and stability. Maybe that is why we seek balance in a work of art, why we feel threatened by instability when balance is absent. *Actual weight,* physical weight in pounds, is important in some types of art, such as sculpture and architecture. All art, however, must deal with the concept of **visual weight.** Visual weight refers to the apparent "heaviness" or "lightness" of forms arranged in a composition. When two sides of a flat composition have the same visual weight, the composition is in balance. Let us see how this works by considering the three types of balance—symmetrical, asymmetrical, and radial.

SYMMETRICAL BALANCE

Symmetry in art means that forms in the two halves of a composition—on either side of an imaginary vertical dividing line—correspond to one another in size, shape, and placement. Sometimes the symmetry is so perfect that the two sides of a composition are mirror images of one another. More often the correspondence is very close but not exact—a situation some writers have called *relieved symmetry*. In either case we consider the composition symmetrically balanced. Since the two sides are identical or nearly so, they have the same visual weight, and therefore they are balanced. The Matisse collage (151) is symmetrically balanced; if you were to fold this image down the middle and match the two sides, they would fit almost exactly. Except for color variations, the forms on one side of the center axis correspond to those on the other side.

Symmetrical balance served the artist Frida Kahlo with exceptional force in *The Two Fridas* (152), for she used it to express the warring duality of her own nature. Kahlo was born in Mexico in 1907, the child of a Hungarian/Jewish father and an Indian/Spanish mother. These two influences—the European and the Mexican—coexisted uneasily in her psyche and her art as long as she lived. We might almost say that Frida Kahlo was Siamese twins who didn't get along. *The Two Fridas* shows this graphically. At left is the "European Frida," dressed in an elegant white gown; at right, the "Mexican Frida" wears a costume suited to that country's natives. Both have their hearts exposed in gory anatomical detail, with veins connecting them. The Mexican Frida holds a tiny portrait of the artist Diego Rivera, to whom Kahlo was married. The European Frida snips the vein connected to the portrait, allowing blood to fall on her skirt. This picture's symmetrical format gives a chilling interpretation to the double identity of its maker.

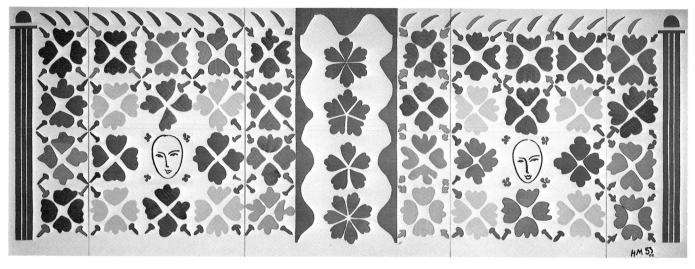

above: 151. Henri Matisse.
Large Composition with Masks.
1953. Paper collage on canvas,
11′7¼″ × 32′8⅛″.
© 1996 Board of Trustees,
National Gallery of Art,
Washington, D.C.
(Ailsa Mellon Bruce Fund).

right: 152. Frida Kahlo.
The Two Fridas. 1939.
Oil on canvas, 5′8½″ square.
Museo de Arte Moderno, Mexico City.

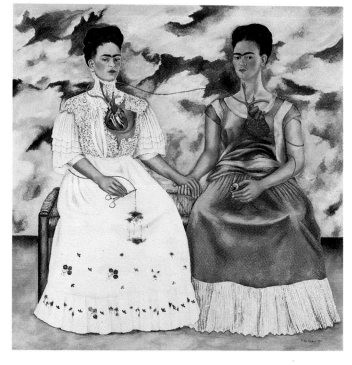

HENRI MATISSE

1869–1954

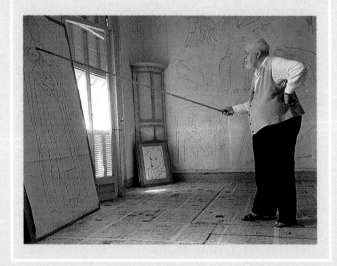

HOW IRONIC IT IS that Matisse, of all people, should have provoked a critic to call him a "wild beast," for, while his art may indeed have seemed a bit wild at first, the artist himself could scarcely have been less so. Cautious, reserved, cheerful, hardworking, dedicated to his family, frugal, painstaking—these are the qualities that describe Matisse. His longtime friend and rival Picasso captured more of the headlines, but the steadfast Matisse created art no less innovative and enduring.

Matisse's father intended him to be a lawyer, but a severe bout of appendicitis at the age of twenty-one changed his life—and changed the course of all modern art. Henri's mother bought him a box of paints as a diversion, and, for once, Matisse reacted strongly. Much later he said of this experience, "It was as if I had been called. Henceforth I did not lead my life. It led me."[1]

Matisse enrolled at the Ecole des Beaux-Arts in Paris and studied with the painter Gustave Moreau, a brilliant teacher who is said to have told his young pupil, "You were born to simplify painting." After a period of experimentation in various styles, Matisse exploded onto the Parisian art scene at the Salon d'Automne (autumn salon) in 1905, when he exhibited, along with several younger colleagues, works of such pure, intense, and arbitrary color that a critic labeled the artists *fauves*—wild beasts. In these early years Matisse did not fare much better with the general public. However, he had the good fortune to attract the attention of certain wealthy Americans who have achieved fame as inspired collectors, including the Stein family (Gertrude and her brothers) and the eccentric Cone sisters of Baltimore.

Considering the period in which he lived, encompassing two world wars, Matisse kept himself remarkably outside the fray. His art did not touch upon politics or social issues. Throughout his life, his favorite subjects remained the human body (usually a beautiful female body) and the pleasant domestic interior. The joys of home life, of family, of cherished objects dominate his expression. In 1898 Matisse married Amélie Parayre, with whom he maintained a contented relationship for many years. Mme. Matisse was lovely, a willing model, charming and lively, and devoted to her husband's career. Their three children all chose art-related lives, Pierre becoming a prominent art dealer in New York.

We think of Matisse as a painter, but he worked in many fields—sculpture, book illustration, architectural design (of a small, jewel-like chapel near his home), and finally in *découpage*. By the early 1930s Matisse had begun to use cut-up paper as a means of planning his canvases, and a decade later the cut paper had become an end in itself. When he was very old and could no longer stand at his easel, Matisse sat in his wheelchair or in his bed, cutting segments of prepainted paper and arranging them into compositions, some of mural size.

Perhaps it was at the end that he came nearest to his goal: "What I dream of is an art of balance, of purity and serenity, devoid of troubling or depressing subject matter, an art which might be for every mental worker, be he businessman or writer, like an appeasing influence, like a mental soother, something like a good armchair in which to rest from physical fatigue."[2]

Henri Matisse, photographed by Robert Capa.

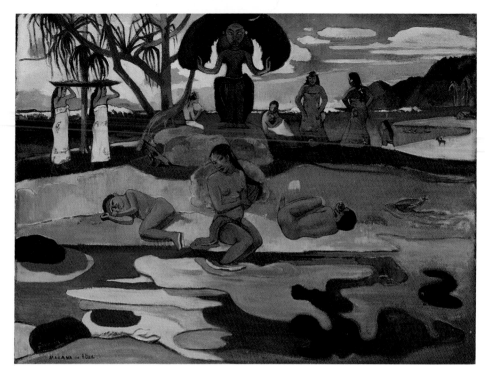

right: **153.** Paul Gauguin. *The Day of the God (Mahana no Atua).* 1894. Oil on canvas, 26⅞ × 36⅛". The Art Institute of Chicago (Helen Birch Bartlett Memorial Collection, 1926).

below: **154.** Sketch showing some of the different factors in visual balance.

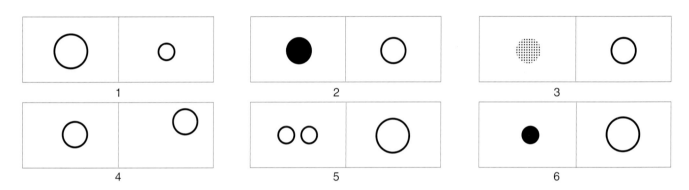

The symmetrical balance in Paul Gauguin's *Day of the God* (**153**) is a little more subtle, but it is nonetheless clear when we study the painting. Here the "god" is centered at the top of the composition, with the main figure directly below flanked by two curled-up reclining bodies. In the background paired figures stand at either side of the god. These major forms establish the symmetry and therefore the essential balance.

When you stand with your feet flat on the floor and your arms at your sides, you are in symmetrical balance. But if you thrust an arm out in one direction and a leg out in the other, your balance is asymmetrical (*not* symmetrical). Of the two, asymmetrical balance is often considered to be the more interesting and dynamic.

ASYMMETRICAL BALANCE

An asymmetrical composition has two sides that do not match. If it seems to be balanced, that is because the visual weights in the two halves are very similar. What looks "heavy" and what looks "light"? Unfortunately, there are no mathematical formulas to follow. The drawing (**154**) illustrates some very general precepts about asymmetrical or ***informal balance***:

1. A large form is visually heavier than a smaller form.
2. A dark-value form is visually heavier than a light form of the same size.
3. A textured form is visually heavier than a smooth form of the same size.

4. A form placed close to the central axis may be visually heavier than a similar form placed near the outer edge of the composition.
5. Two or more small forms can balance a larger one.
6. A smaller dark form can balance a larger light one.

These are only a few of the possibilities. Keeping them in mind, you may still wonder, but how does an artist actually go about balancing a composition? The answer is unsatisfactory but true: The composition is balanced when it looks balanced. An understanding of visual weights can help the artist achieve balance or see what is wrong when balance is off, but it is no exact science.

A fairly straightforward example of small forms balancing a large one (#5 in the drawing) can be found in Paul Klee's *Costumed Puppets* (155). The single large form to the right of the center axis is offset by two smaller forms at the left. Because Klee was a brilliant draftsman and designer, the balance does not seem static. The lower small figure curves in toward the center, and Klee's endlessly inventive pen line animates the entire composition.

For a more complex—and truly elegant—example of asymmetrical balance, we might consider William H. Johnson's painting, *Going to Church* (156). Here the artist has taken an apparently simple scene, a farm family driving in their oxcart from home to church, and transformed it into an abstraction of breathtakingly perfect balance. The main figures, husband and wife, are placed just to right of center. Their children, lower and to the right, are balanced at left by the ox *and* the section of fence. The striped areas, diagonal at left and vertical at right (thought to be inspired by African textiles), are essential to the balance, as are the two tree forms at middle left. In fact, the balance in this work is so masterful that every form counts. If anything were taken away, even the cross atop the church, the balance would be disturbed.

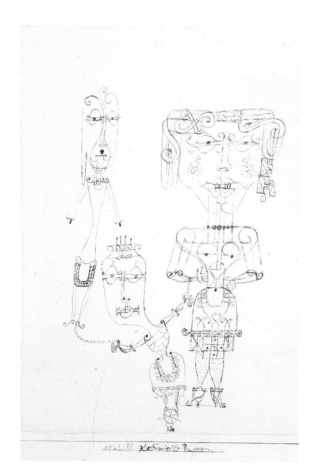

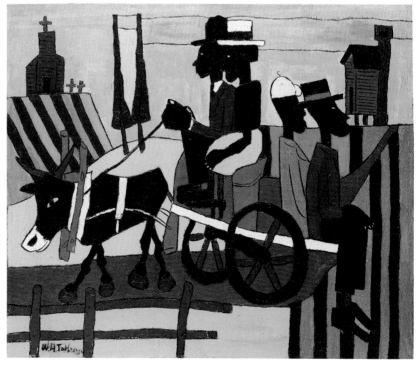

left: 155. Paul Klee.
Costumed Puppets. 1922.
Ink on paper, mounted
on board; 9½ × 6¾″.
Solomon R. Guggenheim Museum,
New York.

right: 156. William H. Johnson.
Going to Church. 1940–41.
Oil on burlap, 38⅛ × 45½″.
The National Museum of American Art,
Washington, D.C.

An equestrian sculpture from Africa also reveals an elegant asymmetrical balance **(157)**. The upraised horse's head and longer front legs balance the form of the rider, who is mounted very far to the rear. Obviously, the Dogon sculptor who made this figurine knew that horses do not have much longer front legs, that people do not have arms twice the length of their legs, and that riders do not sit just over the horse's tail. These features have been adjusted and stylized to create a sculptural balance.

At first glance we might think that Dürer's *Reclining Female Nude* **(158)** is out of balance. Nearly the whole figure, and most of its bulk, lies in the right half of the composition. But the subtitle, *Proportion Study*, gives us a clue to Dürer's intent. He was undoubtedly studying not only the proportions of the human body but also the placement of a figure within the picture space. The figure gazes to the left, and we, as observers, follow her gaze. Thus we find a center of interest in the left side of the drawing when nothing is there! In our minds we fill in the blank of whatever the woman is looking at. This is not imbalance but a daring balance created by conceptual rather than visual cues.

We said at the beginning of this chapter that an artist may choose deliberately to violate the principles of design. Occasionally, asymmetrical balance may be carried to such an extreme that the composition appears unbalanced. We find this often in the work of Chinese and Japanese painters. Nonomura Sotatsu's *Zen Priest Choka* **(159)** shows the priest perched in a tree that barely makes it into the composition. In Asian art as much importance may be placed on what is *not* there as on what is there. The empty space to the right and below may be visually empty, but it is animated by the daring unbalanced design. In looking at this work we feel a tension, a lack of resolution or closure. Imbalance might be compared to someone's starting a story "Once upon a time . . . ," but never getting to " . . . and they lived happily ever after." We are left feeling keyed up, waiting for something to happen.

Another painting **(160)**, this one by a Western artist, is balanced (asymmetrically and perfectly) from left to right, but it seems unbalanced vertically. Nearly all the forms appear in the top half of the composition. This is the reverse of what we expect. We are used to gravity, to heavy things being down. In most works of art of all kinds you will find the greatest weight—visual or

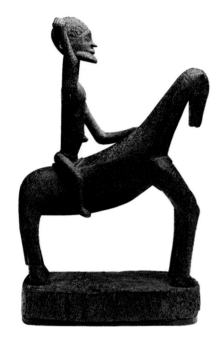

above: 157. *Horse and Rider.* African, Dogon, from Mali. 16th–20th century. Wood, height 27⅛". The Metropolitan Museum of Art, New York (The Michael C. Rockefeller Memorial Collection, bequest, of Nelson A. Rockefeller, 1979).

right: 158. Albrecht Dürer. *Reclining Female Nude (Proportion Study).* 1501. Pen and brush on green paper, 6¾ × 8⅝". Albertina, Vienna.

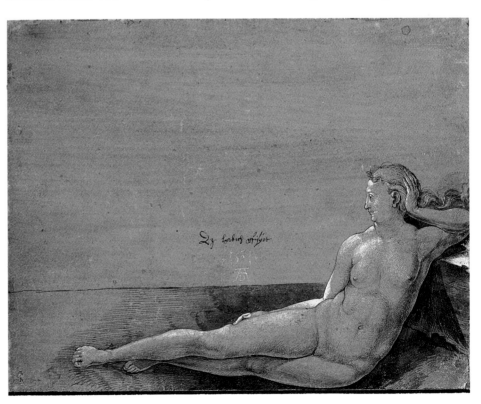

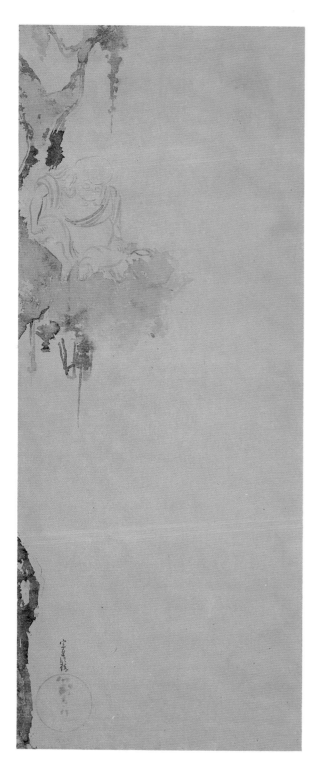

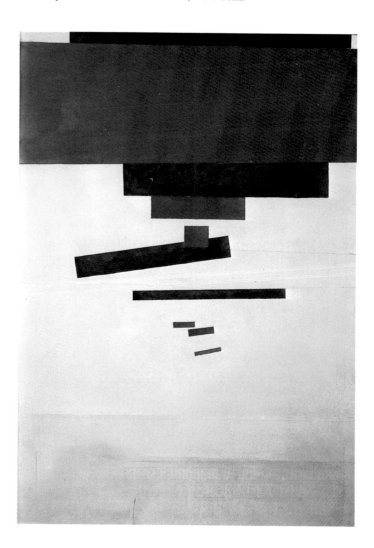

actual—toward the bottom, so that the composition is firmly rooted in the ground. Ilya Chashnik's watercolor catches us, quite literally, off balance. We get a sense of the rectangular shapes falling continuously. The forms never actually fall, of course, but against all reason we feel that they are doing so. By using imbalance artists are able to make us see movement where none exists.

RADIAL BALANCE

There is a third possibility for balance, which is more common in architecture and the crafts than in the pictorial arts. Radial balance means that elements in the composition radiate outward from a central point. A frequent expression

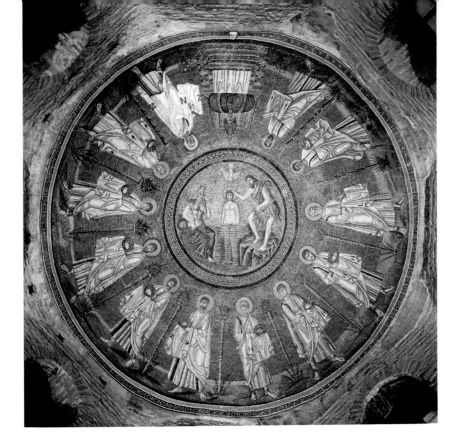

161. *Baptism of Christ and Procession of Twelve Apostles,* dome mosaic. c. 520. Arian Baptistry, Ravenna.

of this is the architectural dome **(161)**. The dome of the Arian Baptistry in Ravenna, Italy, has the scene of Christ's baptism in the center with the twelve apostles arranged in a radial pattern around the outside. Radial balance works especially well with a circular format, and it nearly always focuses attention on the central point.

EMPHASIS AND FOCAL POINT

Emphasis means that the viewer's attention will be centered more on certain parts of a composition than on others. A focal point is a specific spot to which one's attention is directed. Our everyday perception is structured around focal points. Walking down a crowded street, we naturally pick out from the throng the person who is dressed bizarrely, the one person who is exceptionally tall, the person who is waving to attract attention. Not all works of art have a focal point—Warhol's *Soup Cans* **(150)** does not—but the vast majority do have areas of greater emphasis and one or more focal points. Without them, the composition might seem bland and repetitive.

There are numerous methods by which an artist can create a focal point or center of emphasis in a work of art. Grant Wood used several of them in his painting *Parson Weems' Fable* **(162)**. The fable in question is the story of a young George Washington chopping down the cherry tree, then admitting to the evil deed because he "could not tell a lie." Although the boy George is one of the smaller elements in the picture, we have no doubt that he is the center of interest. For one thing, Wood has employed strong directional lines. George's father gestures directly at the boy, and Parson Weems' pointing finger also carries our attention to him. Moreover, the curve of the drapery at the right and the opposing curve of the half-chopped tree frame little George between them. In case we still miss the point, the artist has placed George almost precisely in the middle of the composition and given him a white shirt—the lightest value in the painting. (Although this has little to do with emphasis, we might notice for fun that Wood has painted George's head like that of a full-grown man, the Father of his Country, and put that venerable head atop the body of a boy caught red-handed.)

Another device for creating emphasis is the manipulation of light. We see this in Henry Ossawa Tanner's sensitive portrait of his mother (163). The artist uses a strong light—cutting through prevailing shadow—to focus attention on the woman's face, with its pensive, perhaps weary expression. This light seems to be coming from a source above and outside the picture. It falls also on the drape of a shawl behind the chair, possibly an emblem of motherhood. Because of the subject matter and the pose, we cannot help but be reminded of Whistler's painting of *his* mother (523), but they are very different pictures. Whistler, as we shall see in Chapter 19 (p. 464), was primarily interested in the arrangement of compositional elements. His lighting is general, not focused. Tanner, on the other hand, seems intent on showing the character of his model, and so he shines his clearest light on her face.

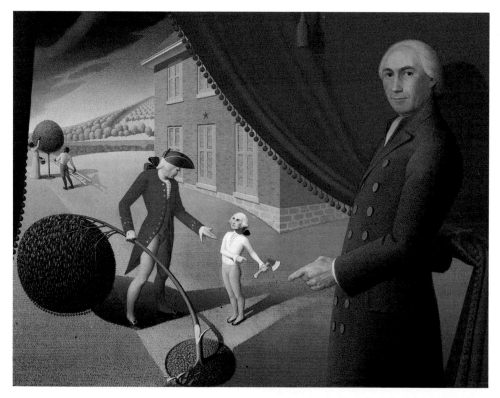

left: 162. Grant Wood.
Parson Weems' Fable. 1939.
Oil on canvas, 3'2⅜" × 4'2⅛".
Amon Carter Museum, Fort Worth.
© 1998 Estate of Grant Wood/
Licensed by VAGA, New York.

below: 163.
Henry Ossawa Tanner.
Portrait of the Artist's Mother.
1897. Oil on canvas, 29¼ × 39¼".
Philadelphia Museum of Art
(partial gift of Dr. Rae Alexander-Minter
and purchased with the W. P. Wilstach
Fund, the George W. Elkins Fund,
and funds contributed by the Dietrich
Foundation and a private donor).

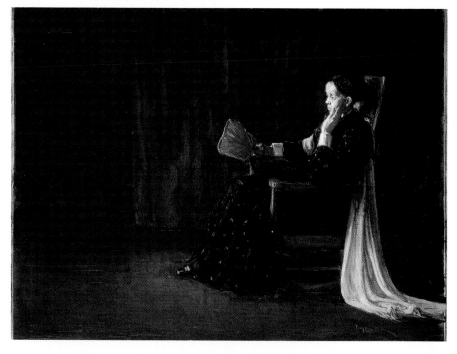

Both directional lines and light create the focal point in Francisco de Goya's *Executions of the Third of May, 1808* **(164)**. The event Goya depicted was the invasion of Spain by Napoleon's armies and their savage execution of Spanish resisters. Our interest is centered on one heroic but doomed Spaniard, his arms raised in a pose of crucifixion. This tragic figure is bathed in light, while most of the rest of the painting remains in shadow. Moreover, the faceless figures of the soldiers point their rifles at him, and even the stance of their bodies focuses our attention on the victim. Goya's sympathies clearly lay with the killed, not the killers. He therefore emphasized the poignant sacrifice of one man, to deemphasize the mechanical slaughter by the others.

Emphasis by placement is evident in Grandma Moses' painting, called *Hoosick Falls in Winter* **(165)**. In this tranquil small-town landscape Grandma Moses has chosen to emphasize the locomotive of the train steaming across

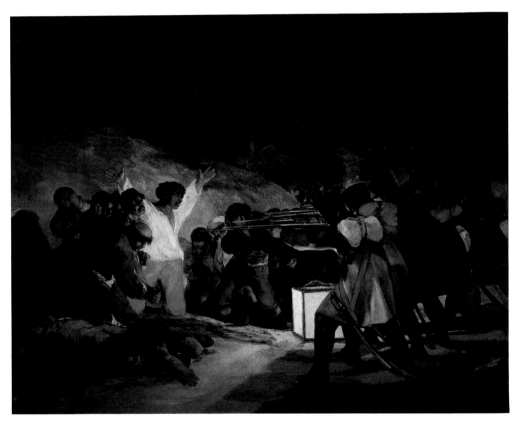

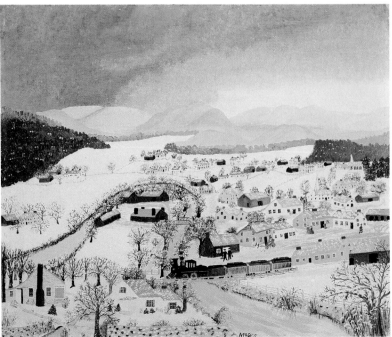

above: 164. Francisco de Goya.
Executions of the Third of May, 1808.
1814–15. Oil on canvas, 8′9″ × 13′4″.
Museo del Prado, Madrid.

left: 165. Anna Mary Robertson
("Grandma") Moses.
Hoosick Falls in Winter. 1944.
Oil on Masonite, 19¾ × 23¾″.
© The Phillips Collection, Washington, D.C.

FRANCISCO DE GOYA

1746–1828

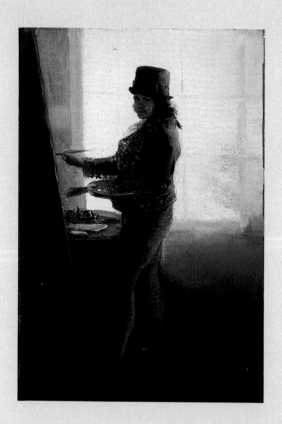

Goya's earliest commissions were for church murals and tapestry cartoons. In 1783 he was launched in one of the two artistic arenas for which he is best known—portraitist to the nobility. Within a few years he was active at the royal court, and in 1799 he was appointed court painter to Charles IV, King of Spain. Some of Goya's portraits, including two of the Duchess of Alba, are exquisitely lovely; others have a darker side to them. According to some critics, Goya's pictures of the royal family, while appearing to flatter, were actually subtle revelations of the subjects' stupidity and corruption.

Goya's other major field of expression was prints, of which he was an unexcelled master. Two major series, each having about eighty images, constitute the bulk of his work: *Los Caprichos*, in which the many follies of human nature are satirized; and *The Disasters of War*, an often brutally explicit catalogue of the cruelties prevalent in wartime.

Goya achieved both fame and financial success relatively early. While his career prospered, however, his personal life was repeatedly marked by tragedy. His marriage to Josefa Bayeu seems to have been more of a convenience than a passion. She bore him many children—perhaps as many as twenty—but only one survived to maturity. In 1792 the artist was struck by a severe illness that left him almost totally deaf. Another near-fatal illness in 1819 increased his isolation and pessimism; Goya bought a home outside Madrid, known as La Quinta del Sordo ("The House of the Deaf Man"), to which he retired and painted a series of works known as the "Black Paintings," for their dark tonality and aura of despair. After all, the artist's relationship with the Duchess of Alba, whatever it might have been (some maintain that they were lovers), seems to have been one of few bright periods in his life.

Goya's education was sketchy, and as an adult he read and wrote with some difficulty. An announcement for *Los Caprichos* probably was written with the help of a friend, but it captures Goya's attitude toward his art: "Painting, like poetry, selects in the universe whatever she deems most appropriate to her ends. She assembles in a single fantastic personage circumstances and features which nature distributes among many individuals. From this combination, ingeniously composed, results that happy imitation by virtue of which the artist earns the title of inventor and not of servile copyist."[3]

WRITERS ON GOYA have long been fascinated by the close friendship between him and the Duchess of Alba, the powerful aristocrat whom many considered the most beautiful woman of her time in Spain. It is a measure of this artist's complexity and uniqueness that the haughty duchess should form a special bond with one who emerged from quite humble origins, whose temperament was often morose and reclusive, and whose imagery could be shockingly gruesome.

Francisco José de Goya y Lucientes was born in a village in the bleak northeast section of Spain. While a young man Goya may have supported himself partially as a bullfighter, but this is one of the many unverifiable stories about his intriguing life. By the age of twenty he was in Madrid.

Francisco de Goya. *Goya in His Studio.* 1790–95.
Oil on canvas, 16½ × 11".
Museo de Bellas Artes de San Fernando, Madrid.

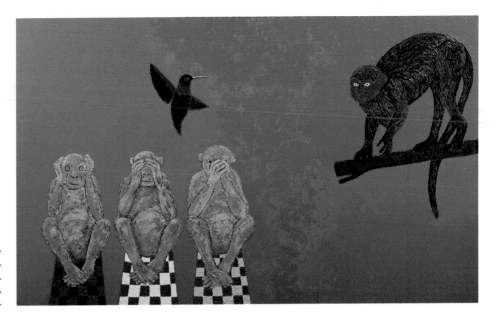

166. Joan Brown.
Out on a Limb. 1986.
Acrylic on canvas, 6 × 10′.
Courtesy Frumkin/Adams Gallery,
New York.

the picture. To accomplish this, she has placed the locomotive just on the bridge crossing the river, with the pale blue of the water acting as a contrasting background. The horseshoe curve of the river also helps to direct our attention to the train.

A variation on emphasis by placement is emphasis by isolation. In Joan Brown's *Out on a Limb* **(166)** we see the traditional Three Wise Monkeys, who "hear no evil, see no evil, speak no evil," clustered together in a fearfully submissive group. We know from their poses and their timid conformity to the group that they are afraid, perhaps of life itself. All alone and daring is the one active monkey, literally out on a limb, precariously supported and ready to take risks. By isolating this one monkey, the artist emphasizes the freedom and danger of being up in the air, on one's own.

Emphasis by contrast works much the same way. Contrast can mean any obvious distinction—dark against light, big against small, textured against smooth, color against gray. Marc Chagall's painting *Woman, Flowers, and Bird* **(167)** is done almost entirely in a neutral bluish gray, with touches of yellow and pale green leaves at the center. There are only two spots of vivid color, the two bright pink flowers, and they attract our attention immediately. This painting is interesting, however, in that the colorful flowers are *not* the main focal point, although they are certainly areas of emphasis. In effect, they are "assistant" focal points. They claim our interest and direct it toward the area they frame—the woman's face, which is the real focal point.

Finally, we should mention emphasis by content. Regardless of other focal devices employed by an artist, certain visual images, when included in a composition, will draw the viewer's attention. Blood and gore attract attention; anything shocking or surprising will act as a focal point. In a figural work the face is nearly always the major focal point, because we are used to looking at people's faces rather than their elbows or hips. And in general, the human figure will tend to draw the viewer's eye.

PROPORTION AND SCALE

Proportion and scale both have to do with size. Sometimes the two words are used interchangeably, but there is a difference. *Scale* means size in relation to some constant or "normal" size. Normal scale is the size we expect something

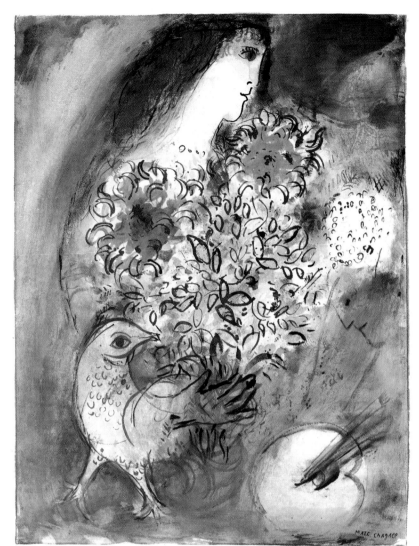

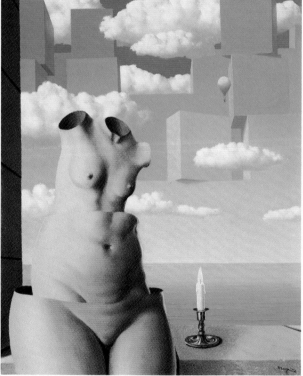

above: 167. Marc Chagall.
Woman, Flowers, and Bird. 1952–53.
Gouache, $25\frac{3}{4} \times 19\frac{7}{8}''$.
Stedelijk Museum, Amsterdam.

left: 168. René Magritte.
La Folie des grandeurs II. 1962.
Oil on canvas, $39\frac{1}{8} \times 32\frac{1}{8}''$.
Hirshhorn Museum and Sculpture Garden,
Smithsonian Institution, Washington, D.C.
(gift of Joseph H. Hirshhorn, 1966).

to be. For example, a model airplane is small-scale in relation to a real air-plane, or to the usual size for an airplane. The 10-pound tomato that wins a prize at the county fair is large-scale.

Proportion, on the other hand, refers to size relationships between parts of a whole, or between two or more items perceived as a unit. Proportion can also mean the size relationship between an object and its surroundings. A very large chair in a very small room seems "out of proportion." René Magritte played with the idea of proportion in *La Folie des grandeurs* **(168)**. The three sections of the nude torso are in different proportions, so they do not fit to-gether at all. Magritte, of course, used this jarring disproportion on purpose to create a startling image.

There are many reasons an artist may choose to violate normal proportions in a work of art. In Morris Hirshfield's *Boy with Dog* **(169)**, for instance, the disproportion was undoubtedly made to serve decorative purposes. Hirshfield, known as a folk or "naive" painter, relished decorative pattern. Here the boy's dog, even if it is a toy poodle (though it looks a bit like a miniature horse), is much too small in relation to the boy. And the boy's arms, hands, and feet are far too small for his body. Yet there is a pleasing sense of flow in the figures of the boy and dog—a flow that echoes the rhythm of the wavelike background. The boy's tiny arm curves downward in an arc, is met by the opposing arc of the leash, and then again by the arc of the dog's body. From head to shoulder to tail we can draw a lovely, undulating S-curve—all of which is mirrored in the background. Similar curving lines move from the boy's hair down through the shirt and coat tails to the legs, and terminate gracefully in the boy's minute feet. If the proportions had been accurate, this decorative effect would have been lost.

The two preceding illustrations both show proportions that are "wrong"—that is, proportions that seem inappropriate, based on our experience of the natural world. In a sense, it is easier to understand the usual applications of proportion by studying the *un*usual, the exceptions. But most artists, most of the time, seek to find the "right" proportions for their work, and the great majority of illustrations in this book have proportions that seem harmonious, seem to mesh with our impressions of the natural world.

Since the time of the ancient Greeks, people have been seeking the "ideal" proportions in art. Much classical Greek figure sculpture was based on a *canon*, or set of rules, of ideal proportions in which the figure's head was to be one-eighth of the total height, the width of the chest one-quarter of the total height, and so on **(170)**. (These proportions would remain the same regardless of the figure's scale.) Similarly, in Greek architecture, vasemaking, and paint-

left: 169. Morris Hirshfield. *Boy with Dog.* 1945. Oil on canvas, 32 × 23". © 1998 Estate of Morris Hirshfield/ Licensed by VAGA, New York.

right: 170. *Poseidon* or *Zeus.* c. 460–450 B.C.E. Bronze, height 6'10". National Museum, Athens.

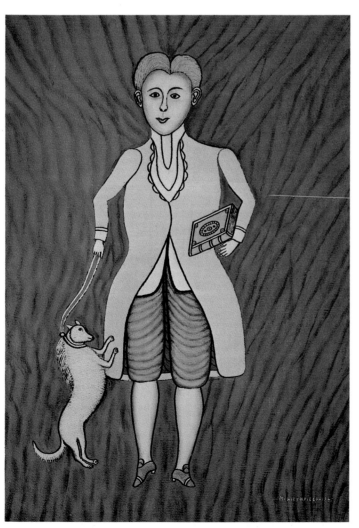

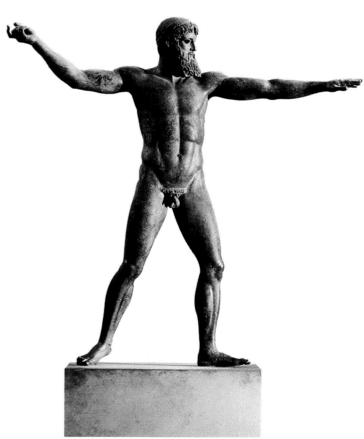

ing, proportions derived from what is known as the ***golden section,*** or ***golden mean.*** Algebraically, the golden mean **(171)** says that $a:b = b:(a + b)$. If a is the width of a temple and b is its length, then the ratio of width to length should be the same as the ratio of length to width-plus-length. For those not mathematically inclined, we can translate this equation into an example. Suppose you want to build a house, and you want it to be 40 feet wide. How long should the house be to fit the "ideal" proportions of the golden section? The answer is about 65 feet. Your house would end up being a rectangle rather like the one shown in the drawing **(171)**.

For mathematicians the golden section, sometimes known as *phi*, has far-reaching implications. The illustration **(171)** shows that every time you cut off a square from one end of a golden rectangle, you are left with another golden rectangle, and so on indefinitely. For artists, as the Greeks knew 2,500 years ago, the golden section "feels right," and to the viewer it "looks right." Many objects in our daily life approximate the golden section in their proportions. The standard 3 × 5 index card is an almost perfect golden rectangle, and the standard playing card comes close. If you were to measure the illustrations in this book, you would find that a large number of them approach the golden mean in their dimensions. Piet Mondrian, that most precise and mathematical of artists, worked within a perfect golden rectangle for his *Composition with Red, Yellow, and Blue* **(101)**. Whatever the reason, this proportion is one we find inherently pleasing and satisfying.

For an entertaining exercise in scale and proportion, we might look at the next illustration, a photograph by Annie Leibovitz **(172)**. Noted for her striking—often startling—portraits of well-known personalities, Leibovitz here brings together the jockey Willie Shoemaker and the basketball star Wilt Chamberlain in a double image that is bound to cause a doubletake. The photograph is real, not distorted or composite. What makes it remarkable is the contrast of proportion and scale. Both men are "correctly" proportioned as individual people; each has a head and arms and legs suited to the body. But Shoemaker is a very small-scale human, and Chamberlain a very large-scale one. Side by side, and dressed alike, they are wildly out of proportion, a jarring unit. It is as though nature was playing a game of scale with these two men, so Leibovitz caught the fun and played a proportion game of her own.

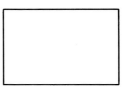

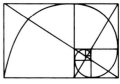

above: 171. Sketches of proportions in the golden section.

left: 172. Annie Leibovitz. *Wilt Chamberlain and Willie Shoemaker.* Photograph.

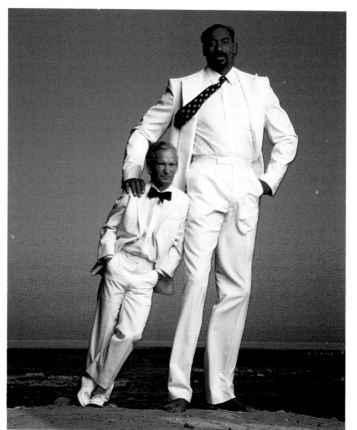

Like proportion, scale is most noticeable when it is "wrong," when it is not what we expect. One artist who is well known for experimenting with distortions of scale is the sculptor Claes Oldenburg, and his approach to scale can only be described as grand. Oldenburg's *Knife Ship* **(173)** is a giant representation in steel of an ordinary pocketknife, with double blade and corkscrew, motorized so that the blades move up and down and the corkscrew turns. The huge size of the sculpture—it is 40 feet long—requires exhibition outdoors or in a large enclosed space, such as the interior of the Guggenheim Museum shown here. By taking an ordinary object, blowing it up to massive scale, and setting it in a public place, Oldenburg makes the form heroic. In effect the artist is saying, "Look at this form, look at it in the new way I have shown it to you." Now, many people have a pocketknife, perhaps a Swiss army officer's knife, and normally this object would not command our attention. But a pocketknife a hundred times the usual size, painted bright red, and equipped with "oars" to make a "ship"—*that* catches our attention. Manipulation of scale—or, for that matter, of any design principle—can make us look at form with fresh perspective.

Proportion and scale must be considered together because they nearly always operate simultaneously. A painting that is, say, 10 feet by 15 feet is certainly large-scale; it is larger than most of the paintings we have seen. We must also take into account, however, where the painting is to be hung. If it is hung in a small house, it will be out of proportion to its surroundings. But if it is hung in a huge auditorium, the proportions may be just right.

Scale and proportion can work side by side *within* a work of art. The figures in Nicholas Africano's *Whiskey per tutti!* **(174)** and the figures in Pieter Bruegel's *Wedding Dance* **(175)** are all small-scale. If you were standing in front of the actual paintings, the figures would be just a few inches tall. The proportions in the two paintings, however, are quite different. Africano's little people are set in a huge, almost empty canvas, so they seem tiny and lost. They are out of proportion to the field they inhabit. Bruegel's painting has many figures, arranged to fill the composition, so its proportions seem perfectly normal. The reason for this discrepancy lies in the different intents of the two artists. Bruegel was drawing a naturalistic festive scene. Africano is aiming at a grand theatrical image, a vision of tiny people lost on an enormous opera stage. Manipulation of scale and proportion serves both these goals.

173. Claes Oldenburg, Coosje van Bruggen, and Frank O. Gehry. *The Knife Ship from "Il Corso del Coltello."* 1985. Steel, 26 × 40′. Installed at the Solomon R. Guggenheim Museum, New York.

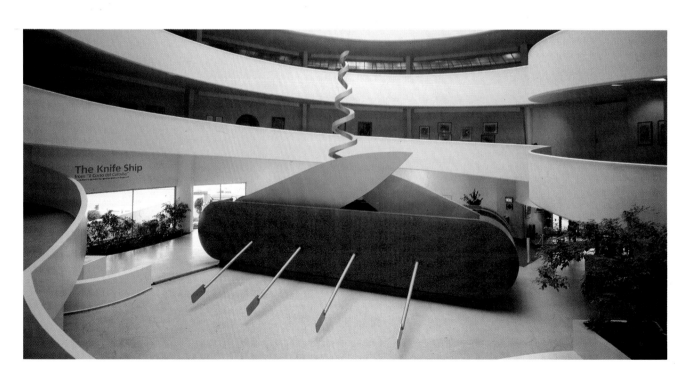

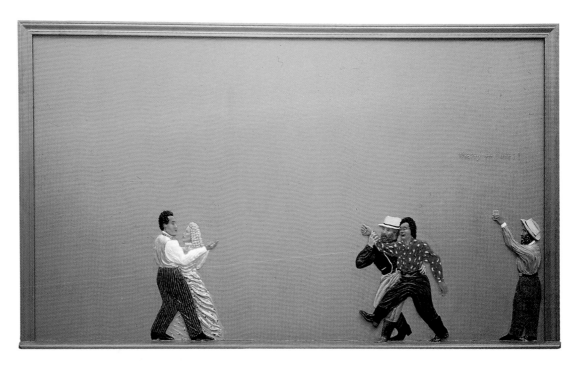

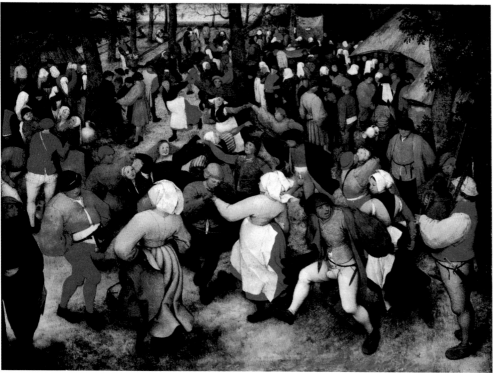

RHYTHM

People who are totally deaf can learn to dance. No one is quite sure how they
keep time when they cannot hear the sounds, but they do. Apparently, they
have some perception of rhythm that is independent of aural cues. All of us are
accustomed to rhythm in music, in dance, in poetry (where it is called meter),
in other aspects of life. Intuitively, we seek rhythm in the visual arts.

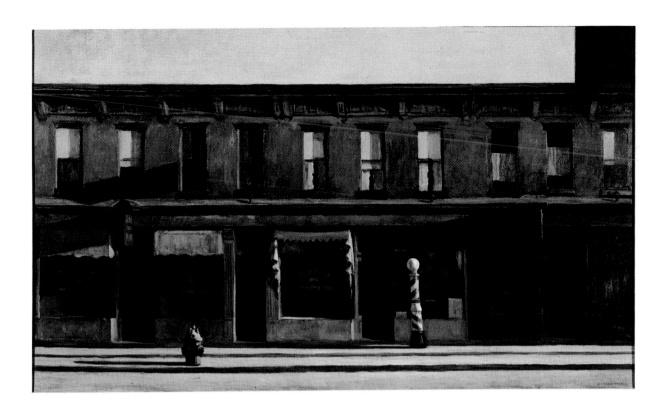

176. Edward Hopper. *Early Sunday Morning.* 1930. Oil on canvas, 2'11" × 5'. Whitney Museum of American Art, New York (purchase, with funds from Gertrude Vanderbilt Whitney).

Visual rhythm depends on the repetition of accented elements, usually shapes. In Edward Hopper's *Early Sunday Morning* **(176)** we find several different rhythms moving horizontally across the canvas **[Overlay 7]**. At top there is the rhythm of the eaves under the roof, and below that the strong rhythmic pulse of the second-story windows alternating with plain wall. At bottom the rhythm of the repeated storefronts counters the two patterns above. Although this is a very repetitive rhythm, we do not find it boring, because there is enough variation of color and light to create interest. The two focal points of fire hydrant and barber pole punctuate the rhythm.

The rhythm in Piet Mondrian's *Composition in Blue B* **(177)** is sharp and staccato. Rectangles of color, many of them overlapping, intersperse with smaller black rectangles that act as weaker beats in the pulse. We can easily imagine this painting to be a visual interpretation of jazz or ragtime music, both of which were in vogue when Mondrian did this painting, and both of which have definite but surprising rhythms. If Hopper's work **(176)** shows the placid rhythms of a small-town street on Sunday morning, Mondrian's conveys the energy and vigor of the city.

Do artists deliberately "put" rhythm into their work, or is that rhythm a natural component of the creative process? Probably some of both, but in the case of our next illustration we might lean toward the latter. Wang Yani, a remarkable artistic prodigy from China, has attracted worldwide fame for the sophisticated brilliance and spontaneity of her painting. Having begun to paint at two and a half, she had her first one-artist show at four. *One Hundred Monkeys* **(178)**, a long handscroll of which we show just a small detail, was painted when Yani was nine and has a favorite theme. Even in this little section the joyful rhythm is immediately evident. Yani's monkeys roll and tumble over themselves and one another. The line of the monkeys' bodies swoops up and down rhythmically. We can almost hear happy circus music in the background. As a teenager Yani traveled widely and often gave public demonstrations of her painting. (If she did not, few would believe such astonishing skill had come from a child.) She works rapidly, her brush moving across the page without indecision. Merely from seeing the results we sense the rhythmic flow of her arm and brush, her internal rhythms translated onto paper.

Just as artists may "put" rhythm into their art either deliberately or intuitively, so also viewers may "find" the rhythm actively or intuitively. Our next two illustrations show an artist's work with a compelling rhythm and the response of a viewer who not only found that rhythm but brought it to life.

From the 1960s into the 1980s the painter Isabel Bishop made a large number of paintings and drawings known collectively as "The Walking Pictures." (One drawing from the series is in Chapter 6, **193**.) Bishop's scenes, set in lower Manhattan, capture people going about their individual business, passing to and fro through the streets, unconnected to each other yet making patterns as they walk, as their paths intersect. Walking is, of course, an inherently rhythmic process—left foot, right foot, left foot, and so on. Bishop, who considered walking "absolutely beautiful," said her goal was to have viewers "believe that this isn't just described movement but movement taking place."[4]

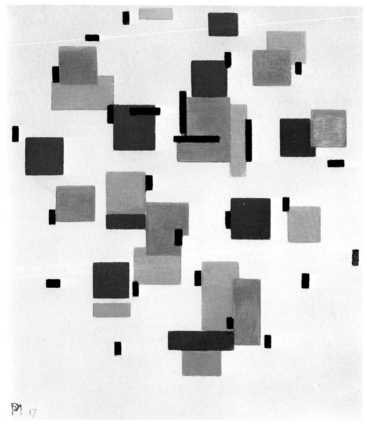

left: 177. Piet Mondrian. *Composition in Blue B.* 1917. Oil on canvas, 24 × 19″. Collection State Museum Kröller–Müller, Otterlo, The Netherlands.

below: 178. Wang Yani. *One Hundred Monkeys*, detail. 1984–85. Handscroll, ink and color on paper; height 1′⅝″, overall length of scroll 34′9⅜″. Collection the artist.

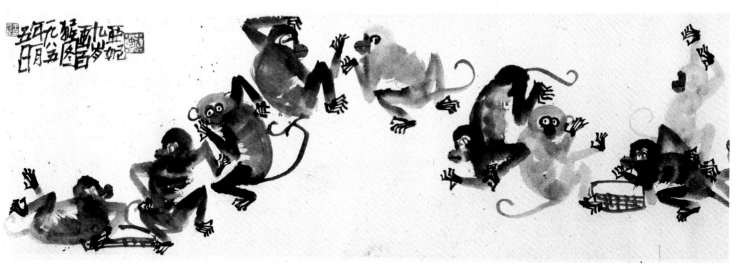

Five Women Walking **(179)** is a splendid realization of that goal, for it is all about movement. Each of the four women shown in profile is portrayed in full stride. As we look at the picture, our minds automatically continue the motion, pulling the back leg forward into the next step. The figure at center heightens this sense of fluid movement. Will she collide with the two women in front of her? No, because by the time she reaches them, they will have crossed and left an open path.

Bishop's painted figures will never move, but, as she intended, our sense of the rhythm in walking makes us believe that movement is taking place. And twenty-five years after Bishop painted *Five Women Walking*, the choreographer Annabelle Gamson actually did make movement take place. Inspired by the Walking Pictures, Gamson created "The Women of Union Square" **(180)**, a dance set to jazz music by Miles Davis. So the rhythm comes full circle: from the real dancelike movement of walkers in Union Square, to the implied movement in Bishop's painting, to the real movement of Gamson's dance.

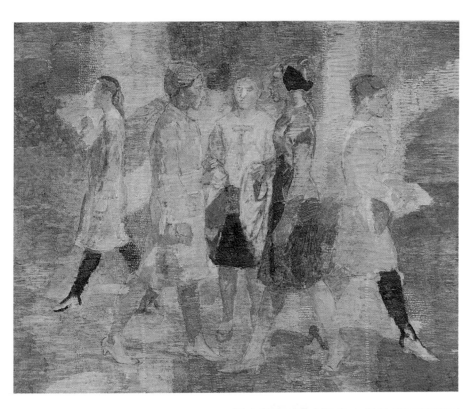

above: 179. Isabel Bishop. *Five Women Walking #2.* 1967. Oil and tempera on gesso panel, 31½ × 39½". Edwin A. Ulrich Museum of Art, The Wichita State University, Wichita, Kan. (gift of Mr. Hebert S. Alder/Endowment Association Art Collection).

right: 180. Lisa Levart. *Emilie Plauché and Pamela Jones Dance "The Women of Union Square."* 1993. Photograph. St. Mark's Church, New York, February 6, 1993. Choreography by Annabelle Gamson, inspired by the Walking Pictures of Isabel Bishop.

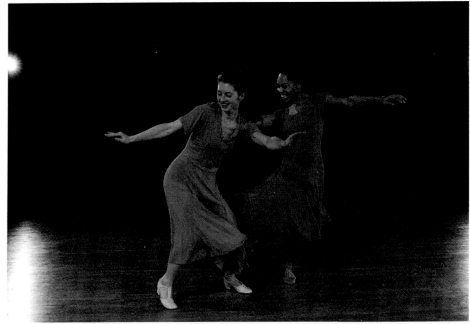

THE GUERRILLA GIRLS

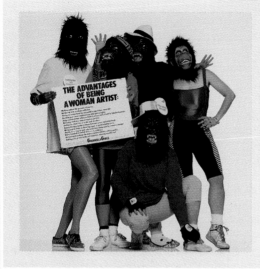

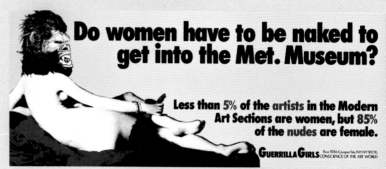

WHO ARE THEY? That's a secret. How many of them are there? That's a secret too. How do you find them? You don't. You leave a message and, if they wish, they'll find you. If you are fostering sexism or racism in the art world, they'll find you whether you like it or not. They strike without warning, often by night, in the manner of guerrilla fighters, wearing the fierce, menacing head masks of gorillas. Each of them is a working artist, and together they have become a force to be reckoned with. They are the Guerrilla Girls.

The Guerrilla Girls came into being in 1985, shortly after the opening of a huge exhibition at New York's Museum of Modern Art. The show, entitled "International Survey of Contemporary Painting and Sculpture," included works by 169 artists, fewer than 10 percent of whom were women. One April morning residents of lower Manhattan, where many artists live and work, awakened to find copies of a distinctive poster plastered on outdoor walls. In bold type the poster inquired, "WHAT DO THESE ARTISTS HAVE IN COMMON?" Underneath were the names of 42 prominent artists—all male. The poster text continued, "They all allow their work to be shown in galleries that show no more than 10 percent women or none at all."

More posters followed. One asked, "DO WOMEN HAVE TO BE NAKED TO GET INTO THE MET. MUSEUM?" Another catalogued "THE ADVANTAGES OF BEING A WOMAN ARTIST," a sweetly sarcastic list that included such benefits as "Working without the pressure of success" and "Seeing your ideas live on in the work of others." Prime targets for the Guerrilla Girls' scorn were art critics, museums, and galleries that concentrate attention on white male artists, all but ignoring women and minority artists. The posters achieved almost instant chic, partly because of their excellent graphic design, partly because of the Guerrilla Girls' aura of mystery.

From posters, the Guerrilla Girls progressed to on-site appearances. Let a museum present a male-dominated exhibition, and the Guerrilla Girls were sure to turn up—wearing their gorilla masks (often with short skirts and lacy stockings), waving bananas, making street theater for an appreciative audience. Given such a cleverly designed campaign, media attention was inevitable. Scores of articles about the Guerrilla Girls have been published in newspapers and magazines. They have been interviewed on television and often speak at colleges.

For ease of communication, each of the Guerrilla Girls has taken the name of a noted woman artist who is dead. (Material for this essay was supplied to the author by "Alice Neel.") It is believed that several members of the group are quite well-known artists, but this cannot be proved, because the women never appear in public as Guerrilla Girls without their masks.

The gorilla masks serve a double purpose. Of course, they protect the wearers' identities, but they also put everybody else at a disadvantage. One knows these are women, so it is more than a little disconcerting to be confronted with a ferocious, toothy ape face. This effect is no doubt intended. Individually, women artists may lack clout, but the Guerrilla Girls, as a group, know a thing or two about power.

There is no way to determine how much influence the Guerrilla Girls have had in improving prospects for women and minority artists. Still, as every reformer knows, the first step toward making a change is getting attention, and that has been taken care of. The Guerrilla Girls have a great many secrets. Just possibly, one of them may be the secret of success.

Some Guerrilla Girls **(left)** and one of their posters **(right)**.

ELEMENTS AND PRINCIPLES: A SUMMARY

In this chapter and the preceding one we have focused one by one on the elements of art and principles of design, isolating each for individual scrutiny. Every member of the ensemble, so to speak, was brought before the curtain and allowed to take a separate bow. Now, to finish this section, we should put the actors back together, reunite the company into a performing unit. By analyzing one work of art in some detail, we can begin to see how the elements and principles interact. It should be clear that we cannot easily talk about one element or principle without involving several of the others. The painting we will analyze is Pablo Picasso's *Girl Before a Mirror* **(181)**.

In *Girl Before a Mirror* a young woman—probably inspired by Picasso's lover at the time, Marie-Thérèse Walter—contemplates her nude image in a mirror (at right) just at the time when she is reaching maturity and realizing her sexual and childbearing capabilities. The reproductive organs are therefore prominent in the image. This is a very brief summary of the painting's content. Now let us consider its visual design **[Overlay 8]**.

Unity is achieved in several ways, including the dominance of curved lines. The straight lines, horizontals and diagonals, serve as a kind of background "filler" to the large swooping curves, and they also provide linear variety. Unity of shape is particularly important to this work. The circle motif—be it face, breast, womb, or buttock—recurs in a rhythmic pattern.

181. Pablo Picasso. *Girl Before a Mirror.* Boisgeloup, March 1932. Oil on canvas, 5′4″ × 4′3¼″. The Museum of Modern Art, New York (gift of Mrs. Simon Guggenheim).

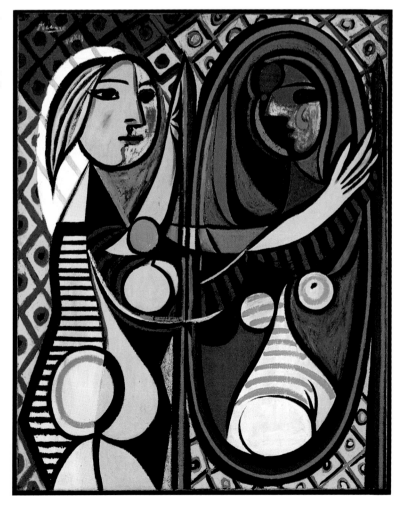

Colors are brilliantly varied, but they fall generally in the same range of values and intensities, thus contributing unity. A skeleton of dark, almost black values in shape and line provides the structure on which the picture is "hung," much as the human body is hung on its bony skeleton.

The balance of *Girl Before a Mirror* is predominantly symmetrical. Picasso has even provided a vertical line in the center of the composition to divide the two halves. Subtle differences between the girl's body and her mirror reflection enliven and relieve the symmetry. There is almost a pendulum effect as our eyes shift back and forth rhythmically between one side and the other—a pendulum effect enhanced by the curve of the arm.

There are several areas of emphasis in *Girl Before a Mirror,* most of which can be found in the shapes painted with the lightest values. Also, the two faces—the light face of the girl and the darker and more menacing one of the reflection—are emphasized by their colors, their placement, and simply by the fact that they *are* faces. Secondary areas of emphasis are the reproductive organs below, shown in a kind of X-ray vision, which gain emphasis by their brightness and by the repetition of the round form. Even with these areas of emphasis, however, it should be borne in mind that the background of this painting is almost as important as the figures. There is no "dead" space, no area of rest for the eyes; every inch of the canvas is important to the artist's expression.

In scale the *Girl Before a Mirror* is rather large, but not unusually so. The proportions are more interesting. Picasso has filled almost the entire space of the composition with the two figures; they jam the picture space from top to bottom and left to right. Also interesting are the proportions of shapes to one another. Small circles and ovals play off against larger and larger circles, to the oval of the mirror image.

Finally, we have alluded before to the rhythms in this work—the rhythm of echoing curved lines, of repeated circular forms, of the pendulum swing from side to side. Besides the pendulum swing, there is a figure-eight rhythm that swoops us through the two figures. By introducing these rhythms Picasso has made what might have been a static image—a girl facing a mirror in a flat space—assume qualities of almost dancelike grace.

Picasso had no program when he painted *Girl Before a Mirror.* He did not stand before his easel with a checklist and make sure that all the visual elements had been accounted for in the proper amounts of unity, variety, balance, scale, proportion, and rhythm. He *knew* what he was doing, but he would not have spelled it out in these terms. Being able to articulate the elements and principles does, however, help the viewer to better understand works of art and to penetrate, a little, the genius of those who make them.

PART THREE

TWO-DIMENSIONAL MEDIA

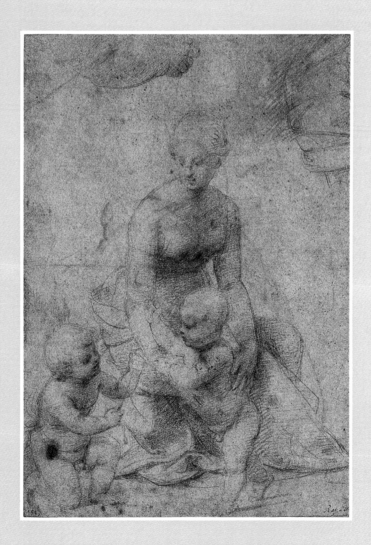

182. Raphael. *Madonna and Child with Infant St. John,*
preparatory drawing for *The Madonna of the Meadows,* **99.**
c. 1505. Red chalk on paper, $8\frac{3}{16} \times 6\frac{1}{4}''$.
The Metropolitan Museum of Art, New York (Rogers Fund, 1964).

CHAPTER SIX

Drawing

E VERYBODY DRAWS. There can scarcely be a person above the age of two who has never made a drawing. Many people take photographs, some paint, a few make sculpture, and a very few may even design a building. But everybody draws. You see a patch of wet sand at the beach, a dusty tabletop, or a blank notepad while you are sitting in class or at a business meeting—and your natural impulse is to draw something.

Children begin to draw long before they begin to write, sometimes before they can talk intelligibly. In drawing far more than in speech, children reveal their fantasies and their fears. Whatever the content, nearly all children draw, which shows how truly universal is this method of expression.

Two qualities often associated with drawing are familiarity and intimacy. Drawing is familiar in that it uses the materials we all are accustomed to—the pencil, the pen, the stick of chalk. There are no mysterious or exotic ingredients. You can pick up a pencil and draw somebody's likeness on paper, and so can a great draftsman like Ingres **(184)**. Your drawing almost certainly will not look as good as his, but it is the same kind of expression.

Drawing seems intimate because it is frequently—although not always—the artist's private note-taking. Many drawings are not intended for exhibition and therefore are not shown publicly during the artist's lifetime. They may be preliminary sketches for some other work of art or just the artist's refined doodling. We think of such drawings as direct expression—from brain to hand—without the intervening censor of desired public approval. In looking at a sketch by Raphael **(182)**, for example, we can speculate about what he was actually thinking as he drew those lines.

The drawing illustrated opposite is a preliminary study for Raphael's painting *The Madonna of the Meadows* **(99)**, apparently the last in a sequence of sketches before the artist committed to working in oils. Comparing the two—the sketch and the finished painting—can be fascinating, offering a glimpse of the artist's developing ideas. Notice how, in the drawing, the figures seem to huddle together in a closed group. For the painting, Raphael made the bodies more upright and tilted all three heads slightly outward, so that we, the viewers, are pulled into the scene. Mary's body, in the drawing, seems rather fragile; the painted version gives her body and garments a sense of monumentality. No background landscape appears in the drawing. Presumably, the artist wanted to be satisfied with his figures before setting them in deep pictorial space. Despite the changes, however, we must not consider this drawing flawed or imperfect. It is a fresh, spontaneous testing of ideas, and very beautiful in its own right.

Other factors may contribute to drawing's sense of intimacy. Most drawings are relatively small (compared with paintings), and many are executed quickly. Drawings are often made in great quantities; some artists do hundreds of drawings for every "finished" work. There are exceptions to this generalization, drawings that are large and/or are executed with painstaking attention to detail, including several examples in this chapter. But part of the charm of drawing as a medium must surely be the fact that, even when a work *is* intended for exhibition, it still retains an air of intimacy.

We usually associate drawings with paper, but, historically, many other surfaces have been used to draw on. The oldest artworks we know of are the cave drawings found in southern France and in Spain **(2)**. (These images are often referred to as paintings, but many have a strong linear quality that would more accurately categorize them as drawings.) The artists who made the cave images worked directly on the stone walls of the caves; archaeologists speculate they drew the outlines either with mats of hair or with charred sticks, then filled in by blowing colors through a hollow pipe. Some 5,000 to 10,000 years after the cave drawings were done, nomadic peoples developed the technique of pottery making. A number of later cultures had strong pottery traditions, including the ancient Greeks **(431,432)** and native peoples of Central and South America. Other cultures worked on papyrus (a paperlike material made from pressed plant stems) or on parchment (treated animal skins). The ancient Chinese drew on silk, their special material, and many Chinese artists still do. However, it is the Chinese who are credited with providing the most common surface for drawing.

According to legend, the Chinese invented paper in 105 C.E. Centuries later the Moslems spread the knowledge of papermaking from the East through Europe and the Mediterranean world. A page from a manuscript of the Koran **(183)**, dated to the 11th century, shows how Moslem scribes in Spain developed **calligraphy,** or "beautiful writing," into an art form. The Koran (or Qur'an) is, of course, the holy book of Islam, the Moslem faith, and the purpose of writing manuscript copies—in this age long before the printed book—was to spread and teach the faith. Yet that higher goal did not preclude giving the sacred words all the decorative beauty at the calligrapher's command. Beyond the flowing script of the text, this unusually lovely page is designed like a picture, with the paper border serving as a frame and the warm color of the paper providing visual richness.

Nowadays, the artist who wants to make a drawing has a dizzying array of surfaces and materials to choose from. Some materials are ancient, while others depend on space-age technology. In this chapter we shall look first at the range of materials used for drawing and the effects each can produce. Then we will explore the various purposes for which a drawing can be made.

MATERIALS FOR DRAWING

Some artists draw almost exclusively in one favorite material, whereas others experiment widely and are eager to try each new medium that comes along. It would be difficult to say how much a choice of material influences the resulting work. Of course, the potential for expression comes from within the artist, not from any substance, but it is nevertheless true that different materials tend to produce particular effects. By "playing" with many tools and papers the artist may be inspired to create new types of imagery.

All drawing media (and, for that matter, all painting media) are based on **pigment**—coloring material in a neutral or some version of a hue that has been ground and mixed with a substance that enables it to adhere to the drawing surface. Drawing materials generally are divided into two categories—dry media and liquid media. The dry media tend to be abrasive. They "scratch" across a paper or some other surface, depositing particles wherever they come

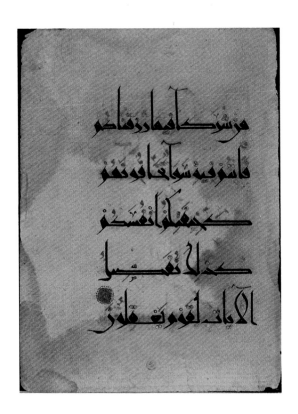

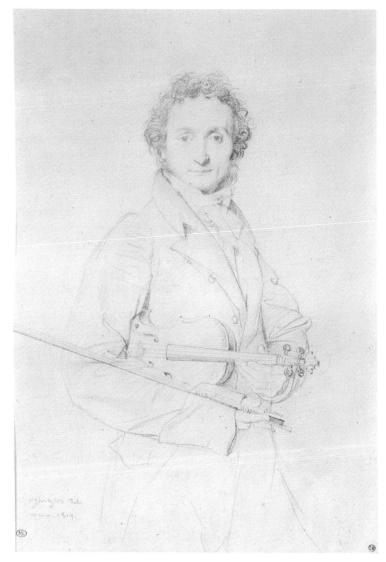

in contact with the surface. Liquid media, in contrast, have particles of pigment suspended in fluid, so they flow onto the surface much more freely.

DRY MEDIA

PENCIL The graphite pencil, sometimes called a "lead" pencil, probably has made more drawings than any other medium. Pencils are cheap, readily available, and easy to work with. Mistakes can be erased. If the drawing turns out badly, it can be thrown away at no great expense.

Despite the pencil's humble status, however, some of the most elegant drawings we know have been done with graphite pencil. The master of this technique was Jean Auguste Dominique Ingres. In 1819 Ingres used the sharp point of a pencil to create a portrait of his friend, the brilliant Italian violinist Nicolo Paganini **(184)**. Paganini was a dynamic character, famed equally for his virtuosity on the violin and his vivid personality. The artist captures both of these qualities. Ingres poses his subject standing proudly erect, the violin and bow poised with the absolute assurance of the master musician. Paganini looks us viewers straight in the eye, showing us his intelligence and zest for life—plus more than a trace of arrogance. The lines of the coat suggest a barely restrained energy in the body underneath. We half expect Paganini to break into a smile, thrust his violin under his chin, and play for us.

left: **183.** Page from a Koran, from Persia. 11th century. Ink and colors on paper, height 7½″. Victoria & Albert Museum, London (by courtesy of the Board of Trustees of the Victoria & Albert Museum).

right: **184.** Jean Auguste Dominique Ingres. *Portrait of Nicolo Paganini.* 1819. Graphite pencil, 11¾ × 8⅝″. Louvre, Paris.

The colored pencils favored by some artists produce a somewhat warmer and softer effect than that of graphite. We see this in a sketch by Henri de Toulouse-Lautrec, called *At the Circus: Trained Pony and Baboon* (185). In his youth, Lautrec had loved the circus. Later, when physical and mental problems forced him into a sanitarium, he took his colored pencils with him and made a series of drawings from memory. This charming work portrays the three circus figures as a performing unit of professionals—three species joined in a working team. Given its subject, the drawing is surprisingly intimate; there are no cheering crowds, no waving banners, no hurly-burly. Lautrec uses his color effects sparingly, to highlight and emphasize. In other hands a circus drawing might be garish or brassy, but this one has the delicacy of a sweetly remembered past.

METALPOINT Metalpoint, the ancestor of the graphite pencil, is an old technique that was especially popular during the Renaissance. Few artists use it now, because it is not very forgiving of mistakes or indecision. Once put down, the lines cannot easily be changed or erased. The drawing medium is a thin wire of metal, often of pure silver (in which case the medium is called ***silverpoint***), mounted in some kind of holding device, such as a wooden shaft or a modern mechanical pencil. The drawing surface must be specially coated with white poster paint or a similar ground—historically, the coating was bone dust and glue—and the lines produced by the metalpoint are typically thin and of uniform width.

Metalpoint drawings are characterized by a fine elegance, a finished perfection. Because of the thin, uniform lines it is somewhat difficult to model rounded forms, so artists often highlighted their drawings in white paint to enhance the illusion of depth, as in Perugino's magnificent *Man in Armor* (186). This drawing was undoubtedly meant to be a finished work, not a preliminary sketch. It is as carefully planned as any painting in its subtle effect of gray line against lovely blue ground.

left: 185.
Henri de Toulouse-Lautrec.
At the Circus: Trained Pony and Baboon. c. 1899.
Colored pencil, black pastel, and graphite, on cream wove paper; $17\frac{1}{4} \times 10\frac{1}{2}''$.
The Art Institute of Chicago (gift of Tiffany and Margaret Blake, 1944).

right: 186. Perugino.
A Man in Armor.
Late 15th–early 16th century.
Metalpoint, heightened with white, on blue ground; $9\frac{3}{4} \times 7\frac{1}{4}''$.
The Royal Collection. © 1997 Her Majesty Queen Elizabeth II.

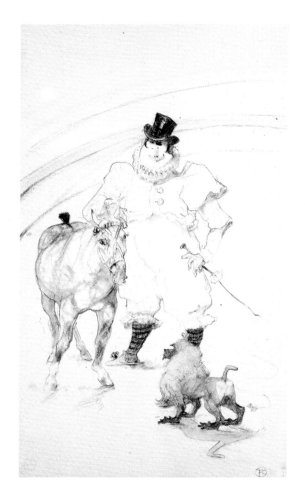

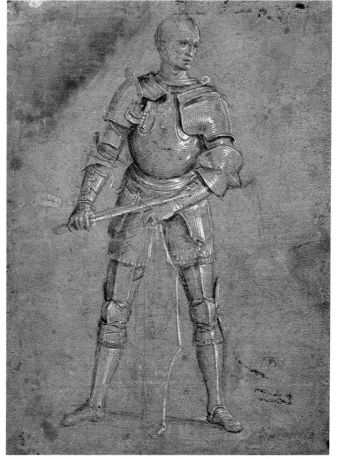

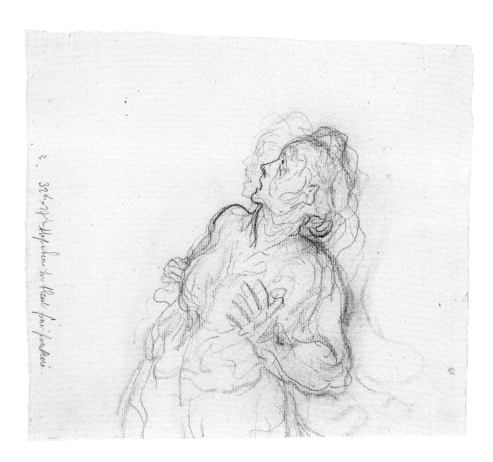

187. Honoré Daumier. *Frightened Woman.* 19th century. Charcoal with black crayon on ivory laid paper, 8¼ × 9⅜″. The Art Institute of Chicago (gift of Robert Allerton, 1923).

CHARCOAL   Charcoal's effects are almost the exact opposite of those offered by metalpoint. Where metalpoint produces a thin, delicate line, charcoal's line is dark, sometimes very soft, occasionally harsh. Charcoal is actually burned sticks of wood—the best-quality charcoal coming from special vine wood heated in a kiln until only carbon remains. Charcoal lines can be thin or thick, pale to velvety black. If charcoal is used on a paper with a "tooth," or heavy grain, the results are textured. Honoré Daumier used charcoal to create the drawing called *Frightened Woman* **(187)**. The undulating charcoal line and repeated form make the figure seem actually to be trembling in fear. No delicate medium could so easily have produced this chilling image.

CHALK AND CRAYON   A wide range of chalks and crayons are available to the artist, and nearly all of them offer color effects. We consider them together here, because there is not always agreement among manufacturers or artists (or even textbook writers) about what to call a given product. Generally speaking, the main difference between chalks and crayons is the ***binder***—the substance that holds particles of pigment together. Chalks have nonfat binders, whereas crayons have a fatty or greasy binder, so there is considerable variation in the way these materials react to contact with paper. If you imagine blackboard chalk and ordinary children's crayons, this difference in effect should be clear.

Chalks and crayons vary in several characteristics. Artists need to experiment with specific products from specific manufacturers to find the effects they want. We can, however, make certain generalizations, bearing in mind they are not hard-and-fast rules. Chalks, being drier and more crumbly, blend well and can be overlaid (two or more colors on top of one another) to produce shaded effects. They usually require a paper with some tooth, are relatively fragile unless covered by a fixative, and offer a limited range of colors. The greasier crayons adhere well to paper and are more permanent, but they are difficult to blend with one another for subtle tones and gradations. (However,

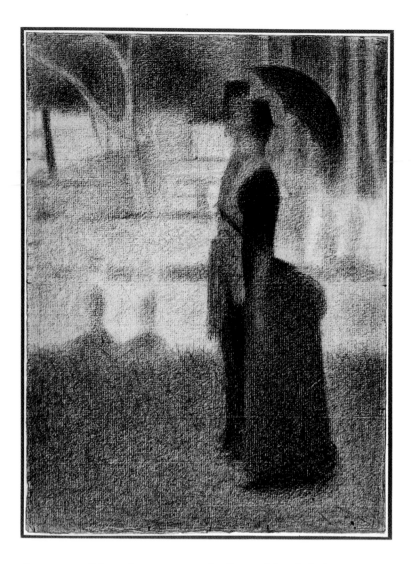

188. Georges Seurat. *The Couple,* study for *A Sunday on La Grande Jatte,* **119.** 1884. Conté crayon, 12¼ × 9¾″. Copyright The British Museum, London.

the newer oil-based crayons can be finger-blended almost as easily as oil paints blend.) Crayons usually offer a wider choice of colors than do chalks, and they come in varying degrees of hardness to permit sharp lines or tonal areas.

Crayon can mean anything from the wax crayons used by children through the lithographic crayon meant for drawing on stone in printmaking (Chapter 8). But the commonest drawing material is **conté crayon**—a fine-textured stick medium available in shades of red, brown, and black.

The artist who comes to mind most readily in discussing conté crayon drawings is Georges Seurat. In Chapter 4 we looked at Seurat's painting technique, called **pointillism,** in which tiny dots of color are massed together to build form. Seurat also did many drawings. By working in conté on rough-textured paper he could approximate the effect of color dots in paint. *The Couple* **(188)** is a preliminary study in crayon for Seurat's landmark oil painting, *A Sunday on La Grande Jatte* **(119).** However, unlike Raphael's sketch for *The Madonna of the Meadows,* this drawing, along with many of Seurat's other studies, is a fully realized work of art. It was Seurat's practice to work out his figures very completely as separate units in drawing and then to transfer them to the painted canvas. This drawing is his study for the male and female figures at far right in the painting **(119)**; it also shows ghost images of the two young women in front of them and the trees in the background.

One other medium that should be mentioned along with the chalks and crayons is **pastel.** Because it is very soft and offers a full range of colors, pastel is often considered a borderline medium, somewhere between painting and drawing. Being fine-textured, it lends itself especially well to the kind of blending of hues that creates gradated tones. Winold Reiss' portrait of *Mary McLeod*

Bethune **(189)** illustrates the great flexibility of this medium. Reiss concentrates on the face of this pioneering educator, modeling her features into full three-dimensionality, capturing his subject's warmth and intelligence. The treatment of the figure, by contrast, is surprisingly modern for a work done in 1925. Bethune's figure and dress are barely sketched, flat and two-dimensional. The artist might be telling us that the substance of this brilliant woman is to be found in her head.

LIQUID MEDIA

PEN AND INK Ink flowing onto paper gives a smooth, uninterrupted line. As with other relatively permanent media, such as silverpoint, there is little possibility for correction once the lines have been inscribed. A major variable in the ink drawing, however, is the relative thickness or thinness of lines, which depends on the pen point used. The lines can be all one width, ranging from fine to heavy, or they can vary. A single line may change, perhaps starting as a fine thread, broadening into thickness, and then tapering down again to a slender mark. Such thick-and-thin lines are referred to as *calligraphic* or *gestural.*

As crayon makes us think of Seurat, pen and ink makes us think of Rembrandt—one of the greatest draftsmen who ever lived. Rembrandt made thousands of drawings during his long career, and he drew almost everything

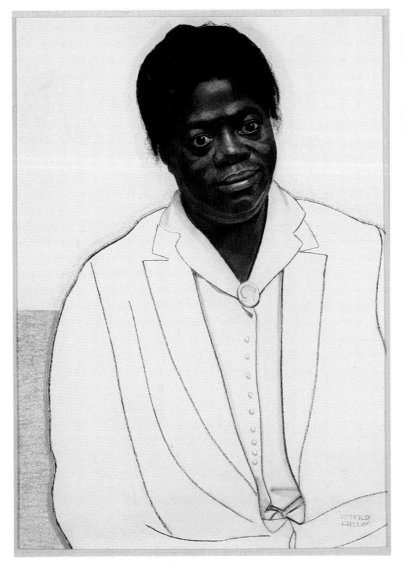

189. Winold Reiss.
Mary McLeod Bethune. c. 1925.
Pastel on artist board,
29⅞ × 21 9/16″.
The National Portrait Gallery,
Smithsonian Institution,
Washington, D.C.
(gift of Lawrence A. Fleischman
and Howard Garfinkle
with a matching grant from the
National Endowment for the Arts).

imaginable. But it is his landscapes that perhaps more than any theme reveal Rembrandt's "handwriting." In *A Thatched Cottage by a Large Tree* **(190)** the curling penwork in the trees and foreground foliage, drawn with a reed pen, is typical of his rapid, sketchy style. The stiff reed point yields a rather bold line with much visual character. We know that trees have leaves, not swirling shapes, and yet ever since Rembrandt this curving line seems to us the very essence of "tree." The drawing may seem sketchy and quick, but the artist has given us a strong sense of forms in space.

Another use of the pen line can be seen in Alexander Calder's circus drawings of the 1930s **(191)**. These drawings are related to Calder's thin wire sculptures from that period **(89)**, and they are just as economical in form, just as uniform in line as the three-dimensional wires. The artist gives us only the barest outlines of the figures, the minimum needed to show shape and position. This type of drawing is a kind of visual shorthand, energetic and playful. The figures are transparent, as they would be when done in wire, but we have no doubt about their arrangement in space. Only a skilled draftsman can give us so much sense of place with so little.

right: 190. Rembrandt.
*A Thatched Cottage
by a Large Tree.* c. 1652.
Reed pen and bistre, $6\frac{7}{8} \times 10\frac{1}{2}''$.
Devonshire Collection, Chatsworth
(reproduced by permission of
the Chatsworth Settlement Trustees).

below: 191. Alexander Calder.
Somersaulters. 1931.
Pen and ink, $22\frac{3}{4} \times 30\frac{3}{4}''$.
Collection Mr. and Mrs.
Alvin S. Lane, Riverdale, N.Y.

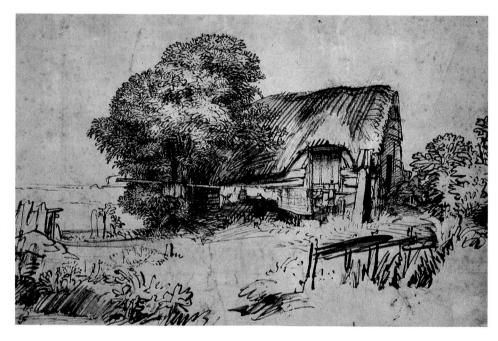

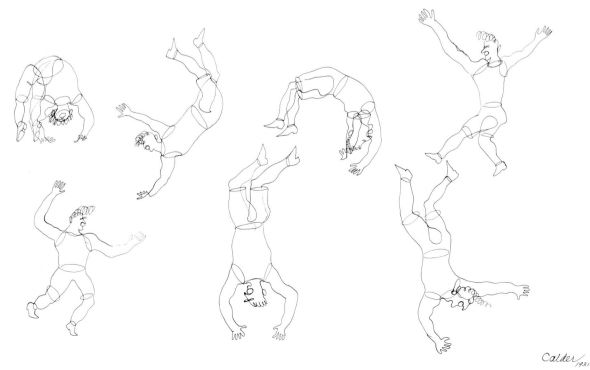

REMBRANDT

1606–1669

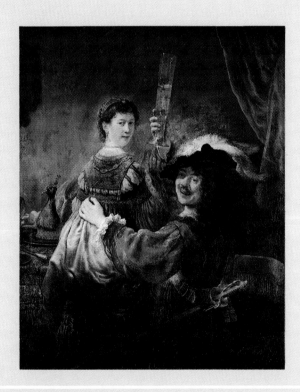

O F THE FEW ARTISTS classified as "greatest of the great," Rembrandt is the most accessible to us. Through more than one hundred self-portraits, we follow his path from the brashness of youth to the high good spirits and prosperity of middle life to the melancholy loneliness of old age. Rembrandt's penetrating self-portraits represent a search for the self, but to the viewer they are a revelation of the self.

Born in the Dutch city of Leiden, Rembrandt Harmensz van Rijn was the son of a miller. At fourteen he began art lessons in Leiden and later studied with a master in Amsterdam. By the age of twenty-two he had pupils of his own. About 1631 he settled permanently in Amsterdam, having by then attracted considerable fame as a portrait painter. Thus began for Rembrandt a decade of

professional success and personal happiness—a high point that would never come again in his life.

In 1634 Rembrandt married Saskia van Uijlenburgh, an heiress of good family, thus improving his own social status. The pair must have been rather a dashing couple-about-Amsterdam. The artist's portraits were in demand, his style was fashionable, and he had money enough to indulge himself in material possessions, especially to collect art. One blight on this happy period was the arrival of four children, none of whom survived. But in 1641 Rembrandt's beloved son Titus was born.

Rembrandt's range as an artist was enormous. He was master not only of painting but of drawing and of the demanding technique of etching for prints. (It is said that Rembrandt went out sketching with an etcher's needle, as other artists might carry a pencil.) Besides the many portraits, the artist displayed unparalleled genius in other themes, including landscapes and religious scenes.

In 1642 Rembrandt's fortunes again changed, this time, irrevocably, for the worse. Saskia died not long after giving birth to Titus. The artist's financial affairs were in great disarray, no doubt partly because of his self-indulgence in buying art and precious objects. Although he continued to work and to earn money, Rembrandt showed little talent for money management. Ultimately he was forced into bankruptcy and had to sell not only his art collection but even Saskia's burial plot. About 1649 Hendrickje Stoffels came to live with Rembrandt, and she is thought of as his second wife, although they did not marry legally. She joined forces with Titus to form an art dealership in an attempt to protect the artist from his creditors. Capping the long series of tragedies that marked Rembrandt's later life, Hendrickje died in 1663 and Titus in 1668, a year before his father.

Rembrandt's legacy is almost totally a visual one. He does not seem to have written much. Ironically, one of the few recorded comments comes in a letter to a patron, begging for payment—payment for paintings that are now considered priceless and hang in one of the world's great museums. "I pray you my kind lord that my warrant might now be prepared at once so that I may now at last receive my well-earned 1244 guilders and I shall always seek to recompense your lordship for this with reverential service and proof of friendship."[1]

Rembrandt. *Self-Portrait with Saskia*. c. 1634. Oil on canvas, 5'3½" × 4'3½". Gemäldegalerie Alte Meister, Staatliche Kunstsammlungen, Dresden.

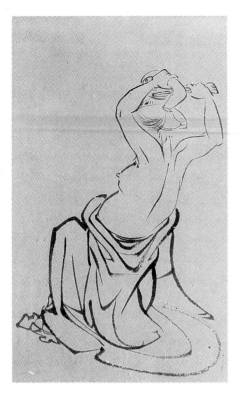

BRUSH AND INK   The brush has long been the favorite drawing tool of Asian artists. Because in the East the brush is commonly used for writing, its handling seems as natural there as using a pencil does to Westerners. When the brush is manipulated in the Asian way, it is the ideal tool (better than a pen) for producing the calligraphic line—thin at the beginning, broadening along its length, and then tapering again to very thin. We see this effect in a marvelous drawing by the Japanese artist Katsushika Hokusai **(192)**. The woman's body is sketched in a few quick calligraphic lines, yet it seems round and full-bodied. One deft stroke down the center of the back, combined with the curve of breast and belly, and Hokusai has made us believe in the three-dimensional form.

When ink is diluted with water and applied with a brush, the result is called a **wash.** Sometimes an artist will combine areas of wash with the pen-and-ink line to impart greater solidity to the forms. We see this in Isabel Bishop's drawing *Students* **(193)**, which is part of the artist's "Walking" series (see also **179**). Here the broad swipes of wash give some weight to the figures, especially the second from left, while Bishop's nervous, scribbly pen-and-ink line fills the drawing with movement. Even though only four figures are included, and one of those is barely sketched, we get the sense of a whole campus full of students milling about, going to and from classes. Bishop is a master of both techniques—the pen line and the brushed-on wash.

Handled somewhat differently, the medium of brush and ink can produce extremely bold effects. Käthe Kollwitz combined touches of wash and thick, aggressive lines of pure black for the powerful image of a *Fettered Man* **(194)**. Kollwitz made a great many drawings, and nearly all of them are in charcoal, a softer medium. For this anguished figure she chose the starker black ink.

above: 192. Katsushika Hokusai.
Woman Adjusting Her Hair. Early 19th century.
Ink on paper, $16\frac{1}{4} \times 11\frac{5}{8}''$.
The Metropolitan Museum of Art, New York
(Charles Stewart Smith Collection, gift
of Mrs. Charles Stewart Smith, Charles Stewart Smith, Jr.,
and Howard Caswell Smith, in memory
of Charles Stewart Smith, 1914).

below: 193. Isabel Bishop. *Students.* c. 1981.
Pen, ink, and ink wash; $4\frac{3}{4} \times 5\frac{1}{4}''$.
Courtesy Midtown Payson Galleries, New York.

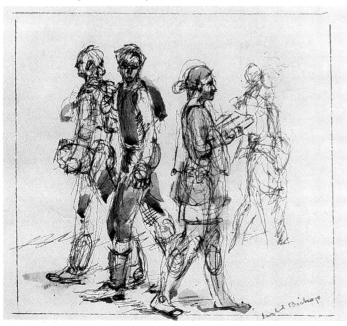

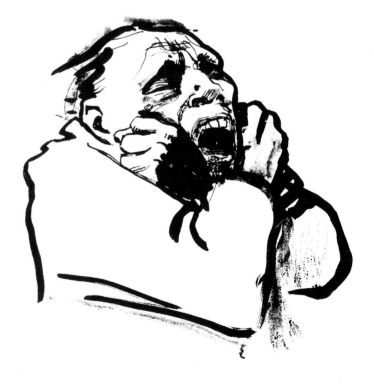

above: 194. Käthe Kollwitz. *Fettered Man.* 1927.
Pen and wash, $17\frac{1}{2} \times 14\frac{1}{2}''$.
Private collection, New York.

KÄTHE KOLLWITZ

1867–1945

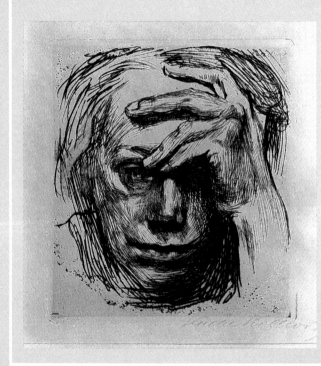

IN A TIME when the word "artist" usually meant a painter or a sculptor, Kollwitz did the bulk of her work in prints and drawings. In a time when vivid, sometimes startling color was preoccupying the art world, Kollwitz concentrated on black and white. And in a time when nearly all artists were men, Kollwitz was—triumphantly—a woman, a woman whose life and art focused on the special concerns of women. This combination of oddities might have doomed a lesser artist to obscurity, but not one of Kollwitz' great gifts and powerful personality.

Käthe Schmidt was born in Königsberg (then in Prussia, now part of Russia), the second child in an intellectually active middle-class family. Her parents were remarkably enlightened in encouraging all their children to take an active part in political and social causes and to develop their talents—in Käthe's case a talent for drawing. Käthe received the best art training then available for a woman, in Berlin and Munich. In 1891, after a seven-year engagement, she married Karl Kollwitz, a physician who seems to have been equally supportive of his wife's career. The couple established themselves in Berlin, where they kept a joint doctor's office and artist's studio for fifty years.

During her student days Kollwitz had gradually focused on line and had come to realize that draftsmanship was her genius. Her conventional artistic training must have intensified the shock when she "suddenly saw that I was not a painter at all."[2] She concentrated then on drawings and prints—etchings and woodcuts early on, lithographs when her eyesight grew weaker.

Five major themes dominate Kollwitz' art: herself, in a great many self-portraits and images for which she served as model; the ties between mothers and their children; the hardships of the working classes, usually interpreted through women's plight; the unspeakable cruelties of war; and death as a force unto itself. As a socialist Kollwitz identified passionately with the sufferings of working people; as a mother she identified with the struggle of women to keep their children safe.

Kollwitz bore two sons—Hans in 1892 and Peter in 1896. The first of many tragedies that marked her later life came in 1914, with the death of Peter in World War I. She lived long enough to see her beloved grandson, also named Peter, killed in World War II. During the almost thirty years between those losses, she continued to work prolifically, but her obsession with death never left her.

Few artists have so touchingly described their attempts to achieve a certain goal, and their continual frustration at falling short. In Kollwitz' case, the artistic goals were generally realized, but the emotional and political goals—never: "While I drew, and wept along with the terrified children I was drawing, I really felt the burden I am bearing. I felt that I have no right to withdraw from the responsibility of being an advocate. It is my duty to voice the sufferings of men, the never-ending sufferings heaped mountain-high. This is my task, but it is not an easy one to fulfill. Work is supposed to relieve you. . . . Did I feel relieved when I made the prints on war and knew that the war would go on raging? Certainly not."[3]

Käthe Kollwitz. *Self-Portrait with Hand on Her Forehead.*
1910. Etching.
Kupferstich-Kabinett, Staatliche Kunstsammlungen, Dresden.

Kollwitz' drawing shows plainly the interaction between drawing medium and imagery. In this case we might suspect that the artist had an image in mind and selected the medium that would best fit that image. Other times the reverse may occur: an artist experiments with a particular medium and thus is inspired with an image idea.

NEW DRAWING MEDIA

Artists today have a broad spectrum of drawing media to work with, and they do not limit themselves to the traditional materials we have just described. In this electronic age drawings are made by computer, by video technology, by all kinds of sophisticated equipment. For instance, if we came upon a reproduction of Barbara Nessim's *Two Shadows Outside Two Women* **(195)**, without looking at the caption we might speculate about what materials the artist used. Perhaps chalk or crayon for the lines, and maybe a colored wash for the pink and blue and purple tones, but how did she get the very fine stippled (dotted) effects in the figures? Actually, this drawing was made on an IBM PC computer terminal, then printed for permanence. Many of us associate computer graphics with business applications, but this delicate and lovely image shows how artists can tap the advanced image-making abilities of the computer.

Side by side with the computer in today's office is the fax machine, and its possibilities for artistic expression have not been neglected. David Hockney, an artist fully comfortable with traditional media, also loves to experiment with new ones. In the late 1980s Hockney began sending fax drawings to his friends. He made the drawings solely for this purpose, so his work cannot be called finished until it has been faxed **(196)**. Of these drawings the artist says, "I realized that if you draw especially for the fax, the prints are perfectly good. The medium is the fax, and if the fax can't read the image, you don't use those techniques."[4] Hockney delights in the fact that these works have no material value; the very act of transmission causes them to "dematerialize." Drawings of this sort force us to reconsider and stretch our definitions of art, because where, after all, *is* the art? In the original drawing? In the recipient's fax print? Or somewhere in the atmosphere?

195. Barbara Nessim. *Two Shadows Outside Two Women.* 1985. Computer drawing, Cibachrome print; 16 × 20″. © Barbara Nessim, 1985.

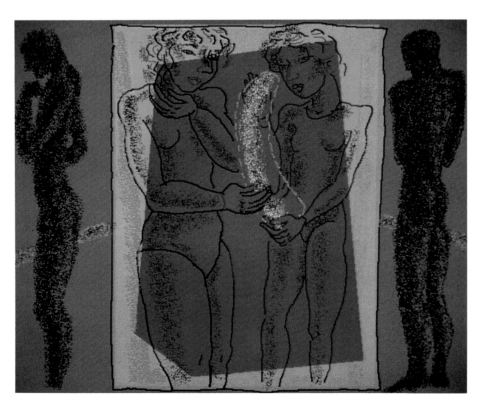

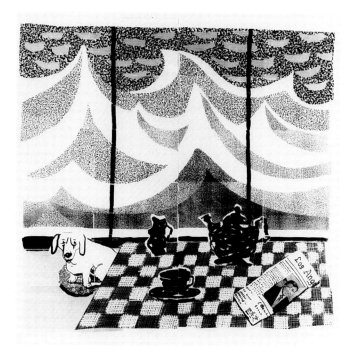

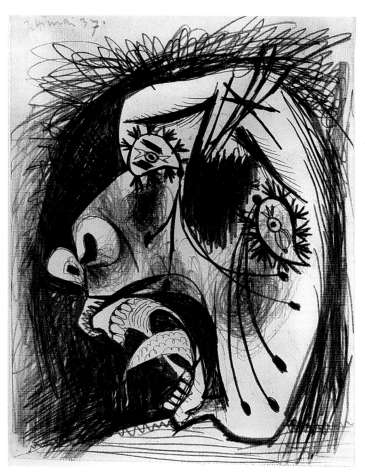

PURPOSES OF DRAWING

PRELIMINARY STUDY

Many of the drawings reproduced in this chapter—including those by Raphael and Seurat—were done mainly as preliminary studies for paintings. Before committing time and material to a finished painting, the artist will often sketch and experiment until the form seems exactly right. Artists working in all fields do the same thing. Sculptors, architects, interior designers, printmakers, landscape architects, and industrial designers—all develop their ideas in preliminary drawings.

In Chapter 3 we examined Picasso's great painting *Guernica* **(58)**, the artist's outraged response to the bombing of a defenseless Basque town by the Nazis in April of 1937. We pointed out that Picasso did not merely spew out his anger onto canvas, but planned the large picture carefully, through many preliminary drawings. It is known that Picasso worked on *Guernica* from May 1 to June 4, 1937. On May 24 he made the drawing shown here **(197)**. We see a disembodied head drawn in heavy pencil, a head all but exploding in violent rage and terror and sorrow. The eyes, transformed into teardrop shapes, are displaced, with one located in the position of an ear. The nose is fragmented, and the mouth gapes open in a soundless shriek. You will not find this head in the finished painting, although there are similarities in the screaming woman with a dead baby at far left. Picasso tried this expression in a sketch and then did not use it. It is as though he needed to explore the many faces of anguish before choosing those that satisfied his vision.

left: **196.** David Hockney. *Breakfast with Stanley in Malibu, August 23, 1989.* 1989. Multi-page fax drawing, black-and-white laser copy, felt marker, gouache, 24 pages; overall size 4′3″ × 4′8″. © David Hockney.

right: **197.** Pablo Picasso. *Head* (study for *Guernica*). May 24, 1937. Pencil and gouache on white paper, $11\frac{1}{2}$ × $9\frac{1}{4}$″. Centro de Arte Reina Sofia, Madrid.

ILLUSTRATION

Another purpose for drawing is illustration, and this field is enormous. Illustrations are made for books, for magazines, for newspapers, for advertising, for fashion displays. Before the advent of the camera, drawn illustrations were the only kind available. Illustrators today still make drawings to record events where the camera is not permitted, such as at many courtroom trials.

One of the most famous illustrators of all time was the 19th-century English artist Aubrey Beardsley. Beardsley was a fascinating character who achieved international recognition by the age of twenty, was enormously productive, and died of tuberculosis at twenty-six. His style is distinctive, bringing together elements of the erotic and the grotesque with ornate, free-flowing decoration. The style has influenced many later illustrators but has never quite been imitated. Beardsley's illustrations for books and magazines **(198)** have strong contrasting areas of black and white. The drawing is broad and exaggerated—in this example almost a caricature. Like any great illustrator, Beardsley went beyond the story he was illustrating to create a whole new world from his own imagination. Once you get to know Beardsley's style, you cannot fail to recognize it. For an illustrator, the style, the personal view of the world, is all important.

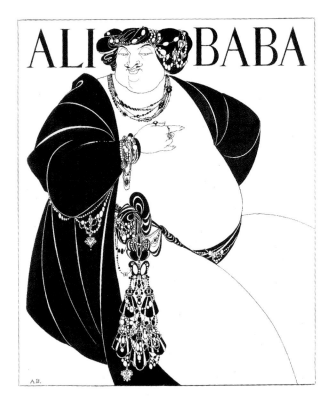

right: 198. Aubrey Beardsley.
Ali Baba, cover design for *The Forty Thieves*. 1897.
Black ink, white gouache,
and graphite on white paper; $9\frac{7}{16} \times 7\frac{13}{16}''$.
Courtesy of The Fogg Art Museum,
Harvard University Art Museums, Cambridge, Mass.
(bequest of Grenville L. Winthrop).

below: 199. Maurice Sendak.
Drawing from *Where the Wild Things Are*. 1963.
Courtesy Harper Collins Publishers, Inc., New York.

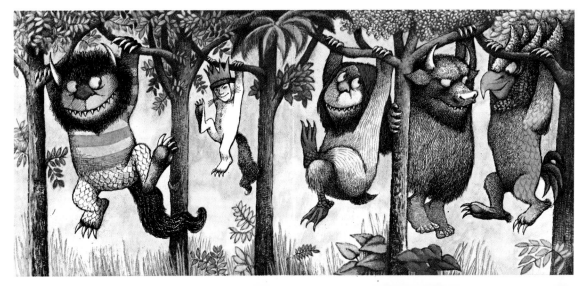

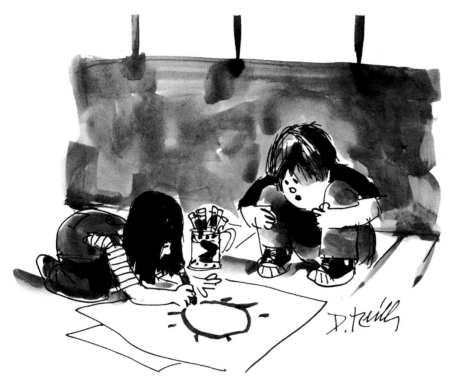

"I only draw with software."

There are some areas in which drawn illustration has never given way to the camera but is still used extensively, such as cartoons and the illustration of children's books. These fields have enjoyed unwavering popularity, and their styles have kept pace with other types of art.

Illustration for children's books has been greatly influenced by the innovative work of Maurice Sendak. Sendak's drawings are not the gentle, benign images that several previous generations had thought appropriate for children. Sendak draws monsters, monsters who dwell somewhere between the naughty and the truly wicked. In his book *Where the Wild Things Are* **(199)** the artist gives concrete form to the dreadful creatures that inhabit children's fantasies. Some critics have attacked the drawings as being too frightening for children. Others suggest that the drawings have psychological value, in that Sendak's stories allow children to confront their monsters and conquer them. From the audience, however, there has never been any argument. Children love the drawings, scary though they be.

There is one more type of drawing associated with illustration—the cartoon. Cartooning is a terrifically demanding art. Most cartoons have specific narrative content, which may be amusing, dramatic, satirical, political, or a combination of these. The artist has to convey this content in one drawing or, in the case of a comic strip, in a few economical drawings. If the cartoon has a caption, it too must be economical. Perhaps more than any other art, the cartoon must live up to the old saying, "One picture is worth a thousand words." Often, the successful cartoon depends on an audience's specialized information; they are made to feel "in on" the joke. For example, it is assumed that readers of *The New Yorker* are knowledgeable about art (nearly every issue has an art-related cartoon) and that they are familiar with current trends in art and computer technology **(200)**.

EXPRESSION

All drawings—in fact, all works of art—are made for the expression of the artist, regardless of any other purpose they might serve, and self-expression was a key motivation for most of the drawings we have seen in this chapter. Artists record on paper what they see, in the unique way they see it. Drawing is just one way in which the imagination takes concrete form.

Contemporary artists have expanded the potential for expression in drawing, as in every other artistic medium. For example, the work by Julian Schnabel (201), which many people would call a painting, actually contains a great many areas that resemble drawing, particularly the nude figure at left. Schnabel's materials—oil and modeling paste on velvet—are not those of drawing; they are not even the materials of conventional painting. But Schnabel's imagery, with its sketchy, linear quality, clearly derives from the world of the sketchbook. Above all, his work shows that the line between drawing and painting, at least for certain artists, has all but disappeared.

With the work of Jonathan Borofsky we have come full circle from the cave drawings of earliest history. Borofsky often draws directly on the walls of a room, and his images are those remembered and recorded from dreams (202). Some historians speculate that the cave artists as well were recording dreams, and their surfaces too were the walls around them. In bypassing conventional surfaces, such as paper, Borofsky shows us that drawing today need accept no limits, no restrictive sizes or shapes. Drawing is so much a natural impulse that it can be around us in the most natural way.

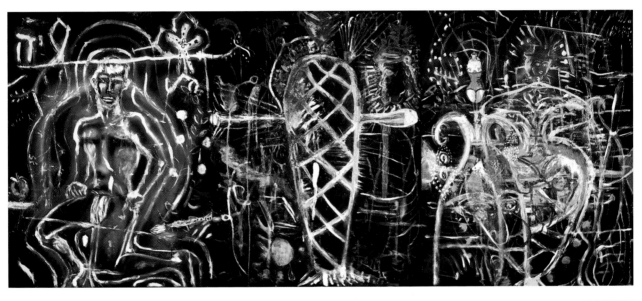

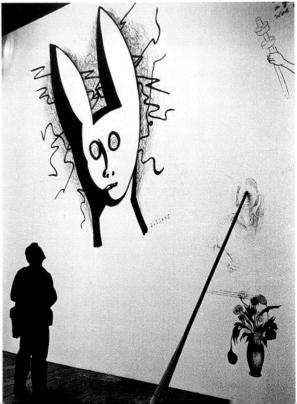

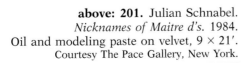

above: 201. Julian Schnabel.
Nicknames of Maitre d's. 1984.
Oil and modeling paste on velvet, 9 × 21′.
Courtesy The Pace Gallery, New York.

right: 202. Jonathan Borofsky. Installation on four walls, floor, and ceiling, Venice Biennale, 1980. Mixed media, wall height 20′.
Courtesy Paula Cooper Gallery, New York.

WHY DO WE LOSE ART?

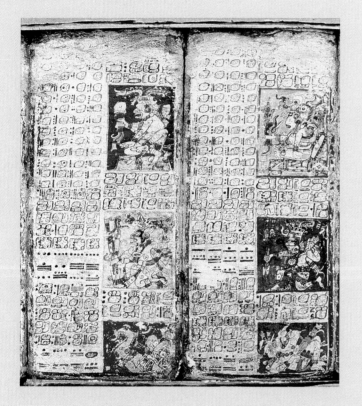

W HEN ART THAT once existed no longer exists, when artworks have been damaged or destroyed, we cannot help but ask, why? What forces removed this art from our cultural heritage? One answer is found in the history of illustrated books.

Bookmaking was a valued art in the ancient Maya civilization, which flourished in Mexico and Central America before the 16th century. The Maya developed an elaborate writing system based on *hieroglyphs*—pictorial symbols for words. They were the only fully literate society in the precolonial Americas, for they could write down any word they could speak. Master astronomers, the Maya devised a calendar much like the one we use now and plotted accurately movements of the sun, Mars, Jupiter, and especially the planet Venus.

The Maya's advanced knowledge of natural phenomena was written down in books, properly called *codices* because they were manuscript, not printed. Each book consisted of long strips of paper made from the bark of the wild fig tree, strengthened with gum substance and coated with a white plasterlike material. Maya scribes wrote their texts onto these sheets and embellished the writing with fine drawings colored in vegetable and mineral dyes. Then the books were folded into what we would call "pages" and bound in stiff covers. The page reproduced here comes from the *Dresden Codex*, the finest surviving Maya book, dated to the 12th century but thought to be a copy of an earlier book from between the 5th and 9th centuries. Its figures are symbolic. For example, the right center drawing shows the serpent god Kukulcan, who represents the planet Venus, pointing darts of death at a frog (lower right drawing), symbol of rain.

Thousands of such books were made during the Maya's long history, but only four are known still to exist. No doubt many of them, being of natural materials, simply rotted away, but the fate of some Maya books is well documented. When conquerors from Spain arrived in Mexico in the 16th century, they destroyed not only the Maya empire but much else as well. One Spaniard in particular, the Franciscan priest Diego de Landa, became both the hero and the villain of Maya chronicles. Fully appreciating the Maya's advanced cultural achievements, Landa recorded them for posterity. At the same time, however, as a Christian, he deplored the Maya's "pagan" religion and writings. In other words, certain Maya artworks violated Landa's sense of moral right, and he was in a position to do something about it. Landa gave the order, and on July 12, 1562, a terrible deed was done, which he himself described this way:

"We found a great number of books in these characters, and, as they contained nothing in which there was not to be seen superstition and lies of the Devil, we burned them all, which [the Maya] regretted to an amazing degree and caused them affliction."[5]

Page from the *Dresden Codex*.
Maya. 12th century (probably copied from a work of the 5th–9th century).
Sächsische Landesbibliothek, Dresden.

CHAPTER SEVEN

Painting

PAINTING IS THE QUEEN of the arts. Ask ten people to form a quick mental image of "art," and nine of them are likely to visualize a painting on a wall. There are several reasons for the prominence of painting. For one thing, paintings usually are full of color, and, as was noted in Chapter 4, color is a potent visual stimulus. For another, paintings usually are framed, some quite elaborately, so that one has the impression of a precious object set off from the rest of the world for our visual excitement. Even without a frame, a painting may seem a thing apart—a focus of energy and life, a universe unto itself. Whatever the painting shows, it establishes its own visual scope, sets its own rules.

If we consider some of the earliest cave images, especially the more elaborate and colorful ones, to be paintings, then the art has been practiced for at least thirty thousand years. During that long history the styles of painting have changed considerably, as have the media in which paintings are done—the physical substances the painter uses. In the latter case it might be more accurate to say broadened, rather than changed, for few media have been completely abandoned, while many new options have been added to the painter's repertoire.

To begin this discussion of painting, we should define certain terms crucial to the understanding of how, physically, such a work of art is put together. As with drawing media (Chapter 6), the color element in paint is the *pigment,* which consists of natural or synthetic color particles. Pigments usually come in the form of a powder, which by itself cannot be spread or made to adhere to the painting surface.

The *medium* or *binder* is the substance in which the pigment is suspended. ("Suspension" here means that the particles are mixed with a liquid or semiliquid material without dissolving or changing chemically.) Linseed oil—as in oil paint—is the best-known medium, but there are many others. A successful medium allows the painter to spread the colors on a surface as desired and, when it dries, adheres securely to the surface. The name of the medium of a particular work is often used to describe the work: an oil painting, a watercolor painting, and so on.

The *solvent* or *vehicle* enables the artist to thin the paint so as to control its flow and also to clean the brushes. A solvent is selected according to whether the paint is ***aqueous*** (water-solvent) or ***nonaqueous*** (dissolved by something other than water). Most of us are familiar with the distinction used for house paints—water-base or oil-base. For water-base paints you can wash the brushes with tap water, but for oil-base paints you need to use turpentine. Much the same distinction applies to artists' paints.

Finally, there is the painting ***support,*** which is the canvas, paper, wood panel, wall, or other surface on which the artist works. The painter may first apply a preliminary coating known as a ***ground*** or ***primer*** to make the support more receptive to the paint and/or to create certain effects.

As suggested earlier, practically every painting medium ever invented is still in use somewhere, by somebody. Artists interested in history or chemistry love to experiment with obscure techniques that went out of fashion centuries ago. Most of the painting media that have fallen out of favor have been abandoned because they were cumbersome or else because they were replaced by similar media that had certain advantages—lower cost, clearer colors, easier preparation, better adherence to the support, quicker drying time, slower drying time—whatever artists might wish.

It is impossible to tell which painting medium is the oldest, but we know that ancient peoples mixed their pigments with such things as fat and honey. Apparently, the first widespread and well-perfected technique came into use in the Classical period, the few hundred years surrounding the year 1 of our era. This was encaustic painting.

ENCAUSTIC

For encaustic, the pigment particles are suspended in hot beeswax, which must be kept at the proper temperature for spreading on a support (often a wood panel). Encaustic is an extremely demanding medium, and few contemporary artists want to cope with its difficulties. However, the wax gives a clear, luminous quality that almost no other medium can rival. The early Christians in Egypt, the Copts, were especially proficient at encaustic painting, and their works retain a splendid brilliance even two thousand years later (**203**).

FRESCO

To make a fresco the artist paints in water-suspended pigment on a surface of freshly spread plaster. As the plaster dries, the colors are absorbed into it, so that the two substances—paint and plaster—fuse. The painting will survive in good condition as long as the plaster remains intact.

Fresco is above all a wall-painting technique, and it has been used for large-scale murals since ancient times. Probably no other painting medium requires such careful planning, such meticulous attention to the chemical properties of the medium, and such hard physical labor. The plaster can be painted only when it has the proper degree of dampness; therefore, the artist must plan each day's work and spread plaster only in the area that can be painted in one session. (Michelangelo could cover about 1 square yard of wall or ceiling in a day.)

There is nothing tentative about fresco. Whereas in some media the artist can experiment, try out forms, and then paint over them to make corrections, every touch of the brush in fresco is a commitment. The only way an artist can correct mistakes or change the forms is to let the plaster dry, chip it away, and start all over again. Usually, the artist begins with a preliminary drawing called a ***cartoon.*** This may be a scaled-down or full-size version of the finished painting. If the cartoon is full size, the artist may cut it up into pieces, each the size

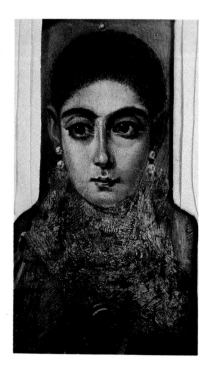

203. *Young Woman with a Gold Pectoral.* Egypto-Roman (Coptic), from Fayoum. 1st–4th century. Encaustic. Louvre, Paris.

of a day's work. Next the artist outlines major forms by placing the cartoon on the surface and poking through its lines with a sharp tool to leave a row of pinholes in the plaster.

There have been three great eras of fresco painting in the history of art: the Classical period in the Aegean and Rome, the Renaissance in 15th- and 16th-century Italy, and the early 20th century in Mexico. Only a few of the Classical frescoes have survived **(443)**; as buildings become ruins, so do their frescoed walls. But among the works we consider the greatest of all in Western art are the magnificent frescoes of the Italian Renaissance.

While Michelangelo was at work on the frescoes of the Sistine Chapel ceiling **(477,478),** Pope Julius II brought in Raphael to decorate the walls of several rooms in the Vatican Palace. Raphael's fresco for the end wall of the Stanza della Segnatura, a room that may have been the Pope's library, is considered by many to be the summation of Renaissance art. It is called *The School of Athens* **(204)** and depicts the Greek philosophers Plato and Aristotle, centered in the composition and framed by the arch, along with their followers and students. The "school" in question means the two schools of philosophy represented by the two Classical thinkers—Plato's the more abstract and metaphysical, Aristotle's the more earthly and physical.

Everything about Raphael's composition celebrates the Renaissance ideals of perfection, beauty, natural representation, and noble principles. The towering architectural setting provides an arena for quiet intellectual debate, and it is drawn in masterful linear perspective (Chapter 4, p. 113; **Overlay 5b**). The figures, perhaps influenced by Michelangelo's figures on the Sistine ceiling, are idealized—more perfect than life, full-bodied and dynamic. *The School of Athens* reflects Raphael's vision of one Golden Age—the Renaissance—and connects it with the Golden Age of Greece two thousand years earlier.

The era that spawned the great fresco artists of Mexico, while scarcely "golden," was a fertile and turbulent one. The Mexican Revolution began in

204. Raphael.
The School of Athens. 1510–11.
Fresco, 26 × 18′.
Stanza della Segnatura,
Vatican, Rome.

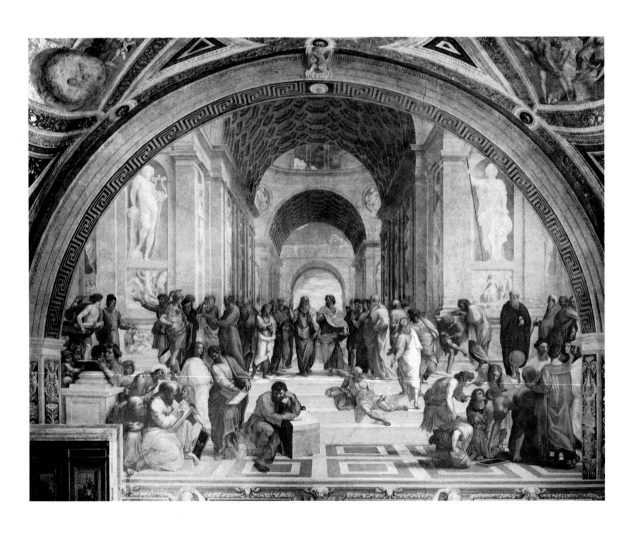

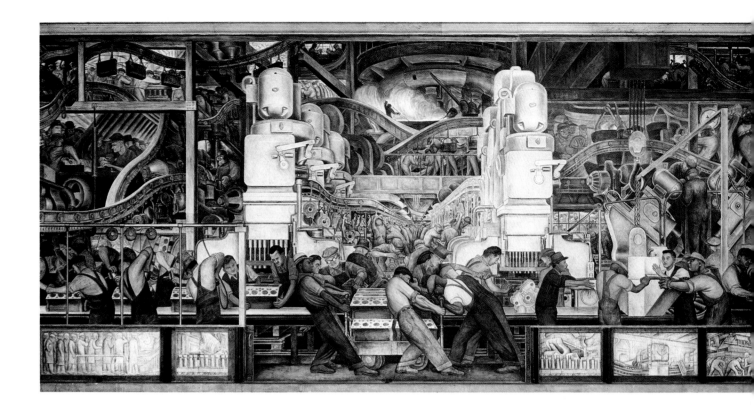

205. Diego Rivera.
Detroit Industry, detail.
1932–33. Fresco, 17'8½" × 45'
(north wall, central panel).
The Detroit Institute of Arts
(Founders Society Purchase,
Edsel B. Ford Fund and gift
of Edsel B. Ford).

1911 and continued for twenty years. It launched a period of great economic and social upheaval, overlapping with the social upheaval of the Depression in the United States. A number of Mexican artists, trained in Mexico but influenced by European art of the time, sought to revive fresco painting, and in this they were supported by the Mexican government.

Diego Rivera's enormous frescoed murals in many public buildings in Mexico and the United States typify this style. *Detroit Industry* **(205)**, an ambitious four-wall panorama at the Detroit Institute of Arts, illustrates the grand scale and monumental quality that often characterize mural painting. Conceived as a tribute to the city and the worker, Rivera's mural has a complex iconography. The detail shown here portrays the manufacture of the 1932 Ford V-8 automobile. Every step of the job, every event in the worker's day is represented, from the punching of the time clock through steel processing, molding, welding, drilling—even the lunch break. The mural treatment bestows a grandeur on the everyday operations of the assembly line. In fact, the frescoed mural probably served Rivera's expressive needs better than any other medium could have done.

EGG TEMPERA

Anyone who has washed breakfast dishes knows about the adhesive strength and quick drying of egg yolk. A painting medium based on egg yolk, called tempera, was preferred by artists throughout the medieval period, until the introduction of oil paint. Egg tempera's yellow color, surprisingly, does not distort a pigment color, and, also surprisingly, tempera works tend to yellow less with age than do those in oil. Paintings done in tempera hundreds of years ago retain their brilliant glow and clear colors. The one disadvantage is that tempera is not as flexible as oil or the synthetics, not nearly as convenient in the application. Oils or acrylics can be laid on in large strokes, small strokes, thick or thin. But in tempera forms must be built up slowly with small, individual brush strokes. For those few contemporary artists who care to take the trouble, the rewards are gratifying.

One such artist is Jacob Lawrence. We saw one of his powerful tempera panels from *The Migration Series* in Chapter 3 **(59)**. Vibrant tempera colors also provide the "raw, sharp, rough" effect the artist has said he wanted in his *Theater* series, from which we illustrate the panel called *Vaudeville* **(206)**. The black community of Harlem, in upper Manhattan, had an exceptionally active theatrical life in the 1940s and early 1950s. Stage shows called vaudeville—combining comedy sketches, musical numbers, and other types of entertainment—were popular. In this work Lawrence presents his two costumed performers against a wildly decorative, multi-patterned backdrop. His colorful patterning shows us that the world of the theater is magical, special, utterly different from the humdrum of everyday existence.

Another 20th-century artist who has made tempera his special medium is Andrew Wyeth. Wyeth's painting *Braids* **(207)** shows the luminous technique at its best. *Braids* is part of a large cache of paintings and drawings that Wyeth had kept secret from most of the art world for fifteen years until a surprise showing in 1986. Nearly all the works depict a woman known as Helga. *Braids* shows Helga's face and upper torso painted in the most painstaking tempera technique. Individual brush strokes highlight single strands of hair, eyelashes, and threads in the sweater, and the face has an almost claylike texture from innumerable tiny strokes of paint. Helga seems natural and lifelike, yet we do not expect her to come to life, to move or turn her head. She is frozen in time by the meticulous rendering of the paint.

right: 206. Jacob Lawrence.
Vaudeville, from the *Theater* series. 1951–52.
Egg tempera on fiberboard, $29\frac{7}{8} \times 20''$.
Hirshhorn Museum and Sculpture Garden,
Smithsonian Institution, Washington, D.C.
(gift of Joseph H. Hirshhorn, 1966).

below: 207. Andrew Wyeth. *Braids.* 1979.
Egg tempera on canvas, $16\frac{1}{2} \times 20\frac{1}{2}''$.
Copyright © 1986 Leonard E. B. Andrews.

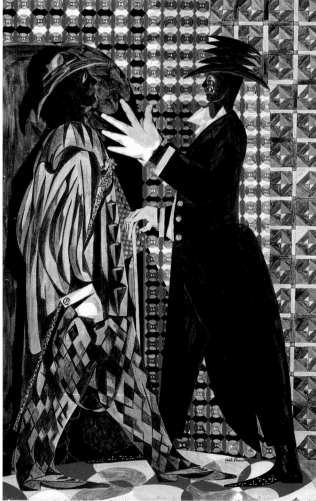

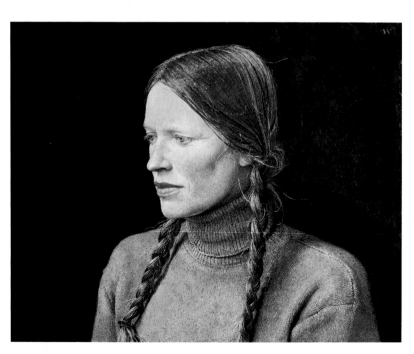

JACOB LAWRENCE

b. 1917

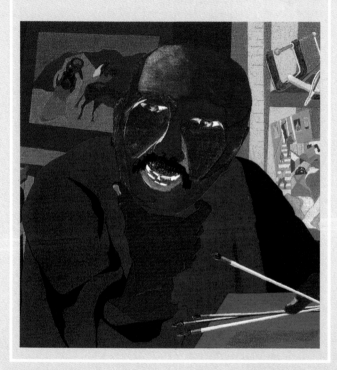

T HE NAME "HARLEM" is associated in many people's minds with hardship and poverty. Poverty Harlem has always known, but during the 1920s it experienced a tremendous cultural upsurge that has come to be called the Harlem Renaissance. So many of the greatest names in black culture—musicians, writers, artists, poets, scientists—lived or worked in Harlem at the time, or simply took their inspiration from its intellectual energy. To Harlem, about 1930, came a young teenager named Jacob Lawrence, relocating from Philadelphia with his mother, brother, and sister. The flowering of the Harlem Renaissance had passed, but there remained enough momentum to help turn the child of a poor family into one of the most distinguished American artists of his generation.

Young Lawrence's home life was not happy, but he had several islands of refuge: the public library, the Harlem Art Workshop, and the Metropolitan Museum of Art. He studied at the Harlem Art Workshop from 1932 to 1934 and received much encouragement from two noted black artists, Charles Alston and Augusta Savage. By the age of twenty Lawrence had begun to exhibit his work. A year later he, like so many others, was being supported by the W.P.A. Art Project, a government-sponsored program to help artists get through the economic void of the Great Depression.

Even this early in his career, Lawrence had established the themes that would dominate his work. The subject matter comes from his own experience, from black experience: the hardships of poor people in the ghettos, the violence that greeted blacks moving from the South to the urban North, the upheaval of the civil rights movement during the 1960s. Nearly always his art has a narrative content or "story," and often the titles are lengthy. Although Lawrence does paint individual pictures, the bulk of his production has been in series, such as *The Migration Series* (59) and *Theater,* some of them having as many as sixty images.

The year 1941 was significant for Lawrence's life and career. He married the painter Gwendolyn Knight, and he acquired his first dealer, when Edith Halpert of the Downtown Gallery in New York featured him in a major exhibition. The show was successful, and it resulted in the purchase of Lawrence's *Migration* series by two important museums.

From that point Lawrence's career prospered. His paintings always have been in demand, and he is sought after as an illustrator of magazine covers, posters, and books. His influence continues through his teaching— first at Black Mountain College in North Carolina, later at Pratt Institute, the Art Students League, and the University of Washington. In 1978 he was elected to the National Council on the Arts.

Many people would call Lawrence's paintings instruments of social protest, but his images, however stark, have more the character of reporting than of protest. It is as though he is telling us, "this is what happened, this is the way it is." What happened, of course, happened to black Americans, and Lawrence the world-famous painter does not seem to lose sight of Lawrence the poor youth in Harlem. As he has said, "My belief is that it is most important for an artist to develop an approach and philosophy about life—if he has developed this philosophy he does not put paint on canvas, he puts himself on canvas."[1]

Jacob Lawrence. *Self-Portrait,* detail. 1977.
Gouache on paper, 23 × 31".
National Academy of Design, New York.

OIL

A popular legend says that oil painting was invented early in the 15th century by the great Netherlandish artist Jan van Eyck, who experimented with it for this portrait **(208)**. However, Van Eyck probably learned the technique from another artist and merely perfected it himself. From that time and for about five hundred years the word "painting" was virtually synonymous with "oil painting." Only in the 1950s, with the introduction of acrylics (plastic resin paints), was the supremacy of oil challenged, and even then many artists clung to their oil paints.

The outstanding characteristic of oil paint is that it dries very slowly. This creates both advantages and disadvantages for the artist. On the plus side, it means that colors can be blended subtly, layers of paint can be applied on top of other layers with little danger of separating or cracking, and the artist can rework sections of the painting almost indefinitely. This same asset becomes a liability when the artist is pressed for time—perhaps when an exhibition has been scheduled. Oil paint dries so *very* slowly that it may be weeks or months before the painting has truly "set."

Another great advantage of oil is that it can be worked in an almost infinite range of consistencies, from very thick to very thin. The German Expressionist painter Oskar Kokoschka often used thick oil paints straight from

left: 208. Jan van Eyck. *Man in a Red Turban (Self-Portrait?).* 1433. Oil on panel, $10\frac{1}{4} \times 7\frac{1}{2}''$. The National Gallery, London (reproduced by courtesy of the Trustees).

right: 209. Oskar Kokoschka. *Self-Portrait.* 1917. Oil on canvas, $31\frac{1}{8} \times 24\frac{3}{4}''$. Von der Heydt Museum, Wuppertal, Germany.

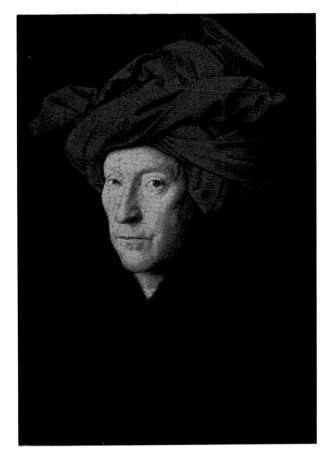

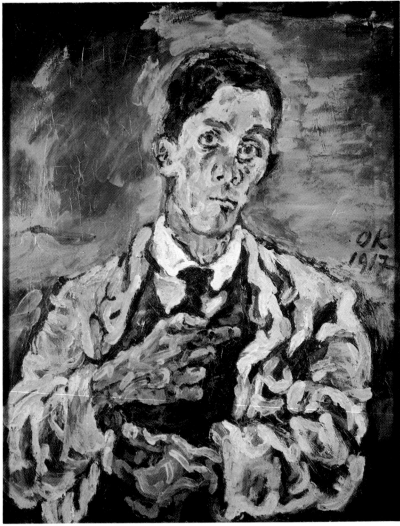

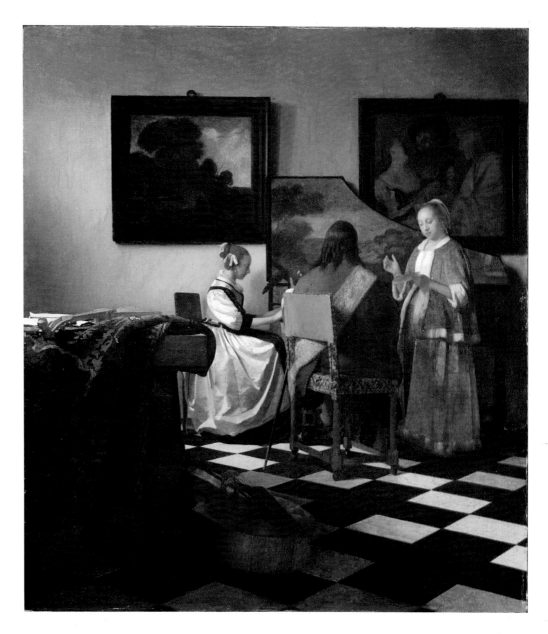

the tube, occasionally squeezing them directly on the canvas without a brush **(209).** He could then mold and shape the thick paint with a palette knife (a spatula-shaped tool) to create actual three-dimensional depth on the canvas. Any thick application of paint is referred to as ***impasto,*** and Kokoschka's is an extreme version of this. The ability to use paint in this way was important for Kokoschka's expression, because the sinewy coils of paint in the *Self-Portrait* trace the artist's passionate exploration of his inner self. Even his coat seems to writhe and twist around him. A smoother medium could not so define his anguished personality.

Oil paint can with equal ease be diluted and applied in very thin layers called ***glazes.*** By painting glaze upon glaze the artist can achieve a sense of depth, a subtle coloration, and a luminous quality that are quite different from the effect of impasto application. This was the technique of many European artists during the 16th and 17th centuries. We find a masterful example in Jan Vermeer's *Concert* **(210).** The warm, rich glow of this work comes from the application of many glazes and is intensified by Vermeer's method of placing tiny light dots of opaque paint as highlights. Like many artists of his time, Vermeer was much concerned with naturalism, and the thin application of oil paint in layers lends itself to lifelike portrayal.

210. Jan Vermeer. *The Concert.* c. 1660. Oil on canvas, 28 × 24¾". Isabella Stewart Gardner Museum, Boston. (Stolen from the museum March 18, 1990; not recovered as of this writing.)

When oil paints were first introduced in the early 15th century, most artists, including Jan van Eyck (208), continued working on wood panels, the surfaces they had been accustomed to using for tempera. Gradually, however, artists adopted the more flexible canvas, which offered two great advantages. For one thing, the changing styles favored larger and larger paintings. Whereas wood panels were heavy and liable to crack, the lighter linen canvas could be stretched to almost unlimited size. Second, as artists came to serve distant patrons, their canvases could be rolled up for easy and safe shipment.

The huge number of "old master" paintings in museums may lead us to think of oil as an old-fashioned medium—out of style and not relevant for artists at the turn of the millennium. Alice Neel's picture of the *Westreich Family* (211) challenges this notion. If we did not know this painting's medium, we might be tempted to say it was one of the newer synthetic paints, especially seeing it in reproduction. The rather flat color areas and sharp defining lines around the figures, the arbitrary blues and greens on flesh—these seem too "modern" somehow for oil paint. But that is just the point: oil has the flexibility to be a great many things. In this thoroughly contemporary painting, oil seems every bit as modern as any substance invented by chemistry.

As is typical of a Neel portrait, this image gives a portrait of the whole body, not just the face, and the group portrait is particularly interesting for its psychological insights into the family dynamic. Neel invites us to study these people and speculate about their relationships. How do these family members feel about each other? Are they close or distant? Are some members bound together while others stand outside the family group? Who are the dominant members? The artist provides us with a number of clues. Notice how the various members of the family hold their hands, their arms, their shoulders, their legs and feet. Observe the ways their bodies lean and the direction of their gaze. See how each of the subjects is dressed. Considered this way, a modern portrait in oil becomes a fascinating study in character.

211. Alice Neel. *Westreich Family.* 1978. Oil on canvas, 3'11" × 5'8". Collection Mrs. T. Westreich, Washington, D.C.

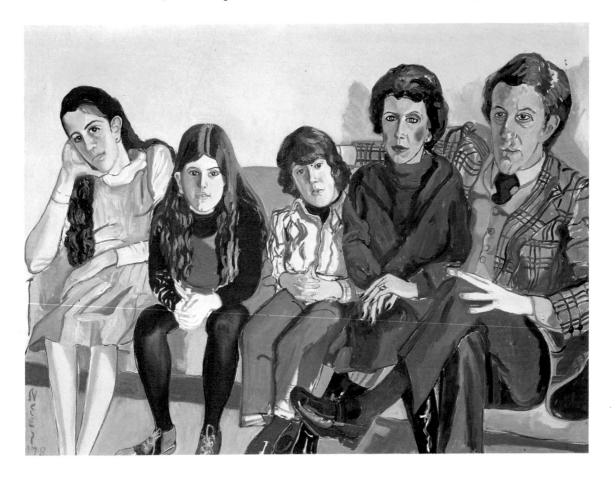

ALICE NEEL

1900–1984

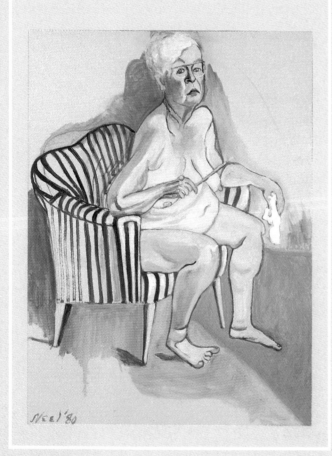

and received a thorough, if conventional, grounding in art techniques.

Her personal life, too, was conventional up to that point, but soon it changed drastically. Neel referred to the men who played important roles in her life by stereotype, rather than by name. Upon leaving art school she married "the Cuban." The couple moved to Havana, where Neel continued to paint and had her first exhibition in 1926. The Cuban marriage eventually broke up, after which Neel returned to New York and worked on the W.P.A. Art Project—the government-sponsored Depression program to help support artists. Along the way she took up with "the sailor," with whom she lived until he cut up and burned all her work. ("You know how men are, they get jealous, they're possessive.") There was also "the Puerto Rican singer." From these liaisons came four children, one of whom died in infancy. Later there would be several grandchildren, who became favorite subjects for Neel's art.

From the beginning Neel was a portraitist, although she preferred to call herself a "people painter," feeling that portraitists are looked down on. This assessment actually proved correct through most of her career. Just at the point when Neel should have been in her artistic prime—the 1940s and 1950s—abstraction had completely taken over the art world. The painter of figures was out of fashion and remained so for at least twenty years. Not until 1974, at the age of seventy-four, did Neel have her first important show—at the Whitney Museum in New York. The show included some fifteen pictures that had not previously been "off the shelf." Alice Neel waited a long time to hear an important critic name her as the best portrait painter of the 20th century, and then she herself did not contradict that statement. The pictures, however, have transcended portrait status in the sense of recording someone's looks. They are major paintings that happen to have people as their subjects.

Quite obviously, Alice Neel was an original, an exceptionally self-directed artist and human being. Neither her personal life nor her career was modeled after any example, nor did she follow anything but her own inclinations: "When they asked me if I had influences I said I never copy anybody. I never did, because I feel that the most important thing about art and in art—and I tell students this—is to find your own road."[2]

W HEN AN ACQUAINTANCE once remarked that Alice Neel painted "like a man," the artist retorted, "No, I don't paint like a man; but I don't paint like they expect a woman to paint." As a matter of fact, this extraordinary woman spent a long lifetime doing the unexpected, with cheerful disregard for the prevailing mores and fashions.

Alice Neel was born in Merion Square, Pennsylvania, the daughter of a proper middle-class family that she described as "anti-bohemian." She studied at what was then the Philadelphia School of Design for Women—"a school where rich girls went before they got married"—

Alice Neel. *Self-Portrait*. 1980. Oil on canvas, 4′6″ × 3′4″.
National Portrait Gallery, Smithsonian Institution, Washington, D.C.

WATERCOLOR

Watercolor is thought of as an intimate art, usually small in scale and executed with great freedom and spontaneity. Watercolor straddles the border between painting and drawing.

The pigments for watercolor are suspended in gum arabic (a gummy plant substance), thinned with water, and painted with a flowing motion onto paper of good quality. Generally, the watercolor is translucent, so that much of the white paper shows through. Watercolors are meant to be done quickly, according to the inspiration of the moment. Mistakes cannot easily be corrected, and overworking spoils the spontaneity of the medium.

Watercolor has been an important part of traditional Japanese painting, where it is often combined with ink or ink washes (sweeps of diluted ink). Japanese brushwork lends itself especially well to a rapid, assured execution. In 15th-century Japan, landscape painting in watercolor and ink reached a high point of development, and the great master of the style was Sesshu. His *Autumn Landscape* **(212)** is a wonderfully composed arrangement of diagonals—one from the trees at upper right to the ground at lower left, another

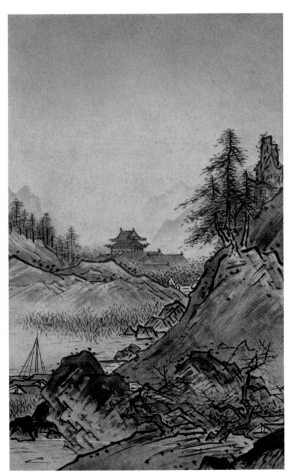

left: 212. Sesshu. *Autumn Landscape.*
Late 15th century.
Ink and color on paper, height 18⅛".
National Museum, Tokyo.

below: 213. John Marin.
From the Bridge, New York City. 1933.
Watercolor on paper, 21⅞ × 26¾".
Wadsworth Atheneum, Hartford, Conn.
(The Ella Gallup Sumner
and Mary Catlin Sumner Collection Fund).

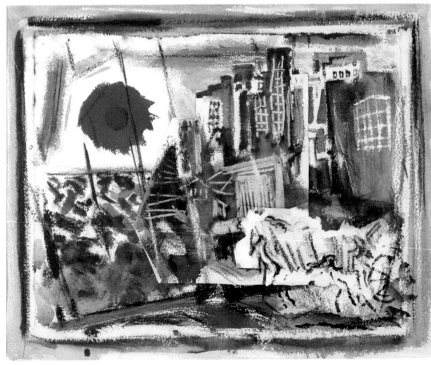

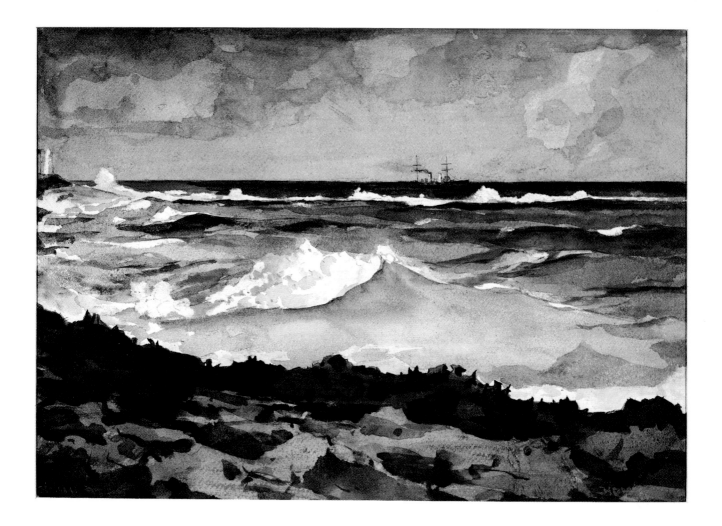

cutting from middle left to intersect with the first and focus attention on the pagoda near the center of the painting. Throughout the painting Sesshu's brushwork is sharp and assured. Only a few strokes are needed to show us the essence of forms.

Like oil, watercolor is a flexible medium, capable of yielding very different effects in the hands of different artists. Two American painters in particular, John Marin and Winslow Homer, were noted for their watercolors; in fact, Marin worked primarily in this medium. Their careers overlapped in time, and both were active at the beginning of this century. But if you compare their paintings, you will see a contrast and understand how each artist drew from the watercolor technique the expression he wanted.

Marin's cityscapes, such as *From the Bridge, New York City* (213), capture the essence and the spirit of the metropolis, rather than its actual appearance. Full of vigor and energy and exciting diagonals, they make us feel the city's pulse, its movement. The brushwork is loose and free, with form only barely sketched in. Marin's style exploits the fluidity of watercolor to its fullest.

Homer's watercolor style could be quite literally "watery," because this artist is famed for his seascapes. In *Shore and Surf, Nassau* (214) he paints the froth and foam of waves breaking over coral reefs onto the rocky coast of the Bahamas. The translucent watercolor medium allows the white of the paper to show through just as natural light might penetrate the brilliant azure and emerald colors of this tropical sea. Although the water and clouds seem turbulent, Homer typically breaks their movement with a serene horizon line, along which, here, a ship steams placidly. His handling of watercolor is more controlled than Marin's, yet it still conveys the excitement of an untamed seacoast.

214. Winslow Homer.
Shore and Surf, Nassau. 1899.
Watercolor, $15 \times 21\frac{3}{8}''$.
The Metropolitan Museum
of Art, New York
(Amelia B. Lazarus Fund, 1910).

GOUACHE

When opaque (nontranslucent) white is added to watercolors, the result is known as gouache. The white may be either mixed with the paints or coated on the support before the watercolors are applied. Because gouache is exceptionally quick-drying, it is well suited for sketches and preliminary drawings, but this also means that brush strokes do not blend well. The artist must adapt to this characteristic by placing colors and forms side by side.

We see this effect of pure color areas in *A Nobleman Riding an Elephant* **(215)**, a splendid miniature painted in India about 1600 by Khem Karan. Both the prancing elephant (with all its finery) and the three figures are described in clear, flat colors like those of a poster. The flatness, however, does not detract at all from the sense of jaunty, spirited movement in this charming work.

SYNTHETIC MEDIA

215. Khem Karan.
A Nobleman Riding an Elephant.
c. 1600. Gouache on paper,
$12\frac{1}{4} \times 18\frac{1}{2}''$.
The Metropolitan Museum of Art,
New York (Rogers Fund, 1925).

The enormous developments made in chemistry during the early 20th century had an impact in artists' studios. All painting media available up to that time showed certain limitations. Oil, the most widely used, had the disadvantage of excessively slow drying time. The new synthetic media offered the promise of more control—control of fluidity, color fidelity, drying time, and durability. It should be noted, however, that there is still no *one* perfect medium for all types of expression and for all artists. The introduction of synthetic media, especially the acrylics, has simply expanded the range of possibilities.

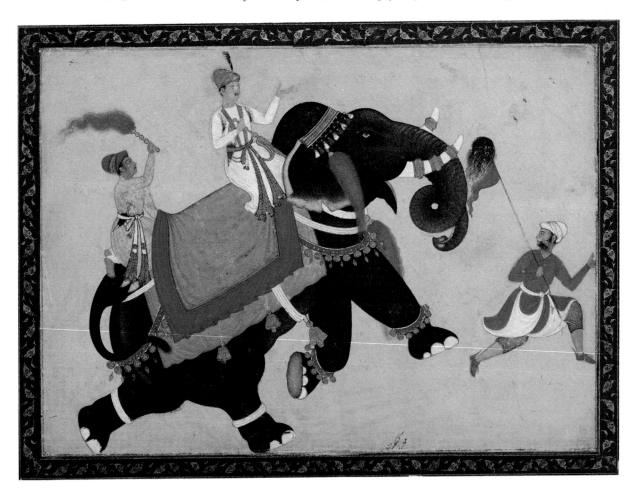

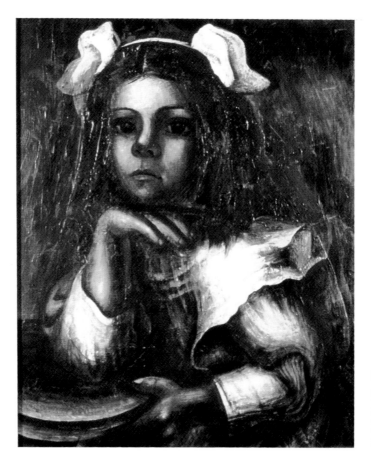

216. David Alfaro Siqueiros. *María Asúnsolo as a Child.* 1935. Duco on plywood, $39\frac{3}{4} \times 29\frac{1}{2}''$. Collection María Asúnsolo, Mexico City.

By the 1930s the chemical industry had learned to make strong, weatherproof paint based on plastic resins, as well as new fadeproof colors for use in industry. The first painter known to have adapted these paints to art was the Mexican artist David Alfaro Siqueiros. In Los Angeles in 1932 Siqueiros organized his students into an industrial crew to paint outdoor murals with plastic resin paints, using slide projectors to transfer designs to the walls and spray guns to apply the paint. The murals, like those of Rivera, were meant to convey a social message. But the most revolutionary part of Siqueiros' work was the way the murals were made. The acrylic paints many artists use today are a development of these early synthetic resins, with similar characteristics of quick drying and resistance to weather and fading.

Siqueiros also pioneered in the use of synthetic paints for smaller works, such as the portrait illustrated here **(216).** The quick-drying Duco paint allowed him to build up rich surface textures, strong value contrasts, and an almost sculptural quality—all of which would be possible but far more laborious in oil.

Synthetic paints were still a novelty in the 1930s, but within twenty years they had become a fact of everyday life and work for artists. The most popular synthetic paints are the water-base acrylics, which were introduced in the 1950s. Acrylics offer quick drying time (though not as unmanageably quick as that of the earlier synthetic resins), pure and intense colors, and great flexibility in methods of application. While many artists still paint with conventional brushes, others have adapted the acrylic medium to pouring, throwing, or dripping. Thinned down, acrylics can be shot through an airbrush—a tool that sprays a controlled mist of paint—as in the work of Audrey Flack **(46).** It has been suggested that the "hard-edge" painting of the 1960s **(550)** could not have been developed without acrylic paints, because they permit the artist to block off areas with masking tape to achieve an absolutely straight line. The masking tape could not be put down on top of slower-drying oils or most other media.

Helen Frankenthaler's painting *Nature Abhors a Vacuum* **(217)** shows how acrylic can behave when it is thinned to the consistency of a dye or stain and poured onto canvas, which partially absorbs the color. In this work there is little actual surface texture; any suggestion of pictorial depth comes from the interplay of colors, not from recognizable shapes. The forms are organic, creating a color landscape of their own within the rectangle of the painting, but they make no specific reference to the natural landscape. Free-flowing washes of paint spread and overlap on the canvas in what appears to be an immediate, spontaneous burst of imagery and color. Like Jackson Pollock **(38,539)**, Frankenthaler often places her canvases flat on the floor, the better to control the flow of paint.

Acrylics also can be applied to many kinds of supports (not just canvas), and they combine well with other techniques and media. For example, Faith Ringgold's *Purple Quilt* **(218)** is actually what the title says—fabrics pieced together and quilted, serving as a framework for the artist's rows of figures painted in acrylic. *The Purple Quilt* is a tribute to Alice Walker's novel *The Color Purple*. One of a series of "painted story quilts," it is meant to celebrate not only women's experience but also black experience. For Ringgold, the quilt format ties contemporary art into the long tradition of (women's) handcraft work, thus breaking down the barrier between "fine" and "applied" arts. This format also provides a grid structure to unify the rows of people, all staring straight ahead, who inhabit the artist's quilts and who, she reports, are representative of the faces she sees while walking through Harlem. Ringgold intends the viewer to "read" her quilt, as one would read a book or play. And, like many contemporary artists, she is pushing out the boundaries of conventional painting media in order to tell her story.

217. Helen Frankenthaler. *Nature Abhors a Vacuum.* 1973. Acrylic on canvas, 8'7½" × 9'4½". Private collection, courtesy André Emmerich Gallery, New York.

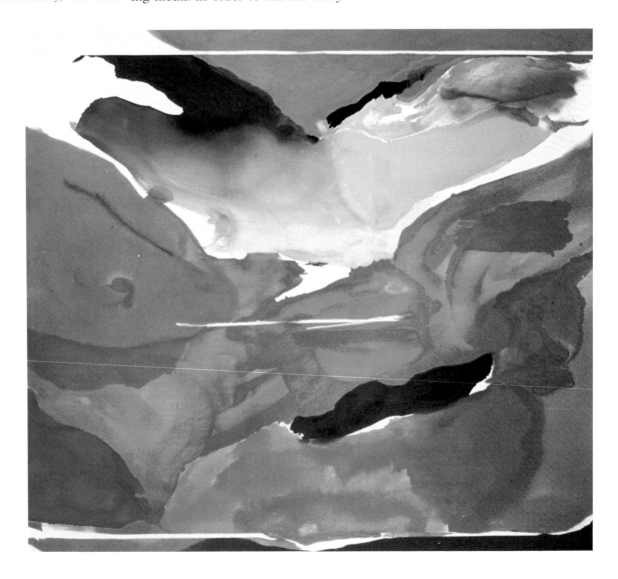

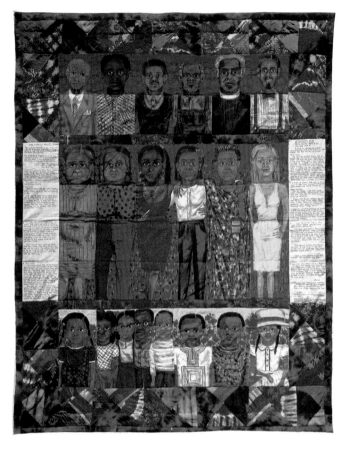

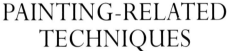

PAINTING-RELATED TECHNIQUES

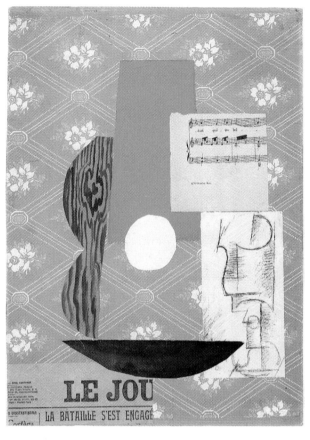

There are several techniques that might be considered cousins of painting, in that they are used to create designs or pictorial images on a predominantly two-dimensional surface. One is *tapestry,* a method employing woven threads, which will be considered in Chapter 12. Two others are *collage* and *mosaic.*

COLLAGE

Collage is a French word that means "pasting" or "gluing." In art terms it refers to the practice of attaching objects, such as bits of paper or cloth, to the surface of a canvas or other support, as well as to the resultant artwork. Nowadays we are accustomed to such works, but there was a time when they seemed revolutionary.

During the early part of the 20th century the artists Pablo Picasso and Georges Braque worked together very closely for several years (pp. 468–469). Their collaboration was fueled by a strong rivalry, with each artist trying to outdo the other in stretching the boundaries of modern art. Apparently it was Braque who first hit upon the idea of pasting real everyday materials onto his canvases, but Picasso wasted no time taking up the challenge.

Guitar, Sheet Music, and Glass **(219)** is one of Picasso's earliest collages, perhaps the very first. In the lower left corner he has pasted a bit of the daily newspaper (in French, *Le Journal*), with the headline *"La Bataille s'est engagé"* (the battle is begun). As printed, the headline referred to the current Balkan wars, but what did Picasso mean? Did he go to battle to enrich the possibilities of art by the then-shocking practice of gluing objects to canvas? Or was his battle that of upstaging his ambitious colleague? Probably some of both. Elsewhere Picasso includes a corner torn from sheet music (both artists were absorbed by musical themes), a wood-grain fragment suggesting a guitar, and a

left: 218. Faith Ringgold.
The Purple Quilt. 1986.
Acrylic on cotton canvas,
tie-dyed, printed, and pieced
fabrics; 7'7" × 6'.
Collection Bernice Steinbaum.

right: 219. Pablo Picasso.
Guitar, Sheet Music, and Glass.
1912. Pasted paper, gouache,
and charcoal; $18\frac{7}{8} \times 14\frac{3}{4}"$.
Collection of the McNay Art Museum,
San Antonio, Tex.
(bequest of Marion Koogler McNay).

sketch of a wine glass. All are pasted on a colored paper resembling wallpaper. Despite Picasso's sly allusion to a "battle," we should not read any deep symbolic significance into this collection of items. The artist's main goal was to assemble forms into a visual composition that satisfied him.

After Picasso and Braque, many artists adopted this method of composing a picture by gathering bits and pieces from various sources. Two of the most prominent, whose work we have already seen in this book, are Romare Bearden **(138)** and Miriam Schapiro **(148)**.

MOSAIC

The mosaic artist "paints" by assembling small colored stones, bits of glass, or colored clay tiles **(tesserae)** into a pattern or pictorial image. Usually, mosaic works are set in a wall or ceiling—or even a floor, because the durability of the material allows it to be walked upon.

Mosaic art is commonly associated with the ancient Romans and with the Byzantine Empire in Europe, starting in the 4th century. We will see a superb example of the Byzantine style, the portrait of Empress Theodora at Ravenna, in Chapter 16 **(450)**. For a Roman example, surprisingly familiar in its imagery, we turn to the villa at Piazza Armerina in Sicily. *Young Women Exercising* **(220)**, dating from the early 4th century C.E., depicts a scene not all that different from what we might see today at the gym or the beach. Three young women, admirably fit and toned, dressed in what we are tempted to call bikinis, go through their workouts. One is clearly running with hand weights. The "painting" style of this work is perhaps a bit crude, especially in the faces, which seem almost a generic version of "female face." Still, the artist, working in tiny stones, has managed a subtle shading in the bodies to show their muscularity, and the figures appear lively and animated.

This brief survey should have demonstrated that the various painting media and the artists who use them yield endless possibilities. It would be difficult to say which comes first—that artist's imagery or the material. Did the first cave artist have the impulse to paint something and search about for a material with which to do it? Or did the cave artist find some pigmented material and then speculate about what would happen if the substance were applied to a wall? The answer is not important, but the two aspects—idea and medium—feed upon each other. No visual image could be realized without the medium in which to make it concrete. And no medium would be of any consequence without the artist's idea—and the compelling urge to paint.

220. *Young Women Exercising,* from the Roman villa at Piazza Armerina, Sicily. Early 4th century C.E. Mosaic.

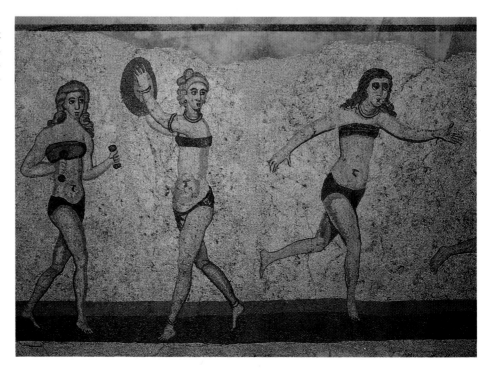

Prints

I F YOU HAVE EVER received a handmade greeting card for Christmas, for a birthday, or as an invitation to a party, then you will appreciate the difference between an art print and a mass-produced reproduction. Commercial greeting cards are cranked out by the thousands, even millions, by the major card manufacturers. But many people like to make their own cards with their own original designs. Usually they will *print* the cards by some type of stamping process. The design is carved out on a printing block made of wood, linoleum, or even the cut side of a potato, leaving some areas raised as in a rubber stamp. Then the printing block is coated with ink and pressed carefully onto paper to make the card.

An image made this way is special. For one thing, the design is unique—a personal expression of the individual who conceived it. Also, each card will be slightly different from all the others because of variations in pressure, inking, placement on the paper, and steadiness of the hand. There is a human touch, which we find missing from commercial products. For each separate image, *one* person made it, judged its quality, and was satisfied. All these factors apply equally to art prints.

Prints differ from most other works of art in two important respects. First, they are made by an indirect process. The artist does not draw or paint directly on the work of art but instead creates the surface that *makes* the work of art. (In some cases the artist may add special touches to each print, but this is not the most common practice.) Second, the printing process results in many nearly identical images, which is why it is called an art of **multiples.** Each image—called an impression—is considered an original work of art. This latter point is crucial to an understanding of art prints, so we need to discuss it more fully.

Before the 1950s there were no strict guidelines for what could genuinely be labeled an "original" print. In the past several decades, however, certain criteria have been established, and the value of contemporary prints has much to do with their adherence to these criteria. The guidelines were set up in an attempt to avoid abuses that had crept into the print market, such as inferior, shoddy, or inauthentic works being passed off as fine art.

Printmaking procedures now are rigidly controlled. The artist works on a plate or stone or some other surface to make the image. Then the image is printed on paper, by hand or by a hand-operated machine, either by the artist or by someone under the artist's immediate supervision. Each print is examined to make sure it meets the artist's standards, and any faulty impressions are destroyed. Usually the artist and printer decide in advance how many impressions will be made—ten, fifty, a hundred or more—and this number is referred to as the **edition.** The size of the edition may be determined by the material used for printing. Hard metal can print many perfect impressions, but a softer material, such as linoleum, will begin to wear down, resulting in a blurred image. Once the planned number of prints has been made, the plate or block is *canceled* (by scratching cross marks on it) or destroyed so that no more prints can be struck. Finally, the artist signs each print individually and numbers each one. For example, if you buy a print marked 10/100, you will know you have the tenth print made in an edition of one hundred. Prints made earlier in the edition are sometimes considered more valuable.

The type of print we are talking about must be distinguished from posters and other reproductions made by mechanical or photographic processes, such as the illustrations in this book. You can buy a color reproduction of a Rembrandt or Picasso painting, or a poster featuring a rock star or film personality, but these are not prints in the sense that we are discussing in this chapter, not original works of art. The artist who made the images has no supervision over the printing process and may not even know about it. The quality of the reproduction is nowhere near as meticulously controlled as that of an art print. Such reproductions are useful for study purposes, and they often give pleasure, but they have little artistic or monetary value.

Today's art print, above all, is designed to *be* a print. It is not a copy of a work done in some other medium, although it may be adapted from an image in another medium. Some artists, for instance, will take a theme they have used in painting and explore its possibilities in prints, but in this case the artist adjusts the image to fit the physical qualities and expressive potential of the particular print medium chosen.

Like drawings, prints are a great boon to the art lover and the collector. At a time when original paintings by well-known artists are beyond the means of any but the very rich, prints by established artists often can be purchased for just a few hundred dollars. (The most fashionable artists command many thousands of dollars for each print, but this price range is limited to a small group.) Young collectors starting out, and even large corporations with huge resources, have eagerly taken to buying prints. They may be a sound financial investment, but far more important is the fact that they give aesthetic pleasure and the joy of owning original art.

There are four basic methods for making an art print (**221**)—relief, intaglio, lithography, and screenprinting. In this chapter we shall look at each in turn and then consider a few advanced and combined techniques.

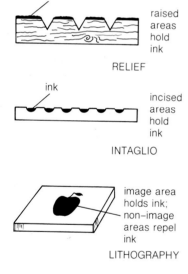

RELIEF

raised areas hold ink

INTAGLIO

incised areas hold ink

LITHOGRAPHY

image area holds ink; non–image areas repel ink

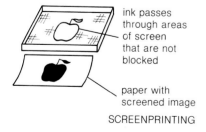

SCREENPRINTING

ink passes through areas of screen that are not blocked

paper with screened image

221. The four basic print methods: relief, intaglio, lithography, and screenprinting.

RELIEF

The term *relief* describes any printing method in which the image to be printed is *raised* from a background (**221**). Think of a rubber stamp. When you look at the stamp itself, you may see the words "First Class" or "Special Delivery" standing out from the background in reverse. You press the stamp to an ink pad, then to paper, and the words print right side out—a mirror image of the stamp. All relief processes work according to this general principle.

Any surface from which the background areas can be carved away is suitable for relief printing. Eskimo artists in Canada's Northwest Territories work with flat stones, cutting and chipping away the background until only the image areas remain in relief. Then the stone is inked, and paper is laid on top and carefully rubbed by hand to make the print.

Stone provides an extremely durable printing surface, capable of yielding a virtually endless number of clear impressions. However, the difficulty of carving stone hampers the creation of fine details. Eskimo prints are valued for their bold and stylized designs (222). When printmakers seek greater flexibility in cutting and image-making, they generally turn to the material most commonly associated with relief printing: wood.

WOODCUT

To make a woodcut the artist first draws the desired image on a block of wood. Then all the areas that are not meant to print are cut and gouged out of the wood so that the image stands out in relief. When the block is inked, only the raised areas take the ink. Finally, the block is pressed on paper, or paper is placed on the block and rubbed to transfer the ink and make the print.

Woodcut is the oldest of the printmaking methods, having been developed in the Western world as soon as paper became available, about 1400. In fact, even before papermaking techniques were introduced in Europe, wood blocks were used to stamp designs on textiles. It was a simple transition from cloth to paper, and so the new art form advanced rapidly.

Early woodcut prints were used for both religious and secular purposes. Until the 15th century only the very rich could afford to own religious pictures, which had to be drawn by hand. Prints put such images into the reach of anyone who wanted them. Similarly, woodcuts ended the upper classes' monopoly on certain games of amusement. Playing cards made from wood blocks were now accessible to the common people. Our illustration (223) shows part of the earliest surviving woodcut "deck" of cards. An anonymous master from south Germany or Austria made these cards about the middle of the 15th century. They depict the various trades—barber, baker, metalsmith—which must have made their users feel right at home while playing games of chance. The little figures, going about their work, are cheerful and charming. And while the drawing style is simple, the bodies and clothing of the tradesmen seem animated; their faces suggest individual personality.

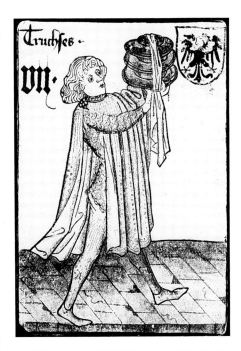

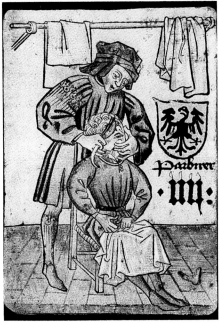

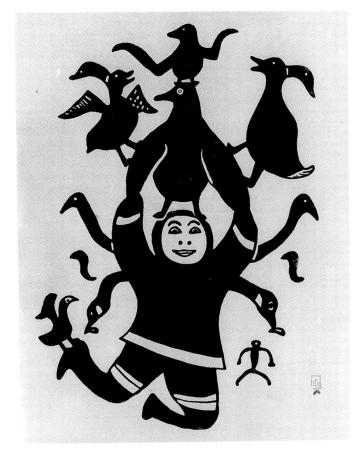

left: 222. Mungituk.
Man Carried to the Moon. 1959.
Stone relief print in black
and gray-orange, $19\frac{1}{8} \times 15''$.
The Brooklyn Museum, New York
(Dick S. Ramsay Fund).

above: 223. "Steward"
and "barber," playing cards
of a courtly pack
with illustrations of trades,
from south Germany or Austria.
1453–57. Hand-colored woodcuts,
each $5\frac{3}{8} \times 3\frac{7}{8}''$.
Kunsthistorisches Museum, Vienna.

The woodcut print reached a high point in Germany and northern Europe during the 15th and 16th centuries, with the work of such masters as Albrecht Dürer. Dürer's *Rhinoceros* **(224)** represents an attempt by a highly imaginative artist to depict a beast he had never seen, but knew only from description. The artist must surely have amused himself very much in creating such wonderful decorative detail, and his results amuse us equally today. (Dürer also worked in other print media; we saw one of his engravings in Chapter 2, **44.**)

By the 17th century prints began appearing in Asia, where Japanese artists, in particular, experimented with the new medium. During the mid-18th century Japanese printmakers perfected the technique of full-color woodcut printing, using several blocks. This method required careful planning in the design and cutting of the wood blocks.

For color printing the artist usually must cut one block for each color that is to appear in the print. On the "red" block, for instance, only the areas that are to print in red are raised; on the "blue" block only the blue areas are raised; and so forth. Then the blocks are printed one color at a time on each sheet of paper in the edition. The impressions made by the various color blocks must be lined up very carefully, one on top of the other, so there are no unintended gaps or overlapping in the finished print. This process of aligning colors is known as **registration.**

The two names most often associated with masterful Japanese woodcut prints are Hiroshige and Hokusai. Ando Hiroshige was renowned for his landscapes, such as *Rain Shower on Ohashi Bridge* **(225)**. As in many of Hiroshige's

left: **224.** Albrecht Dürer. *Rhinoceros.* 1515. Woodcut, 8⅜ × 11⅝". The Metropolitan Museum of Art, New York (gift of Junius S. Morgan, 1919).

right: **225.** Ando Hiroshige. *Rain Shower on Ohashi Bridge.* 19th century. Woodcut, 13⅞ × 9¼". © The Cleveland Museum of Art (gift from J. H. Wade).

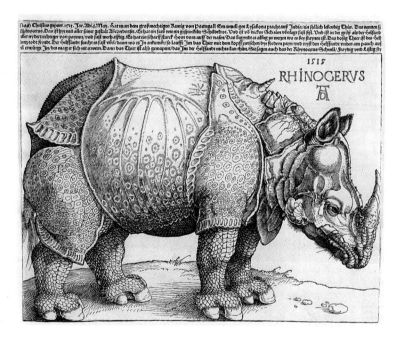

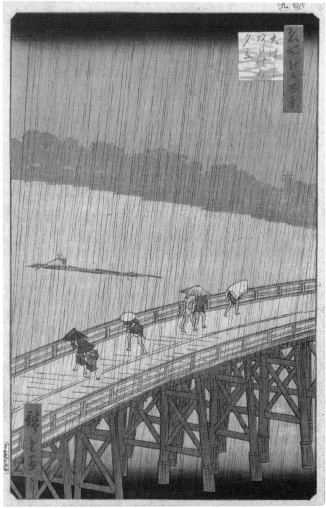

VAN GOGH ON HIROSHIGE

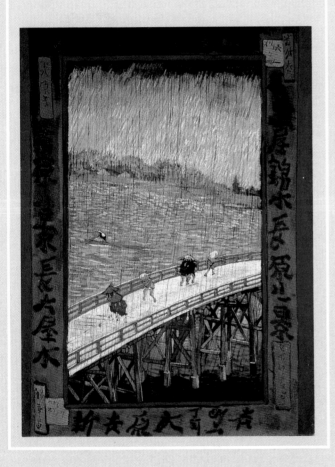

DURING THE TWO YEARS he spent in Paris, from 1886 to 1888, Vincent van Gogh became an avid collector of Japanese prints. Many artists working in France at that time admired the Japanese woodcuts, but Van Gogh, never one to do things by halves, acquired hundreds of them, hung them in his studio and in a nearby café, and made direct copies of several. One such copy is *The Bridge*, after Ando Hiroshige.

We know that Van Gogh actually traced the image from the print directly onto his canvas; some of his tracing papers have been found. This explains the very close replication of Hiroshige's forms. But what of the differences between the two works? Most obviously, the Van Gogh is an oil painting, the Hiroshige a print. On closer inspection we see that Van Gogh's brushwork has finely drawn details, especially in the water and background landscape, that do not appear in the Hiroshige.

The most striking difference, of course, is the decorative border of the painting, which was purely Van Gogh's invention. The artist filled his border with Japanese characters (including the words for "water," "again," and "auspicious"), probably copying them at random from his collection of prints and very likely without knowing their meanings. We can only guess about the aesthetic reasons for this addition. Perhaps Van Gogh wanted to make his painting "more" Japanese. The practical reason, however, was simple: Van Gogh used a standard-size French canvas, 28¾ by 21¼ inches, and he needed some visual device to fill up the spaces around Hiroshige's image area.

Vincent van Gogh. *The Bridge*. 1887. Oil on canvas, 28¾ × 21¼'''.
Vincent van Gogh Foundation,
National Museum Vincent van Gogh, Amsterdam.

prints, the work is composed primarily of diagonals—the bridge slanting from lower left to middle right, the rain slashing down at a different angle, the riverbank cutting across at yet another diagonal. The figures crossing the bridge are small and are depicted not as individuals but as people responding to, and buffeted by, the weather. In a Hiroshige landscape nature is grand and people are small. The long parallel lines of the rain give this print a wonderful rich visual texture, as does the solid understructure of criss-crossing wooden beams supporting the bridge.

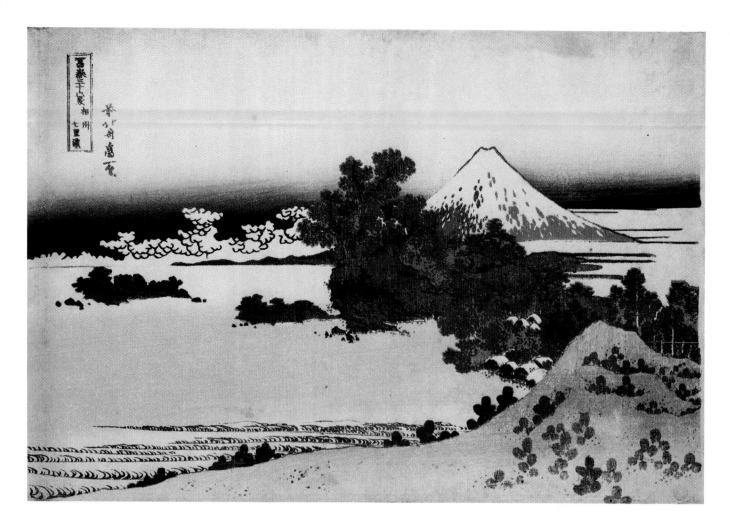

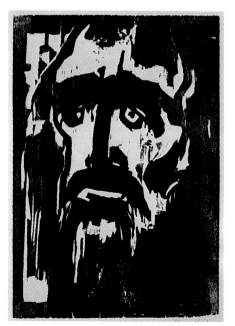

above: 226. Katsushika Hokusai. *View of Fuji from Seven-Ri Beach.* 1823–29. Color woodcut, $10\frac{1}{8} \times 15''$. The Metropolitan Museum of Art, New York (Rogers Fund, 1914).

below: 227. Emil Nolde. *The Prophet.* 1912. Woodcut, $12\frac{1}{2} \times 8\frac{13}{16}''$. © 1997 National Gallery of Art, Washington, D.C. (Rosenwald Collection).

Katsushika Hokusai also made many landscapes during his prolific career. Best known are his numerous views of Mount Fuji—the cone-shaped volcano that is the highest mountain in Japan and is considered a sacred spot to the Japanese. Hokusai drew Fuji in all seasons, in all weathers, and from many vantage points. *View of Fuji from Seven-Ri Beach* (226) presents a vista that seems not entirely of this world. The white cone of the mountain hovers tranquilly in a realm of puffy green foliage and vivid blue clouds.

Japanese woodcut prints were imported to Europe in great quantities during the latter part of the 19th century. Many artists were influenced by aspects of their style, including the emphasis on diagonals, the subtle use of asymmetrical balance (note that Fuji is thrust far to right in the composition and balanced by the calligraphy at upper left), and the areas of flat, unshaded color in many prints. These style characteristics have been absorbed into the mainstream of contemporary art, so they no longer seem "Japanese" but are part of a universal visual expression.

The German Expressionist artists of the early 20th century found in woodcut a medium uniquely compatible with their style. A splendid example is Emil Nolde's *The Prophet* (227). Expressionist imagery is stark, sometimes rough, and occasionally shocking. Woodcut readily lends itself to this style by allowing harsh contrasts of black and white as well as broad—even crude—drawing and cutting. Expressionism is just what its name implies—expressive, and also brooding, emotional, uncompromising. Of all the print methods, woodcut offers the greatest possibilities for that expression.

Because it is such an old technique, woodcut may seem dated, and not suitable for modern imagery. However, several contemporary artists have explored its possibilities. Our next example shows how the concept of the wood block can be expanded into actual three dimensions.

KATSUSHIKA HOKUSAI

1760–1849

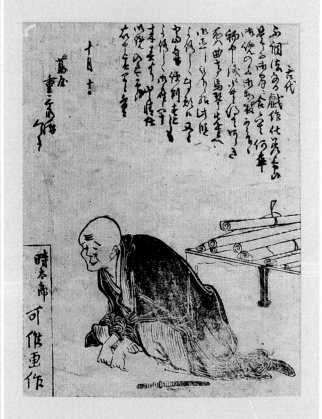

ONE OF THE MOST delightfully eccentric figures in the history of art is the Japanese painter and woodcut designer who has come to be known as Hokusai. During his eighty-nine years Hokusai lived in at least ninety different houses and used some fifty names. The name that stuck for posterity—Hokusai—means "Star of the Northern Constellation."

Hokusai was born in the city of Edo (now Tokyo), the son of a metal engraver. At the age of eighteen he was sent as an apprentice to the print designer Katsukawa Shunsho. So impressed was the master with his pupil's work that he allowed the young man to adopt part of his own name, and for several years Hokusai called himself "Shunro." Later the two quarreled, and Hokusai changed his name.

Even in his early years Hokusai always worked very quickly, producing huge quantities of drawings. As he finished a drawing, he would toss it on the floor, until there were papers scattered all over the studio, making cleaning impossible. When the house got too filthy and disorderly, he would simply move to another, followed by his long-suffering wife.

Hokusai's first book of sketches was published in 1800 and showed various scenes in and around Edo. That same year the artist produced a novel, which he sent off to a publisher accompanied by the self-portrait shown here. (Hokusai's head is shaved in the manner of Japanese artists and writers of that time.) Both books achieved a popular success, but characteristically, Hokusai never bothered to open the packets of money sent by his publisher. If a creditor stopped by, he would hand over a packet or two without counting it. Throughout his life he remained indifferent to money and despite his great accomplishments was usually at the brink of starvation.

As Hokusai's fame spread he was often invited to give public drawing demonstrations. Legends of his virtuosity abound. On one occasion, the story goes, he stood before the assembled crowd outside a temple and drew an immense image of the Buddha, using a brush as big as a broom. Another time he drew birds in flight on a single grain of rice. Hokusai's sense of humor, never far below the surface, came bubbling out when he was asked to perform for the Shogun (the military governor). As onlookers gathered at the palace, Hokusai spread a large piece of paper on the floor, painted blue watercolor waves across it, then took a live rooster, dipped its feet in red paint, and allowed it to run across the painting. Bowing respectfully, he announced to the Shogun that his creation was a picture of red maple leaves floating down the river.[1]

Though well aware of his own skill, Hokusai often amused himself by pretending modesty. In the preface to one of his books he wrote: "From the age of six I had a mania for drawing. At seventy-three I had learned a little . . . in consequence when I am eighty I shall have made still more progress, and when I am a hundred and ten, everything I do . . . will be alive." But the artist did not make it quite that far. As he lay on his deathbed, he cried out: "If Heaven would grant me ten more years!" And then: "If Heaven would grant me *five* more years, I would become a real painter."[2] His grave is marked by a slab on which is carved the last of his names: Gwakio Rojin— Old Man Mad About Drawing.

Katsushika Hokusai. *Kamado Shogun Kanryaku no Maki (Self-Portrait),* from *The Tactics of General Oven.* 1800. Woodcut, $8\frac{7}{8} \times 5\frac{7}{8}$". © 1993 The Art Institute of Chicago (Ryerson Collection).

Sandro Chia's color woodcut *Father and Son Song* **(228)** shows two figures—a colossal father seated in quiet reflection and an adventurous youth trying to climb over him. The image is meant to evoke the struggle of young artists who grapple with the towering legacy of past masters like Michelangelo and, by extension, of all artistic "fathers" and "sons." This print would be compelling in itself, but what makes it especially interesting is the frame, composed of irregular segments of wood, almost like jigsaw puzzle pieces. (Each print in the edition includes these frame pieces.) Chia's work is thus very much about wood—the blocks used for printing on paper and the shaped blocks that both encircle the image and push it out in all directions.

LINOCUT

A linoleum cut, or linocut, is very similar to a woodcut. The major difference is that the material is much softer than wood, which makes it both easier to carve and less durable in printing multiple impressions, resulting in smaller editions. Linoleum has no grain, so it is possible to make cuts in any direction with equal ease. Some artists dismiss linoleum as being suitable only for schoolchildren (or for greeting cards), but Picasso never let such preconceived ideas interfere with his creativity. His color linocut depicting a *Seated Woman (after Cranach)* **(229)** is, as the title implies, an interpretation of a painting by the 16th-century German artist Lucas Cranach, but a more abstract treatment than Cranach could ever have imagined. The splendid colors result from printing with several linoleum blocks, just as is done with color wood blocks. The richly detailed textures in the hair, arm bands, and jewelry may have been made easier to achieve by the relatively soft linoleum.

228. Sandro Chia.
Father and Son Song. 1987–89.
Color woodcut on paper,
with painted oak and plywood frame
and assemblage; 7′1¾″ × 6′3⅝″ × 4¼″.
© Board of Trustees,
National Gallery of Art,
Washington, D.C. (gift of Graphicstudio/
University of South Florida and the Artist
in Honor of the Fiftieth Anniversary
of the National Gallery of Art).
© 1998 Sandro Chia/
Licensed by VAGA, New York.

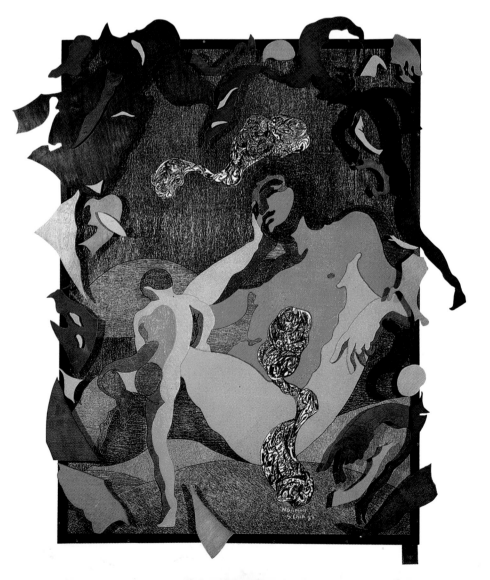

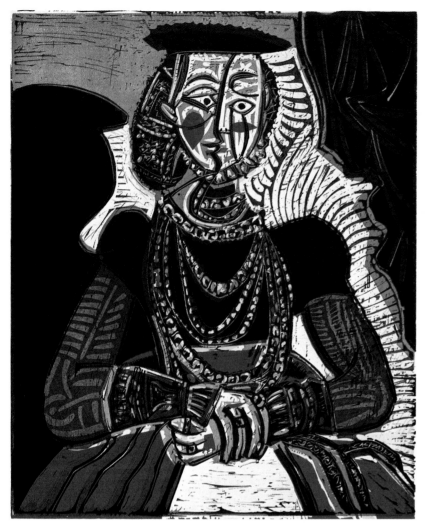

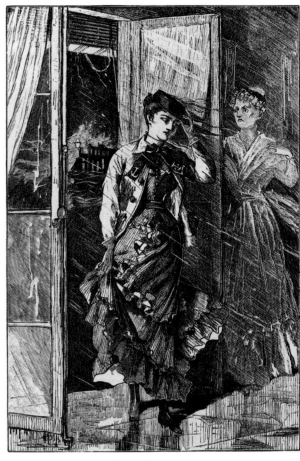

WOOD ENGRAVING

Wood engraving differs in several aspects from woodcut. For one thing, it is done on the end grain of the wood. If you imagine a board, say a 2-by-4, the long, smooth plank sides would be used for woodcut, but the grainy cut end would be used for wood engraving. The end grain can be cut in any direction without chipping or splintering, unlike the plank sides.

A distinctive characteristic of wood engraving is that it is a "white-line" technique. The tool used for cutting makes fine, narrow grooves in the wood, and these grooves, which do not take the ink, result in white lines when the inked wood block is pressed to paper. Woodcut, by contrast, usually has larger, broader, more irregular uninked white areas because of the coarser tools that gouge out background areas.

During the 19th century wood engraving was used widely for printing books and journals. The cut end of the wood could easily be prepared to be "type high"—the same height ($\frac{7}{8}$ inch) as the wooden alphabet letters that printers worked with at the time. Therefore, both images and text could conveniently be printed together. Photography was a young art, and methods for reproducing photographs had not been perfected. Most illustrations still were made in the form of prints. In the United States this art of illustration was dominated by Winslow Homer, who worked for several periodicals during the latter half of the 1800s. Homer depicted events of the Civil War, important political figures, and scenes of everyday life **(230)**.

left: 229. Pablo Picasso. *Portrait of a Young Girl, after Cranach the Younger, II.* 1958. Linoleum cut, printed in color, composition; $25\frac{11}{16} \times 21\frac{5}{16}''$. The Museum of Modern Art, New York (gift of Mr. and Mrs. Daniel Saidenberg).

right: 230. Winslow Homer. *In Came a Storm of Wind, Rain and Spray—and Portia.* Illustration in *The Galaxy,* December 1869. Wood engraving, $6\frac{1}{2} \times 4\frac{3}{8}''$. The Metropolitan Museum of Art, New York (Harris Brisbane Dick Fund, 1933).

INTAGLIO

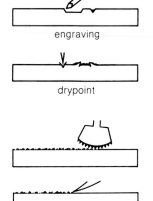

engraving

drypoint

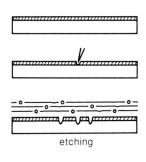

mezzotint

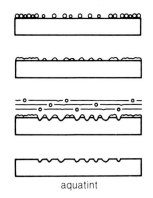

etching

aquatint

The second major category of printmaking techniques is *intaglio* (from an Italian word meaning "to cut"), which includes several related methods. Intaglio is exactly the reverse of relief, in that the areas meant to print are *below* the surface of the printing plate **(221)**. The artist uses a sharp tool or acid to make depressions—lines or grooves—in a metal plate **(231)**. When the plate is inked, the ink sinks into the depressions. Then the surface of the plate is wiped clean. When dampened paper is brought into contact with the plate under pressure, the paper is pushed into the depressions to pick up the image.

There are five basic types of intaglio printing: engraving, drypoint, mezzotint, etching, and aquatint.

ENGRAVING

The oldest of the intaglio techniques, engraving developed from the medieval practice of incising (cutting) linear designs in armor and other metal surfaces. The armorer's art had achieved a high level of expertise, and it was just a short step to realizing that the engraved lines could be filled with ink and the design transferred to paper.

The basic tool of engraving is the **burin,** a sharp, V-shaped instrument used to cut lines into the metal plate **(231)**. Shallow cuts produce a light, thin line, while deeper gouges in the metal result in a thicker and darker line. Engraving is closely related to drawing in pen or sharp pencil in both technique and the visual effect of the work. Looking at a reproduction it is hard to tell an engraving from a fine pen or pencil drawing. As in these drawing media, modeling and shading effects usually are achieved by hatching, cross-hatching, or stippling **(95)**.

During the 18th century engraved copies of well-known paintings became sought-after items for middle-class people. This development came about largely through the efforts of the English artist William Hogarth. Hogarth is best known for three large series of paintings—*The Rake's Progress, The Harlot's Progress,* and *Marriage à la Mode.* Each series was a "picture story" with a moral, and each portrayed the progress of an individual (or, in the last case, a couple) from innocent beginnings through increasing sin to complete

above: 231. Plate-making methods for intaglio printing: engraving, drypoint, mezzotint, etching, aquatint.

right: 232. William Hogarth. *The Marriage Contract,* from *Marriage à la Mode.* 1745. Engraving, $13\frac{15}{16} \times 17\frac{1}{2}''$.

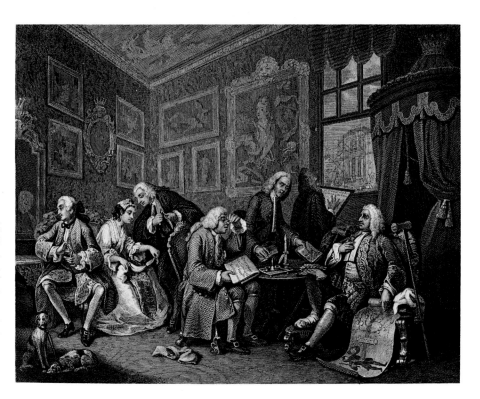

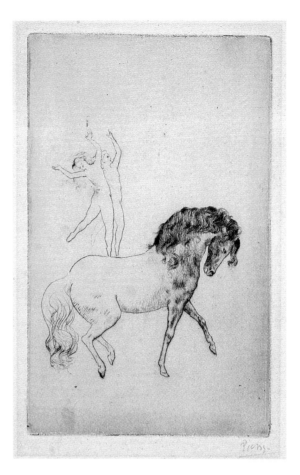

ruin. Being short of funds, Hogarth hit on the idea of making engraved copies of the paintings, copyrighting the engravings, and selling them cheaply in great quantities. This plan worked splendidly for the artist—and for the public as well, since people of limited means could now gain access to fine art.

The first scene in *Marriage à la Mode* **(232)** sets the stage for eventual disaster. A poverty-stricken nobleman is marrying off his son to the daughter of a rich but middle-class merchant. The two fathers settle the details of the marriage contract as they would any business deal. Meanwhile, the engaged couple, at left, ignore each other. Hogarth is not subtle in pointing out that this is not a love match. In fact, the future bride is already responding to the attentions of Counsellor Silvertongue, the lawyer, who will soon become her lover. Later scenes in the series portray infidelities by both partners, great excess of all kinds, a duel, and ultimately the death of the husband.

Hogarth's satire may seem a bit heavy-handed to us today, but his eye for the telling detail—such as the groom's father having a bandaged foot as a result of gout, a disease supposedly caused by excesses of food and drink—must have greatly amused his public. Engraving was the ideal technique for Hogarth, for its precision enabled him to capture a wealth of detail. Not surprisingly, Hogarth's satirical prints were extremely popular with members of the working class.

DRYPOINT

Drypoint is similar to engraving, except that the cutting instrument used is a drypoint needle. The artist draws on the plate, usually a copper plate, almost as freely as one can draw on paper with a pencil. As the needle scratches across the plate, it raises a **burr,** or thin ridge of metal **(231)**. This burr holds the ink, making a line that is softer and less sharply detailed than an engraved line. If engraving is like fine pen drawing, sharp and distinct, then drypoint is more like drawing in soft pencil or crayon, with slightly blurred edges. This soft, sketchy quality is obvious in Picasso's exuberant drypoint, *At the Circus* **(233)**.

MEZZOTINT

Mezzotint is a reverse process, in which the artist works from dark to light. To prepare a mezzotint plate, the artist first roughens the entire plate with a sharp tool called a ***rocker.*** If the plate were inked and printed after this stage, it would print a sheet of paper entirely black, because each roughened spot would catch and hold the ink. Lighter tones can be created only by smoothing or rubbing out these rough spots so as not to trap the ink. To do this, the artist goes over portions of the plate with a burnisher (a smoothing tool) and/or a scraper to wear down the roughened burrs **(231)**. Where the burrs are partially removed, the plate will print intermediate values. Highlights—very light values—print in areas where the burrs are smoothed away entirely.

The major advantage of mezzotint is that it is capable of subtle gradations from dark to light. Whereas engraving and drypoint are predominantly line techniques, mezzotint is based on values. We see this effect in Peter Pelham's portrait *Cotton Mather* **(234)**, one of the earliest prints made in the American colonies. So finely modeled is this portrait of the great Puritan leader that, in reproduction, we might almost mistake it for an oil painting. The face, in particular, is wonderfully naturalistic because of the skillful use of values. This naturalism would be hard to achieve in an engraving or in one of the relief processes.

ETCHING

Etching is done with acids, which "eat" lines and depressions into a metal plate much as sharp tools cut those depressions in the other methods. To make an etching the artist first coats the entire printing plate with an acid-resistant substance called a ***ground,*** made from beeswax, asphalt, and other materials. Next, the artist draws on the coated plate with an etching needle. The needle removes the ground, exposing the bare metal in areas meant to print **(231)**. Then the entire plate is dipped in acid. Only the portions of the plate exposed by the needle are eaten into by the acid, leaving the rest of the plate intact. Finally, the ground is removed, and the plate is inked and printed. Etched lines are not as sharp and precise as those made by the engraver's burin, because the biting action of the acid is slightly irregular.

left: 234. Peter Pelham. *Cotton Mather.* 1727. Mezzotint, 15 × 11″.

right: 235. Rembrandt. *Arnold Tholinx.* c. 1656. Etching, drypoint, and engraving; $17\frac{13}{16} \times 5\frac{7}{8}$″. Musée de la Ville de Paris, Musée du Petit-Palais, Paris.

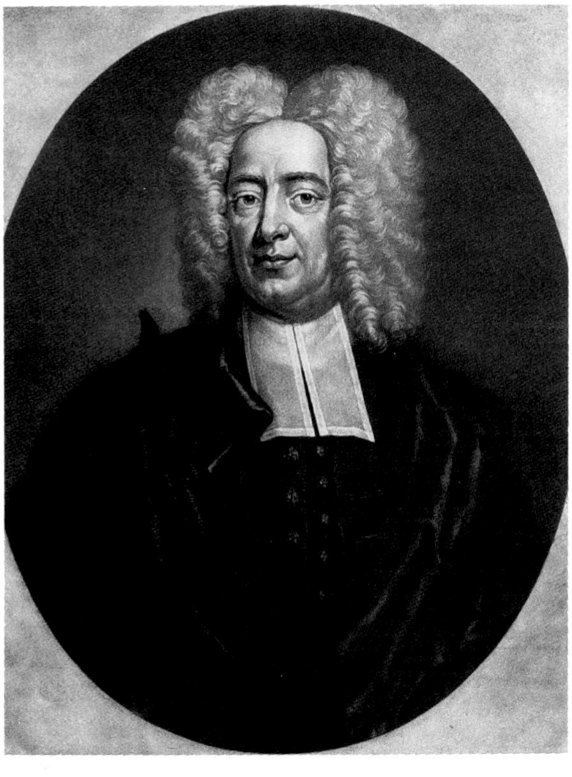

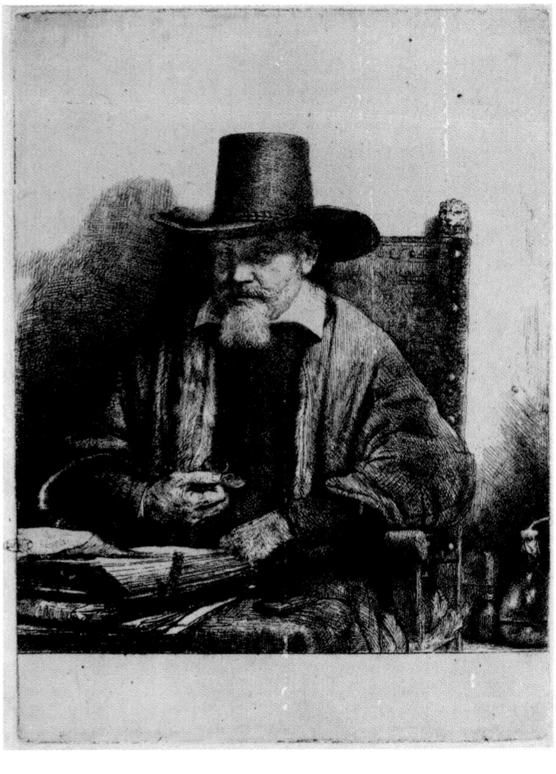

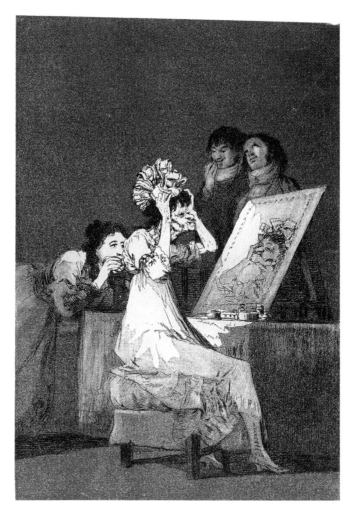

236. Francisco de Goya. *Hasta la Muerte (Until Death),* from *Los Caprichos.* 1797–98. Etching and aquatint, $7\frac{1}{2} \times 5\frac{1}{4}''$. Courtesy of The Fogg Art Museum, Harvard University Art Museums, Cambridge, Mass. (gift of Philip Hofer).

Rembrandt, who was a prolific printmaker, made hundreds of etchings. Unfortunately, many of his plates were not canceled or destroyed. Long after his death, and long after the plates had worn down badly, people greedy to produce yet more "Rembrandts" struck impressions from the plates. These later impressions lack detail and give us little idea of what the artist intended. To get a true sense of Rembrandt's genius as an etcher, we must look at prints that are known to be early impressions, such as the magnificent portrait of *Arnold Tholinx* **(235)**. In this work the artist brought to bear his most refined skills, accomplishing the fully rounded modeling entirely with hatching and cross-hatching **(95)**. The face is serious, the man almost severe, possibly impatient with having his portrait done. Rembrandt's triumph is in conveying not just the physical image but the personality as well. Perhaps no one else could give us such insight into character in this demanding medium.

Another master of the etching technique was the Spanish artist Francisco de Goya. Goya made several ambitious series of prints, and he worked in all the various print media, sometimes, as here, in more than one technique for a single print. The soft, occasionally irregular line of etching gives it a rather "dark," brooding quality, suited to Goya's political and social satire. *Hasta la Muerte (Until Death,* **236**) is from one of his major series, called *Los Caprichos,* meaning caprices, whims, eccentricities, freakishness. We see a grotesque old woman primping absurdly for her seventy-fifth birthday party, reflected even more horribly by her mirror. The look of satisfaction on her face suggests that *she* does not see the ugliness that we and the mocking onlookers see. Goya is poking none-too-gentle fun at her vanity, her girlish costume, her attempt at painting a very faded lily. The message of this print might be: "We do not see ourselves as others see us."

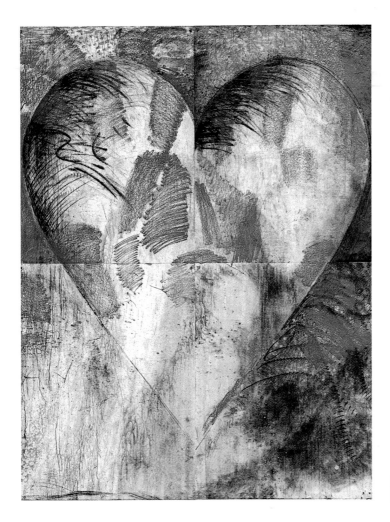

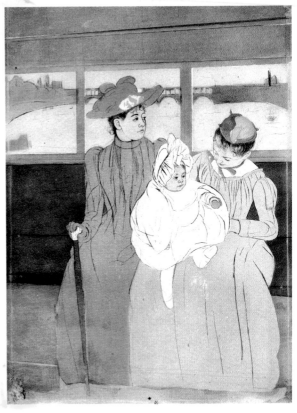

The contemporary American artist Jim Dine, familiar to many as a painter, has been a prodigious printmaker, with more than six hundred editions, in various techniques, to his credit. Often in his art Dine concentrates on emblems, which he develops in several media. For instance, the artist's emblem for himself has been a bathrobe (no body inside, just the robe). Another recurring motif is the heart, associated with Dine's wife, Nancy, and present in paintings, sculpture, drawings, and prints. *The Heart and the Wall* **(237)** is an etching with aquatint and drypoint, made in four sheets joined together because of its enormous size and the limitations of printing presses: Each section is 3½ feet high. The heart may have more nebulous connotations for Dine as well, referring to creativity, romantic love, and feelings in general. He has said: "When I first used the heart I didn't know it would become an abiding theme. Typically, though, I always go where my romance takes me, so it is an emblem that I return to with a lot of affection."[3]

AQUATINT

A variation on the etching process, aquatint is a way of achieving flat areas of tone—gray values or intermediate values of color. To understand why this is desirable, we need only look back at the portrait of *Arnold Tholinx* **(235)**. In that etching Rembrandt created the *illusion* of tone and shading by means of lines, hatched and cross-hatched. But aquatint allows the intaglio printmaker to produce real, not simulated, tone.

To prepare the plate, the artist first dusts it with particles of resin. Several methods are available to control where and how thickly the resin is distributed on the plate. Then the plate is heated, so the resin sticks to it. When the plate is dipped in acid, the acid bites wherever there is no resin, all around the particles **(231)**. For instance, if the particles are thinly dusted and far apart, the acid will be able to bite into larger areas of the plate, but if the particles are close together, the acid will have limited space to penetrate. Different tones, from light to dark, can be produced depending on the density of the particles, the length of time the plate is held in the acid, or the strength of the acid bath.

Because aquatint does not print lines but only areas of tone, it is nearly always combined with one or more of the other intaglio techniques—drypoint, etching, or engraving. The 19th-century American artist Mary Cassatt, who was much influenced by the flat areas of color in Japanese woodcuts, adopted aquatint for a great many of her prints. *In the Omnibus* **(238)** has broad areas of soft tone in the women's dresses, the baby's bunting, and part of the background, but the faces and other details have been precisely rendered in drypoint and etching.

By combining techniques the intaglio artist can get almost any result he or she wishes. Because the artist can achieve effects ranging from the most precisely drawn lines to the most subtle areas of tone, the possibilities for imagery are much greater than in the relief methods. We turn now, however, to a branch of printmaking that is even more flexible in its effects.

LITHOGRAPHY

All the major printmaking categories except one have origins going far back into history, having developed from other art forms, such as decoration of armor and printing on fabrics. That one exception is lithography. Lithography was invented in a particular place at a particular time by a particular individual—a man named Alois Senefelder.

Senefelder was a young German actor and playwright living in Munich during the 1790s. Frustrated by the expense of publishing his plays, he began experimenting with variations on the etching process as a cheap method of reproducing them. He was too poor to invest much money in copper plates, so he tried working on the smooth Bavarian limestones that lined the streets of Munich, which he excavated from the street and brought to his studio. One day, when he was experimenting with ingredients for drawing on the stone, his laundress appeared unexpectedly, and Senefelder hastily wrote out his laundry list on the stone, using his new combination of materials—wax, soap, and lampblack. Later, he decided to try immersing the stone in acid. To his delight he found that his laundry list appeared in slight relief on the stone. This event paved the way for his development of the lithographic process. While the relief aspect eventually ceased to play a role, the groundwork for lithography had been laid.

Lithography is a **planographic** process, which means that the printing surface is flat—not raised as in relief or depressed as in intaglio **(221)**. It depends, instead, on the principle that oil and water do not mix. To make a lithographic print the artist first draws the image on the stone with a greasy material—usually a grease-based lithographic crayon composed of such materials as wax, soap, and shellac. (Senefelder's Bavarian limestone is still in use as a surface, but aluminum plates are also common.) Then the whole stone is treated with a light acid bath to fix the image and is soaked in water. Water is absorbed by the stone only in the areas *not* coated with grease. When the stone is inked, the greasy ink sticks to the greasy image areas and is repelled by the water-soaked background areas. Although the printing surface, stone or plate, is flat, only the image areas print. (This book was printed by a mechanical version of lithography, known as **offset lithography**.)

The potential of lithography was recognized almost immediately. By this method artists could create a wide range of effects, both linear and tonal, with relative ease and consequently low cost. The general public thus could be supplied with inexpensive, high-quality prints suitable for framing. Many companies on both sides of the Atlantic went into the business of making lithographs, but in the United States one firm so dominated the market that its name became almost automatically associated with the word "lithograph." That firm's name was Currier & Ives.

Nathaniel Currier established his lithographic company in New York City in 1834, and in 1857 James Merritt Ives joined him as a partner. During the nearly seventy years the firm was in business it produced an estimated seven thousand lithographs on a wide variety of subjects. There was something for every taste—Civil War battles, landscapes, religious themes, famous disasters (especially fires, which allowed for lurid red effects in the sky), great trains and ships, scenes from the American West, sports (from prizefighting to fishing), and many other categories.

Currier & Ives devised an ingenious system for manufacturing the prints. They employed a great many artists to do the original drawings, after which the image was transferred to stone by professional lithographers. Although color printing, which required several stones, was feasible, Currier & Ives rarely used this expensive method. Instead, after the prints had been run off in black and white, each one was individually hand-colored in assembly-line fashion by platoons of young women sitting at long tables—one color per person. The colorists were supposed to follow color keys supplied by the artist, but quite often—perhaps to break the tedium of the job—they would select colors according to the whim of the moment. A catalogue from 1860 lists prices ranging from 8¢ to $3.75 for each print. In today's auction market a good Currier & Ives lithograph might sell for many thousands of dollars.

One of the most talented and certainly the busiest of Currier & Ives' artists was Flora Bond (Fanny) Palmer. During her career with the firm Palmer made an astonishing number of prints, on all the various subjects. Her detailed drawing style, plus an instinct for what the public would like, put her work greatly in demand. *American Express Train* (239) shows a favorite subject, drawn with her usual attention to detail.

239. Flora Bond (Fanny) Palmer, for Currier & Ives. *American Express Train.* 1864. Color lithograph. Museum of the City of New York (The Harry T. Peters Collection).

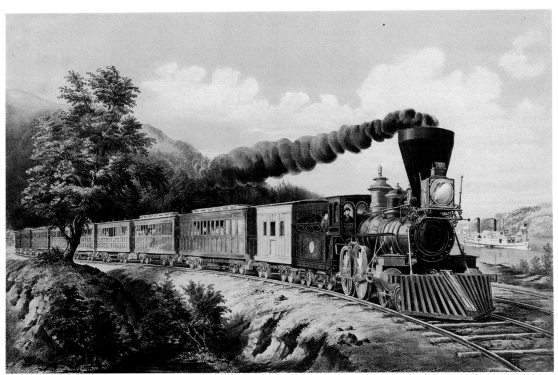

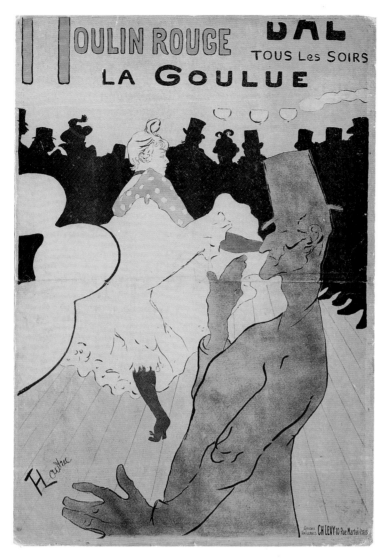

240. Henri de Toulouse-Lautrec.
La Goulue at the Moulin Rouge.
1891. Color lithograph,
5'4¼" × 3'10¾".
Philadelphia Museum of Art
(given by Mr. and Mrs.
R. Sturgis Ingersoll).

Most of the Currier & Ives artists were anonymous. It was the firm name that mattered, not the names of individual artists. Even Fanny Palmer signed few of her lithographs; later experts have identified her prints by analyzing the drawing style. By the end of the century, however, a number of well-known artists, especially in Europe, had taken up the new process. The Frenchman Henri de Toulouse-Lautrec has become closely identified with the lithograph because of one of those rare perfect convergences: He had the right artistic style for the right medium at the right time.

As we saw in Chapter 1, Lautrec practically invented the color lithographic poster, with the designs he made to advertise the Moulin Rouge nightclub and its performers. *La Goulue at the Moulin Rouge* (**240**) is a superior example. One of the featured dancers at the Moulin Rouge, La Goulue (the glutton) is shown doing the can-can before an audience rendered in silhouette. Lautrec understood well that a poster must, above all, catch the eye. Its message is simple: Come to the Moulin Rouge, where you will have a good time. The influence of Japanese prints is obvious in the flattened forms, the broad color areas, and the sharply uptilted perspective, which is visible especially in the floorboards. Despite the apparent foreground (the man in silhouette), middle ground, and background, we get little sense of spatial depth. The composition is meant to be flat and decorative. Lithography provided Lautrec with the means to achieve, with relative ease, both the definite outline and the flat areas of tone. In all, the effect is frivolous, bohemian, and just a trifle sinister—like the Moulin Rouge itself.

Lithography also was well adapted to the stark, intense, brooding imagery of the Norwegian artist Edvard Munch (241). Munch's lithograph *Sin* is done almost entirely in red, symbolic of the title, and we find it shocking to see such an intense color used so freely. Because the green eyes are the only contrast, they rivet our attention. (Red and green, being complementary colors, jar against one another to increase the tension in this print.) The woman's eyes seem at once to be looking inward and gazing at some dreadful horror. This image associates female sexuality with evil and shame—a theme that obsessed Munch throughout his life. Of course, the sense of evil and shame is inherent in the artist, not necessarily in his subjects. Women's hair, especially in quantity as here, was seen by Munch as both an allurement and a potential danger for men. This effect of voluptuous hair—gorgeous yet menacing—was enhanced by the free-drawing capabilities of the lithographic crayon on stone.

Modern techniques for transferring imagery to stone or plate have made it possible to print very complex images by the lithographic process. A good

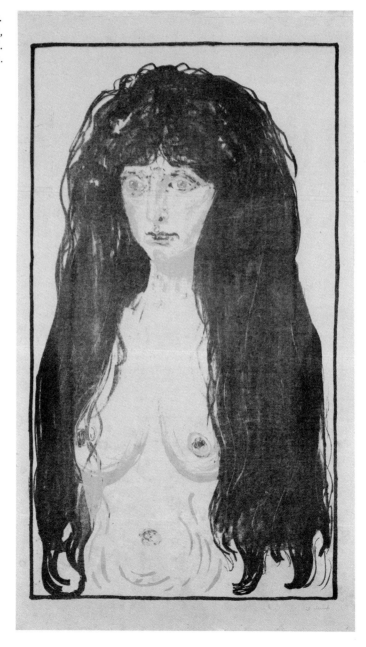

241. Edvard Munch. *Sin.* 1901. Color lithograph, $27\frac{3}{8} \times 15\frac{1}{2}''$. Rijksmuseum, Amsterdam.

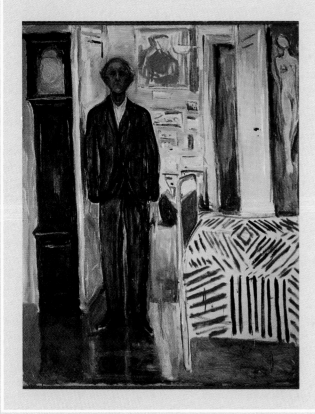

EDVARD MUNCH

1863–1944

anguish and anxiety. At seventeen he began studies in Christiania, becoming involved as well in the rather morbid, sexually permissive bohemian life of the city. In 1885 Munch paid the first of many visits to Paris. There he saw, and was influenced by, the work of the Impressionists and Post-Impressionists, especially that of Paul Gauguin. Although Munch borrowed aspects of painting techniques, his themes remained personal ones—death and dying, generalized anxiety, the despair of loneliness and abandonment, the passions between men and women, the sexual force of Woman as a source of terror.

Munch's first one-artist show, in Berlin in 1892, was a disaster. His powerful subject matter and (to onlookers) harsh painting style caused an uproar, and the show was closed within a week. Nevertheless, the artist decided to take a studio in Berlin, where he remained for several years. The sixteen years following the Berlin exhibition, spent mainly in Germany and Paris, were Munch's most fertile period. It was then that he developed his interest in prints—woodcuts, lithographs, etchings—of which he eventually made more than seven hundred. Prints allowed him to explore, in many variations, the subjects that absorbed him. Often a subject he had tried in painting became starker, more disturbing, more intensely colored in print versions.

By 1908 Munch had gained international fame, but his personal life was far from tranquil. Alcoholic and worn out with hard work, overstimulated by the bohemian clique in Berlin, tormented by at least one miserable love affair—Munch suffered a nervous breakdown and checked himself into a sanitarium in Copenhagen. There he underwent electric shock therapy to counteract effects on his brain of "persistent battering from an obsessive idea."[4]

If there is such a thing as a "Norwegian temperament"—brooding, melancholy, dark as the long nights of northern winter—Munch had it. Certainly it is difficult to visualize imagery like his coming from a French or Italian artist. After the breakdown, Munch's torments eased. However, the output from his later years lacks the power of the Berlin/Paris period. It is as though the therapy that healed him took away all the passion, and the passion was necessary to his art. Perhaps he understood this. As he himself said, "I shouldn't like to be without suffering. How much of my art I owe to suffering!"[5]

T HE PICTURE REPRODUCED HERE, *Self-Portrait between Clock and Bed*, was completed by Edvard Munch two years before his death. Munch chose to portray himself in light of the short time left to him (symbolized by the clock), beside the bed on which he would die. It is not surprising that a man in his eightieth year was anticipating death, but for Munch it was nothing new. Death had obsessed him throughout his life and was an ongoing presence in his art.

Born in a small town in Norway, Munch was raised in Christiania, as Olso was then called. When he was five his mother died, and nine years later his beloved older sister died of tuberculosis. These events haunted the artist **(16)** and no doubt contributed to his extreme

Edvard Munch. *Self-Portrait between Clock and Bed*.
c. 1942. Oil on canvas, 5'7⅞" × 3'11⅞".
Munch Museum, Oslo.

ROBERT RAUSCHENBERG

b. 1925

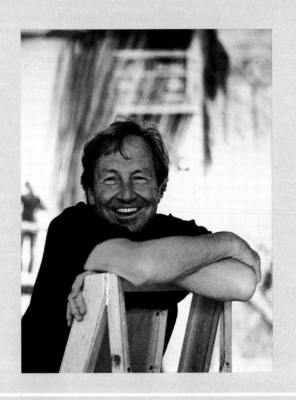

BORN IN Port Arthur, Texas, Milton Rauschenberg—who later became known as Bob and then Robert—had no exposure to art as such until he was seventeen. His original intention to become a pharmacist faded when he was expelled from the University of Texas within six months, for failure (he claims) to dissect a frog. After three years in the Navy during World War II, Rauschenberg spent a year at the Kansas City Art Institute; then he traveled to Paris for further study. At the Académie Julian in Paris he met the artist Susan Weil, whom he later married.

Upon his return to the United States in 1948, Rauschenberg enrolled in the now-famous art program headed by the painter Josef Albers at Black Mountain College in North Carolina. Many of his long-term attachments and interests developed during this period, including his close working relationship with the avant-garde choreographer Merce Cunningham. In 1950 Rauschenberg moved to New York, where he supported himself partly by doing window displays for the fashionable Fifth Avenue stores Bonwit Teller and Tiffany's.

Rauschenberg's work began to attract critical attention soon after his first one-man exhibition at the Betty Parsons Gallery in New York. The artist reports that, between the time Parsons selected the works to be exhibited and the opening of the show, he had completely reworked everything, and that "Betty was surprised." More surprises were soon to come from this steadily unpredictable artist.

The range of Rauschenberg's work makes him difficult to categorize. In addition to paintings, prints, and combination pieces, he has done extensive set and costume design for dances by Cunningham and others, as well as graphic design for magazines and books. "Happenings" and performance art played a role in his work from the very beginning. In 1952, at Black Mountain College, he participated in *Theater Piece #1,* by the composer John Cage, which included improvised dance, recitations, piano music, the playing of old records, and projected slides of Rauschenberg's paintings. Even the works usually classified as paintings are anything but conventional. One has an actual stuffed bird attached to the front of the canvas. Another consists of a bed, with a quilt on it, hung upright on the wall and splashed with paint. Works that might be called sculptures are primarily assemblage; for example, *Sor Aqua* (1973) is composed of a bathtub (with water) above which a large chunk of metal seems to be flying.

In recent years the artist devoted much of his time to ROCI (pronounced "Rocky"), his Rauschenberg Overseas Culture Interchange, which had as its goal promoting international friendship, understanding, and peace. Through ROCI he brought his work to Mexico, Chile, China, Tibet, Germany, Venezuela, Japan, Cuba, and the former Soviet Union.

We get from Rauschenberg a sense of boundaries being dissolved—boundaries between media, between art and nonart, between art and life. He has said: "The strongest thing about my work . . . is the fact that I chose to ennoble the ordinary."[6]

Robert Rauschenberg at home in Captiva,
photograph by Ed Chappell,
June 1992.

example of this complex expression is Robert Rauschenberg's *Centennial Certificate M.M.A.* **(242)**. This print was commissioned of Rauschenberg by the Metropolitan Museum of Art in New York to celebrate its hundredth anniversary, and the museum directors allowed the artist to choose whichever items he wished from the collection to include in the lithograph. Rauschenberg made a collage of reproductions, including: Picasso's portrait of Gertrude Stein (second from top at left, see p. 14); a Rembrandt self-portrait (upper right); a study for Ingres's *Odalisque* (bottom right, see **511**); and a Classical sculpture (lying on its side, above Gertrude Stein). This collage was then transferred photographically to the printing plates. In all, two lithographic stones and two aluminum plates were used to print the image in four colors. One stone carried graph-paper lines and the signatures of museum officials (lower right). At center is a text statement of the museum's goals.

Centennial Certificate M.M.A. is very much a product of the print medium and equally a product of late-20th-century technology. In effect, Rauschenberg created multiple images (an edition of prints) from his multiple image (the collage). This result would not have been possible without the collaboration of photographic and printmaking processes.

SCREENPRINTING

To understand the basic principle of screenprinting, you need only picture the lettering stencils used by schoolchildren. The stencil is a piece of cardboard from which the forms of the alphabet letters have been cut out. To trace the letters onto paper, you simply place the stencil over the paper and fill in the holes with pencil or ink.

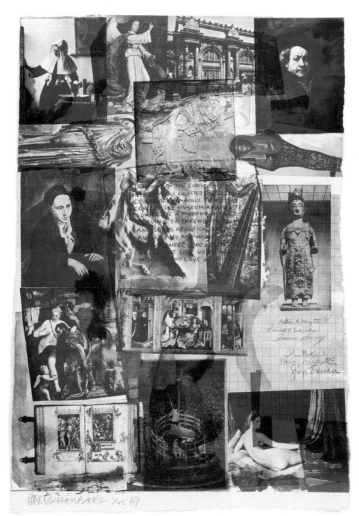

242. Robert Rauschenberg. *Centennial Certificate M.M.A.* 1969. Lithograph, $35\frac{7}{8} \times 25''$. The Metropolitan Museum of Art, New York (Florence and Joseph Singer Collection, 1969). © 1998 Robert Rauschenberg/ Licensed by VAGA, New York.

Today's art screenprinting works much the same way. The screen is a fine mesh of silk or synthetic fiber mounted in a frame, rather like a window screen. (Silk is the traditional material, so the process has often been called **silkscreen** or **serigraphy**—"silk writing.") Working from drawings, the print-maker blocks (*stops out*) screen areas that are *not* meant to print by plugging up the holes, usually with some kind of glue, so that no ink can pass through. Then the screen is placed over paper, and the ink is forced through the mesh with a tool called a **squeegee.** Only the areas not stopped out allow the ink to pass through and print on paper **(221)**.

To make a color screenprint, the artist prepares one screen for each color. On the "blue" screen, for example, all areas not meant to print in blue are stopped out, and so on for each of the other colors. The preparation of multiple color screens is relatively easy and inexpensive. For this reason it is not unusual to see serigraphs printed in ten, twenty, or more colors. This color flexibility would be very difficult to achieve in any of the other methods.

Andy Warhol's portrait of *Marilyn* **(243)** exploits another capability of screenprinting—its potential for flat areas of color. A broad area of unshaded color can be achieved simply by not stopping out the screen in that area. In this portrait of Marilyn Monroe—a favorite and recurring theme—Warhol paints the film star's face in one flat wash of blue to emphasize the eyes and especially the mouth. The background also is flat color, throwing the head into stark contrast, drawing our attention to the famous blond hair (here orange) and the seductive mouth.

Some critics have suggested the colors are meant to show the artificiality of Monroe as sex goddess, the tinsel in the "Tinseltown" of Hollywood. But Warhol himself said this: "As for whether it's symbolical to paint Monroe in such violent colors: it's beauty, and she's beautiful and if something's beautiful it's pretty colors, that's all."[7]

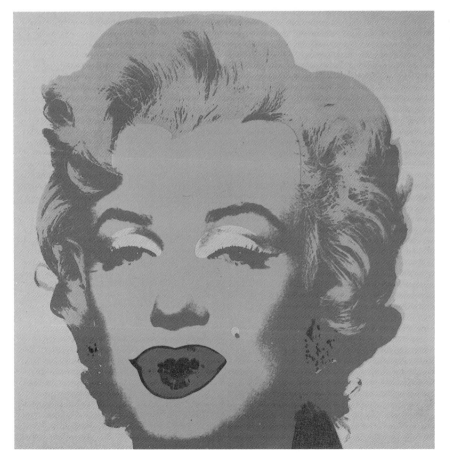

243. Andy Warhol. *Marilyn.* 1967. Serigraph on paper, 36″ square.

ANDY WARHOL

1928–1987

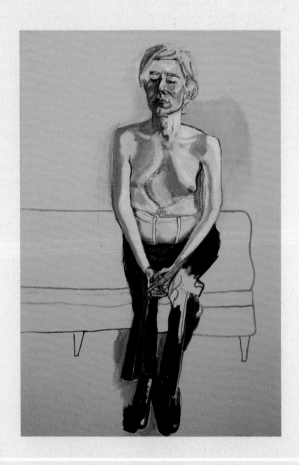

WHEN FRIENDS RECALL the most visible and colorful of the Pop artists, they often remark that he was two people. There was Andy Warhol—media celebrity, high priest of commercial and show-business imagery, wearer of bizarre white wigs, leader to an entourage of quirky New York types, maker of sexually explicit cult films. Then there was Andrew Warhola—child of struggling Czech immigrants, devout Roman Catholic, prolific worker, introvert often paralyzed by shyness, adoring son who, as an adult, brought his mother to live with him for twenty years.

Warhol, born Warhola, grew up in Pittsburgh and attended Carnegie Institute of Technology. After gradua-tion in 1949 he moved to New York, where he launched what would become a highly successful career as a commercial artist. Over the next ten years his employers included most of the chic fashion magazines and elegant Fifth Avenue stores, for which he designed advertisements, promotional pieces, and window displays. He was also—ironically, in view of his later adventures—one of the illustrators for the first edition of *Amy Vanderbilt's Complete Book of Etiquette.*

By 1960 the artist and his style had found each other. Warhol, the gifted commercial artist, slipped into Pop, the "fine art" style of commercial images, without missing a beat. For a decade Pop would remain a dominant art wave in the United States, and Warhol sailed on the crest of that wave. The themes with which he is most closely associated appeared repeatedly in prints and paintings: Marilyn Monroe, Elizabeth Taylor, Jackie Kennedy, and, of course, the famous Coke bottles and Campbell's soup cans **(150)**.

A turning point in Warhol's career occurred in 1963, when the artist moved into a new studio in New York. A friend decorated the entire space in silver paint and aluminum foil, a large group of acquaintances and admirers and hangers-on converged, and thus was born—the Factory. At the Factory Warhol continued his enormous output of prints, paintings, and sculptures. At the Factory he directed the production of many avant-garde (some would say outlandish) films, featuring actors with names like Viva, Ultra Violet, and International Velvet. And at the Factory, in 1968, a woman who announced herself as the founder of SCUM (Society for Cutting Up Men) shot Warhol and nearly killed him.

Many observers felt that Warhol ran out of steam after the shooting, that his art no longer showed the edge and excitement it once had. Nevertheless, he worked steadily, developing his familiar themes and some new ones, until his death at age fifty-eight, of complications following gall bladder surgery.

Warhol often liked to say he was a "machine." He claimed to be devoid of emotion or feeling, just a machine that produced a product, called art, in a place called a Factory. One of his much-quoted statements sums this up. "If you want to know all about Andy Warhol, just look at the surface: of my paintings and films and me, and there I am. There's nothing behind it."[8]

Alice Neel. *Andy Warhol.* 1970.
Oil on canvas, 5′ × 3′4″.
Collection of Whitney Museum of American Art,
New York (gift of Timothy Collins).

SPECIAL TECHNIQUES

There is one major exception to the rule, stated at the beginning of this chapter, that prints are an art of multiples. That exception is the **monotype,** or **monoprint.** Monotypes are made by an indirect process, like any other print, but, as the prefix "mono" implies, only one print results. To make a monotype, the artist draws on a metal plate or some other smooth surface, often with diluted oil paints. Then the plate is run through a press to transfer the image to paper. Or the artist may simply place a sheet of paper on the plate and hand-rub it to transfer the image. Either way, the original is destroyed or so altered that there can be no duplicate impressions. If a series of prints is planned, the artist must do more work on the plate.

Monotype offers several technical advantages. The range of colors is unlimited, as is the potential for lines or tones. No problems arise with cutting against a grain or into resistant metal. One can work as freely as in a direct process like painting or drawing. You may wonder, then, why *not* simply draw or paint? Why bother with the indirect touch of the print? There can be as many reasons as there are monotype artists, but we might list a few. Monotype offers the "accidental" quality of the press as intermediary. Even when the original is finished, one cannot be quite sure how the print will look when it comes through the press. Colors are absorbed into the paper differently, giving a "printed" effect many artists seek. There is the potential for working over the printed image to create a "layered" appearance. Above all, artists love to experiment with techniques that expand their expressive range.

In the last two decades monotype has enjoyed a surge of popularity, encouraging many contemporary artists to explore its effects. Susan Bush made *Woman with Yellow Cage, Bird Dress, Flowers, and Reflections* **(244)** by painting in oils on a sheet of glass, then placing high-quality paper on top and hand rubbing the paper to transfer her image. The broad brush strokes of the artist's painting are clearly visible in the transfer print.

Another realm being explored by contemporary print artists is that of actual three-dimensionality. Most prints are flat, but there is no reason they

left: 244. Susan Bush. *Woman with Yellow Cage, Bird Dress, Flowers, and Reflections.* 1995. Monotype (oil transfer print), 3′9″ × 2′7″. Courtesy the artist.

right: 245. Red Grooms, *Gertrude.* 1975. Color lithograph on Arches-Cover, cut out, glued, and mounted in Plexiglas box; 19¼ × 22 × 10″.

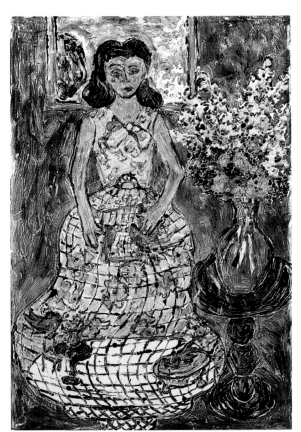

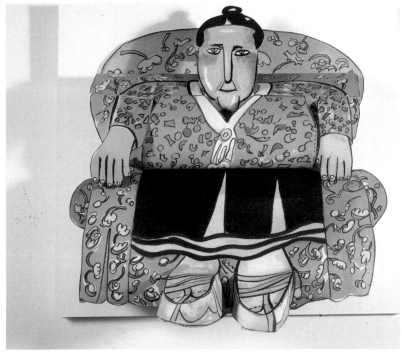

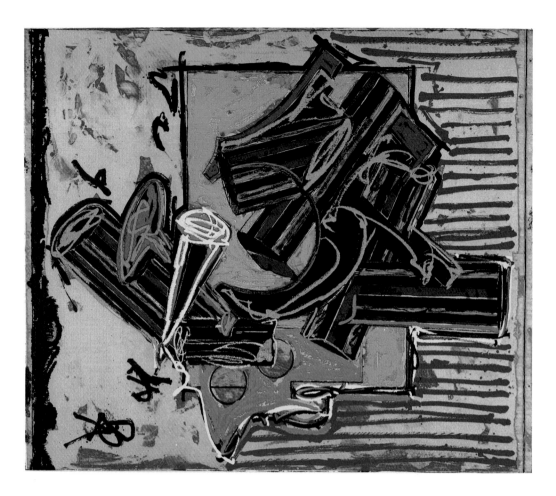

need be. Take an artist whose imagination and sense of humor are manic, who understands the lithographic process, who appreciates pop-up books and paper dolls—and you get *Gertrude* (**245**). Red Grooms made *Gertrude*—the writer and art collector Gertrude Stein (p. 14)—from two lithographic prints, cut, folded, and mounted in three dimensions within an acrylic box. She (we cannot think of this work as "it") is a multiple, but she might just as well have fit into the sculpture chapter of this text. There she sits, pudgy in her flowered blouse in her pudgy flowered chair, an example of where prints can go if artists don't take themselves too seriously.

Until the later 20th century the limitations of printing presses usually restricted an artist to one category of work at a time. A print was either relief *or* intaglio *or* lithography. Now, however, with the increasing sophistication of presses and print workshops, it is possible to combine several print processes in the same image, which broadens the artist's options significantly. Frank Stella's *La penna di hu* (**246**), for instance, was made by combining etching, relief, woodcut, screenprint, and other stencil techniques, in twenty-nine colors. Although not actually three-dimensional (unlike many of Stella's works, which have areas projecting forward in depth), *La penna di hu* has an exceptionally rich surface texture and creates a strong sense of visual three-dimensionality.

Stella's work is printed on handmade paper—an increasingly common practice. We may find it difficult to think of paper as being "made." For most of us, paper comes in tablets or sheets or rolls, and we don't give much thought to how it got that way. But paper is composed of vegetable fibers, pounded into a pulp with water and then pressed into sheets and dried. For special purposes the pulp can be pressed in a mold to take other forms—forms that are quite different from the pages of this text or a memo pad. A reusable mold allows the pressing of multiple forms in an edition.

246. Frank Stella. *La penna di hu.* 1988. Relief, etching, woodcut, screenprint, stencil, hand-colored on white TGL handmade paper; 4′7½″ × 5′6″.
Collection Walker Art Center, Minneapolis, and Tyler Graphic Archives, 1989.

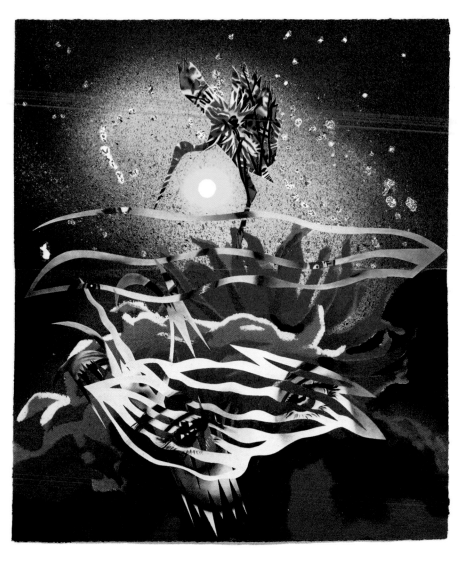

247. James Rosenquist.
The Bird of Paradise Approaches the Hot Water Planet,
from the series
Welcome to the Water Planet.
1988–89. Colored, pressed paper and lithography collage elements on white TGL handmade paper; 8′1″ × 7′1½″.
Printed and published by Tyler Graphics Ltd.
© 1998 James Rosenquist/ Tyler Graphics Ltd./ Licensed by VAGA, New York.

One artist who has done extensive work in pressed paper is James Rosenquist. For more than a year in 1988–89 Rosenquist spent the bulk of his time at Tyler Graphics, a master print studio in Mount Kisco, N.Y., where he and the studio's director, Kenneth Tyler, invented new technology as they went along to satisfy Rosenquist's vision for a print series. A huge mold was built specially to contain the hundreds of gallons of pulp that would be required, and special vacuums were designed to dry and press the pulp into paper. To get the gradated surface effects he wanted, Rosenquist would apply colored pulp with ladles, a spray gun, even an eye dropper. Harder-edged elements printed by lithography were added as collage to the pressed paper. The result was a series called *Welcome to the Water Planet,* from which we illustrate *The Bird of Paradise Approaches the Hot Water Planet* **(247)**. In Rosenquist's iconography, the water planet is Earth, a vivid and beckoning place, and who would not want to dwell among these luscious colors? The print has a rich, velvety surface texture resulting from the color-saturated pulp.

If you had any doubt at the beginning of this chapter that printmaking is a lively art, chances are you have changed your mind by now. In some ways it is an art ideally suited to our life style. The painter, the sculptor, the architect— all these make *one* work of art at a time, that will reside in one place. People who want to see the original must journey to do so. But the print made in an edition of a hundred will reside in a hundred different places and be enjoyed by thousands of people. Truly, the print allows nearly anyone to corner a small piece of the world of art.

The Camera Arts
Photography, Film, and Video

A ROOM WITH A VIEW. This phrase may make you think of real estate or of a classic novel, but we may borrow it here, because it describes the essence of a camera. *Camera* is the Latin word for "room," and it is not farfetched to think of any camera as being a little room with a view—real or imaginary—of the outside world.

The desire to record and preserve images is probably as old as civilization. In the 4th century B.C.E. the Greek philosopher Aristotle understood the most basic principle of the camera, for he noted the ability of light, under controlled circumstances, to duplicate an image. Not until the 16th century, however, did anyone manage to construct a practical device that could harness the image-transferring property of light. That device came to be known as the ***camera obscura.***

You can make a *camera obscura* yourself. Find a light-tight room, even a closet or a very large cardboard box. Arrange for a small hole, no bigger than the diameter of a pencil, in one wall of the room to admit light. Inside, hold a sheet of white paper a few inches from the hole. You will see an image of the scene outside the room projected on the paper—upside-down and rather blurry, but recognizable. That is the principle of the *camera obscura*, which simply means "dark room."

Our illustration **(248)** shows a portable shack serving as a *camera obscura* sketched in cutaway, with one wall and the roof removed for illustra-

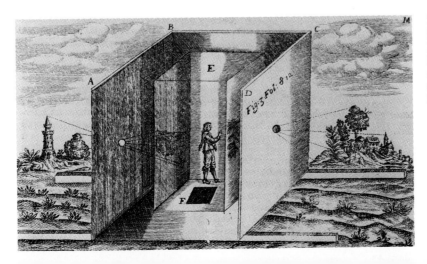

248. *Camera obscura,* in cutaway view. 1646. Engraving. International Museum of Photography at George Eastman House, Rochester, N.Y.

tion purposes. Artists of the Renaissance had welcomed the *camera obscura* with enthusiasm, because it aided them in achieving a major goal—to reproduce the natural world as accurately as possible, with correct proportions and perspective. By the 16th century the mechanism had come into use as a drawing tool. Once an image had been captured in the *camera obscura,* the artist could trace over it, thus ensuring an accurate rendering of the scene.

Today we have come a long way from the *camera obscura,* but its principles remain intact. The modern camera is still dependent on controlled light, and it is still a room with a view. That view may be anything the artist chooses to make it, from a straightforward recording of the natural scene to the most elaborate special effects the mind can conceive. Let us now consider the camera arts—photography, film, and video—and their unique view of the world.

PHOTOGRAPHY

Photography is the art form that best demonstrates a basic truth: Artistry resides not in the hands but in the head. People who cannot draw well sometimes think painters have some unusual skill in their hands, just as a singer may have an exceptional voice. But while some art forms do demand manual skill, the difference between a merely competent mechanical performance and a great work of art lies not in the artist's hands but in the brain—in the artistic inspiration that tells the hands what to do.

It is this confusion between mechanical skill and inspiration that has caused some people to question photography as an art form. After all, painters and sculptors *create* forms; photographers only *find and record* forms. Nevertheless, just as the painter's brain tells the hands what marks to make on canvas, so the photographer's brain interprets what is seen by the eyes and tells the camera what to do. Whereas the average person walks through the world seeing trees and buildings and people, the creative photographer walks through the world seeing compositions—possible photographs. We might almost say that the photographer has an invisible frame somewhere behind the eyes—a frame that is constantly composing pictures.

Two photographs of the same subject will help to show how dependent an image may be on the creative instincts of the artist. Both Sherril V. Schell's picture (249) and David Hockney's (250) show the Brooklyn Bridge, a famous and beautiful structure spanning the East River in New York City. Both artists aimed their cameras down the pedestrian walkway, and the two views have a similar outlook. The two artists' intentions, however, are quite different.

Schell's photograph (249) is not so much "about" the Brooklyn Bridge as it is about geometry and line and pattern. Lines of the steel wires and cables sweep upward to the tower. From this vantage point they appear to cross and intersect, visually filling the open arches with a dense network rather like the mesh of a hammock. The huge, brooding bulk of the stone tower contrasts with this intricate tracery of lines, and shadows cast on the boardwalk add to the geometric complexity. The few people walking across the bridge give us a sense of its scale.

Hockney's treatment of the bridge (250) is a photo-collage, created from dozens of small, individual prints assembled into a single image. We might say this work is "about" movement, about the multiple viewpoints we all accumulate as we walk through the physical world. Hockney has said, "It's our movement that tells us we're alive."[1] And so, as our surrogate, he records the myriad visual impressions we would form as our heads and eyes and bodies moved to take in the scene. Now the stone tower does not seem so imposing. Hockney's many camera angles make it bend inward and tilt backward, like a child's precarious construction. The lines of steel wire are much less important to Hockney than to Schell, so he lets them cluster at the top edges of his image.

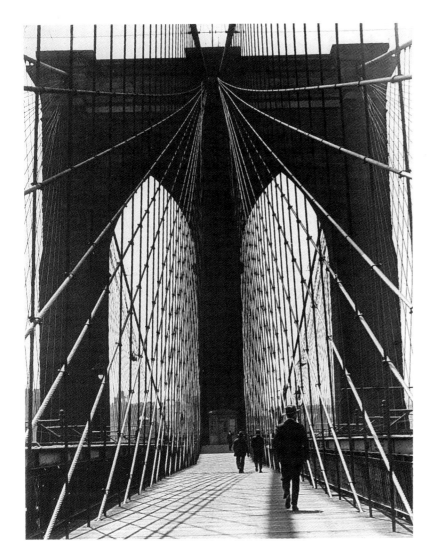

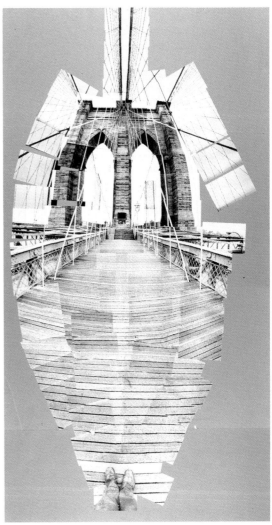

The wooden boardwalk fills nearly half the field, stretching empty except for Hockney's signature touch—his own feet at the very bottom of the picture.

Strangely, neither Schell nor Hockney cared to give any hint of water flowing under the bridge, even though that is the *point* of the bridge, to cross a river. In fact, if you did not recognize the elegant form of the double-arched tower, you might not know this structure for a bridge at all. From these two works we can learn an important lesson: Photographic artistry derives from what is included and emphasized, what is omitted or de-emphasized. Hockney's picture is especially interesting because he shows the bridge empty, which it never is. Only through the collage technique could he eliminate the throngs of walkers and cyclists and skaters who cross the bridge constantly.

An old adage says that "the camera can't lie," and perhaps that is so, but the photographer can. To state that idea more positively, the photographer can show us whatever truth he or she wishes to show, and that is what both Schell and Hockney have done with the Brooklyn Bridge. The "truth" of their pictures is what they chose to make it.

We can apply this same idea to any photographic image, because every situation in the visible world contains many truths, many thousands of details. Each time the photographer points a camera, he or she makes a great many decisions: what to include in the picture, what to leave out beyond the edges, what to emphasize, which angle to shoot from, where to give the sharpest focus. As we shall see throughout this chapter, the truth of a picture is whatever the creative photographer selects for us to see, selects as one particular view of the world.

left: 249. Sherril V. Schell.
Brooklyn Bridge. 1930s.
Gelatin-silver print, 18 × 14″.
© 1993 The Art Institute
of Chicago (Julien Levy
Collection, gift of Jean Levy
and estate of Julien Levy, 1988).
All rights reserved.

right: 250. David Hockney.
*The Brooklyn Bridge,
Nov. 28th 1982.* 1982.
Photographic collage, 9′1″ × 4′5″.
© Copyright David Hockney.

THE STILL CAMERA
AND ITS BEGINNINGS

Despite the amazing sophistication of modern photographic equipment, the basic mechanism of the camera is simple, and it is no different in theory from that of the *camera obscura*. A camera is a light-tight box **(251)** with an opening at one end to admit light, a lens to focus and refract the light, and a light-sensitive surface (today it is usually film) to receive the light-image and hold it. The last of these—the holding of the image—was the major drawback of the *camera obscura*. It could capture an image—and later versions of the *camera obscura* had a lens to focus the image and make it sharp—but there was no way to preserve the image, much less walk away with it in your hand. It was to this end that a number of people in the 19th century directed their attention.

One of them was Joseph Nicéphore Niépce, a French inventor. Working with a specially coated pewter plate in the *camera obscura*, Niépce managed, in 1826, to record a fuzzy version of the view from his window after an exposure of eight hours. Although we may now consider Niépce's "heliograph" (or sunwriting), as he called it, to be the first permanent photograph, the method was not really practical.

Niépce was corresponding with another Frenchman, Louis Jacques Mandé Daguerre, who was also experimenting with methods to fix the photographic image. The two men were cagey with one another, each knowing that whoever was first to develop a simple, inexpensive process would strike a commercial gold mine. Daguerre won the contest. In 1837 he recorded an image of his studio that was clear and sharp, by methods that others could duplicate easily. Daguerre's light-sensitive surface was a copper plate, and he christened his invention the **daguerreotype.** Other pioneers worked with light-sensitive paper (the **calotype**), glass (the **ambrotype**), and dark metal (the **tintype**).

Daguerre's invention caused great excitement throughout Europe and North America. Entrepreneurs and the general public alike were quick to see the potential of photography, especially for portraits. It is hard to realize now, but until photography came along only the rich could afford to have their likenesses made, by sitting for a portrait painter. Within three years after Daguerre made his first plate, a "daguerreotype gallery for portraits" had opened in New York, and such galleries soon proliferated. To our eyes the portraits may seem stiff and posed, which they were. Subjects had to remain motionless, without blinking, for between half a minute and a full minute—the minimum exposure time needed. (If this doesn't seem long to you, try doing it.) What's more, the idea of sitting for a photograph was entirely new and more than a little intimidating to most early subjects. One photographer who managed to capture unstrained poses, often of Native Americans, was the English-born John H. Fitzgibbon, whose sensitive portrait of *Kno-Shr, Kansas Chief* **(252)** has a quiet, almost regal dignity.

The desire to record what people look like remains an important function of photography, for professionals and amateurs alike. Nearly everyone has a drawerful of photographs and slides, recording significant events from birth (some have been photographed *during* birth) through childhood, adolescence, romance, marriage, parenthood, and old age. Despite the popularity of amateur photography, the professional still plays a role in recording what people look like. Portraits constitute a major category in photography.

SUBJECT MATTER
IN PHOTOGRAPHY

PORTRAITS   The professional portrait, at its best, goes beyond merely recording the subject's physical attributes. Like any other photograph, it tells one "truth"—a selected version of all the possible things one could record about the subject. And like any other portrait—an oil painting, for example—it may

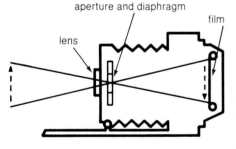

251. The basic parts of a camera.

serve as a revelation of the subject's character. Certain photographers have demonstrated a particular genius for portrait photography.

In the mid-19th century one man, by virtue of creative talent, enterprise, and sheer hard work, dominated the field of photography in the United States. That man was Mathew Brady. Brady opened a daguerreotype studio in New York in 1844, at the age of twenty-one. Later there was a studio in Washington and more studios in New York. From these bases he set out to photograph all the illustrious people of the time, and he very nearly succeeded. He employed many assistant photographers, called "operators," including Timothy O'Sullivan, whose work we shall see later in the chapter **(258)**. In many cases it is impossible to tell which pictures Brady himself took, because his name appears on all products of his studios.

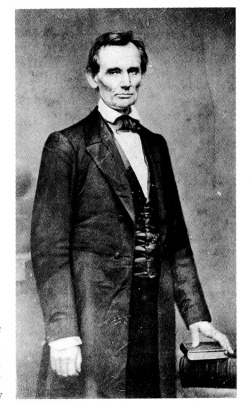

The photograph shown here, however, almost certainly came from Brady's own camera. In 1860, when Abraham Lincoln was running for election to the presidency, he arrived in New York to make a speech at Cooper Union, an important college. During his visit he presented himself at Brady's studio, where this sensitive portrait was made **(253)**. Brady shows us a young Lincoln, clean-shaven, not yet torn by the heartache of war, fresh out of the back country of Illinois. His suit is obviously new, bought for the occasion, with the shirt cuff hanging down awkwardly from the jacket sleeve. Lincoln's facial expression is stern and dignified, but we also sense a bit of apprehension—perhaps caused by the leap into national politics, perhaps caused by the novel experience of having his portrait done.

Lincoln's Cooper Union speech was a success. Brady's photograph was in great demand, and thousands of copies were sold. After the election, Lincoln said, "Brady and the Cooper Union speech made me President."

Another famous portraitist of the 19th century, and an equally fascinating personality, was Julia Margaret Cameron, who, without benefit of multiple assistants, was fully as prolific as Brady. Cameron worked in England in the 1860s and 1870s. She had a wide circle of prominent friends and, by virtue of her strong personality, was able to cajole (or bully) most of them into posing for her. Cameron's photographs have given us likenesses of the great English poet Alfred, Lord Tennyson (her special chum); the American poet Henry Wadsworth Longfellow; naturalist Charles Darwin, who developed the theory

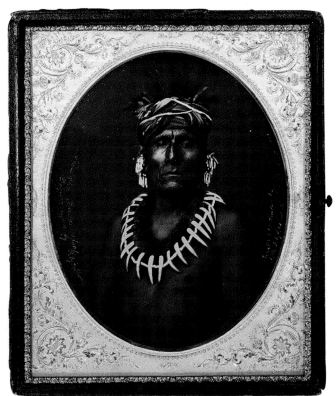

left: 252.
John H. Fitzgibbon.
Kno-Shr, Kansas Chief. 1853.
Daguerreotype, 7 × 5⅞".
Gilman Paper Company Collection.

above: 253. Mathew Brady.
Cooper Union Lincoln Portrait.
1860. Photograph.
Library of Congress, Washington, D.C.

of evolution; and a great many others. The portrait of Darwin **(254)** illustrates many elements of Cameron's unique style: a strong contrast of dark and light, emphasis on the head and face, a soft—faintly blurred—focus, and fondness for the profile view. Over and over Cameron searched out the deepest character of her sitters, and then held that character at a slight distance from us through the soft focus of her lens. Cameron's studies show real people transformed into a photographic ideal.

Some might argue that our next image is not a portrait at all, but rather a documentary photograph—a photograph documenting a *situation*, in this case the harshness of life at the bottom of the economic ladder. But that is not the way the photographer has handled his subject. Gordon Parks' picture called *American Gothic* **(255)** shows a careworn black woman posed, solemn-faced, in front of an American flag. She stands rigidly between her broom and her mop, almost as though she were just another instrument for cleaning. Yet Parks gives the image so much dignity that the woman, Ella Watson, faces us as an individual. Her work is respectable and important; her broom and mop are the tools of her trade, every bit as appropriate to her portrait as a brush and palette would be to the portrait of an artist.

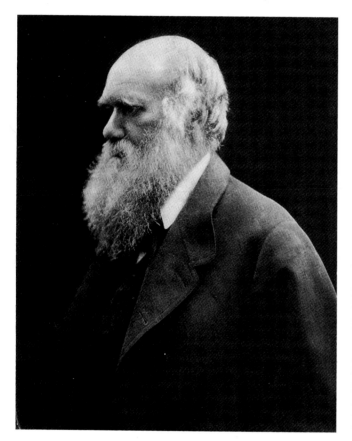

left: 254. Julia Margaret Cameron. *Charles Darwin.* 1868. Carbon print, $10\frac{1}{2} \times 8\frac{1}{4}''$.
The Museum of Modern Art,
New York (gift of Edward Steichen).

---

below: 255. Gordon Parks. *American Gothic.* 1942. Photograph.
Courtesy the photographer.

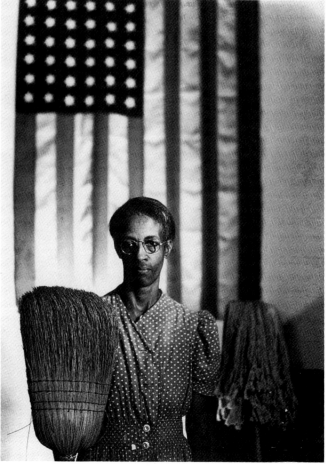

JULIA MARGARET CAMERON

1815–1879

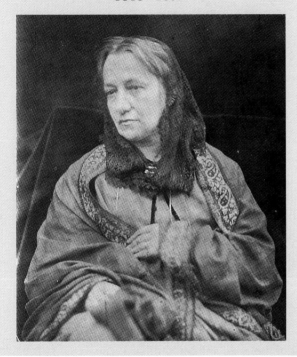

IN A LARGE FAMILY of colorful individuals, Julia Margaret Cameron was the standout. Her great-niece, the writer Virginia Woolf (no stranger herself to unconventional conduct), wrote with a kind of fond awe that Julia Cameron "had a gift of ardent speech and picturesque behaviour." Woolf continues: "There was no eccentricity that she would not have dared. . . ."[2]

Child of a Scottish father and a French mother, Julia Margaret Pattle was born in India, then educated in France and England. Of the seven Pattle sisters, only Julia was plain; the rest were exceptionally lovely. Julia Margaret, however, was not one to allow a lack of physical beauty to cramp her style. Possessed of an exuberant spirit and a zest for life, she set out to *make* beauty wherever she could. At twenty-three she married Charles Hay Cameron, a well-to-do scholar and legal reformer. Their marriage was to be a happy one. The couple settled in England, where they raised eleven children—six of their own and five adopted—while conducting an astonishingly active social life.

Stories abound of Mrs. Cameron's generosity, enthusiasm, energy, and strong will. She maintained a vast correspondence, averaging three hundred letters a month. She collected interesting and talented friends by the score, charming them with her wit and creative escapades, overwhelming them with gifts and favors. Her circle included poets, novelists, scientists, actors, politicians, diplomats—the cream of Britain's intellectual and artistic crop.

In 1863, when Julia Cameron was forty-eight, her daughter bought her a special present: a large wooden box camera and darkroom equipment. From that moment Cameron's life changed, for her energies were channeled into a new passion. A chicken coop on the Camerons' property was converted into a "glass house," or photographic studio. Servants, friends, and relatives were recruited as models, and her demands on them became the talk of the countryside.

Cameron favored long exposure times, so a sitter might be forced to maintain some horribly uncomfortable pose, without moving, for up to ten minutes. If that picture didn't turn out well, there must be another and another, hours of posing without rest, until the model staggered exhausted out of Cameron's "glass house." Virginia Woolf tells us that "Boatmen were turned into King Arthur; village girls into Queen Guenevere. Tennyson was wrapped in rugs; Sir Henry Taylor was crowned with tinsel. . . . She cared nothing for the miseries of her sitters nor for their rank."[3]

Cameron's images mounted to the hundreds, eventually thousands, but she continued to think of herself as an amateur photographer. Although she exhibited her work and had several one-artist shows, she did not sell her photographs. Instead, she gave them away in great bunches to friends, or to whoever took her fancy. Only near the end of her life did Cameron offer for sale a series of photographs, beautifully bound and copyrighted in her name.

In 1865 the Camerons left England and settled in Ceylon (now Sri Lanka), the island nation off the coast of India, where Julia continued to pursue her art in her customary manner. One visitor, a Miss North, complained that "She made me stand with spiky coconut branches running into my head . . . and told me to look perfectly natural."[4] At the age of sixty-three Julia Cameron caught a bad chill and died. She left behind an unfinished memoir entitled "Annals of My Glass House," in which she wrote: "From the first moment I handled my lens with a tender ardour, and it has become to be as a living thing, with voice and memory and creative vigour."[5]

Henry Herschel Hay Cameron. *Julia Margaret Cameron.*
1870. Silver print, $9\frac{3}{4} \times 8\frac{1}{2}$".
Gernsheim Collection, Harry Ranson Humanities
Research Center, The University of Texas at Austin.

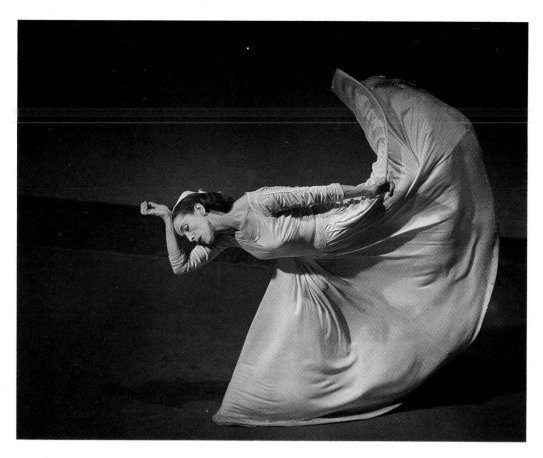

256. Barbara Morgan. *Martha Graham: Letter to the World (Kick).* 1940. Gelatin-silver print. © 1941 by Barbara Morgan.

Now and then a photographer's portrait becomes so closely associated with a given subject that the subject's name automatically triggers a mental image of that portrait. Such is the case with Barbara Morgan's famous study of the dancer Martha Graham **(256).** For anyone who is at all interested in dance, this image *is* Martha Graham. Mention her name, and the mind's-eye sees it: the strong set of the jaw, the impossibly extended neck, the artfully clenched hands, and above all, the great swooping arc of the skirt. Morgan's picture is all studied grace and all arrested motion. We expect the gown to continue its swirl up and over the dancer's head. No subject could ask for a more exquisite capture of the elegant self on film.

We expect a portrait to reveal individual personality, and so we automatically associate this type of photography with people, but there are exceptions. Battina is an exception. She is an individual, she has a lot of personality, she even has star quality. The only thing a little exceptional is that Battina is a dog. Photographer William Wegman has made a great many portraits of Battina **(257),** his own Weimaraner, posed in whimsical situations, sometimes with a prop or costume. Here Battina assumes the role of Lolita, the fictional young temptress of Vladimir Nabokov's novel, and as such she does a send-up of every "sexy" movie starlet's pose ever recorded. The photographs are spare and elegant, the situations silly, the dog maintaining her dignity in spite of the silliness. Only the most stony-hearted dog hater would deny that Battina understands she is "sitting" for her portrait, and responds to the camera with appropriate panache.

LANDSCAPE From the first, landscape has been a popular subject for photographers, whether the natural beauty of the countryside or the constructed landscape of the city. Some early photographers, like Timothy O'Sullivan, went to great extremes to capture nature's forms. Hauling what was then very cumbersome photographic equipment through mountains and desert presented a real challenge, but the results were well worth the effort.

In 1867 O'Sullivan signed on as official photographer to an expedition commissioned by the federal government to explore the territories of Nevada and Colorado. One of his most dramatic photos from this trip **(258)** shows the mule-drawn ambulance O'Sullivan had hired to carry water for his traveling darkroom. Tiny and stark against the vast shifting dunes, the vehicle looks like a toy. We imagine that the footprints and grooves left by the wheels were the first marks ever made in this spot by anything but the wind.

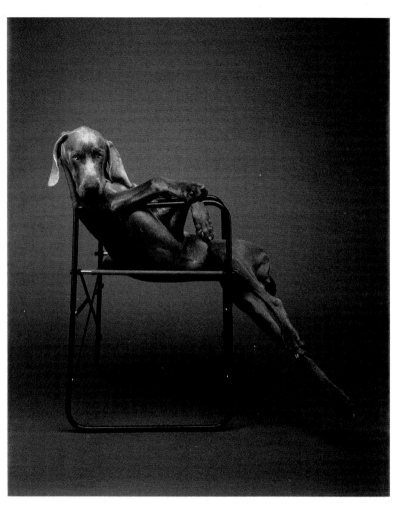

right: 257. William Wegman. *Lolita.* 1990. Polaroid Polacolor, 24 × 20″. Courtesy Pace/MacGill Gallery, New York.

below: 258. Timothy O'Sullivan. *Sand Springs, Nevada.* 1867. Photograph. Library of Congress, Washington, D.C.

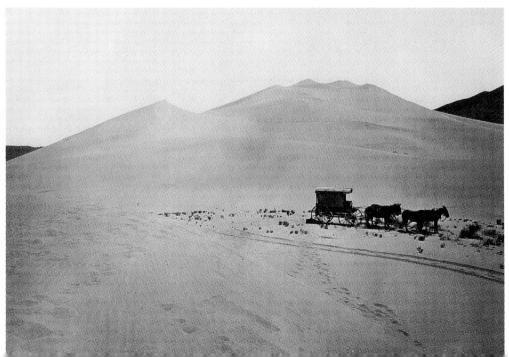

The acknowledged master of 20th-century landscape photography was Ansel Adams. Our illustration **(259)** shows one of his most famous pictures, *Moon and Half Dome*. Although the scene that Adams chose to photograph is undeniably dramatic, that alone does not account for the artistry of this picture. Adams had "set up" the shot by choosing a precise vantage point; by *framing* the photo precisely (that is, including just the portion of landscape he wanted and no more); and by waiting until the moon, light, and shadows seemed just right. The composition is perfectly balanced, with the dark foreground rock at left and the dark shadow at right framing the lighted expanse of the rock known as Half Dome. The brilliant moon at top not only completes the balance of the picture but is its major focal point. Light is used to define natural forms, to create contrast, to pick out textures and details; indeed, light structures the entire photograph. Adams demonstrates that the successful landscape photo, far from being a happy accident, is a demanding art.

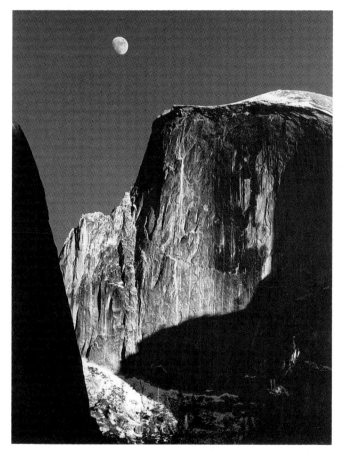

left: 259. Ansel Adams. *Moon and Half Dome.*
1966. Photograph.
Trustees of the Ansel Adams Publishing Rights Trust.
All rights reserved.

below: 260. Berenice Abbott. *Nightview, New York.*
1932. Gelatin-silver print.
Courtesy Berenice Abbott/Commerce Graphics Ltd., Inc.

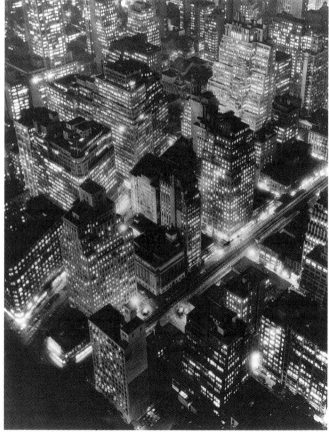

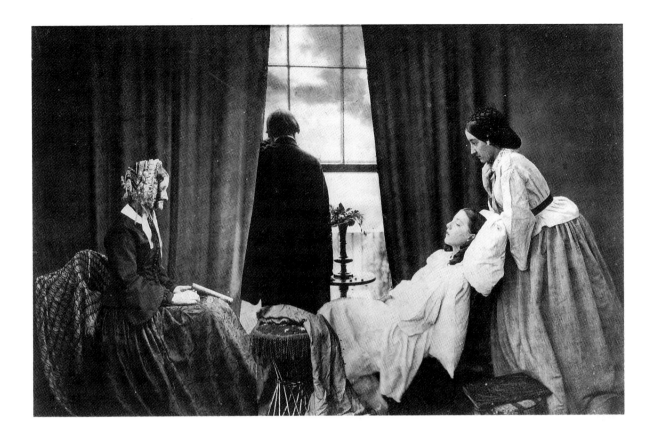

The urban landscape was a favorite theme with Berenice Abbott, who did her most concentrated work during the 1930s. *Nightview, New York* **(260)** shows the city as a gleaming expanse of lights, pulsating with energy, yet clean and pure. No poor people huddle in the streets of this city—although they surely would have done so in this Depression year. No dirty papers collect in the gutters, no taxis blare their horns impatiently, no danger lurks in the dark side streets. To its four edges, this picture is filled with glittering light. Abbott shows us not the harsh reality of the city, but the magic we all hope to find in the metropolis.

GENRE In the visual arts, as we have seen, the theme of genre focuses on everyday life. Usually people are included, but the intention is not to make a portrait of individuals. Instead, a genre photograph captures one of life's "little moments," the tiny dramas that punctuate day-to-day existence.

When photography was new, many assumed that the medium should aspire to duplicate, or even improve upon, the art of painting. The fashion, in that mid-19th-century Victorian age, was for sentimental subjects—the more melodramatic, the more tear-jerking, the more morbid, the better. A style of photograph was developed to satisfy this fashion, and we find a good example in Henry Peach Robinson's *Fading Away* **(261)**. We see a young woman on her deathbed. For all that she is about to expire, she looks remarkably beautiful and remarkably healthy. Her grieving relatives hover at the bedside (one turns toward the window in despair), as our heroine prepares to expel her last shuddering breath. But this scene is not real. It was posed; in fact, it was made as a composite image from five separate negatives. The people are actors, and they were carefully arranged in this stagy genre episode to clutch at the heartstrings of a receptive Victorian audience.

Our next photographer's pictures, while not strictly genre, expand that theme. The work of Diane Arbus concentrated on people who are unusual, apart from the norm—some would say "freaks." Arbus photographed a sword swallower, aging nudists, and people with physical abnormalities of all kinds.

261. Henry Peach Robinson. *Fading Away.* 1858. Albumen composite print, $9\frac{5}{8} \times 15\frac{3}{8}''$. The Royal Photographic Society, Bath, England.

Her goal was to look directly, unflinchingly, at that which others turn away from. Often, her pictures reveal jarring incongruities. *The King and Queen of a Senior Citizens Dance* **(262)** shows a couple decked out in absurdly elaborate robes and crowns, which seem all the more absurd against their banal street clothing. Presumably this is meant to be a festive occasion, but the "king" and "queen" have such mournful expressions that we doubt any pleasure in their monarchy. Their postures are weary, and the woman in particular looks as though she has just plopped herself down in exhaustion, her legs splayed apart. Arbus might be showing us that any attempt to impose gaiety or celebration on this couple will be futile.

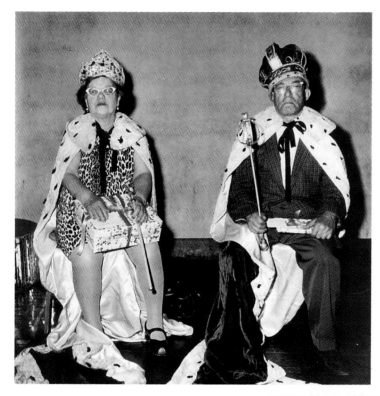

left: 262. Diane Arbus.
The King and Queen of a Senior Citizens Dance, New York City. 1970. Gelatin-silver print, 15 × 11⅜″.
Copyright © The Estate of Diane Arbus, 1971.
The Museum of Modern Art, New York
(Mrs. Armand P. Bartos Fund).

below: 263. John Sexton.
Merced River and Forest, Yosemite Valley, California.
1983. Photograph.
© 1983 John Sexton. All rights reserved.

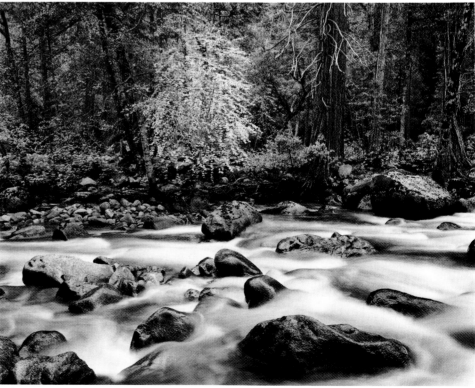

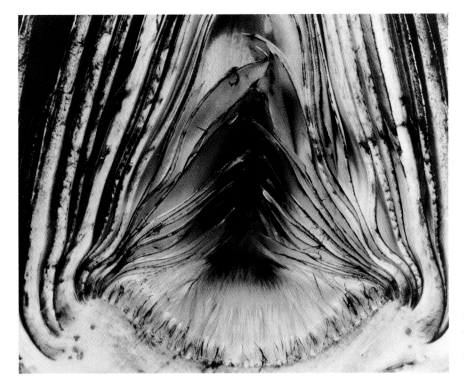

264. Edward Weston.
Artichoke, Halved. 1930.
Photograph.
© 1981 Arizona Board of Regents,
Center for Creative Photography.

ABSTRACTION As has been noted before, abstraction is a process by which natural forms are simplified and reduced to their most characteristic aspects. We might think the camera, which tells only the "truth," cannot do this, but indeed it can. Abstraction in photography can result from viewpoint, angle, distance (including close-up), special lenses, shutter speeds, darkroom techniques, or any combination of these.

A slow shutter speed produced the other-worldly abstraction of John Sexton's *Merced River and Forest, Yosemite Valley, California* **(263)**. What might have been a pretty but commonplace photograph of water rushing through the rapids takes on the quality of a volcanic landscape when the water seems transformed into thick, molten lava. Slow shutter speeds blur the outlines of anything moving quickly. Motionless objects are not affected, but the moisture-soaked rocks appear "smoothed out," as they poke through the ooze and resemble underwater creatures, perhaps a herd of hippopotamuses.

Many of Edward Weston's photographs are extreme close-ups of familiar objects, such as the *Artichoke, Halved,* shown here **(264)**. Without the title, you might not be able to identify the picture's subject matter. By moving in close and picking up the exquisite detail of the vegetable, Weston gives it a majestic quality. All sense of scale is destroyed; this could just as easily be a huge underground cavern or a mysterious growth in a tropical rain forest—or a modern abstract painting. In creating this abstraction Weston challenges our preconceived notion of what an artichoke looks like. He may also encourage us to look beyond the familiar appearance of other common objects and consider their possibilities for abstraction of line, form, and texture.

From the straightforward portrait to a vegetable in disguise, the subject matter of photography includes everything in this world and—since the advent of space travel and sophisticated telescopes—more than a few things that are out of our world. The choice of imagery is limited only by the limits of the photographer's imagination. In some cases, however, the choice of subject matter may be influenced by the photographer's circumstances. Like drawings, photographs often are made for specific applications. The following section explores some of the purposes of photography.

PURPOSES OF PHOTOGRAPHY

Many photographs are made for specific commercial applications, such as publication in books, magazines, and newspapers, and their purpose is primarily illustrative or documentary. Other pictures have no external incentive beyond the photographer's expressive impulse. The dividing line between these two categories is not a rigid one. The photographer on assignment from a magazine may make an image that survives for its artistic qualities long after that issue of the magazine has been forgotten. And, of course, art photographs often are reprinted in books and magazines. Nevertheless, our appreciation of photographs can be enhanced by considering the primary purpose for which each was taken, because this strongly affects the photographer's expression.

THE "ART" PHOTOGRAPH   By art photograph, we mean a picture that is specifically intended for exhibition as art. Such photos are appreciated for their formal qualities and for their expressiveness, rather than for any illustrative value. Almost since the beginnings of the medium photographers have explored the purely expressive potential of the camera. But what we think of as today's art photography owes a great deal to the influence of one man in particular, both because of his own work and because of his efforts to promote photography as an art form. That man was Alfred Stieglitz, and his most famous picture is *The Steerage* (265).

The story of how *The Steerage* was made illustrates our point about photographers moving through the world with an invisible frame behind their eyes. In 1907 Stieglitz was aboard ship on his way to Europe, traveling first class. One day as he was walking the deck, he happened to look down into the lowest-class section, called steerage. Before him he saw a perfectly composed photograph—the smokestack leaning to the left at one end, the iron stairway leaning to the right at the other, the chained drawbridge cutting across, even such details as the round straw hat on the man looking down and the grouping of women and children below. Stieglitz knew he had only one unexposed plate left (the equivalent of one exposure at the end of a roll of film). He raced to his cabin to get his camera. When he returned, the scene was exactly the same; no one had moved. That one plate became *The Steerage*.

265. Alfred Stieglitz. *The Steerage*. 1907. Photograph. The Art Institute of Chicago (Alfred Stieglitz Collection).

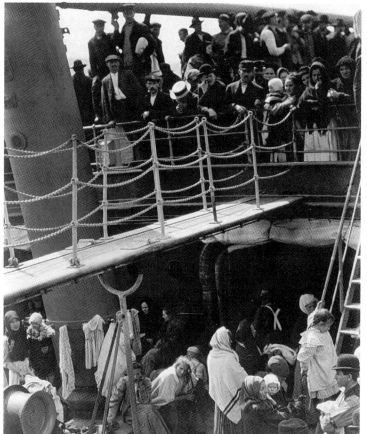

ALFRED STIEGLITZ

1864–1946

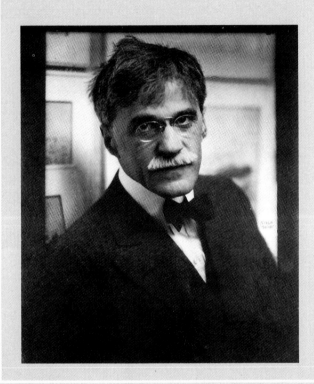

IF ONE HAD TO CHOOSE the individual most responsible for establishing photography as an art form, the strongest candidate probably would be Alfred Stieglitz. Born in Hoboken, New Jersey, Stieglitz was the eldest child of German parents. His youth was spent in travel between Europe and the United States, and he studied at both the City College of New York and the University of Berlin. In 1883, at the age of nineteen, Stieglitz bought his first camera in Berlin; thereafter his life's work seems never to have been in doubt.

Stieglitz settled more or less permanently in New York in 1890, although he continued to travel widely. The first of his major efforts to promote photography as an art form came in 1896, when he was instrumental in founding the Camera Club of New York. The following year he became editor of its quarterly publication, *Camera Notes*. But the group most closely associated with his name was the "Photo-Secession," founded in 1902. A loosely structured national organization of photographers, the Photo-Secession was devoted to promoting exhibitions of photographers, later of contemporary painters and sculptors as well. Stieglitz served as editor of its quarterly, *Camera Work*, which maintained extremely high standards for photographs published and reproduction quality.

As a photographer, Stieglitz dedicated his talents to demonstrating that the medium was accessible to anyone, even those with unsophisticated equipment and little training. He often worked with the simplest cameras, had his photographs printed commercially, and delighted in shooting under difficult conditions—in rain, fog, and darkness. His pictures were exhibited widely and were collected by major museums.

In 1905 Stieglitz, along with photographer Edward Steichen—whose portrait of Stieglitz is shown here—opened the Little Galleries of the Photo-Secession at 291 Fifth Avenue in New York, usually called "291." There the American public viewed the work of "art" photographers and also had its first opportunity to see the paintings of Picasso, Matisse, Cézanne, and other avant-garde European artists, as well as the most innovative Americans. Through his gallery Stieglitz had great influence on the spread of modern art.

Among the artists showing at 291 was the painter Georgia O'Keeffe. In 1918 Stieglitz left his first wife and moved in with O'Keeffe, whom he married after his divorce became final. His photographic portraits of O'Keeffe, including many close-up studies of her hands, are among his most sensitive and striking images. Although Stieglitz and O'Keeffe were frequently apart, often at different parts of the globe (their chronology for the next twenty years or so reads like a travelogue), they remained married until his death at eighty-two.

Stieglitz wrote extensively about his work, but perhaps the most characteristic statement can be found in the catalogue notes he prepared for an exhibition of his photographs in 1921: "My teachers have been life—work—continuous experiment. Incidentally a great deal of hard thinking. Any one can build on this experience with means available to all. . . . I was born in Hoboken. I am an American. Photography is my passion. The search for Truth my obsession."[6]

Edward Steichen. *Alfred Stieglitz at "291."* 1915. Gray pigment gum-bichromate over platinum or gelatin-silver, $11\frac{3}{8} \times 9\frac{9}{16}$". The Metropolitan Museum of Art, New York (Alfred Stieglitz Collection, 1933).

The work of contemporary photographer Cindy Sherman has done much to blur the line between photography and painting. Sherman's photographs are dominated by one model—Sherman herself, disguised in each picture so that her work presents an extremely varied cast of characters. Since her early college days Sherman has been preoccupied with makeup, wigs, costumes, props—all the elaborate trappings of theatrical presentation. Soon she began not only dressing herself up, but photographing the results. In early work Sherman cast herself as characters reminiscent of television programs, films, even commercials. Later she turned her ironic eye to the history of art, specifically to traditional portraits in art history. Transformed by the costumes and wigs—sometimes by fake body parts—Sherman parodied the extremes of high-style portraiture as painted by Old (usually male) Masters **(266)**. According to the artist, "All the women in those paintings were the wives or mistresses of the artists, or the wives of [their] rich patrons. And there was a convention of portraying women that was not real."[7] Sherman thinks of herself as a performance artist (p. 498), because, in a way, she is giving a performance every time she steps in front of her own camera. Her photographs document that performance.

Nan Goldin's work is virtually the antithesis of Sherman's. Although Goldin sometimes turns the camera on herself, more often she directs it toward those in her vast circle of friends. Her settings are casual (even messy), her subjects never seem posed, and the photographs are rarely pretty. Goldin is not interested in artifice but in truth, the truths about people she loves and the real lives they live singly and with one another. *David in My Hallway* **(267)** shows Goldin's best and oldest friend standing in a bare space, gazing intently at the camera. The photograph is apparently simple, yet Goldin has invested it with so much tenderness and affection that we can almost feel the bond between subject and photographer. The more we study it, the more we seem to know David, which is undoubtedly what David's friend meant us to do.

left: 266. Cindy Sherman. *Untitled #193.* 1989. Photograph. Courtesy the artist and Metro Pictures, New York.

right: 267. Nan Goldin. *David in My Hallway, NYC.* 1996. Photograph. Courtesy the artist and Matthew Marks Gallery, New York.

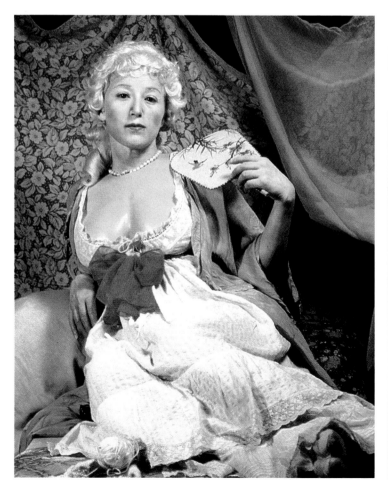

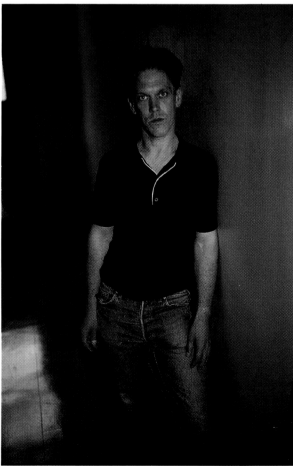

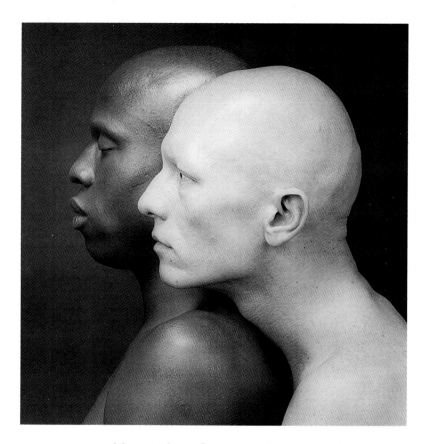

The art pictures of Robert Mapplethorpe are concerned less with truth than with observation of form. Mapplethorpe was a photographer known primarily for his portraits, among them numerous self-portraits (p. 232); for his still lifes, often of flowers; and for his nude figure studies. His style emphasizes elegance of composition and dramatic contrasts of light and dark. We see both in one of Mapplethorpe's best-known images, *Ken Moody and Robert Sherman* **(268)**. Two men are posed with their heads side by side. One is black, one white. Both have shaved heads, and both are apparently nude. Composed in this way, the subjects cease to be men and become statues, carved in marble. We study them for their pure form: the gleam on a shoulder, the intricate curve of an ear, the fleshy thrust of a mouth, the arch of a neck, the speck of an eye's pupil. This picture is about shape against shape, dark against light.

PHOTOJOURNALISM AND EDITORIAL PHOTOGRAPHY Until the 19th century the only pictures that ever appeared in newspapers and magazines were made from drawings or from prints, usually engravings **(230)**. Then photography came along, opening the potential for actual documentation of events. Mathew Brady, whose portrait of Lincoln we saw earlier **(253)**, was among the first to exploit the potential of photographs for journalism. When North and South went to war in 1860, Brady and his team also went to war, carrying their equipment in peculiar horse-drawn wagons that the soldiers dubbed "What-sits." Because his photos still required a fairly long exposure time at sittings, Brady could not photograph actual battles (which obviously would not stand still for the camera), but he recorded scenes of camp life, important generals and their aides, and especially the poignant aftermath of battle. The American Civil War, therefore, was the first major war photographed for posterity.

Because no method had yet been perfected to reproduce the photographs accurately and clearly, early photographs like Brady's were first translated into drawings and then into woodcuts for reproduction. Then, about 1900, the first process for photomechanical reproduction—high-speed printing of photographs along with type—came into being.

CENSORSHIP

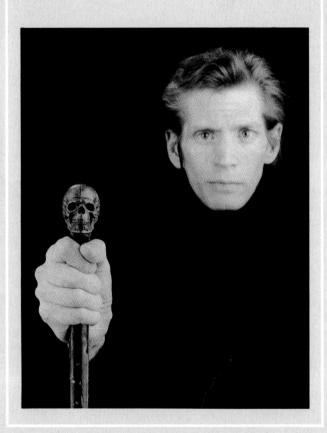

E ACH OF THE ARTS has had its lightning rods—works that, because of their form or content, attract the storm of attention and passion and controversy. These same works usually raise the issue of censorship. In literature it was D. H. Lawrence's *Lady Chatterley's Lover*, which, because of its explicit sex scenes, was banned from publication in the United States for more than thirty years. In theater it was the musical *Hair*, which in 1968 confronted Broadway audiences with a shockingly new sight: the entire cast stark naked. And in photography it was the "X Portfolio" of Robert Mapplethorpe.

Starting in 1976, with his first solo exhibition, Mapplethorpe gained considerable fame, but the fame acquired a troublesome edge when the public at large became aware of his "X Portfolio." For that series of photographs contains images of sadomasochism and homoeroticism, images so frank as to be profoundly disturbing to many (even most) viewers.

Mapplethorpe died of AIDS in the spring of 1989. Soon after, an exhibition of his work was organized, including several examples from the "X Portfolio." The show was planned to tour the United States. Here the saga begins, and it probably will be discussed and debated in art circles for many years to come.

The Mapplethorpe show was scheduled to open at Washington's Corcoran Gallery of Art, a public museum, in the summer of 1989. Before the opening, however, it came to the attention of Senator Jesse Helms, Republican of North Carolina, who denounced the photographs as obscene. Senator Helms' chief objection was that part of the funding for the exhibition had come from the National Endowment for the Arts—in other words, from American taxpayers. His attempt to persuade Congress to prohibit funding for work he considered obscene caused a furor, with intense argument on both sides. In the heat of this controversy, the Corcoran canceled, but the show later opened, to general acclaim, at Washington's Project for the Arts.

After Washington, the Mapplethorpe show moved to Hartford, Connecticut, and Berkeley, California; in both places it ran without major incident or protest. Next on the itinerary, however, was a city well known for its strict opposition to pornography: Cincinnati. And in Cincinnati the controversy became an uproar. No longer was the issue merely public funding. Now it became: Should these photographs be shown at all?

On opening day in Cincinnati, police closed the Contemporary Arts Center while they videotaped the exhibition for evidence. Then the exhibition was reopened, and it played to huge crowds for the duration of its stay. But a grand jury indicted both the gallery and its director on obscenity charges. If convicted, the gallery's director could serve up to a year in jail.

Before discussing the outcome of the trial, it might be well to pause and consider some of the issues involved. Is the Mapplethorpe case really a matter of censorship, and what, in fact, is censorship?

For our purposes here, we will define **censorship** as the supervision by one individual or group over the artistic expression of another individual or group. This definition assumes that person or group A has the power to *control* the expression of person or group B. Usually, the power is exerted for political, religious, or moral reasons. In other words, A can prevent B from making or showing work that conflicts with A's political, religious, or moral point of view.

We expect to find censorship in totalitarian societies, and we are seldom disappointed. Absolute rule survives only *because* it is absolute, so it cannot tolerate other points of view. But in the United States today censorship for political reasons is far less an issue than is censorship concerning religious or moral standards.

We have a pluralistic society, representing many religions, many moral points of view. People of goodwill and thoughtful convictions disagree about what is "right" or "wrong," what should be allowed or not allowed. One of the most explosive areas of disagreement concerns the issue of free expression, specifically as it pertains to the arts. Should artists, writers, and performers be allowed to express whatever they wish? Or should there be limits on that expression to control material that large segments of society consider morally wrong?

Proponents of free expression cite the First Amendment to the Constitution, which states in part: "Congress shall make no law . . . abridging the freedom of speech." Yet that amendment does *not* give you the right to say anything you please. You cannot, for example, deliberately tell a lie about another person, either verbally (slander) or in print (libel). Such lies are prohibited, and the other person could sue you.

In a classic example from the early part of this century, Supreme Court Justice Oliver Wendell Holmes, Jr., said, "No one has a right falsely to shout 'fire' in a crowded theatre." So freedom of speech is *not* absolute; it has limits. Moreover, the Supreme Court historically has held that it is permissible to ban obscene speech, obscene writing, obscene imagery. The problem lies in deciding just *what* is obscene.

As of this writing the Supreme Court standard for obscenity comes from a 1973 case called *Miller v. California*, which held that something is obscene if the "average person applying contemporary community standards" would find it so, and if "the work taken as a whole lacks serious literary, artistic, political or scientific value." Obviously, this judgment raises more questions than it answers. Who is the average person? Which community? Who decides whether the artistic value is serious?

Further complicating the problem is the issue of public funding for the arts. Many people feel that taxpayers' money should not be used to support the arts at all. Others think the government should finance the arts, but not "obscene" art—whatever that is. Those who oppose limits on spending fear that such limits would lead to a situation like the one that has existed in totalitarian societies, where government controls the arts rigidly.

In our system we pay our taxes and allow our elected representatives to decide how the money should be spent. And in 1965 Congress passed the National Foundation on the Arts and Humanities Act, whose declaration of purpose includes this statement: "It is necessary and appropriate for the Federal Government to help create and sustain not only a climate encouraging freedom of thought, imagination and inquiry, but also the material conditions facilitating the release of this creative talent."

Again as of this writing, funding for the National Endowment for the Arts has been sharply curtailed but will continue. The question of funding for "obscene" art—and the method of determining what is "obscene"—remains vague. Of course, there will *never* be absolute answers to any of these questions, answers acceptable to everyone. Readers of this book must make up their own minds, as the courts continue to grapple with these complex issues. That brings us back to the Mapplethorpe case.

Six months after the Cincinnati gallery and its director were indicted on obscenity charges, a jury of local citizens found them not guilty. The jurors were not art experts; most of them had never been in an art museum, knew nothing about art, and cared little about it. Yet they were willing to be guided by the opinions of people who were presented to them as experts, art professionals brought in by the defense. As one juror said afterward, "We had to go with what we were told. It's like Picasso. Picasso from what everybody tells me was an artist. It's not my cup of tea. I don't understand it. But if people say it's art, then I have to go along with it."

Another juror explained his decision this way: "We thought the pictures were lewd, grotesque, disgusting. But like the defense said, art doesn't have to be beautiful or pretty."[8]

The Mapplethorpe jurors were "average persons" who, even when applying the standards of a rather conservative "community," found that the works in question *did* have "serious artistic value." That was the resolution of one case, but there will be many cases, and the question of censorship can never have a definite answer.

Robert Mapplethorpe.
Self-Portrait. 1988. Photograph.
Copyright © 1988 The Estate
of Robert Mapplethorpe.

Today nearly every event that might remotely be considered newsworthy is covered by photojournalists, from the carnage of war to the escape of a pet snake in a residential neighborhood. News photographers must depend to a certain extent on luck. Their best pictures result when they are in the right place at the right time, when some extraordinary event occurs. Nevertheless, it is the photographer's skill that turns a record of an event into a great picture.

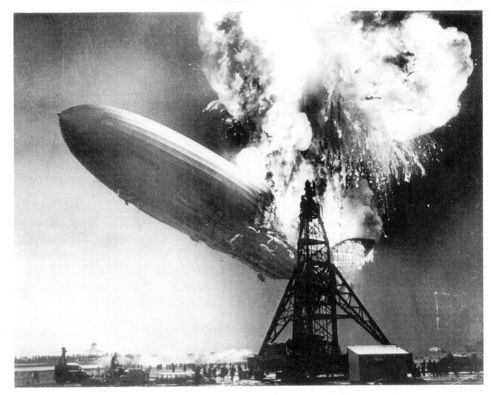

right: 269. Sam Shere. *Explosion of the Hindenburg, Lakehurst, New Jersey.* 1937. Photograph.

below left: 270. Dorothea Lange. *Heading West, Tulare Lake, California.* 1939. Photograph. Library of Congress, Washington, D.C.

below right: 271. Fred R. Conrad. *Kurdish Girl Returning Home.* 1991. Photograph. © Fred R. Conrad.

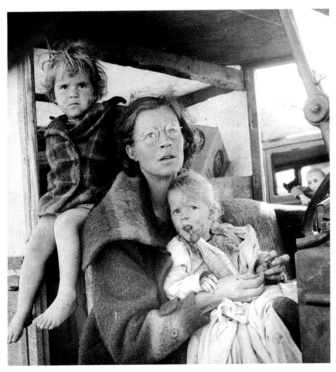

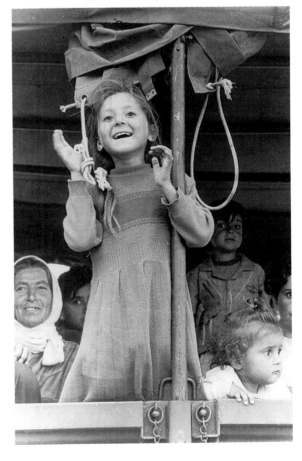

On May 6, 1937, the enormous German airship *Hindenburg* was scheduled to land at Lakehurst, New Jersey. Even though it was the dirigible's seventh transatlantic crossing, the arrival was still considered remarkable enough that a crowd gathered, and twenty-two photographers from the New York and Philadelphia papers had been sent to cover the landing. The photographers were set up to compose shots for feature stories. Just as the giant silver balloon was about to be secured to the mooring tower, it exploded and burst into flames. Of the ninety-two people on board, thirty-six were killed. Every one of the photographers, despite the tremendous heat and danger, managed to snap a few pictures before dashing to cover. Sam Shere's photo, with the tower silhouetted in front of the inferno, is memorable **(269)**.

The burning of the *Hindenburg* was the first disaster to be thoroughly documented in photographs. During the decade of the thirties, however, another kind of disaster—not a sudden one, but a long and painful one—was covered in depth by the most creative photographers of the time. The Great Depression, which began in 1929 and lasted until the onset of World War II, caused hardships for photographers as well as for the population as a whole. To ease the first problem and document the second, the Farm Security Administration (FSA) of the U.S. Department of Agriculture subsidized photographers and sent them out to record conditions across the nation. One of these was Dorothea Lange.

Lange devoted her attention to the migrants who had been uprooted from their farms by the combined effects of Depression and drought. *Heading West, Tulare Lake, California* **(270)** shows a mother and her two children, dirty and disheveled, in a battered truck. Despair is written on all three faces, as the eyes stare off at some distant point that may offer no relief from misery. Lange's masterful composition gives an importance, a universal quality, to the tragedy of one family. The picture's basic structure is a triangle, with the boy's head at the apex, one side running down through his leg, the other diagonal through the mother's head and the younger child, and the base resting on the bottom of the photo (**Overlay 6b;** compare Raphael's *Madonna*, **99**). FSA photos like this one were offered free to newspapers and magazines.

Dorothea Lange's travels for the FSA took her to nearly every part of the country. In one summer alone she logged 17,000 miles in her car. Photojournalism is hard work. It may also be dangerous, as when the *Hindenburg* exploded. But the most difficult and dangerous job, unquestionably, is that of war photographer.

The 1991 war in the Persian Gulf was the most media-intensive conflict in history. Among those covering its aftermath was photographer Fred R. Conrad, whose picture shows how war comes to people, not to armies **(271)**. As battle raged in Iraq, Kurdish families in the north fled to the mountains. Only when their territory had been secured could they return. A young Kurdish girl, framed by Conrad's lens, shows the pure joy of homecoming. Beyond capturing the happiness on the girl's face, Conrad has made a masterful picture. His composition is basically triangular, leading from the face down to the two lower corners. There we see the more subdued pleasure of the woman at left, the apprehensive gaze of the child at right. A nooselike curl of rope dangling beside the girl provides a grim symbol of death—but now it is death conquered by liberation.

The photojournalist, as we said, needs a certain amount of luck. He or she must wait for the picture to happen. There is another branch of journalistic photography, however, that *makes* pictures happen. This is editorial photography. Editorial photographers may deal in fashion, in architecture, in food, or many other areas. Their goal is to make the subject attractive and appealing, or possibly to interpret an idea photographically. Their pictures are "set up" very deliberately to achieve this purpose.

Fashion photography, like fashion illustration, usually aims at creating an illusion—the illusion of an impossible, idealized beauty that the viewer will feel compelled to emulate. No one has mastered this art of illusion better than

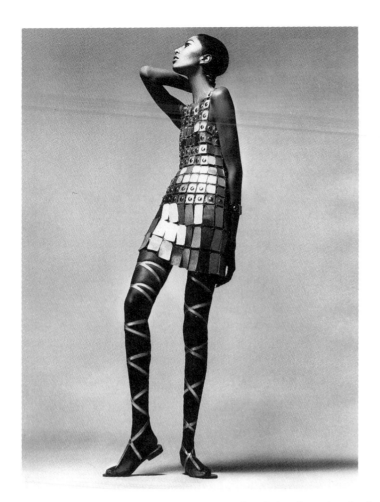

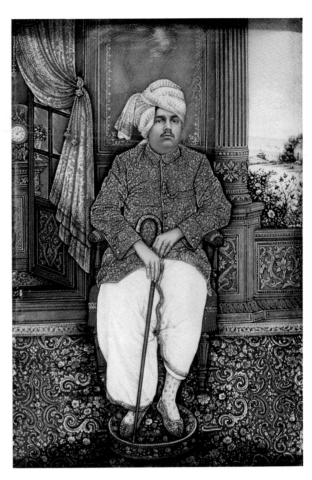

Richard Avedon. Avedon's *Donyale Luna* **(272)** is almost an abstraction. The model, impossibly tall and thin, does not seem to resemble any living creature. We cannot imagine her dashing to catch a bus or sitting down to dinner. Actually, in that dress, we cannot imagine her sitting down at all. But the fashion photographer is not concerned with everyday life. What matters is not reality but a glimpse of unearthly elegance.

Despite its unreal quality, Avedon's photograph is essentially "straight," as are most of the others we have seen so far in this chapter. The camera clicks, and the photographic image is complete. For other photographers, however, the click of the shutter is only the beginning of a process that will create an image very different from that viewed outside the little room of the camera.

SPECIAL EFFECTS AND TECHNIQUES

The idea of using the photographic image only as a starting point is not a new one. We have already explored the question of photography as truth teller. The visual "truth" of a photograph may be influenced by a photographer's inner vision, by prevailing art styles, even by the culture in which photographs are made. We encounter the last of these in seeing how photography developed in a culture apart from Western traditions.

Photography reached India in the 1840s and was eagerly adopted by the populace. The Indian approach to the medium was very different from that in the West, however. Europeans, steeped in Renaissance concepts of depth and perspective, greeted photography as an ever more "real" depiction of the natural world. The Indians, by contrast, had a tradition of miniature painting in which the illusion of deep space was irrelevant. Paintings were flat, all in one plane, and highly decorative. So when they took up photography, the Indians painted over the camera image until it looked "correct" to *them*.

Our illustration shows a splendid example **(273)**. This portrait of a land-owner, taken about 1900, has been meticulously painted all over. While the subject's face and hands retain a suggestion of roundness from the photograph, the rest of his body is flat, thanks to the painting. The chair seems to float in space, while the meeting of patterned rug and wall is just a horizontal division of the picture plane, not an indication that the rug is perpendicular to the picture plane. (Possibly the rug was a plain floor in the photograph; it has been painted with no perspective at all, as though it were parallel to the picture plane.) The background wall—which in the photo must have showed another room opening to the left and a vista out the window at right—now seems more like a painted backdrop for the theater.

There is a lesson to be learned from this approach to photography. Our understanding of how things "are" and how things "should be" has much to do with cultural conditioning. The Indians' cultural heritage predisposed them to the belief that a flat, decorative image is the ideal expression of art; Western cultural heritage predisposes us to believe that the illusion of depth on a flat surface is superior. Actually, neither is right or better. Through understanding and exposure, we can learn to appreciate aesthetic values different from our own. This applies to all aspects of art and culture, not just to photography.

The Surrealist artist Man Ray experimented with several unusual photographic techniques in the 1920s and 1930s. One of them was **solarization,** a process by which an exposed negative is briefly reexposed to light during development. This causes chemical changes in the photographic emulsion—the light-sensitive coating on film. Actually, although Man Ray's name is usually associated with solarization, it may have been his companion at the time, photographer Lee Miller, who discovered the effect—albeit accidentally. She has written:

> Something crawled across my foot in the darkroom and I let out a yell and turned on the light. I never did find out what it was, a mouse or what. Then I realized that the film was totally exposed: there in the development tanks, ready to be taken out, were a dozen practically fully developed negatives of a nude against a black background. Man Ray grabbed them, put them in the [fixer solution] and looked at them.[9]

Miller's own portrait of a woman shows the effect that can be produced when the "accident" is controlled **(274)**. This image combines the visual appearance of a photographic negative *and* a positive print. The ghostly dark shadows around the hand and parts of the face give the woman's portrait a slightly surreal quality.

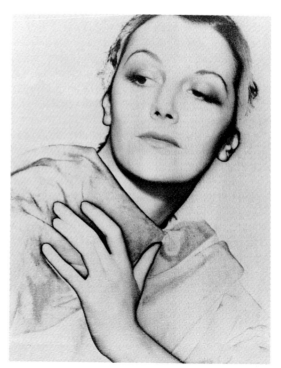

274. Lee Miller.
*Solarized Portrait
of Unknown Woman, Paris.* 1930.
Silver-gelatin print, $9\frac{1}{2} \times 7\frac{1}{2}''$.
Lee Miller Archives,
Chiddingly, East Sussex,
England.
© Lee Miller Archives, 1985.
All rights reserved.

Miller's solarization was a *darkroom* manipulation, which, until just a few years ago, was the chief method available to photographers who wished to enhance or "play with" the images recorded on film. The computer has changed all that. With increasingly sophisticated technology available, the computer has now become—for some photographers—as important a tool as the camera itself.

A pioneer in the field of computer-enhanced photography is Douglas Kirkland, whose portrait of *Cher* is reproduced here **(275)**. This image was made by scanning a "straight" color transparency and then using the computer to manipulate colors, textures, and outlines. The electric result of Kirkland's manipulations is even more Cher-like than Cher herself. Kirkland has written about his work this way:

> I am a photographer using the basics to go where photography alone has not previously allowed me to venture. It may sound odd, but I feel as though the computer is the other half of the camera I've been searching for since I began my photographic career . . . As a photographer, I manipulate the medium to the best of my ability, but nothing I can do manually touches what is possible using skill and judgment at the computer."[10]

At the beginning of this chapter we saw a photo-collage by David Hockney **(250)**, made up of many individual photographs joined to create a composite image. The technique of assembling pieces into a whole also underlies the work of two artists, identical twins, who function as a team—Doug and Mike Starn. The Starn twins are interested in process, in showing the process and the raw materials of photography as a painter might show the process of brush strokes. Their *Double Stark Portrait in Swirl* **(276)**, a portrait of themselves, consists of many pieces of photographic paper, cut and hacked irregularly, taped together (the Scotch tape is usually very obvious), then framed into a composition 8 feet square. Neatness and precision are not what the Starns are about. They smudge and tear and wrinkle their photographic fragments for a deliberate "scarred" effect. Sometimes their works are merely tacked or taped to the wall. Although they may be the art conservator's nightmare of the future, the Starn twins are today's photographic vanguard.

left: **275.** Douglas Kirkland. *Cher.* 1993. Original photograph by the artist, altered using Adobe Photoshop on Apple Macintosh computer. Copyright 1993 Douglas Kirkland.

right: **276.** Doug and Mike Starn. *Double Stark Portrait in Swirl.* 1985–86. Toned silver print and tape, 8′3″ square. Collection Randolfo Rocha, courtesy Stux Gallery, New York.

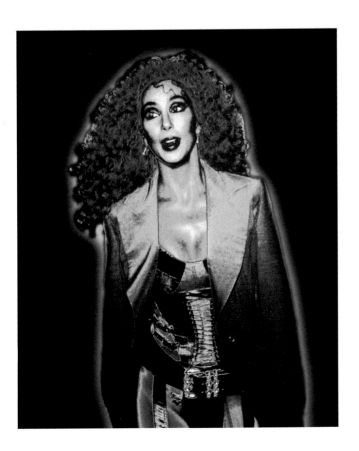

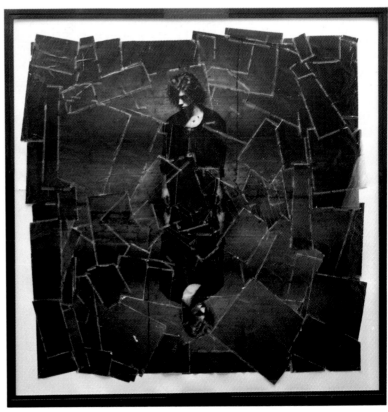

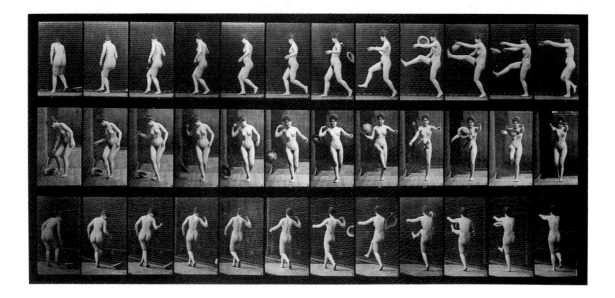

We might very well ask, then, what will photography do next? It is now possible to photograph the vastness of the universe through telescopes and the most minute forms of life through electron microscopes. Just as quickly as scientists have developed new techniques for their studies, creative artists have adapted those techniques for aesthetic purposes. In a mere century and a half photography has come farther and faster than any of the media that have been with us for thousands of years. Where does the camera go now?

One of the places the camera can go is into a realm we have not yet touched upon in this chapter. This realm is not really a new one. It was first explored more than a hundred years ago, but progress since that time has been extraordinary. The camera can seek to capture motion.

PHOTOGRAPHY AND MOTION

Throughout history artists have tried to create the illusion of motion in a still image. Painters have drawn galloping horses, running people, action of all kinds—never being sure that their depictions of the movement were "correct" and lifelike. To draw a running horse with absolute realism, for instance, the artist would have to freeze the horse in one moment of the run, but because the motion is too quick for the eye to follow, the artist had no assurance a running horse ever does take a particular pose. In 1878 a man named Eadweard Muybridge addressed this problem, and the story behind his solution is a classic in the history of photography.

Leland Stanford, a former governor of California, had bet a friend twenty-five thousand dollars that a horse at full gallop sometimes has all four feet off the ground. Since observation by the naked eye could not settle the bet one way or the other, Stanford hired Muybridge, known as a photographer of landscapes, to photograph one of the governor's racehorses. Muybridge devised an ingenious method to take the pictures. He set up twelve cameras, each connected to a black thread stretched across the racecourse. As Stanford's mare ran down the track, she snapped the threads that triggered the cameras' shutters—and proved conclusively that a running horse does gather all four feet off the ground at certain times. Stanford won the bet, and Muybridge went on to more ambitious studies of motion.

In 1887 Muybridge published *Animal Locomotion*, his most important project. Somehow, he persuaded a great many of his friends to take off their clothes and move about doing specific physical activities—in this case, inexplicably, kicking a pith helmet—while he photographed them **(277)**. There were 781 plates in the series—many of nude people, some of clothed people, some of animals—all in motion. For the first time ever the world could see what positions living creatures really assume when they move.

277. Eadweard Muybridge. *Woman Kicking,* Plate 367 from *Animal Locomotion.* 1887. Collotype $7\frac{1}{2} \times 20\frac{1}{4}''$. The Museum of Modern Art, New York (gift of the Philadelphia Commercial Museum).

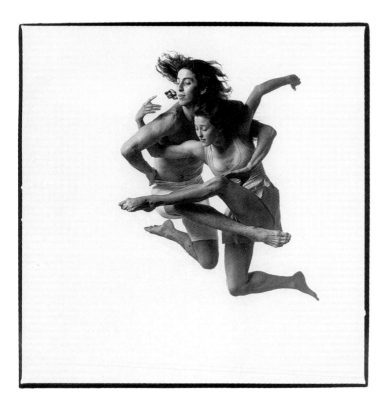

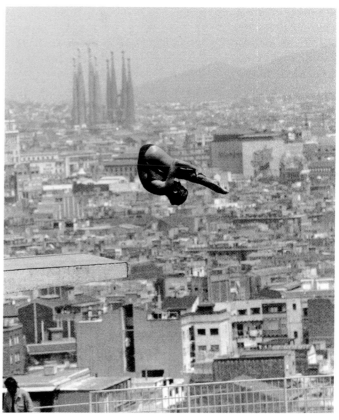

left: **278.** Lois Greenfield.
Daniel Ezralow & Ashley Roland.
1988. Gelatin-silver print.
© Lois Greenfield, 1988.

above: **279.** Barton Silverman.
Ellen Owen at the 1992 Summer Olympics.
1992. Photograph.
© 1998 Barton Silverman/Licensed by VAGA, New York.

The decades following Muybridge's experiments saw increasing sophistication in photographic equipment. As both films and cameras became faster, photographers discovered the ability to *stop* motion to the split second. Capturing one perfect moment in a fluid motion offers much dramatic potential, and that potential has been exploited most particularly in dance and in sports.

Earlier in this chapter we saw Barbara Morgan's picture of Martha Graham **(256)**. Although Morgan froze a moment in Graham's dance, the photograph is a portrait; it is *about* Martha Graham, not about dance in general. Our next image is something quite different. Lois Greenfield's photograph **(278)** is *about* dance—its grace, its physical energy, its defiance of earthly gravity. Amazingly, Greenfield has caught the dancers Daniel Ezralow and Ashley Roland in the split second when they are free in the air, their bodies and limbs intertwined yet never touching! It seems unreasonable to talk of composition when we know the picture was a click in mid-flight, yet somehow this photograph is brilliantly composed. The taut muscularity of the dancers forms a core at center, while their outflung arms and legs and feet and hair create the effect of a pinwheel.

Photographs of athletes in motion can be equally dramatic. Even sports fans long accustomed to stop-action photography can thrill at Barton Silverman's picture of the diver Ellen Owen at the 1992 Summer Olympics **(279)**. For this extraordinary shot Silverman took advantage of the fact that the divers' practice pool was on a high hill overlooking the city of Barcelona. He deliberately kept his focus sharp on the diver and softened the background cityscape so that Owen, tucked into her dive, seems impossibly suspended above a vast landscape. (We have to look hard to see the diving platform, at middle left, from which Owen has just launched herself; Silverman doesn't let us see the pool at all.) This photo becomes all the more fascinating because the background skyline is dominated by Gaudí's Church of the Holy Family, with its many fanciful towers.

Eadweard Muybridge's experiments in the 1880s had two direct descendants. One was stop-motion photography, such as we have seen in the last two examples. The other was *continuous*-motion photography. Undoubtedly, Muybridge had whetted the public's appetite to see *real* motion captured on film. The little room with a view had glimpsed a different world, a world that does not stand still but spins and moves and dances, and the public wanted more of this. The public did not have long to wait.

FILM

On the night of December 28, 1895, a small audience gathered in the basement of a Paris café, which was to become the first commercial movie theater in history. The audience viewed several very short films, including one of a baby being fed its dinner, another of a gardener being doused by a hose. One film in particular caused a strong reaction. *L'Arrivée d'un train en gare (The Arrival of a Train at the Station)* set the audience to screaming, ducking for cover, and jumping from their seats, because it featured a train hurtling directly toward the viewers. Never before, except in real life, had people seen anything of the kind, and they responded automatically. From the beginning, motion pictures could make an image on a screen seem real indeed.

THE ORIGINS OF MOTION PICTURES

Film depends on a phenomenon called **persistence of vision.** The human brain retains a visual image for a fraction of a second longer than the eye actually records it. If this were not true, your visual perception of the world would be continually interrupted by blinks of your eyes. Instead, your brain "carries over" the visual image during the split second while the eyes are closed. Similarly, the brain carries over when still images are flashed before the eyes with only the briefest space between them. Motion-picture film is not real motion but a series of still images projected at a speed of 24 frames per second, which makes the action seem continuous.

Interest in moving pictures really predates the development of the still camera. As early as 1832 a toy was patented in Europe in which a series of drawn images, each slightly different from the next, was made to spin in a revolving wheel so that the image appeared to move. Eadweard Muybridge later applied this principle to his multiple photographic images, spinning them in a wheel he called the *zoopraxiscope*.

Commercial applications of the motion picture, however, awaited three major developments. In 1888 the American George Eastman introduced celluloid film, which made it possible to string images together. Another big step was taken by Thomas Edison, the famous American inventor. It was in Edison's laboratory, in 1894, that technicians created what was apparently the first genuine motion picture. Lasting only a few seconds, the film was made on celluloid. Its "star" was one of Edison's mechanics, a man who could sneeze amusingly on command. Its title: *Fred Ott's Sneeze.*

One major problem remained. There was no satisfactory method for projecting the films to an audience. Here the challenge was taken up by two Frenchmen, brothers appropriately named Lumière (*lumière* means "light"), who in 1895 succeeded in building a workable film projector. The films shown in that Paris café were made by the brothers Lumière. From that point the motion-picture industry was off and running.

The fabulous era of silent films began with the Lumières' movie snippets, and it lasted for just over thirty years. During that time a wholly new creature—the movie star—came into being. Silent-film stars filled a gap in the American consciousness, for they lived and behaved like royalty. Some would have long careers in the cinema. Others fell victim to the next major breakthrough in film technology. Sound film was introduced in 1927, and not all stars of the silent era could make the transition, for their voices did not match their physical attributes. Quite a few virile leading men and sultry leading ladies were discovered to have squeaky little voices.

By the late 1920s the camera—the little room with a view—had come of age. Soon it would see things undreamed of before. Filmmaking of the twenties and thirties seems amazing in at least three respects: the tiny budgets; the rapid production times—perhaps just two or three weeks of shooting; and the small number of people involved. Today a major film may cost tens of millions, be in production for a year or more, and involve hundreds of people. But from the beginning of motion-picture history the greatest films, the classic films, have often been the product of one creative imagination. Usually, though not always, the creative force behind an important film is its director. Let us turn now to a brief survey of classic films and the creative artists who made them.

FILMS AND FILMMAKERS

The word "epic," in films, suggests a picture that is long, crowded, and grand. Usually, an epic film has a story taken from some significant point in history, or perhaps from the Bible. It will employ many actors—the proverbial "cast of thousands"—in climactic scenes with considerable action, such as battles, riots, or natural disasters. Often, the epic film has a moral to preach to its audience. Through the history of film there have been many epics, but the pioneer of the form was a man named David Wark Griffith.

D. W. Griffith began his movie career in 1908 as a director of very short (ten-minute) silent films cranked out at the rate of two a week. This apprenticeship taught him much about the mechanics of filmmaking, so that by the

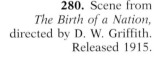

280. Scene from *The Birth of a Nation,* directed by D. W. Griffith. Released 1915.

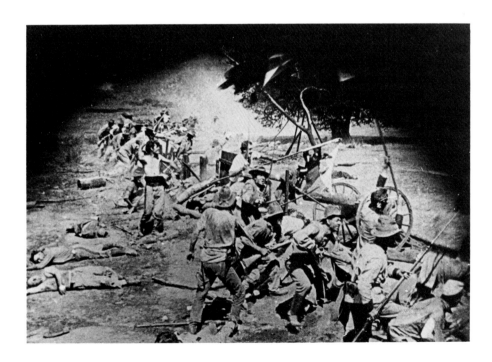

time Griffith had attained greater creative independence, he was ready for it. In 1914 the producer-director shot his first feature-length picture, and even its title proclaims an epic: *The Birth of a Nation* **(280)**. Griffith took his story from a contemporary novel. *The Birth of a Nation* is set in the American South before, during, and after the Civil War. In a now-familiar device, it interweaves the histories of two families—one northern, one southern—whose paths cross and whose members fall in love with one another. The plot allowed for many battle scenes and a particularly effective staging of President Lincoln's assassination. We must remember that this was a *silent* film. All action, all plot, all emotions had to be conveyed by visual images only, without dialogue or sound effects. (There was usually live musical accompaniment in the early movie theaters.)

Most viewers today would find it difficult to sit through *The Birth of a Nation*, for when it is not exaggerated in style it is offensive in its racial prejudice and simplistic morality. Even in its day some audiences reacted strenuously to these aspects of the movie. Reviewing the film on March 4, 1915, *The New York Times* complained about "melodramatic and inflammatory material." The *Times*, however, went on to evaluate "the film as a film" and deemed it "an impressive new illustration of the scope of the motion picture camera."[11] So it was, for Griffith had revolutionized the mechanics of filmmaking.

Each unbroken sequence of movie frames, with the camera rolling, is called a **shot.** Before Griffith, the standard in films had been the **full shot,** showing actors from head to toe. Griffith preferred to experiment with a full range of shots for dramatic effect: the **medium shot** (from the waist up), the **close-up** (head and shoulders), the **extreme close-up** (part of a face), and the **long shot** (seen from the distance). Dissatisfied with the camera as immobile observer of a scene, Griffith developed the **pan shot** (camera moving from side to side) and the **traveling shot** (camera moving from back to front on a track). He also perfected the technique of **cross-cutting,** in which two or more scenes are alternated to advance the action of the film. For example, he might film scenes of a heroine in distress and her hero rushing to save her, then cut back and forth rapidly between the two in order to build suspense.

This last shows Griffith's mastery of film **editing,** or assembling the film creatively after all scenes have been photographed. In *The Birth of a Nation* Griffith also made effective use of the **iris shot (280),** in which the edges of the film are blacked out to create a circle of interest. *The Birth of a Nation* even has **flashbacks,** or cuts to episodes that are supposed to have taken place before the main action of the film. To sum up, Griffith had virtually written a menu of possibilities for future filmmakers.

The mechanics of filmmaking being in place, other creative movie people could focus on story line. The next great genius of the film was a man who tapped the endlessly entertaining possibilities of the human condition—of laughing at oneself and the ridiculous situations one encounters in daily life. His name was Charles Chaplin.

Chaplin began his career as an actor. Sometime in the years 1913–14 he began to develop the character of "Charlie," the Little Tramp, whom he played in most of his films. Physically, Charlie was what today we might call a "wimp"—undersized, clumsy, comical in appearance, wearing shoes and trousers far too big for him, sporting an absurd derby hat and a cane. Charlie was inevitably the one who got the pie in the face, the splash of slush from a passing streetcar, the foot caught in a goldfish bowl. He was the perennial outsider, always looking in wistfully at people who were rich, graceful, beautiful, and successful. But Charlie had courage, and he had a heart of gold. He would rush to save a maiden in trouble, only to lose her affections to the handsome leading man. Charlie was Everyman adrift in a world where anything could go wrong, anybody could trip him up.

Through many silent films Chaplin refined the character of Charlie and also honed his skills as a filmmaker. Soon he was not only acting but writing, directing, and producing as well. By the 1930s Chaplin was at the top of his

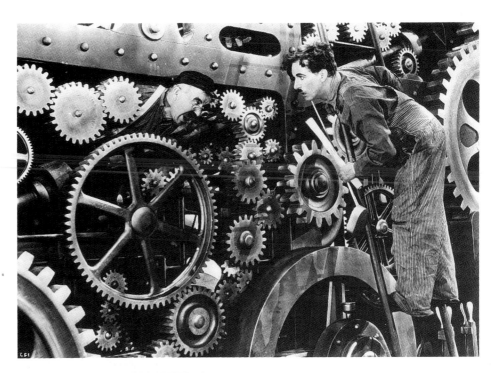

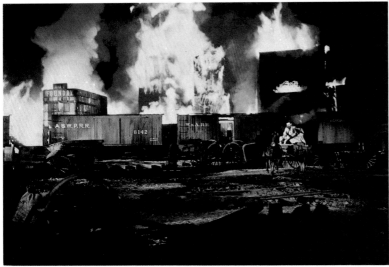

top: 281. Charles Chaplin as "Charlie," the Little Tramp, in a scene from *Modern Times,* directed by Charles Chaplin. 1936.

above: 282. "The Burning of Atlanta," scene from *Gone with the Wind,* produced by David O. Selznick. 1939. © Selznick International Pictures, Inc., ren. 1967 Metro-Goldwyn-Mayer, Inc.

form. *Modern Times* **(281)** is considered by many to be his greatest film. In this movie Chaplin pits himself against the modern assembly line and, predictably, loses the contest. Chaplin's inventive genius goes into high gear, so to speak, as Charlie struggles against the machine and the machine fights back. *Modern Times* continues the battle of the odd little hero against adversity, but now his opponents are mechanical, not human. As with all his films, Chaplin concealed a message in *Modern Times*—that our fast-paced world is hard on innocent nonconformists—but the message is presented with side-splitting humor.

Color photography for films was feasible in the early 1930s. By the end of that decade it had been perfected sufficiently to be available to master producer David O. Selznick when he set out to film *Gone with the Wind,* Margaret Mitchell's spectacularly best-selling novel of the Civil War. Filming *Gone with the Wind* presented a special problem. Mitchell's book had so thoroughly captivated the imaginations of millions of readers that a potential audience *knew* exactly what the movie should look like. Selznick took full charge of the project, overwhelming writers and directors, and he delivered. The movie of *Gone with the Wind* was, and remains, a tremendous success with audiences.

The color effects in *Gone with the Wind* are always vivid **(282)**. For the most intense scenes, such as the burning of Atlanta, Selznick poured on a saturated red. Red worked for Selznick and the film on different levels. It is associated with the clayey soil of Georgia, where the story takes place. It is inherently dramatic. It often symbolizes passion, in this case the passions of war and the passion between those two classic lovers, Scarlett O'Hara and Rhett Butler. To our eyes now, accustomed to color films, the "scorched" effects of *Gone with the Wind* may seem a little exaggerated, but for that time and that movie they were exactly right.

Selznick's control of *Gone with the Wind* was considerable, but it may seem modest compared with the creative involvement by the next filmmaker we shall study. In 1941 R.K.O. released a film created almost single-handed by a twenty-six-year-old "boy genius" who played the starring role, produced and directed the film, co-authored the screenplay, supervised the editing and set design, and, it is said, even sewed some of the costumes himself. The film was not a success with contemporary audiences or critics. Today, however, when movie people compile lists of the "ten best" filmmakers and films, we are sure to find the names of Orson Welles and his masterpiece, *Citizen Kane* **(283)**.

Welles based his story, loosely, on the life of the newspaper publisher William Randolph Hearst, here renamed Charles Foster Kane (played by Welles). What could have been a simple biography of a powerful man was turned by Welles into a startling cinematic achievement. *Citizen Kane* was innovative on a number of levels. Its structure, at first glance an ordinary flashback, begins with Kane's death, then traces his life from childhood and youth up through old age and back to his death again. But the actual telling of the story is far more complex than that. Kane's life on film is divided into five sections—the first played out in blaring newsreel films, the other four narrated in turn from the points of view of four people involved with Kane. Welles begins with a superficial outside view of the brash, successful young Kane, then gradually probes deeper and deeper into Kane's psychic center, as that center slowly disintegrates into lonely, bitter old age.

Cinematically, the movie opens the filmmaker's grab bag of tricks—all meant to highlight Kane's personality. There are ***low-angle shots*** (to show a towering Kane), dramatic long shots, and many traveling shots intended to convey physical and emotional separation. For instance, as Kane's relationship with his first wife becomes cooler, the camera shows the couple farther and farther apart at the ends of an ever-lengthening dinner table. Welles calcu-

283. Orson Welles as Charles Foster Kane and Ruth Warrick as his first wife in a scene from *Citizen Kane*, produced and directed by Orson Welles. 1941.

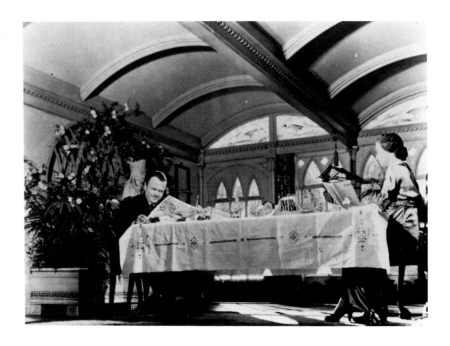

lated every shot to convey the mood, the emotional symbols, the portrait of a character he intended. *Citizen Kane* could not be a stage play. It is too dependent on film techniques for its impact. More than any filmmaker before him, Welles had shown what the camera, used imaginatively, could do.

With a few exceptions, American filmmakers dominated the industry in the early days, but by the 1950s and 1960s critical attention began to focus on European directors with serious aims. Two of these—one Swedish, one Italian—attracted special attention in the United States: Ingmar Bergman and Federico Fellini.

Ingmar Bergman's first internationally successful film, and some would say his greatest, was *The Seventh Seal*, made in 1957. *The Seventh Seal* is an allegory, a story filled with religious and macabre symbolism, a kind of morality play, set in the 14th century apparently in Sweden. As it begins, a knight returning from the Crusades is met on the beach by the figure of Death **(284)**, who announces that the knight's time has come. Stalling for time, the knight challenges Death to a game of chess, and they agree that Death will not claim him until the game is over. The knight hopes to use this borrowed time to find some meaning in life, to accomplish some deed that he cannot name. As the game goes on intermittently, the knight and his squire, with other characters they meet, journey toward the knight's castle. Along the way they encounter a young couple, Jof (Joseph) and Mia (Mary) and their baby son—undoubtedly symbolic of the Christ child and his parents. In the end Death wins the chess game and calls the knight and his party to darkness, but the knight tricks Death into sparing the innocent couple and their baby.

Bergman, who both wrote and directed *The Seventh Seal*, was able to put an unusually personal stamp on this and all his films, because over the years he developed a close-knit repertory company of actors and supporting crew, accustomed to him and to one another. Both he and Welles are examples of what is called an **auteur.** The French word *auteur* translates literally as "author," but in relation to films it implies a great deal more. A cinematic *auteur* has maximum control over a film's production and imparts an individual style to a film or series of films. He or she often writes the screenplay—or closely supervises its writing—and may draw upon personal imagery, dreams, obsessions, fears, memories, beliefs, or loves as subject matter. This was certainly true of Ingmar Bergman, and it was equally true of his counterpart in Italy, Federico Fellini.

284. The figure of Death in an early scene from *The Seventh Seal,* directed by Ingmar Bergman. 1957.

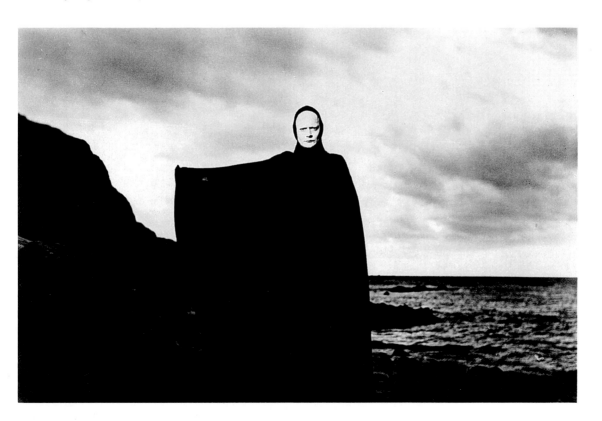

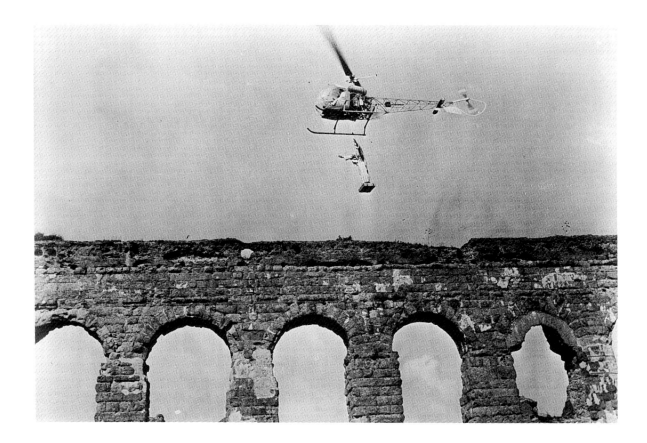

285. Opening sequence of
La Dolce Vita, directed
by Federico Fellini. 1959.

Where Bergman is somber and melancholy, Fellini is flamboyant. His films may at first seem lighthearted, but there is a darker quality beneath the surface. A good example of this complexity is found in one of Fellini's best-known films, *La Dolce Vita*. The title, translated as "the sweet life," surely is ironic, for Fellini's camera zeroes in on people for whom life has become a series of superficial, momentary pleasures, carried to the extreme of depravity. Contrasts are made throughout the film between the old, stable values and society's new focus on instant sensual gratification. Fellini establishes this in his opening sequence, when a huge Christ figure is carried dangling from a helicopter over the city of Rome **(285)**. A number of young women in bikinis, sunbathing on a rooftop, rise to wave at it. The symbolism is apt. Rome is, after all, a city of many churches, the seat of the Roman Catholic Church. But the Romans caught by Fellini's camera are more interested in indulgences of the flesh. They are rich, privileged, idle, and dissolute. Major events in the film include a suicide and an orgy. Fellini's message seems to be that this "sweet life" is not sweet at all, but poisonous; its participants not alive, but acting out a living death.

Despite the prominence of European filmmakers, Hollywood still could support a serious filmmaker, indeed an *auteur*, and it found its own in the person of a transplanted English director named Alfred Hitchcock. We might describe Hitchcock as the "purest" of filmmakers in the sense that his fascination lay almost entirely with the techniques of the camera. Hitchcock had limited interest in story line, even less in dialogue, and he did not much care to direct his performers in interpreting their lines. Actually, by the time the cameras were ready to roll and the actors were in position, most of his creative work was over—a remarkable stance for a director. For Hitchcock, by then, would have plotted every shot to the last detail, established the camera angles and cuts, visualized the completed film. No editor could tamper with his work afterward, because, contrary to the usual practice, he did not shoot several versions of each scene. He shot only what he wanted in the film, what he had determined beforehand.

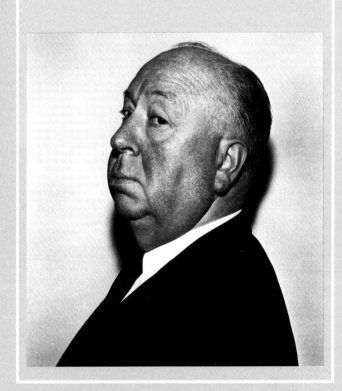

ALFRED HITCHCOCK

1899–1980

IN THE FIRST SCENE of the film *North by Northwest* a man misses a bus and the doors slam in his face. He appears on screen for only a few moments and is never again seen in the movie. But in a very real sense the man missing the bus is the star of the picture. Making the "cameo" appearance that was his trademark in nearly every film, that man is the director—Alfred Hitchcock.

Born in a poor section of London, Hitchcock—who as an adult was always called "Hitch"—was the son of a greengrocer and his wife. His formal schooling ended at age fourteen, after which he worked at assorted jobs to help support his family. When he was twenty he got a job with an American film company based in London. The film industry then was very new, and the roles of participants tended to overlap. Hired as a designer of title cards, Hitchcock soon found himself filling in as a scriptwriter, set designer, supervisor of costumes, production man-

ager, and director. No better apprenticeship could have been planned for the man who would later be acclaimed as the technical virtuoso of filmmaking.

As the film industry expanded, so did Hitchcock's fortunes. Eventually he would direct nine silent films and fourteen sound features in London. With *The Lodger*, a silent film of 1927, Hitchcock already had begun to attract critical notice. Meanwhile, he had married Alma Reville, who would remain his lifelong creative partner. Their daughter Pat was born in 1928.

By the late 1930s the British film business was faltering. Hollywood had become the colossus of the film world. For a time Hitchcock and Hollywood played out a sort of mating dance. Then they were wed. In March of 1939 the Hitchcocks sailed for the United States, which would become their permanent home. During the balance of that year Hitchcock worked on the first, and one of the most famous, of his American films, *Rebecca*.

Not until 1954, however, did Hitchcock truly hit his stride. Most of the pictures that established his filmmaking genius were made in the decade starting with that year: *Rear Window*, *To Catch a Thief*, *Vertigo*, *North by Northwest*, *Psycho*, and *The Birds*. Hitchcock's themes were usually macabre, featuring suspense, murder, psychosexual madness, or (in *The Birds*) placid nature turned to mayhem. During this decade, too, Hitchcock's major preoccupations got their fullest indulgence. He was a demon practical joker, often turning rather cruel pranks against his actors on the set. His devotion to gourmet foods and fine wines sent his weight soaring over 300 pounds. And he indulged another passion (always intense, always platonic) in his choice of female stars for his films—the cool, distant, aristocratic blonde exemplified by Grace Kelly, the first of Hitchcock's favorites.

After 1964 Hitchcock's concentration seemed to fail. Though he made several more films, almost none attained the quality of those from his prime. Still, until his death, neither the world nor the man himself lost the sense of Hitchcock as the consummate director. As early as 1925 Hitchcock had predicted his role as a creative force in filmmaking. Addressing a meeting of his colleagues, he said, "*We* make a film succeed. The name of the director should be associated in the public's mind with a quality product. Actors come and actors go, but the name of the director should stay clearly in the mind of the audience."[12]

Photograph of Alfred Hitchcock.

We see Hitchcock's masterful control of visual imagery in a classic scene from his thriller *North by Northwest*, released in 1959 **(286)**. The hero, played by Cary Grant, has been duped into riding a bus to an isolated spot in the middle of a cornfield. There he stands, waiting for a supposed meeting with a man he does not know (and who, it turns out, does not exist). As Grant waits in the hot sun, there is no sound but the scrunch of his feet on the ground. Hitchcock gives no "meaningful" background music. Then a small airplane appears in the distance, flies closer, and heads directly for Grant. We realize the plane is trying to mow him down. Again, there is no sound but the airplane's engine and Grant's breathing as he runs this way and that, trying to elude the plane. The scene is eerily terrifying, not least because viewers are unprepared for the spectacle of a man in a business suit, stranded in flat country, trying to escape death from a dive-bombing airplane.

Considered logically, this scene is absurd; businessmen do not get attacked by murderous airplanes. Considered cinematically, it is a triumph—a life-and-death struggle of man against anonymous machine. Hitchcock spoke of how he planned this scene to be the *opposite* of what normally we would expect to be a menacing situation. Most filmmakers, setting up danger, would show darkness, looming buildings, mysterious figures peering from windows. Not Hitchcock. He gave us: "Just nothing. Just bright sunshine and a blank, open countryside with barely a house or tree in which any lurking menaces could hide."[13] That is the genius of Hitchcock's technique. Menace drops out of the sky into ordinary life.

In today's world of dazzlingly high-budget films, with their consequent monetary risk, it is unusual for a filmmaker to have the kind of absolute creative freedom that Hitchcock did. One filmmaker who has managed to maintain the position of *auteur* right up to the present is Woody Allen. Allen, who began his career as a stand-up comic and gag writer, began making films in 1969 and has averaged one a year since then. He first achieved both critical and commercial success with *Annie Hall* in 1977, and since then his reputation as a "genius" filmmaker has grown steadily. Legends gain special privileges, and Allen is aware of his extraordinary position when he says, "I have control of everything, and I mean everything. I can make any film I want to make. Any subject—comic, serious. I can cast who I want to cast."

And Allen *does* make any film he wants to make. Hating to repeat himself, he has experimented with various genres—comedies, dramas, fantasies, a mystery, even a musical. Nearly always, however, there is an aura of glamour, of sophistication, a "sheen" on his films that sets them apart from everyday life. He says: "I've never felt Truth was Beauty. Never. I've always felt that people can't take too much reality. . . . You spend your whole life searching for a way out."[14]

286. Cary Grant in a scene from *North by Northwest,* directed by Alfred Hitchcock. 1959. © 1959 Loew's Incorporated.

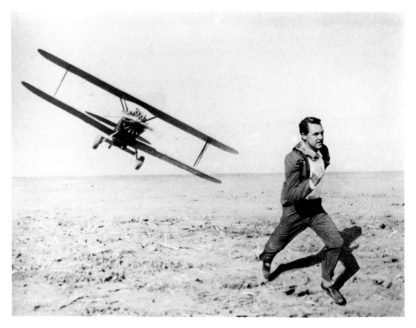

One of Allen's favorite films—and the public's—is *The Purple Rose of Cairo*, released in 1984 **(287)**. In the film a young woman (Mia Farrow), whose life is drab and humdrum, escapes to the movie theater, where, sitting rapt in the dark, she can lose herself in the romantic scenes being played out on the screen. When a movie called "The Purple Rose of Cairo" is playing, she sees it over and over, and falls swooningly in love with its hero (Jeff Daniels). Then an amazing thing happens. While the movie is playing, the hero suddenly steps right off the screen, walks down the theater aisle, and approaches the young woman. He enters her world, and eventually draws her into his fantasy world. In other words, her workaday Truth interacts and collides with his fantasy Beauty. The ensuing developments are both comic and poignant.

Like most of the films we have considered, *The Purple Rose of Cairo* is basically "straight." Its view is of a world that *could* be real, even if it isn't exactly real. Before closing our brief discussion of the film, we should look at another kind of world that is often captured in the camera—a world in which dogs talk, giant apes climb on buildings, creatures from other planets land in the suburbs of California, and galaxies go to war with one another. This is the world of special effects and animation.

SPECIAL EFFECTS AND ANIMATION

King Kong was not the first film to employ special effects, but it was certainly one of the more memorable. Made in 1932, *King Kong* is an adventure story concerning a giant gorilla, some 50 feet tall, which is captured in Africa and somehow transported to New York for display as a curiosity. Also, the film is an odd kind of love story, because when Kong inevitably escapes from his captors, he falls in love with a normal-sized woman and carries her around with him. Mostly, though, *King Kong* was an opportunity to try some of the most imaginative and startling visual effects yet attempted on film.

The model of Kong used for filming was about 18 inches tall. Through trick photography the figure was transformed into a monster capable of climbing the Empire State Building and grabbing at the airplanes that try to shoot him down **(288)**. Effects like these were achieved because filmmakers had become more comfortable with the potential of the camera. No longer need anyone's imagination be limited by physical constraints. A filmmaker could daydream, "What if a giant ape climbed the Empire State Building?" and then proceed to make it happen on film. In life or on the stage, such a feat would present staggering difficulties. In film, anything is possible.

Animation is another tool that expands the filmmaker's range of possibilities. The word **animation** means "bringing to life," and that is precisely what

left: 287. Jeff Daniels and Mia Farrow in a scene from *The Purple Rose of Cairo,* directed by Woody Allen. 1984. Orion (courtesy Kobal).

right: 288. Scene from *King Kong.* 1932.

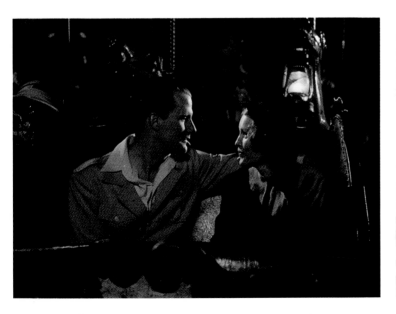

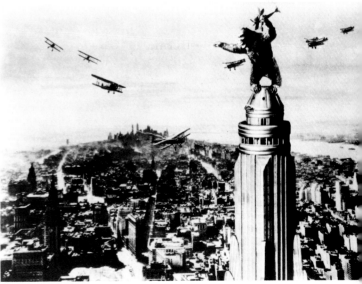

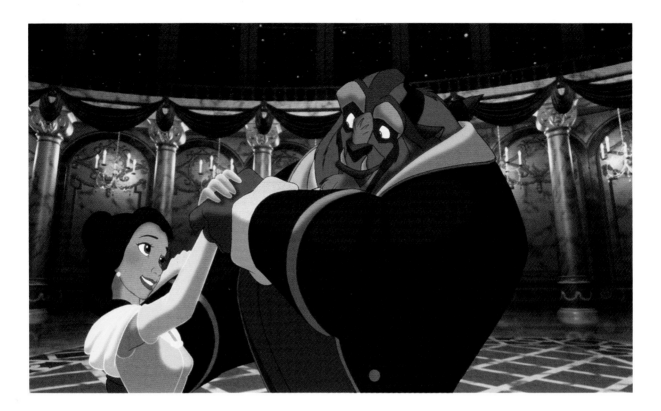

289. Belle and the Beast, in a scene from the animated film *Beauty and the Beast.* 1991. © Disney Enterprises, Inc.

the filmic animator does with drawings of people, animals, and inanimate objects. Animated films are, in principle, little more than sophisticated versions of Muybridge's sequential photographs **(277)** made to spin in a wheel. They involve a series of drawings or cartoons, each slightly different from the next, arranged on film and projected at a speed that makes the drawn figures seem to move. The classic method of animation was perfected by Walt Disney Studios in the late 1920s. You can appreciate how time-consuming this was if you realize how much your body moves just in walking two steps, and consider how many drawings it would take to capture that movement. If the motion is not to seem jerky and unnatural, every shift of position by the merest fraction of an inch requires a new drawing. The smoothest animation, therefore, demanded about 24 different drawings per *second* or some 130,000 drawings for a feature-length film. In its heyday, the 1930s and 1940s, Disney Studios employed armies of illustrators.

Today the mechanics of animation have been simplified by computers. Modern animation is accomplished directly at the computer terminal, using light rather than paint. The artist draws an original picture on the display screen and then programs the computer to "draw" the changing images that simulate action. Images and colors can be varied at will, live action can be combined with animation—the possibilities are literally endless.

One of the most critically acclaimed animated films is Walt Disney's *Beauty and the Beast* **(289)**, released in 1991. Although some think it is meant for children, the film offers much to engage and delight adults. Through sophisticated animation, all sorts of objects come to life and sing and dance—a teapot, a clock, a feather duster, a footstool, an entire set of silverware. In a sly tribute to the pioneers of film, *Beauty's* animated candelabrum is named "Lumière"—a double play on words indicating its light-giving nature.

The possibilities for visual expression in film have expanded tremendously since the brothers Lumière set up their little projector barely a hundred years ago. But another medium, also based on the camera, has come farther and faster in half the time. The video arts—of which television is most prominent—probably touch more people more significantly than all the other media discussed in this book put together.

VIDEO

All art is about communication, but the video arts in particular are about *mass* communication. No other medium even approaches television in its potential for presenting to millions of people the same visual experience at the same moment. A national or international event—such as a grand wedding in the British royal family or the Olympic Games—is telecast simultaneously into homes around the globe, complete with the graphics and other visual trappings devised by the networks to capture our attention. Viewers can, if they wish, compare their responses to an identical visual stimulus. This holds true not only for dramatic one-of-a-kind events, but also for the recurring fare of television. In offices, in supermarkets, in schools across the United States, conversations start with, "Did you see [name a popular show] last night?" For anyone alive now this is normal, but for all the billions of people who populated the earth before the 1950s it would be almost incomprehensible. Thanks to television, living with art has acquired another dimension: It is a mass visual experience.

The first official television broadcast in the United States took place in 1939, in connection with the opening of the New York World's Fair. Few people noticed, however, because there were practically no television receivers to accept the transmission. Not until about 1950 did the television set become an expected fixture in American homes. Now, of course, more homes around the globe have television than have indoor plumbing.

Readers of this book are intimately familiar with commercial television, so there is no need for discussion of its myriad offerings. Less well known, perhaps, is the work of serious video artists, who took up the medium almost from its beginning. In one form of **video art** the image is actually created on the television screen by manipulating dials, selecting colors, combining figures and other elements. Many artists believe this type of expression to be the most valid for our electronic age.

Foremost among video artists working in this realm is Korean-born, New York–based Nam June Paik. Paik envisioned a new art of video technology as

290. Nam June Paik. *Fin de Siècle II.* 1989. Video installation: approximately 300 television sets, 3-channel color video with sound. Collection Laila and Thurston Twigg-Smith; installed at Whitney Museum of American Art, New York, November 9, 1989 to February 18, 1990.

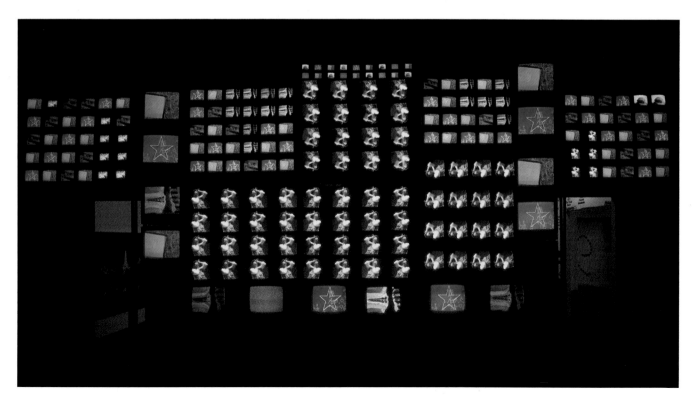

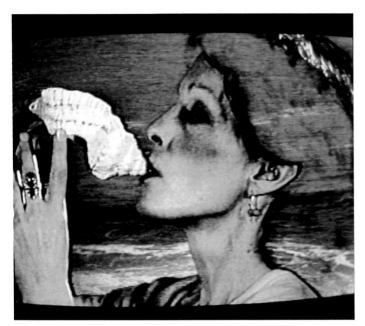 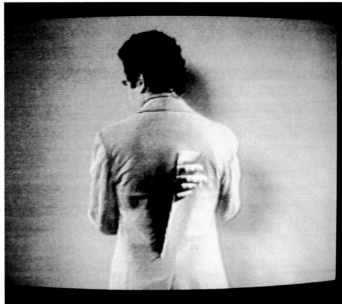

early as 1960. He does not *reproduce* images electronically, as network television might show an image of a painting by Picasso or Renoir. Rather, the image is *produced* and controlled by means of the electronic equipment itself **(290)**. What is especially exciting about this approach is its immediacy, its "aliveness." According to Paik, "Most paintings reflect light. So when it's white paint, for example, you see the white light. Whereas television pictures are glowing light. Light is coming out, sprouting out. So it is much more intense physically. . . ."[15] Paik's video installations are expensive and take up space; they are not the sort of art that most collectors could expect to have in their homes. Still, they draw large crowds at museum exhibitions. We have grown accustomed to television. The fascination of transitory images is inherent in our world. Click—the art is there; click—it's gone; click—it's back again.

Another type of video art is related to filmmaking in the sense that it creates a visual continuum, perhaps even a story. What sets it apart from film is the possibility for electronic manipulation of the imagery, the greater freedom to "play" offered by the video camera. Joan Jonas' *Double Lunar Dogs* **(291)** is based on a science fiction story in which travelers aboard a spaceship, stranded after the apocalypse, grapple with isolation and survival. Special effects condense time and space, turning the voyage into an abstraction.

Peter Campus' *Three Transitions* **(292)**, a classic work in video art, is a very brief (less than five-minute) exercise in electronic displacement of the artist's own face and body. In the first "transition," Campus seems to stab himself in the back, climb out through the wound, then emerge intact on the other side. In the second he wipes away his face with his hand, revealing another same face underneath. And in the last Campus appears to burn his living face as though it were a photograph. These operations are made visually possible—even believable—through sophisticated video technology. Early in this chapter we quoted the adage "The camera can't lie." Video artists like Peter Campus prove that the camera *can* lie—and very creatively.

A room with a view—the camera. What do we see through the peephole of the room? Images from the past, images of the present, images of a possible future. Our fondest memories and our most horrifying nightmares. Colors and shapes known or imaginary. The artistry of those who direct the camera's view need accept no limitations, for the view outside grows bigger all the time.

left: 291. Joan Jonas.
Double Lunar Dogs. 1984.
Video.
Electronic Arts Intermix, New York.

right: 292. Peter Campus.
Three Transitions. 1973.
Video.
Electronic Arts Intermix, New York.

Graphic Design

ALL ART has to do with communication, but this is uniquely true of graphic design. Graphic design has as its goal the communication of some *specific* message to a group of people, and the success of a design is measured by how well that message is conveyed. The message might be "This is a good product to buy," or "You will want to read this book/magazine/article," or "This is an important, respected company," or "This way to the elevators (or rest rooms or library)," or any of countless others. If it can be demonstrated that the public received the intended message—because the product sold well, or the company's stock went up, or the traveler found the right services—then the design has worked.

Not all graphic design has to do with selling, but much of it does, and so for a long time it was known as "commercial art." The term "graphic design" is more inclusive and describes more accurately what artists in this field really do. They create a visual image by some combination of words and/or pictures to communicate a message quickly and effectively. They devise the trademarks and symbols (logos) that construct a special corporate identity for firms doing business around the world. They invent symbols that have the same meaning to people who speak different languages. They provide the colorful images that introduce television programs and movies.

Printed words play an important role in many graphic designs, but designers rely heavily on recognizable visual images as well. Per Arnoldi's poster for Lincoln Center (293) does not even really need the word "dance" for us to grasp its meaning. The artist's two disembodied legs, in brightly colored tights and poised in a classic attitude, immediately suggest the ballet. The image is simple, clean, striking, and witty—all excellent traits for a graphic design.

Because of our constant exposure to television commercials as well as sophisticated magazine advertisements, graphic design seems very much a phenomenon of the 20th century, but in fact it has existed almost since the beginning of civilized life. Street and shop signs were used in ancient Rome and, presumably, continued through subsequent centuries. Over the years graphic design gradually took hold and became a central part of urban life.

Three factors are ultimately responsible for the growing influence of graphic design: the invention of the printing press in the 15th century, the Industrial Revolution in the 18th century, and the revolution in travel and communication in the 20th century.

Anyone can paint one sign, or two or three. The printing press, however, made it possible to reproduce a graphic image many hundreds or thousands of times. This gave designers the *ability* to communicate with a broad public. The *need* for such communication was largely a result of the Industrial Revolution, which began in Europe in the latter part of the 18th century. Before that time, most products were grown or made locally to serve a local population. The person who wanted, say, a new pair of shoes could walk down the road to the village cobbler or perhaps wait for the monthly fair at which cobblers from the neighboring towns might appear, but the choices were fairly limited. With the advent of machines huge quantities of goods were produced in centralized factories for wide distribution, and competition between producers became intense. It was necessary, therefore, to inform the buying public about the availability of certain goods and their relative merits. Graphic design in the form of advertising filled that need.

The history of graphic design for travelers is interesting, too. Some of it is speculative. We wonder, for instance, whether Robin Hood followed signs leading to Nottingham, or whether the pilgrims Chaucer wrote about found signs pointing the way to Canterbury. In the last few decades international travel has increased dramatically. People journey to foreign countries, without knowing the local language, and expect to get around comfortably and safely. Such travel has opened up a whole new realm for the graphic designer.

Nowhere, perhaps, is the need to communicate without words more evident than at the Olympic Games, which draw athletes from scores of countries into one location. Somehow all the athletes must be housed, must find the places where they are supposed to be at various times, and must obtain the services they need. Preparing signs written in all the languages represented would be tedious and cumbersome. So whenever the games are held, graphic images are designed to mark basic areas and functions. The images are designed anew each time, but always they are simple, straightforward, and free of cultural biases. For the 1994 Winter Games at Lillehammer, Norway, IBM created a series of pictograms inspired by an ancient rock carving that depicts a skier **(294)**. Even without captions you should have no difficulty identifying the sports they portray.

So in international travel as well as international commerce the need for graphic design has burgeoned. Fortunately, the *ability* to communicate graphically has also increased, thanks to new mechanical and electronic processes.

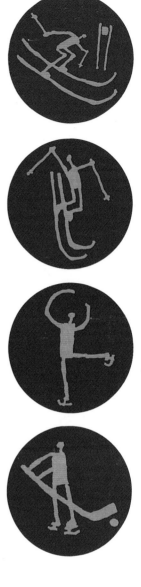

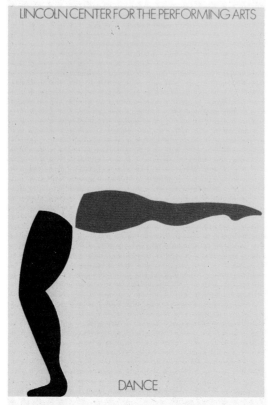

left: 293. Per Arnoldi. *Dance*, poster for Lincoln Center for the Performing Arts. 1986.

above: 294. Pictogram symbols for 1994 Winter Olympic Games at Lillehammer, Norway.

THE TOOLS
OF THE GRAPHIC DESIGNER

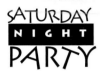

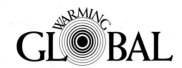

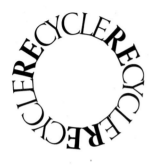

Regardless of the kind of graphic design or the method of reproduction, the graphic designer works with three tools: *type* (printed letters), **photography,** and drawn or painted **illustration.** Every design has at least one of these resources and usually has two or more in combination. We must also take into account the variable of color, because color is often responsible for much of a design's impact.

Type design has come a long way since the invention of movable type about 1450. Contemporary graphic designers have a bewildering array of typefaces and styles to choose from, in an infinite range of sizes. This book, for instance, is printed in a typeface known as *Aster*, which is popular for books because it is easy to read, legible in fairly small sizes, and not tiring to the eyes.

With so many typefaces and sizes to choose from, the designer can select one that best fits the character of the design and the tone of the message to be communicated. Moreover, type design itself has changed radically. In earlier times the letters of type were painstakingly carved out of wood or cast in metal. Today, type is "set"—or created and placed in position—by computer and photographic methods, so it is relatively easy to design an original typeface for a specific purpose. The designer can make a "word picture" that symbolizes the idea of the graphic design **(295).**

A major decision for any graphic designer is whether to use photography or drawn illustration. In either case the options are limitless, and the choice becomes one of finding the image that will best present the idea.

Drawn or painted images are popular for *editorial* illustration—illustrations for newspaper or magazine articles—and it is easy to understand why this is so. A clever illustrator can read the article, digest its ideas, its message, its flavor, then create an original image to express visually what the article says in words. Sometimes the illustration *is* the message. Few words are needed, because the art by itself tells most of the story. For a feature page in The Sophisticated Traveler, a supplement to *The New York Times*, artist Marco Ventura created what the headline announced as "All the Art You'll Ever Need" **(296).** Readers were advised to "study this picture," after which they would "never again need to set foot in any musty old museum." This is instant art history, a crash course in culture, the "Viewer's Digest" guide to art.

With sly wit, Ventura painted a composite of six great masterpieces in Western art history. All of them are illustrated and discussed in this book.

above: 295. Wanda Siedlecka. *Wordplay.* 1990–94. Type designed to create "word pictures."

right: 296. Marco Ventura. *Mona Lisa Contemplating the Bust of Nefertiti as God Creates Order out of Chaos on a Starry Night on the Island of La Grande Jatte as the Infanta Margarita Looks On.* Illustration for The Sophisticated Traveler supplement to *The New York Times*, May 16, 1993.

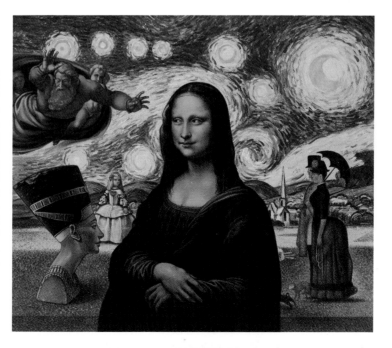

Leonardo da Vinci's *Mona Lisa* **(473)** poses at center, against a background of Vincent van Gogh's painting *The Starry Night* **(15)**. At upper left is the figure of God creating order in the universe, from Michelangelo's frescoes on the Sistine Chapel ceiling **(476)**. Below God are the Egyptian portrait bust of *Queen Nefertiti* **(420A)** and the Infanta Margarita from Velázquez' painting *Las Meninas* **(500)**. At right we see a couple lifted from Georges Seurat's *A Sunday on La Grande Jatte* **(119)**.

The joke of this illustration, of course, lies in the artist's pretending to instruct ignorant viewers. Readers of the *Times'* Sophisticated Traveler section will recognize each of these images instantly, having a shared knowledge of art and having, no doubt, spent quite a lot of time in "musty old museums."

More often, the illustrator's job is to interpret written material with an appropriate image. We find a good example in an illustration for *Union* Magazine **(297)**. The magazine article, entitled "Too Little, Too Late," had this theme: "The insurance industry's cure for the nation's ailing health-care system leaves many consumers standing in the rain." To show this concept, artist Anita Kunz painted a surrealistic hand-face, clearly in distress, clutching a teeny, inadequate umbrella.

The term "drawn illustration" was used earlier to distinguish from photography, but not all illustrations are actually drawn with a pen or crayon. One of the most sought-after illustrators today, Stephen Kroninger, does his "drawing" with scissors. His illustrations for many popular magazines and newspapers are made in the form of collage—cut-up pieces from magazines and other bits of paper, assembled into odd and playful portraits **(298)**. The collage form gives a three-dimensional feel to these illustrations, making them seem like pop-up figures jumping off the page.

Sometimes a photograph is the better choice for a particular design situation, but then the question becomes, what sort of photograph? American Standard is a company that makes bathroom fixtures. A photograph of a sink or tub or toilet would show us the product well enough, but it might not attract our attention as readily as the advertisement shown here **(299)**. This elegant photo of a bathtub drain lever, floating above the water, turns that humble device into a cheery, all-knowing little face. Combined with the caption "It's seen you naked. It's heard you sing," this ad makes us smile—and, ideally, remember the manufacturer's name.

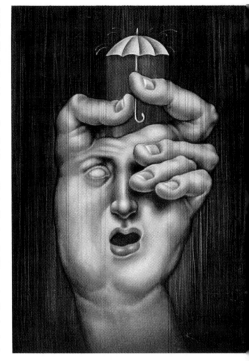

above: **297.** Anita Kunz.
Too Little, Too Late. 1992.
Watercolor and gouache, 11 × 8".
Client: *Union* Magazine.

left: **298.** Stephen Kroninger.
Michael Jackson. 1990.
Collage illustration.
Courtesy the artist.

below: **299.** "It's Seen You Naked.
It's Heard You Sing,"
magazine advertisement
for American Standard.
Art director: Warren Johnson;
writer, Tom Gabriel;
photographer:
Shawn Michienzi, RipSaw.

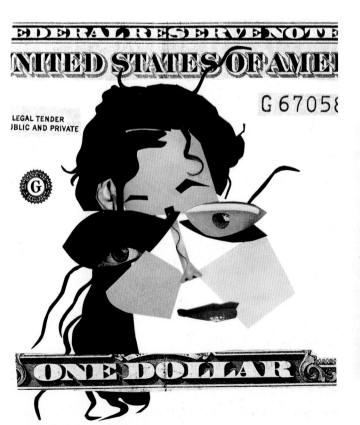

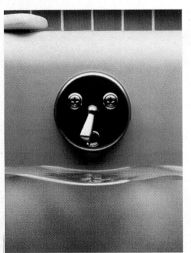

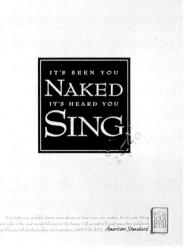

These three tools, then—type, illustration, and photography—lend themselves to literally infinite combinations. The following brief survey of graphic design categories should give some idea of the scope and variety in this field. We begin with the most pervasive design category of modern times.

ADVERTISING

More than at any other time in history we are bombarded from every side by advertising. So many products are made, so many consumers are there to buy them, so many millions of dollars are at stake in bringing the two together. Oftentimes the success of a product has more to do with the advertising campaign than with the product's intrinsic worth. This is especially true when products are alike. How different, really, are household cleaners? All have more or less the same ingredients, and all will get the sink clean. The manufacturer's job, therefore, is to fix the product name in the consumer's mind and have that consumer *perceive* a difference. For this the manufacturer relies on advertising.

What makes a successful advertisement? Why do some ads work better than others? Countless books have been written on this subject, and the answer sometimes involves complex psychological responses. Certain key factors can be identified, however, as contributing to an advertisement's effectiveness.

First of all, the ad must be noticed. Getting the viewer's attention is the advertising designer's first task. One very popular technique for getting atten-

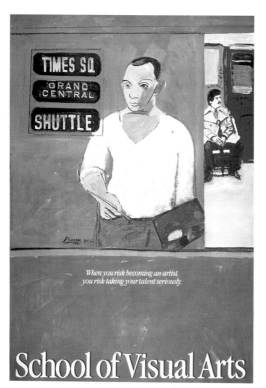

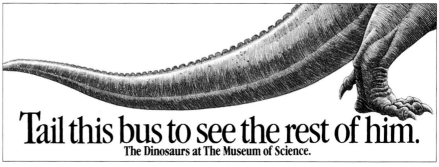

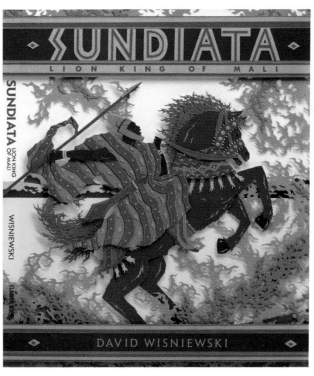

tion is consumer identification, as in ads for expensive items. While flipping through a magazine, you see a picture of an attractive person or group and think to yourself, "I want to be just like that." After a barrage of such ads, you associate the product name with that desirable image.

A related approach is to take the expected and do something unexpected with it. Many people are familiar with Picasso's self-portrait (p. 468), but few are prepared to see Picasso catching the subway at Grand Central Station in New York **(300)**. This poster's visual impact is wonderful in its simplicity, and the message it conveys is understated but clear. The School of Visual Arts teaches courses in art. Probably the majority of its students commute by subway, and that is where the poster has been displayed. Thus, if the artist can take the subway, the subway can take you to art.

Another method of attracting attention is by sheer size. Splashing an advertisement on the side of a bus gives size, and when the bus chugs down a city street, it presents its message to an endless stream of observers. The Museum of Science in Boston used these dual elements of size and motion—plus a good deal of humor—in a series of ads meant to boost museum attendance **(301)**. A science museum may seem, to the public at large, a rather dull and stuffy place. The Boston museum hoped to overcome this stodgy image with a series of ads supervised by creative director Ron Lawner. A giant dinosaur tail goes by, bearing the legend "Tail this bus to see the rest of him." Viewers in the street see the ad, are charmed and amused, and speculate that maybe this museum is more fun than they had imagined. That was the intention, and it seems to have worked. As a result of the ad campaign of which this example was a part, museum attendance actually doubled.

PRINT MEDIA:
BOOKS AND MAGAZINES

Book designers, of all graphic artists, often have the most difficulty making people understand what they do. In this book, for example, the designer selected the typefaces; chose the appropriate sizes of type for text, headings, captions, and so forth; and decided how much space to allow for margins and between various elements. She also devised a way to highlight the "Artists," "Art People," and other special features.

Cover design is another major responsibility of the graphic designer. An old adage says, "You can't judge a book by its cover," but to some extent you can. Certainly for "trade," or general-market books, the cover plays a major part in one's decision whether to buy the book. This is especially true in the highly competitive market for children's books. David Wisniewski's award-winning design for his own book, *Sundiata: Lion King of Mali* **(302)**, illustrates cover art at its best. The African hero is portrayed on a wildly rearing horse, about to throw his spear, his garments flowing out behind him. There is energy and excitement and drama in this image, guaranteed to appeal to youthful readers. The typeface for the book's title is especially appropriate, since it echoes the patterns found in African textiles.

The design of magazine covers, while drawing on the same elements as book cover design (type, photography, illustration), differs in certain respects. One difference has to do with longevity. Books often are kept, in homes and libraries, for many years. Magazines tend to be read quickly and then thrown away. Because of their short life span, magazines can have covers that are contemporary, following up-to-the-minute fashions and events.

Magazine covers are even more influential in a reader's decision to purchase than are book covers. You may be motivated to buy a particular book for any of several reasons—it's on the best-seller list, you heard about it from a friend, your teacher assigned it, and so on. But buying a magazine is more often a spur-of-the-moment decision. You are dashing for the train or waiting to check out at the supermarket. You scan the magazine racks looking for diversion. Chances are, you will buy the magazine whose cover attracts you.

When a drawn illustration is to be used for a cover, the choice of an illustrator is up to the designer of the cover or the magazine's art director—the person in charge of the visual aspects of the whole magazine. Occasionally a particular illustrator is used over and over, has a distinctive style, and therefore becomes closely associated with that magazine. There could be no better example of such a partnership than the one that existed between Norman Rockwell and *The Saturday Evening Post*.

In 1916 a very young Norman Rockwell, just twenty-two years old, presented himself at the Philadelphia offices of *The Saturday Evening Post*, a popular weekly magazine. He carried two paintings meant as potential *Post* covers and a sketch for a third. The *Post*'s art director was impressed and immediately bought the young artist's illustrations, requesting more. Rockwell's first *Post* cover appeared in May of that year, and his covers continued to appear regularly until 1963, when the artist branched out to other magazines. His last *Post* cover was a portrait of President John F. Kennedy, used as a memorial on the December 14 issue—three weeks after the president's assassination. During those forty-seven years Rockwell averaged about six covers each year—an amazing feat when one considers that each of the illustrations was a fully developed painting, often including many characters. Every Rockwell cover was greeted with delight by *Post* readers and guaranteed an increase in sales.

Rockwell's task was not an easy one; working in the magazine's format imposed many restrictions. Obviously, the image had to fit within a certain vertical framework—the shape of the magazine cover (303). Space had to be left at the top for the magazine's title and the date. Sometimes "teaser" blurbs for articles were superimposed over the artwork; Rockwell once mildly complained that the blurbs always seemed to fall just over the spot where he had drawn his most interesting detail. Nevertheless, Rockwell's association with *The Saturday Evening Post* proved to be a long and happy one for all concerned. As with many enduring works of art, his illustrations offered the right style in the right medium at the right time.

303. Norman Rockwell. *The Tom Boy,* cover for *The Saturday Evening Post,* May 23, 1953. Reprinted from *The Saturday Evening Post* © 1953 The Curtis Publishing Company.

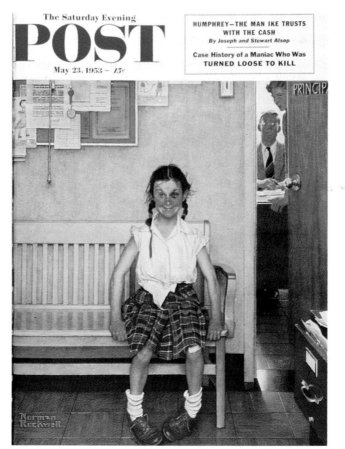

NORMAN ROCKWELL
1894–1978

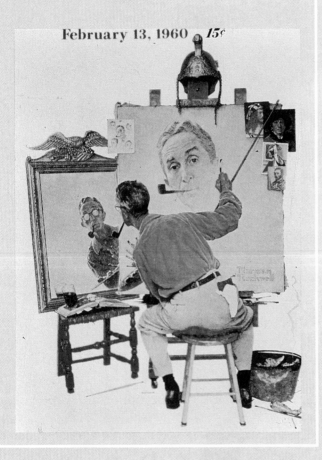

for assignments. His career blossomed, and he remained busy trying to keep up with the demand for his work until the onset of his last illness at the age of eighty-four.

Rockwell's great success was based on the simplest of formulas: He drew ordinary people in ordinary situations doing the sorts of things all the *Post*'s readers were accustomed to doing. He drew them with a gentle humor that poked fun at the situations while never poking fun at people. The magazine's readers could laugh at themselves, at the odd and funny plights they got themselves into, because they sensed the artist was one of *them*, subject to the same foibles as anybody else.

After leaving New York, Rockwell first lived in a suburb of the city, then for many years in Vermont. Ultimately he settled in Stockbridge, Massachusetts, the town with which he is most closely associated. His models for *Post* covers and other illustrations were the townspeople—the mayor, the barber, the village clerk, the children of the neighborhood. In the early years Rockwell painted them from life, but later he developed a system of photographing the scenes and models, then painting from the photographs. Not all Rockwell's subjects were Stockbridge villagers, however. Routinely he was called upon to paint the famous and the mighty—presidents and presidential candidates, from Eisenhower onward; heads of state; sports heroes and astronauts; and many entertainment figures, including Bob Hope, Frank Sinatra, John Wayne, even Lassie.

Rockwell married three times—the latter two marriages were apparently very happy ones—and had three sons. Apart from the sudden death of his second wife, little trouble marred a peaceful, productive life. Although the major art critics always were harsh in their assessment of Rockwell's work, he enjoyed enormous popularity with the general public. In 1969 Rockwell had his first one-artist show of paintings in New York; the local critics savaged the show, but nearly every painting sold at the preview, before the exhibit opened officially.

Actually, the problem of criticism arose only when people tried to evaluate the artist as a *painter;* few ever questioned his gifts as an illustrator. Rockwell commented once on this distinction: "Some people have been kind enough to call me a fine artist. I've always called myself an illustrator. I'm not sure what the difference is. All I know is whatever type of work I do, I try to give it my very best. Art has been my life."[1]

NORMAN ROCKWELL, chronicler of small-town America, was born in New York City and raised in a section known as the Bronx. By the age of fourteen, already determined on a career as an artist, he assumed responsibility for his own education—selecting the art schools he would attend (which eventually included the Art Students League) and finding odd jobs to support himself. One such job was as an extra, often a spear carrier, at the Metropolitan Opera, where he became rather a pet of the legendary tenor Enrico Caruso.

At eighteen Rockwell began to get his first professional commissions, most of them for illustrations in boys' magazines and children's books. Then in 1916 came the first *Saturday Evening Post* cover. After his early triumph at the *Post*, Rockwell never again lacked

THE NEW YORKER ON PICASSO

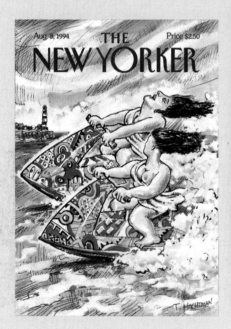

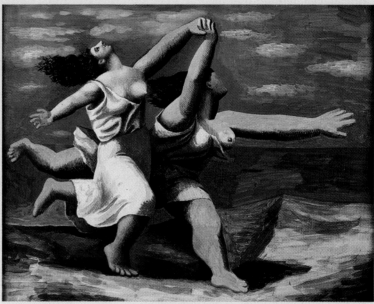

M OST CONTEMPORARY MAGAZINES attempt, through the design of their covers, to establish a certain "tone" or style that is to be associated in the readers' minds with the magazine. A prime example of this approach is *The New Yorker*.

The style of *New Yorker* covers has evolved over the years but has not really changed for decades. Every cover is an illustration, never a photograph, and the tone is droll—always amusing, often irreverent. In recent years many covers have been take-offs (or, more accurately, send-ups) of paintings by well-known artists.

For *New Yorker*'s August 8, 1994, cover, illustrator Tom Hachtman drew *Picasso on the Beach* **(left)**, featuring two ecstatic, barely clad women plunging through the surf on jet skis. Savvy readers of *The New Yorker* made an instant association with Picasso's *Women Running on the Beach* **(right)**. They may not have known the exact painting being spoofed, but the imagery was familiar.

Hachtman's female bodies, like Picasso's, are monumental. (Picasso was in his Neoclassical period at the time of the painting.) And the forward rush of the jet skis gives an even better excuse than a mere run on the beach for the disarray of the women's costumes, the streaming hair, and the rapture in the upturned face. To a point the colors are similar—blue skies, white clouds, pink bodies—except for those wildly patterned jet skis. Why did Hachtman reverse the motion from right to left? Probably because it made a better composition for the vertical format of the magazine. Notice how the lighthouse works conceptually to show the nearby coastline, and visually to balance the picture.

left: Cover drawing
"Picasso on the Beach" by Tom Hachtman.
© 1994 The New Yorker Magazine, Inc.
All rights reserved.

right: Pablo Picasso. *Women Running on the Beach.*
1922. Oil on plywood, $13\frac{3}{8} \times 16\frac{3}{4}"$.
Musée Picasso, Paris.

GRAPHICS AND THE COMPUTER

The computer has done more to influence graphic design than anything since the invention of the printing press. Each of the three tools available to the designer—illustration, type, and photography—can be manipulated in special ways through computer technology.

If the end result is to be a printed design—an advertisement or magazine cover, for example—many graphic designers have replaced their sketch pads with computer terminals. Designing, testing of ideas and forms and colors, is done on the screen with far greater speed than could ever be possible using a crayon or pen. Also, computer-designed typography is now commonplace.

But surely the most exciting new realm for the graphic designer lies in designs made specifically *for* the computer—designs meant to be viewed on one's own computer screen—a field that barely existed just a few years ago. With so many electronic images competing for our attention, graphic designers are called upon to catch our eyes by whatever visual cleverness can be devised. Their designs are essential to the production and marketing of CD-ROMs **(304)** and to the creation of home pages on the World Wide Web **(305)**.

With the computer, there is endless potential for photographic manipulation. One of the masters of this technique is Ryszard Horowitz, whose *Allegory* **(306)** was done on commission for Eastman Kodak Company. Horowitz has been called a "photo-composer," and we can see why from this example. To create his images, Horowitz first photographs the elements he needs—in this case, piano keys, ocean, figures, and so forth. The photographic components are scanned into the computer, then combined and manipulated until the artist achieves the result he wants. *Allegory* is rich and painterly in its effects, exciting in its turbulent movement. It illustrates well a principle that has been emphasized throughout this book: Great art results when the perfect medium and the creative artist come together.

One hesitates to say too much about computer graphics, because this field is evolving so rapidly. In the short time that elapses between the writing of this book and its publication, tremendous expansion of computer art will take place. We are in the middle of another revolution in graphic design.

below: 304. *Dazzeloids*, CD-ROM. 1994. Director and graphics: Rodney Alan Greenblat; animation and design: Jenny Horn and Trish Booten; publisher: Voyager, New York.

bottom left: 305. *Shift Online*, home page, World Wide Web. 1994. Designer identity for Shift Online. © 1994 Jessica Helfand.

bottom right: 306. Ryszard Horowitz, *Allegory*. 1993. Client: Eastman Kodak Company. © Ryszard Horowitz, RGA Print, 1993.

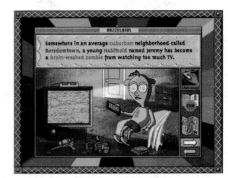

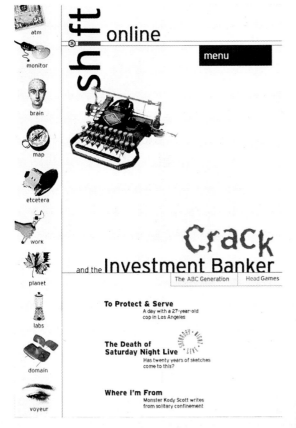

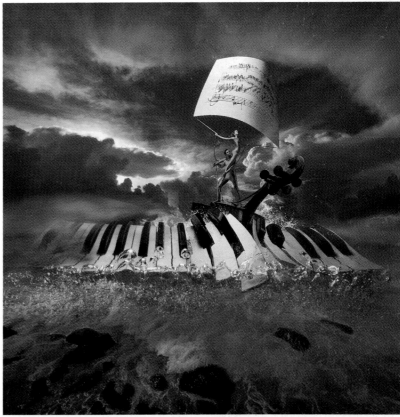

PART FOUR

THREE-DIMENSIONAL MEDIA

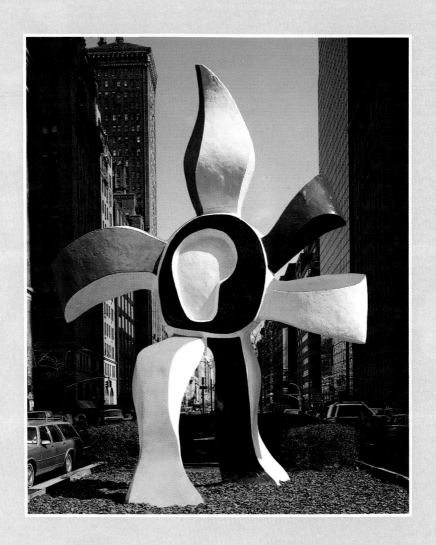

307. Fernand Léger. *The Great Walking Flower (La Grande Fleur Qui Marche).*
1952. Polychrome bronze, height 19′6″.
On site at Park Avenue and 57th Street, New York City.

Sculpture

THE STUDY OF SCULPTURE confronts us with the third dimension, with the concept of *depth*. This seems like an easy and obvious point, but there is more to it than you might imagine. In everyday life we are faced constantly with situations in which our brains have to make adjustments for depth. Just walking down the street requires the brain to make a thousand calculations. How far away is that building? If you misjudge the distance, you may bump into it. How high is the curb? Unless you estimate correctly, you could trip and fall. Driving a car is the experience that causes most of us to be acutely aware of depth. How far away is that huge truck making a left turn across your path? If you miscalculate the distance—the depth in space—you are facing catastrophe.

The media require us to adjust our perceptions of depth in a way that is almost contrary to nature. We see images of people on the movie screen or on television, photographs of people in newspapers and magazines. Even though these are, in reality, flat images, we understand the people to be full-bodied and three-dimensional. This correction for depth becomes automatic, and we don't have to think about it.

As we approach sculpture, however, we might suspend this visual over-drive and train ourselves to be more *actively* aware of depth. A heightened perception of the third dimension is crucial to our full appreciation of sculpture. Sculptures are like our selves, full-bodied and substantial. Usually they look different when viewed from different angles. The experience of looking at a flat painting on a wall is quite unlike the experience of walking up to a freestanding sculpture, circling it, observing it from various viewpoints. If a sculpture is exceptionally large, like Fernand Léger's *Great Walking Flower* **(307)**, we need also to consider it from various *distances*, because we cannot take it in, so to speak, all in one gulp. Only when we integrate many visual perceptions do we begin to reach an understanding of the sculpture as a whole.

This chapter will explore a wide range of three-dimensional forms, from many times and places. Sculpture has one of the longest histories of any art medium, and yet it is especially vital and exciting today. A major reason for this vitality in contemporary sculpture is its use of materials and techniques that were unheard of just a century ago. We will look first at the sculptor's methods, how materials are handled, and how sculptures are designed.

METHODS OF SCULPTURE

There are four basic methods for making a sculpture: modeling, casting, carving, and assembling. Modeling and assembling are considered **additive** processes. The sculptor begins with a simple framework or core or nothing at all and *adds* material until the sculpture is finished. Carving is a **subtractive** process in which one starts with a mass of material larger than the planned sculpture and *subtracts*, or takes away, material until only the desired form remains. Some people consider casting to be an additive process, but in a sense this method occupies a category all its own. Casting involves a mold of some kind, into which liquid or semiliquid material is poured and allowed to harden. Often casting is used to make several identical sculptures.

Let us consider each of these methods in more detail.

MODELING

Modeling is familiar to most of us from childhood. As children we experimented with Silly Putty or clay to construct lopsided figures of people and animals. For sculpture, the most common modeling material is clay, an earth substance found in most parts of the world. Wet clay is wonderfully pliable; few can resist the temptation to squeeze and shape it. As long as clay remains wet, the sculptor can do almost anything with it—add on more and more clay to build up the form, gouge away sections, pinch it outward, scratch into it with a sharp tool, smooth it with the hands. But when a clay form has dried and been *fired*—heated to a high temperature in a kiln (Chapter 12, p. 291)—it becomes hard. Fired clay, sometimes called by the Italian name *terra cotta*, is surprisingly durable. Much of the ancient art that has survived was formed from this material.

A female figure made in Cyprus more than three thousand years ago **(308)** is typical of the fertility images found in most early cultures. The artist who created this little statue had learned to exploit many of the possibilities of clay. After the overall form had been shaped by the fingers, delicate lines defining the form were incised with a sharp tool. The arms and "earrings" were shaped of separate pieces of clay and then added to the main piece.

Throughout their history the Chinese have been masters of ceramic sculpture—sculpture made from clay—but not until fairly recently has the enormous scope of their production been fully appreciated. In 1974 well diggers near the central Chinese city of Xian accidentally uncovered part of the

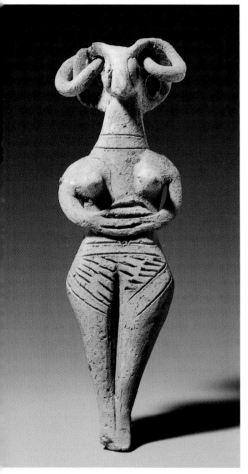

above: 308. Female figure (fertility image?), from Cyprus. c. 1500–1200 B.C.E. Terra cotta, height 6⅛". The Metropolitan Museum of Art, New York (Cesnola Collection; purchased by subscription, 1874–1876).

right: 309. *Cavalryman and Saddle Horse from Earthenware Army of First Emperor of Qin,* excavated at Lintong, Shanxi Province, China. Qin Dynasty (221–206 B.C.E.). Terra cotta, height of man 5'10½". Shanxi Provincial Museum.

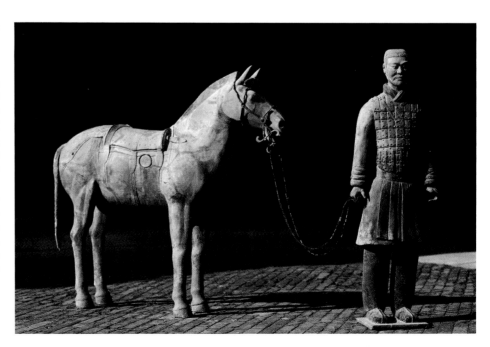

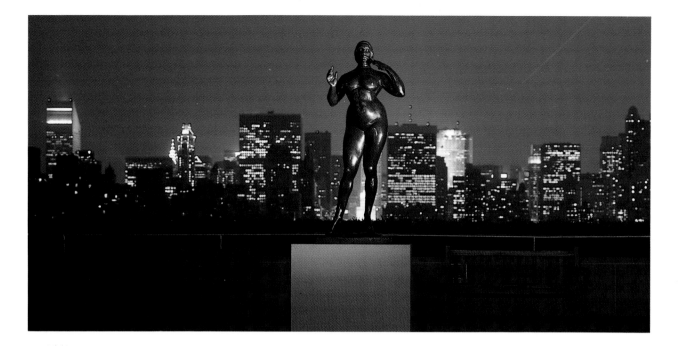

tomb complex of the first emperor of China, Shi Huang Di. Buried since 210 B.C.E., guarding the tomb in military formation, were a whole army of life-size clay soldiers, horses, and attendants—at least seven thousand of them **(309)**. The warriors' faces and bodies are modeled with amazing naturalism, and each variety of provincial headdress is rendered in specific detail. The horses stand waiting to be harnessed and ridden off into battle. More recent digs have unearthed a similar array of scribes, or clerks, suggesting that the entire court, represented in clay, may have gone into the emperor's tomb. We can only speculate how many sculptors labored to build this immense ceramic population, especially in view of the high quality maintained in the figures.

Clay served the Chinese tomb builders well, because of its permanence and potential for naturalism. But later artists have prized clay for other qualities. Sculptors often use clay modeling in the same way that painters traditionally have used drawing, to test ideas before committing themselves to the finished sculpture. As long as the clay is kept damp, it can be worked and reworked almost indefinitely. Even the terminology is the same; we sometimes call a clay test piece a "sketch."

In some ways modeling is the most direct of sculpture methods. The workable material responds to every touch, light or heavy, of the sculptor's fingers, so that the maker and the made become almost one.

CASTING

In contrast to modeling, casting seems like a very *indirect* method of creating a sculpture. Sometimes the sculptor never touches the final piece at all. Metal, and specifically bronze, is the material we think of most readily in relation to casting. Bronze can be superheated until it flows, will pour freely into the tiniest crevices and forms, and then hardens to extreme durability. Even for a thin little projection, like a finger, there is no fear of it breaking off. Also through casting, the sculptor can achieve smooth rounded shapes and a glowing, reflective surface, such as we see in Gaston Lachaise's *Standing Woman* **(310)**. Lachaise exploited the fluidity of metal to capture a fluidity of form. The nude female figure, while surely monumental, has a grace and perfection of form that seems to flow from the head to the pointed toes. Of course, the sculptor could not possibly have known how magically his work would gleam when photographed at night, on the roof garden of the Metropolitan Museum, against the shimmering New York skyline. Captured thus, Lachaise's *Standing Woman* seems the triumphant goddess of the city.

310. Gaston Lachaise. *Standing Woman.* 1927. Cast bronze, height 6'1⅞". The Metropolitan Museum of Art, New York (bequest of Scofield Taylor, 1982). Photographed on the Iris and B. Gerald Cantor Roof Garden. © Scott Frances/Esto.

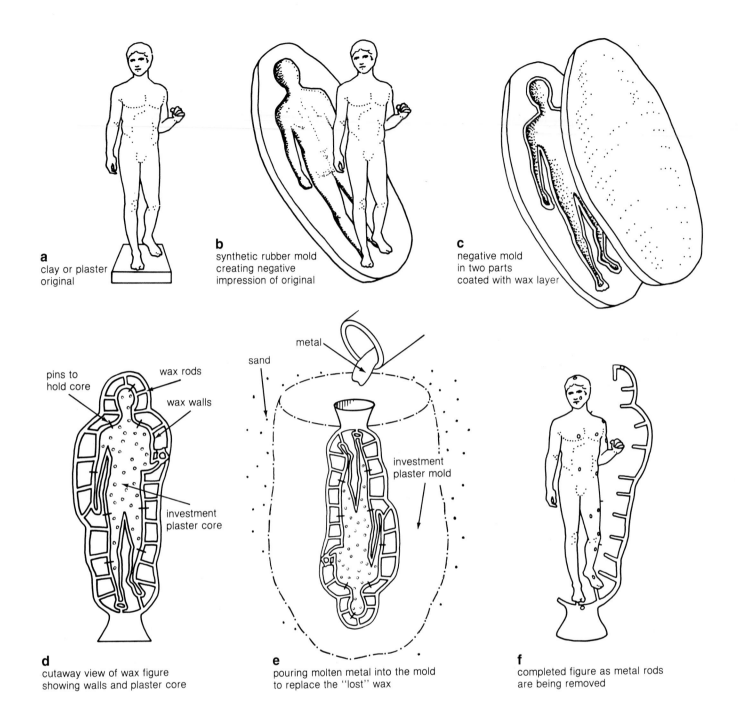

a
clay or plaster
original

b
synthetic rubber mold
creating negative
impression of original

c
negative mold
in two parts
coated with wax layer

pins to
hold core

wax rods

wax walls

investment
plaster core

metal

sand

investment
plaster mold

d
cutaway view of wax figure
showing walls and plaster core

e
pouring molten metal into the mold
to replace the "lost" wax

f
completed figure as metal rods
are being removed

311. Sketch of the major steps
in lost-wax casting.

Besides metal, other materials can be cast, including many plastics and clay. The simplest type of casting is *solid* casting—that is, solid as opposed to hollow. You make a solid cast every time you make an ice cube. You pour liquid material (water) into a mold (the ice-cube tray), cause it to harden (by freezing), and then remove the cast (the ice cube). Novelty ice-cube trays can make cast-ice "sculptures" in the shape of hearts or flowers or any number of other objects. Some plastics are cast by a very similar method. Liquid plastic is poured into a mold and allowed to set, after which the mold is removed.

There are three problems with solid casting. First, it uses quite a lot of material, and this can be expensive, especially with metal. Second, solid-cast objects tend to be very heavy unless they are made of lightweight plastic. Third, many materials, including metal and clay, develop cracks if cast solid. For all these reasons various methods have been developed to make *hollow* casts—that is, casts with an inner core of air.

Metal usually is cast by the ***lost-wax*** method, sometimes known by the French name, ***cire perdue.*** This is an extremely complex process. The following description and the illustrations **(311)** outline its basic principles.

1. The sculptor works either in clay or in plaster to create a full-size model of the intended sculpture **(311a)**. For the sculptor this may end the creative part; very likely specialized technicians will take over afterward to complete the casting.

2. A coating of synthetic rubber is applied to the clay or plaster model. (Earlier generations used other materials.) This rubber coating makes an outside mold of the sculpture's contours that is accurate in every detail **(311b)**. The synthetic rubber mold is removed from the outside of the model.

3. The synthetic rubber mold is now a *negative* or exterior mold of the sculpture **(311c)**. Wax is coated inside the parts of the synthetic rubber mold to a depth of about $\frac{1}{8}$ inch. The wax layer is the exact shape and thickness that is wanted for the final metal sculpture.

4. The space inside the wax layer—what will eventually be the sculpture's hollow core—is filled with a mixture of wet plaster called ***investment,*** which is then allowed to dry **(311d)**. This plaster core is held in place by a series of metal pins. Then the synthetic rubber mold is removed from the outside of the wax layer. A network of wax rods is constructed all over the outside of the wax model. (Later, when the wax is melted away and the metal poured in, these rodlike channels will serve as conduits for the flow of material.)

5. The wax model, complete with rods and plaster core, is coated with another layer of investment plaster, and the assembly is placed in a kiln **(311e)**. The kiln melts away the wax—hence the term *"lost" wax*—leaving an empty space between the inner core and outer layer of plaster that is exactly the shape and thickness of the desired sculpture. (The metal pins maintain the gap between these two sections of plaster, now that the wax is no longer there to hold them apart.) Molten metal is poured into the space that once held the wax, filling every crevice and filling all the rodlike channels. Metal, therefore, has replaced the wax, which is why casting is often known as a ***replacement*** method. Depending on the size of the sculpture, it may take several days for the metal to cool and set.

6. The new metal sculpture is taken from the kiln, and both inner core and outer layer of plaster are removed. Then the rods, now also metal, are cut from the sculpture **(311f)**, rough spots are filed away, and the sculpture is cleaned and polished.

A common application for lost-wax casting has been the large equestrian (rider on horseback) statues we see in parks and plazas. The ancient Romans were masters of the equestrian portrait, and it remained popular for depicting military heroes well into this century. Almost no material except bronze would be strong enough, for the horse and its rider, life-size or larger, must be balanced on slender legs in an animated pose. An outstanding example is the statue of *Colleoni* **(312)** by the 15th-century Italian sculptor Andrea del Verrocchio. The sculptor has shaped the tense muscles and alert poses of both figures with such skill that the horse, although cast in rigid bronze, seems about to leap off its pedestal and gallop away.

Besides providing the necessary strength to make thin forms and projections, cast metal offers the sculptor two other great advantages. First, because the mold is generally reusable, one can make several identical casts of the work. Each is considered an original sculpture, just as each impression of a graphic print is considered an original work of art (Chapter 8). Second, casting makes permanent the most fleeting gesture of the sculptor's hands. The sculptor can work freely in some soft material like clay or wax, and then translate that free expression into a more durable material.

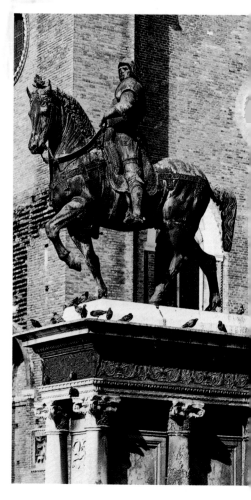

312. Andrea del Verrocchio. *Equestrian Monument of Colleoni.* c. 1483–88. Bronze, height c. 15'. Campo SS. Giovanni e Paolo, Venice.

Still another asset of cast bronze is its resistance to weather. If properly cleaned and cared for, a bronze sculpture installed outdoors not only will withstand the elements but will in time acquire a desirable **patina,** or surface coloring. Bronze was the preferred material of the sculptor Henry Moore **(313)**, whose massive, organic works are displayed in outdoor spaces around the world. Moore's sculptures seem equally at home in a fountain beside a modern building or in a parkland of trees and grass.

CARVING

Carving is more aggressive than modeling, more direct than casting. In this process the sculptor begins with a block of material and cuts, chips, and gouges away until the form of the sculpture emerges. Wood and stone are the principal materials for carving, and both tend to resist the sculptor's tools. When approaching the block to be carved, the sculptor must study the grain of the material—its fibrous or crystalline structure—so as to work *with* that material. Any attempt to violate the grain could result in a failed sculpture.

Wood carving reached an especially high level of expertise in Europe during the Middle Ages and Early Renaissance. A work from 15th-century Germany shows the wood-carver's skill at its most refined. Adriaen van Wesel portrays the *Death of the Virgin* **(314)**, the death of Jesus Christ's aged mother, in an intricate oak carving just 30 inches high. Grouped around the dying Madonna are Christ's twelve Apostles, each showing by individualized facial expression, pose, and gesture his grief at parting from the beloved Mary. Although the space of the carving is shallow, only a few inches deep, the figures do not seem crowded or crammed together, so artfully has the sculptor arranged them. The grain of the oak is apparent throughout the piece, enhancing the texture created by exceptionally fine carving in the hair, faces, and drapery. Given the tendency of wood to chip and split, we marvel at this sculptor's ability to achieve sensitive detail in such a small scale.

left: 313. Henry Moore. *Reclining Figure.* 1963–65. Bronze, length 30′. Lincoln Center for the Performing Arts, New York.

right: 314. Adriaen van Wesel. *Death of the Virgin.* 15th century. Oak, 30 × 21¼″. Rijksmuseum, Amsterdam.

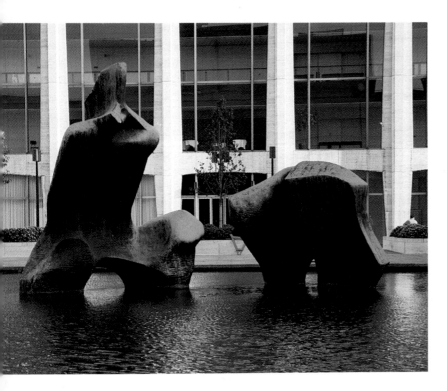

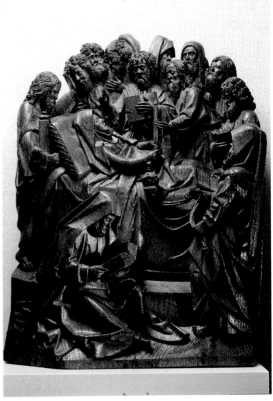

HENRY MOORE

1898–1986

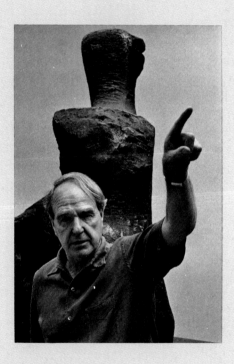

O N THE OCCASION of Henry Moore's eightieth birthday, art critic John Russell wrote that "it is a great thing to be before the public uninterruptedly for the best part of half a century and still stand up, erect and uncontaminated, as a completely honorable human being."[1] Few people would argue with Russell's assessment. If fate smiles on certain individuals, Moore was surely one of them, but one cannot begrudge this "completely honorable" man having enjoyed rich talents as a sculptor and draftsman, international fame, a loving family, respect from his friends, and a long, productive life.

Born in a small mining town in the north of England, Moore was the seventh child of a miner and his wife. Quite early he settled upon the career of sculptor as his goal. ("When I was 11, I was in Sunday school and I heard a story about Michelangelo. I can't remember the story, but what I retained was that Michelangelo was esteemed the greatest sculptor who ever lived. That unremarkable bit of information moved me, then and there, to decide to become a sculptor myself."[2]) After a brief stint in the army during World War I, Moore entered art school in the city of Leeds and first encountered modern art in a private collection there. Later he moved on to London's Royal College of Art.

Henry Moore was no overnight sensation; the type of sculpture he made was too new, too innovative for the public at large to accept. During the 1920s and 1930s Moore patiently laid the groundwork for what would become a world-class career. He worked steadily, exhibited often, taught first at the Royal College and later at the Chelsea School of Art. In 1929 he married Irina Radetzky, a painting student, to whom he remained happily wed all his life. (Their daughter was born in 1946.)

The year 1940 marked something of a turning point for Moore. England was at war, and he became an official war artist. His drawings of Londoners huddled in shelters to escape the Nazi bombing raids have become famous, both because of their unique circumstances and because the artist's sensitive rendering turned the act of hiding underground into a heroic gesture. The English people never forgot that it was Moore who showed them so poignantly in their "finest hour." After the war he was recognized as one of England's foremost artists, and his stature thereafter increased steadily.

Whether in stone or wood or metal, Moore's sculptures focused on three great themes: the family group (or mother and child), the reclining female figure, the form within a form. These sculptures are in the collections—and often adorn the outsides—of the world's great museums, as well as countless other public buildings.

Reflecting on a lifetime devoted to art, Moore retained the joy and excitement that motivated a little boy who learned about Michelangelo: "Art is not practical, and shouldn't be practical. Art is not to earn a living. It's to make the difference between us and animals, like cows. I mean a cow doesn't stop and look at a field and say, isn't it a beautiful green. Painting and sculpture . . . are there to make life more interesting, more wonderful than it would be without them."[3]

Photograph of Henry Moore, 1980.

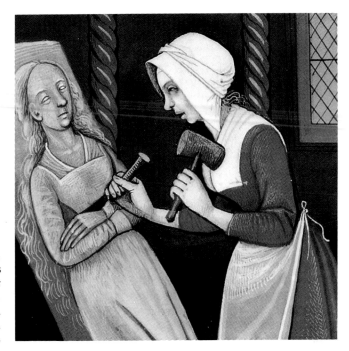

315. *Woman Sculptor at Work,* detail from Boccaccio's *Le Livre des cleres et nobles femmes.* France, late 15th century. Manuscript illustration. Bibliothèque Nationale, Paris.

Medieval carvers also worked extensively in stone; both the number of sculptors and their output became enormous during the great period of cathedral building in Europe from the 12th to the 15th century (p. 389). Contemporary printed sources give us some clues to the carvers' working methods and testify that at least some of them were women **(315)**—which might contradict our stereotyped idea that "heavy" work for women has been a 20th-century innovation.

Stone carving presents an even greater challenge to the sculptor than does wood carving, because the material is scarcer, more expensive, and more resistant to the chisel. A stonecutter of present-day Italy, Pasquinio Pasquini, has spoken eloquently of the risks:

> Sometimes there are surprises in the marble—there can be a defect in it. The hammer is a dangerous instrument: one wrong movement, a statue's finger breaks off, and in a moment the work of months is destroyed. If there's space between arm and body, that's another problem. Delicate parts won't take hammering. There are so many places where danger lurks, where we can't use power tools. Portraits are difficult; one false move banishes resemblance.[4]

Most people consider Michelangelo to have been the greatest genius of stone carving in the history of art; we will see his marble figure of *David* in Chapter 17 **(474)**. According to writings from his day, Michelangelo believed that the sculptor's task is simply to free the subject from its imprisoning block of stone. So perfectly did he visualize the figure inside a block of marble that he announced one had only to cut away those parts of the stone that *weren't* the figure. Few other sculptors would be quite so confident.

One who approached Michelangelo in skill—and took second place to no one in self-confidence—was the 17th-century Italian artist Gianlorenzo Bernini. The portrait bust of his mistress, Costanza Bonarelli **(316)**, would present sufficient answer to anyone who feels that marble cannot be warm and alive. As carved by Bernini, Costanza is not merely alive but sensual and magnetic. The slightly parted lips, the intense eyes, the disarranged bodice of the dress all suggest a woman whose emotions are barely contained within the creamy beige of the stone. Looking at the sculpture, we know it to be stone, but we see hair, flesh, and rumpled linen. In his writings Bernini spoke of the difficulties a sculptor faces when trying to convey personality all in one color

(p. 427). In his portrait of Costanza Bonarelli he shows how he overcame those difficulties. He made Costanza live; we half expect her to breathe.

Sculptors who work in stone are harder to find today than they were in Bernini's time, but they do exist. Even artists who specialize in decidedly 20th-century materials, like steel and plastic, may go back to stone every once in a while, possibly as a way of keeping in touch with their colleagues from earlier times. No other material is so solid and yet so alive, so cold and yet so inviting to the touch, so resistant and yet so satisfying.

ASSEMBLING

Assembling is a process by which individual pieces or segments or objects are brought together to form a sculpture. Some writers make a distinction between *assembling,* in which parts of the sculpture are simply placed on or near each other, and *constructing,* in which the parts are actually joined together through welding, nailing, or a similar procedure. We have chosen to use the term *assemblage* for both types of work, because often the line separating one from the other is a fine one.

The 20th-century American sculptor David Smith came to assemblage in an unusual way. While trying to establish himself as an artist, Smith worked as a welder. Later, when he began to concentrate on sculpture, he readily adapted his welding skills to a different purpose. His mature works broke new ground

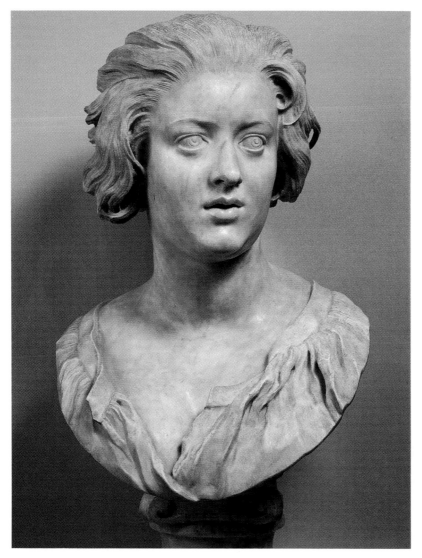

316. Gianlorenzo Bernini. *Costanza Bonarelli.* c. 1635. Marble. Bargello, Florence.

in both materials and forms **(317)**. Sculptures like *Becca* are of steel, which eventually became Smith's favorite material. Steel had long been used for the framework of cars, of refrigerators, of locomotives, but Smith explored its aesthetic potential. He polished the surfaces so they would shine in the sunlight when exhibited outdoors. The form of these works is also daring—slab piled upon slab, the parts joined at seemingly precarious angles. Steel, with its great strength, makes possible the dynamic balance of *Becca,* and assemblage makes possible the soaring composition.

Many sculptures by Deborah Butterfield also are of welded steel, but their effect is quite different from that of Smith's cool, gleaming constructions. *Vermillion* **(318)**, assembled from scrap metal and painted in vivid red, shows a raw power deriving from its abstract shapes and visibly sharp edges. Butterfield's figure is a horse, a recurring theme in the work of this artist, who rides and trains horses in Montana. This horse, however, is not so much lifelike as elemental—expressing the *essence* of an animal, as we might see in a child's drawing or in the cave images from prehistoric times **(2)**. Butterfield's horse embodies "horseness," with its strong flanks, its jaunty tail, its overlong neck, and the proud set of its head.

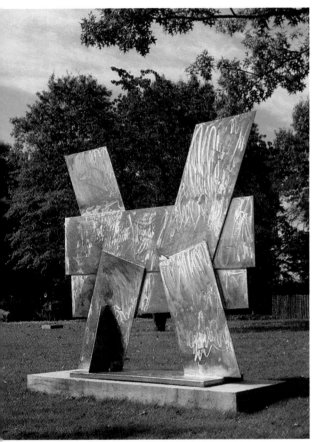

left: 317. David Smith.
Becca. 1965. Stainless steel,
9′5¼″ × 10′3″ × 2′2½″.
The Metropolitan Museum of Art,
New York (purchase, bequest
of Adelaide Milton de Groot,
by exchange, 1972); on loan to
Storm King Art Center,
Mountainville, N.Y.
© 1998 Estate of David Smith/
Licensed by VAGA, New York.

below: 318. Deborah Butterfield.
Vermillion. 1989.
Painted welded steel, height 6′3″.
The Metropolitan Museum of Art,
New York
(gift of Agnes Bourne, 1991).

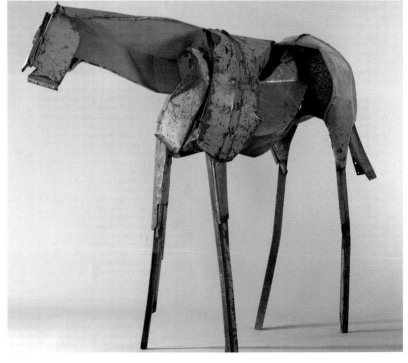

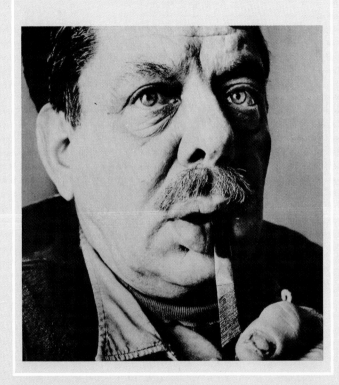

DAVID SMITH

1906–1965

DAVID SMITH holds a special interest for students of art history because, more than most artists of past or present, he was extremely articulate about his work and wrote widely about the business of making art. The man himself was something of a paradox. Physically strong and burly, he personified what we would now call a "macho" life style, having worked as a logger, an oilman, and a welder; as a sculptor his expression depended on the physical skills of the blacksmith. But from the noisy atmosphere of the machine shop Smith produced sculptures of shimmering pure form, and this same macho hero was also a lover of classical music, a lifelong poet, a gourmet cook, and a sensitive father to two daughters.

Smith was born in Decatur, Indiana, where he remained for the first twenty years of his life. By 1926 he was in New York, studying painting at the Art Students League. He took a variety of jobs to support himself, in-

cluding one that proved crucial for his later work—that of metal welder in an automobile factory. In 1927 he married the sculptor Dorothy Dehner; two years later the couple bought the now-famous farm in Bolton Landing overlooking Lake George, New York, where Smith worked until his death and where he displayed quantities of his large sculptures outdoors.

About 1933 Smith turned from painting and collage to sculpture. Influenced by the iron sculptures of Picasso, he focused on metal and began using his welding skills to assemble the forms. Finding a suitable place to work became a problem. As he told it: "One Sunday afternoon we were walking on a navy pier [in Brooklyn]. Down below on the ferry terminal was a long rambly junky looking shack called Terminal Iron Works. Wife said, 'David that's where you ought to be for your work.' Next morning I walked in and was met by a big Irishman named Blackburn. 'I'm an artist. I have a welding outfit. I'd like to work here.' 'Hell! yes—move in.' I learned a lot from those guys."[5]

From that point Smith worked almost exclusively in metal, soon focusing on steel. He had his first exhibition in New York in 1937, after which his reputation as a sculptor grew steadily. Whether in New York or Bolton Landing, he worked prolifically, and he also played with gusto, enjoying a wide range of friendships with many of the most successful artists of the period. After the breakup of his first marriage, Smith married Jean Freas in 1953, and his daughters, Rebecca and Candida, were born in the following two years. The artist's life ended prematurely and tragically when, driving near the farm, he failed to negotiate a turn in the road, crashed his truck, and was killed.

The sculpture of David Smith is represented in nearly every major collection of modern art, but the works housed indoors in museums may strike the viewer as out of place, almost uncomfortable. Smith always preferred his pieces to be displayed outdoors. He wrote: "I like outdoor sculpture and the most practical thing for outdoor sculpture is stainless steel, and I make them and I polish them in such a way that on a dull day, they take on the dull blue, or the color of the sky in the late afternoon sun, the glow, golden like the rays, the colors of nature. . . . They are colored by the sky and the surroundings, the green or blue of water. Some are down by the water and some are by the mountains. They reflect the colors. They are designed for outdoors."[6]

Photograph of David Smith by Irving Penn.

LOUISE NEVELSON

1899–1988

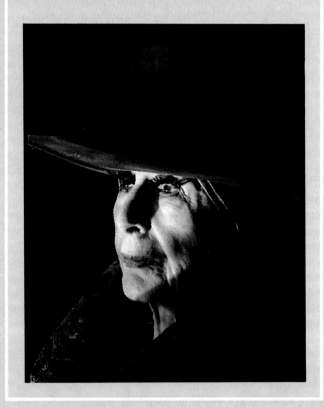

A S A SCULPTOR and as a person, Louise Nevelson always projected the image of royalty. Many of her large works have names suggesting royal subjects—kings, queens, palaces—and the artist made it her personal trademark to dress with an exotic flamboyance suitable for an eastern princess. This preoccupation seems related to her expressed conviction that one can make one's life be anything one chooses. She said that royalty is "dressing beautifully and having comfort and great houses and great art. Who wouldn't want it? Who wants to live in a hut?"[7]

Born Louise Berliawsky in Kiev, Russia, Nevelson emigrated with her family to Rockland, Maine, in 1905.

She claimed she was drawn to art as a child because the schoolhouse in Maine was always cold, and the art room was the only warm place. When she was just twenty-one she married Charles Nevelson. Decades later she would say the marriage was the only thing in her life she would have done differently, because she was not equipped for it. Nevelson's son Mike was born in 1922, but only a few years later the marriage collapsed, and the artist remained single thereafter.

Nevelson attended the Art Students League in New York for three years, then traveled to Europe, where she studied briefly with the painter Hans Hoffmann. Her first one-artist show came in 1941 at an important New York gallery. Despite favorable critical notice, many years passed before the public showed any interest in her work and it became financially sustaining. The artist felt this was because the components of her sculptures have little material value. From her earliest years in New York (where she lived until her death) she formed the habit of picking up cast-off wooden objects in the street—bits of furniture, old tools, sections of architectural elements, and the like. Her most characteristic sculptures are complex assemblages of these "found" objects in shallow, boxlike grids, many of which are wall- or room-size. The assemblages are each spray-painted a uniform color—occasionally white or gold, but most often black, which Nevelson called an "aristocratic" color.

In the late 1960s and 1970s Nevelson experimented with new materials—aluminum and steel—and made several large outdoor sculptures that echo the feeling of her box assemblages (140). She also accepted an unusual commission for the complete interior design of a Christian church (Nevelson was Jewish) in New York, including architectural details, sculptural decoration, even the priest's vestments.

Louise Nevelson was always an extremely prolific worker. All through the years of struggle she continued to produce. She maintained that she had a preconceived blueprint for her life and that, by and large, she had fulfilled it. "I remember my mother telling me, 'You know, art is a very difficult life, and why do you want to choose that? You won't live as well as you could otherwise.' And I said 'It's not how I live, it is how I finish my life.' And I did it."[8]

Photograph of Louise Nevelson.

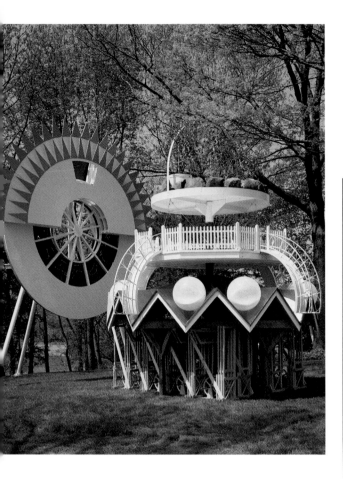

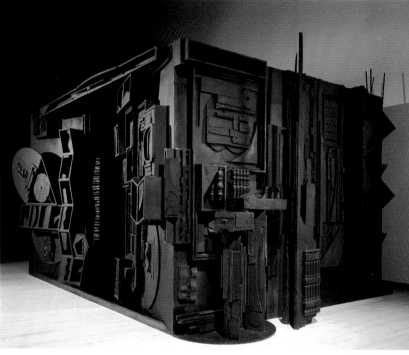

Alice Aycock uses assemblage to create extremely complex sculptures that fulfill her own spiritual and mystical ideals. According to one art critic, her *Fantasy Sculpture I* (319) looks like "a kind of combination Ferris wheel and merry-go-round," but this is only the initial view. As we approach the large work, we are inevitably drawn into Aycock's world of magic, personal symbolism, and cosmic mysteries. We puzzle over the unexpected combinations of forms, the cryptic words stenciled onto the raw wood of the understructure. Unlike most sculpture of this century, Aycock's work has specific and very rich content. It "tells a story," and even if the story isn't fully accessible to us, we are intrigued by it.

The sculptor Louise Nevelson used assemblage as a means of unifying her arrangements of disparate items and shapes into grand constructions. Nevelson was a lifelong collector of ***found objects***—literally objects she found here and there, in the street or the studio or the natural environment. Her sculptures, like *Mrs. N's Palace* (320), consist of odds and ends, mostly pieces of wood, that she accumulated in her studio over many years. Some of the objects are handmade, others machine products. These objects had no connection with one another until the sculptor *gave* them a connection by assembling them, setting up relationships of form that never existed before. Nevelson enhanced the connection by organizing her objects into boxlike structures, then painting the whole a uniform color (often black). So assembled, the objects create a rich, intricate, serene world of their own.

The later sculptures of Nancy Graves also were assembled, but by a technically more complicated process. She, too, began with found objects—some

left: 319. Alice Aycock.
Fantasy Sculpture I. 1990.
Wood, steel, stone, copper,
lucite, moving parts, plants;
20'6" × 18' × 33'.
Lent by the artist for a 1990
installation at Storm King Art
Center, Mountainville, N.Y.

right: 320. Louise Nevelson.
Mrs. N's Palace. 1964–77.
Black painted wood
with black mirror floor,
11'8" × 19'11" × 15'.
The Metropolitan Museum of Art,
New York (gift of the artist, 1985).

organic (leaves, pods, and so forth), others manufactured castoffs (wheels, furniture parts, musical instruments). Once Graves had chosen the components, she had them cast in metal, assembled them into the form she wanted, and finally painted them with bright-hued enamels. We see the results in a work like *Synonymous with Ceremony* (321), a whimsical, delicately balanced, merry construction that shows off some of its original ingredients but joins them in wholly new ways. Graves' constructions make us want to smile, to participate in their colorful and cheerful presence.

SCULPTURE
AND THE THIRD DIMENSION

Most of the sculptures we have looked at are **in the round,** or freestanding and completely finished on all sides. There is another category of sculpture, however, called *relief* sculpture, which is meant to be viewed from one side only. Relief sculptures have three-dimensional depth, but they do not occupy space as independently as sculptures in the round. Often they are used to decorate architecture or functional objects.

If you have a nickel in your pocket, take it out and look at it. On the face you'll see a profile of Thomas Jefferson and on the back an image of his home, Monticello. Both images are in **low relief,** sometimes called by the French name **bas-relief.** The subjects project very slightly from their background. Many kinds of flat surfaces serve as fields for low-relief sculpture—coins, tombstones, walls, decorative plates, book covers. The illustration here (322) shows the back of a throne found in the tomb of the Egyptian king, Tutankhamun (p. 359). A low relief applied to pure sheet gold depicts the young King "Tut" and his queen in graceful poses. The flowing clothes of the two monarchs are of silver, and their headdresses and jeweled collars are inset with colored glass and gemstones.

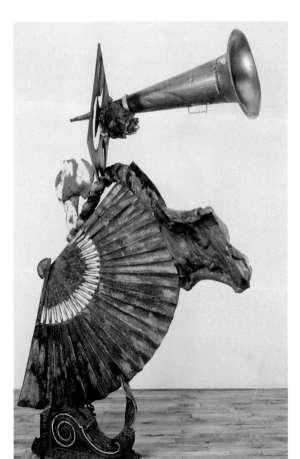

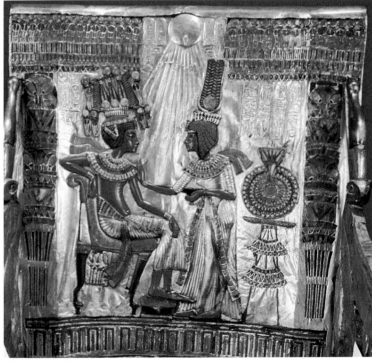

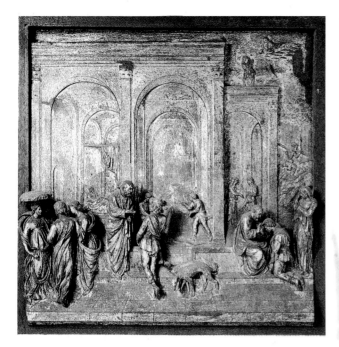

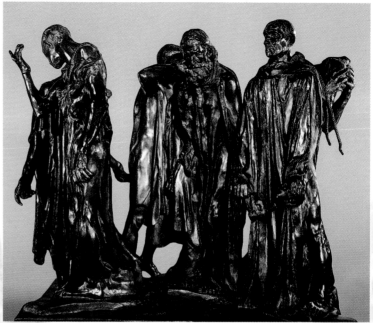

When a sculpture projects more boldly from the background, we call it **high relief** (or **haut-relief**). To fit this category, the sculptured elements should project by at least half their depth, and parts of the figures may be in the round, unattached to the background. The wood carving by Adriaen van Wesel **(314)**, with its rounded heads and torsos of the Apostles, qualifies as moderately high relief. *Mrs. N's Palace* is even higher relief; if the museum guard will let you, you can walk inside it.

Both low and high relief are evident in *The Story of Jacob and Esau* **(323)**, one panel of Lorenzo Ghiberti's famous bronze doors for the Baptistry of Florence Cathedral **(466)**. The arched openings, the figures at upper right, and some of the background figures are in low relief. But nearly all the foreground figures are in very high relief—still attached to the background, but fully round and almost freestanding. Ghiberti used these gradations in relief to create a sense of deep space, which is heightened by the receding perspective of the arches. The impression of depth is enhanced even more by the figures that overlap the frame at left and right, in such a way that they actually seem to advance into our space.

Although we have already looked at several examples of sculpture in the round, it will be useful here to consider one work primarily from the standpoint of its complex interaction with space. Sculpture in the round exists wholly in our world. We can walk around it and see it from every angle. This is a terrific challenge to the sculptor's compositional ability, since every viewpoint must be under control. Even when there is a definite front and back, as there usually is in figurative sculpture, all viewpoints should be interesting. And the fact that the work looks different from every angle makes the observer's experience much richer.

An excellent example of sculpture in the round is Rodin's *Burghers of Calais* **(324)**. Rodin made this sculpture for public display in the city of Calais, in France, and it depicts an episode in the town's medieval history. Six men have offered to give their lives to ransom their city from the English, who hold it captive. Each of them faces certain death, but they confront their sacrifice in different ways. One is angry, one sorrowful, one merely resigned, and so on— but each is unique, facing a personal tragedy amid shared crisis. We can read the men's emotions from their various postures, facial expressions, and gestures. The six hostages march in an irregular circle, some determinedly erect, others drooping in despair. And the viewer must also walk in a circle, because there is no angle from which all faces are visible. Rodin's message is complex, so he expressed it in the complex form of sculpture in the round.

left: 323. Lorenzo Ghiberti.
The Story of Jacob and Esau,
detail from
The Gates of Paradise. c. 1435.
Gilt bronze, 31¼" square.
Baptistry, Florence.

right: 324. Auguste Rodin.
The Burghers of Calais.
1884 (cast 1985).
Bronze, 6'10½" × 7'11" × 6'6".
The Metropolitan Museum
of Art, New York
(gift of Iris and
B. Gerald Cantor, 1989).

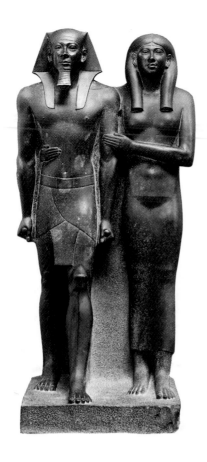

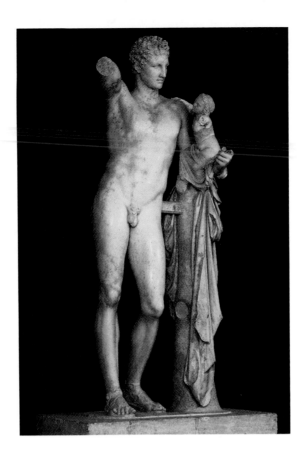

THE HUMAN FIGURE
IN SCULPTURE

We humans tend to be egocentric. We are interested in ourselves, in anything that touches upon our immediate concerns. Artists throughout history have expressed this egocentrism with the self-portrait. So it should come as no surprise that the human figure has always been a basic subject of sculpture. What could be more interesting than oneself—or a figure shaped like oneself? We respond psychologically to the sculpture of a human form much as we would to a real human being. What is that person like? Why does he or she look that way? What is that person thinking?

When children see a figure sculpture, they often arrange their bodies into the same pose as that of the sculpture. As adults we may be tempted to do the same thing, but we have learned to be more inhibited in public. We may be surprised to discover that we have the same impulse to let our bodies mimic the shape of *abstract* sculptures, but this is not really so strange. There is considerable similarity in the way naturalistic and abstract (or nonobjective) sculptures are designed. By studying the figure in sculpture, we can learn much about the way nonfigurative sculptures are designed—how the sculptor handles weights, balances, stresses, and the composition in general. Some nonobjective sculptors go back occasionally to study the human figure, in order to test their understanding of forms in space.

The sculptural treatment of figures throughout history usually has been greatly influenced by the culture in which a particular piece was made. For example, in ancient Egypt figural sculptures, especially those depicting members of the nobility, tended to be somewhat rigid and immobile. Just as the Egyptians built their pyramids for all eternity, so they meant their kings and queens to be posed in eternal serenity. In the sculpture of *Mycerinus and Ka-Merer-Nebty* **(325)** both figures stand proudly erect, facing straight ahead. Although each has the left foot planted slightly forward, there is no suggestion of walking. The shoulders and hips are level, the arms frozen at attention.

In contrast to the formal poses favored by the Egyptians, we find the **contrapposto** perfected by the Greeks in the 5th and 4th centuries B.C.E. Contrapposto means "counterpoise" or "counterbalance," and it is intended to be natural, curving, and relaxed, to imply motion. We have the impression the sculptor has caught the figure in the middle of a movement, and that one second earlier or later the pose would have been different. You can see this effect in *Hermes with the Infant Dionysus* **(326)**, which is probably an original by the famous Greek sculptor Praxiteles. Hermes' weight is on his right foot, so that his right hip is raised and his left leg bent and relaxed. To counterbalance this, Hermes' left shoulder is raised, and the whole figure stands in a gentle S-curve. This elegant curve was Praxiteles' trademark and has been copied ever since. We see exaggerated versions of it today in the poses of such "living statues" as fashion models and professional bodybuilders, who use contrapposto to show off to advantage accomplishments in fabric or muscle tissue.

Eastern art, like its Western counterpart, also presents examples of formal and informal poses. The Buddha, who exists in eternity like the monarchs of Egypt, is routinely depicted in a serene, motionless pose, his arms and legs folded, his face a study in peaceful contemplation **(327)**. But less exalted beings may be modeled in animated motion. Our illustration shows *Shukongojin* **(328)**, a guardian figure known as the "thunderbolt-bearer," who is also associated with Buddhism. This life-size figure stands in the Sangatsu-do (Third Month Hall) of the temple known as Todai-ji at Nara, in Japan. Shukongojin's role is protection. He is meant to ward off demons and evildoers, thus guarding the temple and the faith. His ferocious expression shows that early Japanese sculptors were capable of emotionalism and theatricality, while the S-curve twist to his body demonstrates mastery of the contrapposto pose.

left: 327. *Seated Buddha*, from Gandhara, India (now Pakistan). Kushan period, 2nd–3rd century C.E. Stone, 36 × 22½ × 8″. The Seattle Art Museum (Eugene Fuller Memorial Collection).

right: 328. *Shukongojin*, guardian figure. Nara Period, mid-8th century. Painted clay, height 5′8½″. Sangatsu-do of Todai-ji, Nara, Japan.

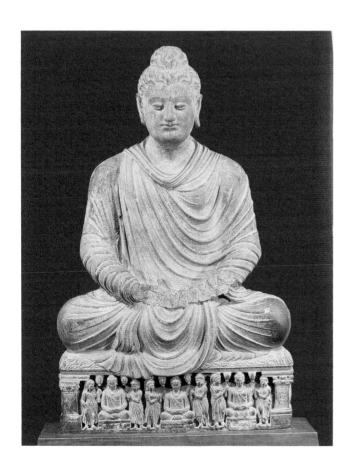

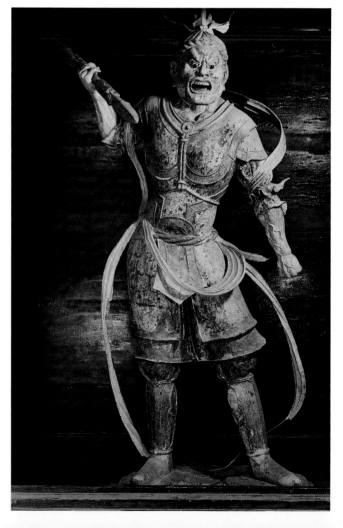

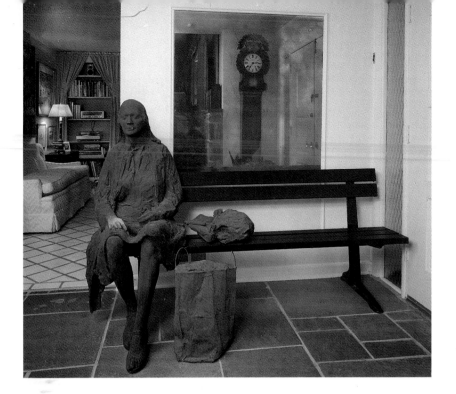

Contemporary sculptors are less committed to specific categories of poses, yet they are no less interested in the human figure as a subject. One modern sculptor who has concentrated on the figure almost exclusively is George Segal. Segal works in plaster, and his figures are cast from living models. The "sculpting" is done by selecting, dressing, and posing his subject. After that, technology largely takes over. The artist pastes plaster-saturated cloth squares over the model to form a perfectly defined shell of the body. After the plaster has hardened, the shell is removed in sections. Later, Segal reassembles the sections and uses this shell as a mold in which to make a plaster cast. Earlier works were left in the pure chalky white of the plaster, but later Segal began to paint some of his people in vivid colors, as evidenced by *Blue Girl on Park Bench* **(329)**.

Segal likes to place his figures in a setting of objects from the real world, such as the actual park bench supporting the *Blue Girl,* which is a component of the sculpture. His expressionless people suggest isolation, boredom, and mental stagnation in a packaged society. The *Blue Girl* might be waiting for a bus, but one has the feeling that if the bus doesn't come, she will go on waiting impassively for all time. These figures are antiheroic. Just as heroic figures show us what we might aspire to be, Segal's people show us what we might fear to become.

The Polish sculptor Magdalena Abakanowicz also shows us what we might fear to become, but she does not necessarily use the entire human figure to do so. Many of Abakanowicz' sculptures consist of body parts, repeated over and over, acquiring power and intensity—even menace—by their very repetition. A well-known piece from the late 1970s consisted of eighty headless human torsos, seated and viewed from behind, called *Backs.* A more recent work, *Infantes* (*Children,* **330**), presents a long, curving row of paired legs, bodies chopped off at the waist. Made of burlap, as are many of Abakanowicz' sculptures, these forms have the texture of skin that is old and wrinkled, possibly burned. One critic has written that the forms suggest victims of a firing squad,[9] and we can readily imagine that some brutal force has shot off the tops of these bodies, leaving the lower halves, inexplicably, standing. The sculptor's title is mysterious. If these are children, are they children of war and violence or perhaps children in a harsh school or prison? Whatever the case, these half-bodies, shorn of their heads and features, acquire tremendous dignity. They reproach us, though we are not sure what we have done to harm them.

SCULPTURE
AND THE ENVIRONMENT

The term "environmental sculpture" may cause some confusion, because it is used in at least three different ways. First, it can refer to sculptures that are large enough for viewers to enter and move about in, sculptures that create their own environments. Second, it can mean large sculptures designed for display in the outdoor environment, such as a sculpture commissioned for a city square. And third, it can be sculptures that are actually a part of the natural environment, such as the presidents' heads carved out of the natural rock of Mount Rushmore. We will look at one or two examples of each type.

Red Grooms has made a kind of specialty of the huge-scale, zany, colorful sculptured environment depicting a place or event. His constructions—always witty and entertaining, always crammed with people, buildings, and things— resemble a cross between an amusement-park funhouse and a comic strip come to three dimensions. In 1975 Grooms lampooned New York City, with comic depictions of a subway car, the Brooklyn Bridge, and other landmarks. In 1982 the city of Philadelphia requested the same madcap treatment, in honor of its three-hundredth birthday. The result was *Philadelphia Cornucopia* **(331)**, a 2,500-square-foot environment installed at the Institute of Contemporary Art. Inspired by the history, romance, and glorious tradition of the city, Red Grooms, as the saying goes, really went to town. His centerpiece is an 11-foot-tall figure of George Washington, proudly standing at the helm of a "ship of state" whose figurehead is an image of Martha Washington. Many other ghosts from Philadelphia's past rise up in colorful caricature, including Benjamin Franklin, Thomas Jefferson, and Betsy Ross.

Grooms' constructions are built of any material at hand—wire, cloth, wood, plastic, metal. And they are painted, but not with naturalistic skin tones. Grooms paints his figures the way a clown puts on makeup—the broader, the more exaggerated, the better. *Philadelphia Cornucopia* demonstrates Grooms' desire for active audience participation in large-scale works of art. Viewers are allowed to walk among the structures and interact with the outlandish creatures who dwell there. To enter this environment is to suspend judgments about reality and let the magic take over.

left: 330.
Magdalena Abakanowicz.
Infantes. 1992.
Burlap and resin; 33 figures,
height of each c. 4'7".
© 1998 Magdalena Abakanowicz/
Licensed by VAGA, New York,
courtesy Marlborough Gallery,
New York.

right: 331. Red Grooms.
Philadelphia Cornucopia, detail.
1982. Mixed media.
Installed at Institute
of Contemporary Art,
University of Pennsylvania,
Philadelphia.

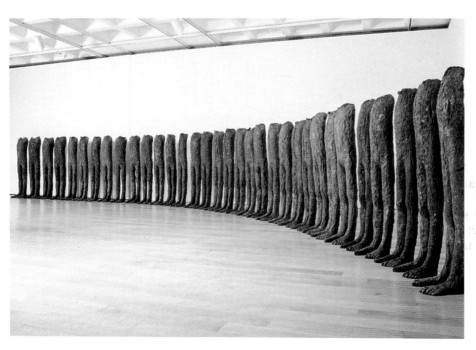

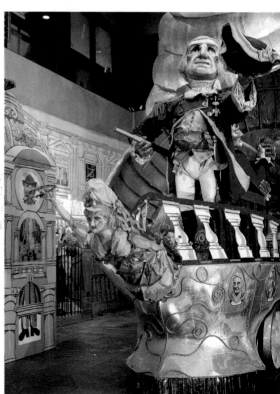

Just down the road from the Institute of Contemporary Art is an environmental sculpture so immense its space could swallow twenty-eight *Philadelphia Cornucopias*. In 1995 artist Judy Pfaff completed her permanent installation of *cirque, Cirque* (332), which extends across the 70,000-square-foot interior of Philadelphia's new Pennsylvania Convention Center. Pfaff's airy construction of steel and aluminum tubes and glass orbs does in fact recall visions of the circus (*cirque*), which is appropriate given that the first circus performance in the United States occurred in Philadelphia, in 1792. Beyond this, Pfaff intended *cirque, Cirque* to evoke a romantic view of the night sky, with its constellations of stars (the glass orbs) and speeding comets. In a huge indoor space, she believes, people naturally want to look up. This artist has given them a dazzling, colorful spectacle to look up at.

Richard Hunt's large work *Jacob's Ladder* (333) is an example of a sculpture designed both physically and iconographically to fit a particular space. Created for the atrium of Chicago's Carter Woodson Library, the sculpture relates, in abstract terms, the story of the biblical patriarch Jacob. While traveling in the desert, Jacob fell asleep one night and dreamed of a ladder reaching from the earth to Heaven. Angels were moving up and down the ladder, and God appeared at the top, speaking to Jacob. "Jacob's ladder" thus becomes a metaphor for the gateway to Heaven.

In Hunt's interpretation, two giant bronze arms reach down from the skylight (symbolically Heaven), and one holds a curving ladder. On the floor below is a bronze sculpture representing an altar in the desert, with Jacob just waking from his sleep. This metaphor, however, has another layer of meaning. The Carter Woodson Library is located in a predominantly black section of Chicago and is staffed and used mostly by blacks. Richard Hunt, who himself is black, intends his "Jacob's ladder" to represent learning, knowledge, literacy—all of which can be acquired in the library—as the gateway to the "heaven" of equality.

Environmental sculpture on a grand scale occurs when an artist sets out to sculpt the earth itself. The idea is an old one—much older, in fact, than recorded history. Some three thousand years ago, highly organized cultures became established in the Ohio River Valley of what is now the United States. People of the Adena and Hopewell cultures, known collectively as the Mound

332. Judy Pfaff.
cirque, Cirque. 1992–95.
Construction of steel
and aluminum tubes,
hand-blown glass orbs,
and other materials.
Permanently installed at Pennsylvania
Convention Center, Philadelphia.

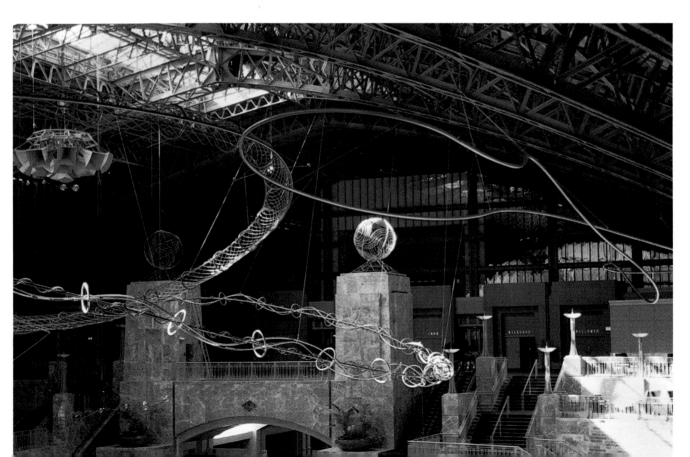

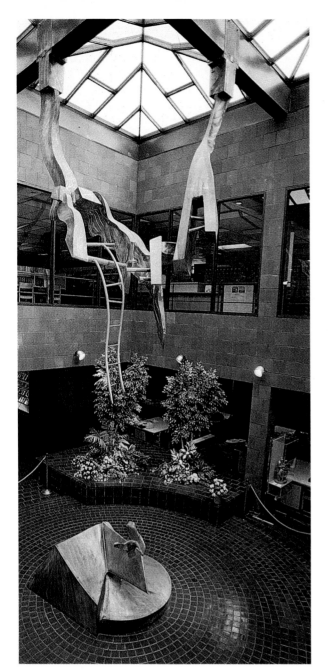

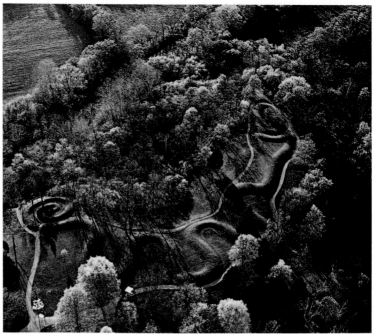

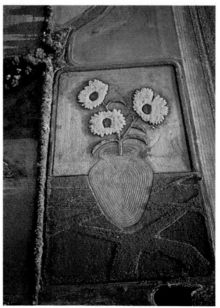

Builders, constructed giant earthworks, often used as burial mounds and sometimes taking the shapes of animals or birds. The most famous of these is the Serpent Mound near Locust Grove, Ohio **(334)**. No one has yet dated this mound precisely, but it was made at least a thousand years ago. Uncoiled, it would measure a quarter mile in length. From the serpent's head, the body curves back and forth along the crest of a hill, then ends in a spiral tail. Just as we do not know the mound's exact age, we do not know how or why it was built. But this splendid creation fascinates us simply because it survives, long after its makers have vanished from the earth they marked.

One intriguing aspect of the Serpent Mound is that its makers *could not see* what they had created. The mound is understood as a serpent only from above, and there are no high elevations in the area. Nowadays, we have airplanes and satellites, a fact likely to stir the earth-marking urge in many souls. Farmers, for instance, constantly mark the earth with their tractors. Combine this activity with an aesthetic impulse, and you get—Crop Art. A fine example is Stan Herd's *Sunflower Still Life* **(335)**, a 20-acre artwork in alfalfa, soybeans, and sunflowers.

left: 333. Richard Hunt.
Jacob's Ladder. 1977.
Bronze,
overall height of space 18′.
Installed at the Carter G. Woodson
Regional Library, Chicago.

top right: 334. Serpent Mound,
near Locust Grove, Ohio.
c. 1000 C.E. or earlier.
Overall length (uncoiled) c. 1300′.

above right: 335. Stan Herd.
Sunflower Still Life. 1986.
Alfalfa, soybeans, and
sunflowers; 20 acres.
Created near Lawrence, Kan.
(later harvested).

For another interpretation of earth-marking, we look to Robert Smithson's *Spiral Jetty* (336), one of the classics of 20th-century sculpture. The *Spiral Jetty* is a 1,500-foot-long ramp of earth and rock—coincidentally almost the same length as the Serpent Mound—bulldozed into position in a secluded part of the Great Salt Lake in Utah. When the *Jetty* was constructed in 1970, the United States was actively involved in space exploration, and for the first time we could see photographs of what our planet looks like from "the outside." We became aware that Earth is always in a state of change, with forms continually building up and breaking down. Smithson's work exemplifies this process on a grand scale; although intended as a permanent structure, the *Spiral Jetty* is no longer visible, because the lake has risen to cover it. The long curl of the spiral also reminds us of old legends about the Great Salt Lake being connected by an underground canal to the Pacific Ocean. According to these legends, the flow of water back and forth created huge whirlpools in the lake, similar to the form of the spiral. Above all, the spiral is a timeless symbol. Smithson took the bold step of carving a giant spiral into the very land we inhabit.

A similarly ambitious work, Christo and Jeanne-Claude's *Running Fence* (337), never was intended to be anything but temporary. Constructed of 18-foot-high nylon panels set on steel posts, *Running Fence* meandered over the hills and fields of northern California for 24½ miles, starting at the Pacific Ocean and then moving inland. It was paid for by the artists and built by their teams of workers, stood for two weeks, and then, as planned, was removed. All that remain are photographs, films, and preliminary drawings. (In photos, *Running Fence* may remind you of China's Great Wall [54], a comparison that surely has occurred to Christo and Jeanne-Claude.)

below: 336. Robert Smithson. *Spiral Jetty.* 1970. Rock, salt crystals, earth, algae; coil length 1500'. Great Salt Lake, Utah (now submerged).

bottom: 337. Christo and Jeanne-Claude. *Running Fence.* 1972–76. Nylon fabric and steel poles, 18' × 24½ miles. Installed in Sonoma and Marin Counties, California, for two weeks, fall 1976.

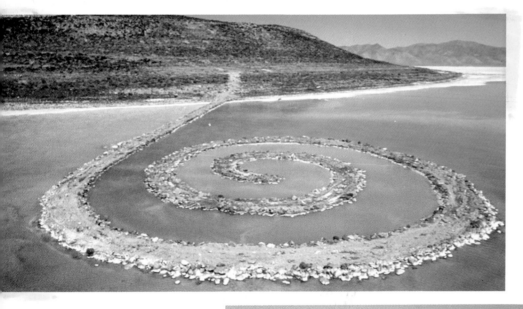

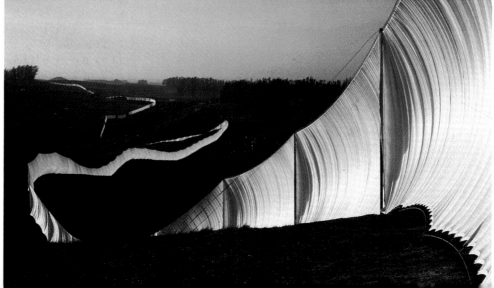

CHRISTO

B. 1935

and

JEANNE-CLAUDE

B. 1935

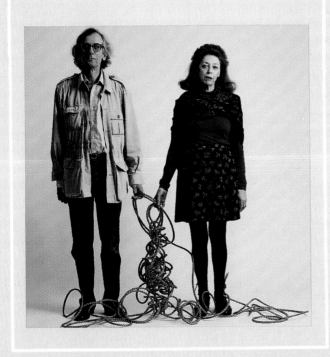

Many artists over time have worked on a grand scale, but none have done so as consistently and as spectacularly as Christo and Jeanne-Claude. Their body of work consists of "projects," most of which have been colossal. Often they wrap things—*large* things—like giant gift packages. They have wrapped a whole section of the Australian coast, cliffs and all, in plastic sheeting. They have wrapped a historic bridge in Paris with 10 acres of silky champagne-colored fabric. In 1995 they wrapped the Reichstag, the German Parliament building in Berlin, with more than a million square feet of shiny aluminum-hued cloth. No passerby could possibly miss these "projects" or ignore them.

Christo and Jeanne-Claude's art is very public, very much out in the open, but the artists themselves remain

something of a mystery. According to the brief and rather formal biography they release, Christo Javacheff was born in 1935 in Bulgaria, in eastern Europe. He studied at the Fine Arts Academy in Sofia, then traveled by way of Prague and Vienna to Paris. It was in Paris, in 1958, that Christo began wrapping, at first on a modest scale. As he tells it, he began with small objects, such as chairs and tables and bottles. In Paris, too, Christo met Jeanne-Claude de Guillebon, born in Casablanca, Morocco, who became his wife and later his partner.

The first of the large-scale wrapped projects was made in Cologne, Germany, in 1961, when Christo allowed his own art exhibition to spill outside a gallery beside the Rhine harbor onto the docks. A stack of barrels and other paraphernalia, plus rolls of industrial paper, became the *Dockside Packages*. Other ambitious wrappings followed, but Christo had yet grander plans. The project that established his international reputation was not, strictly speaking, a wrapping. It was actually more of a *draping*. In 1972 Christo strung a 4-ton orange nylon curtain between two mountains in Colorado, an arrangement that held intact only long enough to be photographed. The artist called it *Valley Curtain*.

Two projects in particular transformed Christo and Jeanne-Claude into media celebrities. The first was *Running Fence*, in the mid-1970s, which set up a white nylon barrier 24½ miles long over the hills of northern California. The other was *Surrounded Islands*, in the early 1980s, for which eleven little islands in Florida's Biscayne Bay were circled with pink polypropylene cloth. Earlier projects had been remarkable, daring, extravagant—but these two were lovely. Even people who had objected to such manipulations of the landscape came to admire them. People had to admire quickly, though, for Christo and Jeanne-Claude's structures are meant to stand physically for only a few days or weeks. After a predetermined period, workers remove them, leaving no trace. The projects live on afterward in the sketches and photographs and recounting of their history.

Some observers have criticized the artists for the transitory nature of their works, but Christo has a ready reply: "I am an artist, and I have to have courage. . . . Do you know that I don't have any artworks that exist? They all go away when they're finished. Only the sketches are left, giving my works an almost legendary character. I think it takes much greater courage to create things to be gone than to create things that will remain."[10]

Christo and Jeanne-Claude
in their studio.

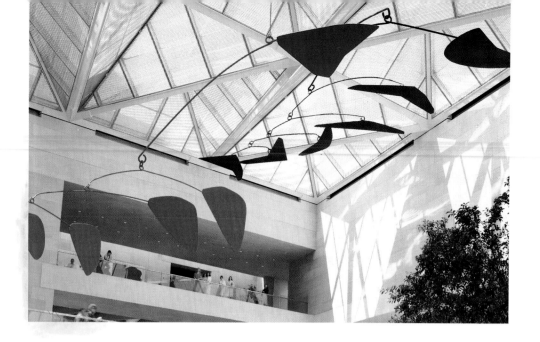

above: 338. Alexander Calder. *Untitled.* 1976. Painted aluminum and tempered steel, 29'10½" × 76'. © 1994 National Gallery of Art, Washington, D.C. (gift of the Collectors Committee).

below: 339. James Turrell. *Afrum-Proto.* 1967. Xenon light projection. Courtesy the artist.

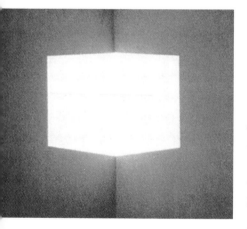

Christo and Jeanne-Claude's work is similar to *Conceptual Art,* a style we shall explore in greater detail in Chapter 20 (p. 491). More important than the physical structure itself is the concept underlying it—in this case the experience of conceiving, planning, building, recording, and removing a monumental work. The sculptures make a mark upon the landscape; they confront nature on a giant scale. The impulse is similar to, though grander than, that of drawing one's initials in wet concrete or painting them on a rock. And yet, after all, one cannot leave a 24½-mile fence across California. The artists deliberately chose to create a structure that had to come down, that had removal built into its concept, in order to focus attention on the process.

MOTION, LIGHT, AND TIME

The world we live in is preoccupied with action—change and movement and energy—so it is only natural that some of our sculpture would reflect this. **Kinetic sculpture** is a broad term generally used to describe works that incorporate motion as part of their artistic expression. The mobiles of Alexander Calder **(338)**, for instance, are light and fluid, balanced so that the slightest current of air will set them moving. In a sense they are *about* motion, which is to say their subject is constant change and a never-ending formation of new relationships in space. Implicit in these mobiles is the element of time. We said of Rodin's *Burghers* **(324)** that you have to move around the sculpture to appreciate it fully. You can also move around a Calder mobile, but *it* is moving too, so the experience of elapsed time, of changing forms and spaces, is even more complex.

Weightless as they seem to be, Calder's mobiles still have substance. If you could touch one, you would feel thin, rigid pieces of metal. Other sculptors have created works based on an element with no substance at all—light. The light sculptures of James Turrell are designed to "make light inhabit space so it feels materially present," according to the artist. In *Afrum-Proto* **(339)**, for instance, we see what appears to be a solid cube hovering in the air. Closer inspection, however, leads us to discover that the cube consists entirely of light. Turrell's work is based on the perception of form, and that perception can be quite persuasive—so much so, in fact, that a 1980 exhibition of his work at the Whitney Museum of American Art resulted in two lawsuits. In both cases, visitors to the exhibition leaned against what seemed to be a wall but was actually a light-form, lost their balance, and fell to the floor.

To the person whose idea of sculpture is the stone carvings of Michelangelo and Bernini, the cast bronzes of Verrocchio or Moore, this conception of light as sculpture may be strange, even shocking. But somehow it seems appropriate that our world should produce sculptures just this transitory and just this susceptible to a modern phenomenon—the power failure.

As a matter of fact, nearly all of us have had experience making sculptures out of materials almost as insubstantial as light—snow and sand. You build a snowman or snowwoman or snowdog; the sun comes out, and it melts. You build a sand castle at the beach; the tide comes in and washes your castle away. Are these really sculptures? Perhaps, by some definitions. They have form, they exist in three dimensions, they are a human creation for the purpose of aesthetic expression. The only thing unusual is that they exist for just a little while and then fade, never to be duplicated exactly.

One of the most talked-about sculptures of the 1990s may not have faded, but, without care, it would certainly have *wilted*. In the summer of 1992 the controversial artist Jeff Koons set up a huge sculpture, nearly 40 feet high, in the courtyard of a Baroque palace in Arolsen, a town in Germany. Built over a framework of wood and steel, the sculpture consisted entirely of flowering plants—petunias, geraniums, begonias, and others in several colors. Its form was that of a sweet, cuddly little dog, sitting obediently and waiting for a pat on the head. The artist called it *Puppy* **(340)**. Needless to say, this sculpture had to be watered on a regular basis. As the plants grew, the puppy's shape inevitably changed. It became more and more of—dare we say it?—a shaggy dog. Nevertheless, while *Puppy* bloomed, people drove from miles around to admire it.

Apart from its sheer charm, *Puppy* makes an important point about the nature of sculpture: We cannot evaluate sculptures according to how long they last. Classical civilizations made sculptures to survive for all eternity, but they will not. Wood sculptures may burn; stone sculptures are eaten away by acid rain and industrial pollution. In times of war metal sculptures have sometimes been melted down to be turned into bullets. What remains, what cannot be taken away, is the sculptor's expression and the experience of the viewer—even if it lasts only for a moment.

340. Jeff Koons.
Puppy. 1992.
Live flowers, earth, wood,
and steel; 39′4″ × 16′5″ × 21′4″.
Courtesy the artist.

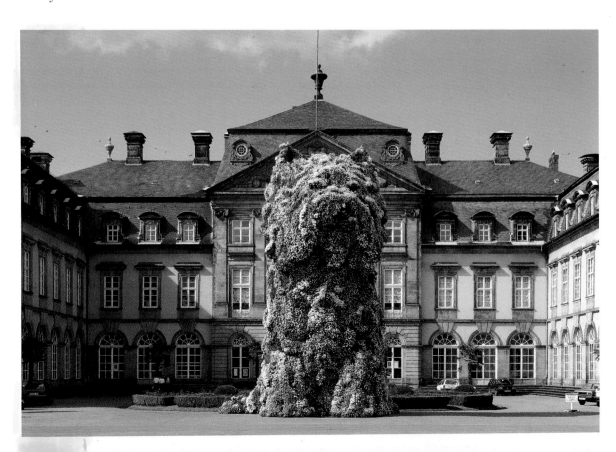

CHAPTER TWELVE

Crafts

THE WORKS OF ART considered in this chapter have certain things in common with one another, but they also share traits with other media, such as sculpture. Most of them have roots in the traditional trades of the Middle Ages—potter, glassblower, blacksmith, woodworker, weaver. It is from this background that the word "craft" derives, referring to expert work done by hand. We still describe as "well-crafted" anything finely made, including a chair, an automobile, a house, even sometimes a painting or sculpture. The specific connotation of craft, however, is an object made by hand, not by machine, and this is true of all the works shown in this chapter.

A common assumption people make about the crafts is that objects are made for some functional use, such as eating, drinking, wearing, or sitting. For this reason they have often been called the "functional arts" or the "applied arts"—that is, applied to everyday necessities. And, to be sure, many of the objects we will look at have that very reason for being. A handmade dinner plate or wine goblet is a craft object, meant to be used for eating or drinking. However, it has never been true that such pieces were supposed to be *only* utilitarian. Hand-crafted objects are made to be beautiful, to be admired for their perfection of form and materials, for the unique expression of their makers. And sometimes an object is *so* special that we are disinclined to use it for any functional purpose.

Consider, for example, our first two illustrations. These ceramic pieces were created some fifteen hundred years and half a world apart. The first is a portrait vessel **(341)** from the Mangbetu people of the African region now part of Congo, made during the last two centuries. The second, a "stirrup vessel" **(342)** dating from about 200–500 C.E., was crafted by the Mochica culture of ancient Peru. Both objects could hold liquids, and both have handles to grip for pouring. The Mochica figure even has a spout (the name "stirrup" comes from the arc-shaped handle-spout). But these works are so masterfully shaped that their forms take precedence over any practical use. Even discounting their historical importance, most people would be more likely to put them on display as art objects than to store them in a kitchen cupboard.

What, then, separates the craft object from the art object? There is no definite line, nor should there be one. Labels are a convenience for talking about art, but they should not force artworks into cubbyholes. What *may* help to distinguish the crafts from the other arts is their emphasis on particular materials. The traditional materials of the crafts are clay, glass, metal, wood, and fiber. Most craft artists concentrate on one material only and have learned to realize its potential for many different kinds of expression. Each of these materials has its own capabilities and limitations, and each lends itself to certain kinds of structural and decorative design. In this chapter we shall consider each of these materials in turn.

CLAY

The craft of *ceramics* involves making objects from clay, a naturally occurring earth substance. When dry, clay has a powdery consistency; mixed with water it becomes *plastic*—that is, moldable and cohesive. In this form it can be modeled, pinched, rolled, or shaped between the hands. Once a clay form has been built and permitted to dry, it will hold its shape, but it is very fragile. To ensure permanence the form must be *fired* in a kiln, at temperatures ranging between about 1200 and 2700 degrees Fahrenheit, or higher. Firing changes the chemical composition of the clay so that it can never again be made plastic. A fired ceramic object, especially one fired at a high temperature, is quite durable. It can be shattered by a hard blow, but the pieces will not disintegrate. A sizable portion of the ancient art that has survived is ceramic, because—unlike wood or fiber—fired clay is highly resistant to the elements. Most large museums have very old ceramic treasures that have been patiently reassembled from the fragments discovered at archaeological sites.

Nearly every culture we know of has practiced the craft of ceramics, and civilizations in the Middle East understood the basic techniques by as early as 5000 B.C.E. The first ceramic ware was undoubtedly made by *pinching*—simple molding and squeezing of a lump of clay between the fingers. This method is adequate for making a small figurine or a miniature bowl, but it would be inefficient to impossible for larger items.

left: 341. Vessel, Mangbetu people, Congo (Zaire). Terra cotta, height 11$\frac{3}{8}$". The Metropolitan Museum of Art, New York (The Michael C. Rockefeller Memorial Collection, bequest of Nelson A. Rockefeller, 1979).

right: 342. Stirrup vessel in the shape of a kneeling warrior with a shield. Mochica culture, Peru, 200–500 C.E. Earthenware with cream slip, height 9$\frac{1}{8}$". The Metropolitan Museum of Art, New York (gift of Nathan Cummings, 1963).

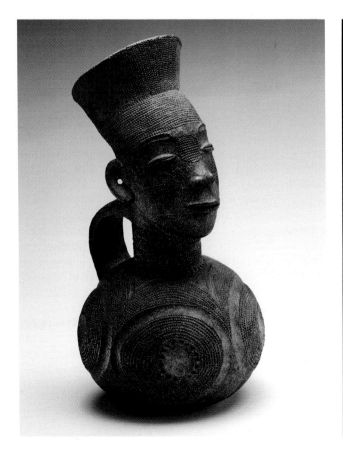

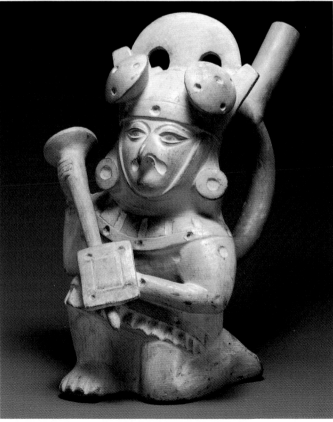

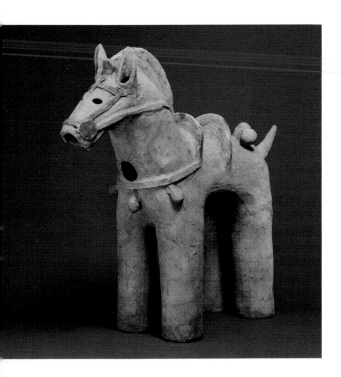

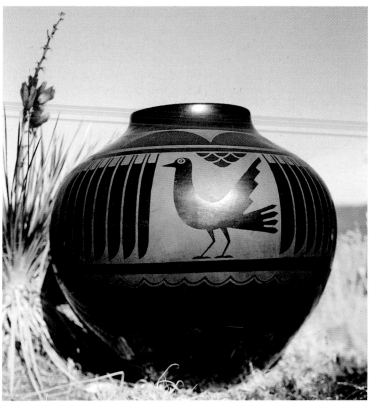

left: **343.** *Haniwa figure: Horse,* from Japan. 5th–6th century. Terra cotta, height 23″. © 1997 The Cleveland Museum of Art (Norweb Collection, 1957).

right: **344.** María Martínez. Black-on-black jar.

A major requirement for most ceramic objects is that they be hollow, that they have thin walls around a hollow core. There are two reasons for this. First, many ceramic wares are meant to contain things—food or liquids, for instance. Second, a solid clay piece is difficult to fire and may very well explode in the kiln. To meet this need for hollowness, ceramists over the ages have developed specialized forming techniques.

One such technique is called ***slab construction.*** The ceramist rolls out the clay into a sheet, very much as a baker would roll out a pie crust, and then allows the sheet to dry slightly. The sheet, or slab, can then be handled in many ways. It can be cut into pieces for assembly into a box form, curled into a cylinder, draped over a mold to make a bowl, or shaped into free-form sculptural configurations. Slab building is usually the method of choice for forming rectilinear objects.

Slab construction was used to create the little horse shown here **(343).** This charming figure is an example of *haniwa*—clay figures placed around Japanese burial mounds between the 3rd and the 6th centuries. *Haniwa* were made to represent many subjects—horses, warriors, birds, and elegant costumed ladies. Usually there was little attempt at naturalism; the subjects were rendered in simple, tubular forms—the word *haniwa* means "circle of clay." This figure intentionally looks more like a toy horse than a real one. The slab construction lends itself readily to the creation of these basic sculptural forms.

Coiling is another technique for making a thin, hollow form. The ceramist rolls out ropelike strands of clay, then coils them upon one another and joins them together. A vessel made from coils attached one atop the other will have a ridged surface, but the coils can be smoothed completely, to produce a uniform, flat wall. The native peoples of the southwestern United States (who never developed the potter's wheel common in most other parts of the world) made extraordinarily large, finely shaped pots by coiling. In this century their craft has been revived by a few supremely talented individuals, including the famous Pueblo potter María Martínez **(344).**

MARÍA MARTÍNEZ

1881(?)–1980

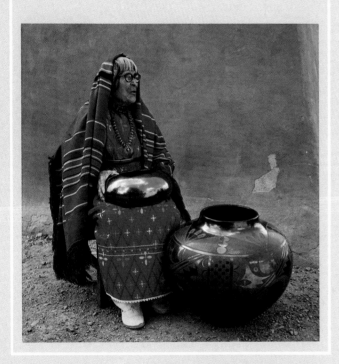

I T IS A LONG WAY in miles and in time between the tiny pueblo of San Ildefonso in New Mexico and the White House in Washington, D.C. But the extraordinary ceramic artist María Martínez made that journey, and many others, in a long lifetime devoted to the craft of pottery making. María—as she signed herself and is known professionally—began her career as a folk potter and ended it six decades later as a first-ranked potter of international reputation.

A daughter of Pueblo people, María most likely was born in 1881, but there are no records. As a child she learned to make pottery, using the coil method, by watching her aunt and other women in the community. Part of her youth was spent at St. Catherine's Indian School in Santa Fe, where María became friends with Julián Martínez. The couple married in 1904.

Although the husband worked at other jobs, the two Martínezes early formed a partnership for making pottery—she doing the building, he the decorating. Between 1907 and 1910 he was employed as a laborer on an archaeological site near the pueblo, under the direction of Dr. Edgar L. Hewett. The amazing career of María Martínez was launched in a simple way: Dr. Hewett gave her a broken piece of pottery from the site and asked her to reconstruct a whole pot in that style using the traditional blackware techniques.

About 1919 the Martínezes developed the special black-on-black pottery that was to make them and the pueblo of San Ildefonso famous. The shiny blackware—created from red clay by a process of smothering the dung-fueled bonfire used for firing—was decorated with matte-black designs. This black-on-black ware was commercially quite successful. María Martínez and her husband became wealthy by the standards of the pueblo and, as was customary, shared that wealth with the entire community.

María bore four sons who survived. Eventually they and their wives and children and grandchildren became partners in her enterprise. One shadow on her domestic life was her husband's serious alcoholism, which began early in their marriage and contributed to his death in 1943. After he was gone, María's daughter-in-law Santana took over much of the decorating of pots, later to be followed by María's son Poponi Da.

As María's fame spread, she traveled widely, giving demonstrations at many world's fairs. Among the awards she received were an honorary doctorate from the University of Colorado and the American Ceramic Society's highest honor for a lifetime of devotion to clay. Her visit to Washington during the 1930s was a highlight. President Franklin D. Roosevelt was not at home, but Mrs. Eleanor Roosevelt was, and she told María, "You are one of the important ones. We have a piece of your pottery here in the White House, and we treasure it and show it to visitors from overseas."

Undoubtedly, María's greatest achievement was in reviving and popularizing the traditions of fine pottery making among the Pueblo people. Not long before her death, according to her great-granddaughter, she said: "When I am gone, essentially other people have my pots. But to you I leave my greatest achievement, which is the ability to do it."[1]

Photograph of María Martínez.

By far the fastest method of creating a hollow, rounded form is by means of the ***potter's wheel*** (345). Egyptian potters were using the wheel by about 4000 B.C.E. Despite some modern improvements and the addition of electricity, the basic principle of wheel construction remains the same as it was in ancient times. The wheel is a flat disk mounted on a vertical shaft, which can be made to turn rapidly either by electricity or by foot power. The ceramist centers a mound of clay on the wheel and, as the wheel turns, uses the hands to shape, "open," and lift the clay form—a procedure known as ***throwing.*** Throwing on the wheel always produces a rounded or cylindrical form, although the thrown pieces can later be reshaped, cut apart, or otherwise altered. Two or more thrown forms can also be joined together.

The most suitable technique, therefore, is one choice the ceramist needs to make in planning a particular work; another choice is the type of clay to be used. Clays differ in their composition, and this in turn affects the character of pieces made from them. Usually a clay is categorized by its firing temperature—the optimum temperature needed to change the clay's chemical composition permanently and make it hard. ***Earthenware*** clays, generally red or brown, fire at the lowest temperatures. Fired earthenware objects are often called ***terra cotta*** ("baked earth"). They tend to be coarse and porous and will not hold liquids unless coated with a glaze (see below). ***Stoneware*** clays, which fire at medium temperatures, are generally brown or grayish. Much commercial dinnerware is made of stoneware, and these clays have been popular among artist-potters.

The aristocrats of clays are the pure white ***porcelains,*** which fire at the highest temperatures. Porcelain is the material of the finest dinnerware and in the past was used for the most elegant of commercial vases and figurines. Chinese porcelains from the Song and Ming dynasties (from the 10th to the 17th century) are thought by many collectors to show the highest level of beauty and refinement ever achieved in ceramic art. The Ming vase shown here (346) is decorated all over with flowing images of the lotus, the sacred flower of Buddhism.

left: 345. Throwing on the potter's wheel.

right: 346. Vase, from China. Ming Dynasty, c. 1522–66. Porcelain, height 8½". Victoria & Albert Museum, London.

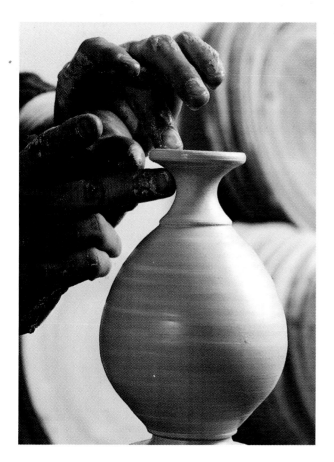

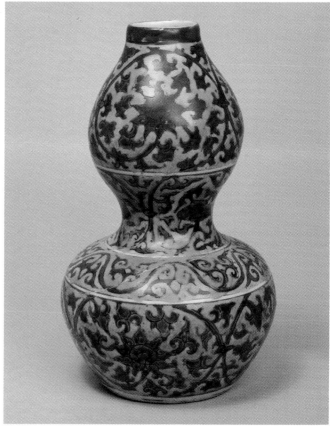

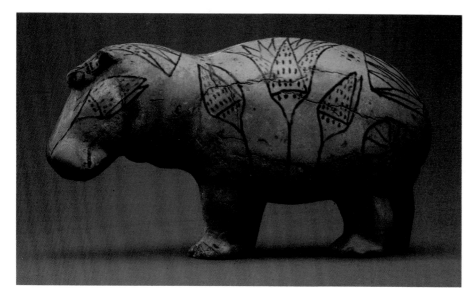

left: 347. *Hippopotamus*,
from the tomb
of Senbi at Meir, Egypt.
XII Dynasty, 2000–1788 B.C.E.
Egyptian faience, height 4⅜".
The Metropolitan Museum of Art,
New York (gift of
Edward S. Harkness, 1917).

below: 348. Linda Arbuckle,
with the technical assistance
of Robert Lyon.
Onward and Upward. 1989.
Thrown terra cotta
with majolica glaze, 13 × 12 × 6".
Collection Ruth and Rick Snyderman,
Philadelphia.

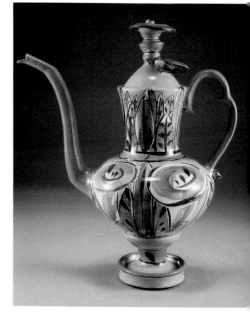

While clays themselves may have interesting colors and textures, much of the potential for decoration in ceramics comes from the glaze. A *glaze* is a glasslike material usually applied to the surface of a ceramic piece and then fired on so as to fuse the glaze with the clay body. Nearly always this is a second firing, which follows the preliminary one to harden the clay. There is virtually no limit to the different effects that can be produced by combination of glazes or by the various methods of applying them. While there are clear glazes, most glazes have color, and this is a major reason for their application. A secondary purpose of the glaze is to make an object watertight and nonabsorbent—especially important for cooking and eating vessels and for the more porous low-fired clays.

One of the earliest glazes, in use by 3000 B.C.E., is known as *Egyptian paste.* Unlike most glazes, this material is mixed into the clay rather than applied on top of it. When the piece is fired (in a single firing), a glassy coating, often turquoise in color, forms on the surface. We see this in the Metropolitan Museum's famous hippopotamus figure, affectionately known as "William" **(347)**.

Conventional glazes can be applied in many ways—by pouring, dipping, or spraying, for example. When properly compounded, glazes can also be painted onto a surface with all the precision and potential for color effects available to an artist using oil paints on canvas. Chinese ceramics are especially valued for the purity and glow of their glazes **(346)**.

Our next illustration, a teapot by Linda Arbuckle **(348)**, brings us back to the discussion at the beginning of this chapter: Is it functional or decorative, art or craft? Ceramic teapots have been made for hundreds of years, and clay is a preferred material for teapots. This particular teapot, however, doesn't look as though it will get much day-to-day service. Arbuckle might almost be poking fun at the traditional utilitarian role of clay pots. The frivolous shape and decoration of *Onward and Upward* should banish any ideas about clay being a heavy or ordinary material.

GLASS

If clay is one of the most versatile of the craft materials, glass is perhaps the most fascinating. Few people, when presented with a beautiful glass form, can resist holding it up to the light, watching how light changes its appearance from different angles.

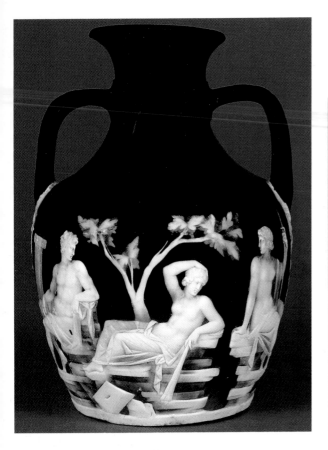

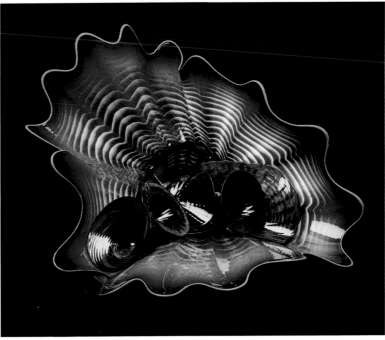

left: **349.** *Portland Vase.*
3rd century C.E.
Cameo-cut glass.
Copyright British Museum, London.

right: **350.** Dale Chihuly.
Violet and Green Persian Set.
1990. Blown glass, 18 × 32 × 32".
Courtesy the artist.

While there are thousands of formulas for glass, its principal ingredient is usually silica, or sand. The addition of other materials can affect color, melting point, strength, and so on. When heated, glass becomes molten, and in that state it can be shaped by several different methods. Unlike clay, glass never changes chemically as it moves from a soft, workable state to a hard, rigid one. As glass cools it hardens, but it can then be reheated and rendered molten again for further working.

Glass as a material holds many risks, both during the creative process and afterward. The shaping of a glass object demands split-second timing— quick decisions and quick handwork—while the glass remains hot. What's more, a finished glass piece is the most fragile of all craft wares. One swift blow can shatter it irreparably. There is something almost heroic about an artist who would spend days, weeks, even months making an object that is so vulnerable.

Glassmaking is nearly as old a craft as ceramics, but it was not until Roman times, near the start of the Common Era, that the first great period of glassmaking as an art began. The Roman era saw the invention of the blow-pipe—an instrument that has changed very little in two thousand years. To blow glass, the artist dips up a portion of molten glass at the end of the pipe and then blows through the pipe to produce a bubble. The bubble can be shaped or cut by various methods while it is still hot. Besides blowing, other ways of forming glass include molding, pressing, and rolling.

The Roman historian Pliny the Elder wrote of large "statues" made from glass, but almost nothing is known about them. It is assumed that they were chiseled out of solid glass blocks and then polished. Although we can only speculate about such pieces, many examples of glassware from the Roman period have survived, including what is perhaps the most famous glass object in the world—the *Portland Vase* **(349)**. The incredible virtuosity displayed in this vessel testifies to long experience in glassmaking. The vase was made in three stages. First the basic form of dark blue glass was blown, and then a layer of semi-opaque white glass was added to the outside. Next the vase was given over to a cameo cutter—a carver of low-relief figural designs—who patiently chipped away the white glass to create a relief design of many gradations. In some areas the dark blue shows faintly through the white to give a shaded effect. Later glass artists have tried to duplicate the remarkable cameo quality of the *Portland Vase* and have failed.

Contemporary glass artists often strive for a balance of form and decoration. Dale Chihuly's designs are exuberant and deliberately sculptural **(350)**. Their decoration seems to evolve from the form itself, rather than being applied to an existing structure. Chihuly's blown-glass works are very thin and translucent; they have a fluid quality that is reminiscent of shapes in the natural world.

A special branch of glass craft, **stained glass** is a technique used for windows, lampshades, and similar structures that permit light to pass through. Stained glass is made by cutting sheets of glass in various colors into small pieces, then fitting the pieces together to form a pattern. Often the segments are joined by strips of lead, hence the term *leaded* stained glass.

Probably our most common association with stained glass is the decorated windows of churches, which often portray religious scenes. Our illustration shows a secular adaptation—Catherine Thompson's panel *The Elephant's Child* **(351)**. Thompson's interest lies in narrative, or storytelling, especially as it relates to fables. Here she interprets the figures of elephant, crocodile, snake, and bird from Rudyard Kipling's classic tale of how the elephant got its trunk. The artist's decorative pattern fills (sometimes overlaps) the border with luminous, jewel-like colors.

METAL

From the most fragile craft material we turn to the most indestructible. Metals rust and corrode under some circumstances, but they do not shatter, chip, or rot away. Indeed, sometimes the action of the elements has a beneficial effect on metals. As was mentioned in reference to cast-bronze sculptures (p. 270), weathering may give metals a surface color, or **patina**, that is more attractive than their original appearance.

Ever since humans learned to work metals, they have made splendid art, as well as functional tools, from this versatile family of materials. Given all the sophisticated technology we have available today, we might think that metalwork would simply get better and better. Yet for sheer beauty of form and decoration, few artists have matched the skill of bronze artisans in China three thousand years ago.

Ornate bronze vessels were made in China as early as the 16th century B.C.E. The *Tiger* illustrated in Chapter 14 **(424)**, dating from the 9th century B.C.E., is thought to have been made as a base support for some large structure, perhaps a throne. Like most works from the period, it is covered with stylized geometric designs in relief. We know that such pieces were **cast** (p. 267) by pouring molten bronze into a mold, but we do not know how ancient Chinese artisans managed to get such elaborate effects from what must have been rather crude molds.

One distinctive aspect of metal is that it is equally at home in the mundane and the sublime—the bridge that spans a river or the precious ring on a finger; the plow that turns up the earth or the crown on a princess' head. Whatever the application, the basic composition of the material is the same, and the methods of working it are similar.

Casting is but one of several methods for working metal. Another ancient technique is **forging**—the art of the blacksmith. Forging involves heating a chunk of metal over a fire until it is red-hot, then beating and shaping it with

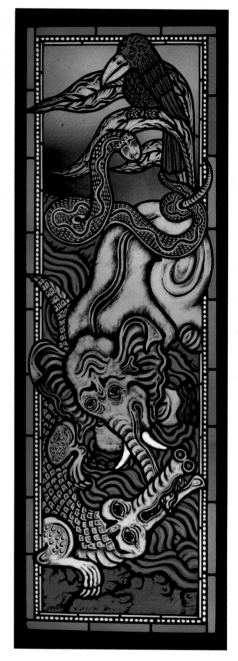

351. Catherine Thompson. *The Elephant's Child.* 1989. Leaded and painted stained-glass panel, 6′4″ × 2′2″. Mountlake Terrace Public Library, commissioned by the Mountlake Terrace Arts Commission, Mountlake Terrace, Wash.

hammers. This is how horseshoes traditionally were made, and it is also the method of making wrought iron, as for balconies and railings.

Some metals, such as copper, are soft enough to be worked cold—cut and hammered into shape without heating. Copper was a favorite material for the weathervanes that adorned the tops of many buildings from the Colonial period in America well into the 19th century. Whimsical figures like the *Angel Gabriel* **(352)** were thin enough to turn at any breeze, pointing the wind's direction, and their shapes made intriguing silhouettes against the sky.

Cold hammering is also the technique of fine silversmiths. The artisan begins with a thin sheet of metal and, working from the back, strikes it repeatedly with small hammers, a method known as ***repoussé.*** In some cases the metal sheet is placed on top of a mold and hammered so as to conform to the shape of the mold. The vase illustrated **(353)** is a wonderful example of this technique. It was made by Tiffany and Company for the World's Columbian Exposition in 1893, and no effort was spared to make it as elaborate—and as uniquely American—as possible. Hammered into relief are flowers and plants from every region of the United States. Both the overall shape of the vase and the handles at the top were inspired by pottery forms from the ancient peoples who once inhabited the Americas.

One of the oldest uses of metal as an expressive medium is for jewelry. This has been true since prehistoric times. Early cultures believed that wearing special stones or special metals could ward off disease and evil spirits—a practice continued today in the wearing of copper bracelets for therapeutic purposes. Apart from its supposed magical powers, metal has great symbolic value. People wear jewelry to symbolize wealth and status. They also wear jewelry to symbolize belonging—to a person (a wedding ring), to an institution (a school ring), to a group (a club or fraternity or religious ring).

Gold and silver have been preferred metals for jewelry since earliest times, partly because of their lustrous sheen and beautiful colors, partly because they are soft enough to be worked into very fine designs. Native peoples

left: 352.
Angel Gabriel weathervane, from Massachusetts. 19th century. Copper. Watercolor rendering by Lucille Chabot, c. 1939. National Gallery of Art, Washington, D.C. Index of American Design.

right: 353.
Tiffany and Company. *Magnolia Vase* made for World's Columbian Exposition, 1893. Silver, gold, and enamel; height 31″. The Metropolitan Museum of Art, New York (gift of Mrs. Winthrop Atwell, 1899).

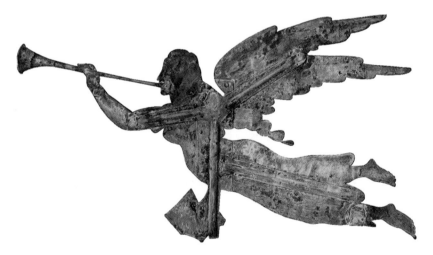

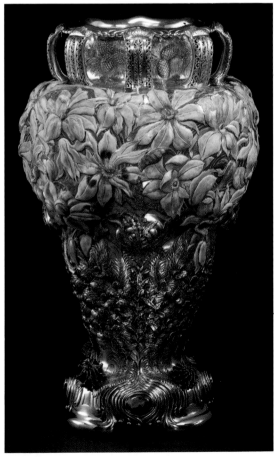

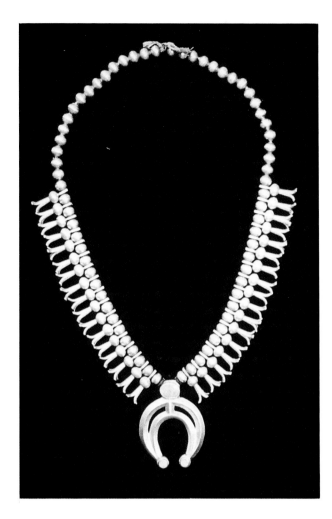

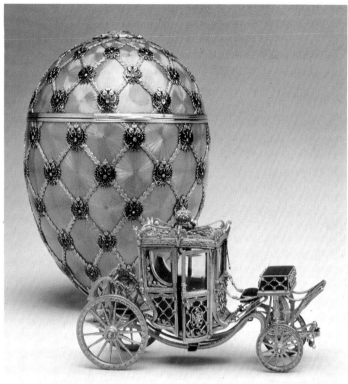

of the American Southwest learned jewelry techniques from the Spaniards and from itinerant Mexican silversmiths in the 19th century. Both silver and turquoise are abundant in the area of Arizona and New Mexico, so we often find them combined in Navajo and Zuni jewelry. The Navajo "squash blossom" necklace (354) is a classic design, with stylized flowerlike projections from a silver-beaded chain and a curved pendant at the bottom.

The use of metals for precious objects has a long history and has attracted many noted practitioners. One name, however, stands out above the rest. Peter Carl Fabergé, a Russian of French descent, established a shop in St. Petersburg in the late 19th century. About 1884 he was named official jeweler and goldsmith to the imperial family. Czar Alexander III was his first patron, followed by Czar Nicholas II. Between 1884 and 1917 Fabergé created numerous pieces in gold, enamels, and gems for his royal clients. His greatest achievement, however, was a series of objects that are unique in all the world. Only 53 are known to exist. They are the imperial Easter eggs (355).

It is a Russian custom to give eggs at Easter. Czar Alexander improved upon the custom by having Fabergé construct, every year, an elaborate metal-and-jeweled egg for presentation to the empress. Each egg was as ornate and lavishly decorated as Fabergé's skilled workers could manage, and each contained a "surprise." When a tiny pearl or diamond on the outside was pressed, the egg opened to reveal a separate, gemlike little object—a portrait, a miniature basket of flowers, or, in the case of the "coronation egg" shown here, a finely detailed gold coach. Alexander's son Nicholas continued the custom, commissioning Fabergé to make Easter eggs for his empress, Alexandra, and for his mother as well. This practice was repeated yearly until the Russian Revolution of 1917 wiped out the imperial family and Fabergé's workshop.

left: 354. Navajo "squash blossom" necklace. Silver and turquoise. National Museum of the American Indian, Smithsonian Institution, New York.

right: 355. Peter Carl Fabergé and workshop. *Coronation Egg.* 1897. Gold, platinum, and enamel with diamonds, rubies, and rock crystal; height of egg 5″. The FORBES Magazine Collection, New York.

WOOD

There are two reasons for the great popularity of wood as a craft material throughout the entire history of art. One is that it is relatively easy to work. The simplest tools will shape it, and there is no need for extreme heat, as with clay, glass, or metal. The second reason is that wood is so widely available. In most inhabited areas of the globe, wood is abundant and easy to obtain.

These two qualities would make wood the ideal material were it not for certain drawbacks. Because of its organic nature, wood is not very durable. Cold and heat distort it, water rots it, and insects can eat it away.

We must assume that only a tiny fraction of the wood objects made over the centuries have survived. Wood was a favorite material in Africa, in the precolonial Americas, and in the South Pacific, but most of the examples we have are fairly recent. One magnificent piece, a mask dating from the 19th century, comes from Bella Coola, on the Pacific Coast of British Columbia, in Canada (356). Representing the sun—the source of warmth and therefore all life—this mask has a central face surrounded by upraised hands, presumably symbolizing the sun's rays.

Wood carving, especially of figures, is a nearly universal art, practiced from earliest times up to the present. And the use of wood for musical instruments is so widespread as to be indispensable. Most of the world's great music would never have been composed without wood instruments on which to play it. From the simplest rattle to the concert grand piano, wood provides a resonance that no other material can duplicate. Combine these two—the carving and the resonance—and you have our next example, a stringed instrument from early-15th-century Italy (357). This beautiful little piece, a relative of the guitar, once had five strings, which were strummed or plucked. Fine carving on the back depicts a young couple, perhaps just betrothed, posing under a tree in which Cupid draws his bow. Plucked instruments of the period were associated with love and springtime. The delicately carved figures reinforce this charming theme.

The carving of wood figures reached a high point in the United States during the 19th century. Certain types of figures flourished: cigar-store Indians and other images that adorned the fronts of shops; magnificent figureheads, usually of women with long, flowing hair, that crowned the prows of sailing ships; and ornate carousel animals. Generations raised on look-alike merry-

left: 356. Bella Coola mask representing the sun, from British Columbia. Before 1897. Wood, diameter 24¾". © American Museum of Natural History, New York.

right: 357. Stringed instrument, from northern Italy. c. 1420. Boxwood and rosewood, length 14⅛". The Metropolitan Museum of Art, New York (gift of Irwin Untermyer, 1964).

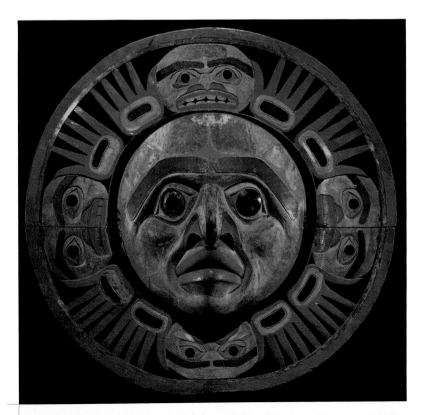

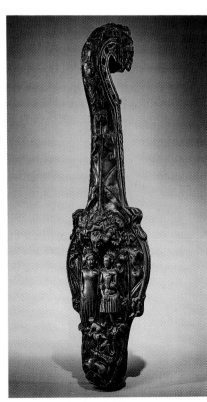

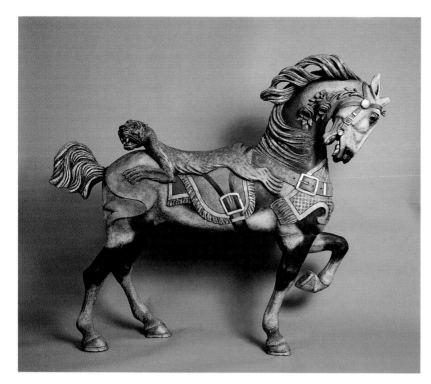

left: **358.** Carousel figure. 19th century.
Wood, length 5'2".
National Museum of American History,
Smithsonian Institution, Washington, D.C.
(Van Alstyne Collection of American Folk Art).

below: **359.** Klindt Houlberg.
Phantasy Plenishing. 1980.
Wood, height 7'.
Courtesy the artist.

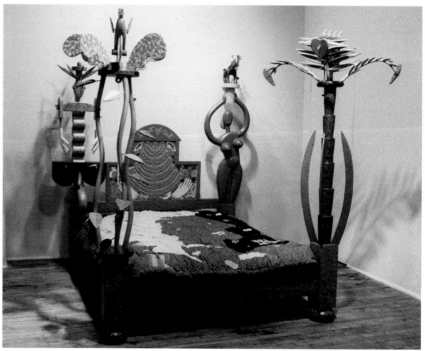

go-round horses can scarcely comprehend the ingenuity of carousel figures carved a century ago. Not only horses, but lions and giraffes and elephants and camels—all were meticulously hand-carved and painted **(358)**. The thrill of the ride came from sitting atop one of these fanciful sculptures in wood.

For most of us, of course, wood is usually associated with furniture, which is generally constructed by a process of nailing and/or gluing. When furniture craft and fine wood carving merge, we may get a zany result like the bedstead illustrated here **(359)**. Klindt Houlberg's *Phantasy Plenishing* looks like a normal, well-crafted bed frame—up to about a foot from the floor. Above that the artist's imagination runs wild. One bedpost is a nude female figure, another a fantasy tree with a bird perched on top, and so on. Houlberg's work makes us realize how rich our environment could be if more everyday objects were treated with this kind of creative expressiveness.

The design possibilities for works of fiber are enormous. By fiber we mean a narrow strand of vegetable or animal material (cotton, linen, wool, silk) or the modern-day synthetic equivalents. Like wood, fiber is widely available and quite perishable, but the construction methods used for fiber are unique to this pliable medium.

For centuries the most common method of working with fiber has been **weaving.** Weaving involves placing two sets of parallel fibers at right angles to one another and interlacing one set through the other in an up-and-down movement, generally on a loom or frame. One set of fibers is held taut; this is called the **warp.** The other set, known as the **weft** or **woof,** is interwoven through the warp to make a fabric. Nearly all fabrics, including those used for our clothing, are made by some variation of this process.

Modern looms are much like computers and, once "programmed," can produce intricate fabrics. But the truly creative artisan really does not require sophisticated technology. Two thousand years ago, weavers of coastal Peru in South America used little more than two sticks to hold the warp taut in making elaborately figured fabrics like the *Paracas Textile* shown here **(360)**. This fabulous cloth, found at a burial site, is loosely woven in wool on cotton. Its central panel of stylized faces is ringed by a border of figures, human and animal, worked in a loop stitch similar to knitting. Fine textiles represented wealth to these ancient peoples, so the expert weaving of this cloth probably indicates that the person with whom it was buried enjoyed high status.

Tapestry is a special type of weaving in which the weft yarns are manipulated freely to form a pattern or design on the front of the fabric. Often the weft yarns are of several colors, and the weaver can use the different-colored yarns almost as flexibly as a painter uses pigment on canvas. Tapestry weaving expe-

left: 360. *Paracas Textile.*
Cabeza Larga, south coast of Peru.
c. 300–100 B.C.E.
Woven cotton with loop stitch
border of wool, 4′11″ × 2′1″.
The Brooklyn Museum, New York
(John T. Underwood Memorial Fund).

right: 361. *The Unicorn Tapestries:
The Unicorn in Captivity.*
Southern Netherlandish,
1475–1500.
Wool, silk, and metallic threads;
12′ × 8′3″.
The Metropolitan Museum of Art,
New York (The Cloisters Collection,
Gift of John D. Rockefeller, Jr., 1937).

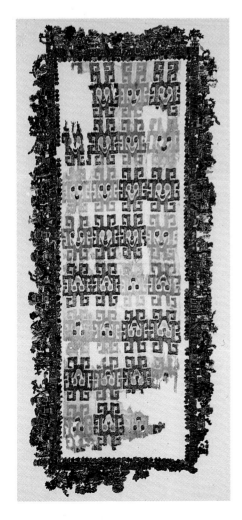

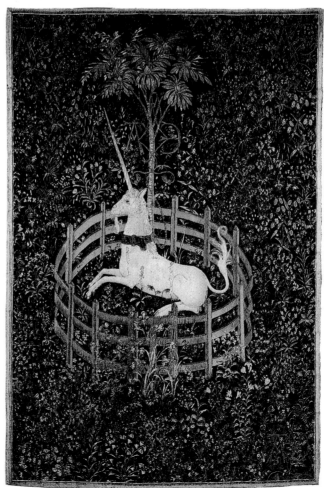

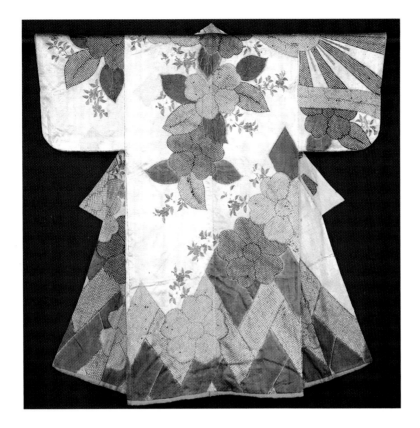

rienced a golden age in Europe from the late 14th century through the 17th. For those who could afford it, tapestry was the art of choice. In place of the paintings we would expect to see now, the castles and great houses of Europe were hung with finely woven cloths, often with elaborate pictorial images.

Among the best-known and most admired of these works are the *Unicorn Tapestries*, a series of seven panels depicting a popular medieval story. According to legend, the unicorn, a wild and fleet one-horned beast, could be tamed only by a virgin. Early panels in the series show the unicorn being hunted by a band of men. When it lays its head in a virgin's lap, it is captured and killed, then brought back to the castle. Finally, the unicorn is restored to life. The final tapestry shows *The Unicorn in Captivity* **(361)**, resting and seemingly contented, in its wooden pen. Medieval art and story-telling often mix mythological and religious themes, and the *Unicorn Tapestries* provide an excellent example. The unicorn legend is intended as a parallel to the Passion of Christ, who assumed a human nature through being born of the Virgin Mary, was killed, and then was resurrected. Yet another layer of meaning shows in the last panel, for the abundant foliage surrounding the captive unicorn was associated with love and fertility, suggesting that these tapestries were woven to celebrate a marriage.

Decorative hangings like the *Unicorn Tapestries* are wonderful to see, but of course the overwhelming majority of works in fibers are meant to be worn as garments. Even clothing, however, offers plenty of opportunity for embellishment. Some of the most luxurious garments in history were crafted in Japan between the 16th and 19th centuries. The *kosode*, a loose one-piece robe worn by both men and women, had short sleeves and was often sashed at the waist. Our example, from the late 17th century, shows a woman's *kosode* lavishly decorated in a variety of techniques **(362)**. Huge stylized cherry blossoms, in subtle colors, form a striking asymmetrical design on the robe's back, and the design is anchored at the hem with a bold zigzag pattern representing a slatted fence, on which more cherry blossoms float. Smaller leaf clusters projecting from the large flowers further enrich this extraordinarily beautiful composition.

362. *Kosode (Woman's Robe).* Japan, Edo Period, late 17th century. Satin, tie-dyed, stitch-resisted, embroidered with silks, and couched with silk yarns wrapped in gold; length 4'5½". The Metropolitan Museum of Art, New York (Purchase, Mary Livingstone Griggs and Mary Griggs Burke Foundation Gift, 1980).

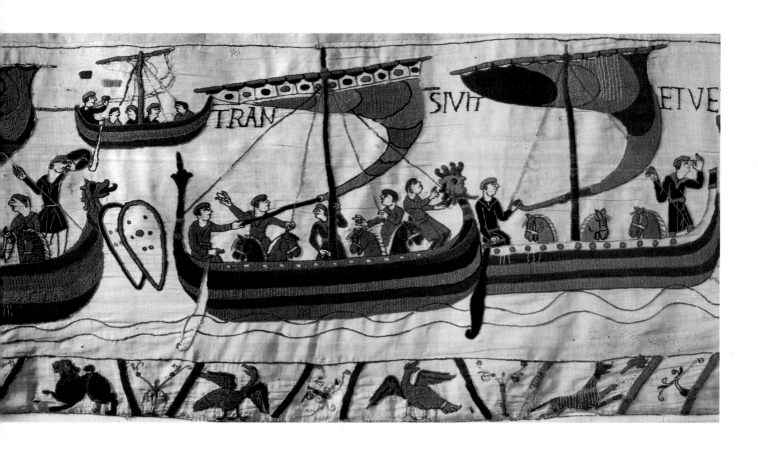

363. *Norman Fleet
Sailing to England,*
detail of the *Bayeux Tapestry.*
c. 1073–88.
Wool embroidery on linen;
height 20″, overall length 231′.
Town Hall, Bayeux,
reproduced with special authorization
of the City of Bayeux.

One of the most famous examples of fiber art in the Western world once hung in the Cathedral of Bayeux and now is preserved in the Town Hall of that French city. This is the *Bayeux Tapestry* **(363)**—misnamed, because it is actually a work of embroidery. (In the past, large-scale fabrics, especially those hung in buildings, often were loosely called "tapestries," regardless of the construction method.) ***Embroidery*** is a technique in which colored yarns are sewn to an existing woven background; frequently the sewing takes the form of decorative motifs or images, as here. The *Bayeux Tapestry* is like a long picture book—20 inches high and 231 feet long—telling the story of the conquest of England by William of Normandy in 1066. The scene illustrated, one of seventy-two separate episodes reading from left to right, shows the Norman boats setting sail to wage war on Saxon England. The fabric's pictorial design is simple and flat. The smaller boat, which is meant to be seen as farther away than the two large ones, does not contribute to any sense of spatial depth; it almost seems to be floating in the air. Despite the charming naïveté of these images, however, scholars have learned more about the events surrounding the Norman Conquest from the *Bayeux Tapestry* than they have from any of the literature of the time.

The illustrations in this chapter cover five different families of materials and four thousand years of human history. They are very different, yet they have certain things in common. Each of them represents a perfect use of the material from which it was made. Each has been formed with the highest possible standards of craftsmanship. Above all, each shows the striving for aesthetic satisfaction that is part of humanity.

Architecture

ARCHITECTURE SATISFIES a basic, universal human need for a roof over one's head. More than walls, more than a chair to sit on or a soft bed upon which to lie, a roof is the classic symbol of protection and security. We've all heard the expression "I have a roof over my head," but it would be unusual to hear someone say, "I'm all right because I have walls around me." Of course, in purely practical terms a roof does keep out the worst of the elements, snow and rain, and in warm climates a roof may be sufficient to keep people dry and comfortable. The roof seems to be symbolic of the nature of architecture.

The walls and roof of a building shape and define space. We can discuss architecture equally in terms of the spaces and volumes created within a structure and in terms of the forms that create those spaces.

More than any of the other arts, architecture demands structural stability. Every one of us daily moves in and out of buildings—schools, houses, offices, stores, churches, bus stations, banks, and movie theaters—and we take for granted, usually without thinking about it, that they will not collapse on top of us. That they do not is a tribute to their engineering; if a building is physically stable, this means it adheres faithfully to the principles of the particular *structural system* on which its architecture is based.

STRUCTURAL SYSTEMS
IN ARCHITECTURE

Any building is a defiance of gravity. Since earliest times architects have tackled the challenge of erecting a roof over empty space, setting walls upright, and having the whole stand secure. Their solutions have depended upon the materials they had available, for, as we shall see, certain materials are better suited than others to a particular structural system. There are two basic families of structural systems: the **shell** system and the **skeleton-and-skin** system.

In the shell system one building material provides both structural support and sheathing (outside covering). Buildings made of brick or stone or adobe fall into this category, and so do older (pre-19th-century) wood buildings constructed of heavy timbers, the most obvious example being the log cabin. The structural material comprises the walls and roof, marks the boundary between inside and outside, and is visible as the exterior surface. Shell construction prevailed until the 19th century, when it began to fall out of favor. Today, however, the development of strong cast materials, including many plastics, has brought renewed interest in shell structures.

The skeleton-and-skin system might be compared to the human body, which has a rigid bony skeleton to support its basic frame and a more fragile skin for sheathing. We find it in modern skyscrapers, with their steel frames (skeletons) supporting the structure and a sheathing (skin) of glass or some other light material. Also, most houses today—at least in Western cultures—are built with a skeleton of wood beams nailed together, topped with a sheathing of light wood boards, shingles, aluminum siding, or the like. Skeleton-and-skin construction is largely a product of the Industrial Revolution; not until the mid-19th century could steel for beams or metal nails be manufactured in practical quantities.

Two factors that must be considered in any structural system are *weight* and *tensile strength*. Walls must support the weight of the roof, and lower stories must support the weight of upper stories. In other words, all the weight of the building must somehow be carried safely to the ground. You can get a sense of this if you imagine your own body as a structural member. Suppose you are lying flat on your back, your body held rigid. You are going to be lifted high in the air, to become a "roof." First you are lifted by four people: One supports you under the shoulders, one under the buttocks, one holds your arms extended above your head, another holds your feet. Your weight is therefore channeled down through four vertical people to the ground, and so you can hold yourself horizontally with some ease. Next you are lifted by two people, one holding your shoulders, another your feet. A lot of your weight is concentrated in the center of your body, which is unsupported, so eventually you sag in the middle and fall to the floor. Then you are lifted by one person, who holds you at the center of your back. The weight at both ends of your body has nowhere to go, nothing to carry it to the ground, and you sag at both ends.

Tensile strength, as applied to architecture, is the ability of a material to span horizontal distances with minimum support from underneath. Returning to the analogy of the body, imagine you are made not of flesh and blood but of strong plastic or metal. Regardless of how you are held up in the air, you can stay rigid and horizontal, because you have great tensile strength.

If you keep these images in mind, you may find it easier to understand the various structural systems we shall consider below. They are introduced here in roughly the chronological order in which they were developed. As was mentioned earlier, all will be of the shell type until the 19th century.

LOAD-BEARING CONSTRUCTION

Another term for load-bearing construction is "stacking and piling." This is the simplest method of making a building, and it is suitable for brick, stone, adobe, ice blocks, and certain modern materials. Essentially, the builder constructs the walls by piling layer upon layer, starting thick at the bottom, getting thinner as the structure rises, and usually tapering inward near the highest point. The whole may then be topped by a lightweight roof, perhaps of thatch

364. Mission St. Francis of Assisi, Ranchos de Taos, New Mexico. c. 1776–80.

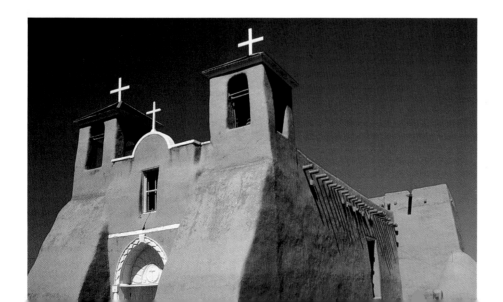

or wood. This construction is stable, because its greatest weight is concentrated at the bottom and weight diminishes gradually as the walls grow higher.

Load-bearing structures tend to have few and small openings (if any) in the walls, because the method does not readily allow for support of material above a void, such as a window opening. This was the system used to construct the Ranchos de Taos church in New Mexico **(364)**, a piled-up mass of adobe, or sun-dried mud. Although the Taos church is hollow, meant to contain worshipers inside, many load-bearing structures are solid all the way through or perhaps have only small open chambers within them.

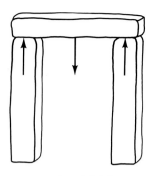

post–and–lintel

POST-AND-LINTEL

After stacking and piling, post-and-lintel construction is the most elementary structural method, based on two uprights (the posts) supporting a horizontal crosspiece (the lintel, or beam). This configuration can be continued indefinitely, so that there may be one very long horizontal supported at critical points along the way by vertical posts to carry its weight to the ground. The most common materials for post-and-lintel construction are stone and wood. Since neither has great tensile strength, these materials will yield and cave in when forced to span long distances, so the architect must provide supporting posts at close intervals.

Post-and-lintel construction has been, for at least four thousand years, a favorite method of architects for raising a roof and providing for open space underneath. In ancient Greece the design of post-and-lintel buildings, especially temples, became rather standardized in certain features. There were three major architectural styles, which appeared in sequence (with some overlapping), and they are known as the **Greek Orders.** The most distinctive feature of each was the design of the column **(365)**. By the 7th century B.C.E. the **Doric** style had been introduced. A Doric column has no base, nothing separating it from the floor below; its **capital,** the topmost part between the shaft of the column and the roof or lintel, is a plain stone slab above a rounded stone. The **Ionic** style was developed in the 6th century B.C.E. and gradually replaced the Doric. An Ionic column has a stepped base and a carved capital in the form of two graceful spirals known as **volutes.** The **Corinthian** style, which appeared in the 4th century B.C.E., is yet more elaborate, having a more detailed base and a capital of delicately carved acanthus leaves.

Possibly the best-known and most impressive post-and-lintel building of all time is the Parthenon in Athens, which is in the Doric style **(366)**. We have already studied the Parthenon as a religious and political structure (Chapter 3, p. 47); here we will focus on its construction. Had the Parthenon been simply an academic exercise in placing horizontal members atop vertical supports—a kind of Classical Age prefabrication—it never would have been so admired for its architectural purity. What sets it apart are the many subtle refinements in its structure.

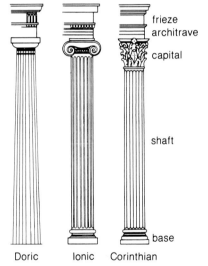

above: 365. Comparison of column styles in the Greek Orders.

left: 366. Ictinus and Callicrates. Parthenon, Athens. 447–432 B.C.E.

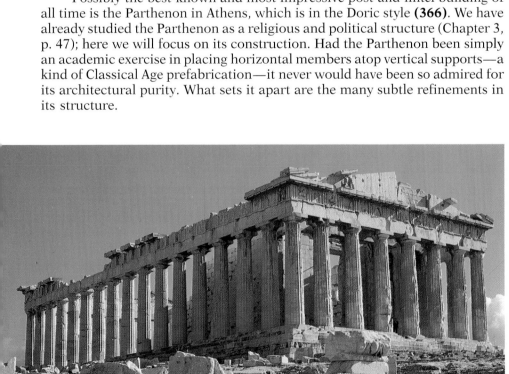

To begin with, the Parthenon has a particularly satisfying proportion of width to length to height—many would say a "perfect" proportion. Legend claims there are no straight lines in the Parthenon, but this is probably a romantic exaggeration. Many of the lines we expect to be straight, however, are not. What the builders did was adjust the physical lines of the temple so they would appear to be straight visually. For example, tall columns that are absolutely straight may appear to bend inward at the center, like an hourglass, so the columns on the Parthenon have been given a slight bulge, known as *entasis*, to compensate for the visual effect. Also, a long horizontal, such as the Parthenon's porch steps, may appear to sag in the middle; to correct for this optical illusion, the level has been adjusted very slightly, rising about $2\frac{1}{2}$ inches to form an arc higher at the center. A large building rising perpendicular to the ground may loom over the visitor and seem to be leaning forward; to avoid this impression, the architects of the Parthenon tilted the whole facade back very slightly. Corner columns, seen against the sky, would have seemed thinner than inside columns, which have the building as a backdrop; therefore, the outside columns were made slightly heavier than all the others. These are only a few of the structural refinements that resulted in a beautiful temple.

Because the Parthenon looks so visually perfect, these optical corrections are not noticeable to the casual viewer. Precise measurements have revealed the secrets of the Parthenon's majesty. The point is, post-and-lintel construction, which at first appears to be so rudimentary, can embody the most sublime forms ever conceived by an architect's mind.

People often assume the Parthenon is a ruin simply because it is old, but this is far from true. Not only is post-and-lintel construction highly stable, but the builders who took such trouble about visual details were equally careful about structural soundness. In fact, were it not for an unfortunate incident in the 17th century, the Parthenon would stand today much as it did twenty-four hundred years ago. In 1687 the Turks, who then controlled Athens and were at war with the Venetians, used the Parthenon as an ammunition dump. The Venetians laid siege to the city, a well-placed shell ignited the ammunition, and the Parthenon blew up. No structural system yet devised can withstand the tragic consequences of conflict between nations.

The post-and-lintel system, then, offers potential for both structural soundness and grandeur. When applied to wood or stone, however, it leaves one problem unsolved, and that is the spanning of relatively large open spaces. The first attempt at solving this problem was the invention of the round arch.

ROUND ARCH AND VAULT

Although the round arch was used by the ancient peoples of Mesopotamia several centuries before our common era **(413)**, it was most fully developed by the Romans, who perfected the form in the 2nd century B.C.E. To get a sense of how the arch works, we might go back to the analogy of the body. Imagine that, instead of lying flat on your back, you are bent over forward into a curve, and again you will be lifted into the air. One person will support your hands, another your feet. As long as your body follows the proper arc—that is, your two supporters stand the correct distance apart—you can maintain the pose for some time. If they stand too close together, you start to topple first one way and then the other; if they move too far apart, you have insufficient support in the middle and plunge to the floor. An arch incorporates more complex forces of *tension* (pulling apart) and *compression* (pushing together), but the general idea is the same.

The arch has many virtues. In addition to being an attractive form, it enables the architect to open up fairly large spaces in a wall without risking the building's structural soundness. These spaces admit light, reduce the weight of the walls, and decrease the amount of material needed. As utilized by the Romans, the arch is a perfect semicircle, although it may seem elongated if it rests on columns. It is constructed from wedge-shaped pieces of

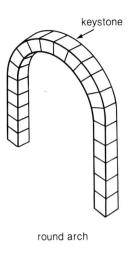

keystone

round arch

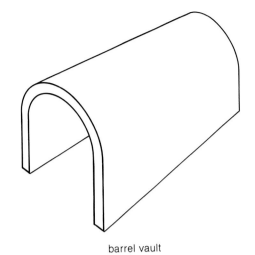

barrel vault

stone that meet at an angle always perpendicular to the curve of the arch. Because of tensions and compressions inherent in the form, the arch is stable only when it is complete, when the topmost stone, the **keystone,** has been set in place. For this reason an arch under construction must be supported from below, usually by a wooden framework.

Among the most elegant and enduring of Roman structures based on the arch is the Pont du Gard at Nîmes, France **(367)**, built about 15 C.E. when the empire was nearing its farthest expansion (see map, p. 375). At this time industry, commerce, and agriculture were at their peak. Roman engineering was applied to an ambitious system of public-works projects, not just in Italy but in the outlying areas as well. The Pont du Gard functioned as an aqueduct, a structure meant to transport water, and its lower level served as a footbridge across the river. That it stands today virtually intact after nearly two thousand years (and is crossed by cyclists on the route of the famous Tour de France bicycle race) testifies to the Romans' brilliant engineering skills. Visually, the Pont du Gard exemplifies the best qualities of arch construction. Solid and heavy, obviously durable, it is shot through with open spaces that make it seem light and its weight-bearing capabilities effortless.

367. Pont du Gard, Nîmes, France. Early 1st century C.E. Length 902'.

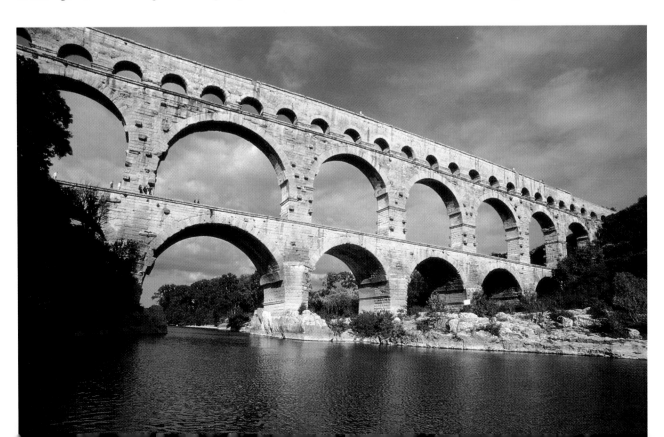

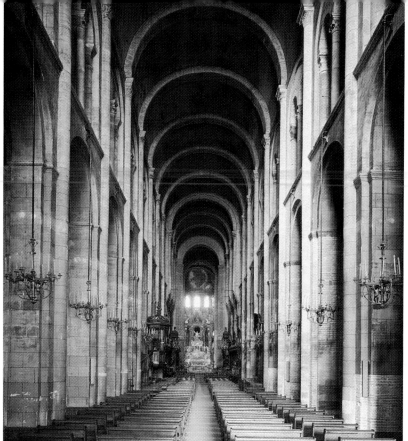

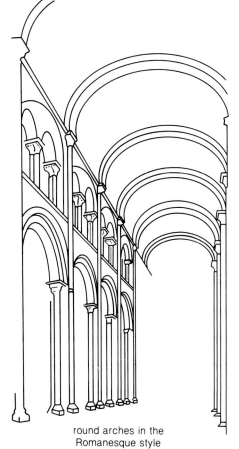

round arches in the
Romanesque style

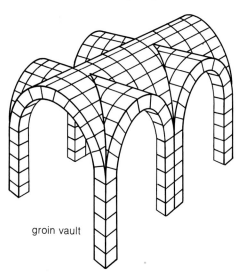

groin vault

When the arch is extended in depth—when it is, in reality, many arches placed flush one behind the other—the result is called a ***barrel vault*** or ***tunnel vault.*** This vault construction makes it possible to create large interior spaces. The Romans made great use of the barrel vault, but for its finest expression we look many hundreds of years later, to the cathedrals of the Middle Ages.

The church of St. Sernin **(368)**, in the southern French city of Toulouse, is an example of the style prevalent throughout Western Europe from about 1050 to 1200—a style known as ***Romanesque.*** Romanesque builders adopted the old Roman forms of round arch and barrel vault so as to add height to their churches. Until this period most churches had beamed wooden roofs, which not only posed a threat of fire but also limited the height to which architects could aspire. With the stone barrel vault, they could achieve the soaring, majestic space we see in the ***nave*** (the long central area) of St. Sernin. Round arches on half columns punctuate the ceiling, leading one's eye to the altar.

On the side aisles of St. Sernin (not visible in the photograph) the builders employed a series of ***groin vaults.*** A groin vault results when two vaults are crossed at right angles to each other, thus directing the weights and stresses down into the four corners. By dividing up a space into square segments known as ***bays,*** each of which contains one groin vault, the architects could cover a long span safely and economically. The arrangement of bays also creates a satisfying rhythmic pattern down the length of the structure.

POINTED ARCH AND VAULT

While the round arch and vault of the Romanesque era solved many problems and made many things possible, they nevertheless had certain drawbacks. For one thing, a round arch, to be stable, must be a semicircle; therefore, the height of the arch is limited by its width. Two other difficulties were weight and darkness. Barrel vaults are both literally and visually heavy, calling for huge masses of stone to maintain their structural stability. Also, the builders who constructed them dared not make light-admitting openings in or around them, for fear the arches and vaults would collapse, and so the interiors of

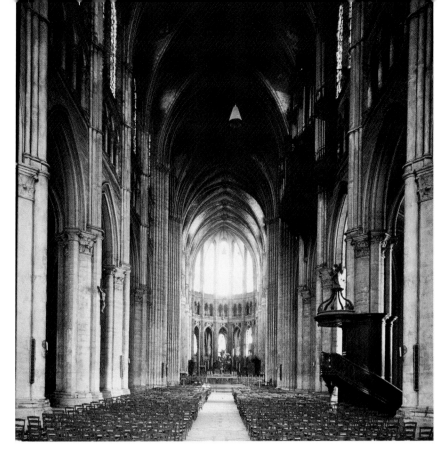

369. Nave,
Chartres Cathedral, France.
c. 1194–1260.

Romanesque buildings tend to be dark. The **Gothic** period in Europe, which followed the Romanesque, solved these problems with the pointed arch.

The pointed arch, while seemingly not very different from the round one, offers many advantages. Because the sides arc up to a point, weight is channeled down to the ground at a steeper angle, and therefore the arch can be taller. The vault constructed from such an arch also can be much taller than a barrel vault. Architects of the Gothic period found they did not need heavy masses of material throughout the curve of the vault, as long as the major points of intersection were reinforced. These reinforcements, called **ribs,** are visible in the nave ceiling of Chartres Cathedral **(369**; see also **49,459)**. The lighter vault also enabled builders to introduce stained-glass windows in the stone walls, and so the Gothic church is much brighter inside than its Romanesque predecessor.

Gothic builders also provided for structural reinforcement outside the churches. Given that the walls were relatively thin, and that arches tend to create a sideways or lateral thrust, there remained the danger that a large cathedral could "lean" outward and collapse. To prevent this, architects developed a system of exterior masonry columns or **piers,** joined to the body of the church by **flying buttresses,** or arched supports. In effect, the flying buttresses (visible in our exterior view of Chartres Cathedral, **459)** "hold in" the walls of the church. As the style progressed, they were increasingly carved and embellished to become decorative outside features of the buildings.

COMPLEX ARCHES

The arch is a graceful and appealing form, so it is no wonder that architects have been drawn to it as a subject for further ornamentation. Islamic architects, in particular, had a special affinity for the arch and remarkable skill for developing it into complex forms. During the period of Islamic influence in Spain, from the 8th to the 15th century, many splendid mosques and palaces were constructed, and these buildings were made all the more splendid by elaborate use of the arch.

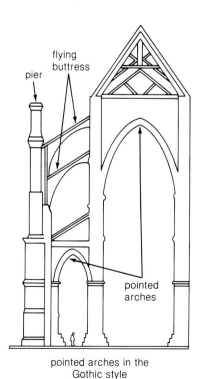

flying
buttress

pier

pointed
arches

pointed arches in the
Gothic style

In Córdoba, once the capital of Moslem Spain, stands the Great Mosque, built in stages between 786 and 987. The mosque's prayer hall **(370)**, meant for communal worship, is a forest of columns supporting double arches arranged piggyback style, one atop the other. Arches in the lower tier are horseshoe-shaped, bending in at the bottom—a signature Moslem design—while those above are round. All the arches are striped, with alternating sections of red brick and white stone. This arrangement transforms the plain, square enclosure into a gaily colored maze, whose repeated arches seem to go on forever. One could imagine oneself in a hall of mirrors, as the arches multiply both vertically and horizontally.

Also in Spain, in the city of Granada, is the Alhambra, a palace complex dating from the 14th century. From outside, the Alhambra looks like a fortress. Inside, around the courtyards and grand rooms **(371)**, the architect's ingenuity has changed the often stolid arch into a lacy, scalloped fantasy, visually as light as the frosting on a wedding cake. In some portions the arches intersect, crossing over one another to create an intricate pattern.

It is interesting to compare these two latter illustrations with those from the preceding sections. At more or less the same time in history, Christian architects in the north of Europe were using the arch to build higher and higher, while Islamic architects in the south were adapting the form to create visual enrichment nearer the ground.

THE DOME

A dome is an architectural structure generally in the shape of a hemisphere, or half globe. One customary definition of the dome is an arch rotated 360 degrees on its axis, and this is really more accurate, because, for example, the dome based on a pointed arch will be pointed at the top, not perfectly hemispherical. The stresses in a dome are much like those of an arch, except that they are spread in a circle around the dome's perimeter. Unless the dome is buttressed—supported from the outside—from all sides, there is a tendency for it to "explode," for the stones to pop outward in all directions, causing the dome to collapse.

left: 370. Prayer hall of Abd al-Rahman I, Great Mosque, Córdoba, Spain. Begun 786 C.E.

right: 371. Detail of arches, the Alhambra, Granada, Spain. c. 1354–91.

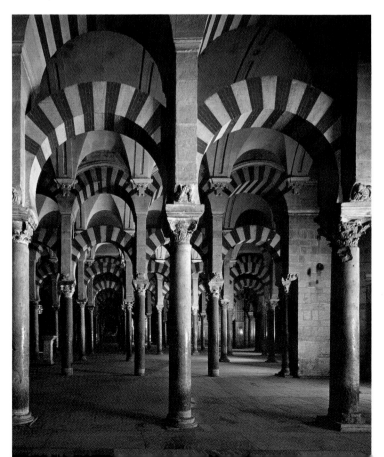

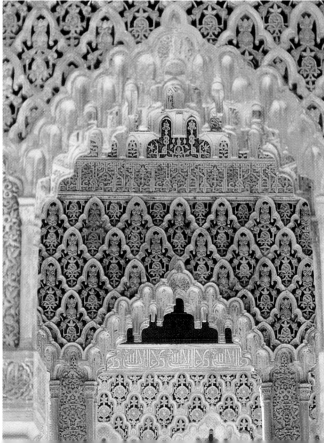

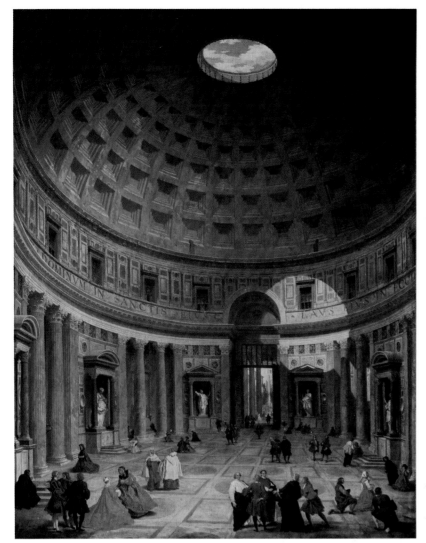

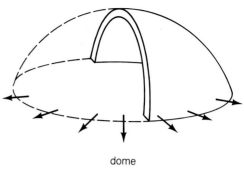

dome

372. Giovanni Paolo Panini.
Interior of the Pantheon. c. 1734–35.
Oil on canvas, 4'2½" × 3'3".
© 1998 National Gallery of Art,
Washington, D.C.
(Samuel H. Kress Collection).

Like so many other architectural structures, the dome was perfected under the incomparable engineering genius of the Romans, and one of the finest domed buildings ever erected dates from the early 2nd century. It is called the Pantheon **(445)**, which means a temple dedicated to "all the gods"—or, at least, all the gods who were venerated in ancient Rome. We reproduce here an 18th-century painting of the interior **(372)** because the circular building is so vast that it is impossible to find a camera angle to convey adequately its shape and scale.

As seen from the inside, the Pantheon has a perfect hemispherical dome soaring 142 feet above the floor, resting upon a cylinder almost exactly the same in diameter—140 feet. At the very top of the dome is an opening 29 feet in diameter called an ***oculus,*** or eye, thought to be symbolic of the "eye of Heaven." This opening provides the sole (and plentiful) illumination for the building. In its conception, then, the Pantheon is amazingly simple, equal in height and width, symmetrical in its structure, round form set upon round form. Yet because of its scale and its classic proportions, the effect is overwhelming. The fact that the Romans, in ancient times, could enclose such a huge space without interior supports today seems extraordinary.

When an architect wishes to set a round dome atop a square building, as is very often the case, the structural problems become more complex. Some transitional device is required between the circle (at the dome's base) and the square (of the building's top), preferably one that bolsters the dome. An elegant solution can be found in Hagia Sophia (the Church of the Holy Wisdom)

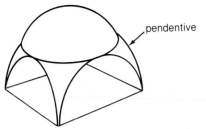

pendentive

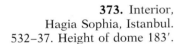

dome with pendentives

in Istanbul **(373**; see also **453)**. Hagia Sophia was built as a Christian church during the 6th century, when Istanbul, then called Constantinople, was the capital of the great Byzantine Empire (p. 382). When the Turks conquered the city in the 15th century, Hagia Sophia became an Islamic mosque, and it is now preserved as a museum. In sheer size and perfection of form it was the architectural triumph of its time and has seldom been matched since then.

The dome of Hagia Sophia rises 183 feet above the floor, with its weight carried to the ground by heavy stone piers—in this case, squared columns—at the four corners of the immense nave. Around the base of the dome is a row of closely spaced arched windows, which make the heavy dome seem to "float" upward. Each of the four sides of the building consists of a monumental round arch, and between the arches and the dome are curved triangular sections known as ***pendentives.*** It is the function of the pendentives to make a smooth transition between rectangle and dome.

Because domes have so much been a feature of public buildings, both religious and political, we may think of them as the capstones of "official" architecture. St. Peter's Basilica in Rome **(479)**, the U.S. Capitol in Washington and its many offshoots in the state capitals, the great cathedrals of London—all are monumental structures topped by imposing domes. One of the loveliest of all domed buildings, however, originally was constructed for a private purpose, and despite its size it has a more intimate quality. This is the famous Taj Mahal at Agra, in India.

The Taj Mahal **(374)** was built in the mid-17th century by the Moslem emperor of India, Shah Jahan, as a tomb for his beloved wife, Arjummand Banu, who died at the age of thirty-nine after having borne fourteen children. Although the Taj is nearly as large as Hagia Sophia and possessed of a dome rising some 30 feet higher, it seems comparatively fragile and weightless. Nearly all its exterior lines reach upward, from the graceful pointed arches, to the pointed dome, to the four slender towers—minarets—poised at the outside corners. The Taj Mahal, constructed entirely of pure white marble, appears almost as a shimmering mirage, which has come to rest for a moment beside the peaceful reflecting pool but may float away at any time.

373. Interior, Hagia Sophia, Istanbul. 532–37. Height of dome 183′.

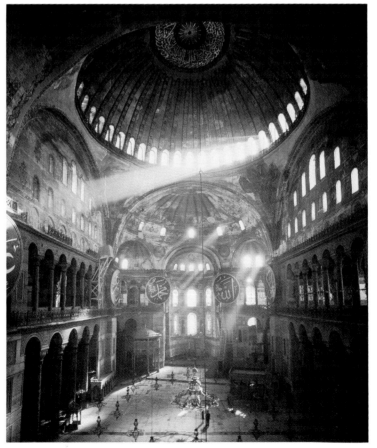

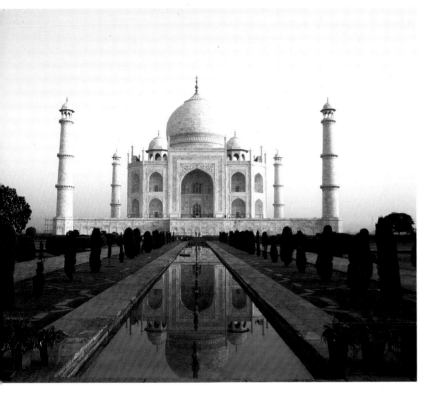

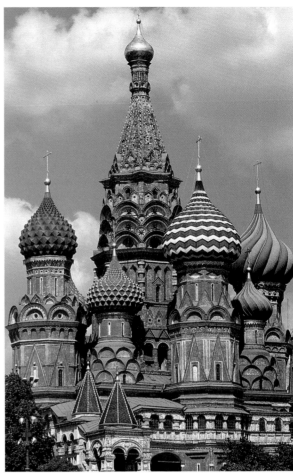

The dome is such a strong architectural feature that we tend to think of it as singular—one huge section of a globe surmounting an important building. For a different approach we might look at traditional Russian architecture, especially the design of churches, in which, typically, many domes are clustered together. The finest example of this style is the Cathedral of St. Basil, in Moscow (375). St. Basil's was built as a Christian church, but its architecture is so ornate and so fanciful as to remind us of a fairy-tale castle. No possible type of decoration has been omitted. Colors and textures and shapes have been laid on with a free hand, and the cathedral sprouts numerous domes, some of them called "onion" domes because of their bulbous shape. Somehow, it all comes together, to create a rich, magnificent effect—so magnificent, in fact, that this structure has become the visual symbol of Moscow.

left: 374. Taj Mahal, Agra, India. 1632–53. White marble.

right: 375.
Cathedral of St. Basil, Moscow. 1555–60.

CAST-IRON CONSTRUCTION

With the perfection of the post-and-lintel, the arch, and the dome, construction in stone and brick had gone just about as far as it could go. Not until the introduction of a new building material did the next major breakthrough in structural systems take place. Iron had been known for thousands of years and had been used for tools and objects of all kinds, but only in the 19th century did architects realize that its great strength offered promise for structural support. This principle was demonstrated brilliantly in a project that few contemporary observers took seriously.

In 1851 the city of London was planning a great exhibition, under the sponsorship of Prince Albert, husband of Queen Victoria. The challenge was to house under one roof the "Works of Industry of All Nations," and the commission for erecting a suitable structure fell to Joseph Paxton, a designer of greenhouses. Paxton raised in Hyde Park a wondrous building framed in cast iron and sheathed in glass—probably the first modern skeleton-and-skin construction ever designed **(376)**. The Crystal Palace, as Paxton's creation came to be known, covered more than 17 acres and reached a height of 108 feet. Because of an ingenious system of prefabrication, the whole structure was erected in just sixteen weeks.

Visitors to the exhibition considered the Crystal Palace a curiosity—a marvelous one, to be sure, but still an oddity outside the realm of architecture. They could not have forseen that Paxton's design, solid iron framework clothed in a glass skin, would pave the way for 20th-century architecture. In fact, Paxton had taken a giant step in demonstrating that as long as a building's skeleton held firm, its skin could be light and non-load-bearing. Several intermediary steps would be required before this principle could be translated into today's architecture.

Another bold experiment in iron construction came a few decades later just across the English Channel, in France, and involved a plan that many considered to be foolhardy, if not downright insane. Gustave Eiffel, a French engineer, proposed to build in the center of Paris a skeleton iron tower, nearly a thousand feet tall, to act as a centerpiece for the Paris World's Fair of 1889. Nothing of the sort had ever been suggested, much less built. In spite of loud protests, the Eiffel Tower **(377)** was constructed, at a cost of about a million dollars—an unheard-of sum for those times. It rises on four arched columns, which curve inward until they meet in a single tower thrusting up boldly above the cityscape of Paris. (The writer Guy de Maupassant claimed that he lunched in a restaurant on the tower as often as possible, because "it's the only place in Paris where I don't have to see it."[1])

The importance of this singular, remarkable structure for the future of architecture rests on the fact that it *was* a skeleton that proudly showed itself

left: 376. Joseph Paxton. Crystal Palace, Hyde Park, London. 1851, destroyed by fire 1936. Contemporary lithograph. by Joseph Nash. Guildhall Library, London.

right: 377. Alexandre Gustave Eiffel. Eiffel Tower, Paris. 1889. Iron, height 934′.

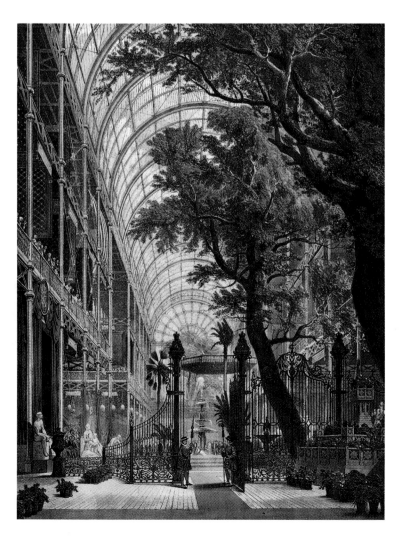

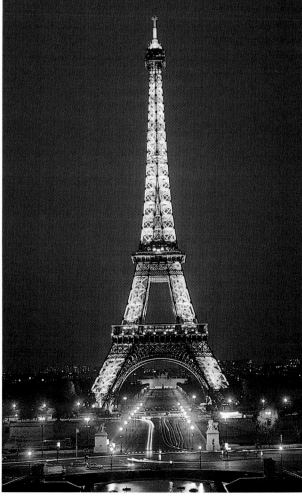

without benefit of any cosmetic embellishment. No marble, no glass, no tiles, no skin of any kind—just the clean lines drawn in an industrial-age product. Two concepts emerged from this daring construction. First, metal in and of itself can make beautiful architecture. Second, metal can provide a solid framework for a very large structure, self-sustaining and permanent. Today the Eiffel Tower is the ultimate symbol of Paris, and no tourist would pass up a visit. From folly to landmark in a century—such is the course of innovative architecture.

Iron for structural members was not the only breakthrough of the mid-19th century. The Industrial Revolution also introduced a new construction material that was much humbler but equally significant in its implications for architecture: the nail. And for want of that simple little nail, most of the houses we live in today could not have been built.

BALLOON-FRAME CONSTRUCTION

So far in this chapter the illustrations have concentrated on grand and public buildings—churches, temples, monuments. These are the glories of architecture, the buildings we admire and travel great distances to see. We should not forget, however, that the overwhelming majority of structures in the world have been houses for people to live in, or **domestic architecture.**

Until the mid-19th century houses were of shell construction. They were made of brick or stone (and, in warmer climates, of such materials as reeds and bamboo) with load-bearing construction, or else they were post-and-lintel structures in which heavy timbers were assembled by complicated notching and joinery, sometimes with wooden pegs. Nails, if any, had to be fabricated by hand and were very expensive.

About 1833, in Chicago, the technique of *balloon-frame* construction was introduced. Balloon-frame construction is a true skeleton-and-skin method. It developed from two innovations: improved methods for milling lumber and mass-produced nails. In this system, the builder first erects a framework or skeleton by nailing together sturdy but lightweight boards (the familiar 2-by-4 "stud"), then adds a roof and sheathes the walls in clapboard, shingles, stucco, or whatever the homeowner wishes. Glass for windows can be used lavishly, as long as it does not interrupt the underlying wood structure, since the sheathing plays little part in holding the building together.

When houses of this type were introduced, the term "balloon framing" was meant to be sarcastic. Skeptics thought the buildings would soon fall down, or burst just like balloons. But some of the earliest balloon-frame houses stand firm today, and this method is still the most popular for new house construction in Western countries.

The balloon frame, of course, has its limitations. Wood beams 2 by 4 inches thick cannot support a skyscraper ten or fifty stories high, and that was the very sort of building architects had begun to dream of late in the 19th century. For such soaring ambitions, a new material was needed, and it was found. The material was steel.

STEEL-FRAME CONSTRUCTION

Although multistory buildings have been with us since the Roman Empire, the development of the skyscraper, as we know it, required two late-19th-century innovations: the elevator and steel-frame construction. Steel-frame construction, like balloon framing, is a true skeleton-and-skin arrangement. Rather than piling floor upon floor, with each of the lower stories supporting those above it, the builders first erect a steel "cage" that is capable of sustaining the entire weight of the building; then they apply a skin of some other material. But if one is going to erect a building of great height, one cannot expect people to walk up ten or more flights of stairs to get to the top floors. Hence, the elevator made its appearance.

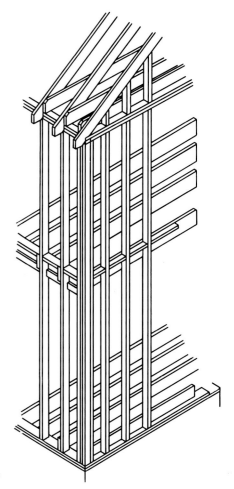

balloon-frame construction

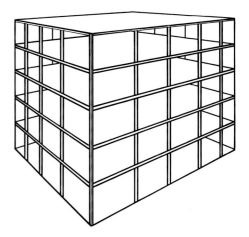

steel–frame construction

What many consider to be the first genuinely modern building was designed by Louis Sullivan and built between 1890 and 1891 in St. Louis. Known as the Wainwright Building **(378)**, it employed a steel framework sheathed in masonry. Other architects had experimented with steel support but had carefully covered their structures in heavy stone so as to reflect traditional architectural forms and make the construction seem reliably sturdy. Centuries of precedent had prepared the public to expect bigness to go hand in hand with heaviness. Sullivan broke new ground by making his sheathing light, letting the skin of his building echo, even celebrate, the steel framing underneath. Regular bays of windows on the seven office floors are separated by strong vertical lines, and the four corners of the building are emphasized by vertical piers. The Wainwright Building's message is subtle, but we cannot mistake it: the nation had stopped growing outward and started growing *up*.

Sullivan's design looks forward to the 20th century, but it nevertheless clings to certain architectural details rooted in classical history, most notably the heavy **cornice**—the projecting roof ornament—that terminates upward movement at the top of the building. In a very few decades even these backward glances into the architectural past would become rare.

Toward the middle of the 20th century skyscrapers began to take over the downtown areas of major cities, and city planners had to grapple with unprecedented problems. How high is too high? How much air space should a building consume? What provision, if any, should be made to prevent tall buildings from completely blocking out the sunlight from the streets below? In New York and certain other cities ordinances were passed that resulted in a number of look-alike and architecturally undistinguished buildings. The laws required that if a building filled the ground space of a city block right up to the sidewalk, it could rise for only a certain number of feet or stories before being "stepped back," or narrowed; then it could rise for only a specified number of additional feet before being stepped back again. The resultant structures came to be known as "wedding-cake" buildings. A few architects, however, found more creative ways of meeting the air space requirement. Those working in the *International* (in fact, European) style designed some of the most admired American skyscrapers during the 1950s and 1960s. International style archi-

left: 378. Louis Sullivan. Wainwright Building, St. Louis. 1890–91.

right: 379. Gordon Bunshaft of Skidmore, Owings, and Merrill. Lever House, New York. 1952.

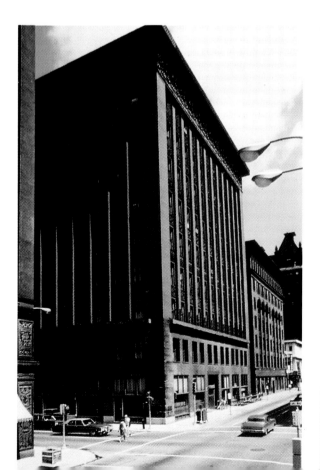

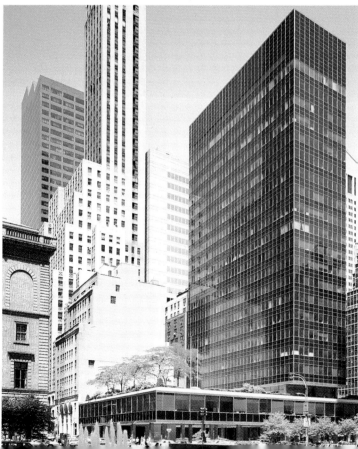

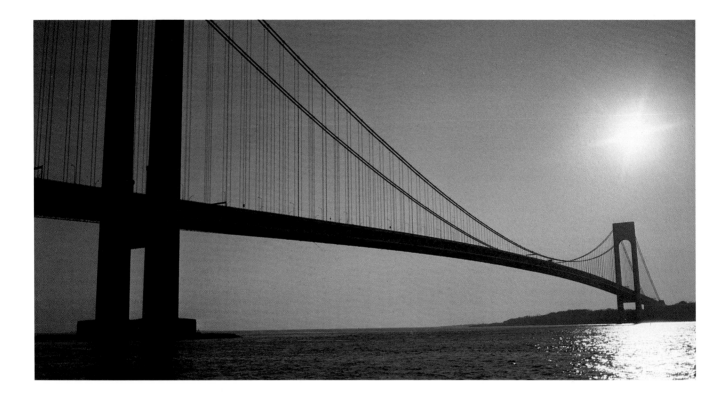

tecture emphasized clean lines, geometric (usually rectilinear) form, and an avoidance of superficial decoration. The "bones" of a building were supposed to show and to be the only ornament necessary. A classic example of this pure style is Lever House.

Lever House in New York **(379)**, designed by the architectural firm of Skidmore, Owings, and Merrill and built in 1952, was heralded as a breath of fresh air in the smog of look-alike structures. Its sleek understated form was widely copied but never equaled. Lever House might be compared to two shimmering glass dominoes, one resting horizontally on freestanding supports, the other balanced upright and off-center on the first. At a time when most architects of office buildings strove to fill every square inch of air space to which they were entitled—both vertically and horizontally—the elegant Lever House drew back and raised its slender rectangle aloof from its neighbors, surrounded by free space. Even its base does not rest on the ground but rides on thin supports to allow for open plazas and passageways beneath the building. Practically no other system of construction except steel frame could have made possible this graceful form.

SUSPENSION

Also made feasible by steel, suspension is the structural method we associate primarily with bridges, although it has been employed for some buildings as well. The concept of suspension was developed for bridges late in the 19th century. In essence, the weight of the structure is suspended from steel cables supported on vertical pylons, driven into the ground. A long bridge, such as the Verrazano-Narrows Bridge in New York **(380)**, may have only two sets of pylons planted in the riverbed, but the steel cables suspended under tension from their towers are strong enough to support a span between them more than four-fifths of a mile long. Suspension structures are among the most graceful in architecture, involving as they do long sweeping curves and the slender lines of the cables. A bridge in particular, suspended over water, may seem almost weightless when viewed from a distance, and there is a sense of flexibility—both visual and physical, because the roadbed may rise and fall several feet depending on winds and passing traffic.

380. Verrazano-Narrows Bridge, New York. 1964. Ammann and Whitney, consulting engineers; John B. Peterkin, Aymar Embury II, and Edward D. Stone, consulting architects.

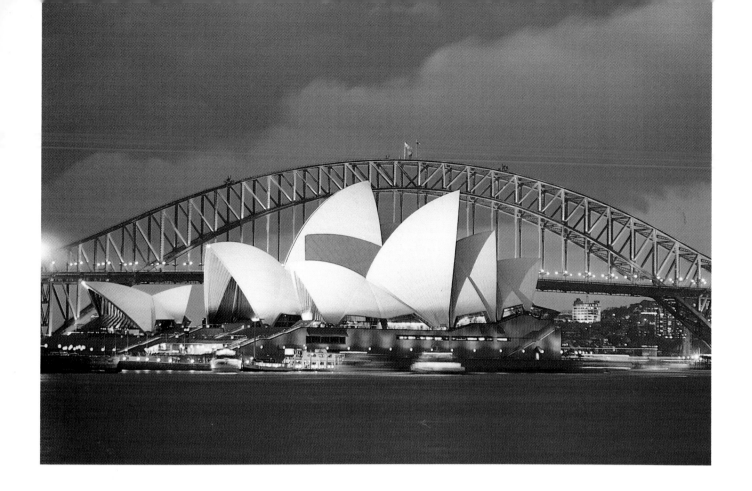

381. Joern Utzon. Sydney Opera House, Australia. 1959–72. Reinforced concrete, height of highest shell 200′.

REINFORCED-CONCRETE CONSTRUCTION

Concrete is an old material that was known and used by the Romans. A mixture of cement, gravel, and water, concrete can be poured, will assume the shape of any mold, and then will set to hardness. Its major problem is that it tends to be brittle and has low tensile strength. This problem is often observed in the thin concrete slabs used for sidewalks and patios, which may crack and split apart as a result of weight and weather. Late in the 19th century, however, a method was developed for reinforcing concrete forms by imbedding iron rods inside the concrete before it hardened. The iron contributes tensile strength, while the concrete provides shape and surface. In the 20th century reinforced concrete, also known as **ferroconcrete,** has been used in a wide variety of structures, often in those with free-form, organic shapes. While it may seem at first to be a skeleton-and-skin construction, ferroconcrete actually works more like a shell, because the iron rods (or sometimes a steel mesh) and concrete are bonded permanently and can form structures that are self-sustaining, even when very thin.

A special kind of ferroconcrete construction—precast reinforced sections—was used to create the soaring shell-like forms of the famous Sydney Opera House in Australia **(381)**. The Opera House, which is really an all-around entertainment complex, is almost as famous for its construction difficulties as it is for its extraordinary design. So daring was its concept that the necessary technology virtually had to be invented as the project went along. Planned as a symbol of the great port city in whose harbor it stands, the Opera House gives the impression of a wonderful clipper ship at full sail. Three sets of pointed shells, oriented in different directions, turn the building into a giant sculpture in which walls and roof are one. Reinforced concrete is the sort of material that allows the builder to experiment and try new techniques, that allows the architect to dream impossible dreams.

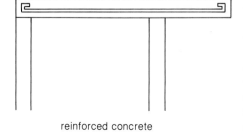

reinforced concrete

GEODESIC DOMES

Of all the structural systems, probably the only one that can be attributed to a single individual is the geodesic dome, which was developed by the American architectural engineer R. Buckminster Fuller. Fuller's dome **(382)** is essentially a bubble, formed by a network of metal rods arranged in triangles and further organized into tetrahedrons. (A tetrahedron is a three-dimensional geometric figure having four faces.) This metal framework can be sheathed in any of several lightweight materials, including wood, glass, and plastic.

The geodesic dome offers a combination of advantages never before available in architecture. Although very light in weight in relation to size, it is amazingly strong, because its structure rests on a mathematically sophisticated use of the triangle. It requires no interior support, and so all the space encompassed by the dome can be used with total freedom. The geodesic dome can be built in any size. In theory, at least, a structurally sound geodesic dome 2 miles across could be built, although nothing of this scope has ever been attempted. Perhaps most important for modern building techniques, Fuller's dome is based on a modular system of construction. Individual segments—modules—can be prefabricated to allow for extremely quick assembly of even a large dome. And finally, because of the flexibility in choice of sheathing materials, there are virtually endless options for climate and light control.

Fuller patented the geodesic dome in 1947, but it was not until twenty years later, when his design served as the U.S. Pavilion at the Montreal World's Fair, that the public's attention was awakened to its possibilities. The dome at Expo 67 **(382)** astonished the architectural world and fair-goers alike. It was 250 feet in diameter (about the size of a football field rounded off) and, being sheathed in translucent material, lighted up the sky at night like a giant spaceship set down on earth.

After Expo 67 some predicted that before long all houses and public buildings would be geodesic domes. This dream has faded considerably, but Fuller's dome has proved exceptionally well suited for government and scientific operations in arctic climates. To build a habitable structure in the freezing

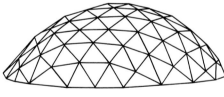

geodesic dome

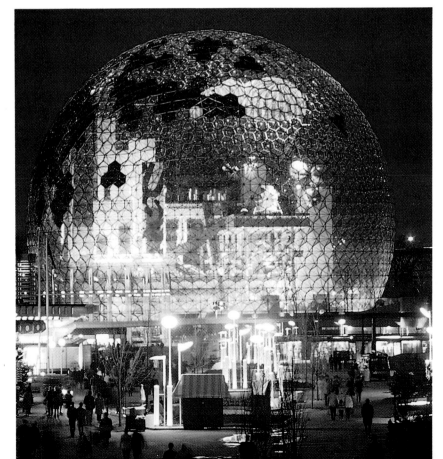

382. R. Buckminster Fuller. U.S. Pavilion, Expo 67, Montreal. 1967. Geodesic dome, diameter 250'.

321

R. BUCKMINSTER FULLER

1895–1983

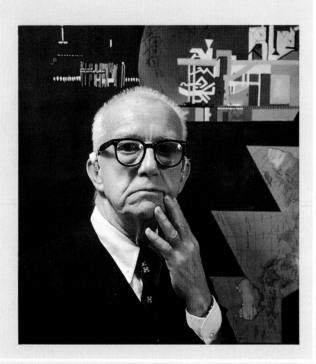

THE TERM "ECCENTRIC GENIUS" might have been coined to describe the 20th-century architect/engineer/inventor/philosopher R. Buckminster Fuller, known to his friends as "Bucky." Whether history will characterize him as more of an eccentric or more of a genius remains to be seen.

Born in a suburb of Boston, Fuller was the black sheep of a distinguished New England family. He attended Harvard University for a short time, but, as he explained afterward, "I cut classes and went out quite deliberately to get into trouble, and so naturally I got kicked out." There followed a variety of odd jobs and a stint in the Navy. After he married Anne Hewlett in 1917, Fuller went into partnership with his father-in-law, an architect, in a building-block company. The year 1922 marked a crisis in his life. The business did not prosper, and the Fullers' daughter Alexandra died on her fourth

birthday. Fuller sank into a terrible depression—working all day and drinking all night. At the lowest ebb he seriously considered suicide. Then in 1927, for some reason, he reached a critical turning point. One night, he later recalled, he found himself saying, "You do not have the right to eliminate yourself. You do not belong to you. You belong to the universe." From that moment he dedicated his life to discovering "the principles operative in the universe and [turning] them over to my fellow men."

The theory Fuller eventually formulated was both simple and extraordinarily grandiose: any problem in the world can be solved by design and technology. He believed wholeheartedly that "there is absolutely nothing that cannot be done." Fuller liked to talk about our planet as "Spaceship Earth" and felt that it should be designed as efficiently as any space vehicle; one of his twenty-five books is entitled *Operating Manual for Spaceship Earth.*

The first practical application of Fuller's theories was the Dymaxion House, patented in 1927. This experimental dwelling had glass walls, rooms hung from a central mast, and such energy-efficient devices as an automatic vacuum-cleaning system. Next came the Dymaxion automobile, a three-wheeled vehicle capable of speeds up to 120 m.p.h. Neither invention achieved any popular success, but in 1947 Fuller patented the design for which he is most famous—the geodesic dome. Based on a system of triangles arranged into four-planed figures, or tetrahedrons, the geodesic dome could enclose a huge amount of space without interior support and allow for total climate control. Thousands of Fuller's domes have been built around the world. One of his most ambitious projects, however—the complete enclosure of midtown Manhattan in a dome 3 miles across—was (understandably) considered impractical.

Fuller remained active until about a month before his death, at the age of eighty-seven. He traveled widely, lecturing about his theories, and particularly enjoyed speaking to college audiences, among whom he attracted rather a cult following. Education was one of his many interests, for, he said: "Every child is born a genius. It is my conviction, from having watched a great many babies grow up, that all of humanity is born a genius and then becomes degeniused very rapidly by unfavorable circumstances and by the frustration of all their extraordinary built-in capabilities."[2]

Photograph of R. Buckminster Fuller.

wastes of Antarctica, for example, one needs a lightweight material that can be shipped and assembled easily, great strength to withstand below-freezing temperatures and high winds, and control of the interior environment. The geodesic dome meets all these requirements.

In this brief survey of the major structural systems we have seen that the form of architecture and its method of construction are largely determined by the materials available. Wood readily lends itself to post-and-lintel construction and balloon-frame construction; stone works for post-and-lintel also, as well as for the arch and dome; metal allows for steel-frame construction, suspension, or reinforced concrete; and so on. But there is another factor—often a more important one—that affects the shape of architecture, and that is the purpose a building will serve. Architecture creates not only an enclosure but an *environment* for living, sometimes extending beyond a single building to a larger design scheme. The functions of architecture and its role in creating an environment will be explored in the rest of this chapter.

PURPOSES
OF ARCHITECTURE

Architecture is seldom miscellaneous. Nearly every structure is designed to serve a specific function, and we evaluate a structure according to the way in which it fulfills its purpose. Although architecture through the ages has been enormously diverse, almost every structure fits into one of just a few major categories: government buildings; other public buildings, such as libraries or museums; commercial buildings, including offices, banks, and shops; buildings for transportation—airline terminals, train stations, and the like; religious buildings; and, of course, residences.

Beyond function, every structure has a particular character or style. It creates a certain environment within its walls and projects a certain image to the broader environment outside. A bank, for instance, may seem grand and imposing, or small-town and friendly, or modern and high-tech. By choosing a style of architecture, the bankers tell us about their self-image and about the customers they hope to attract. Similar effects are evident with other types of structures.

This section will discuss function and style in architecture, concentrating first on individual buildings. Later, we will enlarge our view and look at more complex architectural schemes—the design of whole environments.

Six types of buildings have been chosen for analysis: the house of worship, the museum, the office building, the hotel, the apartment building, and the private residence. For each category we will study two or three examples. These examples don't begin to cover the entire range of possibilities for any given architectural function. Rather, they have been selected because they provide interesting comparisons with one another and because they reveal how architects have attempted to serve the functions at hand in different times, in different places, with different personal styles.

TWO HOUSES OF WORSHIP

Earlier in this chapter we discussed two mighty cathedrals of France—St. Sernin and Chartres **(368,369)**. These are enormous structures, capable of enclosing thousands of worshipers. Here we turn our attention to two much smaller, more intimate religious buildings. Both are considered "pilgrimage churches," in that they are meant to offer spiritual and physical refreshment to travelers, and each will hold about three hundred people. In their styles, however, the two buildings could hardly be more different.

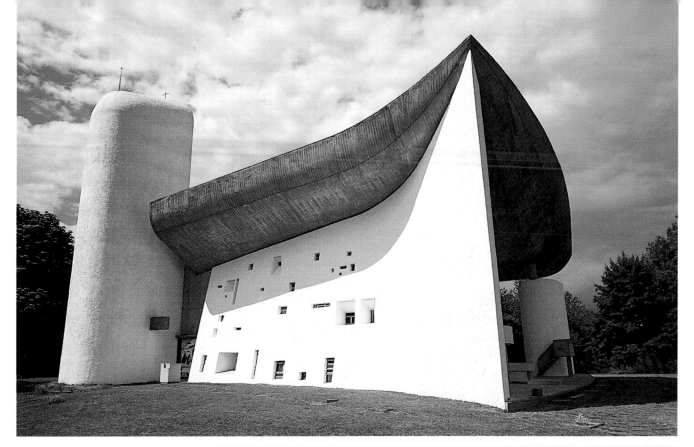

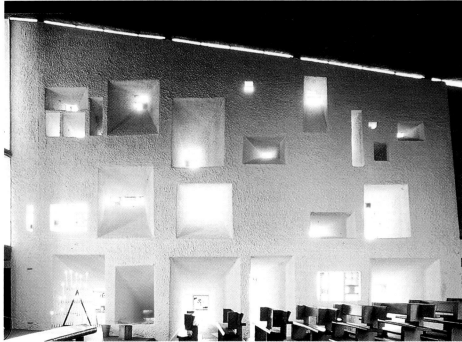

above: 383. Le Corbusier. Notre-Dame-du-Haut, Ronchamp, France. Exterior view from southeast. 1950–55.

right: 384. Le Corbusier. Notre-Dame-du-Haut, Ronchamp, France, interior. 1950–55.

Notre-Dame-du-Haut at Ronchamp, in France, is the masterpiece of the French architect Charles-Édouard Jeanneret, always known as Le Corbusier. Its site is a high, windswept hill in extreme eastern France, near Switzerland, at a spot believed to have been used for religious gatherings since pre-Christian times. Le Corbusier was commissioned to design the chapel to replace a building destroyed in World War II, and his plan was utterly different from its predecessor and unique in all the world.

The exterior of Notre-Dame-du-Haut (roughly, Our Lady of the high place; **383**) cannot be understood from one photograph, since the chapel is different from every angle, but this southeast view hints at the massiveness of the stuccoed, rubble-filled walls pierced by irregular, small openings. The soaring roof of reinforced concrete does not rest on the walls but rides on vertical supports inside the walls. This arrangement leaves a 4-inch space between the roof and walls to create a floating-roof effect and admit some light to the interior **(384)**. Le Corbusier claimed the roof shape was inspired by a crab shell he'd picked up on a beach, but the visitor is more likely to envision a giant sail poised to catch the wind and fly the little church away.

The interior of Notre-Dame-du-Haut has the mystery and solidity of a cave, a shelter in which one can find both safety and privacy. Like the outside, it is unpredictable. No one vantage point gives visitors a sense of the whole, so one must explore as one would explore a cave, trying to understand the unusual sight lines of seating to altar to side chapels. The changing light admitted by small, deep-set windows and the floating roof contributes to Ronchamp's secretive quality.

Another architect's masterpiece provides just about as strong a contrast to Notre-Dame-du-Haut as one could ask for. Thorncrown, a nondenominational chapel in Eureka Springs, Arkansas **(385)**, is the award-winning creation of Fay Jones, an Arkansas native. We need not show two photographs of this building, because the exterior can be readily understood from the inside view. The walls are glass, supported by a forest of wood beams, and natural light floods the interior from all directions. If Ronchamp is a cave, Thorncrown is a tree house, which was the effect Jones intended. It occupies a heavily wooded site, and the architect chose his materials carefully, so builders could carry them along a narrow path and not disturb existing trees. As Ronchamp is complex and unpredictable, Thorncrown is brilliantly simple—a glass shed with clear sight lines. Pilgrims at Thorncrown can be sheltered from the elements, but they are visually, perhaps spiritually, at one with the natural world.

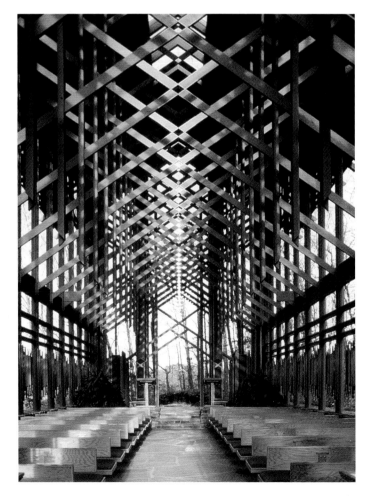

385. Fay Jones and Associates. Thorncrown Chapel, Eureka Springs, Ark. 1980. Overall dimensions 60 × 24′, height 48′.

THREE MUSEUMS

Museums make an interesting study in architectural design, because they are works of art meant to display other works of art or history. How they go about fulfilling this purpose tells us much about the nature of architecture.

In 1989 the architect I. M. Pei installed a sleekly modern glass pyramid in the courtyard of the Louvre Museum in Paris, one of the stateliest, staidest, (some would say) stuffiest museums in the world—a virtual shrine to traditional Old Master art. At first the pyramid, meant as a new main entrance to the Louvre, caused a scandal, but eventually critics and the public came to accept and even applaud the innovative design. Perhaps it was the sense that Pei could pull off anything he undertook to do that led to his selection as architect for a museum of a *very* different character: the new Rock-and-Roll Hall of Fame.

Situated on the shore of Lake Erie in Cleveland, the Rock-and-Roll Hall of Fame and Museum **(386)** could be described as a shrine to rock music—its stars, its songs, its artifacts, its basic culture. Unlike an art museum, in which paintings can be hung demurely on the wall, the Rock-and-Roll Museum needed to be many things at once: a concert hall; a party space complete with the disc jockey's booth; a treasury of film clips and video displays; a research center; a sound chamber—actually, *several* sound chambers—for an ongoing blast of rock music; a repository for costumes, sheet music, famous instruments, and props. Michael Jackson's first glove is there, and so is a piece of Otis Redding's crashed airplane. Needless to say, Elvis (whether alive or dead) is a major presence; on opening day a 16-foot-tall Elvis puppet swiveled down the street to the museum.

To contain all these disparate elements, Pei devised a complex structure. Facing the city is an enormous glass triangle five stories high, which the architect calls a "tent" and which is reminiscent of his Louvre pyramid. Behind the glass triangle rises a tall, square tower, from which other sections jut out over Lake Erie. A drumlike wing perched on a slender column reminds some viewers of early-rock records stacked and playing on a spindle. Pei's challenge in designing the Hall of Fame was to meet two seemingly contradictory goals: to be true to the free spirit of rock-and-roll and to provide a solidity, even a

386. I. M. Pei.
Rock-and-Roll Hall of Fame and Museum, Cleveland.
Completed 1995.
The Rock-and-Roll Hall of Fame and Museum Building is a Registered Trademark in the U.S. Patent and Trademark Office.

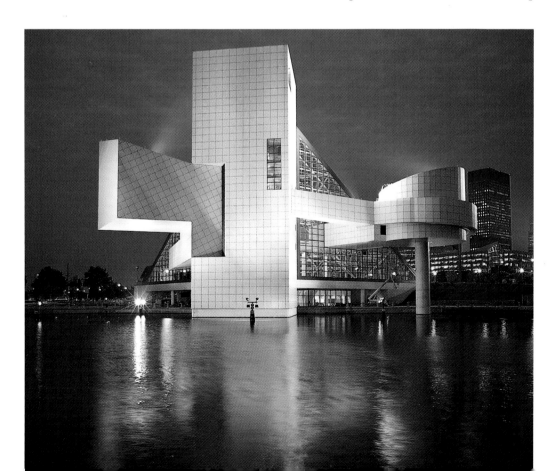

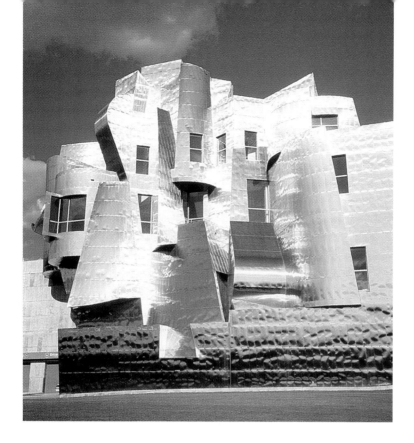

legitimacy, to its history. Most observers agree that, once again, the architect has pulled it off.

The Rock-and-Roll Hall of Fame gave Pei a rare opportunity, which has come to few architects of any era—the chance to design a major museum in its entirety, from the ground up, inside and out. Just a few years earlier a similar dream commission had been awarded for an art museum. The architect was Frank Gehry, and his project was the Frederick R. Weisman Museum of Art at the University of Minnesota in Minneapolis **(387)**.

Gehry is an American usually associated with the **Postmodern** style of architecture. Although highly diverse, Postmodern buildings tend to exhibit certain characteristics. The style emphasizes curves and decorative details, rather than pure straight lines. It is complex rather than simple, warm rather than cool. Its structures are understood gradually, through exploration and study from many angles. Some Postmodern buildings are brightly colored.

For the Weisman Museum project Gehry designed an intricate façade of curves and planes and segmented cones that project outward in many directions. Their gleaming stainless steel reflects light like the facets of a diamond, and since the museum occupies a high bluff over the Mississippi River, the effect is dramatic. Some observers feel the museum's remarkable shape blends perfectly with the fabulous ice sculptures made each year for the Winter Carnival in nearby St. Paul.

Gehry's bold design does not overwhelm the building's role as a functioning art museum. *New York Times* architecture critic Herbert Muschamp writes that the Weisman contains "five of the most gorgeous galleries on earth."[3] Muschamp praises the interior spaces for their hospitality both to museum visitors and to the artworks displayed in the building.

Certain critics have grumbled that Gehry is not an architect but an artist, that his forms are more sculptural than architectural. But this criticism ignores the fact that architects *are* artists; there is no contradiction between the two. A building need not be a simple box to enclose space effectively. Gehry's splendid design for the Weisman Museum brings us back to the point made at the beginning of this section: Art museums are works of art meant to display other works of art.

387. Frank Gehry. Frederick R. Weisman Museum of Art, University of Minnesota at Minneapolis. Completed 1993.

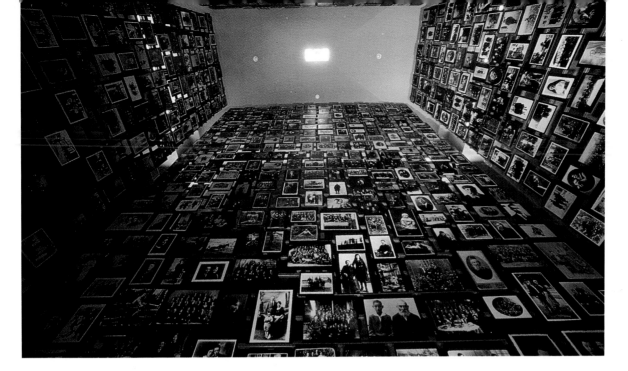

388. Tower of photographs from Ejszyszki, in the United States Holocaust Memorial Museum, Washington, D.C. Completed 1993. James Ingo Freed, of Pei Cobb Freed & Partners, architect.

Our final example in this section is also a new structure, but it is not an art museum. This institution's project director has said, "Most museums deal in the beautiful. We are dealing with the anti-beautiful."[4] The "we" he meant is the United States Holocaust Memorial Museum in Washington, D.C.

The Holocaust Museum, opened in 1993, is a memorial to the millions of Jews and other "undesirables" exterminated by German Nazis during World War II. It has a triple purpose: to inform those who do not know about the Holocaust; to commemorate those who experienced it, both the dead and the survivors; and to thwart those who might wish to repeat it. Put simply, if we know and remember the atrocity, perhaps the atrocity will not happen again.

Most of the museum's space is devoted to a permanent exhibition focusing on aspects of the Holocaust. Its architecture was designed specifically to lead visitors through the exhibits in a planned sequence, as on a journey through horror. One is encouraged to *live* the Holocaust, to walk through its landscape, to witness its agony. There are murals depicting the Jewish ghettos from which innocent people were removed and shipped to the concentration camps. There are the relics, pitiful mountains of small possessions—toothbrushes and dolls and bits of clothing—left behind. There is an actual freight car like the ones used to transport Jews to the camps. There are pieces from the gas chambers, the instruments of mass murder.

Most powerful of all, perhaps, is the tower of photographs from the Polish town of Ejszyszki **(388).** In 1941 Ejszyszki was nearly obliterated by Nazi gun squads. Only twenty-nine people survived the massacre, including a four-year-old girl named Yaffa Sonenson. Sonenson's family escaped to America, and the adult Yaffa Sonenson Eliach spent much of her life collecting some six thousand photographs from relatives and friends of the dead in Ejszyszki.

The faces in these pictures transform the abstraction of "holocaust" into personal tragedy, multiplied over and over. These were real people with real lives, before mindless hatred ended their lives. We see wedding pictures, baby pictures, school pictures, photos of family gatherings, snapshots of young lovers. The sheer number of images, arranged in the museum's tower, is overwhelming. We can perhaps turn away from the abstract concept of the Holocaust. We cannot turn away from the faces.

The Holocaust Museum has already succeeded in part of its mission—to attract visitors who might learn and remember. Half a year after its opening, the museum had to put out a notice asking people please *not* to come for a while. Crowds have been enormous, and the museum cannot accommodate all who wish to enter.

THREE OFFICE BUILDINGS

The architecture of commerce, like that of government, often has strong symbolic value. Its primary purpose is to house offices, but a secondary one may be to make a statement about the firm that owns the building. When a company decides to erect a new office building, its leaders give serious thought to the image that will be projected by that building and lodged in the minds of the public. Unlike the government structure, however, the office building rarely seeks a model in traditional architecture, but rather attempts to convey the impression of dynamic modernism—of a company forging ahead to the future. The office building of the 20th century has therefore tended to be a creature of fashion, taking its design from the trend of the times. Three examples spanning sixty years will illustrate this.

The Chrysler Building in New York, indisputably the gem of early skyscrapers, was completed in 1930 and was the first office building to rise above 1,000 feet. Its slender, elegantly pointed spire **(389)** changed the skyline of New York dramatically and still remains distinctive, in spite of later, taller buildings around it. We might list three elements that contributed to this splendid building: the great success of the automobile industry, which enabled Walter Percy Chrysler to erect a monument to his name; the relative cheapness of fine building materials and labor; and the prevalence of the style known as *Art Deco* **(390)**.

left: 389. William Van Alen. Chrysler Building, New York. Completed 1930.

right: 390. Chrysler Building, New York, interior detail of elevator door.

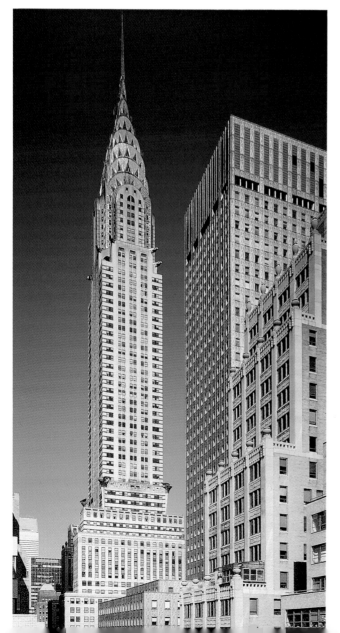

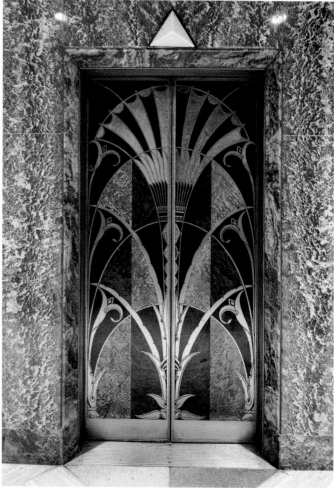

Art Deco, then at the height of fashion, was marked by geometric patterns and a rich display of surface decoration. (The term "deco" came from the Exposition des Arts Décoratifs, held in Paris in 1925, where the style first appeared as a significant force.) Art Deco was definitely a product of the machine age, for its favorite materials were chrome and steel and glass and aluminum—modern materials that glitter and sparkle, preferably in elaborate combinations to dazzle the eye. Its symbolism, unquestionably, is razzle-dazzle, and it celebrates the speed of the automobile and the airplane, people on the move. The top of the Chrysler Building is layered in an overlapping sunburst pattern pierced with triangular windows—a streamlined, geometric sculpture cutting through the sky.

The patterned forms of Art Deco gave way in the 1940s to the pared-down, austere design aesthetic of the International style. In a sense the roots of the International style might be traced back to Louis Sullivan **(378)**, who insisted that "form follows function." In other words, the form of a building or any other object should be expressive of what it is supposed to do, not overlaid with arbitrary decoration. This theme was taken up by two European architects, Le Corbusier and Ludwig Mies van der Rohe, and translated into a style that dominated American architecture through the 1970s. Le Corbusier would eventually discard the geometric simplicity of the International Style in favor of more organic expressions like the Ronchamp chapel **(383)**, but Mies van der Rohe added another catch phrase to the history of art when he made his often-quoted statement: "Less is more." By this he meant that architects (and other designers) must strip their forms to the barest essentials, the parts necessary to the work's function, so as to achieve a more honest, satisfying design.

391. Ludwig Mies van der Rohe and Philip Johnson. Seagram Building, New York. 1958.

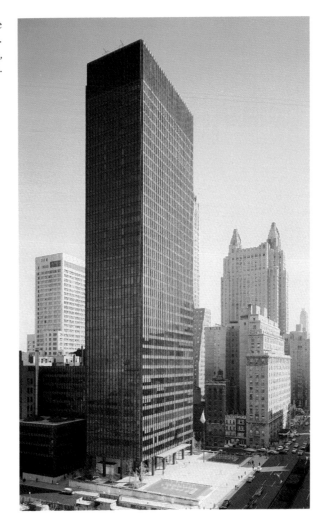

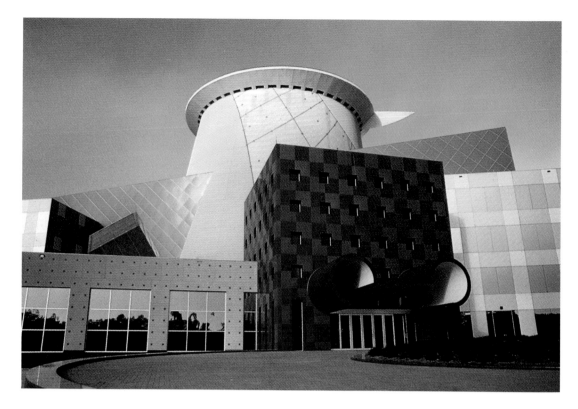

As mentioned earlier, the International style was introduced to the United States by such buildings as Lever House **(379)**. Diagonally across the street from Lever House is a building many consider to be the quintessence of that style. The Seagram Building **(391)**, designed by Mies van der Rohe and Philip Johnson, is almost the direct opposite of the Chrysler Building in its design aesthetic. A stark vertical slab resting on stilts, the Seagram Building rises abruptly from the base and terminates abruptly at the top, with no attempt at accent or decoration. Its form is the extended cube, and much of its visual appeal comes from the combination of bronze-colored steel and amber glass sheathing.

For more than twenty years after the Seagram Building was completed, through the 1970s, the International style held sway as the most luxurious and sophisticated style for skyscraper architecture. Across the United States towers of steel and glass vied with one another for height and simplicity of design. By about 1980 it became clear that some change was due, that the business firm of the 1980s and 1990s would be looking for an image quite different from "the old company that lived in a box." Architects too were ready for change, and so the **Postmodern** style came to corporate America. Not surprisingly, one of the companies that would most ardently embrace Postmodern was the Disney organization.

The Team Disney Building near Orlando, Florida **(392)**, captures the style at its most inventive, being complex, irregular, exuberant, and colorful. The building *does* have cubes, but they are not always vertical, not always parallel to one another, and certainly not a uniform, muted color. Disney's architect, Arata Isozaki, splashed a palette of pink and green and blue and red and yellow over the building's façade, and designed the side wings (which are much longer than this photo shows) to look rather like plaid. The huge central funnel introduces a curving form to play against the square shapes. It is actually a working sundial, the world's largest, inside which Isozaki constructed a Japanese garden of river-washed stones. Above the main entrance projects a stylized, elegant version of—yes—*mouse ears*. This may be an office building where serious business takes place, but it is, after all, an office building at Walt Disney World.

392. Arata Isozaki & Associates. Team Disney Building, near Orlando, Fla. Completed 1991. Used by permission from Disney Enterprises, Inc.

The commercial building, by its design, not only sends a message to the outside world about the image a given company wishes to project. It also sends a message to the people who work inside the building: This is who we want you to be. In the case of Team Disney, we must assume the company wants its employees to be creative, colorful—and a bit outside the traditional mold.

Today's business world demands much of its employees. Many work long hours, and so the office becomes a kind of home away from home. Moreover, with the enormous increase in travel for business and pleasure, one's "home" for any given night may well be a home for hire. We therefore turn for our next section to an architectural category serving the needs of travelers—the hotel.

TWO HOTELS

Choosing a hotel for a brief stay is a little like choosing a costume for a masquerade party. It is temporary, it is special, it is outside everyday life. It gives one the opportunity to say, "What life do I want to live?" or "Who do I want to be?"—for a little while.

The Hotel del Coronado in San Diego is the queen of the 19th-century resort hotels. Designed by architects James and Merritt Reid and completed in 1888, the "Del" wanders amiably across a pretty site overlooking the Pacific Ocean (393). In its heyday the Hotel del Coronado was a favored holiday spot for Victorian ladies and gentlemen, whose "holiday" was not the catch-as-catch-can vacation of today, but a leisurely visit of weeks or months. Daring guests could swim in the sea, but salt-water "bathing tanks" were nearby to accommodate the more timid. The very architecture of the building— rambling, unpredictable, stuck here and there with towers and porches and chimneys—speaks of a bygone time when nobody was in a hurry, when walking the grounds could be a day's activity. The del Coronado has a kind of majesty that says its visitors chose to be there and did not need to be anywhere else. Modern visitors to the "Del" may be seeking the same experience, trying to recapture a time when life was more graceful and much slower.

Drive northeast from San Diego into the desert, and in a few hours you will reach a city that did not even exist when the del Coronado was built—a city where life is seldom called graceful and is much, much faster. From its modest beginnings less than a century ago, Las Vegas has grown to become, arguably, the glitz capital of the world. Once the realm of hard-core gamblers and generally seedy types, Las Vegas now strives to attract a more respectable

393. James and Merritt Reid. Hotel del Coronado, San Diego. 1888.

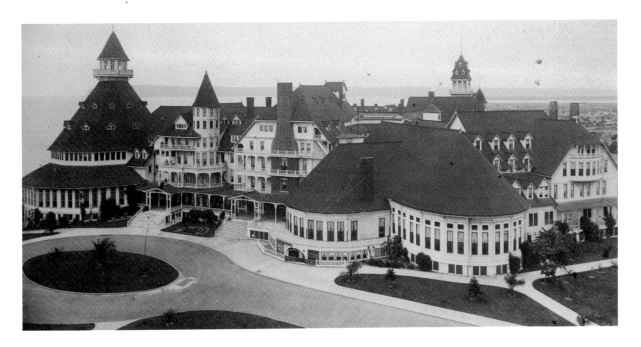

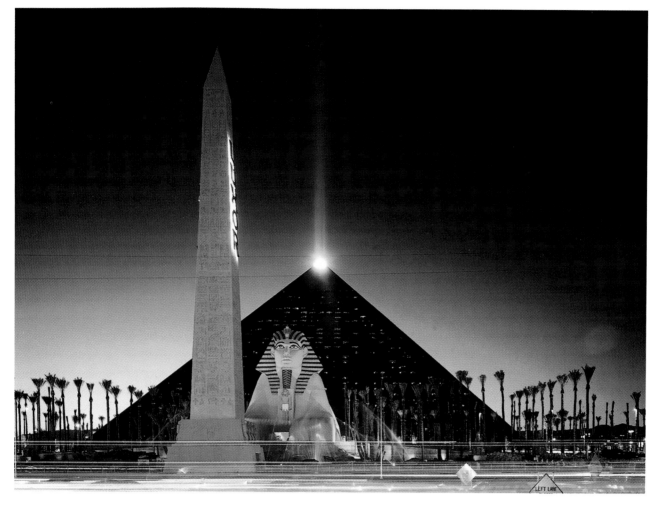

clientele, including families with children in tow. To this end, its developers have competed to erect ever more stupendous hotels often based on "themes." For the student of art, possibly the most interesting of these is the Luxor **(394)**.

To begin, the Luxor is big. Very big. Its more than 2,500 rooms line sloping black glass walls meant to evoke the Great Pyramids at Giza **(53)**, for this hotel's theme is ancient Egypt. One enters, naturally, through a Las Vegas version of the Sphinx **(414)**, which has been spruced up considerably and given a nose (the original's is missing). Also, to create more harmonious size relationships than had occurred to the Egyptians, the Luxor's designers scaled down the pyramid and made their Sphinx twice the original's height. The Sphinx's eyes shoot laser beams at a replica of an Egyptian obelisk, the pointed tower on which the hotel's name is emblazoned. And covering the obelisk, as elsewhere in the hotel, are Egyptian writings, or *hieroglyphs*, which were computer-tested to be meaningless, so that no naughty phrase might be read by a vacationing Egyptologist. There is even a miniature river Nile, complete with barges for hotel guests to ride on.

Is the Luxor art? Is it even architecture as we are considering the subject in this chapter? Perhaps the most appropriate term was coined by Chicago critic Blair Kamin, who called the new Las Vegas hotels "architainment." True, the Luxor provides shelter, as any building should, but its principal function is to ensure that visitors have a good time—and come back often.

The dazzling excesses of the Luxor might cause an observer to say, "It's a nice place to visit, but I wouldn't want to live there." Most of us expect the place where we live, day in and out, to be more serious, more sensible and down-to-earth. As we turn to our next category of buildings, we will find that is usually true. But not always.

394. Luxor Hotel, Las Vegas. Completed 1993.

TWO APARTMENT BUILDINGS

Fanciful architecture was not born yesterday. A century ago the Spanish architect Antoni Gaudí was designing buildings so unusual that their like cannot be found anywhere. Gaudí's masterpiece, the Casa Milá apartment house in Barcelona (395), shows why this architect is not associated with any prevailing style but is one of a kind. The Casa Milá seems almost to have grown on its site, carved out by wind and weather, and this was Gaudí's intention, the "natural" his obsession. The façade of cut stone swirls around windows and balconies in an irregular wavelike pattern. The chimneys on the roof—no two alike—resemble huge organic sculptures. Inside as out, there is scarcely a straight line to be found. Unlike the typical apartment building—where rooms are rectangular, boxes nesting beside, above, and under boxes—the Casa Milá has a completely unpredictable floor plan of free-form rooms clustered around interior patios. As an exercise in multiple dwelling, the Casa Milá would certainly not be for everyone, but for those with a spirit of adventure, life inside this giant cave palace could be *truly* living with art.

At the opposite extreme from the Casa Milá is an apartment complex that actually does consist of boxes nested together. Habitat in Montreal (396), designed by Moshe Safdie, was intended as an experiment in the housing of the future, in both form and construction. Like Fuller's dome (382), it was unveiled at Expo 67, the Montreal World's Fair. The complex consists of 354 prefabricated concrete boxes, stacked one on top of another to form 158 apartments, some on one level, others constructed as duplexes. Although the boxes are of uniform size, they were ingeniously designed for varied uses and floor plans. One box could be a living-dining area with kitchen, another two bedrooms and a bath; some boxes are self-contained units of living room, kitchen, bedroom, and bath. Through this modular system, almost any family size can be accommodated. Each apartment has a private entrance, windows on all sides, and a terrace—the flat roof of one dwelling providing the garden terrace for its neighbor above. In effect, every family lives in the penthouse.

When it first opened, Habitat was considered exciting as a concept but rather sterile as a living environment. It is, after all, so *boxy*. But Habitat has

395. Antoni Gaudí. Casa Milá, Barcelona. 1905–07.

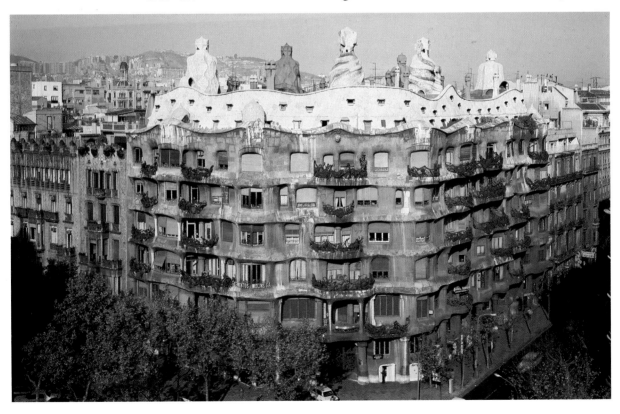

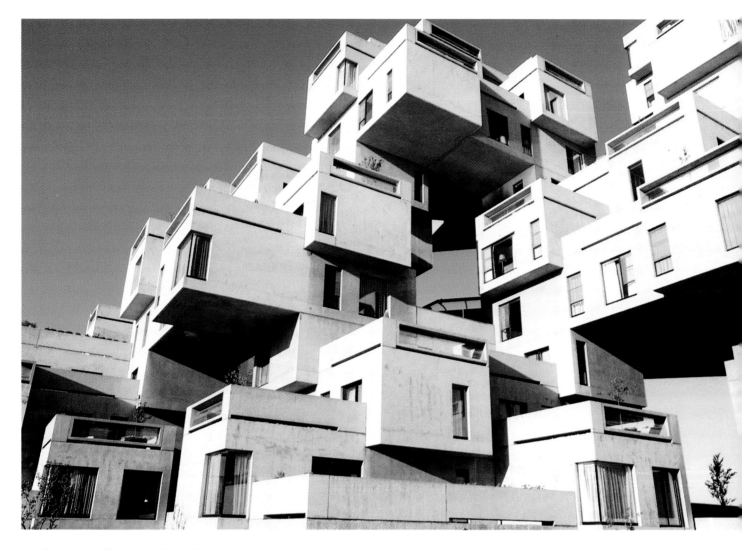

aged quite well in the three decades since, as residents have impressed their human stamp on technology. Some families have added sun porches, some skylights, one a fireplace with a chimney; everywhere there are trees, plants, and flowers. All these touches have turned the apartment house of the future into a sought-after home for the present.

Apartment houses have been with us at least since the time of the ancient Romans, and as space on our planet gets tighter and tighter, they will no doubt proliferate. For the time being, however, most people's dream remains the one-family house, and so we turn to this for our last category.

396. Moshe Safdie.
Habitat, Montreal. 1967.

THREE HOUSES

Ever since humans came down from the trees or out of their caves, most of the architecture built has been in the form of houses. Needless to say, dwellings from different times and places have displayed enormous variety. Each of the three houses considered here reflects a special point of view about what it means to dwell within a building—that is, what kind of roof one should have over one's head.

Master architects usually make their reputations on the "big" commissions—the office buildings, museums, airport terminals, hotels—and only incidentally design private houses. But for the man whom many consider to have been America's greatest architect, the reverse is true. Although he did design important public buildings, Frank Lloyd Wright will always be remembered as the master builder of houses.

Wright's approach to domestic architecture was characterized by two related principles: first, a house should blend with its environment; second, the interior and exterior of a house should be visually and physically integrated. Together, these principles comprised Wright's theory of "organic" architecture. The Kaufmann House in Bear Run, Pennsylvania, usually known as "Fallingwater," is considered to be his masterpiece (397).

Sited beside a stream with a little waterfall, the Kaufmann House was designed to take advantage of the surrounding landscape. Much of the house is built of stone, quarried from the immediate area, so that it seems to grow up from the site, rather than being set down upon it. One departure from this use of natural materials comes in the three terraces of reinforced concrete, two of them *cantilevered* over the waterfall. A cantilever is a horizontal form supported at only one end, jutting out into space at the other. Reinforced concrete, with its high tensile strength, makes such a construction possible, and Wright was among the first to exploit the cantilever for domestic architecture. (We can see examples of the cantilever for a public building in the Rock-and-Roll Hall of Fame [386].) Although not strictly "natural," the concrete cantilevers on the Kaufmann House emphasize the waterfall and make it seem a natural extension of the house.

The interior of "Fallingwater" consists mainly of one large room opening out to the terraces, providing an "organic" flow of spaces with no disruptive partitions. Wright believed that a hearth is the core of a home, so his plans included a massive stone fireplace, the chimney of which is visible in this photograph. As was his custom in private commissions, the architect also designed much of the furniture, building it into the structure so the owners could not tamper with his overall scheme. A master of control over his clients, Wright built his houses not to dominate the landscape but to coexist with it.

397. Frank Lloyd Wright. "Fallingwater" (Kaufmann House), Bear Run, Pa. 1936–37.

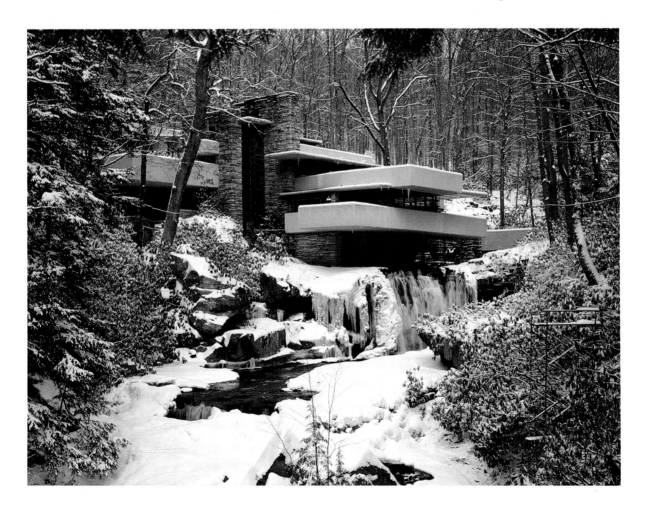

FRANK LLOYD WRIGHT

1867–1959

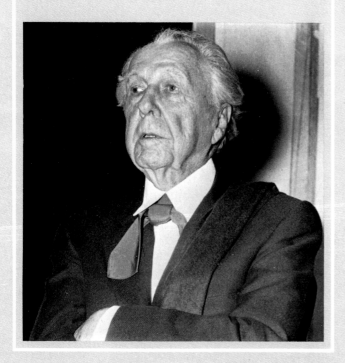

MANY CRITICS CONSIDER Frank Lloyd Wright to have been the greatest American architect of his time; certainly few would dispute the claim that he was the greatest designer of residential architecture. To see a Wright-designed building dating from the first decade of the 20th century is to be shocked by how remarkably modern it seems.

Wright had very little formal education. He attended high school in Madison, Wisconsin, but apparently did not graduate. Later, he completed the equivalent of about one year's course work in civil engineering at the University of Wisconsin, while holding down a job as a draftsman. In 1887 he moved to Chicago and eventually found work in the architectural firm headed by Louis Sullivan, the great designer of early office buildings. Before long Wright had assumed responsibility for fulfilling most of the residential commissions that came into the company, and in 1893 he opened a firm of his own.

During the next two decades Wright refined the principles of the "Prairie houses" that are his trademark. Most are in the Midwest, and they echo that flat expanse of the Great Plains—predominantly horizontal, stretching out over considerable ground area but usually in one story. All expressed Wright's special interest in textures and materials; he liked whenever possible to build with materials native to the immediate surroundings, so that the houses blend with their environments. Interiors were designed in an open plan, with rooms flowing into one another (an unusual practice for the time), and the inside and outside of the house were also well integrated. These ingredients added up to what Wright always referred to as "organic" architecture.

For most of his long life Wright's personal situation was far from tranquil. His parents seem to have had a bitterly unhappy marriage, and they divorced in 1885, when Wright was seventeen—an extraordinary event for that era. Wright himself had a troubled marital history. His first marriage ended when he eloped to Europe with Mamah Brothwick, the wife of a former client, leaving his own wife and six children behind. Five years later, back in Wisconsin, Brothwick was brutally murdered by a deranged servant while Wright was out of the house. This tragedy sent the architect off on a period of wandering through faraway parts of the world. A final marriage in the late 1920s lasted out his lifetime and appears to have given him his first real happiness.

Although he is best known for his domestic architecture, Wright also designed many large-scale commercial and public buildings, including the Solomon R. Guggenheim Museum in New York. His innovative design for the Imperial Hotel in Tokyo, planned to be stable in an area plagued by earthquakes, proved successful when the hotel survived without damage a devastating quake just a year after it was completed.

Wright was the author of several books on his theories of architecture, and always he focused on the organic nature of his work and on his own individuality. "Beautiful buildings are more than scientific. They are true organisms, spiritually conceived, works of art, using the best technology by inspiration rather than the idiosyncrasies of mere taste or any averaging by the committee mind."[5]

Photograph of Frank Lloyd Wright.

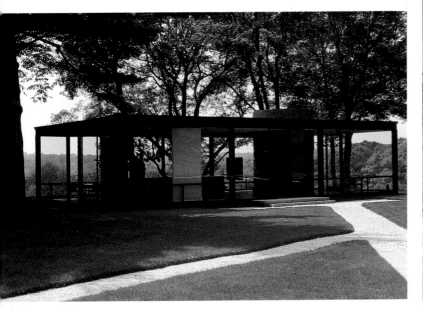

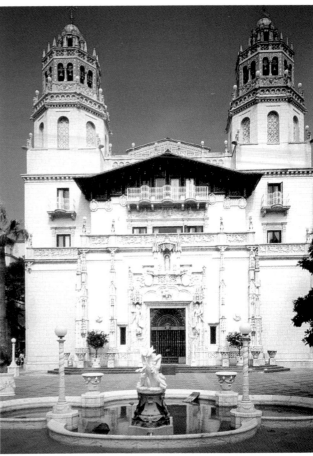

left: 398. Philip Johnson. Glass House, New Canaan, Conn. 1949.

right: 399. Julia Morgan. Casa Grande, Hearst Castle, San Simeon, Calif. 1922–37.

Another house that blends with its natural surroundings—albeit in a drastically different way—is the residence architect Philip Johnson designed for himself in New Canaan, Connecticut. Built in 1949, the house immediately became, and remains, a classic of modern architecture. Most people call it, simply, the Glass House (398). The clean, precise, unadorned, rectilinear lines of this structure place it squarely in the International style, but Johnson's home is obviously unique. All four exterior walls are of clear glass, permitting unobstructed views from the inside out to the surrounding landscape and equally from the outside in. Only the bathroom is enclosed in a floor-to-ceiling brick cylinder. Areas for living, sleeping, and cooking are fully exposed.

Johnson's daring experiment in transparent living naturally gives rise to jokes about people who live in glass houses not throwing stones. (Presumably, the architect never has.) More important, it challenges our customary balance of privacy versus harmony with nature. Most people think of a home as a refuge from the outside world, a place to let down one's hair, to be oneself, to be messy if one chooses. The Glass House is having none of this. It is always "public," always orderly, always on display. By visually dissolving the boundaries between indoors and outdoors, Johnson makes us reconsider the very concept of the house.

There are houses . . . and there are houses. Wright's "Fallingwater" is a house, and so are log cabins and cottages. And so is Casa Grande (399), the centerpiece of William Randolph Hearst's fabulous California estate known as San Simeon. In 1919 the newspaper magnate, who owned an immense ranch on a site overlooking the Pacific Ocean, had become tired of "camping out," as he put it. He therefore hired the San Francisco architect Julia Morgan to "build something a little more comfortable." Morgan, who had been the first woman ever to earn an architectural degree from the prestigious Ecole des Beaux-Arts in Paris, was known for her tenacity, her determination to see a project through to its completion. She would need every bit of that tenacity, for Hearst's project consumed the next eighteen years of her life.

Morgan's supervision of the design was comprehensive. She first had to build wharves at oceanfront to accommodate ships bringing the building materials, as well as roads to transport materials to the site. Next she designed, and supervised the building of, three immense Mediterranean-style guest houses. Eventually she would add hothouses for plants; kennels; two huge swimming pools (one outdoor, one in); a newspaper office and telephone switchboard; a mile-long pergola (a vine-covered archway) so that visitors could ride their horses even in bad weather without getting wet; and an elephant house and bear and lion pits for Hearst's private zoo.

But Casa Grande, the main residence, was Morgan's triumph—and Hearst's as well, for he took an avid interest in the construction. Casa Grande—the translation "big house" is something of an understatement—was intended to have the look and impact of a cathedral. It has more than a hundred rooms, the more public rooms designed on an enormous scale, and is fronted by two 137-foot-high towers copied from the Cathedral of Ronda in Spain. One observer described its architecture as "Bastard-Spanish-Moorish-Romanesque-Gothic-Renaissance-Bull Market-Damn the Expense" style.[6] By all reports, however, Hearst loved it, and so do tourists who flock to see its splendors.

When filmmaker Orson Welles made his thinly disguised biographical movie about Hearst, *Citizen Kane* (283), he called the estate "Xanadu," a reference to the domain of the legendary Chinese emperor Kublai Khan. Hearst himself really was a kind of emperor—an emperor of newspapers. The "something a little more comfortable" that Julia Morgan made may seem to us a palace, but for Hearst it was home.

Morgan's work on the Hearst estate can serve as a transition to the next topic for this chapter. After all, Morgan didn't merely design a building for Hearst to live in. She designed a whole environment to satisfy her client's needs, wishes, and whims. Almost anyone can have a home. William Randolph Hearst had both the impulse and the resources to order up his own little world, designed precisely to his specifications as far as his eye could see.

This impulse for broad-scale design is probably as old as human civilization. Sometimes, as in Hearst's case, it is motivated by a grandiose need for self-gratification. In other cases, however, the impulse comes from an altruistic desire to design a whole environment that is both beautiful and functional. We turn to this ultimate architectural challenge—creating a perfect world.

BEYOND THE BUILDING: ENVIRONMENTAL DESIGN

Environmental design can be defined as large-scale planning to improve the aesthetic and functional qualities of the surroundings in which we live, to make them more habitable. The target environment could be huge or small, anything from a whole city to a little playground or park. This type of design may involve architects, urban planners, landscape designers, and even psychologists and sociologists.

Today's environmental design is as varied as the populations it intends to serve. At its best, it asks many questions before attempting to provide answers. Where is this environment—city, suburbs, or country? What are its geographical location and climate? Who lives in the environment—children, teenagers, young adults, middle-aged adults, elderly people, or a mixed group? How do they move about—on foot, on bicycle, by car, or by mass transit? What do they do in the environment—eat, sleep, work, study, play, or some combination of these? How do the people who plan it, and those who will use it, feel about themselves, and what do they want to show to the world?

To see how designers have grappled with these questions, we will look at a few environmental designs. Some should be familiar to readers of this book.

DESIGN FOR LEARNING:
THREE COLLEGE CAMPUSES

Thomas Jefferson referred to the college campus as an "academical village." This term is apt, because a campus typically possesses most of the characteristics we would find in a traditional village. It is self-contained. It provides nearly all the essentials for daily life—sleeping and eating facilities, work spaces, health care, supplies of goods and services, places for social gathering. Its inhabitants interact closely with one another and have common interests and goals.

The stereotypical view of a college campus evokes the "halls of ivy"—that is, imposing monumental buildings, perhaps in the Gothic style, possibly with ivy growing thickly up the walls. As a matter of fact, some campuses do look like this, at least in their older sections. But campus design is just as diversified as any other. The personality of each college is unique.

There could hardly be a more challenging or interesting task for the environmental designer than planning a college campus. After all, it is much like designing a city from the ground up, and few people in history have had the opportunity to do that. The campus will, presumably, endure for many hundreds of years. It will serve as a working environment and home away from home for a constantly changing population of students and professors. It must be comfortable and efficient, but above all it must express the special personality of the college. It must say through its design: This is who we are. Let us see how three designers tackled this challenge.

Jefferson was not trained as an architect, much less as an environmental designer—if such a term could have existed in the early 19th century. In his day, however, the educated person was expected to be informed on many subjects. Honored now as drafter of the Declaration of Independence and third president of the United States, Jefferson drew more satisfaction from being a cultivated student of the arts and sciences. His great pride was the college he established and whose architecture and overall layout he designed—the University of Virginia **(400)**.

Jefferson's plan for the University of Virginia combined the qualities we admire in the man himself: idealism and practicality. Idealism was embodied in the veneration of knowledge; practicality in the belief that one's surroundings when pursuing knowledge should be comfortable and conducive to study. The university is organized around a rectangle, with a large, grassy lawn at its center. Its focus is the Rotunda, the library, which is modeled after the Pan-

400. Thomas Jefferson. University of Virginia, Charlottesville. 1817–26.

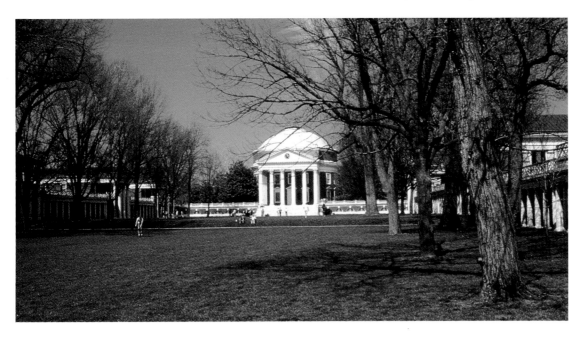

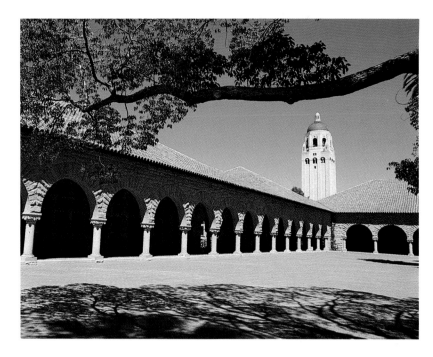

401. Charles A. Coolidge.
Stanford University,
Palo Alto, Calif. Begun 1886.

theon in Rome **(372,445)**, for Jefferson's ideals were rooted in the traditions of ancient Greece and Rome. Strung out along the two sides of the lawn are ten "pavilions," each meant to house the professor of one branch of learning and his college of students. This situation was intended to provide natural and spirited communication between teacher and pupils. (In Jefferson's time education was based on the tutorial system. Each subject had one distinguished professor, around whom students grouped.)

The pavilions are not identical, but each is based on a specific classical prototype, some in the Doric style, some the Ionic **(365)**. Joined to one another by roofed colonnades, the pavilions are planned for an elegant balance between ready access and studious seclusion. Behind the pavilions are formal gardens, then another range of buildings on each side, including "hotels" meant as dining rooms. Overall, Jefferson's design expresses magnificently his concept of "who we are." The "we" in this case—the students and faculty of the University of Virginia—are rational, orderly, and dedicated to learning; they are the enlightened heirs to the great legacy of Greece and Rome.

Just over half a century later, and a continent apart from Virginia, another great university, a very different one, was established and designed. Its patron was Leland Stanford, once governor of California, who endowed the university in memory of his dead son. (We met Governor Stanford earlier in this book, in connection with a bet on his racehorse that inspired Eadweard Muybridge's serial photographs, p. 239.)

In contrast to the University of Virginia, Stanford University is not classical in its design aesthetic. Rather, it draws its inspiration from the Romanesque monastery cloister, but even more specifically from California history. During the 18th and early 19th centuries Spanish Franciscan priests had established a series of mission churches up and down the coast of California. It is this "mission-style" architecture, with its low buildings and red-tiled roofs, that Stanford University emulates **(401)**. Seen from a distance, the university looks rather like a Mediterranean village, growing naturally from the landscape. Its basic motif is not the square post-and-lintel of Jefferson's design, but the graceful arch. For Stanford University, "who we are" is identified with the West, with California, with the legacy of Spanish colonists.

Yet another half century or so brings us to our third campus design—in this instance a design rooted in time and technology rather than place. The U.S. Air Force was organized as an independent branch of the military in

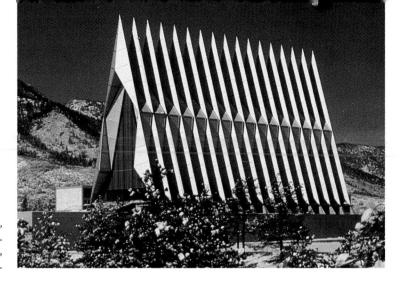

402. Skidmore, Owings & Merrill. United States Air Force Academy, Colorado Springs, Colo. 1956–63.

1947, and in 1954 it established its own service academy **(402)**. Rejecting the architectural examples of its kin—the army academy at West Point (Gothic) and the naval academy at Annapolis (Classical)—the U.S. Air Force Academy sought an environment that would speak to the present and the future. The architectural firm of Skidmore, Owings & Merrill designed for the Colorado Springs site a campus that is consciously modern, sleek as an airplane, boasting of speed, progress, and technological power. For the students and faculty of the Air Force Academy, obviously, "who we are" is a people meant to fly, to be the wave of the future.

Design of the "academical village" is not static. Over the years needs change, student populations grow, buildings must be added. Even Jefferson foresaw this, leaving the grassy central rectangle at the University of Virginia open on one end for possible future expansion. Nevertheless, design of the campus does afford the rare opportunity for total, harmonious environmental planning. And so—to say the very least—does our next design category.

DESIGN FOR SHOPPING: THE MALL

The visionary architect R. Buckminster Fuller (p. 322) once proposed to build a 3-mile-wide geodesic dome over the whole midtown area of Manhattan Island. Fuller probably realized his idea would never be put into practice. New Yorkers are pretty independent people, and it is unlikely they would accept such a drastic change in their everyday lives.

In the abstract, however, the dome concept had its attractions. Think of it: The business district of New York City no longer would be plagued by the stifling heat of August or the cold and slush of January. Snow removal—a huge expense in the city's budget—would become a thing of the past. Individual buildings would not need to be heated or cooled; the entire atmosphere under the dome would be climatically ideal year-round. Air pollution, too, would become obsolete. Flying insects, such as flies and mosquitoes, could be all but eliminated, as could New York's perennial pigeon problem. There would be no more gloomy Mondays. Workers returning from their weekends would be greeted by a light (artificially lighted, if necessary), cheerful environment. Perhaps depressions would lift and crime rates plummet.

In effect, what Fuller dreamed of was turning midtown Manhattan into one giant mall. He was indeed a visionary and well ahead of his time, for, having died in 1983, he had never seen a phenomenon that is now part of our contemporary culture—the MEGAMALL.

The mall has become the equivalent of the old-time village green, a gathering place as comprehensive as the medieval cathedral. Chapter 3 of this book, in its discussion of Chartres Cathedral (p. 49), pointed out the vital role played by the cathedral in people's daily lives. Today, that role has largely been assumed by the mall. Nearly all the social activities one could want are satisfied within the enclosed environment of the mall—sports and entertainment, music and dramatic performances, socializing with friends, having a meal or a snack, and, of course, buying or simply admiring an endless array of consumer goods. The people of medieval Europe walked, so their obvious gathering place was the cathedral in the center of town. The people of suburban North America drive cars; their obvious gathering place is the mall.

A recent entry in the "build-the-megamall" competition is the Mall of America in Bloomington, Minnesota (403). Mall of America is *big*—78 acres, to be exact, or about the size of 88 football fields housed under one roof. For your shopping pleasure there are several department stores and more than 350 shops. If you are hungry, you can choose from among some 40 restaurants. But if you want entertainment, there is always Camp Snoopy, the world's largest indoor amusement park, which features a full-size roller coaster and a four-story waterfall. Movies? Certainly. A 14-screen theater gives you plenty of choice. No matter what the weather outside—and Minnesota has a brutal winter climate—you can pursue whatever activities you fancy under the roof.

We said the people of North America drive cars. They also fly in airplanes. As of this writing, at least one major airline is promoting charter mallflights. For a bargain fare, you can fly into the local airport, board a special bus to the Mall of America, shop till you drop, bus back, and fly home again all in the same day, without ever setting foot in the surrounding countryside. One can't help but think Buckminster Fuller would have loved it. The mall is, after all, one version of life inside the dome.

Architecture and environmental design touch us more directly than any of the other arts. As we move through our everyday lives, we are influenced profoundly by the structures and environments we enter, leave, or pass by.

In years to come these design disciplines will change rapidly, because our lives are changing rapidly. We don't know what factors will influence human life fifty or a hundred years hence, or what functions will need to be served. To be sure, certain conditions are predictable. Population will increase, and there will be a greater need for housing. Industrial pollution must be eliminated or counteracted. But how will the dominance of the computer affect our buildings and our environments? How will space travel influence coming generations? Must we plan now for the eventual colonization of the moon and of distant planets?

Whatever forms architecture and environmental design may take in the future, certain characteristics will remain essential to our buildings and our little worlds: They will still tell us who we are. They will still show us the face we want to present to the world.

403. The Mall of America, Bloomington, Minn. Opened 1992.

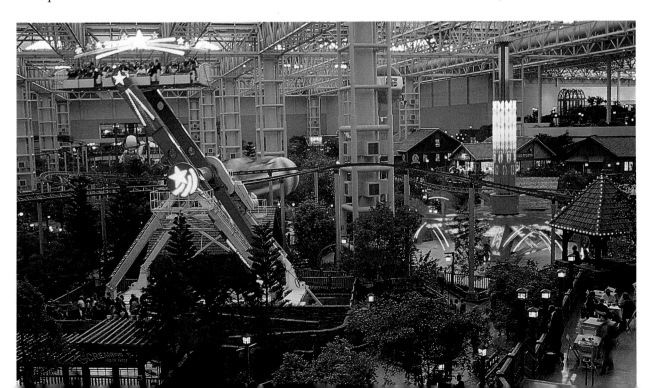

ARTS
IN TIME

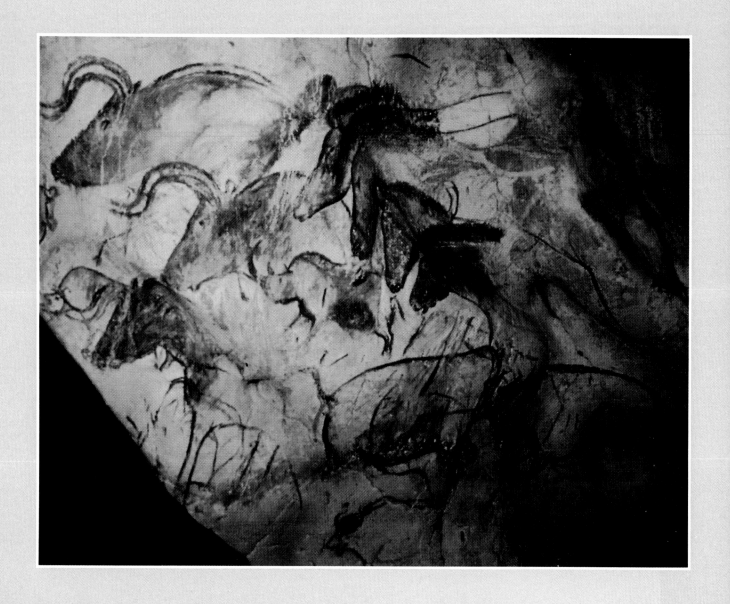

404. *Panel of the Horses,* Chauvet cave, France. c. 30,000 B.C.E.

CHAPTER FOURTEEN

The Ancient World

A MAJOR FACTOR in the understanding and appreciation of art is knowledge of its time frame—when a work of art was made and under what circumstances, how cultural factors of the time may have influenced the artists. For this reason the final part of this book has been devoted to a brief chronological survey, tracing the principal movements in art from earliest times to the present. The eight chapters here should help to place works of art discussed throughout the text in their historical context. Artworks introduced elsewhere in this text obviously fit into a historical chronology, and so they have been cross-referenced in the margins of this section. Chronologies in the chapters list significant dates, styles, and events. As we study the arts in time, however, it should be remembered that the works illustrated here could also be considered primarily for their themes, their design components, and their artistic media.

THE OLDEST ART

On the afternoon of December 18, 1994, two men and a woman, all experienced cave explorers, were climbing among the rocky cliffs in the Ardèche region of southeastern France. From a small cavity in the rock they felt a draft of air, which they knew often signaled a large cavern within. After clearing away some rocks and debris, they were able to squeeze through a narrow channel into what appeared to be an enormous underground room, its floor littered with animal bones. Pressing farther into the cave, the explorers played their lights on the walls and made an astonishing discovery that caused them to overflow "with joy and emotion" and brought "minutes of indescribable madness." The walls were covered with fine drawings and paintings (404)—more than three hundred images as they eventually found—depicting rhinoceroses, horses, bears, reindeer, lions, bison, mammoths, and others, as well as numerous outlines of human hands.

At once the French trio realized their find was important. It was evident that the paintings were extremely old and that the cave had remained untouched, unseen by humans, since prehistoric times. They agreed to name the site after the one in their number who had led them to it, Jean-Marie Chauvet,

C H R O N O L O G Y

	30,000–4000 B.C.E.		4000–500 B.C.E.

Europe

Old Stone Age, 30,000–10,000

New Stone Age, 10,000–4000

    Chauvet cave paintings, c. 30,000
    Venus of Willendorf, c. 23,000
    Lascaux cave paintings, c. 13,000

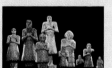

Cave painting, Lascaux

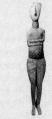

Cycladic *Statuette*

Cycladic culture, Aegean,
  c. 3000–c. 1100

Minoan culture, Crete,
  c. 2000–c. 1100

Mycenaean culture, Greece,
  c. 1600–c. 1100

    Stonehenge, England, c. 2000–1500

**Ancient
Near East**

Statuette, Abu Temple

Ishtar Gate

Sumer, c. 3500–c. 2300
    Square Temple, Tell Asmar, c. 2900–2600

Akkad, c. 2300–c. 2180

First Dynasty of Babylon, c. 1900–c. 1600
    Hammurabi, king of Babylon,
    c. 1792–c. 1750

Assyrian Empire, c. 1000–612

Neo-Babylonia, c. 612–538
    Nebuchadnezzar II, king of Babylon,
    c. 605–562
    Ishtar Gate, c. 575

Africa

Great Pyramids

Mask of Tutankhamun

Nubia, A-Group, c. 3800–c. 3100

Nubia, C-Group, c. 2300–c. 1550

Old Kingdom Egypt, 2686–2181
    Great Sphinx, c. 2530
    Great Pyramids, c. 2500

Middle Kingdom Egypt, 2133–1991

New Kingdom Egypt, 1567–1085
    Amenhotep IV, pharaoh c. 1353–1336
    Tutankhamun, pharaoh c. 1334–1325

Asia

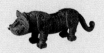

Bronze *Tiger*

Indus Valley Civilization,
  c. 2700–c. 1500

Shang Dynasty, China, 1766–1045

Zhou Dynasty, China, 1045–256

Mesoamerica

Olmec *Colossal Head*

Olmec culture, c. 1500–c. 300

so it is called the Chauvet cave. What they did not realize until months later, after radiocarbon testing had accurately dated the paintings, was that they had just pushed back the history of art by several *thousand* years. The Chauvet images were made about 30,000 B.C.E. and are the oldest paintings we know.

Among many fascinating aspects of the Chauvet cave is the fact that, although the paintings were done some seventeen thousand years before those at Lascaux **(2)**, they do not seem cruder or more "primitive." In fact, some images at Chauvet show a greater drawing sophistication than the much later Lascaux paintings. Moreover, the Chauvet paintings surely did not spring up out of nowhere. They must have been part of a long artistic tradition that stretched back in history and continued for many millennia. For art lovers this raises tantalizing questions: What came before, and between, and where is it?

As we begin this discussion of ancient art, then, it is important to keep in mind that the civilizations covered are not necessarily those in which the *most* art was made or even those in which the *best* art was made. They are, rather, the civilizations whose art *has been found.* Certain conditions foster the preservation of art from a particular culture and therefore give us broad knowledge of that culture's creative expression. At least one of them must be present to save the art for later generations. The conditions are these:

First, the artists worked in durable materials, such as stone and metals and fired clay, rather than more perishable wood or fiber. Second, the local environment is not destructive to artworks; for instance, the hot, dry climate of Egypt provides an excellent milieu for preservation. Third, the culture was highly organized, with stable population centers. Great cities normally house the richest troves of artwork in any culture, for they are where the rulers dwell, the wealth is accumulated, and the artists congregate. Fourth, the culture had a tradition of caching its artworks in places of limited or no accessibility. A huge portion of the ancient art that has survived comes from tombs or underground caves.

This chapter will introduce some of the oldest art we know, dating from the Chauvet cave of about 30,000 B.C.E. to works made a few hundred years before the start of our common era. The locations in which these artworks have been found are widely scattered, in (to use the modern terms) Europe, Asia, Africa, and Mesoamerica (map, below). No doubt art was made in many other places, but it is lost to us or still concealed from our eyes.

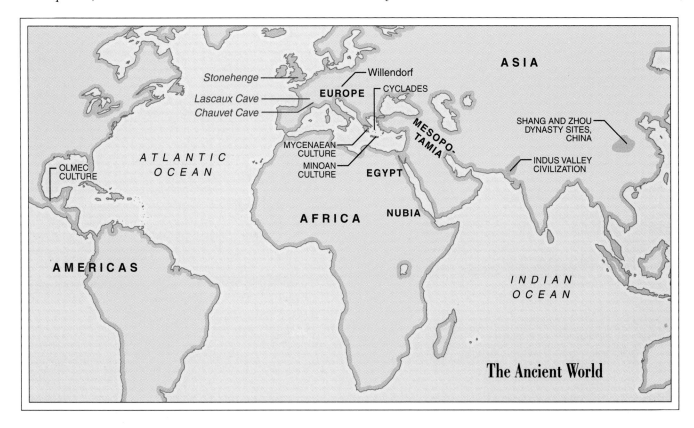

The Ancient World

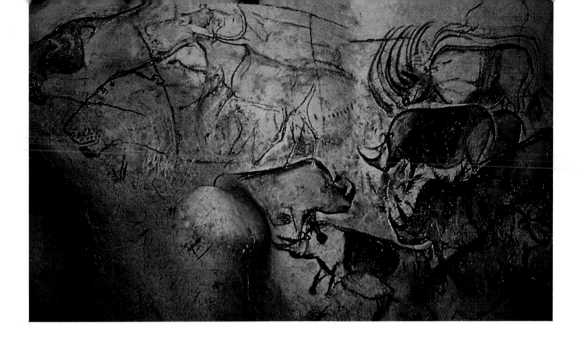

PREHISTORIC ART

405. *Lion Panel,*
Chauvet cave, France.
c. 30,000 B.C.E.

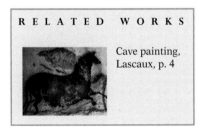

RELATED WORKS

Cave painting,
Lascaux, p. 4

The Chauvet cave paintings date from a time known as the ***Upper Paleolithic Period,*** which simply means the latter part of the Old Stone Age. Archaeologists have formed some tentative conclusions about how the paintings were done. Pigments of red and yellow ochre, a natural earth substance, along with black charcoal, could have been mixed with animal fat and painted onto the walls with a reed brush. In powdered form, the same materials probably were mouth-blown to the surface through hollow reeds. Many of the images are engraved, or scratched, into the rock walls.

More intriguing is the question of *why* the cave paintings were made, why their creators paid such meticulous attention to detail, why they did their work so far underground. As mentioned in Chapter 1, the paintings clearly were not meant to embellish a dwelling space. The cave artists must have lived—slept, cooked their meals, mated, and raised their children—much nearer to the mouths of these caves, close to daylight and fresh air. Until the Chauvet cave was discovered, many experts believed the ancient paintings were done for magical assistance in the hunt, to ensure success in bringing down game animals. But several of the animals depicted at Chauvet, including lions and rhinos and bears, were not in the customary diet of early peoples. Perhaps the artists wished to identify with these wild beasts, but we cannot know for sure.

The one thing we do know is that the paintings are marvelous, made by skilled hands following a developed aesthetic impulse. Our two examples, from the Panel of the Horses **(404)** and the Lion Panel **(405)**, reveal a keen sense of the animals' anatomy and a flair for capturing movement. We see overlapping of figures, a good command of perspective to imply depth, even a richness of textures, as in the horses' manes. Such flourishes as the sweeping curve of a bison's horn or the elegant arch of a horse's neck cannot come from mere observation and recording. They are indicators of true artistic style.

The question of why a work of art was made arises also with ancient sculptures. Nearly as old as the Chauvet cave paintings is a little female statuette that often serves as an emblem of art history's beginnings. She is made of stone, was formed about 25,000 years ago, and was found near a town in present-day Austria. Most people call her the *Venus of Willendorf* **(406)**.

At first the title "Venus" may seem strange, given our usual image of the goddess of love. The name, of course, was applied by modern scholars, possibly supposing that people many thousands of years ago considered this sort of figure a sexual ideal. It seems clear that the statuette was a fertility image, possibly meant to be carried around as an **amulet,** or good-luck charm (the *Venus* is less than 5 inches tall). Only the features associated with childbearing have been stressed—the belly, breasts, and pubic area. Venus' face is obscured. Her arms, crossed above the breasts, are barely defined, and her legs taper off to nothing. If we take this figure literally, she could not see or speak or walk or carry. What she could do was bear and nurture children.

How difficult it is for us living now to imagine what childbirth meant all those millennia ago. On the one hand it must have been a pressing necessity. Children were needed to help in the task of survival, and there may also have been an instinct to continue life through future generations. On the other hand, however, the process by which children are conceived and born was a mystery to these early peoples. The ovum and the sperm were unknown. No wonder elements of magic and ritual became associated with childbirth. Many scholars assume that fertility figures like the *Venus of Willendorf,* which are extremely common in early art, were meant to play a cause-and-effect role. The sculptor would form an image of a woman with exaggerated reproductive features, and this figure would *result* in a child being born. (It would be fascinating to know whether this figure was carved by a woman or a man.)

Much prehistoric art seems to have been created for this purpose—to make sense out of the universe and to exert some control over the forces of nature. Today we have weather forecasters and meteorologists and orbiting satellites and computers—but we still are not absolutely sure whether it will rain tomorrow. Early peoples had none of these, but they made the best out of what they had. Some of their arrangements startle us with their ingenuity.

On a plain in the south of England stand the enormous megaliths known as Stonehenge **(407),** much as they have stood for more than three thousand years. Stonehenge was built over a period of centuries, perhaps beginning as early as 2000 B.C.E. It consists of four concentric rings of stones, the outermost ring being 100 feet in diameter. The basis of the structure is *post-and-lintel* construction (Chapter 13), in which two uprights are surmounted by a horizontal crosspiece, the *lintel.* One of the most fascinating aspects of Stonehenge is the puzzle of *how* it was built. The stones, some weighing 50 tons or more, were quarried many miles away and dragged to the site by whatever primitive means may have been available. Next came the staggering feat of raising the lintels into position, without benefit of the cranes and other modern devices we take for granted. There is no mortar joining these immense rocks. The method used by Stone Age peoples to erect them has stood up ever since.

As with the cave paintings, there is also the fascinating problem of *why* Stonehenge was created. What purpose could have been so compelling as to stimulate this tremendous human effort? For centuries art historians debated the question. Then in 1964 a theory was advanced by astronomer Gerald S. Hawkins that appears to have solved the riddle of Stonehenge. By feeding complex measurements into a computer, Hawkins found that, at the moment of sunrise on the summer solstice (usually June 21), the sun shines through a key opening directly to an altar at the center. Similar computations showed that the position of the stones was organized to predict the winter solstice, the

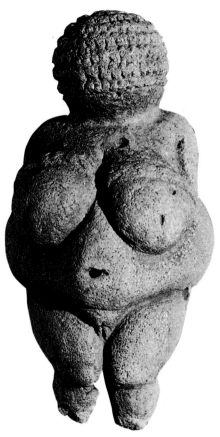

above: 406. *Venus of Willendorf.*
c. 23,000 B.C.E.
Limestone, height 4⅜″.
Natural History Museum, Vienna.

below: 407. Stonehenge.
c. 2000–1500 B.C.E.
Height of stones 13′6″.
Salisbury Plain, England.

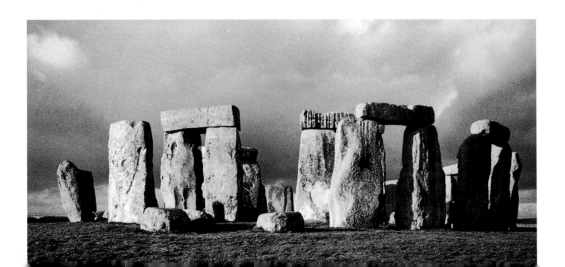

spring and autumnal equinoxes, and even eclipses of the sun and moon. In other words, Stonehenge apparently functioned as a giant calendar, codifying the changes of seasons and stars. Is Stonehenge a religious structure, or the beginning of science, or a link between the two? Whichever the case, it provided the means by which its makers could attempt to tame their world.

For the most part, very early works of art are isolated examples and come from cultures that were essentially nomadic, oriented toward hunting to meet their needs for food. Not until we come to two cultures, both in the Middle East, do we find a coherent, reasonably intact artistic production about which we know a great deal. These are the ancient cultures of Mesopotamia and Egypt—the ancestors of Western art and civilization.

The Mesopotamians and the Egyptians built their societies around mighty rivers, which enabled them to develop agriculture and therefore establish permanent settlements. This permanence, in turn, led to the development of architecture, the standardization of religions and rituals, and the creation of a social climate in which art could flourish. Our study of ancient art, therefore, now turns to the regions of these great rivers—the Tigris and Euphrates in Mesopotamia and the Nile in Egypt.

MESOPOTAMIA

The land we know as Mesopotamia occupied a large, flat area made fertile by its two rivers, the Tigris and the Euphrates, roughly in the area of modern-day Syria and Iraq. Many archaeologists and historians believe that the biblical

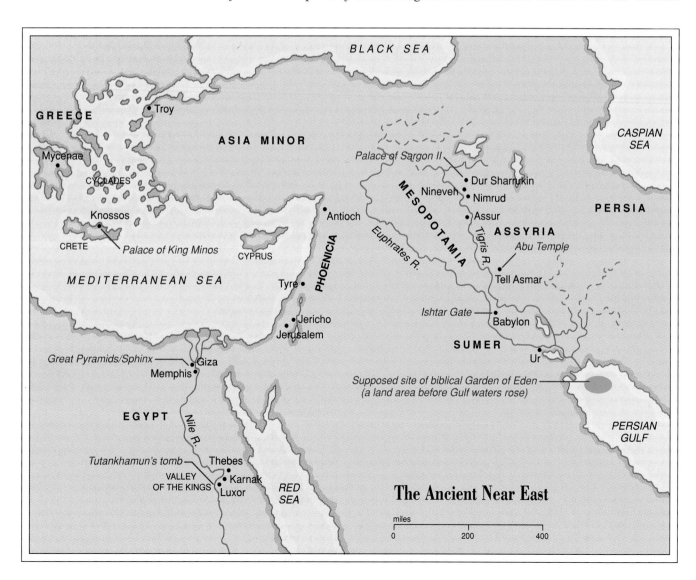

The Ancient Near East

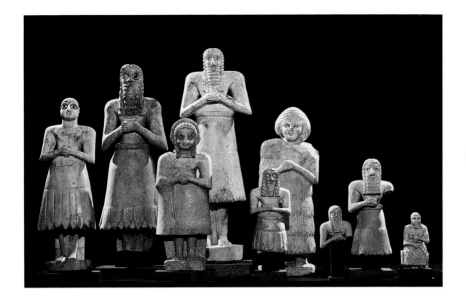

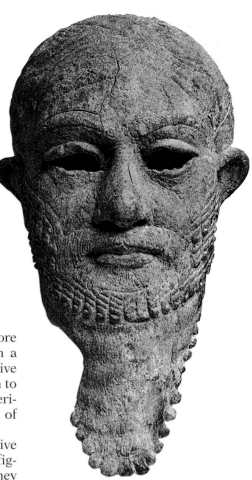

Garden of Eden was located here, at a point near where the rivers join before flowing into the Persian Gulf (map, opposite). Owing to its location on a plain, Mesopotamia had few natural defenses against invasion, and successive waves of people conquered the region. Five kingdoms or peoples are known to us for their distinguished art, and we will consider them in turn: the Sumerians, the Akkadians, the Babylonians, the Assyrians, and a second wave of Babylonians whose culture is referred to as Neo-Babylonian.

The unique character of **Sumerian** art is exemplified by a group of votive statues from the Abu Temple at Tell Asmar **(408)**. The identities of these figures are not clear, but it is assumed they serve Abu, god of vegetation, and they represent priests and worshipers. No real attempt has been made to carve these figures naturalistically; the bodies are extremely stylized, and some of the figures seem rather like decorated cylinders. Each has the hands clasped in the ritual Sumerian gesture of worship. The male figures show the heavily textured beards characteristic of this art, and the lips are curved upward as though to smile—a convention that means those depicted are alive, not dead, though not necessarily happy. But the most extraordinary and riveting feature of each statue is the eyes, which are enormous and carved in a fixed stare. Outlined in black and inset with colored stones and shells, the eyes apparently served as the medium of communication between the worshipers and their gods. They give to these sculptures an exotic appearance very different from that of most Western art from ancient times.

The **Akkadians,** who conquered most of Sumerian territory by about 2300 B.C.E., introduced the concept of loyalty to a specific ruler, rather than to a city-state. We know that their most prominent king was Sargon I, but we do not know the identity of the man depicted in a splendid *Head* found at Nineveh **(409).** Experts assume he was a ruler because of the piece's fine workmanship and costly material (copper). The lifelike features—heavy-lidded eyes, strong nose, sensitive mouth, and outthrust ears—argue that this is a naturalistic portrait of a real person and not a generic or idealized head, and such naturalism is extremely rare in early art. Even though the eyes are but hollows in the metal, we seem to read their expression, to understand this man as a wise, powerful, and dignified leader.

There is no question who was the dominant ruler of the **Babylonians.** Hammurabi, who united Mesopotamia as an empire and reigned from about 1792 to about 1750 B.C.E., has earned a place in history for his comprehensive legal system. The Code of Hammurabi, a collection of laws and edicts, deals with such issues as property rights, financial transactions, and domestic matters. Its underlying values are a stern—yet humane—sense of justice and pro-

left: 408.
Group of votive statuettes, from the Square Temple of the god Abu, Tell Asmar, Iraq. c. 2900–2600 B.C.E. Limestone, alabaster, and gypsum; height of tallest figure 30″. Courtesy of The Oriental Institute of the University of Chicago.

right: 409.
Head of a Dignitary, Akkadian. c. 2000 B.C.E. Copper, height 13½″. The Metropolitan Museum of Art, New York (Rogers Fund, 1947).

tection of the weak from the strong. Hammurabi's Code is inscribed on a stone tablet or **stele,** at the top of which the king is depicted in relief **(410).** We see Hammurabi at left, in a pose of reverential attention, receiving inspiration for his law code from the sun god, Shamash, at right. Seated on a throne meant to represent the holy mountain, with flames of the sun shooting from his shoulders, Shamash extends toward Hammurabi the symbols of divine power, the staff and ring. While Hammurabi is in full profile, the god appears in a combination view—part frontal (the torso), part profile (the head). This latter pose, which shows each body part to its best advantage, plays an important role in Egyptian art as well.

Because Mesopotamia's history over the centuries was a turbulent one marked by almost continual warfare and conquest, a major goal of architecture was the erection of mighty citadels to ensure the safety of temples and palaces. Such a citadel was that of the **Assyrian** ruler Ashurnasirpal II, built at Nimrud in the 9th century B.C.E. Ashurnasirpal's palace had gates fronted by monumental stone slabs carved into enormous human-headed winged beasts, a bull and a lion. The lion **(411)** wears a horned cap indicating divine status, while the animal's body is endowed with a device peculiar to this art style. It has five legs, so that from the front it appears motionless, but from the side it is understood as walking. Visitors to the citadel were meant to be impressed—and no doubt intimidated—by these majestic creatures.

When the Babylonians again came to power in Mesopotamia, late in the 7th century B.C.E., they formed a kingdom we call **Neo-Babylonian.** These "new" Babylonians surely must be ranked among the great architects of the ancient world. They developed a true arch before the Romans did and were masters of decorative design for architecture. Moreover, like their forebears, they had a formidable leader in the person of Nebuchadnezzar, an enthusiastic patron of the arts and architecture who built a dazzling capital city at Babylon.

A genuine planned city, Babylon was constructed as a square, bisected by the Euphrates River, with streets and broad avenues crossing at right angles. Stone is scarce in this region of Mesopotamia, and so the architects made liberal use of glazed ceramic bricks. Babylon must have been a city of brilliant color. Its main thoroughfare was the Processional Way, lined with many ver-

left: 410.
Stele of Hammurabi,
upper part, from Susa.
c. 1780 B.C.E. Basalt,
height of entire stele c. 7'4".
Louvre, Paris.

right: 411. *Human-Headed Winged Lion.* Assyrian, from Nimrud. 883–859 B.C.E. Limestone, height 10'2½". The Metropolitan Museum of Art, New York (gift of John D. Rockefeller, Jr., 1932).

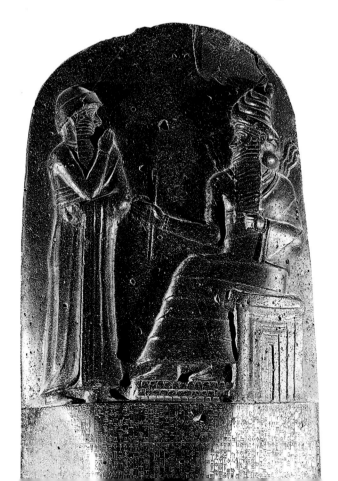

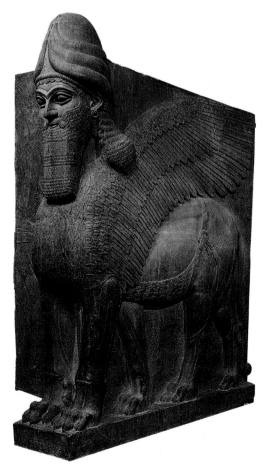

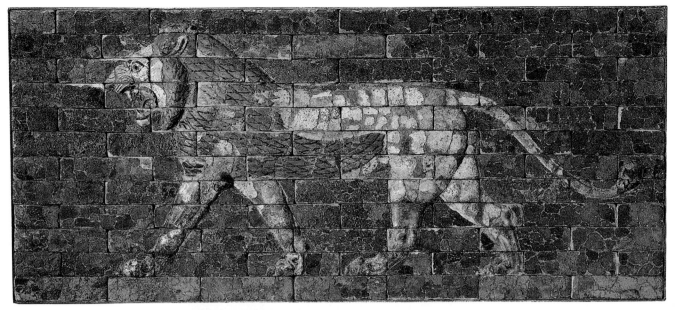

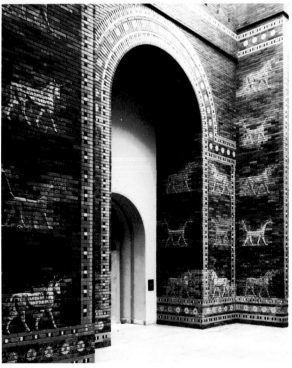

above: **412.** *Walking Lion,*
from Babylon. 6th century B.C.E.
Glazed brick, $3'2\frac{1}{4}'' \times 7'5\frac{1}{2}''$.
The Metropolitan Museum
of Art, New York
(Fletcher Fund, 1931).

left: **413.** Ishtar Gate (restored)
from Babylon, c. 575 B.C.E.
Enameled sun-dried brick,
height 48'9".
Near Eastern Museum,
State Museums, Berlin.

sions of a *Walking Lion* **(412)** molded in relief in reds and yellows against a
blue background. At one end of the Processional Way was the Ishtar Gate
(413), built about 575 B.C.E. and now restored in a German museum. The gate
consists of thousands of glazed mud bricks, with two massive towers flanking
a central arch. On ceremonial occasions Nebuchadnezzar would sit under the
arch in majesty to receive his subjects. The walls of the gate are embellished
with more glazed ceramic animals, probably meant as spirit-guardians.

The history of Mesopotamia parallels in time that of its neighbor to the southwest, the kingdom of Egypt, with which it had regular contacts. In Egypt,
however, we will find considerably less political turmoil. Protected on two
sides by the sea and elsewhere by the desert, Egypt was not subject to the
waves of immigration and invasion that continually transformed Mesopotamia—at least, not during the long period covered by this chapter.

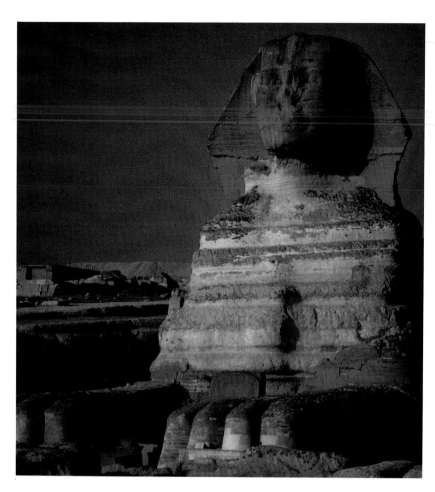

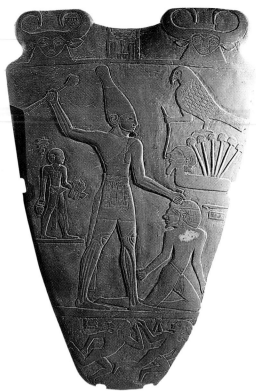

left: **414.** *The Great Sphinx.* c. 2530 B.C.E. Stone, height 65′. Giza, Egypt.

above: **415.** *Palette of King Narmer,* from Hierakonpolis. c. 3100 B.C.E. Slate, height 25″. Egyptian Museum, Cairo.

EGYPT

RELATED WORKS

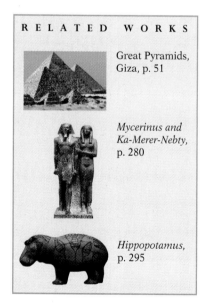

Great Pyramids, Giza, p. 51

Mycerinus and Ka-Merer-Nebty, p. 280

Hippopotamus, p. 295

The principal message of Egyptian art is continuity—a seamless span of time reaching back infinitely into history and forward into the future. The Sphinx **(414)**, the symbol of this most important characteristic of Egyptian art, is the essence of stability, order, and endurance. Built about 2530 B.C.E. and towering to a height of 65 feet, it faces into the rising sun, seeming to cast its immobile gaze down the centuries for all eternity. The Sphinx has the body of a reclining lion and the head of a man, thought to be the pharaoh Chefren, whose pyramid tomb is nearby. Egyptian kings ruled absolutely and enjoyed a semidivine status, taking their authority from the sun-god, Ra, from whom they were assumed to be descended. Power and continuity both are embodied in this splendid monument.

An even earlier relic from Egyptian culture, the so-called *Palette of King Narmer* **(415)**, illustrates many characteristics of Egyptian art. The Greek philosopher Plato wrote that Egyptian art did not change for ten thousand years; while this may be something of an exaggeration, there were many features that remained stable over long periods of time. The palette (so named because it is thought to have been a slab for mixing cosmetics) commemorates a victory by the forces of Upper Egypt, led by Narmer, over those of Lower Egypt, resulting in a unified kingdom. Narmer is the largest figure and is positioned near the center of the palette to indicate this high status. He holds a fallen enemy by the hair and is about to deliver the death blow. In the lowest sector of the tablet are two more defeated enemies. At upper right is a falcon representing Horus, the god of Upper Egypt. In its organization of images the palette is strikingly logical and balanced. The central section has Narmer's figure just to left of the middle, with his upraised arm and the form of a servant filling the space, while the falcon and the victim complete the right-hand side of the composition.

Narmer's pose is typical of Egyptian art and of art styles in other ancient cultures. When depicting an important personage, the Egyptian artist strove to show each part of the body to best advantage, so it could be "read" clearly by the viewer. Thus, Narmer's lower body is seen in profile, his torso full front, his head in profile, but his eye front again. This same pose recurs throughout most two-dimensional art in Egypt. It is believed that the priests, who had much control over the art, established this figure type and decreed that it be maintained for the sake of continuity. Obviously, it is not a posture that suggests much motion, apart from a stylized gesture like that of Narmer's upraised arm. But action was not important to Egyptian art. Order and stability were its primary characteristics, as they were the goals of Egyptian society. We see this in official sculptures, such as the double portrait of *Mycerinus and Ka-Merer-Nebty* in Chapter 11 **(325),** and also in less formal works.

A common sculpture type from the same period as the *Mycerinus* figure is the *Seated Scribe* **(416),** depicting a high court official whose position might be explained as "professional writer." In an era when literacy was rare, the scribe played a vital role in copying important documents and sacred texts, and his work commanded much respect. This sculpture, while somewhat more relaxed than standing pharaoh portraits, is still symmetrical and reserved. The scribe's face shows intelligence and dignity, and his body is depicted realistically as thickening and rather flabby, no doubt a sign of his age and sedentary occupation, perhaps also an indicator of wisdom.

Much of our knowledge about Egyptian life comes from a remarkable collection of small wooden models found in a tomb at Thebes, dating from about 1990 B.C.E. The tomb, uncovered in 1920, was that of Mekutra, a chancellor who served several pharaohs. To ensure his prosperity in the afterlife, Mekutra was buried with models of his house, his garden, the shops on his estate, his herd of cattle, and his fleet of boats **(417),** the last of these demonstrating the importance of the Nile River. The models are wonderfully detailed and crafted, painted in naturalistic colors.

below: 416. *Seated Scribe,* from Saqqara. c. 2400 B.C.E. Limestone, height 21". Louvre, Paris.

bottom: 417. *Model of a Boat,* from the tomb of Mekutra, Thebes. c. 1990 B.C.E. Gessoed and painted wood, height 14⅝". The Metropolitan Museum of Art, New York (Rogers Fund and Edward S. Harkness Gift, 1920).

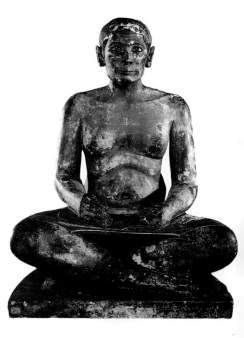

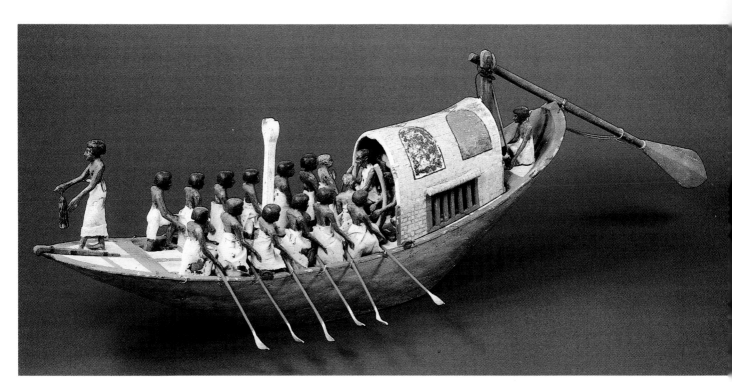

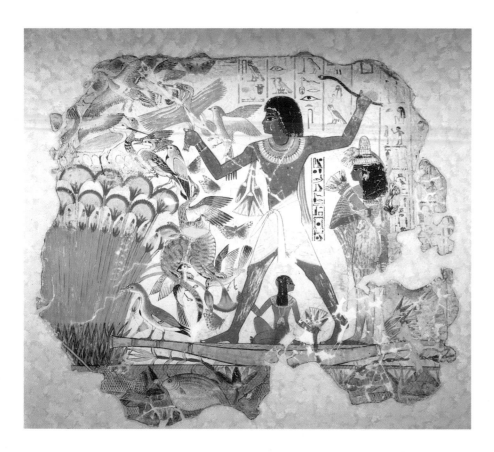

Egyptian painting reveals the same clear visual design and illustrative skill as the works in stone. A wall painting from Thebes **(418)**, depicting a hunting scene, poses the main figure very much like the figure of Narmer, although the two works are separated in time by some 1,650 years. Again the hunter's body is stylized: his head, eyes, torso, and legs are each shown from the most advantageous viewpoint. In keeping with the Egyptians' love of exact detail, this painter draws the birds and other creatures with almost biological precision. If we recognize the species, we can identify them. Even the fish are rendered meticulously; we don't see them as we would through a blur of water, but rather as we *know* the fish to look.

We know other things as well. We know that the hunter, probably a nobleman, is the most important figure in the composition, because he is the biggest. (This is called **hierarchical scale.**) Apart from clues provided by clothing, we know that he is a man and the figure at right is a woman. By convention, regardless of race or complexion, the Egyptians painted men darker (reddish) and women lighter (yellowish).

Above all, this work is beautifully composed. The artist has balanced the dominant figure of the hunter against a richness of sea, plant, and animal life. No area is left "empty." Our eyes find some subject of interest in every part of the painting, yet it doesn't seem crammed or busy or chaotic. In this instance the Egyptians' art shows both unity and a plentiful variety.

One brief period in the history of Egyptian culture stands apart from the rest and therefore has fascinated scholars and art lovers alike. This was the reign of pharaoh Amenhotep IV **(419)**, who came to power about 1353 B.C.E. For a civilization that prized continuity above all else, Amenhotep was a true revolutionary. He changed his name to Akhenaten and attempted to establish monotheism (belief in one god) among a people who had traditionally worshiped many gods. He built a new capital at what is now called Tell el-Amarna, so historians refer to his reign as the Amarna period. Akhenaten's dedication to truth (*maat*) led him to insist upon naturalistic depictions—rather than heroic ideals—of himself and his court, thus fostering a more relaxed style in art.

Nowhere is this more apparent than in the famous portrait bust of his queen, Nefertiti **(420A)**. While enchanted by Nefertiti's beauty, the modern viewer is perhaps even more taken by how contemporary she seems, how she appears to bridge the gap of more than three thousand years to our own world. With her regal headdress and elongated neck, Nefertiti presents a standard of elegance that is timeless. Despite her cool pose, however, she seems knowable, approachable, a woman who might smile and speak to us. Obviously, when the opportunity arose, the Egyptian sculptor was capable of great humanity and warmth, of letting a subject's real characteristics transcend convention.

Our image of Nefertiti has been so conditioned by the bust, reproduced in countless books, that we may be taken aback at seeing a statuette of the queen made just five or six years later, when she was perhaps forty **(420B)**. The long neck and the head thrust proudly forward are still there, but this is an older Nefertiti. She wears a caplike crown and a very thin linen garment. Signs of aging are evident throughout the figure: a softening jawline, sagging shoulders, drooping breasts, protruding belly. Why would the queen allow herself to be sculpted this way? One theory suggests that, since Nefertiti had become a co-ruler with Akhenaten, she had attained the status of "wise woman," and the bodily decline was considered appropriate to that prestigious role.

We are fortunate that so much art from ancient Egypt has been preserved, and the reason is that Egyptian culture meets all four of the conditions listed at the beginning of this chapter. The artists worked in durable materials, the climate is hot and dry, and the population was stable. Above all, the Egyptians buried the finest of their art with their dead.

Custom decreed that an important personage, especially a king, must be fitted out lavishly for the afterlife, with furnishings, jewelry, and artifacts of all kinds, made from the richest materials available. These objects were supposed to remain entombed with the dead pharaohs for all eternity. From earliest times, however, grave robbers have coveted that buried treasure—and not for its artistic merits. Most of the royal tombs uncovered in the Valley of the Kings, across the Nile from Luxor, were found nearly empty, stripped of their wealth. Only in this century, in 1922, did the full splendor of Egyptian art reveal itself to modern eyes. For in that year archaeologists located the one tomb that had remained virtually intact—the tomb of Tutankhamun.

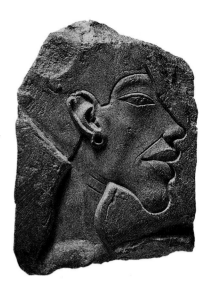

419. *Akhenaten (Amenhotep IV).* c. 1345 B.C.E. Limestone, height 3⅛". Egyptian Museum, State Museums, Berlin.

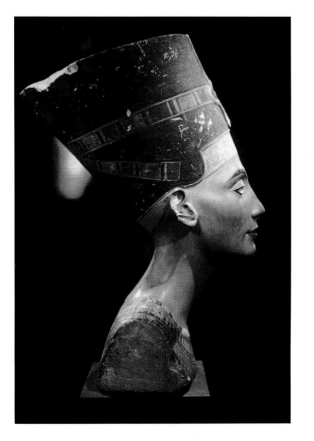

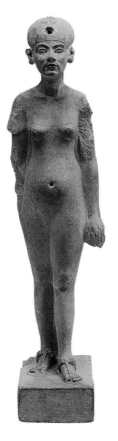

left: 420A. *Queen Nefertiti.* c. 1345 B.C.E. Limestone, height 20". Egyptian Museum, State Museums, Berlin.

right: 420B. *Statuette of Nefertiti.* c. 1340 B.C.E. Limestone, height 15¾". Egyptian Museum, State Museums, Berlin.

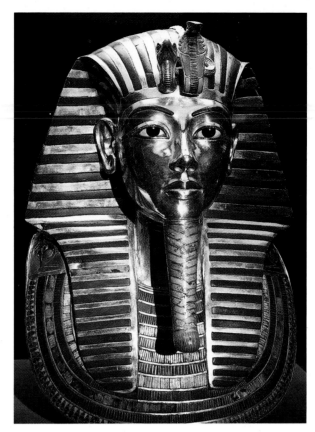

421. Burial mask of the pharaoh Tutankhamun. c. 1325 B.C.E. Gold, inlaid with blue glass and semiprecious stones; height 21¼″. Archaeological Museum, Cairo.

RELATED WORKS

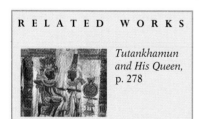

Tutankhamun and His Queen, p. 278

King "Tut," as the 1922 newspapers quickly dubbed him, was married as a young child to a daughter of Akhenaten and Nefertiti, and he succeeded Akhenaten to the throne. Crowned in about 1334 B.C.E. at the age of nine, he died just nine years later. Modern scholars knew of his existence and sought his tomb, wondering whether it, too, had been pillaged by grave robbers. One man in particular, an Englishman named Howard Carter, had spent ten years searching and was running out of time. His sponsor, the Earl of Carnarvon, intended to withdraw financial support. Three weeks before the deadline, Carter's workers found the entrance to the tomb. With Lord Carnarvon behind him, Carter made a hole in the door and stuck in a lighted candle. Unable to stand the suspense, Carnarvon cried, "Can you see anything?" "Yes," replied Carter, "wonderful things!"

Yes, the diggers had found wonderful things—things that had remained untouched even by light for more than three thousand years. Although a very young king, Tutankhamun had been sent into the hereafter in extraordinary style. His tomb was a veritable warehouse of priceless objects, made with superb craftsmanship, created from alabaster, precious stones, and above all gold—gold in unimaginable quantities. We saw the back of the pharaoh's throne, with its relief sculpture in gold, in Chapter 11. Tutankhamun's body, mummified to preserve it from decay, was encased in three coffins, nested one inside the other, the innermost crafted of solid gold. But perhaps most splendid of all the artworks is Tutankhamun's burial mask, which rested atop the mummy's head and shoulders **(421)**. Also of solid gold, ornamented with blue glass and semiprecious gems, the mask is thought to be a faithful depiction of Tutankhamun (insofar as the mummy remains agree), if somewhat idealized. The sculptor's hand was sure in molding the soft gold into a vibrant likeness.

Owing to extensive archaeological work in the area, we know more about ancient Egypt than about almost any early civilization. Gradually, however, we are learning more about Egypt's neighbor to the south, which in time may reveal a similarly brilliant artistic legacy.

WHOSE GRAVE IS THIS ANYWAY?

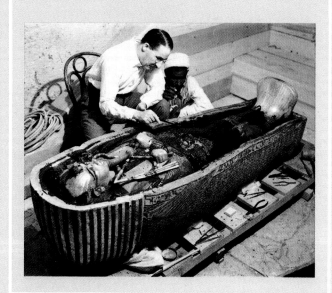

W HEN HOWARD CARTER and his party opened the tomb of the Egyptian king Tutankhamun in 1922, there was rejoicing around the world. The tomb was largely intact, not seriously pillaged by ancient grave robbers, so it still contained the wonderful artifacts that had been buried with the young king more than three millennia earlier. Over the next several years Carter and his team systematically photographed and catalogued the objects from the tomb, then transported them to the Cairo Museum.

There is a certain irony in this story that raises complex ethical questions. Why are Carter and his party not called grave robbers? Why are their actions in stripping the tomb acceptable—even praiseworthy—when similar behavior by common thieves would be deplored? No matter who opens a tomb and takes away its contents, that person is violating the intentions of those who sealed the tomb originally. No matter what the motivation, a human body that was meant to rest in peace for all time has been disturbed. Should this not make us feel uncomfortable?

From the beginning some were uneasy about the propriety of unearthing Tutankhamun's remains. When Lord Carnarvon, Carter's sponsor, died suddenly from a mosquito bite, and several others connected with the project experienced tragedies, rumors arose about the "curse of King Tut." But Carter himself died peacefully many years later, and the talk subsided.

Perhaps it is the passage of time that transforms grave robbing into archaeology. Carter would no doubt have been outraged if, say, his grandmother's coffin had been dug up to strip the body of its jewelry. But after three thousand years Tutankhamun has no relatives still around to protest.

Perhaps it is a question of the words we use to describe such ancient finds. We speak of Tutankhamun's "mummy," and mummy is a clean, historical-sounding word. Parents bring their children to museums to see the mummies and mummy cases. We can almost forget that a mummy is the embalmed body of a dead human being, pulled out of its coffin so that we can marvel at the coffin and sometimes the body itself.

Or, perhaps the difference between grave robbing and archaeology lies in the motives of the perpetrators. Common thieves are motivated by greed, by their quest for money to be made by selling stolen objects. Carter and his team did not sell the treasures from Tutankhamun's tomb but stored them safely in the Cairo Museum, where art lovers from around the world can see them. They were, in effect, making a glorious gift to the people of our century and centuries to come (while at the same time, one must point out, acquiring significant glory for themselves).

The basic issue is a clash of cultural values. To the Egyptians, it was normal and correct to bury their finest artworks with the exalted dead. To us, the idea of all that beauty being locked away in the dark forever seems an appalling waste. We want to bring it into the light, to have it as part of our precious artistic heritage. Almost no one, having seen these magnificent treasures, would seriously propose they be put back in the tomb and sealed up.

In the end, inevitably, our cultural values will prevail, simply because we are still here and the ancient Egyptians are not. After three thousand years, Tutankhamun's grave really isn't his anymore. Whether rightly or wrongly, it belongs to us.

Howard Carter and an assistant unwrapping the innermost of Tutankhamun's three nested coffins. The third coffin is solid gold and contained the king's mummified body.

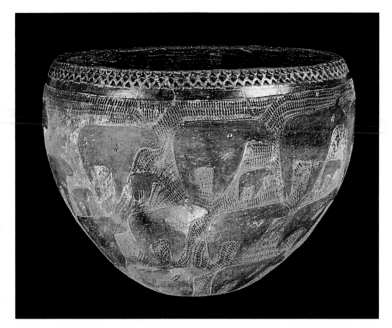

422. *The "Chicago Cattle Bowl."*
Nubian, found at Adindan.
c. 1900–1650 B.C.E.
Terra cotta with red slip,
diameter 5½″.
Courtesy of the Oriental Institute
of the University of Chicago.

NUBIA

The old kingdom of Nubia lay directly to the south of Egypt, occupying an area that stretches a thousand miles along the Nile River (map, p. 347) in what is now southern Egypt and northern Sudan. Scholars have long debated whether the Egyptians were racially black, with many arguing they were of mixed African, Mediterranean, and Asian descent. But there is no argument about the Nubians, who were unquestionably black Africans. Writing in the 5th century B.C.E., the Greek historian Herodotus asserted that the Nubians were the "tallest and handsomest" people on earth. The Romans described a southern Nubian empire ruled by queens. Nubian culture first emerged about 3800 B.C.E. and lasted well into our common era. Only in recent decades have Nubian studies begun to reveal the high level of sophistication this civilization attained.

Because their lands abutted and they shared a river, the Nubians and Egyptians had steady contacts. Nubia was apparently the source of most of Egypt's gold, as well as other precious commodities such as incense, ebony, and ivory. Nubia may also have been the inspiration for Egypt's political system. It is believed that Nubia pioneered in fidelity to a single ruler, divinely ordained, and that Egypt adopted this idea in establishing its pharaohs.

The climate of Nubian territory is exceptionally unwelcoming, for it is the hottest and driest on earth. This factor has no doubt contributed to the relatively scant archaeological work done at Nubian sites—scant, that is, compared to excavations in Egypt. An American archaeologist working in the early 20th century bestowed the unfortunately colorless names still used to designate two major Nubian cultures that have been identified: the A-Group and the C-Group.

The A-Group occupied Nubia from about 3800 to 3100 B.C.E. Evidence from a cemetery suggests this culture had powerful rulers and considerable wealth. From about 2300 to 1550 B.C.E. Nubia was dominated by the so-called C-Group, who are known to have been skilled cattle herders. A splendid ceramic bowl from this culture **(422)** is decorated with images of cattle, leading scholars to suspect the C-Group Nubians worshiped their gods through a cattle cult.

At present, only a few museums have collections of Nubian artwork, but this situation will likely change as excavations continue *and* as curators take a second look at some objects now labeled "Egyptian."

INDUS VALLEY

Far to the east, on the Indian subcontinent, another great culture formed around a mighty river, the Indus. We know very little about the people of what is called the Indus Valley Civilization, except that they built large, well-structured cities, the two most thoroughly excavated to date being Harappa and Mohenjo-Daro (map, p. 347). Their culture emerged about 2700 B.C.E. and flourished until about 1500 B.C.E., so they coexisted with the older Egyptian dynasties and with the Akkadian and Babylonian kingdoms in Mesopotamia.

Relatively few artworks from this civilization have been found, the most famous a tiny male torso from Harappa **(423)**. Some scholars dispute the date of 2000 B.C.E. for this figure, but if it is accurate the torso would be roughly contemporary with the Akkadian copper head **(409)**. Although it is less than 4 inches high, the little figure is modeled with amazing naturalism and well-observed musculature. The protruding abdomen has been interpreted as showing the breath control of a yogi, while the polished surface of the stone convincingly mimics the warm texture of human flesh.

CHINA

Developed civilization in China can be traced to at least 2000 B.C.E., and there were settlements even earlier in an area of northeast China now in Henan Province (map, p. 347). The first clear historical record, however, dates from the Shang Dynasty, which began about 1766 B.C.E. Shang rulers and those of the ensuing Zhou Dynasty, which took power about 1045 B.C.E., built large walled cities, grand palaces, and enormous tombs at a series of capitals in the Yellow River valley.

Shang and Zhou artists are best known for their sophisticated work in bronze casting of sculpture and ritual vessels. The *Tiger* shown here **(424)**, from the 9th century B.C.E., is thought to have been used as a base support for some large structure, perhaps a throne. Like most works from the period, it is covered with ornate geometric designs in relief. Chapter 11 (p. 268) explained the process of lost-wax casting. The Shang and Zhou bronzes were cast by a far more demanding method. Archaeologists speculate that the Chinese metalworkers were able to build multiple-section molds having a hollow core without benefit of any wax layer to hold the sections apart—an astonishing feat for any time. This tiger is elegantly stylized and has a wonderful balance of form, with its outthrust head poised to counterweigh the jauntily curling tail.

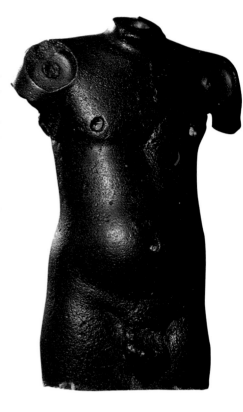

above: **423.** Torso, from Harappa, Indus Valley Civilization.
c. 2000 B.C.E.
Red sandstone, height 3¾".
National Museum, New Delhi.

below: **424.** *Tiger*, from China.
Late Zhou Dynasty,
9th century B.C.E.
Bronze, length 29⅝".
Courtesy of Freer Gallery of Art,
Smithsonian Institution,
Washington, D.C.

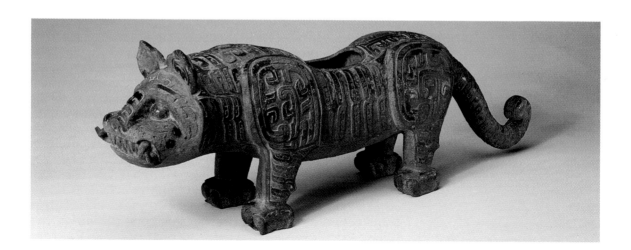

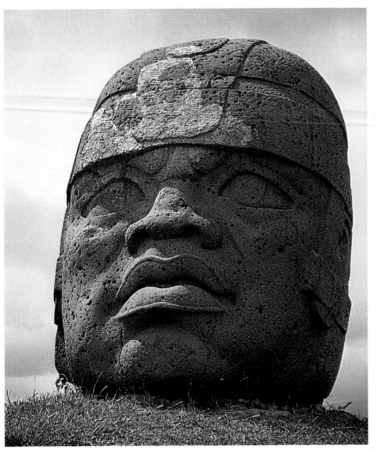

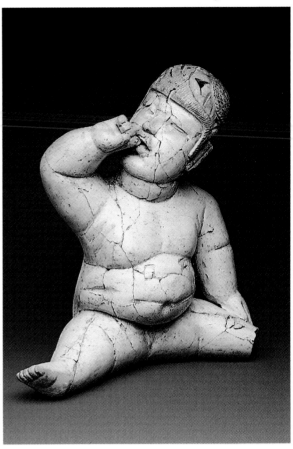

MESOAMERICA

Our discussion of the world's oldest art now moves half a world away, to one of the few very early cultures in the Western Hemisphere. In the fertile lowland on the Gulf coast of Mexico (maps, pp. 347, 522) a still-mysterious people called the Olmec flourished for more than a thousand years, beginning about 1500 B.C.E. The Olmec were farmers, widely dispersed through the region, but their society had certain religious and political centers, notably San Lorenzo and La Venta. At these two sites archaeologists have discovered a dozen huge heads carved from basalt, a very dense and hard stone **(425)**.

The heads are thought to be portraits of rulers, but there is no corroborating evidence for this theory. They may instead represent Olmec gods. Measuring up to 8 feet in height and weighing some 10 tons apiece, the heads have stylized features—broad, flat noses, heavy lips, hooded eyes. Each wears a caplike headdress with a distinctive design, no two alike. Basalt is not available in the area where the heads were found. The nearest source for the stone lies in the mountains at least 60 miles away. We know, then, that some compelling purpose caused the Olmec to drag these immense boulders over a great distance and then carve their surfaces into human form, but we do not know what that purpose was.

The Olmec also worked in ceramics, and a common form is the so-called "baby" figure **(426)**, of which several examples have been found. Almost life-size, the figure can be understood easily: a chubby infant sucking its finger. This one sports either a helmet or a fancy hair arrangement, which has been colored reddish-pink. No one knows why the Olmec crafted these baby figures. Some speculate they were little gods, or that they represented royal inheritance, but we can never be sure.

THE AEGEAN

For our last culture area in this chapter, we return to the place where we started: the southern regions of Europe near the Mediterranean Sea. If we were to sail northwest from Egypt, or west-northwest from Mesopotamia, we would reach the Aegean Sea, an arm of the Mediterranean separating Greece from what is now Turkey. Around the Aegean we find an important focus of early artistic production.

The artistic cultures of the Aegean parallel in time those of Egypt and Mesopotamia, for the earliest begins about 3000 B.C.E. There were three major Aegean cultures: the *Cycladic,* centered on a group of small islands in the Aegean; the *Minoan,* based on the island of Crete at the southern end of the Aegean; and the *Mycenaean,* on the mainland of Greece (maps, pp. 347, 367).

Cycladic art is a puzzle, because we know almost nothing about the people who made it. Nearly all consists of nude female figures like the one we saw in Chapter 2—simplified, abstract, composed of geometric lines and shapes and projections. The figures vary in size from the roughly 2-foot height of our example to approximately life-size, but they are much alike in style. Presumably they were meant as fertility images, although they are a far cry from the fleshier "Venuses" found earlier in the north **(406)**.

A rarer form in Cycladic art is the musician figure, such as the splendid seated *Harp Player* illustrated here **(427)**. This graceful statuette shows a compact composition and a lively immediacy. Simple as the carving is, we really *believe* the harpist is playing his instrument. The sculptor has lengthened the musician's arms to curve into the harp and given the arms a subtle musculature. And, although the face is almost as stylized as that of the female figure, we sense this musician is carried away by the pleasure of his music. To modern eyes the Cycladic figurines seem astonishingly sophisticated in their ability to reduce anatomical forms to the essence of shape.

The *Minoan* culture on Crete can be traced to about 2000 B.C.E. and centers around the great city of Knossos. We take the name from a legendary king called Minos, who supposedly ruled at Knossos and whose queen gave

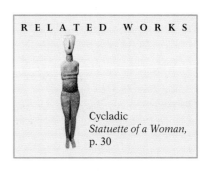
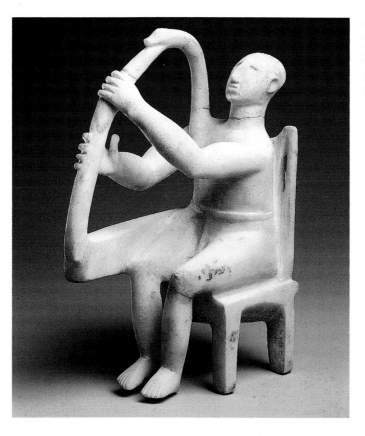

427. *Harp Player,* Cycladic.
c. 2700 B.C.E.
Marble, height 11½".
The Metropolitan Museum
of Art, New York
(Rogers Fund, 1947).

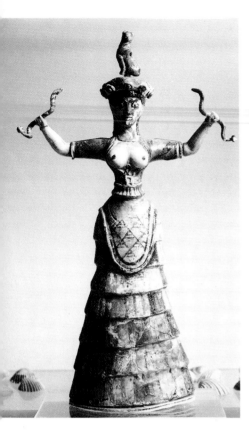

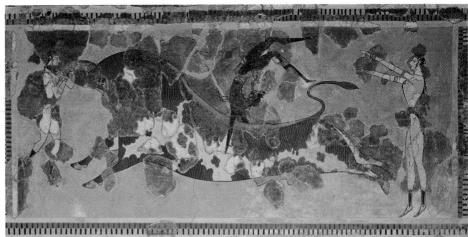

birth to the dreaded creature, half-human, half-bull, known as the Minotaur. The Minoans, being island dwellers, were a seafaring people, and much of their art depicts sea creatures—fishes and dolphins and octopuses. It is believed the Minoans worshiped a female deity, and this may be the identity of the *Snake Goddess* **(428)**, one of two similar figures discovered at the Palace of Knossos. With her bared breasts, tiny waist, and elaborate skirt, this figure resembles then-fashionable ladies of the court, yet she holds a wriggling snake in each hand. Some writers have suggested she is a priestess associated with a snake-handling cult, or perhaps a queen.

The Minoans were also skilled painters. Numerous frescoes survive at Knossos—some fragmentary, some restored—and from these we have formed an impression of a lighthearted, cheerful people devoted to games and sport. Among the finest wall paintings is a work known as the *Toreador Fresco* **(429)**, featuring the Minoans' special animal, the bull. This modern title suggests the Spanish sport of bullfighting (a *toreador* being a bullfighter), but we can see that the Minoans' game was unique to them. A young male acrobat vaults over the back of the racing bull; he will be caught in the waiting arms of the young woman at right. Another female player, at left, grasps the bull's horns; perhaps she is ready to take her turn somersaulting over the animal. Most striking here is the contrast between the hefty, charging bull and the lithe, playful flip of the acrobat. The composition is marvelously balanced, with the women at both sides serving as anchors, the tumbling male figure and the curving tail counter-weighing the massive bull's head. Many graceful curves—of the bull's back, the bull's underbelly, the tumbler's arched body—reinforce our experience of motion, captured to the split second.

Mycenaean culture, so called because it formed around the city of Mycenae, flourished on the south coast of the Greek mainland from about 1600 to 1100 B.C.E. Like the Minoans, the Mycenaeans built palaces and temples, but they are also noted for their elaborate burial customs and tombs—a taste apparently acquired from the Egyptians, with whom they had contact. It seems probable that Egypt or Nubia was also the source of the Mycenaeans' great supplies of gold, for they alone among the Aegean cultures were master goldsmiths. Burial places in and around Mycenae have yielded large quantities of exquisite gold objects, such as the *rhyton*, or drinking cup, in the shape of a lion's head **(430)**. The craftsmanship of this vessel is wonderful, contrasting smooth planar sections on the sides of the face with the more detailed snout and mane. The Mycenaeans also used gold for masks, jewelry, and weapons.

Each of the culture regions introduced in this chapter started a path of artistic development stretching from the misty beginnings of ancient history to our own time. In the following chapters, we will follow these paths, concentrating first on the one most familiar to us—the tradition of Western art history.

above: 428. *Snake Goddess*, Minoan, from Knossos, Crete. c. 1600 B.C.E. Terra cotta, height 17½". Archaeological Museum, Herakleion, Crete.

above right: 429. *Toreador Fresco*, from the Palace of King Minos at Knossos, Crete. c. 1500 B.C.E. Fresco, height c. 32". Archaeological Museum, Herakleion, Crete.

below: 430. Rhyton in the shape of a lion's head, from Mycenae. c. 1550 B.C.E. Gold, height 8". National Museum, Athens.

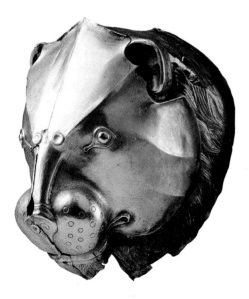

CHAPTER FIFTEEN

Greece
and Rome

Wᴴᴇɴ ᴡᴇ ᴜsᴇ the word "Classical" in connection with Western civilization, we are referring to the two cultures discussed in this chapter—ancient Greece and ancient Rome. The term itself indicates an aesthetic bias, for anything "classic" is supposed to embody the highest possible standard of quality, to be the very best of its kind. If true, this would mean that Western art reached a pinnacle in the few hundred years surrounding the start of our common era and has not been equaled in the millennium and a half since then. This is a controversial idea that many would dispute vehemently. Few can deny, however, that the ancient Greeks and Romans *intended* to achieve the highest standards. Art and architecture were matters of public policy, and it was accepted that there could be an objective, shared standard for the best, the purest, the most beautiful. Except for the Renaissance period in Italy, no other Western culture has undertaken the quest for artistic excellence so deliberately and self-consciously as those long-ago citizens of Greece and Rome.

GREECE

No doubt a major reason we so respect the ancient Greeks is that they excelled in many different fields. Their political ideals serve as a model for contemporary democracy. Their poetry and drama and philosophy survive as living classics, familiar to every serious scholar. Their architecture and sculpture have influenced most later periods in the history of Western art.

It is assumed the Greeks' genius shone equally in painting, but we know very little about this because most painted works have been lost. We would know even less were it not for the large number of painted clay vases that were produced from about the 8th century B.C.E. In Chapter 11 we noted that terra cotta (baked clay) is an extremely durable material; it can shatter but will not disintegrate, and so the pieces can be reassembled. For this reason a large quantity of Greek art has survived to our day.

Few cultures can match the Greeks in the elaborate painting of vases, which represent a major part of their artistic output. These terra cotta vessels served as grave monuments, storage urns for wine or oil, drinking cups, and so forth. An early example is the so-called *Dipylon Vase* **(431)**, named for the cemetery in Athens where it was found. Made in the 8th century B.C.E., the *Dipylon Vase* offers a superb example of the *geometric style* of vase painting, the first clearly defined style we know the Greeks to have followed. The reason for this term is obvious. Much of the vase's decoration consists of geometric lines and patterns, including the "meander" pattern that runs around the top just under the rim. Images of people are little more than stick figures, and they are integrated wonderfully in the overall geometric design.

The *Dipylon Vase* provides an interesting commentary on the burial customs of the Greeks, especially as contrasted with the Egyptians. The pharaoh Tutankhamun's tomb was elaborately fitted out for a prestigious afterlife, since that is what the Egyptians expected. The Greeks were not so optimistic. To them, life beyond the grave was a gray and shadowy place, of little interest. A funerary urn like the *Dipylon Vase* was placed above the burial spot to receive liquid offerings and was intended to show the respect of the deceased's relatives. A funeral procession is painted on the vase. But there is no provision for enjoyment of the next world, only recognition of the one left behind.

Through later centuries Greek vase painting prospered. Our next illustration **(432)** shows a *kylix* (a drinking cup) representing *Eos and Memnon*. The painting is in the *red-figure style,* which developed late in the 6th century B.C.E. A background of black was created from the glaze, leaving the figures in the natural red color of the clay. Despite this technically difficult technique, the painting is remarkably fine. Eos, the goddess of dawn, holds the body of her dead son, Memnon, who has been killed by the hero Achilles. There is a suggestion of depth in the overlapping of Memnon's body in front of Eos and in the crossed legs; the dangling arms of the body visually balance Eos' outspread wings. Finely drawn textures of gown, hair, and wings reveal the skill of the painter's brush. As a mark of the esteem in which vase painters were held, and their pride in the work, this kylix is signed by the painter, Douris.

While all Greek and Roman art is broadly termed Classical, one particular Greek era, the 5th and 4th centuries B.C.E., is (somewhat confusingly) known as the *Classical period.* At that time Greece consisted of several independent city-states, often at war among themselves. Chief among the city-states—from an artistic and cultural point of view, if not always a military one—was Athens.

left: 431. *Dipylon Vase,* Greek, from Athens. 8th century B.C.E. Terra cotta, height 42⅝". The Metropolitan Museum of Art, New York (Rogers Fund, 1914).

right: 432. Douris. *Eos and Memnon,* interior of an Attic red-figure kylix. c. 490–480 B.C.E. Terra cotta, diameter 10½". Louvre, Paris.

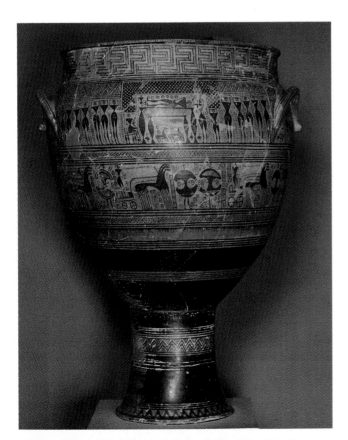

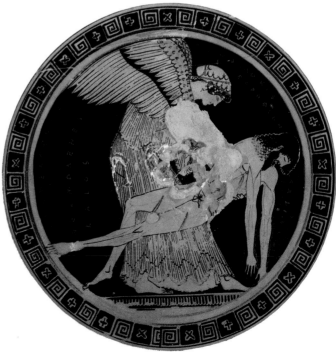

C H R O N O L O G Y

	800–400 B.C.E.	400 B.C.E.–150 C.E.
Style/Period	Geometric period, Greece, c. 800–c. 650 Etruscan period, Italy, c. 700–c. 500 Archaic period, Greece, c. 650–c. 500 Roman Republic, 510–27 Classical period, Greece, c. 500–c. 320	Roman Republic, 510–27 B.C.E. Hellenistic period, Greece, c. 320–30 B.C.E. Roman Empire established, 27 B.C.E.

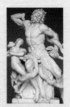

Laocoön Group

| **Political/
Social Events
and
Personalities** | Rome founded, c. 753
Pericles, ruler of Athens, c. 449–429 | Augustus, emperor of Rome,
  27 B.C.E.–14 C.E.
Jesus Christ (c. 4 B.C.E.–c. 29 C.E.)
Pompeii destroyed, 79 C.E.
Trajan, emperor of Rome, 72–80 C.E. |

Wall painting, Pompeii

| **Monuments
and
Major Artists** | Parthenon, Athens, 447–432
Phidias (d. 432) | *Laocoön Group*, late 2nd century
  B.C.E.
Pont du Gard, France,
  1st century B.C.E.
Augustus of Prima Porta, c. 20 B.C.E.
Colosseum, Rome, 72–80 C.E.
Pantheon, Rome, 118–125 C.E.
Praxiteles (c. 390–c. 330 B.C.E.) |

Pont du Gard

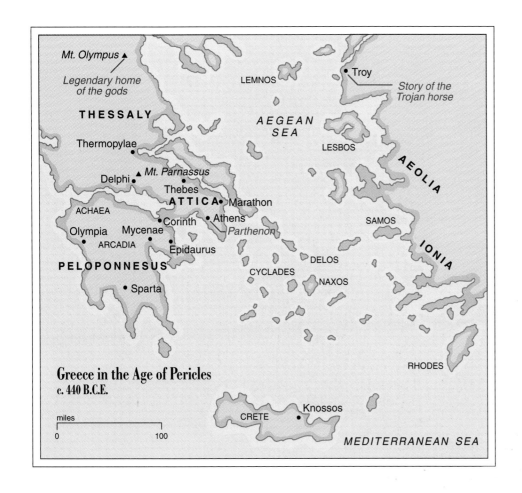

Greece in the Age of Pericles
c. 440 B.C.E.

miles
0   100

Like many Greek cities, Athens had been built around a high hill, or *acropolis*. Ancient temples on the Acropolis had crumbled or been destroyed in the wars. About 449 B.C.E. Athens' great general Pericles came to power as head of state and set about rebuilding. He soon embarked on a massive construction program, meant not only to restore the past glory of Athens but to raise it to a previously undreamed-of splendor.

Pericles' friend, the sculptor Phidias, was given the job of overseeing all architectural and sculptural projects on the Acropolis. The work would continue for several decades, but it took an amazingly short time given the ambitious nature of the scheme. By the end of the century the Acropolis probably looked much like the reconstruction shown here (433). The large columned building at lower right in the photo is the Propylaea, the ceremonial gateway to the Acropolis through which processions winding up the hill would pass. At left in the photo, the building with columned porches is the Erechtheum, placed where Erechtheus, legendary founder of the city, supposedly lived.

But the crowning glory of the Acropolis was and is the Parthenon (434). In previous chapters we have considered the Parthenon as a monument to religious devotion (47) and as an example of post-and-lintel architecture (pp. 307–308). Here let us examine it as the pinnacle of Greek art in what we have come to think of as its Golden Age.

Dedicated to the goddess Athena *parthenos*, or Athena the warrior maiden, the Parthenon is a Doric-style temple (p. 307) with columns all around the exterior and an inner row of columns on each of the short walls. The roof originally rose to a peak, leaving a triangular area or *pediment* (visible in the reconstruction) at each end. The pediments were decorated with sculptures, as was the *frieze*, the narrow band running all around the building just under the roof. In the manner of Greek temples, the Parthenon was

below: 433.
Model reconstruction of the Acropolis, Athens, viewed from the northwest. Courtesy of the Royal Ontario Museum, Toronto.

bottom: 434.
Ictinus and Callicrates. Parthenon, Athens. 447–432 B.C.E.

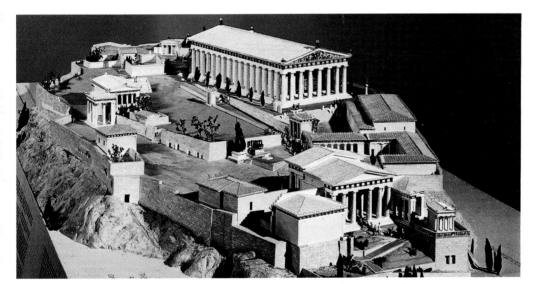

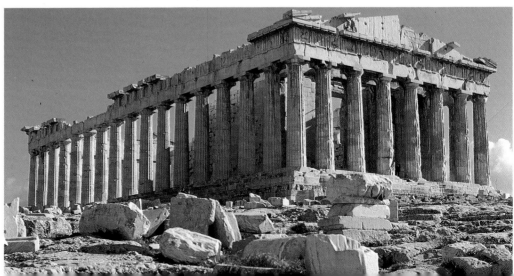

368

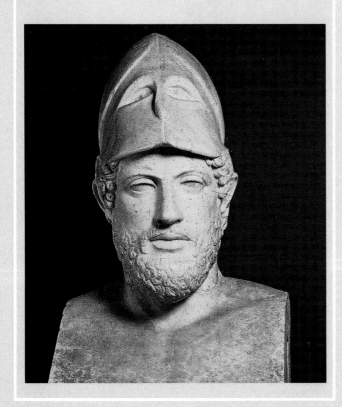

PERICLES

After an early military career, he became active in the government of Athens. About 449 B.C.E. Pericles was elected head of state, a post he held until his death.

An arranged marriage to a cousin produced two sons but little domestic happiness. All sources agree that the companion of Pericles' heart was the beautiful and brilliant Aspasia, a *hetaera*, or upper-class courtesan, with whom he lived openly for many years. Aspasia was possessed of wit and charm that drew to her side (and therefore to Pericles' side) the great artists and thinkers of the day, even Socrates himself. She seems also to have been a clever political adviser.

According to the ancient biographer Plutarch, Pericles excelled not only as a general and statesman but also as an orator, whose "tongue was armed with thunder and lightning." But for our purposes in this book another trait stands out: Pericles had both the means and the vision to become an incomparable patron of the arts.

Soon after assuming power in Athens, Pericles gave his friend, the sculptor Phidias, the task of rebuilding the temples on the Acropolis—but rebuilding them on a far more elaborate scale. Under Pericles' sponsorship, Plutarch remarks, "many edifices, each of which would seem to have required the labor of several successive ages, were finished during the administration of one prosperous man."[1] The jewel of these was, of course, the Parthenon (**434**), built with hand labor and embellished with many sculptures in just fifteen years.

Pericles took a lively interest in the other arts as well. The theater, offering both dramas and comedies, prospered in that time, and Pericles saw to it that all citizens received free tickets. He built a music hall, the Odeum, and personally judged the musical contests held each year. This exhilarating climate for the arts continued until a plague swept Athens in 430 B.C.E. Although Pericles recovered from the disease, he was weakened and died the next year.

We who so highly value the Parthenon, even in its ruined state, cannot imagine it not existing, yet Pericles' building program was not universally popular. Critics charged he had emptied the treasury to serve his own ambitions. But Pericles' ambitions were not for himself. They were for Athens, for her glory in those times and her glory down through the ages. He spoke of it this way: "What I would prefer is that you should fix your eyes every day on the greatness of Athens as she really is, and should fall in love with her."[2]

HIS ENEMIES CALLED HIM "onionhead." Contemporary writers tell us that Pericles had an unusually high, sloping brow reaching up to a domed crown of the head, and that he is always portrayed wearing a helmet to cover this supposed deformity. For modern students, however, the term "onionhead" may take on another meaning. We peel away layer after layer, yet we never fully understand this complex man who is so admired 2,400 years after his death.

Pericles was born about 495 B.C.E., son of the Athenian general Xanthippus. Being of a noble family, he received a thorough education, first from Damon, the master of music—"music" in those times understood to include reading, writing, mathematics, singing, and poetry. Later he studied with the master philosopher Anaxagoras. Under these teachers Pericles developed habits of independent thought, enormous self-discipline, and (even his rivals admitted) unblemished integrity.

Pericles. Roman copy after a Greek original of c. 429 B.C.E., probably by Kresilas. Marble. Vatican Museums, Rome.

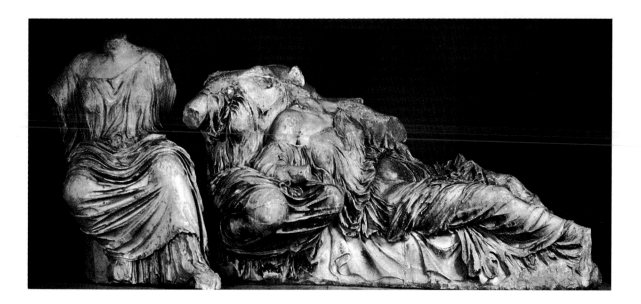

painted in vivid colors, principally red and blue. The architects Ictinus and Callicrates, directed by Phidias, completed the structure in just fifteen years.

The inner chamber of the Parthenon, called the **cella,** once housed a monumental statue of the goddess, made by Phidias himself of gold and ivory and standing 30 feet tall atop its pedestal. Contemporary sources tell us Phidias was an artist of unsurpassed genius, but we must take their word for it, since neither the Athena statue nor any of his original sculptures are known to survive (although copies exist). Many other sculptures from the Parthenon have been preserved, however, and these were probably made by Phidias' students, under his supervision.

One existing sculpture group, now in the British Museum, depicts *Three Goddesses* **(435)**. In Pericles' time this group stood near the far right side of the pediment; if you imagine the figures with their heads intact, you can see how they fit into the angle of the triangle. Carved from marble and now headless, these goddesses still seem to breathe and be capable of movement, so convincing is their roundness. The draperies flow and ripple naturally over the bodies, apparently responding to living flesh underneath.

The Parthenon sculptures represent a high point in the long period of Greek experimentation with carving in marble. We can trace this evolution from the 6th to the 2nd century by comparing three treatments of a favorite Greek sculpture type—the nude male figure. While many marble statues were of females, the most typical Greek figure is male, a nude superbly proportioned to indicate an ideal of physical perfection.

The Greeks' approach to sculpture was a radical departure from artistic precedents in other parts of the Mediterranean world. Egyptian sculptures more often were attached to a support; Greek figures generally are freestanding, in the round. Egyptian figures usually were clothed; the Greeks introduced total nudity in the male figure and in later centuries moved toward increasing nudity in female statues **(50)**. Most of the Egyptian sculptures we know are of pharaohs, their queens, their children, and other members of the court. The Greeks seem to have been far more interested in physical beauty than in high status. To be sure, some of their finest sculptures represent gods, but they are gods in human form—magnificent human form. And many are depictions of anonymous young men, to whom scholars have given the name **kouros,** meaning "youth" or "boy."

The reasons for this new approach to sculpture are clear from Greek philosophy and literature. Whereas the Egyptians emphasized continuity of the state, the Greeks sought perfection of the state *through* perfection of the individual. The ideal human body symbolized an ideal divine soul, dedicated to the highest principles. If perfection could be chiseled into marble, then perhaps the sought-after perfection in human affairs could be attained.

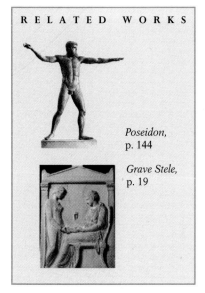

Three figures, made over a period of about 150 years, will show the enormous progress of Greek sculptors in striving toward an ideal of naturalism and physical perfection. The first is a *kouros* that dates from the early **Archaic** period, around 600 B.C.E. **(436)**. This work is a fairly crude attempt at freeing the nude body from its original block of stone. We can almost envision the cube of marble the sculptor began with from the square appearance of the form. Although more than 6 feet tall, the figure seems puny and underdeveloped, its torso too small and slender, its shoulders too narrow. The hair is a stylized braid, the eyes blank and staring, the feet featureless slabs with rigid cylinders for toes. Nevertheless, this sculptor has made great strides toward a natural approach, especially when we compare the *kouros* with earlier Egyptian figural statues **(325)**. The musculature of arms and legs has been studied carefully, the legs separated from one another, the arms separated from the body.

Another *kouros*, carved some seventy-five years later but still in the Archaic period **(437)**, shows considerable progress toward naturalism. This body is far better proportioned, the hips and torso broader, the arms and legs well-developed. We can easily believe a human body might be shaped like this, which is hard to imagine of the earlier *kouros*. In spite of these advances, however, the sculpture retains a blocklike quality, is still imprisoned in the cube of stone. The left foot is set slightly forward to suggest motion, but we do not really believe in that motion because the hips and shoulders are level and the arms held rigidly at the sides. If you try to assume this pose, you will find it almost impossible, for when you take a step forward with one foot, the opposing hip and shoulder go up, and your arms move in counterbalance. There is no indication of this in the statue. On the *kouros'* face is an expression that has been dubbed the "archaic smile"—a rather forced grimace apparently meant to convey animation. (Compare the "smiles" on the Sumerian figures **[408]**, which indicate the people are alive, not dead.)

Now let us compare the *Spear Bearer* by the great sculptor Polyclitus **(438)**, made yet another seventy-five years or so later, in the **Classical** period of the 5th century B.C.E. (Like so many Greek statues, the original bronze of the *Spear Bearer* has been lost and is known to us only through later, and probably inferior, Roman copies in marble.) Here we find the *contrapposto* of a figure in motion (p. 281). With the weight on the right foot, the left knee is bent, the left hip and shoulder rise, the arms reach outward from the body, and the whole form stands in a relaxed S-curve suggestive of movement. The musculature of

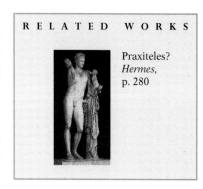
left: 436. *Kouros.* c. 600 B.C.E. Marble, height 6′4″. The Metropolitan Museum of Art, New York (Fletcher Fund, 1932).

center: 437. *Kroisos (Kouros from Anavysos).* c. 525 B.C.E. Marble, height 6′4″. National Museum, Athens.

right: 438. *Doryphorus (Spear Bearer).* Roman copy after a Greek original of c. 450–440 B.C.E. by Polyclitus. Marble, height 6′6″. National Museum, Naples.

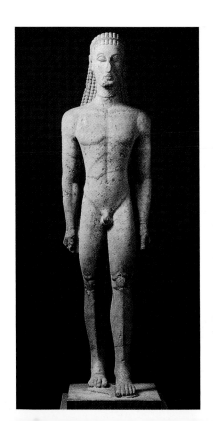

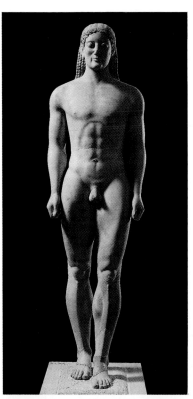

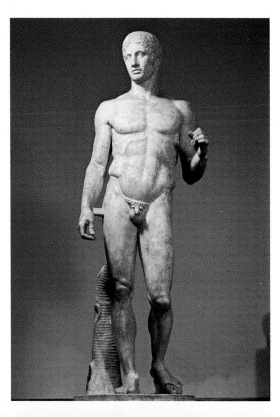

RELATED WORKS

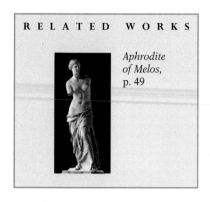

*Aphrodite
of Melos,*
p. 49

a well-developed body has been carefully observed and recorded. Gone is the archaic smile, to be replaced by a natural, pensive expression. We must consider this sculpture in terms of what the Greeks had set out to do. They intended to show a perfectly formed body, at the peak of its youthful strength, rendered in as lifelike a manner as possible. At this they succeeded admirably.

The last phase of Greek art, occurring roughly in the three hundred years B.C.E., is known as **Hellenistic**—a term that refers to the spread of Greek culture eastward to Mesopotamia and Egypt. Hellenistic sculpture tends to be more dramatic and emotional than that of the Classical 5th century; it has more of a tendency to push out into space and is more dynamic. One of the best-known examples of this style is the *Laocoön Group* **(439)**, dated to the late 2nd century B.C.E.

Laocoön was a priest of the sun-god, Apollo, and his story involves one of the most famous events in Greek mythology. In the last year of the war between the Greeks and the Trojans, the Greeks devised a fabulous ruse to overrun the city of Troy. They built a giant wooden horse, concealed inside it a large number of Greek soldiers, and wheeled it up to the gates of Troy, claiming it was an offering for the goddess Athena. While the people of Troy were trying to decide whether to admit the horse, their priest, Laocoön, suspected a trick and urged the Trojans to keep the gates locked. (Here is the source of the well-known warning about "Greeks bearing gifts.") This angered the sea-god, Poseidon, who held bitter feelings toward Troy, and he sent two dreadful serpents to strangle Laocoön and his sons. The sculpture depicts the priest and his children in their death throes, entwined by the deadly snakes.

Compared with statues from the Classical period, such as the *Spear Bearer*, the *Laocoön Group* seems almost theatrical. Its subject matter, filled with drama and tension, would have been unthinkable three centuries earlier. The Classical sculptor wanted to convey an outward serenity, and thus showed the hero in perfection but not in action, outside of time, not throwing the spear but merely holding it. Hellenistic sculptors were far more interested than their predecessors in how their subjects reacted to events. Laocoön's reaction is a violent, anguished one, and the outlines of the sculpture reflect this. The three figures writhe in agony, thrusting their bodies outward in different directions, pushing into space. Unlike earlier figures, with their dignified reserve, this sculpture projects a complicated and intense movement.

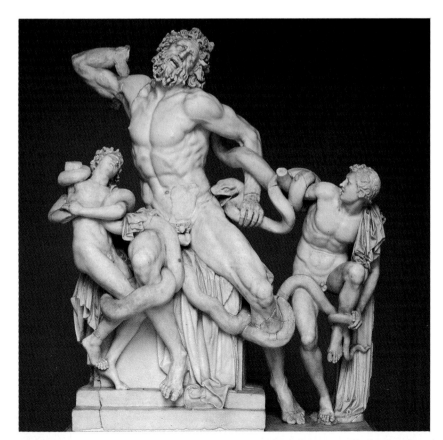

439. Agesander, Athenodorus, and Polydorus of Rhodes. *Laocoön Group.* Late 2nd century B.C.E., or possibly Roman copy of 1st century B.C.E. Marble, height 8'. Vatican Museums, Rome.

RESTORATION

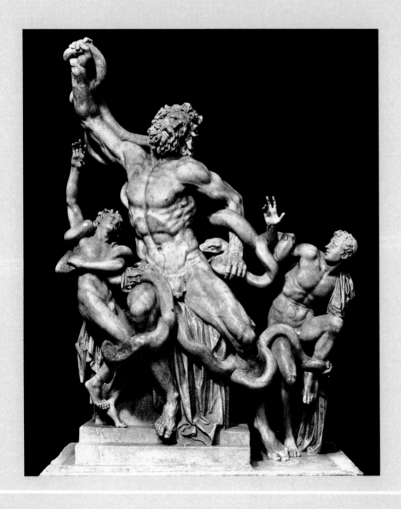

Arguments are most likely to rage when nobody knows exactly what a particular work of art looked like in its original condition. The *Laocoön* statue from 2nd-century B.C.E. Greece is often given as the extreme example of restoration gone wild, and also of the tendency for restorations to mirror the prevailing fashions and tastes of a given period.

When the *Laocoön* sculpture was found in Italy in 1506, it was already damaged; the right arms of all three figures in the group were missing. Since then, no fewer than six restorers have, so to speak, taken a crack at repairing the sculpture, with mixed results. The first major restoration was done in 1532–33, at which time the figures were provided with outstretched arms much like those in our illustration. Art historians generally agree that restorers of the Renaissance viewed themselves as creative "remodelers," rather than mere repair technicians, so they considered it entirely correct to do over a statue to their own satisfaction. From that point the story becomes complicated.

New plaster arms were made in the 17th century, but they were superseded by marble arms attached in the 18th century. During the 19th century earlier versions of the two sons' arms were replaced, as was a terra cotta version of the 16th-century arm made for Laocoön. To satisfy the prudish sensibilities of the 19th century, "fig leaves" were added to cover the men's nakedness. Finally, in 1954 a thorough study of the statue was undertaken, and all the restorations were removed in 1960. As of that date—that is, as of the mid-20th century—classical experts feel the *Laocoön* is as close as possible to the sculptors' original intent. Naturally, the 21st century may have different ideas.

The *Laocoön Group*
with early restorations (now removed).

W HEN ARTWORKS have been harmed, or have deteriorated with age, or have somehow been broken, there is a natural desire to fix them—to undo the damage and restore works to their original states. The general term for this process is *restoration*. In theory restoration sounds idealistic and desirable, but in practice it is often highly controversial. A major area of contention usually revolves around the question: How much? Or, more broadly, how much restoration work should be done, and what kind, and who decides?

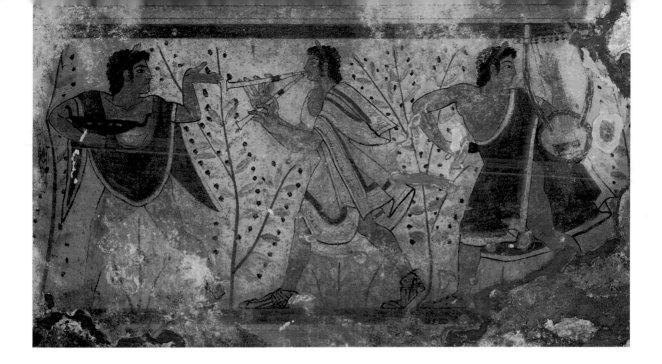

440. *Cup Bearer and Musicians,* from the Tomb of the Leopards, Etruscan Necropolis, Tarquinia. c. 480–470 B.C.E. Fresco, height 3′6″.

According to legend, the Trojans disregarded Laocoön's warning and brought the wooden horse into their city. That night the Greek soldiers slipped out of the horse, pillaged Troy, and destroyed it. Only a few of the Trojans escaped, including Aeneas, who sailed away and, after many adventures, landed at the mouth of the Tiber River and founded the city of Rome. Whether or not one chooses to believe the old myths, it is nevertheless true that the history of Western art and civilization now shifts westward, to the Italian peninsula. There we encounter a people whose culture was contemporary with that of the Greeks but about whom we know comparatively little, very likely because their home territory was soon to be thoroughly dominated by the mighty empire of Rome.

THE ETRUSCANS

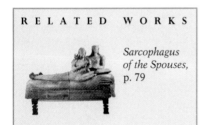
The Etruscans inhabited the Italian peninsula from about the 7th century B.C.E. or earlier. They remain mysterious to us, because no written records or literature has survived. Most of what we know, in fact, comes from Etruscan tombs, which explains why any discussion of the Etruscans' art tends to emphasize burial customs.

At the risk of being too casual, we might say that the Etruscans loved a good funeral. Apparently, they had a rather cheerful idea of death and the afterlife, markedly in contrast to the Greeks. In Chapter 3 we saw an Etruscan sarcophagus, or burial coffin, on which sculptured images of a dead couple recline gracefully, enjoying a pleasant life beyond the grave. Wall paintings from Etruscan tombs testify to that same optimistic point of view.

At Tarquinia, on the west coast of Italy above Rome, are many tombs containing a wealth of frescoed murals. Our example, from the Tomb of the Leopards **(440)**, shows a merry scene, part of the funeral banquet. The young man at left holds a cup, while the other two play, respectively, a double pipe (the Etruscans' favorite instrument) and a lyre. When compared with the figure-painting style of the Greeks during this period, as in Douris' vase painting **(432)**, the Etruscan work seems stylized and relatively crude. Yet how lively the figures are, how colorful and animated. We sense their dancing movements from the swirl of the draperies, the vigor of the poses. There is warmth and humanity in these painted people, and even humor—a quality we seldom find in the art of the Greeks.

The Etruscans flourished in Italy for at least two hundred years. By the early 5th century B.C.E., however, they came under increasing pressure from the people who would eventually conquer not only Italy and Greece but most of Europe and the entire Mediterranean world—the Romans.

ROME

The year 510 B.C.E. is usually cited as the beginning of the Roman era, for it was then, according to ancient historians, that the Roman Republic was founded. There followed a long period of expansion and consolidation of territories brought under Roman rule. Roman legions swept eastward through Greece into Mesopotamia, west and north as far as Britain, across the sea to Egypt, throughout the rim of northern Africa. In 27 B.C.E., when Augustus took the title of "caesar," Rome became officially an empire.

There can be no doubt that the Romans greatly admired the work of their conquered subjects. They made numerous copies of Greek sculptures (including our example of the *Spear Bearer*) and imitated the Greek style for much of their "official" sculpture, such as emperor figures. The *Augustus of Prima Porta* (**55**), for instance, surely derives from Greek precedents. But it may have been Etruscan art, with its evident warmth and humanity, that inspired a special

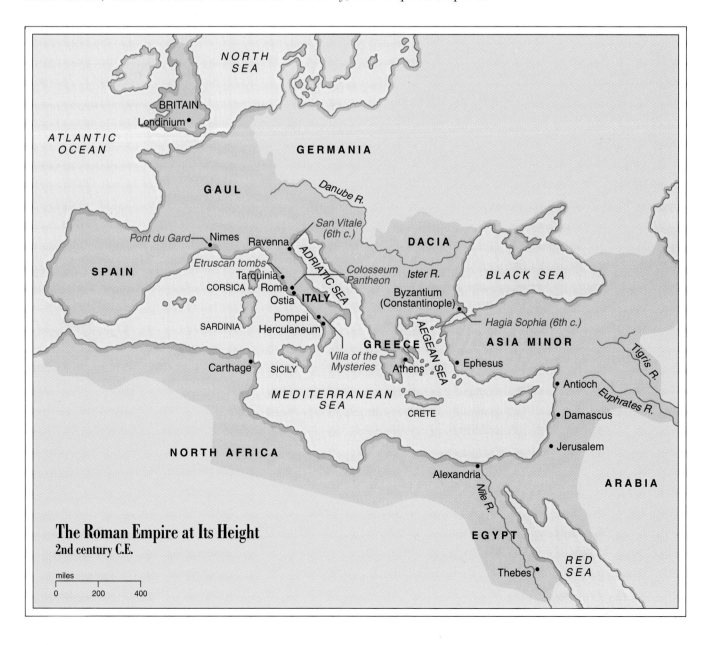

The Roman Empire at Its Height
2nd century C.E.

miles
0   200   400

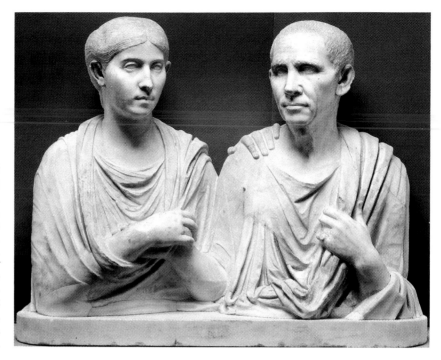

right: 441. *Double Portrait of Gratidia M. L. Chrite and M. Gratidius Libanus.* Last quarter of 1st century B.C.E. White marble with traces of color, height 23¾". Vatican Museums, Rome.

below: 442. Column of Trajan, Rome, detail of relief carvings. 106–113 C.E. Marble; height of frieze band 4'2", height of column 97', on 18' base.

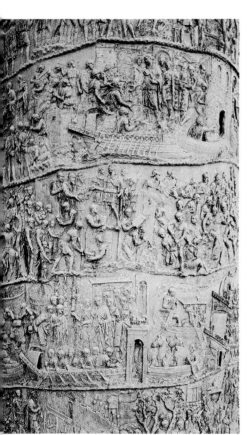

category of sculpture in which the Romans came to excel—the portrait bust of an ordinary citizen.

One such example **(441)** is a portrait of a Roman husband and wife who are fully realized as individuals. Obviously, we cannot know what these people actually looked like, but it is safe to assume the sculptor made a good likeness, with a minimum of idealizing. The husband is old, the creases in his face well defined, his expression patient; we might read from his image a long experience in the trials of the world and gentle resignation to those trials. His wife seems stronger, less marked by pain, and her supportive clasp of the husband's hand is touching. Scholars have read into this pose the highly esteemed Roman virtues of *fides* (faith or fidelity) and *concordia* (harmony). Whereas the Greek sculptures and many of the Roman ones seem to exist in a world apart, these portrait busts are wonderfully accessible. They allow us to identify with people who have been dead for two thousand years.

Like other ancient cultures, the Romans often applied sculpture to architecture, in the form of carved figures in relief. However, our next example, the Column of Trajan **(442)**, is exceptional. Trajan came to power as emperor of Rome in 98 C.E. His role was not only political but also military—expanding the empire's territories and protecting it from outside invaders. Early in his reign Trajan went to war against the Dacians, a people of central Europe who had made periodic raids against the empire. His victory was celebrated by the erection of a triumphal column in the city of Rome.

Trajan's column stands 115 feet tall including its base, and in Roman times it was capped by a monumental statue of the emperor. An overall photograph does not do it justice. We illustrate a closeup of one section to focus on details, because the main feature of Trajan's column is a spiral sculptured band in low relief, running around and around the column, telling the story of Trajan's Dacian campaign. The relief band is about 50 inches high. If we could unwrap it from the column and stretch it out, it would be 656 feet long—about the length of two football fields.

The sculptured band takes the form of ***continuous narrative,*** beginning at the bottom with Trajan setting out for war, ending at the top with his conquest of the Dacians. In between are some 150 episodes, each self-contained yet flowing smoothly into the next. Needless to say, Trajan is the hero of the story, appearing prominently in most of the scenes, but he has a large supporting cast of characters. In all, more than 2,500 human figures are carved into the relief, to say nothing of horses, chariots, boats, and all the paraphernalia of war. For a parallel to this achievement we must look nearly a thousand years later, to the *Bayeux Tapestry* (363), in which many episodes of a historical event are stitched into cloth, not carved into marble.

The anonymous sculptor (or sculptors) who made the Trajan Column's relief had superior gifts at both storytelling and composition. Figures and architectural details are arranged to keep the narrative flowing, to provide basic information about what is going on in each scene. Although the relief is fairly shallow (compare **323**), we get a real sense of spatial depth, even when many figures are clustered together. Perhaps most striking is the fineness of the carving, which gives convincing realism to draped clothing and armor, faces and hair and musculature, bricks and waves in the water. Moreover, the precise carving is carried through to the very top of the column. This last fact raises an intriguing question. Why did the sculptor lavish so much attention on a work that no one could see properly? Above the third or fourth turn of the spiral, the Trajan carvings become a blur to anyone standing on the ground. In Trajan's day there was a courtyard at the base of the column, with smaller columns supporting a balcony from which visitors could get a better view.

The Romans were equally masterful at painting, but were it not for a tragedy that occurred in 79 C.E., we would know little more about Roman painting than we do about the Greek. In that year Mt. Vesuvius, an active volcano, erupted and buried the town of Pompeii, about a hundred miles south of Rome, along with the neighboring town of Herculaneum. The resulting lava and ashes spread a blanket over the region, and this blanket acted as a kind of time capsule. Pompeii lay undisturbed, immune to further ravages of nature, for more than sixteen centuries. Then in 1748 excavations were undertaken, and their findings were made public by the famous German archaeologist Joachim Winckelmann. Within the precincts of Pompeii the diggers found marvelous frescoes that were exceptionally well preserved. Pompeii was not an important city, so we cannot assume that the most talented artists of the period worked there. In fact, there is some evidence to suggest that the fresco painters were not Roman at all, but immigrant Greeks. Nevertheless, these wall paintings do give some indication of the styles of art practiced within the empire at the time.

One fresco, from a house known as the Villa of the Mysteries (443), shows a scene believed to represent secret cult rituals associated with the wine god Dionysus. The figures stand as though on a ledge, in shallow but convincing space, interacting only slightly with one another. Although the artist has segmented the mural into panels separated by black bands, the figures overlap these panels so freely that there is no strong sense of individual episodes or compartments. Rather, the artist has established two rhythms—one of the figures and another of the dividing bands—giving a strong design unity.

RELATED WORKS

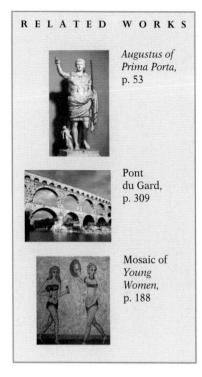

Augustus of Prima Porta, p. 53

Pont du Gard, p. 309

Mosaic of *Young Women*, p. 188

443. Wall painting, from the Villa of the Mysteries, Pompeii. c. 50 B.C.E. Fresco.

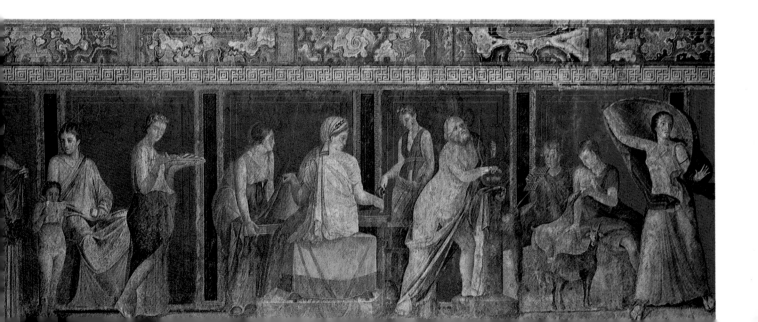

For all their production in sculpture and painting, the Romans are best known for their architecture and engineering. We saw one of their engineering masterpieces, the Pont du Gard (367), in Chapter 13. But the most familiar monument—indeed, for many travelers the very symbol of Rome—is the Roman Colosseum (444).

The Colosseum was planned under the Emperor Vespasian and dedicated in 80 C.E. as an amphitheater for gladiatorial games and public entertainments. A large oval covering 6 acres, the Colosseum could accommodate some fifty thousand spectators—about the same number as most major-league baseball stadiums today. Few of the games played inside, however, were as tame as baseball. Gladiators vied with one another and with wild animals in extraordinarily bloody and gruesome contests, made possible because an extensive system of sewers under the Colosseum could drain away the gore. On special occasions the whole structure could be filled with water for quite realistic naval battles.

While the Colosseum served as headquarters for some rather bloodthirsty activity, its architectural achievement represented the highest ideals of the Romans. Even in its ruined state this structure displays the genius of the Romans as builders. The Colosseum rises on three tiers of arches, each of the levels distinguished from the next by a different style of column between the arches—Doric on the lowest level, Ionic on the second, and Corinthian on the third (365). Around the base are eighty arched openings for entry and exit; it is said that the entire building could be emptied in a matter of minutes. Above all, the structure is logical and coherent. Roman architects tell us in visual detail exactly how the building is organized—which parts are separate from other parts, where to enter, where to go, and so on. The exterior view gives us a clear sense of the inside, the walkways, the scheme as a whole. Today the Colosseum seems romantic; tourists dream of exploring it by moonlight. In its prime, it must have been the crown of the empire.

Second only to the Colosseum for architectural grandeur in Rome is the Pantheon (445), the temple to "all the gods." The Pantheon was built in the reign of Trajan's successor, the emperor Hadrian, who had an avid interest in

444. Colosseum, Rome. 72–80 C.E. Concrete; height 160', diameters 620' and 513'.

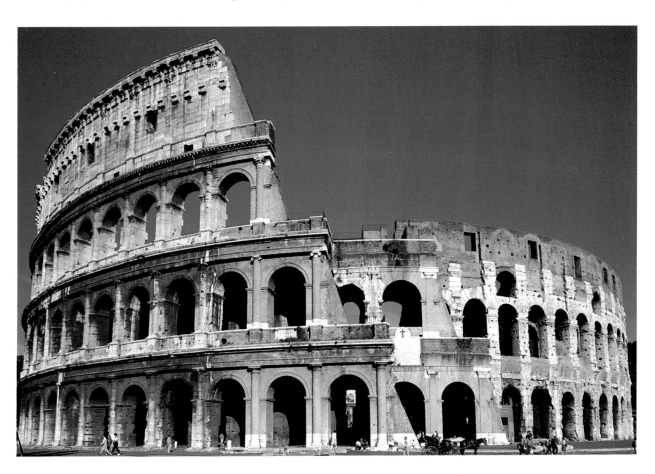

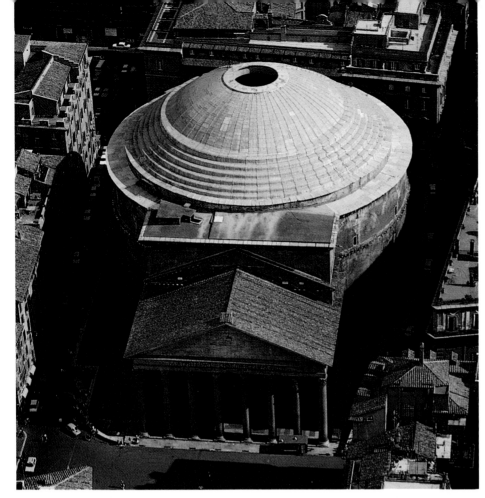

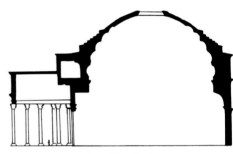

section of the Pantheon

architecture and apparently took a hand in the design. In form the building is simple though massive: a cylinder, topped by a hemispherical dome, fronted by a columned rectangular porch **(445)**. From the outside it may seem clumsy, almost like an immense oil-storage drum with a classic temple porch stuck incongruously on one end. What we see today, however, is not quite what the architects intended. In Roman times the surrounding streets were much lower; a flight of steps leading to the porch was exposed, and this probably contributed to the design harmony. Still, we might suspect that the Pantheon's architects deliberately kept the exterior plain so as not to spoil the "surprise." For the truly spectacular effect of the building comes from walking inside, from suddenly being within the huge space the walls enclose.

The interior of the Pantheon, as we saw from Panini's painting in Chapter 13 **(372)**, is impressive even by today's standards—142 feet high and 140 feet across. Around the base are seven niches that originally held statues (visible in the painting, but now gone) of the "sky" gods: the Sun, the Moon, Mercury, Venus, Mars, Jupiter, and Saturn. Above this level the dome stretches up in a perfect half sphere, carved out with recessed squares called **coffers,** which lighten the dome both visually and structurally. As noted in Chapter 13, the only opening is a 29-foot-wide **oculus,** or eye, at the very top of the dome. Visitors familiar with today's giant indoor spaces, such as the sports stadiums, should bear in mind that the Romans did not have space-age materials. The Pantheon is built of simple concrete. And we can marvel at the engineering genius needed to enclose a space of this size in concrete—and keep it enclosed for nearly two thousand years.

The Pantheon has been in use continually to the present day. Early in the 7th century it became a Christian church, which it remains. This fact points up the first of two changes that will lead our brief chronological survey of art into new areas. One is the increasing importance of the Christian faith; the other, the shift in power within the Roman Empire from the city of Rome to the East.

left: 445. Pantheon, Rome. 118–125 C.E.

above: 446. Section drawing of the Pantheon.

RELATED WORKS

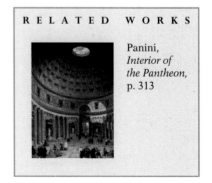

Panini, *Interior of the Pantheon,* p. 313

CHAPTER SIXTEEN

Christian Art in Europe

The Early Church, Byzantium, and the Middle Ages

According to tradition, Jesus, known as the Christ or "anointed one," was born in Bethlehem during the reign of Emperor Augustus. In time his followers would become so influential in world affairs that our common calendar takes as its starting point the presumed date of Jesus' birth, calling it "year 1." As a matter of fact, the 6th-century calendar makers who devised this plan were wrong in their calculations. Jesus probably was born between four and six years earlier than they had supposed, but the calendar has nevertheless become standard.

The faith Jesus preached spread throughout the Mediterranean world— that is, through the Roman Empire—at a surprisingly rapid rate. Although we could cite numerous reasons for the decline and eventual collapse of the Roman Empire, the growing strength of this new *monotheistic* (worshiping one god) religion was surely among them. Within a very few centuries Christianity would dominate Europe, not just spiritually but culturally and politically as well. As a consequence, art and architecture in Europe—as well as music and literature—would be overwhelmingly dedicated to the Christian church for well over a thousand years.

THE EARLY CHRISTIANS

The Roman Empire reached its greatest extent early in the 2nd century, in approximately 117 C.E. Coincidentally, it was just at this time that the Christian church was beginning to make its power felt. By about the year 111 the Emperor Trajan felt it necessary to issue an order to his provincial governors allowing them to punish citizens who openly practiced Christianity. The new

CHRONOLOGY

	150–800	800–1400
Style/Period	Roman Empire, 31 B.C.E.–c. 500 C.E. Byzantine Empire (Europe-Asia), c. 400–1453 Islamic Empire, c. 622–900	Islamic Empire, c. 622–900 Romanesque period, Europe, c. 1050–c. 1200 Gothic period, Europe, c. 1200–c. 1500

Bayeux Tapestry

Political/ Social Events and Personalities	Constantine, emperor of Rome, 306–337 Nomadic migrations, Europe, 4th–5th centuries Justinian, emperor of Byzantium, 527–565 Mohammed (c. 570–632)	Charlemagne, Holy Roman Emperor, 800–814 Crusades, Europe, 1096–1270 Hildegard of Bingen (c. 1098–1179) Marco Polo journeys to China, 1271–1295 Black Death in Europe, 1348–1357

Empress Theodora,
Ravenna

Monuments and Major Artists	San Vitale, Ravenna, 527–547 Hagia Sophia, Istanbul, 532–537 Sutton Hoo Ship Burial, 625–633	*Bayeux Tapestry*, c. 1073–1088 St. Sernin, Toulouse, France, c. 1080–1120 Chartres Cathedral, France, c. 1194–1260 Duccio (active 1278–1318) Giotto (c. 1267–1337)

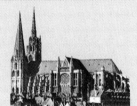
Chartres Cathedral

religion presented a threat to the empire for several reasons, including the fact that it challenged the concept of emperor worship built into the older Roman faith. For more than two hundred years Christians were actively persecuted under the banners of Rome. As a result, they took their religion underground—quite literally. In complex networks of dugout tunnels called **catacombs** the early Christians retreated from danger, buried their dead, and sometimes assembled for worship.

Early in the 4th century the Christians' situation changed abruptly when Emperor Constantine came to power **(447)**. Far more than his predecessors, Constantine was sympathetic to the Christian religion. Under the influence of his mother, Helen, a devout Christian, he was baptized in the faith just before he died. Two actions by Constantine would have a profound effect on the art and culture of the time.

The first came in 313, when the emperor issued an edict of tolerance for all religions. Christians could come out from their underground hiding places and begin to build real churches. We might think, given that the Christian religion was so newly released from persecution, that the first churches would be modest in scale and humble in construction, but such was not the case. Many were built under Constantine's patronage, and, while the emperor took care to select sites outside the city walls so as not to offend the more conservative members of the Roman Senate, he spared no expense. Moreover, the church builders had ample inspiration for grand design in the Roman temples and public buildings all around them. The early churches followed the **basilica** plan—a plan based on a large oblong—of Roman meeting halls, with the entrance at one end and the altar at the other. So spacious were their interiors that some could accommodate more than ten thousand worshipers.

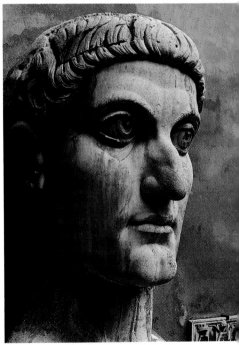

447. *Constantine the Great.*
325–26 C.E. Marble,
height of head 8'6".
Palazzo dei Conservatori, Rome.

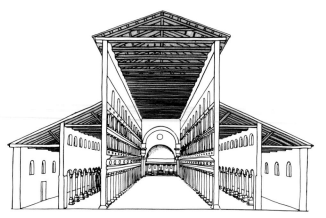

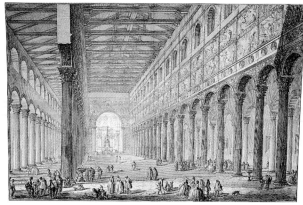

left: 448. Reconstruction of Old St. Peter's, Rome. Begun c. 320.

right: 449. St. Paul's Outside the Walls, Rome. Begun c. 385. Engraving by Giovanni Battista Piranesi.

Foremost among the Early Christian churches was Old St. Peter's, built on the spot where it was believed that Peter, Jesus' first Apostle, had been buried. This structure was demolished in 1506 to erect the "new" St. Peter's now in Rome **(479)**, but contemporary descriptions and drawings have enabled scholars to make informed guesses about its design **(448)**. A similar church built some sixty years later, St. Paul's Outside the Walls, stood intact until the 19th century, and an artist's rendering gives testimony to its grandeur **(449)**.

Constantine's second pivotal act occurred in 330, when he abandoned Rome and moved his capital eastward. He named his new capital city after himself—Constantinople. Today we call it Istanbul. But the ancient world knew it as Byzantium.

BYZANTIUM

450. *Empress Theodora and Retinue.* c. 547. Mosaic. San Vitale, Ravenna.

Byzantine art differs from its Greek and Roman precursors in two distinct ways. First, it is an art based on Christianity. No longer was art diffused into the portrayal of many gods and ideals. One god, one faith, one tradition—these became the standards of Byzantine art. Second, Byzantine art has an

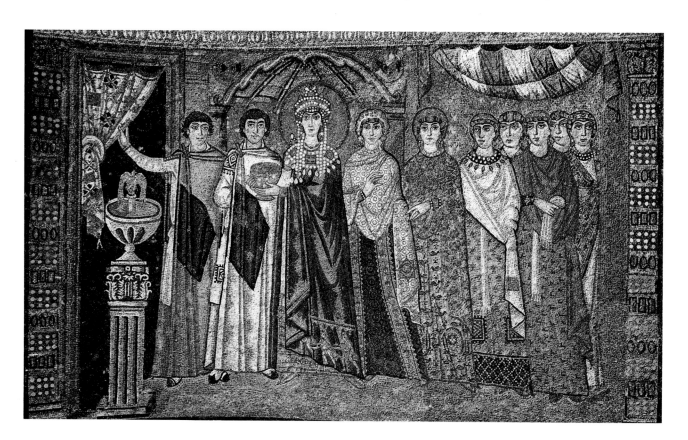

Eastern flavor in both style and materials. The Byzantine style is essentially flat, with an emphasis on elaborate decoration rather than naturalistic depiction. And whereas the Greek or Roman artist might prefer to work in paint or marble, the Byzantine artist was particularly skilled in the art of **mosaic**—small stones or pieces of tile or glass arranged in a pattern.

We see an excellent example of this mosaic art in the portrait panel of *Empress Theodora* (450), wife of the 6th-century emperor Justinian. The *Theodora* mosaic is especially splendid in its rich, vibrant colors and sumptuous decorative details. Many scholars feel the panel was intended to reinforce the royal status of—perhaps even give religious status to—the queen, who was of low birth and had been an actress before her marriage. Thus, Theodora is garbed in purple, the color of royalty, and there is a lavish use of gold throughout the picture. The "halo" effect around the queen's head has suggested to some writers that she was supposed to be identified with the Virgin Mary, mother of Jesus.

The design character of Byzantine art is well illustrated by this mosaic. Theodora is meant to be in procession, with her retinue trailing behind her, but we get little sense of this movement. Also, while the artist has used some overlapping, especially in the attendants at right, all the figures appear to be in the same plane, and that plane is identical with the ornately decorated background. But neither motion nor the sense of rounded figures in depth was important to Byzantine artists or the intended audience. Far more compelling was the impression of quiet dignity, the appearance of an empress in majesty accepting the homage of her subjects, and these qualities are conveyed splendidly. The effect seems even more remarkable when we remember this image was put together from tiny pieces, like a giant picture puzzle.

Theodora's mosaic is housed in a building that represents one of the high points of Byzantine architecture—the church of San Vitale (451), built in the early 6th century. At this point Eastern styles in art and architecture had spread westward; San Vitale is in the Italian city of Ravenna. Its ground plan (452) reveals its somewhat unusual spatial organization—unusual, that is, for a church in Western Europe. Most Early Christian churches were simple rectangles; later, churches in the West adopted the cross plan, consisting of a long main section intersected by a shorter section at right angles to the first. In either of these plans one enters through a door at one end, and straight ahead at the other end is the altar. The axis, or main line of sight, is from door to altar, horizontally through the church. San Vitale, with its Eastern character, is not like that. It is a central-plan church, built in the form of an octagon, and so the focus of attention is in the center of the building, immediately under the

RELATED WORKS

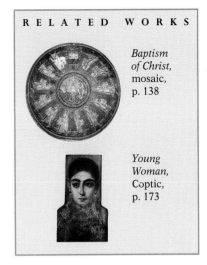

Baptism of Christ, mosaic, p. 138

Young Woman, Coptic, p. 173

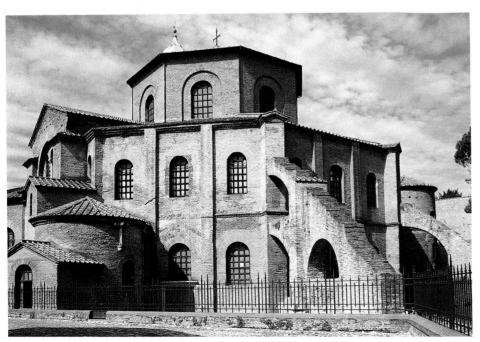

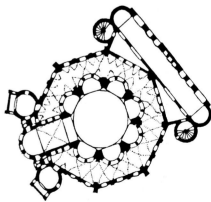

left: 451. San Vitale, Ravenna, exterior of apse. c. 527–47.

above: 452. Plan of San Vitale, Ravenna.

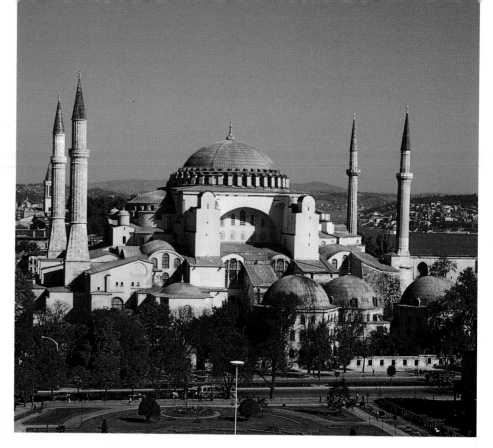

453. Hagia Sophia, Istanbul. 532–37. Height of dome 183′.

RELATED WORKS

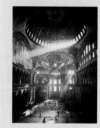

Hagia Sophia, interior, p. 314

dome. The major axis, therefore, is vertical, from floor to dome (or earth to Heaven), with the altar off to one side. The central plan remained a feature of Eastern churches long after the cross plan had become firmly established in the West.

San Vitale is fairly small, a perfect little jewel of a church. At least five of its size could be contained within another Byzantine church built just at the same time—the magnificent Hagia Sophia in Constantinople **(453)**. We saw the interior of Hagia Sophia in Chapter 13 **(373)**. Our view of the outside gives a better sense of the building's massive scale and helps to show why it is considered the masterpiece of Byzantine architecture. The mighty dome, floating 183 feet above floor level, dominates the landscape, testifying as much to the glory of the empire as to the faith celebrated within. In time that faith would change. The pointed towers at the four corners, called **minarets,** are not original but were added in the 15th century when Hagia Sophia became an Islamic mosque.

Byzantine art would continue to flourish in Eastern Europe for another thousand years. Meanwhile, however, great changes were under way in the western portion of the continent. By the time San Vitale and Hagia Sophia were built, the old Roman Empire had effectively ceased to exist. New groups of people were settling and establishing their own cultures throughout Western Europe. Inevitably, they brought with them their own styles of art. It is to these people that we now turn our attention.

THE MIDDLE AGES
IN EUROPE

The authors of history books give us labels, convenient terms for naming things. Some time ago historians agreed that the "old" world ended just about when Hagia Sofia was built, in the mid-6th century. They also agreed that the "new" world began some eight hundred years later with the Renaissance. Nowadays such tidy cubbyholes seem naive, but labels can be hard to shake off. Although we may no longer refer to these periods as old and new, we still call the intervening time "middle."

THE EARLY MIDDLE AGES

The kingdoms of the early Middle Ages in Europe were inhabited by descendants of migratory tribes that had traveled southward and westward on the continent during the 4th and 5th centuries. Ethnically Germanic, these peoples emerged, for the most part, from the north-central part of Europe, or what today we would call northern Germany and Scandinavia (map p. 387). The Romans referred to them as "barbarians" (meaning "foreigners") and considered them crude—with some justification, for, being nomadic, they had a considerably lower level of culture than did the settled citizens of the empire. Moreover, it was continual invasion by the "barbarians" that brought about the empire's ultimate collapse, near the end of the 5th century.

By the year 600 the migrations were essentially over, and kingdoms whose area roughly approximated the nations of modern Europe had taken form. Their inhabitants had steadily been converted to Christianity. For purposes of this discussion, we will focus initially on the people who settled in three areas—the Angles and Saxons in Britain, the Norsemen in Scandinavia, and the Franks in Gaul (modern France).

On the island of Britain north of London (then Londinium) was Sutton Hoo, where the grave of an unknown 7th-century East Anglian king has been found. Objects discovered at the burial site include a superb gold and enamel purse cover **(454)**, with delicately made designs. The motifs are typical of the *animal style* prevalent in art of northwestern Europe at that time—a legacy, very likely, from the migratory herdsmen who were these people's ancestors. The term "animal style" came to refer not only to the actual depiction of animals but also the intricate tracery of lines and bands that often accompanies the animal images. We can see this tracery clearly in the upper left and right medallions of the Sutton Hoo purse cover.

Animal-style art also flourished in Scandinavia. A particularly rich trove of carved-wood objects was found at Oseberg in southern Norway, in a buried Viking ship dating from the early 9th century. The Oseberg ship, itself made of wood and decorated with a wonderfully carved prow, is believed to have been a luxury vessel intended for cruising the coastline and rivers. Among its contents was a splendid animal head **(455)** that adorned the top of a post—the sort of post probably carried in religious processions. The animal style is evident in the ribbonlike tracery of the creature's head and neck—astonishingly skillful for carving in wood.

left: **454.** Purse cover, from the Sutton Hoo Ship Burial. 625–33. Gold with garnets and enamels, length 7½". Copyright The British Museum, London.

right: **455.** *Animal Head*, from Oseberg Burial Ship, Norway. c. 825. Wood, overall height c. 18". University Museum of National Antiquities, Oslo.

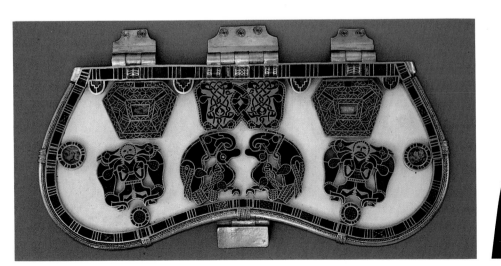

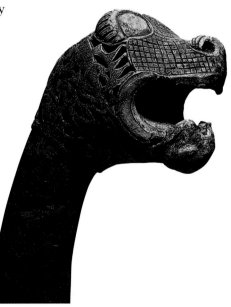

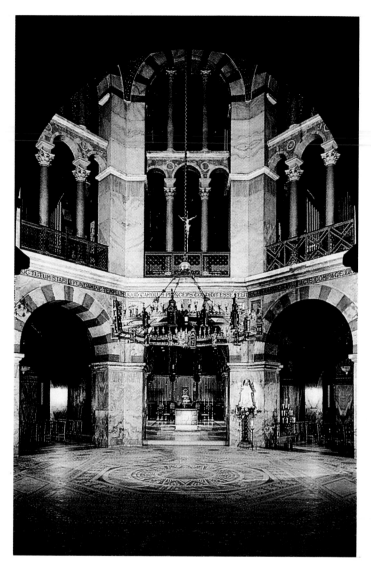

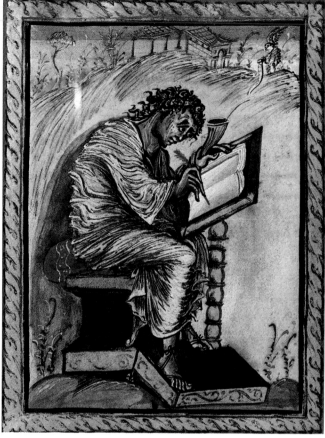

left: 456. Palace Chapel of Charlemagne, Aachen. 792–805.

right: 457.
St. Matthew the Evangelist, from *The Gospel Book of Archbishop Ebbo.* Before 823. Illumination, $10\frac{1}{4} \times 7\frac{7}{8}''$. Bibliothèque de la Ville, Epernay.

In France a different style of art was taking root, called **Carolingian** after the emperor Charlemagne. Charlemagne, or Charles the Great, was a powerful Frankish king whose military conquests eventually gave him control over most of Western Europe. On Christmas Day of the year 800 the Pope crowned Charlemagne Holy Roman Emperor—making him the first of many rulers to bear that title. The title is significant because it united two major forces. Charlemagne was *Roman* in that he thought of himself as inheriting the legacy of the old Roman Empire. He was called *holy* for being a Christian king, the dominant Christian king.

Charlemagne seems to have been much aware of past glories in the old Roman Empire, and he wished to imitate or surpass them in his own reign, his own empire. Following the example of Roman emperors before him, he took an active interest in artistic and cultural matters. At his capital, Aachen, Charlemagne ordered built a splendid Palace Chapel to be his personal place of worship **(456)**. The architecture of the chapel gives several clues to his ambitions. Its basic design is modeled after San Vitale in Ravenna **(451)**, which Charlemagne apparently had seen and admired. Very likely he wished to copy the perfection of that octagonal church, to match the architectural ideals of Byzantium. At the same time, however, the details of the Palace Chapel are much heavier, more solid, more *Roman*, especially the robust Roman arches. Charlemagne—the Frankish king from the north—intended to be a Roman emperor, even to the design of his holy place.

Carolingian art is a mixture of northern and southern influences. Such painting as we know from the early Middle Ages is mostly in manuscripts, a form we associate primarily with the North. And most manuscripts were created in the service of the Christian church. Christianity centers on the Bible, a collection of sacred writings put down over many centuries and collected into one book (the word "bible" comes from the Greek and Latin words for "book"), probably in the 8th century. For the teaching and practice of faith, it was essential to possess a Bible, and in this era, long before the invention of the printing press, manuscripts had to be copied laboriously by hand. Most of the work was done by monks, who toiled in special writing centers known as *scriptoria.* In the finest examples, the prose manuscripts were decorated, or *illuminated*, with drawings, paintings, and elaborate capital letters.

The *St. Matthew* page from *The Gospel Book of Archbishop Ebbo* (457) provides a fine example of Carolingian manuscript styles. It depicts St. Matthew hard at work transcribing what would become the first book of the Bible's New Testament. Everything about Matthew suggests a frenzy of creative inspiration, from the agitated drapery of his clothing to the intense concentration on his face. Even his feet and toes seem tensed by the effort of his project. Although this image of the Gospel writer may seem stylized, we can see hints of Roman influence in the roundness of the body, the convincing wrinkles of the garment, and the artist's attempt to place Matthew in a natural setting.

Some writers consider Charlemagne's coronation day to be the end of the early Middle Ages. The emperor was crowned not by his own people but rather by the Pope, the leader of the Christian religion, and he was crowned *Holy* Roman Emperor. For the first time a political ruler had the sanction of the Church of Rome, and this opened a new chapter in European history.

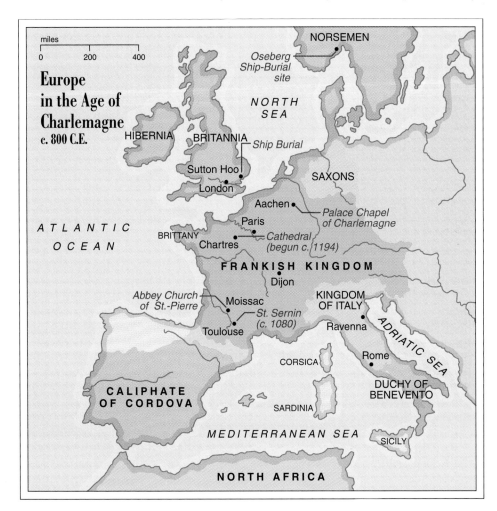

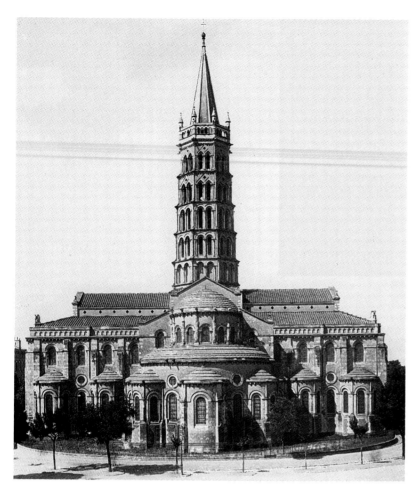

458. St. Sernin, Toulouse, France, view toward the apse. 1080–1120.

The Christian faith was not the only one practiced in Europe. Older religions retained their adherents in the north, and Jews were settled throughout Europe. The Islamic Empire took control of Spain in the early 8th century, retaining a stronghold there into the 15th century. But Christianity was dominant, and the next several centuries would bring its greatest period of strength—and its greatest period of building.

THE HIGH MIDDLE AGES

The Middle Ages was a time of intense religious preoccupation in Europe. It was during this era that most of the great cathedrals were built. Also, a major portion of the art that has come down to us is associated with monasteries, churches, and cathedrals.

Historians generally divide the art and architecture of the high Middle Ages into two periods: the **Romanesque,** from about 1050 to 1200, based on southern styles from the old Roman Empire; and the **Gothic,** from about 1200 into the 15th century, which has more of a northern flavor. (The term "Gothic" derives from the Goths, who were among the many nomadic tribes sweeping through Europe during the 4th and 5th centuries. It was applied to this style by later critics in the Renaissance, who considered the art and architecture of their immediate predecessors to be vulgar and "barbarian.")

Although there was no sharp dividing line between the Romanesque and the Gothic, we can find many differences in their characteristic styles. These differences should be evident as we compare examples from each, first in architecture, then in sculpture.

In Chapter 13 we studied the interiors of two grand French cathedrals—St. Sernin in Toulouse and Chartres (368,369). Now let us consider the outsides of these two structures, in views focused toward the **apse**—the main altar area—of each.

The Cathedral of St. Sernin is a splendid example of the Romanesque style **(458)**. Although the interior of the nave **(368)** soars upward to a breathtaking height, from the outside the church seems to hug the ground—solid, durable, *Roman*. The plan is absolutely symmetrical, with a single tower rising from the center. (The tower is of a later date and has some Gothic influence.) Arches around the windows are classic round Roman arches, and they are arranged in a regular, logical progression, with columns in between (compare the Colosseum, **444**). Also, we see a minimum of decorative detail on the façade; most statuary is inside the building. This cathedral was meant to turn inward, to gather worshipers inside its core and shelter them there. St. Sernin gives us an impression of stability, of a church firmly rooted and dependable, representing a faith meant to endure forever.

Chartres Cathedral **(459)**, some 300 miles to the north and begun a century or so later, is very different in its lofty Gothic design. As St. Sernin hugs the earth, Chartres reaches upward to the heavens. As St. Sernin appears solid and durable, Chartres was intended to seem weightless. From the outside, Chartres looks to be all points and spires and intricate decorative detail. The exterior of the cathedral is embellished with more than two thousand carved figures **(461)**—not visible in this overall photograph—which serve as a transition between the town and the church, a welcoming committee, so to speak, for the faithful as they enter.

Chartres has two tall spires, notable for their very different designs and the consequent lack of symmetry. Its arches are not the round ones of a Romanesque building, but rather the pointed arches developed in the Gothic period **(369)**. Another innovation of Gothic architecture was the flying buttress (p. 311), an exterior support meant to control the outward thrust of thin masonry walls built very high. The flying buttresses around the apse of Chartres are plainly visible in the photograph **(459)**. All in all, the Gothic cathedral, as interpreted at Chartres, reveals an architecture of soaring ambitions, celebrating a faith that simultaneously reaches outward to the townspeople and up to the skies.

The sculpture of the high Middle Ages offers similarly interesting comparisons between the Romanesque and Gothic styles. As suggested earlier, most of it focused on religious themes and was made to embellish church buildings. The sculptors who created these carvings were itinerant stonecutters, who traveled about Europe from job to job, working on whichever church was currently in progress. Judging by the sheer number of sculptures, there must have been virtual armies of skilled carvers.

RELATED WORKS

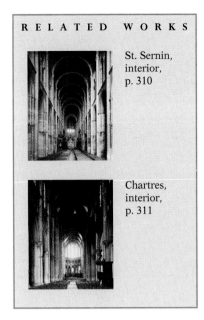

St. Sernin, interior, p. 310

Chartres, interior, p. 311

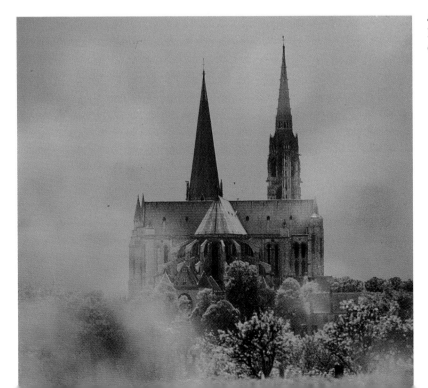

459. Chartres Cathedral, France, view toward the apse. c. 1194–1260.

RELATED WORKS

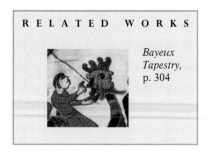

Bayeux
Tapestry,
p. 304

At Moissac, in southwestern France, is the abbey church dedicated to St. Peter, or in French St.-Pierre, built from the late 11th century onward. The memorial portrait of its abbot, *Durandus* (460), is carved as a shallow relief and is in the Romanesque style. Durandus' figure stands contained within the round Roman arch, his shoulders and vestments echoing the arch. His pose is fully frontal, almost perfectly symmetrical. The low-relief carving and delicate lines were influenced by manuscript illumination styles, with their flattened, decorative imagery. Romanesque sculptors seem more interested in relating the carving to the architecture than in creating rounded, naturalistic forms.

Barely a hundred years later the stonecarvers of the Gothic period had "opened up" their figures, to give them more volume and greater independence from the architectural supports. The illustration shows a group of column sculptures from the north porch of Chartres Cathedral, representing the Old Testament prophets Melchizedek, Abraham, and Moses (461). Each of the figures is attached to a column, but they are not imprisoned by the columnar structure. They are convincingly rounded bodies, individuals with their own personalities, looking out, perhaps, to greet the visitors who will pass through the cathedral's doors.

The medieval carver's task was not only artistic but also instructional. For a largely illiterate populace, the sculptors had to interpret the Bible stories clearly, to make the figures recognizable. For example, in this grouping from Chartres, the figure of Abraham is identified by his son Isaac held before him. The most familiar story about Abraham tells of God testing the prophet by asking that he sacrifice the child (see also 465). Similar clues are provided for the other figures. Beyond the teaching function, however, these personalizing touches may cause us to relate to the sculptures more actively. They seem less like architectural enrichment, more like people.

Our comparison of Romanesque and Gothic sculptures shows the trend toward naturalism, toward greater volume and roundness. Sculptures were beginning to come down off the wall and inhabit their own space. Much the same tendency is evident in painting of the period, as the decorative flatness of manuscript styles gave way to a search for pictorial depth. We see a hint of this depth in the illustration from Hildegard of Bingen's *Scivias* (opposite). The trend would accelerate in the 14th century, for we are approaching the era when naturalism in art would be more important than ever before or since.

left: 460.
Tomb of Abbot Durandus,
relief at St.-Pierre de Moissac,
France. 1100.

right: 461.
*Melchizedek, Abraham,
and Moses,*
column sculptures
from North Porch
of Chartres Cathedral.
c. 1220.

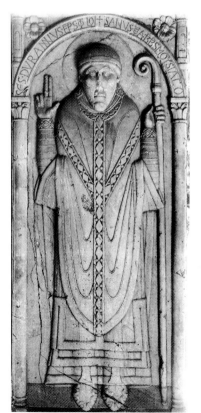

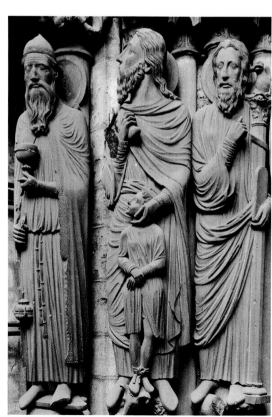

HILDEGARD OF BINGEN

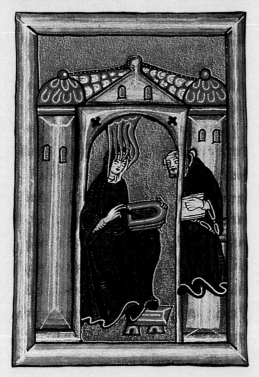

IN SUMMER of the year 1098, in the German town of Bermersheim, a knight called Hildebert and his lady Mechthilde welcomed their tenth and last child, a daughter, whom they named Hildegard. The little girl was frail in health, but from early childhood she showed unusual spirituality. At about age five, as she would tell it much later, young Hildegard experienced a mystical vision of brilliant light, accompanied by images from Heaven. It was this combination of fragility and religious devotion, apparently, that caused her parents to place Hildegard in a convent at the age of seven or eight.

At the convent Hildegard was tutored in Latin, music, the scriptures, and religious studies. She took her vows as a nun when she was about eighteen. Little is known of her life for the next twenty years, until 1136. In that year Hildegard, at age thirty-eight, was elected abbess of the convent.

Perhaps her new status gave Hildegard the courage to confide in others, to reveal the secret she had kept for so long—that she was subject to visions of God, Christ, the cosmos, biblical events, and religious symbols. In any case, she did so, and she was taken seriously. Encouraged by her churchly mentors, Hildegard began to write.

Her first major work, started in 1142, was called *Scivias*, which translates from the Latin as *Know the Ways (of the Lord)*. In this book, a ten-year project, Hildegard tells of her visions, describing them in exact detail and illustrating them with painted illuminations that are startlingly modern in their simplicity. Some believe she made the paintings herself, but it is more likely they were done by others under her close supervision.

Vision two, shown here, is a portrait of Hildegard at the moment of her spiritual awakening. Seated in a small room, dressed in the robes of a courtly woman, Hildegard is struck by heavenly tongues of fire, which engulf her head. She is poised ready to record the event, as is her secretary, Volmar, standing awestruck at right. Symbolically, the spiritual flames will unloose Hildegard's own tongue, inspiring her to speak of God's ways.

Mystical though she may have been, Hildegard was no stranger to worldly concerns. She seems to have been an exceptionally good administrator, strong-willed and skillful at getting her own way. For long years her nuns had occupied the tiny women's quarters of a monastery, forced to endure domination and crowding by the monks. When she proposed to leave and establish a separate convent, she met bitter opposition from the men, who would thus lose the considerable wealth the nuns had brought to the community. Hildegard was undeterred. Taking care to enlist the protection of highly placed clergy and nobility, she departed with her nuns, about 1150, for a new convent site at Rupertsberg, near the town of Bingen.

Hildegard's last decades were extremely productive. Several other books followed the *Scivias*, including a medical text and a nine-book treatise on botany, biology, geology, and astronomy. She wrote the music and text for some sixty-three hymns and also a miracle play, which was performed as an opera. All the while she maintained a vast correspondence, exchanging letters with monarchs and church leaders, scholars and ordinary people. In her last years she traveled rather widely, and she was called to preach in the great cathedrals. Her services were much in demand as an exorcist, capable of driving out evil spirits.

Many contemporary accounts about Hildegard report her recurring, serious illnesses, but we do not know how she died. We have only the date. The extraordinary life of Hildegard of Bingen, spanning eighty-one years, came to an end on September 17, 1179.

Illustration (folio Ir.) from Hildegard of Bingen's *Scivias*.
1142–52. Manuscript illumination.
Formerly Wiesbaden Hessische Landesbibliothek;
destroyed in World War II.

THE LATE MIDDLE AGES

Claus Sluter, a Flemish sculptor who worked in France in the late 14th century, brought his figures even farther off the wall than had the artisans of Chartres. Sluter's most ambitious project was the so-called *Moses Well* (462), a six-sided stone pedestal featuring life-size portraits of six Old Testament prophets, carved in very high relief. The view illustrated here shows Moses on the left, David on the right. Perhaps the word "portraits" seems unusual, since no one really knows what the patriarchs looked like. But Sluter has taken pains to depict them as individual personalities, vibrant and animated, so that we feel he has captured the character of each. The prophets do not stand rigidly, bonded to their background, but instead reach out to interact with one another and with the viewer.

The prophets at Chartres (461), while fully rounded, have a columnar aspect. Their bodies are compressed—shoulders rigid, arms close to the torso, legs straight—and their garments fall in orderly pleats. If one could take them down from the columns, they would still look rather like columns themselves. But Sluter's figures have a presence of their own, independent of any backing. Their heads lean forward, shoulders twist, arms are bent at the elbow—in short, we sense that they *could* walk down off the wall.

Beside the Chartres sculptures, Sluter's figures are monumental, seeming especially massive because they are encased in a heavy swirl of drapery. This last point is the key to why the *Moses Well* appears in this chapter rather than the next one. Sluter's work serves as a bridge between the art of the Middle Ages and the art of the Renaissance. In true Renaissance style the sculptor has carved lifelike, mobile figures; yet so profuse is the mountain of drapery swirling around the figures that we have a limited sense of the body underneath. It remained for the next generation to strip away the garments and study the human form.

462. Claus Sluter. *Moses Well*. 1395–1406. Stone, height of figures c. 6′. Chartreuse de Champmol, Dijon.

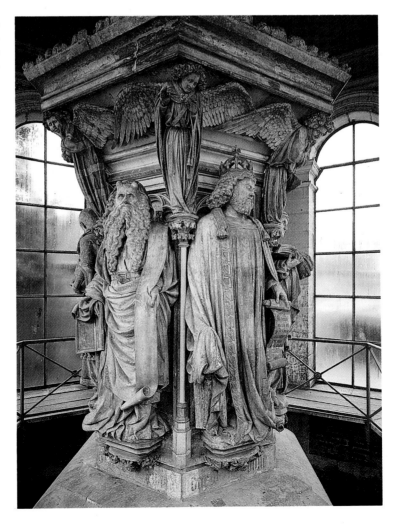

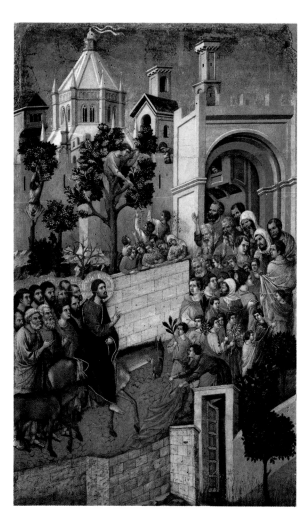

463. Duccio.
Christ Entering Jerusalem,
detail of *Maestà Altar.*
1308–11. Panel, 40 × 21".
Cathedral Museum, Siena.

Some scholars would argue that the last two artists in this chapter belong in the next, as pioneer masters of the Renaissance. Like Claus Sluter, both were transitional artists, both were influential in making the shift from art styles of the Middle Ages to the quite different styles of the Renaissance. We place them here mainly because their major sources of inspiration were the vestiges of Byzantine art to the east and the medieval Gothic tradition to the north. Succeeding generations of artists would look to Greece and Rome.

Duccio was an artist of Siena, in Italy. His masterpiece was the *Maestà Altar,* a multisection panel meant to be displayed on the altar of a church, of which we illustrate the part showing *Christ Entering Jerusalem* **(463)**. What is most interesting about this painting is Duccio's attempt to create believable space in a large outdoor scene—a concern that would absorb painters of the next century. Christ's entry into the city, celebrated now on Palm Sunday, was thought of as a triumphal procession, and Duccio has labored to convey the sense of movement and parade. A strong diagonal thrust beginning at the left with Christ and his disciples cuts across the picture to the middle right, then shifts abruptly to carry our attention to the upper left corner of the painting— a church tower that is Christ's presumed goal. The architecture plays an important role in defining space and directing movement. This was Duccio's novel, almost unprecedented, contribution to the art of the period, the use of architecture to enclose and demarcate space rather than to act as a simple backdrop for the figures.

Duccio's contemporary, a Florentine artist named Giotto, made an even more remarkable break with art traditions of the Middle Ages. Most of Giotto's best work was in fresco (Chapter 7), and the most notable examples are in a

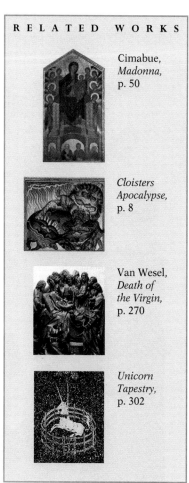

RELATED WORKS

Cimabue,
Madonna,
p. 50

*Cloisters
Apocalypse,*
p. 8

Van Wesel,
*Death of
the Virgin,*
p. 270

*Unicorn
Tapestry,*
p. 302

small church in Padua called the Arena Chapel. *The Lamentation* **(464)**, a work depicting Mary, St. John, and others mourning the dead Christ, illustrates Giotto's highly original use of space in painting. The scene has been composed as though it were on a stage and we the viewers are an audience participating in the drama. In other words, space going back from the picture plane seems to be continuous with space in front of the picture plane, the space in which we stand. Accustomed as we are now to this "window" effect in painting, it is difficult to imagine how revolutionary it was to medieval eyes, used to predominantly flat, decorative space in painting **(457,** p. 391). Moreover, Giotto seems to have developed this concept of space largely on his own, with little artistic precedent. The figures in *The Lamentation* are round and full-bodied, clustered low in the composition to enhance the effect of an event taking place just out of our reach.

Giotto's grouping of the figures is unusual and daring, with Christ's body half-hidden by a figure with its back turned. This arrangement seems casual and almost random, until we notice the slope of the hill directing attention to Christ's and the Virgin's heads, which are the focal point. Yet another innovation—perhaps Giotto's most important one—was his interest in depicting the psychological and emotional reactions of his subjects. The characters in *The Lamentation* interact in a natural, human way that gives this and the artist's other religious scenes a special warmth.

Neither Duccio nor Giotto had an especially long career. Each did his most significant work in the first decade of the 14th century. Yet in that short time the course of Western art history changed dramatically. Both artists had sought a new direction for painting—a more naturalistic, more human, more engaging representation of the physical world—and both had taken giant steps in that direction. Their experiments paved the way for a flowering of all the arts that would come in the next century and that its practitioners would name a "rebirth"—the Renaissance.

464. Giotto. *The Lamentation.* 1305–06. Fresco, 7'7" × 7'9". Arena Chapel, Padua.

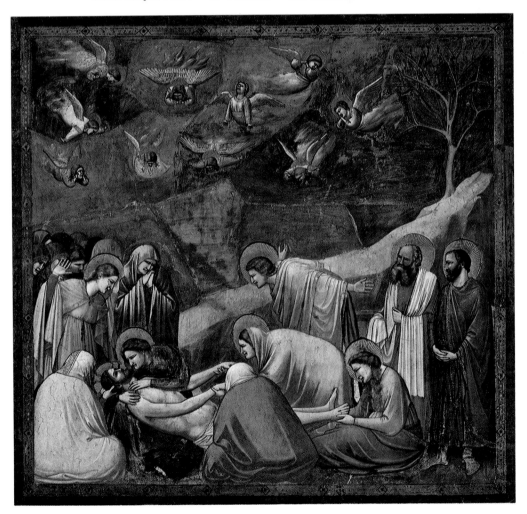

The Renaissance

T HE RENAISSANCE was the first period in Western art history to name itself, for its time and for posterity. We call the art of ancient Greece and Rome "Classical," but the Greeks and Romans didn't call it that. We call the art of northern Europe in the 13th and 14th centuries "Gothic," but the people making the art didn't call it that. This may seem to be a trivial point, a quibble about word meanings, but it is not. Artists of the Renaissance were *self-conscious*, aware of their work as being different from that of the past many centuries. They strove deliberately to create a golden age in the arts, and they called it a *renaissance*—a *rebirth*—of the era they most admired: the Classical period of Greek and Roman art that had begun nearly two thousand years earlier. Today we still call 15th- and 16th-century European history "the Renaissance," and to a large extent we still accept the prideful belief of its makers that it was indeed a golden age.

The Renaissance brought a revolution in the world of art, a clear break with the immediate past. Nearly everything about art changed, and changed quickly—the types of art being made, the way works of art looked, the materials used, the role of the artist, the identities and influence of patrons, and the artistic precedents that served as inspiration.

Before discussing the stylistic components of the Renaissance, we might address the question of why it occurred, especially why it began at the time and place it did. Italy in the 15th century offered a perfect combination of circumstances. For one thing, the conditions for artistic patronage were unusually favorable. Italy had developed powerful city-states engaged in extensive trade and banking. The members of the merchant class, at the head of this commerce, had a great deal of money to spend, were well educated, and were highly motivated for reasons of prestige and temperament to invest in art. Also, the Christian church was centered in Italy, and it provided another important source of patronage.

Besides the abundance of customers for art, there was ready inspiration for art. During this period a growing interest in the past led to the excavation of Classical Greek and Roman ruins, which revealed architecture and sculpture that had not been seen for centuries. Many of the leading artists of the Renaissance studied these works and took them as models.

CHRONOLOGY

	1400—1450	1450—1500
Style/Period	Renaissance, Italy, c. 1400–c. 1550 Gothic period, northern Europe	Renaissance, Italy, c. 1400–c. 1550 Renaissance, northern Europe, c. 1450–c. 1600
Political/ Social Events and Personalities	Joan of Arc burned at the stake, 1431 Printing press invented, c. 1450	Lorenzo de' Medici, ruler of Florence, 1469–1492 Christopher Columbus lands in the Americas, 1492
Monuments and Major Artists	Jan van Eyck (1370?–1440?) Lorenzo Ghiberti (1378–1455) Donatello (1386–1466) Rogier van der Weyden (1400–1464) Masaccio (1401–1428)	St. Peter's, Vatican, Rome, begun c. 1450 Piero della Francesca (1416?–1492) Giovanni Bellini (c. 1430–1516) Sandro Botticelli (1444?–1510) Hieronymus Bosch (c. 1450–1516) Leonardo da Vinci (1452–1519)

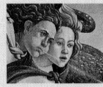

Botticelli, *The Birth of Venus*

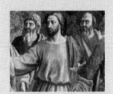

Masaccio, *The Tribute Money*

Finally, we might be tempted to say that the Renaissance began in Italy in the 15th century because Michelangelo, Leonardo, Raphael, and others were there. But perhaps another age with the same social and historical advantages would have spawned artists of equal genius. We cannot know for sure, but the problem is intriguing. Let us now sum up the changes that took place in art; we will refer to them again as they are illustrated in specific examples. Some have already been mentioned in previous chapters.

The types of art made during the Renaissance included all those that had been popular during the Middle Ages—sculpture, architecture, tapestry, and so forth—but there was a much greater emphasis on painting. Throughout the medieval period, painting had taken rather a back seat to the other arts. Although miniatures and frescoes continued to be made, artists of the Middle Ages showed little interest in the "easel painting," the precious object to be hung on the wall for its own sake. But in the Renaissance painting came to life, with an energy perhaps never before seen. The Renaissance has been called "the age of painting"; this may be an overstatement in view of the splendid sculpture and architecture it produced, but the phrase is certainly true when we compare the Renaissance with the several centuries preceding it.

For the first time since the Classical periods of Greece and Rome the quest for "realism"—the faithful representation of the natural world—

1500—1550	1550—1600

Renaissance, Italy, c. 1400–c. 1550
Renaissance, northern Europe,
   c. 1450–c. 1600
	Mannerism, Italy, c. 1550–c. 1620
	Renaissance, northern Europe,
	   c. 1450–c. 1600

Holbein, *Henry VIII*

Henry VIII, king of England,
   1509–1547
Martin Luther, beginning of Protestant
   Reformation in Europe, 1517
Charles V, Holy Roman Emperor,
   1519–1558
	Elizabeth I, queen of England,
	   1558–1603
	William Shakespeare (1564–1616)

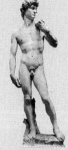

Michelangelo, *David*

Titian, *Charles V*

Sistine Chapel frescoes, Rome,
   1508–1512
Leonardo da Vinci (1452–1519)
Matthias Grünewald (c. 1470–1528)
Albrecht Dürer (1471–1528)
Michelangelo (1475–1564)
Giorgione (1476/78–1510)
Raphael (1483–1520)
Titian (c. 1490–1576)
Hans Holbein the Younger
   (1497/8–1543)

Michelangelo (1475–1564)
Titian (c. 1490–1576)
Tintoretto (1518–1594)
Pieter Bruegel the Elder (1525–1569)
Sofonisba Anguissola (1535?–1625)
El Greco (1541?–1614)

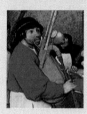

Bruegel, *Peasant Wedding*

dominated art. Painters and sculptors dissected corpses to better understand the mysteries of human anatomy. Elaborate studies of perspective were undertaken (p. 114) to create the illusion of accurate three-dimensional space. It was during the Renaissance that the notion of art as mirror of the physical world became set, a notion that persists in some people's minds even today.

Since painting was newly popular, artists took great interest in its physical properties, and the materials of that medium changed radically. Oil paint, which had been introduced in the 14th century, soon eclipsed the more cumbersome tempera (Chapter 7, p. 175). New techniques of fresco painting were perfected. On the whole, there was a great deal of experimentation with materials, some of it rewarding, some of it disastrous. Leonardo da Vinci, whose curiosity about the world seems to have been boundless, was most prone to try new techniques, and some of his best-known works, including *The Last Supper* **(134)**, have deteriorated badly. Nevertheless, the experimentation led to some extraordinary developments.

The changing role of the artist is a fascinating aspect of the Renaissance. Up until that time the vast majority of Western artists had been anonymous. In isolated cases we may have a name; we know, for example, that Praxiteles was a great genius of Greek sculpture, and we know what his work looked like **(326)**. Beyond that, we have little information about the man himself. Even this much is an advantage over our knowledge of most artists in the 13th and 14th centuries. The medieval artist, in general, was considered a skilled craftsman, little more. A talented wood- or stone-carver might be given the same respect that today is accorded to a first-rate carpenter—valuable, indispensable when needed, forgotten when the job is finished. Of course, there were exceptions, and a few names have come down to us, but not many.

Starting with the great masters of the Renaissance we suddenly have rather complete portraits of the artists—who they were, how they lived and worked, what they thought about art and life in general. For the first time artists were considered a breed apart, comprising a class of their own that transcended the social class determined by birth—not nobility, not bourgeoisie, not clergy, but a separate and elite category of people respected not because of who they were, but because of what they could *do*. They lived in the courts of the nobles and popes, they moved freely in good society, their company was sought after, their services in demand.

The character of art patronage reflected the changing times. Before the Renaissance only two groups of people could afford to be art patrons—the nobility and the clergy. Both continued to be active sponsors of art, but they were joined in the 15th century by a new class of merchant-rulers, very rich, socially ambitious, fully able to support extravagant spending on art. The climate could not have been more fertile for a flowering of art: the best artists were available, and virtually unlimited funds existed to support them.

One more element is needed to complete our picture of the Renaissance artist—the changing sources of inspiration. Renaissance artists cast their eyes backward to those they considered their natural teachers—the great masters of ancient Greece and Rome. To their everlasting credit these later artists were not satisfied merely to imitate; they forged a new style of art that at least equaled the standards of the Classical world. With this preamble, then, let us look at the artists of the Renaissance.

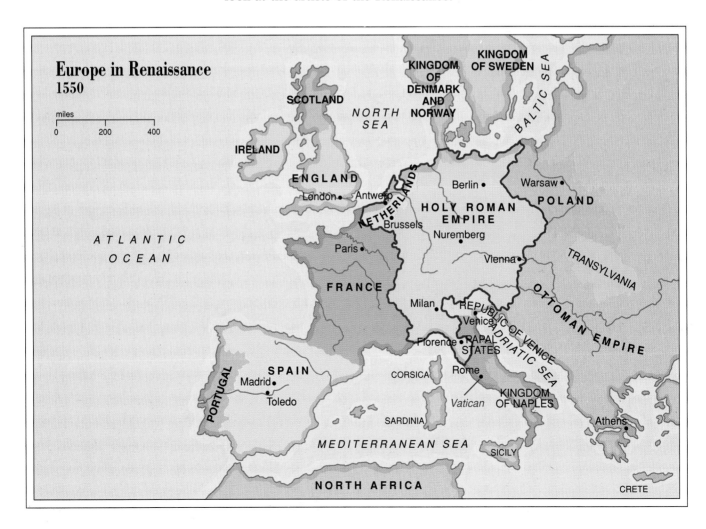

Europe in Renaissance 1550

THE RENAISSANCE
IN ITALY

In 1401 the city of Florence announced an artistic competition, the winner of which would be awarded the commission for making sculptured bronze doors to decorate the Baptistry of the Cathedral. At least six artists were invited to submit trial pieces. The subject was to be the sacrifice of Isaac, from the biblical story in which God tested the faith of Abraham by requiring him to slay his son, Isaac. (At the last moment the Lord, convinced of Abraham's obedience, spared the boy.) Among those submitting designs to the competition was a twenty-three-year-old goldsmith, Lorenzo Ghiberti. Ghiberti's trial panel **(465)** shows a strong sense of composition; its action is compact, with a subtle curving rhythm from lower right to upper left, and the figures of Abraham and Isaac at middle right are emphasized to create a focal point. Isaac's nude body reveals Ghiberti's admiration for ancient statues and is a true Renaissance figure. Ghiberti won the prize and spent much of the next two decades working on the doors.

Shortly after the doors were installed, Ghiberti was asked to make another set, this time for the east side of the Baptistry, and this time without any need to prove himself in competition. The east doors were more than twenty-five years in the making and finally were installed in 1452. So marvelous were their design and craftsmanship that Michelangelo termed them the "Gates of Paradise," and so they have been called ever since **(466)**.

Between the time of the first competition and the completion of the "Gates of Paradise"—half a century—Ghiberti's style had matured considerably. We saw one panel of the later doors in Chapter 11 **(323)**. The artist had made extensive studies of perspective, allowing him to create the illusion of

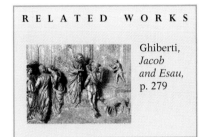

RELATED WORKS

Ghiberti, *Jacob and Esau,* p. 279

left: **465.** Lorenzo Ghiberti. *Sacrifice of Isaac.* 1401. Gilt bronze, 21 × 17½″. Museo Nazionale del Bargello, Florence.

right: **466.** Lorenzo Ghiberti. "Gates of Paradise," east doors of the Baptistry, Florence. 1425–52. Gilt bronze, height 18′6″.

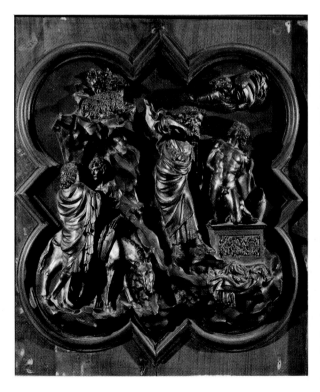

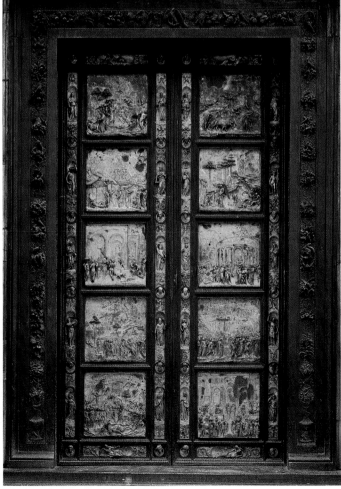

spatial depth on the shallow bronze doors. And he is in full control of three-dimensional volumes; some of the figures on the east doors are virtually in the round. The composition is simplified, less cluttered, easier to understand. In the span of time from the trial panel to the "Gates of Paradise," Ghiberti made the transition from the first gropings of the Renaissance to a more assured style that foreshadowed the sculptures of Michelangelo's generation.

While Ghiberti was working on the first set of bronze doors for the Baptistry, he was assisted by, among others, the young sculptor Donatello. Donatello was born in Florence about 1386 and was apprenticed to Ghiberti by the age of seventeen. During his long career he worked in many different styles and in all the sculptural media then available—wood, stone, and metal. An early work, the statue of *St. Mark* in Florence **(467)**, depends on Donatello's familiarity with two sources of inspiration—ancient Greek and Roman sculptures and the scriptures. The figure is as naturalistic as any of the Greek statues, yet there is a stamp of individual personality in both face and body that may have come from Donatello's reading of Mark's Gospel.

St. Mark shows many of the characteristics that came to typify Donatello's work and helps to explain why some writers consider Donatello to be the founder of modern sculpture. This statue is enclosed within a niche but is by no means dependent on the architectural framework for support. Unlike the vast majority of medieval sculptures, *St. Mark* is totally self-sustaining—fully rounded and capable of standing on its own. Moreover, Donatello's figure is remarkably lifelike. St. Mark seems caught in the act of movement, and his body underneath the garments seems real, substantial, made of flesh and bone. If you compare this statue with the figures on Sluter's *Moses Well* **(462)**, carved a mere decade earlier, you will appreciate Donatello's originality. Sluter's prophets are wrapped in massive drapery that has a life of its own, independent of the body. But St. Mark's clothing responds to the form underneath. Where the left knee bends outward, the robe falls back; where the right arm is pressed to the body, the sleeve wrinkles. We know that if St. Mark moved, the garments would move with him.

467. Donatello. *St. Mark.* 1411–13. Marble, height 7′9″. Or San Michele, Florence.

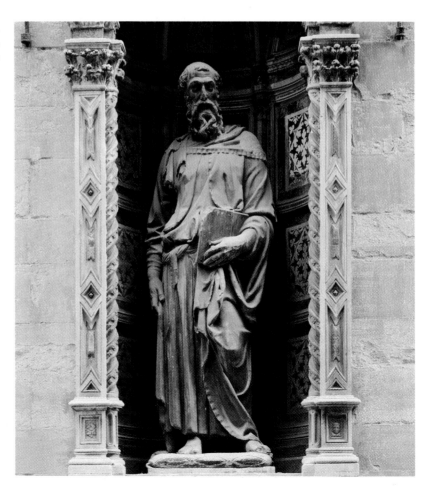

At the same time that Donatello was exploring the potential for naturalism and animation in sculpture, the early painters of the Renaissance were grappling with the problems of conveying these qualities on a flat surface. Among the first of those who could indisputably be called a Renaissance artist was the young genius known as Masaccio, whose name has been variously translated as "wicked Tom" and "slovenly Tom." Masaccio lived for only twenty-seven years, and there are just four works that can be attributed to him definitely. Nevertheless, his contribution to the development of Early Renaissance art was immense.

Masaccio's best-known painting is *The Tribute Money* **(468)**, a fresco in the Brancacci Chapel in Florence. The story related in this fresco is taken from the Gospel of St. Matthew and concerns an event in the life of Christ. Christ's disciples, especially Peter, had questioned whether it was proper to pay taxes to the Roman government, considering that Christ was the Messiah and above such authority. But Christ pointed out the difference between earthly and spiritual obligations and counseled that the taxes be paid, saying "Render therefore unto Caesar the things which are Caesar's; and unto God the things that are God's" (Matthew 22:21). He urged Peter to go and catch a fish, which would have a coin in its mouth, and to pay the tax collector.

To portray this fairly complicated story, Masaccio has employed the device of **continuous narrative,** by which different parts in a sequence of events are shown in the same work. We saw this technique in the *Bayeux Tapestry* **(363)** and in the sculptured reliefs on Trajan's Column **(442)**. Masaccio has selected three episodes from the story of the tax collector for his painting. In the center, Christ is conferring with his disciples and instructing Peter to pay the tax. At left, Peter goes fishing and finds the coin; at right, he turns the coin over to the Roman tax official. Such a running narrative might have seemed awkward were it not for Masaccio's compositional powers and his mastery of spatial perspective. The most important scene is the conference among Christ and his twelve Apostles, just off center in the composition. Here the figures are drawn together in dramatic tension by their grouping and their gestures. The fishing segment is least important; Masaccio thrusts it far to the left. For the paying of tribute money, the climax of the event, Masaccio has separated the two key figures—Peter and the tax collector—by an architectural background.

All of Masaccio's figures are well constructed, standing in relaxed *contrapposto* poses (p. 281). This effect is especially apparent in the legs of the tax collector in his two appearances. Like Donatello's *St. Mark*, the figures have real, living bodies under their garments, bodies that seem to have the muscle and bone to move. A comparison of this work with Duccio's *Christ Entering Jerusalem* **(463)**, painted just a little over a century earlier, will show that great strides had been made in using linear perspective to depict architecture in three-dimensional space. Also, Masaccio's shading and treatment of drapery

468. Masaccio.
The Tribute Money. c. 1427.
Fresco, 8′2⅜″ × 19′8¼″.
Brancacci Chapel, Sta. Maria del Carmine, Florence.

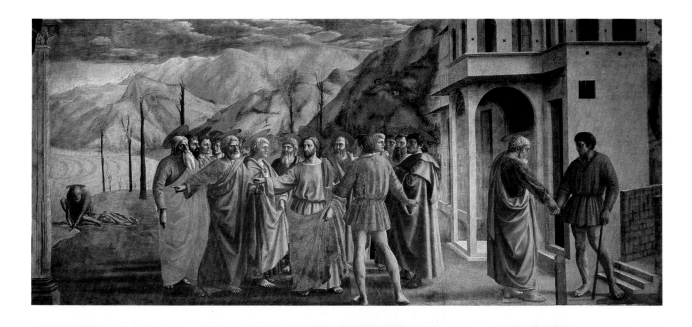

RELATED WORKS

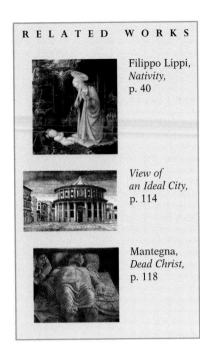

Filippo Lippi,
Nativity,
p. 40

*View of
an Ideal City*,
p. 114

Mantegna,
Dead Christ,
p. 118

give convincing roundness to the bodies. The figures have a dignity and gravity that mark them as true products of the Renaissance.

Masaccio's art had a profound influence on another Florentine painter, who came into prominence about a generation later—Piero della Francesca. In Piero's fresco *The Resurrection* **(469)** we can see the artist's debt to Masaccio in the sure handling of linear perspective and the wonderful roundness of the bodies. Piero, however, was a skilled mathematician, and that is one of the things that sets his composition apart from the work of the earlier master. This picture is constructed as a triangle, with Christ's head at the apex. The triangle moves down to the two lower corners of the painting and cuts across the bottom, pulling the figures of Christ and the sleeping soldiers into one coherent group **[Overlay 9a].** A vertical axis runs from Christ's face straight down to the bottom of the painting. In spite of this structure, the picture does not seem rigid. The poses of the soldiers, as they lie sprawled in sleep, are by no means stiff. Also, Piero has introduced elements of asymmetrical balance to offset the predominantly symmetrical balance of the triangle. Christ's upraised arm with the banner juts out to one side of the central axis, while his bent left knee pushes out to the other side. At their best, Renaissance painters imposed an order, often a geometrical order, on their compositions, but they did not let that order overwhelm their art.

Yet another Florentine painter, a quarter-century younger than Piero, was Sandro Botticelli. Botticelli was rather more sophisticated and worldly than most of his artist-contemporaries. While he painted many religious subjects, his earlier works took their themes from Greek and Roman culture and the Classical myths. Also, he had a special fascination with detail and with the depiction of women as graceful, exquisite beings, so weightless they often

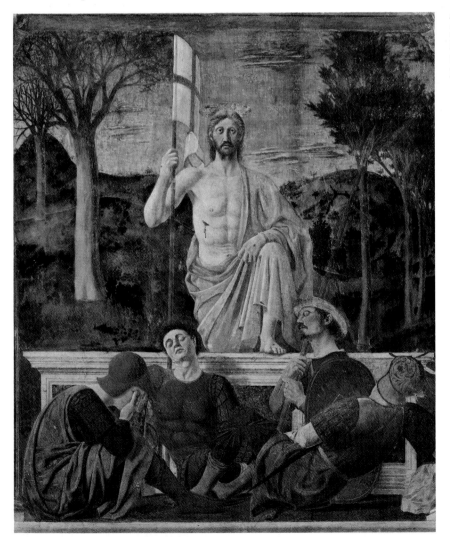

469. Piero della Francesca.
The Resurrection. c. 1460.
Fresco, 9'6" × 8'4".
Gallery, Palazzo del Commune,
Borgo San Sepolcro, Italy.

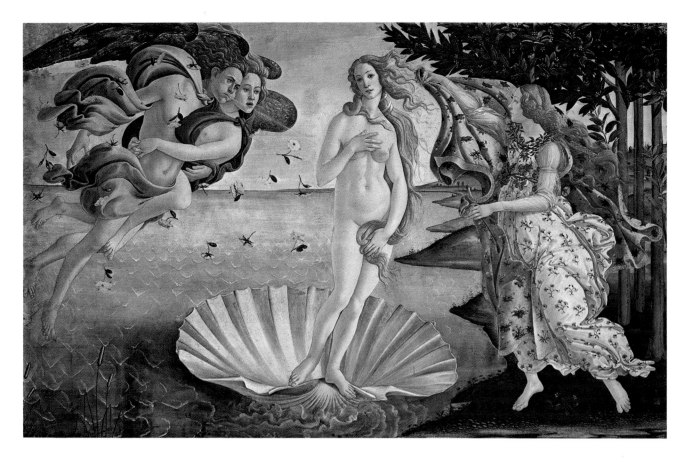

seem about to float out of the paintings. Early in his career Botticelli had the great fortune to enjoy the patronage of the Medici, the ruling merchant family of Florence. Sometime in the 1470s, it is believed, the Medici commissioned Botticelli to paint two large works as decoration for their family villa. One of these works was *The Birth of Venus* (**470**).

Venus was the Roman goddess of love and beauty. According to legend, she was born from the sea, and so Botticelli depicts her floating upward on a shell. Two Zephyrs, or wind gods, blow her gently toward the shore, where a figure representing spring waits ready to clothe Venus in a flowing garment. The portrayal of Venus establishes Botticelli's credentials as a Renaissance artist in two respects. For one thing, Venus is a "pagan" figure, not a Christian one, and her choice as a subject for art was a telling sign of the times. For another, Botticelli paints the goddess in the nude, with strategically placed hands and a tress of hair the only concessions to modesty. Such a large-scale depiction of the female nude in art had been virtually unknown since Classical times. Venus' pose is modeled after a Roman sculpture of the goddess, which Botticelli had studied in the Medici collection, but her lightness, her fragile quality, her delicate beauty and billowing hair—these are Botticelli's own.

As we can see in *The Birth of Venus*, Botticelli has mastered the technique of painting round, full-fleshed bodies. However, he is not nearly as interested as later artists would be in showing deep, three-dimensional space. The space in *The Birth of Venus* is actually quite shallow, with the sea and horizon and trees serving as a backdrop, almost a stage set, and the figures all inhabit the same plane. These characteristics mark Botticelli as an artist of the Early Renaissance. Painters of the next generation would strive to set their figures more naturally, in a deeper landscape.

While Botticelli was at work in Florence, painting in Venice was dominated by the Bellini family: the father Jacopo, his sons Gentile and Giovanni. Venetian artists were especially interested in depictions of the natural landscape, with an emphasis on atmosphere created by light and color. We see

470. Sandro Botticelli. *The Birth of Venus.* c. 1480. Tempera on canvas, 6′7″ × 9′2″. Uffizi, Florence.

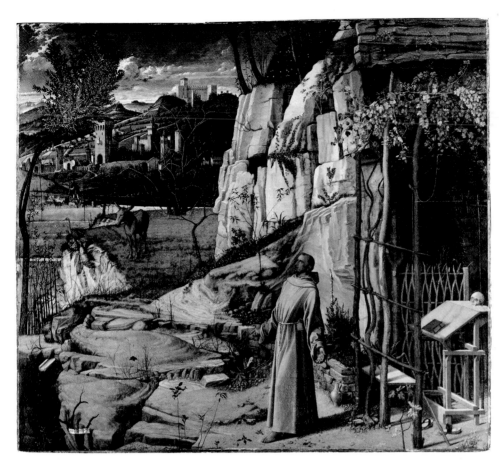

471. Giovanni Bellini.
St. Francis in the Desert. c. 1485.
Oil on panel, $4'\frac{1}{2}'' \times 4'7''$.
Copyright the Frick Collection,
New York.

these effects in a painting by the most influential member of the dynasty, Giovanni Bellini's *St. Francis in the Desert* **(471)**.

Francis was a holy man, a monk and preacher, born in the Italian town of Assisi in the late 12th century. According to legend, he was able to converse with the birds and animals, in a language both man and creatures understood freely. Francis' goodness was so profound that God bestowed upon him the *stigmata*—marks or wounds upon his hands and feet like those Christ had suffered when he was nailed to the cross at his Crucifixion. The artist Bellini has chosen to capture the moment when Francis received the stigmata, a moment of intense pain and great joy. A brilliant golden light bathes the scene, presumably the light of God shining down on the holy man. Francis stands in awe of the light, his arms outstretched, his gaze cast upward, welcoming this sign of God's favor.

Bellini has employed a favorite device to structure this scene. He frames the saint in a protective craggy foreground landscape, then shows us another layer of landscape in the far distance. Again, as with Botticelli, we might view this arrangement almost as a stage set. The far landscape could be a painted backdrop, the rocky cave a construction on the stage. There is little sense of one progressing naturally to the other. Still, Bellini had made great strides toward portraying a fully three-dimensional landscape, and his ideas would be developed further by his two greatest pupils: Giorgione **(480)** and Titian **(482)**. A great many painters of the next generation would be indebted to Bellini's example for the warmth of light and color he mastered.

We come now to a period known as the *High Renaissance*—a brief but glorious time in the history of art. In barely twenty-five years, from shortly before 1500 to about 1525, some of the most celebrated works of Western art were produced. Many artists participated in this brilliant creative endeavor, but the outstanding figures among them were unquestionably Leonardo da Vinci and Michelangelo.

The term "Renaissance man" is applied to someone who is very well informed about, or very good at doing, many different, often quite unrelated, things. It originated in the fact that several of the leading figures of the Renaissance were artistic jacks-of-all-trades. Michelangelo was a painter, sculptor, poet, architect—incomparably gifted at all. Leonardo was a painter, inventor, sculptor, architect, engineer, scientist, musician, and all-around intellectual. In our age of specialization these accomplishments seem staggering, but during the heady years of the Renaissance nothing was impossible.

Leonardo is the artist who most embodies the term "Renaissance man"; many people consider him to have been the greatest genius who ever lived. Leonardo was possessed of a brilliant and inquiring mind that accepted no limits. Throughout his long life he remained absorbed by the problem of how things work, and how they might work. A typical example of his investigations is the well-known *Study of Human Proportions* **(472)**, in which the artist sought to establish ideal proportions for the human body by relating it to the square and the circle. Above and below the figure is Leonardo's eccentric mirror writing, which he used in his notes and journals.

Leonardo's interest in mathematics is also evident from his careful rendering of perspective. In Chapter 4 we examined his masterpiece, *The Last Supper* **(134)**, which uses one-point linear perspective to organize the many figures in the composition and set them into deep space. Yet another interest, experimental painting techniques, served the artist less well in *The Last Supper*. Rather than employing the established fresco method (Chapter 7), Leonardo worked in a medium he devised for the *Last Supper* project, thus dooming his greatest work to centuries of restoration (p. 115).

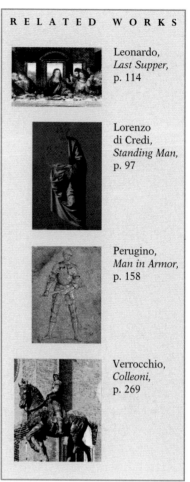

RELATED WORKS

Leonardo,
Last Supper,
p. 114

Lorenzo
di Credi,
Standing Man,
p. 97

Perugino,
Man in Armor,
p. 158

Verrocchio,
Colleoni,
p. 269

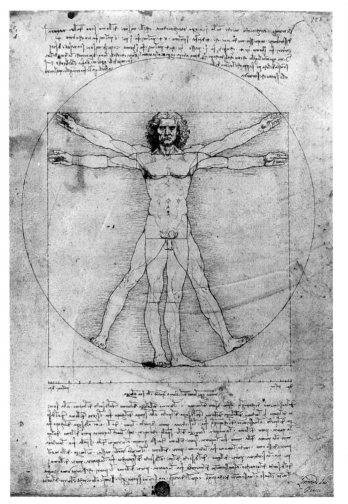

472. Leonardo da Vinci.
*Study of Human Proportions
According to Vitruvius.*
c. 1485–90.
Pen and ink, $13\frac{1}{2} \times 9\frac{3}{4}''$.
Academy, Venice.

In spite of his vast accomplishments, Leonardo often had difficulty completing specific projects. Many of his most ambitious works were left unfinished, including his best-known painting, the *Mona Lisa* **(473)**. *Mona Lisa* has been the object of special fascination ever since it was painted. Songs, poems, and treatises have been written about the sitter's smile, and her image often turns up in remarkably unexpected contexts. Just what is so magical about this painting is hard to define. Certainly the "mysterious" smile on the woman's face contributes to the *Mona Lisa*'s special aura, but it alone is not sufficient to explain the painting's fascination. For this work Leonardo was in masterful control of a newly developed technique known as **sfumato** (deriving from the Italian for "smoke"), which involves painting in thin glazes to achieve a hazy, cloudy atmosphere and a sense of three-dimensional form. Behind the model is a fantasy landscape, vague and undefined, another element of the painting's mystery. Some of the intrigue of the *Mona Lisa* must lie in its contradictions. It presents to us a Florentine matron, not at first glance beautiful, posed almost rigidly in the exact center of the painting, showing little of her emotions. Yet further acquaintance with the subject reveals beauty so unique as to ignore conventional ideas of beauty, a pose that is not rigid but serene, and a personality which, though elusive, draws us to her.

During the years when Leonardo was painting the *Mona Lisa*, Michelangelo, a quarter-century younger, also was in Florence, at work on one of the projects for which he is best known. Michelangelo had established his reputation as a sculptor by the age of twenty-five. A year later he received the

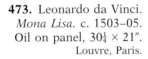

473. Leonardo da Vinci. *Mona Lisa.* c. 1503–05. Oil on panel, 30¼ × 21″. Louvre, Paris.

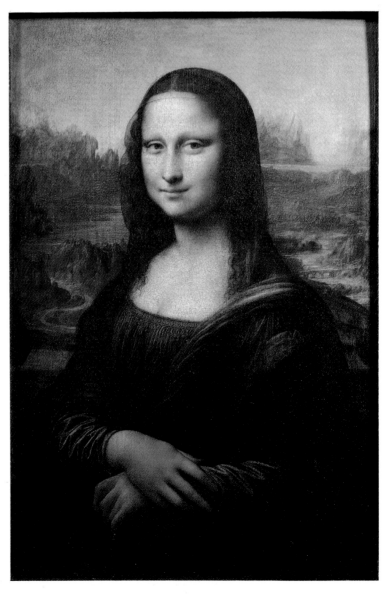

LEONARDO DA VINCI

1452–1519

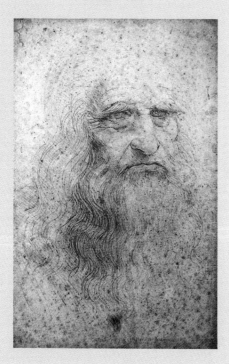

N O CLUES ARE OFFERED by the scant knowledge about Leonardo's origins to explain what spawned perhaps the most complex imagination of all time. Leonardo was the illegitimate son of a peasant woman known only as Caterina and a fairly well-to-do notary, Piero da Vinci. He was raised in his father's house at Vinci and, when he was about fifteen, apprenticed to the Florentine artist Andrea del Verrocchio, in whose workshop he remained for ten years. It is said the pupil's talent so impressed his master that Verrocchio gave up painting forever.

In 1482 Leonardo left Florence for Milan, where he became official artist to Lodovico Sforza, duke of that city. There the artist undertook many projects, foremost among them his famous painting of the *Last Supper*. Leonardo remained with Sforza until the latter's fall from power in 1499, after which he returned to Florence.

Sketches and written records indicate that Leonardo worked as a sculptor, but no examples remain. Only about a dozen paintings can be definitely attributed to him, and several of these are unfinished. There are, however, hundreds of drawings, and the thousands of pages from his detailed notebook testify to the man's extraordinary genius. If Leonardo completed relatively few artistic works, this can only be ascribed to the enormous breadth of his interests, which caused him repeatedly to turn from one subject to another. He was a skilled architect and engineer, engrossed in the problems of city planning, sanitary disposal, military engineering, and even the design of weapons. He made sketches for a crude submarine, a helicopter, and an airplane—with characteristic thoroughness also designing a parachute in case the airplane should fail. He made innovative studies in astronomy, anatomy, botany, geology, optics, and above all mathematics. His contemporaries reported his great talent as a musician—he played and improvised on the lute—as well as his love of inventive practical jokes.

In 1507 Leonardo was appointed court painter to the King of France, Louis XII, who happened to be in Milan at the time. Nine years later the aging artist was named court painter to Louis's successor, Francis I. Francis seems to have revered him for his towering reputation as an artist and his crisp intellect, but to have expected little artistic production from the old man. The king provided comfortable lodgings in the city of Amboise, where Leonardo died.

Solitary all his life, Leonardo did not marry, and he formed very few close attachments. His obsession seems to have been with getting it all down, recording the fertile outpourings of his brain and hand. In his *Treatise on Painting*, assembled from his notebook pages and published after his death, he advised painters to follow his method: "You should often amuse yourself when you take a walk for recreation, in watching and taking note of the attitudes and actions of men as they talk and dispute, or laugh or come to blows with one another . . . noting these down with rapid strokes, in a little pocket-book which you ought always to carry with you . . . for there is such an infinite number of forms and actions of things that the memory is incapable of preserving them."[1]

Leonardo da Vinci. *Self-Portrait*. c. 1512.
Chalk on paper, 13 × 8¼″. Biblioteca Reale, Turin.

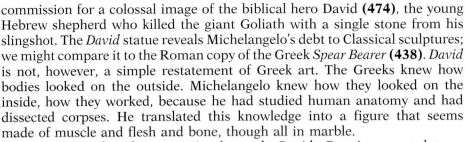

commission for a colossal image of the biblical hero David **(474)**, the young Hebrew shepherd who killed the giant Goliath with a single stone from his slingshot. The *David* statue reveals Michelangelo's debt to Classical sculptures; we might compare it to the Roman copy of the Greek *Spear Bearer* **(438)**. *David* is not, however, a simple restatement of Greek art. The Greeks knew how bodies looked on the outside. Michelangelo knew how they looked on the inside, how they worked, because he had studied human anatomy and had dissected corpses. He translated this knowledge into a figure that seems made of muscle and flesh and bone, though all in marble.

There are other characteristics that make *David* a Renaissance sculpture, not a copy of a Greek one. For one thing, it has a tension and energy that are missing from Greek art. Some writers have suggested that the statue is a self-portrait—not so much that it duplicates Michelangelo's features, but that it expresses the creative tension of its maker. The hands especially are taut and strong, held at the ready for action. Another Renaissance quality is the expression on David's face. Classical Greek statues generally bore an expression of beatific calm, showing the subject to be above earthly concerns. But David is young and vibrant—and angry, angry at the forces of evil represented by the giant Goliath. Michelangelo equated perfect beauty with perfect truth and honor. He seems to have found these qualities in the story of David and to have embodied them in his statue of the young conqueror.

Soon after the completion of *David*, Michelangelo was in Rome, working on sculptures for the tomb of Pope Julius II, which was to be completed during the pope's lifetime. Julius interrupted this project because another idea had captured his imagination. He proposed to employ his young protégé not as a sculptor but as a painter. The artist, whose distaste for painting is well documented, rebelled against the plan, but in the end he was forced to capitulate. Michelangelo would spend the next four years standing in an uncomfortable half-crouch on a scaffold 68 feet above the floor, creating the masterpiece for which he will always be most admired: the ceiling frescoes of the Sistine Chapel in the Vatican.

The Sistine Chapel **(475)**, named after an earlier pope called Sixtus, has a high vaulted ceiling 128 feet long and 44 feet wide. Julius required that Michelangelo cover this entire expanse, 700 square yards, with a painted decoration based on religious themes. Fresco was the only practical medium, and the

below: **474.** Michelangelo. *David.* 1501–04. Marble, height 18′. Academy, Florence.

right: **475.** Sistine Chapel, Vatican, Rome. 1473–80. Ceiling frescoes painted 1508–12.

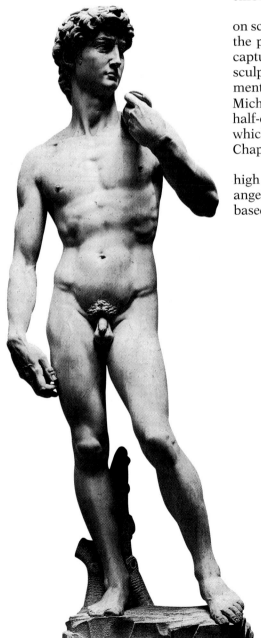

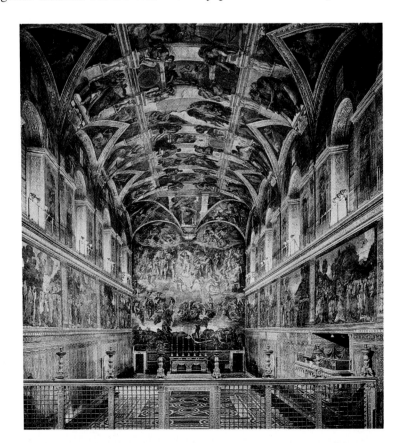

MICHELANGELO

1475–1564

He traveled to Venice and Bologna, to Florence, then finally to Rome, where he attracted the first of what would become a long list of patrons among the clergy. A *Pietà* (Virgin mourning the dead Christ) made in 1500 and now in the Vatican established his reputation as a sculptor. Within a dozen years after that he had completed the two works most closely associated with his name: the *David* statue **(474)** and the ceiling frescoes in the Sistine Chapel **(476)**.

From his teen years until his death Michelangelo never lacked for highly placed patrons. He served—and survived—six popes, and in between accepted commissions from two emperors, a king, and numerous members of the nobility. All his life he struggled to keep a balance between the work he wanted to do and the work demanded of him by his benefactors. His relationships with these powerful figures were often stormy, marked by squabbles about payment, insults given and forgiven, flight from the scene followed by penitent return.

Michelangelo served these masters, at various times, as painter and architect, but he considered himself above all to be a sculptor. Much of his time was spent supervising the quarrying of superior stones for sculptural projects. His greatest genius lay in depictions of the human figure, whether in marble or in paint. Vasari writes that "this extraordinary man chose always to refuse to paint anything save the human body in its most beautifully proportioned and perfect forms." To this end Michelangelo made extensive anatomical studies and dissected corpses to better understand the inner workings of the body.

Michelangelo, who is presumed to have been a homosexual, formed a number of passionate attachments during his life. These inspired the artist, always a sensitive and gifted poet, to write numerous sonnets. One of his most poignant verses, however, was written as a commentary on his labors up on the scaffold under the Sistine Chapel ceiling. We might find it amusing if it were not so heartfelt:

> I've grown a goiter by dwelling in this den—
>   As cats from stagnant streams in Lombardy,
>   Or in what other land they hap to be—
>   Which drives the belly close beneath the chin;
> My beard turns up to heaven; my nape falls in,
>   Fixed on my spine; my breast-bone visibly
>   Grows like a harp: a rich embroidery
>   Bedews my face from brush-drops thick and thin. . . .[2]

H E IS BEYOND LEGEND. His name means "archangel Michael," and to his contemporaries and those who came after, his stature is scarcely less than that of a heavenly being. He began serious work as an artist at the age of thirteen and did not stop until death claimed him seventy-six years later. His equal may never be seen again, for only a particular time and place could have bred the genius of Michelangelo.

Michelangelo Buonarroti was born in the Tuscan town of Caprese. According to his devoted biographer and friend, Giorgio Vasari, the young Michelangelo often was scolded and beaten by his father for spending too much time drawing. Eventually, however, seeing his son's talent, the father relented and apprenticed him to the painter Domenico Ghirlandaio. At the age of fourteen Michelangelo was welcomed into the household of the wealthy banker Lorenzo de' Medici, who operated a private sculpture academy for promising young students. There he remained until Lorenzo's death, after which Michelangelo, just seventeen years old, struck out permanently on his own.

Anonymous artist. *Portrait of Michelangelo.* 16th century.
Staatliche Museen Preussischer Kulturbesitz, Berlin.

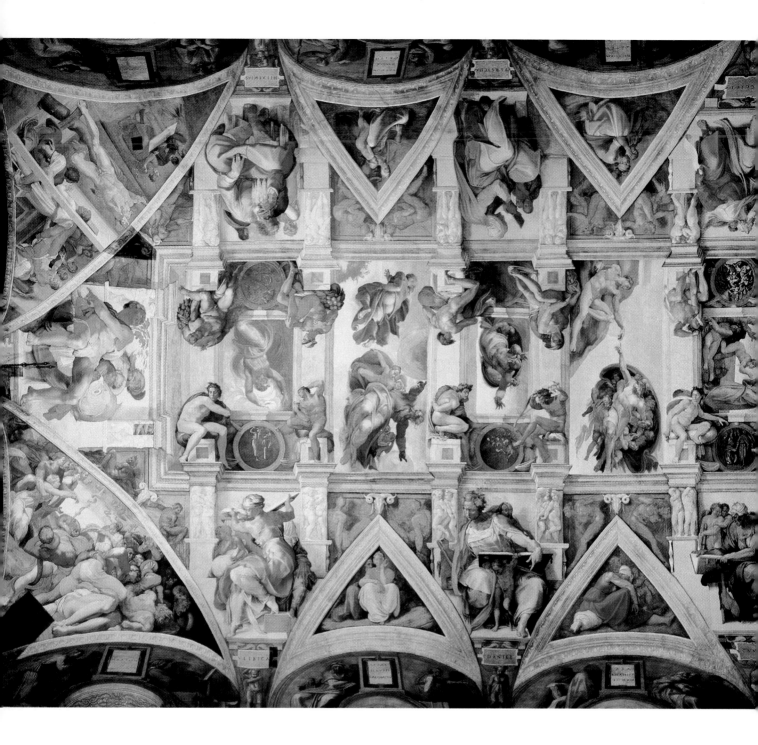

difficulties of this technique are considerable (Chapter 7). Paint must be applied to fresh plaster just when it has the proper degree of dampness; only a small area can be covered at a time; and the painting must be done directly, with no allowance for correction of mistakes. For this project the artist had to work in a cramped position, with paint and plaster continually dripping in his face. So situated, he was only inches away from the working surface, yet the paintings had to be readable and compelling to a viewer standing on the floor, nearly 70 feet below.

Even more overwhelming than the physical constraints was the challenge of making a coherent composition in such a huge area. Michelangelo organized the ceiling into a painted architectural framework of squares, rectangles, and triangles **(476)**. These segments depict Old Testament stories of the crea-

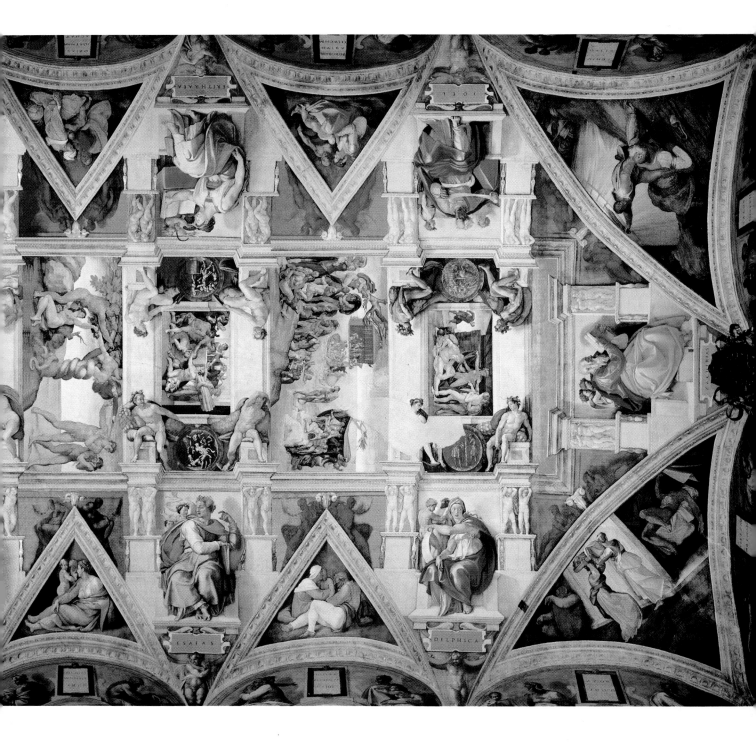

tion of the world, the creation of Adam and Eve, the Fall of Man, and other biblical events. Some figures on the ceiling are from Greek and Roman mythology, for Michelangelo meant to connect the older Classical cultures with Christian theology of his own time.

Each of the segments is self-contained, yet the panels flow gracefully from one to the next, thanks to the artist's placement of overlapping *ignudi* (nude youths) in the spaces between them. The iconographic identity of the *ignudi* is unknown. Some historians have called them angels, but the idea of nude, heavily muscled, wingless angels seems a little far-fetched. Throughout the composition Michelangelo's painted figures have the same anatomical fullness and muscular energy as his sculptures. In fact, many have called the figures "painted stone."

476. Michelangelo. Ceiling, Sistine Chapel. 1508–12. Fresco, 44 × 128′. Vatican, Rome.

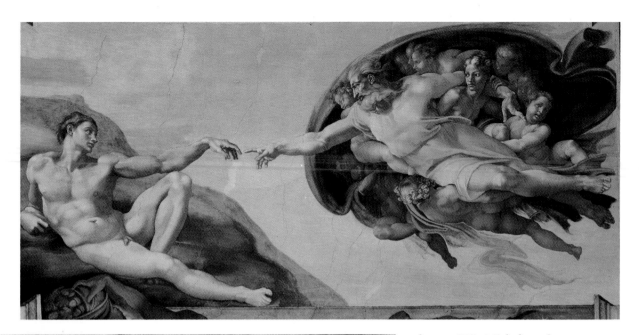

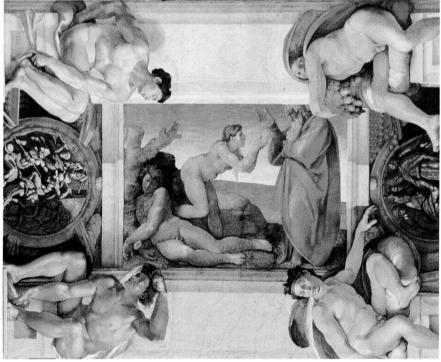

above: 477. Michelangelo.
Creation of Adam,
detail of Sistine Chapel ceiling.
1511. Fresco. Vatican, Rome.

left: 478. Michelangelo.
Creation of Eve,
detail of Sistine Chapel ceiling.
1509–10. Fresco. Vatican, Rome.

The *Creation of Adam* **(477)** is the most familiar of the ceiling images. Based on the biblical book of Genesis, this scene shows Adam, the first man, reclining on a rock. He is well-formed but listless; the spirit of life—the soul—has not yet been breathed into him. At right the dynamic figure of God sweeps toward Adam, wrapped in a symbolic cloak of Heaven. God's left arm embraces a woman thought to represent Eve, the first woman, who at this point in the story is still an idea in God's mind. His left forefinger points to a child, probably meant to be the Christ child, who will come much later to redeem the world. The focal point of this composition is the two hands, stretching toward one another. In a split second they will meet, and the long history of humankind will begin. Michelangelo's genius is nowhere clearer. He does not show us the consummation. He shows us, rather, the thrilling potential.

Because the *Creation of Adam* is reproduced more often than any of the other frescoes, many people assume it is at the center of the ceiling, but it is not. Michelangelo reserved the central position for the *Creation of Eve* **(478)**. Why did the artist place Eve at the very heart of his complex scheme? We don't know, but we assume he had serious theological reasons, perhaps dictated by the clergy. In Christian doctrine Eve, the first woman, prefigures the Virgin Mary, who would give birth to the Christ child. Mary is the foundation of the Christian church, and here she is represented by Eve—at the center of the pope's chapel. This panel (which is surrounded by four *ignudi*) shows Eve being called into life by a benevolent and paternal God. Adam lies asleep at left. We know from the scripture that God has cast Adam into a deep sleep to take one of his ribs, from which Eve was formed. Unlike Adam in his creation scene, Eve does not wait for the enlivening touch. On her own she moves forward, toward the beckoning hand of the Lord.

The ceiling frescoes were an immediate success, and Michelangelo continued as a papal favorite, although his commissions were not always in his preferred line. Just as Pope Julius had urged the sculptor to work as a painter, one of Julius' successors, Pope Paul III, encouraged the sculptor to work as an architect. In 1546 Paul named Michelangelo the official architect of the new St. Peter's, the ceremonial cathedral that is the "headquarters" of the Roman Catholic Church. This structure would be erected on the site of *old* St. Peter's **(448)**, dating from the Early Christian era in the 4th century. By the time he began work on the project, Michelangelo was an old man, well into his seventies and physically tired, but his creative vigor was undiminished. He designed a majestic cross-shaped building **(479)** that now comprises the **apse** of St. Peter's (the section containing the altar) and topped it with a towering dome, which he did not live to see completed. Even at his advanced age Michelangelo refused to relax his lifelong perfectionism. He studied the engineering problems, and he mastered them. Today Michelangelo's dome stands as the world symbol for the church of Rome.

Besides Leonardo and Michelangelo, three other painters, each just a few years younger than Michelangelo, made far-reaching contributions to the art of the High Italian Renaissance. They are Giorgione, Raphael, and Titian.

479. Michelangelo.
St. Peter's, apse and dome.
1546–64. Vatican, Rome.

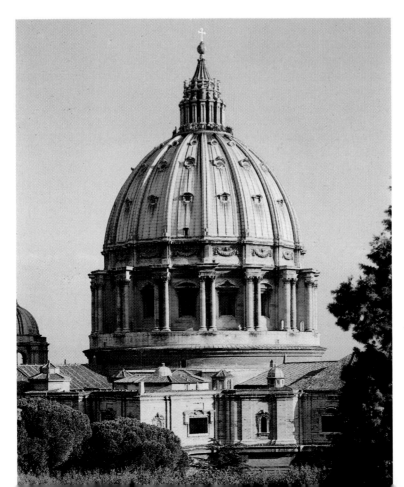

413

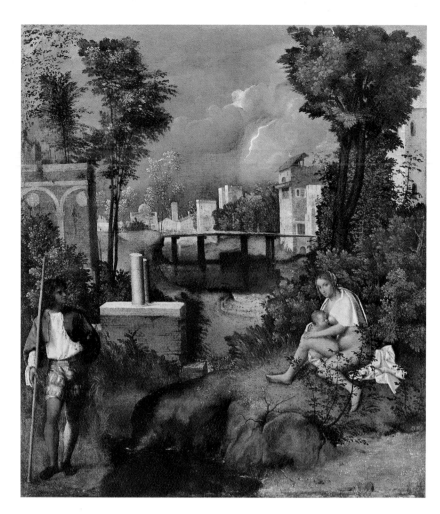

480. Giorgione. *The Tempest.*
c. 1505. Oil on canvas,
$32\frac{1}{4} \times 28\frac{3}{4}''$.
Academy, Venice.

The iconography of Giorgione's painting *The Tempest* **(480)** is unknown. Even the artist's contemporaries seem not to have known what story he was depicting or to have been able to identify the nude woman nursing a child at right and the soldier (or shepherd) at left. Most likely Giorgione was making reference to some event in Greek or Latin poetry, or perhaps he was trying to evoke a classical mood. But regardless of the meaning of its subject, *The Tempest* makes an important contribution to Renaissance art in the way it is composed. Artists of earlier generations, as late as Botticelli **(470)**, would compose a scene by concentrating on the figures and painting the landscape as a kind of backdrop. Giorgione, however, has started by constructing a landscape and then placing his figures in it naturally. This approach paved the way for the great landscape paintings of the centuries to follow.

In *The Tempest,* as the title implies, the subject is really the approaching storm, which closes in dramatically over the city while the two foreground figures are still bathed in sunlight. The artist's debt to his teacher, Bellini, will be obvious if you compare this work with the older master's *St. Francis in the Desert* **(471)**, which also shows a highlighted foreground figure and a distant landscape. Giorgione, however, is less concerned with the human experience. His principal interest seems to have been the contrast of bucolic foreground against the city rendered in careful perspective, with the two drawn together by the violent effects of nature. The storm and the lush vegetation create a world in which nature dominates, not people, and the painting evokes a powerful, compelling mood of apprehension and anticipation.

Raphael also was capable of placing figures in a believable setting, as we saw in his brilliant fresco *The School of Athens* **(204)**. But for the painting illustrated here, *Pope Leo X with Two Cardinals* **(481)**, the artist has deemphasized the architectural setting and moved in close to create a true and perceptive portrait. As Julius II had been Michelangelo's great patron, Leo X was

Raphael's. Leo was the son of Lorenzo de' Medici, and the cardinals on either side of him are his nephews. Raphael has not flattered the pope. The pontiff we see is seriously overweight and has a puffy face and rather coarse features. Despite its unflinching realism, the portrait conveys Leo's majesty and power, emanating not just from the office of pope but from the man.

Even before Raphael painted the portrait of Leo X, the artist Titian, Raphael's contemporary, had declined to become the pope's official artist. Possibly Titian hoped that a career of greater scope awaited him. If so he was not disappointed, for Titian eventually achieved an international reputation, numbering among his many royal patrons King Philip II of Spain, King Francis I of France, and, above all, the Holy Roman Emperor Charles V.

The term "Roman" here requires some explanation. In the mid-16th century the Holy Roman Empire comprised an area of Europe reaching from the borders of France at the west to Poland and Hungary in the east—roughly the size of modern-day Germany, Austria, and parts of northern Italy (map, p. 398). Its ruler, Charles V, was not Roman at all but Austrian, and he reigned as the most powerful monarch in the West.

After a time the emperor refused to be painted by anyone *but* Titian. In *Charles V at Mühlberg* (482) the artist has created the image of a great hero—majestic yet honorable, stalwart yet kind, the defender of the Catholic faith on the field of battle. We know that Charles was quite short in stature, and so the artist has cleverly bowed the horse's head to make its rider more imposing. Unlike Raphael, Titian did not limit himself to a strict duplication of his subject's features. He certainly improved a bit on nature in drawing the emperor's face. Also, he made sure to pose Charles in splendid royal armor, on a prancing horse, isolated against a vivid sky—all of these factors designed to enhance the ruler's aura of power.

In the service of his noble clients Titian painted many grand and heroic pictures, but his influence on later artists derives largely from more intimate

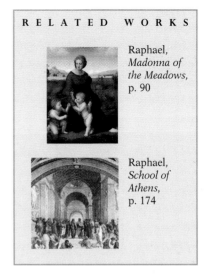
left: **481.** Raphael.
Pope Leo X with Two Cardinals.
c. 1518. Oil on wood, 5'3⅛" × 3'8⅞".
Uffizi, Florence.

right: **482.** Titian.
Charles V at Mühlberg.
1548. Oil on canvas,
10'10¾" × 9'1⅞".
Copyright © Museo del Prado,
Madrid.

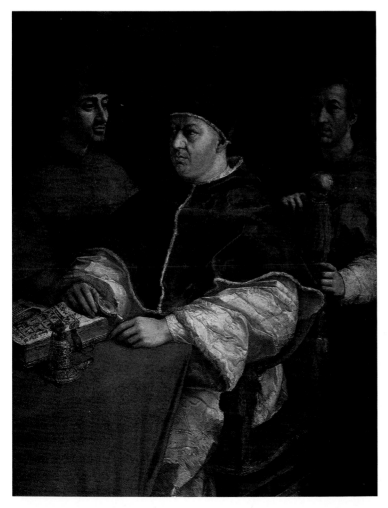

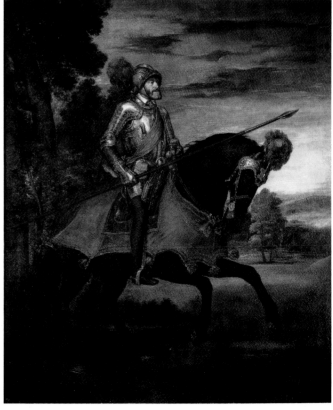

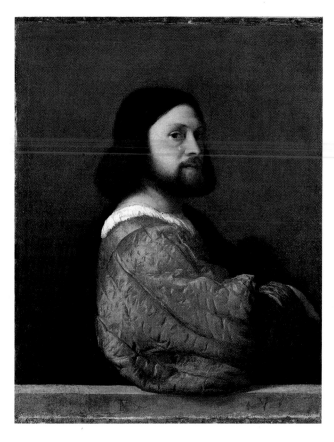

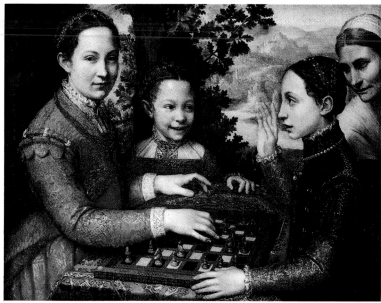

portraits, such as the *Portrait of a Man* shown here **(483)**. The artist had at his command a wide repertoire of poses—copied by artists even today—that flattered his sitters and gave them a self-assured dignity. Among Renaissance artists, Titian is thought of as the greatest colorist. The lush blue sleeve in this portrait, for instance, is iridescent with tonal shadings and highlights. The sleeve is treated with such importance, it seems almost to form a pedestal for the sitter's head.

Another noted portraitist of the period was Sofonisba Anguissola, the first woman artist known to have achieved celebrity among her contemporaries. Anguissola was born about 1535 in Cremona, the eldest of six sisters. She was well educated and was trained in painting; by about age twenty-two she had attracted the admiring attention of Michelangelo.

Anguissola's masterpiece, *The Chess Game* **(484)**, dates from 1555, when the artist was about twenty. It portrays two of her sisters engaged in a playful game outdoors on a balmy afternoon, while another sister and their maidservant look on. A misty landscape is seen in the distance. At left is Lucia, who gazes toward us serenely as she makes her move, to the apparent consternation of Minerva, at right. In the center little Europa displays her impish amusement at her older sister's downfall on the chess board. To understand Anguissola's originality, we might compare *The Chess Game* with Raphael's *Pope Leo X* **(481)**. Raphael poses his three subjects formally, with no interaction among them. By contrast, Anguissola, while giving us fully realized portraits of her sisters, also sets them in motion, gives them something to do, shows us their relationships and their feelings. The apparent casualness of the chess game provides the medium for a form that was evidently new to Italian art. Because of Anguissola's focus on the activities of everyday life—the *storia*, or action—many scholars consider *The Chess Game* to be a genre painting.

By the mid-15th century the style that can be identified as Renaissance had begun to spread outward from the Italian peninsula. When Renaissance ideals penetrated the North—Germany, Switzerland, northern France, and the Netherlands—they changed the look of art and swept away the last vestiges of the Middle Ages.

THE RENAISSANCE IN THE NORTH

The first half of the 16th century was a time of tremendous spiritual, intellectual, and artistic upheaval in northern Europe. The Protestant Reformation was in full swing, bringing with it the establishment of new Christian denominations—Anglican, Lutheran, and Calvinist—which would split away large numbers of people from the Church of Rome. Literary and philosophical explorations emphasized the Greek and Roman classics and gave rise to the movement known as *humanism.* And Renaissance styles in art, which had appeared in Italy a half century earlier, now sprang up in the North. This activity can be traced in part to the new ease of communication. The printing press, developed in the mid-15th century, made possible a dramatic increase in the spread of books and artistic images. Travel throughout Europe became far more common, not just for trade but for pleasure and study.

Northern art of the Renaissance differs in several respects from its Italian counterpart, perhaps the most important being the Northern artist's love of detail. Meticulous rendering of details was a trademark of Robert Campin, a prominent artist in the city of Tournai. The subject of Campin's *Mérode Altarpiece* **(485)** is the Annunciation, the biblical event in which the Angel Gabriel came from Heaven to tell Mary she would become the mother of God. Campin placed this scene in a typical middle-class Flemish house of his time (ignoring the fact that Mary was a Jewish maiden in 1 C.E.). He is obviously familiar with perspective to create the illusion of deep space, but he has not elected to use the technique. The table at center, for instance, tilts so sharply it looks ready to dump its contents. Far more important is the precise replication of objects.

The Annunciation setting is replete with symbols, most of them referring to Mary's purity: The lilies on the table, the just-extinguished candle, the white linen, among others. At upper left, between two round windows, the tiny figure of a child carrying a cross flies down a light ray toward the light starburst on Mary's gown, signifying that the infant Jesus will enter Mary's womb through God's will, not through human impregnation. The right wing of the altarpiece shows Joseph, who will become Mary's husband, at work in his carpenter shop. By tradition, Joseph is making a mousetrap, symbolic of the soon-to-come Jesus' "trapping" the Devil, bringing good to banish evil. In the left wing the donors, who commissioned the painting, kneel to witness the holy scene.

No recitation of this picture's details should overshadow its sheer beauty. Mary's face, modest above her crimson gown, is among the loveliest in all

485. Robert Campin.
Mérode Altarpiece. c. 1426.
Oil on panel, $25\frac{3}{16} \times 24\frac{7}{8}''$ (center),
$25\frac{3}{8} \times 10\frac{3}{4}''$ (each wing).
The Metropolitan Museum
of Art, New York
(The Cloisters Collection, 1956).

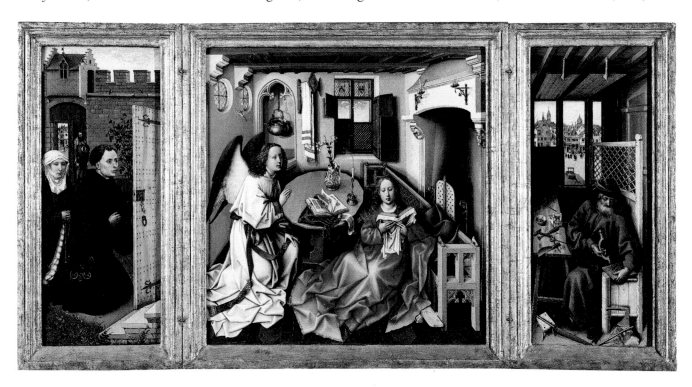

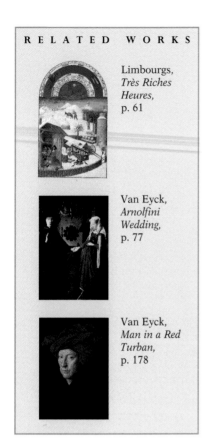

Renaissance art. The angel, while strangely full-bodied for a heavenly being, displays an unearthly radiance owing to his luminous face and brilliant gold wings. Both central figures wear robes that flow into rivers of soft drapery. The *Mérode Altarpiece* is only about 2 feet in height. Its exquisitely rendered details, its clear colors, and the artist's skillful placement of light and shadow combine to give it a jewel-like quality.

Northern artists' preoccupation with decoration and surface and *things* derives naturally from their heritage. The North had a long tradition of painted miniatures, manuscript illuminations, stained glass, and tapestries—all decorative arts with a great deal of surface detail. Whereas the Italian masters were obsessed with structure—accurate perspective and the underlying musculature of the body—Northern artists perfected their skill at rendering the precise outer appearance of their subjects. And they were unsurpassed at capturing in paint the textures of satin or velvet, the sheen of silver and gold, the quality of skin to its last pore and wrinkle. And they loved to fill their pictures with a perfect riot of forms—people, animals, objects of every sort.

In figure painting, including portraits, Northern artists were less committed than their Italian colleagues to showing an idealized image. The Northerner preferred to strive for a *realistic* view, an exact resemblance to the living subject. We have already seen this tendency in works by one of the greatest of Northern masters, Jan van Eyck. Here we turn to Rogier van der Weyden, a Netherlandish artist who was influenced by Van Eyck and whose style exhibits characteristics we associate particularly with the Northern Renaissance.

In *St. Luke Drawing the Virgin* (486) Rogier paints an imaginary scene. At left is the Virgin Mary nursing the infant Jesus. At right is St. Luke, author of one of the four Gospels in the Bible, who could not possibly have known about the birth of Jesus when it occurred and would at most have been an infant himself at the time. Nevertheless, Rogier shows us the adult Luke, special saint of artists, drawing the mother and child in silverpoint (p. 158). The two larger figures are carefully balanced in an architectural setting, behind which, through a window, we glimpse a landscape in depth. Typical Northern touches

486. Rogier van der Weyden. *St. Luke Drawing the Virgin.* c. 1435. Oil and tempera on panel, 4'6⅛" × 3'7⅝". Courtesy of Museum of Fine Arts, Boston (gift of Mr. and Mrs. Henry Lee Higginson).

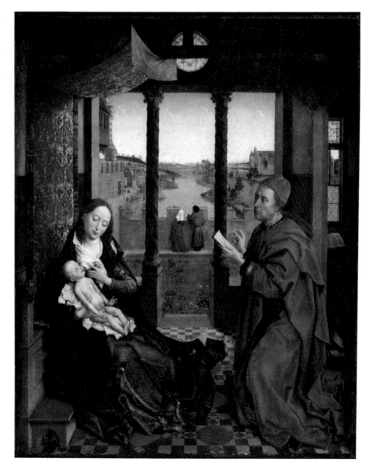

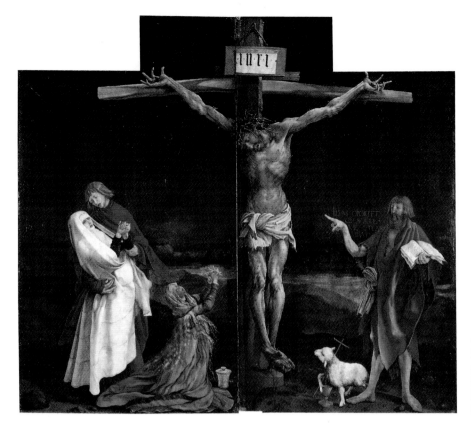

487. Matthias Grünewald. *The Crucifixion,* center panel of the *Isenheim Altarpiece* (exterior). Completed 1515. Panel, 8'10" × 10'1". Musée d'Unterlinden, Colmar.

include Rogier's minute attention to details in the room—woodwork, tiles, canopy, window panes; wonderfully lavish drapery in the garments; rich colors; and faces so finely modeled and human we can think of them as portraits. There is great emotional warmth in this picture. The Virgin and child exchange tender glances, while St. Luke, in his effort to capture their likeness, seems almost overcome with reverence and love.

While Rogier's painting is gentle, religious art of the Northern Renaissance could also be harsh in its emotionalism—far harsher than that of Italy. This has less to do with the Reformation than with the Northern temperament. Northern art abounds in truly grim Crucifixions, gory martyrdoms of saints, and inventive punishments for sinners. Italian artists did sometimes undertake these subjects, but they never dwelt so fondly on the particulars.

Matthias Grünewald, a German artist active in the early 16th century, painted the Crucifixion of Christ as the center of his great masterpiece, the *Isenheim Altarpiece* **(487)**. Originally, the altarpiece reposed in the chapel of a hospital devoted to the treatment of illnesses afflicting the skin, including syphilis. This helps to explain the horrible appearance of Christ's body on the cross—pockmarked, bleeding from numberless wounds, tortured beyond endurance. Without question the patients in the hospital could identify with Christ's sufferings and thus increase their faith.

In Grünewald's version of the Crucifixion, the twists and lacerations of the body speak of unendurable pain, but the real anguish is conveyed by the feet and hands. Christ's fingers splay out, clutching at the air but helpless to relieve the pain. His feet bend inward in a futile attempt to alleviate the pressure of his hanging body. To the left of the Cross the Virgin Mary falls in a faint, supported by St. John, and Mary Magdalene weeps in an agony that mirrors Christ's own. To the right John the Baptist offers the only sign of hope. He points calmly at the dying Savior in a gesture that foreshadows Christ's Resurrection. Grünewald's interpretation of the Crucifixion is in keeping with a stark Northern tradition in which depictions of extreme physical agony were commonplace.

Another German artist of the period, Hans Holbein the Younger, cultivated a less dramatic style and is best known for his portraits. Holbein was

RELATED WORKS

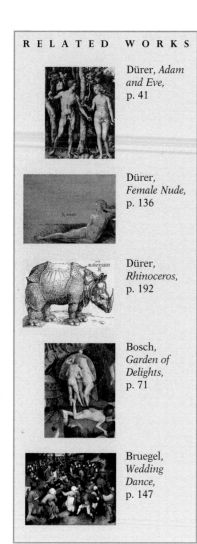

Dürer, *Adam and Eve*, p. 41

Dürer, *Female Nude*, p. 136

Dürer, *Rhinoceros*, p. 192

Bosch, *Garden of Delights*, p. 71

Bruegel, *Wedding Dance*, p. 147

among the first of the true cosmopolitans—well educated, well traveled, at home in many cities. Born in Augsburg, in southern Germany, Holbein eventually settled in London, where he became court painter to King Henry VIII. It is largely through Holbein that we have a visual record of that most intriguing of monarchs (488). The painting shows two characteristics of the style that made Holbein one of the greatest portraitists ever. On the one hand, every aspect of the subject's appearance is rendered in careful detail, from the hairs in his beard to the textures of skin, clothing, and fur. On the other hand, the artist has penetrated surface appearance to give us an imposing character study. He has posed the monarch full front, so that he dominates and fills the picture space, the very image of arrogant kingship at the height of its powers. Henry confronts and overwhelms the viewer—much as he must have confronted the papacy, his own ministers in England, and, for that matter, all six of his wives.

Pieter Bruegel the Elder, an artist who worked in Antwerp and Brussels, also was well educated and well traveled, but his work took an opposite path from that of Holbein. Whereas Holbein concentrated on extravagant portraits of the nobility, Bruegel is best known for his animated genre scenes of the peasantry at work and play. *Peasant Wedding* (489) depicts the celebration, held in a barn, after the nuptials of a young couple. Just to right of center a hanging cloth, on which is suspended something like a crown, isolates the bride, who sits looking rather pleased with herself—presumably because she has made a good match. There is disagreement about which figure is the groom; some art historians identify him as the man in dark clothing leaning backward just at the center of the composition.

Bruegel employed an interesting compositional device [Overlay 9b]. The table, slanting diagonally from lower right to upper left, pulls together a large number of people in conviviality but without confusion. His special talent, however, lies in painting these people as *types*—as "cheerful peasants"—yet also as individuals. If you examine each character, you begin to speculate about emotions, thoughts, reactions. The bagpiper at center left: Surely he wishes he could stop playing and eat some of the delicious food going by. The

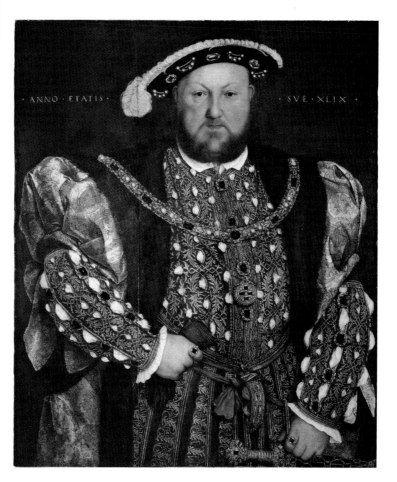

488. Hans Holbein the Younger. *Henry VIII.* 1540. Panel, $32\frac{1}{2} \times 29''$. National Gallery, Rome.

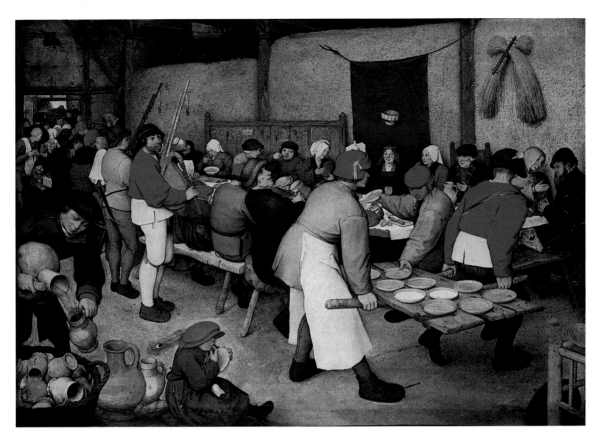

pair at far right: Are they discussing the details of the marriage contract and assessing the match? The couple immediately to the bride's left, variously identified as her parents or the groom's: They don't look especially happy. In fact, they look downright grim. Have they made a poor bargain, or are they pessimistic about the outcome of this marriage? All in all, *Peasant Wedding* is a marvelous study in personality and in visual organization.

By the second half of the 16th century the artistic energies that had fueled the Renaissance were essentially spent. Artists had developed Renaissance principles to the extent they wished and were ready for change. As it happened, that change mirrored social and religious trends evident throughout Europe.

489. Pieter Bruegel the Elder. *Peasant Wedding*. c. 1565. Oil on panel, $3'8\frac{7}{8}'' \times 5'4''$. Kunsthistorisches Museum, Vienna.

LATE 16TH-CENTURY EUROPE

The Protestant Reformation in northern Europe was extremely successful and drew large numbers of people away from the Roman Catholic Church. Deeply wounded, the Church of Rome regrouped itself and struck back. The Catholic Counter-Reformation, begun in the second half of the 16th century and continuing into the 17th, aimed at preserving what strength the Church still had in the southern countries and perhaps recovering some lost ground in the North. Spain and Italy were two major centers of the Counter-Reformation, and some artists were deeply involved in its activities.

Two artists in particular are associated with the Counter-Reformation and can serve as a transition from the 16th century to the 17th. They are difficult to categorize, because their styles, while very different from those of the High Renaissance, do not fit either with the Baroque style, which we shall consider in the next chapter. Some writers label their work, and that of their contemporaries, *Mannerist*.

Mannerism is a term few art historians agree about. Certainly it is considered a reaction to the Renaissance, a rejection of the scientific theories so popular with Renaissance artists and of compositions based on mathematical principles. Stylistic traits most often associated with Mannerism are a dramatic use of space and light and a tendency toward elongated figures. But whether any particular artist can be called Mannerist is a matter of debate.

The first of the two artists was the Italian master Tintoretto, born in Venice. His *Last Supper* **(490)** makes an interesting comparison with Bruegel's *Peasant Wedding*. Like Bruegel, Tintoretto has organized a large group of people by means of a table set in a sharply diagonal composition. The mood of the two paintings, however, could hardly be more different. Bruegel's atmosphere is one of lighthearted celebration. But Tintoretto's picture portrays a religious subject, and he has given it a dramatic and mystical treatment.

The scene of the *Last Supper* takes place a few days before Christ's death and depicts the moment when Christ breaks bread and gives it to his disciples to eat—the basis for the sacrament of Holy Communion. Christ's head is brilliantly lighted, and clouds of angels waft toward him, making it clear that a supernatural event is taking place in this ordinary setting. The serving attendants, who are tied to earthly concerns, go about their business, oblivious to the spiritual drama, but Christ's disciples are very much caught up in the great mystery. Small halos of light form around all their heads to indicate their holiness—except for Judas, who will soon betray Christ.

The artist most closely associated with the Catholic Counter-Reformation was Doménikos Theotokópoulos, known as El Greco. Born on the Greek island of Crete (hence, "the Greek"), El Greco traveled as a young man to Venice and Rome, where he studied the works of Michelangelo and Titian. Eventually he moved on to Spain, settling permanently in Toledo, an intensely Catholic center of the Counter-Reformation. One of his most important commissions, executed for a chapel in that city, was *The Burial of Count Orgaz* **(491)**. The count in question, an extremely pious man, had actually died and been buried some 250 years earlier, but El Greco depicts the burial as though it were taking place at the time of the painting. The nobility and clergy of Toledo, many of them El

490. Tintoretto. *The Last Supper.* 1592–94. Oil on canvas, 12′ × 18′8″. San Giorgio Maggiore, Venice.

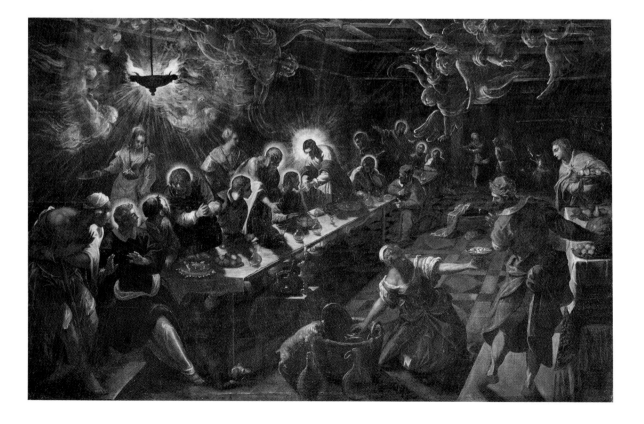

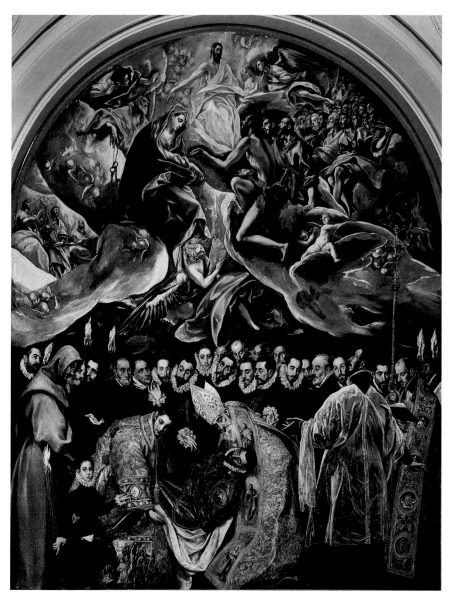

491. El Greco.
The Burial of Count Orgaz.
1586. Oil on canvas,
16′ × 11′10″.
Santo Tomé, Toledo, Spain.

Greco's patrons, are portrayed as graveside mourners. So holy was Count Orgaz that St. Stephen and St. Augustine have miraculously appeared to lower the body into its tomb. At the center of the composition, above the mourners' heads, an angel holds a wispy white form, meant to represent the count's soul.

Catholic Spain turned its eyes upward, to the heavens rather than the earth, and forward, to eternal life rather than the earthly one. *The Burial of Count Orgaz* illustrates this tendency perfectly, with a sharply divided composition. The living are grouped in a static row, earthbound, the line of their heads forming a barrier between earth and sky, life and the hereafter. Above them, the heavens open into a turbulent vision of Paradise. The figures of Christ and the Virgin, saints and angels, are dramatically elongated and flame-like. Below all is stillness and sorrow; above, movement and ecstasy.

Tintoretto's and El Greco's works have some elements in common, especially in their emphasis on the spiritual, but we cannot link them with each other as easily as we could match the products of Renaissance artists. The last half of the 16th century and beginning of the 17th was a period of much experimentation in art but no single coherent trend. Not until about the second decade of the 17th century can we again identify a definite style and give it a label. That label is Baroque.

VINCENZO PERUGIA

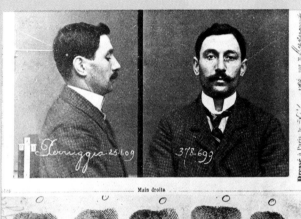

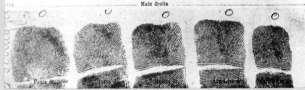

AT 7:20 ON THE MORNING of August 21, 1911, three members of the maintenance staff at the Louvre paused briefly in front of the *Mona Lisa*. The chief of maintenance remarked to his workers, "This is the most valuable picture in the world." Just over an hour later the three men again passed through the Salon Carré, where Leonardo's masterpiece hung, and saw that the painting was no longer in its place. The maintenance chief joked that museum officials had removed the picture for fear he and his crew would steal it. That joke soon proved to be an uncomfortably hollow one. *Mona Lisa* was gone.

Thus begins the story of the most famous art theft in history, of the most famous painting in the world, and of the man who would inevitably become the most famous art thief of all time: Vincenzo Perugia.

French newspapers announced the catastrophe under the banner headline "Unimaginable!" All during the weeks that followed, rumors abounded. A man carrying a blanket-covered parcel had been seen jumping onto the train for Bordeaux. A mysterious draped package had been spotted on a ship to New York, a ship to South America, a ship to Italy. The painting had been scarred

with acid, had been dumped in the sea. All clues, however far-fetched, were followed up, but no trace of *Mona Lisa* could be found.

More than two years would pass before the thief surfaced. Then, in November of 1913, an art dealer in Italy received a letter from a man who signed himself "Leonard." Would the dealer like to have the *Mona Lisa?* Would he. Of course it was a joke. But was it? The dealer arranged to meet "Leonard" in a hotel room in Florence. "Leonard" produced a wooden box filled with junk. The junk was removed, a false bottom came out of the box, and there, wrapped in red silk and perfectly preserved, was the smiling face of *Mona Lisa.* The dealer swallowed his shock and phoned for the police.

"Leonard" was actually an Italian named Vincenzo Perugia—a house painter who had once done some contract work in the Louvre. As he told the story of the theft, it was amazingly simple. On the morning in question Perugia, dressed in a workman's smock, walked into the museum, nodded to several of the other workers, and chose a moment when no one else was in the Salon Carré to unhook the painting from the wall. Then he slipped into a stairwell, removed the picture from its frame, stuck it under his smock, and walked out. Stories that Perugia had accomplices have never been proved.

What were the thief's motives? And why, after pulling off what can only be described as the heist of the century, did he so naively offer the painting to the Italian dealer? Perugia claimed he was motivated by patriotism. *Mona Lisa* was an Italian painting by an Italian artist. Believing (mistakenly) that it had been stolen by Napoleon to hang in France, he wanted to restore it to its rightful home. At the same time, however, he expected to be "rewarded" by the Italian government for his heroic act and thought $100,000 would be a good amount. No one shared this point of view.

Perugia was tried, convicted, and sentenced to a year in prison. After his release he served in the army, married, settled in Paris, and operated a paint store. Soon Perugia, who had so briefly captured the world's headlines, settled back into the obscurity from which he had emerged.

And *Mona Lisa?* After a triumphal tour of several Italian museums, she was returned to France. She hangs—at least as of this writing—safely in the Louvre. Romantics say her smile is even more enigmatic than before.

"Mug shot" of Vincenzo Perugia (with the name misspelled) after his arrest in 1913.

The 17th and 18th Centuries

THE PERIOD ENCOMPASSING the 17th and 18th centuries in Europe has often been called "The Age of Kings." Some of the most powerful rulers in history occupied the thrones of various countries during this time: Frederick the Great of Prussia, Maria Theresa of Austria, Peter the Great and Catherine the Great of Russia, and a succession of grand kings named Louis in France, to name but a few. These monarchs governed as virtual dictators, and their influence dominated social and cultural affairs of the time as well as political matters.

This same period could equally be called "The Age of Colonial Settlement." By the early 17th century the Dutch, the English, and the French had established permanent settlements in North America. (Spain and Portugal had earlier laid claim to much of Central and South America.) The first successful English colony was at Jamestown, in Virginia, where a party led by John Smith arrived in 1607. Thirteen years later the plucky little ship *Mayflower* made landing in what is now Massachusetts. The settlers endured many hardships as they struggled through their first winters in the New World. At Jamestown the colonists went through a period still known as the "starving time." Ironically, the "starving time" in North America coincided exactly with a European style so opulent that its name is now synonymous with extravagance: the Baroque.

THE BAROQUE STYLE IN EUROPE

Baroque art differs from that of the Renaissance in several important respects. Whereas Renaissance art stressed the calm of reason and enlightenment, Baroque art is full of emotion, energy, and movement. Colors are more vivid in Baroque art than in Renaissance, with greater contrast between colors and between light and dark. In architecture and sculpture, where the Renaissance sought a classic simplicity, the Baroque favored ornamentation, as rich and complex as possible. Baroque art has been called dynamic, sometimes even theatrical. This theatricality is clearly evident in the work of the Baroque's leading interpreter, the artist Gianlorenzo Bernini.

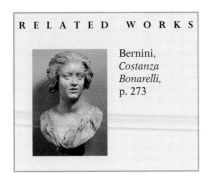
Bernini would have been a fascinating character in any age, but if ever an artist and a style were perfectly suited for one another, this was true of Bernini and the Baroque. With a taste for drama and overstatement, a flair for the grand gesture, Bernini found great success in an era that appreciated such expression. Bernini's background was in the theater, in stage and scene design; he was also an unsurpassed sculptor and architect. All these talents were brought to bear in his masterpiece, the Cornaro Chapel in the church of Santa Maria della Vittoria in Rome **(492)**. The chapel itself, shown here in an 18th-century painting, is a brilliantly integrated scheme of architecture, painting, sculpture, and lighting. On the ceiling is painted a vision of heaven, with angels and billowing clouds. At either side of the chapel sit sculptured figures of the Cornaro family, donors of the chapel, in animated conversation, watching the drama before them as though from opera boxes. The whole arrangement is lighted dramatically by sunlight streaming through a yellow-glass window.

The centerpiece of the chapel is Bernini's sculptured group known as *St. Teresa in Ecstasy* **(493)**. Teresa was a Spanish mystic, founder of a strict order of nuns, and an important figure in the Counter-Reformation. She claimed to be subject for many years to religious trances, in which she saw visions of Heaven and Hell and was visited by angels. It is in the throes of such a vision that Bernini has portrayed her. Teresa wrote:

Beside me, on the left hand, appeared an angel in bodily form, such as I am not in the habit of seeing except very rarely. . . . He was not tall but short, and very beautiful; and his face was so aflame that he appeared to be one of the highest rank of angels, who seem to be all on fire. . . . In his hands I saw a great golden spear, and at the iron tip there appeared to be a point of fire. This he plunged into my heart several times so that it penetrated to my entrails. When he pulled it out, I felt that he took them with it, and left me utterly consumed by the great love of God. The pain was so severe that it made me utter several moans. The sweetness caused by this intense pain is so extreme that one cannot possibly wish it to cease. . . . This is not a physical, but a spiritual pain, though the body has some share in it—even a considerable share.

left: 492. Anonymous artist, 18th century. *Cornaro Chapel, Santa Maria della Vittoria, Rome.* Oil on canvas. Staatliches Museum, Schwerin, Germany.

right: 493. Gianlorenzo Bernini. *St. Teresa in Ecstasy.* 1645–52. Marble and gilt bronze, lifesize. Cornaro Chapel, Santa Maria della Vittoria, Rome.

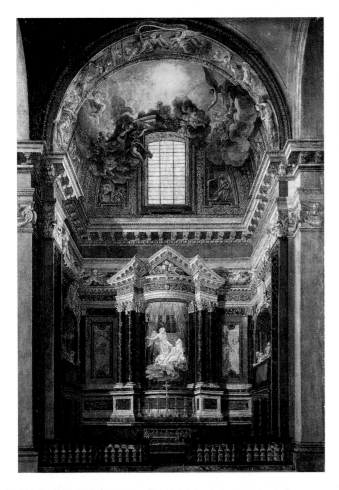

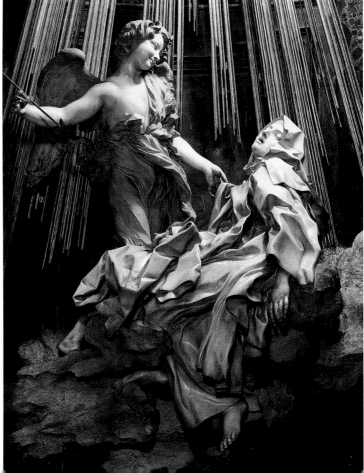

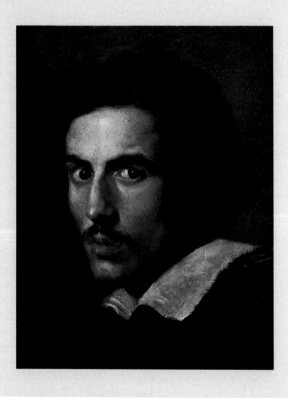

GIANLORENZO BERNINI

1598–1680

GIANLORENZO BERNINI falls into a category we find fascinating in all the arts—the youthful prodigy. Born in Naples, he trained with his father, Pietro, a talented sculptor, and by the age of seventeen he had received a commission from the pope. Too late in history to be a man of the Renaissance, Bernini was nonetheless a Renaissance man—sculptor, painter, architect, stage designer, playwright, composer of music, and, by all accounts, a great wit. He lived into his eighties and displayed throughout his life enough energy and enthusiasm and inventiveness for a dozen ordinary people.

Nearly all of Bernini's life was spent in Rome, and he outdid even his great predecessor Michelangelo in papal patronage, serving seven popes over a period of half a century. Master always of the grand design, he executed many huge projects, including the Cornaro Chapel group with *St. Teresa in Ecstasy* and the piazza and colonnade of the Vatican. Several outdoor fountains in Rome—elaborate figural sculptures—are also of his design. This last is typical of Bernini, for, grand showman that he was, he loved to incorporate such effects as light, smoke, or in this case water in his creations. Often he was called upon to plan important public events, such as state funerals or celebrations in honor of the saints.

As a sculptor, Bernini excelled at the portrait bust— the head-and-shoulders likeness in marble of an individual. One of the loveliest of these depicts Costanza Bonarelli **(316)**, the wife of Bernini's assistant who was also Bernini's mistress. Sometime in the mid-1630s the current pope, Urban VIII, urged the artist to terminate this relationship and take a wife. So in 1639 Bernini, then forty-one years old, married a young woman half his age, Caterina Tezio. The story is told that Bernini felt compelled to give away the portrait bust of Costanza Bonarelli, which until then he had kept in his home. The artist's wife eventually bore him eleven children, nine of whom survived to maturity.

Bernini's fame as an architect and sculptor spread throughout Europe. In 1665 Louis XIV, king of France, summoned the artist to Paris to work on a new design for the Louvre palace. The trip was not a success. Bernini's plan for the Louvre was rejected, and the artist alienated his hosts by expressing his preference for Italian art and contempt for French art. He returned to Rome, where he remained until his death.

One major work did result from Bernini's sojourn in Paris—a splendid portrait bust of Louis carved after Bernini had made numerous sketches of the king going about his daily activities. It was in Paris, too, that the artist reportedly explained the problems of portrait sculpture: "If a man whitened his hair, beard, eyebrows and—were it possible—his eyeballs and lips, and presented himself in this state to those very persons that see him every day, he would hardly be recognized by them. . . . Hence you can understand how difficult it is to make a portrait, which is all of one color, resemble the sitter."[1]

Gianlorenzo Bernini. *Self-Portrait.* c. 1625. Oil on canvas. Galleria Borghese, Rome.

CHRONOLOGY

	1600—1650		1650—1700
Style/Period	Baroque period, Europe Colonial period, North America	Bernini, *St. Teresa in Ecstasy*	Baroque period, Europe Colonial period, North America

**Political/
Social Events
and
Personalities**
	Catholic Counter–Reformation
	   in Europe
	Jamestown (Virginia) settled, 1607
	Mayflower lands on coast of North
	   America, 1620
			Catholic Counter–Reformation
			   in Europe
			Louis XIV, king of France, 1643–1715

Monuments and Major Artists	Cornaro Chapel, Rome, 1645–1652 Caravaggio (1571–1610) Peter Paul Rubens (1577–1640) Artemisia Gentileschi (1593–c. 1652) Nicolas Poussin (1593/94–1665) Gianlorenzo Bernini (1598–1680) Diego Velázquez (1599–1660) Rembrandt (1606–1669) Judith Leyster (1609–1660)	Rembrandt, *The Night Watch*	Versailles Palace, France, 1661–1688 Gianlorenzo Bernini (1598–1680) Rembrandt (1606–1669) Jacob van Ruisdael (1628/9–1682) Jan Vermeer (1632–1675)

Bernini shows the saint in a swoon, ready for another thrust of the angel's spear. She falls backward, yet is lifted up on a cloud, the extreme turbulence of her garments revealing her emotional frenzy. We can almost hear the moans Teresa spoke of in describing her passionate experience. The angel, wielding his spear, has an expression on his face of tenderness and love; in other contexts he might be mistaken for a Cupid. A work like *St. Teresa in Ecstasy* could never have emerged from the Renaissance. Artists of the Renaissance looked backward to the cool, restrained style of Greece in the Classical period. But the Baroque artist was far more interested in the later Hellenistic period of Greek art, typified by the *Laocoön Group* **(439)**. Both in composition and in the intensity of emotion portrayed, there is a kinship between the *Laocoön* and *St. Teresa* sculptures.

The Baroque fondness for dramatic composition and lighting revealed in the Cornaro Chapel also is apparent in works by two of Bernini's contemporaries—Artemisia Gentileschi and Caravaggio. In Gentileschi's *Judith and Maidservant with the Head of Holofernes* **(494)**, pose, gesture, and light are used much as they would be in the theater. The artist took her subject from the biblical story of Judith. According to the scripture, Judith, a pious and beautiful Israelite widow, volunteered to rescue her people from the invading armies of the Assyrian general Holofernes. Judith charmed the general, accepted his invitation to a banquet, waited until he drank himself into a stupor, then calmly beheaded him, wrapped up his head in a sack, and escaped.

Other of Gentileschi's paintings show the decapitation in progress. Here she focuses on the moments after the gory deed is done. She poses Judith tensely, caught in the wavering light from a single candle, one hand still clutching the bloody sword, the other poised in a gesture of silence. These

1700–1750	1750–1800
 Pelham, *Cotton Mather* Rococo style, Europe, c. 1700–1775 Colonial period, North America	Rococo style, Europe, c. 1700–1775 Neoclassicism, begins c. 1750 Revolutionary period, North America
Louis XV, king of France, 1715–1774	 Vigée-Lebrun, *Marie Antoinette* Louis XVI, king of France, 1774–1792 American Declaration of Independence, 1776 American Revolution, 1775–1783 French Revolution, begins 1789

Watteau, *Gersaint's Signboard*
 	
Antoine Watteau (1684–1721)
Jean Baptiste Siméon Chardin
    (1699–1779)
François Boucher (1703–1770)
	
	David, *The Death of Marat*
	
	Jean Baptiste Siméon Chardin
	    (1699–1779)
	François Boucher (1703–1770)
	John Singleton Copley (1738–1815)
	Francisco de Goya (1746–1828)
	Jacques Louis David (1748–1825)
	Elisabeth Vigée-Lebrun (1755–1842)

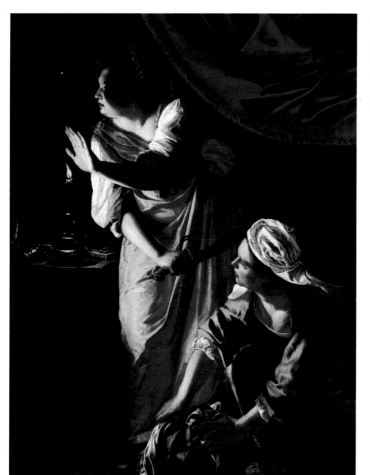

494. Artemisia Gentileschi. *Judith and Maidservant with the Head of Holofernes.* c. 1625. Oil on canvas, 6′½″ × 4′7¾″. © The Detroit Institute of Arts (gift of Mr. Leslie H. Green).

429

Baroque devices heighten the sense of danger, the urgency of deeds committed in the dark of night.

Caravaggio, too, focuses on a suspended moment after violent death. His magnificent *Deposition* (**495**) shows the crucified Christ being removed from the Cross and prepared for burial. The body is lowered by two of Christ's followers—his disciple St. John and the Jewish ruler Nicodemus, to whom Christ had counseled that a man must be "born again" to enter Heaven. The group also includes the three Marys—Christ's mother, the Virgin Mary, at left; Mary Magdalene, center; and Mary Cleophas, at right—who look on in despair. Caravaggio's structure is a strong (though complex and twisting) diagonal leading from the upraised hand at top right down through the cluster of figures to Christ's face. The light source seems to be coming from somewhere outside the top left edge of the picture. Light falls on the participants in different ways, but always enhances the sense of drama. Mary Magdalene's face, for example, is almost totally in shadow, but a bright light illuminates her shoulder to create a contrast with the bowed head. Light also catches the pathetic outstretched hand of the Virgin. Christ's body is the only figure lit in its entirety; the others stand in partial darkness.

When one sees this painting, the most immediate impact comes from the stark dead-white of Christ's form, in contrast to the vivid garments and flesh tones of the others. The viewer's experience of this poignant scene is intensified by the fact that we observe it from "a worm's-eye view," from a position below that of the participants in the drama, who stand on a stagelike slab. Certain elements of the composition almost seem to project forward out of the painting—the corner of the slab, Christ's feet, Nicodemus' elbow. Because the deposition group breaks out of the picture plane, we are drawn into the scene; we become a part of it.

left: **495.** Caravaggio. *The Deposition.* 1604. Oil on canvas, 9'9⅛" × 6'7¾". Pinacoteca, Vatican, Rome.

right: **496.** Peter Paul Rubens. *The Raising of the Cross.* 1609–10. Oil on panel, 15'2" × 11'2". Antwerp Cathedral.

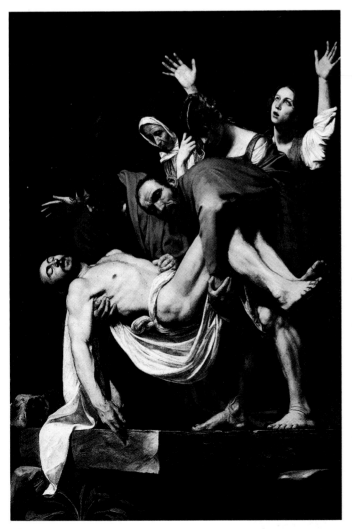

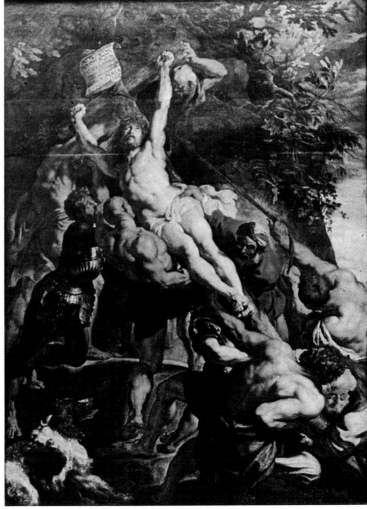

We might compare Caravaggio's *Deposition* with a work painted just a few years later, *The Raising of the Cross* (496) by the Flemish artist Peter Paul Rubens. Although he spent most of his life in Antwerp (in modern Belgium), Rubens had traveled to Italy and studied the works of Italian masters, including Caravaggio. There are similarities between these two paintings—in the sharply diagonal composition and dramatic lighting—but we also find several differences in the two masters' styles. Caravaggio's figures seem almost frozen in a moment of anguish, but Rubens' painting teems with movement and energy, each of the participants balanced precariously and straining at his task. While the Caravaggio group projects from the picture plane, its action is contained on four sides within the frame of the canvas. But Rubens' figures burst outside the picture in several directions, suggesting that the action continues beyond the painting. In addition, Rubens, like other Northern artists, is far more interested than Caravaggio in textural details—precise rendering of foliage, hair, the curly dog, and so on. Rubens' lifelike treatment of musculature recalls Michelangelo's paintings on the Sistine Chapel ceiling (477), but the writhing S-curve of Christ's body is typically Baroque.

Baroque painting in mid-17th-century France seems relatively subdued in contrast to the work of Southern artists of this period and even to that of Rubens. This was due to the French interest in Classical Greek and Roman art, particularly evident in the paintings of Nicolas Poussin. Poussin, born a Frenchman, spent much of his career in Rome, but he struck a different path from that of the Italian artists. His *Rape of the Sabine Women* (497) depicts a famous episode in Roman myth. Romulus, the legendary founder and first king of Rome, was concerned that the men of his city had no wives and so could not establish families. To remedy this problem, he announced a festival and invited the people from the neighboring region of Sabina to attend. Poussin shows us the climax of this event. Romulus, standing at upper left on the steps of the temple, gives a signal—opening his cloak—and each of the Roman men seizes a Sabine woman to carry off, killing the Sabine men.

Despite the violent and dramatic nature of the occasion, Poussin's treatment seems curiously restrained and reflects his admiration for Classical art. Poussin based his background on what he believed to be authentic Roman architecture, and he modeled his figures after ancient Greek and Roman sculptures. The two women at left, with their arms upraised, strike us more as carefully posed statues than as terrified maidens about to be carted away into wedlock by rather brutish strangers. There is little sense of continuous action. We almost have the impression that these are actors, arranged into a living

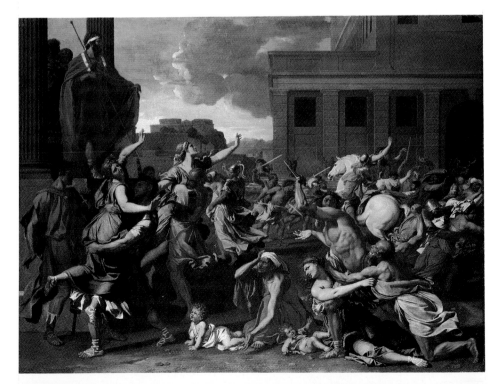

497. Nicolas Poussin.
The Rape of the Sabine Women.
1634. Oil on canvas,
$5'7\frac{7}{8}'' \times 6'10\frac{5}{8}''$.
The Metropolitan Museum of Art,
New York
(Harris Brisbane Dick Fund, 1946).

PETER PAUL RUBENS

1577–1640

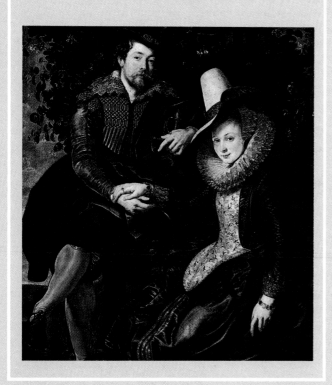

IN ALL THE HISTORY of art, one of the most civilized figures was the Flemish painter Peter Paul Rubens. Rubens was born in the German town of Siegen, but he returned with his mother at the age of ten to her native Antwerp (then in the Spanish-controlled Netherlands, now a city of Belgium) after the death of his father. There he was placed as a page in a wealthy home—a post that seems to have taught him the tact and courtly manners that would serve him well in the years to come. Coupled with these was an innate intelligence and pleasant disposition, all of which contributed to an enormously productive, rewarding life.

Rubens began his art studies in Antwerp. At the age of twenty-two, however, he set out for Italy, where he was to remain for eight years. During this time he traveled widely through all the major cities, studied the works of the great Italian masters, and was employed as court painter by the Duke of Mantua.

When the final illness of Rubens' mother called him home in 1608, the artist fully expected to return to Italy. But several inducements persuaded him to remain in Antwerp, which became his base for the rest of his life. For one thing, he was immediately successful as an artist and found many lucrative commissions. For another, the political and intellectual climate satisfied him. Perhaps most important, Rubens met, fell in love with, and married a young woman of Antwerp, Isabella Brant. This union lasted for seventeen years, produced three children, and was an extremely happy one. Rubens painted their wedding portrait, a detail of which is shown here.

In an atmosphere of domestic fulfillment, Rubens settled down to work. He became court painter to the Archduke Albert and his wife (also named Isabella), who were at the time rulers of the Netherlands. Over many years he also served them as political emissary and diplomat to foreign courts, often being entrusted with the most secret of negotiations. Artistic commissions poured in from all parts of Europe. Rubens was able to fulfill them mainly because he had a well-organized studio and many assistants. For certain large works, Rubens would make preliminary drawings, assistants would execute routine parts of the canvas, and then the master would make corrections and provide finishing touches.

Rubens' personal life took a stunning blow in 1626, when his wife died suddenly. Four years later, however, the artist remarried. His second wife was Hélène Fourment, and at the time of their marriage she was sixteen, Rubens fifty-three. This marriage, too, seems to have been a most successful one and produced five children. It was cut short by the artist's death, at sixty-three, from heart failure caused by gout.

The workshop approach perfected by Rubens occasionally got him into trouble. In 1621 he was forced to write this letter to a dissatisfied client: "I am quite willing that the picture painted for My Lord Ambassador Carleton be returned to me and that I should paint another . . . making rebate as is reasonable for the amount already paid, and the new picture to be entirely by my own hand without admixture of the work of anyone else, which on the word of a gentleman I will carry out."[2]

Peter Paul Rubens. *The Honeysuckle Bower (Self-Portrait with Wife)*, detail. c. 1609. Oil on canvas, 5'10½" × 4'5½". Bayerische Staatsgemäldesammlungen, Munich.

tableau with appropriate facial expressions, who will momentarily break the pose and go about their business. Poussin's art is above all rational and intellectual. He wants us to understand the dramatic import of the scene from his careful composition and ordering of the figures, not from any overt display of passion. The "classicizing" tendencies of Poussin had much influence on French artists for the next century.

To grasp fully the flavor of the Baroque in France, we should look once again at a king who for all time exemplifies the term "absolute monarch"—Louis XIV. In Chapter 3 we discussed how Louis's portrait by Rigaud both captured and enhanced the ideal of regal power. But in Louis's reign official portraiture was, so to speak, just the tip of the iceberg. Every aspect of the king's life and environment was calculated to present the image of divine rule. Louis's statement *"L'Etat c'est moi"* ("I am the state") was not just an expression of ego. It was the truth.

Louis ascended the throne of France in 1643, at the age of four. He assumed total control of the government in 1661 and reigned, in all, for seventy-two years. During that time he made France the artistic and literary center of Europe, as well as a political force to be reckoned with. Showing the unerring instincts of a master actor, he created an aura around his own person that bolstered the impression of divinity. Each day, for example, two ceremonies took place. In the morning half the court would file into Louis's chambers, in full pageantry, to participate in the king's *lever*—the king's "getting up." At night the same cast of characters arrived to play ritual roles in the king's *coucher*—his "going to bed."

A life in which the simple act of climbing in and out of bed required elaborate ceremony surely also needed an appropriate setting, and Louis did not neglect this matter. He summoned Bernini from Rome to Paris to work on completion of the Louvre palace (although the final design of the building was the work of others). But Louis's real love was the Palace of Versailles, in a suburb of the capital, which he substantially rebuilt and to which he moved his court in 1682. It was from this remarkable structure that the power of kingship flowed forth.

In all, Versailles occupies an area of about 200 acres, including the extensive formal gardens **(498)**. The complex embraces several grand châteaux, used at various times by one or the other of Louis's mistresses and their children, who were accorded quasi-royal status. There was also the Orangerie, a massive and elegant building in which the king kept his orange trees, and the king's stables—capable, it is said, of accommodating some twelve thousand

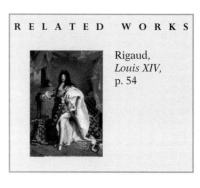

RELATED WORKS

Rigaud,
Louis XIV,
p. 54

498. Pierre Patel.
Bird's eye view of the château and park of Versailles, 1668, viewed from the East.
Musée du Château, Versailles.

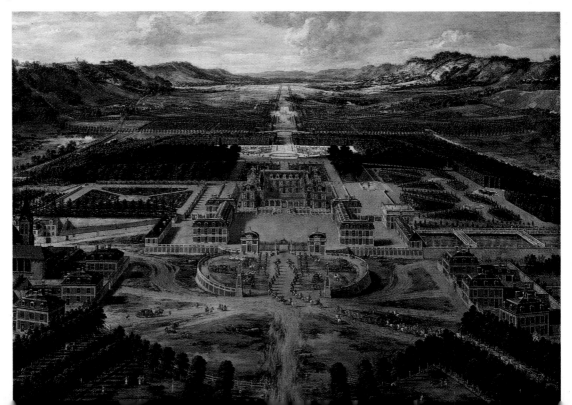

horses. A system of reservoirs, constructed at huge expense, provided water for innumerable fountains and a mile-long "Grand Canal." Louis's plans greatly expanded the Menagerie, or zoo, which provided rooms for dining overlooking the animals' cages.

The palace itself, redesigned and enlarged during Louis's reign, is an immense structure, more than a quarter of a mile wide. Of the countless rooms inside, the most famous is the Hall of Mirrors **(499)**, 240 feet long and lined with large reflective glasses. In Louis's time the Hall of Mirrors was used for the most elaborate state occasions, and even in our own century it has served as the backdrop for momentous events. The treaty ending World War I was signed in the Hall of Mirrors.

At the beginning of this discussion we said the Baroque style was characterized by ornamentation, dynamism, theatricality, and overstatement. What could better exemplify this style than the reign of Louis XIV and the Palace of Versailles?

The French court clearly was a model of pomp and pageantry, and the Spanish court to the south was eager to emulate that model. King Philip IV of Spain reigned for a shorter time than his French counterpart and could not begin to match Louis in either power or ability. Philip had one asset, however, that Louis never quite managed to acquire—a court painter of the first rank. That painter was one of the geniuses of Spanish art—Diego Velázquez.

In his capacity as court painter Velázquez created his masterpiece, *Las Meninas (The Maids of Honor)* **(500)**. At left we see the artist, working on a very large canvas, but we can only guess at the subject he is painting. Perhaps it is the young princess, the *infanta*, who stands regally at center surrounded by her attendants ("*las meninas*"), one of whom is a dwarf. Or perhaps Velázquez is actually painting the king and queen, whom we see reflected in a mirror on the far wall. Their participation is clear, but where are they standing? Possibly they are outside the picture, standing next to us, the observers. This ambiguity

left: 499.
Jules Hardouin-Mansart
and Charles Lebrun.
Hall of Mirrors, Versailles Palace.
Begun 1676.
Length 240′, height 43′.

right: 500. Diego Velázquez.
Las Meninas
(The Maids of Honor). 1656.
Oil on canvas, 10′5¼″ × 9′3¾″.
© Museo del Prado, Madrid.

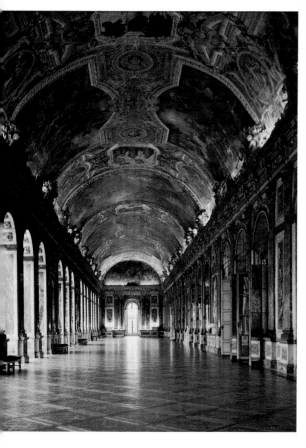

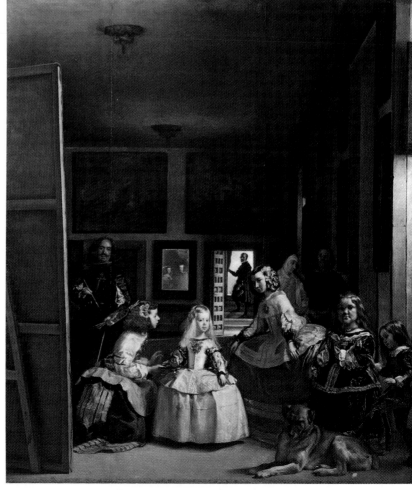

PICASSO ON VELÁZQUEZ

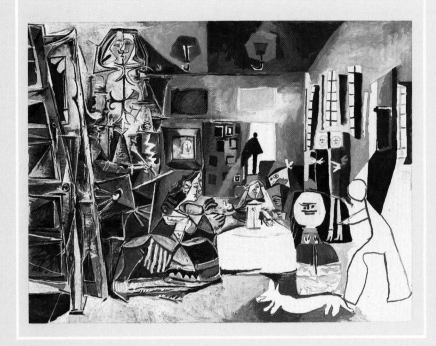

Pablo Picasso. *Las Meninas (after Velázquez).*
1957. Oil on canvas, 6'4⅜" × 8'6⅜". Museo Picasso, Barcelona.

ALMOST EXACTLY THREE HUNDRED YEARS after Velázquez painted *Las Meninas,* another Spaniard undertook the same subject. Here are all the familiar elements of Velázquez' masterpiece: the easel at left with a large work in progress, the little *infanta,* the maids in waiting, the dog, the dwarf, the mysterious figure at the open door in the background. It is unmistakably *Las Meninas*—and unmistakably Picasso.

One cannot resist the temptation of thinking Picasso had a wickedly good time with this painting, sparring against his great compatriot. His free play with Velázquez' forms is endlessly inventive. The figure of the artist, not conspicuous in the original, now looms large and has taken on a jaunty, convivial air. The dog becomes a pale dachshund, the maid behind the *infanta* a cartoon horse, the two figures at right playing-card images. With his impish sense of fun—and, no doubt, a vigorous competitive spirit—Picasso has sought out minor details in the Velázquez (such as the ceiling fixtures) and sifted them through his own style to pull our eyes into every part of this busy composition. Picasso is paying witty tribute to his great predecessor, while at the same time making sure—as always—that we know who holds the brush now.

is part of the picture's fascination, as is the dual nature of the scene. Although it shows a formal occasion, the painting of an official portrait, Velázquez has given the scene a warm, "everyday" quality, almost like that of a genre painting. Some experts believe Velázquez is painting the king and queen, and the little *infanta* has just wandered in to disrupt the proceedings.

Like Caravaggio, Velázquez uses light to create drama and emphasis, but light also serves here to organize and unify a complex space. The major light source comes from outside the top right corner of the painting, falling most brilliantly on the *infanta,* leaving the others in various degrees of shadow. Another light source illuminates the mysterious figure in the open doorway at back. Velázquez may have put him there to direct attention to the reflected images of the king and queen. Light also strikes the artist's face and the mirror reflection. What could have been a very disorderly scene has been pulled together by the device of spotlighting, much as a designer of stage lighting would control what the audience sees. The theatricality of the Baroque is more subtle in Velázquez than in Bernini, but it is no less skillful.

To end this discussion of 17th-century art, we move north, to the Netherlands. The Dutch Baroque, sometimes called the "bourgeois Baroque," is quite different from Baroque movements in France, Spain, and Italy. In the North, Protestantism was the dominant religion, and the outward symbols of faith—imagery, ornate churches, and clerical pageantry—were far less important.

RELATED WORKS

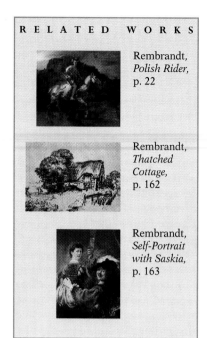

Rembrandt,
Polish Rider,
p. 22

Rembrandt,
*Thatched
Cottage*,
p. 162

Rembrandt,
*Self-Portrait
with Saskia*,
p. 163

Dutch society, and particularly the wealthy merchant class, centered not on the church but instead on the home and family, business and social organizations, the community. We see this focus in the work of two Dutch artists with very different styles—Rembrandt and Judith Leyster.

This text has already considered several works by Rembrandt, who was master of so many media that we return to him again and again in discussions of art. His place in the Dutch Baroque was a special one because he not only enjoyed the patronage of the prosperous middle class but also cultivated membership in that class himself. During Rembrandt's prime years, he and his wife, Saskia van Uijlenburgh (p. 163), maintained the lifestyle of an elegant and worldly Amsterdam couple, so that when the rich merchants of the city commissioned a picture, they were dealing with one of their own.

If you go to Amsterdam and visit the state museum, you will see a great many group portraits of Dutch gentlemen from this period. Often, the men are arranged at a banquet table or simply posed in a row, like sparrows on a wire. As our next illustration demonstrates, this is not at all the way Rembrandt handled a group portrait.

Sortie of Captain Banning Cocq's Company of the Civic Guard **(501)** shows a kind of private elite militia guard going out on an exercise. Actually, the group had little if any military significance. Like contemporary Americans who don costumes and restage Revolutionary War battles, Captain Cocq's troop apparently relished the fun of dressing up and playing war games. For this picture, then, Rembrandt has poured on the theatrical effects. He groups the figures naturally, in deep space, with Captain Cocq, resplendent in a red sash, at the center. The composition builds on a series of broad V-shapes, pointing upward and outward **[Overlay 10a].** The nested V-shapes make the picture seem to burst out from its core—and may have made its subjects feel they were charging off heroically in all directions, into battle. Lest this geometric structure seem rigid, Rembrandt has "sculpted" it into greater naturalness through his dramatic lighting of the scene. Light picks out certain individuals:

501. Rembrandt.
*Sortie of Captain Banning Cocq's
Company of the Civic Guard
(The Night Watch).* 1642.
Oil on canvas, 12'2" × 17'7".
Rijksmuseum, Amsterdam.

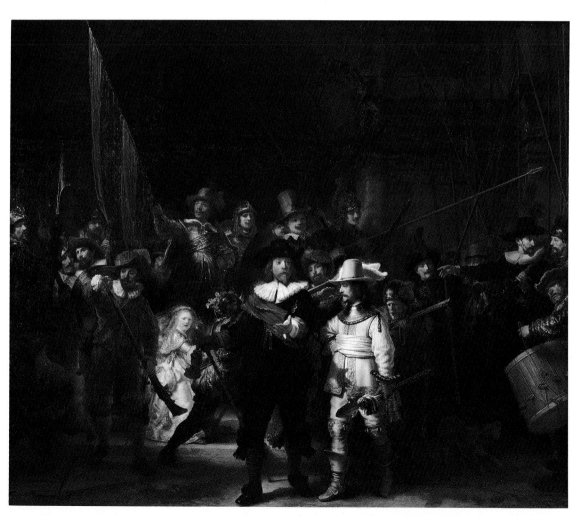

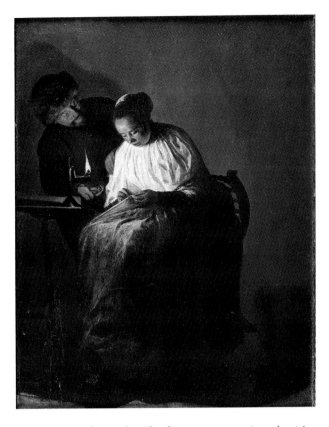

502. Judith Leyster.
The Proposition. 1631.
Oil on canvas, $11\frac{7}{8} \times 9\frac{1}{2}''$.
Mauritshuis, The Hague.

Captain Cocq himself; the drummer at far right; the lieutenant at Cocq's side, awaiting orders; and especially the little girl in a golden dress, whose identity and role in the picture remain a mystery.

For many years Rembrandt's painting was known as *The Night Watch*, and it still is informally called by that name. The reason has nothing to do with the artist's intent. A heavy layer of varnish applied on top of the oil paint, combined with smoke from a nearby fireplace, had gradually darkened the picture's surface, until it seemed to portray a nighttime scene. No one alive remembered it any differently. During World War II Rembrandt's masterpiece was put away for safekeeping. Before it was returned to exhibition after the war, the varnish was removed and the surface thoroughly cleaned. What emerged was a painting very different from the one art lovers had become accustomed to. *The Night Watch* is, in fact, a "day watch," and the restorers who scrubbed away centuries of soot had uncovered a picture shot through with dazzling Baroque light.

Baroque light is also a prominent feature in works by Judith Leyster, a Dutch portraitist and genre painter who was almost exactly contemporary with Rembrandt. The 17th century was the great age of Dutch genre painting—painting that focused on scenes of everyday life—and during her lifetime Leyster was one of the most highly regarded artists in that style. After her death, however, she was virtually forgotten. Paintings from her hand made their way into important collections and museums, but many seem to have been attributed to another (in our time, far better known) Dutch painter, Frans Hals. Leyster's disappearance from art history prevailed for some two centuries. Then, in 1893, a Dutch art historian who had just sold a "Hals" to the Louvre museum in Paris discovered Leyster's distinctive monogram on the canvas. Since then, other works by "Hals" have been reattributed to Leyster.

The Proposition (502), a genre painting from 1631, shows Leyster's mature style at its best. A young woman sits quietly, intent on her sewing. Behind her shoulder looms a crude, rough-looking man who offers her gold coins to buy her sexual favors. The man's left hand rests possessively on the woman's arm, but she does not look up from her work. One can almost hear her thinking, "If I ignore him, he will go away. *Please* go away!" Typically, the artist has placed a candle in a strategic position to light this scene. Light shines on the

RELATED WORKS

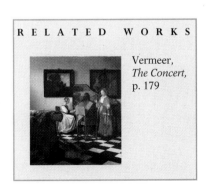

Vermeer,
The Concert,
p. 179

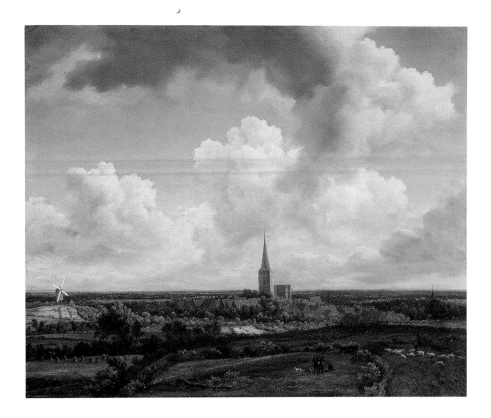

503. Jacob van Ruisdael. *Extensive Landscape with a View of the Town of Ootmarsum.* 1660s. Oil on canvas, 23¼ × 28⅞". Alte Pinakothek, Munich.

woman's face and casts a sheen on her smooth forehead. Her white blouse, surely a symbol of purity and virginity, is brightly illuminated. The lustful man, however, lurks in the gloom outside the candle's glow, and his shadow is thrown menacingly on the wall behind him. For this painting, then, Leyster manipulates light to show the sharpest of polarities: good versus evil.

The 17th century was also a great period for landscape painting in the Netherlands. Of course, Rembrandt drew and painted many landscapes **(190)**, but his style in this area as in every other was a personal one. More typical of the Dutch landscape painting was the work of Jacob van Ruisdael. Van Ruisdael's *Extensive Landscape with a View of the Town of Ootmarsum* **(503)** shows not only the famed flatness of the Dutch landscape, but also the artist's reaction to that flatness as an expression of the immense, limitless grandeur of nature. The artist makes a contrast between the land—where human order has been established in the form of buildings and cultivation—and the sky, with its billowing clouds, yielding to the wind, which mere people can never tame. The horizon line is set quite low, and, significantly, only the church steeple rises up in silhouette against the sky, perhaps symbolizing that humankind's one connection with the majesty of nature is through the church.

Despite this emphasis on the church building, Van Ruisdael's art is essentially secular, as is that of Leyster and Rembrandt. Although religious subjects continued to appear in art—and do so even now—never again would religious art dominate as it did in the Renaissance and Italian Baroque periods. No doubt this is largely because of the change in sponsorship; popes and cardinals became less important as patrons, while kings, wealthy merchants, and the bourgeoisie became more so. We can follow this increasing secularization of art as we move out of the 17th century into the 18th.

THE 18TH CENTURY

The first half to three-quarters of the 18th century is often thought of as the age of **Rococo**—a development and extension of the Baroque style. The term "rococo" was a play on the word "baroque," but it also refers to the French words for "rocks" and "shells," forms that appeared as decorative motifs in architecture, furniture, and occasionally in painting. Like the Baroque, Rococo is an extravagant, ornate style, but there are several points of contrast. Baroque, especially in the South, was an art of cathedrals and palaces; Rococo is more intimate, suitable for the aristocratic home and the drawing room (although there are a number of very grand Rococo buildings). Baroque colors are intense; Rococo leans more toward the gentle pastels. Baroque is large in scale, massive, dramatic; Rococo has a smaller scale and a lighthearted, playful quality. And, as suggested earlier, the Baroque—at least in its origins—was a religious art; Rococo is far more secular and, in its extreme forms, charmingly romantic.

The Rococo style of architecture originated in France but was soon exported. We find some of the most developed examples in Germany, especially in Bavaria. The Mirror Room of the Amalienburg, a little house in Nymphenburg Park near Munich **(504)**, should demonstrate amply why the word "rococo" has come to mean "elaborate and profuse." Designed by a Frenchman, François Cuvillies the Elder, the Mirror Room is a perfect riot of sinuous, twisting, almost visibly *growing* decorative forms. The line between walls and ceiling has been obscured deliberately to create the illusion of "sky" above the room. Large arched mirrors multiply the effect of playful design everywhere the eye might focus. Rococo was above all a sophisticated style, and the Amalienburg shows us the height of that sophistication.

504. François Cuvillies the Elder. Mirror Room, Amalienburg. 1734–39. Nymphenburg Park, Munich.

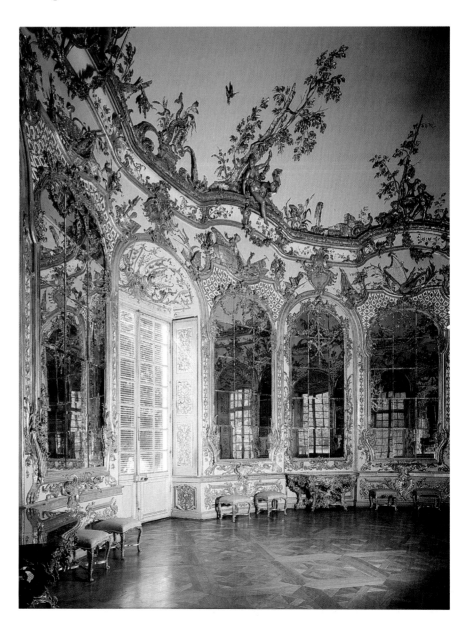

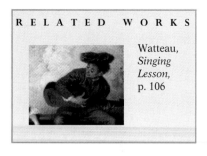
Sophistication was paramount in painting as well. The art of Antoine Watteau is typical of the carefree, aristocratic impulse of the Rococo. We considered Watteau's use of romantic, pastel colors in Chapter 4. Here, in a more ambitious work called *Gersaint's Signboard* (**505**) the artist gives us a picture of fashionable French society out for a day of shopping—shopping for artworks to decorate the opulent home. All is elegance, verging on the pretentious—the men in their powdered wigs, the women in their silks, everyone maintaining a pose of bored nonchalance. At right the gallery owner, Gersaint, displays a painting to prospective customers, while the adjacent group seems more taken with a smaller work of art. At left, paintings are being crated, presumably for shipment to purchasers, and a woman gowned in shimmering pink silk pauses to glance at them. Watteau celebrates in painting a class of people whose most serious concern was maintaining a chic life style.

Somewhat outside this predominant trend toward aristocratic art was another French artist, younger by about fifteen years than Watteau, the painter Jean Baptiste Siméon Chardin. Chardin specialized in the still life and the middle-class genre scene. His typical works have a quiet, meditative appeal and show ordinary people in ordinary activities. Pictures of children at play, as in *The House of Cards* (**506**), were a favorite theme. Here the boy, dressed in the very proper middle-class attire of the day, is caught up in the concentration of building his card house. There is a tension between his still pose and the precarious balance of the cards. Like the card house, Chardin's picture is perfectly but precariously balanced. The boy leans into his project, and Chardin's masterfully calculated light strikes three areas—the face, the upright cards, and the half-open drawer—to create a tight triangle of interest **[Overlay 10b]**. The fact that this triangle is balanced on one of its points adds subtly to the tension of the moment.

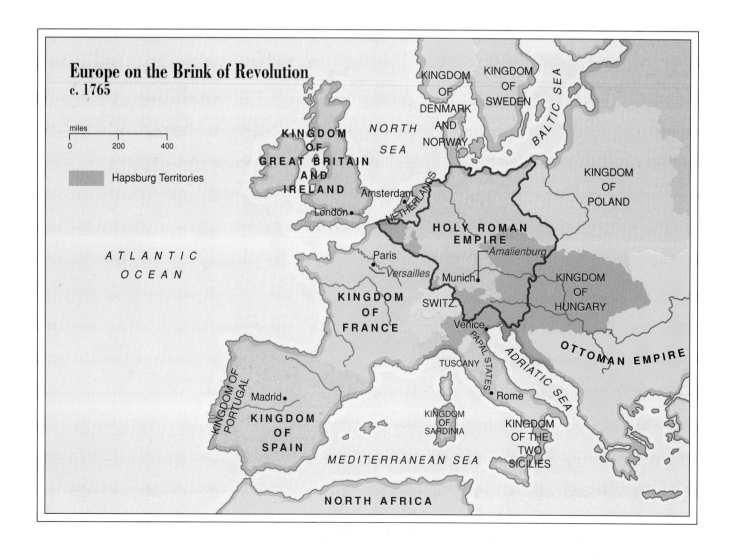

Europe on the Brink of Revolution
c. 1765

miles
0   200   400

Hapsburg Territories

KINGDOM OF GREAT BRITAIN AND IRELAND

Amsterdam

London

ATLANTIC OCEAN

NORTH SEA

KINGDOM OF DENMARK AND NORWAY

KINGDOM OF SWEDEN

BALTIC SEA

NETHERLANDS

HOLY ROMAN EMPIRE

Amalienburg

KINGDOM OF POLAND

Paris

Versailles

Munich

SWITZ.

KINGDOM OF FRANCE

KINGDOM OF HUNGARY

Venice

PAPAL STATES

ADRIATIC SEA

OTTOMAN EMPIRE

KINGDOM OF PORTUGAL

Madrid

KINGDOM OF SPAIN

TUSCANY

KINGDOM OF SARDINIA

Rome

KINGDOM OF THE TWO SICILIES

MEDITERRANEAN SEA

NORTH AFRICA

Closer to Watteau in spirit is another French artist whose name has become almost synonymous with the Rococo—François Boucher. To admirers Boucher's art is sumptuous and delightful; to detractors it is frivolous and decadent. In Boucher's paintings the people are pretty. The women are frequently nude and, if so, are very pink and voluptuous. If the women are dressed, they are stunningly dressed. Everybody is in love.

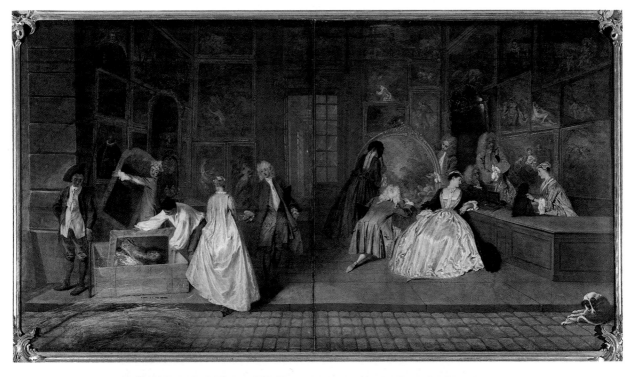

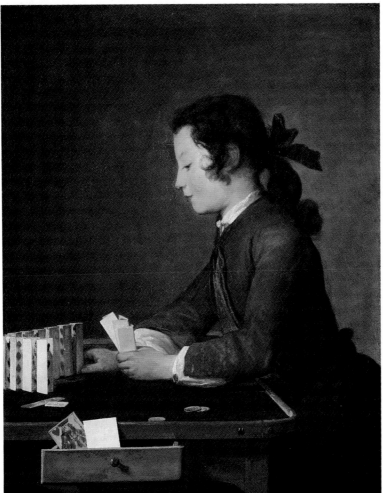

above: 505. Antoine Watteau. *Gersaint's Signboard*. 1720–21. Oil on canvas, 5'3⅞" × 10'1". Staatliche Museen, Berlin.

left: 506. Jean Baptiste Siméon Chardin. *The House of Cards*. c. 1735. Oil on canvas, 32⅜ × 26". © 1993 National Gallery of Art, Washington, D.C. (Andrew W. Mellon Collection).

Boucher's art suited perfectly the ideals of the French court presided over by Louis XV, great-grandson of the builder of Versailles. Form without substance, beauty without character, extravagance with little regard for paying the bills—such was the reign of Louis XV, and so it was chronicled by Boucher. In 1759 Boucher painted the *Marquise de Pompadour* (507), Louis's mistress and influential adviser. How beautiful she looks, how charming—posed languidly in her lace-frilled dress, resting lightly against a classical statue. Boucher flattered her physically (she was a good deal fatter and less gifted with regular features), and he failed to record the steely political brain that lurked behind the soft face. During the reign of Louis XV, the government of France was on the brink of collapse. The king himself is reputed to have said, *"Après moi, le déluge"* ("After me, the flood"). But for a little while—with Louis XV on the throne, the Marquise de Pompadour at his side, and Boucher at his easel—appearances were kept up.

The lower classes did not participate in this world. They could not afford to wear lace-frilled dresses and had no time to be charmingly in love. Many, in fact, were on the brink of starvation. Louis—if he really said it—was right. The flood was coming. France would endure only one more self-indulgent Louis before taking up arms.

Louis XVI, grandson of his predecessor, came to power in 1774. His queen, Marie Antoinette, probably never did say "The people have no bread? Let them eat cake!" However, history has marked her forever with the callous attitude implied by this remark. In a portrait done by Elisabeth Vigée-Lebrun, her favorite painter, the queen certainly does not look preoccupied with the suffering of her oppressed subjects (508). Gowned sumptuously in red satin,

507. François Boucher. *Marquise de Pompadour.* 1759. Oil on canvas, $35\frac{7}{8} \times 27\frac{1}{4}''$. The Wallace Collection, London.

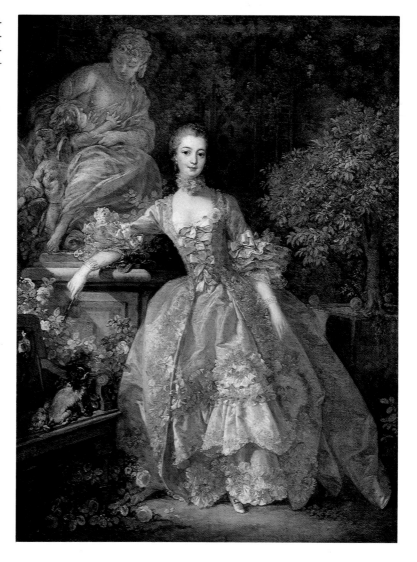

442

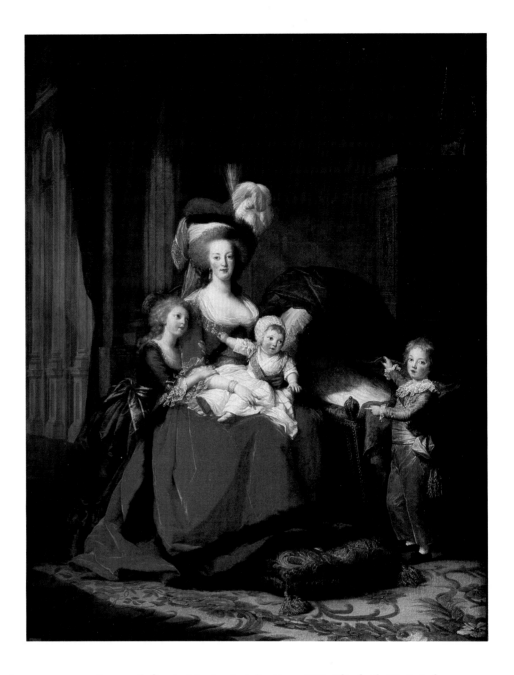

she poses in a setting so regal as to seem almost defiant. Marie Antoinette might be saying, "Everything is all right, the monarchy is intact, nothing to worry about." Her surroundings are indeed regal—a grand salon in the Palace of Versailles, with the Hall of Mirrors visible at left. And the queen sits among her children, the supposed future of the nation, arranged in sentimental attitudes. Her son, the *dauphin* (or crown prince), points to the empty cradle of Marie's youngest child, who has just died.

Vigée-Lebrun always flattered her sitters, and never more so than in this portrait. Such extravagant flattery, however, did not enhance the queen's popularity in a nation on the brink of financial disaster. Vigée-Lebrun herself tells us that when the large canvas was carried into the palace, she heard angry voices crying *"Voilà la déficite"* ("There is the deficit").

Although Vigée-Lebrun later made several copies of her own portraits of the queen, she never again painted Marie Antoinette from life. Within two years revolution had swept the country, ultimately destroying the monarchy and the aristocracy. The artist fled and took refuge outside France. The queen died by the guillotine.

508. Elisabeth Vigée-Lebrun.
Marie Antoinette and Her Children. 1787.
Oil on canvas, 8'8" × 6'10".
Palace of Versailles, France.

ELISABETH VIGÉE-LEBRUN

1755–1842

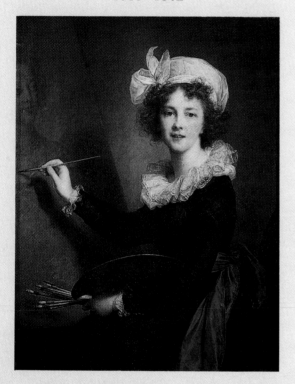

From her self-portrait she gazes directly at us, her viewers—calm, self-possessed, sure of her talent, sure of her place in the world. Her brush is poised over the canvas; we have momentarily interrupted her work on a portrait of her great patron, the Queen of France. She will not be interrupted for long. Throughout her remarkable life, Elisabeth Vigée-Lebrun knew where she was going and remained steadfast on that path.

Born in Paris, the daughter of a portrait painter, Elisabeth Vigée was convent-educated and encouraged from an early age to draw and paint. At eleven she began serious art studies. After her father's untimely death, Elisabeth resolved to work as a painter, and by age fifteen she was her family's chief financial support. Patrons flocked to her studio, eager to have their portraits done by the young artist, and her fees multiplied.

One dark spot was her mother's remarriage, to a man who seems mainly to have coveted his step-daughter's income. Because of this unpleasant circumstance, Elisabeth made the one real mistake of her life. Although she "felt no manner of inclination for matrimony," she succumbed to her mother's urgings and accepted the proposal of Jean Baptiste Pierre Lebrun, hoping "to escape from the torture of living with my stepfather." Alas for the twenty-year-old artist, she had merely "exchanged present troubles for others." Lebrun was "quite an agreeable person," but, his wife soon discovered, "his furious passion for gambling was at the bottom of the ruin of his fortune and my own." The happiest result of the union was Vigée-Lebrun's only child, her daughter Julie.

Neither marriage nor motherhood interfered with the artist's burgeoning career and social life. By all evidence she was lovely, witty, charming, and perfectly at home in any company. Quite independent of her husband, she entertained a growing circle of aristocratic friends, many of whom commissioned portraits. In 1779 a summons came from the Palace of Versailles. Marie Antoinette sought her services, and Vigée-Lebrun made the first of some twenty portraits of the queen. The two women became friends—a splendid advantage for the artist initially, but a dangerous liability as resentment of the monarchy grew. When revolution came in 1789, Vigée-Lebrun fled the country, taking Julie with her. Lebrun was left behind forever.

Then commenced Vigée-Lebrun's twelve years of "exile" from France. And what an exile it was! She traveled first to Rome and Vienna, then to St. Petersburg and Moscow, spending six years altogether in czarist Russia. Wherever she went she was treated like visiting royalty, entertained lavishly, invited to join the local painters' Academy. Wherever she went she was overwhelmed with portrait commissions. Kings and queens, princesses, counts, duchesses—she painted them all, in between the elaborate dinners and balls to which they invited her. In her memoirs she tells us she missed painting Catherine the Great because the empress died just before the first scheduled sitting.

In 1801, the furies of the revolution having abated, Vigée-Lebrun returned to Paris. She had not, however, quite satisfied her urge to travel. Only after a three-year stay in London and two visits to Switzerland did she finally settle down to write her memoirs and paint the survivors of the French nobility. She died in her eighty-seventh year, having painted more than 660 portraits. Her memoirs conclude with these words: "I hope to end peacefully a wandering and even a laborious but honest life."[3] And she did.

Elisabeth Vigée-Lebrun. *Self-Portrait at the Easel.*
c. 1789. Oil on canvas. Uffizi, Florence.

REVOLUTION

Repeatedly in this book we have pointed out that art responds to the culture from which it emerges. To get a sense of how dramatic was the revolution that shook France in 1789 (and its implications for much of Western civilization), we might compare Vigée-Lebrun's painting with a work done in France just six years later, when the revolution had reached its height.

Jacques Louis David began his career as a Rococo painter, having studied briefly with Boucher, his great-uncle. Two forces caused him to change his artistic direction. The first of these was the French Revolution, whose ideals David embraced. Eventually, the artist became an important propagandist for the anti-aristocracy forces. The other was the newly revived fascination with Classical antiquity. Just as Renaissance leaders, three centuries earlier, had turned admiring eyes back toward ancient Greece and Rome, so too did revolutionary leaders in France. David's evolving style reflected this preoccupation.

Working in a manner that came to be known as **Neoclassicism,** or "new classicism," David structured his compositions along very precise, often geometric lines. Emotions are restrained, outlines are clear, colors are cool, figures have the full-bodied muscularity of Classical sculptures. In a determined rejection of Rococo frivolity, David's works appeal to the viewer's reason, logic, and high moral principles. We see these qualities in a picture that many consider to be the artist's finest, *The Death of Marat* (509).

Jean-Paul Marat, a major figure in the revolution, pursued the goal of wiping out France's greedy and corrupt aristocracy. He was responsible for the execution by guillotine of hundreds of people. Because of a painful skin ailment Marat spent his days in the bathtub, which was fitted out with a writing desk so he could work, and there he received callers. A woman named Charlotte Corday, incensed by Marat's excesses with the guillotine, gained entry to

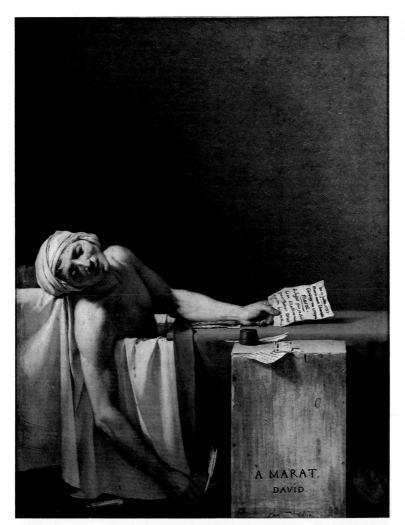

509. Jacques Louis David. *The Death of Marat.* 1793. Oil on canvas, 5′5″ × 4′2½″. Musées Royaux des Beaux-Arts de Belgique, Brussels.

his apartment and stabbed him to death. As a memorial to his friend, David painted the scene.

In lesser hands Marat's demise could have been laughable—a naked man murdered in his tub by a furious woman caller. But David has invested the event with all the pathos and dignity of Christ being lowered into his tomb. (Compare Caravaggio's *Deposition*, **495**.) Marat is shown, in effect, as a kind of secular Christ martyred for the revolution. All the forms are concentrated in the lower half of the composition, and light bathes the fallen leader in an unearthly glow, both of these devices contributing to the sense of tragedy. Marat's face and body could be those of a fallen Greek warrior, sculpted in marble by an ancient master. It is probably safe to conclude that David's purpose in this work was to transform a man whom many considered Satan himself into a sainted hero.

Most of David's art is politically aware. And although the term certainly didn't exist in his time, it is always "politically correct." The French Revolution was built on goals like those David attributed to Marat—liberty, equality, fraternity, and participation by all levels of society in the government and economy of France. In practice, however, the noble ideals of the revolution soon disintegrated into wholesale slaughter of aristocrats (including the royal family) and, in time, of anyone who disagreed with those momentarily in power. Art such as David's projected the *image* the leaders of the revolution wished to have of themselves, just as Vigée-Lebrun's art had projected the image desired by the French monarchs.

510. John Singleton Copley. *Paul Revere.* 1768–70. Oil on canvas, 35 × 28½". Courtesy, Museum of Fine Arts, Boston (gift of Joseph W., William B., and Edward H. R. Revere).

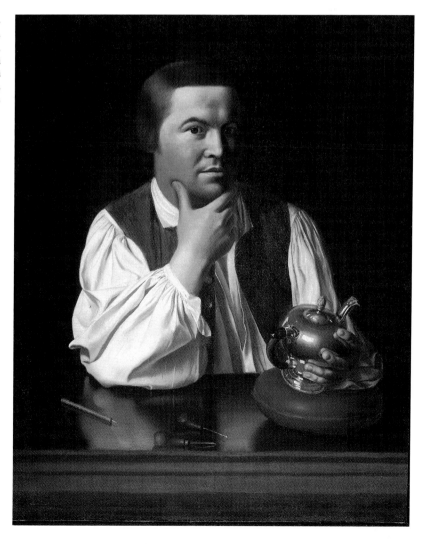

Two other revolutions occurred at more or less the same time as that in France. One was the American Revolution, preceding the French by thirteen years. During the relatively brief period covered by this chapter, the American colonists had progressed from the "starving time" of Jamestown to a nation of people capable of independence and self-government. During that time also the area that was to become the United States had developed its own artistic styles. And by the eve of the Revolution the colonies had their own master artist, born on home soil—John Singleton Copley.

Born in Boston, Copley grew up in the home of his stepfather, the artist Peter Pelham, whose portrait of *Cotton Mather* we saw in Chapter 8 **(234)**. Copley would paint many people who later became heroes of the Revolution, including *Paul Revere* **(510)**. Legend and poetry have preserved the image of Paul Revere taking his "midnight ride" on horseback, from Boston to Concord, to warn his fellow colonists that "the British are coming!" In his day, however, Revere was better known as an exceptionally gifted silversmith. The artist poses him with a silver teapot in one hand, the tools of his trade scattered elegantly on the table.

Copley's portrait is in much the same Neoclassical style as David's tribute to Marat. The subject sits quietly behind his table, gazing straight toward us. We as viewers might be seated just opposite him. Although he is dressed informally, Revere shows great dignity and an obvious pride in his work. Copley has rendered his subject's features, the garments, and the polished tabletop with wonderful realism. We sense fullness, a three-dimensional volume, in the body and especially in the hand clasping the teapot.

The third revolution of this time was not a political uprising but an economic and social upheaval. Many would argue that the Industrial Revolution, which began slowly in the last half of the 18th century, is still going on.

It is difficult to overestimate the impact—social, economic, and ultimately political—of the change from labor done by hand to labor done by machine. Within the space of a few decades the machine drastically altered a way of life that had prevailed for millennia. People who had formerly worked in their homes or on farms suddenly were herded together in factories, creating a new social class—the industrial worker. Fortunes were made virtually overnight by members of another new class—the manufacturers. Naturally, all this upheaval was reflected in art. At the beginning of the 19th century, then, Western civilization faced a totally new world.

CHAPTER NINETEEN

The Modern World: 1800–1945

A CHAPTER COVERING the art of the 19th and early 20th centuries presents certain difficulties, not the least of which is its title. Many writers designate the art of this period as "modern," a term that means "characteristic of the present or of the recent past," and so it will be called in this text. However, this poses a problem: When did "modern" start? There are those who would say that truly modern art did not exist until the Impressionists in the 1870s, or until the period just before World War I, or even until the late 1940s. Some artists working today would maintain that "modern" didn't exist until last week, at the very earliest. Moreover, we must remember that people in other periods of history undoubtedly thought of their own art as "modern," and perhaps even called it that.

If modern refers to the present and the recent past, we are faced with another puzzle: When does "modern" stop? In other words, what do we call everything that follows the present? Some writers, clearly at a loss for new labels, have coined the terms "postmodern" and "antimodern" to indicate a change in style, but these designations are unsatisfactory at best. They do not evoke any particular style characteristics, as "Renaissance" and "Baroque" do. All they tell us, really, is that the period called "modern" could not go on indefinitely, and that new art styles replaced those once considered to be "modern." Future generations will no doubt think up better, more revealing names for "modern" art and its aftermath.

Whatever we call it, we cannot ignore the fact that the art produced during the 19th and early 20th centuries offers a variety of expression unprecedented in the history of art. A second dictionary definition of "modern," especially as the word applies to art, is "characteristic of styles that reject traditionally accepted forms and emphasize individual experimentation and sensibility." This definition may prove more useful, because as we move farther into the chapter, we will indeed see an increasing rejection of traditional forms and a search for personal expression.

We begin our discussion at the turn of the 19th century, when the seeds of modern art movements were sown. The center of Western art was France, and so it remained (with a few digressions) until the onset of World War I.

FRANCE, EARLY 19TH CENTURY: NEOCLASSICISM, ROMANTICISM, REALISM

As we have seen in earlier chapters, most periods in the history of art had one dominant style—the High Renaissance style or the Baroque style, for instance—that major artists of the time followed. But French art of the early 19th century is not like that. It is customarily divided into three broad categories: classic, romantic, and realist. The fact that artists of the first rank were working in each of these styles gives a hint of the great diversity that was soon to come.

Representing the classic style—or, as it is usually called, **Neoclassical** ("new classical")—was the work of Jean Auguste Dominique Ingres; we saw one of his drawings in Chapter 6 **(184)**. Ingres was a pupil of Jacques Louis David **(509)**, and he inherited his master's admiration of ancient Greek and Roman art, as well as David's preference for sharp outline, reserved emotions, and studied (often geometric) composition—all characteristics of the Neoclassical style. We see these qualities in *La Grande Odalisque* **(511)**. "Odalisque" is a French word derived from the Turkish, meaning a concubine in a harem. It is typical of Ingres that, in portraying the nude figure, he placed it in an exotic situation. The nude was acceptable to contemporary standards of morality only when separated from everyday life. This nude, while unquestionably sensual, seems also rather distant and aloof. In Classical Greek art and in much art of the High Renaissance a cool detachment was deemed ideal. The Neoclassical style followed this trend. Ingres has outlined this figure very clearly, isolating it from its background, and the composition is perfectly balanced—the drape at right offsetting the raised torso on the left. Although a classicist, Ingres was capable of certain romantic touches. Here the figure of the odalisque has been adjusted in its proportions. The long curving spine gives the figure an unearthly elegance, and the graceful arm that connects the two halves of the composition surely outreaches that of any human female.

511.
Jean Auguste Dominique Ingres.
La Grande Odalisque.
1814. Oil on canvas,
2′11¼″ × 5′3¾″.
Louvre, Paris.

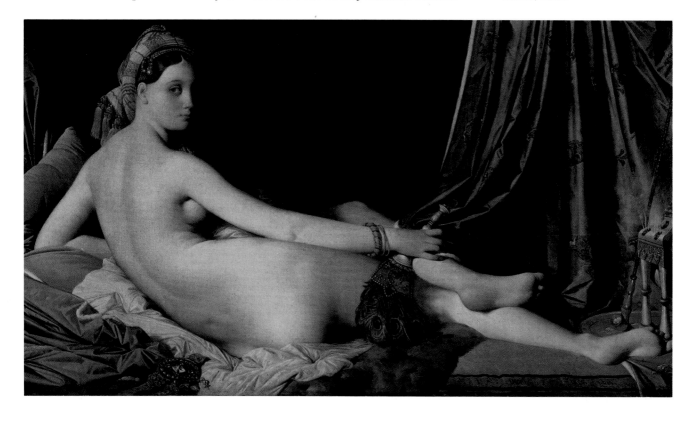

C H R O N O L O G Y

	1800—1850	1850—1900
Style/Period	Neoclassicism, France, early 19th century Romanticism, France, early 19th century Realism, France, mid-19th century Federal style and Classic Revival, United States	Impressionism, France, c. 1875–1900 Post-Impressionism, France, c. 1880–1900 Romanticism, United States

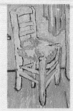

Van Gogh,
The Artist's Room

| **Political/ Social Events and Personalities** | Napoleon I, emperor of France, 1804–1814
War of 1812, United States, 1812–1814
Invention of photography by Daguerre, 1837 | Victoria, queen of England, 1837–1901
Admiral Perry visited Japan, 1853
American Civil War, 1861–1864
First public showing of motion pictures, 1895 |

Brady,
Abraham Lincoln

| **Major Artists** | Jacques Louis David (1748–1825)
J. M. W. Turner (1775–1851)
Jean Auguste Dominique Ingres (1780–1862)
Théodore Géricault (1791–1824)
Eugène Delacroix (1798–1863)
Honoré Daumier (1808–1879) | Gustave Courbet (1819–1877)
Rosa Bonheur (1822–1899)
Edouard Manet (1832–1883)
James Abbott McNeill Whistler (1834–1903)
Edgar Degas (1834–1917)
Winslow Homer (1836–1910)
Paul Cézanne (1839–1906)
Auguste Rodin (1840–1917)
Claude Monet (1840–1926)
Berthe Morisot (1841–1895)
Pierre-Auguste Renoir (1841–1919)
Thomas Eakins (1844–1916)
Mary Cassatt (1845–1926)
Paul Gauguin (1848–1903)
Vincent van Gogh (1853–1890)
John Singer Sargent (1856–1925)
Georges Seurat (1859–1891)
Henri de Toulouse-Lautrec (1864–1901) |

Manet, *Le Déjeuner
sur l'herbe*

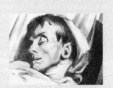

Daumier, *Murder in
the rue Transnonain*

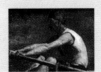

Eakins, *The Biglin
Brothers Racing*

1900–1925

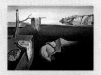

Dali, *The Persistence of Memory*

Expressionism, Europe, c. 1900–1920
Fauvism, France, begun 1905
Cubism, France, c. 1907–1914
Dada, Europe, c. 1916–1922
Surrealism, Europe, begun 1924

1925–1945

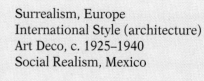

Chrysler Building

Surrealism, Europe
International Style (architecture)
Art Deco, c. 1925–1940
Social Realism, Mexico

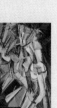

Duchamp, *Nude Descending a Staircase*

Wright brothers' first flight, 1903
Armory Show, New York, 1913
World War I, 1914–1918
Russian Revolution, 1917
Bauhaus, Germany, 1919–1933
Tutankhamun's tomb found, 1922
Harlem Renaissance, New York, 1920s

Lange, *Heading West*

Great Depression, 1929–1941
Spanish Civil War, 1936–1939
Television broadcast from New York
    World's Fair, 1939
World War II, 1939–1945

Picasso, *Les Demoiselles d'Avignon*

Edvard Munch (1863–1944)
Alfred Stieglitz (1864–1946)
Wassily Kandinsky (1866–1944)
Käthe Kollwitz (1867–1945)
Henri Matisse (1869–1954)
Piet Mondrian (1872–1944)
Pablo Picasso (1881–1973)
Georges Braque (1882–1963)

Picasso, *Guernica*

Frank Lloyd Wright (1867–1959)
Henri Matisse (1869–1954)
Constantin Brancusi (1876–1957)
Paul Klee (1879–1940)
Ernst Ludwig Kirchner (1880–1938)
Pablo Picasso (1881–1973)
Edward Hopper (1882–1967)
Diego Rivera (1886–1957)
Georgia O'Keeffe (1887–1986)
Marcel Duchamp (1887–1968)
Jean Arp (1887–1966)
Marc Chagall (1887–1985)
Joan Miró (1893–1983)
Norman Rockwell (1894–1978)
Aaron Douglas (1899–1979)
Salvador Dali (1904–1989)
Frida Kahlo (1907–1954)

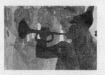

Douglas, *Aspects of Negro Life*

Kahlo, *The Two Fridas*

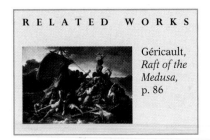
Ingres's lifelong rival was Eugène Delacroix, champion of the **Romantic** movement. The Romantic ideal stressed drama, turbulent emotions, and complex composition, all of which are evident in Delacroix's masterpiece, *Liberty Leading the People* **(512)**. In 1830 France was rocked by a brief uprising of the people, an aftershock of the French Revolution forty years earlier. Although not personally involved, Delacroix chose to depict an imaginary moment in this uprising as a statement of sympathy with the democratic ideals of the Revolution. Prominent in the composition is the figure of a woman, symbolizing Liberty and France—powerful, striding across the barricades, holding aloft the tricolor flag of France. Participants in the uprising stream behind her, following her lead—the artist does not tell us where, but presumably to the abstract goal of Freedom.

If we compare this passionate scene with the polished perfection of Ingres, the differences are obvious. Ingres's figure is motionless, languid; Delacroix's picture seethes with energy and violence. Ingres's *Odalisque* is beautifully contained within the frame of the picture, whereas Delacroix's figures marching toward us in a diagonal movement seem about to burst out of the composition, giving the impression of one frame in a continuous drama. Ingres's outlines are clear and refined; Delacroix's free brush strokes give us a sense of blurred motion, of flickering light and confusion. Yet, in spite of its dynamism, Delacroix's painting is every bit as carefully composed as that of Ingres. The composition is stable, based on a triangle, with the apex in the hand and flag of Liberty, and the two sides moving down through the upraised rifle at left, the boy's arm and pistol at right. In their concern for the structure

512. Eugène Delacroix. *Liberty Leading the People, 1830.* 1830. Oil on canvas, 8′6″ × 10′10″. Louvre, Paris.

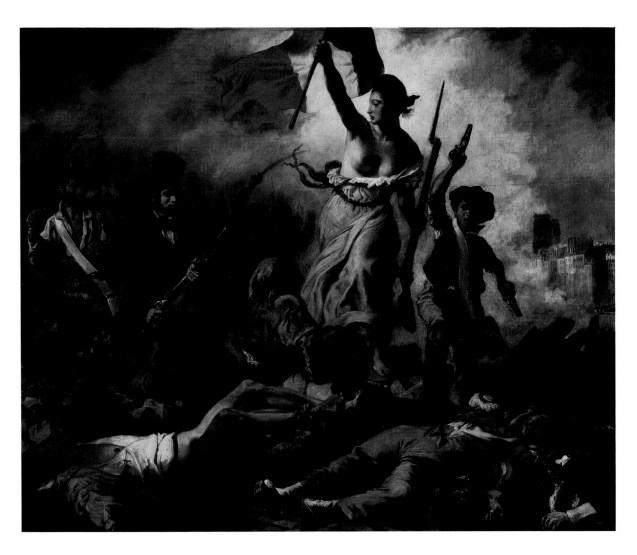

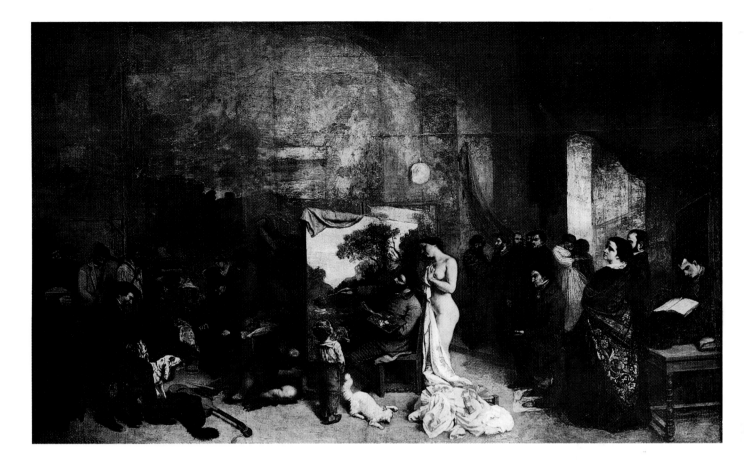

of painting Ingres and Delacroix were not as far apart as they appeared, but—because of the bitterness of their rivalry—neither would have admitted it.

The **Realist** movement in French art came somewhat later than Neoclassicism and Romanticism and was, in effect, a reaction against both. Realist artists sought to depict the everyday and the ordinary, rather than the heroic or the exotic. Their concerns were very much rooted in the present. One of the leaders of the Realist movement was Gustave Courbet, who in 1855 exhibited a huge painting, *The Artist's Studio* **(513)**, subtitled *A Real Allegory Summing Up Seven Years of My Life as an Artist.* To this day, more than a century later, art historians debate the meanings of the "allegory," or symbolic story.

At the center of the canvas sits Courbet himself, at work on a landscape painting. Although a great many people crowd into the studio, the artist seems aloof from them, as though his aesthetic concerns are all-consuming. A little boy (usually identified as Innocence) gawks up at the work in progress. Behind the artist stands a nude model, whom some consider to be his Muse, or inspiration, others the personification of Truth (that is, the "naked truth"). All the figures to the left of the composition are common people; they are "types," not individuals, derived from Courbet's origins in a rural village. At right are the artist's "intellectual" friends, many of them identifiable figures—his patrons, other artists, writers, and so on. Perhaps Courbet is saying the artist represents a special elite, fed by his origins and by his comrades, but apart from them, alone with Innocence and Truth. We know from Courbet's work as a whole that here the artist was trying to make a particular point—that everyday activities, such as an artist working at his easel or peasants toiling in the fields, were fit subject matter for grand-scale art. In an age when only paintings of religious or historical or mythological scenes were considered "great art," this was a revolutionary idea.

Another Realist artist of the time, and one of the greatest animal painters of any time, was Rosa Bonheur. Bonheur's best-known work—almost exactly

513. Gustave Courbet.
*The Artist's Studio:
A Real Allegory Summing Up
Seven Years of My Life
as an Artist.* 1855.
Oil on canvas,
11′9¾″ × 19′6⅝″.
Musée d'Orsay, Paris.

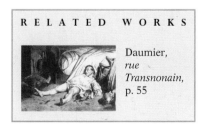

RELATED WORKS

Daumier,
*rue
Transnonain,*
p. 55

contemporary with Courbet's *Artist's Studio* and nearly as large—is *The Horse Fair* **(514)**. But while the Courbet work is very still and placid, Bonheur's painting teems with action. The Parisian horse fair was an event at which horses were traded and sold. Some of them, obviously, are barely tamed. Bonheur delights in portraying their wild freedom and power. Her extremely naturalistic depiction of the animals' anatomy came partly from the artist's frequent visits to the stockyards and slaughterhouses, partly from her lifelong love of animals. We as viewers seem to see the working of taut muscles, as the horses gallop and rear through this complex, dramatic composition. The figures of the men are much less important. Bonheur did not often focus on people and perhaps was less interested in them than in her beloved wild creatures. Many believe, however, that the man in blue at center, next to the rearing white horse, is a woman in disguise and is the artist's self-portrait.

Three of the four paintings we have considered so far in this chapter include a nude or seminude woman. Why are the women unclothed? Their nudity has a specific, accepted purpose—the exotic (Ingres's odalisque is a harem woman); the heroic (Delacroix's Liberty is bare-breasted as a mythical Amazon); the allegorical (Courbet's model may be the nude figure of Truth). These conventions satisfied contemporary tastes. But eight years after Courbet exhibited *The Artist's Studio*, a painting was placed on display in Paris that portrayed female nudity without any apparent justification at all. It caused a terrific scandal—the first of many artistic scandals that would shock the art world in the decades to come. The artist responsible for setting off this earthquake was a mild, conventional, well-to-do gentleman: Edouard Manet.

FRANCE, LATE 19TH CENTURY: MANET

514. Rosa Bonheur.
The Horse Fair. 1853–55.
Oil on canvas, 8′1¼″ × 16′7½″.
The Metropolitan Museum of Art,
New York (gift of
Cornelius Vanderbilt, 1887).

In 19th-century France the mark of an artist's success was acceptance at the annual Salon, a state-sponsored exhibition of paintings. Artists submitted their work for consideration by an official jury, whose members varied from year to year but tended to be conservative, if not downright stodgy. Art critic John Russell has described an ideal Salon painting of the period as containing the following ingredients:

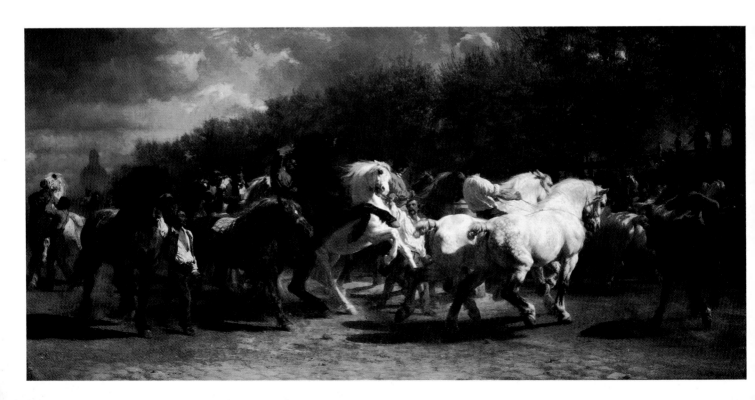

ROSA BONHEUR

1822–1899

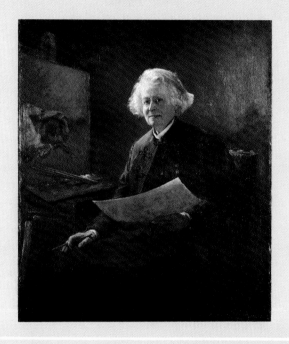

FOR PEOPLE WHO RECOGNIZE her name, an automatic word-association is "horses." Schoolchildren often are shown reproductions of her monumental painting *The Horse Fair.* But a closer look at this artist, one of the most successful and decorated of her time, reveals there is much more to Rosa Bonheur than horses.

The name Bonheur means "happiness," and during most of her life the artist seems to have enjoyed a good deal of that. Born in 1822 and christened Rosalie, she was the eldest child of Raimond Bonheur, a painter and art teacher, and Sophie Marquis Bonheur, who had been his pupil. All four of the Bonheur children became artists, but Rosalie—who later changed her signature to Rosa—was the standout. She earned her first money as an artist at age twelve; at nineteen she exhibited at the Salon, the annual showing of professional artists in Paris. Over the next several years Bonheur would exhibit frequently, win increasingly prestigious awards, and garner many commissions from buyers.

In her teens Bonheur formed a close friendship with Nathalie Micas, the daughter of one of her father's friends. The two women would eventually establish a home together, and they lived as companions until Micas's death in 1889. Meanwhile, Bonheur was beginning

to attract considerable attention—part admiring, part scandalized—for her eccentric ways.

Bonheur frequented the horse-trading fairs and slaughterhouses in order to gain intimate knowledge of animal anatomy. On these excursions she dressed in male clothing—a practice so unusual for women in her day that she needed a special license from the police to avoid arrest. She rode horses astride, rather than in the "ladylike" sidesaddle, and smoked cigars or a pipe. Surprisingly, in view of her shocking conduct, Bonheur was welcomed and admired by the Empress Eugénie of France and even by that most puritanical of monarchs, Queen Victoria of England.

The house Bonheur and Micas shared was at Fontainebleau, near Paris. There they collected a menagerie that at various times included lions, an otter, sheep, goats, an ostrich, plus numerous horses and dogs. All the animals seem to have had the run of the place—even the lions, which would follow Bonheur around like pussycats. The artist loved them and painted them; it was said that Micas could entrance the creatures with her gaze, so they would hold still for Bonheur to catch their likeness.

By 1887, at the age of sixty-five, Bonheur was financially and professionally secure. Her work was represented in many fine collections. Micas's death two years later was a severe blow. Only one event raised her spirits, and that was the arrival in Paris of the American showman Colonel William Cody, known as "Buffalo Bill," with his touring Wild West show. Long an admirer of America in general and the American West in particular, Bonheur was fascinated by Buffalo Bill's "cowboys and Indians" extravaganza. She made a great many sketches, entertained Buffalo Bill at her studio, and painted him on a prancing white horse.

When Bonheur was seventy-six, a young American painter, Anna Klumpke, arrived to make a portrait of the aging artist. Klumpke stayed on and soon earned her mentor's intense devotion. Just about a year later Rosa Bonheur died, quietly, of lung congestion. She was buried alongside Nathalie Micas, but she left her estate to Anna Klumpke.

Rosa Bonheur's life was one of passion, of great individuality—a life with art. Near the end, she described it this way: "Art is a tyrant. It demands heart, brain, soul, body. . . . I wed art. It is my husband, my world, my life dream, the air I breathe. I know nothing else, feel nothing else, think nothing else."[1]

Anna Elizabeth Klumpke. *Rosa Bonheur.* 1898.
Oil on canvas, 46⅛ × 38⅝".
The Metropolitan Museum of Art, New York
(gift of the artist in memory of Rosa Bonheur, 1922).

... a knight in armor, a group of cardinals, some tropical vegetation, some counterfeit stained glass, a medieval feast with every dish and goblet shown in meticulous detail, a distant view of Constantinople through a window in the background, and in the foreground, three or four naked women, dancing.[2]

Russell wrote this description with tongue in cheek, but there can be no doubt the Salon pictures followed a predictable formula.

In 1863 the Salon jury rejected four thousand of the submitted paintings, which caused such an uproar among the spurned artists and their supporters that a second official exhibition was mounted—the "Salon des Refusés" (showing of those who had been refused). Among the artists who were refused were Whistler and Cézanne. Among the works in the "refused" show—and very soon the most notorious among them—was Edouard Manet's painting *Le Déjeuner sur l'herbe* (515).

Luncheon on the Grass, as it is usually translated, shows a kind of outdoor picnic. Two men, dressed in the fashions of the day, relax and chat in a woodland setting. Their companion is a woman who has, for no apparent reason, taken off all her clothes. In the background another woman, wearing only a filmy garment, bathes in a pool. With this one painting Manet had broken several "rules" held dear by French artists and art lovers alike, and it would be difficult to decide which transgression shocked the public most.

The nude woman is not a goddess, not a harem slave, not an allegorical figure. Then why is she naked, and why sitting nonchalantly with two men who are clothed? Why does she gaze out at the viewer so calmly and matter-of-factly? Nudity in some classical guise was quite acceptable to Manet's audience, but nudity for its own sake was not. With the wisdom of hindsight we can now understand that Manet regarded the nude figure as a study in painted form, an exercise to display his newfound insights into light and shape. His contemporaries had no such understanding. To make matters worse, Manet had "borrowed" certain compositional elements from well-known masterpieces of the past—not an unusual practice among artists but considered presumptuous in the hands of such a "bad" painter as Manet.

515. Edouard Manet. *Le Déjeuner sur l'herbe.* 1863. Oil on canvas, 7′ × 8′10″. Musée d'Orsay, Paris.

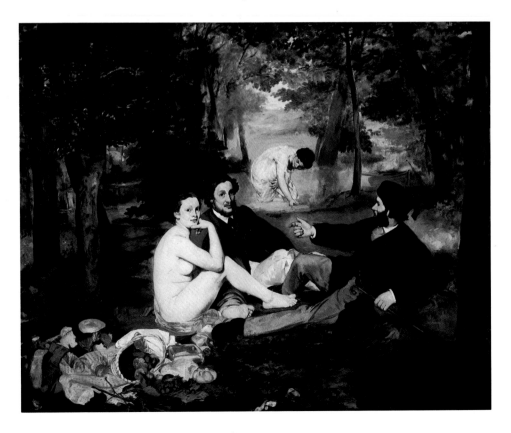

EDOUARD MANET

1832–1883

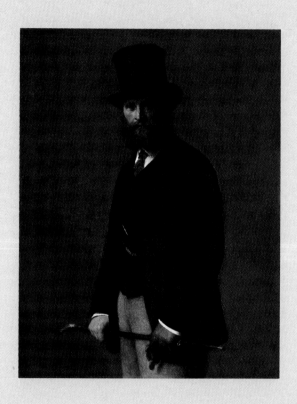

Dutch and Spanish art, particularly the paintings of the great Spanish artist Diego Velázquez. In 1859, when he was just twenty-seven, Manet submitted work to the Salon, the annual government-sponsored art exhibition. This submission was rejected, but two years later Manet placed two paintings in the Salon, one of them a portrait of his parents. Then in 1863 came the great scandal of *Le Déjeuner sur l'herbe*, which was rejected by the Salon, hung in the Salon des Refusés, called "immodest" by the French emperor, and heaped with abuse by critics and the public alike. Nevertheless, Manet continued to send paintings to the Salon each year, considering it the only true "field of battle" for an artist.

Surprisingly little is known about Manet's private life. He married Suzanne Leenhoff, who had been his piano teacher, in 1863. Though he earned little money from his art, his private means were sufficient to enable him to live comfortably. From time to time he traveled in Europe, but he always returned quickly to Paris, his spiritual as well as actual home. Manet was the quintessential Parisian. The well-dressed, well-mannered, well-spoken artist played an important role in intellectual society of the time. His closest friends were the writer-journalist Emile Zola and the poet Charles Baudelaire. Although he never exhibited with the Impressionist painters—most of whom were younger than he—Manet was considered by the Impressionists to be their natural leader and inspiration.

Sometime in the early 1880s Manet was struck by a serious illness, the exact nature of which is unknown. This illness resulted in the amputation of a gangrenous leg, and ultimately in his death at the age of fifty-one. As has happened with so many artists, recognition came to Manet just a bit too late. Seven years after his death, his painting *Olympia* was accepted by the Louvre.

Manet never got over his surprise at the public's contempt for his art, nor his bitterness about the rejection. In 1878 he wrote to Edgar Degas: "If there were no rewards, I wouldn't invent them: but they exist. And one should have everything that singles one out . . . when possible. It is another weapon. In this beastly life of ours, which is wholly struggle, one is never too well armed. I haven't been decorated? But it is not my fault, and I assure you that I shall be if I can and that I shall do everything necessary to that end."[3]

E DOUARD MANET was a gentleman. That old-fashioned word aptly describes one of the most civilized, elegant figures in the history of art. Unfortunately for Manet, through most of his career he was also a gentleman scorned. Few artists have had to endure as much public derision and abuse as Manet did, and few have been as poorly equipped to tolerate abuse as he. To the end of his life he sought popular success for his art, but always it eluded him.

Manet was born in Paris of well-to-do parents. At first he contemplated a naval career, but after two unsuccessful attempts to gain admittance to the naval academy, he turned to painting. He studied at the Ecole des Beaux-Arts and also in the studio of the painter Thomas Couture, but the major influences on his work were

Henri Fantin-Latour. *Edouard Manet.*
1867. Oil on canvas, 46 × 35½".
The Art Institute of Chicago (Stickney Fund).

Bad, indeed, his technical skills must have seemed to the Salon jurors, for Manet was breaking new ground in the way he interpreted forms on canvas. The artist simplified round, three-dimensional shapes into a series of flat planes. He took a fresh look at the way light strikes a subject, concentrating on brilliant highlights and deep shadow, all but eliminating the middle transitional tones. The image seems to have been caught in an instantaneous flash of brilliant light.

Today's viewer sees *Le Déjeuner sur l'herbe* as one of the first steps toward concerns that would dominate 20th-century art, especially in the use of light and shadow and in the de-emphasis of absolute naturalism. Manet's contemporaries, on the whole, thought him just a clumsy painter. Poor Manet was subjected to a storm of outrage and scorn from critics and the art-viewing public alike. We find it ironic, therefore, that little over a hundred years later, when a major Manet exhibition was organized in Paris and then moved to the United States, *Le Déjeuner sur l'herbe* was not included in the traveling show. The painting is considered priceless—and far too precious to leave France.

IMPRESSIONISM AND POST-IMPRESSIONISM

During the years following Manet's sensation in the Salon des Refusés, young French artists increasingly sought alternatives to the Salon. One group in particular looked to Manet as their philosophical leader, although he never consented to exhibit with them. The group was formed in 1874 and staged private showings each year until 1886. Because of the diversity of their techniques, the artists had difficulty finding a name for their association. Then a critic, after seeing a painting by Claude Monet (a member of the group) entitled *Impression: Sunrise*, scornfully dubbed the artists "impressionists." Rather than taking offense, the group happily adopted the name; their work was known thereafter as **Impressionism.**

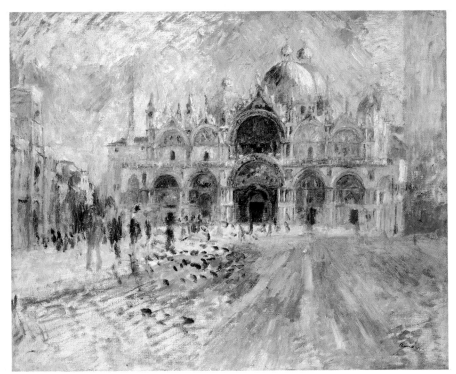

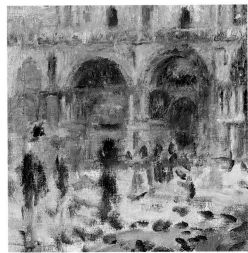

left: 516. Pierre-Auguste Renoir. *Piazza San Marco.* 1881. Oil on linen, 25⅝ × 32″. Minneapolis Institute of Arts (John R. van Derlip Fund).

below: 517. Detail of Renoir's *Piazza San Marco,* **516.**

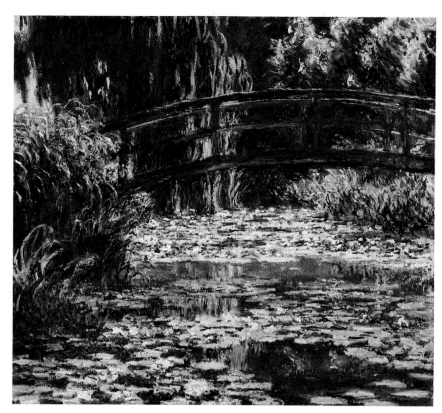

518. Claude Monet. *Water Lily Pool.* 1900. Oil on canvas, $35\frac{3}{8} \times 39\frac{3}{4}''$. The Art Institute of Chicago (Mr. and Mrs. Lewis Larned Coburn Memorial Collection).

The Impressionists attempted to paint what the eye actually sees, rather than what the brain interprets from visual cues. For example, if you look at a house in the distance and you know intellectually that the house is painted a uniform color of yellow, you might "see" all one shade of yellow, because your brain tells you that is correct. In purely visual terms, however, your eyes register many variations of yellow, depending on how light strikes the house and the shadows it creates. This is what the Impressionists were after—the true visual impression, not the version that is filtered through the knowing brain.

If you look closely at a small section of an Impressionist painting, you will see many individual brush strokes of varying colors, placed side by side with no blending—a jumble of color daubs. But when you move farther away, your eyes "mix" the colors to produce a recognizable subject with shimmering effects of light. Pierre-Auguste Renoir's painting of the *Piazza San Marco* illustrates this effect **(516,517)**. As rendered in the Impressionist style, St. Mark's is not the massive Byzantine cathedral we may know it to be, but a light-as-air palace wavering in the heat of a Venice summer.

Claude Monet, who gave Impressionism its name, is perhaps the artist who best typifies that style. (Despite the similarity of the names, Manet and Monet were not related.) Monet preferred to work outdoors, in daylight, and labored diligently to record on canvas the exact "impression" created by light striking a surface. Best known of Monet's paintings—and those showing the most developed Impressionist style—were the canvases of the water garden he built outside his home, the famous "water lilies" series **(518)**. Although we can identify trees, reeds, a bridge, the floating lily pads, our overall impression is of shimmering light and color, the sparkling effect produced by sunlight reflecting off the water. Monet's technique of combining many small, vivid brush strokes of pure color gives a dazzling brilliance.

Another artist associated with the Impressionist group, and one firmly dedicated to its goals, was Berthe Morisot. Morisot had an early success in the Salon and exhibited in this "establishment" forum several years running, but after she took up with the Impressionists she refused ever again to submit

RELATED WORKS

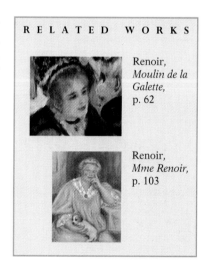

Renoir, *Moulin de la Galette,* p. 62

Renoir, *Mme Renoir,* p. 103

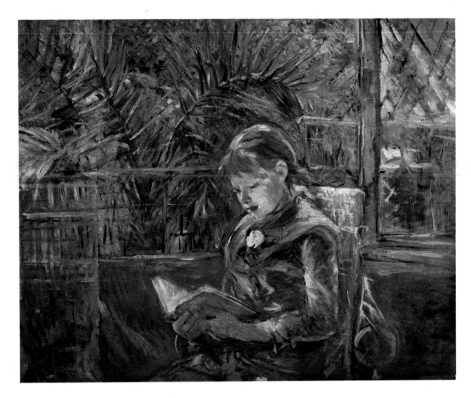

519. Berthe Morisot.
La Lecture. 1888.
Oil on canvas, 29¼ × 36½".
Museum of Fine Arts,
St. Petersburg, Fla.

RELATED WORKS

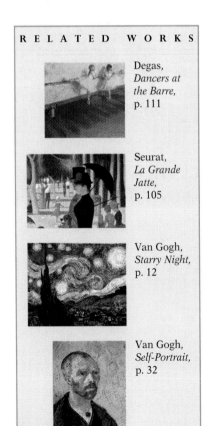

Degas,
*Dancers at
the Barre,*
p. 111

Seurat,
*La Grande
Jatte,*
p. 105

Van Gogh,
Starry Night,
p. 12

Van Gogh,
Self-Portrait,
p. 32

work to the Salon. Like Monet's, Morisot's paintings are suffused with light; they sparkle with the immediacy of the quick glimpse. Morisot, however, was not so committed as Monet to painting outdoors. Often she posed her figures in a charming room or on a balcony, as in *La Lecture* **(519)**. Her brushwork is somewhat freer than Monet's and is sometimes described as "nervous," with its long flamelike flicks of color. But according to Edgar Degas, whose praise was highly valued, Morisot's airy style "conceals the purest draftsmanship."

Degas was well equipped to comment on Morisot's draftsmanship, being the finest, most sure-handed draftsman of the Impressionist group. Considering his great interest in line, some critics question whether he can be called an Impressionist at all. Yet Degas's concerns were similar to those of Renoir and Monet and Morisot—to record the fleeting moment, to capture on canvas an instantaneous perception of the eye. As we have noted in other chapters, Degas was absorbed by the unusual angle of sight, the "peephole" view of a scene, and his composition was strongly influenced by the complex spatial relationships in Japanese prints. *The Tub* **(520)**, a work painted in the mid-1880s, shows the artist in masterful control of these effects. We see a nude at her bath, viewed from above. We glimpse her as though we are quickly looking in a window while passing by. She is crouched rather awkwardly, scrubbing her shoulder, her body almost filling the left side of the canvas. On the right is a table or shelf that increases the picture's spatial ambiguity. We assume that it is above the figure, but the space is so compressed that the left and right sections might be in the same plane. These spatial relations appear to be haphazard, but actually they reflect a meticulously planned composition. To appreciate the originality of Degas's conception, we might speculate how Ingres or Delacroix might have posed a nude bathing, barely half a century earlier.

The Impressionists profoundly influenced the major artists who followed them, especially in the lightness and brightness of colors. However, the work of the members of this next generation is so diverse in so many respects that no one stylistic label seems to fit all of them, and they generally are known as the **Post-Impressionists.** They include Vincent van Gogh, Paul Cézanne, Paul Gauguin, and Georges Seurat.

We have already considered a number of works by Van Gogh in this book. His style is characterized by intense, high-key colors; loose brushwork, often with a heavy impasto; a swirling, agitated composition; and a subject matter emphasizing those things closest to him—the landscapes he inhabited, buildings in which he dwelled, his friends, himself. Among his best-known paintings is *The Artist's Room at Arles* **(521)**, a study of his own bedroom in a little house he rented. Van Gogh identified so closely with the bedroom that it is virtually a self-portrait. The narrow room, empty except for the bed, two straight chairs, a small table, and, significantly, several paintings on the wall, speaks eloquently of a lonely artist dedicated to his work. The composition is an unusual one. Nearly half the canvas is devoted to bare floor and the blank footboard of the bed. All the main items of interest—Van Gogh's toilet articles on the table, his clothes on a peg, his looking glass, the pillows on his bed, and above all his paintings—are clustered (we might even say crammed) into the top half of the composition. The artist might be showing us that he lived in a compressed world—the world of his mind and his extraordinary art.

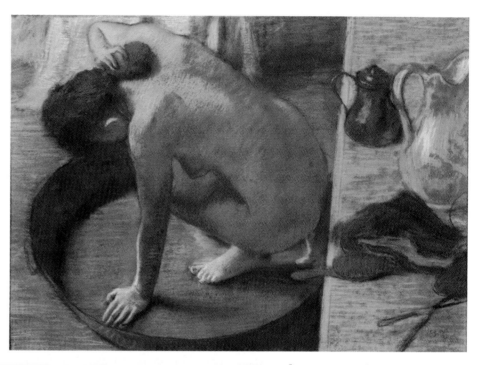

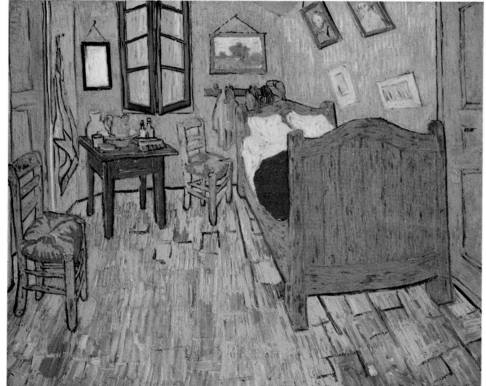

above: 520. Edgar Degas.
The Tub. 1886.
Pastel, $23\frac{1}{2} \times 32\frac{1}{8}''$.
Musée d'Orsay, Paris.

left: 521. Vincent van Gogh.
The Artist's Room at Arles.
1888–89. Oil on canvas, $29 \times 36''$.
The Art Institute of Chicago
(Helen Birch Bartlett
Memorial Collection).

461

RELATED WORKS

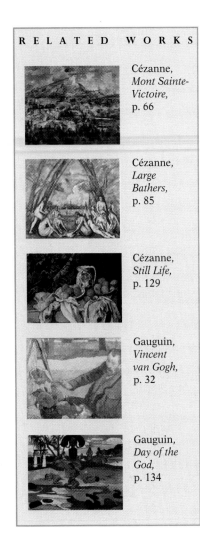

Cézanne, *Mont Sainte-Victoire*, p. 66

Cézanne, *Large Bathers*, p. 85

Cézanne, *Still Life*, p. 129

Gauguin, *Vincent van Gogh*, p. 32

Gauguin, *Day of the God*, p. 134

Paul Cézanne took a different approach in building on the work of the Impressionists. His search was for a solidity and a geometric order in the visual world, and he explored this problem in landscapes, in figural compositions, in still lifes, even in portraits. A solitary and uncommunicative figure nearly all his life, Cézanne had enormous influence on artists of succeeding generations.

Paul Gauguin worked in the Impressionist style early in his career, but he soon became dissatisfied. Like Van Gogh and Cézanne, he felt the need for more substance, more solidity of form than could be found in optical perceptions of light. Beyond this, Gauguin was interested in expressing a spiritual meaning in his art. All these he sought on the sun-drenched islands of the South Pacific. Gauguin's paintings made in Tahiti have brilliant high-keyed colors, thus revealing his debt to the Impressionists. But to this color effect he has added his own innovations: flattened forms and broad color areas, a strong outline, a taste for the exotic, an aura of mystery, a quest for the "primitive."

Nafea Faaipoipo (When Are You To Be Married?) **(522)** was painted soon after the beginning of Gauguin's first long stay in Tahiti, and it shows all these characteristics. The figures of the two young women are so flat that we feel we almost could cut around them as if they were paper dolls and pull them out of the painting. Strong outlines define them; this is especially apparent in the skirt and face of the woman at left. The landscape is rendered in broad, flat color areas receding backward: green grass of the foreground, a large yellow middle ground, deep blue shadow under the trees, purple mountain in the background. We know that the women of Tahiti, especially the young girls,

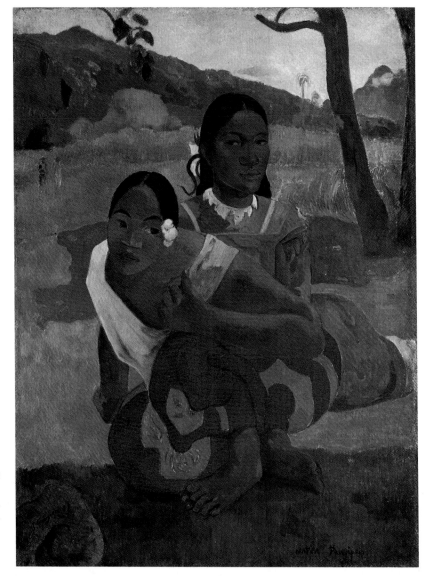

522. Paul Gauguin. *Nafea Faaipoipo (When Are You To Be Married?)*. 1892. Oil on canvas, $41\frac{1}{4} \times 30\frac{1}{2}''$. Rudolf Staechelin Foundation, Basel.

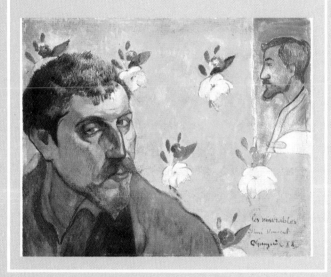

PAUL GAUGUIN

1848–1903

W HEN GAUGUIN SET SAIL from France in 1891, headed for the remote island of Tahiti in the South Pacific, he wrote a new chapter in the legend of the romantic, bohemian artist. To this day the legend persists. Many people want an artist to be—and Gauguin himself perhaps wanted to be—a dramatic, tormented soul who turns away from the comforts of modern civilization, who is not subject to society's conventions, who thrives in an exotic climate.

Paul Gauguin's origins gave but little hint of what was to come. Born in Paris, he spent part of his childhood in Peru, then returned with his family to France. After a stint in the merchant marine, he settled down and established himself as a stockbroker in Paris. When his career prospered, he married a young Danish woman, Mette Gad, who eventually bore him five children. Sometime in this period he took up painting as a hobby.

Over the years this hobby gradually came to be an obsession. In 1883, when he was thirty-five, Gauguin suddenly announced to his wife that he intended to quit his job and become a full-time painter. His attempts to support himself in this profession were not rewarding; eventually, Gauguin's wife rejoined her family in Denmark, taking the children, and the couple never lived together again. In 1886 Gauguin made the first of three visits to Brittany, the westernmost province of France. By this time he had already begun to establish his style of painting in broad shapes and flat color areas. A year later the artist journeyed to the island of Martinique, in the Caribbean, where the lush tropical colors heightened his palette even further. Late in 1888 Gauguin paid a brief—and disastrously unpleasant—visit to Van Gogh in the south of France. Finally, disillusioned with Western society and its values, Gauguin departed for Tahiti.

In Tahiti, Gauguin "went native." He lived in a grass hut and took as his *vahine*, or woman, a thirteen-year-old Tahitian girl, who gave birth to his son. At first all seemed idyllic, but even in the tropics one could not live for free, and Gauguin's finances were tight. He returned to Paris in 1893, hoping to sell his paintings, but the trip was not a success. Two years later Gauguin again set sail for Tahiti—never to return home.

During the second Tahitian period, Gauguin's fortunes went from bad to ghastly. He was wracked by a severe case of syphilis, suffered from a broken ankle that would not heal, and was desperately poor. At lowest ebb he attempted suicide, but the arsenic he swallowed was vomited up, causing him great agony. In 1901 he made his final voyage, to the Marquesas Islands, where—after a series of strokes—he died, penniless and completely alone. Three years after his death a memorial exhibition of Gauguin's work was organized in Paris. The show was a triumph. Gauguin was recognized as one of the great artists of his time.

Through all his ordeals, Gauguin seems to have considered the sacrifice worth it—necessary to achieve the vision he sought in art. As he wrote to his wife, "I am a great artist. . . . I am a great artist and know it. It is because of what I am that I have endured so many sufferings so as to pursue my vocation, otherwise I would consider myself a rogue."[4]

Paul Gauguin. *Les Miserables (Self-Portrait).*
1888. Oil on canvas, 28 × 35″.
Rijksmuseum Vincent van Gogh, Amsterdam.

were usually slender and lithe. Gauguin has given them a heavy, monumental solidity in keeping with his interest in broad form, and perhaps also because it fulfilled his fantasies about what a "noble savage" ought to look like. Mystery and magic are conveyed by the stylized gesture of the woman at right and the secretive expressions of both women. Perhaps the magic was more in Gauguin's mind than in the subjects he painted. Nevertheless, in the South Pacific he found the ideal environment to foster his unique artistic vision.

When Gauguin moved to this remote island thousands of miles from France, he still kept in touch with his colleagues and dealers in Paris—an indication that we are approaching 20th-century standards of travel and communication. Of course, artists always have traveled. Even the ancient Greek sculptors occasionally set out on the "wine-dark sea" celebrated by the poet Homer. But at the turn of the 20th century, travel across the great oceans had become so convenient and commonplace as to be taken for granted. This ease of movement gave rise to a new phenomenon—transatlantic cultivation of the arts. American artists and writers flocked to London and Paris to learn from the masters there. European artists and writers flocked to the United States, where they found an eager market among certain discerning collectors. Two worlds were rapidly becoming one.

BRIDGING THE ATLANTIC: LATE 19TH CENTURY

RELATED WORKS

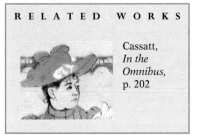

Cassatt, *In the Omnibus,* p. 202

Since the early days of the Colonies, American artists had journeyed to Europe, the better to learn their craft. Toward the end of the 19th century, however, the pace of traveling accelerated. Some artists based in the United States, including Winslow Homer and Thomas Eakins, made brief visits to Europe and then returned home. Others, born in the United States and considered to be American artists, actually spent much of their working lives in Europe. This latter group includes Mary Cassatt, James Abbott McNeill Whistler, and John Singer Sargent.

Whistler was born in Massachusetts but eventually settled in London. His most famous painting (523) has been done a great injustice—and become a cliché—through generations of use on Mother's Day cards, advertisements, and comic posters, thus earning the unfortunate title *Whistler's Mother.* But the artist himself wondered aloud why anyone should care about the identity of the model; his own title, *Arrangement in Gray and Black, No. 1,* speaks far more to Whistler's intent. This image, which has entered the public consciousness as an expression of a son's sentimental devotion to his aged mother, actually was meant, and succeeds, as a subtle study of formal composition, light, and color.

Whistler's harmony of values—principally soft black and grays—gives the painting a warm, mellow quality. But even more striking is the composition's exquisite visual balance—the elderly woman arranged in profile at right, balanced against the drape at left, the perfect placement of the picture on the wall a bit off center, even the second picture barely visible at upper right. If any of these elements were changed or removed, Whistler's elegant composition would fall apart. (Indeed, the drape at left is often cropped out in commercial reproductions; you can see how awkward the picture becomes if you cover this portion with your hand.) *Arrangement in Gray and Black* demonstrates a new interest among artists in using the visual elements for their own sake, not just to serve the needs of a particular subject matter.

Although John Singer Sargent was an American citizen, he actually spent very little time in the United States. Born in Italy to American parents, Sargent established his primary studio in London, with only occasional trips to New

below: 523.
James Abbott McNeill Whistler.
*Arrangement in Gray and Black,
No. 1 (The Artist's Mother).*
1871. Oil on canvas, 4'9" × 5'4½".
Musée d'Orsay, Paris.

right: 524. John Singer Sargent.
Madame X (Mme Pierre Gautreau).
1884. Oil on canvas,
6'10¼" × 3'11¼".
The Metropolitan Museum of Art,
New York (Arthur H. Hearn Fund, 1916).

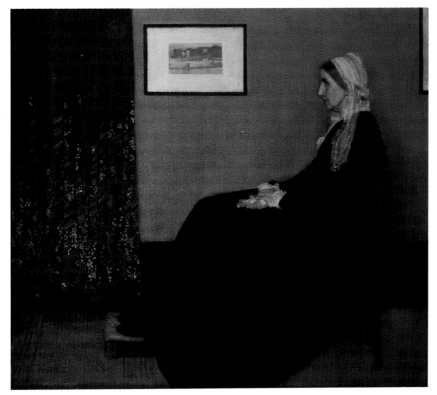

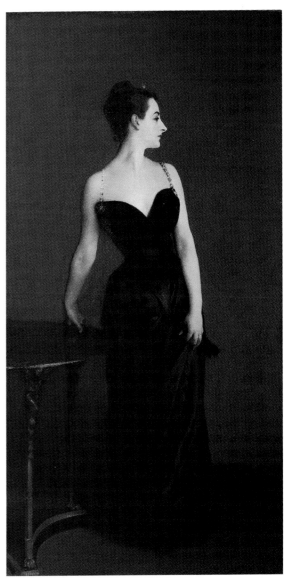

York and Boston. He made his reputation early as a portrait painter, and throughout his career he remained wildly in demand by the rich and fashionable on both sides of the Atlantic. The best of Sargent's portraits succeed because they create an aura of elegance and aristocratic glamour. A typical example is the notorious *Madame X* (524), painted in 1884.

Sargent's portrait of Mme Gautreau, an American society woman, caused a scandal when it was exhibited in Paris, in equal parts because of the subject's low-cut dress—quite daring for a "nice" woman of the time—and her haughty expression. A century later, however, we see both of these factors as contributing to the effectiveness of the picture. Mme Gautreau's pose, the essence of grace, is enhanced by the elegant full profile of her head. The abundance of creamy white skin contrasts dramatically with the velvety tones of her dress. Shocking as the portrait might have been, we can well imagine that wealthy women of the period would pay handsomely to be made to look like this.

If Paris was startled by *Madame X*, worse upsets were soon to come. Change was everywhere, signaled by the Impressionists and the Post-Impressionists. How far and how fast art was moving will be obvious when we look at the next "portrait" illustrated here, a work painted just twenty-one years after *Madame X*.

FRANCE,
EARLY 20TH CENTURY:
FAUVISM, CUBISM,
AND OTHER MOVEMENTS

RELATED WORKS

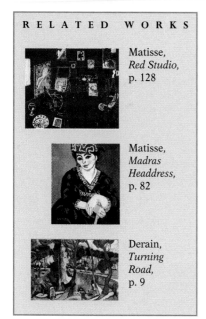

Matisse,
Red Studio,
p. 128

Matisse,
*Madras
Headdress,*
p. 82

Derain,
*Turning
Road,*
p. 9

A public that could be shocked by *Madame X*—to our eyes a lovely but rather conventional painting—was hardly prepared for the explosion that shook the art world soon afterward. In 1903 the Salon d'Automne (autumn salon) was organized in Paris as an alternative to the establishment Salon. Two years later the Salon d'Automne exhibited the work of a new group of artists whose style caused a critic to label them *fauves*—"wild beasts"—and the label stuck. Among the artists who evoked this angry response was an unlikely candidate for wildness—Henri Matisse.

The Matisse painting illustrated here **(525)** is technically a portrait of the artist's wife, Amélie, but it is known by a more descriptive title, *The Woman with the Hat*. Gertrude Stein (p. 14), who saw the painting at the Salon d'Automne and, with her brother Leo, bought it for 500 francs (about $100), later wrote that "people were roaring with laughter at the picture and scratching at it." Characteristically, Gertrude Stein remarked that she herself thought *The Woman with the Hat* "perfectly natural."[5] No doubt she was unique among observers of 1905 in finding the picture "natural," for Matisse, building on precedents Gauguin had explored a generation earlier **(522)**, painted this image in purely arbitrary colors, or colors unrelated to the natural appearance of his subject. Mme Matisse wears a hat piled high with flowers, and the riotous, exuberant colors in the hat are carried through the rest of the canvas—the background, the dress, the fan, even the model's face. It is as though Matisse made his entire painting a bouquet of glorious blooms, arranging his saturated hues according to the inspiration of the moment. In *The Woman with the Hat,* and other paintings of this time, Matisse showed that color is a tool, one of many tools in the artist's kit, to be used as the artist sees fit.

The Fauve movement did not last very long, a mere three years or so. Matisse went on to explore other aspects of painting, as did his fellow exhibitors at the 1905 Salon d'Automne. Yet the Fauve experiment was crucial for the development of modern art, in that it broke once and for all a longstanding taboo about the boundaries and conventions of art. Never again would artists feel they must confine themselves to replicating the "real" colors of the natural world, although they might do so if they wished. The artistic bag, so to speak, was open.

No sooner had the color rule been broken than artists began to break more daringly than ever before with conventions of shape and space. At the forefront of this experimentation was an artist, just a dozen years younger than Matisse, who broke nearly every rule art had long followed and who emerged as one of the greatest masters of all time: Pablo Picasso. Many consider a painting done early in the artist's career to be pivotal in the development of 20th-century art. That painting is *Les Demoiselles d'Avignon* **(526)**.

Les Demoiselles d'Avignon was not Picasso's title but was given to the painting years later by a friend of his. It translates literally as "the young women of Avignon" and refers to the prostitutes of Avignon Street, a notorious district of Barcelona. In early sketches for the painting Picasso included a sailor entering at left to purchase the prostitutes' services, but in the finished canvas the sailor has been omitted. Picasso had become so involved with the formal components of his painting—the relations of form and space—that he all but forgot its original content.

If these are prostitutes, then how extraordinary they are! They are far from enticing. Picasso has chopped them up into planes—flat, angular segments that still hint at three-dimensionality but have no conventional modeling. Almost as an affront to traditional pictures of curvaceous nude bathers, the artist has defined his nudes in sharp geometric shapes. Figure and ground lose their importance as separate entities; the "background"—that is, whatever is not the five figures—is treated in much the same way as the women's bodies. As a result, the entire picture appears flattened; we have no sense of looking "through" the painting into a world beyond, as with Delacroix or even Manet.

To many people who see *Les Demoiselles* for the first time, the faces cause discomfort. The three at left seem like reasonable enough, if abstract, depictions of faces, except for the fact that the figure at far left, whose face is in profile, has an eye staring straight ahead, much as in an Egyptian painting. But the two faces at right are clearly masks—images borrowed from "primitive" art—and they create a disturbing effect when set atop the nude bodies of European females.

In *Les Demoiselles* Picasso was experimenting with several ideas that he would explore in his art for years to come. First, there is the inclusion of nontraditional elements. Picasso had recently seen sculptures from ancient Iberia (Spain before the Roman Empire), as well as art from Africa. In breaking with Western art conventions that reached back to ancient Greece and Rome, Picasso looked for inspiration from other, equally ancient, traditions. Second, there is the merging of figure and ground, reflecting the assumption that all portions of the work participate in its expression. And third, there is fragmenting of the figures and other elements into flat planes, especially evident in the breasts of the figure at upper right and the mask just below. This last factor proved especially significant for an artistic journey on which Picasso was soon to embark—the movement known as **Cubism.**

Picasso's partner in this venture was the artist Georges Braque. Braque met Picasso in 1907 and saw *Les Demoiselles* in Picasso's studio. By all reports, Braque was at first dismayed and puzzled by the painting, but later he came to understand Picasso's goals. Both artists had been strongly influenced by the

left: 525. Henri Matisse. *The Woman with the Hat.* 1905. Oil on canvas, 31¾ × 23½". San Francisco Museum of Modern Art (bequest of Elise S. Haas).

right: 526. Pablo Picasso. *Les Demoiselles d'Avignon.* Paris, June–July 1907. Oil on canvas, 8′ × 7′8″. The Museum of Modern Art, New York (acquired through the Lillie P. Bliss Bequest).

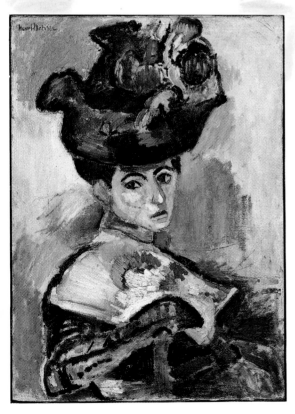

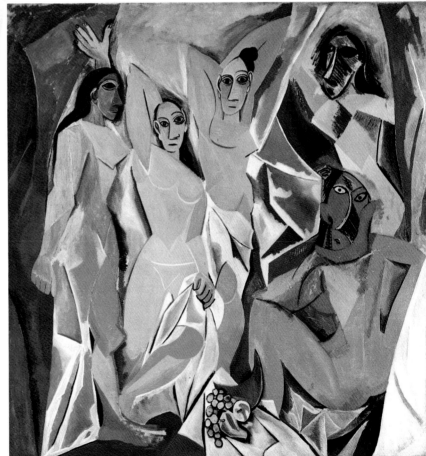

PABLO PICASSO

1881–1973

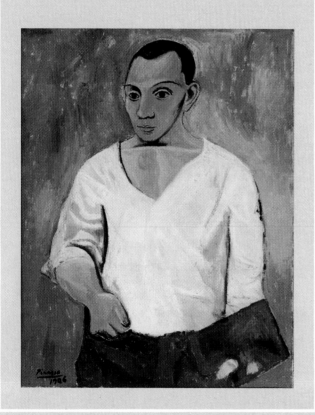

Although Picasso worked in many different styles throughout his life, much of his art is classifiable into the well-known "periods": the "Blue" period, when his paintings concentrated on images of poverty and emotional depression; the "Rose" period, whose paintings included depictions of harlequins and acrobats; the Cubist period, when he worked with the painter Georges Braque; and the "Neoclassical" period, in which the figures took on qualities resembling ancient Greek sculptures.

Success came early to Picasso. Except for brief periods when he was short of funds (usually because of some romantic entanglement), he lived well and comfortably, traveled widely, and enjoyed a large circle of friends. His work was always in demand, whether in painting, sculpture, prints (of which he made thousands), theatrical design, murals, or ceramics (he took up ceramic art in 1947 and decorated some two thousand pieces in a single year).

It would be impossible to discuss Picasso's life without reference to the women who shared it, because they are a constant presence in his art. Picasso married only twice, but he maintained long, occasionally overlapping, liaisons with several other women. His attachments included Fernande Olivier; Eva Gouel; Olga Koklova, his first wife and the mother of his son Paulo; Marie-Thérèse Walter, mother of his daughter Maïa; Dora Maar; Françoise Gilot, who bore him Claude and Paloma, then later wrote a scandalous memoir of her years with the artist; and finally Jacqueline Roque, whom he married in 1961, in his eightieth year.

Despite his international celebrity, Picasso gave almost no interviews. One of the few took place in 1935 and included this insight into the nature of art: "Everyone wants to understand art. Why not try to understand the song of a bird? Why does one love the night, flowers, everything around one, without trying to understand them? But in the case of a painting people have to understand. If only they would realize above all that an artist works of necessity, that he himself is only a trifling bit of the world, and that no more importance should be attached to him than to plenty of other things which please us in the world, though we can't explain them. People who try to explain pictures are usually barking up the wrong tree."[6]

Pablo Picasso. *Self-Portrait with Palette.* 1906.
Oil on canvas, 36¼ × 28¾."
Philadelphia Museum of Art (The A. E. Gallatin Collection).

T HE LIFE OF Picasso defies summary in a one-page biography. Few artists have lived so long; none have produced such an immense volume of work in so diverse a range of styles and media; and only a rare few can match him in richness and variety of personal history.

Pablo Ruiz y Picasso was born in the Spanish city of Málaga. He attended art schools in Barcelona and Madrid but became impatient with their rigid, academic approach and soon abandoned formal study. After two trips to Paris—where he saw the work of Van Gogh, Gauguin, and Lautrec—he settled permanently in that city in 1904 and never again lived outside France.

late works of Paul Cézanne **(69)** and by Cézanne's idea that natural forms could be reduced to geometric solids—the cone, the sphere, and the cylinder. Picasso and Braque also were interested in the geometry of forms, but they took as their starting point an angular, rather than a curved, solid—the cube.

In 1909 Braque and Picasso began working closely together, and they continued to do so for several years. By 1910 their experiments were so closely intertwined that the two artists' styles became virtually one, and it is often difficult even for experts to tell their work apart. This parallel development will be evident from two paintings of the same date, Picasso's *Accordionist* **(527)** and Braque's *Man with a Guitar* **(528)**. Both works, from their titles, claim to depict someone playing a musical instrument. The close observer will find many fragments that suggest musical symbols or that hint at an arm or fingers. But the announced subject, for both artists, is merely a starting point for the exploration of form.

Cubism is an art of facets, like the facets in a diamond. Forms are flattened into planes, broken apart, and reassembled to make a striking visual (but abstract) reality. We see the same form from different angles simultaneously; top, bottom, side, and frontal views may be combined into one image. Figure and ground are treated in the same way and have equal weight in the composition, blending together into a coherent whole. As Cubism developed, both Braque and Picasso began introducing bits of the "real world" into their canvases—stenciled letters and numbers or even pasted-on newspaper and fabrics. The psychological tension produced in the viewer by merging "real" with "not real" (the illusory world of paint on canvas) would have important implications for the artists of the Dada movement (p. 475) and for many artists of the later 20th century.

Cubism was a final, dramatic declaration of independence from Renaissance ideals of natural representation and linear perspective (p. 114). Picasso's and Braque's paintings are clearly *not* an attempt to show us exactly what the model looked like. Instead, they represent a study of forms for their aesthetic possibilities, a statement that a work of art has its own reality and need not be a mirror of the natural world. Neither Braque nor Picasso completely abandoned naturalism. Some of Picasso's works after Cubism **(27)** are as faithful representations of the natural world as anyone could ask for. However, with Cubism the principle was firmly established that a painting is *paint on canvas*—an arrangement of shapes and colors and lines chosen to suit the artist's expressive purpose, whatever that might be.

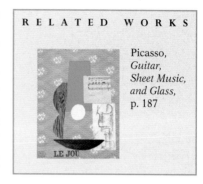

RELATED WORKS

Picasso, *Guitar, Sheet Music, and Glass,* p. 187

left: 527. Pablo Picasso. *The Accordionist.* 1911. Oil on canvas, 4'3¼" × 2'11¼". Solomon R. Guggenheim Museum, New York (gift, Solomon R. Guggenheim, 1937).

right: 528. Georges Braque. *Man with a Guitar.* 1911–12 (begun Céret, summer 1911; completed Paris, early 1912). Oil on canvas, 45¾ × 31⅞". The Museum of Modern Art, New York (acquired through the Lillie P. Bliss Bequest).

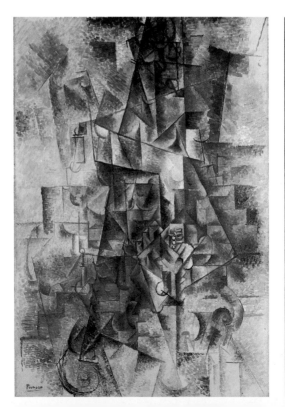

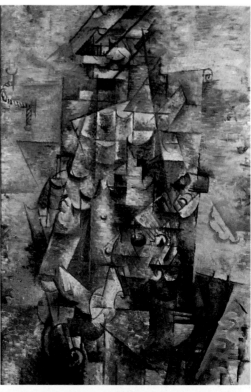

EARLY
20TH CENTURY:
EXPRESSIONISM

R E L A T E D   W O R K S

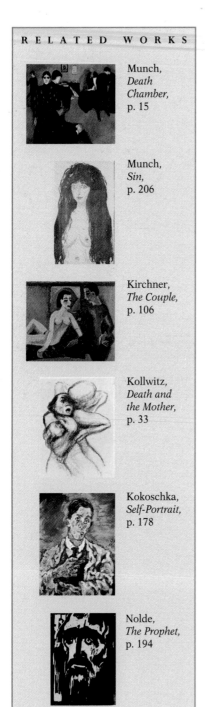

Munch,
*Death
Chamber,*
p. 15

Munch,
Sin,
p. 206

Kirchner,
The Couple,
p. 106

Kollwitz,
*Death and
the Mother,*
p. 33

Kokoschka,
Self-Portrait,
p. 178

Nolde,
The Prophet,
p. 194

If Picasso and Braque in this period were experimenting with a purely visual reality, some of their contemporaries were more interested in exploring a psychological one. During the first two decades of this century a movement developed in Germany that came to be known as *Expressionism.* Centered around a group of artists based in Dresden who called themselves **Die Brücke** ("the bridge"), Expressionism had many roots. It was strongly influenced by Van Gogh and Gauguin, took its intense color effects from Fauvism, and admired the stark, deeply emotional works of the Norwegian artist Edvard Munch. At the time when Expressionism flourished, Sigmund Freud was active in Vienna, publishing his new theories about the role of the unconscious, the meaning of dreams, and the practice of psychoanalysis. The Expressionists were entirely in sympathy with Freud's goal of probing the unconscious and hoped to take the process one step further—to translate their inner explorations into a meaningful art.

Ernst Ludwig Kirchner, a leader of *Die Brücke,* gives us a haunting image of urban loneliness in *Street, Dresden* **(529)**. Isolation was an important theme for Kirchner, whether it was the isolation of individuals living together in the metropolis or the emotional isolation of lovers from one another **(122)**. His street in Dresden is peopled by gaunt, troubled figures, each caught in personal sorrow and interacting not at all with those around them. Kirchner's debt to the Fauve artists is clear in his intense, arbitrary colors. Edvard Munch's influence is also evident, for Munch often painted solitary, tormented figures trapped inside a group that offers no comfort. Munch's anguish, however, seems more personal. The Expressionists were pessimistic about the human condition in general—that is, about life itself.

The painting styles of the Expressionist artists are often dissimilar, but their thread of connection is the desire or need to probe their deepest emotions and to express those emotions in their work. Other artists generally associated with the Expressionist movement include Käthe Kollwitz, Oskar Kokoschka, and Emil Nolde.

SYNTHESIS
AND AWAKENING:
THE ARMORY SHOW

European art, by the second decade of the 20th century, had run through a series of "isms"—Impressionism, Post-Impressionism, Fauvism, Cubism, Expressionism. The artists connected with these styles certainly were aware of each other's work and were influenced by one another. But each group tended to exhibit with other members of that group—Impressionists with Impressionists, Cubists with Cubists, and so on. Never had the various movements been brought together in one place to make the statement that *here* is modern art—or, rather, here are the many directions of modern art. Moreover, this extraordinary activity in European art had gone mostly unnoticed in the United States. Some few American artists and collectors had followed the new styles, but the public at large was unaware of them. All this changed abruptly in 1913. In that year a show of European and American art was organized by a group of progressive American artists. The show opened at the 69th Regiment

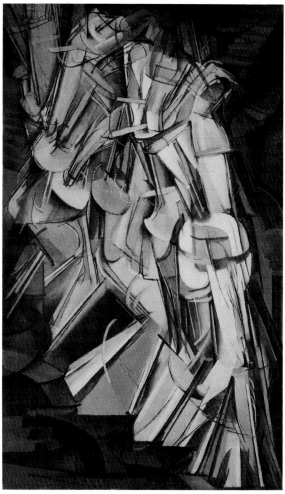

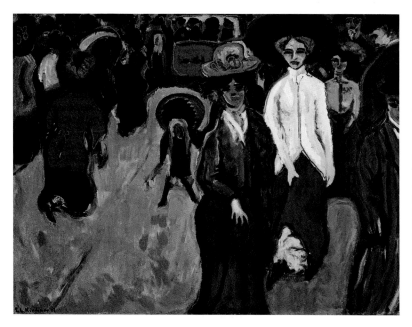

Armory in New York, and although there have been many art exhibitions in many armories, this one is still known as the Armory Show.

European art of the previous four decades was well represented, and the show caused an immediate sensation. So abusive was the press in its criticism that the general public became intrigued and flocked to the Armory to laugh at the art (and its makers). The critics singled out one work in particular for their greatest scorn, and that work soon became the star attraction. It is a Cubist-derived painting by the Frenchman Marcel Duchamp known as *Nude Descending a Staircase* (530).

As in a more "orthodox" Cubist painting, Duchamp has taken an image, here the nude figure, and flattened it into planes, which are then reshuffled and rearranged. However, he has also repeated the image many times over, creating a sharp, choppy rhythm that makes the figure appear to descend the staircase. When we first look at *Nude Descending a Staircase,* we may be tempted to echo the comment of a viewer at the Armory Show, who called the painting "an explosion in a shingle factory." But on closer inspection the forms begin to emerge, although they are abstracted: the rounded shape moving diagonally across the center of the canvas is a hip, the lower section of the painting a series of repeated legs. Duchamp had adopted the rather static forms of Cubism and set them in motion.

Another artist represented in the Armory Show was the Romanian-born sculptor Constantin Brancusi. Brancusi worked briefly in the studio of the great French sculptor Auguste Rodin (324) but soon departed with the now-famous statement, "No other trees can grow in the shadow of an oak tree." By 1910 Brancusi's work had become simplified and abstract, as evidenced by

The Kiss **(531)**, from a series of sculptures on this theme. *The Kiss* represents two of Brancusi's main preoccupations—fidelity to materials and a search for the essence of form. Here Brancusi's material is stone, and he has carved it in such a way that we are very much aware of its nature as stone, not as an attempt to mimic flesh. So highly simplified is the shape that the kiss itself, the union of two souls and bodies, becomes more important than the individuals who take part in it. Even sex differences between the two are barely suggested (the woman, at left, by longer flowing hair and a rounded breast). Brancusi said: "Simplicity is not an end in art, but one arrives at simplicity in spite of oneself, in approaching the real sense of things."

We can see how far Brancusi has moved from the style of his teacher—how nearly he had arrived at simplicity—by comparing a work of Rodin's, also called *The Kiss,* carved just about a decade earlier **(532)**. Rodin's version of the same subject is far more naturalistic, the figures modeled to a smooth perfection and grace. The embrace of the lovers is both romantic and erotic—qualities missing from Brancusi's interpretation.

The Armory Show introduced not only French artists to the United States, but Russian as well, most notably Wassily Kandinsky. Born in Moscow, Kandinsky spent long periods of time in both Paris and Munich. He was influenced by the Post-Impressionists and the Fauves, but by about 1905 he had begun to move toward a much greater abstraction than that attempted by either group. *Picture with an Archer* **(533)**, painted in 1909, is contemporary with both Matisse's *Woman with the Hat* and Picasso's *Les Demoiselles d'Avignon,* yet it is remarkably different in approach. Neither Picasso nor Matisse ever completely abandoned figural references in their work, but Kandinsky strove increasingly to eliminate representation. His canvases explode with color and energy derived from his own emotional experience—an expression of "inner necessity"—and he considered subject matter "detrimental" to this expression. For this artist, "The harmony of color and form must be based solely upon the principle of proper contact with the human soul."

left: 531. Constantin Brancusi. *The Kiss.* c. 1908. Stone, height 19¾″. Musée d'Art Moderne, Paris.

right: 532. Auguste Rodin. *The Kiss.* 1886–98. Marble, height 5′11¼″. Musée Rodin, Paris.

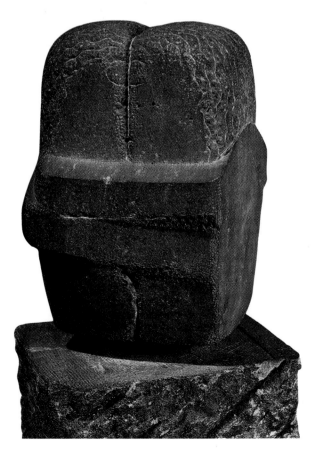

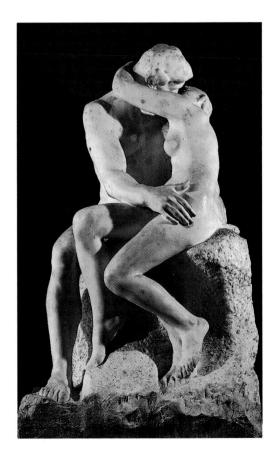

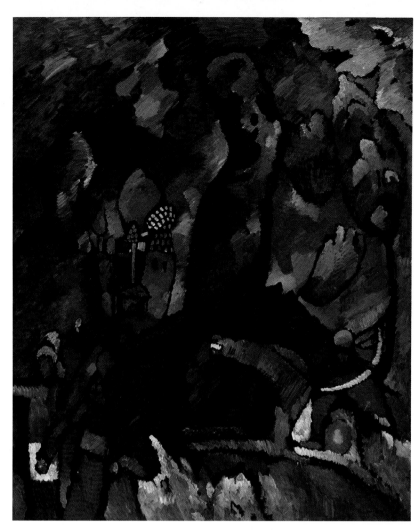

533. Wassily Kandinsky.
Picture with an Archer.
1909. Oil on canvas, 5′9″ × 4′9″.
The Museum of Modern Art,
New York (fractional gift
of Mrs. Bertram Smith
to The Museum of Modern Art, New York).

While the Armory Show attracted much negative criticism, it was a commercial success; about 350 works were sold. Moreover, the show firmly established the position of modern art and introduced its principles to the United States. New York was soon to become the hub of the American art world and eventually of the international art scene, but this latter circumstance was some three decades in the future. Meanwhile, just a few years after the Armory Show, one small, self-contained neighborhood of New York City became the focal point for a splendid flowering of all the arts among a certain group of people—black Americans.

NEW YORK IN THE TWENTIES: THE HARLEM RENAISSANCE

Harlem is the northeast section of Manhattan Island. It was and is home to many black Americans, of all economic classes. During the decade of the 1920s Harlem served as a magnet for some of the greatest talents of that generation—artists, musicians, composers, actors, writers, poets, scientists, and educators. Louis Armstrong came to Harlem, and so did Duke Ellington. The writer Langston Hughes and the poet Countee Cullen were in residence. Creative energy was in the air, and for a time it seemed as though almost every Harlemite was doing something wonderful—a book, a play, a Broadway show, a sculpture series, a jazz opera, a public mural. This phenomenon came to be called the Harlem Renaissance.

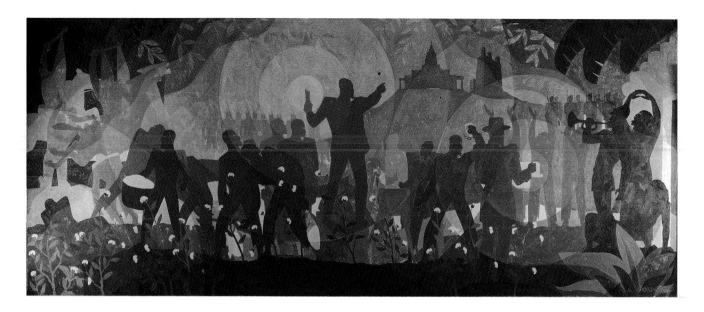

534. Aaron Douglas.
*Aspects of Negro Life:
From Slavery
Through Reconstruction.*
1934. Oil on canvas, 5′ × 11′7″.
Schomburg Center for Research
in Black Culture,
The New York Public Library
(Astor, Lenox and
Tilden Foundations).

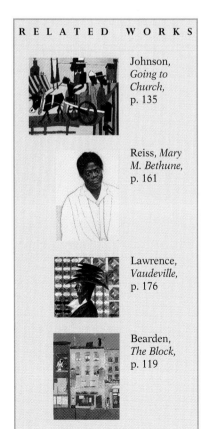

RELATED WORKS

Johnson,
*Going to
Church,*
p. 135

Reiss, *Mary
M. Bethune,*
p. 161

Lawrence,
Vaudeville,
p. 176

Bearden,
The Block,
p. 119

The name, of course, refers to the European Renaissance of the 15th and 16th centuries, when a similar flowering of the arts and sciences occurred. Whenever creative people converge in one place, their talents are mutually supportive and their ideas mutually inspiring. For the black culture centered in Harlem of the twenties, moreover, there was a special agenda. Much of the spirit embodied in the Harlem Renaissance had to do with merging three experiences: the rich heritage of Africa, the ugly legacy of slavery in America (ended barely more than fifty years earlier), and the realities of modern urban life.

There is no single style associated with artists of the Harlem Renaissance. Their work, like that of their colleagues in the other arts, is extremely varied. William H. Johnson, whose *Going to Church* was discussed in Chapter 5 **(156)**, is perhaps best known of the painters. But another artist, the painter and illustrator Aaron Douglas, may be more representative of the spirit and aspirations of the group.

Douglas, who was born in Kansas, moved to Harlem in 1924. During the Harlem Renaissance years he gradually developed a style he called "geometric symbolism." He worked prolifically through the twenties but is perhaps most noted for a series of murals done a few years later, for the 135th Street branch of the New York Public Library. The series is called *Aspects of Negro Life;* our illustration shows the segment that Douglas called *From Slavery Through Reconstruction* **(534).**

Several of Douglas' influences are evident in the mural. The artist had been befriended by Albert Barnes, an important collector of modern and African art, and therefore had access to the Barnes Collection—an opportunity few others enjoyed. Douglas' simplification and stylization of forms surely derived from his studies of West African sculpture. Space is flattened, as in the paintings of modern masters like Gauguin **(522)**, and the palette of colors is limited, as in Cubism **(527,528)**. This section of the mural shows a progression from left to right and (as the title implies) from slavery to freedom. At left, the silhouette figures seem bowed down and fearful. One plays a drum, symbolic of the African heritage. At right, the figures are upright and proud and joyful. One plays a trumpet, symbolic of the Jazz Age and of black musical brilliance. The dominant center figure synthesizes these polarities. He points upward, toward freedom.

The Harlem Renaissance, as a movement, lasted only a decade. Its momentum was stopped by the stock market crash of 1929 and the ensuing Great Depression of the 1930s. Clearly, however, its energy lingered in the work of artists like Aaron Douglas, and it was a source of inspiration for younger artists of the next generation, especially Jacob Lawrence and Romare Bearden.

EUROPE DURING
AND AFTER WORLD WAR I:
DADA AND SURREALISM

During World War I in Europe there arose an art movement known as **Dada,** which came into being as a reaction against the unprecedented carnage of world war. The artists associated with Dada felt that any civilization that could tolerate such brutality must be swept away, and all of its institutions, including traditional art, along with it. Dada, therefore, was anti-everything, even anti-meaning (the name "dada" is said to have been chosen at random from a French dictionary). Representative of Dada's art is Marcel Duchamp's work known as *L.H.O.O.Q.* **(535).** Duchamp selected the one painting that for the Western world symbolizes art with a capital *A* and gleefully drew a moustache and goatee on a reproduction of *Mona Lisa*. As if that irreverence were not enough, he penciled in the letters at the bottom, which, when pronounced the French way, make a vulgar pun suggestive of nymphomania. *L.H.O.O.Q.* is thus a kind of artistic blasphemy—poking fun at one of the most cherished institutions of art.

 Surrealism, as we have seen (p. 73), is an art based on the unconscious, often taking its subject matter and its imagery from dreams and fantasies. Conceived as a reaction to the more "intellectual" art movements, such as Cubism, Surrealism—according to its manifesto published in 1924—aimed at

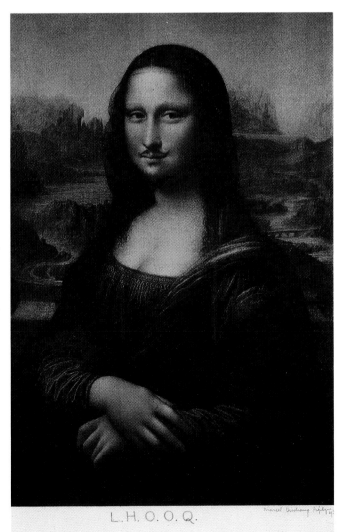

535. Marcel Duchamp. *L.H.O.O.Q.* 1919. Rectified ready-made, pencil on reproduction of Leonardo's *Mona Lisa;* $7\frac{3}{4} \times 4\frac{7}{8}''$. Private collection.

536. Salvador Dali.
The Persistence of Memory. 1931.
Oil on canvas, $9\frac{1}{2} \times 13''$.
The Museum of Modern Art,
New York (given anonymously).

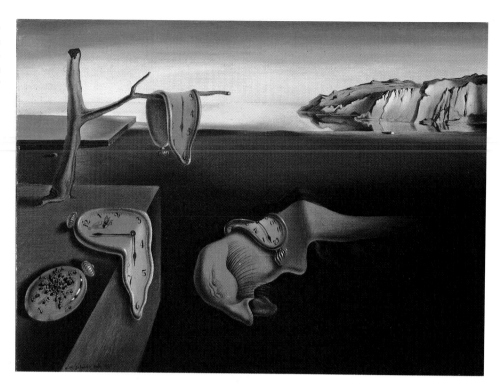

RELATED WORKS

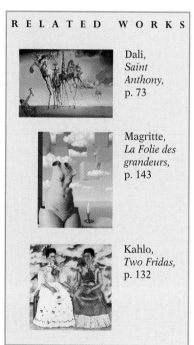

Dali,
*Saint
Anthony,*
p. 73

Magritte,
*La Folie des
grandeurs,*
p. 143

Kahlo,
Two Fridas,
p. 132

"pure psychic automation by which one intends to express verbally, in writing, or by other method, the real functioning of the mind." Artists who worked in the Surrealist mode are generally separated into two categories—those whose imagery is predominantly figural, including Salvador Dali and René Magritte, and those following a more abstract style, such as Joan Miró.

Possibly the most famous of all Surrealist works is Dali's *Persistence of Memory* **(536)**, a small painting that many people call simply "the melted watches." Dali's art, especially here, offers a fascinating paradox: His rendering of forms is precise and meticulous—we might say *super*realistic—yet the forms could not possibly be real. *Persistence of Memory* shows a bleak, arid, decayed landscape populated by an odd, fetal-type creature (some think representative of the artist) and several limp watches—time not only stopped but melting away. Perhaps in this work Dali's fantasy, his dream, is to triumph once and for all over time. Earlier in this book we have seen images connected with "time running out"—in the egg timer and watch of Audrey Flack's *Marilyn* **(46)** and the bedside clock of a dying Edvard Munch (p. 207). Dali's melted watches cannot move, so the artist may hope to capture time and gain artistic immortality.

Joan Miró's *Carnival of Harlequin* **(537)**, representing the abstract phase of Surrealism, shows us not the oddly distorted landscape of a Dali work but rather a completely invented landscape—and one teeming with life. Miró's fantasy world is aswarm with odd little creatures—animals and fish and insects and perhaps a snake or two—as well as nameless abstract forms that participate in the artist's madcap party. Much of Miró's imagery suggests a cheerful sexuality, as though the whole space of the universe were occupied with lighthearted erotic play and reproduction. In contrast to the utter stillness of Dali's *Persistence of Memory,* Miró's *Carnival* is all movement. There are even a few musical notes at the top to accompany the dance. As interpreted by Miró, Surrealism's dreams are lively ones.

While both Dada and Surrealism, as movements, were relatively short-lived, they had great influence on artistic developments in the second half of this century. Meanwhile, another aesthetic—one equally dedicated to altering the course of modern art—had taken root in Germany. It centered on what is perhaps the most famous of all art schools: the Bauhaus.

BETWEEN WORLD WARS: THE BAUHAUS

The **Bauhaus** was founded as a school of design in 1919 in Weimar, Germany. It moved to Dessau in 1925 and then briefly to Berlin, before being closed by the Nazis in 1933. Throughout its short existence, a mere fourteen years, it had an enormous impact on all the art and design of its time, and the influence of the Bauhaus continues to be felt in many fields. Actually, the Bauhaus was less important as a school than as an *idea*. Although its faculty included some of the most noteworthy names in 20th-century art and architecture, it produced few students of particular talent. But many of the principles that guided its curriculum are alive and well today.

Architect Walter Gropius founded the Bauhaus, and he was also the prime theorist in the development of the school's philosophy. Briefly, the Bauhaus hoped to erase the lines separating painters, sculptors, architects, craft artists, and industrial designers. All artists and designers, whatever their form of expression, were considered essentially craftsmen committed to using materials and forms in the most straightforward manner, without artificially applied decoration. The word "Bauhaus" translates roughly as "building house," and its leaders sought to "build" a new guiding principle of design compatible with 20th-century technology. In its later years the school focused more and more on architecture and industrial design, with a view toward reconciling aesthetic design to the capabilities of machine production. Structures, rooms, furniture, and everyday household objects were stripped of superficial embellishment, pared down to the lines necessary for functional use.

Despite this emphasis on industrial design, the painting faculty retained a strong voice. Wassily Kandinsky taught at the Bauhaus for eleven years, and he is only one of several noted artists whose names are associated with the school. Another was Josef Albers, who later emigrated to the United States. Albers' most representative work was done in the 1950s and 1960s, so he will be considered in the next chapter **(544)**.

Also on the painting faculty was the Swiss artist Paul Klee. Klee's work is among the most difficult to categorize in the history of art. Most art historians consider him among the great painters of the century, yet he fits no niche or

537. Joan Miró. *Carnival of Harlequin.* 1924–25. Oil on canvas, 26 × 36⅝". Albright-Knox Art Gallery, Buffalo, N.Y. (Room of Contemporary Art Fund, 1976).

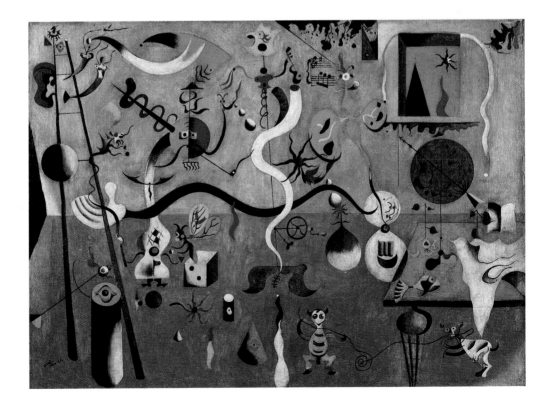

538. Paul Klee.
Dance You Monster to My Soft Song!
1922. Watercolor and oil
transfer drawing
on plaster-primed gauze
bordered with watercolor
on paper mount;
overall size $16\frac{5}{8} \times 12\frac{7}{8}''$.
Solomon R. Guggenheim Museum,
New York
(gift, Solomon R. Guggenheim,
1938).

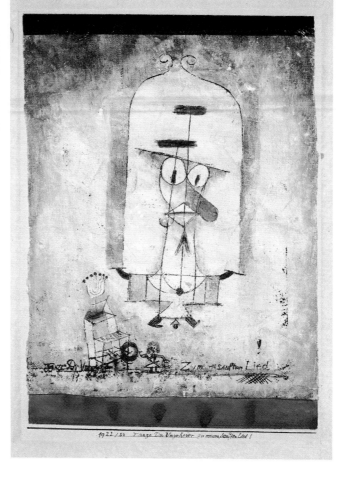

RELATED WORKS

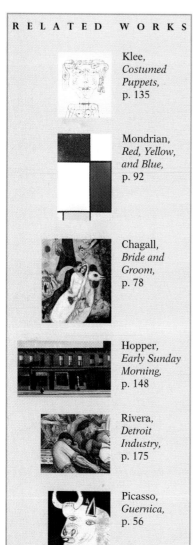

Klee,
*Costumed
Puppets,*
p. 135

Mondrian,
*Red, Yellow,
and Blue,*
p. 92

Chagall,
*Bride and
Groom,*
p. 78

Hopper,
*Early Sunday
Morning,*
p. 148

Rivera,
*Detroit
Industry,*
p. 175

Picasso,
Guernica,
p. 56

"ism"; there is really no one like Klee. A common first reaction to a Klee painting is, "That looks like a child's drawing!" And, indeed, the artist took much of his inspiration from the art of children, but behind the childlike imagery is a technique and sensibility of great sophistication. The apparent playfulness masks a deeply complex, subtle imagination. *Dance You Monster to My Soft Song!* **(538)**, a mixed-media watercolor, was done two years after Klee joined the Bauhaus staff. Here the delicate line drawing is masterfully controlled to express the idea of a quite friendly monster dancing away to the tune played by a little girl at a transparent piano. Klee's genius lies in combining inventive imagery with a sure command of line, color, and design.

Except for Dada and Surrealism, few major art movements emerged during the period between the world wars, although individual artists pursued their own styles. Piet Mondrian was at work in Holland and Marc Chagall in France. In the United States Edward Hopper painted his lonely, penetrating visions of the American scene, while the Mexican muralists were creating grand-scale images of the social scene both above and below the border. Of course, Picasso and Matisse continued to develop their art throughout the period.

Following World War I Europe remained in a state of social and economic turmoil, joined by the United States in 1929, when the entire Western world plunged into the Great Depression. World War II, beginning in 1939 in Europe, 1941 for the United States, brought organized activity in Western art almost to a standstill. Certainly, art was made during the war years, but attention was focused on the conflict, and many of the artists were on the battlefield. When the Western nations emerged from war in 1945, it was discovered that the art capital of the Western world somehow had moved across the ocean—from Paris to New York.

Art Since 1945

THE ART MADE in Europe and North America since the end of World War II is dizzying in its variety and complexity. Nevertheless, we as viewers have one great advantage in approaching this art. We live now. All the artworks considered in this chapter were made during the lifetimes of people still alive today. While we can have only limited success in getting "inside" the minds of Michelangelo or Rembrandt, we inhabit the same world as contemporary artists. We have walked the same streets, watched the same movies and television programs, experienced the same world events. We share a culture with contemporary artists, and so this is *our* art. If we take the trouble to look and study, we may find it is the art with which we feel most connected.

The year 1945 is considered a turning point in the history of Western art. For long years most of the world had been preoccupied with killing and death and hardship—the horrors of World War II. When hostilities ended in late summer of 1945, there was a natural yearning to start afresh, to redirect energies toward creating rather than destroying. But another factor in this turning point was the shift in focus from the old world to the new. Since the time of the ancient Greeks the great centers of Western art had been in Europe—Athens, Rome, Florence, Paris, London. Now, suddenly, the art capital had crossed an ocean and settled in North America. Its hub was New York City.

NEW YORK: 1945—1960

In the aftermath of World War II most of Western Europe was completely devastated. The United States, while exhausted, was not. No bombs had fallen or battles been fought in New York, as they had in London and Paris and Amsterdam and most of the cities in Germany. When the time came to resume the normal activities of life, New York became the center of a vibrant art revival. Many of the most progressive European artists had immigrated to the United States, and they served as teachers and inspiration for a new generation of artists—most of them American—who gravitated to New York. In fact, painters associated with the first major postwar art movement are referred to as the *New York School.*

Not a school in the sense of an institution or of instruction, the New York School was a convenient label under which to lump together a group of painters also known as the *Abstract Expressionists.* Primary among them were Jackson Pollock and Willem de Kooning; the group also included Franz Kline and Lee Krasner. Abstract Expressionism had many sources—Surrealism,

CHRONOLOGY

STYLE/PERIOD	MAJOR ARTISTS

Pollock, *Blue Poles*

Smith, *Becca*

Abstract Expressionism, c. 1945–1960
Minimal Art, 1960s
Pop Art, 1960s

Warhol, *Campbell Soup Cans*

New Realism, 1970s–1990s
Neo-Expressionism, 1980s–1990s
Conceptual Art, 1970s–1990s
Computer Art, 1980s–present
Performance Art, 1970s–1990s
Post-Modern Art, 1980s–1990s

Johns, *Target with Four Faces*

Pablo Picasso (1881–1973)
Josef Albers (1888–1976)
R. Buckminster Fuller (1895–1983)
Henry Moore (1898–1986)
Mark Rothko (1903–1970)
Willem de Kooning (1904–1997)
David Smith (1906–1965)
Philip Johnson (b. 1906)
Lee Krasner (1908–1984)
Jackson Pollock (1912–1956)
Romare Bearden (1914–1988)
Jacob Lawrence (b. 1917)
Louise Nevelson (1899–1988)
Alice Neel (1900–1984)
Franz Kline (1910–1962)
I. M. Pei (b. 1917)
Lucian Freud (b. 1922)
Robert Rauschenberg (b. 1925)
Helen Frankenthaler (b. 1928)
Jasper Johns (b. 1930)
Andy Warhol (1930–1987)
Frank Stella (b. 1936)
David Hockney (b. 1937)
Anselm Kiefer (b. 1945)
Susan Rothenberg (b. 1945)
Cindy Sherman (b. 1954)

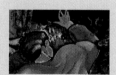

Chia, *Café Tintoretto*

Cubism, the early works of Kandinsky (**533**), and in some cases even Eastern art. The artists involved had less in common than seems apparent at first. One unifying thread is that their paintings, on the whole, are very large in scale, tending to overwhelm the viewer in their dynamic—even violent—presence. Most of the works are entirely nonrepresentational, but de Kooning for one retained figural elements in many of his paintings and thus fits better the technical definition of "abstract." Abstract Expressionism was characterized by bold, passionate painting—sometimes achieved with sweeping brush strokes, at other times produced by the artist hurling paint on the canvas, as Pollock did. The sheer power and energy of this technique caused it to be known as ***action painting.***

The quintessential Abstract Expressionist was Jackson Pollock, who had perfected his technique of "drip painting" by the late 1940s (pp. 34–35, and

38). *Blue Poles* **(539)** shows Pollock's typically dense interweaving of lines and colors, here punctuated by the almost vertical "poles," which are themselves criss-crossed with intricate patterns of dripped and spattered paint. Even in reproduction this canvas vibrates with energy, so that one can imagine the impact of the 7-by-16-foot painting on a viewer standing before it.

Lee Krasner, who was married to Pollock, came to Abstract Expressionism at about the same time as her husband. Krasner's work, as exemplified by *The Bull* **(540)**, has bolder areas of color and is often characterized by bulbous shapes that seem to burst out at the viewer. There is a fierce quality in Krasner's work, deriving from the strong colors and tensely drawn—not spattered—lines. In *The Bull* the rhythms are mostly circular, except for the totem-like image at right.

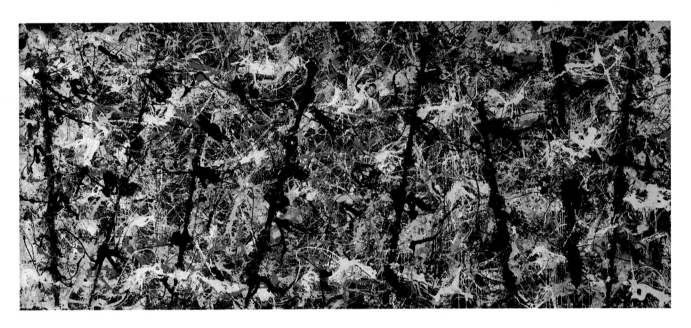

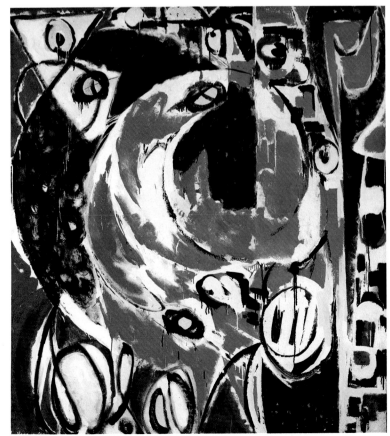

above: 539. Jackson Pollock. *Blue Poles.* 1952. Oil, enamel, and aluminum paint, glass on canvas; 6'11½" × 16'½". Australian National Gallery, Canberra (purchased 1973).

left: 540. Lee Krasner. *The Bull.* 1958. Oil on cotton duck, 6'5" × 5'10⅛". Courtesy Robert Miller Gallery, New York.

LEE KRASNER

1908–1984

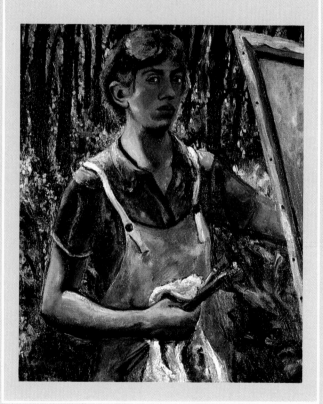

IN OCTOBER OF 1983 the first major retrospective show of paintings by Lee Krasner opened at the Museum of Fine Arts in Houston. Later, the same exhibition toured the United States. Krasner did not live to see it arrive in New York—once the hub of the Abstract Expressionist movement—because she died just eight months after the Houston opening. Amazingly, this remarkable woman, whom critics now consider "an artist of the first rank," expressed little bitterness about the fact that she worked so long under the shadow of Abstract Expressionism's "golden boy"—Jackson Pollock.

Krasner, born Lenore, was the sixth child of Russian immigrant parents who had settled in Brooklyn. By the age of thirteen she had decided to become an artist. She enrolled first at Cooper Union, later at the Art Stu-

dents League in New York. She also studied for several years with the painter Hans Hofmann, from whom she learned the principles of Cubism, and under whose tutelage she took her first steps toward Abstract Expressionism. Like many other young artists of the Depression period, Krasner supported herself by working for the government-sponsored Federal Art Project. Her first exhibition—part of a group show—took place in 1937, in New York.

In 1942 Krasner, having heard about the work of Jackson Pollock, went to his studio one day and introduced herself. Soon the couple were living together, and in 1945 they married. This union proved to be a successful working partnership. Wherever they lived, in New York or at their house on Long Island, Krasner and Pollock maintained joint studios. While their painting styles usually remained separate, the two seemed to sustain and encourage each other's work.

Unfortunately for Krasner, the climate of the times was not receptive to a woman who painted in such an assertive style as Abstract Expressionism. Of the New York School of artists she later said, "There were very few painters in that so-called circle who acknowledged I painted at all." Krasner was relegated to the status of "Pollock's wife." Not long afterward, in 1956, she was assigned the role of "Pollock's widow," when her husband was killed in a car crash.

Gradually, after Pollock's death, the critics began to take a fresh look at the work of Lee Krasner, to evaluate it for its own sake. Through it all she continued to paint and to exhibit. And she remained true to the principles of Abstract Expressionism. Other fashions came and went, but this artist continually sought the development of her personal style. By the late 1970s "Pollock's widow" was again Lee Krasner.

Krasner's ideas about painting were her own, not an echo of Pollock's. "Painting, for me, when it really 'happens' is as miraculous as any natural phenomenon—as, say, a lettuce leaf. . . . One could go on forever as to whether the paint should be thick or thin, whether to paint the woman or the square, hard-edge or soft, but after a while such questions become a bore. . . . The painting I have in mind . . . transcends technique, transcends subject and moves into the realm of the inevitable—then you have the lettuce leaf."[1]

Lee Krasner. *Self-Portrait.*
c. 1930. Oil on linen, 30⅛ × 25⅛".
Courtesy Robert Miller Gallery, New York.

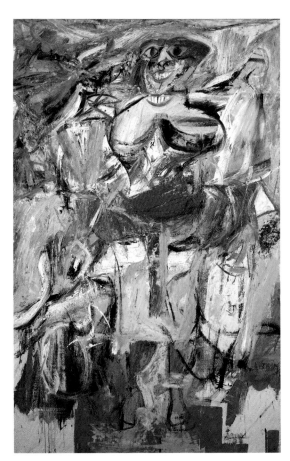

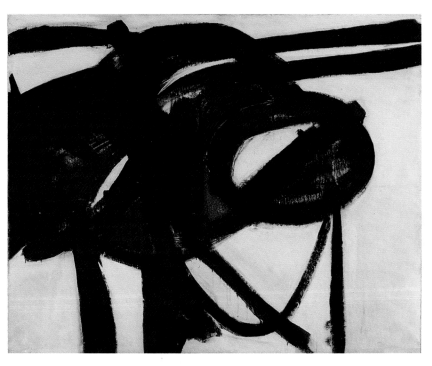

left: **541.** Willem de Kooning.
Woman and Bicycle. 1952–53.
Oil on canvas, 6'4½" × 4'1".
Whitney Museum of American Art,
New York (purchase).

below: **542.** Franz Kline.
Chief. 1950.
Oil on canvas, 4'10⅜" × 6'1½".
The Museum of Modern Art,
New York (gift of
Mr. and Mrs. David M. Solinger).
© 1998 Estate of Franz Kline/
Licensed by VAGA, New York.

Willem de Kooning often used figural images in his paintings, especially in his famous "Woman" series from the early 1950s, of which *Woman and Bicycle* **(541)** is typical. De Kooning's women throughout the series are predatory monsters—all eyes and teeth and huge engulfing breasts. The artist himself said that he always began with an image of a young, beautiful woman, only to see it transformed on canvas, as he worked, into a hideous nightmare creature. We have a sense of de Kooning struggling against this woman in his painting, struggling to carve her up and subdue her, using the weapons of harsh, slashing brushstrokes and intense colors. But the more he cuts, the more menacing his woman-monster becomes, until she threatens to destroy the artist who created her. *Woman and Bicycle* is clearly abstract, and it is just as clearly an expression of de Kooning's conscious and unconscious feelings about women.

Krasner, de Kooning, and Pollock usually worked in color, but other Abstract Expressionists—notably Franz Kline—are more closely identified with the bold use of black. Kline's painting *Chief* **(542)**, named after a locomotive that passed through the Pennsylvania town where the artist was born, resembles an actual locomotive only in its raw, almost menacing power. Above all, Kline's art is based on the gesture—the tense sweep of a broad brush held at arms' length, the dramatic contrast of black against white in large scale.

Another form of abstraction that came into prominence in the postwar period is known as **Color Field** painting. As the name implies, imagery is reduced to a large "field" or area of color, in some cases one pure color filling the entire canvas. In contrast to the dynamic emotionalism of Abstract Expressionism, Color Field paintings have a meditative tranquillity that draws the viewer in and invites contemplation. The work of Mark Rothko in the late forties through the sixties **(543)** usually features one or more soft-edged color rectangles floating in the larger color rectangle of the canvas. The inner rectangle has sides parallel to the canvas edges, and its boundaries are blurred and gently blended, causing the inner sections to float. Very large scale is also characteristic of Rothko's work, so the viewer is enveloped in sensuous color.

Superficially the work of Josef Albers **(544)** seems much like that of Rothko, especially when reproduced in a book. In fact, the two artists' paintings have very little in common. Rothko's canvases are huge, Albers' rather small. Rothko's edges are soft and blurred, Albers' precise. Most important, Rothko's expression is emotional, Albers' more intellectual. In the 1950s Albers began a long series of paintings—finally there were hundreds—all entitled *Homage to the Square*. All are "nests" of three or four squares centered in the canvas. What varies is the color, and this was Albers' chief preoccupation. Albers hoped to show the dynamic interaction of colors—how they work together when placed side by side, how some colors advance while others recede, how colors intensify or deintensify each other (pp. 98–107). By restricting himself to the square, he avoided distractions of form, so that the viewer can concentrate on the pure, saturated color. Because it is a series, *Homage to the Square* makes the point that there is no one "best" way a painting can be done, but many different possibilities.

left: 543. Mark Rothko. *Orange and Yellow.* 1956. Oil on canvas, 7'7" × 5'11". Albright-Knox Art Gallery, Buffalo, N.Y. (gift of Seymour H. Knox, 1956).

right: 544. Josef Albers. *Homage to the Square: Ascending.* 1953. Oil on composition board, 43½" square. Whitney Museum of American Art, New York (purchase).

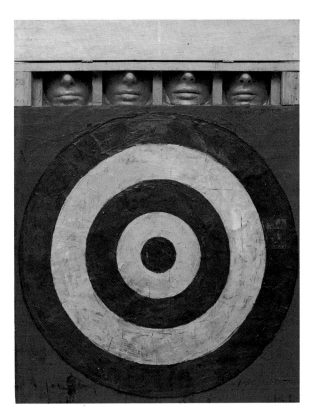

right: 545. Jasper Johns. *Target with Four Faces.* 1955. Assemblage: encaustic and collage on canvas with objects, 26″ square, surmounted by four tinted plaster faces in wood box with hinged front; overall dimensions with box open 33⅝ × 26 × 3″. The Museum of Modern Art, New York (gift of Mr. and Mrs. Robert C. Scull). © 1998 Jasper Johns/ Licensed by VAGA, New York.

far right: 546. Robert Rauschenberg. *Bed.* 1955. Combine painting: Oil and pencil on pillow, quilt, and sheet on wood supports; 6′3¾″ × 2′7½″ × 8″. The Museum of Modern Art, New York (gift of Leo Castelli in honor of Alfred H. Barr, Jr.). © 1998 Robert Rauschenberg/ Licensed by VAGA, New York.

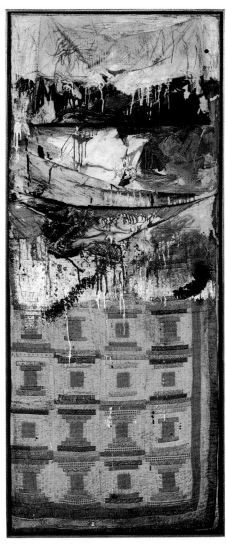

By the time Rothko and Albers painted the works shown here, in the mid-1950s, abstractionism had held sway for more than fifteen years, and the art world was ready for a change of pace. The return of representational art was signaled by two artists who appeared on the scene about 1955—Robert Rauschenberg and Jasper Johns.

Jasper Johns chose as his subjects some of the most familiar images one could imagine—the American flag, a map of the United States, numbers, letters of the alphabet. All are rendered accurately, in true proportions, but in a freely brushed, painterly style. His *Target with Four Faces* **(545)** may remind us of a shooting gallery in an amusement park. The inclusion of actual three-dimensional heads with the painting owes a debt to Dada, which often pushed into the third dimension, and to the earlier collage work of Picasso and Braque. Here the target is drawn precisely, the four identical faces seem waiting for bullets to hit them, yet there is no sense of menace in this work. By painting the target so matter-of-factly, Johns has taken away the menace. The target and faces are no longer objects to be shot at, but images to be studied for their own visual interest. This artist sought the familiar, stripped it of its familiar associations, and shows it to us as art.

Johns' friend and rival Robert Rauschenberg also took the usual and made it unusual. One of his best-known creations from the 1950s at first attracted mockery and outrage but now is considered among the pivotal works of mid-century art. *Bed* **(546)** is actually the artist's own bedding (quilt, pillow, blanket) stretched as though they were canvas, hung on the wall vertically, and painted over to make what Rauschenberg called a **combine painting.** People react strongly to *Bed,* no doubt because its disheveled condition and rather lurid dripped paint make it resemble the scene of a ghastly crime, but the artist himself called it "one of the friendliest pictures" he'd ever painted. Over time, *Bed* really has come to seem friendlier, as we are no longer startled by odd, even gory transformations of everyday objects.

With their works of the fifties, Johns and Rauschenberg anticipated what would become an important art style of the 1960s—Pop Art.

RELATED   WORKS

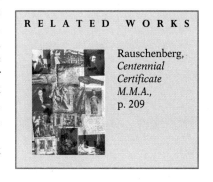

Rauschenberg, *Centennial Certificate M.M.A.,* p. 209

ART STYLES
OF THE SIXTIES
AND SEVENTIES

RELATED WORKS

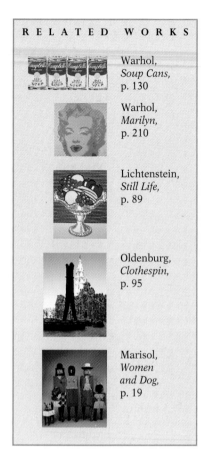

Warhol,
Soup Cans,
p. 130

Warhol,
Marilyn,
p. 210

Lichtenstein,
Still Life,
p. 89

Oldenburg,
Clothespin,
p. 95

Marisol,
*Women
and Dog*,
p. 19

POP ART Pop Art was both startling and controversial. As Dada had done nearly half a century earlier, it broke the rules about what constituted fitting material for serious art. Pop drew its subject matter from the most mundane objects of mass-produced culture—billboards, commercial packages, and the like. Andy Warhol's *100 Campbell Soup Cans* and images of Marilyn Monroe were examples of this trend. Whereas Abstract Expressionism was a style of passion and intensity, whose artists seemed to *hurl* their emotions onto canvas, Pop artists tend to be rather cool and restrained. We sense an emotional distance from their subjects, which they present to us in an almost matter-of-fact fashion.

Roy Lichtenstein, whose still life we saw earlier, often based his imagery on the comic book. Many of Lichtenstein's paintings **(547)** are huge, meticulously rendered frames adapted from comic strips, accurate down to the dialogue in "balloons" and the dot pattern of cheap newspaper reproduction. The artist did not hesitate to introduce a touch of irony by poking fun at himself and the art world in proclaiming this work a "masterpiece." Pop Art attempted to show that a detached look at the overfamiliar objects of daily life could give them new meaning as visual emblems.

The English artist David Hockney is often associated with the British Pop Art movement, although his work is individual and has maintained a consistent and personal style over many decades. Hockney settled in Los Angeles in 1964 and proceeded to paint his version of the "good life," southern California style. As interpreted by Hockney, California living was a kind of sanitized, unchanging paradise, and the swimming pool was its temple. *A Bigger Splash* **(548)** refines paradise to its basic elements: the bland, salmon pink house with sliding glass doors; a single deck chair perched on the equally bland patio; two stilt-like palm trees—emblems of California; a diving board; and the splash left by an unseen swimmer who has gone into the pool. Hockney's painting

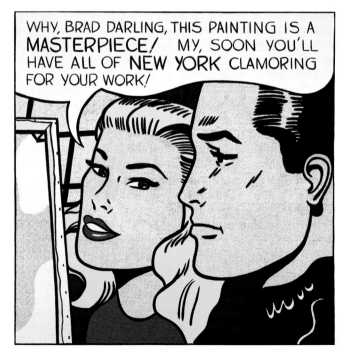

547. Roy Lichtenstein.
Masterpiece. 1962.
Oil on canvas, 4′6″ square.
© Roy Lichtenstein.

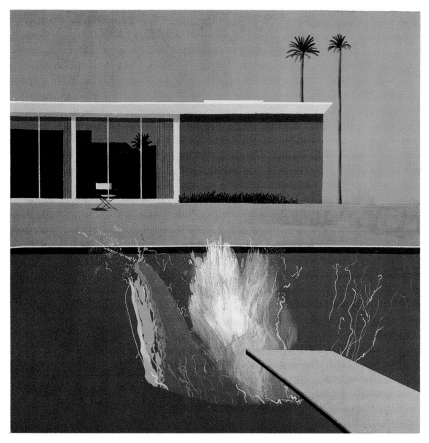

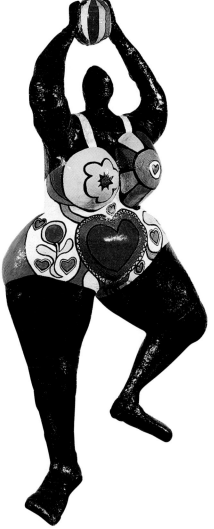

style in this work shows the exaggerated realism of a magazine illustration or advertisement. His colors are flat and unmodulated, and most of his lines are severe verticals and horizontals. The sharp diagonal of the diving board leads to the single irregular form—the titular splash, which is the residue of an invisible human presence.

Another artist sometimes associated with Pop could almost be described as "anti-Pop" (or "pro-Mom"), although her forms are compatible with Pop imagery. Several male artists of the Pop movement painted women as caricatured pin-ups—voluptuous, "sexy," passive, and available. Niki de Saint-Phalle's huge female figures, called *Nanas,* are voluptuous and sexy, but they are anything but passive. *Black Venus* **(549)**, a painted polyester sculpture more than 9 feet tall, exhibits a sexuality that is both powerful and buoyantly cheerful. The figure almost bursts out of a sort of bathing suit gaily colored in hearts and flowers, clutching a beach ball. Her breasts and hips and thighs are enormous (remember the *Venus of Willendorf,* **406**), but her pose is dynamic; she stands ready to run or jump or dance to happy music. Saint-Phalle's *Venus* is an earth mother, but an earth mother who wants to play.

As an identifiable movement, Pop Art ended with the 1960s, but it has never really gone away. Its underlying premise, that images from the popular culture are fit subject matter for "fine" art, remains a part of the contemporary artist's array of options.

MINIMAL ART Coexisting with Pop in the 1960s was a diametrically different movement called Minimal Art, which sought to reduce the art elements to a "minimum"—simple (often geometric) shapes and sometimes color. Minimal Art can be seen as a kind of celebration of the artist's basic materials. A painting is paint on canvas, a sculpture is metal or stone or wood or similar medium. By stripping art down to these substances, the Minimal artists attempted to reaffirm the worth of art for its own sake, not as a reflection of anything else.

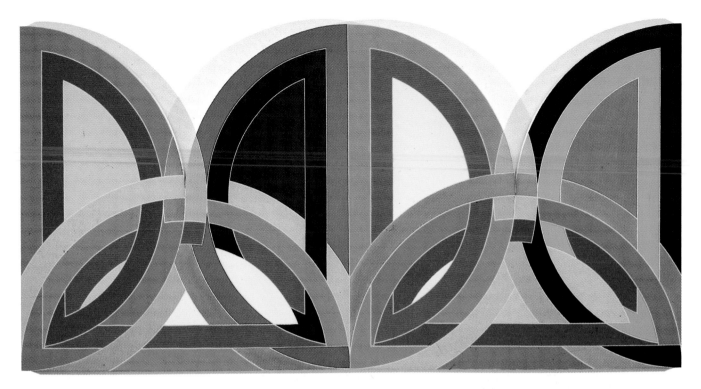

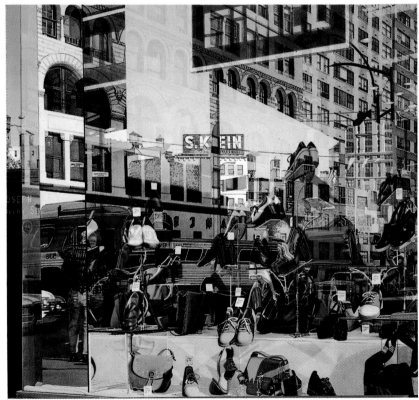

In painting the Minimal style is often referred to as "hard-edge." Lines
are drawn as though with a ruler, colors are pure and unshaded, shapes are
precise. Frank Stella's *Takht-i-Sulayman 1* **(550)** illustrates these characteristics. Its shapes are as regular as those drawn with a compass and a protractor,
its rhythms simple and repetitive. Geometric shape in one way or another has
been a part of painting for centuries. The overlays accompanying this book
show that a great many artists have structured their compositions around the

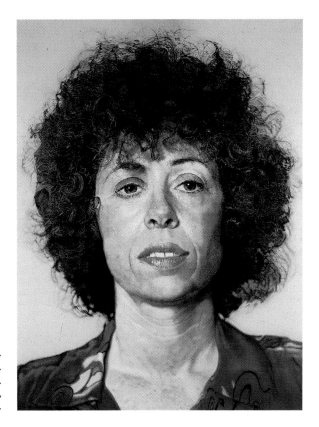

552. Chuck Close. *Linda.* 1975–76. Acrylic on canvas, 9 × 7'. Courtesy Pace Wildenstein, New York.

triangle, the straight diagonal, the rectangle. What the Minimalists of the sixties did was strip away the figural references to concentrate on the geometry.

REALISM Oddly enough, at the same time the Minimalists were removing figural references from their work, other artists, equally prominent, were rediscovering figural imagery and carrying that imagery to new heights of Realism. During the years when Abstract Expressionism dominated the art world, representation of people or things had been considered unsophisticated, if not amateur. Pop Art, with its soup cans and targets and cartoon characters, made it once again acceptable for artists to explore recognizable subject matter, and the Realist artists of the late 1960s and the 1970s took up this new interest with enthusiasm.

Certain artists carried this interest to such an extreme, rendering forms with such meticulous attention to detail, that their paintings seem almost indistinguishable from photographs. Their style has been called **Photorealism.** Don Eddy's *New Shoes for H.* **(551)**, an acrylic painting on canvas, captures precisely the image we might see while walking past a shop window on a sunny day. A display of women's shoes becomes all the more complex when overlaid with reflections from the plate glass. We can't tell exactly where we, as viewers, are standing, nor can we be sure which portions of the scene are viewed first-hand, through the window, or mirrored by the glass.

To enhance the effect of photographic immediacy, some artists, notably Audrey Flack and Chuck Close, worked from *actual* photographs to make their paintings. The photos, greatly enlarged, were projected onto canvas, after which the artist would blow paints through an airbrush (a spraying device) to match the forms and colors in the projected image. Close's *Linda* **(552)** shows one result of this process—a portrait that is by no means conventionally beautiful but is certainly realistic. Presented in this scale (the painting is 9 feet high) and without benefit of any artistic prettifying, Linda's face, surrounded by a wild tangle of hair, confronts us with its every pore, line, and wrinkle. Strangely, the almost brutal realism of the portrait gives it a kind of majestic quality, a take-me-as-I-am self-assurance.

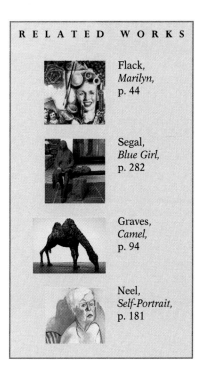

RELATED WORKS

Flack, *Marilyn,* p. 44

Segal, *Blue Girl,* p. 282

Graves, *Camel,* p. 94

Neel, *Self-Portrait,* p. 181

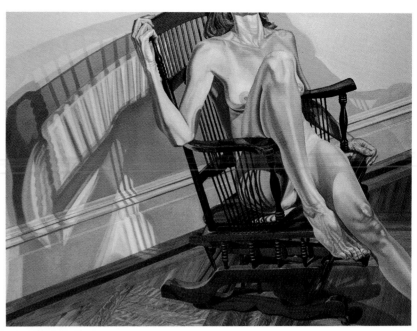

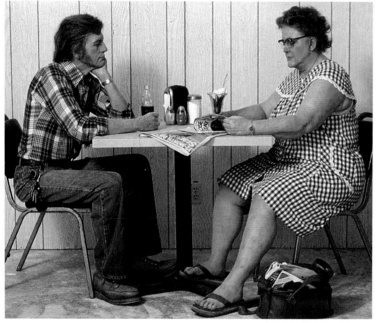

above: 553. Philip Pearlstein.
Female Nude on a Platform Rocker.
1977–78. Oil on canvas, 6'¼" × 8'.
The Brooklyn Museum, New York
(John B. Woodward Memorial Fund,
Augustus Healy Fund,
Dick S. Ramsay Fund,
and Other Restricted Income Funds).

---

left: 554. Duane Hanson.
Self-Portrait with Model. 1979.
Painted polyester and mixed media, lifesize.
Courtesy the artist.

Another type of uncompromising reality can be found in the paintings of Philip Pearlstein, who depicts the nude figure in a *super*realistic style that might more accurately be described as "naked" **(553)**. Pearlstein's nudes, both female and male, are rendered with meticulous accuracy, sparing none of their bulges, wrinkles, warts, hairs, and general imperfections. The "peephole" point of view, in which we see the models at odd angles and abruptly cut off by the edges of the canvas, is reminiscent of works by Degas **(520)**. The interplay of textures is important for Pearlstein. In *Female Nude on a Platform Rocker* we see the shadows cast on the wall by an apparently rocking chair, the smooth wood of the chair, the polished parquet floor, the prominent bones and sinews of hands and feet. One could not call this figure erotic. Pearlstein considers the body an *object* to be studied in light of its forms, juxtaposed with other forms.

Realism in sculpture is best illustrated by the work of Duane Hanson, whose figures have caused many a museum-goer to do a double and triple take. *Self-Portrait with Model* **(554)** looks almost as convincing in the "flesh," so to speak, as it does in this reproduction. Both figures are made of polyester and fiberglass. Like the plaster people of George Segal **(329)**, Hanson's figures are cast from life, but they are painted to be as naturalistic as possible and have been dressed in real clothes and hair and positioned at a real table. The "model" in this work is typical of Hanson's subjects: middle-aged, middle class, middle (at least) weight, perhaps a stereotype of Middle America. From her housedress to her comfortable spread-legged pose to her flip-flops to her tabloid newspaper, she is the image of somebody's Aunt Gertrude. The sculptor puts himself in this construction (his plastic self, remember), contemplating his model not with scorn, but with affection.

CONCEPTUAL ART AND SITE WORKS   Some people would say that Conceptual Art is the polar opposite of Realist art, for while Realist art strives to mimic forms in the physical world, Conceptual Art *has* no physical form. It is based primarily or solely on an *idea,* and while there may be recording of the idea—photographs or films—that recording is not the art. The idea is the art. If this sounds confusing, we can turn to an example, and we find a good one in the work of Sol LeWitt.

The illustration (555) is a photograph of LeWitt's 1971 work entitled *Wall Drawing 111—A Wall Divided Vertically into Five Equal Parts, with Ten Thousand Lines in Each Part: 1: 6″ Long.* You could not visit a museum or gallery and see this work—at least, not in this exact form. It exists solely as the idea of drawing ten thousand lines on a wall. Suppose a collector decides to "buy" this *Wall Drawing.* What the collector gets is a certificate entitling him or her to have a draftsman—not LeWitt, not necessarily a trained artist—come into the collector's home and draw ten thousand lines on a blank wall, using a ruler and pencil. If the collector subsequently "sells" the work, the wall must be painted over and the certificate transferred to a new owner. Or, suppose a museum owns the work. It can display the work whenever it wishes to, then simply have the wall painted over to make room for a new exhibit. There is no storage problem. Needless to say, each time the work is redrawn on a wall, it looks different. The appearance doesn't matter; only the idea matters.

Site works also are motivated by the ideas behind them, but they have physical substance, often temporary but usually on a grand scale. Examples seen earlier in this book include Christo's *Running Fence,* which expressed the idea of setting up a nylon barrier across 24½ miles of California, and Robert Smithson's *Spiral Jetty,* which expresses the idea of the whirlpool or spiral as a timeless symbol.

The art styles of the sixties and seventies—Pop Art, Minimal Art, Realism, Conceptual Art, and site works—all enjoyed a brief heyday as movements. But by about 1980 those movements had essentially ended. Still, each of these styles left a trail behind it, and so as we consider the art of the near past and present, we will find traces of their influence in contemporary art.

RELATED   WORKS

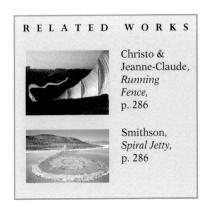

Christo & Jeanne-Claude, *Running Fence,* p. 286

Smithson, *Spiral Jetty,* p. 286

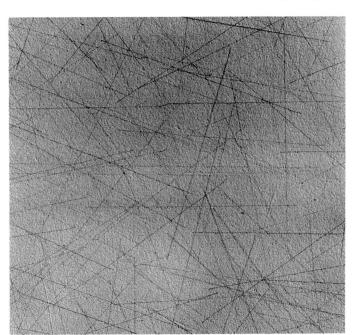

555. Sol LeWitt. *Wall Drawing 111— A Wall Divided Vertically into Five Equal Parts, with Ten Thousand Lines in Each Part: 1: 6″ Long.* 1971. Pencil applied directly to wall. First installation: John Weber Gallery, New York, September 1971. Dimensions of all five parts: 9′4″ × 46′8″. Courtesy John Weber Gallery, New York.

ART OF THE EIGHTIES AND NINETIES

RELATED WORKS

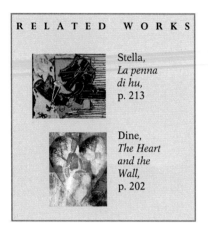

Stella,
*La penna
di hu,*
p. 213

Dine,
*The Heart
and the
Wall,*
p. 202

556. Frank Stella.
Pergusa. 1981.
Mixed media on etched
magnesium panel,
6′1″ × 7′8″ × 2′.
Collection Graham Gund,
Cambridge, Mass., courtesy
M. Knoedler & Co., New York.

A good way to introduce the art of our own time is to look at another work by Frank Stella, this one made thirteen years after *Takht-i-Sulayman 1* **(550)**. Stella's later work still embodies the artist's preoccupation with interwoven curvilinear forms, yet he has transformed hard-edge geometry into a more painterly and complicated tracery. Creative artists, in general, build on what they have done before. Stella has taken his Minimal expressions of the sixties and developed them into a joyous visual exuberance for the eighties. *Takht-i-Sulayman*'s movement is slow and measured; our eyes move rhythmically around and through its precise curves. *Pergusa* **(556)** pulses with energy, a roller-coaster ride of shapes. There is another big difference between the two works. *Takht-i-Sulayman* of the sixties is two-dimensional. *Pergusa* of the eighties has moved out into the third dimension. It has elements of relief attached to the background surface and projecting to almost 2 feet.

Like many works of contemporary art, *Pergusa* is difficult to categorize. It looks like a painting when reproduced in this book, and sections of it are painted, but it has more depth than many sculptures. Strictly speaking, it is neither a painting nor a sculpture, but a little of both. Stella's prints show a similar versatility in the combination of several techniques. As we move through the nineties, we see an increasing trend toward a "no-holds-barred" approach to material and method. For the contemporary artist any medium, any process, anything at all is fair game if it results in the desired expression.

The variety of options extends also to the styles in which contemporary artists work. Earlier periods in the history of art often pitted fashion against anti-fashion. As recently as the 1950s, when Abstract Expressionism held sway, few important museums or galleries would mount shows by contemporary artists working in a naturalistic style, because such work was considered old-fashioned, even trivial. Now the situation has changed dramatically. A

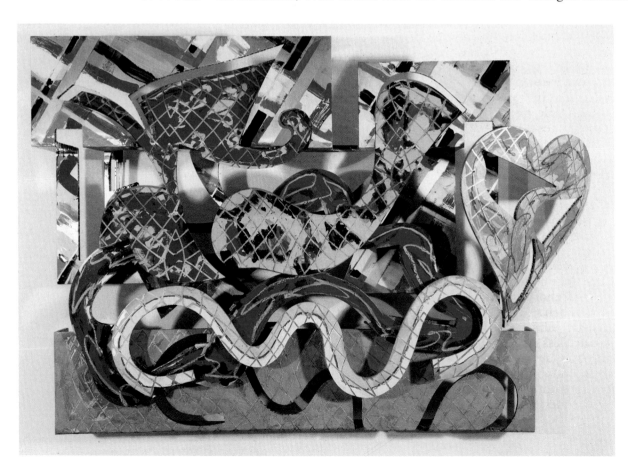

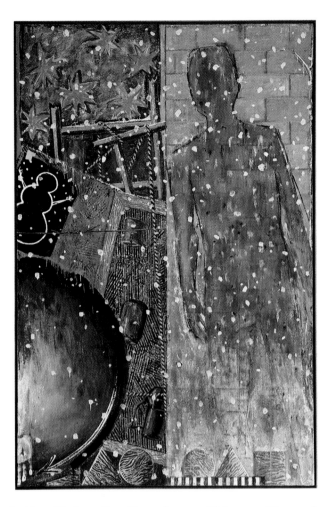

557. Jasper Johns.
Winter, from *The Seasons.* 1987.
Oil on canvas, 6'3" × 4'2".
© 1998 Jasper Johns/
Licensed by VAGA, New York.

tour of the major galleries in New York or San Francisco or Chicago will reveal an astonishing range of styles—all fashionable, all taken seriously by critics and the art-viewing public. In the next few pages, then, we will look at some of the styles of today.

THE FIGURE AS SYMBOL The human figure seldom disappears from art, and when it does—as in the Color Field painting of the sixties—it soon comes back. Artists are people, and as such many return over and again to images of themselves. Sometimes the figure is lifelike, as we saw in the previous section. But other artists take the figure only as a starting point, then distort and abstract its contours to give it symbolic and even magical importance.

In Jasper Johns' *Winter* (557) the shadowy, snow-dappled form at right represents the artist. *Winter* is one of four large paintings in a series called *The Seasons,* each of which contains the shadowy form. The series was done more than thirty years after *Target with Four Faces* (545), which helped to usher in the Pop Art movement. A comparison of the two works will show that Johns has traveled far from the blank, robotlike impersonality of the "four faces" to a more intimate expression. The *Seasons* paintings are considered to be autobiographical, but since Johns is a very private person, his allusions to himself are enigmatic. The ghostly figure crammed into the right side of the painting recalls Edvard Munch's claustrophobic self-portrait (p. 207) and was also inspired by a Picasso painting in which that artist depicted himself as a shadow. Other symbols are less obvious. The snowman at left is an emblem of winter, but the cut-off circular form at bottom left has no immediate reference. Perhaps it is an echo of Johns' earlier paintings, such as *Target.* We sense the artist taking stock, sifting through his artistic attic, reworking imagery that he has developed for decades.

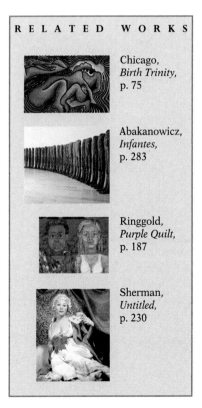

R E L A T E D W O R K S

Chicago,
Birth Trinity,
p. 75

Abakanowicz,
Infantes,
p. 283

Ringgold,
Purple Quilt,
p. 187

Sherman,
Untitled,
p. 230

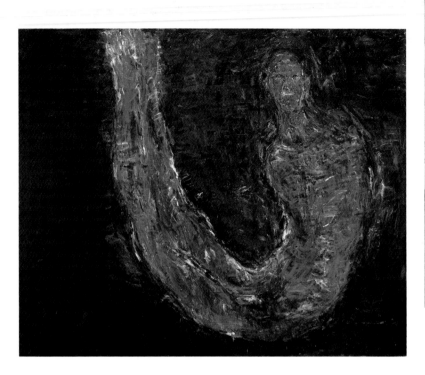

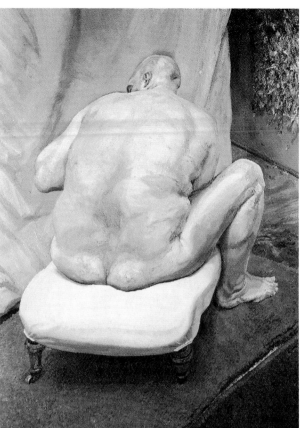

The painter Susan Rothenberg, long associated with images of a single horse, turned in the late 1980s to explorations of the human—or humanoid—form. *Blue U-Turn* (558) places a huge-scale, deep-blue figure of indeterminate gender in an apparently liquid environment. The figure is stretched-out and rubbery. Its sketchy features gaze at us with a fixed stare, yet we sense that its elongated body is in constant motion, curling and drifting through its watery space. What does this figure symbolize? The title of the painting is descriptive and gives no clue. Rothenberg's sinuous blue person could be swimming in the womb, in the depths of the ocean, in the farthest reaches of the cosmos. The figure is powerful but not menacing. Its graceful curve and implied movement offer promise of harmony with the universe.

THE FIGURE FOR ITS OWN SAKE Every now and again the knowing voices of the art world proclaim that figure painting—the natural rendering of the human body—is finished, over, dated, boring. And just as often those knowing voices have to eat their words. One of the most respected painters working today is the English artist Lucian Freud, who is the grandson of the pioneer psychoanalyst Sigmund Freud, and who is himself a master painter of figures.

Freud is best known for his nudes, and he approaches the nude in a way quite unlike any artist before him. *Naked Man, Back View* (559) is typical of his style. The huge body is so plastic, one feels one could actually reach out and squeeze the rubbery flesh, and that it would be warm to the touch—although one might shudder at the prospect of touching this body. The sheer *fleshiness* of the subject, rendered in exacting detail, both fascinates and repels the viewer. With his merciless eye Freud discovers every bump and bulge and blotch on the sitter's body. The American painter Philip Pearlstein does this too, but if you flip back and forth between Pearlstein's *Female Nude* **(553)** and Freud's *Naked Man*, you will see an enormous difference. Pearlstein's figure is cool and detached, an object to be scrutinized from afar. Freud's *Naked Man* is anything but cool. He is a human mountain, a thundering presence who seems to inhabit the viewer's own space and to dominate that space.

ABSTRACTION Abstraction is still an important current in present-day art, and among the most innovative of its practitioners is Elizabeth Murray. *Painter's Progress* **(560)** is typical of Murray's exuberant shaped canvases, rather like a brilliantly colored Cubist painting in which the facets have been cut apart and allowed to slip and slide and collide with one another. Here the basic form is a painter's palette, shattered and then reassembled. As in a Cubist work, we can find references to the human figure, but Murray's forms are not only more joyous but more outward-turning, seeming to ricochet off each other like a vivid musical animation.

The later work of Frank Stella **(556)** also fits the category of abstraction, as do many other contemporary examples in this text.

NEO-EXPRESSIONISM Early in the 1980s there came into prominence a group of artists who were called "new" Expressionists, or *Neo-Expressionists*. Mostly Germans and Italians, these artists were young children during and after World War II. Their work reflects the consciousness of nations that fought the great war, lost, and began to pick up the pieces afterward.

Neo-Expressionist art is basically representational and often contains figures, but its intensity of form and energy makes it quite different from the Realist paintings of the 1970s. Neo-Expressionist works are full of passion and

RELATED WORKS

Frankenthaler, *Nature Abhors a Vacuum*, p. 186

Starn Twins, *Double Portrait*, p. 238

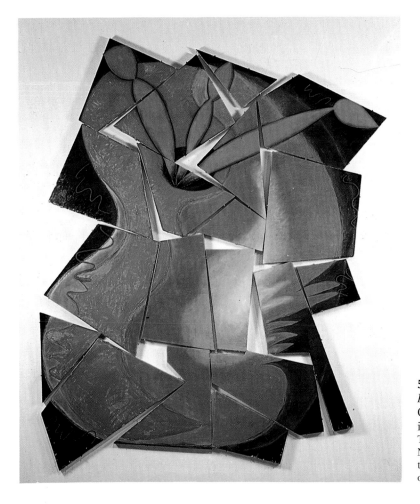

560. Elizabeth Murray. *Painter's Progress*. 1981. Oil on canvas, in 19 parts; 9'8" × 7'9". The Museum of Modern Art, New York (acquired through the Bernhill Fund and gift of Agnes Gund).

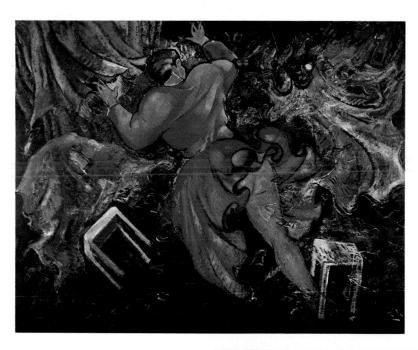

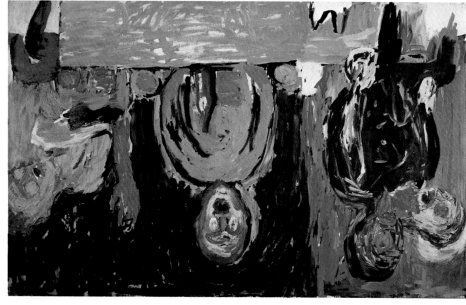

above: **561.** Sandro Chia. *Incident at the Café Tintoretto.* 1981. Oil on canvas, 8′5″ × 11′2″. © 1998 Sandro Chia/ Licensed by VAGA, New York.

right: **562.** Georg Baselitz. *Nachtessen in Dresden.* 1983. Oil on canvas, 9′2″ × 14′9″. Collection Doris and Charles Saatchi, London, courtesy Xavier Fourcade, Inc., New York.

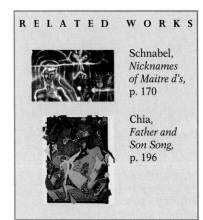

R E L A T E D   W O R K S

Schnabel, *Nicknames of Maitre d's,* p. 170

Chia, *Father and Son Song,* p. 196

symbolism, occasionally even story line. We can see this in *Incident at the Café Tintoretto* **(561)**, by the Italian artist Sandro Chia. Chia paints everyday events and invests them with cosmic importance. The "incident" depicted in this work might be an ordinary fight in a café, but Chia gives it the drama of a scene from Dante's *Inferno.* Part of the reason for the painting's impact is its dense, seething composition, showing turmoil in every part of the large canvas. Another contributing factor is the vivid, clashing color, which almost shrieks at us to compel attention.

The German artist Georg Baselitz not only finds intensity in everyday events but also turns such events quite literally upside down. *Nachtessen in Dresden* **(562)** is printed correctly in this book, and the huge canvas is hung this way on a gallery wall. The painting's title translates simply as "supper in Dresden," but its strange inverted composition creates a jarring effect.

Best known of the German Neo-Expressionists is Anselm Kiefer, whose enormous paintings often include direct references to the horrors of Nazi power under Adolf Hitler and the atrocities of World War II. *Interior* **(563)**, for example, was copied from a photograph of Hitler's Chancellery (or office of

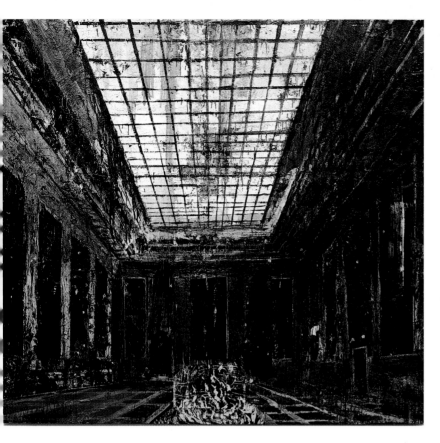

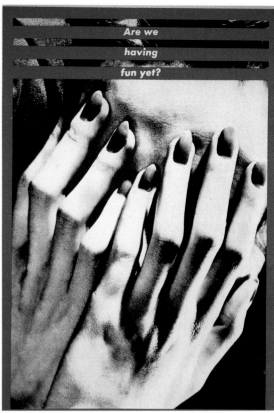

state), a building designed by the ambitious Nazi architect Albert Speer. In Kiefer's work the Chancellery, rendered in dramatic perspective, is abandoned and decaying. A fire burns in the center of the room; perhaps it will destroy the building and the regime it represents. Most critics have read Kiefer's work as a kind of exorcism—an attempt to drive out the evil spirits of Germany's past. And, to be sure, the artist's vast theatrical spaces, almost like stage sets, are empty. The actors are gone.

By the mid-1980s several American (New York-based) artists had become associated with the Neo-Expressionist movement. Prominent among them are Julian Schnabel and Eric Fischl. Whether they would label themselves as Neo-Expressionists remains unclear, but their work is disturbing and expressive. Because Fischl often makes reference to earlier styles, he will be considered in the next section.

REFERENCE, QUOTATION, AND APPROPRIATION When an artist consciously borrows from a preexisting source—whether in style, imagery, or medium—we call that borrowing a ***reference*** to the earlier work, or a ***quotation*** of that work. Another word you may hear is ***appropriation,*** which means literally taking something made by another for one's own. Most of the time there is nothing dishonest or unethical about this approach, nor is there any attempt to conceal the source of the reference. Artists throughout history have paid tribute thus to their predecessors, as the "Artists on Artists" boxes in this text reveal. Among contemporary artists, there is a special interest in ***transformation*** of existing art to make a fresh and original statement.

Barbara Kruger appropriates photographs from commercial sources, such as magazines and newspapers, and blows them up to billboard size. She then overlays the photographs with messages drawn from advertising, politics, or popular jargon. *Are We Having Fun Yet?* **(564)** juxtaposes that ironic question with an anguished picture of hands pressed to a face. Kruger's images are stark and even shocking, especially so in view of their size. There is a tension, a biting clash between picture and words, a mockery of mass-produced values like "having fun."

left: **563.** Anselm Kiefer.
Interior. 1981.
Oil, paper, and straw
on canvas; 9'5¼" × 10'2½".
Collection Stedelijk Museum,
Amsterdam.

right: **564.** Barbara Kruger.
Untitled (Are We Having Fun Yet?).
1987. Photographic silkscreen/
vinyl, 12'3½" × 8'7".
Courtesy Mary Boone Gallery,
New York.

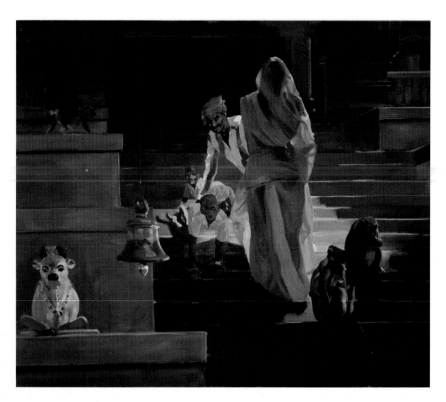

565. Eric Fischl.
On the Stairs of the Temple.
1989. Oil on linen, 9'7" × 11'8".
National Gallery of Art,
Washington, D.C., courtesy
Mary Boone Gallery, New York.

Recent works by Eric Fischl show an appropriation not of subject matter or form, but of style. In a series of paintings resulting from a trip to India, Fischl evokes the heroic, allegorical style of such 19th-century French artists as Delacroix and Courbet **(512,513)**, even to the majestic composition and dramatic lighting. *On the Stairs of the Temple* **(565)** shows a veiled woman descending the stairs, a turbaned man, two apparently injured boys, a pair of monkeys, a hanging bell, a small white cow figure. In a 19th-century painting all these images would *mean* something; there would be a story or moral or allegory. In Fischl's work they probably do *not* mean anything. The allegory is presented for its own visual sake, with no hidden significance.

The American artist Pat Steir has carried the idea of artistic quotation to marvelous heights in a complex work known as *The Brueghel Series* **(566)**. Steir, who lives part of the year in Holland, conceived the project after viewing a still-life painting of flowers by Jan Brueghel the Elder in a Dutch museum. Having bought a poster of the Brueghel painting, she then cut the poster into small pieces and used each piece as the basis for a separate painting. When hung together in a prearranged pattern, the sixty-four panels—completed over a period of two years—echo the form of the original flower painting. Each panel, however, is executed in a different style, which explains the work's subtitle, *A Vanitas of Style*. In effect, *The Brueghel Series* is a painting about painting, about all the rich variety of styles that have been practiced by artists for the last several centuries, ranging from Rembrandt to Steir herself. A small book reproduction of this work, which in life is nearly 20 feet tall, makes it difficult to identify the individual styles, but we might recognize the style of Jackson Pollock (far left, third from top), of Franz Kline (top row, second from right), and of Piet Mondrian (top row, third from left). Other artists represented include Botticelli, Picasso, Watteau, Matisse, O'Keeffe, Degas, and Gauguin. Taken as a piece, *The Brueghel Series* is a wonderful summation of the best in Western art history.

PERFORMANCE, INSTALLATIONS, AND COMBINATIONS During the 1970s the phenomenon known as ***Performance Art*** emerged. Performance Art undoubtedly took its inspiration from the "Happenings" of the 1950s and 1960s, one of which is described on page 208. ***Happenings*** are difficult to define; they are visual events in which some activity occurs, often with several people par-

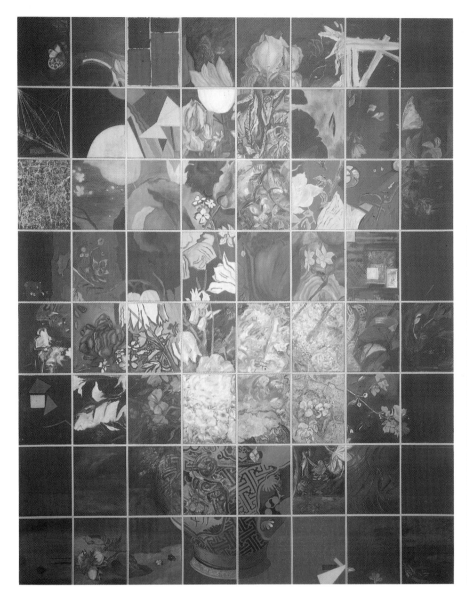

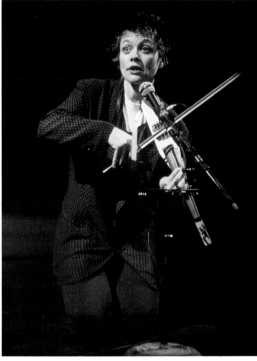

ticipating, often with audience involvement. They may include music, dance, mime, art, reading, or none of these. Imprecise as it may sound, Happenings are things that happen.

Performance artist Laurie Anderson developed this idea considerably through the 1980s. In *Empty Places*, a performance work first presented in 1989, the artist herself is at the center of the action **(567)**. She tells stories and she sings, sometimes in her own clear soprano voice, sometimes through an electronic device that alters the sound. She plays a keyboard and a violin (Anderson is a classically trained violinist). Meanwhile, on a series of screens—two of them 20 feet tall—are projected still and moving images that change at a dizzying pace. The slides and films, most of which were shot by Anderson, may be keyed to the stories and the music (or they may not). In broadest terms, the theme of *Empty Places* is the American scene, but it is a scene filtered through the artist's own experience.

Like the Conceptual Art discussed earlier, Performance Art has no physical substance in the sense of an object you could buy or hang on the wall. In Performance Art the art is the artist. If you take away the artist, there is no more art. This is a far cry from the art of the Middle Ages, in which the artworks endure and are valued while the names of the artists have been mostly forgotten. In a very real sense, Performance Art is the triumph of the artist over the material object.

left: **566.** Pat Steir.
*The Brueghel Series
(A Vanitas of Style).*
1982–84. Oil on canvas;
64 panels, each $28\frac{1}{2} \times 22\frac{1}{2}''$.
Courtesy the artist
and Michael Klein, Inc., New York.

right: **567.** Laurie Anderson
in performance, *Empty Places.*
1989.

RELATED WORKS

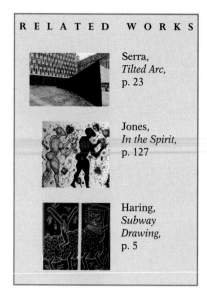

Serra,
Tilted Arc,
p. 23

Jones,
In the Spirit,
p. 127

Haring,
*Subway
Drawing*,
p. 5

Installations are works that achieve their intended form only when they are set into a planned environment. The art medium—whether painting, sculpture, fiber art, or whatever—becomes one with the environment to fulfill the artist's expression. Works by Richard Serra, Ben Jones, and Judy Pfaff, seen earlier in the book, fit this category. We might even include the drawings of Keith Haring, since they were "installed" in the New York subway system.

Jenny Holzer is another artist who often works in installations, and Holzer's medium is words. Specifically, she deals in slogans—short, pithy statements like "Lack of charisma can be fatal," and "Money creates taste," and "A name means a lot by itself," and "You are trapped on the earth so you will explode." Quite a lot of people think Holzer's slogans are trite and childish. They grumble that the slogans might have come out of a fortune cookie, but this criticism doesn't bother Holzer in the least. She has said, "I want to make art that's understandable, has some relevance and importance to almost everyone. . . . I like fooling with different presentations and modes. I like to make it turn purple and go upside down."[2]

Holzer's art is unabashedly popular. Set into gaudy electronic letters that flash or travel in a running band, her slogans might seem most at home in New York's Times Square or on the strip in Las Vegas—and, in fact, they *have* appeared in both places. But one of Holzer's best-known sites was the Guggenheim Museum in New York, where her installation took over the museum for two months in 1989–90 **(568)**.

The Guggenheim, with its mushroom shape and tiers of ramps, is not always the most hospitable setting for every type of art, but Holzer's moving red, yellow, and green slogans fit in as though the museum had been designed for that purpose. (One critic remarked that the museum "never looked better"— all the while allowing that the architect, Frank Lloyd Wright [p. 337], might be spinning in his grave.) This art, obviously derived from television and advertising and computers, speaks directly to our time.

Our next artist, Jennifer Bartlett, is extremely difficult to categorize. To get a meaningful sense of her range, the viewer should see a wide selection of

568. Jenny Holzer. *Selections from Truisms, Inflammatory Essays, The Living Series, The Survival Series, Under a Rock, Laments, and new writing.* Installation, December 12, 1989–February 11, 1990. Extended helical tricolor L.E.D. electronic display signboard, 11″ × 162′ × 4″. Solomon R. Guggenheim Museum, New York (partial gift of the artist, 1989).

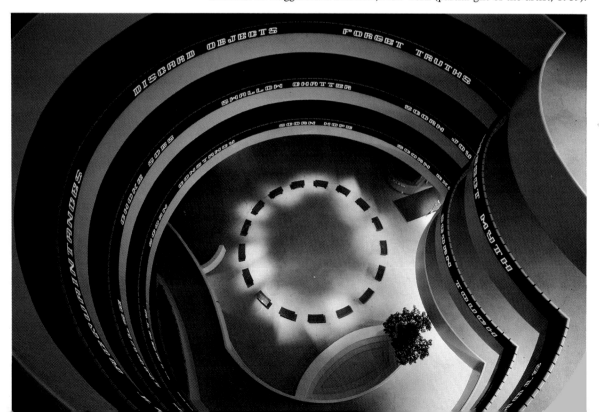

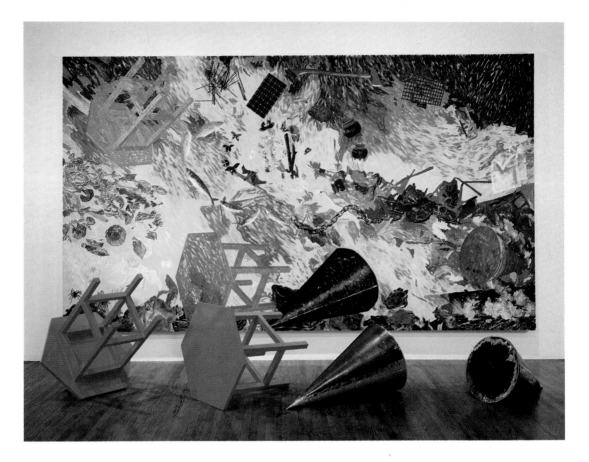

her works, and here we can show only one. Bartlett's sources are eclectic—everything from Impressionism to Expressionism to the various styles of the 1960s—and her subjects are equally wide-ranging. She has worked in practically every known medium: oil, pastel, charcoal, fresco, ceramic, enamel, steel plates, wood, and so on.

Spiral: An Ordinary Evening in New Haven **(569)** could be called a ***combination*** work, because the sculptural forms and the huge painted canvas are meant to be inseparable. The canvas shows a giant firestorm, a blazing inferno that sweeps everything in its path, including some tipped-over tables and two large gray cones. Sculptured versions of the tables and cones rest on the floor in front of the painting. Perhaps these are the survivors of the firestorm, the pure objects that endure when the rest of the world is burnt away.

569. Jennifer Bartlett.
Spiral: An Ordinary Evening in New Haven. 1989.
Painting: oil on canvas, 9 × 16′;
tables of painted wood,
one with steel base;
cones of break-formed
hot-rolled welded steel.
Private collection, Greenwich, Conn.,
courtesy Paula Cooper Gallery, New York.

TOWARD THE MILLENNIUM

Milestones always inspire us to look backward and forward. Whether it is a zero-year birthday, a big anniversary, the turn of a decade or century, we cannot help comparing our present situation with conditions in place at the last milestone, and wondering what the future will bring for the next milestone. The turn of a millennium is, obviously, a stupendous milestone. Counting backward under the terms of our common calendar, the vast majority of humans who have lived—and the vast majority of artists who have worked—never experienced such an event. In fact, it is difficult to find any artist in history whose name we know who ever saw a millennium turn. And it is fascinating to speculate how many artists now prominent, and which ones, will be known by name a thousand years hence.

The last millennium has witnessed enormous changes in the way art is created and the way it is perceived. Nevertheless, one can still find examples that seem to have some elements in common. Two images are shown here—one made just before the year 1000, another made just before the year 2000.

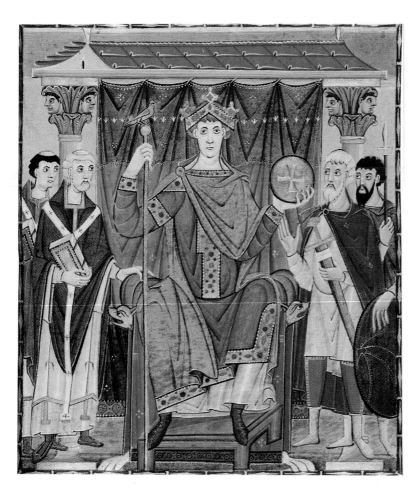

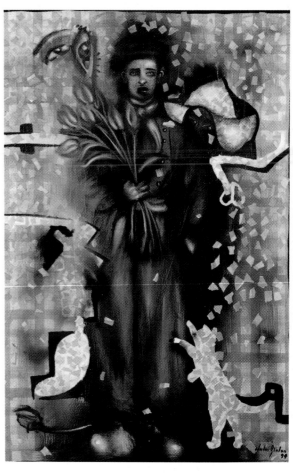

left: 570. *Otto III Enthroned Receiving the Homage of Four Parts of the Empire,* from the *Gospel Book of Otto III.* 997–1000. Manuscript illumination, height of image c. 9″. Bayerische Staatsbibliothek, Munich.

right: 571. Julio Galán. *The Great Haircut (El gran corte de pelo).* 1994. Collage, oil, and spray paint on canvas; 5′3″ × 4′3¼″. Collection Isabella del Frate, courtesy Annina Nosei Gallery, New York.

Otto III Enthroned **(570)** was painted about 997–1000 by an unknown manuscript artist, probably a monk, in the area of what is now western Germany. *The Great Haircut* **(571)** was painted in 1994 by Julio Galán, an artist born and educated in Mexico, who has exhibited both in his home country and in the United States. What are the factors that distinguish or unite these works done a thousand years apart?

Quite different purposes motivated the artists who made these paintings. The anonymous monk who portrayed Otto III was charged with glorifying a royal patron, the emperor himself. Galán, like most artists today, worked principally for his own self-expression. The picture of Otto was meant for only a few privileged eyes; it is part of the emperor's *Gospel Book,* a vehicle for private religious devotions. Galán's painting, on the other hand, appeared in a major museum exhibition in New York and was viewed by tens of thousands of people. In scale the two works are very dissimilar. *Otto III* is a miniature about 9 inches high, while *The Great Haircut* measures more than 5 feet in height. Why then should we compare them, why set them side by side on a page of this book?

The common factor is that both images feature a dominant human figure—in both cases a man, as it happens—centered in the composition and posed frontally. And, although there are other figures in each work, it is the face of the central character that draws our attention. Most particularly, it is the eyes, looking straight out at us from a thousand years ago or just a few years ago. We try to read their expressions, to know what these painted people are thinking and feeling. In other words, we look for communication, with both the subjects and those who created them.

When art does not communicate anything to us, when it does not speak to us in some way, we pass it by. Over the millennia generations of artists have chosen the human form as a favorite medium of communication. Will artists of the year 3000 still be painting human images, and will the eyes seek those of viewers a thousand years from now? Possibly they will, or possibly artists of the future will find some new way, as yet undreamed of, to live with art.

DOROTHY AND HERBERT VOGEL

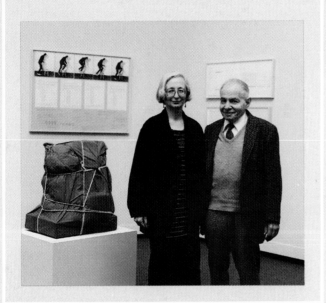

ART COLLECTORS ARE RICH. Art collectors are glamorous. Art collectors are members of the upper classes or the nobility, or else they are important business leaders. Everybody knows these facts, but apparently nobody bothered to inform Dorothy and Herbert Vogel of New York City. The Vogels—she a retired librarian, he a retired postal worker—are not rich, and their life style is modest. They are the sort of people one can't help but call "ordinary." One fact about the Vogels is undeniably *extra*ordinary: They have been collecting art on an ambitious scale for more than thirty-five years.

Everybody in the fashionable art world of New York, it seems, knows the unfashionable Herbert and Dorothy. The Vogels attend as many openings as possible, they regularly visit several artists' studios, they study the art seriously—and they buy. Their small Manhattan apartment eventually became crammed to ceilings with some seventeen hundred original works of art, emphasizing the Minimal, Conceptual, and Post-modern artists. This collection was acquired almost entirely on Herbert's salary from the post office. Dorothy's income pays the couple's living expenses.

The odds against two such . . . well . . . *ordinary* people becoming important art collectors seem formidable. Herbert, the son of a tailor, grew up in New York and started work for the post office after high school and the army. Dorothy, born in Elmira, New York, earned a master's degree in library science and took a librarian's job in Brooklyn. The couple met at a singles' party, dated for a year, then married in 1962. Their plunge into the art world was led by Herbert, who had taken some art courses at New York University, had made friends with young artists, and aspired to be an artist himself. Soon Herbert got Dorothy involved, and the two decided collecting would be more to their taste.

The Vogels began slowly. Rushing from their respective jobs in the evening, they would rendezvous in a subway station, then go off to a gallery to study the art and consider possible purchases. At first, dealers and gallery habitués wondered, "Who on earth *are* those people?" The Vogels do not look like one's usual image of collectors. Soon, however, their clever and persistent buying attracted attention; soon their appearance in a gallery created a stir. As their collection grew, so did their reputation. Artists accept them as friends because their love of the work is so sincere.

No doubt an important factor in the Vogels' success has been their single-mindedness. Dorothy and Herbert have no children, though they have turtles and fish in quantity and—as of this writing—six cats (Picasso, Renoir, Manet, Degas, Cézanne, and Corot; since our last edition, Dorothy reports, Whistler has died). Nearly all their time is devoted to the collection. They are shrewd buyers, stretching their limited budget to the utmost.

The value of the Vogels' collection was demonstrated in 1992, when the National Gallery of Art in Washington announced it would acquire the collection as part-purchase, part donation. Once the art was moved out for inventory, the Vogels had their apartment painted for the first time in decades—and went back to buying art.

Most people pretty much live out the lives they were born to, but Herbert and Dorothy Vogel obviously are made of stronger stuff. The postal worker and the librarian—together they invented a special life for themselves, a life with art. Seeing them, talking with them, one cannot doubt they are enjoying every moment of it.

Collectors Dorothy and Herbert Vogel at the exhibition "From Minimal to Conceptual Art: Works from The Dorothy and Herbert Vogel Collection," at the National Gallery of Art, May 29 through November 27, 1994.

CHAPTER TWENTY-ONE

Art Around the World

T HERE IS NO PLACE on earth where humans have lived without objects that could properly be called art. Living with art is not a modern innovation or a special fancy of people associated with Western culture. Art has flourished from earliest times, in all centers of civilization.

It is not surprising that those of us raised in Western culture—that is, in Europe or North America—would consider our own artistic traditions to be familiar and accessible, and to think of everything else as "foreign." Human beings, by their very nature, are most comfortable with the familiar, the known, and they tend to assume their own ways are superior to all others. It is easy to forget that what is normal and familiar to oneself may seem "foreign" to others.

Because this book is intended primarily for students in North America, it has emphasized the arts in Western tradition—art styles having their roots in ancient Egypt and Mesopotamia, then progressing through the Classical Greeks and Romans in a fairly straight line to our own time. That approach has been standard for many generations, but nowadays it needs considerable adjustment. The ease of travel and communication we now take for granted forces us to question whether any traditional values can still be treated as standard. Large segments of the population in North America come from cultures outside the European base. Large numbers of European-descended North Americans travel abroad to meet cultures different from their own.

The world of art has produced many lines of artistic development, some of them crossing or touching upon the Western, some quite independent. There is a rich heritage of art to be found in Asia, in Africa, in the ancient Americas, and in Oceania. Earlier chapters of this book have introduced plentiful examples of these art styles, because they can be examined alongside Western specimens in terms of their themes, their design factors, and their media. Then in Chapter 14 we began a journey through time, seeking the very earliest art we know made in various parts of the world. Subsequent chapters followed the path of Western art from these beginnings to the present. Here we take up, in turn, the other paths we identified, through the art traditions of Asia, the ancient Americas, Africa, and Oceania. These journeys will be briefer but no less thrilling, for the works illustrated and discussed in this chapter stand among glories of world art.

THE ARTS OF ASIA

CHINA

China occupies a vast area in the eastern part of Asia (map, below). Over the centuries its boundaries have shifted continually as a result of wars, periods of expansion, and periods of invasion. The Great Wall, illustrated in Chapter 3, was an early attempt to stabilize China's northern border.

As noted in Chapter 14, the first period for which we can identify a coherent art style was the Shang Dynasty, dating from about 1766 B.C.E. A dynasty is a succession of rulers who pass power from one hand to the next in their family line. China's history is marked by a series of dynasties, starting with the Shang and covering three and a half millennia into the 20th century. Shang artists were known for their intricate bronze casting **(424)**, but the early Chinese also demonstrated great skill at ceramic art. Decorated pottery has been found in very old tombs, and the potter's wheel was in common use. We know that ceramic sculpture had attained a high degree of expertise by the 3d century B.C.E., because of the armies of life-size clay figures unearthed near Xian, in central China. The superb modeling of these figures testifies to a long period of prior development.

Buddhism was introduced to China from India in the 1st century C.E., during the Han Dynasty. The new religion caused profound change in Chinese

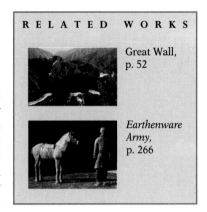
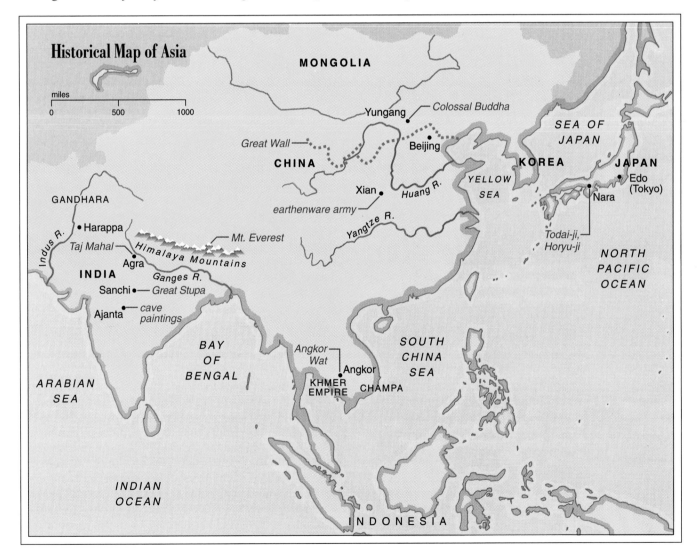

Historical Map of Asia

C H R O N O L O G Y

	3000 B.C.E.–1 C.E.	1–900 C.E.
China	Shang Dynasty, 1766–1045 Zhou Dynasty, 1045–256 Qin Dynasty, 221–206 Han Dynasty, 206 B.C.E.–220 C.E.	Han Dynasty, 206 B.C.E.–220 C.E. Six Dynasties, 220–589 Tang Dynasty, 618–907

Tang *Camel*

India	Indus Valley Civilization, c. 2500–c. 1500	Andhra Period, c. 70 B.C.E.–3d century C.E. Gandhara style c. 150–500 Gupta Period, 320–647 Medieval Period, c. 600–1500

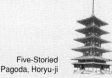
Seated Buddha

Japan	Archaic Period	Archaic Period, to 552 Asuka Period, 552–645 Nara Period, 645–794 Heian Period, 794–1185

Five-Storied
Pagoda, Horyu-ji

Mesoamerica	Olmec, c. 1500–300	Teotihuacán, to c. 600 Classic Maya, c. 300–900

South America		Mochica, c. 1–600 Huari-Tiahuanaco, c. 500–900

Mohica
stirrup vessel

North America	Northwest Coast cultures Eastern Woodlands (mound builders) Southwest cultures	Northwest Coast cultures Eastern Woodlands (including Cole culture) Southwest cultures

Head, Cole culture,
Ohio

Africa and Oceania	Egypt, Old Kingdom, 2686–2181 Egypt, Middle Kingdom, 2133–1991 Egypt, New Kingdom, 1567–1085 Nubia, c. 3800 B.C.E.–c. 200 C.E.	Islamic era (north), beginning c. 700

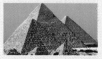
Great Pyramids

900–1500

Ladies Preparing
Newly Woven Silk

Song Dynasty, 960–1279
Yuan Dynasty, 1280–1368
Ming Dynasty, 1368–1644

Krishna as
the Butter Thief

Medieval Period, c. 600–1500

Sesshu, *Autumn*
Landscape

Heian Period, 794–1185
Kamakura Period, 1185–1392
Muromachi (Ashikaga) Period,
    1392–1573

Post-Classic Maya, c. 900–1525
Aztec, c. 1350–1525

Musician,
Chimú

Chimú, c. 1300–1425
Inca, c. 1425–1550

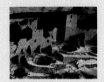

Cliff Palace, Mesa Verde

Northwest Coast cultures
Eastern Woodlands cultures
California cultures
Plains cultures
Southwest cultures (including Anasazi
    and Mogollon)

Stone images,
Easter Island

Islamic era (North Africa)
Easter Island

1500–1900

Guanyin

Ming Dynasty, 1368–1644
Qing Dynasty, 1644–1912

Taj Mahal

Mughal Dynasty, 1526–1756
Rajput style, c. 1500–1900

Hokusai, *View of Fuji*

Momoyama Period, 1573–1615
Tokugawa (Edo) Period, 1615–1868

Spanish colonial period

Spanish colonial period

Colonial period

Brass plaque,
Benin Chief

Akan
Dogon
Bambara
Yoruba
Dahomey
Bamum
Lega
Luba (Baluba)
Benin (kingdom c. 1550–1680)

art, which would be dominated for several centuries by Buddhist imagery. A *Colossal Buddha* **(572)**, carved of sandstone and measuring 45 feet high, fills the mouth of a cave at Yungang, in northeast China. Probably sculpted about 460 C.E., this figure is considered archaic (or old-style) for the simplicity of its form. The drapery falls in a series of regular, almost geometric folds, and the face is modeled in smooth planes. The Buddha wears an expression of beatific serenity, his half-smile reminiscent of the "archaic smile" of early Greek sculptures **(437)**. What is most striking about this figure is its sheer size, and the sense of it emerging, almost growing, from the living rock.

The Tang Dynasty (618–907) was a period of great political stability and exceptional cultural brilliance in China. The arts of painting and ceramics, in particular, flourished in that time. A masterpiece of Tang painting is the *Scroll of the Emperors,* dated to the 7th century. The ***handscroll*** is a particularly Asian form of art, virtually unknown in the West. It is meant for personal viewing and is held in the hands, rather like a book. Instead of having pages, however, the handscroll is one long horizontal piece of material, often silk, rolled from end to end. The viewer gradually unrolls the work, revealing one section at a time. The *Scroll of the Emperors* is attributed to Yan Liben, who was both a government official and a court artist. In all it measures 18 feet in length and depicts thirteen Chinese emperors. We illustrate the section showing *Emperor Wen Di* **(573)** with two of his attendants.

Wen Di is seated on his dais, or low throne, in a calmly regal pose. The artist has captured both the ease of the emperor's body and the soft drape of his clothing. It is believed the artist meant this image as a portrait of Wen Di, rather than just as a conventional emperor "type." The two court ladies behind the emperor provide an exceptionally elegant balance to the composition, filling out a triangle of interest. One faces toward the emperor, but the other looks away, mirroring the emperor's downcast gaze at the other side of the pyramid of figures. This is a tranquil scene but not a static one. We almost sense that the emperor is moving forward, as though drawn on a sled or rolling platform. This impression of movement owes partly to the isometric perspective (p. 117), partly to the women's poses and the graceful swirl of their skirts.

left: 572. *Colossal Buddha,* Cave 20, Yungang, Shanxi, China. Six Dynasties period, second half of 5th century. Stone, height 45′.

right: 573. Yan Liben (attrib.). *Emperor Wen Di of the Chen Dynasty,* from *Scroll of the Emperors.* China, Tang Dynasty, 7th century. Section of a handscroll, ink and color on silk; height 20⅛″. Courtesy of Museum of Fine Arts, Boston (Denman W. Ross Collection).

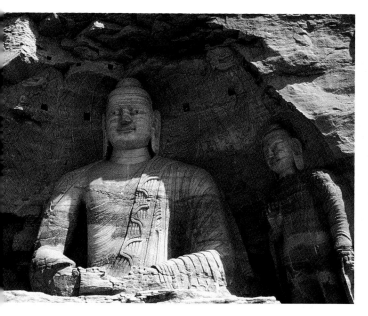

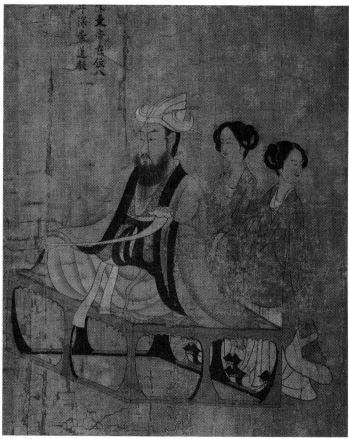

Tang ceramics are among the finest ever made, in any time or place. The *Camel* shown here **(574)** demonstrates that Tang artists had mastered the elements of figural ceramic work—purity of form, control of projecting sections, articulation of fine details, and brilliance of glaze colors. The camel is portrayed in midstride, with its elongated neck swooping up and backward, its head thrust toward the sky, its mouth open in an almost audible roar. Clay is plastic when wet and not especially strong until it has dried and been fired (Chapter 12). This fact makes it all the more remarkable that the ceramic sculptor managed to balance a rounded body and heavy flanks over the knobby knees and spindly lower legs that are so typical of camel anatomy. Fine surface details are everywhere, from the hairs on the camel's thighs and neck to the elaborate riding seat crowning the single hump.

The Tang Dynasty was followed by a brief period of political turmoil called the Five Dynasties. Order was restored under the Song Dynasty (960–1279), which witnessed another golden age of Chinese art.

Figural sculpture was exceedingly fine in the Song Dynasty, and much of its imagery continued to refer to the religion of Buddhism. Chapter 3 explained the importance of *bodhisattvas* in Buddhist theology. They are subdeities, or Buddhas-to-be, who have deferred their goal of *Nirvana*—or freedom from the cycle of birth, death, and rebirth—to help others attain that goal. In other words, they are intercessors for humans. Most beloved and powerful of the bodhisattvas is Guanyin (or Kuan-Yin), who is known as Avalokiteśvara in India and Kannon in Japan. Bodhisattvas are without sex—or, rather, they encompass both sexes—so you may encounter depictions of Guanyin that seem gracefully female in body and pose, while others have the more robust musculature of the male. (The same is true of angels in Christian theology.)

A *Guanyin* dating from about 1100 **(575)**, carved from wood and richly painted and gilded, captures this personage in an especially elegant guise. Guanyin sits easily, in a pose called *maharaja-lila*, the pose of an Indian prince, which combines other-worldly peace with compassion for human affairs. As a work of sculpture, this figure is expertly composed. The pure vertical line of head, torso, and left leg anchors Guanyin's body on its ornate throne, while the bent knee and outthrust arms—especially the right arm, with its gracefully

left: **574.** *Camel.* China, Tang Dynasty, early 8th century. Glazed terra cotta, height $34\frac{3}{4}''$. Los Angeles County Museum of Art (William Randolph Hearst Collection).

right: **575.** *Guanyin.* China, Song Dynasty, c. 1100. Painted wood, height 7'11". The Nelson-Atkins Museum of Art, Kansas City (purchase: Nelson Trust).

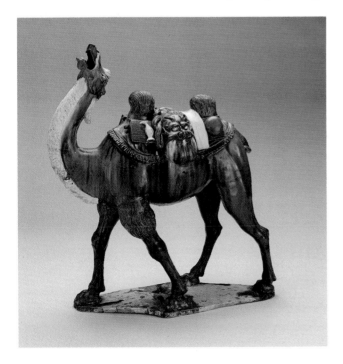

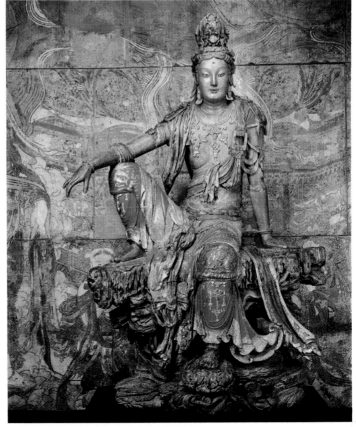

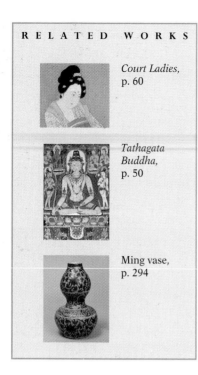
extended fingers—create a perfect asymmetrical balance. The swirl of draperies animates this serene figure, giving it the look of calm within the storm.

Exceptionally fine ceramics in the form of elegantly shaped bowls and vases were a hallmark of the Song era, and the tradition of figure painting continued in such works as *Court Ladies Preparing Newly Woven Silk*, which we saw in Chapter 3. But the glory of Song art was its landscape painting, and one of the great masters of landscape was Li Cheng. Li Cheng's career spanned a period from the later Five Dynasties into the Song Dynasty. The artist is associated with the so-called Monumental style favored in landscape painting, of which *A Solitary Temple amid Clearing Peaks* (**576**) is a splendid example.

In *A Solitary Temple* we see three distinct areas in depth: a foreground of rocks and gnarled trees, a middle ground where the temple reposes, and a background of towering, almost mystically grand mountains. We as viewers are expected to walk into this landscape—but only to a point. We can imagine crossing the bridge and proceeding to the temple, even climbing to the pagoda atop its hill. But the notion of scaling those steep-faced, craggy mountains in the background seems impossible. Even though Li Cheng has joined the background to the temple area with a waterfall at left, the mountains rise up as a barrier, stopping our progress into the landscape. Characteristic of the artist's style is the meticulous attention paid to every twisted branch and tree, every seam in the rocks. And, as is usual in a landscape work of this period, the

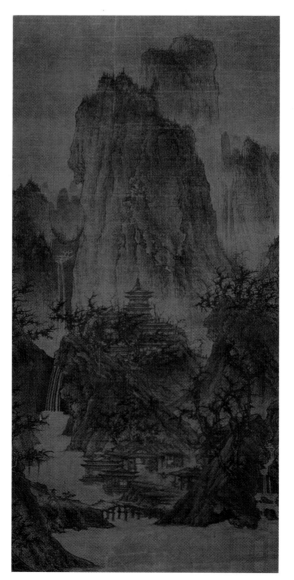

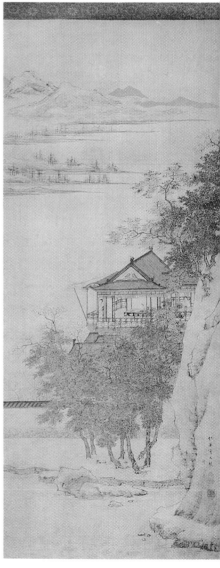

right: 576. Li Cheng (attrib.).
*A Solitary Temple
amid Clearing Peaks*.
China, Five Dynasties period
or early Song Dynasty,
c. 940–967.
Hanging scroll, ink and
slight color on silk, height 44″.
The Nelson-Atkins Museum of Art,
Kansas City (purchase: Nelson Trust).

far right: 577. Qiu Ying.
*A Lady in a Pavilion
Overlooking a Lake*.
China, Ming Dynasty, c. 1552–60.
Hanging scroll, ink and color
on paper; height 35¼″.
Courtesy of Museum of Fine Arts, Boston
(Chinese and Japanese Special Fund).

buildings are very small and the people almost invisibly tiny. Despite its title, this painting's subject is not really the temple. The temple gives scale and focus to the real subject, which is nature at its most magnificent.

The Song Dynasty collapsed under conditions the Great Wall was designed to prevent—invasion from the north. Mongols led by Genghis Khan, and later by his grandson Kublai Khan, overran China and established their imperial rule for almost a century, a period the Chinese call the Yuan Dynasty. Yuan art is magnificent but somewhat outside the mainstream of Chinese styles. Once native Chinese rule had been reestablished, another golden age of Chinese art came into being. That age was the Ming Dynasty.

Many people automatically associate the Ming Dynasty (1368–1644) with porcelain ceramics. In fact, to some collectors the word "Ming" is almost a necessary adjective preceding the word "porcelain" (although others insist that Tang and Song pieces are superior). Ming porcelain wares have a purity of form and often highly ornate decoration, as can be seen from the example in Chapter 12.

Ming landscape painters looked back to their predecessors of the Song Dynasty for inspiration, but the later masters sometimes took a more intimate approach. Qiu Ying's hanging scroll, *A Lady in a Pavilion Overlooking a Lake* (**577**), makes an interesting comparison for Li Cheng's *Solitary Temple* (**576**), painted some six hundred years before. Like the earlier work, the Ming *Pavilion* has three areas in depth: the foreground rocks, the middle ground with a pavilion nestled in a clump of trees, and distant mountains. Now, however, the architecture has assumed greater importance. It is the focus of our interest. The background mountains do not loom or create an obstacle to our passage but are simply part of a tranquil long vista. Our chief hesitation about walking into this landscape is that it seems so unreal, so dreamlike. The pavilion, which would be our presumed goal if we were travelers, appears to float above the ground, suspended like a balloon on its cushion of fluffy trees. The Song and Ming paintings, nevertheless, share one important characteristic: People are small in relation to the grandeur of nature. The "lady" of the Ming painting's title, sitting in her pavilion, playing her harp, is so tiny we need a magnifying glass to see her properly.

The Qing Dynasty, established in 1644, was the last of the traditional Chinese dynasties, ruling until China was declared a republic in 1912. During the early years of the dynasty large quantities of fine porcelain objects were made for export, chiefly to Europe. The creamy white porcelain figures came to be known in French as *blanc-de-Chine* (white China ware), although they are more correctly called by their Chinese name, *Dehua*. Our example shows a figure of *Guanyin the Merciful* (**578**), now a feminized version of the bodhisattva who appears so often in Asian art. In contrast to the princely Song image (**575**), this Guanyin seems contained, modest, and delicate. Her designation as "the merciful" reflects her popularity as an object of prayers and petitions, for this later Guanyin was worshiped especially by mothers. The naturalistic, almost fluid draperies swirling around the figure are typical of the Dehua style and indicate a masterful control of ceramic modeling.

Painting in the Qing Dynasty became more intimate and less "monumental" than it had been in earlier centuries. Nature remained a focus of attention, but as often as not the focus was narrower. Figures, whether people or animals, assumed more importance. We saw one expression of this style in Chapter 3, with Ren Xia's *Cat on a Rock*, in which the cat, the rock, and the banana leaves combine to form a still-life arrangement.

With the establishment of the Republic in 1912 and the communist People's Republic in 1949, the climate for art in China changed dramatically. As never before, art was viewed as an instrument for social reform rather than as an end unto itself. Still, an art tradition that has endured for some four thousand years cannot be diverted in a mere half century. The spirit and vitality of Chinese art remain alive in the work of the young, including that remarkable child prodigy, Wang Yani.

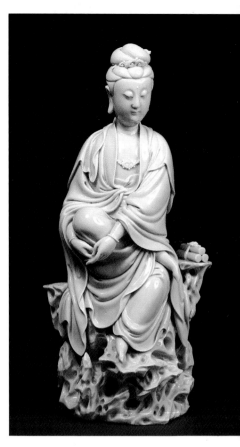

578. *Guanyin the Merciful.* c. 1700. *Blanc-de-Chine* porcelain, height 15″. Victoria & Albert Museum, London (Salting Bequest).

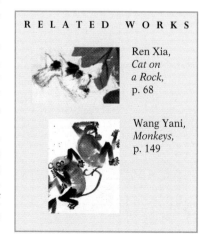

RELATED WORKS

Ren Xia, *Cat on a Rock*, p. 68

Wang Yani, *Monkeys*, p. 149

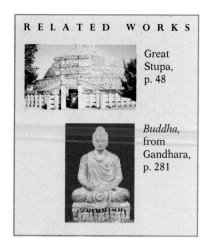
INDIA AND SOUTHEAST ASIA

The area of India's historical territories is so large and so self-contained that it is often referred to as a "subcontinent," jutting out from the south of Asia into the Indian Ocean (map, p. 505). The Himalayas, the highest mountain range in the world (of which Mt. Everest is a part), create a natural and formidable northern boundary, separating India from China.

Developed civilization in India can be traced back even farther than it can in China. As discussed in Chapter 14, by about 2400 B.C.E. a culture known as the Indus Valley civilization was established in the northwest region around the Indus River. Few works of art survive from the early centuries of India's history, probably because most were made from wood and other perishable materials.

For this brief survey of Indian art, we begin with works inspired by one of India's most important early religions—Buddhism. Gautama Siddhartha, later called the Buddha, was born in India about 563 B.C.E. His teachings attracted many followers, and by about the 3d century B.C.E. Buddhist imagery and architecture had begun to appear. In Chapter 3 we considered the Great Stupa, a major Buddhist shrine at Sanchi, for its role as a religious structure. Here we might look a little closer and focus on one detail of the shrine.

The Great Stupa has four gateways, each of them richly embellished with sculptures carved from sandstone. Our example shows a portion of the East Gate, featuring a *yakshi*, or female fertility spirit **(579)**. Yakshis and their male counterparts, called *yakshas*, were actually holdovers from an ancient religion of nature gods, now incorporated into Buddhism. The yakshi is shown embracing a tree, for her touch was supposed to cause the tree to flower. As befits a fertility figure, her body is voluptuous—full-breasted and broad-hipped—and it curves into a graceful twisting pose. This body type and sinuous posture would remain characteristic of Indian figural sculpture for centuries.

From the early centuries of our era the northwest region of Gandhara (now parts of Pakistan and Afghanistan) had extensive contacts with the Roman Empire. As a result, Greek and Roman styles greatly influenced the sculpture of the period, even of such innately Indian figures as the Buddha. A *Head of the Buddha* **(580)**, dating from the 5th century, shows this influence in

579. *Yakshi*,
detail of East Gate,
Great Stupa, Sanchi, India.
Early Andhra Period,
1st century B.C.E. Sandstone,
height of figure c. 5'.

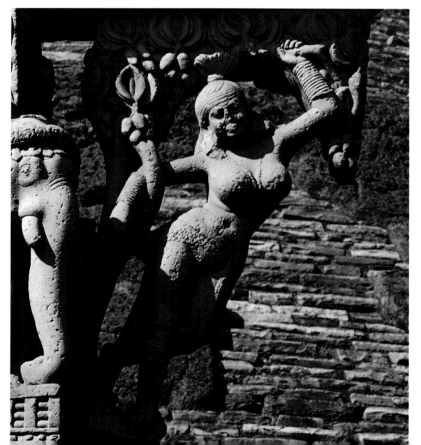

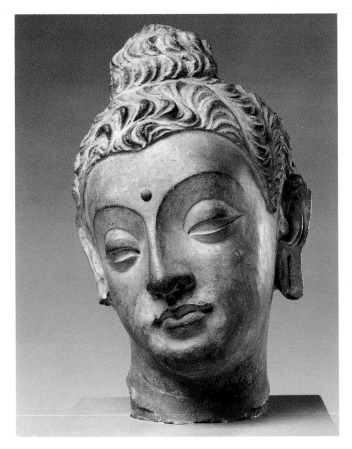

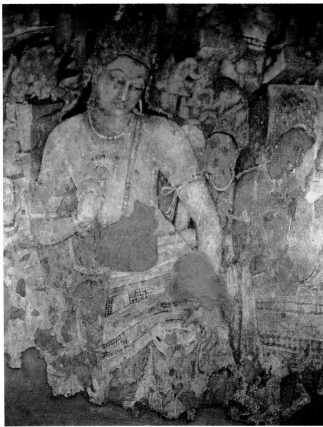

the slightly tilted angle of the head, the Western-style hair, and especially the strong linear carving of the eyebrows, nose, and lips. Full-length figures of the Buddha, such as the one we saw in Chapter 11 **(327)**, often were wrapped in graceful swirls of Greco-Roman-style draperies.

Surviving examples of early Indian painting are scarce. We know, however, that the art of painting was highly developed by the 5th century, because the few remaining works give evidence of a rich heritage. At Ajanta, in central India, a complex network of caves was carved out of the rock between the 1st and the 6th centuries. The caves—twenty-nine in all—were organized as both a religious retreat (there are living quarters for monks) and a pilgrimage site. For reasons that remain unclear, the caves were subsequently abandoned, and they apparently lay untouched for many hundreds of years. Not until 1819, when a hunting party of British officers came upon the caves by chance, did the modern world learn of the marvelous artworks preserved inside.

Many sculptures adorn the rooms and corridors at Ajanta, but by far the most exciting images inside the caves are the magnificent wall paintings depicting Buddhist personages and stories. The illustration shows an image of the bodhisattva Padmapani, a figure so lovely and graceful that modern scholars have called it *The "Beautiful Bodhisattva"* **(581)**. Padmapani, in Buddhist iconography, is a special form of Avalokiteśvara (or Guanyin) known as the lotus-giver. In this painting he holds a blue lotus blossom in his hand and wears the ornate crown of a prince. His serene face and downcast eyes perfectly express the compassion of the bodhisattva for humankind.

The "Beautiful Bodhisattva," dated to about 500 C.E., reflects the courtly style of the Gupta dynasty (320–647), a kind of golden age of enlightened political rule and art patronage. The Gupta period also marked the end of Buddhism as a major religion in India. By this time Buddhism had spread to most parts of east Asia, but it was supplanted on home soil by a revival of Hinduism, which became, and remains, the dominant religion of India.

left: **580.** *Head of the Buddha.* India, Gandhara style, 5th century. Stucco, height 9¾". Victoria & Albert Museum, London (by courtesy of the Board of Trustees).

right: **581.** *The "Beautiful Bodhisattva" Padmapani,* from Cave 1, Ajanta, India. c. 500. Fresco, detail.

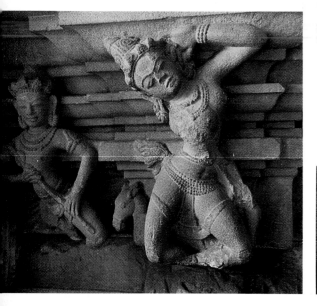

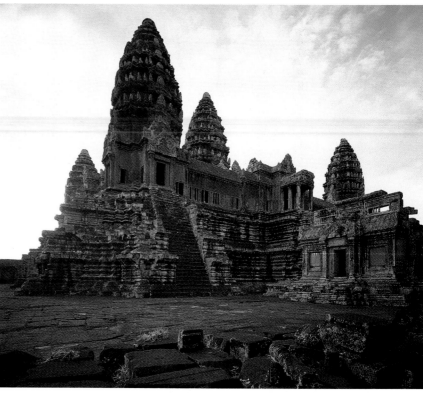

left: 582. *Celestial Dancer,* from Champa (Vietnam). 10th century. Sandstone, height c. 36″. Museum at Da Nang, Vietnam.

right: 583. Angkor Wat, Cambodia. 12th century. Height of central tower 213′.

The Gupta style is often called "international," because its influence extended throughout much of East and Southeast Asia. This influence is apparent in a carved sandstone figure of a *Celestial Dancer* **(582)** from Champa, a kingdom dating from the 3d to the 15th century in what is now part of Vietnam. The dancer is more animated than the bodhisattva at Ajanta, yet we can find similarities in the sharply defined facial features, the lavish crown and ornaments, the graceful curve of the body, and the stylized arm posture.

Just west of Champa lay the domain of the Khmer people, whose empire dominated what we now call Cambodia and much of the surrounding area from the 9th to the 15th century. The capital of the Khmer Empire was Angkor, a term that means simply "the city." At Angkor, over a period of several hundred years, a succession of Khmer kings built their palaces, temples, roads, and extensive canals used for both travel and irrigation. Eventually, the vast Angkor complex covered 75 square miles.

From the Indians, the Khmer had adopted the Hindu religion, and it was usual for each of their kings to identify with one or another of the Hindu gods, most often Shiva or Vishnu. The king thus became a sort of god-king, ruling by divine authority and goodness. When the king erected a temple to one of the gods, it was simultaneously a temple to himself as the earthly personification of that god. There are many such temples at Angkor, but the most famous—and the most beautiful—is Angkor Wat.

Angkor Wat, dedicated to the god Vishnu, was built by King Suryavarman II in the early 12th century. It is meant to represent Meru, the legendary mountain home of the gods, and its five pineapple-shaped towers symbolize Meru's five peaks **(583)**. Steep flights of steps lead to a terrace, at the center of which is a dominant tower rising more than 200 feet. The other four towers occupy the four corners of the structure and are connected by a network of covered galleries. Some scholars believe the arrangement has astronomical significance, and that, like Stonehenge in England **(407)**, its sight lines were planned to calculate planetary movements and events in the calendar. Both outside and in, the temple buildings are richly embellished with sculptures portraying Vishnu and other Hindu deities.

RESTORATION

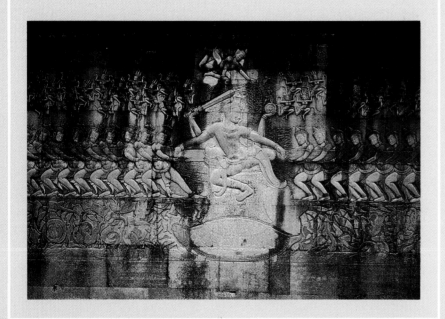

HERE IS THE CHALLENGE:
An ancient temple, magical in its beauty and thick with magnificent sculptures, is located deep inside a jungle. The climate is tropical—hot, humid, subject to monsoon rains. Algae and fungi grow unchecked, loving the moist atmosphere. Plants of all kinds flourish, boring their roots under and around temple stones, climbing the walls, penetrating every crevice. Bats proliferate, and their acidic droppings eat away the rock. Colonies of insects build their nests in the ground, in the cracks, in the delicate features of stone reliefs. When the rains come, water seeps through any opening, causing further erosion of the stone.

To make matters worse, the temple attracts other sorts of predators, predators encouraged not by the climate but by the treasures to be found inside. Because the temple complex is very large and difficult to guard, thieves regularly plunder the site for whatever artworks they can cut and carry away to sell to eager collectors. If a whole sculpture cannot be removed conveniently, looters simple slice off a portion. There are many headless statues in this temple.

Is that all? No, not quite. This temple happens to be located in Cambodia, in an area that has endured warfare variously involving government troops, the communist Khmer Rouge, the Vietnamese, and even the Americans. Bullet holes and mortar wounds give testimony to the fact that Angkor Wat stands in a battle zone.

The Khmer people abandoned their old capital at Angkor in the 15th century. Apparently, the site was more or less forgotten until 1861, when the French, who had colonized the region, rediscovered Angkor and literally hacked it out of the jungle. By then the jewel of the city, the temple called Angkor Wat, was in ruins. Sporadic attempts were made to preserve and restore the structures, but political turbulence over a long period made any real progress impossible. Finally, in the late 1980s, hostilities had declined to the point where restoration seemed feasible. A team of experts from India was selected for the project, but their task is daunting.

Some parts of Angkor Wat are so badly damaged that they must be completely dismantled and reassembled, stone by stone. Weed-killer and other chemicals will be used in great quantities to drive back the tropical growth. Ditches and conduits must be built to drain away excess water. And, of course, every inch of Angkor Wat and its sculptures will need to be scrubbed, to clean away centuries of nature's jungle coating. Recently, the restorers at Angkor Wat have drawn criticism from those who feel the scrubbing entails too much elbow grease and too little care—in other words, that untrained workers are throwing out the artworks with the algae. Angkor Wat, needless to say, is very fragile. As with any restoration project, it is hard to say when *enough* work is too much.

Perhaps the greatest challenge facing the restorers is one they cannot control. Unless peace can be maintained in the region, Angkor Wat is doomed. No temple, however magical, can survive the brutal assault of war.

Bas-relief sculpture at Angkor Wat, depicting the god Vishnu
in the story called "Churning the Sea of Milk."
The relief has been partially cleaned.

RELATED WORKS

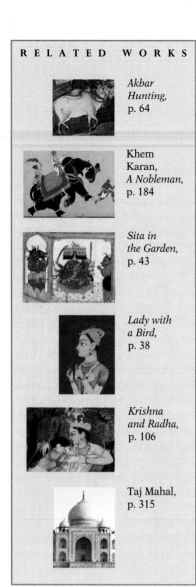

Akbar Hunting, p. 64

Khem Karan, A Nobleman, p. 184

Sita in the Garden, p. 43

Lady with a Bird, p. 38

Krishna and Radha, p. 106

Taj Mahal, p. 315

When Hinduism regained its ascendancy in India, displacing Buddhism as a dominant religion, styles of art changed accordingly. The Hindu gods are considerably more active than their counterparts, the serene Buddha and bodhisattvas. Depictions in art reflect this animation. In this book we have already met Krishna, who is—to put it as simply as possible—an incarnation or evolving form of Vishnu. We saw Krishna keeping a rendezvous with his beloved, Radha, as painted in an 18th-century Indian miniature **(121)**. Here we consider an image of Krishna that is both earlier in art history and earlier in the god's eventful life, in his childhood **(584)**. The Krishna legend is full of tales about his boyish pranks and escapades. A bronze sculpture from the 13th century depicts Krishna as "the butter thief," stealing butter from his cowherd foster parents. The child god dances impishly as he runs away with the butter. Although made of rigid bronze, this little figure projects a great deal of implied movement. Krishna's weight is balanced on one leg with the other bent, and his arms thrust out in counterbalance. We half expect him to dance right off the pedestal in delight at his trick.

While India maintained its Hindu culture, lands to the north and west were solidly Muslim. Starting in the 11th century, the territories of India were repeatedly invaded by Muslim forces, and by 1526 these forces had conquered most of the subcontinent. Under a king named Babur they established the Mughal Dynasty, which would rule India for more than two hundred years. (The word "Mughal" has come into our language as "mogul," meaning a powerful or important person.)

Mughal art is often secular, not religious, and it was strongly influenced by Persian styles. It flourished under three great emperors of the Mughal Dynasty, all of whom were devoted patrons of the arts. The first was Akbar,

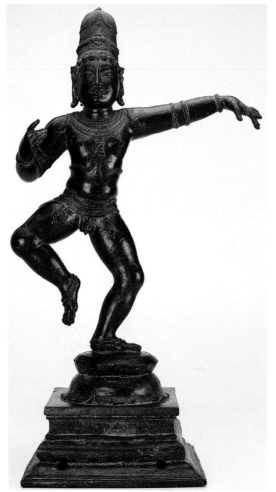

584. *Krishna as the Butter Thief,* from Tanjore, India. 13th century. Bronze, height 26″. The Nelson-Atkins Museum of Art, Kansas City (purchase: Nelson Trust).

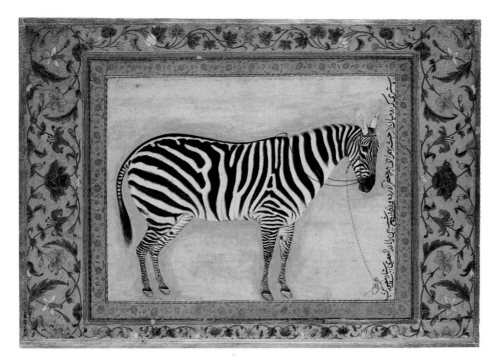

grandson of the conqueror Babur, who commissioned the series of miniature paintings known as the *Akbar Nama* (history of Akbar), discussed in Chapter 3 **(66)**. Akbar did not impose Muslim beliefs on his subjects. In fact, he married a Hindu princess and hoped to reconcile the two religions.

Akbar's son Jahangir both admired and imitated his father's art patronage. A dedicated amateur naturalist, Jahangir had court artists follow him around so as to record the exact appearance of plants, birds, and animals that took his interest. In *Emperor Jahangir's Zebra* **(585)** the painter Mansur has obviously captured the image of the beast, down to the last stripe. Zebras are native to Africa and do not live naturally in India. It is said that when this painting was presented at court, onlookers thought the artist had taken liberties with the coloring. But those of us who know the zebra from zoos or circuses can see that Mansur knew how to get a likeness.

Jahangir's son Shah Jahan also supported painting, but that is not the contribution to art for which he is best known. It was Shah Jahan who, grieving for his dead queen, commissioned one of the most beautiful buildings in the world, the Taj Mahal **(374)**.

JAPAN

The island nation of Japan, floating in the Pacific Ocean off the east coast of Asia, is tiny in comparison with the two huge land masses we have just considered (map, p. 505). That its influence far exceeds its size is no less true historically than it is now, no less true in art than in political or economic matters.

Fine ceramic vessels dated to at least 3000 B.C.E. have been discovered in Japan, indicating that developed cultures inhabited the islands from early times. Japanese expertise in working with clay—which continues to the present—would manifest itself centuries later in the stylized *Haniwa* figures placed around grave sites, such as the horse illustrated in Chapter 12.

The Buddhist religion migrated to Japan, by way of Korea, in the mid-6th century. Through the first two eras of recorded Japanese history—the Asuka Period (552–645 C.E.) and the Nara Period (645–794 C.E.)—Japanese Buddhist architecture tended to mimic Chinese styles. This influence is evident in the temple complex called Horyu-ji, built in the old capital city of Nara during the 7th century.

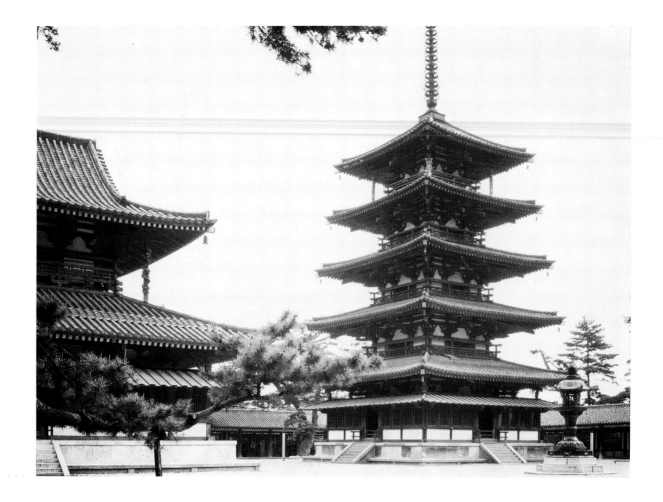

586. Five-Storied Pagoda of Horyuji, Nara, Japan. Asuka Period, 7th century.

Horyu-ji (the suffix -*ji* means "temple") consists of a cluster of buildings, of which we illustrate the Five-Storied Pagoda **(586)**, one of the oldest wooden structures in the world. A pagoda is a tower with many rooflines. Originally, the pagoda seems to have had a defensive purpose, offering a high vantage point for warding off invaders. With the advent of Buddhism the pagoda became a sacred building, and Horyu-ji's pagoda was constructed for worship. Its five tiled roofs sweep upward gracefully, their visual lightness seeming to deny the solid post-and-lintel construction (p. 307) that supports the weight of the pagoda. The "sacred tree" form capping the pagoda can be seen as an extension of the three-part "umbrella" that crowns the Great Stupa at Sanchi, in India **(48)**.

There are many temple complexes in the old capital city of Nara. Another of them, Todai-ji, dates from about a hundred years later, in the Nara Period. Todai-ji contains numerous splendid figural sculptures of the period, including the *Shukongojin*, or guardian figure, illustrated in Chapter 11.

Painting flourished in Japan during the Heian Period (794–1185), and by this time Chinese influence had declined in favor of native Japanese styles. For a marvelous example of Japanese narrative painting, we can examine one of a series of images made to illustrate *The Tale of Genji*.

The Tale of Genji, or *Genji Monogatari*, written by Lady Murasaki Shikibu in the 11th century, is often called the first novel in world literature. It relates the adventures of Prince Genji, outlining his many romantic (i.e., sexual) entanglements. Genji's exploits serve Lady Murasaki as a device for exploring some of the most profound human emotions, passions, and relationships. Along the way she provides vivid descriptions of court life in that time—the scandals and intrigues, the elaborate code of dress, the minute points of etiquette that must be observed.

RELATED WORKS

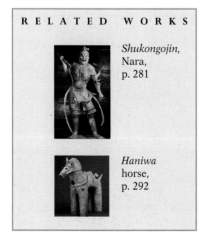

Shukongojin, Nara, p. 281

Haniwa horse, p. 292

A series of handscrolls painted in the 12th century, probably by several artists, highlight key episodes in the story **(587)**. The image shown here portrays a group of court ladies and their maids, apparently engaged in quiet domestic activity. One, at lower left, is having her hair combed, while another looks at an album of paintings and a third reads from a book. In fact, the tranquillity of the scene is deceptive. One of the ladies, Ukifume (at upper left), was assaulted, almost raped, just a few hours earlier, and the other ladies are trying to calm her. It is believed that the structure of this picture, with its many nonparallel diagonals, is meant to convey the underlying tension and barely controlled emotions in the scene.

The painting's space is extremely complex. Although the room is drawn in careful isometric perspective (p. 117), a large screen cutting through the foreground at a diagonal that is *not* consistent with the perspective partially blocks two of the figures. This form is meant to be understood as hanging near the ceiling. A painted screen in the background actually leads to another room, but it creates the impression of looking outside to a garden. All the figures are drawn in a classically Japanese style. The women's features are barely defined in stark white faces, and their bodies are encased in a voluminous swirl of draperies that reveal nothing of the form underneath. This style for painting the human figure, with a head or hand or foot emerging mysteriously from a mountain of garments, would endure in Japanese art for many centuries.

During the Kamakura Period (1185–1333) the relatively peaceful aristocrats of Heian were replaced by a military ruling class. Kamakura is thought of as a robust, dynamic, and even warlike era. We can find indications of this temperament in a classic series of painted handscrolls called the *Heiji Monogatari*. Whereas many earlier handscrolls, such as *The Tale of Genji*, tended to be episodic, showing one closed scene at a time, Kamakura artists embraced the handscroll as a means of depicting an ongoing narrative, a continuous stream of action. The subjects for their action painting were readily at hand in the many uprisings and feuds and wars of the time.

RELATED WORKS

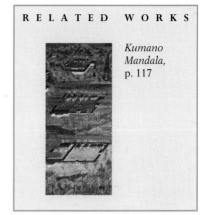

Kumano Mandala, p. 117

587. Illustration from *The Tale of Genji*. Heian Period, 12th century. Handscroll (now preserved in sections), ink and color on paper; height 8½″. Tokugawa Art Museum, Nagoya, Japan.

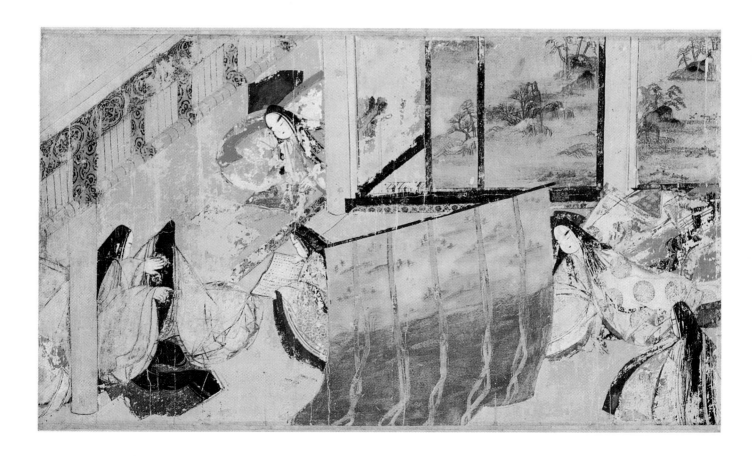

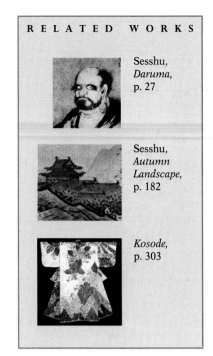
The Burning of Sanjo Palace **(588)**, one section of the *Heiji Monogatari*, is justly famous among the narrative Kamakura handscrolls. Artists of all kinds (including photographers and filmmakers), from all times and places, have always known that a great fire makes for a dramatic picture. In this scene we observe a little of the palace at upper left, drawn in the diagonal of isometric perspective (p. 117). From lower right a throng of mounted soldiers charge in at an opposing diagonal, flashing their swords and bows. Great red flames of fire and belching smoke threaten to engulf everything in their path. We can almost hear the screams of men and horses as they tumble over one another, racing ahead of the inferno. The scene is frenzied, and yet, artistically speaking, it is a controlled frenzy. Strong visual lines demarcate areas of interest—the palace, the charging row of soldiers, the fire. What gives the picture its energy is that we know the lines will dissolve in the next instant. The soldiers will scatter or converge in a messy heap, the fire will surge forward, and the two leaping horses, poised dramatically at center, will land.

The art of the Kamakura Period is thought by many experts to be the most quintessentially *Japanese* of art styles in that nation's history—not only expressive of Japanese culture but relatively free of Chinese influence. But it was the following period, known as Muromachi or Ashikaga (1392–1573), that produced one of the greatest masters in all Japanese art, the painter Sesshu. We have seen two examples of Sesshu's work earlier in this book: his picture of the Zen patriarch *Daruma* and his tranquil *Autumn Landscape*.

During the Edo Period (1615–1868) economic prosperity fed the taste for works in which sheer visual loveliness expressed pride in Japan's cultural heritage. Sumptuously embellished garments, such as the *kosode* shown in Chapter 12, were a major art form, as was decorative painting. A master

588. *The Burning of Sanjo Palace,* from the *Heiji Monogatari.*
Kamakura Period, late 13th century. Handscroll (detail),
ink and color on paper; height 16¼″, overall length 22′9″.
Courtesy Museum of Fine Arts, Boston (Fenollosa-Weld Collection).

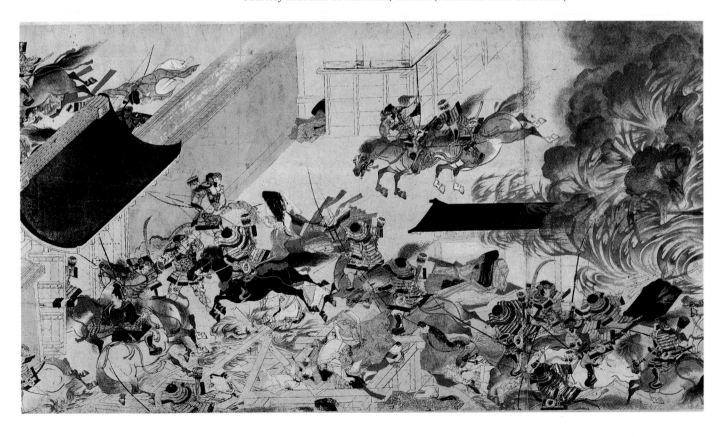

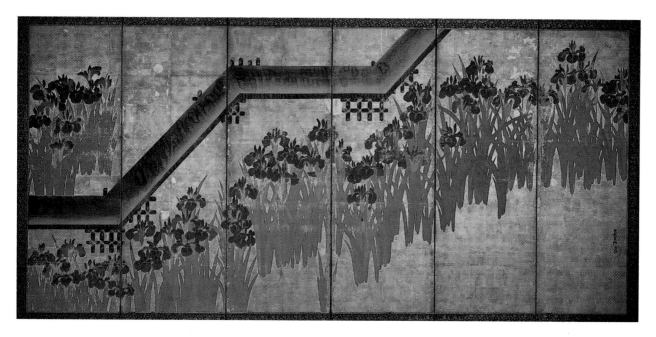

589. Ogata Korin. *Iris and Bridge,* six-fold screen.
Edo period, early 18th century.
Ink, color, and gold leaf on paper; 5'10½" × 12'2¼".
The Metropolitan Museum of Art, New York
(purchase, Louisa Eldridge McBurney Gift, 1953).

artist of this style was Ogata Korin, whose six-fold screen *Iris and Bridge* is illustrated here **(589)**. (A detail of the painting appears on the back cover of this book.) To Western eyes, Korin's image is simply a beautiful painting of flowers, but the Japanese viewer would recognize certain narrative content. The picture alludes to a classic collection of poem-tales written in the 10th century known as the *Ise Monogatari,* or *Tale of Ise,* which provided inspiration for many artists of later generations.

In one episode of the *Tale of Ise* the courtier Narihira has been banished from the capital of Kyoto to the provinces, following an ill-advised romantic affair with a noble lady of the court—the Emperor's beloved. During his travels, he stops by the Eight-Plank Bridge, and the nearby flowers make him nostalgic for home and the friends he has left behind. (It has been suggested that the artist identified with the poem's wanderer, since he himself was forced to leave Kyoto to seek clients for his work.)

The story's reference to irises by the bridge is fleeting, and Korin does not attempt to illustrate the scene in any detail. The zigzag of the wooden bridge echoes the upward path of the flowers, but it does not give us any sense of real space or landscape. We are meant to enjoy, for its own sake, the display of gorgeous colors and shapes set off against a rich gold-leaf background. Korin's luxuriant sweep of irises, with deep green foliage and vivid blooms, creates a certain mood, a flavor that the Japanese people have come to associate with their national spirit.

The extraordinary history of Japanese woodcut printing began in the 17th century and reached a peak of excellence during the later Edo Period. We have studied two of the outstanding 19th-century masters in Chapter 8: Ando Hiroshige **(225)** and Katsushika Hokusai **(226** and p. 195). As noted in that chapter, Japanese woodblock prints were imported in huge quantities to Europe and exerted a profound influence on Western art styles. Not long afterward, Japanese collectors began acquiring Western art, so the process of cross-fertilization accelerated. Although we can still, to this day, identify an entity called Japanese art, the styles emerging from that culture have become part of the collective consciousness of artists around the world.

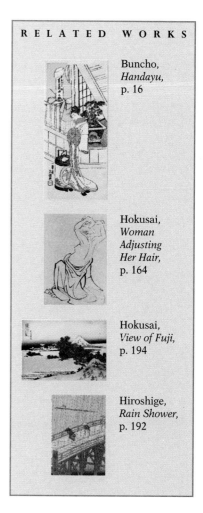

RELATED WORKS

Buncho,
Handayu,
p. 16

Hokusai,
Woman Adjusting Her Hair,
p. 164

Hokusai,
View of Fuji,
p. 194

Hiroshige,
Rain Shower,
p. 192

THE ARTS
OF THE AMERICAS

No one knows for sure when humans first occupied the double continent of the Americas or where those people came from. The most popular theory supposes that migrants from Asia crossed a now-submerged land bridge linking Siberia with Alaska, then gradually pushed southward, seeking hospitable places in which to dwell. Certainly, the Americas were populated—albeit in widely separated regions—by 7000 B.C.E.

By 3000 B.C.E, we can identify developed cultures in three important centers (map, below): the Northwest Coast of North America, the fertile plateaus and coastal lowlands of Mesoamerica, and along the Pacific Coast of South America. During the ensuing centuries several cultures in these territories (and others) created extremely rich and sophisticated artistic expressions. Their art has sometimes been called "pre-Columbian," referring to Columbus' voyages to the Americas, but this term no longer seems appropriate. Columbus, after all, never made landfall in any of the areas we shall discuss, and even if he had done so, it makes little sense to designate several long and splendid art traditions only as having come *before* one explorer's journeys.

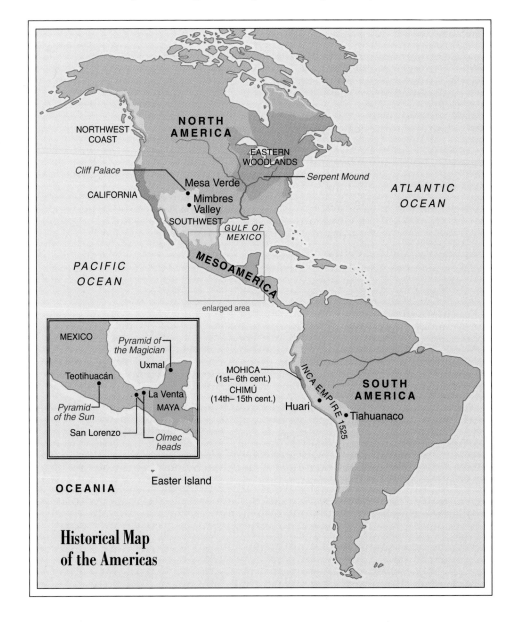

**Historical Map
of the Americas**

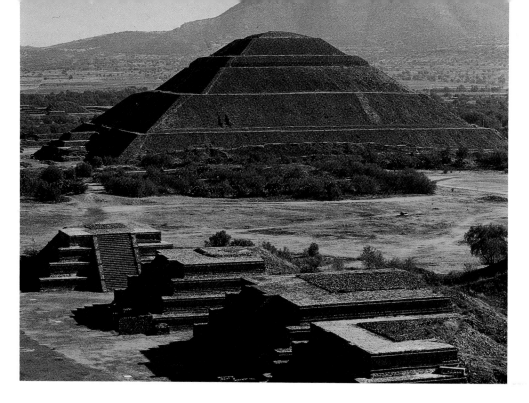

To be sure, the arrival of Europeans in the Americas, beginning with Columbus, effectively ended the flowering of native art styles in many parts of the Western Hemisphere. But let us not dwell on the ending. Let us rather look at the periods when these art styles arose and flourished. We take up the story in the geographic center of the hemisphere, in Mesoamerica.

590. Pyramid of the Sun, Teotihuacán, Mexico. 50–200 C.E.

MESOAMERICA

The term "Mesoamerica" refers to the territory of present-day Mexico, as well as the narrow strip of land joining the continents of North and South America. Earliest of the documented culture groups in the area was that of the Olmec, who occupied a region on the Gulf coast of Mexico for perhaps a thousand years, beginning about 1500 B.C.E. We saw two examples of their extraordinary art in Chapter 14 **(425,426)**.

Northwest of the Olmec lands, near present-day Mexico City, lie the remains of the greatest city in the ancient Americas: Teotihuacán. The center of a powerful empire, Teotihuacán was occupied from a few decades B.C.E. to about 600 of our calendar, so its period of dominion coincides almost exactly with that of the Roman Empire in Europe. Like Rome, Teotihuacán was a grand and efficient capital. At the height of the empire's power, its population may have numbered as many as a quarter million. The city covered 9 square miles and was laid out on a grid pattern, with streets crossing at right angles. Teotihuacán had many characteristics of a modern metropolis. Archaeologists have identified the elite sectors, where wealthier citizens lived in spacious square buildings, as well as the poorer districts far from the city's center, which housed the humbler workers in tiny rooms.

Towering over the city is the Pyramid of the Sun **(590)**, a massive stone and brick structure more than 200 feet high. The exact purpose of the pyramid is unknown. Certainly its nature was religious, and later cultures believed it was meant for worship of the sun (hence the name), but the specifics remain unclear. Excavations beneath the pyramid have revealed a natural cave, reached by a tunnel, directly under the pyramid's center. Perhaps the Teotihuacanos thought this hollow to be a kind of "cave-womb" from which their ancestors emerged, and that is why they built their pyramid on the spot.

While we know relatively little about the people who built and inhabited Teotihuacán, we know a great deal about their neighbors to the south and

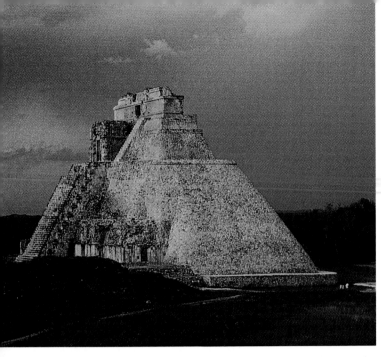

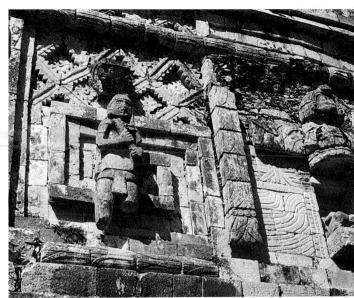

east—the Maya—because the latter group left extensive records to tell us about themselves. The Maya were based in the lower part of Mexico, especially the Yucatán peninsula, and in what is now Guatemala. They emerged as a culture by about 200 B.C.E., flourished during what is called the Classic Period (300–900), and did not really disband as a cultural entity until the Spanish conquest in the mid-16th century.

Unquestionably, the Maya had the most advanced and complex civilization in the ancient Americas. Like their counterparts in Europe, the Greeks and Romans, they excelled in many areas—science, engineering, architecture, painting and sculpture, writing. As was noted in Chapter 6, the Maya were fully literate, having developed a system of **hieroglyphs**, or pictorial symbols, that could record any word in their language. Although the Spanish invaders burned a great many Maya books, the few surviving ones, plus extensive stone inscriptions at Maya sites, have enabled modern scholars to learn much about the society.

The Maya religion was **polytheistic**, worshiping many gods, mostly nature gods—gods of wind and rain, stars and planets, animals and birds. Earthly rulers, who were usually male but occasionally female, identified closely with these gods, and both—rulers and gods—demanded human sacrifice. Part of the reason, no doubt, why we find the Maya so fascinating is the contrast between their rather bloodthirsty rituals and their superb intellectual and artistic achievements. The Maya excelled at mathematics and astronomy. During the Classic Period they devised a calendar more accurate than any that would come into use, anywhere on earth, for about a thousand years.

Among the most beautiful of Maya sites is Uxmal, in the northwest part of Yucatán (map, p. 522). At Uxmal can be found a cluster of magnificent stone buildings dominated by the Pyramid of the Magician (**591**). The pyramid (whose name is modern and probably inappropriate) rises from an elliptical base to a height of 84 feet. A graceful small temple at the summit is reached by two extremely steep flights of stairs—so steep that one wonders how the short-statured Maya managed to climb them at all, much less in dignified procession. The temple itself is richly ornamented with stone carvings, as is a nearby structure that has been dubbed the Nunnery (**592**) because of its rows of tiny cell-like rooms. Actually, the Nunnery most likely served as living quarters for priests who officiated at ceremonies in the pyramid-temple. Precisely what those ceremonies may have involved is unknown, but Maya inscriptions from many sources provide clear evidence that ritual bloodletting and the cutting out of human hearts played an important role in religious observance.

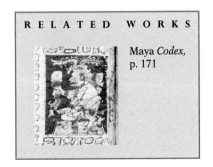

The Maya were also highly skilled ceramic artists. Especially noteworthy are the many clay figurines found on Jaina Island, off the coast of Yucatán not far from Uxmal. Jaina apparently was a cemetery for the Maya aristocracy, since the clay figures appear at burial sites. Our example depicts the *Fat God* **(593)**, a figure who turns up often in Jaina clay sculptures. Like many Jaina images, he is polychromed (many-colored) and elaborately decorated, with his feathered headdress, patterned robe, and much ornate jewelry. The god's features bear the stamp of individual personality. In fact, his scowl seems almost comical, and this effect may have been intended.

All in all, the ancient Mesoamerican civilizations endured for some three thousand years. During the same time span complex civilizations were evolving in what we now call South America, and these cultures, too, have left us artworks of the highest quality. This brief survey will focus on a few of them.

SOUTH AMERICA

The earliest known inhabitants of South America occupied a region along the Pacific coast, west of the Andes Mountains, principally in modern-day Peru (map, p. 522). Some experts believe the area was populated as early as 10,000 B.C.E., but to find well-documented cultures we must look much later.

Among the first of these cultures were the Mochica (or Moche), who flourished from about the year 1 of our era until about 600 C.E. The Mochica are renowned for their decorative arts—metalwork (in gold and silver), weaving, and especially pottery. Many consider them to have been the finest ceramists in the Western Hemisphere—if not in the world—at their time. We saw a splendid example in the stirrup vessel illustrated in Chapter 12.

Farther south and high in the mountains lie Huari and Tiahuanaco, which were flourishing settlements from the 6th through the 9th century. Their two cultures are often linked in discussion because Huari and Tiahuanaco artworks share many characteristics and motifs. The mosaic mirror illustrated here **(594)** is typical of the style. Mosaic is an art form that involves piecing together bits of material, usually stones or glass, to form a pattern or picture. In this case, however, the material is pyrite, a lustrous metallic min-

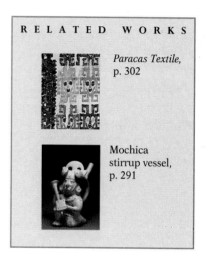
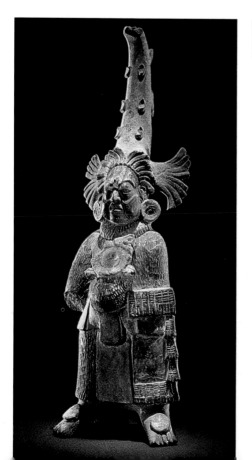

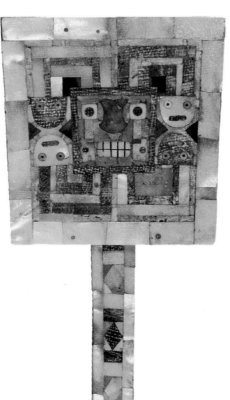

far left: 593. *The Fat God,*
figurine from Jaina Island,
Mexico. Maya,
Late Classic Period, c. 700–900.
Polychrome ceramic.

left: 594. Mosaic mirror,
from Huari-Tiahuanaco, Peru.
c. 500–800. Pyrites, turquoise,
and shell; height 9½″.
Dumbarton Oaks Research Library
Collections, Washington, D.C.

eral, and the arrangement is geometric. A central face, presumably a god, has highly abstract features—circle eyes, an almost cartoon nose, and mock-ferocious square teeth. On either side are paired abstract faces floating, disembodied, in hourglass shapes. If you did not know that this mirror is more than a thousand years old, you might easily mistake it for a modern piece, perhaps based on the imagery of Paul Klee (compare **538**). The subtle interplay of colors against the reflective surface makes this work a small gem.

The Chimú of coastal Peru, and the Inca who followed them, were master goldsmiths and metalsmiths. Abundant supplies of gold and silver in the region were wrought into jewelry, ceremonial vessels, and figurines. A *Figure of a Musician* **(595)** is believed to have come from a tomb at Chan Chan, the great city of the Chimú. This jaunty little statuette, lifelike down to its fingernails, shows the Chimú skill to excellent advantage.

Relatively few gold and silver pieces survive from the many thousands we know were made by ancient peoples, and the reason for this is a sad one. The precious metals that gave these cultures their wealth also caused their destruction. When expedition parties from Spain began arriving in what they called the New World in the early 16th century, their quest was for *plata y oro*, silver and gold. Having little or no appreciation for art styles so different from the ones they knew, the Spaniards shipped home vast quantities of fine works, to be melted down for the metal. The Spaniards had one commodity the native people lacked, and that was gunpowder. Within a surprisingly few years the local societies had been crushed, to be replaced by Spanish rule.

Descendants of the Maya, the Chimú, the Inca, and others still live today in the regions their ancestors once dominated. But their kingdoms and their empires are long gone.

NORTH AMERICA

It might be expected that those of us who live in North America would have a clearer picture of our own continent's art history than of that in other regions, since we are, after all, right here on the spot. Unfortunately, we do not. In general, the ancient arts of North America are much less available to us than

left: 595. *Figure of a Musician,* from Peru. Chimú, 14th–15th century. Silver and turquoise, height 8¼″. The Metropolitan Museum of Art, New York (The Michael C. Rockefeller Memorial Collection, gift of Nelson A. Rockefeller, 1969).

right: 596. *Head,* possibly representing an ancestral figure. Cole culture, Ohio, c. 600 C.E. Stone, height c. 6″. Ohio Historical Society, Columbus.

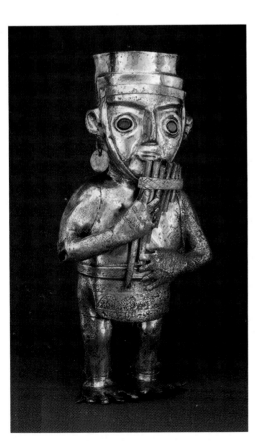

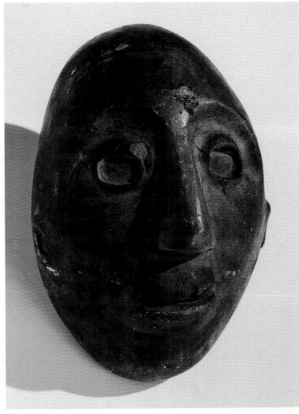

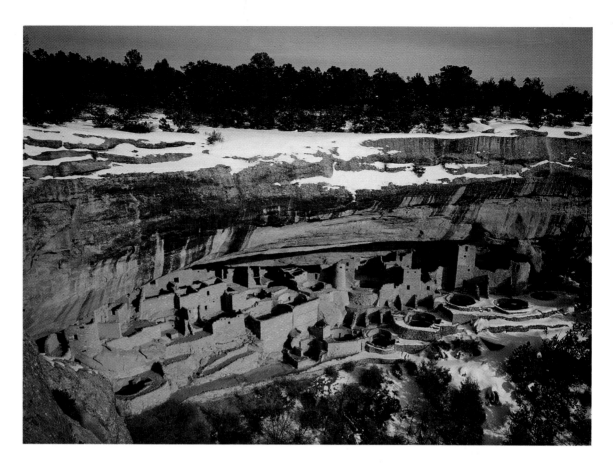

those of many other parts of the world. Partly this is because the early inhabitants seem to have made their artifacts from perishable materials, such as wood and fiber. Partly it is due to the absence of large, complex population centers. There was no great city even remotely equivalent to Teotihuacán in North America.

The first clearly identifiable culture group populated an area known as the Eastern Woodlands—in parts of what are now Ohio, Indiana, Kentucky, Pennsylvania, and West Virginia—starting about 700 B.C.E. Several cultures in the region are known collectively as the "mound builders," because they created earthworks, some of them burial mounds, in geometric forms or in the shapes of animals. The Serpent Mound in Ohio, which we saw in Chapter 11, is the most famous of the mounds still visible.

In the same general area of present-day Ohio, at the beginning of the 7th century, there lived a people known as the Cole culture, about whom very little is known. A marvelous stone *Head* **(596)** from a Cole burial site is thought to represent an ancestral figure. The face is stylized, especially in the jutting nose leading up to elegant eyebrow ridges and in the round, pupil-less eyes. Yet the sculptor of this tiny image had a gift for capturing a human likeness, for there is warmth and expressiveness on the face. The mouth almost seems ready to speak, to tell us, perhaps, about the history and ways of long-dead people.

Ancient North America may not have had cities, but in the southwest part of the United States can be found communal dwelling sites so ambitious that modern admirers have dubbed them "palaces." The Cliff Palace at Mesa Verde in Colorado **(597)** is one such structure. Mesa Verde was the home of a people called the Anasazi, who populated the region beginning several centuries B.C.E. Around the 12th century C.E. they began clustering their buildings in protected sites on the undersides of cliffs and making access to them quite difficult through a complex system of handholds and footholds. (Modern tourists have been provided an easier way in.) This arrangement allowed the Anasazi to ward off invaders and maintain a peaceful community life.

597. Cliff Palace,
Mesa Verde, Colo.
Anasazi culture, Pueblo Period,
c. 1200 C.E.

RELATED WORKS

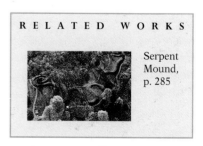

Serpent Mound, p. 285

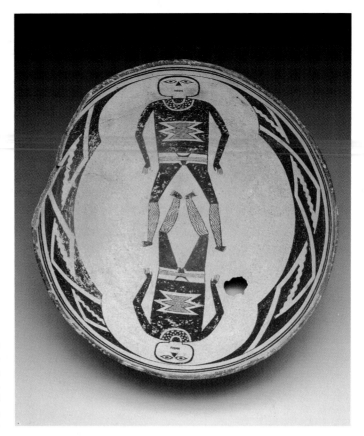

598.
Bowl with Two Human Figures,
Mimbres. 1000–1150 C.E.
Ceramic, diameter 13″.
Dallas Museum of Art
(Foundation for the Arts Collection,
anonymous gift).

Cliff Palace, dated to about 1200 C.E., has more than two hundred rooms organized in apartment-house style, most of them living quarters but some at the back meant for storage. In addition, there are twenty-three *kivas*—large, round chambers, mostly underground and originally roofed, used for religious or other ceremonial purposes. The structures are of stone or adobe with timber, and so harmonious is the overall plan that many scholars believe a single architect must have been in charge. The Cliff Palace was occupied for about a hundred years. Early in the 14th century it was abandoned, for reasons that remain unclear.

The Anasazi's neighbors in the Southwest were a people whose culture is called the Mogollon. Mogollon tradition flourished in the Mimbres Valley of what is now New Mexico from about the 3d century into the 12th. Today we associate the word "Mimbres" with a certain type of ceramic vessel developed about 1000 C.E. and meant to be placed on graves. Mimbres jars and bowls were decorated with geometric designs or with stylized figures of animals, fish, insects, and humans. Often the images featured two paired figures— possibly symbolizing life and death **(598)**. A distinctive feature of this pottery is the "kill-hole," which was punched deliberately into each piece to allow the vessel's essence to join with the spirit of the deceased.

Far north of the Mimbres Valley, in a region bordering the Pacific Ocean, we find evidence of the oldest settlements in the Americas. An area called the Northwest Coast—comprising parts of Alaska, British Columbia (in modern Canada), and the state of Washington (map, p. 522)—gave rise to many sophisticated cultures with well-developed art styles. Unfortunately, many of these cultures' artifacts were made of wood, and the older ones have perished, so most surviving examples are fairly recent.

Masks played an important role in the religious-artistic traditions of Northwest cultures. We saw a splendid example in the Bella Coola mask shown in Chapter 12. A neighboring people, the Kwakiutl, produced the mask illustrated here **(599)**, which represents the female spirit Dzonokwa. Meant to

RELATED WORKS

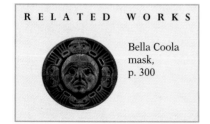

Bella Coola
mask,
p. 300

be used in the Ghost Dance, a ceremonial visit to the land of the dead, the mask of Dzonokwa shows her fierce and bloodthirsty side, especially in the scarlet-ringed mouth and wild hair. Dzonokwa was believed to roam the dark woods, snatching and eating babies. If pleased, however, she could bestow wealth on her favorites, so either way she was a force to be reckoned with.

Roughly contemporary with the two masks—that is, from the late 19th century—is a delightful little figure carved by the Tlingit people, who dwelt in the northernmost part of the Pacific Coast region. *Owl Man Perching on a Raven* (600) was made to commemorate the death of a certain man. His clan symbols were the owl and the raven, so both creatures are represented. The carving is fairly basic, but brilliant colors animate the image, and the stylized features of the face manage to be at once forceful and amusing. Real human hair provides a jaunty cap for the figure.

We know quite a bit about the Haida people, who occupied an island off the coast of Canada, thanks in part to an extremely talented wood carver named Charles Edenshaw. Edenshaw, the nephew of a great Haida chief, was both knowledgeable about his people's traditions and able, through his carving skill, to interpret and preserve those traditions. About 1901 he carved a wood model of the Myth House his uncle had built in the mid-19th century

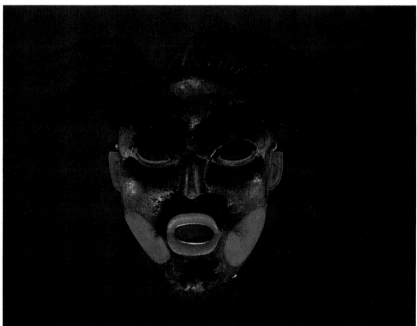

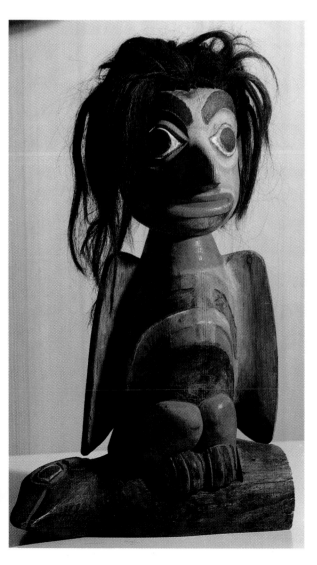

above: 599. Mask representing the female spirit Dzonokwa. Kwakiutl, before 1899. Wood, $11\frac{3}{4} \times 9\frac{1}{2}''$. American Museum of Natural History, New York.

left: 600. *Owl Man Perching on a Raven.* Tlingit, Yakutat, Alaska. After 1891. Painted wood, with human hair, height $17\frac{1}{2}''$. Portland Art Museum, Portland, Ore. (Rasmussen Collection of Northwest Indian Art).

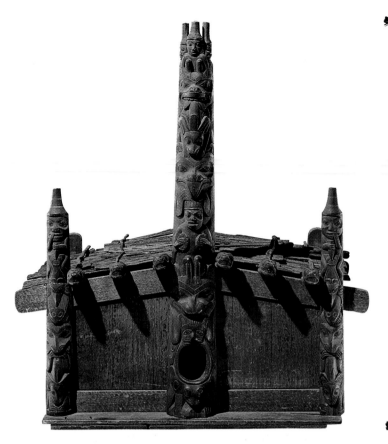

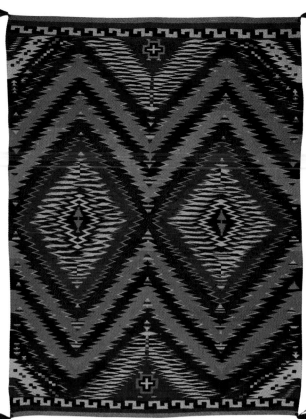

left: **601.** Charles Edenshaw.
*Chief Albert Edenshaw's
Myth House of Kiusta*, model.
Haida, c. 1901. Wood,
height of center pole 36⅛".
American Museum
of Natural History, New York.

right: **602.** *Eye-Dazzler Blanket.*
Navajo, c. 1890.
Wool and cotton, 6'2¾" × 4'8¾".
Dallas Museum of Art
(Textile Purchase Fund and gifts from
the Eugene McDermott Foundation,
Silas R. Mountsier III,
and anonymous donor).

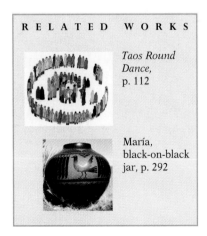

RELATED WORKS

*Taos Round
Dance,*
p. 112

*María,
black-on-black
jar,* p. 292

(601). Figures on the central pole depict the "lazy son-in-law" story, a complicated tale that can be told only in digest form here. When a certain woman accused her son-in-law of laziness, the man took revenge thus: He captured and killed a lake serpent, wore the serpent's skin to catch a huge number of fish, then deposited the fish outside his mother-in-law's house. The mother-in-law, thinking her own spiritual powers had attracted the fish, bragged publicly about this feat. When her son-in-law told her their true source, she died of shame. On the tall pole of the model, the mother-in-law is the seated figure with raised knees near the roofline, and the son-in-law appears, wearing the lake serpent's skin, second from top.

When Chief Edenshaw had completed the full-size original of his Myth House, the occasion called for a **potlatch,** a ritual feast unique to the Haida and some of their Northwest Coast neighbors. At a potlatch, the host would give to the invited guests not only quantities of food but also a substantial amount of his wealth and worldly goods. The guests were expected to reciprocate later by hosting potlatches and giving away *their* wealth to others. Because it was unthinkable to refuse the host's gifts, potlatches became an exercise in one-upmanship of generosity. Whoever gave away the most wealth acquired the highest prestige. Regrettably, this practice has died out.

The peoples of the Northwest Coast made numerous artworks in wood for the obvious reason that wood was plentiful in their territory. Far to the south, in the region of what is now the southwestern United States, forests are not so abundant. The native peoples of this area—the Navajo, Hopi, and others—made art from what they had, and their media included silver, clay, and fiber. We have already seen examples of silver and clay works in this book.

The Navajo in particular were (and are) expert weavers. Working with relatively simple looms, they turned out spectacular pieces like the *Eye-Dazzler Blanket* illustrated here **(602).** This title needs no explanation. The blanket all but pulsates with intricate zigzag patterns in the vivid colors of the Southwest desert landscape, especially the reds and oranges one might see when the setting sun bathes outcroppings of rock. No European-based precedents can account for this bold design. Its sophistication is original and, yes, dazzling.

AFRICA

The history of human civilization begins in Africa. Although experts squabble continually about dates, there is no serious disagreement that the first creatures who could truly be called human developed in Africa, then migrated north into Europe, spread through Asia, and eventually reached the Americas.

For art historians, Africa presents much the same problems as does North America. Most of the artifacts are of wood, and there are few written records to establish dates or define the iconography, few great cities to be excavated for their treasures. Chapter 14 touched upon the ancient kingdom of Nubia, which flourished in northeast Africa from about 3800 B.C.E. into the beginning of our common era. Between that time and the 19th century, relatively little concrete evidence has been discovered, and therefore the dates of most artworks illustrated in this section are vague or unknown.

The *Commemorative Head* illustrated here (603) comes from the Akan people who inhabited present-day Ghana in the 17th century. Such heads, of terra cotta, were sculpted by women as memorials to be placed on the graves of high-ranking people. They probably are not portraits, in the sense that they mimic the features of the departed, but rather are meant to capture the essence of the subject and to convey respect. This particular head is beautifully abstracted into a series of graceful curves—the pure oval of the face, the sweeping arc of the hairline, the more delicate curls of eyebrows and beard, the oval mouth, the rounded ears. A strong triangular nose punctuates the face and gives it character.

603. *Commemorative Head.*
Akan, Adansi Fomena (Ghana),
17th century (?).
Terra cotta, height 12″.
The Metropolitan Museum
of Art, New York
(The Michael C. Rockefeller
Memorial Collection, gift of
Nelson A. Rockefeller, 1964).

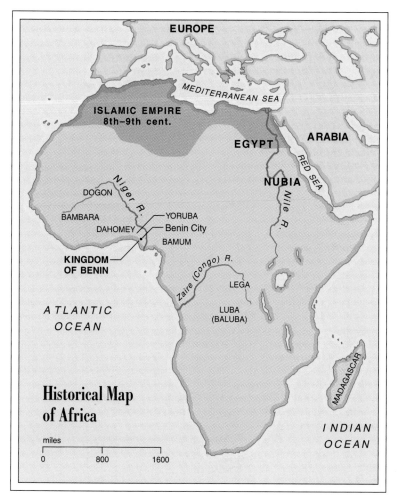

Historical Map of Africa

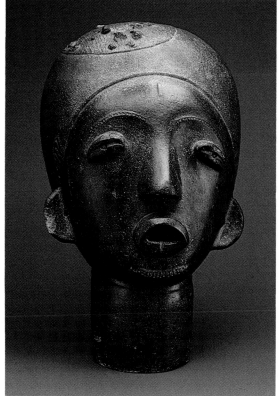

RELATED WORKS

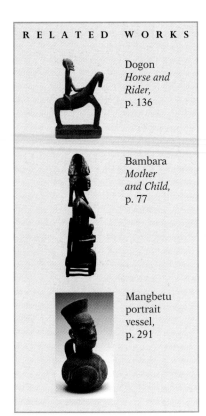

Dogon
*Horse and
Rider,*
p. 136

Bambara
*Mother
and Child,*
p. 77

Mangbetu
portrait
vessel,
p. 291

Earlier in this text we saw a little wood sculpture of a horse and rider from the Dogon people in what is now Mali, which displayed a fine mastery of asymmetrical balance. Here we consider another sculpture, also Dogon, carved in elegant symmetrical balance **(604)**. This double-figure piece depicts a woman and a man, perched side by side on a round stool, who may represent ancestor figures. The man's right arm encircles the woman and rests on her breast, while his left hand points to his own genitals. These gestures are understood to signify his role as protector and begetter, hers as mother and nurturer. The long tubular figures, with their exaggerated arms and torsos and their parallel tubular legs, are almost mirror images except for certain details—the man's jutting beard, the woman's earring and lip plug, her developed breasts. While the man's encircling arm has symbolic importance, it also serves the sculptor's compositional needs. It closes the square, giving a horizontal anchor near the top of the figures to balance the horizontal stool near the bottom.

A figure from the Luba people, who live in the area of modern Congo, shows a sensitive command of wood carving. *Kneeling Woman Presenting a Bowl* **(605)** is both stylized and warmly human. The Luba sculptor has made the head and hands far too large for the normal proportions of a body, indicating that the head and the act of holding the bowl are the most important

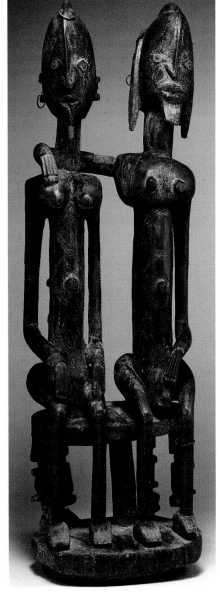

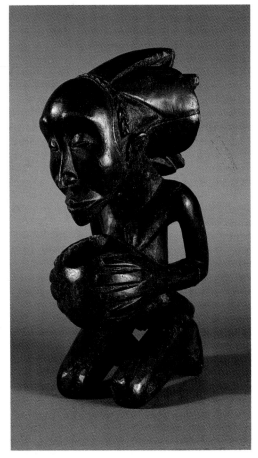

right: 604. *Seated Couple,*
Dogon, from Mali.
Wood and metal, height 29″.
The Metropolitan Museum
of Art, New York
(gift of Lester Wunderman, 1977).

far right: 605. *Kneeling Woman
Presenting a Bowl,*
Luba, from Congo (Zaire).
Wood, height 17⅛″.
© Africa-Museum, Tervuren, Belgium.

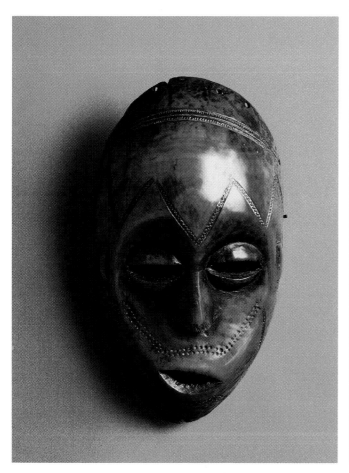

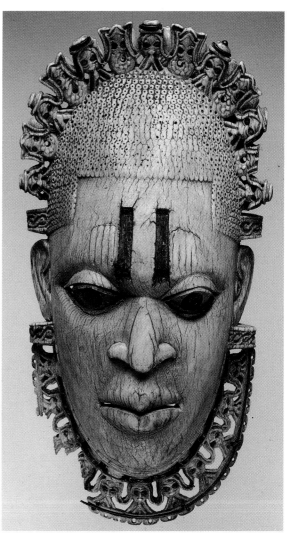

elements in the composition. This woman may have been an ancestor figure, and her elaborate headdress suggests high rank. Her expressive face is carved in what is called the "long-face" style.

Masks play an extremely important role in African tribal culture, being associated with the dance and with rituals connected to birth, puberty, death, and seasonal events. The example shown here **(606)**, from the region of Kinshasa in Congo, was carved from ivory. Like the Akan *Head* **(603)**, it is a pure oval with well-defined elliptical eyes and mouth, a strong jutting nose, and incised details. A zigzag line across the forehead highlights the smooth facial planes, and a high polish on the surface almost gives this mask the appearance of leather.

The best-preserved and best-documented artworks from Africa originate in the kingdom of Benin, which dominated the Niger River area of Nigeria from the 15th to the 18th century. In the late 15th century Benin was visited by traders and missionaries from Portugal, and the two nations established a more-or-less peaceful relationship that endured for some time. Portuguese references often show up in Benin art, as in an exquisite ivory mask from the 16th century **(607)**. The mask is quite small, meant to be worn not on the face but on a belt at the hip, and it probably represents a queen mother. Surrounding her face are tiny carved figures of mudfish and Portuguese men. Both symbolize the Benin king's dual nature as human and divine, because the mudfish can live on land and water, while the Portuguese came across water to bring wealth to Benin lands. The carving on the mask's face is unusually fine. We can read humanity and warmth in its serene expression.

left: 606. Mask, Lega, Congo-Kinshasa. 19th–20th century. Ivory, height 10½″. The Metropolitan Museum of Art, New York (The Michael C. Rockefeller Memorial Collection, gift of Nelson A. Rockefeller, 1969).

right: 607. *Pendant Mask*, Court of Benin. Early 16th century. Ivory, iron, and copper; height 9⅛″. The Metropolitan Museum of Art, New York (The Michael C. Rockefeller Memorial Collection, gift of Nelson A. Rockefeller, 1972).

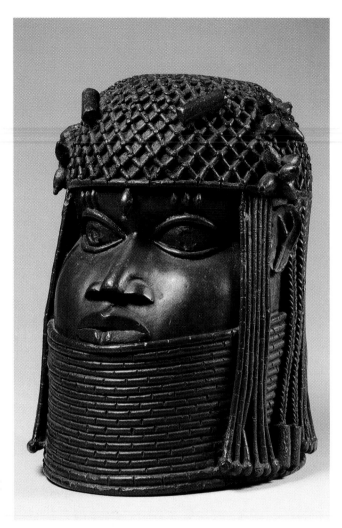

608. *Head*, Court of Benin, Bini culture, Nigeria. c. 1550–1680. Brass, height 10¾″. The Metropolitan Museum of Art, New York (The Michael C. Rockefeller Memorial Collection, gift of Nelson A. Rockefeller, 1979).

RELATED WORKS

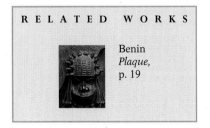

Benin *Plaque,* p. 19

Benin artists worked in many media, but they are especially famed for their mastery of metal casting, in bronze and brass, using the lost-wax method (Chapter 11). We saw a superb example of Benin metalwork in the complex figural plaque in Chapter 2. Among the most striking of Benin sculptures are the royal heads, representing kings and queens. The illustration (608) is a king, wearing a high bead collar and a beaded crown. The face is generally naturalistic except for the oversize eyes, which are a feature of this style. Heads like this one were placed on altars to commemorate past *obas*, or kings, and to pay tribute to their achievements. They were not meant to duplicate the features of any particular king but rather celebrate the general condition of kingliness. It is believed that only the head was included and not a complete figure, because the head is the center of life, power, and intelligence.

The kingdom of Dahomey, lying west of Benin lands in the region of present-day Ivory Coast and Ghana, was established early in the 17th century. Typical Dahomean artworks include wood carvings that have been *cladded*, or coated, with metal sheeting. A *Lion* from the treasure of King Gbehanzin (609) has sheet silver closely hammered to the wood form and is studded with silver nails. The fierce lion, with its sharp teeth, represents the power of kingship.

Wood and metal are also combined in a superb mask from the Bamum people of Cameroon (610). This image's features, while stylized, are more naturalistic than those of many other African artworks. The protruding ears and upturned mouth give it a celebratory appearance, and the modeling of the face seems almost to create a portrait. A colorful and festive part-oval head-dress mirrors the oval of the face.

For the last illustration in this survey of African art, we turn to an art form that comes from the earth itself—the art of *bogolanfini*, or mud-dyeing of fabrics. Practiced for centuries by Bamana women is what is now Mali, mud-dyeing is a painstaking process in which iron-rich, near-black mud is applied freehand with wooden sticks to a prepared cloth. Traditional motifs are abstract and geometric (611), creating an intricate black-and-white pattern on the fabric. Unlike most of the art forms discussed in this section—and, for that matter, most styles presented in this chapter—*bogolanfini* has not withdrawn into the closed world of museum exhibition. Skilled artisans at work in Mali today are keeping the tradition alive.

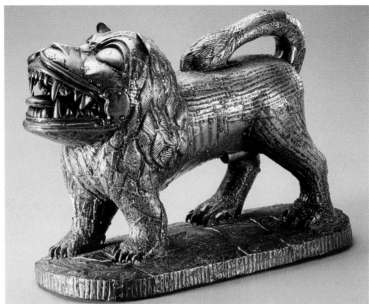

left: 609. *Lion,* from the treasure of King Gbehanzin of Dahomey. 18th–19th century. Wood with silver sheet, length 17¾". Dapper Museum, Paris.

below left: 610. Mask, Bamum, from Cameroon. Wood, copper, and other materials; height 26". The Metropolitan Museum of Art, New York (The Michael C. Rockefeller Memorial Collection, gift of Nelson A. Rockefeller, 1969).

below: 611. Nakunte Diarra. *Display Cloth, tapis.* 1992. Mud-dyed cloth, 6'1½" × 4'7". Indiana University Art Museum, Bloomington.

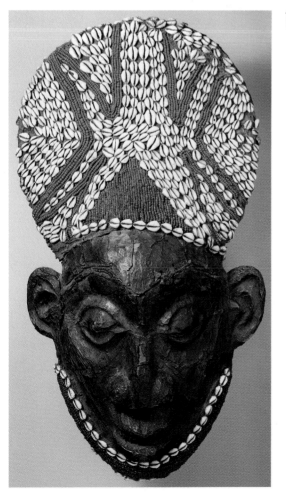

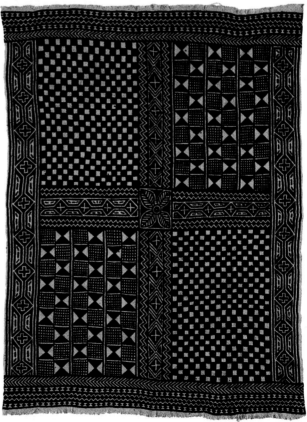

OCEANIA

To find the last culture area in this survey, and the last illustration in this book, we travel to a tiny island in the South Pacific Ocean, thousands of miles from any major land mass. A Dutch expedition landed there on Easter day in 1722 and called it Easter Island, but the natives had their own name: *Te-Pito-o-te-Henua*, which means "The Navel-of-the-World" (map, p. 522).

Easter Island would probably be no more interesting than any other speck in the vast ocean, except for one remarkable circumstance. On the island are hundreds of huge figures, carved from stone and weighing as much as 90 tons apiece **(612)**. The faces are distinctive, with strongly jutting noses, prominent brow lines, and long ears. Originally each was capped with a red-stone topknot several feet high, but these have been toppled off. Who carved these images? And when? And why? All these questions remain unanswered. Nor do we know why, after such a colossal effort went into their creation, these giants were knocked over and their headdresses scattered around the island. Archaeological work continues, and some of the statues have been restored to their earlier positions, but it is doubtful that all the mysteries of Easter Island will ever be explained.

The Easter Island figures make a fitting conclusion to this book. At the very beginning of Chapter 1 we stated the book's underlying premise: that everybody lives with art, and that art is inextricably connected to human existence. Now, more than five hundred pages later, we have explored through the centuries and the continents, we have visited the cities and towns and open lands. At every time, in every place, we have found works that we can properly call art—works made for aesthetic expression. We end up on a tiny island in the middle of a vast ocean, and here as well the premise holds true. Even in a place as remote as Easter Island, even in the "navel of the world," long-ago people were living with art.

612. Stone figures, Easter Island. 15th century or earlier.

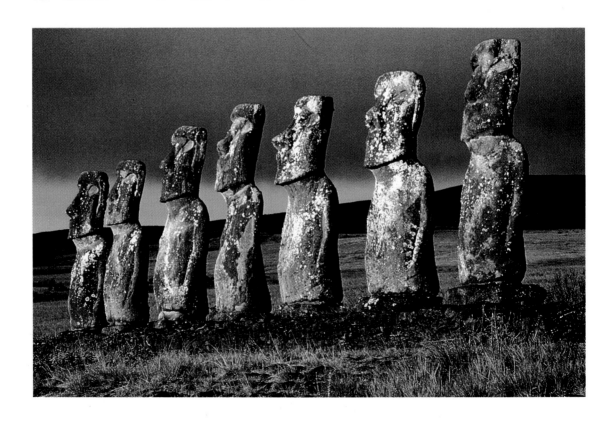

PRONUNCIATION GUIDE

This guide is meant to provide the reader with an acceptable pronunciation for names and other words that may be unfamiliar to native speakers of English. It is not perfect. It ignores the nasal sounds of the French *en, in, ain,* as well as the guttural German consonants, giving instead the nearest English equivalents. These sounds are difficult to render phonetically and difficult to pronounce for those who have not studied the languages. But no reader should be embarrassed by using these pronunciations.

In many cases there are two or more pronunciations for a particular artist's name, both or all of which are in common use and considered "correct." The pronunciations in this guide are those most often heard among English-speaking North Americans, and a few alternates have been provided. Some instructors may prefer variant pronunciations of certain artists' names; these may be equally correct but inadvertently omitted from the list.

The phonetic system employed for this guide is meant to be as simple as possible. Its conventions include those listed in the margin.

an—plan, tan
ay—play, day, stay
ah—spa, hurrah
eh—pet, get
er—her, fur
oh—toe, show, go
ohn—phone, moan
ow—cow, how
uh—bus, fuss
ye—pie, sky

Abakanowicz, Magdalena   mahg-dah-LAY-nuh ah-bah-kah-NOH-vich
Angkor Wat   ANG-kohr WAHT, or ANG-kohr VAHT
Akhenaten   ah-keh-NAH-ten
Anguissola, Sofonisba   soh-foh-NEES-bah ahn-gwee-SOH-lah
Aphrodite   aph-roh-DYE-tee
Arcimboldo, Giuseppe   jyoo-SAY-pee ahr-cheem-BOHL-doh
auteur   oh-TER
Avalokiteśvara   AH-vah-loh-kih-TESH-vahr-uh
Baldovinetti, Alesso   ah-LESS-oh bal-doh-veen-ETT-ee
Balla, Giacomo   JAH-koh-moh BAH-lah
Baselitz, Georg   GAY-ohrg BAZ-eh-litz
bas-relief   BAH   ree-leef
Bellini, Giovanni   jyoh-VAHN-ee bell-EE-nee
Benin   beh-NEEN
Bernini, Gianlorenzo   jahn-loh-REN-zoh bayr-NEE-nee
bodhisattva   boh-dih-SAHT-vuh
Bonheur, Rosa   buhn-ER
Bosch, Hieronymus   heer-AHN-ih-mus BOSH
Botticelli, Sandro   SAN-droh boht-ee-CHEL-ee
Boucher, François   frahn-SWAH boo-SHAY
Brancusi, Constantin   KAHN-stan-teen BRAHN-koosh (more often in the U.S.: brahn-KOO-see)
Braque, Georges   zhorzh BRAHK
Bruegel, Pieter   PEE-tur BROO-g'l (often: BROY-g'l)
camera obscura   KAM-er-uh ob-SKOOR-uh
Campin, Robert   roh-BAYR kahn-PAN
Caravaggio   kah-rah-VAH-jyoh
Cellini, Benvenuto   ben-ven-OO-toh chel-EE-nee
Cézanne, Paul   POHL say-ZAN
Chardin, Jean Baptiste Siméon   zhahn ba-TEEST see-may-OHN shar-DAN
Chartres   SHAR-tr'
Chauvet cave   shoh-VAY
Chia, Sandro   SAN-droh KEE-ah
chiaroscuro   kee-ah-roh-SKOOR-oh

Cimabue   chee-mah-BOO-ay
cire perdue   seer payr-DOO
contrapposto   kohn-trah-POH-stoh
Copley, John Singleton   KOP-lee
Courbet, Gustave   goos-TAHV koor-BAY
Daguerre, Louis Jacques Mandé   loo-ee ZHAHK man-DAY dah-GAYR
Dahomey   deh-HOH-mee
Dali, Salvador   sal-vah-DOHR DAH-lee, or dah-LEE
Daumier, Honoré   ohn-ohr-AY dohm-YAY
David, Jacques Louis   zhahk loo-EE dah-VEED
Degas, Edgar   ed-GAHR deh-GAH
de Kooning, Willem   VILL-um duh KOON-ing
Delacroix, Eugène   uh-ZHAYN duh-lah-KRWAH
Delaunay, Sonia   SOHN-yuh deh-loh-NAY
Derain, André   ahn-DRAY deh-RAN
Donatello   dohn-ah-TELL-oh
Dubuffet, Jean   zhahn dyu-boo-FAY
Duccio   DOO-chyo
Duchamp, Marcel   mahr-SELL doo-SHAHN
Dufy, Raoul   rah-OOL dyu-FEE
Dürer, Albrecht   AHL-brekht DOOR-er
Eakins, Thomas   AY-kins
Fabergé, Peter Carl   fab-er-ZHAY
Fauve   fohv
Frankenthaler, Helen   FRANK-en-thahl-er
Gaudí, Antoni   ahn-TOH-nee gow-DEE
Gauguin, Paul   POHL goh-GAN
Genji Monogatari   GEHN-jee mohn-oh-geh-TAHR-ee
Gentileschi, Artemisia   ahr-tuh-MEE-zhyuh jen-till-ESS-kee
Géricault, Théodore   tay-oh-DOHR zheh-ree-COH
Ghiberti, Lorenzo   loh-REN-zoh ghee-BAYR-tee
Giacometti, Alberto   ahl-BAYR-toh jah-coh-MET-ee
Giorgione   johr-JYOHN-ay
Giotto   JYOH-toh
gouache   gwahsh
Goya, Francisco de   frahn-SISS-coh day GOY-ah (in Spain: frahn-THEES-coh)
Grünewald, Matthias   mah-TEE-ess GROON-eh-vahlt
Guanyin   gwahn-YEEN

537

haut-relief   OH   ree-leef
Heiji Monogatari   HAY-jee   mohn-oh-geh-TAHR-ee
Hiroshige, Ando   AHN-doh   heer-oh-SHEE-gay
Hokusai, Katsushika   kat-s'-SHEE-kah   HOH-k'-sye
Holbein, Hans   HAHNS   HOHL-byne
Houdon, Jean Antoine   zhahn   ahn-TWAHN
   oo-DOHN
Huari   HWAHR-ee
Inca   ING-keh
Ingres, Jean Auguste Dominique   zhahn
   oh-GOOST   dohm-een-EEK   AN-gr'
intaglio   in-TAHL-yoh   (sometimes anglicized to
   in-TAG-lee-oh)
Kandinsky, Wassily   vah-SEE-lee   kan-DIN-skee
Kirchner, Ernst Ludwig   AYRNST   LOOT-vik
   KEERSH-nur
Klee, Paul   KLAY
Klimt, Gustav   goos-TAHV   KLEEMT
Knossos   KNAH-sohs
Kokoschka, Oskar   koh-KOHSH-kah
Kollwitz, Käthe   KAY-tuh   KOHL-vitz
Korin, Ogata   oh-GAH-tah   KOHR-een
Kupka, František   frahn-TEE-shek   KOOP-kuh
Lachaise, Gaston   gas-TOHN   lah-SHEHZ
Laocoön   lay-AH-coh-un
Lascaux   las-COH
Laurencin, Marie   lohr-ahn-SAN
Lautrec, Henri de Toulouse-   ahn-REE   deh
   too-LOOS   loh-TREK
Léger, Fernand   fayr-NAHN   lay-ZHAY
Leonardo da Vinci   lay-oh-NAHR-doh   dah
   VEEN-chee   (often in U.S.: lee-oh-NAHR-doh)
Leyster, Judith   YOO-dit   LYE-stur
Limbourg   lam-BOOR
Magritte, René   reh-NAY   ma-GREET
Manet, Edouard   ayd-WAHR   ma-NAY
Mantegna, Andrea   ahn-DRAY-uh   mahn-TAYN-yah
Mapplethorpe, Robert   MAY-p'l-thorp
Marisol   mah-ree-SOHL
Masaccio   mah-ZAH-chyoh
Matisse, Henri   ahn-REE   ma-TEES
Maya   MAH-yah
Mesa Verde   MAY-suh   VAYR-day
mezzotint   MET-zoh-tint
Michelangelo   mye-kel-AN-jel-oh,
   or mee-kel-AN-jel-oh
Mies van der Rohe, Ludwig   LOOT-fik   mees   van
   der   ROH-eh
Mimbres   MIM-bres
Miró, Joan   HWAHN   meer-OH
Mochica   moh-CHEE-kuh
Modersohn-Becker, Paula   MOH-der-zun   BEK-er
Modigliani, Amedeo   ahm-ay-DAY-oh
   moh-deel-YAHN-ee
Moghal   MOH-g'l
Mondrian, Piet   PEET   MOHN-dree-ahn
Monet, Claude   CLOWD   moh-NAY
Morisot, Berthe   BAYR-t'   mohr-ee-ZOH
Munch, Edvard   ED-vahrd   MOONK
Muybridge, Eadweard   ED-werd   MY-bridj
Mycenae   my-SEEN-ay, or my-SEEN-ee
Olmec   OHL-mek

Piero della Francesca   PYAYR-oh   DEL-lah
   fran-CHESS-kuh
pointillism   PWAN-teel-izm   (sometimes anglicized
   to POYN-till-izm)
Pollock, Jackson   PAHL-uck
Polyclitus   pahl-ee-KLY-tus
Pompeii   pahm-PAY, or pohm-PAY
Pont du Gard   pohn   dyu   GAHR
Poussin, Nicolas   nee-coh-LAH   poo-SAN
Praxiteles   prak-SIT-uh-leez
Qiu Ying   chyoo-YING
Raphael   RAFF-yell, or RAF-fye-ell, or raf-fye-ELL
Rauschenberg, Robert   ROW-shen-burg
Redon, Odilon   oh-deel-OHN   reh-DOHN
Ren Xia   rehn   SHAH
Renoir, Pierre-Auguste   pyayr   oh-GOOST
   rehn-WAHR
repoussé   reh-poo-SAY
Rigaud, Hyacinthe   ee-ah-SANT   ree-GOH
Rococo   roh-coh-COH
Rodin, Auguste   oh-GOOST   roh-DAN
Rogier van der Weyden   roh-JEER   van   dur
   VYE-den
Rousseau, Henri (le Douanier)   ahn-REE   roo-SOH
   (luh   dwahn-YAY)
St. Sernin   san   sayr-NAN
San Vitale   san   vee-TAHL-ay
Sesshu   SESS-yoo
Seurat, Georges   zhorzh   syoo-RAH
Siqueiros, David Alfaro   see-KAYR-ohs
Sotatsu, Nonomura   noh-noh-MOOR-ah
   SOH-taht-s'
Stieglitz, Alfred   STEEG-litz
Taj Mahal   tahzh   meh-HAHL
Teniers, David, the Younger   ten-EERZ, or TEN-yerz
Teotihuacán   tay-OH-tee-hwah-CAHN
Tiahuanaco   tee-ah-hwah-NAH-coh
Titian   TISH-an, or TEE-shan
Todai-ji   toh-DYE-jee
trompe-l'oeil   trump-LOY
Tutankhamun   toot-an-KAH-mun
Uxmal   oosh-MAHL
Van Eyck, Jan   YAHN   van   IKE
Van Gogh, Vincent   van   GOH   (in the U.S.; the
   Dutch pronunciation is nearly impossible to render
   phonetically for English speakers)
Van Ruisdael, Jacob   YAH-cub   van   ROYS-dahl
Vasari, Giorgio   JOHR-jyoh   va-SAHR-ee
Velázquez, Diego   DYAY-goh   vay-LASS-kess
   (usually in the U.S.; in Spain, vay-LATH-keth)
Vermeer, Jan   YAHN   vayr-MEER, or vayr-MAYR
Verrocchio, Andrea del   ahn-DRAY-uh   del
   vayr-OHK-yoh
Versailles   vayr-SYE
Vigée-Lebrun, Elisabeth   ay-leez-eh-BETT
   vee-ZHAY   leh-BRUN
Watteau, Antoine   ahn-TWAHN   wah-TOH,
   or vah-TOH
Willendorf   VILL-en-dohrf
Yucatán   yoo-cuh-TAN
Zaire   zye-EER
Zhou Dynasty   ZHOH

BIBLIOGRAPHY AND SUGGESTED READINGS

GENERAL REFERENCES

Beardsley, John, and Jane Livingston. *Hispanic Art in the United States*. New York: Abbeville Press, 1987.

Chadwick, Whitney. *Women, Art, and Society*. London: Thames and Hudson, 1990.

Cummings, Paul. *Artists in Their Own Words*. New York: St. Martin's, 1982.

Fleming, William. *Arts & Ideas*, 9th ed. Fort Worth, Tex.: Harcourt Brace, 1995.

Goldwater, Robert, and Marco Treves, eds. *Artists on Art: From the Fourteenth to the Twentieth Century*. New York: Pantheon, 1974.

Gombrich, E. H. *The Story of Art*, 16th ed. Englewood Cliffs, N.J.: Prentice-Hall, 1996.

Harris, Ann Sutherland, and Linda Nochlin. *Women Artists: 1550–1950*. New York: Knopf, 1977.

Heller, Nancy G. *Women Artists: An Illustrated History*. New York: Abbeville, 1987.

Honour, Hugh, and John Fleming. *The Visual Arts: A History*, 4th ed. Englewood Cliffs, N.J.: Prentice-Hall, 1996.

Janson, H. W. *History of Art*, 5th ed. rev. by Anthony Janson. Englewood Cliffs, N.J.: Prentice-Hall, 1996.

Jones, Lois Swan. *Art Information: Research Methods and Resources*, 3d ed. Dubuque, Iowa: Kendall/Hunt, 1990.

Kleiner, Fred S., Richard G. Tansey, and Diane Kirkpatrick. *Gardner's Art Through the Ages*, 10th ed. Fort Worth, Tex.: Harcourt Brace, 1996.

Lee, Sherman. *A History of Far Eastern Art*, 5th ed. Englewood Cliffs, N.J.: Prentice-Hall, 1993.

Piper, David, ed. *Random House Library of Painting and Sculpture*, 4 vols. New York: Random House, 1981.

Stangos, Nikos. *The Thames and Hudson Dictionary of Art and Artists*, rev. ed. New York: Thames and Hudson, 1994.

Stokstad, Marilyn, et al. *Art History*. New York: Abrams, 1995.

CHAPTER ONE
LIVING WITH ART

CHAPTER TWO
WHAT IS ART?

Arnheim, Rudolf. *Visual Thinking*. Berkeley: University of California Press, 1980.

Four Americans in Paris: The Collections of Gertrude Stein and Her Family. New York: Museum of Modern Art, 1970.

Hammacher, A. M., and Renilde Hammacher. *Van Gogh: A Documentary Biography*. New York: Macmillan, 1982.

Lipman, Jean, and Tom Armstrong, eds. *American Folk Painters of Three Centuries*. New York: Hudson Hills and Whitney Museum of American Art, 1980.

Mendelowitz, Daniel M. *Children Are Artists*. Stanford, Calif.: Stanford University Press, 1963.

Nelson, George. *How To See: A Guide to Reaching Our Manmade Environments*. Boston: Little, Brown, 1979.

Sonnenburg, Hubert von, et al. *Rembrandt/Not Rembrandt*. New York: Metropolitan Museum of Art, 1995.

CHAPTER THREE
THEMES AND PURPOSES OF ART

Bloemink, Barbara J. *The Life and Art of Florine Stettheimer*. New Haven, Conn.: Yale University Press, 1995.

Bradley, William. *Art: Magic, Impulse, and Control: A Guide to Viewing*. Englewood Cliffs, N.J.: Prentice-Hall, 1973.

Clark, Kenneth M. *Civilization: A Personal View*. New York: Harper & Row, 1970.

Elsen, Albert E. *Purposes of Art*, 4th ed. New York: Holt, Rinehart and Winston, 1981.

Lisle, Laurie. *Portrait of an Artist: Georgia O'Keeffe*. New York: Seaview Books, 1980.

CHAPTER FOUR
THE VISUAL ELEMENTS

CHAPTER FIVE
PRINCIPLES OF DESIGN IN ART

Albers, Josef. *Interaction of Color*, rev. ed. New Haven, Conn.: Yale University Press, 1975.

Boase, T. S. R. *Giorgio Vasari: The Man and the Book*. Princeton, N.J.: Princeton University Press, 1979.

Frayling, Christopher, Helen Frayling, and Ron van der Meer. *The Art Pack*. New York: Knopf, 1992.

Itten, Johannes. *The Art of Color*. New York: Van Nostrand Reinhold, 1973.

———. *Design and Form: The Basic Course at the Bauhaus and Later*. New York: Van Nostrand Reinhold, 1975.

Kettenmann, Andrea. *Frida Kahlo: Pain and Passion*. Cologne: Taschen, 1992.

Lauer, David. *Design Basics*, 3d ed. Fort Worth, Tex.: Harcourt Brace, 1990.

CHAPTER SIX
DRAWING

Betti, Claudia, and Teel Sale. *Drawing: A Contemporary Approach*, 3d ed. Fort Worth, Tex.: Harcourt Brace, 1992.

Chaet, Bernard. *The Art of Drawing*, 2nd ed. New York: Holt, Rinehart and Winston, 1983.

Edwards, Betty. *Drawing on the Right Side of the Brain*, rev. ed. Los Angeles: Tarcher, 1989.

Gill, Robert W. *Basic Perspective*. London: Thames and Hudson, 1980.

Goldstein, Nathan. *The Art of Responsive Drawing*, 4th ed. Englewood Cliffs, N.J.: Prentice-Hall, 1991.

Mendelowitz, Daniel M., and Duane Wakeham. *A Guide to Drawing*, 4th ed. Fort Worth, Tex.: Harcourt Brace, 1988.

Nicolaides, Kimon. *The Natural Way to Draw*. Boston: Houghton Mifflin, 1975.

CHAPTER SEVEN
PAINTING

Chaet, Bernard. *An Artist's Notebook: Techniques and Materials.* New York: Holt, Rinehart and Winston, 1979.

Cockcroft, Eva, John Weber, and James Cockcroft. *Toward a People's Art: A Contemporary Mural Movement.* New York: Irvington, 1987.

Goldstein, Nathan. *Painting: Visual and Technical Fundamentals.* Englewood Cliffs, N.J.: Prentice-Hall, 1979.

Hills, Patricia. *Alice Neel.* New York: Abrams, 1983.

Hoopes, Donelson F. *Winslow Homer Watercolors.* New York: Watson-Guptill, 1976.

Mayer, Ralph. *The Artist's Handbook of Materials and Techniques,* 5th ed. New York: Viking, 1991.

Wheat, Ellen Harkins. *Jacob Lawrence: American Painter.* Seattle: Seattle Art Museum, 1986.

CHAPTER EIGHT
PRINTS

Fine, Ruth E., and Mary Lee Corlett. *Graphicstudio.* Washington, D.C.: National Gallery of Art, 1991.

Mayor, A. Hyatt. *Prints and People.* Princeton, N.J.: Princeton University Press, 1980.

McShine, Kynaston, ed. *Andy Warhol: A Retrospective.* New York: Museum of Modern Art, 1989.

Peterdi, Gabor. *Printmaking.* New York: Macmillan, 1986.

Pratt, John Lowell, ed. *Currier and Ives: Chronicles of America.* Maplewood, N.J.: Hammond, 1968.

Rauschenberg, Robert. *An Interview with Robert Rauschenberg by Barbara Rose.* New York: Elizabeth Avedon Editions, 1987.

Saff, Donald, and Deli Sacilotto. *Printmaking: History and Process.* New York: Holt, Rinehart and Winston, 1978.

CHAPTER NINE
THE CAMERA ARTS

Bernard, Bruce. *Photodiscovery: Masterworks of Photography 1840–1940.* New York: Abrams, 1980.

Ewing, William E. *Breaking Bounds: The Dance Photography of Lois Greenfield.* San Francisco: Chronicle, 1992.

Gutman, Judith Mara. *Through Indian Eyes.* New York: Oxford University Press, 1982.

David Hockney: A Retrospective. Los Angeles: Los Angeles County Museum of Art, 1988.

Horan, James D. *Mathew Brady: Historian with a Camera.* New York: Bonanza, 1955.

Kirkland, Douglas. *Icons: Creativity with Camera and Computer.* San Francisco: Collins, 1993.

Livingston, Jane. *Lee Miller: Photographer.* New York: The California/International Arts Foundation, 1989.

London, Barbara, with John Upton. *Photography,* 5th ed. New York: Harper/Collins, 1993.

Newhall, Beaumont, and Nancy Newhall, eds. *Masters of Photography.* New York: A & W, 1983.

Shipman, David. *The Story of Cinema.* New York: St. Martin's Press, 1986.

Spoto, Donald. *The Dark Side of Genius: The Life of Alfred Hitchcock.* Boston: Little, Brown, 1983.

Szarkowski, John. *Looking at Photographs: One Hundred Pictures from the Collection of the Museum of Modern Art.* New York: Museum of Modern Art, 1973.

CHAPTER TEN
GRAPHIC DESIGN

Buechner, Thomas S. *Norman Rockwell: A Sixty Year Retrospective.* New York: Abrams, 1972.

Glaser, Milton. *Graphic Design.* Woodstock, N.Y.: Overlook, 1983.

Heller, Steven, ed. *Innovators of American Illustration.* New York: Van Nostrand Reinhold, 1986.

Lupton, Ellen. *Mixing Messages: Graphic Design in Contemporary Culture.* New York: Cooper-Hewitt National Design Museum, 1996.

CHAPTER ELEVEN
SCULPTURE

Beardsley, John. *A Landscape for Modern Sculpture: Storm King Art Center.* New York: Abbeville, 1985.

———. *Earthworks and Beyond.* New York: Abbeville, 1989.

Gray, Cleve, ed. *David Smith by David Smith.* New York: Holt, Rinehart and Winston, 1968.

Kaprow, Allan. *Assemblage, Environments and Happenings.* New York: Abrams, 1966.

CHAPTER TWELVE
CRAFTS

Charleston, Robert J., ed. *World Ceramics.* Avenal, N.J.: Outlet, 1991.

Nelson, Glenn C. *Ceramics: A Potter's Handbook,* 5th ed. New York: Holt, Rinehart and Winston, 1984.

Nordness, Lee. *Object U.S.A.* New York: Viking, 1970.

Waller, Irene. *Textile Sculptures.* London: Studio Vista, 1977.

CHAPTER THIRTEEN
ARCHITECTURE

Bennett, Corwin. *Spaces for People: Human Factors in Design.* Englewood Cliffs, N.J.: Prentice-Hall, 1977.

Boutelle, Sara. *Julia Morgan, Architect.* New York: Abbeville, 1988.

Dunlop, Beth. *Building a Dream: The Art of Disney Architecture.* New York: Abrams, 1996.

Fuller, R. Buckminster, and Robert W. Marks. *The Dymaxion World of R. Buckminster Fuller.* New York: Reinhold, 1960.

Hitchcock, Henry Russell. *In the Nature of Materials: The Buildings of Frank Lloyd Wright, 1887–1941.* New York: Da Capo, 1975.

Mehrabian, Albert. *Public Places and Private Spaces: The Psychology of Work, Play and Living Environments.* New York: Basic Books, 1980.

Rudofsky, Bernard. *Streets for People: A Primer for Americans.* New York: Doubleday, 1969.

Safdie, Moshe. *Form and Purpose: Is the Emperor Naked?* Boston: Houghton Mifflin, 1982.

CHAPTER FOURTEEN
THE ANCIENT WORLD

Arnold, Dorothea. *The Royal Women of Amarna: Images of Beauty from Ancient Egypt.* New York: Metropolitan Museum of Art, 1996.

Chauvet, Jean-Marie, et al. *Dawn of Art: The Chauvet Cave.* New York: Abrams, 1996.

Edwards, I.E.S. *Tutankhamun: His Tomb and Its Treasures.* New York: Metropolitan Museum of Art, 1977.

Hawkins, Gerald S. *Stonehenge Decoded.* New York: Delta, 1965.

Strouhal, Eugen. *Life of the Ancient Egyptians.* Norman, Okla.: University of Oklahoma Press, 1992.

CHAPTER FIFTEEN
GREECE AND ROME

Boardman, John. *The Parthenon and Its Sculptures.* Austin, Tex.: University of Texas Press, 1985.

Paris-Rome-Athens: Travels in Greece by French Architects in the Nineteenth and Twentieth Centuries.. Houston: Museum of Fine Arts, 1982.

Pedley, John Griffiths. *Greek Art and Archaeology.* New York: Abrams, 1993.

CHAPTER SIXTEEN
CHRISTIAN ART IN EUROPE

Chastel, André. *French Art: Prehistory to the Middle Ages.* Paris and New York: Flammarion, 1994.

Evans, Helen C., and William D. Wixom, eds. *The Glory of Byzantium.* New York: Metropolitan Museum of Art, 1997.

Flanagan, Sabina. *Hildegard of Bingen: A Visionary Life.* London and New York: Routledge, 1989.

Holme, Bryan. *Medieval Pageant.* New York: Thames and Hudson 1987.

Illuminations of Hildegard of Bingen, with commentary by Matthew Fox. Santa Fe, N.M.: Bear & Company, 1985.

Stokstad, Marilyn. *Medieval Art.* New York: Harper & Row, 1986.

Swann, Wim. *The Gothic Cathedral.* Garden City, N.Y.: Doubleday, 1969.

CHAPTER SEVENTEEN
THE RENAISSANCE

Cuttler, Charles D. *Northern Painting: From Pucelle to Bruegel.* New York: Holt, Rinehart and Winston, 1968.

Ferino-Pagden, Sylvia, and Maria Kusche. *Sofonisba Anguissola: A Renaissance Woman.* Washington, D.C.: National Museum of Women in the Arts, 1995.

Hartt, Frederick. *History of Italian Renaissance Art,* 4th ed. Englewood Cliffs, N.J.: Prentice-Hall, 1994.

Leonardo da Vinci. *Notebooks,* ed. E. MacCurdy. New York: Braziller, 1955.

Panofsky, Erwin. *The Life and Art of Albrecht Dürer.* Princeton, N.J.: Princeton University Press, 1955.

Vasari, Giorgio. *Lives of the Artists,* trans. George Bull. New York: Penguin, 1966.

CHAPTER EIGHTEEN
THE 17TH AND 18TH CENTURIES

Held, Julius S., and Donald Posner. *17th and 18th Century Art.* New York: Abrams, 1979.

Levey, Michael. *Rococo to Revolution.* New York: Praeger, 1966.

Walton, Guy. *Louis XIV's Versailles.* Chicago: University of Chicago Press, 1986.

CHAPTER NINETEEN
THE MODERN WORLD

Arnason, H. H. *History of Modern Art: Painting, Sculpture, Architecture, Photography.* New York: Abrams, 1986.

Ashton, Dore. *Rosa Bonheur: A Life and a Legend.* New York: Viking, 1981.

Brettell, Richard, et al. *The Art of Paul Gauguin.* Washington, D.C.: National Gallery of Art, 1988.

Dachy, Marc. *The Dada Movement.* New York: Rizzoli, 1990.

Harlem Renaissance: Art of Black America. New York: The Studio Museum and Abrams, 1987.

Hughes, Robert. *The Shock of the New.* New York: McGraw-Hill, 1991.

Lanchner, Carolyn. *Joan Miró.* New York: Museum of Modern Art, 1993.

Roskill, Mark, ed. *The Letters of Vincent Van Gogh.* New York: Atheneum, 1977.

Rubin, William, ed. *Pablo Picasso: A Retrospective.* New York: Museum of Modern Art, 1980.

Rubin, William. *Picasso and Braque: Pioneering Cubism.* New York: Museum of Modern Art, 1989.

Rubin, William S. *Dada and Surrealist Art.* New York: Abrams, 1969.

CHAPTER TWENTY
ART SINCE 1945

Anderson, Laurie. *United States.* New York: Harper & Row, 1984.

Ashton, Dore. *The New York School: A Cultural Reckoning.* New York: Penguin, 1980.

Battcock, Gregory. *Super Realism: A Critical Anthology.* New York: Dutton, 1975.

———. *Minimal Art: A Critical Anthology.* New York: Dutton, 1968.

Chicago, Judy. *The Dinner Party: A Symbol of Our Heritage.* Garden City, N.Y.: Doubleday, 1979.

Fineberg, Jonathan. *Art Since 1940: Strategies of Being.* Upper Saddle River, N.J.: Prentice-Hall, 1995.

Seitz, William C. *Abstract Expressionist Painting in America.* Cambridge, Mass.: Harvard University Press, 1983.

Stella, Frank. *Working Space.* Cambridge, Mass.: Harvard University Press, 1986.

Varnedoe, Kirk. *Jasper Johns: A Retrospective.* New York: Museum of Modern Art, 1996.

CHAPTER TWENTY-ONE
ART AROUND THE WORLD

Baker, Joan Stanley. *Japanese Art.* London: Thames and Hudson, 1984.

Coe, Michael, Dean Snow, and Elizabeth Benson. *Atlas of Ancient America.* New York: Facts on File, 1986.

Dwyer, Jane Powell, and Edward B. Dwyer. *The Traditional Art of Africa, Oceania, and the Americas.* San Francisco: Fine Arts Museum of San Francisco, 1973.

Ezra, Kate. *Royal Art of Benin: The Perls Collection.* New York: Metropolitan Museum of Art and Abrams, 1992.

Furst, Peter T., and Jill L. Furst. *North American Indian Art.* New York: Rizzoli, 1982.

Jonaitis, Aldona. *From the Land of the Totem Poles.* New York: American Museum of Natural History, 1988.

Lee, Sherman. *A History of Far Eastern Art,* 5th ed. Englewood Cliffs, N.J.: Prentice-Hall, 1993.

Murray, Jocelyn, ed. *Cultural Atlas of Africa.* New York: Facts on File, 1981.

Pacific Islands, Africa, and the Americas, The. New York: Metropolitan Museum of Art, 1987.

Phillips, Tom, ed. *Africa: The Art of a Continent.* Munich and New York: Prestel, 1995.

Schele, Linda, and David Freidel. *A Forest of Kings: The Untold Story of the Ancient Maya.* New York: William Morrow, 1990.

Stuart, Gene S., and George E. Stuart. *Lost Kingdoms of the Maya.* Washington, D.C.: National Geographic, 1993.

Vanished Civilization of the Ancient World, ed. Edward Bacon. New York: McGraw-Hill, 1963.

Weidner, Marsha, et al. *Views from Jade Terrace: Chinese Women Artists, 1300–1912.* Indianapolis: Indianapolis Museum of Art, 1988.

CHAPTER ONE

1. Calvin Tomkins, "The Time of His Life," *The New Yorker* (July 8, 1996), p. 66.
2. Quoted in Don Lambert, "Reflections of Genius," *Saturday Review* (January-February 1984), p. 22.
3. Quoted in Donatella Lorch, "Survival Found at the Tip of a Paintbrush," *The New York Times* (July 28, 1996), pp. 25–26.
4. Adapted from Sidney J. Parnes and Harold F. Harding, eds., *A Source Book for Creative Thinking* (New York: Scribner's, 1962); and Daniel M. Mendelowitz, *Children Are Artists*, 2d ed. (Stanford, Calif.: Stanford University Press, 1963).
5. Mark Roskill, ed., *The Letters of Vincent van Gogh* (New York: Atheneum, 1977), p. 188.
6. P. Huisman and M. G. Dortu, *Lautrec by Lautrec* (New York: Viking, 1964), p. 164.

CHAPTER TWO

1. Paul Gray, "Attention Name Droppers," *Time* (February 5, 1996), p. 77.
2. For more detail about *The Polish Rider* and the Rembrandt Research Project, see Anthony Bailey, "A Young Man on Horseback," *The New Yorker* (March 5, 1990), pp. 45–77.
3. Douglas C. McGill, "Artists and Officials Argue over Removing Sculpture," *The New York Times* (March 7, 1985), p. B1.
4. "Intrusive Arc," *The New York Times* (May 31, 1985), p. A26.
5. Catherine Barnett, "Mischief with Mummies," *Art & Antiques* (September 1988), p. 71.
6. Robert Goldwater and Marco Treves, eds., *Artists on Art: From the Fourteenth to the Twentieth Century* (New York: Pantheon, 1972), p. 417.
7. Quoted in Irving Sandler, *The Triumph of American Painting: A History of Abstract Expressionism* (New York: Harper & Row, 1976).
8. Goldwater and Treves, p. 82.
9. Vincent van Gogh, *The Complete Letters;* quoted in Ronald Pickvance, *Van Gogh in Saint-Rémy and Auvers* (New York: The Metropolitan Museum of Art and Harry N. Abrams, Inc., 1986), p. 219.

CHAPTER THREE

1. Paul Zanker and John Pollini, quoted in "Scholar-Detectives Learn How Augustus Idealized His Image," *The New York Times* (January 10, 1984), p. C3.

2. Charles Blitzer and the Editors of Time-Life Books, eds., "Age of Kings," *Great Ages of Man: History of the World's Culture* (New York: Time-Life, 1967), p. 62.
3. Henry Kamm, "Rauschenberg Show Heralds Union of the Arts in Berlin," *The New York Times* (March 10, 1990), p. 11.
4. Gerstle Mack, *Paul Cézanne* (New York: Knopf, 1936), p. 199.
5. Exhibition catalogue statement, Anderson Galleries, January 29, 1923; quoted in Laurie Lisle, *Portrait of An Artist: Georgia O'Keeffe* (New York: Seaview Books, 1980), p. 66.
6. Kathleen Jessie Paine, *William Blake* (New York: Praeger, 1970), p. 148.
7. Statement by the artist written for Peter Selz, *New Images of Man* (New York: Museum of Modern Art, 1959), p. 60.

CHAPTER FOUR

1. Goldwater and Treves, op. cit., p. 74.
2. Benoit B. Mandelbrot, "Fractals and an Art for the Sake of Science," in *LEONARDO, Computer Art in Context, Supplemental Issue* (1989), pp. 21–22.
3. Quoted in Ken Shulman, "Monumental Toil to Restore the Magnificent," *The New York Times* (July 2, 1995), pp. 31, 34.
4. Peter de Polnay, *Enfant Terrible: The Life and Work of Maurice Utrillo* (New York: Morrow, 1969), p. 190.

CHAPTER FIVE

1. John Russell and the Editors of Time-Life Books, eds., *The World of Matisse* (New York: Time-Life, 1969), p. 9.
2. Goldwater and Treves, op. cit., p. 413.
3. Ibid., pp. 203–204.
4. Quoted in Helen Yglesias, *Isabel Bishop* (New York: Rizzoli, 1989), p. 120.

CHAPTER SIX

1. Joan Kinneir, *The Artist by Himself* (New York: St. Martin's, 1980), p. 101.
2. Martha Kearns, *Käthe Kollwitz: Woman and Artist* (Old Westbury, N.Y.: Feminist Press, 1976), p. 48.
3. Ibid., p. 164.
4. B. J. Roche, "The Soul of a New Machine: David Hockney and His Art for the Faxes," *The Washington Post* (September 3, 1989), p. G5.
5. This statement has been quoted in many sources, including Victor Wolfgang von Hagen, *The Ancient Sun Kingdoms of*

the Americas (Cleveland and New York: World, 1961), p. 387.

CHAPTER SEVEN

1. Black Mountain College Records, 1946; quoted in Ellen Harkins Wheat, *Jacob Lawrence: American Painter* (Seattle: Seattle Art Museum, 1986), p. 73.
2. Barbaralee Diamonstein, *Inside New York's Art World* (New York: Rizzoli, 1979), pp. 261–262.

CHAPTER EIGHT

1. Elizabeth Ripley, *Hokusai: A Biography* (Philadelphia: Lippincott, 1968), p. 24.
2. Ibid., pp. 62, 68.
3. Quoted in Ruth E. Fine and Mary Lee Corlett, *Graphicstudio* (Washington, D.C.: National Gallery of Art, 1991), p. 85.
4. Kinneir, op. cit., p. 107.
5. Piri Halasz, "An Artist's World of Passion, Pain and Weird Beauty," *Smithsonian* (December 1978), p. 94.

6. Robert Rauschenberg, *An Interview with Robert Rauschenberg by Barbara Rose* (New York: Elizabeth Avedon Editions, 1987), p. 59. Information in this biography is adapted from *Robert Rauschenberg* (Washington, D.C.: National Collection of Fine Arts, 1976).
7. Gretchen Berg, "Andy: My True Story," *Los Angeles Free Press* (March 17, 1967), p. 3; quoted in Kynaston McShine, ed., *Andy Warhol: A Retrospective*, (New York: Museum of Modern Art, 1989), p. 460.
8. Ibid.

CHAPTER NINE

1. *David Hockney: A Retrospective* (Los Angeles: Los Angeles County Museum of Art, 1988), p. 58.
2. *Victorian Photographs of Famous Men and Fair Women by Julia Margaret Cameron* (Boston: Godine, 1973), p. 13.
3. Ibid., p. 18.
4. Ibid., p. 19.
5. Helmut Gernsheim, *Julia Margaret Cameron* (New York: Aperture, 1975), p. 180.
6. Sue Davidson Lowe, *Stieglitz: A Memorial Biography* (New York: Farrar Straus Giroux, 1983), pp. xxiii, 441.
7. Glenn Collins, "A Portraitist's Romp Through Art History," *The New York Times* (February 1, 1990), p. C17.

8. Isabel Wilkerson, "Obscenity Jurors Were Pulled 2 Ways," *The New York Times* (October 10, 1990), p. A12.

9. Jane Livingston, *Lee Miller: Photographer* (New York: The California/International Arts Foundation, 1989), p. 35.

10. Douglas Kirkland, *Icons: Creativity with Camera and Computer* (San Francisco: Collins, 1993), p. 12.

11. *The New York Times Film Reviews, 1913–1970* (New York: Arno Press, 1971), p. 6.

12. Donald Spoto, *The Dark Side of Genius: The Life of Alfred Hitchcock* (Boston: Little, Brown, 1983), p. 73.

13. François Truffaut, *Hitchcock*, rev. ed. (New York: Simon and Schuster, 1983), p. 256.

14. Quoted in John Lahr, "The Imperfectionist," *The New Yorker* (December 9, 1996), pp. 68, 70, 73.

15. Kerry Green, "Nam June Paik," *Video Systems* (July 1982), p. 53.

CHAPTER TEN

1. Donald Walton, *A Rockwell Portrait* (Kansas City: Sheed Andrews & McMeel, 1978), p. 7.

CHAPTER ELEVEN

1. John Russell, "Henry Moore at Eighty—Many Happy Returns," *Smithsonian* (August 1978), p. 75.

2. Carll Tucker, "Henry Moore," *Saturday Review* (March 1981), p. 44.

3. Ibid., p. 46.

4. Israel Shenker, "A Sculptor's Heaven on Earth Is Italy's City of Holy Stone," *Smithsonian* (February 1989), p. 108.

5. Cleve Gray, ed., *David Smith by David Smith* (New York: Holt, Rinehart and Winston, 1972), p. 25.

6. Ibid., p. 123.

7. Vicki Goldberg, "Louise Nevelson," *Saturday Review* (August 1980), p. 36.

8. Diamonstein, op. cit., p. 271.

9. Robert Hughes, "Dark Visions of Primal Myth," *Time* (June 7, 1993), p. 64.

10. Steven R. Weisman, "Christo's Intercontinental Umbrella Project," *The New York Times* (November 13, 1990), p. C13.

CHAPTER TWELVE

1. Susan Peterson, *The Living Tradition of María Martínez* (New York: Kodansha International, 1977), p. 191.

CHAPTER THIRTEEN

1. Quoted in Stanley Meisler, "Long Live Paris, with Her Pleasures and Complexities," *Smithsonian* (August 1991), p. 44.

2. *The New York Times* (July 3, 1983), p. 17.

3. Herbert Muschamp, "Frank Gehry Lifts Creativity Out of the Box," *The New York Times* (December 12, 1993), Sect. H., p. 44.

4. Quoted in Michael Kerman, "A National Memorial Bears Witness to the Tragedy of the Holocaust," *Smithsonian* (April 1993), p. 60.

5. Frank Lloyd Wright, *A Testament* (New York: Horizon Press, 1957), p. 64.

6. Quoted in Patricia Failing, "She Was American's Most Successful Woman Architect," *ARTnews* (January 1981), p. 70.

CHAPTER FIFTEEN

1. *Life Stories of Men Who Shaped History, from Plutarch's Lives*, Eduard C. Lindeman, ed. (New York: The New American Library, 1950), p. 73.

2. Thucydides, *The Peloponnesian War*, trans. Rex Warner (Baltimore: Penguin, 1954), pp. 118, 121.

CHAPTER SEVENTEEN

1. Quoted in Robert Wallace and the Editors of Time-Life Books, eds., *The World of Leonardo* (New York: Time Incorporated, 1966), p. 17.

2. Goldwater and Treves, op. cit., pp. 60–61.

CHAPTER EIGHTEEN

1. Goldwater and Treves, op. cit., p. 134.

2. Ibid., pp. 145–146.

3. *Memoirs of Madame Vigée Lebrun*, trans. Lionel Strachey (New York: Braziller, 1989), pp. 20, 21, 214.

CHAPTER NINETEEN

1. Dore Ashton, *Rosa Bonheur: A Life and a Legend* (New York: Viking, 1981), p. xii.

2. John Russell and the Editors of Time-Life Books, eds., *The World of Matisse* (New York: Time-Life, 1969). p. 17.

3. Nicholas Wadley, *Manet* (London: Paul Hamlyn, 1967), pp. 25–26.

4. Daniel Guerin, ed., *The Writings of a Savage: Paul Gauguin* (New York: Viking, 1974), p. 54.

5. Gertrude Stein, *The Autobiography of Alice B. Toklas* (New York: Vintage, 1990), p. 35.

6. Goldwater and Treves, op. cit., p. 421.

CHAPTER TWENTY

1. Barbara Rose, *Lee Krasner: A Retrospective* (Houston: Museum of Fine Arts; New York: Museum of Modern Art, 1984), p. 134.

2. Grace Glueck, "And Now, a Few Words from Jenny Holzer," *The New York Times Magazine* (December 3, 1989), p. 110.

G L O S S A R Y

Words in *italics* are also defined in the glossary.
Numbers in **boldface** following the definitions
refer to the numbers of figures in the text
that best illustrate the definitions.

abstract Characteristic of art in which natural *forms* are not rendered in a *naturalistic* or *representational* way, but instead, are simplified or distorted to some extent, often in an attempt to convey the essence of form. Compare *nonobjective*. **(33)**

Abstract Expressionism Painting style of the late 1940s and 1950s in which *abstract* or *nonobjective forms* were used to convey emotional *content*. Abstract Expressionism emphasized spontaneity and often employed bold colors and/or strong *value* contrasts; the paintings were usually quite large in *scale*. Because this art often involved energetic physical movement by the artist, it is also referred to as *action painting*. **(38)**

acrylic A plastic substance commonly used as a *binder* for paints and as a *casting* material for sculpture.

action painting Any painting style calling for vigorous physical activity; specifically, *Abstract Expressionism*.

aesthetic Pertaining to the beautiful, as opposed to the useful, scientific, or emotional. An aesthetic response is an appreciation of such beauty.

afterimage An image that persists after the visual stimulus for that image has been removed. In colors, the tendency of the eyes to see a *hue* after having looked for a time at the *complementary* hue. **(117)**

aquatint An *intaglio printmaking* method in which areas of tone are created by dusting resin particles on a plate and then allowing acid to bite around the particles. Also, a *print* made by this method. **(231)**

arch A curving architectural *form* usually made of bricks or other masonry, often in the shape of a semicircle but sometimes rising to a point at the top. **(367)**

Archaic style In Greek art, the style prevalent from the 8th to the 6th century B.C.E. **(436)**

armature A rigid framework, often of wood or steel, used to support a sculpture or other large work while it is being made.

Armory Show An art exhibition held in 1913 at the 69th Regiment Armory in New York, at which avant-garde European art was introduced to the United States.

Art Deco An art style of the 1920s and 1930s based on modern materials (steel, chrome, glass) and repetitive geometric patterns. **(390)**

Art Nouveau An art style of the 1890s featuring curvilinear shapes based on plant forms.

assemblage The technique of creating a sculpture by joining together individual pieces or segments, sometimes "found" objects that originally served another purpose. Also, a sculpture made by this method. **(321)**

asymmetrical Not *symmetrical*. **(154)**

atmospheric perspective A device for suggesting three-dimensional depth on a two-dimensional surface. Forms meant to be perceived as distant from the viewer are blurred, indistinct, and misty.

auteur A filmmaker who exercises maximum control over a film's production and imparts an individual style to a film, often drawing upon personal imagery, dreams, obsessions, fears, memories, or loves as subject matter.

axis A straight line, often an imaginary vertical line.

Baroque A style dominant in European art during the 17th century, characterized by strong colors and *value* contrasts, bold *scale*, dramatic use of light, elaborate ornamentation, great emotionalism, even theatricality. **(492)**

barrel vault A *vault*, or masonry roof, based on an extension of the round *arch;* in effect, many round arches placed one behind the other. **(368)**

bas relief Also known as low relief, sculpture in which figures project only slightly from a background, as on a coin. **(322)**

Bauhaus A school of design in Germany from 1919 to 1933, best known for its attempts to adapt design principles to machine technology.

binder A substance in paints that causes particles of *pigment* to adhere to one another and to a *support*.

calligraphy The art of "beautiful writing." Specifically, a style of decorative penmanship highly developed in Asia, featuring a flowing, controlled line, often with gradations from thick to thin. **(183)**

cantilever A horizontal architectural *form* projecting beyond its supports. **(397)**

cartoon 1. A simple drawing with humorous or satirical *content*. 2. A preparatory drawing for a *mural, fresco,* or other large work.

casting The process of making a sculpture or other object by pouring liquid material—clay, metal, plastic—into a mold and allowing it to harden.

ceramic Made from fired ("baked") clay.

chiaroscuro Literally, "light-dark." In two-dimensional art, the use of different *values* to create *modeling* and to simulate the effects of light and shadow in nature. **(109)**

chroma See *intensity*.

cire-perdue See *lost wax*.

Classical style In Greek art, the style of the 5th century B.C.E. Loosely, the term "classical" is often applied to all the art of ancient Greece and Rome, as well as to any art based on logical, rational principles and deliberate *composition*. **(438)**

collage A work of art made by pasting bits of paper, cloth, or other material onto a flat surface. **(219)**

Color Field painting A style of painting prominent from the 1950s through the 1970s, featuring large "fields" or areas of color, meant to evoke an *aesthetic* or emotional response through the color alone. **(543)**

color wheel A circular arrangement of *hues* based on some particular color theory. Often, an arrangement of the hues in a rainbow, plus intermediary colors. **(111)**

544

complementary colors *Hues* directly opposite one another on the *color wheel* and therefore assumed to be as different from one another as possible. When placed side by side, complementary colors are intensified; when mixed together, they produce a *neutral*. **(111)**

composition The organization of lines, shapes, colors, and other art elements in a work of art. More often applied to two-dimensional art; the broader term is *design*.

computer art Art generated electronically, within the computer. **(195)**

Conceptual Art An art form in which the underlying idea or concept and the process by which it is achieved are more important than any tangible product. **(555)**

content The message conveyed by a work of art—its subject matter and whatever the artist hopes to convey by that subject matter.

continuous narrative A device by which two or more episodes in an event are portrayed in the same work of art. **(468)**

contrapposto Literally, "counterpoise." A method of portraying the human figure, especially in sculpture, so that it is apparently relaxed and mobile. The result is often a graceful S-curve. **(326)**

cross-cutting In filmmaking, a technique of alternating two or more scenes or shots to advance the action.

cross-hatching An area of closely spaced lines intersecting one another, used to create a sense of three-dimensionality on a flat surface, especially in drawing and *printmaking*. See also *hatching, stippling*. **(95)**

Cubism A style of art pioneered in the early 20th century by Pablo Picasso and Georges Braque. In the most developed type of Cubism, *forms* are fragmented into *planes* or geometric facets, like the facets in a diamond; these planes are rearranged to foster a pictorial, but not *naturalistic*, reality; forms may be viewed simultaneously from several vantage points; figure and background have equal importance; and colors are deliberately restricted to a range of *neutrals*. **(527,528)**

Dada A movement that emerged during World War I in Europe that purported to be anti-everything, even anti-art. Dada poked fun at all the established traditions and tastes in art with works that were deliberately shocking, vulgar, and nonsensical. **(535)**

daguerreotype The earliest form of photograph, invented by Louis Jacques Mandé Daguerre, in which the photographic image is made permanent on a copper plate.

design The planned organization of lines, shapes and masses, colors, textures, and space in a work of art. In two-dimensional art, often called *composition*.

dome An architectural structure generally in the shape of a hemisphere or half globe; theoretically, an arch rotated 360 degrees on its vertical *axis*. **(373)**

drypoint An *intaglio printmaking* technique, similar to *engraving*, in which a sharp needle is used to draw on a metal plate, raising a thin ridge of metal that creates a soft line when the plate is printed. Also, the resultant *print*. **(231)**

earthenware *Ceramic* ware, usually coarse and reddish in color, fired in the lowest temperature ranges.

edition In *printmaking*, the number of images made from a single plate and authorized by the artist.

encaustic A painting *medium* in which the *binder* is hot beeswax. **(203)**

engraving An *intaglio printmaking* method in which a sharp tool called a burin is used to scratch lines into a metal plate. Also, the resultant *print*. **(231)**

entasis In *Classical* architecture, the slight swelling or bulge built into the center of a column to make the column seem straight visually.

environmental art 1. Art that is large enough for viewers to enter and move about in. 2. Art designed for display in the outdoor environment. 3. Art that actually transforms the natural landscape. **(336)**

etching An *intaglio printmaking* method in which lines and image areas are created by first coating a plate with an acid-resistant substance, then scratching through the substance with a sharp needle, and finally immersing the plate in acid, which "bites" depressions into the exposed sections. Also the resultant *print*. **(231)**

Expressionism Any art that stresses the artist's emotional and psychological expression, often with bold colors and distortions of form. Specifically, an art style of the early 20th century followed principally by certain German artists. See also *Abstract Expressionism*. **(227)**

Fauvism A short-lived painting style in early-20th-century France, which featured bold, clashing, arbitrary colors—colors unrelated to the appearance of *forms* in the natural world. Henri Matisse was its best-known practitioner. The word *fauve* is usually translated as "wild beast." **(525)**

ferroconcrete Reinforced concrete; a building material that has metal rods or steel mesh embedded in concrete to provide strength. **(381)**

figure-ground relationship In two-dimensional art, the relationship between the principal *forms* and the background. Figure-ground ambiguity suggests equal importance for the two. **(103)**

flashback In filmmaking, a cut to a scene or episode that is supposed to have taken place before the main action of the film.

foreshortening A method of portraying *forms* on a two-dimensional surface so that they appear to project or recede from the *picture plane*. **(137)**

forging Shaping metal with hammers while it is hot; the method for making wrought iron.

form 1. The physical appearance of a work of art—its materials, style, and *composition*. 2. Any identifiable shape or mass, as a "geometric form."

fresco A painting *medium* in which colors are applied to wet plaster, thus bonding the image with the painting surface; most often used for *murals*. **(204)**

Futurism Art movement founded in Italy in 1909 and lasting only a few years. Futurism concentrated on the dynamic quality of modern technological life, emphasizing speed and movement. **(143)**

genre Art that depicts the casual moments of everyday life and its surroundings. **(62)**

geodesic dome An architectural structure invented by R. Buckminster Fuller, based on triangles arranged into tetrahedrons (or four-faceted solids). **(382)**

glaze 1. A coating of glassy, often colored material bonded by heat onto a *ceramic* object. 2. Paint applied in a very thin layer.

golden section Also called the "golden mean," a system of proportions developed by the ancient Greeks in which sections of a line or shape were related to one another according to an "ideal" expressed algebraically as $a:b = b:(a + b)$. **(171)**

Gothic A style of architecture and art dominant in Europe from the 12th to the 15th century. Gothic architecture features pointed *arches*, ribbed *vaults*, and often large areas of stained glass. **(369)**

gouache A painting *medium* similar to *watercolor* but with the addition of opaque white. **(215)**

groin vault A *vault*, or masonry ceiling, resulting when two *barrel vaults* intersect. Often used in medieval architecture to roof a square area.

ground 1. A substance applied to a painting or drawing *support* in preparation for the pigmented material. 2. The preparatory substance used as a coating for a *printmaking* plate. 3. The background in a work of two-dimensional art. See also *primer, figure-ground relationship.*

happening An event performed by artists, usually spontaneous and unrehearsed, that may include music, dance, mime, art, reading, or any combination of these.

hard-edge A style of art, principally painting, of the mid-20th century in which *forms* are depicted with precise, geometric lines and edges. **(550)**

hatching An area of closely spaced parallel lines used to create a sense of three-dimensionality on a flat surface, especially in drawing and *printmaking*. See also *cross-hatching, stippling.* **(95)**

haut-relief Also known as high relief, sculpture in which figures are attached to a background but project substantially from that background, usually by at least half their normal depth. **(323)**

Hellenistic style In Greek art, the style of the 3rd to 1st centuries B.C.E., characterized by drama and emotionalism and, in sculpture, a tendency for *forms* to push out boldly into space. **(439)**

hue The property of a color that distinguishes it from others in the *color wheel;* the name of a color. **(111)**

iconography Loosely, the "story" depicted in a work of art; people, places, events, and other images in a work, as well as the symbolism and conventions attached to those images by a particular religion or culture.

illumination Hand-drawn decoration or illustration in a manuscript, especially prevalent in medieval art. **(457)**

impasto A thick application of paint to canvas or other *support*. **(209)**

Impressionism An art style of the late 19th century, principally in France, in which artists tried to capture in paint the fleeting effects—or impressions—of light, shade, and color on natural *forms*. **(516)**

inlay In woodworking, a technique in which small pieces of wood, often with varying grains and colors, are glued together to make a pattern.

intaglio Any *printmaking* technique in which the lines or image areas to be printed are recessed below the surface of the printing plate. The intaglio techniques are *aquatint, drypoint, etching, engraving,* and *mezzotint.* **(221)**

intensity The degree of purity or brilliance of a color. Also known as *chroma* or *saturation.* **(112)**

isometric perspective A system for depicting three-dimensional depth on a two-dimensional surface, especially common in Eastern art. Isometric perspective resembles *linear perspective*, except that parallel lines do not converge. Instead, they are parallel to one another, but at an angle to the *picture plane.* **(136)**

kinetic Of or relating to movement. Kinetic art is art that incorporates movement as part of its expression. **(141)**

kore Greek for "maiden"; an ancient Greek sculpture of a young woman, usually clothed.

kouros Greek for "youth" or "boy"; an ancient Greek sculpture of a nude young man. **(437)**

linear perspective System for depicting three-dimensional depth on a two-dimensional surface. Linear perspective has two main precepts: 1) *forms* that are meant to be perceived as far away from the viewer are made smaller than those meant to be seen as close; 2) parallel lines receding into the distance converge at a point on the horizon line known as the *vanishing point.* **(132)**

linocut Also known as linoleum cut, a *relief printmaking* technique in which a block of linoleum is carved so as to leave image areas raised above the surface of the block; in function, similar to a common rubber stamp. Also, the resultant *print.* **(229)**

lintel A beam; a horizontal architectural member usually supported by vertical posts. See also *post-and-lintel.*

lithography A *planographic* (or flat-surface) *printmaking* technique, based on the premise that oil and water do not mix. Image areas are drawn in greasy crayon on a stone or plate, and the greasy ink used in this method adheres to those areas. **(221)**

lost-wax casting Also known by the French term *cire-perdue*, a method for *casting* metal sculptures and other objects. Positive and negative *molds* are built around a layer of wax that exactly duplicates the shape and size of the desired sculpture. When this arrangement is heated, the wax melts out (is "lost") and then molten metal is poured into the mold to replace it. **(311)**

Mannerism A term sometimes applied to art of late 16th and early 17th-century Europe, characterized by a dramatic use of space and light and a tendency toward elongated figures. **(491)**

mass Three-dimensional *form*, often implying bulk, density, and weight.

medium 1. The material used to create a work of art. 2. The *binder* for a paint, such as oil. 3. An expressive art form, such as painting, drawing, or sculpture.

metalpoint A drawing technique, especially popular in the *Renaissance*, in which the drawing material is a thin wire of metal. See also *silverpoint.* **(186)**

mezzotint An *intaglio printmaking* method in which the printing plate is first roughened all over with a sharp tool called a rocker to create a pattern of burrs. *Values* from light to medium dark are created by smoothing away the burrs in relative degree. Also, the resultant *print.* **(231)**

Minimal Art A style of painting and sculpture in the mid-20th century in which the art elements are restricted to an extreme "minimum"—lines, simple (often geometric) shapes, and sometimes color. **(550)**

mixed media Descriptive of any work of art employing more than one *medium*—for example, a work that combines painting, *collage*, and *screenprinting.*

mobile A sculpture that incorporates movement, usually effected by air currents. **(338)**

modeling 1. In sculpture, shaping a *form* in some *plastic* material, such as clay, wax, or plaster. 2. In drawing, painting, or *printmaking*, the illusion of three-dimensionality on a flat surface created by simulating effects of light and shadow. **(109)**

mold A hollow or negative *shape* used for *casting* liquid clay, metal, or *plastic.*

monochromatic Having only one color. Descriptive of work in which one *hue*—perhaps with variations of *value* and *intensity*—predominates.

monotype A *printmaking* method in which only one impression results. **(244)**

mosaic An art form in which small pieces of tile, glass, or stone are fitted together and embedded into a background to make a pattern or image. Often used for floor and wall decoration. **(220)**

mural Any large-*scale* wall decoration in painting, *fresco, mosaic,* or other *medium.* **(205)**

naturalistic Descriptive of a work of art that closely resembles *forms* in the natural world. Synonymous with *representational.*

nave The long central section of a church or cathedral where the congregation stands or sits. **(369)**

Neoclassicism "New" classicism—a style in 19th-century Western art that referred back to the *Classical* styles of Greece and Rome. Neoclassical painting is marked by sharp outline, reserved emotions, deliberate (often geometric) *composition*, and cool colors. **(509)**

Neo-Expressionism "New" Expressionism—a term originally applied to works by some European artists, primarily German and Italian, who came to maturity in the post-World War II era; expanded in the 1980s to include certain American artists. Neo-Expressionist works have much emotion and symbolism, sometimes unconventional *media*, and often intense colors and turbulent composition. **(563)**

neutral Having no *hue*—black, white, or gray; sometimes a tannish color achieved by mixing two *complementary colors*.

New York School See *Abstract Expressionism*.

nonobjective Descriptive of works of art that have no reference to the natural world of images. Composed of lines, shapes, and sometimes colors, chosen and arranged for their own expressive potential. Synonymous with *nonrepresentational*. Compare *abstract, stylized*.

nonrepresentational See *nonobjective*.

Op Art Short for optical art, a style popular in the 1960s and based on optical principles. Op Art deals in complex color interactions, to the point where colors and lines seem to vibrate before the eyes. **(142)**

optical color mixture The tendency of the eyes to blend patches of individual colors placed near one another so as to perceive a different, combined color. Also, any art style that exploits this tendency, especially the *pointillism* of Georges Seurat. **(118)**

painterly Descriptive of paintings in which *forms* are defined principally by color areas, not by lines or edges.

palette 1. A surface used for mixing paints. 2. The range of colors typically used by an artist or group of artists.

pastel 1. A soft, chalky crayon used for drawing; also, the resultant drawing. 2. A light-*value* color.

patina A surface coating that develops on metals, particularly copper and bronze, through exposure to weather and oxides, or by the deliberate application of corrosive chemicals.

pediment The triangular area above the porch on a Greek temple, often decorated with sculptures. **(433)**

pendentive In architecture, a curving, triangular section that serves as a transition between a *dome* and the four walls of a rectangular building. **(373)**

performance art Similar to a *happening*, art in which there is no concrete object, but rather, a series of events performed by the artist in front of an audience, possibly including music, sight gags, recitation, audio-visual presentations, or other elements.

perspective Any system for depicting the illusion of three-dimensional space on a two-dimensional surface. See *atmospheric perspective, isometric perspective, linear perspective*. **(132)**

Photorealism A painting style of the mid-20th century in which people, objects, and scenes are depicted with such naturalism that the paintings resemble photographs. **(551)**

pictorial space The illusory space in a painting or other work of two-dimensional art that seems to recede backward into depth from the *picture plane;* the "window" effect in a painting.

picture plane An imaginary flat surface that is assumed to be identical to the surface of a painting. *Forms* in a painting meant to be perceived in deep three-dimensional space are said to be "behind" the picture plane. The picture plane is commonly associated with the foreground of a painting.

pigment A coloring material made from various organic or chemical substances. When mixed with a *binder*, it creates a drawing or painting *medium*.

plane A flat surface. See *picture plane*.

planography A *printmaking* technique in which the image areas are level with the surface of the printing plate; *lithography*. **(221)**

plastic 1. Capable of being molded or shaped, as clay. 2. Any synthetic polymer substance, such as *acrylic*.

pointillism An art style of the late 19th century, particularly associated with Georges Seurat, in which small patches or "points" of color are placed close together to build *form*. See also *optical color mixture*. **(118)**

Pop Art An art style of the 1960s, deriving its imagery from the popular, mass-produced culture. Deliberately mundane, Pop Art focused on the overfamiliar objects of daily life to give them new meanings as visual emblems. **(150)**

porcelain A *ceramic* ware, usually white, firing in the highest temperature ranges and often used for fine dinnerware, vases, and sculpture.

post-and-lintel In architecture, a structural system based on two or more uprights (posts) supporting a horizontal crosspiece (lintel or beam).

Post-Impressionism A term applied to the work of several artists—French or living in France—from about 1885 to 1900. Although all painted in highly personal styles, the Post-Impressionists were united in rejecting the relative absence of *form* characteristic of *Impressionism*. The group included Vincent van Gogh, Paul Cézanne, Paul Gauguin, and Georges Seurat.

primary color A *hue* that, in theory, cannot be created by a mixture of other hues. Varying combinations of the primary hues can be used to create all the other hues of the spectrum. In pigment the primaries are red, yellow, and blue. **(111)**

primer A preliminary coating applied to a painting *support* to improve adhesion of paints or to create special effects. A traditional primer is gesso, consisting of a chalky substance mixed with glue and water. Also called a *ground*.

print An image created from a master wood block, stone, plate, or screen, usually on paper. Prints are referred to as multiples, because as a rule many identical or similar impressions are made from the same printing surface, the number of impressions being called an *edition*. A print is considered an original work of art and, today, is customarily signed and numbered by the artist. See *relief, intaglio, lithography, screenprinting*. **(221)**

printmaking The art of making *prints*.

proportion Size relationships between parts of a whole, or between two or more items perceived as a unit; also, the size relationship between an object and its surroundings. Compare *scale*. **(168)**

radial Projecting outward from a central core like the spokes in a wheel. **(161)**

Realism Broadly, any art in which the goal is to portray forms in the natural world in a highly *representational* manner. Specifically, an art style of the mid-19th century, identified especially with Gustave Courbet, which fostered the idea that everyday people and events are fit subjects for important art. **(513)**

refraction The bending of a ray of light, for example, when it passes through a prism. **(110)**

registration In *printmaking*, the precise alignment of impressions made by two or more printing blocks or plates on the same sheet of paper, as when printing an image in several colors.

relief Anything that projects from a background. 1. Sculpture in which figures or other images are attached to a background but project from it to some degree. See *bas-relief, haut-relief.* 2. A *printmaking* technique in which portions of a block meant to print are raised above the surface. See *woodcut, linocut, wood engraving.* **(221)**

Renaissance The period in Europe from the 14th to the 16th century, characterized by a renewed interest in *Classical* art, architecture, literature, and philosophy. The Renaissance began in Italy and gradually spread to the rest of Europe. In art, it is most closely associated with Leonardo da Vinci, Michelangelo, and Raphael.

representational Descriptive of a work of art that closely resembles *forms* in the natural world. Synonymous with *naturalistic.*

Rococo A style of art popular in Europe in the first three-quarters of the 18th century. Rococo architecture and furnishings emphasized ornate but small-*scale* decoration, curvilinear *forms,* and *pastel* colors. Rococo painting, also tending toward the use of pastels, has a playful, light-hearted, romantic quality and often pictures the aristocracy at leisure. **(504)**

Romanesque A style of architecture and art dominant in Europe from the 9th to the 12th century. Romanesque architecture, based on ancient Roman precedents, emphasizes the round *arch* and *barrel vault.* **(368)**

Romanticism A movement in Western art of the 19th century, generally assumed to be in opposition to *Neoclassicism.* Romantic works are marked by intense colors, turbulent emotions, complex *composition,* soft outlines, and sometimes heroic subject matter. **(512)**

salon 1. A fashionable gathering of artists, writers, and intellectuals held in a private home. 2. In France, a state-sponsored exhibition of art, held in Paris, controlled by the Academy of Fine Arts. Starting in 1863, opposition to the restrictive, overly conservative jurying of the Salon resulted in alternative exhibitions.

sarcophagus A stone or *ceramic* coffin, sometimes decorated with sculpture. **(84)**

saturation See *intensity.*

scale Size in relation to some "normal" or constant size. Compare *proportion.*

screenprinting A *printmaking* method in which the image is transferred to paper by forcing ink through a fine mesh in which the areas not meant to print have been blocked; a stencil technique. **(221)**

secondary color A *hue* created by combining two *primary colors,* as yellow and blue mixed together yield green. In pigment the secondary colors are orange, green, and violet. **(111)**

serigraphy See *screenprinting.*

sfumato From the Italian word for "smoke," a technique of painting in thin *glazes* to achieve a hazy, cloudy atmosphere, often to represent objects or landscape meant to be perceived as distant from the *picture plane.* **(473)**

shape A two-dimensional area having identifiable boundaries, created by lines, color or *value* changes, or some combination of these. Broadly, *form.*

silkscreen See *screenprinting.*

silverpoint A variation of *metalpoint* in which the drawing material is a thin silver wire.

simultaneous contrast The tendency of *complementary colors* to seem brighter and more intense when placed side by side.

still life A painting or other two-dimensional work in which the subject matter is an arrangement of objects—fruit, flowers, tableware, pottery, and so forth—brought together for their pleasing contrasts of shape, color, and texture. Also, the arrangement of objects itself. **(147)**

stippling A pattern of closely spaced dots or small marks used to create a sense of three-dimensionality on a flat surface, especially in drawing and *printmaking.* See also *cross-hatching, hatching.* **(95)**

stupa A shrine, usually dome-shaped, associated with Buddhism. **(48)**

style A characteristic, or a number of characteristics, that we can identify as constant, recurring, or coherent. In art, the sum of such characteristics associated with a particular artist, group, or culture, or with an artist's work at a specific time.

stylized Descriptive of works based on *forms* in the natural world, but simplified or distorted for *design* purposes. See also *abstract.*

support The surface on which a work of two-dimensional art is made; for example, canvas, paper, or wood.

Surrealism A painting style of the early 20th century that emphasized imagery from dreams and fantasies, as well as an intuitive, spontaneous method of recording such imagery. **(536)**

suspension A structural system in architecture, most common in bridges, in which the weight of a horizontal member is suspended from steel cables supported by uprights called pylons. **(380)**

symbol An image or sign that represents something else, because of convention, association, or resemblance.

symmetrical Descriptive of a design in which the two halves of a composition on either side of an imaginary central vertical *axis* correspond to one another in size, shape, and placement. **(152)**

tempera A painting *medium* in which the *binder* is egg yolk. **(206)**

tensile strength In architecture, the ability of a material to span horizontal distances with minimum support from underneath.

terra cotta Italian for "baked earth." A *ceramic* ware, usually reddish, fired in the low temperature ranges and somewhat porous and fragile; *earthenware.* **(343)**

trompe-l'oeil French for "fool-the-eye." A painting or other work of two-dimensional art rendered in such an extremely *naturalistic* manner that the viewer is "tricked" into thinking it is three-dimensional. **(32)**

value The relative lightness or darkness of a *hue,* or of a *neutral* varying from white to black. **(108)**

vanishing point In *linear perspective,* the point on the horizon where parallel lines appear to converge. **(132)**

vault A masonry (brick or concrete) roof or ceiling, especially in medieval architecture. See also *groin vault, barrel vault.* **(368)**

volume Similar to *mass,* a three-dimensional *form* implying bulk, density, and weight; but also a void or empty, enclosed space.

wash Ink or *watercolor* paint thinned so as to flow freely onto a *support.*

watercolor A painting *medium* in which the *binder* is gum arabic.

woodcut A *relief printmaking* method in which a block of wood is carved so as to leave the image areas raised from the background. Also, the resultant *print.* **(221)**

wood engraving Similar to *woodcut,* a *relief printmaking* process in which the image is cut on the end grain of a wood plank, resulting in a "white-line" impression.

I N D E X

All references are to page numbers.
Numbers in **boldface** indicate an illustration on that page.

Aachen, Palace Chapel of Charlemagne, **386**
Abakanowicz, Magdalena, *Infantes*, 282–**283**
Abbot Durandus, medieval tomb sculpture, **390**
Abbott, Berenice, *Nightview, New York*, **224**–225
abstract art, defined, 30
Abstract Expressionism, 479–483
abstraction, in late-20th-century art, 495; in photography, 227
Abu Temple, Tell Asmar, Iraq, votive statuettes, **351**
Acropolis, Athens, model reconstruction, **368**
action painting, 34, 480
Adams, Ansel, *Moon and Half Dome*, **224**
advertising, graphic design for, 257–259
Aegean art, 363–364
Aeneas, 374
African art, 531–535; Akan *Commemorative Head*, **531**; Bambara *Mother and Child*, 76–**77**; Bamum mask, 534–**535**; Benin *Head*, **534**; Benin *Pendant Mask*, **533**; Benin plaque, *Warrior Chief, Warriors, and Attendants*, 18–**19**; Dahomey *Lion*, 534–**535**; Diarra, mud-dyed cloth, **535**; Dogon *Horse and Rider*, **136**; Dogon *Seated Couple*, **532**; Lega ivory mask, **533**; Luba *Kneeling Woman Presenting a Bowl*, **532**–533; Mangbetu portrait vessel, 290–**291**
Africano, Nicholas, *Whiskey per tutti!*, 146–**147**
afterimage, in colors, **104**
Agesander, Athenodorus, and Polydorus of Rhodes, *Laocoön Group*, **372**–373
Agra, India, Taj Mahal, 314–**315**
AIDS Memorial Quilt, 80–**81**
Ajanta, India, The "*Beautiful Bodhisattva,*" cave painting, **513**
Akan art, Ghana, *Commemorative Head*, **531**
Akbar Hunting with Trained Cheetahs (Lal and Sanwlah), **64**–65
Akhenaten, pharaoh of Egypt, 356–**357**
Akkadian art, *see* Mesopotamian art
Albers, Josef, *Homage to the Square: Ascending*, **484**
Alhambra, Granada, Spain, **312**
Allen, Woody, 249–250; *The Purple Rose of Cairo*, **250**
Amalienburg, Munich, Mirror Room (Cuvilliés), **439**
ambrotype, 218
Amenhotep IV, *see* Akhenaten
American Revolution, 447
American Standard advertisement, "It's Seen You Naked, It's Heard You Sing," **257**
Anasazi culture, Cliff Palace, Mesa Verde, Colo., **527**–528
Anderson, Laurie, *Empty Places*, **499**

Angel Gabriel weathervane, **298**
Angkor Wat, Cambodia, **514**; restoration, **515**
Anguissola, Sofonisba, *The Chess Game*, **416**
animal style, in medieval art, 385
animation, in films, 250–251
Aphrodite of Melos, **49**
aquatint, 202–203
Arbuckle, Linda, *Onward and Upward*, **295**
Arbus, Diane, *The King and Queen of a Senior Citizens Dance, New York City*, 225–**226**
arch construction, 308–312
Arcimboldo, Giuseppe, *Summer*, **8**–9
Armory Show, 1913, 470–473
Arnoldi, Per, *Dance* poster, 254–**255**
Arp, Jean, *Collage Arranged According to the Laws of Chance*, **111**
Art Deco, 329–330
assembling, for sculpture, 273–278
Assyrian art, *see* Mesopotamian art
Augustus of Prima Porta, **53**
Avedon, Richard, *Donyale Luna, Dress by Paco Rabanne, New York Studio*, **236**
Aycock, Alice, *Fantasy Sculpture I*, **277**

"Baby" Figure, Olmec, **362**
Babylonian art, *see* Mesopotamian art
balance, asymmetrical, 134–137; as design principle, 131–138; radial, 137–138; symmetrical, 131–134; visual, **134**
Baldovinetti, Alesso, *Portrait of a Lady in Yellow*, **38**–39
Balla, Giacomo, *Dynamism of a Dog on a Leash*, **124**
balloon-frame construction, **317**
Bambara art, *Mother and Child*, 76–**77**
Bamum art, Cameroon, mask, 534–**535**
Baptism of Christ and Procession of Twelve Apostles, dome mosaic, Ravenna, **138**
Baroque art, in Italy, 425–435; in the Netherlands, 435–438
Bartlett, Jennifer, *Spiral: An Ordinary Evening in New Haven*, **501**
bas relief, 278
Baselitz, Georg, *Nachtessen in Dresden*, **496**
Bauhaus, 477–478
Bayeux Tapestry, **304**
Bearden, Romare, *The Block*, **119**
Beardsley, Aubrey, *Ali Baba*, cover for *The Forty Thieves*, **168**
"Beautiful Bodhisattva" Padmapani, Ajanta, India, **513**
Beauty and the Beast, animated film, **251**
Bella Coola mask, Northwest Coast, **300**
Bellini, Giovanni, *St. Francis in the Desert*, 403–**404**
Benin art, *Head*, **534**; *Pendant Mask*, **533**; *Plaque: Warrior Chief, Warriors, and Attendants*, 18–**19**
Bergman, Ingmar, *The Seventh Seal*, **246**

Bernini, Gianlorenzo, biography, 427; Cornaro Chapel, **426**; *Costanza Bonarelli*, 272–**273**; *St. Teresa in Ecstasy*, **426**–428; *Self-Portrait*, **427**
Bingen, Hildegard of, Art People, 391
Bingham, George Caleb, *Fur Traders Descending the Missouri*, 61, **62**, 63
birth, as a theme in art, 74–76
Birth of a Nation, The (Griffith), **242**–243
Bishop, Isabel, *Five Women Walking #2*, 149–**150**; *Students*, **164**
Blake, William, *Satan Watching the Caresses of Adam and Eve*, **72**–73
boat model, from Thebes, **355**
Bonheur, Rosa, biography, 455; *The Horse Fair*, 453–**454**
books, Maya, **171**
Boring, E. G., ambiguous figure, **11**
Borofsky, Jonathan, installation drawing at 1980 Venice Biennale, **170**
Bosch, Hieronymus, *The Garden of Earthly Delights*, **71**
Botticelli, Sandro, *The Birth of Venus*, **402**–403
Boucher, François, *Marquise de Pompadour*, **441**–442
Brady, Mathew, *Cooper Union Lincoln Portrait*, **219**
Brambilla, Pinan (Barcilon), *Last Supper* restoration, **115**
Brancusi, Constantin, *The Kiss*, **471**–472
Braque, Georges, *Man with a Guitar*, **469**
Brown, Joan, *Out on a Limb*, **142**
Brücke, Die, 470
Bruegel, Pieter, the Elder, *Peasant Wedding*, **420**–421; *Wedding Dance*, 146–**147**
brush and ink, 164
Buddha, colossal sculpture, Yungang, **508**; Gandhara-style *Head*, **513**; Gandhara-style figure, **281**; painting from Tibet, **50**
Buddhism, 48, 505, 509
Buncho, Ippitsusai, *The Actor Handayu in a Female Role*, **16**
Bunshaft, Gordon, Lever House, New York, **318**–319
Burning of Sanjo Palace, from *Heiji Monogatari*, **520**
Bush, Susan, *Woman with Yellow Cage, Bird Dress, Flowers, and Reflections*, **212**
Butterfield, Deborah, *Vermillion*, **274**
buttresses, in architecture, 311
Byzantine art, dome mosaic, Ravenna, **138**; *Empress Theodora and Retinue*, **382**–383; Hagia Sophia, Istanbul, **384**; San Vitale, Ravenna, 383–384

Calder, Alexander, *Cow*, **84**–85; *Somersaulters*, **162**; *Untitled* (National Gallery), **288**
Calle de Sueños (Dream Street), children's art, **5**
Callicrates, *see* Ictinus
calligraphy, 156–**157**
calotype, 218

Cambodia, Angkor Wat, **514–515**
Camel, Tang ceramic sculpture, **509**
camera, basic parts, **218**
camera obscura, **215**–216
Cameron, Henry Herschel Hay, *Julia Margaret Cameron*, **221**
Cameron, Julia Margaret, biography, 221; *Charles Darwin*, 219–**220**
Campin, Robert, *Merode Altarpiece*, **417**
Campus, Peter, *Three Transitions*, **253**
Canaletto, *View of Venice: Grand Canal Looking Southwest from Near the Rialto Bridge*, **116**–117
cantilever, 336
Caravaggio, *The Deposition*, **430**
Carolingian art, 387
carousel horse, 300–**301**
Carter, Howard, and Tutankhamun's tomb, 358–**359**
cartoon, magazine, Reilly, **169**; as preparatory drawing, 173–174
carving, for sculpture, 270, 272–273
Casa Milá, Barcelona (Gaudí), **334**
Cassatt, Mary, *In the Omnibus*, 202–203
casting, for sculpture, 267–270
cast-iron construction, 315–317
Cavalryman and Saddle Horse from Earthenware Army of First Emperor of Qin, **266**–267
cave paintings, Chauvet, **344**–345, 347, **348**; Lascaux, **4**–5
Celestial Dancer, from Champa (Vietnam), **514**
censorship, 232–233
ceramics, 291–295
Cézanne, Paul, biography, 67; *The Large Bathers*, **85**; *Mont Sainte-Victoire*, **66**; *Self-Portrait with a Beret*, **67**; *Still Life with Curtain and Flowered Pitcher*, **129**
Chagall, Marc, *The Bride and Groom of the Eiffel Tower*, **78**–79; *The Painter and His Wife*, **103**; *Woman, Flowers, and Bird*, 142–**143**
chalk, 159
Champa (Vietnam), *Celestial Dancer*, **514**
Chaplin, Charles, *Modern Times*, 243–**244**
charcoal, 159
Chardin, Jean Baptiste Siméon, *The House of Cards*, 440–**441**
Charlemagne, Palace Chapel, Aachen, **386**
Chartres Cathedral, France, 48–49, **311**, **389**–390; column sculptures, **390**
Chashnik, Ilya, *Floating Suprematist Forms*, 136–**137**
Chauvet cave, France, *Lion Panel*, **348**; *Panel of the Horses*, **344**–345, 347
Chefren, pharaoh of Egypt, pyramid, 51–52
Cheops, pharaoh of Egypt, pyramid, 51–52
Chia, Sandro, *Father and Son Song*, **196**; *Incident at the Café Tintoretto*, **496**
chiaroscuro, 97
Chicago, Judy, *Birth Trinity*, **75**
Chihuly, Dale, *Violet and Green Persian Set*, **296**–297
children's art, *Calle de Sueños (Dream Street)*, **5**
Chimú art, *Figure of a Musician*, **426**
Chinese art, 505–511; *Camel*, Tang ceramic sculpture, **509**; *Colossal Buddha*, Yungang, **508**; *Court Ladies Preparing Newly Woven Silk*, 60; *Great Wall*, **52**; *Guanyin*, Song Dynasty, **509**–510; *Guanyin the Merciful*, Qing Dynasty,

511; Li Cheng, *A Solitary Temple amid Clearing Peaks*, **510**–511; Ming vase, **294**; Qiu Ying, *A Lady in a Pavilion Overlooking a Lake*, **510**–511; Ren Xia, *Cat on a Rock*, **68**; *Tiger*, **361**; tomb sculptures, **266**–267; Yan Liben, *Scroll of the Emperors*, **508**
Chiu-Tah, *Taos Round Dance*, **112**–113
Christians, early, 380–382
Christo, biography, 287; *Running Fence*, **286**, 288
chroma, as property of color, 101
Chrysler Building, New York (Van Alen), **329**–330
Cimabue, *Madonna Enthroned*, **50**
Circle That Isn't There, perception drawing, **11**
cire-perdue casting, 268–269
Citizen Kane (Welles), **245**–246
Classical Period, in Greek art, 365–372
clay, as craft material, 291–295
Cliff Palace, Mesa Verde, Colo., **527**–528
Cloisters Apocalypse, **8**
Close, Chuck, *Linda*, **489**
Cole culture, Ohio, *Head*, **526**–527
collage, 187–188
color, as design element, 98–107; emotional properties, 105–107; optical effects, 104–105
color chart, showing hue, value, and intensity, **100**
Color Field painting, 484
color harmonies, 102–103
color mixture, optical, 104
color theory, 99–101
color wheel, **99**
colors, complementary, 101; primary, 99; secondary, 101; tertiary, 101
Colossal Buddha, Yungang, China, **508**
Colosseum, Rome, 378
Column of Trajan, Rome, 376–377
Commemorative Head, Akan, from Ghana, **531**
composition, defined, 36
computer graphics, 263
Conceptual Art, 491
Conrad, Fred R., *Kurdish Girl Returning Home*, **234**–235
Constable, John, *The White Horse*, **64**–65
Constantine, emperor of Rome, 381–382; portrait head, **381**
Constantinople, *see* Istanbul
content, and form, defined, 36
continuous narrative, *Bayeux Tapestry*, **304**; Masaccio, **401**; Trajan's Column, **376**–377
contrapposto, 281
Coolidge, Charles A., Stanford University, Palo Alto, Calif., **341**
Copley, John Singleton, *Paul Revere*, **446**–447
Coptic art, *Young Woman with a Gold Pectoral*, **173**
Córdoba, Spain, Great Mosque, **312**
Corinthian style, in Greek architecture, **307**
Cornaro Chapel, Santa Maria della Vittoria, Rome (Bernini), **426**
Cornell, Joseph, *The Hotel Eden*, **130**–131
Courbet, Gustave, *The Artist's Studio: A Real Allegory Summing Up Seven Years of My Life as an Artist*, **453**
Court Ladies Preparing Newly Woven Silk (attrib. Hui-zong), 60
crayon, 159–160

creativity, 9–10
cross-hatching, **88**
Crystal Palace, London (Paxton), 315–**316**
Cubism, 467–469
Cup Bearer and Musicians, Etruscan wall painting, **374**
cupid, attrib. Michelangelo, **21**
Currier & Ives, **204**–205
Cuvillies, François, the Elder, Mirror Room, Amalienburg, Munich, **439**
Cycladic art, *Harp Player*, **363**; *Statuette of a Woman*, **30**
Cypriot sculpture, **266**

Dada, 475
Daguerre, Louis Jacques Mandé, 218
Dahomey art, *Lion*, from treasure of King Gbehanzin, 534–**535**
Dali, Salvador, *The Persistence of Memory*, **476**; *The Temptation of Saint Anthony*, **73**
Daumier, Honoré, *Frightened Woman*, **159**; *Murder in the rue Transnonain*, **55**–56
David, Jacques Louis, *The Death of Marat*, **445**–446
Dazzeloids, CD-ROM, **263**
death, as a theme in art, 79–80
Degas, Edgar, *Dancers Practicing at the Barre*, **111**–112; *The Tub*, 460–**461**
de Kooning, Willem, painted toilet seats, **21**; *Woman and Bicycle*, **483**
Delacroix, Eugène, *Liberty Leading the People*, **452**
Delaunay, Sonia, *Electric Prisms*, **128**–129
Derain, André, *The Turning Road, l'Estaque*, **9**–10
Diarra, Nakunte, mud-dyed cloth, **535**
Dine, Jim, *The Heart and the Wall*, **202**
Dipylon Vase, 366
Disney Building, Orlando, Fla. (Isozaki), **331**
Dogon art, Mali, *Horse and Rider*, **136**; *Seated Couple*, **532**
Dolce Vita, La (Fellini), **247**
dome construction, 312–315; geodesic, 321, 323
Donatello, *St. Mark*, **400**
Doric style, in Greek architecture, **307**
Doryphorus (Spear Bearer), copy after Polyclitus, **371**–372
Douglas, Aaron, *Aspects of Negro Life: From Slavery Through Reconstruction*, **474**
Douris, *Eos and Memnon*, red-figure kylix, **366**
Dragon and the Beasts Cast Into Hell, The, from *Cloisters Apocalypse*, **8**
Dresden Codex, Maya art, **171**
drypoint, 199
Dubuffet, Jean, *Childbirth*, **75**–76
Duccio, *Christ Entering Jerusalem*, **393**
Duchamp, Marcel, *L.H.O.O.Q.*, **475**; *Nude Descending a Staircase, No. 2*, **471**
Dufy, Raoul, *Regatta at Cowes*, **108**
Dürer, Albrecht, *Adam and Eve*, **41**, 43; biography, 42; *Reclining Female Nude (Proportion Study)*, **136**; *Rhinoceros*, **192**; *Self-Portrait*, **42**

Eakins, Thomas, *The Biglin Brothers Racing*, **86**–87; *The Concert Singer*, **96**
Early Christian art, 380–382; *Constantine the Great*, **381**; Old St. Peter's, Rome (reconstruction), **382**; St. Paul's Outside the Walls, Rome, **382**

earthworks, Herd, *Sunflower Still Life*, **285**; Serpent Mound, Locust Grove, Ohio, **285**; Smithson, *Spiral Jetty*, **286**

Easter Island, stone figures, **536**

Eastern Woodlands, Cole culture, *Head*, **526**–527

Eddy, Don, *New Shoes for H*, **488**–489

Edenshaw, Charles, 529–530; *Chief Albert Edenshaw's Myth House of Kiusta*, **530**

edition, in printmaking, 190

egg tempera, 175–176

Egyptian art, 354–359; *Akhenaten* portrait, 356–**357**; Great Pyramids, Giza, **51**–52; *Great Sphinx*, **354**; *Hippopotamus*, **295**; *Model of a Boat*, from Thebes, **355**; *Mycerinus and Ka-Merer-Nebty*, 280–281; *Nefertiti*, portrait bust, **357**; *Nefertiti*, statuette, **357**; *Palette of King Narmer*, **354**–355; *Seated Scribe*, from Saqqara, **355**; Tutankhamun, burial mask, **358**; *Tutankhamun and His Queen*, relief sculpture, **278**; Tutankhamun tomb, opening, **359**; wall painting, from Thebes, **356**; *Young Woman with a Gold Pectoral*, Coptic, **173**

Eiffel, Alexandre Gustave, Eiffel Tower, Paris, **316**–317

El Greco, *The Burial of Count Orgaz*, 422–**423**

emphasis, as design principle, 138–142

Empress Theodora and Retinue, mosaic at Ravenna, **382**–383

encaustic, 173

engraving, 198–199; wood, 197

environmental design, 339–343

environmental sculpture, 283–286, 288

Escher, M. C., *Symmetry Drawing E 67 (Study of Regular Division of the Plane with Horsemen)*, **94**

Eskimo art, Munguituk, **191**

etching, 200–202

Etruscan art, 374–375; *Cup Bearer and Musicians*, wall painting, **374**; *Sarcophagus of the Spouses*, **79**

Expressionism, 33, 462–463; Abstract, 34, 479–483; German, 33, 194

Eye-Dazzler Blanket, Navajo, **530**

Fabergé, Peter Carl, *Coronation Egg*, **299**

"Fallingwater" (Kaufmann House), Bear Run, Pa. (Wright), **336**

Fantin-Latour, Henri, *Edouard Manet*, **457**

Fat God, Maya, Jaina Island, Mexico, **525**

Fauvism, 9–10, 466

fax drawing (Hockney), 166–**167**

Fellini, Federico, *La Dolce Vita*, **247**

ferroconcrete, 320

fiber, as craft material, 302–304

figure-ground relationship, 94

Fischl, Eric, *On the Stairs of the Temple*, **498**

Fitzgibbon, John H., *Kno-Shr, Kansas Chief*, 218–**219**

Flack, Audrey, *Marilyn*, **44**

flying buttresses, 311

focal point, as design principle, 138–142

foreshortening, 118

form, and content, defined, 36

fractal imagery (Mandelbrot), **102**

Frankenthaler, Helen, *Nature Abhors a Vacuum*, **186**

Freed, James Ingo, United States Holocaust Memorial Museum, Washington, D.C., **328**

French Revolution, 442–446

fresco, 173–175

Freud, Lucian, *Naked Man, Back View*, **494**–495

Fuller, R. Buckminster, biography, 322; U.S. Pavilion, Expo 67, Montreal, **321**, 323

Futurism, 124

Galán, Julio, *The Great Haircut (El gran corte de pelo)*, **502**

Gamson, Annabelle, "The Women of Union Square" (inspired by Isabel Bishop), **150**

Gaudí, Antoni, Casa Milá, Barcelona, **334**

Gauguin, Paul, biography, 463; *The Day of the God (Mahana no Atua)*, **134**; *Les Miserables (Self-Portrait)*, **463**; *Nafea Faaipoipo (When Are You To Be Married?)*, **462**, 464; *Vincent van Gogh*, 32

Gehry, Frank O., *The Knife Ship from "Il Corso del Coltello,"* **146**; Frederick R. Weisman Museum of Art, University of Minnesota at Minneapolis, **327**

Genji Monogatari, handscroll illustration, 518–**519**

genre art, in painting, 60–63; in photography, 225–226

Gentileschi, Artemisia, *Judith and Maidservant with the Head of Holofernes*, 428–**429**

geodesic domes, 321–323

geometric style, in Greek art, 366

Géricault, Théodore, *The Raft of the Medusa*, 86–87

Ghiberti, Lorenzo, "Gates of Paradise," **399**–400; *Sacrifice of Isaac*, **399**; *The Story of Jacob and Esau*, **279**

Giacometti, Alberto, *The Nose*, 84–85

Giorgione, *The Tempest*, **414**

Giotto, *The Lamentation*, 393–**394**

Giza, Egypt, Great Pyramids, **51**–52; Sphinx, **354**

glass, as craft material, 295–297; stained, 297

Glass House, New Canaan, Conn. (Johnson), **338**

golden mean (section), **145**

Goldin, Nan, *David in My Hallway, NYC*, **230**

Gone with the Wind (Selznick), 244–245

Gospel Book of Archbishop Ebbo, **386**–387

Gospel Book of Otto III, **502**

Gothic style, 389–390; in architecture, 310–311, 389; Chartres Cathedral, 48–**49**, **311**, **389**

gouache, 184

Goya, Francisco de, biography, 141; *Executions of the Third of May, 1808*, **140**; *Goya in His Studio*, **141**; *Hasta la Muerte (Until Death)*, from *Los Caprichos*, **201**

Granada, Spain, Alhambra, **312**

Grave Stele of Hegeso, 18–**19**

Graves, Nancy, *Camel VI, VII, & VIII*, **94**; *Synonymous with Ceremony*, 277–**278**

Great Mosque, Córdoba, Spain, **312**

Great Pyramids, Giza, Egypt, **51**–52

Great Sphinx, Giza, Egypt, **354**

Great Stupa, Sanchi, India, 48; *Yakshi* detail on east gate, **512**

Great Wall of China, **52**

Greek art, 365–374; *Aphrodite of Melos*, **49**; *Dipylon Vase*, **366**; Douris, *Eos and Memnon*, **366**; *Grave Stele of Hegeso*, 18–**19**; *kouros*, Archaic, **371**; *Kroisos (Kouros from Anavysos)*, **371**; *Laocoön Group*, **372**–373; Parthenon, **47**, 307–308, **368**–370; Polyclitus, *Spear Bearer* (copy), **371**–372; Praxiteles, *Hermes with the Infant Dionysus*, 280–281; *Three Goddesses*, Parthenon sculptures, **370**

Greek Orders, **307**

Greenfield, Lois, *Daniel Ezralow & Ashley Roland*, **240**

Griffith, D. W., *The Birth of a Nation*, **242**–243

Grooms, Red, *Gertrude*, **212**–213; *Philadelphia Cornucopia*, **283**

Gropius, Walter, 477

Grünewald, Matthias, *The Crucifixion*, from *Isenheim Altarpiece*, **419**

Guanyin, wood, Song Dynasty, **509**–510

Guanyin the Merciful, Qing Dynasty porcelain, **511**

Guernica (Picasso), protection of, 57

Guerrilla Girls, Art People, **151**

Guggenheim Museum, New York (Wright), **110**–111; Holzer installation; **500**; *The Knife Ship* installation, **146**

Guilbert, Maurice, *Lautrec par lui-même*, **17**

Haas, Richard, *trompe-l'oeil* mural, Cincinnati, **30**

Habitat, Montreal (Safdie), **334**–335

Hachtman, Tom, *Picasso on the Beach*, cover for *The New Yorker*, **262**

Hagia Sophia, Istanbul, **314**, **384**

Haida art, Northwest Coast, *Chief Albert Edenshaw's Myth House of Kiusta*, **530**

Hall of Mirrors, Versailles Palace, **434**

Hammurabi, ruler of Babylonia, 352–353; *Stele of Hammurabi*, **352**

haniwa figure, *Horse*, **292**

Hanson, Duane, *Self-Portrait with Model*, **490**–491

Happenings, 498–499

Hardouin-Mansart, Jules, Hall of Mirrors, Versailles Palace, **434**

Haring, Keith, *Subway Drawing*, **5**

Harlem Renaissance, 177, 473–**474**

Harp Player, Cycladic, **363**

haut relief, 279

Hawkins, Gerald S., and Stonehenge, 349–350

Head, Benin, **534**

Head, Cole culture, Ohio, **526**–527

Head, Olmec, from La Venta, **362**

Head of the Buddha, Gandhara style, from India, **512**–513

Head of a Dignitary, Akkadian, **351**

Hearst Castle, San Simeon, Calif. (Morgan), **338**–339

Heiji Monogatari, **520**

Hellenistic style, in Greek art, 372

Herd, Stan, *Sunflower Still Life*, **285**

Hermes with the Infant Dionysus (attrib. Praxiteles), 280–281

hierarchical scale, 356

Hildegard of Bingen, Art People, 391

Hippopotamus, ceramic figure from Egypt, **295**

Hiroshige, Ando, *Rain Shower on Ohashi Bridge*, **192**–193; Van Gogh painting after, **193**

Hirshfield, Morris, *Boy with Dog*, **144**

Hitchcock, Alfred, 247–249; biography, 248; *North by Northwest*, **249**

Hockney, David, *A Bigger Splash*, 486–**487**; *Breakfast with Stanley in Malibu, August 23, 1989*, 166–**167**; *The Brooklyn Bridge*, 216–**217**

Hogarth, William, *The Marriage Contract*, from *Marriage à la Mode*, **198**–199

Hokusai, Katsushika, biography, 195; *Self-Portrait*, **195**; *View of Fuji from Seven-Ri Beach*, **194**; *Woman Adjusting Her Hair*, **164**

Holbein, Hans, the Younger, *Henry VIII*, 419–**420**

Holocaust Memorial Museum, Washington, D.C. (Freed), **328**

Holzer, Jenny, *Selections from Truisms, Inflammatory Essays, The Living Series, The Survival Series, Under a Rock, Laments, and new writing*, **500**

Homer, Winslow, *In Came a Storm of Wind, Rain and Spray—and Portia*, 197; *Shore and Surf, Nassau*, **183**

Hopper, Edward, *Early Sunday Morning*, **148**

Horowitz, Ryszard, *Allegory*, **263**

Horse and Rider, Dogon, from Mali, **136**

Horyu-ji, Nara, Japan, Five-Storied Pagoda, **518**

Hotel del Coronado, San Diego (Reid), **332**

Houdon, Jean Antoine, *La Frileuse (Winter)*, **30**

Houlberg, Klindt, *Phantasy Plenishing*, **301**

Huari, Peru, mosaic mirror, **525**–526

hue, as property of color, 101

Hui-zong, emperor of China, 60

Human-Headed Winged Lion, Assyrian, **352**

Hunt, Richard, *Jacob's Ladder*, 284–**285**

iconography, 40–**44**

Ictinus and Callicrates, Parthenon, Athens, **47**, 307–308, 368–370

illumination, of books and manuscripts, 60–61, 387; *Cloisters Apocalypse*, **8**; *Gospel Book of Archbishop Ebbo*, **386**–387; *Gospel Book of Otto III*, **502**; Koran page, 156–**157**

illusionistic art, defined, 28

illustration, 168–169

imaginative art, 70–74

impasto, 179

Impressionism, 63, 458–460

Indian art, 512–517; *Akbar Hunting with Trained Cheetahs* (Lal and Sanwlah), **64**–65; *The "Beautiful Bodhisattva,"* from Ajanta, **513**; Great Stupa, Sanchi, **48**; *Head of the Buddha*, Gandhara style, 512–**513**; Karan, *A Nobleman Riding an Elephant*, **184**; *Krishna as the Butter Thief*, **516**; *Krishna and Radha in a Grove*, 106–**107**; *Lady with a Bird*, **38**–39; Mansur, *Emperor Jahangir's Zebra*, **517**; *Portrait of a Landowner*, 236–**237**; *Seated Buddha*, from Gandhara, **281**; *Sita in the Garden of Lanka with Ravana and His Demons*, **43**; Taj Mahal, 314–**315**; *Yakshi*, detail of Great Stupa, **512**

Indus Valley Civilization, torso from Harappa, **361**

Industrial Revolution, 447

Ingres, Jean Auguste Dominique, *La Grande Odalisque*, **449**; *Portrait of Nicolo Paganini*, **157**

installations, 500–501

intaglio printmaking, 198–203; plate-making methods, **198**

intensity, as property of color, 101

International style, in architecture, 318–319, 330–331

Ionic style, in Greek architecture, **307**

Ishtar Gate, from Babylon, **353**

Islamic art, Alhambra, Granada, Spain, **312**; Great Mosque, Córdoba, Spain, **312**; Koran, calligraphy page, 156–**157**; Taj Mahal, Agra, India, 314–**315**

isometric perspective, *see* perspective

Isozaki, Arata, Team Disney Building, Orlando, Fla., **331**

Istanbul, Hagia Sophia, 314, **384**

Jaina Island, Mexico, Maya *Fat God*, **525**

Japanese art, 517–521; *haniwa* figure, *Horse*, **292**; *Heiji Monogatari*, **520**; Horyu-ji, Nara, **518**; Korin, *Iris and Bridge* screen, **521**; *Kosode (Woman's Robe)*, **303**; *Kumano Mandala*, **117**; Sesshu, *Autumn Landscape*, **182**–183; Sesshu, *Daruma*, **27**; *Shukongojin*, guardian figure from Nara, **281**; Sotatsu, *The Zen Priest Choka*, 136–**137**; *The Tale of Genji*, 518–**519**; *see also* Hiroshige, Hokusai

Jeanne-Claude, biography, 287; *Running Fence*, **286**, 288

Jefferson, Thomas, University of Virginia, Charlottesville, **340**–341

Johns, Jasper, *Target with Four Faces*, **485**; *Winter*, from *The Seasons*, **493**

Johnson, Philip, Glass House, New Canaan, Conn., **338**; Seagram Building, New York, **330**–331

Johnson, William H., *Going to Church*, **135**

Jonas, Joan, *Double Lunar Dogs*, **253**

Jones, Ben, *In the Spirit*, **127**

Jones, Fay, Thorncrown Chapel, Eureka Springs, Ark., **325**

Kahlo, Frida, *The Two Fridas*, **132**

Kandinsky, Wassily, *Picture with an Archer*, 472–**473**

Karan, Khem, *A Nobleman Riding an Elephant*, **184**

Kaufmann House ("Fallingwater"), Bear Run, Pa. (Wright), **336**

Kiefer, Anselm, *Interior*, 496–**497**

kinetic sculpture, 288

King Kong, **250**

Kirchner, Ernst Ludwig, *The Couple*, **106**–107; *Street, Dresden*, 470–**471**

Kirkland, Douglas, *Cher*, **238**

Klee, Paul, *Costumed Puppets*, **135**; *Dance You Monster to My Soft Song!*, 477–**478**

Klimt, Gustav, *Expectation*, **109**

Kline, Franz, *Chief*, **483**

Klumpke, Anna Elizabeth, *Rosa Bonheur*, **455**

Kneeling Woman Presenting a Bowl, Luba, from Congo (Zaire), **532**–533

Kokoschka, Oskar, *Self-Portrait*, **178**–179

Kollwitz, Käthe, biography, 165; *Death and the Mother*, **33**; *Fettered Man*, **164**; *Self-Portrait with Hand on Her Forehead*, **165**

Koons, Jeff, *Puppy*, **289**

Koran, calligraphy page, 156–**157**

Korin, Ogata, *Iris and Bridge* screen, **521**

Kosode (Woman's Robe), from Japan, **303**

Kouros, Archaic Greek, **371**

Krasner, Lee, 35; biography, 482; *The Bull*, **481**; *Self-Portrait*, **482**

Krishna as the Butter Thief, from Tanjore, India, **516**

Krishna and Radha in a Grove, Indian painting, 106–**107**

Kroisos (Kouros from Anavysos), **371**

Kroninger, Stephen, *Michael Jackson*, **257**

Kruger, Barbara, *Untitled (Are We Having Fun Yet?)*, **497**

Kumano Mandala, **117**

Kunz, Anita, *Too Little, Too Late*, advertisement, **257**

Kupka, František, *Prometheus in Red and Blue*, 108–**109**

Kwakiutl art, mask representing Dzonokwa, 528–**529**

Lachaise, Gaston, *Standing Woman*, **267**

Lady with a Bird, Indian painting, **38**–39

Lal and Sanwlah, *Akbar Hunting with Trained Cheetahs*, **64**–65

Landa, Diego de, and Maya art, 171

Lange, Dorothea, *Heading West, Tulare Lake, California*, **234**–235

Laocoön Group, **372**–373; restorations, 373

Lascaux, France, cave art, **4**–5

Last Supper, The (Leonardo da Vinci), restoration, **115**

Las Vegas, Luxor Hotel, **333**

Laurana, Luciano, *View of an Ideal City*, **114**

Laurencin, Marie, *Group of Artists*, **112**–113

Lautrec, Henri de Toulouse-, *At the Circus: Trained Pony and Baboon*, **158**; biography, 17; *L'Estampe originale*, **16**; *La Goulue at the Moulin Rouge*, **205**; photograph, 17

La Venta, *Colossal Head*, Olmec, **362**

Lawrence, Jacob, biography, 177; *One of the Largest Race Riots Occurred in East St. Louis*, **58**; *Self-Portrait*, **177**; *Vaudeville*, **176**

Layton, Elizabeth, *Garden of Eden*, **6**

Lebrun, Charles, Hall of Mirrors, Versailles Palace, **434**

Le Corbusier, Notre-Dame-du-Haut, Ronchamp, France, **324**–325

Lega art, Congo-Kinshasa, ivory mask, **533**

Léger, Fernand, *The Great Walking Flower (La Grande Fleur Qui March)*, **264**–265

Leibovitz, Annie, *Wilt Chamberlain and Willie Shoemaker*, **145**

Leonardo da Vinci, biography, 407; *The Last Supper*, **114**–116, 405; *Mona Lisa*, **406**; *Self-Portrait*, **407**; *Study of Human Proportions According to Vitruvius*, **405**; theft of *Mona Lisa*, 424

Levart, Lisa, *Emilie Plauché and Pamela Jones Dance "The Women of Union Square,"* (dance by Annabelle Gamson), **150**

Lever House, New York (Skidmore, Owings, and Merrill), **318**–319

LeWitt, Sol, *Wall Drawing 111—A Wall Divided Vertically into Five Equal Parts, with Ten Thousand Lines in Each Part: 1:6" Long*, **491**

Leyster, Judith, *The Proposition*, **437**–438

Li Cheng, *A Solitary Temple amid Clearing Peaks*, **510**–511

Lichtenstein, Roy, *Masterpiece*, **486**; *Still Life with Crystal Bowl*, **89**

light, as design element, 95–96

Limbourg brothers, *Les Très Riches Heures du Duc de Berry*, 60–**61**

Lin, Maya Ying, Vietnam Memorial, Washington, D.C., **80**

line, as visual element, 83–92

linear perspective, *see* perspective

linocut, 196

Lion, Dahomey, from the treasure of King Gbehanzin, 534–**535**

Lippi, Fra Filippo, *Nativity*, **40**–41

lithography, 203–209

load-bearing construction, 306–307

Lorenzo di Credi, *Drapery for a Standing Man, Represented Frontally*, **97**–98

lost-wax casting, 267–270

Louis XIV, king of France, 54–55, 433–434

Louis XV, king of France, 434

Louis XVI, king of France, 434

Luba art, Congo (Zaire), *Kneeling Woman Presenting a Bowl*, **532**–533

Lumière brothers, *L'Arrivée d'un train en gare*, 241–242

Luxor Hotel, Las Vegas, **333**

Magnolia Vase (Tiffany and Company), **298**

Magritte, René, *The Blank Cheque*, **8**–9; *La Folie des grandeurs II*, **143**

Mall of America, Bloomington, Minn., **343**

Man Ray, and photography, 237; photograph of Gertrude Stein and Alice B. Toklas, **14**

Mandelbrot, Benoit B., *A Fractal Dragon*, **102**

Manet, Edouard, biography, 457; *Le Déjeuner sur l'herbe*, **456**–458

Mangbetu portrait vessel, 290–**291**

Mannerism, 422–423

Mansur, *Emperor Jahangir's Zebra*, **517**

Mantegna, Andrea, *Dead Christ*, **118**–119

manuscript illumination, *see* illumination

Mapplethorpe, Robert, and censorship, 232–233; *Ken Moody and Robert Sherman*, **231**; *Self-Portrait*, **232**

María, *see* María Martínez

Marie Antoinette, queen of France, 442, **443**, 444

Marin, John, *From the Bridge, New York City*, **182**–183

Marisol, *Women and Dog*, 18–**19**

marriage, as a theme in art, 76–79

Martínez, María, biography, 293; black-on-black jar, **292**; photograph, 293

Masaccio, *The Tribute Money*, **401**–402

masks, Bamum, 534–**535**; Bella Coola, **300**; Benin, **533**; Kwakiutl, 528–**529**; Lega, **533**

mass, as design element, 92–94

Massys, Quintin (copy after), *Grotesque Old Woman*, 24–25

Matisse, Henri, biography, 133; *Large Composition with Masks*, **132**; *Mme Matisse Madras rouge (The Red Madras Headdress)*, **82**–83; photograph by Capa, **133**; *The Red Studio*, **128**–129; *The Woman with the Hat*, **466**–467

Maya art, 524–525; destruction of, 171; *Dresden Codex*, **171**; *Fat God*, Jaina Island, **525**; Nunnery, Uxmal, relief carvings, **524**; Pyramid of the Magician, Uxmal, **524**

Mesa Verde, Colo., Cliff Palace, **527**–528

Mesopotamian art, 350–353; *Head of a Dignitary*, Akkadian, **351**; *Human-Headed Winged Lion*, Assyrian, **352**; Ishtar Gate, from Babylon, **353**; *Stele of Hammurabi*, **352**; votive statuettes from Tell Asmar, Sumerian, **351**; *Walking Lion*, from Babylon, **353**

metal, as craft material, 297–299

metalpoint, 158

Mexican art, ancient, 522–525

Meyerowitz, Joel, *St. Louis Gateway Arch*, **92**

mezzotint, 200

Michelangelo, biography, 409; *Creation of Adam*, detail of Sistine Chapel ceiling, **412**; *Creation of Eve*, detail of Sistine Chapel ceiling, **412**–413; cupid attrib. to, **21**; *David*, 406, **408**; *Head of a Satyr*, **88**; portrait, **409**; St. Peter's Basilica, apse and dome, **413**; Sistine Chapel ceiling frescoes, **408**, 409, **410**–**412**, 413

Mies van der Rohe, Ludwig, Seagram Building, New York, **330**–331

Miller, Lee, *Solarized Portrait of Unknown Woman, Paris*, **237**

Mimbres bowl, Mogollon culture, **528**

Ming vase, China, **294**

Minimal Art, 487–489

Minoan art, *Snake Goddess*, **364**; *Toreador Fresco*, at Knossos, **364**

Miró, Joan, *Carnival of Harlequin*, 476–**477**

Mission St. Francis of Assisi, Ranchos de Taos, N.M., 306–307

Mitchell, Joan, *Lucky Seven*, **31**

mobile, Calder, National Gallery, **288**

Mochica art, stirrup vessel, 290–**291**

modeling, for sculpture, 266–267

Modern Times (Chaplin), 243–**244**

Modersohn-Becker, Paula, *Mother and Child*, **76**–77

Modigliani, Amedeo, *Female Nude, Kneeling*, **84**

Moghal art, *see* Indian art

Mogollon culture, Mimbres bowl, **528**

Moissac, France, abbey church of St.-Pierre, relief sculpture, **390**

Mona Lisa (Leonardo da Vinci), **406**; theft of, 424

Mondrian, Piet, *Composition in Blue B*, 148–**149**; *Composition with Red, Yellow, and Blue*, **92**–93

Monet, Claude, *Water Lily Pool*, **459**

monoprint, 212

Moore, Henry, biography, 271; *Reclining Figure*, **270**

Morgan, Barbara, *Martha Graham: Letter to the World (Kick)*, **222**

Morgan, Julia, Hearst Castle, San Simeon, Calif., **338**–339

Morisot, Berthe, *La Lecture*, **459**–460

mosaic art, 188; *Baptism of Christ and Procession of Twelve Apostles*, Ravenna, **138**; *Empress Theodora*, Ravenna, **382**–383; *Young Women Exercising*, **188**

Moscow, Cathedral of St. Basil, **315**

Moses, Anna Mary Robertson ("Grandma"), *Hoosick Falls in Winter*, **140**, 142

Mother and Child, Bambara, from Mali, **76**–77

motion, as design element, 122–124

mud-dyed cloth (Diarra), from Mali, **535**

multiples, 189

Munch, Edvard, biography, 207; *Death in the Sickroom*, **15**; *Self-Portrait between Clock and Bed*, **207**; *Sin*, **206**

Mungituk, *Man Carried to the Moon*, **191**

Murasaki, Lady (Shikibu), *The Tale of Genji*, 518–**519**

Murray, Elizabeth, *Painter's Progress*, **495**

Museum of Science, Boston, bus advertisement, **258**–259

musical instrument, Early Renaissance, **300**

Musician figure, Chimú, **426**

Muybridge, Eadweard, *Woman Kicking*, from *Animal Locomotion*, **239**

Mycenaean art, lion's-head Rhyton, **364**

Mycerinus, pharaoh of Egypt, pyramid, **51**–52; *Mycerinus and Ka-Merer-Nebty*, **280**–281

naive art, 27–29

Names Project, *AIDS Memorial Quilt*, 80–**81**

Nara, Japan, Horyu-ji, **518**

National Endowment for the Arts, 232–233

naturalistic art, defined, 28

nature and art, 63–70

Navajo art, *Eye-Dazzler Blanket*, **530**; "squash blossom" necklace, **299**

Neel, Alice, *Andy Warhol*, **211**; biography, 181; *Self-Portrait*, **181**; *Westreich Family*, **180**

Nefertiti, queen of Egypt, **357**

Nelson, Joan, *Untitled (#227)*, **70**

Neoclassicism, 445–446, 449

Neo-Expressionism, 495–497

Nessim, Barbara, *Two Shadows Outside Two Women*, **166**

Nevelson, Louise, biography, 276; *City on a High Mountain*, **122**; *Mrs. N's Palace*, **277**; photograph, **276**

New York School, 479–483

New Yorker, The, cartoon by Reilly, **169**; cover illustration by Hachtman, **262**

Niépce, Joseph Nicéphore, 218

Nîmes, France, Pont du Gard, **309**

Noguchi, Isamu, *Black Sun* (study), **110**–111

Nolde, Emil, *The Prophet*, **194**

nonrepresentational art, defined, 31

North by Northwest (Hitchcock), **249**

Northwest Coast, Americas, Bella Coola mask, **300**; Kwakiutl mask, 528–**529**; Haida model, *Chief Edenshaw's Myth House of Kiusta*, **530**; Tlingit *Owl Man Perching on a Raven*, **529**

Notre-Dame-du-Haut, Ronchamp, France (Le Corbusier), **324**–325

Nubian art, cattle bowl, **360**

Nunnery, Uxmal, Mexico, relief carvings, **524**

Oceania, 536

oil painting, 178–180

O'Keeffe, Georgia, 229; biography, 69; *Black Hollyhock, Blue Larkspur*, **68**; photograph by Alfred Stieglitz, **69**

Old St. Peter's, Rome (reconstruction), **382**

Oldenburg, Claes, *Clothespin*, **95**–96; *The Knife Ship from "Il Corso del Coltello,"* **146**

Olmec art, *"Baby" Figure*, **362**; *Colossal Head*, **362**

Olympic games, 1994, pictogram symbols, **255**

Orlando, Fla., Team Disney Building (Isozaki), **331**

Oseberg Burial Ship, animal head, **385**

O'Sullivan, Timothy, *Sand Springs, Nevada*, **222**–**223**

Otto III Enthroned Receiving the Homage of Four Parts of the Empire, **502**

Owl Man Perching on a Raven, Tlingit, Northwest Coast, **529**

Paik, Nam June, *Fin de Siècle II*, **252**–253

Palette of King Narmer, **354**–355

Palmer, Flora Bond (Fanny), *American Express Train*, **204**

Panini, Giovanni Paolo, *Interior of the Pantheon*, **313**

Pantheon, Rome, **378**–379; Panini painting of interior, **313**

Papa, Anthony, *15 Years to Life*, **6**

Paracas Textile, from Peru, **302**

Parks, Gordon, *American Gothic*, **220**

Parthenon, Athens (Ictinus and Callicrates), **47**, **307**–308, **368**–370; pediment sculptures, **370**

pastel, 160–161

Patel, Pierre, view of Versailles palace and gardens, **433**

patina, 270

Paxton, Joseph, Crystal Palace, London, 315–**316**

Pearlstein, Philip, *Female Nude on a Platform Rocker*, **480**

Pei, I. M., Rock-and-Roll Hall of Fame and Museum, Cleveland, **326**–327

Pelham, Peter, *Cotton Mather*, **200**

pen and ink, 161–162

pencil, graphite, 157–158

pendentives, **314**

Penn, Irving, photograph of David Smith, **275**

perception, 11–12

Perez, Pedro F., *Los Marielitos*, **93**–94

Performance Art, 498–499

Pericles, 368–370; *Art People*, **369**; portrait bust, **369**

Persian art, page from a Koran, 156–**157**

perspective, atmospheric, 118; isometric, **113**, 117; linear, **113**–117

Peru, ancient, Chimú *Musician* figure, **526**; Huari mirror, **525**–526; Mochica stirrup vessel, **290**–291; *Paracas Textile*, **302**

Perugia, Vincenzo, *Art People*, 424

Perugino, *A Man in Armor*, **158**

Pfaff, Judy, *cirque, Cirque*, **284**

Phidias, 368–370

photojournalism, 231, 234–235

Photorealism, 488–489

Picasso, Pablo, *The Accordionist*, **469**; *Au Cirque (At the Circus)*, **199**; biography, 468; *Les Demoiselles d'Avignon*, **466**–**467**; *Dora Maar Sitting*, **26**; *Girl Before a Mirror*, **152**–153; *Guernica*, **56**–58; *Guitar, Sheet Music, and Glass*, **187**–188; *Head*, study for *Guernica*, **167**; *Las Meninas (after Velázquez)*, **435**; *Olga Picasso in an Armchair*, **26**; *Portrait of a Young Girl, after Cranach the Younger, II*, **196**–**197**; *Self-Portrait* (1901), **27**; *Self-Portrait with Palette*, **468**; *Women Running on the Beach*, **262**

pictogram symbols, 1994 Winter Olympic Games, **255**

picture plane, defined, 112

Piero della Francesca, *The Resurrection*, **402**; *View of an Ideal City*, **114**

pigment, 156

Pippin, Horace, *John Brown Going to His Hanging*, **7**

Piranesi, Giovanni Battista, engraving of St. Paul's Outside the Walls, **382**

playing cards, woodcut, **191**

pointillism, 104, 160

political art, 51–59

Pollock, Jackson, 482; biography, 35; *Blue Poles*, **481**; *Convergence*, **34**; photograph by Hans Namuth, **35**

Polyclitus, *Spear Bearer* (Roman copy), **371**–372

Pompeii, wall painting, Villa of the Mysteries, **377**

Pont du Gard, Nîmes, France, **309**

Pop Art, 486–487

Portland Vase, **296**–297

Portrait of a Landowner, early Indian photograph, **236**–237

portrait bust, Roman, **376**

Poseidon or *Zeus*, Greek sculpture, **144**

post-and-lintel construction, 307–308

Post-Impressionism, 460–464

Postmodern style, in architecture, 327, 331

potter's wheel, **294**

Poussin, Nicolas, *The Rape of the Sabine Women*, **431**, 433

Praxiteles (?), *Hermes with the Infant Dionysus*, **280**–281

prehistoric art, cave paintings, Chauvet, **344**–345, 347, 348; Lascaux, **4**–5; Serpent Mound, Locust Grove, Ohio, **285**; Stonehenge, **349**–350; *Venus of Willendorf*, **348**–349

prism, color refraction, **98**–99

proportion, as design principle, 142–146

public art, *Tilted Arc* (Serra), **23**

Purple Rose of Cairo, The (Allen), **250**

Pyramid of the Magician, Uxmal, Mexico, **524**

Pyramid of the Sun, Teotihuacán, Mexico, **523**

pyramids, Giza, Egypt, **51**–52

Qiu Ying, *A Lady in a Pavilion Overlooking a Lake*, **510**–511

Queen Nefertiti, portrait bust, **357**; statuette, **357**

Ramáyana, Indian epic poem, 43

Ranchos de Taos, N.M., Mission St. Francis of Assisi, **306**–307

Raphael, biography, 91; *Madonna and Child with Infant St. John*, **154**–155; *The Madonna of the Meadows*, **90**; *Pope Leo X with Two Cardinals*, **414**–**415**; *The School of Athens*, **174**; *Self-Portrait* (detail of *School of Athens*), **91**

Rauschenberg, Robert, *Bach's Rocks*, **59**; *Bed*, **485**; biography, 208; *Centennial Certificate M.M.A.*, **209**

Ravenna, *Baptism of Christ* mosaic, **138**; *Empress Theodora* mosaic, **382**–383; San Vitale, **383**–384

Realism, in French art, 453–454; in late-20th-century art, 489–491

red-figure style, in Greek vase painting, 366

Redon, Odilon, *Orpheus*, **74**

Reid, James and Merritt, Hotel del Coronado, San Diego, **332**

reinforced-concrete construction, 320

Reiss, Winold, *Mary McLeod Bethune*, 160–**161**

relief printmaking, 190–197

relief sculpture, 278–279

religion and art, 47–51

Rembrandt, *Arnold Tholinx*, **200**–201; biography, 163; *The Polish Rider*, **22**; *Self-Portrait with Saskia*, **163**; *Sortie of Captain Banning Cocq's Company of the Civic Guard (The Night Watch)*, **436**–437; *A Thatched Cottage by a Large Tree*, **162**

Rembrandt Research Project, 22

Ren Xia, *Cat on a Rock Beneath Banana Palms*, **68**

Renoir, Pierre-Auguste, *Le Moulin de la Galette*, **62**–63; *Piazza San Marco*, **458**–459; *Portrait of Madame Renoir*, **103**

representational art, defined, 28

restoration, Angkor Wat, **515**; *Laocoön Group*, **373**; *Last Supper*, **115**

Revolution, American, 447

Revolution, French, 443–445

Reynolds, Joshua, *Mrs. Mary Robinson (Perdita)*, **39**

Rickey, George, *Double L Excentric Gyratory II*, **123**

Rigaud, Hyacinthe, *Louis XIV*, **54**–55

Riley, Bridget, *Current*, **123**–124

Ringgold, Faith, *The Purple Quilt*, **186**–**187**

Rivera, Diego, *Detroit Industry*, **175**

Robinson, Henry Peach, *Fading Away*, **225**

Roche-Rabell, Arnaldo, *The Spirit of the Flesh*, **102**

Rock-and-Roll Hall of Fame and Museum, Cleveland (Pei), **326**–327

Rockwell, Norman, biography, 261; *The Tom Boy*, **260**; *Triple Self-Portrait*, **261**

Rococo art, 107, 438–443

Rodin, Auguste, *The Burghers of Calais*, **279**; *The Kiss*, **472**

Rogier van der Weyden, *St. Luke Drawing the Virgin*, **418**–419

Roman art, 375–379; *Augustus of Prima Porta*, **53**; Colosseum, **378**; Column of Trajan, **376**–377; *Constantine the Great*, **381**; Pantheon, **313**, 378–379; Pompeii, wall painting, **377**; Pont du Gard, Nîmes, France, **309**; *Portland Vase*, **296**–297; portrait bust, **376**; *Young Women Exercising*, mosaic, **188**

Romanesque style, 388–389; in architecture, 310; St. Sernin Cathedral, Toulouse, France, **310**, **388**–389

Romanticism, in French art, 452

Ronchamp, France, Notre-Dame-du-Haut (Le Corbusier), **324**–325

Rosenquist, James, *The Bird of Paradise Approaches the Hot Water Planet*, **214**

Rothenberg, Susan, *Blue U-Turn*, **494**

Rothko, Mark, *Orange and Yellow*, **484**

Rousseau, Henri, biography, 29; *The Dream*, **27**–28, 30–31; *Myself, Portrait-Landscape*, **29**; *A Wedding in the Country*, **78**

Rubens, Peter Paul, biography, 432; *The Honeysuckle Bower (Self-Portrait with Wife)*, **432**; *The Raising of the Cross*, **430**–431

Safdie, Moshe, Habitat, Montreal, 334–**335**

St. Basil's Cathedral, Moscow, **315**

St. Matthew the Evangelist, from *The Gospel Book of Archbishop Ebbo*, **386**–387

St. Paul's Outside the Walls, Rome, **382**

St. Peter's Basilica, Rome, **413**

St. Peter's, Old, Rome, **382**

Saint-Phalle, Niki de, *Black Venus*, **487**

St.-Pierre de Moissac, France, relief sculpture, **390**

St. Sernin Cathedral, Toulouse, France, **310**, **388**–389

San Simeon, Calif., Hearst Castle (Morgan), **338**–339

San Vitale, Ravenna, **383**–384

Sanchi, India, Great Stupa, **48**; *Yakshi* sculpture, **512**

Santa Maria della Vittoria, Rome, Cornaro Chapel (Bernini), **426**

Sarcophagus of the Spouses, Etruscan, **79**

Sargent, John Singer, *Madame X (Mme Gautreau)*, **465**

saturation, as property of color, 101

Saturday Evening Post, cover illustrations (Rockwell), **260**–261

Schapiro, Miriam, *Children of Paradise*, **130**–131

Schell, Sherril V., *Brooklyn Bridge*, 216–**217**

Schnabel, Julian, *Nicknames of Maitre d's*, **170**

School of Visual Arts, subway poster, **258**–259

screenprinting, 209–210

Scroll of the Emperors (Yan Liben), **508**

Seagram Building, New York (Mies van der Rohe and Johnson), **330**–331

Seated Buddha, from Gandhara, **281**

Seated Couple, Dogon, from Mali, **532**

Seated Scribe, from Saqqara, **355**

Segal, George, *Blue Girl on Park Bench*, **282**

Selznick, David O., *Gone with the Wind*, **244**–245

Sendak, Maurice, drawing from *Where the Wild Things Are*, 168–**169**

Senefelder, Alois, 203

serigraphy, 209–210

Serpent Mound, Locust Grove, Ohio, **285**

Serra, Richard, *Tilted Arc*, **23**

Sesshu, *Autumn Landscape*, **182**–183; *Daruma*, **27**

Seurat, Georges, *The Couple*, study for *A Sunday on La Grande Jatte*, **160**; *A Sunday on La Grande Jatte*, 104–**105**

Seventh Seal, The (Bergman), **246**

Sexton, John, *Merced River and Forest, Yosemite Valley, California*, **226**–227

sfumato, 406

Shahn, Ben, *Miners' Wives*, **37**

shape, as design element, 92–94

Shere, Sam, *Explosion of the Hindenburg, Lakehurst, New Jersey*, **234**–235

Sherman, Cindy, *Untitled #193*, **230**

Shi Huang Di, emperor of China, 52

Shift Online, home page design, **263**

Shukongojin, guardian figure from Nara, Japan, **281**

Siedlecka, Wanda, *Wordplay* type designs, **256**

silkscreen, 209–210

Silverman, Barton, *Ellen Owen at the 1992 Summer Olympics*, **240**–241

silverpoint, 158

simultaneous contrast, in colors, 104

Siqueiros, David Alfaro, *María Asúnsolo as a Child*, **185**

Sistine Chapel, Vatican, **408**; Michelangelo frescoes, 409, **410**–**412**, 413

Sita in the Garden of Lanka with Ravana and His Demons, Indian painting, **43**

site works, 491

skeleton-and-skin construction, in architecture, 306

Skidmore, Owings & Merrill, Lever House, New York, **318**–319; United States Air Force Academy, Colorado Springs, Colo., **342**

Sluter, Claus, *Moses Well*, **392**

Smith, David, *Becca*, **274**; biography, 275

Smithson, Robert, *Spiral Jetty*, **286**

Snake Goddess, Minoan, **364**

solarization, in photography, 237

Solomon R. Guggenheim Museum, *see* Guggenheim Museum

Sotatsu, Nonomura, *The Zen Priest Choka*, 136–**137**

space, as design element, 110–120

Spear Bearer, copy after Polyclitus, **371**–372

Sphinx, Giza, Egypt, **354**

Stanford University, Palo Alto, Calif. (Coolidge), **341**

Starn, Doug and Mike, *Double Stark Portrait in Swirl*, **238**

Statuette of a Woman, Cycladic, **30**

steel-frame construction, 317–319

Steichen, Edward, *Alfred Stieglitz at "291,"* **229**

Stein, Gertrude, Art People, 14

Steir, Pat, *The Brueghel Series (A Vanitas of Style)*, **498**–**499**

Stele of Hammurabi, **352**

Stella, Frank, *La penna di hu*, **213**; *Pergusa*, **492**; *Takht-i-Sulayman 1*, **488**

Stettheimer, Florine, *Lake Placid*, **63**

Stieglitz, Alfred, biography, 229; *Georgia O'Keeffe*, **69**; *The Steerage*, **228**

stippling, **88**

Stonehenge, **349**–350

style, 36–40

stylized art, defined, 30

subject matter, defined, 36

Sullivan, Louis, Wainwright Building, St. Louis, **318**

Sumerian art, *see* Mesopotamian art

Sundiata: Lion King of Mali, book cover, **258**–259

Surrealism, 73, 475–476

suspension, in architecture, 319

Sutton Hoo Ship Burial, purse cover, **385**

Sydney Opera House, Australia (Utzon), **320**

Taj Mahal, Agra, India, 314–**315**

Tale of Genji, The, handscroll illustration, 518–**519**

Tang Dynasty ceramics, *Camel*, **509**

Tanner, Henry Ossawa, *Portrait of the Artist's Mother*, **139**

Taos, N.M., Mission St. Francis of Assisi, **306**–307

Tarquinia, Etruscan wall painting, **374**

Tathagata Buddha, Tibetan painting, **50**

Team Disney Building, Orlando, Fla. (Isozaki), **331**

Tell Asmar, Iraq, votive statuettes from Square Temple, **351**

tempera, 175–176

Teniers, David, the Younger, *The Picture Gallery of the Archduke Leopold*, **2**–3

tensile strength, in architecture, 306

Teotihuacán, Mexico, Pyramid of the Sun, **523**

terra cotta, 294

texture, as design element, 107–109

Thebes, Egypt, boat model, **355**; wall painting, **356**

Thompson, Catherine, *The Elephant's Child*, **297**

Thorncrown Chapel, Eureka Springs, Ark. (Jones), **325**

Three Goddesses, Parthenon sculptures, **370**

throwing, for ceramics, **294**

Tiahuanaco, Peru, *see* Huari

Tibetan art, *Tathagata Buddha*, **50**

Tiffany and Company, *Magnolia Vase*, **298**

Tiger, Chinese bronze, **361**

time, as design element, 120, 122

Tintoretto, *The Last Supper*, **422**

tintype, 218

Titian, *Charles V at Mühlberg*, **415**; *Portrait of a Man*, **416**

Tlingit art, *Owl Man Perching on a Raven*, **529**

toilet seats, de Kooning, **21**

Toklas, Alice B., **14**

Toreador Fresco, Minoan, **364**

Toulouse, France, St. Sernin Cathedral, **310**, **388**–389

Toulouse-Lautrec, *see* Lautrec

Trajan's Column, Rome, **376**–377

Très Riches Heures du Duc de Berry, Les (Limbourgs), 60–**61**

trompe-l'oeil, 28; Richard Haas mural, **30**

Turner, J. M. W., *Rockets and Blue Lights (Close at Hand) to Warn Steamboats of Shoal Water*, **65**

Turrell, James, *Afrum-Proto*, **288**–289

Tutankhamun, pharaoh of Egypt, burial mask, **358**; relief sculpture on throne, **278**; tomb opening, **358**–359

Unicorn in Captivity, The, from *The Unicorn Tapestries*, **302**–303

United States Air Force Academy, Colorado Springs, Colo. (Skidmore, Owings & Merrill), **341**–342

United States Holocaust Memorial Museum, Washington, D.C. (Freed), **328**

U.S. Pavilion, Expo 67, Montreal (Fuller), **321**, 323

unity, as design principle, 127–131

University of Virginia, Charlottesville (Jefferson), **340**–341

Utzon, Joern, Sydney Opera House, Australia, **320**

Uxmal, Mexico, Nunnery carvings, **524**; Pyramid of the Magician, **524**

Valadon, Suzanne, biography, 121; *Reclining Nude*, **120**; *Self-Portrait*, **121**

value, as design element, 96–98; as property of color, 101

value scale, **97**

Van Alen, William, Chrysler Building, New York, **329**–330

Van Bruggen, Coosje, *Clothespin*, **95**–96; *The Knife Ship from "Il Corso del Coltello,"* **146**

Van der Weyden, Rogier, *see* Rogier
Van Eyck, Jan, *Man in a Red Turban,* **178**; *Portrait of Giovanni Arnolfini (?) and His Wife, Giovanna Cenami (?),* 76–**77**
Van Gogh, Theo, Art People, **45**
Van Gogh, Vincent, *The Artist's Room at Arles,* **461**; biography, 13; *The Bridge (after Hiroshige),* **193**; *Old Vineyard with Peasant Woman,* **87**–88; *Self-Portrait* (1889), **13**; *Self-Portrait Dedicated to Paul Gauguin,* **32**; *The Starry Night,* **12**
Van Ruisdael, Jacob, *Extensive Landscape with a View of the Town of Ootmarsum,* **438**
Van Wesel, Adriaen, *Death of the Virgin,* **270**
vanishing point, 113
variety, as design principle, 127–131
Vasari, Giorgio, Art People, 125; *Self-Portrait,* **125**
Vatican, Rome, St. Peter's Basilica, apse and dome (Michelangelo), **413**; Sistine Chapel, **408**; Michelangelo frescoes, 409, **410**–**412**, 413
vault construction, in architecture, 310–311
Velázquez, Diego, *Las Meninas (The Maids of Honor),* **434**–435
Ventura, Marco, *Mona Lisa Contemplating the Bust of Nefertiti as God Creates Order out of Chaos on a Starry Night on the Island of La Grande Jatte as the Infanta Margarita Looks On,* **256**–257
Venus de Milo, **49**

Venus of Willendorf, 348–**349**
Vermeer, Jan, *The Concert,* **179**
Verrazano-Narrows Bridge, New York, **319**
Verrocchio, Andrea del, *Equestrian Monument of Colleoni,* **269**
Versailles Palace, France, **433**–434; Hall of Mirrors, **434**
video art, 252–253
Vietnam Memorial, Washington, D.C. (Lin), **80**
Vietnamese art, *see* Champa
Vigée-Lebrun, Elisabeth, biography, 444; *Marie Antoinette and Her Children,* 442–**443**; *Self-Portrait at the Easel,* **444**
Villa of the Mysteries, Pompeii, wall painting, **377**
Vogel, Dorothy and Herbert, Art People, **503**

Wainwright Building, St. Louis (Sullivan), **318**
Walking Lion, from Babylon, 352–**353**
Wang Yani, *One Hundred Monkeys,* 148–**149**
Warhol, Andy, biography, 211; *Marilyn,* **210**; *100 Campbell Soup Cans,* **130**–131
watercolor, 182–183
Watteau, Antoine, *Gersaint's Signboard,* 440–**441**; *The Singing Lesson,* **106**–107
weathervane, *Angel Gabriel,* **298**
Wegman, William, *Lolita,* 222–**223**
Weisman Museum of Art, University of Minnesota at Minneapolis (Gehry), **327**

Welles, Orson, *Citizen Kane,* 245–246
Weston, Edward, *Artichoke, Halved,* **227**
Whistler, James Abbott McNeill, *Arrangement in Gray and Black, No. 1 (The Artist's Mother),* 464–**465**
Woman Sculptor at Work, manuscript illustration, **272**
wood, as craft material, 300–301
wood engraving, 197
Wood, Grant, *Parson Weems' Fable,* 138–**139**
woodcut, 191–196; Japanese, 192–194; playing cards, **191**
Woodrow, Stephen Taylor, *The Living Paintings,* **20**
Woolf, Virginia, 221
Wright, Frank Lloyd, biography, 337; "Fallingwater" (Kaufmann House), Bear Run, Pa., **336**; Solomon R. Guggenheim Museum, New York, **110**–111
Wyeth, Andrew, *Braids,* **176**

Yakshi, sculpture at Great Stupa, Sanchi, India, **512**
Yan Liben, *Emperor Wen Di of the Chen Dynasty,* from *Scroll of the Emperors,* **508**
Young Woman with a Gold Pectoral, Coptic painting, **173**
Young Women Exercising, Roman mosaic, **188**

Zeus, or *Poseidon,* Greek sculpture, **144**

PHOTOGRAPHIC CREDITS

All references are to figure numbers.
The following abbreviations have been used throughout:
AR: Art Resource, New York
ARS: Artists Rights Society, New York
RMN: Service de Documentation Photographique de la Réunion des Musées Nationaux, Paris.

back cover: © 1993 The Metropolitan Museum of Art.

Chapter 1: 1, Erich Lessing/AR; **2,** Jean Vertut, Issy-les-Moulineaux, France; **5,** Don Lambert, Topeka, Kan.; **9,** © 1996 Charly Herscovici/ARS; **10,16,** Scala/AR; **11,** © 1996 ARS/ADAGP, Paris; **14,15,** © 1998 The Museum of Modern Art, New York; **p. 14,** © 1996 ARS/ADAGP/Man Ray Trust, Paris.

Chapter 2: 19, Nimatallah/AR; **21,** Robert E. Mates, New York; **22,** Robin Holland; **23,** Najlah Feanney/SABA; **24,** © The Willem de Kooning Revocable Trust/ARS, photo Tony Jerome, NYT Pictures; **27,30,** RMN; **31,** © 1998 The Museum of Modern Art, New York; **32,** courtesy Brooke Alexander, New York; **33B,** Schecter Lee; **34,** Lee Stalsworth; **37,** © President and Fellows, Harvard College, **38, p. 35,** © 1996 The Pollock-Krasner Foundation/ARS; **43,** Jörg P. Anders; **p. 23,** © 1996 Richard Serra/ARS, photo courtesy Gagosian Gallery, New York; **p. 29,** AR.

Chapter 3: 47,48,55,84, Scala/AR; **49,** Francisco Hidalgo/The Image Bank; **50,54,81,** Erich Lessing/AR; **52,** AR; **53,** Derek Berwin/The Image Bank; **56,** RMN; **58,** © 1996 Estate of Pablo Picasso, Paris/ARS; **59,** © 1998 The Museum of Modern Art, New York; **62,82,** Giraudon/AR; **70,** from *Views from the Jade Terrace,* Indianapolis Museum of Art, 1988, © Indianapolis Museum of Art, photo K. Culbert-Aguilar, Chicago; **71; p. 69,** © 1996 The Georgia O'Keeffe Foundation/ARS; **75,** © 1996 Demart Pro Arte®, Geneva/ARS; **78,** © 1996 ARS/ADAGP, Paris, photo © 1998 The Museum of Modern Art, New York; **80,** Freie Hansestadt Bremen (Stadtgemeinde) und Bundesrepublik, Deutschland; **83,** © 1996 ARS/ADAGP, Paris, photo Philippe Migeat © Centre Georges Pompidou; **85,** Mark Segal/Panoramic Stock Images; **86,** Paul Margolies, © 1996 NAMES Project Foundation; **p. 57, left:** Spanish Ministry of Culture; **right:** AP/Wide World Photos.

Chapter 4: 87, © 1996 Succession H. Matisse/ARS; **88,** by permission of Fond Mercator Paribas, Antwerp; **89,** © ARS/ADAGP, photo © The Museum of Modern Art, New York; **90,** © 1996 ARS/ADAGP, photo Lee Stalsworth; **93,137, p. 91, p. 125,** Scala/AR; **96,120,** Giraudon/AR; **105,** Graydon Wood, Philadelphia; **109,122,** RMN; **114,** John Betancout, courtesy Galeria Botello, Hato Rey, Puerto Rico; **115,123,124,130,139, p. 121,** © 1996 ARS/ADAGP; **118,119,** photo © The Art Institute of Chicago. All Rights Reserved; **125,** with permission of Galerie Welz, Salzburg; **126,** David Heald, © Solomon R. Guggenheim Foundation, New York; **128,** © 1996 ARS/VG Bild-Kunst, Bonn, photo © 1998 The Museum of Modern Art, New York; **133,134,** Alinari/AR; **140,** Jerry L. Thompson; **141,** Malcolm Varon, 1986; **142,** © The Museum of Modern Art, New York; **p. 115, left:** Maki Galimberti/NYT Permissions; **right:** Ing. C. Olivetti, & C., S.p.A.

Chapter 5: 145, ARS/Giraudon/AR; **146,** © 1996 Succession H. Matisse/ARS, photo © 1998 The Museum of Modern Art, New York; **147,170,** Erich Lessing/AR; **148,** George Holzer; **150,** © 1996 The Andy Warhol Foundation for the Visual Arts/ARS; **151,** © 1996 Succession H. Matisse/ARS; **152,** Schalkwijk/AR; **153,** photo © 1990, The Art Institute of Chicago. All Rights Reserved; **155,173,** David Heald, © The Solomon R. Guggenheim Foundation, New York; **156,** AR; **160,** Otto E. Nelson, New York; **161,** Scala/AR; **165,** © 1996 Grandma Moses Properties Co., New York; **166,** Jim Strong; **167,** © 1996 ARS/ADAGP; **172,** © 1989 Annie Leibovitz/Contact Press Images; **174,** D. James Dee; **176,** © 1996 Whitney Museum of American Art; **181,** © 1998 The Museum of Modern Art, New York; **p. 133,** © 1996 Succession H. Matisse/ARS, photo Robert Capa/Magnum; **p. 151, left:** © 1994 Deborah Feingold; **right:** courtesy Guerrilla Girls, Conscience of the Art World, New York.

Chapter 6: 184, Giraudon/AR; **187,** © 1997 The Art Institute of Chicago. All Rights Reserved; **189,** AR; **190,** Chatsworth Photo Library © 1993; **191,** © 1996 ARS/ADAGP; **197,** © 1996 Estate of Pablo Picasso/ARS.

Chapter 7: 203, Giraudon/AR; **204,** Scala/AR; **205,** © 1994 The Detroit Institute of Arts; **206,** Lee Stalsworth, courtesy Francine Seders Gallery; **207,** Leonard E. G. Andrews; **209,** © 1996 ARS/Pro Litteris, Zurich, photo Giraudon/AR; **210, p. 181,** AR; **211,** © The Estate of Alice Neel, courtesy of Robert Miller Gallery, New York; **213,** courtesy John Marin Estate/Kennedy Galleries, Inc., New York; **216,** reproduction authorized by Instituto Nacional de Bellas Artes y Literatura; **220,** Erich Lessing/AR.

Chapter 8: 222, Robert E. Mates, New York; **229,** © 1998 The Museum of Modern Art, New York, **232,** The Bettmann Archive; **234,** courtesy Kennedy Galleries, New York; **235,** Photothèque; **241, p. 207,** photo Munch Museum, reproduced by permission of the Estate of Edvard Munch, BONO, Oslo; **243,** © 1996 The Andy Warhol Foundation for the Visual Arts/ARS; **244,** George Roos, New York; **245,** © 1996 Red Grooms/ARS; **247,** Steven Sloman, New York; **p. 195,** photo © 1993 The Art Institute of Chicago. All Rights Reserved; **p. 208,** Ed Chappell, Naples, Fla.; **p. 211,** © 1996 The Andy Warhol Foundation for the Visual Arts/ARS, photo Geoffrey Clements, New York.

Chapter 9: 254,277, © 1998 The Museum of Modern Art, New York; **256,** reprinted by permission of McIntosh & Otis, Inc., New York; **262,** by permission of John Pelos, for the Estate of Diane Arbus; **268, p. 233,** Art & Commerce Anthology, Inc.; **269,** UPI/Bettmann Newsphotos; **271, 279,** NYT Pictures; **276,** © 1996 Mike & Doug Starn/ARS; **280,281,283,285,288,** Museum of Modern Art Film Stills Archive; **282,286,** Turner Entertainment Company; **284,** Janus Films; **290,** David Allison; **p. 248,** The Bettmann Archive.

Chapter 10: 294, Design Gruppen '94 for Lillehammer Olympic Organizing Committee; **296,** courtesy of the artist, Milan; **301,** permission to reprint from Arnold Fortuna Lawner & Cabot Inc. Advertising; **303,** printed by permission of the Norman Rockwell Family Trust, © 1953 the Norman Rockwell Family Trust; **306,** © Ryszard Horowitz, R/GA Print, 1994. Electronic Imaging: Robert Bowen & Joseph Francis; **p. 261,** printed by permission of the Norman Rockwell Family Trust, © 1960 the Norman Rockwell Family Trust; **p. 262, right:** RMN, Arnaudet.

Chapter 11: 307, photo Zindman/Fremont, courtesy Marisa del Re Gallery, New York, © 1996 ARS/ADAGP; **308,** © 1997 The Metropolitan Museum of Art; **309,** Dept. of Asian Art, The Metropolitan Museum of Art; **312,316,323,** Scala/AR; **313,** Jacqui Wong, New York: **317,** David Finn; **319,** Jerry L. Thompson; **320,324,** Lynton Gardiner; **322,** Boltin Picture Library; **326,** Erich Lessing/AR; **328,** Sakamoto Photo Research Laboratory; **330,** Ted Thai/Time Magazine; **331,** © 1996 Red Grooms/ARS; **332,** Sara Krulwich/NYT Pictures; **333,** © Michael Melford, Mount Kisco, N.Y.; **334,** © 1989 Tony Linck; **335,** Daniel Dancer; **336,** Gian Franco Gorgoni © 1984/Contact Press; **337,** © Christo 1998, photo by Jeanne-Claude; **338,** © 1996 ARS/ADAGP; **339,** John Cliett; **p. 271,** Sanford H. Roth, Rapho/PR; **p. 275,** Condé Nast Publications; **p. 276,** Richard Schulman/Gamma Liaison; **p. 287,** Snowdon/Camera Press/Retna Ltd.

Chapter 12: 344, Jerry Jacka, Phoenix, courtesy Museum of New Mexico, Santa Fe; **345,** The Image Bank; **351,** Michael Seidl; **352,** Dean Beasom; **355,** Larry Stein; **356,** A. Singer, courtesy Library Services, American Museum of Natural History; **358,** Richard W. Strauss, Arlington, Va.; **p. 293,** Jerry Jacka, Phoenix.

Chapter 13: 364, courtesy New Mexico Magazine, photo Mark Nohl; **366,** William Katz/Photo Researchers; **367,** Lionel Isy-Schwart/The Image Bank; **368,369,370,** Scala/AR; **371,** Guido Alberto Rossi/The Image Bank; **373,** Erich Lessing/AR; **374,** Comstock; **375,** Gary Gladstone/The Image Bank; **376,** Bridgeman/AR; **377,** Harold Sund/The Image Bank; **378,** Hedrich Blessing, courtesy Chicago Historical Society; **379,** © 1989 Nong-Fei Louie, New York; **380,** Chris Minerva/FPG International; **381,** © 1992 Tibor Bognar/The Stock Market; **382,** David Maclean/Shostal Associates; **383,** © David Sailors/The Stock Market; **384,** © Alfred Wolf/Photo Researchers; **385,** Fay Jones; **386,** © Brownie Harris/The Stock Market; **387,** © 1993 Don F. Wong, Minneapolis; **388,** © 1993 Robert C. Lautman, Washington, D.C.; **389,** Peter Mauss/ESTO; **390,398,** © Norman McGrath, New York; **391,** Ezra Stoller/ESTO; **392,** © 1991 The Walt Disney Company; **393,** Culver Pictures; **394,** © Henry Groskinsky, New York; **395,** © MAS, Barcelona; **396,** Armen Kachaturian/Gamma Liaison; **397,** Michael Freeman, courtesy Fallingwater/The Western Pennsylvania Conservancy; **399,** © Hearst San Simeon State Historical Monument, photo John Blades; **400,** © University of Virginia; **401,** Kent Reno/Jeroboam; **402,** courtesy Skidmore, Owings & Merrill, photo Hedrich Blessing; **403,** Bill Pugliano/Gamma-Liaison; **p. 322,** John Loengard, Life Magazine © Time Inc.; **p. 377,** UPI/Bettmann Newsphotos.

Chapter 14: 404,405, Jean Clottes, Ministere de la Culture/SYGMA; **406,410,421,** Erich Lessing/AR; **407,** Jon Davison/Stockphotos/The Image Bank; **408,** Victor J. Boswell, 1982; **414,** Comstock; **415,** Werner Forman/AR; **416,** Giraudon/AR; **419,420B,** Bildarchiv Preussischer Kulturbesitz, Berlin; **420A,** Vanni/AR; **423,** Borromeo/AR; **425,** Lee Boltin/Boltin Picture Library; **426,** Schecter Lee; **428,** Nimatallah/AR; **429,** Scala/AR; **430,** ICONA, Rome; **p. 359,** Egyptian Expedition, The Metropolitan Museum of Art.

Chapter 15: 432, RMN, Mr. Chuzeville; **434,** William Katz/Photo Resource; **435,** AR; **436,** Schecter Lee; **437,** Nimatallah/AR; **438,442,443, p. 369,** Scala/AR; **439,441,** ICONA, Rome; **440,** Hirmer Fotoarchiv, Munich; **444,** Alann Becker/The Image Bank; **445,** Blaine Harrington/The Stock Market; **p. 373,** Anderson/AR.

Chapter 16: 447, Erich Lessing/AR; **448,** Figure from *Gardner's Art Through the Ages,* Ninth Edition, by Horst de la Croix, Richard G. Tansey, and Diane Kirkpatrick, copyright © 1991 by Harcourt Brace & Company, reproduced by permission of the publisher; **449,** Prints Division, The New York Public Library; **450,463,464,** Scala/AR; **451,** Gerard Mathieu/The Image Bank; **453,** Erich Lessing/Magnum Photos, Inc.; **455,** Werner Forman/AR; **456,** AR; **458,** © ND-Viollet; **459,** Gerald Brimacombe/The Image Bank; **460,461,** Foto Marburg/AR; **462,** G. Dagli Orti, Paris; **p. 391,** Otto Müller Verlag, Salzburg.

Chapter 17: 465,473,484, Erich Lessing/AR; **466,467, 469,470,474,475,479,480,481,488,490, p. 407,** Scala/AR; **468,** courtesy Olivetti, photo Antonio Quattrone, Florence; **472,** Anderson/AR; **476,477,478,** Nippon Television Network; **487,** Giraudon/AR; **491,** Lauros-Giraudon/AR; **p. 424,** The Bettmann Archive.

Chapter 18: 492,499, p. 432, Erich Lessing/AR; **493,495, p. 444,** Scala/AR; **496,** courtesy Belgium Tourist Office; **498,** Giraudon/AR; **504,** BSV/L, Weiss, 1984, Bayerischen Verwaltung der Staatlichen Schlosser, Garten und Seen Museumstabteilung; **508,** RMN; **p. 427,** AR.

Chapter 19: 511,512,515, RMN; **513,** Scala/AR; **519,** courtesy Hirschl and Adler Galleries, Inc., New York; **520,531,** Giraudon/AR; **522,** Hans Hinz, Allschwil; **523,532,** Erich Lessing/AR; **525,** © 1997 Succession H. Matisse/ARS; **526,** © Estate of Pablo Picasso/ARS, photo © 1998 The Museum of Modern Art, New York; **527,** © 1997 Estate of Pablo Picasso/ARS, photo David Heald, © Solomon R. Guggenheim Foundation; **528,529,533,** © The Museum of Modern Art, New York; **530,** © 1997 ARS/ADAGP/Estate of Marcel Duchamp; **534,** Manu Sassoonian; **535,** Cameraphoto/AR; **536,** © 1997 Demart Pro Arte, Geneva/ARS, photo © 1998 The Museum of Modern Art, New York; **538,** © 1997 ARS/VG Bild-Kunst, Bonn, photo Lee B. Ewing, © Solomon R. Guggenheim Foundation; **p. 463,** Vincent van Gogh Foundation; **p. 468,** © Estate of Pablo Picasso/ARS.

Chapter 20: 539,540, p. 482, © 1997 The Pollock/Krasner Foundation/ARS; **541,** © 1997 The Willem de Kooning Revocable Trust/ARS; **542,545,546,560,** © 1998 The Museum of Modern Art, New York; **543,** © Kate Rothko-Prizel & Christopher Rothko/ARS; **544,** © 1997 ARS/VG Bild-Kunst, Bonn; **547,** Robert McKeever; **549,** © 1997 ARS/ADAGP, photo © 1997 Whitney Museum of American Art; **550,** © 1997 Frank Stella/ARS, photo Hickey-Robertson, Houston; **555,** © 1997 Sol LeWitt/ARS; **556,** © 1997 Frank Stella/ARS; **562,** Bruce C. Jones, New York; **567,** Martha Swope, Life Magazine, © Time Inc.; **568,** © 1990 The Guggenheim Foundation/photo David Heald; **569,** Andrew Moore; **p. 503,** Lorene Emerson, © National Gallery of Art.

Chapter 21: 572, Inge Morath/Magnum; **574,** © 1993 Museum Associates, Los Angeles County Museum of Art. All Rights Reserved; **575,584,** © 1994 The Nelson Gallery Foundation. All Reproduction Rights Reserved; **579,** Wendy Holden, University of Michigan; **581,** Eliot Elisofon/Life Magazine © Time Inc.; **582,** courtesy Mme Loan de Fontbrune, Chargée de mission, Section Chine Musée National des Arts Asiatiques-Guimet; **583, p. 515,** © 1994 Michael Freeman, London; **586,** The Bridgeman Art Library/AR; **590,591,** Werner Forman Archive, London/AR; **592,** Fred J. Damerau, North Salem, N.Y.; **593,** Lee Boltin/Boltin Picture Library; **597,** Terrence Moore, Tucson, Ariz.; **599,601,** Jim Coxe, © American Museum of Natural History; **603,** Schecter Lee, © 1986 The Metropolitan Museum of Art; **604,607,** © 1993, 1995 The Metropolitan Museum of Art; **606,** Stan Ries; **609,** Bruno Albertoni; **611,** Michael Cavanagh & Kevin Montague; **612,** Harald Sund/The Image Bank.

The "Living with Art" Team

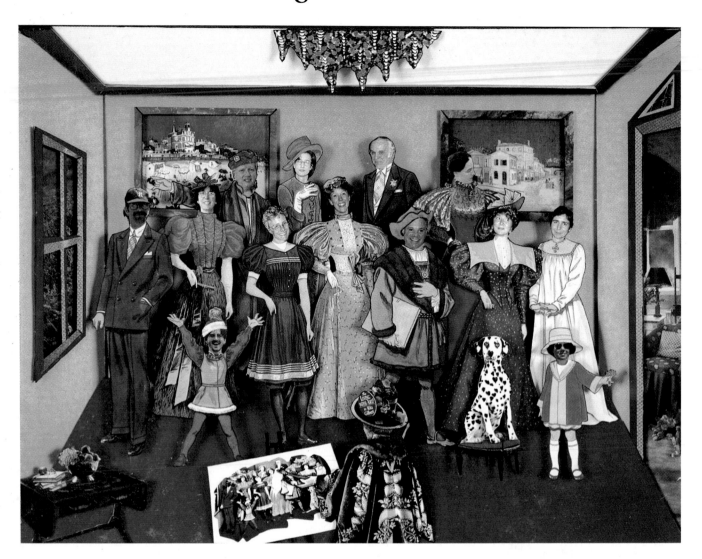

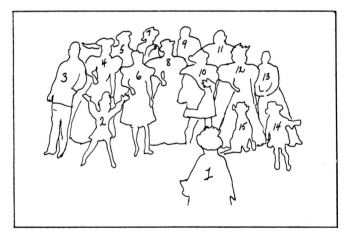

1, Rita Gilbert; 2, Jeff Brick; 3, Curt Berkowitz; 4, Kathy Bendo;
5, Phil Butcher; 6, Nancy Blaine; 7, Cynthia Ward; 8, Margaret Metz;
9, Joe Murphy; 10, Rich Ausburn; 11, Mia Galison; 12, Wanda Lubelska;
13, Wanda Siedlecka Kossak; 14, Peggy Mullaney; 15, "Art," the team mascot.

Jeff Brick. *The "Living with Art" Team*. 1995.
Box assemblage of photographs, found paper dolls,
color Xerox, cardboard, Plexiglas, magazine clippings,
and other materials; $18\frac{1}{4} \times 24\frac{1}{4} \times 1\frac{1}{2}''$.
Collection Rita Gilbert. © 1995 Jeff Brick, photo © 1995 Richard Koser.

The "Living with Art" Team *is a work of art created
by Jeff Brick. Like any work of art, it presents an artistic
truth that is meaningful to the artist, but it does not
duplicate precisely the "truth" of the "real world."
For one thing, the people depicted do not customarily
dress this way, and the room in which they stand
does not exist. For another, several of those portrayed
did not actually work on this edition of* Living with Art*,
while others, not included, did. But* The "Living with
Art" Team *perfectly captures the spirit of our group,
and it demonstrates that we practice what I preach:
We really do live with art.*

R. G.